Emergency:—
Quick Meals 35 to 45 Minute
menus, Pages 1443-74

Measurements and Equivalents
Pages 154-159

Carving Poultry p. 1075,
Meat p. 912

Frozen Foods and Freezing
Pgs. 136-139

S0-EBY-594

OVEN TEMPERATURES
Roast Beef
       pgs. 804
Spring Lamb
   pgs. 840-43
Roast Veal
      p. 875
Pork p.854
   Poultry
    p. 1044

Make
Double Stew
Freeze
    half—

pg. 136

Plan Menus for
Next week

Pages
49-67

Boss for
Dinner Wednesday

Read Over
Table Setting and
Service
Page 1414

What a triumph to place such beautiful food before your most treasured friends. This luscious crown roast, p 863, Crunchy Tomato Broil, p 1402, Zucchini au Gratin, p 1401, and homemade bread will go far in establishing your reputation as an excellent cook. Photo, courtesy Kraft Kitchens.

An efficient kitchen eliminates much of the work in preparing varied and delicious meals for the family.

Meta Given's

MODERN
ENCYCLOPEDIA
OF COOKING

A modern cook book, complete in every detail, brings the latest developments in home economics into your kitchen for a simpler, better and richer life. **NEW REVISED EDITION VOLUME ONE**

Published by

J. G. FERGUSON PUBLISHING COMPANY · CHICAGO

Distributed to the Book Trade by Doubleday & Company, Inc.

Total copies in use
Over One Million Books

TABLE OF CONTENTS

VOLUME ONE

Charts and Tables vii

List of Illustrations and Color Plates xi

Acknowledgments xiii

Foreword xiv

The Meal Planner's Creed 1
    The Diet Pattern 3
    Food for Children 45
    Why Use Menus? 49
    How to Use These Menus 51
    Menu Suggestions by the Month 55

The Food Shopper's Creed 68

Homemaker's Handbook 69
    Stretching the Food Dollar 70
    Purchasing Fruits and Vegetables 75
    Buying Staples 105
    Freezing Foods 136
    Care of Food in the Home 140
    Measurements and Equivalents 154
    Tin and Glass Jar Sizes 160
    Puzzling Kitchen Jobs 161

The Cook's Creed 171
    Appetizers 173
    Beverages 212
    Breads 232
    Cake 308
    Candy 400
    Cereals 420
    Cheese 435
    Cookies 454
    Croquettes 501
    Desserts 509
    Eggs 656
    Fish 687

VOLUME TWO

Foreign Foods 737
Frying with Deep Fat 738
Game 741
Garnishing 783
Meat 788
Variety Meats 890
How to Carve Meats 912
Pastry and Pies 921
Poultry 1028
How to Carve Chicken and Turkey 1075
Preserves and Pickles 1078
Salads 1114
Salad Dressings 1196
Sandwiches 1208
Sauces 1237
Soups 1263
Timbales 1301
Vegetables 1304

The Family Hostess' Creed 1411
  The Social Use of Food 1412
  Table Setting and Service 1414
  Buffet Service 1420

Glossary of Terms Used in Cooking 1423

Your Kitchen 1431

Kitchen Equipment . . . . *facing page* 1438

Casserole Suggestions . . . . . . *between pages* 1438 *and* 1439

Altitude Cookery . . . . *between pages* 1438 *and* 1439

Picnics and Special Meals 1439

Quick Meals for Homemakers in a Hurry 1443

Index 1475

HOW TO USE THIS BOOK

The *encyclopedia arrangement* of this book makes it the easiest-to-use cook book ever published.

It is *alphabetically* arranged by chapters, by subjects within chapters, by recipes within subjects, cross referenced by actual page numbers to charts, necessary general information, other recipes, etc.

Also there is a complete detailed Index of both Volumes found at the end of Volume Two.

CHARTS AND TABLES

VOLUME ONE

TABLE   PAGE

Basic Four Food Groups 7
Menu Planning Guide 8
Menu Plans for One Week 9
Recommended Daily Dietary Allowances 10
Nutrients in Basic Four Food Groups (One Day's Selection) . . . 11
Desirable Weights for Heights 14
Calorie Allowances for Various Body Weights 14
Normal Rate at Which Children Should Gain Weight 14
Protein and Calorie Values of Selected Foods 16
Cholesterol Content of Selected Foods 19
Ascorbic Acid (Vitamin C) and Calorie Values of Selected Foods . 24
Thiamine (Vitamin B_1) and Calorie Values of Selected Foods . . 26
Riboflavin (Vitamin B_2) and Calorie Values of Selected Foods . . 30
Niacin and Calorie Values of Selected Foods 32
Vitamin A and Calorie Values of Selected Foods 36
Calcium and Calorie Values of Selected Foods 38
Iron and Calorie Values of Selected Foods 39
Sodium Content of Selected Foods 43
Outline for Planning Adequate Diets for Children 1 to 5 Years Old 48
Homemaker's Guide for Buying Vegetables 79
Homemaker's Guide for Buying Fruits 89
When Fresh Fall and Winter Pears Are Best for Eating 95
Orange Sizes 96
Lemon Sizes 96
Average Vitamin Values of 100 Grams of Dried Fruit 97
Homemaker's Guide for Buying Apples 97
Homemaker's Guide for Buying Common Dried Fruit Products . . 102
Olive Table 124
The Homemaker's Spice Guide, Description, Source and Uses . . 128
Freezing Foods 136
Equivalent Weights and Measurements 154
Frequently Used Substitutions and Equivalents 155
Number of Units Per Pound of Common Foods 156

(continued on page x)   vii

Group 1. Milk Group

Group 3. Vegetable Fruit Group
Photos, courtesy Wheat Flour Institute

(For explanation, see page 7)

FOOD GROUPS

Tin Can and Glass Jar Sizes 160
Syrup for Canning or Plumping Fruit 169
Enrichment Standards 233
Yeast Doughs and Possible Variations 266
Cooking Temperatures for Candy 402
The Answers to Your Questions About Cheese 448
Know Your Fish 691

VOLUME TWO

Cuts for Making Soups 797
Timetable for Broiling Beef 800
Beef Chart 801
Timetable for Roasting Beef 804
Timetable for Braising Beef 806
Lamb Chart 839
Timetable for Broiling Lamb 840
Timetable for Roasting Lamb 840
Timetable for Braising Lamb 843
Pork Chart 853
Timetable for Broiling Ham and Bacon 854
Timetable for Braising Pork 856
Timetable for Roasting Pork 863
Veal Chart 874
Timetable for Roasting Veal 875
Timetable for Braising Veal 875
Variety Meats 891
Timetable for Variety Meats 892
Pastry Ingredients, 6, 8, and 9 Inch Double Crust Pies 924
Pastry Ingredients, 6, 8 and 9 inch Single Crust Pies 928
Timetable for Thawing Poultry in Refrigerator 1029
Buying and Cooking Guide for Chicken 1035
Timetable for Roasting Chicken 1044
Timetable for Roasting Turkey 1070
Extracting Fruit Juices 1080
Other Jellies 1087
Cooking Methods Suitable for Various Vegetables 1307
Altitude Cookery . . . . *between pages* 1438 *and* 1439

LIST OF ILLUSTRATIONS

VOLUME ONE

CROWN RIB ROAST MENU (in color)   Frontis

THE BASIC FOUR   viii

BAKED ALASKA PIE and LEMON CHIFFON PIE (in color)   xvi

APPETIZERS BEVERAGES BREADS   *Between pages 192–193*

Hot appetizers (in color)
Appetizers for special parties
Cocktails with canapés
Lemonade for hot day
Pineapple sodas
How to measure
How to cut shell-shaped pastry

How to make baking powder
   biscuits
How to make basic white bread
How to shape and proof yeast
   bread
How to make attractive rolls
Interesting yeast dough rolls
Corn sticks and muffins (in color)

CAKES CANDIES COOKIES DESSERTS   *Between pages 384–385*

German chocolate cake (in color)
Stollen (in color)
Popcorn balls and candied orange
   peel
Tray of confections
How to quick-mix cakes
How to mix conventional cakes
Cake with chocolate frosting
Bride's cake
Cookies
Cocoa Indians

Griddle cakes (in color)
Baked Alaska
Chocolate blanc mange
How to bake custard
How to make soft custard
How to make steamed custard
Steamed fruit pudding
Fancy sugar cookies
Snow pudding, Valentine's day
Snow pudding, custard sauce
Cheese soufflé (in color)

COOKIES DESSERTS CEREALS CHEESE EGGS FISH
Between pages 672–673

Candy-like brandy snaps
Assorted cookies and fruit
How to fill Vienna tarts
How to make fruit filled cookies
Strawberry shortcake
Sugared fruits
Cheese soufflé
Rice croquettes with jelly
Cheese pudding
Macaroni and cheese
Sunday night supper
Bacon and eggs, tomatoes
Scrambled eggs and bacon

Outdoor barbecue dinner
   (in color)
Eggs Benedict
Poached eggs on cereal
Omelet with shrimp sauce
Casserole, sliced egg garnish
How to know your eggs
Deviled eggs, cold cuts
Deviled eggs in casserole
Fish fillets, Spanish sauce
Fish roll-ups
Baked fish, quick Spencer method
Frying whole small fish

GARNISHING GAME MEAT PASTRY   *Between pages 894–895*

Broiled T-bone steak (in color)
Edible garnishes
Spanish pork chops
Leg of lamb
Standing rib roast (in color)
Pork chops
Tuna salad, accompaniments
Pan-broiled liver sausage
Heart sauerbraten

Pheasants on rice
Wild duck
How to make pastry
How to make pie shells
Apple pie, turkey cut-outs
Pumpkin pie, cheese pumpkins
Cream puff swans
How to weave lattice crust
Chocolate cream pie (in color)

POULTRY SALAD SANDWICHES SOUPS   *Between pages 1054–1055*

Roast turkey, fruit garnish
How to stuff a chicken
How to truss poultry
Oven-fried chicken with potatoes
Roast chicken with peaches
Oven-fried chicken halves
Pan-fried chicken, Southern style
Tossed salad
Marinated shrimp with aspic
Formal salad platter
Horseshoe salad
Turkey dinner (in color)
Citrus salad plate

Shredded salad
Potato salad, cold cuts
Arrangement of cold cuts
How to make mosaic sandwiches;
   checkerboard sandwiches
Grapefruit avocado mold
Glazed ham, cornucopias
Ham sandwiches, unusual
Sandwich bar
Split pea soup
Cold beat borsch
How to stuff peppers (in color)
Tomato and onion salad (in color)

VEGETABLES   *Between pages 1310–1311*

Colorful vegetables (in color)
Pea and potato casserole
Asparagus, pan-broiled tomatoes
Deluxe vegetable plate
Baked acorn squash
Onions and green beans,
   dill sauce
Okra, Texas style
Frankfurters lima bean casserole
Stuffed cabbage rolls
Vegetable plate, bacon garnish
Blackeyed peas, boiled tongue
Macaroni salad
Tomato cheese luncheon dish
Shredded cabbage in aspic

Diced beets in aspic
Fresh fruits for buffet (in color)
Chicken shortcake
Meat croquettes, mustard sauce
Party luncheon plate
Plum kuchen
Candied grapefruit shells
Gold cake glorified
Decorative butter
Fruit nut centerpieces
Halloween desserts
Child's lunch box
Fruit and nuts for hospitality
Good old-time picnic foods
Fruits for any meal

YOUR KITCHEN EQUIPMENT   *Between pages 1438–1439*

The Electric Range
Pressure Saucepans
An Efficient Kitchen

Gas Wall Ovens
Broiling Steak in Electric Ovens
Frying Doughnuts

ACKNOWLEDGMENTS

BUILDING a cook book is much like building a house: both must be large, functional and modern enough to serve one's needs for practical and pleasant ways of living. First the builder goes through a stage of dreaming. Then he collects all the worthwhile ideas he can find from houses he and his acquaintances have built as well as those from architects and building specialists. When he finally decides to build his house, a blueprint is drawn, embodying the practical features dreamed up, those gleaned from observations of other houses, and those contributed by experts consulted.

When the blueprint is completed, capable workmen are called in and the house begins to grow slowly but surely. As work progresses, friends and neighbors drop in, giving the builder the benefit of their experience, knowledge and skill, pointing out weak spots and ways of strengthening them, adding their bit to the dreams and plans of the builder. So when the house is finished, it bears the mark of many minds and hands.

Anyway, that is much the way it has been with the production of this cook book. Three home economics teachers, successful in their profession because of their thorough training, broad experience, and a desire to teach others, gave wise counsel on the features needed to make the book of value to students and inexperienced housewives. One of these teachers with others of my experimental kitchen assistants became the construction staff. After the material began to take shape, friends scientifically trained and especially skilled in the techniques of food preparation came along from time to time to observe our structure and make recommendations for its improvement. Their discriminating judgment was highly beneficial when we were ready to do the final polishing of our recipe and editorial material. For many of the good features in this book, the credit goes to all these helpers; for all that is faulty, I take the blame.

Not only acknowledgment but special mention is due those who assisted me so wholeheartedly. In the more than two years which were required to bring forth this book, a number have participated. Each was assigned to that part of the job for which she was best fitted. Some worked constantly for months, others intermittently for shorter periods.

Before any of the components could be woven together, however, it was necessary to take an inventory and evaluate critically the material I had accumulated. Louise Leavitt, formerly an instructor at the University of Minnesota and well qualified for the task, did this important job. Later on as the book developed, she drafted and composed our Kitchen chapter and organized and edited the definitions of food terms used in the Glossary. Catherine Zander, an instructor in Nutrition, also of the University of Minnesota, did a special job of analyzing and outlining the material for our Nutrition chapter. Elvera Rest who came from the staff of the department of home economics at the University of Illinois became my chief cook book builder assistant. For more than sixteen months she applied herself capably and unstintingly to the serious business of revising old material, helping to write the new, editing and putting the copy together in logical order. Mata Friend, formerly a home economics teacher in the Laboratory School at the University of Chicago, ably assisted me in experimental work. Janet Webster was assigned to the tedious but highly important details involved in getting the copy ready for the printer and reading all the proof carefully and critically. Ann Satter and Mildred Stull tested and checked recipes for some sections of the book. Mary Newby assisted in recipe work and used her capable hands to model our pastry and yeast bread technique pictures. Charlotte Schaeffer drew the pen sketches. Hendrick Dahl made most of the black and white pictures used in the book. Dr. Margaret Doyle, formerly of the University of Chicago, made some important revisions in the Diet chapter. Flossie Derryberry and Ivah McWilliams gave capable assistance typing recipes and reading proof. Mrs. Sammie K. Burden, Mrs. Lucille Bethke Bateman and Mrs. Sarah Adams double checked our Quick Meals, and Elaine Bechtel did editorial work.

I also wish to acknowledge the help of my professional friends who have been generous in supplying specialized information for the chapters within their provinces. They are as follows: Katherine Niles, formerly of the Poultry and Egg National Board, Reba Staggs of the National Live Stock and Meat Board, Agnes Reasor, formerly of the Cereal Institute, Margaret Buchan, formerly with Northwestern Yeast Company, Harriet T. Barto, Associate Professor of Dietetics of the University of Illinois, Dr. J. R. Chittick, formerly of the Jaques Manufacturing Company, Dr. Sleeter Bull, formerly of the University of Illinois, Dr. L. Jean Bogert, author of *Nutrition and Physical Fitness* and other nutrition textbooks, Essie Elliott, formerly of the California Fruit Growers Exchange, L B. Williams, formerly of the California Food Research Institute, Venona Swartz, formerly of the American Meat Institute, Mary Wright, formerly of the U. S. Advertising Agency, Elaine Norden, formerly of Campbell Mithun, Inc., Clara Snyder, formerly of the Wheat Flour Institute, Frank G. Ashbrook and Edna N. Sater, authors of *Cooking Wild Game,* Herta Breiter, formerly of the National Dairy Council.

Organizations that have contributed much to the attractiveness of this cook book by permitting me to use photographs, charts or tables owned by them are: Armour and Company, Kraft Kitchens, National Dairy Council, The Pillsbury Company, Self-Rising Flour and Corn Meal Program, Inc., The Borden Company, National Live Stock and Meat Board, Sealtest Laboratory Kitchen, General Foods, Independent Grocers' Alliance, Wheat Flour Institute, The Cereal Institute, California Foods Research Institute, Oregon Pear Bureau, National Research Council, American Meat Institute, Russell Miller Milling Company, *Woman's Day* Magazine.

META GIVEN

Orlando, Florida

Foreword

EVERY homemaker, whether her family numbers two or ten, needs a cook book that is *complete*—one that will assist her with any type of meal-making problem. A good cook book is like an extra pair of hands to help with your cooking, a personal shopper to direct your buying, and a friendly dietitian to guide your meal-planning. Through its wise use the members of your family not only enjoy the meals you prepare, but reflect the health and good spirits that come from well-balanced meals, properly cooked.

A *complete* cook book is to you as a homemaker what a dictionary and an encyclopedia are to a writer. No matter what problem confronts you, the answer will nearly always be found between its covers. . . . For instance, perhaps company drops in on Sunday night and every store is closed. A quick glance through the sandwich chapter turns up combinations for which you're almost certain to have the "makings" on your shelves. Or maybe year-old Bill is becoming a feeding problem. The chapter on child feeding offers practical, proved methods of transforming mealtime from fretful chaos to tranquil harmony. Or, if teen-age daughter wants to try her hand at baking, she turns to the chapter on pies, cakes, cookies, or breads and following its detailed instructions and step-by-step illustrations, she proceeds from an uninitiated start to a successful finish without help from anyone.

If your pies or biscuits aren't all they should be, if a good neighbor brings you a venison steak or a wild duck, if you're planning a special party, looking for a rare cheese, or simply stumped about what to feed your family for dinner, a good cook book will come to your rescue every time.

Of course, a host of really good recipes is the most important contribution of such an "encyclopedia" for your kitchen. You'll value *one* book that contains at least one recipe for every type of food you may want to try, from simple everyday stews and vegetables, to fancy bride's cakes. You'll want every recipe to produce an eye-appealing, appetite-stimulating product, as well as to include newest approved techniques, labor-saving methods, and suggestions for money and time-economy in cooking.

Producing recipes that meet this standard is very serious business. They must first be developed in a modern laboratory-kitchen by a person trained in experimental cooking. They must then be tested and re-tested, tasted and re-tasted by a trained staff to make certain that they'll be enjoyed by a wide variety of people. Finally, they must be written accurately and clearly.

A cook book that offers all this is not written in a month or even in a year. It grows slowly and gradually with but a small beginning and no ending. Probably a truly good cook book can be written only by a person who has what is called a "feeling" for food, an impelling interest which prompts such a person to work with recipes and to learn more about cooking techniques. It calls for study in many fields—home economics, dietetics, nutrition, chemistry, bacteriology, physiology, art, and economics.

But the end of formal education is only the beginning for a cook book author-to-be. For years she must work in her chosen field of foods, profiting from her mistakes, perfecting her skills, teaching others and learning from them. Finally, one day she realizes that the information she has gathered through the years will be helpful to others and she decides to write it all down. And so—after months of organization, additions, deletions, and revisions—a new cook book is born.

Such is the background for *The Encyclopedia of Cooking*, second book to be written by Meta Given for homemakers. Her first—*Modern Family Cook Book*—was published in 1942.

Meta Given began cooking as a small girl on a Missouri hill farm where folks had good food but little variety. The women were forced to be resourceful in presenting the same simple foods in a variety of interesting ways. She watched food grow on her family's farm, learned to store and preserve a summer's plenty to last through the winter months.

This early interest in foods led the author to an extensive study of home economics, and later to teaching. As a home economics specialist, she tested new varieties of foods and food products, created fresh ways for using old favorites, prepared food to be photographed for magazines and advertisements, and wrote about recipes, nutrition, shopping, and kitchen equipment.

But there comes a time in every woman's life when she feels the need for taking life a little easier and passing the reins of responsibility to another in whom she has complete confidence. That time has come to Meta Given and she has chosen, as the person to keep her *Encyclopedia of Cooking* up to date, Mary Lawton Wright, Associate Professor of Home Economics at Arizona State University, Tempe, Arizona. Like Meta Given, Mary Wright began life on a farm, in central Iowa. She taught Home Economics in high school and at Purdue University before her marriage. She has one daughter and six grandchildren. She is a member of the American and Arizona Home Economics Associations and former president of the Illinois Home Economics Association, and is listed currently in *Who's Who among Women* and *Who's Who in the West*. She also worked with Meta Given professionally.

In taking this book into your kitchen, you are bringing to your aid in meal-planning, cooking, serving, and even cleaning up, the wise and friendly counsel of Meta Given herself. In it, she presents "cooking" in its modern sense—as a science and an art. The first recipe you try may surprise you by the smoothness and speed of its preparation, the small number of dishes used, and the deliciousness of the finished product. But only after years of continued use will you fully appreciate the worth of a book especially written to answer your meal-making problems both of today and of many, many tomorrows.

ELVERA REST

ABOVE: *Baked Alaska, p 610, becomes this Baked Alaska Pie when the ice cream is put in a baked pie shell instead of on a cake base. Slightly soften the ice cream before putting it into the pie shell and freeze hard before adding next layer. Swirl on the meringue and brown just before serving using 3 egg whites, 6 tbsp. sugar, ⅛ tsp. salt, ½ tsp vanilla. Photo, courtesy American Dairy Association.*

BELOW: *It's more fun to entertain if much of the work can be done the day before. This Lemon Chiffon Pie, p 943, and the Baked Alaska, above, will help you do just that. And please the most finicky palate, besides. Photo, courtesy The Pillsbury Company.*

The Meal Planner's Creed

The health of my family is in my care; *therefore*—

> *I will spare no effort in planning meals containing the right kinds of food in the right amounts.*

Spending the food dollar to get the most for it is my job; *therefore*—

> *I will choose foods from a wide variety, variously priced to save money without sacrificing health.*

My family's enjoyment of food is my responsibility; *therefore*—

> *I will increase their pleasure by preparing a variety of dishes attractive in color and form and pleasing in flavor and texture.*

My family's health, security, and pleasure depend on my skill in planning meals; *therefore*—

> *I will treat my job with the respect due it.*

The Diet Pattern

This vital chapter might have been called "What Every Meal-Planner Should Know." In it are facts about foods and their nutritive values. These are presented in a down-to-earth manner, taking them out of the laboratory and bringing them right into your kitchen! You, as meal-planner and cook, should know these basic facts in order to choose foods and diets to bring exuberant health to your family.

FEEDING the family an adequate diet has been greatly simplified in recent years. Volumes have been written on nutrition and countless hours have been spent in research on which these volumes are based. Fortunately, we do not have to read all of this material in order to feed our family adequately. Why? Because trained nutritionists have organized the necessary information into a simplified form. If you follow the recommendations given here conscientiously you can be assured of a diet which is as adequate as present knowledge can make it.

The Institute of Home Economics recommends planning the daily family meals around four food groups, commonly known as The Basic Four, which are listed in Table 1, page 7. Used in recommended amounts daily, for each person, with as much variety as possible within each group, the Basic Four Food Groups supply all the essential nutrients except vitamin D. This vitamin is not present naturally in any foods except in very small amounts, and so other plans must be made to insure an adequate supply, see page 37. By improving eating habits it is possible to not only add years to our life but life to our years.

TIPS FOR EASE AND INTEREST IN PLANNING MENUS

So many times women are heard to say, "I wouldn't mind cooking if I only knew what to fix." Menu planning can be easy—yes, and fun—if you will do two things:

(1) Always plan your menus when you are hungry, and

(2) Plan menus for one week, or at least three or four days, at a time.

This makes shopping easier, assures you that ingredients will be on hand when needed, and makes it easier to follow the Basic Four to insure good nutrition. A good routine is to coordinate the time for menu planning with the day the grocery stores run food advertisements. These advertise-

3

ments are a good indication of what fresh foods are in season and reasonable; and taking advantage of sale prices in staples is often a morale booster when money is scarce.

Next, settle yourself comfortably at a large table or desk with your favorite recipe book at your side and a classified list of your family's favorite dishes. If you have never assembled such a list, a suggestion for an easy way to do so is given in Table 2, page 8. This done, rule a sheet of regular 8½ x 11-inch typing paper in columns like Table 3, page 9, using the entire sheet so spaces will be larger than on the sample chart. With the Basic Four Food Groups, Table 1, page 7, in front of you, you are now ready to plan menus for a whole week.

Probably you will find it easier to get variety into meals and days if one meal, such as dinner, is planned for the entire week first; then plan the breakfasts for the week; and then the lunches (or suppers). First, consulting the Basic Four, make your selections from the Meat Group for all the dinners. Try to get in one fish and one variety meat such as liver each week. One pork, one beef and one chicken dish per week will give good variety. A lamb and a veal dish, if available in the local market, would give further variety. If such variety is offered every week, your children will never embarrass their hostess when they are guests by informing her they don't like lamb, or fish, or whatever she serves. Not only does a weekly variety in the family meal develop sophisticated appetites but the more variety in meals from day to day the more likely a person will get all of the nutrients needed for an adequate diet.

After the meats have been selected for all the dinners, then fill in the vegetables, then the salads, then the desserts (it may well be a simple fruit or fruit and cheese) and beverage. As you are selecting the various foods, consult (1) the newspaper advertisements to see what foods are available at prices within your budget and (2) your own list of family favorites, fashioned after Table 2, page 8. Also consult the foods listed in the tables between pages 16–39, which show the foods highest in the various nutrients.

Next plan the breakfasts across the page. If a full glass of orange juice (¾ measuring cup or 6 oz.) or a half grapefruit is served as the breakfast fruit, that will furnish enough vitamin C for the day. If citrus fruit is not served, consult table on page 24 to be sure you get enough vitamin C in your meals.

And now comes the last meal of the day—lunch or supper, depending on your meal pattern. Instead of being a catch-as-catch-can meal, the menu for this meal should be checked carefully to be sure it supplies all the nutrients not furnished in sufficient amount in the other two meals.

Looking down the column for the first day's meals (probably this will be Saturday), which foods in the Basic Four have not been used in amounts needed? The answer to this gives you the clue or clues for the menu for lunch. Easy, isn't it? After planning all the lunches (or suppers), the job is done for the week.

Next comes the grocery list. There is much in favor of planning two grocery lists—one for staples and one for perishables. If a special pad is placed on the kitchen wall on which staples are listed before the supply is depleted, and that list is transferred to the marketing list weekly, one will never run out of staples.

One advantage of listing the perishables (and staples not usually kept on hand) for the day in the lower space of the menu sheet is that, if you find it advisable to shop for perishables twice during the week you can easily see which items you will need on each trip. If all the marketing for the week is done at one time, care will need to be taken when planning the menus to put the most perishable foods on the first few days and those which do not deteriorate so fast the latter part of the week. This will prevent waste and help keep the cost down.

PREPARATION AND VARIETY ARE IMPORTANT

Serving the correct food and having the family eat it are two different things. Of greatest importance is preparing the food so that it is tasty and appetizing. Serving the food attractively and in a friendly atmosphere is also very important in stimulating enthusiasm for food. In most cases, the less said about eating, the better children will eat. It is most important to the health of the family that adults do not show evidence of any food prejudices.

A young child is likely to form good food habits which will continue to adulthood if he is given special consideration when he starts to eat. He prefers food at room temperature at first, rather than hot or very cold. When a new food is introduced, give him only a few tastes the first time, gradually increasing the size of the serving. Do not show undue concern if he does not eat it with relish at first. After a few trials, the taste will seem less strange and he will gradually learn to like it. Add new foods to his diet early and regularly (but not too frequently) so he will learn to like a variety of foods.

When planning menus, other things as well as nutritive value should be kept in mind, such as (1) variety in texture, shape, color, flavor and temperature; (2) seasonal foods, and (3) amount of money available for food.

Variety in flavor. Foods must first taste good; there should be balance between mild and strong, sweet and piquant foods. Avoid repeating one flavor or food in the same meal such as tomato juice, tomato salad or spaghetti with tomato sauce. If one food is highly flavored, let that suffice and plan milder flavors for the other dishes in the course. Care should be taken to season foods only enough to bring out the natural flavors, not to hide them.

Variety in color. White foods such as mashed potatoes look more appealing if served with colorful foods, such as broccoli, beets, bright carrots or red jelly. Colors in food served in the same course should also be harmonious. The red of tomatoes and the green of broccoli are attractive together but try red tomatoes with pickled beets or carrots and the effect is not so pleasing. Garnishes are valuable in adding color contrast. A strip of pimiento across the broccoli, a spoonful of red jelly atop a tapioca pudding are two examples of adding color interest easily. Color in dishes and table linen should also be considered in planning a menu. Occasionally foods, such as cake icings and whipped cream may be colored with a few drops of food coloring. For greatest eye appeal, the resulting colors should be very light as intense colors in most foods are not appetizing.

Variety in texture and consistency. If you can use contrasting adjectives to describe the texture and consistencies of the foods served in a course, you will have achieved this goal. These might include soft and firm; pliable and crisp; thin and thick; moist and dry. A piece of crisp, crunchy celery gives pleasing contrast to the softness of mashed potatoes; a moist sauce offers relief to the dryness of rice, etc. However, one sauce in a course is usually sufficient.

Variety in temperature. Even on a cold day, a cold salad direct from the refrigerator is a delightful contrast to a bowl of hot stew, just as hot coffee is an excellent accompaniment to a frozen dessert. Most foods have an ideal temperature at which they taste best and care should be taken to serve them at that temperature. Hot foods should be served hot and cold foods should be served cold. Having plates and serving dishes for hot foods heated and dishes for salads and frozen foods chilled makes a meal more appealing to the discriminating person.

Variety in methods for preparation. All boiled foods in one meal are monotonous as are all fried or all baked foods. A delicious New England boiled dinner is appreciated even more if accompanied by crispy hot rolls.

There are many excellent food combinations for casserole dishes; also for fruit salads, vegetable salads, etc. However, when planning one dish which is a combination of several foods, it is best to have most of the other dishes of the meal of one food only.

Variety in shapes is important too. A variety of round, flat, oblong, spherical and other shapes is more appealing in food than the use of similar shapes. If scalloped potatoes are to be served, why not serve the zucchini stuffed rather than sliced and the tomatoes for salad cut in wedges?

TABLE 1. BASIC FOUR FOOD GROUPS

For Adequate Nutrition, Eat These Foods Every Day:*

Group 1. Milk Group

Children under 9 years, 2 to 3 cups†
Children 9 to 12 years, 3 or more cups
Teenagers, 4 or more cups
Adults, 2 or more cups

† 1 cup is considered 8 oz., one full measuring cup.

Equivalent in calcium value:
  1" cube cheddar cheese = ⅔ cup milk
  ½ cup cottage cheese = ⅓ cup milk
  2 tbsp. cream cheese = 1 tbsp. milk
  ½ cup ice cream = ¼ cup milk

Group 2. Meat Group

2 or more servings or its equivalent (at least one of meat, poultry or fish) alternates—dry beans, dry peas or nuts

1 serving = 2 to 3 oz. lean cooked meat, poultry or fish, all without bone
1 serving = 2 eggs
1 serving = 1 cup cooked dry beans, dry peas or lentils
1 serving = 4 tbsp. peanut butter

Group 3. Vegetable Fruit Group

4 or more servings, including:
  1 serving citrus fruit or other fruit or vegetable important for vitamin C**
  1 dark green or deep-yellow vegetable for vitamin A,*** at least every other day
  2 or more servings of other vegetables and fruits, including potatoes

1 serving = ½ cup vegetable or fruit or an ordinary size serving as 1 apple, ½ grapefruit

Group 4. Bread Cereal Group

4 or more servings; check labels to be sure they are whole grain, enriched or restored

1 serving = 1 slice bread
1 serving = 1 oz. ready-to-eat cereal
1 serving = ½ to ¾ cup cooked cereal, cornmeal, grits, macaroni, noodles, rice or spaghetti

---

* Plus other foods as needed to round out meals, provide additional calories if needed, and to satisfy the appetite, such as butter, margarine, other fats, oils, sugars and unenriched refined grains.

** FRUITS AND VEGETABLES IMPORTANT FOR VITAMIN C. (SEE ALSO TABLE ON P 24):

Cantaloupe	Fresh pineapple	Cauliflower
Grapefruit	Watermelon	Green peppers
Oranges	Broccoli	Kohlrabi
Strawberries	Brussels sprouts	Potatoes
Raspberries	Cabbage, raw	Tomatoes

*** See Vitamin A foods, table on p 36, for fruits and vegetables highest in this vitamin (many of these are also high in iron).

TABLE 2. MENU PLANNING GUIDE (*My family's favorite dishes*)

First Course	Meats	Meats	Poultry, Fish	Vegetables	Salads	Accompaniments	Desserts
Soups	*Beef*	*Lamb*	*Chicken*	Asparagus	*Tossed*	*Breads*	Custard
Beef Vegetable	Swiss steak	Curry	Oven fried	Newburg	Wilted lettuce	Pecan rolls	Bread Pudding
Chicken	Pepper steak	Irish stew	A la King	Polonaise	Cole slaw	Streussel coffee cake	Apple Dumplings
Corn	Short ribs	Pilaf	Pie	Green beans	Mixed fruit	Garlic bread	Apple Crisp
Chowder	Stew	Leg of lamb	'n Dumplings	Au gratin	Waldorf	English Muffin	Baked Apples
Clam	Stroganoff	Creole	Chop Suey	Savory	Carrot raisin	Cinnamon Toast	Bavarian Cream
Chowder	Liver		Curry	Beets, Harvard		Nut bread	Lemon Fluff
Cream of tomato	*Ground Beef*	*Miscellaneous*	Roast	Cabbage	*Molded*	Pan rolls	Peach Cobbler
French Onion	Chili con carne	Franks	*Fish, Sea foods*	au gratin	Perfection		Prune Whip
Navy bean	Cheeseburgers	Bologna cups	Shrimp curry	'n Corned Beef	Sunshine	*Pickles*	Strawberry Shortcake
Oyster MG 1472	Spaghetti	Sweetbreads	Halibut steaks	red, with apples	Cranberry	Watermelon	Tapioca Pudding
Potato	Meat loaf	Broiled	Scalloped	Cauliflower	Bing Cherry	Beet	
Split Pea	Stuffed Peppers	Creamed	Oysters	F. F.		Peaches	
		Oxtails	Codfish balls	with cheese sauce	*Hearty*		*Pies*
Appetizers	*Pork*	*Dried Beef*	Fried Oysters	Corn	Chicken	*Relishes*	Lemon Meringue
Chicken Livers	Roast	On toast	Fried scallops	greenpepper	Potato	Three Bean	Pecan
Clam Dip	Chops	Souffle	F. F. shrimp	Onions	Kidney Bean	Cranberry	Apple
Deviled Eggs	Spareribs	Noodle casserole	F. F. perch	creamed	Crab Louis		
Garlic Olives	Chop Suey		Salmon Loaf	fried		*Jams, Jellies*	Ice Cream
	Ham slice	*Veal*	Salmon Cakes	Parsnips	*Dressings*		Sundaes
Cocktails	Ham loaf	Paprika	Salmon Souffle	Potatoes	French		
(non-alcoholic)	Sausage	Veal Birds	Souffle	baked	Blue cheese		Fresh Fruit
Clam Juice	Boiled dinner	Scallopini	Tuna	scalloped	Italian		with cheese
Tomato Juice		Sub gum	Casserole	au gratin	Lime Honey		
Fruit cup				new, with peas	Cooked Fruit		
Melon balls				Sweet Potatoes			
Rhubarb shrub				Baked			

Probably you will not need recipes for many of your family's favorites, but for those you do, if you indicate the location of them on this sheet it will save you much time when planning menus and grocery list (for instance, MG1472 after Oysters under Soups indicates the recipe will be found in this book page 1472, MG being used for Meta Given's Encyclopedia of Cooking; F might be used for your own menu file; MB might be used for "my book" if you have a book in which you have copied recipes; etc. (It would be a good idea to keep a record of your abbreviations just in case you might forget.)

TABLE 3. MENU PLAN FORM FOR ONE WEEK

Plan Wisely if You Would Save Time, Energy and Money

	Menu	Saturday	Sunday	Monday	Tuesday	Wednesday	Thursday	Friday
Breakfast	Fruit Cereal Egg Bread Beverage							
Lunch	Protein Salad Bread Beverage							
Dinner	Meat Potato Vegetable Salad Bread Beverage Dessert							
	Market List, Perishables							

TABLE 4. RECOMMENDED DAILY DIETARY ALLOWANCES[1], REVISED 1963

Food and Nutrition Board, National Research Council

DESIGNED FOR THE MAINTENANCE OF GOOD NUTRITION OF PRACTICALLY ALL HEALTHY PERSONS IN THE U.S.A.

(Allowances are intended for persons normally active in a temperate climate)

	Age[2] Years from to	Weight kg. (lbs.)	Height cm. (in.)	Calories[3]	Protein gm.	Calcium gm.	Iron mg.	Vitamin A Value I U	Thiamine mg.	Riboflavin mg.	Niacin Equiv.[4] mg.	Ascorbic Acid mg.	Vitamin D I U
Men	18-35	70 (154)	175 (69)	2,900	70	0.8	10	5,000*	1.2	1.7	19	70	
	35-55	70 (154)	175 (69)	2,600	70	0.8	10	5,000	1.0	1.6	17	70	
	55-75	70 (154)	175 (69)	2,200	70	0.8	10	5,000	0.9	1.3	15	70	
Women	18-35	58 (128)	163 (64)	2,100	58	0.8	15	5,000	0.8	1.3	14	70	
	35-55	58 (128)	163 (64)	1,900	58	0.8	15	5,000	0.8	1.2	13	70	
	55-75	58 (128)	163 (64)	1,600	58	0.8	10	5,000	0.8	1.2	13	70	
	Pregnant (2nd and 3rd trimester)			+ 200	+20	+0.5	+5	+1,000	+0.2	+0.3	+3	+30	400
	Lactating	8 (18)		+1,000	+40	+0.5	+5	+3,000	+0.4	+0.6	+7	+30	400
Infants[5]	0- 1			kg.x115 ±15	kg.x2.5 ±0.5	0.7	kg.x1.0	1,500	0.4	0.6	6	30	400
Children	1- 3	13 (29)	87 (34)	1,300	32	0.8	8	2,000	0.5	0.8	9	40	400
	3- 6	18 (40)	107 (42)	1,600	40	0.8	10	2,500	0.6	1.0	11	50	400
	6- 9	24 (53)	124 (49)	2,100	52	0.8	12	3,500	0.8	1.3	14	60	400
Boys	9-12	33 (72)	140 (55)	2,400	60	1.1	15	4,500	1.0	1.4	16	70	400
	12-15	45 (98)	156 (61)	3,000	75	1.4	15	5,000	1.2	1.8	20	80	400
	15-18	61 (134)	172 (68)	3,400	85	1.4	15	5,000	1.4	2.0	22	80	400
Girls	9-12	33 (72)	140 (55)	2,200	55	1.1	15	4,500	0.9	1.3	15	80	400
	12-15	47 (103)	158 (62)	2,500	62	1.3	15	5,000	1.0	1.5	17	80	400
	15-18	53 (117)	163 (64)	2,300	58	1.3	15	5,000	0.9	1.3	15	70	400

[1] The allowance levels are intended to cover individual variations among most normal persons as they live in the United States under usual environmental stresses. The recommended allowances can be attained with a variety of common foods, providing other nutrients for which human requirements have been less well defined. See text for more detailed discussion of allowances and of nutrients not tabulated.

[2] Entries on lines for age range 18-35 years represent the 25-year age. All other entries represent allowances for the midpoint of the specified age periods, i.e., line for children 1-3 is for age 2 years (24 months); 3-6 is for age 4½ years (54 months), etc.

[3] Tables 1 and 2 and figures 1 and 2 in text show calorie adjustments for weight and age.

[4] Niacin equivalents include dietary sources of the preformed vitamin and the precursor, tryptophan, 60 mg tryptophan represents 1 mg niacin.

[5] The calorie and protein allowances per kg for infants are considered to decrease progressively from birth. Allowances for calcium, thiamine, riboflavin, and niacin increase proportionately with calories to the maximum values shown.

* 1,000 I U from preformed Vitamin A and 4,000 I U from beta-carotene.

TABLE 5. NUTRIENTS IN BASIC FOUR GROUPS

(One Day's Selection)

	Amount	Calories	Protein grams	Vit C mg	Vit B₁ mg	Riboflavin mg	Niacin mg	Vit A IU	Calcium mg	Iron mg
Milk	2 cups	320	18	4	.16	.84	0.2	700	576	0.2
Lean Beef	2.5 oz	140	22	—	.04	.16	3.3	10	10	2.7
Beef Liver (fried)	3 oz	195	22	22	.22	3.55	14.1	45,420	9	7.5
Grapefruit	½ med	55	1	52	.05	.02	.2	10	22	.6
Broccoli spears	1 cup	40	5	135	.14	.29	1.2	3,750	132	1.2
Apple, Raw	1 (⅓ lb)	70	tr	3	.04	.02	.1	tr	8	.4
Potato, baked	1 (⅓ lb)	90	3	20	.10	.04	1.7	0	9	.7
Cornflakes*	1 oz	110	2	0	.12	.02	.6	tr	5	.4
Bread***	3 slices	180	6	tr	.18	.12	1.5	tr	48	1.8
Totals		1180	79	236	1.05	5.06	22.9	49,940	819	15.5
Recommended***		2600	70	70	1.0	1.6	17	5,000	800	10.

* Enriched.
** Made with 1% to 2% non-fat dry milk. If skim milk is used, this reduces calories to 150 without reducing other nutrients except vitamin A (to 20 I U) which is far in excess of needs in this selection.
*** Recommended allowance for a man age 35-55 weighing 154 lbs, for others, see Table 4, p 10.
Because liver and broccoli are both high in vitamin A, it would be just as well to serve another vegetable not so high in this nutrient; broccoli was used here to show that on days when liver is not served, a dark green (or yellow vegetable) would furnish a sufficient quantity of vitamin A. If neither were served, vitamin A would be quite deficient in this selection. Since excess vitamin A is stored in the body, it is not important that each day's selection meet the recommended allowance if on other days it is exceeded sufficiently.

ELEMENTS OF THE DIET

A homemaker can rest assured she will be feeding her family an adequate diet if she follows the simple directions mentioned on pages 3 to 7. Nevertheless, some women, and men too, are deeply concerned with the "hows and whys" of nutrition.

A well-balanced diet is made up of a great variety of foods, from which the body contains the elements it requires for growth, maintenance and repair. If one or more of these elements is persistently lacking or present in insufficient quantity, the health suffers—not suddenly or dramatically, but gradually, over a long period. Nutritionists call this "hidden hunger" which is not revealed by hunger pangs but by such signs as lowered vitality, lowered resistance to disease, fatigue, poor teeth, anemia, and in more acute stages by deficiency disease, such as scurvy, pellagra, and beriberi. "Hidden hunger" may be present even when the appetite is satisfied.

Essential food elements supplied by an adequate diet fall into 5 classes:

1. Protein—builds and repairs body tissues; an excess furnishes heat and energy, see p 15.

2. Carbohydrates—furnish heat and energy; an excess over needs will be stored in the form of body fat.

3. Fats—same as carbohydrates, above. Some fats also serve as a carrier for fat soluble vitamins A, D, E and K; help the body use these vitamins; and furnish essential fatty acids, see p 18.

4. Minerals—build and repair teeth, bones and blood and help regulate body functions, see p 20.

5. Vitamins—promote growth and maintain health and vigor, see p 20.

Besides these food elements, it is also essential to supply *bulk* which aids in elimination of body waste and *water* which aids in regulation of body functions such as digestion and elimination of body waste.

Table 4, page 10, gives the *Recommended Daily Dietary Allowances* of calories, protein, minerals and vitamins according to sex and age.

TAKE THE GUESS WORK OUT OF MEAL PLANNING

Probably one of the first things that come to the mind of a person who wants to learn more about the food value of the meals she feeds her family is: How can I satisfy myself that I have included all the nutrients needed if I do select foods as recommended in the Basic Four Food Groups?

In Table 5, p 11, is listed one day's selection from the foods recommended in the Basic Four (Table 1, page 7) as any homemaker might select, the amounts of each in a standard size serving and the nutrients each furnishes. These figures were obtained from the tables between pages 16 through 39. In the last two lines are given the total of each of the nutrients and the amounts recommended for a man of 35 to 55 years of age weighing 154 pounds in Table 4, page 10.

This shows that a man this age and size can get all the nutrients needed in 1,170 calories; to get enough calories to maintain his desirable weight, he will need to add more food to supply 1,430 more calories. This could include butter for the bread and baked potato (or gravy should the potato be boiled), sugar on the cereal, salad dressing, more bread or larger servings of any food desired.

You may make a selection for a day's dietary as recommended in the Basic Four Food Groups and calculate its food value in the same way. It is much simpler to do it with the basic foods than with complicated recipes.

CALORIES

Obesity* is America's number one health problem. Yet it is possible to eat all the foods necessary for optimum health and still keep the calorie consumption low enough to maintain a desirable weight, see tables on pages 11 and 14.

A diet which maintains the adult body at a constant desirable weight is supplying the correct number of calories. To be utilized in the most efficient manner, however, the diet must also supply sufficient quantities of the essential proteins, minerals and vitamins.

Most physicians agree that up to 30 years of age, it is desirable to be slightly overweight rather than slightly under; after that age, it is usually safer to be slightly underweight. The variation from normal weight, however, should usually not exceed 10 per cent in either direction.

To reduce small amounts it is only necessary to cut down sharply on concentrated fuel foods (sugars, starches and fats), being sure to meet all the other requirements of the Basic Four, p 7.** (However a reducing diet should include enough fat to curb the appetite and carry a sufficient amount of fat-soluble vitamins and essential fatty acids. Otherwise a person is likely to nibble between meals and often foods available at such times, especially if one is away from home, are likely to be high in calories.) By dieting correctly in this fashion, a new habit of eating will be cultivated which will hold over after dieting is no longer necessary. No one should begin a strict diet without first consulting a physician who will keep close watch on physiological changes during the campaign as well as offer dietary advice.

* Overweight means an excess of 10 to 20% in body weight. When overweight exceeds 20% of desirable weight, the condition is referred to as obesity. It is well to remember that one can gain 10 lbs a year by drinking only 1 bottle of soft drink (105 cal) each day beyond body needs.
** Avoid these high calorie foods as much as possible: fat on meat, cooking fats, salad oils, mayonnaise, gravies, rich sauces, nuts, pastries, cakes, cookies, candies, jellies, jams and sugar sweetened beverages.

DESIRABLE WEIGHTS FOR HEIGHT*

Height in inches	Weight in pounds	
	Men	Women
58	....	112±11
60	125±13	116±12
62	130±13	121±12
64	135±14	128±13
66	142±14	135±14
68	150±15	142±14
70	158±16	150±15
72	167±17	158±16
74	178±18	....

* In cases where weight must be reduced or increased due to pronounced variation from the normal, it is always wise to consult a physician, since other factors besides diet may play a part in causing the abnormality. It is safe to say, however, that in both reducing and gaining diets, and especially in the former, care must be taken to see that the full daily requirement of protein, vitamins and minerals is met. In a reducing diet *only total calories* should be decreased. *All* the other recommended dietary allowances *must be met* to maintain health.

CALORIE ALLOWANCES FOR INDIVIDUALS* OF VARIOUS BODY WEIGHTS

[At mean environmental temperature of 68° F. and assuming moderate physical activity]

MEN

Desirable weight Pounds	Calorie allowances		
	25 years	45 years	65 years
110	2,500	2,350	1,950
121	2,700	2,550	2,150
132	2,850	2,700	2,250
143	3,000	2,800	2,350
154	3,200	3,000	2,550
165	3,400	3,200	2,700
176	3,550	3,350	2,800
187	3,700	3,500	2,900

WOMEN

	25 years	45 years	65 years
88	1,750	1,650	1,400
99	1,900	1,800	1,500
110	2,050	1,950	1,600
121	2,200	2,050	1,750
128	2,300	2,200	1,800
132	2,350	2,200	1,850
143	2,500	2,350	2,000
154	2,600	2,450	2,050
165	2,750	2,600	2,150

NORMAL RATE AT WHICH CHILDREN SHOULD GAIN IN WEIGHT.*

	BOYS			GIRLS		
	Approximate average gain				Approximate average gain	
Age, *years*	Per month, *ounces*	Per year, *pounds*	Age, *years*	Per month, *ounces*	Per year, *pounds*	
0-1	16	11-13	0-1	16	11-13	
1-2	7	6	1-2	7	5½	
2-3	6	5	2-3	6	4½	
3-8	6⎱	Avg. gain of about	3-8	6⎱	Avg. gain of about	
8-12	8⎰	4½ lbs. a year	8-12	8⎰	4½ lbs. a year	
12-14	12	9	12-14	12	10	
14-16	16	13	14-16	8	7	
16-18	8	6	16-18	4	3	

* From *Nutrition and Physical Fitness,* Seventh Edition, 1960, by L. Jean Bogert. Published by W. B. Saunders Company, Philadelphia and London.

It has been found that the health of children can be gauged by the rate at which they gain in weight. The preceding table is one which you

can safely use in checking your child's rate of growth. It is based on measurements of more than 167,024 boys and girls with no serious physical defects.
The child's diet should be such as to increase the weight at an average or
better than average rate rather than just to maintain it. See table on p 14.

PROTEIN

Muscles and all body tissues, except fat, are made up chiefly of protein.
Their growth, upkeep and repair require that they be supplied daily with
an adequate amount of protein in the food consumed.

Proteins are made up of different combinations of 22 amino acids. The
body can make over half of these amino acids but the remaining ones,
known as the essential amino acids, must be supplied as such by food. To
make the best use of these *essential amino acids,* the body needs all 22
amino acids together at one time.

The best quality proteins, often called *complete proteins,* are those
which have all the essential amino acids present in goodly amounts. Foods
which contain these high-quality proteins are from animal sources such as
meat, poultry, fish, eggs, milk and cheese. It is wise to include some of
these foods in each meal.

Second-best foods for protein include soybeans, nuts, dry beans and
dry peas. When these are used as a main dish, some food from the complete
protein list (above) should be used in the same meal, even though the
quantity is small.

A still lower quantity and quality of protein is supplied by cereals,
bread, vegetables and fruit. However, if some of the complete proteins are
served in the same meal, they will make the less complete proteins more
valuable than if eaten alone.

Normal healthy adults will obtain enough protein if the diet is
selected according to the Basic Four Food Groups, Table 1, page 7, since
it includes adequate amounts of *protein-rich* foods. It will be noticed that
boys between the ages of 12 to 18 years and expectant and nursing mothers
need extra protein. They should have an extra-generous supply of milk and
eggs, which, in addition to protein, supply many of the bone and blood
building materials.

By consulting table on p 16, one can determine quickly the approximate protein content of one meal or of the day's dietary. If the total for the
day is lower than Table 4, page 10, advises for your age, sex and weight,
look for foods which have a higher protein content per serving—or add
protein by drinking more milk (each adult should have at least 1 pint daily
to insure enough calcium) or adding an extra egg for breakfast.

The following table shows approximately the number of grams of
protein in single servings of foods which are important sources of protein,
as well as the number of calories each serving supplies.

PROTEIN AND CALORIE VALUES OF SELECTED FOODS
Recommended Daily Dietary Allowance of Protein for Normal Adults: 58 to 80 gms.
(See Table 4, page 10 for other ages)

Practical Sources	Average Serving	Protein Grams	Calories
Dairy Products			
Cheese, Cottage, uncreamed	½ cup	17.5	98
Milk, whole	1 cup	9.0	160
Buttermilk, cultured, from skim milk	1 cup	9.0	90
Milk, skim and nonfat dry reconstituted	1 cup	9.0	90
Milk, nonfat dry	⅓ cup	8.3	83
Milk, evaporated, undiluted	½ cup	9.0	172
Milk, chocolate drink	1 cup	8.0	190
Cheese, American cheddar	1-inch cube	4.0	70
Cheese, American cheddar, process	1 oz	7.0	105
Cheese, Swiss	1 oz	8.0	105
Cheese, blue or Roquefort	1 oz	6.0	105
Cheese, cream	1 oz	2.0	105
Ice milk	½ cup (⅛ qt)	4.5	143
Ice cream, hand packed	½ cup (⅛ qt)	6.2	215
Ice cream, factory packed	⅛ of qt bulk	3.0	145
Eggs, large (24 oz per dozen) :			
Eggs, whole	1 (1.8 oz)	7.0	75
Egg white	1 (1.1 oz)	4.0	15
Egg yolk	1 (0.7 oz)	3.0	60
Fish			
Bass, baked	3½ oz (3x3x¾-in)	20.5	75
Bluefish, baked or broiled	3 oz	22	135
Clams, meat only	3 oz	11	70
Clams, canned, solids and liquid	3 oz	7	45
Crabmeat, canned or cooked	3½ oz (¾ cup)	17	100
Fish, lean, raw (cod, haddock, sole, etc.) **	3½ oz (3x3x⅜-in)	16-19	75
Fish, lean, raw, fried	3½ oz (raw)	16-19	165
Fish, med fat, raw (shad, halibut, mackerel)	3½ oz (3x2x1-inch)	16-19	140-200
Lobster, canned	3½ oz (⅔ cup scant)	18.4	32
Oysters, raw, meat only	½ cup	10.0	80
Salmon, canned, pink	3 oz	17	120
Shrimp, canned, meat only	2.2 oz (½ cup)	15.4	75
Tuna, canned in oil, drained	3 oz (¾ cup)	24	170
Meat, Poultry			
Beef, trimmed to retail basis*			
Lean and fat, pot roasted	3 oz	23	245
Lean only	2 oz	22	140
Hamburger, market ground, broiled	3 oz	21	245
ground lean	3 oz	23	185
Roast, oven cooked, no liquid added Relatively fat, such as rib			
Lean and fat	3 oz	17	375
Lean only	1.8 oz	14	125

Practical Sources	Average Serving	Protein Grams	Calories
Relatively lean, such as round			
Lean and fat	3 oz	25	165
Lean only	2.7 oz	24	125
Beef			
Steak, broiled			
Relatively fat, such as sirloin			
Lean and fat	3 oz	20	330
Lean only	2 oz	18	115
Relatively lean, such as round			
Lean and fat	3 oz	24	220
Lean only	2.4 oz	22	130
Corned Beef, canned	3 oz	22	185
Liver, fried	3 oz	22	195
Tongue, simmered	3 oz	18	205
Beef, dried or chipped	1 oz	9.5	58
Bologna	2 oz	7	175
Frankfurters, cooked	1 large (9 per lb)	6	155
Lamb, lean only, roast or broiled	2.6 oz	21	140
Pork, fresh, cooked, trimmed to retail basis*			
Chop, thick, with bone	1 chop, 3.5 oz	16	260
Roast, oven cooked, no liquid added			
Lean and fat, no bone	3 oz	21	310
Lean only	2.4 oz	20	175
Ham, smoked, lean and fat	3 oz	18	290
Luncheon meat, cooked ham, sliced	2 oz	13	170
Luncheon meat, spiced or unspiced	2 oz	8	165
Veal, cutlet, broiled, no bone	3 oz	23	185
Veal, roast medium, med fat	3 oz	23	305
Poultry			
Chicken, cooked			
Flesh and skin, broiled, no bone	3 oz	23	185
Breast, fried, with bone	½ breast, 3.3 oz	25	155
Breast, fried, flesh and skin only	2.7 oz	25	155
Leg, fried (thigh and drumstick) with bone	4.3 oz	27	245
Leg, fried, (drumstick only) with bone	2.1 oz	12	90
Chicken, canned, boneless	3 oz	18	170
Legumes, Nuts			
Beans, lima cooked	½ cup	8	130
Beans, dry, cooked (navy, pinto, kidney)	½ cup	7.5	115
Cowpeas, black-eye peas, dry, cooked	½ cup	6.5	95
Split peas, dry, cooked	½ cup	10	145
Almonds	¼ cup	6.5	212
Brazil nuts	¼ cup	5	228
Cashew nuts, roasted	¼ cup	5.7	190
Peanuts, roasted, shelled (halves)	¼ cup	9.2	210
Peanut butter	1 tbsp	4	95
Pecans, halves	¼ cup	2.5	190
Walnuts, black, chopped	¼ cup	6.5	195
Walnuts, English or Calif., halves	¼ cup	3.8	162

* Outer layer of fat removed to within approximately ½ inch of the lean. Deposits of fat within cut were not removed.
** When dipped in egg and crumbs and fried, add 75 calories per serving.

CARBOHYDRATE AND FAT

Unlike protein, no recommended daily dietary allowance has been established for either carbohydrate or fat, one of whose chief functions is to furnish calories for body energy. In 1962, carbohydrates furnished 47% and fats 41% of all calories consumed in the United States. In 1909, fat consumption was only 32% of the dietary calories.

Carbohydrates are essential in the diet as a source of energy for the brain and for other specialized purposes. Excess carbohydrate is readily converted to fat in the body but the reverse is not true.

Fat has several important functions in the body besides supplying energy: (1) it serves as a carrier of the fat-soluble vitamins A, D, E and K; (2) certain fats (especially those containing highly unsaturated fatty acids) are a source of essential fatty acids, a deficiency of which cause dermatitis, impairment of growth and reproductive capacity, and loss of efficiency of energy utilization; (3) it contributes to palatability of the diet; and (4) it is stored in the body to supply energy for later use and to serve (a) as padding around organs which helps absorb shocks, (b) as protection for nerves and (c) as insulation to help keep body temperature normal. The quantity of essential fatty acids (see 2 above) is not large and since they are widely distributed among common foods, most abundantly in edible oils, it seems probable that a mixed diet adequate in other nutrients will also supply an adequate amount of these essential fatty acids.

Cholesterol, a fatty substance of many foods, has attracted much attention in recent years as it is one of the materials found in deposits clogging the artery walls of victims of atherosclerosis. However, it is important to remember that cholesterol is essential to life; part of the body cholesterol comes from food eaten but by far the largest amount is produced in the body itself. The richest food sources of cholesterol are egg yolk, kidney, liver, sweetbreads, heart and fish roe. For other sources, see table on p 19.

Many factors are implicated in atherosclerosis besides cholesterol level of the blood stream, prominent among them being lack of exercise, overweight, excessive eating, glandular irregularity including diabetes, heredity, high blood pressure, excessive smoking, and stress of daily living.

There is insufficient evidence to indicate a drastic reduction in fat consumption for the population in general but a moderate reduction in fat and substitution of some polyunsaturated fats (as in vegetable oils) for saturated fats (as in solid fats) may be indicated. A moderate reduction of total fat consumption to around 25 or 30% of total calories can be accomplished by using a minimum of butter or margarine, cream, salad dressings, ice cream, pie and other rich desserts, but one should be sure to get sufficient protein in the diet by using skim milk, poultry, fish and lean meats. Any drastic change in diet or exercise should be under the supervision of a physician.

CHOLESTEROL CONTENT OF SELECTED FOODS*

Food	Size Serving	Cholesterol Milligrams	Food	Size Serving	Cholesterol Milligrams
Beef, raw, without bone	3½ oz	70	Lamb, raw, without bone	3½ oz	70
Brains, raw	1¾ oz	1,000	Lard and other animal fat	1 tbsp	15
Butter	1 tbsp	36	Liver, raw	3½ oz	300
Cheese, cheddar	1 oz	28	Lobster, meat only	1¾ oz	100
Cottage cheese, creamed	¼ cup	8	Margarine		
Cream cheese	2x1x¾"	36	All vegetable fat		0
Cheese spread	1 oz	19	⅔ animal fat, ½ veg fat	1 tbsp	9
Chicken, flesh only, raw	3½ oz	60	Milk		
Crab, meat only	1¾ oz	63	Fluid, whole	1 cup	27
Egg whole	1	248	Fluid, skim	1 cup	7
Egg white	1	0	Mutton, no bone	3½ oz	65
Egg yolk	1	248	Oysters, meat only	1¾ oz	100
Fish, steak	3½ oz	70	Pork, no bone	3½ oz	70
, fillet	3½ oz	70	Shrimp, flesh only	3½ oz	125
Heart, raw	3½ oz	150	Sweetbread (thymus)	3½ oz	250
Ice cream	4 oz	51	Veal, no bone	3½ oz	90
Kidney, raw	1¾ oz	188	Yeast, brewers	1 oz	204

* Calculated from Table 4, Composition of Foods, Agriculture Handbook No. 8, Agricultural Research Service, United States Department of Agriculture.

VITAMINS AND MINERALS

The body is quick to show any deficiency of calories in the diet by a loss of body weight; but it can go along for days, even for several weeks, with an inadequate supply of vitamins or minerals, with no noticeable effect. Yet a deficiency of vitamins or minerals continued over a period of time may cause even more serious consequences to health than the lack of sufficient calories.

To the scientists, vitamins are no longer mysterious substances, for they have been isolated, their chemical structures are known, and many have been produced in the laboratory. As these vitamins have become available, it has been possible to learn more about how each functions. There is still a lot to be learned, however, especially about how all the vitamins, minerals and other nutrients work *together* in the smoothly functioning machinery of our body.

The vitamins which require particular consideration in planning our diets are *vitamins A, D, C* (ascorbic acid), and *thiamine, riboflavin* and *niacin.* The last 3 are members of the "B-complex," which also includes such vitamins as *pyridoxine* (vitamin B_6), *pantothenic acid, para-amino benzoic acid, biotin, inositol, choline, folic acid* and *vitamin B_{12}.* All these vitamins serve important functions, and are considered to be essential for humans. For the normal, healthy individual, however, a diet supplying the first 6 vitamins mentioned above, and which is adequate in other respects, will undoubtedly meet the needs for all these lesser-known vitamins.

FUNCTIONS OF MINERALS

Minerals are building materials and are essential to body growth, maintenance and repair; and they are also important in regulating the functions of the body. There are only 3 minerals in which the diet is likely to be lacking: *Calcium, Iron* and *Iodine.*

Calcium and phosphorus work together in bone building with the help of vitamins A, C and D. These minerals are vital for the young child, the adolescent, and the pregnant and nursing mother. In the child and adolescent, they are needed to make hard, straight bones and sound teeth. In pregnancy and lactation, they are required to give the baby a good start and also to preserve the mother's health, since she must share her own body calcium with her child. A super-generous supply of calcium and phosphorus during pregnancy will help to put an end to the old superstition that the mother must lose "a tooth for every child." Adults require these same minerals to help *keep* their teeth and bones sound and healthy.

In nutritional anemia, the supply of hemoglobin (the red part of the blood) is low. *Iron and copper* are partners in the formation of this hemoglobin. New red cells must continually be manufactured by the body, and this is impossible without a sufficient supply of iron. Nutritional anemia is the most conspicuous result of iron deficiency, and many persons suffer from mild anemia which reveals itself chiefly in lowered vitality and a tendency to easy fatigue.

Iodine is needed by the thyroid gland to help keep it functioning normally, and it is the activity of the thyroid that regulates the utilization of the foods we consume. Excessive thyroid activity causes the metabolic rate (the rate at which food is converted into energy by the body) to go up, with resulting nervousness and loss of weight; subnormal thyroid activity causes it to go down, usually followed by a gain in weight and often by lethargy or overrelaxation. Sufficient iodine to maintain normal thyroid activity and normal metabolism is found in sea foods and in garden produce and drinking water in coastal areas. In the Great Plains area in the center of the country, and around the Great Lakes, it is desirable to supplement the diet with iodine. Sea foods and iodized salt are the only practical sources of iodine in these areas, where the soil and water are lacking in this mineral.

A number of other minerals, such as *manganese, cobalt, fluorine, silicon, zinc, nickel,* and *aluminum* are also found in the body. Some of these such as manganese and cobalt, are considered to be nutritionally essential, although their functions are not clearly defined. Cobalt has been found to form a part of the vitamin B_{12} molecule. Fluorine is found in the teeth, and a *certain limited amount* is believed to be helpful in preventing tooth decay. It is not known whether the other minerals are really "essential"—it is unlikely that the diet will fail to supply sufficient quantities of these trace elements, however.

FOOD SOURCES OF THE VITAMINS AND MINERALS

It is possible for normal individuals, under normal conditions, to get an adequate amount of all the vitamins and minerals in a well-balanced diet of natural foods with the possible exception of vitamin D. This vitamin is available in very few foods, such as vitamin D-enriched milk and certain enriched breads and breakfast cereals. It is found abundantly in fish liver oils.

Just what constitutes an adequate supply of vitamin D for adults has not been established. But 400 International units daily is the amount suggested for children and expectant and nursing mothers. To be on the safe side, this should be supplied by fish liver oil (on the advice of a physician, only) or by consuming one quart of vitamin D milk. Theoretically, it can be discontinued safely during the summer months if the child is much in the sun; but in practice, the sunshine is not always of good quality, due to smoke and haze, and the body may fail to manufacture sufficient vitamin D even when frequently exposed directly to the sun.

The foods listed in the following tables are the "practical" sources of the various vitamins and minerals. These figures are averages, and are presented to show the *approximate* amount supplied by one serving of the food. In interpreting this information, several factors must be considered. Different *varieties* of the same fruit or vegetable will vary in the amounts of minerals and vitamins they contain, and milk or eggs produced at different *seasons* of the year will also differ nutritionally. Even two tomatoes from the same vine will not contain exactly the same amounts of nutrients. Even if foods could be produced with identical food values, other factors such as *storage conditions* after harvesting, methods of storing in the home, the *method of cooking,* and length of *time between cooking and serving* will alter amounts of vitamins and minerals that will be available when food is eaten.

It is obvious, therefore, that figures could be presented which would differ from those given here. New research on vitamins and minerals constantly brings information to the attention of nutritionists. No attempt is made to list *all* of the foods that contain a particular vitamin or mineral. We have chosen to present only what we call "practical" sources.

A PRACTICAL SOURCE of a vitamin or mineral is a food that fits the following outline in every respect.

1. It must contain sufficient amounts of the vitamin or mineral in *one* serving to make a substantial contribution toward the recommended daily allowance; or it must be served often enough (for example, bread) so that the amount eaten during *one* day will make a worthwhile contribution to the recommended goal.

2. The food must be generally obtainable and commonly eaten to be considered practical.

3. The vitamins and minerals must be available to the human body: for example, spinach contains large amounts of calcium, but this calcium is in a form which cannot be assimilated by the human body, so it cannot be considered a practical source of this mineral. (However, spinach should not be shunned for it is an excellent source of iron.)

4. The minerals and vitamins must be present in such a form that they can be depended upon to be there in significant amounts when the food is eaten. For example: some foods contain sufficient amounts of vitamin C in the raw state to be considered a practical source, but because the food is always stored and then cooked, and because the vitamin may be partially destroyed by cooking and storing, the amount left at the time the food is eaten is not sufficient to call it a dependable and practical source.

So remember when reading the charts that follow, many foods that do not appear on the list may contain small amounts of the vitamins and minerals, and will add up and increase the day's total intake. For example: apples are not rich in vitamin C, but when citrus fruits are scarce or too expensive, the eating of several raw apples a day would contribute a worthwhile and significant amount of this vitamin. It is easy to make the mistake of thinking that if a food does not contain large amounts of a certain vitamin or mineral, it is not a good food. There are five essential food elements (protein, carbohydrates, fats, minerals and vitamins), and a mixed diet of many foods is absolutely essential to supply all of these elements in an adequate diet.

If information is desired on nutritive value of more foods than are given on pages 16 to 39, a copy of No 4 below (from which most of these figures were taken) may be obtained for 20 cents by writing to Superintendent of Documents, U.S. Government Printing Office, Washington 25, D.C.

REFERENCES FOR INFORMATION ON NUTRITION

1. Food. The Yearbook of Agriculture, 1959. United States Department of Agriculture, Washington, D.C.

2. Laboratory Handbook for Dietetics. Revised by Clara Mae Taylor, Ph.D. and Grace Mae Leod, Ph.D., Columbia University, 1959. The Macmillan Company, New York.

3. Nutrition and Physical Fitness. L. Jean Bogert, Ph.D. Seventh Edition, 1955. W. B. Saunders Company, Philadelphia, Pennsylvania.

4. Nutritive Values of Foods. Home and Garden Bulletin No. 72, 1964. United States Department of Agriculture, Washington, D.C.

5. Recommended Dietary Allowances. National Research Council, Publication 1146. Revised 1964. Washington, D.C.

6. Composition of Foods. Agriculture Handbook No. 8, 1963. Agricultural Research Service, United States Department of Agriculture.

ASCORBIC ACID
(Vitamin C)

When You Think of
ASCORBIC ACID
Think of These
Citrus Fruits and Tomatoes   Green and Leafy Vegetables
Other Fruits and Vegetables

Special attention should be paid to the amount of vitamin C in meals served as the American Diet is likely to be low in this important vitamin which contributes so much to health. In addition to this, ascorbic acid (vitamin C) is the most easily destroyed of all the vitamins. It dissolves in the cooking water; it is partially destroyed by heat; and it deteriorates on standing when exposed to the air. Cooking should be done quickly with small amounts of water, and this water served with vegetables. Soda is especially destructive to this vitamin, and should never be added when cooking green vegetables. A slight amount of acid in the food helps to preserve ascorbic acid which explains why citrus fruits and tomatoes are particularly valuable sources. To help prevent losses of ascorbic acid, foods should be stored covered and at a low temperature. If juice is squeezed the night before using, it should be kept refrigerated and with as little space as possible between juice and cover.

When marketing, select fruits and especially vegetables which have been stored at a low temperature or on crushed ice.

ASCORBIC ACID (VITAMIN C) AND CALORIE VALUES OF SELECTED FOODS

Recommended Daily Dietary Allowance for Normal Adults: 70 milligrams

(See Table 4, page 10 for other ages)

Practical Sources	Average Serving	Vitamin C† Mg.	Calories
Fruits			
Oranges*			
Whole, fresh	1 med (3-inch diam)	75	75
Juice, fresh; frozen, conc., diluted	1 cup (8 oz)	112-125	110
Grapefruit*			
Whole, fresh	½ med (4¼-inch diam)	50	50
Juice, fresh; frozen, conc., diluted	1 cup	95	100
Sections, fresh	1 cup	72	75
Sections, canned, sweet'd, solids and liquid	1 cup	75	175
Tomatoes*			
Whole, fresh	1 med (3 per lb)	35	30
Canned or cooked	½ cup	20	24
Juice, canned	1 cup	38	50
Tangerines*			
Whole, fresh	1 med (4 per lb)	26	40
Lemon juice, fresh	2 tbsp	14	10
Lime juice, fresh	2 tbsp	10	8
Strawberries, fresh*	1 cup	88	55
Strawberries, frozen	2½ oz	37	75
Melons, cantaloupe*	½ med (5-inch diam)	63	60
watermelon	2 lb with rind	30	115
Papaya, raw, ½-inch cubes	1 cup	102	70
Pineapple, raw, diced	1 cup	24	75
Pineapple, canned	1 large slice, 2 tbsp juice	8	90
Pineapple, juice	6 oz	16	100
Apples, fresh	1 med (3 per lb)	3	70
Apricots	3 med (12 per lb)	10	55
Bananas	1 med (3 per lb)	10	85
Cherries, fresh, sweet	½ cup	6	40
Peaches, fresh	1 med (4 per lb)	7	35
Raspberries, fresh	1 cup	31	70

Practical Sources	Average Serving	Vitamin C† Mg.	Calories
Green and Leafy Vegetables			
Broccoli spears, cooked*	1 cup, 3 med flowers	135	40
Brussels sprouts*	1 cup	113	45
Cabbage, raw, fresh, green, shredded*	1 cup (3½ oz)	50	25
Cabbage, cooked, 7 min*	1 cup	53	40
Green beans, cooked short time	½ cup	8	15
Green beans, canned, drained	½ cup	4	20
Green peppers, raw	1 med (6 per lb)	80	15
Green, spinach, kale, chard, etc, cooked	½ cup	25	20
Peas, green, cooked	½ cup	16	55
Lettuce, head	¼ lb	7	15
*Other Vegetables***			
Cauliflower, raw	¼ cup	22-30	9
Cauliflower, cooked	⅔ cup	44	17
Kohlrabi, cooked	¾ cup	35	15
Lima beans, fresh, immature, cooked	½ cup	14	90
Rutabagus, cooked	½ cup	12-24	17
Sweet potatoes, peeled after cooking	1 med (6 oz, raw)	24	160
Sweet potatoes, canned, solid	½ cup	15	118
White potatoes, peeled after cooking	1 med (6 oz, raw)	20	90
White potatoes, mashed, with milk	¾ cup	14	109

† The vitamin C values given for cooked foods are for foods cooked under favorable conditions (small amount of water, short cooking time, etc.). As much as 70 to 90% may be lost by improper cooking and discarding cooking water.
* These foods are the best sources of ascorbic acid. They contain large amounts of the vitamin in the raw state. The skin protects the vitamin from air, the acid in the fruit helps preserve the vitamin, and they are most generally eaten raw.
** These foods will supply the day's ascorbic acid allowance in the summer when generous amounts of fresh fruits and vegetables are available and are eaten in the raw state. At other seasons they should not be depended upon regularly for the complete allowance. One serving of citrus fruit or tomato supplemented by these other foods is the safest and wisest rule to follow.

Functions: Ascorbic acid plays an important role in tooth and bone formation, facilitates absorption of iron into blood stream, has a positive effect on mineral retention, helps in metabolic use of folic acid, is active in the healing of wounds and research *indicates* that a consistently high daily intake will defer the process of aging. Lack of sufficient vitamin C has been associated with low hemoglobin levels (a measure of one kind of anemia); greater liability to infections such as pulmonary tuberculosis, diphtheria, rheumatism and pneumonia; lack of energy; fleeting pains in the joints; and bleeding gums. A severe deficiency causes scurvy. Large doses of vitamin C over prolonged periods show no harmful effects.

THIAMINE

(Vitamin B$_1$)

When You Think of
THIAMINE
Think of These

Meat, Fish and Poultry   **Cereals Whole or Enriched**
Vegetables   **Eggs and Dairy Products**   **Fruits and Nuts**

Thiamine is fairly resistant to dry heat but some is destroyed by roasting (meats) and toasting (breads). This vitamin is not found in large amounts in most foods and it is necessary to include several foods from the following list in the diet every day to insure meeting the recommended allowance.

There may be considerable loss of thiamine in the preparation and cooking of food. Care should be taken not to soak fruits and vegetables in water as thiamine is soluble even in cold water. Such foods should be cooked quickly in as little water as possible and the cooking liquid used in sauces and gravies. Thiamine is less quickly destroyed when cooked in a liquid which is slightly acid but an alkaline liquid (such as hard water or water to which soda has been added) causes rapid loss.

THIAMINE (Vitamin B$_1$) AND CALORIE VALUES OF SELECTED FOODS

Recommended Daily Dietary Allowance for Normal Adults: 0.8 to 1.2 milligrams

(See Table 4, page 10 for other ages)

Practical Sources	Average Serving	Thiamine Mg.	Calories
Meat, Poultry			
Pork, fresh, trimmed to retail basis*			
Chop, thick with bone, cooked	1 chop, 3.5 oz	.63	260
Roast, oven cooked, no liquid added			
Lean and fat, no bone	3 oz	.78	310
Lean only	2.4 oz	.73	175
Simmered, no bone, lean only	2.4 oz	.46	148
Bacon, broiled or fried crisp	2 slices	.08	100
Ham, smoked, lean and fat	3 oz	.40	245
Luncheon meat, boiled ham, sliced	2 oz	.25	135
Luncheon meat, canned, spiced or unspiced	2 oz	.18	165
Beef hearts, trimmed of fat, braised	3 oz	.21	160
Beef liver, fried	3 oz	.22	180
Beef tongue, simmered	3 oz	.04	210

* Outer layer of fat removed to within approximately ½ inch of the lean. Deposits of fat within cut were not removed.

Practical Sources	Average Serving	Thiamine Mg.	Calories
Lamb, lean only, no bone, cooked	2.6 oz	.11	140
Veal, roasted, med done, med fat	3 oz	.11	230
Bologna, (2 slices 4x4x0.1-inch)	2 oz	.09	175
Frankfurter (9 per lb)	1 large	.08	155
Chicken, leg, thigh and drumstick	4.3 oz	.05	245
breast (both fried)	3.3 oz	.04	155
canned, boneless	3 oz	.03	170
Fish and Shellfish			
Mackerel, Atlantic, broiled	3 oz	.13	200
Oysters, meat only (6-10 med selects)	½ cup	.16	80
Shad, baked	3 oz	.11	170
Whole Grain and Enriched Cereals			
Bread, cracked wheat (20 slices per lb loaf)	1 slice	.02	60
Bread, whole wheat, graham	1 slice	.03	55
Bread, whole wheat, graham, toasted	1 slice	.03	55
Bread, white, enriched	1 slice	.06	60
Cornflakes, enriched	1 oz	.12	110
Cornmeal, whole ground	1 cup	.45	420
Cornmeal, degermed, enriched	1 cup	.64	525
Corn, puffed, enriched	1 oz	.12	110
Farina, cooked, enriched	1 cup	.11	105
Macaroni, enriched, cooked until tender	1 cup	.19	155
Macaroni, (enriched, cooked 8-10 min.) and cheese, baked	1 cup	.22	475
Muffins, with enriched flour	1 (2¾-inch diam)	.11	135
Noodles, egg, enriched, cooked	1 cup	.23	200
Oatmeal, regular or quick, cooked	1 cup	.19	130
Rice, puffed, enriched	1 cup (½ oz)	.06	55
Rice, parboiled type, cooked	1 cup	.10	185
Rice, cooked, white	1 cup	.19	185
Rice flakes, enriched	1 cup (1 oz)	.10	115
Rolls, of enriched flour	1 roll (12 per lb)	.11	115
Spaghetti, enriched, cooked tender	1 cup	.19	155
Wheat, puffed, enriched	1 oz	.15	105
Wheat, puffed, enriched, presweetened	1 oz	.14	105
Wheat flakes, enriched	1 oz	.18	100
Whole wheat flour, hard, stirred	1 cup (¼ lb)	.66	400
All purpose flour, enriched, sifted	1 cup	.48	400
Wheat germ, stirred	1 cup	1.39	245
Vegetables			
Asparagus, cooked, cut spears	½ cup	.13	17
Bean sprouts (soybeans), raw	1 cup	.12	30
Broccoli spears, cooked	1 cup	.14	40
Collards, cooked	½ cup	.13	28
Cowpeas, cooked, immature	½ cup	.25	88
Dandelion greens	½ cup	.12	30
Peas, green, cooked	½ cup	.22	57
Peas, green, canned, solids and liquid	½ cup	.11	82
Potatoes, baked, medium	1 (3 per lb)	.10	90
Sweet potatoes, baked, small	1 (3 per lb)	.10	155

Practical Sources	Average Serving	Thiamine Mg.	Calories
Sweet potatoes, boiled (peeled after boiling)	1 (3 per lb)	.13	170
Soybeans, cooked	½ cup	.45	105
Spinach, cooked	½ cup	.06	20
Spinach, canned, drained, solids	½ cup	.03	22
Tomatoes, raw (med, 3 per lb)	1 med	.10	35
Tomatoes, cooked or canned	1 cup	.13	50
Tomato juice	1 cup	.13	45
Turnip greens, cooked, small amount of water	½ cup	.10	15
Fruits			
Avocados, raw, 3⅓x4¼" peeled	½	.12	185
Cantaloupe, med. 5" diam, about 1⅔ lb	½ melon	.08	60
Cherries, raw, sweet	1 cup	.06	80
Cherries, canned, red sour pitted	1 cup	.07	105
Dates, "fresh" and dried, pitted, cut	1 cup	.16	490
Grapefruit			
Raw sections	½ cup	.07	75
4½" diam, size 64 red or white	½ fruit	.05	55
Canned, syrup, solid and liquid	1 cup	.07	175
Canned, water pack, solid and liquid	1 cup	.07	70
Grapefruit juice			
Fresh	1 cup	.09	95
Canned, unsweetened	1 cup	.07	100
Canned, sweetened	1 cup	.07	130
Frozen, concentrate, unsweetened, diluted	1 cup	.10	100
Frozen, concentrate, sweetened, diluted	1 cup	.08	115
Grape juice, bottled	1 cup	.10	165
Oranges, raw, 3" diam, size 88	1	.12-.16	75
Orange juice, fresh	1 cup	.21	110
Orange juice, frozen concentrate, diluted (3 parts water : 1 part juice)	1 cup	.21	110
Papaya, raw, ½-inch cubes	1 cup	.07	70
Pineapple, raw, diced	1 cup	.12	75
Pineapple, canned, slices	1 large, 2 tbsp juice	.09	90
Pineapple, juice, canned	1 cup	.12	135
Prunes, cooked, unsweetened, med.	17-18 prunes (1 cup)	.08	295
Raisins, dried	1 cup	.18	460
Watermelon, raw, 4x8-inch wedge	2 lbs with rind	.13	115
Legumes, Nuts			
Almonds, shelled	¼ cup	.09	212
Beans, canned, navy, Great Northern, red	1 cup	.13	230
Beans, lima, cooked	1 cup	.26	260
Brazil nuts, broken pieces	¼ cup	.33	225
Cashews, roasted	¼ cup	.14	190
Cowpeas or black-eye peas, dried, cooked	1 cup	.41	190
Peanuts, roasted, shelled, halves	¼ cup	.11	210
Peanut butter	1 tbsp	.02	95
Peas, split, dry, cooked	1 cup	.37	290
Pecans, halves	¼ cup	.24	185
Walnuts, black, chopped	¼ cup	.07	195
Walnuts, English	¼ cup	.08	162

Practical Sources	Average Serving	Thiamine Mg.	Calories
Eggs and Dairy Products			
Milk, whole	1 cup	.08	160
Milk, skim	1 cup	.10	90
Buttermilk	1 cup	.09	90
Evaporated milk, diluted (equal parts)	1 cup	.05	172
Nonfat dry milk, not reconstituted	1 cup	.28	251
Egg yolk, large (24 oz per dozen eggs)	1 yolk	.04	60

Function: Thiamine or vitamin B_1 is essential for a normal rate of growth in children, for normal appetite, a healthy nervous system and full utilization of food eaten. A low intake of thiamine may result in such symptoms as nervous irritability, fatigue, lassitude, loss of interest in food, depressed mental state, dizziness, insomnia, loss of weight and lowered blood pressure. Since the enrichment of cereals and grain products with thiamine and other nutrients, beriberi, the extreme deficiency disease due to lack of vitamin B_1, is no longer common in the United States.

RIBOFLAVIN

(Vitamin B_2, formerly called G)

When You Think of
RIBOFLAVIN
Think of These

Eggs and Dairy Products   **Meat, Fish and Poultry**
Vegetables   **Cereal Products**

Riboflavin is not affected by heat to any great extent, and it is not destroyed by contact with air, but it is destroyed by light. Foods such as milk, therefore, suffer nutritional losses when allowed to stand in the sunshine, the loss depending on the time of standing and the quality of the sunshine. Riboflavin does dissolve in water. For this reason, vegetables should be cooked in small amounts of water, and the leftover liquid from vegetables, as well as gravies and juices from meats, should *always* be served. No doubt many persons on low-cost diets (and some who spend more money for food) do not get enough riboflavin. Without a liberal use of milk, eggs, leafy vegetables and legumes, there is likely to be a deficiency in this vitamin.

RIBOFLAVIN (Vitamin B₂) AND CALORIE VALUES OF SELECTED FOODS

Recommended Daily Dietary Allowance for Normal Adults: 0.8 to 2.0 milligrams

(See Table 4, page 10 for other ages)

Practical Sources	Average Serving	Riboflavin Mg.	Calories
Meat, Fish and Poultry			
Liver, beef, fried	3 oz	3.55	195
Heart, beef, braised, fat trimmed off	3 oz	1.04	160
Tongue, beef, simmered	3 oz	.25	210
Veal, roasted med done, med fat	3 oz	.26	230
Lamb, leg, roasted, lean and fat	3 oz	.23	235
Lamb, leg, roasted, lean only	2.5 oz	.21	130
Ham, lean and fat	3 oz	.16	245
Luncheon meat, boiled ham, sliced	2 oz	.09	135
Luncheon meat, canned, spiced or unspiced	2 oz	.12	165
Pork chop, thick, with bone	3.5 oz	.18	260
Pork roast, oven cooked, no liquid added			
Lean and fat, no bone	3 oz	.22	310
Lean only	2.4 oz	.21	175
Pork cuts, simmered			
Lean and fat	3 oz	.21	320
Lean only	2.2 oz	.19	135
Beef trimmed to retail basis*			
Relatively fat, such as rib			
Roast (dry heat), lean and fat	3 oz	.13	375
Roast (dry heat), lean only	1.8 oz	.11	125
Relatively lean, such as round			
Lean and fat	3 oz	.19	165
Lean only	2.5 oz	.18	125
Beef, chipped or dried	2 oz	.18	115
Bologna, 2 slices, 4x4x0.1-inch	2 oz	.12	175
Frankfurter cooked (9 per lb)	1 large	.10	155
Chicken, leg and thigh, fried			
with bone	4.3 oz	.18	245
without bone	3.1 oz	.18	245
Chicken breast, fried, with bone, ½ breast	3.3 oz	.17	155
Fish and Shellfish			
Mackerel, Atlantic, broiled	3 oz	.23	200
Oysters, meat only (7-10 med selects)	½ cup	.21	80
Salmon, pink, canned	3 oz	.16	120
Shad, baked	3 oz	.22	170
Dairy Products and Eggs			
Milk, whole	1 cup	.42	160
Milk, skim	1 cup	.44	90
Buttermilk, cultured	1 cup	.44	90
Milk, dry, nonfat (not reconstituted)	⅓ cup	.41	83
Cream, half and half	¼ cup	.09	81
Cream, coffee	¼ cup	.09	126
Cheese, cheddar	1-inch cube	.08	70
Cheese, cottage, creamed	½ cup	.28	120

* See * page 26.

Practical Sources	Average Serving	Riboflavin Mg.	Calories
Eggs, large (24 oz per doz)	1 large	.16	75
Egg white	1 large	.09	15
Egg yolk	1 large	.07	60
Vegetables			
Soybeans, cooked	½ cup	.23	105
Turnip greens, canned, solids and liquid	½ cup	.10	20
Turnip greens, fresh, cooked	½ cup	.18	15
Collards, cooked	½ cup	.18	28
Spinach, cooked	½ cup	.12	20
Asparagus, cooked, cut spears	½ cup	.16	18
Peas, green, cooked	½ cup	.08	58
Broccoli spears, cooked	1 cup	.29	40
Mushrooms, canned, solids and liquid	¼ cup	.15	8
Fruits			
Avocados, 3 by 4-inches	½ avocado	.21	185
Avocados, ½-inch cubes	1 cup	.30	260
Orange juice	1 cup	.06	100
Grapefruit juice	1 cup	.04	95
Papayas, ½-inch cubes	1 cup	.08	70
Peach, med, 2-inch diam (4 per lb)	1 med	.05	35
Peaches, dried, cooked, unsweetened	½ cup	.07	110
Prunes, dried, cooked, unsweetened	½ cup (9 prunes, 3 tbsp syrup)	.09	150
Raspberries, red, raw	1 cup	.11	70
Strawberries, raw, capped	1 cup	.10	55
Watermelon, raw, wedge 4x8"	2 lbs with rind	.13	115
Nuts and Legumes			
Almonds, shelled	¼ cup	.33	212
Beans, dry, canned (navy, Great Northern, red, etc.)	1 cup	.10	230
Beans, lima, cooked	1 cup	.12	260
Cashews, roasted	¼ cup	.12	192
Peanuts, roasted, shelled	¼ cup	.05	210
Split peas, dry, cooked	1 cup	.22	290
Whole Grain and Enriched Cereals			
Bread, white, enriched	1 slice	.04	60
Bread, cracked wheat	1 slice	.02	60
Bread, whole wheat and grahams	1 slice	.03	55
Macaroni, enriched, cooked tender	1 cup	.11	155
Macaroni, enriched, and cheese, baked	1 cup	.46	475
Noodles (egg), cooked, enriched	1 cup	.14	200
Noodles (egg), cooked, not enriched	1 cup	.03	200
Wheat germ, stirred	1 cup	.46	245

Function: B_2 (vitamin G), or riboflavin, is associated with normal growth, general health, successful reproduction and better utilization of all food eaten. A deficiency of riboflavin results in such symptoms as cracks or fissures at the corner of the mouth, and an oily dermatitis around the folds of the nose and mouth. Certain changes may also take place in the eyes, which may be indicated by sensitivity to light or excessive production of tears.

NIACIN

When You Think of

NIACIN

Think of These

Meat, Fish and Poultry	Cereal Products
Vegetables	Fruits and Nuts

Niacin, the third member of the B-complex, is not affected by heat to any great extent, and is not destroyed by contact with the air. However, it does dissolve in water. Therefore, it is important to cook in small amounts of water and to use the cooking liquid from vegetables and the gravies and juices from meats.

The *niacin "equivalent,"* as noted in Table 4, page 10, needs some explanation. It is now known that tryptophane, one of the essential amino acids, is partially converted to niacin in the body. Food tables do not include this source of niacin as yet but a fairly accurate way has been found to compute the niacin equivalent furnished by the rest of the food consumed: Add the total grams of protein in the diet for the day and divide by 6 to get the total number of milligrams of niacin equivalent furnished by the protein. Add to this the amount of niacin in the food eaten as given in the table below. Milk furnishes even more niacin equivalent than average protein because of its extremely high quality protein. One quart of milk contains only 1.1 mg. of niacin as such, but contains enough tryptophane to make 8.0 mg. of niacin or a total of 9.1 mg. of niacin equivalent.

If milk, meats, whole grains or enriched cereals, leafy and other vegetables are used freely, the diet will supply a sufficient amount of niacin; if not, the amount of niacin consumed is likely to be less than will cause buoyant health although it is not likely to be so low as to cause symptoms of pellagra, which has practically disappeared from the United States since the cereal and bread enrichment program was started in 1941.

NIACIN AND CALORIE VALUES OF SELECTED FOODS
Recommended Daily Dietary Allowances for Normal Adults:
13-19 mg Niacin Equivalent**

(See Table 4, page 10 for other ages)

Practical Sources	Average Serving	Niacin Mg.	Calories
Meat, Poultry			
Bacon, broiled or fried crisp	2 slices	.8	100

Practical Sources	Average Serving	Niacin Mg.	Calories
Beef, trimmed to retail basis,* cooked			
Heart, fat trimmed off, braised	3 oz	6.5	160
Liver, fried	3 oz	14.1	195
Tongue, simmered	3 oz	3.0	210
Cuts, braised, simmered or pot roasted			
Lean and fat	3 oz	3.5	245
Lean only	2.5 oz	3.3	140
Hamburger, broiled			
Market ground	3 oz	4.6	245
Ground lean	3 oz	5.1	185
Roast, oven-cooked, no liquid added			
Relatively fat, as rib			
Lean and fat	3 oz	3.1	375
Lean only	1.8 oz	2.6	125
Relatively lean, such as round			
Lean and fat	3 oz	4.5	165
Lean only	2.5 oz	4.3	125
Steak, Sirloin, lean and fat	3 oz	4.0	330
Steak, Sirloin, lean only	2 oz	3.6	115
Steak, Round, lean and fat	3 oz	4.8	220
Steak, Round, lean only	2.4 oz	4.1	130
Corned beef	3 oz	2.9	185
Dried beef, (or chipped)	2 oz	2.2	115
Chicken, cooked			
Broiled, no bone	3 oz	7.4	115
Breast, fried, ½ breast			
with bone	3.3 oz	11.2	155
without bone	2.7 oz	11.2	155
Drumstick, fried, with bone	2.1 oz	2.7	90
Canned, boneless	3 oz	3.7	170
Lamb, trimmed to retail basis, cooked			
Chop, thick, with bone, broiled			
Lean and fat	4.8 oz	5.6	400
Lean only	2.6 oz	4.5	140
Leg, roasted, lean and fat	3 oz	4.7	235
Lean only	2.5 oz	4.4	130
Pork, fresh, trimmed to retail basis, cooked			
Chop, thick, with bone	3.5 oz	3.8	260
Lean and fat	2.3 oz	3.8	260
Lean only	1.7 oz	3.3	130
Roast, oven-cooked, no liquid added			
Lean and fat	3 oz	4.7	310
Lean only	2.4 oz	4.4	175
Pork, cured. Ham, lean and fat	3 oz	3.1	245
Luncheon meat, boiled ham, sliced	2 oz	1.5	135
Luncheon meat, canned, spiced or not	2 oz	1.6	165
Bologna, slice 4x4x0.1-inch	2 slices	1.5	172
Frankfurter, cooked, 9 per lb	1 large	1.3	155
Veal, cutlet, broiled, no bone	3 oz	4.6	185
Veal, roast, med fat, med done	3 oz	6.6	230
Fish and Shellfish			
Bluefish, baked or broiled	3 oz	1.6	135
Clams, raw, meat only	3 oz	1.1	65
Clams, canned, solids and liquid	3 oz	.9	45
Crabmeat, canned or cooked	3 oz	1.6	85
Haddock, fried	3 oz	2.7	140

Practical Sources	Average Serving	Niacin Mg.	Calories
Mackerel, Atlantic, broiled	3 oz	6.5	200
Mackerel, Pacific, canned, solids and liquid	3 oz	7.4	155
Ocean Perch, breaded, fried	3 oz	1.5	195
Oysters, raw	½ cup	3.0	80
Salmon, pink, canned	3 oz	6.8	120
Sardines, Atlantic, canned, drained	3 oz	4.6	175
Shad, baked	3 oz	7.3	170
Shrimp, canned, meat only	3 oz	1.5	100
Swordfish, broiled with butter	3 oz	9.3	150
Tuna, canned in oil, drained	3 oz	10.1	170
Nuts, Legumes			
Almonds	¼ cup	1.2	212
Peanuts, roasted, shelled, halves	¼ cup	6.1	210
Peanut butter	1 tbsp	2.4	95
Beans, dry, canned, navy, red	1 cup	1.5	230
Peas, split, dry, cooked	1 cup	2.2	290
Vegetables			
Asparagus, cut spears	½ cup	1.2	18
Asparagus, canned	6 spears	.8	20
Lima beans, immature, cooked	½ cup	1.0	90
Sweet corn, cooked, ear 5 by 1¾-inch	1 ear	1.0	70
Sweet corn, canned, solids and liquid	½ cup	1.2	85
Mushrooms, canned, solids and liquid	¼ cup	1.2	8
Peas, green, cooked	½ cup	1.8	55
Peas, green, canned, solids and liquid	½ cup	1.1	85
Potatoes, Baked, med, 3 per lb	1 med	1.7	90
Potatoes, peeled before boiling	1 med	1.4	80
Cooked Soybeans	½ cup	1.3	105
Tomato juice, canned	1 cup	1.8	45
Fruits			
Avocados, raw (3x4-inches)	½	1.7	185
Avocados, ½-inch cubes	1 cup	2.4	260
Cantaloupe, med, 5-inch diam	½ melon	1.2	60
Orange juice	1 cup	.9	100
Peaches, whole, raw, 4 per lb	1 peach	1.0	35
Peaches, canned, solids and liquid	½ cup	.7	100
Prunes, cooked, not sweetened	½ cup	.9	150
Raspberries, raw	1 cup	1.1	70
Strawberries, raw	1 cup	1.0	55
Whole Grain and Enriched Products			
White bread, enriched (20 slices per lb)	1 slice	.5	60
Whole-wheat bread	1 slice	.7	55
Rye bread	1 slice	.3	55
Cornflakes	1 oz	.6	110
Farina, enriched, cooked	1 cup	1.0	100
Macaroni, enriched, cooked until tender	1 cup	1.5	155
Noodles, egg, enriched, cooked	1 cup	1.8	200
Rice, parboiled, cooked	1 cup	2.0	185
Rice, white, cooked	1 cup	1.6	185
Spaghetti, enriched, cooked	1 cup	1.5	155
Cornmeal, dry, whole ground	1 cup	2.4	420
Cornmeal, dry, degermed	1 cup	5.1	525

Practical Sources	Average Serving	Niacin Mg.	Calories
Rice flakes, enriched	1 cup	1.6	115
Wheat, puffed, enriched	1 oz	2.2	105
Wheat, shredded, plain (all shapes)	1 oz	1.2	100
Wheat flakes, enriched	1 oz	1.4	100
Wheat flours			
whole wheat, hard, stirred	1 cup	5.2	400
all-purpose, or self-rising, enriched	1 cup	3.8	400
Wheat germ	1 cup	2.9	245
Soups, canned; ready-to-serve			
Bean with pork	1 cup	1.0	170
Clam chowder	1 cup	1.0	85
Pea	1 cup	1.0	130
Yeast, Compressed	1 oz	3.2	25
Dry, active	1 oz	10.4	80
Brewer's dry	1 tbsp	3.0	25

* See * page 26.
** Niacin equivalents include dietary sources of preformed vitamin and the precursor, trypto-phane (one of the amino acids). Niacin figures only are given in this table. Among the best sources of tryptophane are milk, eggs, legumes and nuts. A diet which contains a generous amount of protein, provides enough tryptophane to increase the niacin value by about one-third.

Function: Niacin (formerly called nicotinic acid) is associated with normal growth and a healthy nervous system. A severe deficiency of this vitamin results in the disease pellagra.

VITAMIN A

When You Think of

VITAMIN A

Think of These

Green and Yellow Vegetables Yellow and Yellow-Red Fruits
Eggs and Dairy Products

Vitamin A is the most stable of the vitamins. It is not destroyed by acid or alkali. It is not dissolved in water. It does not deteriorate on exposure to air except in the presence of rancid fat. Vitamin A may be formed in the body from carotene, the yellow coloring, which occurs in most *yellow fruits and vegetables*. Green and green leafy vegetables are also good sources of carotene. In general, the deepest color indicates the highest carotene content and the greatest potential vitamin A value. This vitamin is fairly stable to all cooking procedures, but since many of the other vitamins are also found in the same foods with vitamin A, proper cooking of all vegetables and the use of cooking liquid is still just as important.

VITAMIN A AND CALORIE VALUE OF SELECTED FOODS

Recommended Daily Dietary Allowance for Normal Adults: 5000 I U

(*See Table 4, page 10 for other ages*)

Practical Sources	Average Serving	Vitamin A* IU	Calories*
Vegetables: Dark Green, Leafy and Yellow			
Spinach, cooked	½ cup	7,290	20
Carrots, cooked, diced	½ cup	7,610	22
Carrots, raw	1 (1x5½-inches)	5,500	20
Sweet potato, baked	1 med (4 per lb)	8,970	155
Sweet potato, canned, solid pack	½ cup	8,500	117
Squash, yellow, winter, baked, mashed	½ cup	4,300	65
Curly endive, escarole	2 oz	1,870	10
Broccoli, cooked	1 cup	3,750	40
Kale, cooked	½ cup	4,070	15
Asparagus, green, cooked	½ cup	790	17
Tomatoes	1 med (3 per lb)	1,350	35
Pumpkin, canned	⅙ cup	2,430	13
Peas, green, fresh cooked or canned	½ cup	430-560	55-85
Beans, green, fresh cooked or canned	½ cup	340	15-22
Parsley	1 tbsp, chopped	300	1
Okra, cooked	8 pods, 3x⅝-inch	420	30
Tomato juice	1 cup (8 oz)	1,940	45
Tomatoes, canned	½ cup	1,090	25
Turnip greens, cooked or canned	½ cup	4,570-5,450*	15-20
Fruits: Yellow and Yellow-Red			
Apricots, dried, cooked, unsweetened	½ cup	4,275	120
Apricots, fresh	3 med (12 per lb)	2,890	55
Cantaloupe, med, 5½-inch diam	½	6,540	60
Papaya, raw, ½-inch cubes	1 cup	3,190	70
Watermelon	2 lb with rind	2,530	120
Peach, fresh, yellow	1 med (4 per lb)	1,320	35
Peaches, canned, slices	½ cup	550	100
Tangerine juice, canned, frozen, diluted	1 cup	1,020	105-115
Prunes, dried, cooked, unsweetened	½ cup, 3 tbsp juice	930	150
Cherries, canned, red sour, pitted	½ cup	840	115
Orange juice, fresh or frozen, diluted	1 cup	500	100-110
Eggs and Dairy Products			
Egg yolks (24 oz per doz eggs)	1 med	580	60
Cream, half-and-half	¼ cup	290	81
Butter or margarine**	1 tbsp	460	100
Whole milk	1 cup	350	160
Cheese, cheddar or American	1-inch cube	220	70
Cheese, blue or Roquefort	1 oz	350	105
Meats			
Liver, beef, fried	3 oz	45,500	195
Liver Sausage	2 oz	3,000	190
Fish Liver Oils	on advice of physician only	see container	see container

* Second figure is for canned food including both solids and liquid.
** Based on deep yellow color.

Function: Vitamin A helps to keep the skin and mucous membranes of the body in good condition, and by so doing helps build up resistance to disease. It prevents certain eye diseases (it is a specific remedy for some forms of night blindness); aids in bone growth, maintaining tooth enamel and helps prevent degenerative changes in nerves.

VITAMIN D

Vitamin D is known as the "sunshine" vitamin, because it can be produced by the action of sunshine, or ultra-violet light on certain substances in the skin. It is most important during the growth period, when its presence is essential to enable the body to use its supply of calcium and phosphorus efficiently in building strong bones and teeth. Absence of vitamin D from the diet in childhood may produce rickets. Vitamin D is not present naturally in any foods except in extremely small amounts but it may be obtained from fish liver oils and from milk enriched with vitamin D. The decline in rickets in recent decades can be credited in large part to the fortification of cow's milk and a few other foods with vitamin D.

It is not definitely known how important vitamin D is in the diet of the adult, but it seems that a certain amount is necessary to enable the body to make use of the calcium and phosphorus supplied by food. It is thought that most adults will receive enough vitamin D from exposure to sunlight but those who do not go out in the sun, such as invalids or nightworkers, should supplement their diet with vitamin D.

THE VITAMIN FAD

Since science has discovered how to prepare vitamin concentrates, either from natural foods or with synthetic vitamin compounds, it has become popular to "take" all the vitamins in tablets, pills or capsule form. This practice, according to recent studies, may actually be harmful to health as well as to the budget, and it certainly is not desirable. If necessary to take vitamins in this form, it should be done only under a physician's supervision.

All of the vitamins, except vitamin D, can be obtained in adequate amounts from an ordinary adequate diet by a healthy individual. Unless there is an abundance of sunshine, or an adequate amount of fortified milk is consumed, it may be necessary to take vitamin D in the form of a fish liver oil or some other preparation (others are sometimes recommended by the physician for various reasons), which may be considered to be a supplementary food, rather than a medicine.

CALCIUM AND IRON

CALCIUM AND IRON

When You Think of Calcium,
think of —
MILK, CHEESE, ICE CREAM

When You Think of Iron,
think of —
MEAT, EGGS, GREENS

CALCIUM AND CALORIE VALUE OF SELECTED FOODS

Recommended Daily Dietary Allowances for Normal Adults: 0.8 grams

(See Table 4, page 10 for other ages)

Practical Sources	Average Serving	Calcium Grams	Calories
Dairy Products			
Whole milk	1 cup	.28	160
Skim milk; buttermilk; yoghurt	1 cup	.29	90
Nonfat dry milk (no water added)	⅓ cup	.30	83
Cheese, blue, Roquefort	1 oz	.09	105
Cheddar or American	1-inch cube	.13	70
Cottage, creamed	½ cup	.10	120
Swiss	1 oz	.26	105
Ice cream, factory packed	⅛ quart	.08	145
Ice milk	⅛ quart	.14	142
Fish			
Oyster, meat only	½ cup	.11	80
Salmon, pink, canned (bone included)	3 oz	.16	120
Sardines, canned, drained	3 oz	.37	175
Vegetables			
Collards, cooked	½ cup	.14	28
Dandelion greens, cooked	½ cup	.12	30
Kale, cooked	½ cup	.07	15
Mustard greens, cooked	½ cup	.09	17
Spinach,* cooked	½ cup	.08	20
Turnip greens, cooked	½ cup	.13	15

* Calcium of spinach may not be usable because of presence of oxalic acid.

IRON AND CALORIE VALUES OF SELECTED FOODS
Recommended Daily Dietary Allowances for Normal Adults: 10 to 15 milligrams
(See Table 4, page 10 for other ages)

Practical Sources	Average Serving	Iron Mg.	Calories
Meats, Poultry			
Liver, Pork, fried	3 oz	18.1	195
Calf, fried	3 oz	10.6	195
Beef, fried	3 oz	7.5	195
Heart, Beef, trimmed of fat, braised	3 oz	5.0	160
Beef, trimmed to retail basis,* cooked			
Cuts, braised, simmered, roasted			
Lean and fat	3 oz	2.9	245
Lean only	2.5 oz	2.7	140
Hamburger, market ground	3 oz	2.7	245
ground lean	3 oz	3.0	185
Tongue, simmered	3 oz	1.9	210
Chicken, flesh only, broiled	3 oz	1.4	115
Lamb, roasted, lean only, no bone	2.5 oz	1.4	130
Pork, fresh, trimmed, cooked			
Chop, thick, with bone	3.5 oz	2.2	260
Roast, oven-cooked, no liquid added			
Lean and fat	3 oz	2.7	310
Lean only	2.4 oz	2.6	175
Pork, cured, ham, lean and fat	3 oz	2.2	245
Luncheon meat, boiled ham, sliced	2 oz	1.6	135
Luncheon meat, canned, spiced or not	2 oz	1.2	165
Bologna, 4x4x0.1-inches	2 slices	1.0	172
Frankfurter (9 per lb)	1 large	.8	155
Fish and Shellfish			
Clams, raw, meat only	3 oz	5.2	65
Clams, canned, solids and liquid	3 oz	3.5	45
Oysters, meat only, raw	½ cup	6.6	80
Eggs, large (24 oz per dozen)			
Whole, without shell	1 large	1.1	75
Yolk	1 large	.9	60
Nuts, Legumes			
Almonds, shelled	¼ cup	1.7	212
Brazil nuts, broken pieces	¼ cup	1.2	226
Cashew nuts, roasted	¼ cup	1.3	190
Peanuts, roasted, shelled, halves	¼ cup	.8	210
Peanut butter	1 tbsp	.3	95
Pecans, halves	¼ cup	.6	185
Walnuts, black	¼ cup	1.9	197
Walnuts, English	¼ cup	.8	162
Vegetables			
Asparagus, spears, cooked	½ cup	.5	17
Lima beans, immature, cooked	½ cup	2.0	90
Broccoli spears, cooked	1 cup	1.2	40
Celery cabbage, raw, 1-inch pieces	½ cup	.3	7

Practical Sources	Average Serving	Iron Mg.	Calories
Collards, cooked	½ cup	.5	28
Cowpeas, cooked, immature seeds	½ cup	1.7	87
Dandelion greens, cooked	½ cup	1.6	30
Mustard greens, cooked	½ cup	1.2	17
Peas, green, cooked	½ cup	1.5	55
Peas, green, canned, solids and liquid	½ cup	2.1	85
Potato, peeled before boiling	1 med (3 per lb)	.6	80
Soybeans, cooked	½ cup	2.5	105
Sweet potatoes, baked	1 med (4 per lb)	1.0	155
Spinach, cooked	½ cup	2.0	20
Tomatoes, raw (3 per lb)	1	.8	35
Tomatoes, canned	½ cup	.6	25
Tomato juice	1 cup	2.2	45
Turnip greens, cooked	½ cup	.7	12
Fruits			
Apricots, dried, small	¼ cup	1.0	97
Blackberries, raw	1 cup	1.3	85
Blueberries, raw	1 cup	1.4	85
Cantaloupe, 5-inch diam	½ melon	.8	60
Dates, pitted, cut	½ cup (⅕ lb)	2.6	245
Peaches, dried, not cooked	¼ cup	2.4	105
Prunes, med, unsweetened, cooked	½ cup	2.2	150
Prune juice, canned	½ cup	5.2	100
Raisins, dried	¼ cup	1.4	115
Raspberries, red, raw	1 cup	1.1	70
Strawberries, red	1 cup	1.5	55
Watermelon, 4x8-inch wedge	2 lb with rind	2.1	120
*Whole Grain and Enriched Cereals***			
White bread, enriched	1 slice	.6	60
Whole wheat, bread	1 slice	.5	55
Rye bread	1 slice	.4	55
Cornflakes, enriched	1 oz	.4	110
Wheat, puffed, enriched	1 oz	1.2	105
Farina, cooked, enriched	1 cup	.7	100
Macaroni, enriched, cooked until tender	1 cup	1.3	155
Noodles, egg, enriched, cooked	1 cup	1.4	200
Oatmeal or rolled oats, cooked	1 cup	1.4	130
Spaghetti, enriched, cooked	1 cup	1.3	155
Whole wheat flour, stirred (from hard wheat)	1 cup	4.0	400
All-purpose flour, enriched, sifted	1 cup	3.2	400
Wheat germ, stirred	1 cup	6.4	245

* See * page 26.
** Based on minimal level of enrichment.

TEN WAYS TO GET THE HIGHEST FOOD VALUES FROM FRUITS AND VEGETABLES:

1. Choose fruits and vegetables which are fresh, or which have been well refrigerated and cared for in storage.
2. Use as soon after marketing as possible. If necessary to store for any time, refrigerate properly. If frozen foods should thaw, *do not re-freeze!*
3. Peel, or pare very thinly; scraping may be all that is necessary.
4. Cook in the smallest possible amount of water.
5. Save and use all cooking water.
6. Cover during cooking to prevent oxidation; cook quickly and do not overcook.
7. Do not use soda in cooking green vegetables or to make tomato soup.
8. Do not overcook. Vegetables should still retain some of their original crisp texture and raw, fresh flavor.
9. Prepare all salads just before serving.
10. Avoid excess handling, such as chopping, mashing and grating.

HOW WELL ARE WE FED?

According to surveys, 10% of the families in the United States have poor diets. However, many other families are deficient in one or more individual nutrients. In general, families often consume more calories than are required (as evidenced by overweight), nearly half of the calories coming from fat in such foods as meat, milk, ice cream, cheese, baked goods and food mixtures, foods not often considered as main sources of fat.

Calcium and vitamin C (ascorbic acid) are the nutrients most likely to be in short supply when compared with daily recommended allowances, see Table 4, page 10. In the latest government nutrition survey, about 30% of the families fell short of the calcium recommendation and 25% were low in vitamin C. It is extremely difficult to get enough calcium into the diet without using milk and other dairy products. However, if milk is consumed liberally as a beverage, there is no problem as 1 quart of milk will provide 1.14 grams of calcium, which is sufficient for all children except those between 12 and 18. The small amount extra needed for this age, see Table 4, page 10, is readily obtained from the rest of the diet, chiefly from ice cream, cheese and dark green, leafy vegetables. By checking your menu with this table, it is easy to see if your family is getting the amount of vitamin C it needs for positive health. Select one member of the family (say yourself). No matter what your age you will require 70 mg. of ascorbic acid (table on page 24). One half grapefruit will provide 50 mg. and ⅔ cup cooked cauliflower will provide 22 mg. to make your total 72. Without a citrus fruit or tomatoes or dark green leafy vegetables (cooked quickly), however, it does take planning to be sure you supply the required 70 mg. of ascorbic acid per person. As mentioned above, 25% of the families in the latest survey did not reach the desired goal in vitamin C.

From 15 to 20% of the families surveyed had diets providing less than the recommended quantities of vitamin A, thiamine and riboflavin. Approximately 9% of the families were low in protein; nearly all diets which were low in protein were also deficient in at least three other nutrients. This was not surprising because the foods that contribute most of the proteins (see table on page 16) also supply a considerable quantity of minerals and vitamins.

Although one-third of the families with the highest incomes had diets which were higher in practically all the nutrients, the greatest improvement in diets in the United States between 1936 and 1948 was in the low income families. The reason for this is that low income families eat more grain products and thus have benefited more from the enrichment program. They also made larger gains in the amount of meat and citrus fruits eaten. As much as it helps, a high income does not insure an adequate diet. Only 63% of the city families with an annual income of $6,000 or more had diets that measured up to the recommended levels in all nutrients. It takes knowledge and the willingness to plan diets carefully to ensure an adequate diet. But it can be done even with limited means if one is intent on giving her family the correct food for positive health.

A study of the tables between pages 16–39, which show the foods which are highest in the individual nutrients, will aid in planning adequate diets without necessarily increasing the cost.

LOW SODIUM (NA) OR SODIUM-RESTRICTED DIETS

Sodium-restricted (so-called low salt) diets of various levels of restriction are used for the prevention, control and elimination of edema (water retention in tissues causing swelling) in many pathological conditions as well as for the alleviation of hypertension. The degree of restriction may vary from a very low sodium diet (250-mg sodium), a strict sodium restriction (500-mg sodium), a moderate sodium restriction (1,000-mg sodium) to a mild sodium restriction (2,400 to 4,500 mg sodium). A normal diet contains about 3,000 to 6,000 mg of sodium daily although a liberal intake of salty foods may result in much higher sodium intake.

In a mild sodium-restricted diet, it may be necessary only to eliminate the use of table salt and monosodium glutamate in cooking food and at the table. By far the most liberal source of sodium in the diet is from the table salt (sodium chloride). However, the use of salty foods such as ham, dried fish, brined pickles, corned beef and sauerkraut should also be avoided.

In diets with severe sodium restriction, the sodium content of the natural foods must be taken into account. The physician of such patients will furnish them lists of foods with approximate sodium content of average size servings.

The following table indicates the approximate amount of sodium in general classes of food.

APPROXIMATE SODIUM CONTENT OF SELECTED FOODS

Food	Average Serving	Sodium Grams	Foods to avoid
Milk, whole	1 cup	120	Ice cream, sherbet, all milk drinks un-
skim	1 cup	120	less made with low-sodium milk.
low-sodium whole or skim	1 cup	7	
Meat or poultry	1 oz cooked	25	Bacon, all canned (except low-sodium),
Chicken or turkey	1 oz cooked	25	all manufactured or smoked meats, all
Fish	1 oz cooked	25	shellfish and all canned fish except di-
Salmon, tuna canned, low-sodium	1 oz	25	etetic low-sodium.
Cottage cheese, unsalted	¼ cup	25	
Cheese, low-sodium	1 oz	25	
Peanut butter, low-sodium	2 tbsp	25	
Vegetables Group A*	½ cup	9	Greens of all kinds except turnip greens;
Group B**	½ cup	5	celery, sauerkraut, brined pickles and
Fruits	Varies***	2	olives, all canned vegetables except di- etetic (low-sodium).
Low-Sodium Breads	Varies	5	Self-rising flour or corn meal.
Low-Sodium Cereals	¾ cup	5	All ready-to-eat cereals *except* Puffed Rice, Puffed Wheat and Shredded Wheat —or dietetic cereals containing less than 6 mg per 100 gm cereal as noted on label.
			All commercial salad dressings except low-sodium.

FRUITS AND VEGETABLES GROUPED BY APPROXIMATE SODIUM CONTENTS

* Group A, containing approximately 9 mg Sodium per ½ cup serving. Asparagus, broccoli, Brussels sprouts, cabbage, cauliflower, chicory, cucumbers, endive, escarole, green beans, lettuce, mushrooms, okra, onions, peppers, pumpkin, rutabaga, radishes, squash, tomatoes, turnip greens, wax beans.

** Group B, containing approximately 5 mg Sodium per serving. Dried lima or navy beans, lentils, split peas, cowpeas, parsnips, potatoes (small), sweet potatoes (¼ cup).

*** Fruits Grouped by Size Servings to give approximately 2 grams Sodium. 1 small: apple, orange, peach (med), pear; ½ small banana, grapefruit, mango. ½ cup: apple sauce, mixed fruit, grapefruit juice, orange juice, diced pineapple. ⅓ cup: apple juice or cider, pineapple juice.

Miscellaneous:

Apricots, 4 halves dried†, 2 med fresh, ¼ cup nectar; 1 cup blackberries; ⅔ cup blueberries; ¼ small cantaloupe, 10 large cherries; 2 dates; 1 fig; 12 grapes; ¼ cup grape juice, ⅛ med honeydew melon, 2 med plums or prunes, ¼ cup prune juice, 2 tbsp raisins, 1 cup strawberries, 1 large tangerine, 1 cup watermelon.

Sodium is negligible in lemons, limes, cranberries and rhubarb.

† Check to be sure sodium sulphite has not been used in processing.

It is possible to buy many low-sodium foods and substitutes for foods containing large amounts of sodium in the special diet sections of large chain stores and in dietetic food stores. Potassium carbonate can be used instead of baking soda (sodium carbonate) and a sodium-free baking powder containing potassium carbonate may be used in place of regular baking powder which contains sodium carbonate. If none can be located, a pharmacist can mix one using this formula: 69 grams potassium carbonate, 56 grams cornstarch, 15 grams tartaric acid and 112 grams potassium bi-tartrate. Substitute 1½ tsp of this baking powder for 1 tsp of regular baking powder. This amount will make a little more than ½ lb.

One may also buy low-salt bread and unsalted butter (often called sweet butter since it is made of sweet cream) and unsalted margarine. Often these are kept in the freezer cases as they are more perishable than the salted products.

When buying foods for a salt-restricted diet, watch the labels and do not select foods which contain ingredients which include sodium in the name, such as sodium acetate, sodium alginate, sodium benzoate, monosodium glutamate, etc. Likewise, do not use foods whose labels include salt or leavening.

Food for Children

No pumpkin pie for the very young children—not even on Thanksgiving! But the youngsters won't feel slighted if you'll bake some of the pumpkin custard filling without spice in custard cups and dress it up with some dainty special garnish, so they can have their VERY OWN dessert on the great day. This is just one of many suggestions you'll find in this chapter for fitting the family's regular menus to Junior's measure, to his benefit and yours.

IN MOST homes it is not convenient or practical for the children to eat meals entirely different from those that are prepared for the grown-ups. From the time the baby begins to receive solid food, the objective should be to teach him to like and to eat all the foods that are good for him. This does not mean that he will eat everything his parents eat, and in just the same form; for actually a child's meals should be tailored to fit him just as his clothes are. What it does mean is that food prejudices should not be allowed to develop in the growing child, if he is to grow up healthy, well-nourished and happy.

One of the most important influences on the child's attitude toward food is his parents' attitude. If the father dislikes vegetables and says so, the child is likely to copy his father's dislike and refusal of vegetables. If the mother dislikes some particular food and never serves it at home, the child will not become acquainted with it and may never learn to like it.

Parents who conquer their own food dislikes lest they influence the children, are benefiting not only the youngsters but themselves in the long run, since it is difficult to eat a well-balanced diet if one has a number of food prejudices, to say nothing of the social embarrassments they cause to both guest and hostess.

FEEDING THE PRE-SCHOOL CHILD

The youngster from babyhood to five or six years of age is being introduced to a great variety of unfamiliar foods. Foods which the child welcomes from the very first are meats, which he will be served daily, and sweets, which he should be given very sparingly and only after meals. Most other foods he will like as he becomes familiar with them.

45

To introduce a child to a new food, give him a small quantity of it—not more than a taste at first—then feed him his regular meal. After two or three trials he should be ready to accept the new food as an old friend. Don't try to start him on more than one new food at a time.

The adult taste cannot be depended upon to judge the proper seasonings for children. As a rule, children dislike any food that is not bland. Cereals should be only very slightly sweetened, if at all. A small amount of salt is all that will be required to make most vegetables palatable. Pepper and other spices are not required by a perfectly healthy, unsophisticated palate, and should never be given to the little child except in the smallest amounts, and then only on very special occasions.

Other taboos for the pre-school child are coffee or tea in any form; they should not be used even as flavoring in such foods as puddings or sauces for the child. Rich gravies should be avoided, and the child should get no pastry. Both contain a large proportion of fat which slows down the time of digestion. When other members of the family have pie, some of the filling may be saved out for the child, unless it is too rich in itself. A custard cup of baked filling will be more acceptable to any child than the filling scooped out of a piece of pie, because it seems more like his own.

It is desirable for the pre-school child to have his heaviest meal in the middle of the day rather than with the rest of the family in the evening. His evening meal may be light, with a milk soup, cereal and milk, or even bread and milk, as its basis. And it may be more convenient for him to finish his meal and be put to bed before the rest of the family has dinner.

FEEDING THE SCHOOL CHILD

After his school life begins, the child's diet will gradually begin to conform more closely to the grown-up pattern, though condiments, stimulants such as tea and coffee, and rich foods like pastry should still be avoided.

From eight or nine years on, the growing child's caloric requirements will be nearly the same as an adult's, and during adolescence the boy's requirement often exceeds his father's, unless his father is very active.

If the child has been trained from babyhood to accept and enjoy a variety of foods, including the important vegetables, both raw (in salads) and cooked, he will present no special feeding problems during the school years or afterward.

Breakfast is an important meal for the child, and he should *never* be allowed to hurry off without it in the morning. It must be remembered that breakfast, even when the child declares that he is not hungry for it, must be depended on to supply at least one-quarter of the day's vitamins, minerals and calories. If it is omitted, the dietary lack must be made up at the other meals, or nutrition will suffer.

Preferably the breakfast should contain at least one hot dish. Especially in cold weather, an all-cold breakfast does not give the quick warmth and energy that should help to start the day right. Hot whole-grain or enriched cereal, with plenty of whole milk or cream and a little sugar, is a good every-day breakfast dish. If the hot cereal is omitted, a cup of hot cocoa or hot milk should be included in the breakfast menu for the child.

A child who is never hungry for breakfast will find his appetite stimulated by getting up half an hour earlier than usual and taking some brisk exercise. His morning household tasks, if done before breakfast, will prove a great appetizer.

In schools where a Lunch A is served, the day's dietary of the children is more likely to be adequate. However, some children still find it necessary to "take" their lunch. It should be planned just as carefully as a home luncheon, to provide its fair share of the day's requirement. Sandwiches should be made with whole-grain or enriched white bread. Sandwich fillings should not be limited to the simple sliced meat, or cheese, jelly or jam, which are the easiest things to prepare. There are many delicious chopped raw vegetable spreads which are high in food value; and combinations of these with meat and cheese are especially good. The lunch box should always contain fruit, either an apple, orange or banana, or other fruit which may be conveniently eaten from the hand, or a little covered jar of stewed or canned fruit.

The lunch box should contain a thermos bottle. In cold weather, the thermos should provide a hot milk soup, or a hot milk drink. In hot weather, a cold milk beverage, or cold milk may be more refreshing.

The following chart provides a diet pattern for adequate diets that will supply the recommended daily allowances for children from 1 to 5 years. (See page 48.) It also shows clearly the gradual increase in the amounts and kinds of foods eaten by children through these years. Last, but probably most important, it emphasizes the similarity in the diet of a year-old child to one of five, or for that matter of any age. Only the variety and quantity of foods change as our appetites increase and our palates become more sophisticated; but, the foods that are needed for an adequate diet at thirty are the same foods with slight modifications that are needed at two.

OUTLINE FOR PLANNING ADEQUATE DIETS FOR CHILDREN 1 TO 5 YEARS OLD*

Amounts Usually Recommended per day	At 1 year	At 2 years	At 3 years	At 4 years	At 5 years
Milk	1 quart	1 quart	1 quart	1 quart	1 quart
Cereal	2-4 T. strained, no sugar	1/4-1/2 c. unstrained, no sugar	1/4-1/2 c. unstrained, no sugar	1/4-3/4 c., no sugar	1/2-1 c., no sugar
Bread	1/2-1 slice white	1-3 slices white or whole wheat	1-3 slices white or whole wheat	2-4 slices	2-4 slices
Citrus fruit juice	3-4 T.	4-8 T.	4-8 T.	4-8 T.	1/4-1/2 c.
Additional fruit	1 kind (2-4 T.)	2 T. pulp strained (1 or 2 kinds daily)	3-4 T. pulp strained or chopped (1 or 2 kinds daily)	3-4 T. pulp strained or chopped raw or cooked	1/4-1/2 c. peeled and mashed, or finely cut
Potatoes		1/2-1 medium	1/2-1 medium	1 medium	1 medium
Additional vegetables	2 T. strained pulp twice daily	2-4 T. strained or chopped	2-4 T. strained or chopped	2-4 T. chopped or mashed	1/4 c. chopped or mashed
Eggs	1/2-1 yolk	1 yolk or 1 egg	1 whole egg	1 whole egg	1 whole egg
Meat	"Liver soup" or "beef soup" 2-4 T.	1 or 2 T. chopped liver or ground lean beef instead of egg	3 T. chopped liver or lean beef or lamb or fish	4 T. chopped liver or lean beef, lamb, or fish	1-2 oz. lean tender beef, lamb, chicken, liver
Fish liver oil	1-2 t.	1-3 t.	1-2 t.	?	?
Butter, cream, bacon			1 T. butter	2 T. butter or 2 T. cream or 2 slices bacon	2-3 T. of butter and cream or 2 slices of bacon
Milk and vegetable soup			cream soup	cream soup	cream soup
Puddings			tapioca, junket, custard, gelatin, rice, cornstarch	tapioca, junket, custard, gelatin, rice, cornstarch	tapioca, junket, custard, gelatin, rice, cornstarch
Sherbet & custard, ice cream				sherbet, frozen custard	small amount plain ice cream
Cookies				graham cracker, arrow root, vanilla wafer	plain sugar cookies, molasses cookies

NOTE: Amounts of foods recommended here apply to the average or normal child. Some children eat as much and some eat more. All foods should be bland in flavor.
* From University of Illinois, Urbana, Ill., by permission of Harriet T. Barto, Associate Professor of Dietetics.

Why Use Menus?

"Our grandparents got along all right without worrying about balanced menus. They didn't even know about vitamins and minerals, and weren't any the worse for it. So why should I fuss about what MY *family eats, so long as they get filled up?" This is the substance of a recent protest against the modern emphasis on balanced meals, and represents the attitude of many otherwise up-to-date homemakers. The answer to the question "Why use menus?" is given in detail in this chapter.*

ONE of the reasons grandmother's unscientific method of filling up her family and letting it go at that was nutritionally successful in so many cases is that in those days folks had bigger appetites. Everyone worked harder—physically harder—than most of us do now. Ninety years ago, 80 per cent of the population lived on farms; and in those days there were few of the labor-saving devices which all of us take for granted in this age of electricity and diesel engines. Men and women, boys and girls, all worked with their hands and it made them hungry. They lived in colder, draftier houses too, and needed food to keep them warm as well as to make energy. Vitamins and minerals are found rather sparingly in most foods, and the smaller the meals we eat the more difficult it is to get these nutrients in sufficient quantities for health. Our grandparents ate more food and automatically obtained more of these precious food elements.

But it should not be overlooked that many of the diseases now proven to be caused by dietary deficiencies were not recognized at that time, even though they *did exist;* our forebears may have suffered from these symptoms of vitamin and mineral deficiencies in the diet, and blamed it on other causes.

Another thing that influences present-day diets to a great extent, both for the worse and for the better, is that a vastly greater variey of foods is available to us. Grandmother had only a few basic foods to work with, and if her family wanted enough to fill them up, they had to eat what was set before them. If Johnny didn't like greens, Johnny had no other choice and therefore any food dislike was quickly discouraged. Today it is all to easy to replace a food disliked by some member of the family with another food which may be less valuable nutritionally. To this extent the wide variety of foods which we enjoy may affect our diet for the worse.

On the other hand, the possibilities of good nutrition are increased today because we can have access to many foods which were formerly not available at all in many parts of the country, or were available only for brief seasons. For example, when grandfather was a boy, oranges were such a rarity in the North and East that many children saw them only in the toes of their Christmas stockings, whereas today we can drink fresh orange juice every day of the year if we wish. The same is true to a smaller extent of many other fresh fruits and vegetables, and even of dairy products, and of canned and frozen foods of all kinds. If we use this variety wisely we can not only improve our nutrition but make our meals more attractive. Our untrained tastes and preferences, however, cannot be depended upon as a reliable guide to a wise choice of nutritionally sound meals, even amongst this abundance. This is where scientifically planned menus are needed.

We are inclined to think that food prices are high today but studies show that the average take-home pay per hour of factory workers will buy more of almost any food today than it would in 1947 or before the war. In many families, however, the proportion of income spent for food may have increased (1) due to use of convenience foods (which must include the cost of services in manufacturing) and (2) because their diets have been upgraded in quality.

Thus the changing conditions of life which have made us an urban instead of a rural nation have added the extra task of *meal-planning for health* to the homemaker's essential activities. It is with the object of lightening her burden that the following menus have been planned for one week of each month of the year.

Here are the ways in which our carefully worked-out menus, p 56-67, help both the homemaker herself and her whole family:

1. They outline a day-by-day diet which provides the essential food elements in quantities sufficient to develop and maintain buoyant health. Because of the smaller quantities of food which almost all of us consume nowadays, and because of the smaller vitamin and mineral content of much of that food, it is difficult to do this by haphazard selection of the foods the family happens to fancy.

2. They provide for a reasonable variety, not only in the foods themselves but in their methods of preparation. Thus the family may be kept interested in the basic protective foods which must be eaten daily for health.

3. They utilize seasonable foods. The summertime season for fresh fruits and vegetables is so short that it is a good practice to serve them very often while they last. Few families would object to strawberry shortcake or strawberries and cream every day during their brief season. This is also an economy measure, for fresh foods in season are usually low in price.

4. They suggest ways of using inexpensive foods, especially inexpensive cuts of meat, with which many women are unfamiliar. These are just as delicious, satisfying, and digestible as the more expensive ones, when properly cooked. The frequent use of these inexpensive cuts will make it possible to enjoy the choicer ones on special occasions—on holidays, and when "company" comes.

5. They call the homemaker's attention to new recipes, new food combinations, uses of leftovers, perhaps even to foods which she has never tried before; and thus they build up her recipe repertoire, make her a more versatile cook, and satisfy her with a sense of new achievement.

6. They answer that daily recurring question: "What shall I serve today?" which becomes a nightmare to so many women—and they answer it so reliably that the homemaker no longer needs to be uncertain about her choice of food.

In short, these menus are designed to help women deal confidently and successfully with the changing world in which they live, so far as food and nutrition are concerned.

HOW TO USE THESE MENUS

The menus you will find in the pages of this book are not meant for "slavish" following. You may want to vary them, to exercise your own imagination and ingenuity, and to adapt them to your family's preferences and to the food supply available to you. For example, if you raise your own corn or strawberries, you will probably serve corn or strawberries during their season much oftener than they are called for here. If you have your own chickens, you may be able to serve eggs or egg dishes every day instead of 3 or 4 times a week, and to indulge in a chicken dinner much oftener than we have allowed it. But regardless of your supply, if Susie happens to be allergic to strawberries, you will have to skip strawberries for Susie even in their season, and give her instead some other fresh fruit in season at the same time.

These menus will free you from the pressure of having to plan 3 meals a day every day of the week. Even though you prefer to make your own adjustments, they furnish a basic plan to guide you.

The menus are designed to give satisfactory nutrition at medium to low levels of cost, to suggest variety, methods of preparation and service which will enable the family to enjoy their meals day after day.

Should you desire to make a few changes in these menus, use all of the above factors to guide you.

1. HOW TO BEGIN MEAL PLANNING

Due to shortage of space in this book, representative *menus* have been planned for but *one week in each month of the year*. These are merely to give you a *right start* in meal planning. Here are 2 suggestions:

1. Use these menus as a guide in connection with the Basic Four Food Groups, the Menu Planning Guide and Menu Planning Form for One Week, Tables 1, 2 and 3, pages 7, 8 and 9.

2. Repeat these menus when practical. When food is well cooked and attractively served, the average healthy family does not tire of meals repeated occasionally when each repetition is a week apart. One advantage in such repetition is:

(a) That the seasonal foods will continue in season and enable you to take advantage of them.

(b) That it saves the homemaker time in making up menus from scratch. However, it isn't much of a trick to make substitutions now and then to give the meal a *"new look,"* or to change days so that the family will not expect to get the same food, say cooked cereal, each Tuesday.

2. HOW TO MAKE SUBSTITUTIONS OF FOODS

You may occasionally wish to substitute other foods for those in a given menu, whether because strawberries give Susie the hives, or because pork chops are not the best meat buy on the day they are suggested, or because you have less, or even more to spend than usual. This can easily be done, but to keep the menu well balanced nutritionally, be sure to substitute something from the same class of food. That is, if you take out a fresh fruit, put another fresh fruit in, not a pudding; if you take out a leafy green vegetable, substitute another vegetable of the same type, such as cabbage for lettuce or spinach for broccoli.

3. HOW TO ADJUST QUANTITIES

The recipes have been designed for a family of five—husband, wife and three children. If there are fewer in your family, you can adjust the amounts of food you allow in proportion. A family consisting of father, mother and only one child will consume roughly about three-fifths—slightly over one half—as much food as a family of five. But where this is difficult or impossible, or if you simply prefer not to bother with changing recipes, you can make the full amount and count on serving the leftovers at another meal, replacing some food of the same type called for in the menu for that meal. If what is left over is vegetable, let it replace a vegetable, not meat or eggs or a citrus fruit. Utilizing leftovers intelligently is a real art, involving careful storing, careful re-heating, and careful serving to make them as attractive as they were the first time. But if your family doesn't like to eat leftovers, it will pay you to practice reducing recipes to fit the number of mouths you have to feed, so that all will be consumed in the first meal. The supposition is that father and his adolescent son will want larger servings, mother and little sister smaller ones, than the average figured on, depending of course upon their physical activity.

A number of times the menus suggest a recipe which will be sufficient for two meals, based on average appetites. Perhaps for your particular family the quantities may be too skimpy, or too large, according to the food needs and the activities of the various members. You will probably be able to judge from the recipes whether quantities are about right, or whether they need to be adjusted.

Of course it is often convenient to have a little too much, in case unexpected guests drop in about dinner time; and perhaps Junior may have been playing football, thus acquiring a double-barreled appetite. On the other hand, sometimes a rather small meal provides welcome opportunity for using up leftovers.

Since all the recipes are based on what we assume to be average folks with average activities and average appetites, there is very likely to be some deviation from the needs of your family. So it is up to you, as you use the book, to exercise your native ingenuity in adapting both menus and recipes to the special needs of your special household.

4. HOW TO SWITCH MENUS

If the noon meal is the big meal of the day in your home, in most cases you can simply switch the dinner and luncheon menus, and serve dinner at noon and luncheon as the evening supper.

If your husband's employer or some other special guest is coming to dinner on a week-day evening and you want to do something extra for him which doesn't appear on the menu for the day, perhaps you can switch it with Sunday's dinner. This usually provides for something a little "special" and may just fill the bill. In making such exchanges from day to day, you need to plan carefully about leftovers—both those already on hand and those which you will have as a result of the switch. This may mean adjustments for two or three days—but you have the menus to use as a basis and a little juggling will usually do the trick successfully.

5. HOW TO PLAN AHEAD WITH THE MENUS

Don't be content to study the menus just one day at a time. Look ahead to the next day—that will enable you to get ready in advance if there is any preliminary preparation to be done, and will save you work. For example, there may be a dried bean dish tomorrow, and in that case the beans should be put to soak overnight.

If you have storage facilities for more than enough food for a day or two, study the whole week's menus at a time. Then make a list of the foods required for each menu, referring to the individual recipes for exact amounts when it is necessary, then make your market list for the whole week, or for half the week, according to your convenience. Some homemakers form a habit of making 2 lists. On one they put staple items and canned or packaged foods which can safely be bought and stored, and on the other, foods like meats, fruits and fresh vegetables, which should be bought more frequently.

Sometimes you will be able to make considerable savings by buying enough potatoes or apples for a whole week, or a month, or even longer. But this is never practical unless you have suitable and sufficient storage space to take care of them.

Another advantage in planning ahead is that it helps you to arrange for family assistance. You will know which meals require help and be able to assign tasks in advance, so other members of the family can plan their activities accordingly.

6. HOW TO ADJUST THE MENUS TO YOUR FREEZING AND CANNING PROGRAM

If you are in a position to can or freeze fruits and vegetables yourself, you will save money and will have greater variety, and in some cases better flavor.

Where home canning has been done, keep a list of the products you have on hand, and check off each jar or can as it is used. Try to use them according to a schedule, so your strawberry jam will not be all gone while you still have a big supply of grape jelly on hand. Unless you have reason to suppose that the strawberry jam won't keep well this year, due to some seasonal difference in the fruit, this is an unnecessary sacrifice of variety.

The daily menus in this book have been planned to include the basic foods which supply the normal individual's daily needs for protein, minerals, vitamins and energy. The menus meet the Recommended Dietary Allowances adopted by the Food and Nutrition Board of the National Research Council.

menu suggestions by the month

MONDAY
Breakfast—Orange Juice
Rolled Oats with Thin
  Cream
Toast with Butter, Jelly
Coffee for Adults
Milk for Children

Luncheon—Cream of
  Navy Bean Soup
Hot Corn Bread and Butter
Raw Apples
Tea for Adults
Milk for Children

Dinner—Poached Eggs on
  Beef Hash
Baked Acorn Squash
Head Lettuce, French
  Dressing
Bread and Butter
Whipped Strawberry
  Gelatine
Vanilla Crisps
Coffee for Adults
Cocoa for Children

TUESDAY
Breakfast—½ Grapefruit
Hot Whole Wheat Cereal
  with Thin Cream
Cinnamon Toast
Coffee for Adults
Milk for Children

Luncheon—Spinach
  Chowder
Toasted Cheese
  Sandwiches
Fresh or Canned Pears
Tea for Adults
Milk for Children

Dinner—Curried Lamb
Baked Potatoes Butter
Buttered Parsley Carrots
Stuffed Prune Salad
Bread and Butter
Pumpkin Custard
Coffee for Adults
Milk for Children

WEDNESDAY
Breakfast—Freshly Sliced
  Oranges
Poached Eggs on Toast
Jelly
Coffee for Adults
Cocoa for Children

Luncheon—Tomato
  Rarebit

Shredded Cabbage and
  Celery Salad
Sliced Bananas with Thin
  Cream
Tea for Adults
Milk for Children

Dinner—Pan-fried Liver
Mashed Potatoes
Green Onions
Creamed Peas
Whole Wheat Bread and
  Butter
Butterscotch Pudding
Coffee for Adults
Milk for Children

THURSDAY
Breakfast—Grapefruit
  Juice
Hot Rice with Brown
  Sugar and Thin Cream
Whole Wheat Toast with
  Butter
Coffee for Adults
Milk for Children

Luncheon—Baked Beans
Boston Brown Bread
Pickles and Celery
Stewed Apricots
Cocoa for All

Dinner—Escalloped
  Potatoes and Ham
Buttered Onions
Grated Carrot and Raisin
  Salad
Bread and Butter
Apple Dumplings
Coffee for Adults
Milk for Children

FRIDAY
Breakfast—Grapefruit
  Juice
Scrambled Eggs
Whole Wheat Toast and
  Butter
Coffee for Adults
Cocoa for Children

Luncheon—Spicy Bread
  Crumb Griddle Cakes,
  Syrup
Pork Sausage Patties
Grape Tapioca
Tea for Adults
Milk for Children

Dinner—Veal a la King
American Fried Potatoes

Buttered Spinach
Olives and Radishes
Bread and Butter
Cupcakes (Half for
  Saturday)
Coffee for Adults
Milk for Children

SATURDAY
Breakfast—Tangerines
Whole Wheat Muffins with
  Butter
Fried Sliced Luncheon
  Meat
Jelly
Coffee for Adults
Cocoa for Children

Luncheon—Macaroni
  with Cheese Sauce
Stewed Tomatoes
Celery Cabbage, Raw
Bread and Butter
Cupcakes
Tea for Adults
Milk for Children

Dinner—Quick-baked
  Pike
Parsley Buttered Potatoes
Green Beans with Onions
Bread and Butter
Peach Salad
Cocoa Puff
Coffee for Adults
Milk for Children

SUNDAY
Breakfast—Grapefruit
  Halves
Prepared Cereal with
  Thin Cream
Toast with Butter
Jam
Coffee for Adults
Milk for Children

Dinner—Baked Ham Slice
Baked Sweet Potatoes
Buttered Brussels Sprouts
Bread and Butter
Crabapple Pickles
Dried Fruit Whip
Coffee for Adults
Milk for Children

Supper—Molded
  Vegetable Salad
Bacon Muffins with
  Butter
Cocoa for All

MONDAY
Breakfast—Stewed Dried
Peaches
Soft-cooked Eggs
Toast with Butter, Jelly
Coffee for Adults
Milk for Children

Luncheon—Tomato and
Cabbage Soup
Crackers
Whole Wheat Bread and
Butter
Cottage Cheese with
Marmalade
Tea for Adults
Milk for Children

Dinner—Meat Soufflé
Buttered Carrots
Green Pepper Sticks
Radishes
Creamed Potatoes
Bread and Butter
Lemon Fluff
Coffee for Adults
Milk for Children

TUESDAY
Breakfast—Tangerines
Prepared Cereal with
Milk
Toast with Butter, Jelly
Coffee for Adults
Cocoa for Children

Luncheon—Kidney Bean
Loaf with Chili Sauce
Lettuce Sandwiches
Fruit Cocktail, or Fruit
Cup
Hermits
Tea for Adults
Milk for Children

Dinner—Braised
Spareribs with Gravy
Mashed Potatoes
Butter Beets
Celery
Bread and Butter
Dutch Apple Pie
Coffee for Adults
Milk for Children

WEDNESDAY
Breakfast—Grapefruit
Halves
Scrambled Eggs
Biscuits and Butter, Jam
Coffee for Adults
Cocoa for Children

Luncheon—Spinach
Chowder
Melba Toast
Cranberry Sauce
Oatmeal Drop Cookies
Tea for Adults
Milk for Children

Dinner—Meat Balls,
Sauerkraut
Potato Dumplings
Bread and Butter
Shredded Lettuce with
Mayonnaise
Fresh Red Raspberry
Bavarian
Coffee for Adults
Milk for Children

THURSDAY
Breakfast—Applesauce
Bran Muffins and Butter
Broiled Bacon
Jelly
Coffee for Adults
Milk for Children

Luncheon—Hot Tomato
Bouillon
Grilled Cheese Sandwiches
Sliced Bananas in Orange
Juice
Tea for Adults
Milk for Children

Dinner—Pot Roast of
Veal with Gravy
Carrot Sticks
Baked Potatoes
Buttered Spinach
Bread and Butter
Brown Sugar Custard
Coffee for Adults
Milk for Children

FRIDAY
Breakfast—Prune Juice
Rolled Oats with Thin
Cream
Toast with Butter
Jam
Coffee for Adults
Milk for Children

Luncheon—Baked Eggs
in Bacon Rings
Toast and Butter
Orange Waldorf Salad
Peanut Butter Cookies
(Save Half for Saturday's
Luncheon)
Chocolate Ice Cream
Tea for Adults

Milk for Children
Dinner—Lamb Patties
Quick Escalloped Potatoes
Buttered Peas
Bread and Butter
Baked Apples
Coffee for Adults
Milk for Children

SATURDAY
Breakfast—Tomato Juice
Griddle Cakes
Syrup
Coffee for Adults
Cocoa for Children

Luncheon—Beans au
Gratin
Bread and Butter
French Bowl Salad
Peanut Butter Cookies
Stewed Dried Apricots
Tea for Adults
Milk for Children

Dinner—Heart Chop Suey
Boiled Rice
Lettuce
1000 Island Dressing
Bread and Butter
Frozen Berries and
Cookies
Coffee for Adults
Milk for Children

SUNDAY
Breakfast—Grapefruit
Halves
Broiled Bacon
Scrambled Eggs
Toast and Preserves
Coffee for Adults
Milk for Children

Dinner—Braised Pork
Chops
Gravy
Mashed Potatoes
Buttered Broccoli
Head Lettuce
Russian Dressing
Bread and Butter
Cottage Pudding with
Lemon Sauce
Coffee for Adults
Milk for Children

Supper—Cottage Cheese
Salad
Jelly Sandwiches
Cookies
Tea for Adults
Milk for Children

MONDAY
Breakfast—Freshly Sliced
  Pared Oranges
Poached Eggs
Toast
Butter
Coffee for Adults
Milk for Children

Luncheon—Oyster Stew
Soda Crackers
Date Nut Bread
Applesauce
Tea for Adults
Milk for Children

Dinner—Veal Paprika
Mashed Potatoes
Buttered Green Beans
Celery Hearts
Whole Wheat Bread
  and Butter
Golden Feather Cake
  (Save Half for Tuesday
  Dinner)
Raspberries Frozen or
  Canned
Coffee for Adults
Milk for Children

TUESDAY
Breakfast—Sliced
  Bananas
Whole Wheat Cereal and
  Cream
Toast with Butter and
  Bacon
Jelly
Coffee for Adults
Milk for Children

Luncheon—Grilled Cheese
  Sandwiches
Bread and Butter Pickles
Lettuce with French
  Dressing
Applesauce
Gum Drop Cookies
Cocoa for All

Dinner—Lamb Shanks
Pepper Gravy
Hashed Brown Potatoes
Cucumber and Onion Salad
Bread and Butter
Snow Pudding with
  Lemon Sauce
Coffee for Adults
Milk for Children

WEDNESDAY
Breakfast—Stewed
  Prunes

Scrambled Eggs and
  Bacon
Toast with Butter
Coffee for Adults
Cocoa for Children

Luncheon—Creamed
  Tuna on Toast
Stewed Tomatoes
Molded Peach Fig Salad
Tea for Adults
Milk for Children

Dinner—Frankfurter and
  Lima Bean Casserole
Buttered Cabbage
Cranberry Relish
Bread and Butter
Chocolate Blanc Mange
Coffee for Adults
Milk for Children

THURSDAY
Breakfast—Grapefruit
  Halves
French Toast and Bacon
Syrup
Coffee for Adults
Milk for Children

Luncheon—Split Pea
  Soup
Soda Crackers
Carrot Coconut Salad
Doughnuts
  (Save Half for Friday
  Dinner)
Apple Juice or Milk for
  Children

Dinner—Spanish Sausage
Mashed Potatoes
Buttered Green Beans
Whole Wheat Bread and
  Butter
Canned Plums and Cookies
Coffee for Adults
Milk for Children

FRIDAY
Breakfast—Orange Juice
Rolled Oats with Thin
  Cream
Toast with Butter
Jam
Coffee for Adults
Milk for Children

Luncheon—Eggs Benedict
Celery
Canned Pears
Tea for Adults

Milk for Children

Dinner—Codfish Balls
Harvard Beets
Celery Cabbage Salad
Bread and Butter
Sugar Cookies
Baked Apples
Coffee for Adults
Milk for Children

SATURDAY
Breakfast—Sliced
  Bananas
Farina with Thin Cream
Toast with Butter
Honey
Coffee for Adults
Milk for Children

Luncheon—Peanut Butter
  and Watercress
  Sandwiches
Orange and Coconut Salad
Cocoa for All

Dinner—Hamburger
  Patties
Creamed Potatoes
Head Lettuce with 1000
  Island Dressing
Bread and Butter
Mincemeat Custard
Coffee for Adults
Milk for Children

SUNDAY
Breakfast—Canned
  Grapefruit Juice
Quick Streusel Coffee Cake
Pan-fried Canadian Bacon
Coffee for Adults
Milk for Children

Dinner—Beef Sauerbraten
Potato Dumplings
Buttered Cauliflower
Pickled Crabapples
Whole Wheat Bread and
  Butter
Mince Pie
Coffee for Adults
Milk for Children

Supper—Cream of Carrot
  Soup
Soda Crackers
Waldorf Salad
Ginger Ice Box Cookies
  (Save Half for Monday)
Tea for Adults
Milk for Children

MONDAY
Breakfast—Orange Juice
Bran Muffins
Pan-broiled Link Sausage
Apple Butter
Coffee for Adults
Cocoa for Children

Luncheon—Beef Bouillon
Crackers
Kidney Bean Salad
Canned Pineapple and
  Cookies
Tea for Adults
Milk for Children

Dinner—Barbecued
  Spareribs
Parsley Buttered Potatoes
Creamed Celery
Vegetable Slaw
Bread and Butter
Bread Pudding
Coffee for Adults
Milk for Children

TUESDAY
Breakfast—Pineapple
  Juice
Rolled Oats with Milk
Toast with Butter
Jelly
Coffee for Adults
Milk for Children

Luncheon—Cream of
  Tomato Soup
Crackers
Peanut Butter Sandwiches
Prune Whip
Tea for Adults
Milk for Children

Dinner—Pot Roast of
  Veal with Gravy
Boiled Potatoes
Buttered Green Cabbage
Olives and Radishes
Bread and Butter
Tapioca Cream
Coffee for Adults
Milk for Children

WEDNESDAY
Breakfast—Tomato Juice
Poached Eggs on Toast
Bacon
Coffee for Adults
Cocoa for Children

Luncheon—Cream of Beet
  Soup

Crackers
Grapefruit Avocado Salad
Oatmeal Cookies
  (Save Half for Thursday)
Tea for Adults
Milk for Children

Dinner—Lamb Patties
Creamed Potatoes
Buttered Carrots
Wilted Lettuce
Bread and Butter
Cherry Pie
Coffee for Adults
Milk for Children

THURSDAY
Breakfast—Stewed
  Raisins
French Toast and Bacon
Jelly
Coffee for Adults
Milk for Children

Luncheon—Cream of
  Potato Soup
Crackers
Stewed Apricots
Oatmeal Cookies
Tea for Adults
Milk for Children

Dinner—Pineapple Juice
Old-fashioned Baked
  Beans
Boiled Potatoes
Cole Slaw
Whole Wheat Bread and
  Butter
Grapefruit Shortcake
Coffee for Adults
Milk for Children

FRIDAY
Breakfast—Sliced
  Bananas on Prepared
  Cereal with Milk
Toast with Butter and
  Bacon
Jelly
Coffee for Adults
Cocoa for Children

Luncheon—Green Beans
  au Gratin
Melba Toast
Pineapple Date Salad
Tea for Adults
Milk for Children

Dinner—Tomato Juice
Cocktail

Braised Pork Shoulder
  Steak
Mashed Potatoes
Carrot Slaw
Whole Wheat Bread and
  Butter
Rice Pudding
Coffee for Adults
Milk for Children

SATURDAY
Breakfast—Freshly Sliced
  Peeled Oranges
Cooked Whole Wheat
Cereal with Thin Cream
Scrambled Eggs
Toast with Butter
Coffee for Adults
Milk for Children

Luncheon—Ham and
  Cheese Sandwiches
Hot Cauliflower Salad
Applesauce
Tea for Adults
Milk for Children

Dinner—Tuna and Celery
  Fondue
Buttered Green Beans and
  Potatoes
Raw Spinach Salad
Cornsticks and Butter
Lemon Chiffon Pudding
Coffee for Adults
Milk for Children

SUNDAY
Breakfast—Canned
  Grapefruit Sections
Wheat Biscuits with Milk
Toast with Butter
Quince Honey
Coffee for Adults
Cocoa for Children

Dinner—Beef and
  Vegetable Pie
Big Wig's Salad
Whole Wheat Bread and
  Butter
Peach Cobbler
Coffee for Adults
Milk for Children

Supper—Denver
  Sandwiches
Bread and Butter Pickles
Fruit Buttermilk

MONDAY
Breakfast—Stewed
  Rhubarb
Prepared Cereal with Milk
Bacon and Toast with
  Butter
Coffee for Adults
Cocoa for Children

Luncheon—Cold Fruit
  Platter with Cottage
  Cheese
Crackers
Chocolate Blanc Mange
Milk for All

Dinner—Meat Croquettes
Parsley Buttered Potatoes
Creamed Green Beans
Green Onions
Radishes
Bread and Butter
Strawberry Shortcake
Coffee for Adults
Milk for Children

TUESDAY
Breakfast—Stewed Prunes
Scrambled Eggs and Bacon
Whole Wheat Toast with
  Butter
Coffee for Adults
Milk for Children

Luncheon—Potato Carrot
  Soup
Croutons
Cabbage and Apple Salad
Canned Sliced Peaches
Tea for Adults
Milk for Children

Dinner—Baked Liver and
  Vegetables
Buttered Asparagus
Bread and Butter
Radishes and
  Green Onions
Lemon Pie
Coffee for Adults
Milk for Children

WEDNESDAY
Breakfast—Sliced
  Bananas on Prepared
  Cereal with Thin Cream
Toast with Butter
Bacon
Coffee for Adults
Cocoa for Children

Luncheon—Pineapple
  Date Salad

Ham Salad Sandwiches
Tea for Adults
Milk for Children

Dinner—Veal Fricassee
Buttered New Peas
Hot Rolls and Butter
Cornstarch Pudding
Coffee for Adults
Milk for Children

THURSDAY
Breakfast—Tomato Juice
Poached Eggs on Toast
Bacon
Coffee for Adults
Milk for Children

Luncheon—Printemps
  Chowder
Peanut Butter Jelly
  Sandwiches
Sugared Fresh Pineapple
Vanilla Crisps
(Save ⅔ for Friday and
  Sunday)
Tea for Adults
Milk for Children

Dinner—Baked Macaroni
  and Cheese
Vegetable Slaw
Buttered Beets
Whole Wheat Bread and
  Butter
Strawberry and Banana
  Fruit Cup
Coffee for Adults
Milk for Children

FRIDAY
Breakfast—Sugared
  Strawberries
Rolled Oats with Milk
Cinnamon Toast
Bacon
Coffee for Adults
Milk for Children

Luncheon—Creamed
  Spinach on Noodles
  with Cheese
Bread and Butter
Applesauce
Vanilla Crisps
Tea for Adults
Milk for Children

Dinner—Country Fried
  Steak
Mashed Potatoes

Escalloped Tomatoes
Wilted Lettuce
Bread and Butter
Stewed Rhubarb and
  Sponge Cake
Coffee for Adults
Milk for Children

SATURDAY
Breakfast—Grapefruit
  Juice
French Toast
Canadian Bacon
Syrup
Coffee for Adults
Milk for Children

Luncheon—Olive and Egg
  Sandwiches
Finger Salads
Banana-Vanilla
  Refrigerator Cake
Tea for Adults
Milk for Children

Dinner—Braised Spanish
  Pork Chops
Buttered Fresh Asparagus
Pickled Peaches
Bread and Butter
Frozen Raspberries and
  Butter Cookies
Tea for Adults
Milk for Children

SUNDAY
Breakfast—Sugared
  Fresh Pineapple
Soft-cooked Eggs
Whole Wheat Toast with
  Butter
Coffee for Adults
Milk for Children

Dinner—Stuffed Lamb
  Breast
Boiled Rice
Buttered New Peas and
  Carrots
Tomato and Lettuce Salad
Refrigerator Rolls
(Save Part of Dough for
  Monday)
Strawberries and Cream
Vanilla Crisps
Coffee for Adults
Milk for Children

Supper—Salted Crackers
Cheese
Fruit Cup
Milk for All

MONDAY

Breakfast—Canned Orange and Grapefruit Juice
Prepared Cereal with Milk
Toast with Butter
Bacon
Coffee for Adults
Milk for Children

Luncheon—Red Raspberry and Cottage Cheese Salad
Toast and Butter
Cinnamon Blanc Mange
Tea for Adults
Milk for Children

Dinner—Cold Meat Loaf
Escalloped New Cabbage
American Fried Potatoes
Sliced Tomatoes and Cucumbers
Whole Wheat Bread and Butter
Applesauce
Oatmeal Cookies (Save Half for Tuesday Lunch)
Iced Tea for Adults
Milk for Children

TUESDAY

Breakfast—Stewed Prunes
Soft-cooked Eggs
Bacon
Whole Wheat Toast with Butter
Coffee for Adults
Milk for Children

Luncheon—Cream of Pea Soup
Soda Crackers
Strawberries with Cream
Oatmeal Cookies
Tea for Adults
Milk for Children

Dinner—Pot Roast of Veal with Gravy
Parsley Buttered Potatoes
Savory Green Beans
Hot Baking Powder Biscuits and Butter
Tomato and Lettuce Salad
Sugared Fresh Pineapple
Coffee for Adults
Milk for Children

WEDNESDAY

Breakfast—Applesauce
French Toast and Butter
Honey
Broiled Bacon
Coffee for Adults
Milk for Children

Luncheon—Creamed Peas
Carrot Sticks
Potted Meat Sandwiches
Eleanor's Fluffy Creamed Rice
Tea for Adults
Milk for Children

Dinner—Short Ribs Pot Roast
Boiled Potatoes
Bread and Butter
Grated Carrot and Raisin Salad
Cherry Cobbler
Coffee for Adults
Milk for Children

THURSDAY

Breakfast—Strawberries with Cream
Scrambled Eggs
Toast with Butter
Jelly
Coffee for Adults
Milk for Children

Luncheon—Bacon and Peanut Butter Sandwiches
Wilted Lettuce
Canned Pears
Chocolate Sauce
Tea for Adults
Milk for Children

Dinner—Pork Chop Suey
Rice
Whole Wheat Bread and Butter
Sliced Tomatoes and French Dressing
Brown Sugar Custard
Coffee for Adults
Milk for Children

FRIDAY

Breakfast—Tomato Juice
Rolled Oats with Thin Cream
Toast with Butter
Jelly
Coffee for Adults
Milk for Children

Luncheon—Cream of Asparagus Soup
Soda Crackers
Buttered Beets
Sugared Fresh Pineapple
Tea for Adults
Milk for Children

Dinner—Quick-baked Fish
Escalloped Potatoes
Buttered Spinach
Cornbread and Butter
Radishes and Green Onions
Sliced Bananas with Top Milk
Coffee for Adults
Milk for Children

SATURDAY

Breakfast—Sugared Strawberries with Cream
Prepared Cereal with Milk
Cinnamon Toast
Sausage
Coffee for Adults
Milk for Children

Luncheon—Green Beans on Toast with Welsh Rarebit
Radishes
Bread and Butter
Stewed Rhubarb
Cookies
Tea for Adults
Milk for Children

Dinner—Swiss Steak
Mashed Potatoes
Creamed New Cabbage
Lettuce with Russian Dressing
Whole Wheat Bread and Butter
Watermelon
Coffee for Adults
Milk for Children

SUNDAY

Breakfast—Sugared Red Raspberries
Poached Eggs
Toast with Butter
Jam
Coffee for Adults
Milk for Children

Dinner—Roast Leg of Lamb
Buttered New Peas
Whole Wheat Bread and Butter
Raw Cauliflower Salad
Fresh Strawberry Pie
Coffee for Adults
Milk for Children

Supper—Watercress and Bacon Sandwiches
Tossed Vegetable Salad
Cantaloupe Wedges
Iced Tea or Coffee
Milk

MONDAY
Breakfast—Cantaloupe
  Wedges
Pan-broiled Sausage Links
Toast with Butter
Preserves
Coffee for Adults
Milk for Children

Luncheon—Jellied
  Tomato Bouillon
Crackers
Kohlrabi with Cheese
  Sauce
Whole Wheat Bread and
  Butter
Red Plums
Chilled Cocoa for All

Dinner—Meat Soufflé
Quick Escalloped Potatoes
Broiled Tomatoes
Head Lettuce
French Dressing
Bread and Butter
Sugared Fresh Sour
  Cherries
Coffee for Adults
Milk for Children

TUESDAY
Breakfast—Sliced
  Bananas on Prepared
  Cereal with Milk
Poached Eggs on Toast
Coffee for Adults
Milk for Children

Luncheon—Cucumber,
  Onion and Pickle
  Sandwiches
Cottage Cheese
Orange Jelly
Milk for All

Dinner—Curried Lamb
Boiled Rice
Buttered Peas
Tomato and Lettuce Salad
Whole Wheat Bread and
  Butter
Red Raspberries and
  Cream
Coffee for Adults
Milk for Children

WEDNESDAY
Breakfast—Sugared Fresh
  Blackberries
Bacon
Whole Wheat Toast with
  Butter
Marmalade

Coffee for Adults
Milk for Children

Luncheon—Tomato and
  Cabbage Soup
Crisp Crackers
Fresh Fruit Salad
Iced Tea for Adults
Milk for Children

Dinner—Boiled Fresh
  Tongue
Buttered Spinach
Hashed Brown Potatoes
Grated Carrot and Raisin
  Salad
Bread and Butter
Röd Gröd
Cream
Coffee for Adults
Milk for Children

THURSDAY
Breakfast—Chilled New
  Apple Sauce
Scrambled Eggs and
  Sausage
Toast with Butter
Coffee for Adults
Milk for Children

Luncheon—Kidney Bean
  Salad
Bacon Sandwiches
Cantaloupe Wedges
Iced Tea for Adults
Milk for Children

Dinner—Baked Pork
  Chops with Caraway
  Seed
Creamed Potatoes No. 1
Creole Wax Beans
Whole Wheat Bread and
  Butter
Jelly Roll
Hot or Iced Coffee
Milk for Children

FRIDAY
Breakfast—Canned
  Grapefruit Sections
Prepared Cereal with
  Cream
Toast with Butter
Jelly
Coffee for Adults
Milk for Children

Luncheon—Fresh Corn
  and Tomato Casserole
Bread and Butter
Cantaloupe Balls and
  Cherry Salad

Cold Baked Custard
Hot or Iced Tea
Milk for Children

Dinner—Lamb Patties
Parsley Buttered Potatoes
French Bowl Salad
Bread and Butter
Peach Shortcake
Hot or Iced Coffee
Milk for Children

SATURDAY
Breakfast—Plums, Fresh
  Red or Blue
Soft-cooked Eggs
Toast with Butter
Jelly
Coffee for Adults
Milk for Children

Luncheon—Baked Beans
  in Tomato Cups
Rye Melba Toast
Blackberries with Cream
Iced Tea for Adults
Milk for Children

Dinner—Veal a la King
Buttered or Crisp Noodles
  or Toast
Cole Slaw
Rye Bread and Butter
Chocolate Marshmallow
  Pudding
Coffee for Adults
Milk for Children

SUNDAY
Breakfast—Sliced
  Peaches on Prepared
  Cereal with Thin Cream
Toast with Butter
Jam
Coffee for Adults
Milk for Children

Dinner—Rolled Steak
Mashed Potatoes
Fried Corn
Whole Wheat Bread and
  Butter
Celery and Radishes
Devil's Food Cake and
  Ice Cream
Coffee for Adults
Milk for Children

Supper—Tossed Vegetable
  Salad
Melba Toast and Butter
Fresh Apricots
Iced Tea for Adults
Milk for Children

MONDAY
Breakfast—Stewed Fresh
  Plums
Fried Eggs and Bacon
Toast with Butter
Jam
Coffee for Adults
Milk for Children

Luncheon—Creamed
  Carrots and Celery on
  Toast
Sliced Tomatoes
Pears
Hot or Iced Tea
Milk for Children

Dinner—Pan-fried Liver
  and Bacon with Onions
Riced Potatoes
Buttered Green Beans
Bread and Butter
Cucumber and Radish
  Salad
Pineapple Bavarian
Coffee for Adults
Milk for Children

TUESDAY
Breakfast—White Grapes
Prepared Cereal with Milk
Toast with Butter
Sausage
Jelly
Coffee for Adults
Milk for Children

Luncheon—Cabbage au
  Gratin
Sliced Tomatoes with
  French Dressing
Whole Wheat Bread and
  Butter
Watermelon
Hot or Iced Tea
Milk for Children

Dinner—Stuffed Veal
  Rolls with Gravy
Boiled Potatoes
Pickled Beets and Onions
Bread and Butter
Fresh Peach Cobbler
Coffee for Adults
Milk for Children

WEDNESDAY
Breakfast—Sliced
  Peaches
Prepared Whole Cereal
  with Thin Cream
Toast with Butter
Broiled Bacon

Coffee for Adults
Milk for Children

Luncheon—Parsley
  Butter Sandwiches
Orange Waldorf Salad
Caramel Blanc Mange
Hot or Iced Tea
Milk for Children

Dinner—Braised Beef
  Balls
Creamed Potatoes
Buttered Spinach
Bread and Butter
Baked Fresh Pears
Coffee for Adults
Milk for Children

THURSDAY
Breakfast—Grapefruit
  Juice
Soft-cooked Eggs
Bacon
Cinnamon Toast
Coffee for Adults
Milk for Children

Luncheon—Beet Borsch
Crisp Crackers
Sliced Bananas with
  Lemon Sauce
Hot or Iced Tea
Milk for Children

Dinner—Roast Boston
  Style Pork Butt
Roast Potatoes
Buttered Peas
Whole Wheat Bread and
  Butter
French Bowl Salad
Cantaloupe Wedges
Coffee for Adults
Milk for Children

FRIDAY
Breakfast—Cantaloupe
Prepared Cereal with
  Top Milk
Toast with Butter
Jam
Bacon
Coffee for Adults
Milk for Children

Luncheon—Creamed Eggs
  on Toast
Sliced Tomatoes and
  Lettuce Wedges
French Dressing
Fresh Pears
Hot or Iced Tea

Milk for Children

Dinner—Cold Sliced Fresh
  Boston Style Pork Butt
Corn on the Cob
Okra and Tomatoes
Cabbage, Carrot and
  Raisin Salad
Bread and Butter
Fresh Peach Tarts
Coffee for Adults
Milk for Children

SATURDAY
Breakfast—Grapefruit
  Juice
Prepared Cereal with Milk
Toast with Butter
Broiled Bacon
Coffee for Adults
Milk for Children

Luncheon—Tuna Salad
Buttered Summer Squash
Whole Wheat Bread and
  Butter
Fresh Plums
Chilled Cocoa for All

Dinner—Irish Stew
Lettuce with French
  Dressing
Bread and Butter
Fresh or Canned Apricots
Brownies
Coffee for Adults
Milk for Children

SUNDAY
Breakfast—Sliced
  Bananas with Milk
French Toast
Syrup
Coffee for Adults
Milk for Children

Dinner—Chicken
  Fricassee
Mashed Potatoes
Corn on the Cob
Whole Wheat Bread and
  Butter
Tomato and Cucumber
  Salad
Peach Blossom Pie
Coffee for Adults
Milk for Children

Supper—Olive and Egg
  Sandwiches
Prune Milk Shake
Cookies

MONDAY
Breakfast—Melon Wedges
Cooked Whole Wheat
Cereal with Thin Cream
Toast with Butter
Broiled Bacon
Coffee for Adults
Milk for Children

Luncheon—Cream of
Lima Bean and Carrot
Soup
Whole Wheat Toast and
Butter
Lettuce with French
Dressing
Fruit Cup
Coconut Fingers
Tea for Adults
Milk for Children

Dinner—Hot Beef
Sandwiches
Gravy
Parsley Buttered Carrots
Mashed Potatoes
Celery
Caramel Mousse
Iced Tea for Adults
Milk for Children

TUESDAY
Breakfast—Sliced
Peaches
Prepared Cereal with Milk
Toast with Butter
Orange Marmalade
Coffee for Adults
Milk for Children

Luncheon—Stuffed
Tomato Salad
Carrot Butter Sandwiches
Fresh Pears
Tea for Adults
Milk for Children

Dinner—Braised Spareribs
Creamed Potatoes
Buttered Peas
Whole Wheat Bread and
Butter
Tossed Vegetable Salad
Apple Crumble
Coffee for Adults
Milk for Children

WEDNESDAY
Breakfast—Concord
Grapes
Griddle Cakes and Bacon

Syrup
Coffee for Adults
Milk for Children

Luncheon—Baked Eggs
in Tomato Cups with
Bacon
Whole Wheat Bread and
Butter
Baked Prune Pudding
Milk for All

Dinner—Steak and
Kidney Pie
Buttered Summer Squash
Cole Slaw
Bread and Butter
Apple Snow
Coffee for Adults
Milk for Children

THURSDAY
Breakfast—Melon Wedges
Rice Cooked in Milk
Toast with Butter
Jelly
Coffee for Adults
Milk for Children

Luncheon—Stuffed Green
Peppers No. 4
Finger Salad
Bread and Butter
Baked Peaches
Milk for All

Dinner—Veal Chop Suey
Pan-broiled Tomatoes
Whole Wheat Bread and
Butter
Shredded Lettuce with
French Dressing
Lemon Fluff
Coffee for Adults
Milk for Children

FRIDAY
Breakfast—Grape Juice
Rolled Oats with Top Milk
Poached Eggs on Toast
Coffee for Adults
Milk for Children

Luncheon—Salmon Salad
Muffins Butter
White Grapes
Milk for All

Dinner—Beef Pot Roast
Roast Potatoes
Buttered Green Beans
Tomato and Lettuce Salad

Bread and Butter
Fresh Peach Ice Cream
Coffee for Adults
Milk for Children

SATURDAY
Breakfast—Sliced
Bananas in Freshly
Squeezed Orange Juice
Prepared Cereal with Milk
Toast with Butter
Jelly
Coffee for Adults
Milk for Children

Luncheon—Creamed
Chipped Beef on Toast
Celery Carrot Sticks
Baked Apples No. 1
Tea for Adults
Milk for Children

Dinner—Lamb Shanks
with Vegetables
Baked Potatoes
Cucumber and Radish
Salad
Buttered Spinach or
Mustard Greens
Bread and Butter
Baked Custard
Coffee for Adults
Milk for Children

SUNDAY
Breakfast—Frozen
Orange and
Grapefruit Juice
Prepared Cereal with
Thin Cream
French Toast Syrup
Coffee for Adults
Milk for Children

Dinner—Stuffed Veal
Rolls
Creamed Potatoes
Fried Eggplant
Tomato and Lettuce Salad
Whole Wheat Bread and
Butter
Plum Dumplings
Coffee for Adults
Milk for Children

Supper—Parsley Omelet
Bread and Butter
Angel Food Cake with
Lemon Sauce
Tea for Adults
Milk for Children

MONDAY

Breakfast—Freshly
Sliced Oranges
Cooked Cracked Wheat
Cereal
Toast with Butter, Jelly
Coffee for Adults
Milk for Children

Luncheon—Cream of
Tomato Soup
Orange Bread with
Cream Cheese
Red and Green Salad
Grapes
Tea for Adults
Milk for Children

Dinner—Fresh Pig Hocks
Boiled Potatoes
Buttered Rutabaga
Lettuce with French
Dressing
Bread and Butter
Baked Apples
Coffee for Adults
Milk for Children

TUESDAY

Breakfast—Orange Juice
Rolled Oats with Milk
Toast with Butter
Jam
Coffee for Adults
Milk for Children

Luncheon—Corn Fritters
with Sausage
Celery
Poached Pears
Tea for Adults
Milk for Children

Dinner—Boiled Bologna
Baked Potatoes
Escalloped Tomatoes
Bread and Butter
Lettuce with French
Dressing
Brown Sugar Custard
Coffee for Adults
Milk for Children

WEDNESDAY

Breakfast—Stewed Prunes
French Omelet
Toast with Butter, Jelly
Coffee for Adults
Milk for Children

Luncheon—Macaroni,
Tomato and Green
Pepper Casserole
Toast with Butter, Honey
Concord Grapes
Tea for Adults
Milk for Children

Dinner—Spanish Liver
Buttered Parsnips
Whole Wheat Bread and
Butter
Cole Slaw
Sliced Bananas with
Lemon Sauce
Coffee for Adults
Milk for Children

THURSDAY

Breakfast—Grapefruit
Juice
Prepared Cereal with Milk
Toast with Butter, Jam
Bacon
Coffee for Adults
Cocoa for Children

Luncheon—Vegetable
Soup
Crisp Crackers Butter
Oatmeal Cookies
Applecot Sauce
Tea for Adults
Milk for Children

Dinner—Lamb Shoulder
Chops with Dressing
Creamed Potatoes
Buttered Spinach
Whole Wheat Bread and
Butter
Frosted Cup Cakes
(Save Half for Saturday)
Coffee for Adults
Milk for Children

FRIDAY

Breakfast—Freshly Sliced
Oranges
Hot Whole Wheat Cereal
with Thin Cream
Toast with Butter, Jelly
Coffee for Adults
Milk for Children

Luncheon—Leek and
Potato Soup
Crisp Crackers or Toast
Lettuce Wedges with 1000
Island Dressing
Pears
Tea for Adults

Milk for Children

Dinner—Stewed Chicken
and Dumplings
Buttered Carrots
Bread and Butter
Sliced Cucumber Salad
Cherry Tapioca
Coffee for Adults
Milk for Children

SATURDAY

Breakfast—Tomato Juice
French Toast
Syrup
Broiled Sausages
Coffee for Adults
Milk for Children

Luncheon—Eggs a la
Goldenrod on Toast
Tomato Aspic Salad
Sliced Pineapple
Tea for Adults
Milk for Children

Dinner—Salmon Loaf
Potatoes O'Brien
Buttered Peas
Whole Wheat Bread and
Butter
Celery and Radishes
Frosted Cup Cakes
Coffee for Adults
Milk for Children

SUNDAY

Breakfast—Orange Juice
Poached Eggs with Bacon
Toast with Butter, Jam
Coffee for Adults
Cocoa for Children

Dinner—Tomato Juice
Cocktail
Roast Duck with Gravy
Mashed Potatoes
Buttered Rutabaga
Radishes
Whole Wheat Bread and
Butter
Grape Bavarian
Coffee for Adults
Milk for Children

Supper—Date, Cream
Cheese, and Shredded
Lettuce Salad
Bread and Butter
Pineapple Buttermilk

MONDAY
Breakfast—Sliced
  Bananas on Prepared
  Cereal with Milk
Cinnamon Toast Bacon
Coffee for Adults
Cocoa for Children

Luncheon—Boston Clam
  Chowder
Crisp Crackers or Toast
Jam Meringue Puff
Tea for Adults
Milk for Children

Dinner—Meat Loaf
Quick Escalloped Potatoes
Baked Hubbard Squash
Whole Wheat Bread and
  Butter
Shredded Lettuce with
  Dressing
Apple Sauce Cake
(Save Half for Tuesday
  Dinner)
Coffee for Adults
Milk for Children

TUESDAY
Breakfast—Tomato Juice
Rolled Oats with Thin
  Cream
Toast with Butter
Marmalade
Coffee for Adults
Milk for Children

Luncheon—Tuna Fish
  Salad
Bread and Butter
Stewed Dried Apricots
Tea for Adults
Milk for Children

Dinner—Roast Fresh
  Boston Style Pork Butt
Mashed Potatoes
Savory Creamed Spinach
Bread and Butter
Apple Sauce Cake
Coffee for Adults
Milk for Children

WEDNESDAY
Breakfast—Freshly Sliced
  Peeled Oranges
Soft-cooked Eggs Bacon
Toast with Butter, Jelly
Coffee for Adults
Milk for Children

Luncheon—Oxtail Soup
Carrot Raisin Sandwiches
Baked Apricot Whip
Tea for Adults
Milk for Children

Dinner—Beef Stew with
  Vegetables
Cole Slaw
Whole Wheat Bread and
  Butter
Rice Pudding
Coffee for Adults
Milk for Children

THANKSGIVING DAY
Breakfast—Grapefruit
  Halves
Prepared Cereal with Thin
  Cream
Toast with Butter, Jam
Coffee for Adults
Cocoa for Children

Thanksgiving Dinner—
  Roast Turkey with
  Dressing and Gravy
Mashed Potatoes
Buttered Onions
Cranberry Sauce
Head Lettuce with 1000
  Island Dressing
Whole Wheat Bread and
  Butter
Pumpkin Pie
Coffee for Adults
Milk for Children

Supper—Oyster Bisque
Crisp Crackers or Toast
Canned Peaches
Milk for All

FRIDAY
Breakfast—Stewed Prunes
Cooked Whole Wheat
  Cereal with Thin Cream
Toast with Butter Jam
Coffee for Adults
Milk for Children

Luncheon—Turkey a la
  King, Toast
Head Lettuce, French
  Dressing
Cranberry Sauce
Tea for Adults
Milk for Children

Dinner—Baked Fish
Tartar Sauce

Mashed Potatoes
Stewed Tomatoes
Grapefruit Salad
Bread and Butter
Apple Dumplings
Coffee for Adults
Milk for Children

SATURDAY
Breakfast—Hot Rolled
  Oats with Milk
Fried Apples Bacon
Toast with Butter, Jelly
Coffee for Adults
Milk for Children

Luncheon—Escalloped
  Cabbage with
  Broiled Bacon
Bread and Butter
Waldorf Salad
Ginger Crisps
(Save Some for Sunday)
Tea for Adults
Milk for Children

Dinner—Chicken Broth
  with Rice
Croutons
Pea and Potato Casserole
Carrot and Cabbage Salad
Bread and Butter
Lemon Cake Custard
Coffee for Adults
Milk for Children

SUNDAY
Breakfast—Tomato Juice
Scrambled Eggs
Toast with Butter
Broiled Bacon
Coffee for Adults
Milk for Children

Dinner—Chicken Pie
Candied Sweet Potatoes
Buttered Green Beans
Whole Wheat Bread and
  Butter
Lettuce Wedges with 1000
  Island Dressing
Pineapple Upside Down
  Cake
Coffee for Adults
Milk for Children

Supper—Peanut Butter
  and Jelly Sandwiches
Ginger Crisps
Canned Peaches
Cocoa for All

MONDAY

Breakfast—Grapefruit
  Halves
Griddle Cakes Sausage
Syrup
Coffee for Adults
Milk for Children

Luncheon—Bacon Omelet,
  Tomato Sauce
Bread and Butter
Canned Fruit Salad
Chocolate Marshmallow
  Pudding
Tea for Adults
Milk for Children

Dinner—Diced Meat
  Roast
Mashed Potatoes
Buttered Rutabaga
Tossed Vegetable Salad
Bread and Butter
Dried Apricot Bavarian
Coffee for Adults
Milk for Children

TUESDAY

Breakfast—Stewed Dried
  Apricots
Cooked Whole Wheat
  Cereal Milk
Toast with Butter, Jelly
Coffee for Adults
Milk for Children

Luncheon—Beef Broth-
  Noodle Soup
Crisp Crackers
Lettuce, 1000 Island
  Dressing
Dutch Apple Cake with
  Lemon Sauce
Tea for Adults
Milk for Children

Dinner—Beef and
  Vegetable Pie
Orange Waldorf Salad
Bread and Butter
Floating Island
Coffee for Adults
Milk for Children

WEDNESDAY

Breakfast—Freshly Sliced
  Oranges
Poached Eggs on Toast
Bacon
Coffee for Adults
Milk for Children

Luncheon—Broccoli with
  Cheese Sauce

Toast and Butter
Celery
Sugar Cookies for Children
  (Save Half for Saturday's
  Lunch)
Fruit Cup
Holiday Fruit Cake for
  Adults
Tea for Adults
Milk for Children

Dinner—Braised Pork
  Chops
Gravy
Mashed Potatoes
Buttered Carrots
Cole Slaw
Whole Wheat Bread and
  Butter
Scalloped Apples
Coffee for Adults
Milk for Children

THURSDAY

Breakfast—Dates in
  Cooked Wheat Cereal
  with Milk
Toast with Butter, Jelly
Coffee for Adults
Milk for Children

Luncheon—Cream of
  Tomato Soup
Melba Toast with Butter
Sweet Potato Salad
Canned Peaches
Tea for Adults
Milk for Children

Dinner—Creamed Shrimp
Boiled Rice
Buttered Spinach
Whole Wheat Bread and
  Butter
Prune in Orange Jelly
Coffee for Adults
Milk for Children

FRIDAY

Breakfast—Freshly
  Sectioned Grapefruit
Pan-fried Mush Bacon
Honey and Butter
Coffee for Adults
Milk for Children

Luncheon—Carrot Soufflé
Watermelon Pickles
Celery
Whole Wheat Bread and
  Butter
Pears
Cocoa Indians

Tea for Adults
Milk for Children

Dinner—Spanish Sausage
Riced Potatoes
Pan-fried Onions
Bread and Butter
Shredded Lettuce with
  Mayonnaise
Apple Cobbler
Coffee for Adults
Milk for Children

SATURDAY

Breakfast—Dried Fruit
  Compote
Prepared Cereal with Milk
Toast with Butter, Jam
Bacon
Coffee for Adults
Cocoa for Children

Luncheon—Green Beans
  in Egg Sauce
Bread and Butter
Orange Coconut Salad
Sugar Cookies
Tea for Adults
Milk for Children

Dinner—Braised Spareribs
Savory Sauerkraut No. 1
Parsley Buttered Potatoes
Bread and Butter
Lemon Grapenut
  Pudding
Coffee for Adults
Milk for Children

SUNDAY

Breakfast—Baked Apples
Broiled Sausage Patties
Toast with Butter, Jelly
Coffee for Adults
Milk for Children

Dinner—Roast Chicken
Dressing Gravy
Mashed Potatoes
Creamed Brussels Sprouts
Whole Wheat Bread and
  Butter
Tomato Aspic Salad
Lettuce
Fruit Nut Pudding with
  Hard Sauce
Coffee for Adults
Milk for Children

Supper—Egg Salad
  Sandwiches
Dill Pickles
Pears
Cocoa for All

The Food Shopper's Creed

The health of my family is in my care; *therefore*—

> *I will base my market list on meals planned according to the "diet pattern."*

> *I will choose foods of the qualities and in the quantities to provide the nutritive elements required for a good diet.*

Stretching the food dollar is part of my responsibility; *therefore*—

> *I will take advantage of what the markets offer in the way of variety, quality and price, to the end that I may exchange my dollar for maximum food values.*

My family's enjoyment of food is my responsibility; *therefore*—

> *I will use the possibilities of the market to provide variety, excellent quality, and novelty within the limits of my food budget.*

Purchasing food for the feeding of my family is an important business transaction; *therefore*—

> *I will make every effort to weigh possibilities offered by various markets, by various foods, and the forms in which they are offered from season to season, to the end that I may take pride in a job well done.*

Homemaker's Handbook

The information in the following chapters has been summarized from the best sources available. Some of it has been obtained directly from the manufacturer, other parts have been adapted from recent government publications, and all of the tabulated material has been supplemented by the laboratory work and experience of home economics co-workers and myself. My hope is that it will answer your questions about "stretching the food dollar," about "purchasing fruits and vegetables," about "purchasing staples," such as chocolate, flour, milk, shortenings, sugar, etc., and about "commercially canned foods and their contents." It is designed to supplement the knowledge of experienced housewives, to pass on to the new bride the benefit of our experience, and to provide accurate data to all of you who are studying, or are just vitally interested in the challenging job of FEEDING THE MODERN FAMILY.

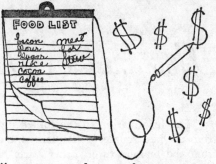

Stretching the Food Dollar

Memorize this brief chapter if you want to be a good manager. Adopt it as your homemaking creed, and put it into practice every day, for it will help you stretch your food budget so both ends will meet every time.

THERE are various ways to make the budget allowance for food go farther. By putting them into action you may be able to shave a dollar or two a week from your estimated weekly food budget. All of the following suggestions will help you to "stretch your food dollar"; certain ones will apply more than others to the type of community in which you live and to your individual family.

MAKE IT YOURSELF

Ready-to-eat foods such as cooked meats, salads, bakery goods and foods packaged in fancy wrappings are usually more expensive than similar products made at home. In buying these products, you pay not only for the food itself, but for the time and labor that go into the preparation and packaging of it.

However, some convenience foods cost very little more than similar food prepared in the home and some actually cost less. Among the latter, according to a study published in June 1963,[1] are orange juice concentrate compared with an equal amount of juice from fresh oranges, canned peas (rather than fresh), and instant coffee which costs about half as much as regular ground coffee for an equal amount of brew. Baking powder biscuits made from a mix and a home recipe cost practically the same, within 1/10 of one per cent for 6 servings. Ready-to-serve and frozen cakes cost more than recipe-cakes made at home but some cakes made from mixes cost about the same and in some cases less than the recipe-cake. The same is true of many other baked products. The spread between tea bags and loose tea was greater than between instant tea and loose tea, although the instant tea was almost twice as costly as the loose tea leaves. Often it costs as much or more to make your own pickles, jams, etc. but many good cooks take pride in making their own and even in making their favorite specialties for gifts.

[1] Comparative Costs to Consumers of Convenience Foods and Home Prepared Foods. Marketing Research Report No. 609, 1963, United States Department of Agriculture.

70

Ready-to-eat foods and packaged mixes have a time-saving value, especially on extra-busy days, and are convenient to use in those unforeseen emergencies that arise in every family. On these occasions, such foods seem like life savers.

CHOOSE A DEPENDABLE MARKET

When there are several stores in your neighborhood, it is usually a good idea to shop around and find which stores give you the best values for different foods; one store may carry the best meat, and another the freshest fruits and vegetables, while still another may make a specialty of staple items and canned goods. *The least expensive merchandise is not always the best buy.* When comparing costs you need to consider also the amount of waste of the purchased food, the cleanliness and care of the food in the store, the dependability of the quality of the merchandise from day to day, and your own time spent in shopping. Once you have determined which stores are most satisfactory, it will be to your advantage to buy there regularly.

BUY GRADED MERCHANDISE

Many foods—fruits and vegetables (fresh, canned, frozen and dried), meats, poultry, eggs, butter, cheese, honey and rice—may now be graded according to federal specifications by trained government inspectors. The top grades are those foods most perfect in shape, color, size, and flavor; with certain other physical characteristics, depending on the type of food, that make them superior in quality. The top grades, however, are no more nutritious or wholesome than the lower grades.

All of the grades have their place; the highest grades for special occasions where perfect appearance and the highest quality are desired, the medium grades for everyday use, and the lower grades for thrift, when appearance is less important. It is unwise, for example, to buy the highest grade, whole, solid packed canned tomatoes, at a high price, and then use them to make a tomato sauce in which the lower-priced cut tomatoes would have served as well. The same reasoning applies to all foods. It is extravagant to buy choice quality, when the lower quality will serve the same purpose.

You can make a considerable saving by learning the differences between the various government grades of foods, and then choosing between them wisely.

BUY IN QUANTITY

Every woman knows that in buying hand lotion, for example, a bottle containing twelve ounces should cost much less than twice as much as a bottle containing six ounces. Exactly the same principle applies to food. A ten-pound bag of sugar costs less per pound than ten pounds bought one pound at a time. In buying the one pound you are paying not only for the food itself, but for the same amount of labor in packing and labeling that went into the larger bag. Whenever you are choosing between the various sizes of packaged foods, compare the net weights, and figure for yourself the most economical size.

More or less the same principle applies to fresh foods, such as apples and potatoes. If you buy a sack of potatoes all at once, rather than two or three pounds every day, it saves a lot of handling by the retailer, and may save you several cents per sack. Form the habit of ordering bulk foods by weight, rather than by volume or number, whenever possible. It is simpler to compare the price of lemons in two different stores, for example, when the price is given by pound rather than by dozen; since a dozen lemons may include fruit of a great range in size.

Many housewives have storage facilities for purchasing canned food by the case, and a few staple foods in advance, and if menus are planned ahead, they will know what they need. The savings when added up at the end of the year, will mount to a tidy sum to spend on the occasional extras which make living a little more luxurious.

BUDGET YOUR INCOME

Quantity buying is frequently difficult because a larger amount of cash is needed to pay for the food all at once, than to buy small amounts from day to day. The only way to meet this problem is by a system of budgeting, firmly followed.

A simple budget system can be planned by keeping a careful account of a month's expenditures, and then dividing the next month's income into portions to meet the various large items. A convenient way of doing this, is to have a group of envelopes labeled with the family's big expenses: rent, gas, light and heat; groceries, meat and milk; taxes; clothing for the various members of the family; and so on. Divide the actual cash of the income between these envelopes, and make the expenditures fit the allowance. Not all the expenses will need to be considered every month. A fraction of the whole sum should be put aside each month for those obligations which must be met at a future date. By following this plan faithfully one will have the money needed to pay for food in large as well as in small sums, providing the monthly total is not exceeded. The same system could be followed on a weekly basis.

This simple budget system has the advantage of being based on past experience of *your* family, rather than on some theory of a remote budget-planner who never had to deal with Junior's shoes or Sister's tooth-straightening.

HAVE YOUR OWN GARDEN

Not everyone is fortunate enough to have a large back yard or a convenient spot for a big garden. But many people can locate a place for a small kitchen garden. Here with the expense of a few seeds, some good outdoor exercise, and a lot of fun, the family can raise many of their vegetables for summer use.

The "victory-gardens" of the war years proved to thousands of families the advantages, even in a large city, of having a small garden. They have experienced the thrill of eating fresh vegetables all summer, and have learned the economy of wisely preserving any excess by freezing, canning, or drying.

MAKE USE OF LEFTOVERS AND AVOID WASTE

There are some old proverbs, "waste makes want" and "a penny saved is a penny earned," that apply to food as well as to money. The intelligent housewife recognizes that preventing any possible food waste is the best known way of stretching the food dollar.

For example, a small rubber scraper should be used to remove every trace of batter, dough, or sauce, etc., from bowls and pans before they are placed in the sink for washing. Dry bread, rolls, and cake should be made into crumbs instead of being discarded or allowed to mold. Crumbs, made quickly in an electric blender and frozen, keep indefinitely. The good outer envelope leaves of cabbage, lettuce, etc., should be saved and combined with spinach or other cooked greens. Fruits or vegetables should be pared as thinly as possible, if at all. Chicken wings and necks, as well as other parts of the animal's carcass, even though they may contain little visible meat, may be used for preparing delicious soups. Food leftovers may be regarded as clear gain or as clear loss, according to whether your family has learned to accept them gracefully in a new dress, or insists that leftovers are only good for chicken feed. The way leftovers are presented will usually determine the amount of enthusiasm they can be expected to arouse. An ancient, dried-out dab of meat or vegetable can't possibly rate more than a cool reception, but a well-stored tasty leftover used in the preparation of a new and interesting "dish" will be received with an enthusiastic welcome.

Meats are the most generally accepted leftovers, and some people go so far as to choose a larger pot roast, or a larger ham or turkey than the family requires, in order to have some left for sandwiches, hash, croquettes or for various casserole dishes the next day. These are popularly called planned-overs.

One example will illustrate how a big meat cut can be economically and appetizingly used, for even a small family. Have the butcher saw a small whole ham in two and cut two half-inch steaks from the center to be broiled for the first night's dinner. For the next day, roast the butt end—a fine main dish for Sunday dinner. *Several* days later prepare a boiled dinner with the shank end; or cut off thin slices to pan-broil for breakfast or for sandwiches, and use the bone for making bean or pea soup.

Vegetable leftovers are less easily used, because usually only small amounts are left. However, two or even more kinds may be combined to be served hot as a vegetable or in soup, or chilled for salad. When leftover vegetables must be reheated, some of their pot liquor should be left on them and they should be heated in this, or if there is none, in a little milk and butter.

Leftovers should be cooled and placed in closed containers, air-tight if possible, to prevent the absorption of any foreign odors and flavors and to prevent drying out. Then be sure that the food goes straight into the refrigerator and is used as soon as possible. If good care is given to the foods while they are stored, they will remain in good condition till the next day; but it should be remembered that part of the vitamin content will lessen on standing.

It should become a fixed habit to check the refrigerator daily for leftovers that can be incorporated in the day's meals, and never to allow these leftovers to deteriorate unused. Avoid any excess chopping or cutting of leftovers. Let the pieces be large enough to be readily identifiable. Do your disguising in some way other than making the food itself unrecognizable.

In the recipe section of this book will be found leftover dishes to meet most situations. This leaves the housewife only the responsibility of keeping track of what leftovers she has on hand and of using them while they still retain their flavor, form, color, and vitamin content.

For further information on the care of leftovers and vitamin losses, see the chapters on "Care of Food in the Home" and "The Diet Pattern."

Purchasing Fruits and Vegetables

Have you ever bought apples for a pie and been disappointed because the filling was too mushy and entirely lacking in that good tart apple flavor? ... Do you lack imagination when it comes to planning for and finding variety in vegetables at any season of the year? ... Do you know the government grades and seasons of abundance for all the fruits and vegetables? For help, read on.

THE modern retail market offers a great abundance of fresh fruit and vegetables at any season. Many that were strictly seasonal crops a few years ago are now available all year, thanks to shipments from California, the southern states, and even from Mexico and South America. New methods of refrigeration, modern high-speed transportation, and scientific methods of ripening after harvesting, have all combined to provide the housewife of today with more fresh foods over longer seasons than her mother and grandmother ever dreamed of having.

In general, prices of fruits and vegetables shipped in from the South and West are not prohibitive, except when compared to home-grown products at the height of their season. Quality in many cases is excellent. Exceptions are fruits such as figs and apricots, which are so perishable that it is almost impossible to ship them successfully.

The market-wise housewife is likely to get better quality at lower cost than an inexperienced buyer. She knows in general the peak seasons of the various products she buys and can tell when a fruit or vegetable is as abundant and as inexpensive as it will become. She recognizes the quality of any given food and knows when a bargain is a bargain, and when it is a means of disposing of inferior stock. She is familiar with varieties, and can tell whether a handsome apple is good for cooking or only for eating from the hand, and whether it is worthwhile to lay in a big supply. She has learned how many servings to expect from a given weight, and buys accordingly, with little waste of perishable foods.

This knowledge is usually accumulated through years of experience as a food buyer, but the information in the buying guides that follow will help even the inexperienced shopper to determine what fruits and vegetables to buy, when they are most plentiful and most likely to be inexpensive, and how to care for them once they are in the home.

ORANGES, LEMONS AND GRAPEFRUIT

Since oranges and grapefruit are so extensively used in our country, some detailed information about these fruits should be of particular interest to housewives. The dietary recommendation to serve a citrus fruit or tomato every day means that oranges and grapefruit may be served 200 days of the year in most families, either as a tall six to eight oz glass of juice, or in salads, fruit cups, or desserts.

Good quality oranges are firm and heavy for their size. They need not be large, in fact, small oranges are very economical for juice, but they should never be spongy or have soft or decayed spots. A small spot of decay ruins the flavor of the whole orange. Surface blemishes, such as scars, scratches, and slight discolorations, greenish areas, or russeting on the skin do not affect the quality.

The greater part of the market supply of oranges and lemons is from Florida and California, but Texas is also shipping large quantities each year. The two chief California varieties of oranges are the Valencia and the Washington Navel. Valencias are abundant in June and July and then again in September through November. The Washington Navel is a seedless orange, and its season begins in November and continues until about May. The Florida varieties are the Valencia, Parson Brown, Pineapple, and Seedling. The Parson Brown is in season during October and early November, the Pineapple from January to the middle of March, and the Valencia from March through May. All these oranges can be used for juice, or for slicing and dicing, but the Washington Navel is the only one that can be divided into large attractive sections.

Tangerine and Satsuma varieties come chiefly from the Gulf States. They have a thin loosely fitting skin, which is easily removed, and the sections may be separated readily.

The number that appears on the end of a crate of oranges indicates the size. It is based on the number of oranges of uniform size that will fit into a standard sized crate. The largest size is 92 for Florida oranges and 100 for those from California. The smallest is 324 from Florida and 344 from California. The crates from California and Florida are not exactly the same size, so the same number of oranges from the two states will differ somewhat in size. Numbers 150–176 are best for eating, but the cost of the juice is somewhat less when the smaller sizes are used. To save time when reaming the small oranges, cut only a thin slice from the stem end, instead of cutting the orange in half, and ream the whole orange in one operation. *See Chart 10, p 96.*

Grapefruit is on the market most of the year, but storage fruit furnishes most of the summer supply. Quality in grapefruit may be judged by practically the same standards as for oranges: good quality grapefruit is firm, globe-shaped, and heavy for its size, thin-skinned and juicy. Pointed fruits are apt to be thick skinned. The skin may be clear yellow, or russet, but surface discolorations in no way mar the quality. The pink fleshed fruit is less acid than the white.

The size of grapefruit is numbered the same as oranges and lemons, see Charts 9 and 10, p 96, the numbers ranging from 36, the largest, to 150, the smallest. Corresponding numbers from California and Arizona will be a trifle smaller than from Florida, since the crate sizes are different.

Both fruits may be practically stored by the crate or half crate, especially by large families. They should be sorted and stored at 40° F to 60° F and each fruit should be individually wrapped in paper. They should be sorted regularly, and any with soft spots removed.

The federal grades for grapefruit, lemons, and oranges are listed in Table 7, p 89.

WHAT IS MEANT BY QUALITY APPLES?

An apple that is hefty and solid must of necessity have fine firm texture and be full of juice; and the apple that is firm in texture is also crisp and crunchy; if it is satisfying to the palate, its juice must have a lively flavor. Apples that are fragrant are those that have only recently ripened and have not been long removed from the tree. The skins are sturdy enough to make a good protective covering for tender juicy flesh, and are of sufficient strength and closeness of texture to take a high polish; but not sturdy enough to be tough.

We approve of the brilliant red apple, and the picture of a lovely child eating an apple could not be perfect without the spot of red color. But a few varieties of rich golden apples, or those with streaks of gold and red are just as delicious as any all-red apple. The best eating apples mature in the autumn or early winter.

Quality in cooking apples demands some of the characteristics of eating apples with a few additional ones. Those essential for making elegant pie have been graphically narrated by a famous American of Civil War days—Henry Ward Beecher. Mr. Beecher was so impressed by his mother's wonderful apple pie that he vocally expressed the essential requirements at a public meeting in one of the most famous of his essays or sermons. Beecher understood the importance of knowing varieties in apples. He chose Spitzenbergs when his mother sent him to the cellar for apples. He observed that the right varieties of apples do not cook to a mush in the pie, but hold their shape so the slices in the finished pie appeared "like ghosts of their former selves." He knew that the baked pie should still have the tart and natural apple flavor. He appreciated the value of an apple being juicy, when he says that even the "mouth" of the apple pie was "watering" when it emerged from the oven. All this makes for appetizing pie. The varieties that are best for pie mature in the autumn.

Apples that make good pie are also excellent for stewing, frying, and for making dumplings or bettys. Apples for sauce need to be tart and juicy, and should mush up when heated through. Those best for sauce mature in summer and early fall. Apples for baking should hold their shape until thoroughly cooked. Among the superior pie or stewing apples are the Gravenstein, Jonathan, Northern Spy and Wealthy. The Jonathan, Wealthy, Greening, and Rome Beauty are excellent for baking. Early Harvest, Duchess and Greening are among the best for making sauce. See Table 7, p 89, and Homemakers Guide for Buying Apples, Table 11, p 97.

HOW TO STORE

If planning to store apples for fairly long periods, varieties which keep well such as Delicious, Rome Beauty, Winesap, or Yellow Newton should be chosen. Apples keep well when stored in a cool dry place, and may be purchased by the box, peck, or bushel by a family which uses them generously, and has adequate cooler capacity or a cool cellar for storage. For the smaller family, about 4 to 6 pounds is about as many as can be kept conveniently in the refrigerator. Every variety of apple keeps best when bought and stored at the height of its season, when it is at its prime. For best storage results, all decayed fruit should be sorted out regularly and the apples separated as much as possible by putting paper between the layers.

Before buying in quantity, it is a good idea to sample the apples. If they are to be used for eating raw, a single apple may be tried; and if they are required for all-purpose use, it is a good plan to bake or stew a few to learn something of their cooking qualities. In many respects, appearance and quality are closely associated, but fine appearance does not always signify fine quality. Sometimes a good looking apple will lack flavor because it is over ripe or has been improperly stored.

Table 11, page 97, the Guide for Buying Apples, describes only the most commonly available commercial varieties. It gives information on the main market seasons and best possible uses for each variety.

TABLE 6 — HOMEMAKER'S GUIDE FOR BUYING VEGETABLES *

Vegetable	Purchase Unit	Yield Per Purchase Unit	Market Season	Federal Grades	Quality Standards	Approximate Per Cent Waste	Storage *
Artichoke, French or Globe	By Unit	One artichoke per serving (1/4 lb.)	Nov. to June	U. S. No. 1 U. S. No. 2 Unclassified	Cone shape or rounded. Bright green, scales fleshy and tightly clinging. Compact and heavy. Open or spreading scales indicate overmaturity. Avoid those with worm injury at base.	52	Very perishable; use immediately to prevent toughening. Refrigerate.
Artichokes, Jerusalem	By lb. or qt.	1 lb. contains 5 med. tubers and serves 4-5	Sept. to Feb.	None	Heavy for size. Smooth surface. Larger tubers more economical.	31	Store in cool, dark, dry place, with good air circulation.
Asparagus	By bunch (1 to 3 lb. each) or by lb.	15 to 22 med. stalks per lb., or 2 cups diced. 1 lb. serves 2-4	March to Aug., Oct. to Nov. from Calif.	U. S. No. 1 U. S. No. 2 Unclassified	Stalks should be straight, fresh, tender, not woody. Tips compact and unbroken. Stalk size varies considerably. Spreading tips indicate lack of freshness or overmaturity.	25	Refrigerate covered to prevent drying.
Beans, lima	By lb. (unshelled) or pt. (shelled)	1 lb. (well filled) in shell makes 1/3 lb. (1 cup) shelled or 2 servings. 1 lb. shelled is 2¾ cups or 4-5 servings	July to Oct.	U. S. No. 1 U. S. Combination U. S. No. 2 Unclassified	Pods well-filled but not bulging. Light green pods, free from yellow color. Crisp not flabby. Shelled beans are usually salvaged from old stock and are not recommended for purchase.	60	Refrigerate unshelled beans and shell just before using. Very perishable after shelling.

* For more complete information on storage of vegetables— see chapter "Care of Food in the Home,"

Vegetable	Purchase Unit	Yield Per Purchase Unit	Market Season	Federal Grades	Quality Standards	Approximate Per Cent Waste	Storage
Beans, string or snap (Green or Wax)	By lb. (about 1 qt.)	4-5 servings per lb. (3½ cups).	All year. Most plentiful from April to Oct.	U. S. Fancy U. S. No. 1 U. S. Combination U. S. No. 2 Unclassified	Pods either flat or rounded depending on variety. Should be bright green, young, tender, crisp, not wilted, rusty or spotted. Should snap quickly when bent. May be stringless or have an easily removed string. Bulging, whitish colored pods indicate overmaturity.	10	Refrigerate covered to prevent drying.
Beets	Young beets by bunch. Matured beets topped, by lb.	3-4 medium beets per bunch; 5 medium per lb. 1 lb. diced makes 1¾ cups and serves 3-4.	All year. Most plentiful June to Sept.	U. S. No. 1 Unclassified	Beets of 2-3 inches diameter or smaller are best. Larger ones or those with deep leaf scars or rough ridges are usually tough and woody. Should be firm, with fresh unwilted tops.	25	Remove tops and refrigerate in hydrator.
Broccoli	By lb.	1 lb. serves 4-5.	All year. Most plentiful Nov. to June.	U. S. Fancy U. S. No. 1 U. S. No. 2 Unclassified	Heads vary greatly in size, but should be compact with tender stalks, relatively free from leaves. Bright green. Avoid overmature heads with open buds, showing yellow or purple blossoms.	25	Refrigerate, covered to prevent drying.

Brussel Sprouts	By qt. or lb.	1 qt. weighs 1 lb. and serves 4-5. (25-40 sprouts).	Sept. to April	None	Sprouts should be hard, with fresh green color. Yellow, spotty appearance or worm holes indicate poor quality. Improved by frost.	23	Refrigerate covered.
Cabbage	By lb. or head	1 lb. shredded makes 4 cups raw or 2-3 cups cooked.	All year.	U. S. No. 1 U. S. Commercial. Unclassified	Shape depends on variety. Head should be solid and heavy with no yellow leaves. Worm injury or decay at core indicates poor quality.	27	Refrigerate covered or store in cool, dark, dry place, with good air circulation.
Carrots	With tops by bunch 5 - 6. Without tops by lb., qt., pk. (12 lb.) or bu. (50 lb.)	4 large carrots per lb. 1 lb. serves 4.	All year.	U. S. No. 1 Unclassified	Well shaped, fresh, firm, clean, smooth and bright in color. Tops should be fresh and green. Pale color, or coarse green shoulders indicate poor quality.	37 (with tops)	Remove tops and refrigerate covered. Store topped carrots in cool, dark, dry place.
Cauliflower	By head or lb.	1 small head weighs 1 lb. and serves 4-5.	All year. Most plentiful June to Dec.	U. S. No. 1 Unclassified	Head should be compact. Flowers should be white or creamy, clean, and free from black specks. Leaves should be fresh, bright and trimmed long to protect head. Spreading clusters indicate overdevelopment.	55 (per cent waste may be decreased by using peeled stems and tender leaves.)	Refrigerate in hydrator or wrap securely in waxed paper untrimmed. Wash and trim just before using.
Celery and Celeriac	By stalk and by root	2 small stalks weigh about 1 lb., and will make 4 servings of hearts plus about 1 cup diced.	All year.	U. S. Fancy U. S. No. 1 U. S. Combination U. S. No. 2 Unclassified	Stalks may be green or white depending on variety. Should be crisp, thick, solid, and free from blemishes. Individual branches not too large. Celery hearts, best for eating raw; untrimmed celery for other uses is most economical. Note: celeriac is a variety of celery with a large root which tastes like celery.	37	Do not remove root end. Refrigerate in hydrator.

Vegetable	Purchase Unit	Yield Per Purchase Unit	Market Season	Federal Grades	Quality Standards	Approximate Per Cent Waste	Storage
Chinese Cabbage or petsai (Celery Cabbage)	By head or lb.	Med. size head weighs about 2 lbs. Serves 8-10 raw.	Sept. to Dec.	None	Head should be firm, leaves crisp and tender and free from discoloration at tips. Color varies from white to pale green.	13	Same as celery.
Corn	By dozen or unit	1 doz. med. sized ears make 3 cups corn cut from cob. 1 dozen makes 4-6 servings.	July to Sept.	U. S. No. 1 U. S. Fancy Unclassified	Ears should have fresh, green husks; plump, well-filled kernels should be soft and milky. Very small, soft kernels indicate immaturity; hard glazed kernels without milk indicate over-ripeness. Sweet corn, either yellow or white is sweeter than field corn. For best flavor, corn should be eaten 2-3 hrs. after picking; quality deteriorates rapidly as sugar is converted to starch. Avoid insect and worm injury. Tips cut off in store indicate worm injury and poor quality.	62	Very perishable; use immediately. If stored, leave husks on to protect kernels. Wrap ears separately in cellophane or put into plastic bags, close and refrigerate, the least possible time.
Cucumbers	By unit (for slicing). By pk. (15 lb.) or bu. (60 lb.) for pickling	9-inch cucumber weighs 1 lb. and makes 25-30 slices.	All year but best during late fall and winter.	U. S. Fancy U. S. No. 1 U. S. No. 2 Unclassified	Straight, not too thick, with rounded rather than tapering ends. Fresh, firm, not shriveled. Bright green. Over mature cucumbers are dull, puffy, and yellow.	30	Refrigerate.

	Unit of purchase	Amount	Season	Grades	Buying guide	Page	Care
Eggplant	By unit or by lb.	1 lb. egg-plant makes 3 cups diced, serves 3-4.	All year, most plentiful from Aug. to Sept.	U. S. No. 1 / U. S. No. 2 / Unclassified	Uniform, dark purple; free of brown spots on skin. Should be firm, glossy, solid, not wilted or shriveled. Good size is 6-9 inches in diameter.	13	Refrigerate covered.
Greens: Beet Greens, Chard, Collards, Dandelions, Kale, Mustard Greens, Spinach, Turnip Greens, etc.	By lb. or pk. (3 lb.)	1 lb. makes 2 cups cooked.	Varying season for each kind of green; some kind available all year.	U. S. No. 1 / U. S. Commercial / Unclassified	Fresh, young green, and tender. Should not be excessively dirty or coarse. Avoid insect injury.	15 to 30 depending on kind	Trim off damaged leaves. If dirty, store in paper bag. Refrigerate in hydrator. Wash just before using.
Kohlrabi (Cabbage-Turnip)	By bunches of 4-6 or by lb.	4 med. Kohlrabi per lb. makes 2 cups diced.	July to Sept.	None.	Pale green bulbs of 2-3-inch diameter preferable. Large bulbs tough and woody. If tops are fresh, use for greens.	46	Refrigerate covered.
Lettuce	By head, bunch, or lb.	1 large head weighs 1 lb. and has 20 to 30 leaves. Serves 4-5.	All year.	*Head* U. S. Fancy / U. S. No. 1 / U. S. Commercial / U. S. No. 2 / *Leaf* U. S. Fancy / U. S. No. 1 / Unclassified	Head lettuce should be firm, fresh, crisp, and heavy for size. Leaf lettuce should be fresh and crisp. Leaves should be green and not excessively dirty.	31	Trim off all soiled leaves. Wash and store separately. Wash head an hour or two before needed and return to hydrator or damp cloth to crisp.

Vegetable	Purchase Unit	Yield Per Purchase Unit	Market Season	Federal Grades	Quality Standards	Approximate Per Cent Waste	Storage
Mushrooms	By lb.	1 lb. contains 20-30 medium-size mushrooms. 1 lb. serves 5-10.	All year.	U. S. No. 1 Unclassified	May be immature "buttons", with unopened caps or "open caps" in which the cap has expanded, breaking the veil which joins it to the stem, and exposing the gills. There is slight if any difference in flavor. Stems should be trimmed to 1¼ inches. Color ranges from white to deep cream or brownish shade, depending on variety. Spotted appearance indicates decay.	5	Store in refrigerator in tightly covered dish, without washing.
Okra	By lb. or qt.	1 lb. contains about 35 three-inch pods, and makes 2¾ cups cut. Serves 4-6.	August to October.	U. S. No. 1 Unclassified	Pods vary in length, depending on variety. Should be young, crisp, and tender, easily pierced with thumb nail. Older pods are woody and seeds hard.	12	Refrigerate in hydrator. Wash just before using. Fairly perishable.
Onions Leeks Garlic Chives Shallots Green Onions	By lb. or pk. (14 lb.) or bu. (56 lb.) Large Spanish onions, by unit. Green onions by bunch. Chives by the pot.	4-5 dry onions, per lb. 10-12 green onions per bunch. 1 lb. onions serves 4-5.	Domestic onions all year. Bermudas from March to June. Green onions Dec. to Aug.	Onions U. S. No. 1 U. S. No. 2 U. S. Commercial U. S. Combination Unclassified	Dry should be bright, hard, clean, with dry skins. Onions with a seed stem are usually poor in quality. No decay should be evident. Bermuda onions are flat, white or yellow, medium in size. Spanish onions are large, globular or oval in shape. Domestic onions are	Dry 6 Green 59	Place green onions in hydrator. Store dry onions in cold, dark, dry place, well ventilated.

mild, yellowish brown or white, globular, with yellow, red, brown or white skins. White varieties are milder in flavor. Green necks should be of medium size with little or no bulb formation, and white up to 2-3 inches from root. Tops should be fresh, green, tender, and crisp. Leeks look like giant green onions—the green tops are usually tough and should be discarded.

	Purchase	Yield / Serving	Season	Grades	How to Select		Care
Parsnips	By lb. or by bunches of 5-6 parsnips.	4 med. topped parsnips per lb. 1 lb. cleaned and cut into strips makes 2¾ cups. Serves 4-5.	Sept.-May	None	Smooth, firm, well-shaped parsnips of small to med. size are best. Large, soft, flabby roots may be pithy or decayed; mis-shapen ones are wasteful.	22	Hold in a cool, dark place. Not susceptible to cold; frozen parsnips retain full flavor.
Peas	By lb. (in pods.)	1 lb. shelled makes 1⅛ cups peas, and serves 2.	All year, most plentiful from April to Sept.	U. S. No. 1 U. S. Fancy Unclassified	Size of peas depends upon variety. Pods should be bright green, crisp, well-filled, free from blemishes. Peas should be tender and sweet. Sprouted peas or presence of mold indicates overmaturity or long storage.	55	Refrigerate covered in pods; do not shell until ready to be used.
Peppers, green	By unit or lb.	2-3 medium peppers per lb.	All year. Most plentiful June to Nov.	U. S. Fancy U. S. No. 1 U. S. No. 2 Unclassified	Firm, thick-fleshed, glossy, bright green, crisp and of fresh appearance. Blemishes, discoloration, sunken spots, etc.—may indicate decay. Mis-shapen peppers are wasteful.	16	Perishable. Refrigerate. Excessive dryness makes peppers wither; moisture makes them become slimy.
Potatoes, Irish	By lb., pk. (15 lb.) bu. (60 lb.) or sack (100 lb.)	4 medium potatoes per lb. 1 lb. peeled and cubed measures 2⅓ cups. Serves 2-3.	All year.	U. S. Fancy U. S. Extra No. 1 U. S. No. 1 U. S. Commercial U. S. No. 2 Unclassified	Smooth surface with shallow eyes, reasonably clean, free from blemishes. Not withered, soft, or sprouted. When buying in large quantities, look for presence of dry rot (hollow brown spots in center of potato.) Green spots beneath skin may cause bitter flavor.	16	Store in cool, dark, dry place, where there is good air circulation. Hold above freezing temperature, and protect potatoes from drafts. Do not store new potatoes.

Vegetable	Purchase Unit	Yield Per Purchase Unit	Market Season	Grades Federal	Quality Standards	Approximate Per Cent Waste	Storage
Potatoes, sweet	By lb.	2 large or 4 medium potatoes per lb. 1 lb. serves 4.	July to April.	U. S. Fancy U. S. Extra No. 1 U. S. No. 1 U. S. No. 2 Unclassified	Firm, sufficiently regular in shape to avoid waste in peeling. Look for discolored spots, mold, or other signs of decay. Wrinkled ends indicate lack of freshness. *Jerseys:* pale yellow with dry, mealy but firm flesh. *Yams:* deep orange, with moist, soft, sweet flesh.	15	Store at 55° to 60° F. with little humidity. Buy in small quantities as they deteriorate quickly.
Pumpkin	By lb. or unit.	1 lb. makes ¾ cup cooked pulp. Serves 2.	Sept. to March	None	Deep yellow, fine-grained flesh. Larger varieties may be covered with russet netting. Smaller pumpkin preferable.	31	Store in cool, dark, dry place, with good air circulation.
Radishes	By bunch.	6-12 radishes per bunch.	All year. Most plentiful April-Oct.	U. S. No. 1 Unclassified	Firm, crisp, well-formed, smooth, with leaves green and fresh. Red or white. Shape and color depends on variety.	51	Remove tops and refrigerate covered.
Salad Vegetables Endive Escarole Parsley Romaine Watercress	By head, bunch or lb.	1 large head endive weighs 1 lb. and makes 6-8 salads. 1 med. bunch cress will garnish 4-5 salads.	All year.	U. S. No. 1 Unclassified	Crisp, fresh, leaves bright green. Avoid insect injury.	10	Refrigerate covered.

Salsify (Oyster plant)	By bunches 10-12 roots	5 med. roots per lb. 1 lb. yields 2 cups diced. Serves 4-5.	July-October.	None	Smooth, well-shaped roots, resembling small parsnips.	24	Refrigerate covered.
Squash, summer	By unit or by lb.	1 medium size squash makes 1½ cups. Serves 2.	July to Sept.	None	3 types: (1) *Crook neck*, usually deep yellow, warted with long curved neck. (2) *Marrows*, cylindrical, smooth, and tapering toward stem end, dark green with light stripes running lengthwise. (3) *Flat scalloped*, smooth skinned, pale green to white in color. Avoid squash with shells that cannot be easily pierced with thumbnail.	3	Refrigerate covered.
Squash, fall and winter	By unit or by lb.	1 lb. yields 1 cup cooked. Serves 2.	Sept. to March.	None	3 types: (1) *Acorn*, dark green, medium size (½-¾ lb., fluted, acorn-shaped. (2) *Sweet Potato*, light green with white stripes running from stem to blossom end. Medium size (½-¾ lb.) (3) *Hubbard*, *dark green warty and smooth silver skin.* Large 3-10 lbs. Oval tapering at both ends. All have yellow flesh and must have a very hard shell for *good keeping* quality.	26	Store in cool, dark, dry place with good air circulation.

Vegetable	Purchase Unit	Yield Per Purchase Unit	Market Season	Federal Grades	Quality Standards	Approximate Per Cent Waste	Storage
Tomatoes	By lb. or bushel (56 lb.)	3-5 per lb.	All year. Most plentiful July to Nov.	U. S. Fancy U. S. No. 1 U. S. No. 2 Unclassified	Solid, well-colored, glossy, with smooth, unblemished skins. Heavy for size. Stem ends should be free from open cracks and ridges.	2	Ripen at room temperature. Store in refrigerator or in cool, dark, dry place. For long periods of storage wrap tomatoes separately.
Turnips, white Rutabaga, (yellow turnip)	By bunch (with tops) or by lb. peck (14 lb.) or bu. (56 lb.)	4 medium turnips per lb.	All year. Most plentiful from Sept. to May.	U. S. No. 1 Unclassified	Tops should be fresh, green, young, and crisp; roots firm, smooth, with few leaf scars around crown and very few fibrous roots. Very large turnip may be tough, woody, pithy, hollow or strong in flavor.	13	Refrigerate covered. Rutabagas may be wax-dipped and stored in cool, dark, dry place, with good air circulation.

REFERENCES USED IN PREPARING TABLES ON BUYING VEGETABLES AND FRUITS.

1. Better Buymanship, Fresh Fruits and Vegetables. Household Finance Corporation, 919 N. Michigan Avenue, Chicago.
2. Food Buying and Our Markets by Monroe, Kyrk, and Stone. M. Barrows and Co., Inc., N. Y.
3. Produce Guide, National Assoc. of Retail Grocers, 360 N. Michigan Ave., Chicago.
4. A Fruit and Vegetable Buying Guide for Consumers by R. G. Hill. U.S.D.A. Misc. Publ. No. 167.
5. Food Standard Handbook for Quantity Cookery by Dahl and Breland. The Dable, Stanford, Connecticut.
6. Legal Weights Per Bushel for Various Commodities, U. S. Dept. of Commerce, (Circular C425 of National Bureau of Standards.)

TABLE 7   HOMEMAKER'S GUIDE FOR BUYING FRUITS

Fruit	Purchase Unit	Servings Per Unit	Market Season	Federal Grades	Quality Standard	Percentage of Waste	Storage *
Apples	By unit, lb., peck (12.5 lb.), box (44 lb.), barrel (140 lb.), bushel (48 lb.). Peck contains about 40 medium apples; bushel about 150.	3 medium apples per lb., 2½ to 3 lb. makes 1 qt. apple sauce.	See separate chart on apples, Table 11	U. S. Fancy U. S. No. 1 U. S. No. 1 Early U. S. Commercial U. S. Utility U. S. Utility Early U. S. Combination U. S. Hail Unclassified	See separate chart on apples, Table 11	12	Refrigerate or store in cold, dry, dark place, above freezing temperature. For long storage, wrap or pack in shredded waxed paper.
Apricots	By lb., doz., basket (6 lb.), crate (22 lb.), lug (26 lb.)	8 to 12 apricots per lb., 2 to 3 fruits per serving.	May to August.	U. S. No. 1 U. S. No. 2 Unclassified	Should be plump, fairly firm, and of uniform golden color. Must be picked slightly immature in order to reach market in good condition. Tree-ripened fruit is of better quality.	6	Refrigerate ripe fruit, covered. Slightly green fruit may be ripened at room temperature. Very green fruit will become shriveled when stored.
Avocados or Alligator Pears	By unit (5 oz. to 3 lb. each) or box (12 to 15 lb.)	2 to 5 servings for average - size avocado.	All year. Most plentiful in fall and winter.	None	May be spherical or pear shaped. Color varies from green to dark mahogany. Skin may be smooth and paper-thin, or thick, leathery and pebbled. Flesh should be almost as soft as a ripe pear. Flavor delicate and nutlike.	25	Ripen in warm, humid room. If ripe, refrigerate but do not place on ice. Coat cut surface with citrus fruit juice to prevent darkening. Wrap cut pieces in waxed paper.

* For further information on storage, "Care of Food in the Home," p 140. Table 11 is on p 97.

Fruit	Purchase Unit	Servings Per Unit	Market Season	Federal Grades	Quality Standard	Percentage of Waste	Storage
Bananas	By lb., doz., or hand (10 to 20).	5 very small, 3 medium, or 2 large bananas per lb.	All year.	None.	Plump and well developed. For cooking, buy yellow - ripe or green - tipped fruit; for eating raw, buy full-ripe, brown flecked fruit. Avoid bruised fruit.	33	Store in dry moderately warm room. Do not refrigerate, as flavor will be poor and discoloration will result.
Berries, Blackberries Blueberries Boysen-berries Dewberries Gooseberries Huckle-berries Loganberries Raspberries Youngberries	By half-pint, pint, or quart.	1 qt. without caps measures 3¾ cups and will serve 4 to 6.	June to August.	U. S. No. 1 U. S. No. 2 U. S. Combination Unclassified	Bright, clean, fresh appearance. Individual berries plump. Free from adhering caps (an indication of maturity). Stained boxes indicate damaged berries. Watch for mold.	4	Spread berries on shallow tray without washing. Remove soft or moldy berries. Cover with waxed paper. Refrigerate. Very perishable. Wash just before using.
Berries, Cranberries	By lb. or quart.	1 lb. measures 1 qt. and makes 3-3½ cups of cooked sauce.	October to February.	None	Should be lustrous and firm to point of hardness. Color varies from bright to dark red. Dark fruit usually sweeter.	4	Sort without washing. Place in bowl or glass jar. Cover loosely and refrigerate. Wash just before using.
Berries, Strawberries	By half-pint, pint, or quart.	1 qt. hulled makes 3 cups	December to July, but most plentiful May and June.	U. S. No. 1 U. S. No. 2 U. S. Combination Unclassified	Berries firm, well colored, free of white, green or darkened tips. Hulls should be attached.	4	Same as for other berries.

Cherries, Sour Red Sweet Black Sweet White	By lb., quart, or lug (15 lb.)	1 lb. sweet cherries stemmed and pitted measures 2¾ cups and serves 4 to 5. 1 qt. sour cherries pitted makes 2 cups.	May to August	None except for black cherries U. S. No. 1 Unclassified	Bright, fresh appearance, plump, good color, fairly firm, juicy, good flavor. Examine at stem end for worm injury, decay, and bruises. Sweet cherries (Royal Anne or White cherries; Bing, Republican, etc., or Black cherries) used primarily for eating fresh. Sour red cherries (Montmorency, Richmond, English Morello) for cooking.	6	Wash. Wormy cherries will float. Drain well and spread on shallow tray in refrigerator.
Currants	By half-pint, pint, or qt.	1 qt. stemmed measures 3 cups.	June to July	None	Same as for berries above.	10	Same as for berries.
Dates	By package or lb.	6 to 8 servings per pound	August to Dec.	None	Plump, lustrous, golden brown color. Smooth skin.	25-40	Refrigerate or store in cool, dry place.
Figs	By unit, doz., lb., or box (10 lb.)	10 to 12 figs per pound.	June to August.	None	Should be fully ripe, fairly soft, but not mushy. Color varies from green-yellow to purple or almost black. Size varies. Look for mold.	8	Use soon after purchasing. Refrigerate. Ripened figs ferment readily.
Grapefruit	By unit, doz., lb., or box. See special section on grapefruit	2 servings per grapefruit. About 12 sections per fruit.	All year, but best from Sept. to May.	U. S. Fancy U. S. No. 1 U. S. No. 2 U. S. Combination Unclassified Culls	See special section on grapefruit	34	See special section on grapefruit

Special section on Grapefruit is found on pp 76-7.

Fruit	Purchase Unit	Servings Per Unit	Market Season	Federal Grades	Quality Standard	Percentage of Waste	Storage
Grapes	By lb., 2, 4, or 12 qt. basket; crate (20 lb.) or box (34 lb.)	3 to 4 servings per lb.	Western grapes, June to December. Eastern grapes Sept. to Oct.	U. S. Fancy U. S. No. 1	Flesh firmly attached to stem. Plump, of high color and good flavor. Bunches should be compact. Note evidence of decay at stem end of grape.	22	Examine and snip out any damaged grapes. Refrigerate or store in cool, dry place, where air circulation is good, on shallow trays. Sort frequently. Wash just before using.
Kumquats	By qt. basket.	8 to 12 servings per qt. as salad.	Dec. to Jan.	None	Same as oranges. Both rind and pulp used.	6	Secure waxed paper over top of basket. Refrigerate or store in cool, dry, dark place.
Lemons	By doz., lb., box (Nos. 210 and 588 fruits— 76 lb.)	3 to 4 tablespoons of juice per lemon.	All year.	U. S. No. 1 U. S. No. 2 U. S. Combination U. S. No. 3 Unclassified	Fine textured skin, heavy for size. Deep yellow fruits are usually thinner skinned, juicier but less acid.	38	Refrigerate in hydrator, or wrap individually in tissue or waxed paper and store in cool, dry place.
Limes	By unit, doz., box (80 lb.)	1 to 2 tablespoons of juice per lime.	All year, but most plentiful June to August.	U. S. No. 1 U. S. No. 2 U. S. Combination Unclassified	Green in color, heavy for size. Yellow fruits lack acidity.	24	Same as lemons.
Melons, Watermelon	By unit or lb., 15 to 35 lb. each, average size.	15 to 20 servings per watermelon.	May to October.	U. S. No. 1 U. S. No. 2 U. S. No. 3 Unclassified	Symmetrical in shape. Fresh bloom over surface. If cut or plugged, melon should show flesh crisp, free from fibers, ripe and sweet. Avoid decay at stem end.	54	Refrigerate, turning melon occasionally.

	Sold by	Amount / Servings	Season	U.S. Grades	What to look for		Care
Melons, Cantaloupe, Muskmelon	By unit or crate (60 lb.)	1 small melon serves 2. 1 large melon, 4 to 6.	April-October.	U. S. No. 1 Commercial Unclassified	Honey dew has smooth surface, cantaloupe should have the rind heavily netted. Melons picked at the proper stage of maturity have an indented "scar" of darker appearance at stem end showing it was not forced from vine. Ripe melons have a pronounced aroma typical of the variety.	53	Hold in cool, dry place or wrap in several layers of waxed paper or in an oil silk bag and refrigerate. For best flavor, remove from refrigerator an hour or so before serving, should be cool but not ice-cold.
Honey Dew Honey Ball		1 small melon serves 2. 1 large melon serves 4 to 8.	All year. Most plentiful June to July.	U. S. No. 1 Commercial U. S. No. 2 Unclassified			
Oranges	By doz., lb., or box. See special section on oranges.	1 orange per serving. 1 lb. makes about 1 cup juice. About 9-12 sections per fruit.	All year. Tangerines, Nov. to May. See section on oranges.	U. S. Fancy U. S. No. 1 U. S. No. 2 U. S. Combination U. S. No. 3 Unclassified	See special section on oranges	22-28	See special section on oranges
Nectarines	By lb., doz., or basket, (6 lb.)	1 lb. sliced makes 4 servings.	May to October.	U. S. Fancy U. S. Extra No. 1 U. S. No. 1 U. S. No. 2 U. S. Combination Unclassified	Firm flesh, free from small punctures. Avoid decayed spots. Smooth skins, otherwise similar to a peach.	12	Under-ripe fruit can be ripened in warm room. Green fruit will shrivel rather than ripen. Refrigerate sound tree-ripened fruit, covered. Serve any bruised fruit at once.
Peaches	By lb., basket, box, (20 lb.) or bushel (48 lb.)	1 lb. sliced makes 2-3 servings. 2-2½ lb. makes 1 qt. sauce. 3 medium peaches per lb.	May to October.	U. S. Fancy U. S. Extra No. 1 U. S. No. 1 U. S. No. 2 Unclassified	Flesh firm, not hard. White or yellow depending on variety. Not green, blush is not good indication of maturity. Free from small punctures through which gum exudes, as these may indicate worms. Avoid decayed spots.	12	Sort out any bruised fruit, and use at once. Under der ripe fruit may be ripened in a warm room. Refrigerate ripe fruit covered.

Special section on Oranges is found on p 76.

Fruit	Purchase Unit	Servings Per Unit	Market Season	Federal Grades	Quality Standard	Percentage of Waste	Storage *
Pears, Late Summer (Bartlett)	By lb., doz., box (46 lb.) or bushel (50 lb.)	3 pears per lb. 2 to 2½ lb. makes 1 qt. sauce.	July to October.	U. S. No. 1 U. S. No. 2 U. S. Combination Unclassified	Regardless of color or variety, pears are ready to eat when flesh yields readily to gentle pressure at stem end. Not wilted or shrivelled.	17	Ripen fruit at 60° to 70° F. in humid place. Refrigerate ripe fruit, or store in cool, dark, dry place.
Pears, Winter			Sept. to April. See special chart on Pears	U. S. Extra No. 1 U. S. No. 1 U. S. No. 2 U. S. Combination Unclassified	See special chart on Pears		
Persimmons	By unit.	2 servings per large fruit.	October to February.	None	Flesh very sweet and very soft when ripe. Unripe fruit is very acid and puckery.	18	Ripen at room temperature, store in cool, well-ventilated place, sorting frequently.
Pineapples	By unit, lb., or crate (18 to 42 fruits 70 lb.)	6 servings per medium fruit.	March to June, most abundant. Almost all year at fancy grocers.	U. S. Fancy U. S. No. 1 U. S. No. 2 Unclassified	Heavy for size. Free of soft spots. Golden orange color when ripe, and leaves pull out readily. Look for signs of decay at bottom.	39	Ripen at 65° to 70° F. covered with heavy paper. Store ripe fruit in refrigerator.
Plums and Fresh Prunes	By lb., basket—6 lb., lug—16 lb., crate—20 lb. or bushel—56 lb.	15 to 20 per lb., 1½ to 2 lb. makes 1 qt. sauce.	May to November.	U. S. Fancy U. S. No. 1 U. S. No. 2 Unclassified	Plump, fresh skins, free from scars or skin defects.	15	Refrigerate, or hold in cool, dark, humid place.

Special table 8 on Pears is found on p 95.

	By unit	Servings	Season	Grades	Quality		Storage
Pomegranates	By unit.	2 servings per medium fruit. 1 fruit will garnish 12 salads.	Sept. to November.	None	Hard, tough, leathery rind. Color varies from reddish brown to deep red.	36	Store in cool, dry, place.
Quinces	By unit, lb., peck—12 lb. or bushel—48 lb.	3 medium fruit per pound.	Sept. to November.	None	Greenish-yellow to yellow, firm but not hard consistency. The presence of worms are shown by punctures in the skin. Bruises or spots should be avoided.	12	Avoid bruising. Store in cool, dry, dark place.
Rhubarb	By lb., carton (2 to 10 lbs.) or box (15) to 20 lbs.)	1 lb. makes 4 to 6 servings. (2 cups sauce)	May to August	U. S. Fancy U. S. No. 1 U. S. No. 2 Unclassified	Fairly thick stalks, which are fresh and crisp, not wilted or flabby. Large leaves indicate old stalks. Color varies with variety.	32	Refrigerate, or hold in cool place. Cover with damp cloth to retain crispness.

TABLE 8   WHEN FRESH FALL AND WINTER PEARS ARE BEST FOR EATING *

Variety	Characteristics	MARKET SEASON									
		Sep.	Oct.	Nov.	Dec.	Jan.	Feb.	Mar.	Apr.	May	June
Bosc	Russet variety; long tapering neck.	●	●	●	●	●					
Comice	Green-skinned, famous for size. Long famous for its superb quality and beauty		●	●	●	●					
Anjou	A fruit every member of the family will enjoy. Green-skinned, fine-grained, spicy.		●	●	●	●	●	●	●	●	
Nelis	Rough outside but with a heart of gold. Russet variety; small, very sweet.					●	●	●	●	●	●

Shipping season is scientifically determined in order to place pears in the hands of consumers at best eating time. For maximum flavor and money value, it is important that the right variety of pear be used at the right season. The solid pears on the chart above show the months when the four major varieties of fall and winter pears are at their best and are most plentiful in the markets.

* Courtesy Oregon-Washington-California Pear Bureau, Hood River, Oregon.

Chart 9   ORANGE SIZES

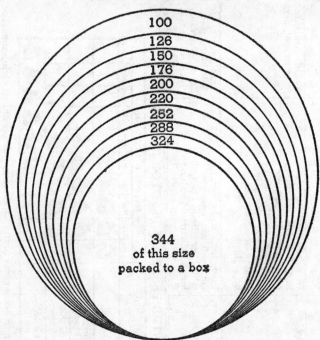

100
126
150
176
200
220
252
288
324

344
of this size
packed to a box

Chart 10   LEMON SIZES*

* See next page.

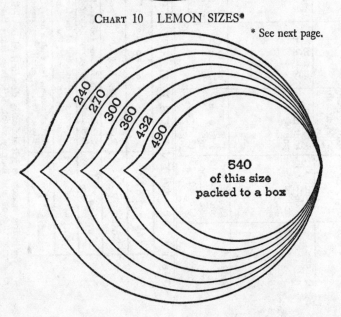

240
270
300
360
432
490

540
of this size
packed to a box

The quality of lemons is best judged by their weight and the texture of their skin. High quality lemons are heavy for their size, the skin is thin and fine grained and their color ranges from a clean yellow to yellow that is heavily russeted. The largest sized lemons from California are numbered 240 and the smallest 540. The largest from Florida are 210 and the smallest 288. Sizes 300 and 360 are as a rule the ones which yield the most juice.

NUTRITIVE TABLE 8
AVERAGE VITAMIN VALUES OF 100 GRAMS OF DRIED FRUIT *
(About 3.5 oz.)

	A (I.U.)	B₁ (mg.)	C (mg.)	G (mg.)
Dried Apricots (sulfured)	8913	.09	8	.28
Dried Figs	64	.09	0	.11
Dried Peaches (sulfured)	3550	.04	20	.20
Prunes	1603	.17	5	.53
Raisins	105	.12	0	.13

* Nutritional information supplied by the California Foods Research Institute: references in bibliography at end of section, p 104.

HOMEMAKER'S GUIDE FOR BUYING APPLES *

TABLE 11

Variety	Characteristics	Main Market Season	Best Uses
Baldwin	Medium to large apple. The light yellow or greenish skin is blushed and mottled with bright red, indistinctly striped with carmine and covered with a scattering of conspicuous gray or white dots. The flesh is yellowish, juicy, mildly acid; firm, crisp, rather tender. Quality good to very good.	November-April	Dessert, (eating raw) Applesauce Pie, cobbler Apple betty, etc.
Delicious	Medium to large apple. Red and yellow striped skin. Five characteristic points on the blossom end. Fine grained, yellowish white flesh; juicy, fragrant, mildly acid, firm, crisp, and tender. Quality good to very good.	October-February	Dessert, (eating raw)
Duchess	Medium apple. Red striped skin. Attractive color effect caused by pale yellow or greenish yellow skin being mostly covered with irregular splotches and stripes of bright red mottled with carmine. Flesh tinged with yellow; juicy, somewhat acid for eating raw. Rather firm, crisp, tender. Quality fair to good.	July-October	Applesauce Baking Pie, cobbler Apple betty, etc.
Golden Delicious	Medium to large apple, yellow to solid gold-colored skin. Flesh is rich, juicy, almost spicy in flavor. Crackling texture. Quality good to excellent.	October-January	Dessert, (eating raw) Applesauce Baking

* Adapted from "A Fruit and Vegetable Buying Guide for Consumer," Miscellaneous Publication No. 167, United States Department of Agriculture.

Variety	Characteristics	Main Market Season	Best Uses
Gravenstein	Medium to large apple. Yellow with red stripes on skin. Greenish with orange-yellow skin overlaid with broken stripes of light and dark red. Yellowish flesh, juicy, slightly acid, firm, crisp, fragrant. Quality good to very good.	July-September	Dessert, (eating raw) Applesauce Pie, cobbler Apple betty, etc.
Grimes Golden	Medium apple. Deep clear yellow skin with pale yellow or russet dots. Yellow flesh, moderately juicy, firm, crisp, tender and fragrant. Quality good to excellent.	October-January	Dessert, (eating raw) Applesauce Pie, cobbler Apple betty
Hubbardston	Medium to large apple. Yellow skin mingled with red. The yellowish skin is blushed with red which varies from a dull brownish to a clear bright red and is more or less marked with deep carmine. Whitish flesh, slightly tinged with yellow; juicy, slightly acid, fairly firm, crisp, tender, fragrant. Quality good to very good.	October-January	Useful for all purposes.
Jonathan	Small to medium apple. Deep lively red skin. One side bright yellow splotch overlaid with lively red and striped with carmine. Whitish flesh slightly tinged with yellow; juicy, slightly acid, fairly firm, crisp, tender, fragrant. Quality very good to excellent.	September-December	Dessert, (eating raw) Applesauce Pie, cobbler etc.
McIntosh	Medium to large apple. Bright deep red skin striped with carmine. Highly colored specimens become dark almost purplish-red overspread with thin lilac bloom. White flesh sometimes veined with red; juicy, slightly acid, becoming mild and nearly sweet when very ripe; firm, crisp, fine textured, fragrant. Quality good to excellent.	October-January	Useful for all purposes.
Northern Spy	Large to very large apple. Bright skin striped red. The clear pale yellow skin is nearly concealed with bright pinkish red, mottled and splashed with carmine and overspread with a thin delicate bloom. Yellowish flesh; very juicy, rather firm, crisp, very tender, fragrant. Quality very good to excellent.	October-March	Dessert, (eating raw) Applesauce Pie, cobbler Apple betty, etc.
Rhode Island Greening	Medium to large apple. Green or yellowish skin sometimes has a brownish red blush. Yellowish flesh; juicy, slightly acid, firm, crisp, tender, rich. Quality good to very good.	October-March	Applesauce Baking Pie, cobbler Apple betty, etc.

Variety	Characteristics	Main Market Season	Best Uses
Rome Beauty	Large apple. Yellow mingled with red. The yellowish or greenish skin is more or less mottled with bright red striped with carmine. Nearly white flesh with slight yellow or greenish tinge; juicy, mildly acid, rather crisp, moderately fine textured. Quality fair to good.	November-May	Applesauce Baking Pie, cobbler Apple betty, etc.
Spitzenberg	Medium to large apple. Bright red skin conspicuously striped with darker red which may become almost a purplish blush. White flesh tinged with yellow; juicy, slightly acid; firm, crisp, rather tender, aromatic. Quality very good to excellent.	October-February	Useful for all purposes.
Tompkins King	Large to very large apple. Attractive skin, red over yellow. The fine yellow color is washed and mottled with orange-red, striped and splashed with bright carmine and covered with numerous white or russet dots. Yellowish flesh, juicy, slightly acid; crisp, tender, rather coarse, aromatic. Quality very good to excellent.	November-February	Dessert, (eating raw) Applesauce Pie, cobbler Apple betty, etc.
Wagener	Medium apple. Bright light red skin with some contrasting yellow. The skin is bright, pinkish-red striped with bright carmine over a clear pale yellow background. Whitish flesh with a yellowish tinge; very juicy, slightly acid; moderately firm, crisp, tender. Quality good to very good.	November-January	Dessert, (eating raw) Applesauce Pie, cobbler Apple betty, etc.
Winesap	Small to medium apple. Bright deep red skin, indistinctly striped with dark purplish red overspread with a faint brown and marked with small scattered whitish dots. Flesh tinged with yellow, sometimes veined with red; very juicy, slightly acid, very firm, moderately crisp. Quality good to very good.	November-June	Useful for all purposes.
Yellow Newton	Medium to large apple. Greenish yellow to yellow often showing slight brownish or brownish pink color. Flesh distinctly tinged with yellow; juicy, mildly acid; firm, crisp, tender, highly aromatic. Quality very good to excellent.	January-May	Dessert, (eating raw) Applesauce Pie, cobbler Apple betty, etc.
Yellow Transparent	Small to medium apple. Greenish white to greenish yellow skin. White flesh, juicy, sharply acid until fully ripe; pleasant but not high flavor. Quality fair to good.	July-August	Applesauce Pie, cobbler Apple betty, etc.

DRIED AND DEHYDRATED FOODS

The terms "dried" and "dehydrated" are often used interchangeably, but foods preserved by both methods are not the same. In dehydration, moisture is removed under controlled conditions of temperature, humidity and air circulation. In drying, the moisture is removed naturally by sun and air, with little control of temperature, humidity and air circulation.

Drying is a very old form of food preservation. In fact its origin in antiquity is not even known. The quality of those old foods varied greatly and depended entirely on sanitary and weather conditions. Some of them were excellent, for example the old time dried corn, apples and fruit leathers. Others were very poor being unattractively dark in color and with little of the true fruit or vegetable flavor. The modern dried foods are much superior in flavor, color, and keeping quality, because the choice of good fresh foods and the techniques in preparation and storage have been greatly improved.

Dehydration is a modern method of food preservation and is now used to preserve a greater variety of foods than was ever attempted with drying. Because the techniques are rigidly controlled, the resulting foods may be of superior color and flavor. Some of these foods, both sun dried and dehydrated, are pasteurized at the end of the dehydration, then are put into sanitary packages that bring them to the consumer in a most attractive form.

Dried and dehydrated foods have several advantages over foods preserved in other ways. They need no refrigeration or special care until package is opened. They are less bulky and weighty; the weight ranges from one-fourth to one-ninth of the original. With present or improved standards of dehydration and packaging the future use of dried foods seems assured.

Both dried and dehydrated fruits and vegetables differ considerably from the fresh in flavor, aroma and appearance. Many of them have even greater appeal than the original food. Dried apricots have a more beautiful rich color, and a flavor with more character than is found in the fresh product. And many people feel the same way about the modern tenderized and pasteurized dried prune, which is so delicious as it comes from the package, that there is no point in cooking it to enhance its appetite appeal.

There is some destruction of vitamins in the dehydration and drying of foods, the exact amount depending upon the quality of the original food and the care used in preparation for drying as well as in the actual moisture-removing process. The exact vitamin content of commercially dried fruits and vegetables is not entirely agreed upon at present. Research has shown, however, that there is considerable variation in the losses among the fruits. In general the losses of vitamin A, thiamine, and ascorbic acid seem to be the most important ones. There is evidence that prolonged sun drying destroys fairly large amounts of vitamin A and that sulfuring treatment with drying causes losses of thiamine, but this is not an important constituent of the cut fruits. Ascorbic acid destruction varies considerably with the fruit as well as the exact treatment. Studies have shown that sulfuring helps to preserve this vitamin. Prunes, raisins and figs are seldom sulfured. Sulfuring cut fruits, such as apricots, peaches, pears and apples retains their color and flavor. See Nutritive Table 8, p 97, and Homemakers Guide for Buying Common Dried Fruit Products, Table 12, p 102.

There is even less conclusive data available for vegetables. It appears that vitamin A is retained well, that thiamine loss is somewhat greater, but in most cases is not serious. Ascorbic acid, however, is almost totally destroyed by some drying methods.

"The principal values of dried fruits lie in their high energy values, as the sugars in dried fruits are simple sugars. They require no digestive action in the body—are assimilable as is, immediately upon being eaten. All dried fruits are high in iron and are alkaline in their end reaction. Dried apricots and peaches are outranked only by liver and kidney in their capacity for blood regeneration in anemic conditions caused by nutritional deficiencies, according to Dr. George H. Whipple of the University of Rochester."

Dried fruits and vegetables should be stored in a cool, dark, dry place, in moisture proof and insect proof containers. Glass or moisture proof bags that can be tightly sealed are suitable containers; ordinary paper sacks are not satisfactory.

The following vegetables are naturally dried after they mature on vine or stalk:

> *Beans: navy, kidney, chile, pinto, soy, black eye, lima, black eye peas, lentils, popcorn.*

Commercially dried parsley and onion flakes of good quality have been on the market for a number of years, and others like mint, celery and green pepper have made their appearance on the grocer's shelves recently.

Dried fruits that are available commercially have been listed in the following table (No 12, p 102) with information on the product varieties and the government or commercial grades.

SOME HINTS ON BUYING FRESH FRUITS AND VEGETABLES

1. Personally select your own fruits and vegetables; ordering them by telephone may prove disappointing and costly.

2. Scrutinize a "bargain" carefully. If it is damaged stock, determine whether the waste will offset the reduction in price. If the price is low because of a temporary over-supply of the food, the reduced price may represent a real bargain.

3. Do not judge quality by size. Overgrown fruits and vegetables are seldom of top quality. In many cases a safer standard is weight; for example, a small grapefruit which is heavy for its size will hold more juice than a larger grapefruit of the same weight.

4. When buying by measure rather than weight, be sure that you get full measure. Small fruits, such as berries and cherries, and some small vegetables, are often packed in containers of various kinds. These may be packed very loosely; and sometimes the container is "faced" with specimens of excellent quality which conceal the poor quality of the rest of the pack.

5. Remember that beauty is often only skin deep, and that blemishes may affect only the surface appearance of a fruit or vegetable.

6. Be considerate of other buyers by handling fruits and vegetables very carefully when it is necessary to test quality by handling. Tomorrow you may be the last shopper, and find nothing but pinched, bruised and rejected fruit in the grocer's trays.

7. Learn the names and how to identify common varieties of fruits and vegetables. Then you will be sure to get the kind that you want, and will not be disappointed when using them.

8. Study the market columns regularly for information regarding available supply and current prices. Knowledge of this type is helpful in securing value for money spent.

HOMEMAKER'S GUIDE FOR BUYING
COMMON DRIED FRUIT PRODUCTS

TABLE 12

Fruit	Product and Pack Varieties	Grading	General Information
Apples	Apple nuggets Apple powder		Contain about 3% moisture. For pie and sauce. A specialty with limited use.
	Apple quarters Apple rings Apple slices	Agricultural Marketing Administration (USDA) 1. U.S. Grade A-Fancy 2. U.S. Grade B-Choice 3. U.S. Grade C-Standard 4. Off-grade dried apples which are wholesome and edible but do not meet U.S. Standard	Apples are usually dehydrated instead of sundried. They are sulfured before drying to prevent oxidation. Certain varieties of apple are more suitable than others for dehydration. Moisture should not exceed 24%.
Apricots	Apricot halves (Usually unpeeled)	Agricultural Marketing Administration (USDA) (Tentative) 1. Extra Fancy 2. Fancy 3. Extra Choice 4. Choice 5. Standard Ungraded slabs	May be sun-dried in June, July and August or dehydrated. The fruit is usually sulfured. The moisture content is usually 20-25%. Apricots are graded for size to make them more easily handled.
Bananas	Banana powder Banana flakes	None	Useful in preparing beverages. Also used therapeutically. Moisture content from 3-6%. The fruit may be either sundried or dehydrated.

Fruit	Product and Pack Varieties	Grading	General Information
Dates	Fard Persian Hallowi Khadrawi Deglet Noor California Mission (Dates are sold pitted and unpitted)	Commercial Grades: 1. Extra Fancy 2. Fancy 3. Choice Grades are based on size, firmness and uniformity	There are two general types of dates: 1. The black, sweet and meaty date with a thin skin. The Fard is an example of this type. 2. The golden brown date with a coarse texture and a larger seed. The Persian, Hallowi and Khadrawi are examples. The Deglet Noor is a black date from Africa but the California Mission date is somewhat similar.
Figs	Black Mission White: Smyrna (Calimyrna) White Adriatic Figs are sold in bulk, pulled in squares or rounded and sold in boxes; and pressed and sold in bricks.	California Grade Sizes: 1. Extra Fancy 2. Fancy 3. Extra Choice 4. Choice 5. Standard	Black Mission are small and tender and of good flavor. Smyrna and the White Adriatic are larger, sweeter and have a thin skin. Figs are usually sun-dried but may be dehydrated. The least expensive form of figs is sold in bulk in natural form.
Peaches	Clingstone Freestone	California Grade Sizes: 1. Jumbo 2. Extra Fancy 3. Fancy 4. Extra Choice 5. Choice 6. Standard Slabs or Pie Fruit	Peaches are both sun-dried and dehydrated. The Clingstone variety is dehydrated and Freestone sun-dried. Freestone varieties such as Elberta and Muir are considered very desirable. Grades in addition to size are based on flavor, uniformity, maturity, and freedom from extraneous matter.
Pears	Bartlett is one of the most common varieties	Agricultural Marketing Administration (USDA) 1. Grade A-Fancy 2. Grade B-Choice 3. Grade C-Standard Sizes: 1. Jumbo 4. Medium 2. Extra 5. Small large 6. Extra 3. Large small	Pears are both sun-dried and dehydrated. They have a moisture content of not more than 24%.

Fruit	Product and Pack Varieties	Grading	General Information
Prunes	California Varieties: French-Petite Imperial Sugar Silver Oregon Varieties: Italian	California Grade Sizes determined by number of prunes per lb. 20-30 70-80 30-40 80-90 40-50 90-100 50-60 100-110 60-70 110-120	Prunes are less expensive than most other dried fruits. The California varieties, in general, are more sweet and tender than the large tart Italian prune from Oregon. Prunes are both sundried and dehydrated. Tenderized prunes have had moisture added. Small prunes are less expensive than large prunes and usually give "more meat" for the same amount of money.
Raisins	Seedless: Sultana Thompson's Seedless Sultanina Seeded: Malagas Muscats (also called Muscatel or Alexandria raisins)	Grade Sizes: Cluster and seeded raisins: Four crown Three crown Two Crown One Crown Seedless Raisins: Bakers Choice Fancy	Seeded raisins have a more pronounced flavor than the seedless. The grapes are seeded after drying. Thompson's Seedless are sometimes sulfur-bleached to give the light amber color frequently seen.

References:

"Drying and Dehydration of Foods," by Harry W. von Loesecke. Reinhold Publishing Company, New York.

"Food Buying and Our Markets," by Day Monroe, Hazel Kyrk and Ursula Stone. Barrows and Company, New York.

Reprints, University of California—Agnes Fay Morgan.

Nutrition and Physical Fitness—L. Jean Bogert.

Food Values of Commonly Used Portions—Bowes & Church.

Chemistry of Food and Nutrition—Henry C. Sherman.

Nutrition and Diet in Health and Disease—James McLester.

Buying Staples

THIS chapter is a series of handy reference guides designed to answer questions about various staple items: chocolate and cocoa, fats, oils and other shortenings, flours, leavening agents, milk and milk products, nuts, olives and pickles, sugars and syrups, spices, herbs, extracts and vinegars.

It is more factual material than you would probably enjoy reading at one stretch, but every page contains facts about commonly used foods that would be of interest and practical help to everyone who is buying food, or planning to buy it one day. Just a casual turning of the next ten or fifteen pages will bring to your attention numerous little-known facts about many of these foods, and we feel sure will encourage you to turn to these pages often when you are seeking an answer to some question.

Remember these pages when you are tasting an exotic dish in an unusual restaurant: the spice chart will suggest the spice to go with different kinds of foods. Remember these pages when you are wondering how cocoa is made, or why you can keep the hydrogenated shortenings at room temperature, or the difference between brown sugar, granulated, powdered and confectioners'. These and numbers of other questions can be answered by reading the readily accessible material in this chapter.

THE ANSWERS TO YOUR QUESTIONS ABOUT CHOCOLATE AND COCOA

Chocolate and Cocoa are produced from the roasted beans of cacao trees, grown in the tropical belt near the equator. These beans are the seeds of the fruit from the cacao tree. At the present time, millions of pounds of chocolate and cocoa are used annually in this country.

Chocolate is made by grinding the fermented, roasted, shelled cacao beans. Different flavorings such as vanilla may be added, and many special processes are employed to give a smooth mellow product. The resulting chocolate mass is then molded into the familiar bars, squares, etc. Chocolate contains about 50 per cent of cocoa butter, about the same amount as the original bean. The degree of roasting brings out the flavor, and accounts in part for differences in flavor.

The difference between Bitter, Semi-sweet, Sweet, and Milk Chocolate is based on the amount of sugar and milk that is added to the chocolate. *Bitter chocolate* contains 5 to 20 per cent sugar, *Semi-sweet* from 20 to 40 per cent sugar, and *Sweet* from 40 to 65 per cent sugar. *Milk chocolate* contains about 12 per cent whole milk solids and from 35 to 50 per cent sugar.

Cocoa is made by removing about one-half of the cocoa butter from the ground chocolate. The remaining mixture contains about 22 per cent of the original cocoa butter. It is hardened into a cake, then pulverized.

Dutch Process cocoa is chemically treated to darken and enrich the color. Dutch process cocoa is also said to dissolve more easily and has less tendency to settle out when made into a beverage.

Cocoa and chocolate may be used interchangeably if the following adjustments are made. Three level tablespoons of cocoa plus two teaspoons of shortening are approximately equal to one ounce of baking chocolate. Chocolate should be melted over hot water or cut and added to liquid and heated until it melts, then cooled and added to the other ingredients. Cocoa may be sifted with dry ingredients, or mixed with a cold liquid first.

Both cocoa and chocolate should be stored in a fairly cool place. If the temperature is above 85° F, chocolate usually becomes crumbly and grayish, because some of the cocoa butter separates out and accumulates on the surface. When the chocolate cools, the surface butter looks whitish.

A chocolate in liquid form has come on the market recently under several brand names in a carton containing 8 1-oz packets. It gives results comparable to solid chocolate except in recipes where the chocolate must harden, such as in nut or cereal clusters or toffee topping.

THE ANSWERS TO YOUR QUESTIONS ABOUT
FATS, OILS AND OTHER SHORTENINGS

Fats, oils and other shortenings are important in the preparation of foods of many kinds. All are important nutritionally for their caloric value, and some contribute vitamins and other growth and health promoting substances. They give a sense of satisfaction after eating, because of their richness and "staying" quality. In addition, butter, olive oil, and meat drippings add their distinctive flavor to many kinds of foods. They all contribute shortness and pleasing texture to baked products, and aid in developing delicate crusty coatings when foods are fried. All fats except the all-hydrogenated lard and vegetable fats must be covered closely to prevent the absorption of other flavors, and should be stored in the refrigerator.

Butter is made by churning pasteurized sweet or soured cream until the particles of butterfat cling to each other and the buttermilk can be washed out. Salt is then added and the butter "worked" to remove air and most of the water. The federal standard requires that butter contain at least 80 per cent butter fat, with the remaining 20 per cent of water, salt and curd. The presence of water keeps butter plastic. It is extremely important that butter be handled carefully and cleanly to prevent contamination and changes in flavor during its preparation and storage. Large quantities of butter are carried in cold storage to make equal amounts available the year around.

Because of its fine characteristic flavor, butter is valued as a spread for breads, for making butter cakes and for flavoring vegetables, sauces, icings, and confections. Since butter contains water and milk proteins, it is not suitable for deep fat frying and because its shortening power is lower than most other fats, it does not make economical or tender pastry.

Butter is a particularly valuable source of vitamin A. Its vitamin content varies, being high when cows are on pasture, and low when on dry feed. The color also varies depending on the feed, and in winter a harmless pure food coloring is added to give butter more appetite appeal.

Salted butter is most commonly sold, but "sweet" or unsalted butter is also available. Sweet butter has an especially pleasing butter flavor, but it is perishable and quickly loses its fine flavor.

Butter becomes soft at room temperature. It should be refrigerated in a covered container to keep it firm and preserve its delicate flavor.

Margarine is the chief fat other than butter used as a spread and for cooking. It is made from either vegetable or animal fats other than butterfat. In processing, margarine is churned in pasteurized milk, which causes it to take up milk solids and to acquire butter flavor. Margarine now must be fortified by adding a minimum of 15,000 U.S.P. units of vitamin A per pound, and some brands contain even more. The vitamin A value of fortified margarine is comparable to the average vitamin A content of butter throughout the entire year. Scientific tests also show margarine to be about the equal of butter in digestibility, caloric and nutritive value. And good margarine is far superior to poor butter in eating quality.

On July 1, 1950, the federal tax on colored margarine was repealed by Congress. Since then, yellow margarine has become available in all the States. Eliminating the extra work of coloring margarine has increased its popularity which is reflected in increased sales. The coloring added is similar to that used in coloring some butter. Margarine of good quality is a wholesome fat and may be used wherever butter is used. It costs much less than butter because the processes of production are less expensive.

SHORTENINGS

There are three types of shortening on the market: *Lard, Emulsified* and *Non-Emulsified Shortenings.*

Lard is made by rendering the leaf, visceral and back-fat of healthy hogs over low heat. To obtain creamy white lard, delicate in odor and sweet in flavor, the fat is freed from blood by thorough washing, and from muscular tissue by careful trimming. It takes care and skill to make top-quality lard, and quality is only maintained by proper storage in a cool place; stored in a warm place, it soon becomes rancid and is unfit for food use. Even at room temperature lard becomes very soft so it must be stored in a place cool enough to keep it firm for best cooking results. Commercial packers scientifically process their lard, thus making it uniformly higher in quality than farm-made lard. The packer treatment of lard deodorizes it, reduces its tendency to become rancid and insures its uniform plasticity and consistency.

Lard is a favorite shortening of many experienced cooks and of those from farms where good lard was made. Lard ranks high in shortening power and as a deep-fat frying medium. Pie, biscuits, yeast breads, cookies, doughnuts and crullers made with good lard are hard to match in eating quailty.

The smoke point of lard ranges from 350° to 365° F and when heated above this point, a black smoke with an acrid odor is given off. This indicates the product is disintegrating and no longer is fit for use. Lard is important nutritionally; it is an animal fat containing fatty acids essential for growth.

Emulsified Shortenings include *hydrogenated pure vegetable shortenings* and *shortening compounds.* By adding emulsifying agents such as mono- and di-glycerides to these shortenings they are able to produce the large volume and fine texture in quick-mix cakes. An emulsified shortening produces a strong emulsion in the quick-mix batters which contain a higher proportion of liquid and sugar. This batter structure differs from batter produced with butter or plain lard.

A hydrogenated pure vegetable shortening is made by treating pure vegetable oils with hydrogen to harden them enough not to melt at room temperature or to become rancid. The process of hydrogenation is so carefully and completely controlled that the shortening always stays the same consistency. After hydrogenation, these shortenings are creamed to a smooth texture; they are pure white, odorless and flavorless. These features make them desirable in foods which depend on other ingredients for flavor and aroma.

Shortening Compounds are usually made by combining a hard fat with a soft fat or oil to give the desired "body" to the final product. Shortening compounds are produced from all-vegetable fats, or from all-animal fats, or from a combination of the two. Compounds are also pure white, bland in flavor, odorless and of good keeping quality.

There is little or no difference in the smoke points of *Emulsified* hydrogenated vegetable shortenings and the *Emulsified* shortening compounds—which range from 360° to 370° F. When an emulsified shortening is heated to these temperatures, there is first a sweet-smelling vapor given off. This indicates the burning off of the glycerides, but when these shortenings are heated until darkly discolored, they no longer do a top-quality deep-fat frying job.

Non-Emulsified shortenings may be either *hydrogenated pure vegetable shortenings* or a *shortening compound.* At present there are but few non-emulsified shortenings on the market; the trend is toward all shortenings being emulsified. Top-quality shortenings of this class are also pure white, odorless and flavorless. The smoke point ranges from 400° F to well above 400° F, and such shortenings naturally have a long life for deep-fat frying. *Read Labels* to learn whether shortening is *Emulsified* or *Non-Emulsified.*

Oils are used chiefly in American cookery for salad dressings, and are especially suitable for this use as they are liquid at room temperatures. They are convenient to use in many recipes calling for shortenings, but when used in baked products as cake and pastry, they sometimes give a crumbly texture and an oily appearance. Vegetable oils of domestic origin on the retail market are cottonseed, corn, peanut, soy and olive oils. The oils are pressed out of the seeds or fruit (usually with the aid of heat) and the expressed oils are refined to remove objectionable colors, odors and flavors. These oils may be marketed pure or blended in different proportions. *Olive oil* is imported in large quantities. Its color is usually an indication of its quality, a golden straw color characterizes the high grades, and a greenish tint the inferior grades. If labeled "olive oil" it is never mixed with other oils, but may be a mixture of various grades of olive oil. It is a good plan to read the labels.

Bacon, ham, sausage and roast pork drippings are excellent for panfrying various foods, for greasing the griddle, for making cream sauce, for seasoning some vegetables such as green and lima beans, and for shortening in some hot breads such as corn bread, biscuits and plain muffins.

Cracklings are the solid residue left from tried-out pork or chicken fat and are especially flavorsome in hot breads. They add flavor not duplicated by any other shortening in such food as "cracklin' corn bread," p 241.

Beef drippings, especially if they contain some of the brown juice, are also excellent for sautéing, and for making gravy and cream sauce.

Lamb drippings are too tallowy to be desirable for cooking, but if allowed to accumulate they can be used to make soft laundry soap.

Mineral oil was formerly used by uninformed persons in making low-calorie salad dressing. This is an unwise practice as it tends to deplete the body of the fat-soluble vitamins. The use of mineral oil is illegal in commercial products. The oil has neither nutritive nor caloric value.

THE ANSWERS TO YOUR QUESTIONS ABOUT FLOURS

*All-purpose flour** is a relatively low protein flour and is made by blending hard and soft wheat flours. Hard wheat is a spring-sown wheat raised in the northern states, while the soft wheat is sown in the fall in the middle and more southerly states. This flour is designed for general baking use to make quick and yeast breads, pastries, cookies, and some cakes.

Barley flour is made by removing the outer coat from barley and then putting the barley through a pearling machine a number of times. The shelled off coats are sifted together and sold for flour. It has limited uses, but is used as a thickener in soup mixes.

Bread flour is made by milling hard wheat, and has a higher percentage of protein—11 to 12.5 per cent—and a lower percentage of starch than flours made of the soft wheats. Because it has greater power to absorb liquid, it will produce more loaves of bread from a given weight than does an all-

---

* *Variations* occur in this flour. In the South, where quick breads, cakes and biscuits comprise the largest part of baking, some manufacturers use a larger proportion of soft wheat in their all-purpose flour. Since such flour has a higher moisture content than flours manufactured for markets in the North, it may be necessary to use either a smaller proportion of liquid or a larger amount of flour in a recipe.

purpose or soft-wheat flour. It is sold unblended, chiefly to commercial bakeries for making only bread and rolls.

Buckwheat flour is a mixture of ground buckwheat seeds and white flour. Buckwheat is an herb rather than a cereal grass. Its seeds are ground and sifted through a coarser bolting cloth than that used for cereal flours, which allows particles of hull to pass through, and gives the flour its characteristic flavor and dark color. The white flour is added to modify the naturally strong, bitter flavor of buckwheat.

Cake flour is milled especially from the highest grade of soft wheat for the chief purpose of making fine cakes. It contains a high percentage of starch and a low percentage of the protein, gluten.

Corn flour is finely ground and sifted corn meal. It is one of the flours used to replace wheat flour in the diet of those with wheat-flour allergy.

Enriched flour is white flour with added specified amounts of the essential nutrients thiamine, niacin, riboflavin and iron. Calcium and vitamin D are permitted optional additions. The addition of these nutrients was recommended by nutritionists and other agencies concerned with shortages in the national diet, with exact proportions established on the basis of popular need. Flour and bread were chosen as carriers because they are widely available and inexpensive. The addition of these nutrients at levels specified in food and drug regulations does not alter the taste, color, texture, baking quality or caloric value of the flour or the final baked product. See page 233 for enrichment standards.

Gluten flour is made by washing some of the starch from high protein flour, drying the remainder and regrinding it to make a product containing over 40 per cent protein. It may be added to regular flour to improve its baking qualities or to produce gluten bread of high protein content. By more complete starch removal, products containing 75 to 85 per cent protein are obtained. When used in foods, this product is called "vital gluten."

Instantized, instant blending or quick mixing flours are prepared by either a selective grinding and bolting procedure, to produce a free flowing granular product, or by agglomeration—a process in which regular flour is first subjected to a controlled amount of atomized moisture which causes the flour to clump or agglomerate. The product is then dried to a normal moisture level and sieved for uniformity.

If these flours are enriched, they contain the amounts of thiamine, niacin, riboflavin and iron specified by the Food and Drug Administration. They may also carry the permitted optional enrichment ingredients, calcium and vitamin D. These flours may be plain or self-rising.

Instantized, instant blending or quick mixing flours offer advantages to the consumer. They disperse instantly in cold water; they are free-pouring like salt and dust-free compared to regular flour. They eliminate the need for sifting because they do not pack down in the package and they pour through a screen or sieve. However, in some products, different results are obtained than with regular all-purpose flour.

Potato flour, prepared from dehydrated potatoes, is a white velvety flour especially suited for making muffins and sponge cakes, and for a thickening agent in pies and fruit sauces. It may be combined with other flours to provide a change in flavor and texture.

Pumpernickel flour is a coarsely ground rye meal, comparable to coarsely ground whole wheat.

Rice flour is milled from the cracked particles, incompletely debranned, and otherwise imperfect rice grains left from making head rice. It is practically pure white in color. For best results, rice flour should be combined with other flours, or used in combination with eggs and milk. If not used in this way, a grainy heavy product results.

Rye flour is a mixture of milled rye with enough gluten added from hard wheat flour to enable it to rise when made into yeast doughs. White rye flours are made from the inner part of the kernel, whereas the dark rye flours are taken from the outer portions of the kernel.

Self-rising flour is all-purpose flour blended with a leavening and salt in exact proportions. Enriched self-rising flour has the addition of thiamine, niacin and riboflavin plus iron and calcium in exact proportions as required by the Food and Drug Administration.

Stone-ground whole wheat and Buckwheat flour are prepared by grinding the grain or seeds between stones rather than between steel rollers. The heart or germ is left in as these flours are not bolted (sifted).

Soy flour manufacture began as a by-product in the extraction of oils used in producing foods, paints, etc. from soy beans. These flours are designated as full-fatted, low-fat, and defatted. The full-fat flour contains all the natural oil of the bean, the low-fat has 5 to 7 per cent of the oil, and the defatted, 1 to 3 per cent of the oil, and most of the coloring matter removed. The low-fat flour is most commonly used in the home; the full-fat flour is sold in largest quantities to the food industry. There is relatively little of the defatted flour on the market. Soy flour is used alone, or in combination with wheat flour in the making of quick and yeast breads, cakes, cookies, and pastry; and it is commonly used as a meat "extender." It has a high protein content, and is highly recommended as a source of this and other essential nutrients.

Whole wheat or graham flour is made by grinding the entire wheat grain. Loaves of bread made from whole wheat tend to be smaller and heavier than loaves made from enriched white flour. The bran in whole wheat limits the rising power of the dough, probably by cutting the gluten strands that form the cellular network of bread. Sometimes white flour is mixed with whole wheat flour to produce a loaf lighter in color and texture and of larger volume.

THE ANSWERS TO YOUR QUESTIONS ABOUT LEAVENING AGENTS

Bread and biscuits rise, popovers pop, and soufflés puff, because of the magic influence of leavening agents. Steam, air and gas are the three agents that leaven or lighten all baked foods.

Steam alone stretches the elastic walls of cream puffs and popovers, and makes them expand and lighten. Steam helps to leaven all baked foods.

Air is actually a leavening in any batter that is beaten, since the beating motion incorporates air into the mixture. The air expands during baking and lightens the product. Eggs, particularly egg whites, have the physical ability to incorporate especially large amounts of air. Beaten egg whites should be stiff and hold their shape, but never dull or dry. If they are over-beaten to the dry stage, the structure loses most of its elasticity, and is not able to stretch, expand and lighten when heated.

Gas is set free whenever baking powder, soda and acid, or yeast is used. This gas is always in the form of carbon dioxide, and disappears from the food when it is baked. The action of baking powder, soda, and yeast is somewhat more involved than that of steam or air, and requires further explanation.

CAUTION!

All baking powder used in recipes in this book is double action, the sulphate-phosphate type. Increase the amount by ¼ if you have only the phosphate, or tartrate type. Read the label.

BAKING POWDER

Two different types of baking powder are commonly used in the home, both containing baking soda and cornstarch, plus certain acid reacting compounds which vary in nature and amount. The powders derive their names from the acid reaction ingredients. They are: (1) sulfate-phosphate, so-called combination (or double-action) baking powder, containing sodium aluminum sulfate and calcium acid phosphate. (2) Tartrate baking powder, containing cream of tartar and tartaric acid, and phosphate baking powder, containing calcium acid phosphate. Since food laws in general require that the ingredients be named on the label, you can readily determine which type of baking powder you are using.

The leavening gas given off by both types is the same, but the rate of formation and residue varies considerably. Baking soda is the alkaline compound in baking powder which, in the presence of water, reacts with the acid ingredients of baking powder to form carbon dioxide, which is a gas. In this reaction the batter or dough is permeated with very fine bubbles of the gas which make the batter light. The only function of the cornstarch is to keep the active chemical ingredients separated and inactive while in the container. It has been found that a major portion of the cornstarch formerly used in combination-type baking powders may be replaced with a specially precipitated calcium carbonate, which, not only keeps the baking powder stable but also has the health advantage of enrich-ing baked foods with substantial amounts of much needed calcium.

The rate of gas formation differs according to the type of baking powder. Sulfate-phosphate (combination type) baking powders have their lesser action in the cold batter, with the greatest action in the oven. That is why these baking powders can be sifted with the dry ingredients. Such batters or doughs, after being poured, or rolled out and cut, may stand a short time without much effect on the leavening power. Tartrate and phosphate baking powders have the major portion of their action in the cold batter and the lesser action in the oven. For this reason, these baking powders are sprinkled over cake or other batters the last minute of beating. As soon as the beating is finished, the batter is promptly poured into the pans and is promptly placed in the oven.

To preserve the strength of baking powder, it is essential to keep it dry. Keep the container tightly closed and in a dry place where the temp is uniform; never let it stand open in a humid kitchen, and never put a wet spoon into the powder. Baking powder remains active longest in a dry climate. It usually can be depended upon for at least two years. When it fails to give the required volume to a baked product, it should be replaced with fresh powder. Slight deterioration is indicated when the powder con-tains soft lumps; a hard caked condition indicates advanced deterioration.

Careful measurement is very important. Any type of baking powder is fluffy and will settle and pack in the container when subjected to vibration, as occurs in shipment. It is, therefore, advisable to shake the package well before the initial opening to insure more accurate measurement. Always measure baking powder by the level teaspoon.

IMPORTANT!

In substituting one type of baking powder for another it must be re-membered that ¼ more tartrate or phosphate baking powder must be used than of the double action (D.A.) type to obtain uniform results. For ex-ample, if a recipe calls for 1 tsp of D.A. baking powder, it will be necessary to use 1¼ tsp of the tartrate or phosphate type, or if the recipe calls for 1½ tsp D.A. baking powder it will be necessary to use 1⅞ tsp (a scant 2 tsp) of tartrate or phosphate powder. An excess of any baking powder tends to produce coarse texture and dryness. When buttermilk is used in a recipe, as a rule both baking powder and soda are used. In this case the soda serves to neutralize the acidity of the milk. Therefore avoid excess amounts, that is, more than can be neutralized. Excess amounts of soda impair the odor and flavor of the baked product and will darken the color.

Advance preparation, if desired, is satisfactory with batters and doughs made with baking powder. The batter or dough may be mixed a few hours in advance of baking, and stored in the refrigerator. When this is done, cake batter should be poured into the pans, and biscuits shaped before storing, to avoid manipulation after storing. In waffle and griddle cake batter, which is stirred and poured as it is baked, with the result that some leavening is lost, a combination (sulfate-phosphate) baking powder is preferable.

Note: At high altitudes, the atmospheric pressure is less than at sea level so the leavening gas expands more with the same amount of leavening. Recipes must be adjusted for use in localities in high altitudes; the method of adjustment is usually explained in the various state bulletins distributed by the state colleges and extensions services.

BAKING SODA

Before the days of baking powder our ancestors made their own leavening by using soda with some acid, either soured milk, soured cream, or molasses. The soda reacted with the acid and set free the gaseous carbon dioxide. One-fourth tsp of soda and ½ cup of soured milk are about equivalent to the reaction of one tsp of baking powder. The molasses used today is much more mild and much less acid than the old fashioned type, and no exact equivalents can be given. When soda is used in a recipe, it is a good rule to mix it with the dry ingredients so that release of gas is delayed until the liquid is added in the final mixing. However, in some very good recipes, soda is added to the milk or molasses. In some cases soda is added to hot water which is thoroughly stirred into the batter just before it is poured into the baking pans. When soda is added directly to the liquid it serves mainly to neutralize the acid rather than as a leavening agent.

CREAM OF TARTAR

Before the commercial manufacture of baking powder, many recipes called for baking soda and cream of tartar. The cream of tartar was the acid ingredient used to combine with soda to form carbon dioxide gas. It is used today in the tartrate baking powders, sometimes in combination with tartaric acid. The chief use of cream of tartar now is in the baking of angel food cakes. An angel cake baked without it is cream colored instead of pure white, and is less tender. It gives a slight acid reaction to the batter, and affects the color and tenderness of the flour and egg white proteins.

YEAST

Yeast is a microscopic plant which under proper conditions causes fermentation and liberates carbon dioxide. The various procedures in making yeast breads and rolls set up the proper conditions in the dough for the fermentation process. As the liberated carbon dioxide increases in amount and expands, the bread rises. The heat of baking stops the fermentation process and the carbon dioxide passes off as vapor. *Compressed yeast* is moist and very perishable. It must be refrigerated or it will weaken and spoil. It is convenient and quick to use, but it must be fresh. It is usually more expensive than the other forms. *Dry yeast* is obtainable in granular and cake form. *Dry cake yeast* acts more slowly than the compressed, and must be used in larger amounts than compressed; however, this yeast keeps for months but keeps best if refrigerated. *Granular dry yeast* is used like compressed yeast. It is much less perishable, keeps for several weeks but best with refrigeration. The newest type of *active dry yeast* does not need to be dissolved in liquid before it is added to the other dry ingredients.

MILK AND MILK PRODUCTS

Great strides have been made during the past few decades in improving the production and distribution of milk and other dairy products. Every possible precaution is now taken so that the milk delivered to the grocery store and your door is sanitary and retains its fresh flavor and quality. It is then the responsibility of the homemaker to refrigerate these important dairy products as quickly as possible. A *storage temperature of 40°F* is most desirable to protect flavor and food value. It is vitally important to the health of her family that every homemaker be sure the milk she buys is pasteurized.

Pasteurized Milk. Milk is pasteurized to destroy all disease-producing organisms which might be present. Pasteurization also improves the keeping quality of milk without changing the food value significantly. The most common method of pasteurizing milk is by heating it to at least 160° F for not less than 15 seconds in approved equipment, properly operated, and then promptly cooling it to 40° F. When properly done, pasteurization destroys all disease-producing organisms as well as most of the other bacteria present, including lactic acid bacteria, the bacteria which causes milk to sour. Consequently, pasteurized milk does not sour naturally. If sour milk is needed for a recipe, use buttermilk or stir one tablespoon vinegar or lemon juice into each cup of milk. Cream may be "soured" the same way.

Raw milk (unpasteurized), which is still used on farms occasionally and is also sold in certain rural communities, is dangerous to drink. Diseases such as bovine tuberculosis, typhoid and undulant fever may be transmitted by untreated raw milk. It can be made safe by boiling 5 minutes before using or by pasteurizing in home pasteurization equipment which is available from mail order companies catering to farm trade.

Homogenized milk has its fat globules—the cream—uniformly dispersed throughout the milk so cream does not rise to the top. This is done most commonly by forcing the milk through a small opening under high pressure. This gives the milk a slightly "richer" taste and causes a smaller curd to form during digestion.

Certified milk is milk which is produced and distributed under conditions which conform with the high standards for cleanliness set forth by the American Association of Medical Milk Commissions. Most certified milk is also pasteurized, which is essential for safety. It is generally somewhat more expensive than ordinary pasteurized milk, since it must carry the added costs of special supervision.

Concentrated fresh milk—Fresh milk is concentrated by removing ⅔ of the water at low temp under vacuum, pasteurizing at 150°–155° F for 30 min, then homogenizing. While perishable, a concentrated milk may retain its flavor and sweetness in a properly cooled household refrigerator for about two weeks.

Concentrated frozen milk—To increase the keeping quality of fresh concentrated milk, it may be quickly frozen and held at −10° to −20° F until ready for use. Like other frozen foods, it must be used soon after defrosting.

Vitamin D milk has had its natural content of vitamin D increased by adding 400 U.S.P. units of vitamin D per quart. Natural foods are poor sources of vitamin D, although small amounts are present in egg yolk, liver and some fish. Much fresh whole and skim milk as well as evaporated milk is now also enriched with 2000 units of vitamin A. Since all children need 400 U.S.P. units of vitamin D daily, one quart of Vitamin D milk a day will take care of the vitamin D requirements.

Buttermilk originally was the by-product from churning sour cream to make butter. Cultured buttermilk, the product which is now universally available, may be made of skim milk, partially skimmed milk, sweet cream buttermilk, reconstituted soluble dried skim milk or reconstituted plain condensed skim milk. Uniformly fresh, clean milk is heated to 180° to 190° F for 30 min, cooled to 68° to 72° F, cultured chiefly with Streptococcus lactis, and incubated at this temp until the acidity is 0.8 to 0.9 per cent. The butterfat content of these milks varies between 0.1 and 1.5 per cent. The concentration of milk solids not fat is similar to that of whole milk. Salt is sometimes added to accentuate flavor.

Acidophilus milk—Freshly separated sweet skim milk, heated to 190° F for 1 hr, cooled to 100° F, cultured with Lactobacillus acidophilus and incubated at this temp, results in the product acidophilus milk. Because lactose and dextrin are believed to favorably influence the intestinal flora, 5 to 10 per cent of one or the other is added after the milk is cooled.

Yogurt—With a consistency resembling custard, yogurt is manufactured from concentrated whole milk fermented by a mixed culture of one or more strains of such organisms as Streptococcus, Thermophilus, Bacterium bulgaricum, and Plocamo-bacterium yoghourtii. The milk is usually homogenized before pasteurization, inoculated and incubated in wide mouthed jars or paper containers at a temp between 112° and 115° F. The final product is acid in flavor, contains between 19 and 20 per cent total milk solids and little or no alcohol.

Skim Milk is milk with almost all the cream removed. Most skimmed milk shows a fat content of about o.1 per cent. Since only butter fat is removed, the remaining milk contains almost all the minerals, proteins and water soluble vitamins. The caloric value is only half of whole milk. Since its vitamin A content is negligible due to its lack of butter fat, many diaries add 2000 units of vitamin A and 400 vitamin D units per quart to make its vitamin content equal to whole vitamin D milk. Skim milk is pasteurized and is desirable in low calorie diets.

High Protein Skim Milk is quite popular now. It has had the fat content reduced to 2 per cent or lower and the protein increased from 3.5 to around 10 per cent. It has also been pasteurized, homogenized and some have been fortified with 2000 I.U. of vitamin A and 400 I.U. of vitamin D per quart. Check the label. The added protein not only aids in nutritive value of reducing diets but causes the milk to taste much more like whole milk.

Graded milk—In states or communities where milk is graded, only Grade A pasteurized and Certified milk are allowed.

Chocolate milk is also available; it is made from whole milk. *Chocolate drink* may be made from partially skimmed or skimmed milk.

Soft curd milk is milk that has been treated by a special process so that the curd formed during digestion will be more tender. This type of milk is sometimes used in baby formulas, since it is easier to digest. It is also prescribed in the treatment of certain digestive disorders.

Evaporated milk is made from fresh whole milk of high quality by evaporating 60 per cent of the water content. The milk is then sealed in cans and sterilized by heat. Most of the food value remains, but variable amounts of Vitamins B_1 (thiamine) and C are lost. Its fat content is about 7.9 per cent, and it contains not less than 25.9 per cent total milk solids. Practically all evaporated milk has a vitamin D concentrate added. It forms a fine soft curd during digestions. Since all brands of evaporated milk must conform to federal standards, they are similar, and this uniformity makes them particularly useful for baby formulas. With the addition of an equal measure of water it may be used in almost all kinds of cookery to replace whole fresh milk. Nondiluted, very cold evaporated milk will whip like cream. Since it keeps almost indefinitely when unopened, it is convenient for emergencies and as a supplement to fresh milk. It is usually priced somewhat lower than an equivalent quantity of fresh milk. No sugar is added.

Condensed milk should not be confused with evaporated milk. It is made by evaporating about one-half of the water content from a mixture of whole milk and sugar. It contains about 40 per cent sugar and at least 28 per cent total milk solids and not less than 8.5 per cent butter fat. It is not sterilized, but depends upon the sugar for preservation. Sweetened condensed milks are used mostly to make bakery goods, desserts, and candy. It is more expensive than an equivalent amount of fresh milk, but has an individual flavor and other properties that make it pleasing to use in many foods.

Malted milk powder is made by drying and grinding a mixture of whole milk and the liquid separated from a mash of barley malt and wheat flour with additions of small amounts of salt and soda. It contains at least 7.5 per cent of butter fat. Malted milk powder is sold in both tablet and powder form.

Nonfat dry milk solids (dried skimmed milk) are identified by the government as "the product resulting from the removal of fat and water from milk." These solids contain the lactose, milk proteins, and milk minerals in the same relative proportions as they were contained in the fresh milk from which the solids were made. "It contains not over 4 per cent by weight of moisture, and not over 1½ per cent fat, unless otherwise indicated." The use of dried skim milk is an easy and economical way to improve the flavor and nutritional value of foods. It is used chiefly in cookery by sifting it with other dry ingredients to make breads, cakes, biscuits, bread puddings, and as a constituent of many commercially prepared mixes. It can be used to advantage in cooked cereals, ground meat mixtures, or sausage products. It can be used to prepare whipped chilled gelatin or frozen desserts by adding the required amount of ice water and beating. To reconstitute nonfat dry milk, follow package directions. Unused portions should be kept in a cool dry place, not refrigerated, with package reclosed. After water or other liquid has been added to nonfat dry milk, it should be given the same care as other fluid milk products.

Instant nonfat dry milk—Most of the nonfat dry milk on the market now dissolves instantly. There are several processes by which this is accomplished, varying with the processor. This type of nonfat dry milk is rather coarse, creamy-white and free-flowing.

Dry whole milk is identified by the government as "the product resulting from the removal of water from milk and contains not less than 26 per cent milk fat, and not more than 5 per cent moisture." It is not generally available in the U. S. market.

Cream is defined "as a portion of milk which contains not less than 18 per cent butter fat." In general the same rules of safety and quality that apply to market milk apply to cream. Light cream or coffee cream usually runs from 18 to 25 per cent butter fat, whipping cream from 30 to 40 per cent, or even higher in the "extra heavy type." Cream of 30 per cent butter fat whips well. The percentage of butter fat of the cream usually appears on the bottle or carton, and since it is usually true that the higher the butter fat content the more expensive the cream is, it is well to check to see that you are getting the highest butter fat content for the money.

Sour or cultured soured cream must contain at least 18 per cent butter fat. Like cultured buttermilk, commercial sour cream is made by adding a bacterial culture to pasteurized cream so that flavor and acidity can be controlled. Never buy sour cream in bulk, since its safety for more than a short period cannot be assured, due to hazards of contamination. See Index for Sour Cream recipes.

SOME FACTS AND HINTS ABOUT MILK
AND MILK PRODUCTS

1. Milk is not only one of the most important foods in the diet from a nutrition standpoint, it is also one of the most economical. A quart of milk per day furnishes over half the protein recommended for all ages except boys from 12 to 18; all the calcium and riboflavin recommended for all ages except for boys and girls from 12 to 18; and more than one-fourth of the vitamin A recommended for all ages (unless skim milk is used).

2. On a nation wide basis the actual consumption of milk and milk products in 1955 provided about two-thirds of the total calcium in our diets, nearly half the riboflavin and more than one-fifth of the protein.

3. The wise housewife will never allow a drop of milk or cream to spoil or otherwise be wasted. Since light destroys both riboflavin and vitamin C, milk should be taken in promptly if delivered, and refrigerated or stored in a cool dark place as soon as possible. It should be kept in the refrigerator when not being used, and closely covered at all times to prevent contamination. Adding old milk to fresh will hasten the spoilage of the fresh, and should only be done if the entire amount is to be used at once. Developing the habit of placing the new fresh milk behind bottles or cartons of older milk will assure the use of the older milk before it has a chance to spoil.

4. In using buttermilk or sour cream in recipes, the commercial type should always be bought. The flavor and acidity are more nearly standardized in commercially prepared buttermilk and sour cream, and can be depended upon to produce a fine cooked product. Milk that sours in the home and that has an unpleasant flavor should not be used for beverages or in cooking.

5. If your family does not enjoy the flavor of buttermilk, and there is some remaining from baking a gingerbread or devil's food cake, try some of the refreshing buttermilk drinks with added fruit juices and other flavorings to be found on pp 224 to 227. It can also be used in biscuits, p 236.

6. It is almost impossible in many areas to buy milk which is not homogenized, so all cream needed by the family for cereal (usually half and half), coffee (usually called light cream, containing 18½ per cent fat), and for whipping needs to be purchased as such. If enough cream is used by the family and if each person gets his fair share, then there is no reason why skim milk cannot be used for cooking and for drinking if desired, providing fortified skim milk is used (containing vitamins A and D) or some other plan is used for supplying these important vitamins.

TRUE STATEMENTS TO COUNTERACT FALLACIES
ABOUT MILK

1. There is no physiological or chemical evidence to support the theory that milk and fish or ice cream and fish should not be eaten at the same meal.

Milk and fish are entirely compatible, and are eaten together in fish chowders and oysters stews with no ill effects whatever.

2. *Milk is not a fattening food.* The pint of milk a day, which is the recommendation for adults, contributes a little over 335 calories. Since the average adult man requires about 3000 calories, this is only 11 per cent of his total caloric need. The pint of milk, however, provides three-fourths of his need for calcium, and about one-half of his phosphorus need, besides contributing significant amounts of several vitamins. On very strict reducing diets, it is sometimes advisable to use skimmed milk; this provides only about one half the amount of calories and about the same amount of B vitamins and minerals. Skim milk contains very little vitamin A, since this nutrient is found in the cream fraction only. However, a well-planned diet is not likely to be deficient in vitamin A.

3. *Milk and acid fruits can be mixed with no ill effect.* Actually the curd formed by the action of an acid on milk probably aids in the digestion of milk because curd forms naturally when milk reaches the stomach.

ANSWERS TO YOUR QUESTIONS ABOUT NUTS

1. *What Are the Most Generally Used Nuts in the United States?*

Almonds: Used in soups, fish, chicken and vegetable sauces and casseroles; in cakes, confectionery and pastries.

Brazil nuts: Used untoasted in fruit-nut bread, cookies and poultry stuffing; toasted, as garnish for coffee cake.

Butternuts: Used chiefly in cakes and candies.

Cashews: Used chiefly as salted nuts for snacks. May be substituted for pecans in pecan pie.

Chestnuts: Used chiefly in poultry stuffing. May be boiled and pureed and used in cakes, croquettes, jams, soups and soufflés.

Coconuts: Grated and used in cookies, cakes, cake fillings and frostings, meringues and cream pies. Milk used in curry sauces.

Filberts: Used chiefly in confectionery; may also be used in soups and hors d'oeuvres.

Hickory nuts: Used chiefly in cakes and candies.

Peanuts: Used in candies, especially in peanut brittle, in cookies and peanut butter, and for snacks.

Pecans: Used in pies, fruit-nut bread, waffles, muffins, sweet rolls, candies, ice cream, cakes, cookies and conserves.

Pine nuts: Used chiefly in rice and pasta dishes and confectionery.

Pistachio nuts: Used chiefly in ice cream and for snacks.

Walnuts (black): Used chiefly in chocolate cookies, cakes and candies, such as brownies and fudge.

Walnuts (white): Used in Waldorf and other fruit salads, cookies and fruit cakes.

2. Where Are These Nuts Grown?

The peanut, white or English and black walnut, pecan, almond and filbert are grown on a fairly large scale in this country. Brazil nuts come from South America, cashews from India and chestnuts from Southern Europe.

3. Are Nuts of Any Value Nutritionally?

Nuts are a concentrated food and most of them contain proteins of good quality. They are so rich in fat, however, that they are not entirely satisfactory as animal protein substitutes. They are a high energy food and fairly rich in phosphorus. Some contain appreciable ammounts of iron and are good sources of the B-complex vitamins. See Tables, pages 28, 31, 34 and 39.

4. Why Do Nuts Become Rancid and Also Turn Purplish in Some Foods?

Flavor of nuts depend on presence of various kinds of oils and tannin. These oils are present in relatively large amounts in all kinds of nuts and they become rancid just as other fats do. This accounts for the disagreeable flavor and odor of stale nuts. To prevent rancidity, store nuts in airtight containers in a cool, dry, fairly dark place. Tannin gives nuts such as walnuts a puckery taste and causes them to turn a purplish color in nut bread or Waldorf salad. If apples are cut with an iron knife, the acid and enzyme act on the iron to produce iron salts, and when coming in contact with the tannin, develop a purplish color in the nuts. Therefore, chop nuts with a stainless steel or plastic knife.

5. Why Are Some Nuts Roasted?

Roasting develops the flavor and improves the texture of mild-flavored nuts such as almonds, hickory nuts and white walnuts. Browning in the oven or frying in a small amount of fat alters the raw flavor in a very pleasing way. Be careful not to scorch.

6. What Is Blanching?

Blanching is removing skin from smooth-surfaced nuts. To blanch almonds, pistachios or walnuts, pour boiling water over them, simmer 2 or 3 min, then drain and slip skins off. Rinse nuts in cold water and spread out on absorbent paper, and dry at room temp several hours before storing in a jar. Cut nuts while moist, right after blanching.

7. What Are Nut Butters and Pastes?

Nuts are ground medium fine to make butters and very fine for pastes. Peanut butter is usually ground roasted peanuts with nothing added except salt. Some have small bits of nuts throughout, while others are "homogenized" to a very smooth consistency. The most common paste is almond. This may be made of plain ground almonds or it may contain other ingredients, such as sugar or flavorings. It is used in macaroons and other baked products.

8. Is It More Economical to Buy Shelled or Unshelled Nuts?

Shelled nuts save time and labor but nuts in the shell keep better, are less expensive and not as easily contaminated by insects or by handling.

9. How Are Chestnuts Prepared?

Make slit on each side of nut with sharp-pointed paring knife and drop into enamel saucepan. Cover with boiling water, boil gently 20 min. Remove from heat; take one or two chestnuts at a time from water. Use knife to strip off shell and thin brown-skin covering meat. Dip nut from time to time in cold water to remove shell and skin more easily. Leaving in hot water keeps shells and skins soft and the cleaning job is more easily done.

BREAKING, CHOPPING, GRINDING AND GRATING NUTS

Experimental cooks now believe that the best way to prepare walnuts or pecans to be used in baked foods, salads, candy, etc. is to break them with the fingers to the desired size.

Chopped nuts rank next to broken ones in quality. The most satisfactory way to chop nuts is to put not more than a cupful onto a good-sized chopping board. Use a large French knife for chopping. With the fingers of left hand on the tip of the knife and the handle in the right hand, cut down through the pile of nuts 3 or 4 times. Then hold the tip of the knife firmly on the board and rotate the handle of the knife through a quarter of a circle, cutting rapidly up and down through the nuts as the knife is rotated. Never lift the handle of the knife more than 2 or 3 inches from the board as you cut.

Nuts ground in a food chopper are not desirable for any use because such grinding presses the oil from the nuts and leaves a greasy mass of particles that are too irregular in size. Nuts put through a food mill are not oily and the particles obtained are much more regular in form and size. To do a good job of grinding nuts through a food mill put not more than ¼ cupful at a time into the food mill. Have the bottom screw very loose. Place food mill over a flat bottom bowl or pan that fits the food mill. Then slowly with a strong arm press the nuts through.

Nuts may be grated fine on a medium grater. Rub the nuts only in one direction—downward on the grater. Grated nuts are desirable for some cookies, especially Christmas Stars.

GETTING FRESH COCONUT READY TO USE

There is nothing equal to fresh-grated coconut for pie, cake and ambrosia. Use a large nail or metal skewer to puncture the 3 spots on end of coconut not covered with the hard shell; then turn it over a glass to drain out the milk. This can be combined with milk for liquid in cake or in filling for coconut cake. Heat drained coconut in a moderate oven (350° F) 30 min or until shell cracks in several places. Remove and cool slightly. Tap coconut with hammer all over to finish cracking, then pry off shell with a sturdy knife. Pare off brown skin thinly with a sharp knife. Grate fine on a sharp grater or shred medium fine on a sharp shredder. Grate or shred onto waxed paper, transferring gratings to bowl frequently to keep fluffy. Cover to keep moist. Use promptly, or place in jar, seal tightly and quick-freeze.

ANSWERS TO QUESTIONS ABOUT OLIVES AND PICKLES

The olives packed commercially are grown in California or in Spain. The bulk of the California crop is made into ripe olives, minor portions being cured as green olives and green-ripe olives. The olives grown in Spain are cured as green olives and are finished either with the pit or stuffed with pimiento. Olives are usually picked by hand. All are bitter when picked and are cured in a pickling solution to make them palatable.

Ripe Olives are royal purple when picked. In the pickling process they are held in a special brining solution. But at intervals they are removed from this brine and are subjected to jets of air which causes oxidation and develops their rich black color. After sufficient treatment they are packed in fresh brine in glass or tin, sealed and sterilized. Ripe olives are packed whole or chopped. Size and number in pack are indicated on labels.

Green-ripe Olives are picked ripe and pickled and brined similarly to the ripe olives. However, they are not brought into contact with air and their color ranges from a light green to a mottled brown. They are somewhat richer in oil than are other types of olives.

Green or Spanish Olives are picked green and held in a curing solution for a short time, then rinsed and held in a salt brine. After several weeks, they are packed in a light brine and shipped to this country where the brine is brought to the required strength. Olives are packed and sealed, but do not require sterilization. (Always packed in glass.) *Queen olives* are the large variety, *Manzanilla* the smaller. Either may be packed with pits or stuffed with pimiento. The size of the olive largely determines its price. Green olives sometimes develop scum when held for some time. This does not indicate spoilage, but is a natural brine development. Olives keep well as long as they are covered with brine, but darken and spoil when exposed to the air.

PICKLES

Commercially packed pickles are made from cucumbers cured many months in brine. A smaller amount of quick-cure dill and sweet and sour pickles are also produced. To cure pickles, young cucumbers are picked when they reach the desired stage of maturity and are sorted into different grades according to size, shape and color. They are then washed and packed into wooden tanks in brines of different strengths and held from six months to two years, depending upon supply and market price. Curing gives pickles

TABLE 13
OLIVES ILLUSTRATED SHOW AVERAGE SIZES OF VARIOUS GRADES *

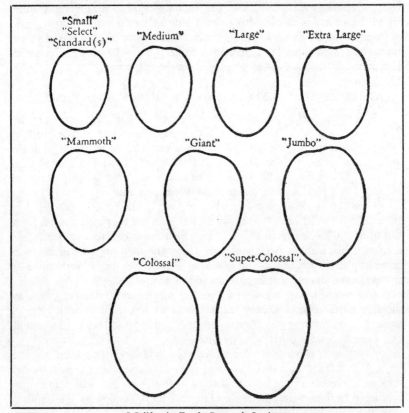

* California Foods Research Institute

bright green color and firm texture. They are then "freshened" in fresh water until salt is removed, then are packed with the various combinations of vinegar, spices, dill and other herbs, sugar and vegetables to make different varieties and packs.

The largest cucumbers, 800–1800 to the 40 gallon cask, are used to make dill pickles. The midget size, 20,000 to the 40 gallon cask, is used to make sweet pickles. The in-between sizes are used for sweet, mixed and sliced pickle mixtures.

THE ANSWERS TO YOUR QUESTIONS ABOUT
SUGARS AND MOLASSES

Cane sugar is made from juice pressed from sugar cane stalks. The juice is first clarified with sulfur and lime, then it is centrifuged, percolated through charcoal, and heated at 63° F until concentrated enough for a certain percentage of sugar to crystallize out. This is called "first" sugar. The drained off liquid containing considerable sugar is called "first" or light molasses. Part of the "first" molasses is added to fresh cane juice and reworked like first batch of juice to obtain a "second" sugar. The liquid left is called "second" or dark molasses. Part of the "second" molasses is diluted with water, reboiled to obtain a "third" sugar. The liquid left is called "third" or black strap molasses.

All extracted sugars are washed, dried, then screened to separate into crystals of extra fine, fine, medium and standard granulations. These sugars are run into barrels, bags and boxes for distribution. Granulated sugar is pure carbohydrate with only caloric value.

Molasses remaining at the end of the three sugar extractions contains considerable calcium and iron. Research shows black strap molasses contains more than three times the iron of light molasses. However, iron in black strap is only 54 per cent usable, while in light molasses 97 per cent usable. Since light molasses has a milder flavor than the dark, most people eat more light and obtain as much iron as eating less of the dark.

Beet sugar is made from juice pressed from sugar beets. The process of purification and crystallization is similar but less elaborate than that of making cane sugar. The composition of beet and cane sugar is the same. They sweeten identically and may be used interchangeably in cooking, baking, and making candies and jellies.

Brown or soft sugars are made from syrups left after different extractions of granulated sugar. These syrups are evaporated at a low temp to make fine crystals with syrup adhering to them. *Dark-brown sugar* has a more clinging syrup than the *light-brown sugar.* These sugars add distinctive flavor to cooked and baked foods and contain small amounts of calcium and iron depending on the percentage of syrup clinging to crystals.

Corn sugar is made by evaporating corn syrup to the point of crystallization. It is ⅗ as sweet as cane sugar, yellowish in color, and is sold in both lump and granular forms. It is used commercially in baking bread and making ice cream. In the household it is used for preparing food for special diets.

Corn syrup is made by cooking cornstarch under high pressure in the presence of acid (hydrolizing), which turns the starch to a liquid. Up to 10 per cent cane sugar is added to make *white corn syrup* and up to 10 per cent refiners molasses is added to make *dark corn syrup.* A maple-flavored corn syrup is also on the market. *Double-sweetness corn syrup* is made from refined cornstarch through the action of enzymes or by the use of lime. It tastes sweeter than other corn syrup since it contains a chemically different sugar.

Domino or cube sugars are made by pressing moist granulated sugar crystals into slabs. After slabs dry, they are sawed and clipped into dominoes, cubes or other shapes. Special machines also press the moist crystals into desired forms. Dominoes and cubes are convenient for sweetening beverages.

Honey is a syrup condensed by bees from flower nectar. Its color, flavor and aroma depend on the kinds of flowers visited. Recognized wild flower honeys are goldenrod, and aster. Fruit tree blossoms and field crops also contribute their flavors. White clover, alfalfa, buckwheat and basswood honeys are famous for their distinctive flavors. With occasional exceptions the lighter colored honeys are of a higher grade than the dark. Honey is sold in the comb, strained, and in a homogenized form especially for table use. It serves as a spread and contributes its unusual flavors to cooked and baked dishes and in sauces and dressings. Honey naturally granulates but can be restored to liquid form by placing container in hot (not boiling) water.

Maple sugar is made from the sap of hard maple trees. The juice is filtered and concentrated by low heat until it will crystallize into a solid cake. Maple sugar contributes a delicate flavor to custards, candies, icings and other confections. *Maple syrup* is made by filtering maple sap and evaporating it to a concentration of 64 per cent sugar. Such a syrup weighs 11 lbs per gallon. *Maple-sugar syrup* is made by dissolving maple sugar in water. Both syrups have fine characteristic maple flavor. As a rule maple syrup is sweeter and milder than maple-sugar syrup.

Pulverized sugar may be either *powdered or confectioners'*. Both are made by grinding ordinary granulated sugar and sifting it through bolting cloths of different degrees of fineness. Powdered sugar is coarser than confectioners', and is used to bake fine textured cakes, to make icings, and to sift over desserts, strawberries, grapefruit, and other fresh fruit. Very fine confectioners' sugar, XXXX to XXXXXX may be pure sugar or sugar mixed with three per cent cornstarch to keep from caking. It is used to make butter icings, quick candies, and to sift over cakes, cookies, candies and chewing gum.

Sorghum is made of the juice pressed from fresh green stalks of sorghum cane, a relative of sugar cane, grown in the middle-western and southern states. This juice is usually evaporated in open pans and cooked down to the consistency of molasses. The color of sorghum varies from a beautiful amber color to a dark reddish tan, depending upon the quality of the cane and the uniformity of the slow cooking process. Sorghum adds a characteristic flavor to cakes, candy, cookies, etc., and is used as a table syrup.

THE ANSWERS TO YOUR QUESTIONS ABOUT
SPICES, HERBS, EXTRACTS AND VINEGARS

A dash of nutmeg in the cream for your oatmeal! A breath of fresh mint flavor in your pale green-tinted whipped cream or meringue! A pinch of sage in meat loaf, a mere trace of marjoram in escalloped tomatoes! The most glamorous ingredients which can go into cookery are the spices and herbs. It was for spices that Europeans first sailed to the Indies, and the glamor of those days when the East was a fabulous and far-off place still clings to spices which we buy in matter-of-fact little tin cans.

Most all the spices are grown in the tropical regions of the Orient, and in the islands of Madagascar, Zanzibar and Pemba off the coast of East Africa. The "Spice Islands" are still the islands of the Dutch East Indies. Allspice, mustard and chili are the most common of the very few spices native to the western hemisphere.

Some herbs used for seasoning and flavoring foods are imported from various regions of Europe. Unlike the spices, herbs can be grown in this country, and many more of them will be home-grown in the future.

Flavoring extracts are largely of domestic origin. The favorite, vanilla, is made from a tropical American plant. Extracts add as much appetite appeal to foods as exotic spices, but they lack the romantic appeal of spices.

Vinegars may be made from practically any fruit by fermenting the juice to make alcohol, then oxidizing the alcohol to make acetic acid. Vinegar may also be made from corn sugar or syrup, molasses, cereal grains such as barley malt, or from dilute alcohol. In wine producing countries, wine vinegar is commonly made from grapes; in our own country, apple cider vinegar is found more than any other kind. Some vinegars are also named for the flavoring they may contain such as basil, tarragon, garlic, etc.

HOW TO BUY AND USE SPICES

Even though spices are one of the oldest known cooking aids, don't make antiques of them. Spices used for cooking should be fresh and full-flavored. It is advisable to buy them in small quantities and to replace them as often as two or three times a year, even if all the spice has not been used. A dust-like aroma readily reveals when the spice has lost its rich fresh potency.

Most spices are now packed in metal boxes with a patented top which may be opened for sprinkling and then tightly closed. The can containing any sort of spice should never be allowed to stand open. Form the habit of closing the top the moment you set the box down, and you will never waste its fragrance on the pantry air. Keep spices in a dry cool place. And remember that spices are like rare perfume—once the scent is gone they are worthless.

The amounts of spices to be used in cooking can be adjusted to suit the individual taste. If you were to decide to put an extra egg into your favorite recipe you might get into trouble; and varying the amount and kind of spice may change the product favorably or unfavorably. The more spice used in cookies, cake or puddings, the drier the product is.

The amount of spice specified in any of our tested recipes is designed to please the average palate. You and your family will probably not want less but you may like more. Just remember that subtlety should be your watchword in using spices: use enough to make your guests wonder, not enough to make them jump!

The following table gives sources and uses of familiar spices and herbs.

TABLE 14. THE HOMEMAKER'S SPICE AND HERB GUIDE. DESCRIPTION, SOURCE AND USES OF FAMILIAR SPICES*

Name	Description and source	Uses
Allspice	Dried berry of pimento (not pimiento) tree, grown in West Indies. Flavor resembles blend of cinnamon, nutmeg and cloves, hence the name.	Used whole in pickling, stews, soups, preserved fruit, boiling fish, spicing meat and gravy. The ground, used to season pot roasts, baked goods, apple butter, conserves, catchup, mincemeat.
Anise	Dried seed of plant belonging to celery family. Grows in Southern Europe, Tunis, India, Chile and Mexico.	Sprinkled on coffee cake, sweet rolls, cookies; in sweet pickles; flavoring cough syrups, licorice products, some candies, and in chocolate cake icing.
Balm	A lemon-scented herb. Cultivated in Europe, grows wild in U. S. Also cultivated for bees.	Pleasant seasoning for broiled fish, meats, salads, soups, sauces. Few bruised leaves in cold tea and punch add nice touch.
Basil, Sweet	Belongs to mint family; one of the best known of herbs. Grown in Europe and U. S.	Famous in tomato dishes; bean, mock turtle and potato soups; good in potato, spaghetti, egg dishes, steaks, venison, wild duck.
Bay Leaf	Dried leaves of laurel. Grows in many parts of world. Leaves from shrubs of Eastern Mediterranean considered best.	Famous in pickled beets, stews, gravies, relishes, spiced vinegar or marinade, in meats, as sauerbraten, etc.
Borage	A rough, hairy, blue-flowered European plant, cucumber odor.	Used to season cucumber salad, string beans and green salads.
Burnet	Belongs to the rose family.	Flavoring green salads, vinegar.
Caraway Seed	Dried pungent seeds from herb of the carrot family. Grows in Holland, Russia, Poland.	In rye bread, baked goods, kraut, cabbage, potatoes, roast pork, goose, cheese, cake, cookies.
Capers	Low growing shrub of the Mediterranean. Green flower buds and young berries of shrub are pickled.	In fish, chicken, potato, green salad. Sauces for fish, lamb, mutton, heart, cold tongue, and as garnish.
Cardamon	Belongs to ginger family. Seeds enclosed in small pod. Grows in Malaya, India, Ceylon. Seed and pod may be ground together, or only seeds are ground. Put seeds between folds of muslin and pound to powder.	Seeds in pod used in pickling; ground adds delectable flavor to Danish pastry, coffee cake, fancy rolls. Bruised seeds in coffee is delicious.
Cassia Bark	From cassia tree. Grown in Malaya, China. Resembles cinnamon flavor. Called Chinese cinnamon.	For pickling, preserving. Ground in combination with allspice, nutmeg, clove. Used in mincemeat.

* Adapted from *"Spices—and How to Use Them,"* published by American Spice Trade Association, New York City.

Name	Description and source	Uses
Cassia Buds	Dry unripe fruit of cassia tree.	Pleasing, sweet pickling spice.
Cayenne	Smallest, hottest member of red pepper family. Grown in Africa.	Used sparingly to season meats, fish, sauces, egg dishes, mayonnaise.
Celery Salt	Made by grinding celery seed and fine salt together.	In soups, cream sauces, salads, dressings; on roast poultry, meats.
Celery Seed	Pungent seed from plant similar to garden celery. Comes from India.	Croquette mixtures, stews, slaw, potato salad, salad dressing, pickles, cheese, fish, meat spreads.
Chervil	Aromatic herb of carrot family, like parsley but more delicate.	Used fresh or dry in salads, soups, egg and cheese dishes.
Chile Peppers	A fine satiny surfaced red pepper. Grown in Mexico and Southwest U. S.	Used to make chili powders for chili con carne, tamales, pickles, cooking dried beans. Both green and ripe peppers pickled and used to make hot sauces.
Chile Tepines	Very, very hot tiny red peppers. Grown in Mexico.	Used in preparing hot Mexican foods such as meat and egg dishes.
Chili Powder	A blend of chili, red peppers, cumin seed, oregano, garlic powder, salt, etc.	Most widely used in chili con carne. Also used in cocktail sauces, gravies, stews, appetizers.
Chives	Grows indoors or outdoors from clumps of small onion-like bulbs. Has mild, onion-like flavor.	Adds color and flavor to cottage and cream cheese, egg and potato dishes, soup and vegetable garnish.
Cinnamon	Bark of true cinnamon tree that grows in Ceylon. Milder in flavor and thinner than cassia bark.	To flavor pickles, preserves, fruits, hot drinks and as "spoons" for after-dinner coffee. Ground in baked goods, puddings, cake, mincemeat.
Cloves	Nail-shaped dried flower bud of the clove tree. Rich and pungent in flavor.	Whole in baked ham, pickling, and drinks. Ground in cakes, cookies, conserves, desserts.
Coriander	Bible-time aromatic herb of carrot family. Grows in India, Morocco. Flavor like lemon peel and sage.	Spicy seeds used in curry powder, oriental candy, pickles, meat products and frankfurters.
Cumin or Comino	Native of Palestine, of carrot family. Esteemed by Jews. An Italian and Mexican favorite. Aromatic seeds with bitter warm flavor.	In Curry Powder; cookies, egg and cheese dishes, sauerkraut, soup, meat, rice, pickles, sausage, Chili Con Carne, Hot Tamales.
Curry Powder	Blend of spices from India. By varying proportions of 16 spices, different flavored curries are produced. Contains turmeric, ginger, red pepper, cumin, coriander, etc.	Used to make curries of meat, fish, eggs, chicken; curry sauce and flavoring gravies. Adds Oriental touch to rice, veal, shrimp, chicken dishes.

Name	Description and Source	Uses
Dill	Herb of carrot family with aromatic leaves, seeds and stem. Grows widely in Europe and U. S.	Fresh leaves in sauces for potatoes, beans, fish, lamb, veal; fresh seed heads make lovely garnish. Dried or green heads and stems in pickles.
Dill "Seed"	Dried tiny fruit of dill plant. Pleasant pungent flavor.	Good in pickles and to garnish split pea and lentil soup.
Fennel Seed	From plant of carrot family. Aromatic, resembles anise and dill, but has distinct flavor of its own.	Popular with Italians and Scandinavians. For rolls, rye bread, other baked goods, bean and lentil soup.
File	A powder made from dried tender sassafras leaves and other herbs. It thickens and flavors.	Used in Creole cookery in place of okra to thicken gumbos.
Garlic	Potent flavored bulb of onion family. Flavor either very popular or unpopular. Enjoyable if used with discretion.	Used either fresh or dried to enrich flavor of salad dressing, meat, many cooked vegetables.
Ginger	Dried root of subtropical plant grown in China, Japan, India, British West Indies. Warm in flavor.	Cracked root used in pickles, preserves, chutney. Ground root in cake, gingerbread, cookies, puddings, soups, pot roasts.
Juniper Berries	Dried berries of evergreen shrub, with warm, pungent flavor.	Used sparingly for epicure's touch to roast venison, lamb, duck, goose and some stews.
Lovage	European herb of carrot family. Pronounced, rich celery flavor.	Used to flavor tomato juice, soups, stews and gravies.
Mace	Lacy covering on inner shell holding nutmeg. Nutmeg tree grows in East and West Indies. Flavor more delicate than nutmeg.	Ground mace good with chocolate. Used in Pound and other yellow cake, oyster stew, spinach. Whole in pickling, preserving and fish sauces.
Marjoram	One of best known herbs; belongs to mint family. Grown mostly in Europe. Potent in flavor.	Dried, good pounded into veal, used in meat, potato, spinach, cheese, egg and fish dishes; chicken or green vegetable salads. Season poultry stuffings, sausage, stews, soups. Use sparingly. Often used with other herbs.
Mint	A widely grown herb with a delightfully cool, pungent flavor. Obtainable in dried form.	Popular in sauce or jelly with roast lamb. Used chopped as edible garnish on carrots, beets. Delicious in iced tea and fruit beverages.

Name	Description and Source	Uses
Mono Sodium Glutamate (Not a spice)	Neutral salt of glutamic acid which is one of twenty odd amino acids — the building blocks of all proteins. Is extracted from wheat protein and sugar beets.	Used to heighten flavor in meat, poultry, fish and vegetable dishes.
Mustard Seed	Seed of mustard plant grown in England, Europe and the U. S. Prepared mustard is ground seed blended with other spices and vinegar.	Whole seed in pickles, boiled with beets, cabbage, sauerkraut. Smart salad garnish. Ground mustard flavors sauces, gravies. Prepared mustard in salad dressing, on ham, frankfurters, cheese.
Nasturtium	Leaves and seeds of the common nasturtium flower.	Leaves in salads and sandwiches. Seeds used to flavor vinegar.
Nutmeg	Kernel of fruit of the Nutmeg tree. Grown in Dutch East Indies and British West Indies. One of the oldest known spices.	Traditional flavoring for baked custard and other desserts. Also used in cream soups, sauces, stews, vegetables such as spinach.
Oregano	Is wild marjoram. Has a pleasing, pungent fragrance.	Widely used in Mexican and Italian dishes; in meat stews, dried beans, lentils, pizza.
Paprika	A red pepper grown in Hungary or Spain. Rich fiery flavor. Method of grinding determines ultimate flavor. Spanish milder than Hungarian.	Used for color and mild flavor. In fish, shellfish, vegetable and egg dishes and in salad dressing.
Parsley	Widely grown useful herb. Rich in Vitamin A. Good source of vitamin when eaten in salad-like portions. Obtainable dried.	Chopped to season and garnish soups, stews, salads, potatoes, stuffings. Sprigs as salad ingredient and edible garnish.
Pepper, Black and White	Black pepper is dried small, immature berries of climbing vine grown in India and Dutch East Indies. White pepper is mature berries with hulls removed.	Used whole in pickling, soups, gravies and meats. Used ground in most meat, vegetable, fish and egg dishes.
Pimiento	Ripe fleshy fruit of a sweet pepper plant. Packed in small cans in its own viscous juice.	Used for spots of brilliant color, mild flavor in soups, stews, salads; as garnish for green vegetables like asparagus, green beans.
Poppy Seed	Tiny seeds of poppy plant—about 900,000 seeds to the pound. Imported from Holland.	Used whole as topping for breads and cookies; as filling for Kolachy; in cookies and cake. Garnish for noodles.
Poultry Seasoning	A mixture of several spices as sage, pepper, marjoram, savory, thyme, onion powder and celery salt.	Used in poultry, pork, veal and fish stuffings; to season meat loaf, dumplings, biscuit crusts for meat and poultry pies.

Name	Description and Source	Uses
Rosemary	Belongs to mint family. Grown in Southern Europe and Western Asia. Dry, needle-like leaves. Used for flavoring.	Delicious in tomato and egg dishes; soups, fish, roast lamb, pork, beef and duck. Improves stuffings, vegetable and cheese dishes when combined with sage. In biscuit and muffin mixtures.
Rue	A strong scented perennial herb that is woody and bitter in flavor.	A few fresh leaves are an interesting addition to green salads.
Saffron	Dried stigmas of a species of purple crocus. Grown in Mediterranean region.	Used primarily in Scandinavian and Spanish foods for yellow color as well as flavor in yellow rice, breads and pea soup.
Sage	The most familiar of herbs. Dried leaf of shrub belonging to the mint family. Grown in U. S., Yugoslavia and Greece.	Powerful in flavor. Used to season stuffings, sausage, veal and pork dishes, beans, tomatoes and fresh cheese.
Sausage Seasoning	White pepper is chief ingredient. For pork sausage, sage added; for frankfurters, coriander and nutmeg. Other seasonings added for liver sausage and bologna.	Used in seasoning home produced sausages.
Savory	Grown principally in Southern France. Flavor is at its best in early summer, so term, "Summer Savory" denotes top quality. Has a clean balsam fragrance.	Good in boiled fish. Known as the "bean herb." Fine flavor for peas, beans, lentils, fresh or dried; in stuffing, meat balls, croquettes, meat sauces, gravies, egg dishes.
Seasoning Salt	Includes celery, garlic, onion salt, etc. Made by grinding dried, fresh seeds or dried fresh vegetable flakes with pure salt.	Used as an alternate for part or all of the salt. Added to meat, poultry and egg dishes and in stuffings and sauces.
Sesame or Benne Seed	From pods within blossoms of a plant grown in India, China and Turkey. Hulled seeds are pearly white with toasted almond flavor.	Baked on rolls, breads and buns to give rich, nutty flavor to crusts. Used in Jewish candy, Halvah. Sesame oil is used in commercial flour mixtures.
Shallots	Small type onion producing large clusters of small bulbs.	Used like garlic to flavor meats, poultry, sausage, head cheese.
Smoke Salt	A synthetic smoke flavoring ground into salt.	Home-curing meat and seasoning bean, lentil or split pea soups.
Sorrel	Belongs to dock family. Long slender leaves used fresh have pleasant acid flavor.	Shredded and added to lettuce, makes lemon juice or vinegar unnecessary. Also in some soups.
Soy Sauce	Made from soy beans by a long curing process.	A "must" in most all Chinese and Japanese dishes.
Tabasco	Made by macerating fresh picked, small hot Mexican peppers, salting and curing 3 years, blending with vinegar, straining, bottling. Produced in Avery Islands.	Used to season egg dishes, gravies, marinades, salad dressings, sauces, sea foods, poultry and soups.

Name	Description and Source	Uses
Tarragon	Related to wormwood family. Has aromatic leaves of a slightly bitter flavor.	Fresh prized for flavoring vinegar and to shred with lettuce for salad. Fresh or dried adds excitement to fish, egg and chicken dishes, lobster thermidor, fish sauces, beets, spinach, aspics.
Thyme	Grown principally in Southern France. The No. 2 of American favorite herbs.	An essential in the famous New Orleans Cuisine. Present in the French bouquet Garni. Excellent seasoning for Manhattan Clam Chowder, lamb, meat soups, stews. Good on vegetables such as carrots, peas, egg plant, escalloped onions, also in stuffings.
Turmeric	Root of plant belonging to ginger family. Bright yellow with rich appetizing aroma, and a rather sharp, mustardy flavor.	Often combined with mustard for pickling and used in meat and egg dishes. An ingredient of curry powder.

HOW TO CARE FOR AND USE HERBS

Herbs, which are mostly used in dried form, should be fresh. They should be kept tightly covered at all times and replaced often. Some herbs may be easily grown in your garden; a few like parsley and chives may be grown in pots or window boxes. Chives grow well when transplanted from the tiny pots in which they are sold to a window box or garden. Here is a list of herbs which you can grow more or less easily: Caraway, Chervil, Chives, Dill, Garlic, Marjoram, Mint, Parsley, Sage, Shallots, Sorrel, Sweet Basil and Tarragon. (See Table 14.)

To dry garden herbs, choose fresh clean tender leaves. Arrange washed, drained leaves in a single layer on shallow trays; cover with cheesecloth and place in a dry shady place until so dry they crumble when handled. Then pack in clean dry jars with airtight lids and store in a cool dry place. When ready to use, crumble and rub through a fine sieve to remove bits of stem or midribs of leaves.

HOW TO BUY AND USE EXTRACTS

The flavoring extracts which should be on every flavoring shelf are vanilla, lemon, almond and perhaps orange. In purchasing them, select a good brand, for there is considerable difference in the quality and flavor. It is always good economy to buy pure vanilla, the extract of the vanilla bean, rather than any of the synthetic vanillin products, which are stronger and may be unpleasant in flavor. The cost is somewhat higher, but since the vanilla flavor of any product depends at most on only a few teaspoons of the extract it is false economy to use an inferior flavoring. This applies to all flavorings.

There is a great variety of other flavoring extracts. Some of these are peppermint, wintergreen, rose, clove, cinnamon, anise, strawberry, raspberry, pistachio, black walnut, and maple. While it is certainly not practical to keep any large assortment of extracts on hand, it is useful to know the available kinds. Read label to learn whether the flavoring is synthetic or pure.

Like spices, flavoring extracts should be bought in small quantities, with the possible exception of vanilla in households where a good many cakes and puddings are made. Extracts should be kept tightly closed at all times, and re-closed immediately after using, for their flavor is volatile and deteriorates rapidly on exposure to air.

Many combinations of flavorings are possible to produce pleasing flavor variations. Vanilla and lemon, lemon and almond, rose and wine, are some of the most popular. Almond is one of the strongest of the extracts and should be used cautiously; but all the extracts are volatile and some of the flavor is dissipated in baking or cooking. Therefore cakes and baked puddings can take a little more flavoring than puddings and other foods to which the flavoring is added after cooking is completed. Freezing also reduces the intensity of the flavor.

HOW TO BUY AND USE FOOD COLORING

Colorings are sometimes used with flavoring extracts; for example, a cake icing which is flavored with rose extract will be more attractive if it is lightly tinted rose. Coloring that is used in foods should always be pure food coloring. It may be in the form of either a paste or a liquid. The paste is a more concentrated color and should be used cautiously.

Foods should never be brightly colored. Icings, fondant and the like should be tinted very delicately in order to be attractive in appearance. Too bright a color will have a "poisonous" appearance such as is found in very cheap and poor quality candies and icings. To avoid accidental use of too much color, take a little of the substance to be colored into a separate dish and mix some of the coloring with it to give a fairly bright color; then combine this colored material with the rest of the mixture a little at a time. The best way to use paste coloring is to dissolve it in a little water before adding it to the food.

The most frequently used food colors are red, yellow and green. It is rarely desirable to use a color not found in natural foods, such as blue. In fact, the only occasion for using blue and violet is in decorative frostings for making violets and forget-me-nots for fancy cakes.

HOW TO BUY AND USE VINEGARS

For most cooking purposes, the fruit vinegars add a flavor and mellowness not obtained from distilled or white vinegar. White vinegar is useful when it is important not to alter the color in a product. Full fermentation brings cider to a strength of 6 per cent acetic acid. While full strength vinegar may be bought, the usual strengths are 4 per cent and 5 per cent. It is important to read the labels on vinegar, as a 5 per cent vinegar will give a sharper flavor than the same amount of 4 per cent vinegar. A 5 per cent vinegar can be reduced to approximately the same strength as a 4 per cent by adding 1 tbsp of water to ¼ cup of vinegar.

Although vinegar keeps well at room temp, it does not keep indefinitely, and should be replaced from time to time. The "mother" of vinegar which forms as a cloudy slippery mass in the bottle is not harmful in any way, but it indicates that the vinegar is old and has probably become musty and more harsh in flavor. White vinegar does not form a "mother" and keeps almost indefinitely, which is the reason it is preferred by some for pickling and preserving.

Cider vinegar is made by the fermentation of the juice of apples. It is filtered, bottled and pasteurized.

White or distilled vinegar is made from the fermentation of grains, including corn, barley malt, and rye. It is aged in wood to mellow the flavor, and distilled so that the final product is a highly purified acetic acid, of 4 or 5 per cent. It is without fruit flavor, and colorless.

Malt vinegar is made from fermented barley malt, and other cereals. This richly flavored vinegar is used more in England than in this country.

Wine vinegar may be made from either white or red grapes. The white wine vinegar is considered superior to the red. It is made principally in Europe, especially in the wine producing countries such as Italy, Spain, and France. It is used primarily for salad dressing.

Flavored vinegars to be used in salad dressings, such as tarragon, are made by immersing herbs, seeds or other flavoring in either malt, cider, white, or white wine vinegar. To make your own flavored vinegars, merely soak the desired herbs and seasonings in the vinegar until the preferred flavor is obtained. Then strain through a fine cloth to make it clear, and pour into bottles and cork tightly for future use. The following seasonings are particularly pleasing: Tarragon leaves; a mixture of marjoram, savory, cress, and parsley; nasturtium seed pods and leaves, dill seed, garlic, cloves, fennel, mint, or mustard. This is one place your own imagination can be put to work to make you famous for your salad dressing!

FREEZING FOODS

FREEZING ONLY THE BEST IN THE BEST WAY

Freezing is a popular method of preserving food because it retains the fresh flavor, color and nutritive value of the fresh product. Remember, however, that freezing *will not improve* an under-ripe berry or over-ripe fruit. Freezing food is easy, but it is important to use correct freezing methods in order to fill the freezer with best quality products.

Having chosen top-quality foods for freezing, be sure you plan, pack and freeze so as to preserve all their quality. It is impossible to tell you all about freezing in space as brief as this. We can only hit the high spots, so we strongly recommend that you study carefully the directions that came with your freezer. Also, send for free bulletins on freezing foods which are available from the U. S. Government Printing Office, Division of Public Documents, Washington, D.C. 20402, or from your State Agricultural Experiment Station, to supplement the manufacturer's directions.

Wise planning is essential to get maximum value from your freezer. On the basis of your family's size and its tastes, the number of guest meals you are likely to serve, and the size of your freezer, decide what foods and how much of each you want to preserve for weeks or immediate needs.

Pre-cooked and prepared foods including combination meat dishes, sandwich spreads, soups and baked foods can be frozen at any season of the year.

Freeze seasonal foods when supplies are plentiful and prices low. This table is a guide for most parts of the country, most years.

WINTER	SPRING	SUMMER	FALL
Beef	Fish	Chickens	Fish
Lamb	Veal	Beef and Fish	Game
Pork	Pork	Apple Sauce	Stewing and
Turkey	Broilers (chickens	Berries, cherries	roasting
Ducks	and turkeys)	Apricots, peaches	chickens
Game	Asparagus	Fruit pies	Turkey
Cranberries	Green beans	Cauliflower	Squash
Tart Pie apples	Strawberries	Lima and green	Pumpkin purée
Fruit cakes	Rhubarb	beans	Tart apples
Mincemeat pies	Pineapple	Brussels sprouts	Concentrated
Citrus fruits	Early cherries	Broccoli	grape juice
		Sweet corn	or purée
		Crabapple pickles	Plum pudding

Speed the food to the freezer without delay. Keep fresh produce and meat chilled; cool all blanched or cooked foods thoroughly before packaging. Package in freezer wrapping and put into the freezer immediately.

PACKAGING

Choose the right type of container or wrapping material for the food you are freezing, on the basis of specific directions. It is important always to eliminate as much air from the package as possible and to prevent loss of moisture from the food. Fill containers compactly, allowing recommended amount of head space for expansion. Wrap meat or irregularly shaped foods snugly and if desired, mold the wrap even more closely to food with stockinette.

Select containers according to family needs. A pint carton of fruit or vegetables serves 3; quarts are better for larger families or for guest meals. Pack chops, steaks and roasts in meal-sized amounts (for 2 or 3, a family, or guest meals). Separate pieces of meat, fish, etc. with 2 layers of freezer wrap so they can be easily separated before thawing. Ground meat can be tamped into layers right in the carton, separating layers with two layers of freezer wrap.

To seal plastic bags, press out all air possible. Twist ends and double over in a gooseneck, then secure with a rubber or paper-and-metal band.

When filling cartons and bags, keep the sealing surfaces clean by using a wide-mouthed funnel, especially if a heat seal is to be used. Spots of syrup or fruit juice interfere with a perfect seal.

Cellophane and coated paper bags must be heat-sealed to fuse the coatings. First, press out all air possible, then fold open end down snugly against food, seal with an ordinary curling iron, a laundry iron, or heated blade of an old case knife. The iron or knife should be hot enough to melt the coating but not to scorch. Test first on newspaper to be sure it doesn't scorch; then on waxed paper to be sure it fuses the wax. Lay end being sealed on a metal base; an inverted rectangular baking pan will do.

Waxed cartons can be sealed satisfactorily with push-on or snap-in lids if lids fit closely enough. Otherwise, air and moisture passing in and out will cause deterioration. Lids that don't fit snugly should be sealed with freezer tape mitered neatly at corners.

Irregular packages such as roasts, whole chickens or turkey pieces should first be packaged compactly into bags. Then press out all air you can, fold open end, twist it around meat and tie it securely. Heat-seal non-twisted edges for extra protection. If any sharp places protrude, protect them with patches of freeze paper, then draw stockinette snugly over package and tie firmly.

LABEL PACKAGES PLAINLY AND ARRANGE PROPERLY

So as to be able to find quickly the food you want, and to judge the success of method of preparation used, mark or tag each package with this information:

1. Kind of fruit, vegetable or meat, with weight, number of pieces or servings.
2. Date of freezing, to avoid holding too long.
3. Quality and variety of food (to judge which varieties freeze most successfully).
4. Method of preparation.

As you gain experience, you may need only the first two items.

In a *chest-type freezer,* store the heavy, bulky packages on the bottom so as not to shift them each time smaller packages are removed. Place newly packaged foods on bottom and along walls for fast freezing; shift longest-frozen ones toward top. Keep labeled sides up. Baskets at top should hold often-used foods. Do not place unfrozen food in contact with food already frozen.

In an *upright freezer,* group foods of a kind together; meat on one shelf, vegetables on another, etc. Put frequently used foods in the door or on the most convenient shelf, with labels facing out. Little packages that might "get lost" can be collected in a mesh or plastic bag.

INDEX YOUR FREEZER CONTENTS

To know exactly what your freezer holds and how long it has been there, keep an index. This should show, in columns, facts such as: Date in . . . . Kind of food. Amount. Date out. Put your index up on an outside wall of the freezer or nearby, and note on it each package you put in or remove.

COOKING FROZEN FOODS

Cook *vegetables* without defrosting; cooking time is less than for the fresh product. Defrost *meats* before cooking, or cook frozen, if desired. *Fish* and *poultry* should be defrosted before cooking; this may be done in the refrigerator, allowing 4½ to 5 hours per pound, at room temperature for 2 or 3 hours, or in front of an electric fan for ¾ to 1 hour. *Fruits* are best defrosted in the refrigerator, and should be served when they are barely thawed.

FREEZING MISCELLANEOUS FOODS

Eggs: Freeze only perfectly fresh eggs without cracks. Break *whole eggs* into bowl; for each cupbowl, add 1 tablespoon white corn syrup or sugar, or 1 teaspoon of salt, depending on how they will be used. Break yolks with fork; mix thoroughly with whites without incorporating air. Prepare *yolks* like whole eggs. Package *whites* without salt or sweetening and without mixing. Package in moisture-vapor-proof cartons or bags, putting enough in each container for a cake, an omelet, etc. (One medium yolk equals 1½ tablespoons; 1 white equals 2 tablespoons). Seal and freeze promptly.

Butter: Wrap butter (very fresh) in freezer paper, or leave in carton, overwrap, and seal. (Keeps up to 6 months at 0° F.)

Cheese: Cut into sandwich slices; separate slices with freezer wrap. Or cut into wedges of a size to last a day or two. Wrap in moisture-vapor-proof paper and freeze promptly.

Ice Cream: Pack home-made ice cream in moisture-vapor-proof cartons; leave commercial ice cream in its original package. Hold frozen no longer than 2 months.

Canapés: These tidbits can be made a week before a party, laid on cookie sheets or in a flat shallow box with freezer paper between layers and frozen firm, then wrapped and stored in freezer. Olive slices and pimiento garnishes freeze well, but parsley sprigs and sieved or sliced hard-cooked eggs should be added just before serving. Arrange on tray while frozen, cover, and allow an hour for thawing.

Soups: Split pea, bean, chicken, vegetable and cream soups all freeze well. Prepare in concentrated form to save space; add water when ready to heat for serving. Pack in containers holding enough for one meal.

Cooked meat, poultry or fish: Pack choice slices of roast meat or pieces of chicken or turkey compactly together and wrap snugly in freezer paper; freeze promptly. Or pack chunks or small pieces of meat, fish or poultry compactly and wrap for use in casserole dishes. Or grind the cooked meat and prepare salad mixtures for sandwich spreads.

Combination Main Dishes (chili, chop suey, curry, baked beans, gumbo, meat pies, stews, hash, etc.): Make your favorite recipe and cool thoroughly. Turn into freezer containers or line casseroles with freezer wrap before filling. When frozen, turn out and wrap snugly in freezer paper. Store in freezer. To serve, unwrap and replace frozen mass in original casserole for heating. Add cooked potatoes or hard-cooked eggs when reheating. At 400° F, it takes about 45 minutes for pints, 1 hour for quarts to heat through.

Baked goods: Quick and yeast breads, rolls and coffee cakes keep longer and have better quality if frozen after baking. Cool. Wrap in freezer paper. To reheat biscuits and muffins, defrost at room temperature about 1 hour; then bake about 5 minutes at 425° F.

Cakes of all types freeze well. If frosted before freezing, use only butter-type or cooked fudge-type frosting, not seven-minute type. Freeze unwrapped until frosting is firm. Then wrap in freezer paper and seal. If cake is to be kept more than 10 days, seal with freezer tape. Defrost ½ to 1 hour before serving.

Cookies: Baked bar cookies or unbaked refrigerator cookies freeze well. Freeze cookies such as Brownies in their pan after cooling. Shape refrigerator cookie dough into a roll, freeze, wrap in freezer paper and seal with tape. When ready to use, defrost just until the roll can be cut into thin slices.

Pies: Fruit and chiffon pies freeze best; home-made custard and cream pies tend to separate when thawed. Meringue shrinks and becomes tough. Freeze in pans. For unbaked two-crust pies, cut vents when ready to bake. For baked pies, bake only until light brown; then cool, wrap and seal. Bake the frozen unbaked pie at 400° F for 40 to 60 minutes, depending on thickness. Defrost baked pies and reheat at 350° F until browned.

Sandwiches: Make sandwiches of cheese, meat, poultry, fish or peanut butter in the usual way, but without lettuce. Wrap each in waxed paper, then stack enough for a meal together and wrap in freezer paper.

Shelled nuts may be packed in sealed glass jars or freezer bags and stored in the freezer. So can fresh grated coconut. *Bacon or chicken fat* may be frozen in clean glass jars or cans with tight-fitting lids sealed with freezer tape.

Puréed foods for cream soup or baby food may be frozen in suitable-size containers; or frozen solid in ice-cube trays, than unmolded and packed in freezer bags or rectangular cartons.

Care of Food in the Home

Almost as important as the actual cooking of foods is their storage. Many foods are stored in the home for periods varying from a few hours to several weeks or months (as for potatoes and apples); and the manner in which they are cared for influences not only their appearance, flavor, and general quality, but their food value as well.

CARELESSNESS in caring for and storing foods after they are brought into the home may result in various forms of deterioration and spoilage such as withering, discoloration, molding and decay. This brings about marked loss of natural flavor, attractive appearance, and vitamin content, and sometimes the complete loss of the food itself.

In the great majority of cases, only enough of the perishable foods should be brought into the home for one or two days at a time, and they should be stored carefully until used. The kind of storage space a family needs for foods depends upon the source of supply. When families raise their own produce a second refrigerator often reduces waste. However, a farm family, which has a garden planted to provide a succession of fresh vegetables all summer, and which has a large unheated storage cellar for winter vegetables, can get along with one refrigerator for dairy products and the most perishable foods. The storage cellar is a good place to store root vegetables, potatoes, apples and all canned foods in the winter. And in the summer, when rains, heat or draught make it necessary to harvest larger amounts of vegetables than can be consumed in one day, the cellar will keep the excess in good condition for several days. Usually fresh vegetables will require no refrigeration if they are gathered the day they are eaten, with the possible exception of the highly perishable ones such as lettuce, radishes and cucumbers, or foods that are more appealing when chilled, like tomatoes and cucumbers.

The city woman has a different problem in obtaining and caring for foods. Her grocer buys fresh vegetables and fruits daily, and if he has adequate refrigeration facilities for storing them to preserve their freshness, it is to her advantage to purchase these foods shortly before she needs them, and not burden her own refrigerator with them. If she lives in a house rather than an apartment, it may be possible and practical for her, too, to have a storage cellar which will be unheated, as well as an efficient refrigerator. But she is more likely to be entirely dependent on her refrigerator for food storage than is the farm woman. Many foods keep best in the refrigerator, for a low temp slows down the action of organisms and enzymes which cause spoilage. Some foods do not require refrigeration but need a cool dry place; others require a cool moist place, such as a cellar; still others keep well at room temp. Usually it is advisable to clean the foods before storing, and to remove soft or damaged specimens; but sometimes washing is not recommended, as for berries or grapes, until just before serving.

FRESH VEGETABLES*

Salad Greens. Green salad vegetables include lettuce, endive, cress, escarole, romaine, cabbage, parsley, mint, spinach, celery and green onions. When any of these vegetables are brought into the kitchen, they should be trimmed immediately to remove bruised or soiled parts. If they are in tight heads, like *cabbage, head lettuce, celery* or *French endive,* washing is not necessary but trimmed heads should be placed in the hydrator, which has a tight-fitting cover to prevent vegetables from drying out. Plastic or other waterproof bags are good containers for storing bulky fruits and vegetables. The bags should fold together snugly or close tightly with a zipper or drawstring. Lacking a hydrator or crisping bag, wrap trimmed vegetables in cheese cloth wrung out in cold water, then in waxed paper or aluminum foil. If lettuce cups are desired, prepare lettuce 4 to 5 hours before serving by washing heads in cold water and removing a deep core at stem-end. Invert under running water to separate leaves, then drain thoroughly core-end down. For wedges, do not remove core. Wrap lettuce prepared either way in a damp cloth and return to refrigerator to crisp. Wash greens like leaf lettuce and curly endive before storing to remove sand or dirt; remove excess water by shaking gently in a folded towel, then store like head lettuce. Use within a day or so. Wash parsley in the same way and place loosely in a clean jar or shortening can with a wet paper napkin in bottom, cover and store in refrigerator. A hermetically sealing container which stops oxidation and prevents dehydration keeps parsley in good condition for at least 10 days. Spinach requires special care in washing; the roots should be trimmed off and each leaf washed separately to avoid grittiness. Drain well. Washed spinach should be used within a day or so.

Cress (water), one of the most perishable of greens, turns to a motley yellow if not properly cared for. To prolong the life of watercress and have it ready for instant use, untie the bunch, cut off excessively long stems and

* For further information on storing vegetables, see chart "Homemaker's Guide to Buying Vegetables," p. 79.

swish leaves in cold water to clean well. Then stand upright in a jar containing about an inch of water, cover tightly and store in refrigerator.

Mint will keep for several days after it is washed, the excess water shaken off, and stored just like parsley. *Green onions* may be kept in the same way as mint, but not longer than a few days. *Chives,* which are always purchased growing, usually in little pots, may be kept in any cool corner of the kitchen or in a window. They should never be watered from the top, as this causes the spears to turn yellow. To water them, set the pot in a shallow dish of cold water.

Do not allow greens to freeze, for freezing makes the leaves limp and watery. When trimming head lettuce, save 2 or 3 outer leaves—do not wash; wrap these snugly around hole or cut head to retard "pink color." Using the outer leaves of cabbage to wrap the cut head prevents the brown or black discoloration, which causes considerable waste.

Cucumbers and radishes, though not belonging to the family of leafy greens, are favorite salad materials. Cucumbers should be washed, dried, and placed in the refrigerator. If they are to be peeled, it should not be done until time for use. Any unused portion of the cucumber should be cut off and not peeled; a piece of waxed paper may be fastened over the cut end with a rubber band. Radishes also should be washed, and dried and the leaves removed before placing in the refrigerator. The outer fresh leaves of radishes may be cooked with spinach to give a delicious new flavor; the heart leaves may be left attached to the radish when it is served, for they are attractive in appearance and edible, with an appealing peppery flavor. Just before serving, cut off the tap root and if desired, make roses by cutting through the skin and flesh to obtain petals. Radish roses have almost no food value because they are soaked in water and the flavor rapidly deteriorates because of the many cuts on their surface.

Other green vegetables. All green vegetables should be cooked the same day they are bought, if possible, to avoid excessive vitamin loss. *Green beans* should not be washed before storing in the refrigerator; they should be washed, strung and broken or cut into lengths just before cooking time. *Peas* should be left in their pods if they must be stored for a few hours; if the pods are very soiled they may be washed and dried before putting them into the refrigerator. After shelling, peas quickly lose freshness and vitamin content, so they should be shelled just before cooking time. *Asparagus* stalks should be washed clean in cold water after removing scales along the sides of stalk where soil or sand is caught. If not crisp, trim off ends and stand stalks in cold water a few minutes; then drain and place in refrigerator. For best eating, do not store asparagus more than a few hours before cooking.

Tomatoes keep well if not bruised or cracked. If under-ripe, ripen at room temp; if over-ripe or bruised, use at once, and do not allow to stand near sound ones. Wash and dry sound tomatoes before storing in the vegetable compartment. Sort frequently, and use at once if they begin to show soft areas.

Root vegetables, such as potatoes, carrots, turnips, parsnips, and beets should be stored in a cool place where the air is not too dry. In cold weather, storing them is no problem, but in hot weather, refrigeration is desirable for carrots and beets, so buy them in small quantities unless you have a cool cellar or a large refrigerator. When cool storage space is available outside the refrigerator, do not wash root vegetables until just before cooking. When storing carrots and beets, cut carrot tops off close and beet tops about 2½ inches from the beet. The reason for this is, that once root vegetables are out of the soil, food material in the roots starts flowing back into the leaves. This is the opposite of what happens when the roots are growing in soil. Roots which lose this food material, lose color, flavor, texture and food value. Wash young tender beet tops, store and cook like spinach. Wash carrots but do not scrape before storing. Wash beets carefully to avoid breaking skin.

FRUITS*

Apples are a semi-perishable fruit. As long as the waxy, air-tight skin is not bruised, they keep well in the refrigerator or any cool, not too dry place. In winter, both cooking and eating apples keep well in a cool cellar or similar storage place. Experimental tests show that one mellow-ripe apple in a basket of barely ripe ones speeds up the ripening of all in the basket. If weather is warm, apples keep best in the refrigerator. Governmental research proves that apples held at refrigerator temp retain their nutritional value and flavor for long periods. Wash before serving.

Bananas should never be kept in the refrigerator. The cold darkens them. When buying a supply of bananas, buy full-ripe ones to be eaten immediately, yellow-ripe for the next day or two, and green-tipped to be kept longest. They ripen rapidly in a warm room. Ripening may be slowed down by keeping them in a cool place, but not in the refrigerator or in a paper bag.

Berries of all kinds are quite perishable. One or two soft or moldy berries in a basket will spoil others, so it is always best to turn them out of the basket and pick them over as soon as they are brought home. A convenient way is to turn them out on a tray and sort out the soft ones. They can then be covered with waxed paper and stored on the same tray, or put without washing into a clean bowl, covered and placed in the refrigerator. They should not be washed until just before serving. *Raspberries and blackberries,* if hulled, need only to be washed and drained before serving. *Strawberries and dewberries* may be sandy, so *before hulling,* they should be washed as follows: Place the berries in a large bowl and run cold water gently over them; swish them gently through the water and lift them out with outspread fingers to drain in a colander. Badly soiled berries may need several washings, but this should not be done until just before serving time. Any blemishes should be cut out when the berries are hulled. Some people

* For further information on storing fruits, see separate Table 7, p 89.

prefer strawberries left whole, sprinkled with sugar, and served almost immediately; some like them sugared and left to stand until the juice begins to be drawn out; others want their berries sliced or crushed with sugar to make them very juicy. Although some people prefer berries chilled, they have a more intense flavor at room temp. Their flavor deteriorates if they are allowed to stand for more than half an hour after preparing.

Grapes, like berries, should be picked over and any spoiled grapes snipped out with scissors, then stored in the refrigerator *without washing,* in a covered bowl or in the hydrator. When ready to serve, wash by holding the bunch under the cold water faucet, and shake dry in a clean dry towel. Most people will like them chilled in warm weather, and warmed to room temp when the day is cool.

Melons should be kept in the refrigerator if they are fully ripe. If cantaloupe seems hard, it will ripen slowly outside the refrigerator. Since all melons absorb flavors and odors from other food and also give off their own odor, it is desirable to keep them in a large plastic bag or wrapped snugly in aluminum foil. After cutting, pat a piece of waxed paper flat over the cut surface before returning to the bag. For best flavor and appearance, cut a melon just before serving, and serve cool but not ice cold. Never put ice inside a cantaloupe or honey dew to chill it as this dilutes the fine flavor.

Peaches should not be washed or rubbed before storing, as the removal of the bloom (or fuzz) hastens spoiling. Perfectly sound peaches may be kept in the refrigerator for a day or two, but if they show any fresh bruises, they should be consumed the same day. Wash, peel and slice them just before serving. If they are to be sugared, let them stand for a short time after slicing with the sugar on them either in or out of the refrigerator, depending on the temp preferred. Peaches are perishable and need special care to avoid waste. *Apricots, nectarines and plums* require similar care.

Oranges, grapefruit and lemons are best kept covered in the refrigerator, or in a cool place. It is preferable not to cut or squeeze them until just before they are to be served, because the edge of their fine flavor, as well as some vitamin content, may be lost when the juice or cut fruit stands a few hrs.

Dried fruits have such a low moisture content that they keep well at room temp, as long as they are in a sealed container that will prevent insect contamination and excessive drying. If the room is fairly cool and dry, so much the better. Once opened they should be wrapped in waxed paper or moisture-proof cellophane and kept in the refrigerator. If fruit becomes dry and hard, it may develop a white sugar deposit on the surface that is mistaken for mold. Steaming for a few min will restore the original moisture content and dissolve this sugar deposit, but the original high quality is gone.

Canned fruits and vegetables. Commercially canned fruits and vegetables will keep in any cool, dry place. For finest flavor and best color all fruits and vegetables should be consumed within a year after they are packed.

The same applies to home-canned foods put up in tin. Commercial and home-canned foods in glass should be stored in a place that is not only cool, but dark and slightly damp. If the air is too dry, the rubber rings may dry out and crack, permitting organisms to enter. Light bleaches the color of the foods. Therefore, glass jars of canned food which must be stored in a light place either should be wrapped in regular tan-colored heavy wrapping paper or should be shielded from the light by hanging a tan or cream-colored window shade over the front of the shelves.

After cans or jars are opened, they are still the safest containers for the left-over contents, since the inside of the can is more sterile than most bowls or jars. For several reasons however, it may be advisable to transfer the food. If the leftover amount is small, there is no point in allowing it to remain in the original container. Some foods, especially fruit juices, and tomatoes, need to be covered *tightly* in order to prevent flavor changes. After the can is opened, it is best to place the unused portion in a jar or bottle with a screw cap, and of a proper size, so that as little air as possible comes in contact with the food. Store pickles of all kinds in a cool dark place to keep them crisp and to prevent loss of color.

Frozen fruits and vegetables. Keep either commercially or home frozen foods frozen until they are ready to be used. Be sure that your market has adequate storage facilities for frozen food, and keeps it frozen until the moment it is delivered. When you bring packages of frozen food from the store or freezer locker, store them in the freezing compartment of your refrigerator as quickly as possible. Vegetables (except corn on the cob) and rhubarb are kept frozen until ready to cook. Fruits to be eaten raw should be partially thawed before using. For best results the fruit should be left in the original container in the refrigerator to thaw, but not in the freezing compartment. This will take from 6 to 8 hrs. Fruit will thaw more quickly out of the container, and at room temperature, but this gives less perfect results than slow thawing, and should be used only in emergencies.

MEAT

Fresh meat. All fresh meat should be refrigerated, and since under average home refrigeration it loses its fine flavor if kept too long, it is never wise to buy more fresh meat than is needed for two or three days, especially if it is to be kept in the uncooked state. Always place meat in the coldest spot in the refrigerator under the freezing compartment or the ice compartment. It is not harmed by freezing, but once meat has thawed, it should never be refrozen.

The smaller the proportion of cut surfaces exposed on a piece of meat, the better it keeps. Thus meat in one large piece, like a standing rib roast, will keep in good condition in the refrigerator for a longer time than meat cut in small pieces as for stewing. Ground meat, which has a very high proportion of cut surface, loses flavor and juiciness rapidly, and should be used as soon as possible after purchasing.

As soon as fresh meat is brought into the home, it should be unwrapped and wiped off with a damp cloth—never washed in water. Then it may be placed on a clean dry plate or shallow refrigerator dish, and covered lightly or not at all; a piece of waxed paper laid over the meat, or a loosely fitting refrigerator-dish cover may be used. Meat should never be closely covered or tightly wrapped in waxed paper, because a little drying of the surface retards bacterial growth and is therefore desirable. If the meat is left wrapped in the butcher's original paper, cold penetration is slowed up and the paper may absorb some of the meat juices. When meat is placed in the ice compartment to freeze, it should be wrapped completely in waxed paper. Any exposed surface will become dry and will be hard after cooking.

Frozen meat. Either commercially or home frozen meat should be kept frozen until ready for use. Thin cuts of steaks or chops may be cooked without thawing, or only partially thawed, but for best results with all cuts of meat, it is best to thaw before cooking. Thawing should be done in a covered dish or pan in the refrigerator. This may take as long as 24 hrs for large roasts, but with simple planning, it should be no problem to allow the meat to remain in the refrigerator for one day before cooking. Any meat juice that may ooze out into the dish during thawing, should be added to the pan in which the meat is cooked. This will be no more than a tbsp at the most. Frozen meat should never be put into water to thaw. It leaches out the flavor and juices and makes the meat soft and unappetizing. It is possible to cook meat without thawing, but the length of time for cooking is greatly increased, and by the time the inside is cooked to a palatable state, the outer surface is overdone and very dry. Chops that are not thawed do not brown as well as chops that are thawed. Once raw meat has thawed, it should not be refrozen, but should be cooked at once.

Cured meats. Old-fashioned *country style ham* and similar products (smoked picnics and smoked butts) may be kept out of the refrigerator in any dark, cold place, except in hot weather, where refrigeration is desirable. But most hams today have a mild cure and require about the same care as fresh meat before cooking, especially after they have been cut. *Sliced bacon* should be left in its original wrapping, or wrapped in clean waxed paper, and should always be kept dry in refrigerator near the freezing compartment. Only the amount to be used for the meal should be removed from the refrigerator. If the whole package is taken out and allowed to warm up, moisture will condense on the bacon and lessen its keeping qualities. It is not advisable to keep bacon, even in the refrigerator, longer than a week or two, as the fat tends to become hard and easily broken, and both appearance and flavor deteriorate. *Corned beef* should be treated just like fresh meat. *Sliced cold cuts* such as salami and bologna should be stacked compactly, wrapped in waxed paper, and kept in a cold part of the refrigerator.

Ready-to-serve canned meats. If sliced canned meats are left over from one meal to another, the slices should be piled together and wrapped securely in waxed paper before placing in the refrigerator. They should be kept the shortest possible time, for the flavor does deteriorate rapidly.

Cooked meat. After cooking, any meat should be made into the most compact parcel possible, wrapped tightly in waxed paper or foil, or placed in a dish with a tight-fitting cover. Because the surface has already been dried out by cooking, no further drying is desirable, and there may be loss of meat flavor as well as absorption of other flavors if the meat is left uncovered. Leftover cooked meat should be cooled then chilled as soon as possible. If it is filled with dressing, like a stuffed breast of veal, it is best to remove the dressing and store it separately in a covered bowl in the refrigerator.

POULTRY AND STUFFING

Poultry should be cleaned, drawn, washed and thoroughly drained, then stored in the coldest place in the refrigerator. If bird is to be stuffed for roasting, stuff it the day it is cooked. Laboratory studies show it is an unsafe practice to stuff a bird the day before it is cooked even though it is kept chilled. These studies prove that such cooked stuffings often contain harmful organisms which can cause serious illness. When refrigerator is crowded and weather is cold, store in any available place where thermometer reading is 50° F or lower. If bird is cut up for frying, stewing or broiling, place in bowl, cover lightly with waxed paper and store in refrigerator until cooking time. Birds left whole keep better than those cut up. Break leftover cooked poultry into pieces and store compactly in covered bowl in refrigerator. Store stuffing separately.

FISH

Fish is a very perishable food and even though refrigerated, should not be kept any longer than 24 hours after purchase. To keep for longer periods, it should be frozen. Frozen or unfrozen, wrap it carefully in waxed paper to prevent any transfer of odors.

DAIRY PRODUCTS AND EGGS

Fresh milk and cream should always be stored in the original containers, since the bottles or cartons are sterilized before being filled and the inside is therefore as clean as possible. If the outside of the container is soiled, it should be thoroughly washed with cold water, and dried before placing in the refrigerator. Milk and cream belong in the coldest place in the refrigerator, and the manufacturer usually indicates where this place is by making it tall enough to accommodate bottles.

Evaporated and sweetened condensed milk should be kept in the can, in the refrigerator after opening, but the can should be well cleaned on the top and outside before it is opened, and any drip should be wiped off before the opened can is put away. The opening may be covered with a hood of waxed paper fastened on with a rubber band. Sweetened condensed milk will keep almost indefinitely even when open, if it is well cared for. Evaporated milk, however, should be used within a few days, for once opened it is almost as perishable as fresh milk.

Butter should have a special glass or enamelware container with a close-fitting cover, because it absorbs food odors readily. If quarter-pound sticks are wrapped separately in parchment or foil, leave wrapped until needed. Margarine should be given care similar to butter, but it is not as perishable. Both butter and margarine must be refrigerated.

Cheese, whether natural or packaged, requires refrigeration as soon as it is cut. Processed packaged cheeses are pasteurized and change very little, either in aroma or in texture, when kept unopened without refrigeration for several months; but as soon as they are exposed to the air, organisms can enter and the cheese should be refrigerated.

All cut natural cheeses, whether packaged or not, require refrigeration because they are not pasteurized. Natural cheeses such as Camembert, Brie, Roquefort and Liederkranz, which are cut and then packaged, are quite perishable and should be kept in the refrigerator even before opening. If kept cold, they hold their natural flavor well without giving off much aroma. The soft types, like Camembert and Brie, should be allowed to warm up to room temperature before serving, since this semi-liquid softness is characteristic of such cheese when well ripened, and its flavor is best in this soft state. The old way of keeping cheese like cheddar, wrapped in cloth moistened in vinegar is not recommended. If vinegar is strong enough, it helps retard the development of mold. It also changes the appetizing aroma and fine flavor. A more modern way of retarding mold formation is to keep the cheese wrapped in aluminum foil or enclosed in a plastic bag.

Cottage cheese and cream cheese are both very perishable and absorb odors and flavors readily. They should be kept covered and refrigerated, and used as soon as possible after purchasing.

Eggs should be covered and always kept in the refrigerator by the housewife as well as by the poultryman and the dealer. This not only prolongs their freshness, but helps keep the egg yolk in the center of the egg, which is desirable for stuffed eggs or for hard-cooked eggs which are sliced for garnishing. Eggs separate easily while cold—so separate immediately after taking from refrigerator. If yolks are not used at once, put into small jar, add a drop or two of water and seal tightly with screw-top lid; return to refrigerator and use within a day or two. They may also be dropped into simmering water and hard-cooked before storing, then used in salads, creamed dishes or sieved to garnish cooked vegetables or salads. Let whites warm to room temp before beating to get greatest possible volume. Hard-cooked eggs should be cracked, then put under cold running water and peeled. Cool, then place in a refrigerator dish, cover with wet paper toweling, cover and refrigerate. Use within a day or two.

COOKED FOODS

Never buy foods containing custard, such as eclairs, unless the store keeps them in a refrigerator. They should always be refrigerated until used, and it is never wise to keep these foods overnight. The combination of eggs, milk, and sugar is irresistible to bacteria, and serious illness can result from eating the foods in which these bacteria have multiplied rapidly. There is no danger in keeping home-made custard mixtures overnight in the refrigerator, *if* the following precautions are taken into consideration when the custard is made: Baked custards should be removed from the pan of hot water in which they are baked and placed on cake racks till cool; then covered and kept in the refrigerator until they are served. Soft custards may be cooled rapidly by setting the top of the double boiler in a pan of cold water. When cool, pour the custard into a clean jar, cover tightly with a screw-top lid, and place in the refrigerator until serving time. Custard is best both in flavor and in texture if served the same day it is made.

White sauce may often be made conveniently a few hours ahead of time and stored until just before use. The sauce should be cooled thoroughly by placing the pan in cold or iced water, stirring frequently as it cools. This prevents a "skin" from forming on top. Then it may be poured into a clean glass jar and stored like soft custard. When ready to use, reheat over boiling water, add a little milk, if needed to bring it to the desired consistency, and stir thoroughly. Like custard, it is best to use white sauce the day it is made.

Gelatin desserts of the plain fruit variety keep better than those made with whipped cream or whipped evaporated milk, but it is best not to keep even these longer than a day. They should be kept in the refrigerator constantly and, if possible, should be covered to prevent absorption of foreign odors and flavors, and drying out of the surface.

Leftover cooked foods should be placed in clean, covered containers—bowls, refrigerator dishes, or glass jars—and kept in the refrigerator. If small quantities of several vegetables or cooked or canned fruits are left, they may be combined in one container and used for salad or soup. Leftovers should always be used as soon as possible for the sake of flavor, appearance, and nutritive value.

BAKED GOODS

Homemade cake keeps best if it is transferred from the baking pans to cake coolers soon after removal from the oven, and frosted as soon as it is cooled. Frosting helps to keep cake fresh and moist. Of the various types of icings, a cooked fudge or panocha icing will keep in good condition longest; butter icing is next best; and a seven-minute frosting is most perishable—it is at its best for only a few hours. Whether iced or not, the cake itself will keep in best condition if covered so it is virtually air-tight. Cake boards and covers do the job very satisfactorily. But it should be remembered that cake is at its very best when perfectly fresh, as soon as it has lost the oven heat. *Commercially baked cake* should be kept the same way; if possible, it should be left or replaced in its original wrapper.

Cookies should be stored in a cookie jar or covered tin pail. A large glass jar with a screw top lid is also satisfactory. This helps to keep crisp cookies crisp and soft ones soft. Only one kind of cookie should be put into a cookie jar at one time, or there will be interchange of flavors between diffcrent kinds, which makes all of them taste nondescript. It is possible to store more than one kind of cookie in the same jar, if all the cookies of the same type are placed in a tightly sealed cellophane or waxed paper bag. These bags may be purchased new, or may be saved from dried fruits, bought cookies, etc. The cookie jar should be thoroughly washed out, scalded and carefully dried between batches, and all cookies should be well cooled before they are placed in the jar.

Pie should be made in a sufficient quantity for just one meal, if possible, for no pie can be stored with very satisfactory results. The crust becomes soaked on standing, and the filling, whether it is a fruit or custard type, becomes unattractive in appearance and loses the fine edge of its flavor. Mince, pumpkin and fruit pies may, if necessary, be kept overnight in the refrigerator, and reheated before serving. Reheating restores some of the original flakiness to the crust, but it is at its best within a few hours after baking. Chiffon pies should be stored in the refrigerator, and they should be covered. It is highly desirable that they be eaten the day they are made.

Bread keeps best if left in its original wrapping, or if wrapped snugly in waxed paper. Then it should be stored either in a clean dry bread box or, if none is available, in a closed container in the refrigerator. Bread that is kept in the refrigerator shows less tendency to become moldy. If the bread is always kept wrapped, the bread box is much easier to care for than if the unwrapped loaf is placed in it; in the latter case, the box will require frequent scaldings to keep it sweet and free from mold. Bread and cake should never be stored in the same box, as the cake draws the moisture from the bread.

MISCELLANEOUS FOODS

Coffee should preferably be kept in the home not longer than a week, so a family should not purchase more than a week's supply at a time. If the coffee is purchased in a paper sack, transfer it immediately to a clean dry glass or tin container. Cover it tightly, and never leave the cover off for a second longer than necessary when measuring coffee into the pot. The volatile substances which give coffee its flavor and aroma escape very quickly when exposed to air. Keep the tightly closed coffee container in the refrigerator, or other cool dark place. A good plan is to let it stand upside down, so the rising aroma cannot escape through the crack around the lid but will be trapped in the upturned bottom of the container.

Syrups, such as molasses, honey, maple syrup and corn syrup, and also *jellies, jams, preserves and pickles,* need no refrigeration so long as they are unopened, though they keep best in a cool, fairly dry place. After opening, the jars or bottles should be thoroughly cleaned on the outside to remove any sticky smears where bacterial growth might start. The tops should be covered with a layer or two of strong waxed paper, secured with a rubber band or a piece of string. If convenient, they should be stored in the refrigerator; but if the remainder is to be consumed within a few days, this is not necessary, provided a cool place is available outside the refrigerator. Honey should never be kept cold unless you particularly like it very thick. If refrigerated over a long period, it is likely to crystallize. Crystallized honey can be restored to its liquid state by setting the jar in a pan of hot water for a few minutes to melt.

Both *mayonnaise and French dressing,* and the various types of cooked salad dressing (either commercial or homemade), should be stored in the refrigerator, but not in the coldest spot. They should never freeze. Keep them tightly covered and the outside of the container clean. Homemade French dressing should be taken out before using and allowed to warm up enough so that it can be mixed well by shaking before adding to the salad.

Shortenings and oils. Hydrogenated shortenings, especially those made from vegetable oils, are very stable and need no refrigeration to keep them in good condition. These shortenings should be kept tightly covered, for if exposed to the air they will collect dust and will eventually contract and crack on the surface, though they may not become rancid. If their storage place is so hot that they melt at any time, their texture will be changed. After these shortenings have once been melted and used for deep fat frying, they should be carefully strained, cared for in the same way as before using, and not used for any other purpose than frying.

Regular or hydrogenated lard should be stored in the refrigerator, if possible. It is softer than the hydrogenated vegetable fats, and is relatively easy to handle even when chilled.

Cooking and salad oils (olive, cottonseed and corn oils) may be kept in the refrigerator to prevent rancidity, though if they are used within a few weeks, there is little danger of their becoming rancid in any cool place.

Spices and extracts should always be kept tightly covered, in a cool dark dry place. Light and heat affect the volatile substances which give them flavor and aroma. Some manufacturers are putting flavoring extracts in dark bottles to exclude a maximum of light. It is not advisable to buy spices in large quantities, because even under best storage conditions, they lose their potency. Spices should be replaced every six months.

Nuts contain a rather high percentage of oil, and if stored in a warm place, they become rancid and discolored. Place shelled nutmeats in a clean dry glass jar, cover tightly, and store in refrigerator. Keep nuts in the shell in cool, dry place. Do not expect shelled or unshelled nuts to keep indefinitely.

Dry bread crumbs are convenient to have on hand. They are easily made from stale mold-free bread by drying it thoroughly in a very slow oven, then rolling to fine crumbs with a rolling pin, rubbing it over a coarse grater or by pressing the broken dried bread through a food mill with the screw very loose. When rolling bread, crumbs will not scatter if the dry bread is placed in a paper sack and rolled in the sack. Put crumbs immediately into a clean dry glass jar and cover with a screw-top in which several holes have been punched, or with 2 or 3 thicknesses of cheesecloth tied very loosely or fastened securely with a rubber band. Keep in cool dry place. Crumbs should not be stored in an air-tight container, or they will become stale and musty in flavor. Stored as directed, they will keep several weeks without deteriorating.

Dried legumes and cereals. All types of cereals, flour, rice, macaroni, spaghetti, barley, etc., keep well and can be stored at room temp, but they can become infested with tiny insects or weevil. It is false economy to purchase larger amounts of legumes and cereal products than can be conveniently stored. Metal or glass cannisters with tight fitting lids are ideal containers for these foods. Empty coffee jars with screw tops can be decorated and used to hold oatmeal, pancake flour, etc., and even dried beans and peas. They are a decorative as well as a useful addition to the storage shelves. If flour bins or containers should become infested with weevil, it is necessary to wash and scald the containers thoroughly, and dry them in the sun if possible, before re-using. After prepared cereals have been opened, they become rubbery and tough in a relatively short time, if not kept very dry. They can be easily freshened by spreading the cereal on a baking sheet and placing it in a slow oven for a few minutes. On cooling, the cereal will become as fresh and crisp as when it was first opened.

Store plain or flavored gelatin in any dry place and keep it in a tightly sealed container. Never dip into it with a wet spoon.

REFRIGERATION HELPS

The proper care of food in the home is very dependent on an efficiently working refrigerator, either gas, electric, or ice. Don't abuse this important servant in your kitchen. It demands very little care in return for its faithful service in protecting your health and your budget.

KEEP THE REFRIGERATOR COLD!

1. *Keep the temp* of your refrigerator within the safety zone, no lower than 32° F, no warmer than 50° F. Check this with a thermometer.

2. *In an ice refrigerator,* the volume of ice should never fall below one-half of the capacity of the box, for economical operation. The ice should not be wrapped in paper or a blanket; this defeats the principle of cooling by ice.

3. *Don't restrict air* circulation by crowding dishes together in the refrigerator. Proper circulation of air around the food is very essential.

4. *Don't put hot foods* into the refrigerator; it steams the inside of the cabinet and wastes refrigeration. Cool foods to room temperature before

storing. When it is advisable to cool food very quickly, such as custard, the bottom of the pan or bowl can be immersed in cold water or ice, to chill quickly before placing in the box.

5. Keep the doors of the refrigerator closed tightly when not in use. When removing food from the refrigerator, remove as many items at one time as you will need, and close the doors again as quickly as possible. Remember cold air is heavy and literally *tumbles* out when the door opens.

KEEP THE REFRIGERATOR CLEAN!

1. Wash the refrigerator inside and out with a solution of baking soda and water at least once a week to keep it fresh and sweet smelling.

2. Dry the excess moisture from the shelves and walls after washing, as this excess moisture makes convenient spots for yeasts or molds to develop.

3. Put only clean food into the clean refrigerator. Wipe off the outside of such containers as milk bottles, cans, etc., before placing them in the box. Rinse sand and dirt from vegetables.

4. If an accident should occur, be thorough about removing the spilled material, and wash and dry the soiled shelves at once.

DEFROST WHEN NECESSARY!

1. Defrost before the frost builds up to ¼ inch on the freezer. Never "hack" at the frost with any sharp instrument. Consult your instruction book for the recommended method of defrosting.

2. Turn control to least cold "setting" when going away for several days.

REMEMBER THAT SPECIAL FOODS NEED SPECIAL CARE!

1. It is best to cover most foods to prevent their drying out or absorbing odors, but it is especially important to cover strong-smelling foods like sauerkraut, broccoli, and cheese to prevent transfer of odors to other foods.

2. Variety meats, such as liver, kidney, heart, sweetbreads, and brains keep best when frozen. Either freeze them as soon as you get them home, or cook them within 24 hrs after purchase.

3. If you refrigerate with ice, do not put foods in the ice compartment. That part of the refrigerator is not designed for food protection.

4. Ice cream belongs in the freezing compartment until time to serve. If the container is too large, cut it in half without removing the contents and store the half-cartons in ice trays. Melted ice cream should not be refrozen.

5. All frozen packaged foods belong in the freezing compartment until they are to be used. If you only need part of a package, cut it off, and return the unused portions to the freezer.

Measurements and Equivalents

WHEN recipes were written in such terms as "butter the size of a walnut" and "a pinch of this or that," a cook had to depend entirely on her own judgment, developed through years of experience. Today's recipes are developed with standard measurements and standardized equipment, and although judgment is still an indispensable quality in a cook, the novice can more nearly duplicate an experienced cook's products while she is developing her own knowledge and experience.

Modern recipes are worked out in test kitchens where the worker is trained to use accurate measurements. The only way you can possibly benefit by this experience and training is to measure accurately, too.

Cakes made by two persons following the same recipe will always differ to some extent. The two bakers will use different degrees of vigor in beating and mixing, and will spend different lengths of time on the process. They may use sugars of different degrees of fineness, or eggs of a different size. One may use an aluminum baking pan a half-inch wider or a quarter of an inch deeper than the tin or glass pan used by the other. One may have a better insulated oven, with a more constant temp than the other. The cakes of both may be excellent, yet slightly different in texture, color, lightness, and flavor. These variations are part of the charm of home cooked food. However, standardized measurements will considerably lessen the possibility of a "failure" and the resulting waste of precious food.

In the following pages will be found the measures and equivalents of the ingredients used in all types of cooking, the units per lb of commonly used foods, and illustrated directions on proper measuring techniques.

TABLE 16: EQUIVALENT WEIGHTS AND MEASUREMENTS

1 bushel	....	4 pecks
1 peck	....	8 quarts
1 gallon	....	4 quarts
1 quart	....	2 pints
		32 fluid ounces
		4 cups
1 pint	....	16 fluid ounces
		2 cups

EQUIVALENT WEIGHTS AND MEASUREMENTS *(Continued)*

1 cup	8 fluid ounces
	16 tablespoons
¾ cup	12 tablespoons (6 ounces)
⅔ cup	10 tablespoons and 2 teaspoons
½ cup	8 tablespoons (4 ounces)
⅓ cup	5 tablespoons and 1 teaspoon
¼ cup	4 tablespoons (2 ounces)
⅛ cup	1 fluid ounce
	2 tablespoons
1 tablespoon	½ fluid ounce
	3 teaspoons
1 teaspoon	60 drops
1 pound	16 ounces (dry weight)

TABLE 17

FREQUENTLY USED SUBSTITUTIONS AND EQUIVALENTS

¼ pound butter	½ cup
1 ounce baking chocolate (unsweetened)	1 square
1 cup of fresh egg whites	8-10 whites
1 cup of fresh egg yolks	12-14 yolks
1 cup of fresh whole eggs	5-6 eggs
Eggs, dried whites	1 tablespoon dried white plus 2 tablespoons water is equivalent to 1 fresh white
Eggs, dried yolks	1½ tablespoons dried yolk plus 1 tablespoon water is equivalent to 1 fresh yolk
Eggs, dried whole	2 tablespoons egg plus 2 tablespoons water is equivalent to 1 fresh egg
1 ounce salt	2⅛ tablespoons (1 lb. = 2⅜ cups)
1 fluid ounce vanilla	2 tablespoons
1 fluid ounce vinegar	2 tablespoons
½ pint coffee cream	serves 8 for coffee
½ pint whipping cream	makes 2 cups, whipped
1 cup evaporated milk	makes 3 cups, whipped
1 quart skim milk	¾ cup dried milk plus 4 cups water
1 quart whole milk	2 cups evaporated milk plus 2 cups water
1 ounce baking powder	2⅔ tablespoons
1 ounce baking soda	2 tablespoons
⅙ ounce baking soda	1 teaspoon
1 ounce cream of tartar	3 tablespoons
⅑ ounce cream of tartar	1 teaspoon

FREQUENTLY USED SUBSTITUTIONS AND EQUIVALENTS *(Continued)*

8-10 graham crackers .... 1 cup crumbs
 4 ounces bread .... 3 cups soft crumbs

1 cup all-purpose flour minus 2 tablespoons equals 1 cup cake flour (both sifted before measuring).

¼ cup cocoa plus 1½-2 teaspoons shortening equals 1 ounce unsweetened chocolate.

1 cup vegetable shortening plus ½ teaspoon salt is approximately equal to 1 cup butter.

1 cup sweet milk, or ½ cup evaporated milk and ½ cup water, plus 1 tablespoon lemon juice or vinegar, equals 1 cup buttermilk.

1 tablespoon of corn starch........ 2 tablespoons flour (for thickening)
4-6 lemons (No. 300)............. 1 cup juice
 1 lemon (No. 300)............. 3 tablespoons to ¼ cup juice
2-4 oranges (No. 176)............. 1 cup juice
 1 cake compressed yeast.......... 1 package dry granulated yeast
 2 cakes compressed yeast.......... 1 package "Household" yeast
                                    (larger cake)

TABLE 18

NUMBER OF UNITS PER POUND OF COMMON FOODS

FOODS IN POUND (OR STATED MEASURE)	UNITS PER POUND (OR STATED MEASURE)
Beverages	
Chocolate	4 cups (grated)
	(1 ounce, 1 square = ¼ cup grated)
	2 cups (melted)
Cocoa	4 cups—about 64 tablespoons
	(serves about 100)
Coffee, drip	5 cups (fine)—about 80 tablespoons
	(serves about 60)
Coffee, regular	5½ cups (coarse)
Tea	6-8 cups—(serves from 300-400)
Cereal Products and Starches	
Barley, pearl	2-2¼ cups
Bran	8 cups
Bread (1 pound loaf)...........	16 average slices
Cornflakes	16 cups
Cornmeal	2¾-3 cups
Cornstarch	3-3¼ cups
Crackers, graham	40-60 crackers
Crackers, oyster	200-500 crackers
Crackers, saltine	125 crackers
Crackers, soda	70-90 crackers

NUMBER OF UNITS PER POUND OF COMMON FOODS *(Continued)*

FOODS IN POUND (OR STATED MEASURE)	UNITS PER POUND (OR STATED MEASURE)

Cereal Products and Starches (Continued)

Cream of wheat................... 2½-3 cups
Farina......................... 2⅔ cups
Flour, all-purpose (sifted)......... 4 cups
Flour, all purpose (unsifted)....... 3½ cups
Flour, cake (sifted).............. 4½-4⅔ cups
Flour, cake (unsifted)............. 4 cups
Flour, wholewheat (unsifted)....... 3½ cups
Grapenuts (1 lb., 12 ounces)....... 3 cups
Macaroni, elbow (uncooked)....... 4-4½ cups
Noodles (uncooked) .... 5-6 cups
Oatmeal...................... 6 cups
Pop corn (unpopped)............. 2⅔ cups
Rice, brown (uncooked).......... 2-2¼ cups
Rice, white (uncooked)........... 2-2¼ cups
Rice, wild (uncooked)........... 3 cups
Spaghetti (uncooked) .... 4-5 cups
Tapioca, minute (uncooked)........ 2½ cups

Dairy Products

Cheese, American (grated)......... 4 cups
Cheese, cottage .... 2 cups

Fats and Oils

Butter........................ 2 cups
　　　　　　　　　　　　　　　48-60 pats
Hydrogenated vegetable shortening.. 2 cups
Lard......................... 2-2½ cups
Oleomargarine .... 2 cups
Salad oil .... 2⅛-2½ cups

Fruits, Dried

Apples........................ 6 cups
Apricots...................... 3 cups
Currants...................... 3-3⅜ cups
Dates, pitted .... 3 cups
Dates, unpitted .... 2½ cups, 60-70 dates
Figs.......................... 2¾ cups
Peaches....................... 3 cups
Pears......................... 3 cups
Prunes........................ 2-3 cups
Raisins, seeded .... 2-2½ cups
Raisins, seedless .... 2-2½ cups

Fruits, Fresh—See separate chart "Guide for Buying Fruits," Table 7, p 89.

Number of Units per Pound of Common Foods *(Continued)*

Foods in Pound (or Stated Measure)	Units per Pound (or Stated Measure)

Legumes, Dried

Beans, kidney .... 2½-2⅔ cups
Beans, lima .... 2½ cups
Beans, navy .... 2⅓-2½ cups
Beans, soy .... 2½ cups
Lentils......................... 2⅓ cups
Peas, split .... 2¼ cups

Meats—
Beef

Club steak .... 2 servings
Dried beef .... 12-20 servings creamed
Flank.......................... 4-6 servings
Ground .... 4 servings
Porterhouse steak .... 1-2 servings
Round steak .... 2-4 servings
Sirloin .... 2-3 servings
Stew (little or no bone) .... 4 servings
Stew (medium amount of bone) ..... 3 servings
Rib roast .... 1½ servings

Lamb

Boneless rolled roast............. 3-4 servings
Loin chop .... 3 servings
Rib chop .... 3 servings
Leg .... 2 servings

Pork

Bacon, sliced, narrow strips........ 30 slices
Bacon, sliced, wide strips.......... 15-20 slices
Shoulder steaks .... 2-3 servings
Ham, whole .... 2-3 servings
Roast, loin .... 3-4 servings
Chops......................... 3-4 servings
Spare ribs .... 2 servings

Miscellaneous Meats

Frankfurters .... 12-16 weiners

Veal

Chops .... 3-4 servings
Loin roast .... 3-4 servings
Steak .... 3-4 cutlets
                                 4 veal birds
Stew .... 2 servings

Number of Units per Pound of Common Foods *(Continued)*

Foods in Pound (or Stated Measure)	Units per Pound (or Stated Measure)

Nuts

Almonds . . . . 3 cups shelled
Brazil . . . . 1½ cups shelled
Cashew . . . . 4 cups shelled
Chestnuts . . . . 2 cups shelled (3½ cups in shell)
Cocoanut . . . . 6 cups shredded
Filberts . . . . 3½ cups shelled
Peanuts . . . . 3-3½ cups shelled
Pecans . . . . 3-4 cups shelled
Walnuts . . . . 4 cups shelled

Poultry

Broiler (up to 2½ pounds)   Allow ½ bird per person
Fryers (2½ to 3 pounds)   Allow ¾ pound per person
Roaster (3½ pounds and over)   Allow ¾ pound per person
Hens (2½ pounds and over)   Allow ½-¾ pound per person

Fish

Fin fish, whole. . . . . 1-1½ servings
Fin fish, drawn (eviscerated only) . . . 1-2 servings
Fin fish, dressed (eviscerated, head
    and fins removed) . . . . 2-3 servings
Fin fish, steaks. . . . . 2-4 servings
Fin fish, fillets. . . . . 2-4 servings
Fin fish, canned. . . . . 4-6 servings
Oysters, shucked . . . . 1 quart equals 40-60 oysters
                                            1 quart serves 6-8
Shell fish, crab. . . . . 1 cup meat
Shell fish, lobster. . . . . 1 small lobster
Shell fish, shrimp. . . . . 3 servings per pound

Sweetening Agents

Honey . . . . 1 cup weighs 10 ounces
Marshmallows 60-80
Molasses . . . . 1 cup weighs 12 ounces
Sugar, brown, tight pack. . . . . 2¼ cups
Sugar, granulated . . . . 2¼ cups
Sugar, loaf and cube. . . . . 70-116 squares
Sugar, powdered . . . . 2⅓ to 2½ cups, tightly packed

Vegetables—See separate chart "Homemaker's Guide for Buying Vegetables," Table 6, p 79.

*Tin Can and Glass Jar Sizes used for Packing Foods.

Terms used by the industry to designate container sizes such as No. 2 or 303 are being less frequently used now than in years past. The amount of food in the can or jar is generally described on the label by weight and measure.

COMMON CONTAINER SIZES

INDUSTRY DESIGNATION	DESCRIPTION FOR CONSUMER		PRODUCT
	Approx. net weight (check label)	Approx. cups	
No. ¼	3 to 4 oz	½	Tuna, tuna-like fishes, Vienna sausage, potted meats
No. ½	6 to 8 oz	1	Tuna, tuna-like fishes, salmon
No. 1 Tall	9 oz	1	Ripe olives and pears
8 oz or 8Z Tall	8 to 9 oz	1	Fruits, Vegetables, ** specialties
Picnic	10½ oz	1¼	Condensed soups, fruit, vegetables, meat, fish products, ** specialties
12 oz (vacuum)	12 oz	1½	Used mostly for vacuum packed corn
No. 300	14 to 16 oz	1¾	Pork and beans, baked beans, meat products, cranberry sauce, blueberries, ** specialties
No. 303	15½ to 17 oz	2	Fruits, vegetables, meat products, ready-to-serve soups, ** specialties
No. 2	20 oz or 1 pt 2 fl oz, or 18 fl oz	2½	Juices, ready-to-serve soups, a few fruits and vegetables, ** specialties
No. 2½	1 lb 13 oz, 29 oz or 30 oz	3½	Fruits, pumpkin, sauerkraut, greens, tomatoes
No. 3 Cyl.	3 lb 3 oz or 1 qt 14 fl oz, or 46 fl oz	5¾	Fruit, vegetable juices, whole chicken, pork and beans, condensed soup for institutional use
No. 10	***6½ to 6¾ lbs	12 to 13	Fruits, vegetables for restaurant and institutional use

Infants and Chopped Junior foods come in small cans or jars suitable for the smaller servings. The weight appears on the label.

Meat, fish, poultry and seafood are usually advertised and sold under weight terminology.

* Information adapted from publications of National Canners Association, Washington, D.C.

** Combinations as macaroni, spaghetti, Spanish-style rice, Mexican and Chinese type foods, tomato aspic, etc.

*** As a rule used for quantity service.

NOTE: Labels on cans or jars of identical size may show different net weights for different products due to difference in the density of the food. One example, a can of pork and beans weighing 1 lb in a size 303, blueberries in the same size can 14 oz.

Check this table to be sure of buying the right amount of canned food for following recipes in this book.

Puzzling Kitchen Jobs

BROWNING FLOUR

DELICATELY browned flour gives a rich color and a delicious flavor to gravies and some sauces. To prepare it, spread white flour about ¼-inch thick in the bottom of a heavy skillet and place over moderate heat, stirring frequently until flour takes on an even tan color. Cool and store in a glass jar or other moisture-proof can or container. Browned flour has only about ½ the thickening power of white flour, so a sauce or gravy recipe calling for ¼ cup white flour will require about ½ cup browned flour. The browner the flour, the less its thickening power will be.

BUTTER ELABORATION

Butter is more than just a nutritious food with a delicious flavor; it may be highly decorative also, if shaped with imagination. All these attractive little butter pats, balls, curls and blossoms can be made by any enterprising housewife armed with a sharp knife, a pair of wooden paddles, a butter curler, and a mold or two. When directions are followed, they are easy the first time, easier the second and fun no matter how often you make them.

Butter balls: Have butter firm but not so cold that it crumbles. Stand wooden paddles a min or so if used regularly or for 3 or 4 min if they have never been used before in boiling water, then in ice water until ready to use, and return them for a minute to the ice water each time after making a butter ball. Cut butter into 1-inch sq pats about ⅓-inch thick, and quickly press into a rough ball. If weather is warm, butter may be held under ice water while pressing into shape. Place a ball on the grooved side of one paddle, and holding this steady, place the other paddle lightly over the butter. Now roll it round and round, exerting scarcely any pressure until the butter takes a ball shape with burry or waffled markings. A little practice reveals how little pressure is required to shape the balls. Let balls stand in ice water for a few min; then place in refrigerator on waxed paper until ready to use.

Butter roses: Using about ½ tsp butter, make small balls with the paddles. Then turn the paddles over, place a ball on the smooth side of one, and with the smooth side of the other paddle, spank the ball flat, making it

161

a little less than ⅛-inch thick. With fingers, roll up this flat round disc to form a narrow tube to use for center of rose. Make a flattened disc for each petal and arrange around the tightly rolled center, curling tightly or spreading out according to whether a bud or a full-blown rose is desired. After the addition of each petal, drop the rose into ice water. The petals may be handled more easily without breaking if the butter has first been squeezed and worked in ice water until waxy and pliable. Put finished roses on waxed paper and place in the refrigerator until ready to serve. Much larger butter roses may be made in the same way, using more butter for each petal.

Curled butter pats: Have butter well chilled; cut in pats about ⅓-inch thick. Dip a sharp knife into hot water and starting at the corner of pat, shave a thin layer curving upward toward center. The knife should make a 60 degree angle with the butter surface. Do two corners or all four, and decorate center with tiny sprigs of parsley if desired.

Butter curls: Have the butter moderately hard. Work on a ¼-lb stick of butter, drawing the chilled butter curler along the surface to remove about ⅛-inch of the butter. A little practice will enable you to get just the right thickness to curl well.

Butter molds: Prepare butter molds, plunger type, like the wooden paddles, by dipping quickly into boiling, then standing in ice-cold water. Have butter firm but not hard. Cut into pats ½-inch thick and cut out with the chilled mold, holding the plunger up; then lower plunger and press down to mark the design into the surface of the pat. Remove excess butter from mold and release the molded butter on waxed paper; store in refrigerator until ready to serve.

BUTTERING BREAD CRUMBS

Melt 2 to 3 tbsp of butter in a skillet or shallow saucepan. Add ½ cup sifted fresh dry bread crumbs and stir over moderate heat until crumbs are all coated and slightly toasted. Use to sprinkle over au gratin or casserole dishes to give a temptingly toasted, delicate topping.

CARROT STICKS

Choose small or medium-size, tender carrots for sticks. Keep in refrigerator until ready to serve. Wash well and scrape; then cut in quarters lengthwise, then cut the quarters into strips of the desired size. Never soak strips in water. Serve immediately or wrap in a damp cloth and place in the refrigerator. Never store longer than an hr for the freshest appearance and flavor.

CHOPPING PARSLEY

Chopped parsley adds so much to many foods in appetizing color, fresh flavor and food value, parsley is one of the richest sources of vitamin A known, that it is worth while to know a quick and easy way of preparing it. The usual method of chopping it in a wooden bowl or with a knife on a bread board is not as efficient as it might be, and it makes a good deal of dish-washing.

The easiest way is to put the leaves of the washed parsley into a small narrow glass like the typical commercial cheese or jelly glass. Then with a pair of kitchen scissors, snip the parsley leaves until they are finely divided into clean-cut bits. This method prevents the bits from flying about and there is nothing to wash except the glass and the tips of the scissors.

Parsley should preferably be chopped just before using to be at its best in color and food value. The leaves may be stripped from the coarse stems and placed in the glass, and the glass covered and placed in the refrigerator an hr or two ahead of time ready to be quickly snipped up when needed.

FLOUR-WATER PASTE FOR THICKENING GRAVY, ETC.

Sprinkle 2 tbsp flour over ¼ cup cold water in a small jar; cover and shake vigorously until blended. This amount will thicken ¾ cup liquid to average thickness when stirred in, heated to boiling, then simmered 2 or 3 min.

GRATING AND GRINDING FOOD

Food graters come in various sizes, and it is worth while to choose the right size for the food to be grated in order to make it as attractive as possible. And it is most important that they be of metal heavy enough to keep their shape and to retain a good sharp cutting edge. Owning a set of graters and shredders makes it possible to choose a very fine size for grating whole nutmegs, a slightly coarser one for grated orange or lemon rind, a still coarser one for raw carrots, and one with a wide blade-like arrangement on which to shred cabbage to be used in slaw.

Using too fine a grater for carrots and other raw foods, such as raw potatoes and apples, reduces them to a mush and deprives them entirely of the crisp, fluffy, attractive form they should retain. The same effect may be produced by moving the material being grated back and forth over the grater; if it is moved in one direction only, the food remains in beautiful loose shreds.

Grated food should be handled as little as possible, especially if it is to be sprinkled over a dish as a garnish like grated chocolate or cheese. It should be grated just before it is used, for finely divided foods dry out, oxidize, become discolored and lose flavor, attractiveness, and food value much more rapidly than foods in large pieces. If it is necessary to let a grated food such as grated lemon rind stand for a few minutes before using, it should be folded up in waxed paper to prevent loss of aroma and flavor.

Foods are conveniently grated onto waxed paper. This makes the job of measuring and cleaning up easier.

Graters should be made of stainless materials and should be thoroughly cleaned after each use. Every bit of food that may be clinging to the rough side should be carefully removed by rinsing with running water and brushing if necessary. When onion has been grated, it is especially important to remove every trace of odor so none will be imparted to the next food to be grated.

Everything that is true of grating food is also true of grinding. The size of knife used should be carefully chosen, the ground food should be treated in the same way, and the grinder should be cleaned scrupulously, and thoroughly dried to prevent rusting. And it should be remembered that not all foods to be used in a finely divided state should be ground. An example is nuts which should always be chopped, slivered, or shaved rather than ground.

HOW TO GRIND HORSERADISH WITHOUT TORMENTING THE EYES

Scrub the horseradish roots clean in cold water, scraping off the outer thin layer of skin and all discolored spots. Rinse well in cold water. Split large roots. Have food grinder set up and fitted with fine blade. Before starting to grind, cut off a piece of cheesecloth large enough to fold double and tie over the face to cover the eyes and nose. Wet cloth in cold water, wring out and tie over face, then proceed to grind the root. Add enough vinegar to moisten horseradish ground material and pack into clean dry jars. Cover tightly and keep stored in refrigerator. It darkens quickly on standing at room temp.

LARDING MEAT

Larding means introducing into lean meat long narrow strips of fat salt pork or bacon. The strips may be inserted in slashes made with a sharp knife, or a special larding needle may be used to thread the fat into the meat. The inserted fat melts and bastes the lean meat, thus conserving the meat juices and helping to make the meat more tender. Do not lard meat with plenty of fat.

HOW TO MAKE ONION JUICE

1. Cut the unpeeled onion in half crosswise and ream it on a lemon or orange reamer just as you would squeezing lemon juice. The reaming is only harder.

2. Lay a piece of cheesecloth on a piece of waxed paper, then grate the peeled onion on a shredder, letting the gratings and juice fall on the cheesecloth. Then lift up the cheesecloth and squeeze the juice onto the waxed paper. The unpeeled onion with a slice cut off may also be scraped with a paring knife onto the waxed paper. While the commercial onion juice is available everywhere and saves the homemaker of this task, it does not have the fresh zip of the home prepared.

HOW TO PREPARE SCRAPED ONION AND JUICE

Cut an unskinned medium size onion in half crosswise. Hold onion firmly on a sheet of waxed paper cut-side perpendicular to paper and with a paring knife scrape gently up and down to obtain juice and fine particles of onion.

PARBOILING

Parboiling means partially cooking in boiling water. The amount of cooking done in parboiling varies from simmering a few minutes to boiling until not quite tender. For example, green pepper cases which are to be stuffed and baked are usually immersed in boiling water for 2 or 3 min; this intensifies the green color and destroys the enzymes which ordinarily destroy the color during cooking. It also takes out some of the strong flavor. The parboiled peppers are nowhere near to being fully cooked, but the parboiling process contributes to the better appearance, flavor and texture of the finished product.

Potatoes are often parboiled until almost tender, then drained and their cooking finished in the roasting pan with a roast of meat. Onions to be baked may be parboiled until it is easy to push out the centers for stuffing. Dried beans which are to be baked are sometimes parboiled to reduce the baking time.

PLUMPING RAISINS AND CURRANTS

Wash raisins and turn into colander. Cover, place over boiling water and let steam for 5 min. Cool.

CARMELIZING SUGAR FOR CARAMEL SYRUP

Sift 1½ cups granulated sugar slowly into a moderately hot heavy skillet, stirring constantly until all the sugar is melted to a light amber-colored liquid. Carefully add 1½ cups boiling water, stir and simmer until caramel is dissolved and is of a typical syrup consistency. Cool and store in a covered jar to use as coloring for stews and gravies, as a delicious sweetening for custards, ice cream or candy, and as a luscious sauce for ice creams or puddings.

RADISHES AND RADISH "ROSES"

Radishes that are brilliant in color, uniform in shape and have crisp, firm-textured tender flesh are beautiful without any further treatment than washing them very clean and trimming off the tap root and even leaving on some of their central tender green leaves. Served on cracked ice or ice cubes in a relish dish with olives, celery, pickles, etc., they high-light the whole arrangement. But many cooks like to do a little further elaboration to make radish "roses."

A sharp paring knife and a grapefruit knife are all the tools that are required for making roses. One type of rose is made by first slicing off the tap root just down far enough to leave a white dot on the radish about one-fourth inch in diameter. Then remove a thin slice of radish at five points on the side of the radish equal distances apart, and when this slice is removed, it will leave either five round or oval spots on the sides. Then at these points, make thin downward slices parallel to the first slices that were removed, but leaving these slices attached at the bottom for five petals. Drop into ice water so that the petals will curl back to make more realistic roses.

Another kind of rose is made by cutting off the tap root flush with the surface of the radish. Then with a sharp paring knife, mark the radish straight from the root end down into five or six equal sections cutting just through the skin and downward about three-fourths of the way toward the stem end. Now use the curved grapefruit knife to cut through from each side of the sections to loosen the skin neatly from the flesh to make the "rose" petals. If the petals loosened are not uniform in shape, a scissors may be used to trim them uniformly. Drop these also into ice water to curl the petals back.

Radish roses should not be prepared too far ahead and they should remain in ice water until almost serving time to be most beautiful. Their chief value is decorative, since the carving and soaking removes most of their nutritive value.

RE-HEATING QUICK BREADS

Leftover muffins, biscuits and shortcakes may be freshened successfully if they are sprinkled very lightly with water and placed in a paper sack, then snugly closed at the end and heated in a moderately hot oven (400° F) until crust is crisp and they are piping hot all the way through.

Another way of heating them is to split them and toast under the broiler or in a hot oven. This produces a crisper texture and a different flavor from fresh bread, whereas the first method makes them taste like freshly baked breads.

RENDERING CHICKEN OR GOOSE FAT

Put lumps of raw chicken or other poultry fat pulled from the cavity and gizzard into a shallow baking pan and place in a slow oven (250° to 300° F) until fat has tried out. Drain off the accumulated fat from time to time to avoid overheating, and strain. Store in closely covered container in refrigerator. Chicken fat is a delicious substitute for butter in cakes or cookies, for frying potatoes, for making white sauce, or wherever small amounts of fat are used for cooking. *It is not practical to render turkey fat* because of perishability.

SOURING FRESH OR EVAPORATED MILK

When a recipe calls for sour milk or buttermilk and there is none in the house, fresh or evaporated milk in the proper dilution may be soured by adding vinegar. Use 1 tbsp vinegar to each cup of fresh milk or diluted evaporated milk. Stir and use as sour milk.

STEAMING

Steaming means cooking by application of steam rather than by dry heat or heat from boiling water. It is adapted to cooking certain vegetables, especially yellow and white ones, and to fruit puddings and some fruits. In modified form, it is applied to many other foods; for example, baked custards are always placed in a pan of water in the oven.

Special steamers resemble large double boilers in which the upper pan has perforations in the bottoms permitting the steam to circulate through. These are a great convenience, but if the budget or the storage space will not permit the purchase of one, it is possible to improvise a steamer with equipment which may be already on hand. A good-sized saucepan, a flat-bottomed colander which fits inside it, and a lid which will cover the pan tightly with the colander in place, will make a satisfactory steamer for many foods. The water in the saucepan should never be permitted to touch the bottom of the colander when steaming is being done.

A covered roasting pan may be converted into an oven steamer by placing a trivet or wire rack in the bottom to lift the foods above the surface of the water. This is useful for puddings and other steamed foods. Steaming may also be done in an ordinary double boiler when the water is not permitted to touch the upper pan. Excellent steamed pudding may also be made by pouring the batter directly into the top of the double boiler, covering it, and cooking over shallow boiling water until done.

To steam puddings, fill the mold two-thirds full of batter, fit cover on mold and place in the steamer. If mold, such as a clean tin can, has no lid, a piece of muslin folded two or three times to form a square may be tied over top of can in such a manner as to allow for generous rising and rounding up of pudding at the top. Tie muslin securely around top of the can with twine. Then place a square of aluminum foil over muslin and press around sides. Proceed to follow direction in recipe for required time for steaming.

SUBSTITUTING EVAPORATED FOR FRESH MILK

If you wish to use evaporated milk in a recipe for baked goods which calls for fresh milk, dilute the evaporated milk with water in the proportion of 2 parts water to 1 part evaporated milk. For example, in a cake or biscuit recipe calling for 1 cup fresh milk, use ⅓ cup evaporated milk diluted with ⅔ cup water.

For other cooked foods such as custards and sauces, dilute the evaporated milk with an *equal* quantity of water. This produces a milk which is the equivalent in food value of the same amount of fresh milk. For example, in a recipe for cocoa calling for 1 qt fresh milk, use 2 cups evaporated milk diluted with 2 cups water.

For whipping and generally when evaporated milk is being substituted for cream, it should be used full strength.

USE OF CANNED FRUIT JUICES

When canned fruits are drained for use in salads, the juice is sometimes a problem for the homemaker to dispose of. Here are some suggestions:

1. Use instead of water in making fruit gelatins.

2. Combine with water or ginger ale and a little lemon or lime juice as a beverage.

3. Combine with milk or buttermilk to make a nutritious and flavorful after-school beverage for children.

4. Thicken with cornstarch and use as a sauce for cornstarch pudding or leftover cake.

5. Use instead of water to moisten prepared mincemeat.

6. If several kinds of fruit juices are on hand at one time, mix them together as an appetizer-cocktail.

7. Use to make boiled dressing or mixed with mayonnaise to be served over fruit salad.

USES OF STALE BREAD

Stale bread should not be allowed to become moldy. Even when it is quite hard and old, it may still be used for toast; or if this is not practical, it may be placed in a slow oven (250° to 300° F) and dried out until very hard and crisp. Then it may be placed in a large paper sack and rolled with a heavy rolling pin until it forms fine crumbs. These may be sieved if desired, and they will be as good as purchased crumbs. Store in jar with perforated top.

Slightly stale bread which is neither hard nor moldy, though it may have lost its appeal for eating as bread, may be used with complete satisfaction in bread puddings, escalloped tomatoes, stuffings for meat or poultry and many other cooked dishes.

WHIPPING EVAPORATED MILK

Have the evaporated milk thoroughly chilled. This may be done by any of several methods: (*1*) Pack the unopened can in ice and salt as for freezing ice cream. (*2*) Place the unopened can in the freezing compartment of a mechanical refrigerator. (*3*) Pour the milk out into a bowl surrounded by ice and salt. (*4*) Pour the milk out into a freezing tray. Chill until ice cold and mushy.

Have bowl and beater chilled. Pour milk out into the cold bowl, do not dilute, and whip immediately and rapidly. Addition of 1 to 2 tsp of lemon juice to each cup of milk before or after it becomes stiff, and continued beating will make it hold its stiffness better. Sugar may be beaten in just as with whipped cream.

Evaporated milk will not turn to butter no matter how long beating is continued. If it fails to whip successfully, it needs to be colder. You can rechill and re-whip it without fear of its turning to butter.

Evaporated milk increases in volume about three times when whipped while whipping cream doubles in bulk when whipped.

TABLE 19   SYRUP FOR CANNING OR PLUMPING FRUIT

Density of Syrup	Sugar (parts)	Water or Fruit Juice (parts)
Thin	1	3
Medium	1	2
Heavy	1	1
Extra Heavy	1½	1

WHIPPING CREAM

Anyone who tries to whip cream under various conditions knows that a number of factors influence the results. The quality of cream is important. Cream that contains from 30 to 35 per cent butterfat whips up quickly into a smooth, stiff mass and will drain out very little milk on standing. The type of whipper also counts. An egg beater is not nearly so satisfactory as a turbine beater with blades that revolve close to the bottom of the bowl. The amount of cream whipped at one time needs also to be regulated. When a large quantity is to be whipped, one saves time and obtains better results by doing successive whippings in smaller amounts. Both whipper and bowl should be chilled in refrigerator. A deep bowl with rather straight sides is much better for whipping than a broad, shallow one. The cream should be whipped rapidly. In two or three min one should be able to whip a half pt perfectly. Whipping should stop at the right time. When the cream becomes stiff and is still smooth, it is time to stop. When whipped too long, it is lumpy and a large amount of milk drains from it. If underwhipped, the cream drains out and it has the appearance of unwhipped cream. When properly whipped, the cream will hold up for several hrs if it is stored in refrigerator, but if it is held too long, it will dry out on the surface and will change in flavor.

HOW TO MEASURE

Use standard measuring utensils. Nested aluminum cups and spoons are best for dry ingredients and solid fats; a glass measuring cup which extends a short distance above the 1-cup mark to prevent spillage and with a lip for pouring is best for liquids such as milk and oil.

Granulated sugar: Since this type of sugar does not pack, the measuring cup may be put directly into the sugar cannister and used as a scoop. Fill to overflowing, then level off with the *straight* edge of a spatula or knife. If sugar is lumpy, sift before measuring.

Confectioners' sugar packs upon standing and also forms tiny lumps occasionally, so sift before measuring. Sift once onto a square of waxed paper, then with a scoop or spoon pile it lightly into measuring cup of correct size to overflowing. Next, level off with the straight edge of a spatula or knife.

Cornstarch, baking powder and soda pack upon standing. To measure, stir contents of carton to loosen slightly, then dip measuring spoon into carton and fill it heaping full. Level with straight edge of spatula. Some cartons, e.g. baking powder, have a paper cover with a straight line marked on it which, if cut accurately, may be used for leveling the measurement.

Brown sugar: If brown sugar is lumpy, roll it first. Then pack firmly into the measuring cup with the back of a sturdy tablespoon and level off.

Shortening: Pack solidly into proper size measuring cup with the back of a sturdy tablespoon to eliminate air pockets. Then level off.

Butter which is packed in ¼-lb stick may be cut quite accurately. One ¼-lb stick is equivalent to ½ cup or 8 tbsp.

Flour settles so it should be sifted once before measuring. Then pile lightly into the proper size measuring cup to overflowing and level off.

Liquids: It is more accurate to measure 4 tbsp of liquid in a ¼ cup measure than by tablespoons. If you fill a tbsp measure with liquid you will notice that it rounds up slightly—and the thicker the liquid the more it rounds up. If you have a bit extra for each of four tablespoons it could make quite a difference in the total amount, especially with thick liquids like molasses.

Milk and all other liquids are most conveniently measured in a glass measuring cup which has the 1-cup mark about ½ inch below the rim. Place the cup on a level surface, then read at eye level to obtain an accurate measure.

Oil, syrup and molasses: Follow directions for milk, above. In addition, because of their tendency to cling to the cup, use a rubber spatula, preferably a narrow one, to scrape the last drop out when adding to other ingredients. Time will be saved if molasses is measured in the cup in which oil or shortening has been measured, as the syrup will pour from the cup more easily.

Half an egg: Beat the egg gently with a fork to break white and mix thoroughly with yolk. Be careful not to make the white foam as this complicates accurate measuring. Then divide in half or take half of the following measurements for medium eggs, after beating gently: 1 medium egg = 3⅓ tbsp; 1 medium egg *white* = 2 tbsp; 1 medium egg *yolk* = 1⅓ tbsp.

The Cook's Creed

Maintaining the health of my family depends in a large measure on the food I serve; *therefore—*

> *I will take care to prepare and cook all foods in a way to preserve a maximum of their nutrients.*

My family's enjoyment of food is in my care; *therefore—*

> *I will prepare and serve all foods as appealing to the eye and palate as I can.*

Stretching the food dollar is part of my responsibility; *therefore—*

> *I will take such care of foods that none will spoil.*
>
> *I will use left-overs with thought and skill.*

Well-prepared foods and appetizing meals are creative achievments; *therefore—*

> *I shall enjoy doing that important work well.*

Good food is the inalienable right of all who work; *therefore—*

> *I shall bring food to the table that satisfies and pleases my family.*

Appetizers

APPETIZERS include canapés, hors d'oeuvres, dips or dunks, cocktails and shrubs. Appetizers are tasty small portions of food attractively designed to whet the appetite. They are served before formal and informal dinners and buffet suppers. Semi-solid cocktails and shrubs are served at the table. Canapés, hors d'oeuvres and dips are usually served on a tray in the living room where guests help themselves. This informality helps to create a friendly atmosphere. While the guests enjoy these tidbits, the hostess can return to the kitchen to add the last-minute touches to foods for the next course, and place them on the table.

EASY TO MAKE WHEN THE JOB IS PLANNED FROM START TO FINISH

First, read this chapter through carefully to help you decide which appetizers you wish to serve, then estimate the number you will need. *Remember* appetizers are "meal-starters" only, not the whole meal. Five or 6 kinds of appetizers are permissible when served for parties or receptions of over 100, otherwise use 2 or 3 fillings, and allow not more than 3 or 4 appetizers for each guest. Check the recipes selected. List all ingredients and quantity required to make the butters, fillings, garnishes, bread-cuts, etc. Shop ahead of time. Prepare and store in refrigerator foods whose flavors will not be impaired with 6 to 8 hours of standing. For example, prepare the butters, fillings and dip mixtures. Leave out a spoonful of each butter and filling to practice with, then cover remainder closely and refrigerate. Hollow out vegetables like beets, lay in a flat dish, drizzle with French Dressing, cover and chill. Hard-cook eggs, peel, cool, cover and store. Slice close-textured bread uniformly thin, never thicker than ¼", then cut it into desired shapes, keeping each shape together. If you are inexperienced, leave one of each pattern out on the table; stack the rest, wrap in waxed paper, cover with a damp towel and store in refrigerator. *Remember,* make bread cutouts for canapés small. Canapés, like hors d'oeuvres, are never more than 2 mouthfuls. Now take the "left-out" bread cutouts, butters and fillings and practice spreading the cutouts until you can estimate the amount of butter and fillings needed for each canapé, and can do the work quickly and neatly. Then practice garnishing until you obtain canapés you like best. Look at the Canapé Illustrations in this chapter for ideas. Put these "practice samples" in a covered container in a cool place to bring out for observation when you start assembling canapés for serving. These samples will help you work speedily and spontaneously, which is essential to produce fresh-looking, alluring canapés. *Next, prepare the garnishes* p 783.

ORGANIZE THE PREPARATION THIS WAY

1. Make one variety of appetizer at a time. For instance, when making canapes, use only one shape of bread cutout. Spread this shape with one variety of butter and filling. Remove all cutouts and fillings from refrigerator. Butters and fillings at room temperature spread easily.

2. Toast all cutouts to a delicate brown on *one side only.* Toast cutouts on a cookie sheet under broiler or in a little butter heated in a heavy skillet. Cover toasted cutouts loosely with waxed paper until ready to spread.

3. An hour before serving time, lay toasted cutouts, untoasted side up, on a flat tray or cookie sheet with an all-around rim. Quickly spread all with the chosen butter to prevent drying out.

4. Drop needed amount of filling from spoon onto each cutout before spreading; then spread quickly but lightly to avoid a "packed or handled" look.

5. Wrap tray in waxed paper, or slip it into a plastic bag and place in refrigerator. Before starting next variety, remove all leftovers and clean table, then proceed with next shape in same orderly routine.

6. Lay on garnishes quickly and lightly. Do not press down too firmly.

7. The final but important step is the arrangement on the serving tray. By following certain rules and being guided by your own artistic sense, you can arrange the tray to "look like a picture." These are the rules:

(a) Keep all canapes and hors d'oeuvres of the same pattern together to avoid a spotty appearance.

(b) Place canapes with dark fillings on the outside, but harmonize the colors and balance the shapes.

(c) Serve immediately after arranging for that freshest appearance possible.

Use a similarly organized method to make hors d'oeuvres.

HOW TO MAKE THOSE PRETTY LITTLE SHAPES
TO GARNISH CANAPÉS

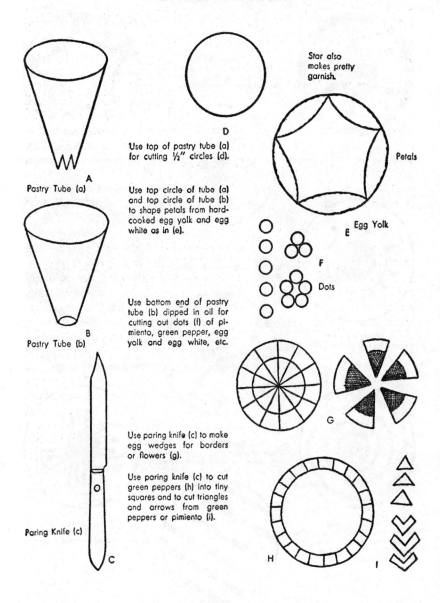

Pastry Tube (a)

Use top of pastry tube (a) for cutting ½" circles (d).

D

Star also makes pretty garnish.

Petals

Use top circle of tube (a) and top circle of tube (b) to shape petals from hard-cooked egg yolk and egg white as in (e).

E   Egg Yolk

Pastry Tube (b)

Use bottom end of pastry tube (b) dipped in oil for cutting out dots (f) of pimiento, green pepper, egg yolk and egg white, etc.

F   Dots

Use paring knife (c) to make egg wedges for borders or flowers (g).

G

Use paring knife (c) to cut green peppers (h) into tiny squares and to cut triangles and arrows from green peppers or pimiento (i).

Paring Knife (c)

C

H   I

NO SPECIAL TOOLS ARE REQUIRED FOR MAKING BEAUTIFUL CANAPÉS
(*Use a 2 inch biscuit cutter*)

Figure 3 (Below)
a) Petals cut from sliced egg yolk using olive pitter to cut them. b) Caviar or chopped pimiento in center.

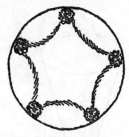

Figure 1 (Above)
a) Thin strips pimiento. b) Fine chopped parsley around edge. c) Thin slice egg yolk.

Figure 2 (Above)
a) Parsley leaflet. b) Cream cheese piping.

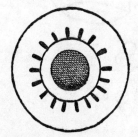

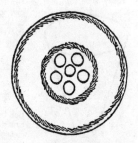

Figure 6 (Below)
a) Small cut-outs from sliced egg yolk. b) Small triangles and thin strips green pepper.

Figure 4 (Above)
a) Thin strips ripe olive. b) Whole egg slice.

Figure 5 (Above)
a) Inner and outer circles piped around with parsley butter. b) Polka dots cut from egg white.

Figure 9 (Below)
Stripes made of thin strips of ham, American cheese or piped cream cheese.

Figure 7 (Above)
Colored cream cheese on a combination of sieved egg yolk and mayonnaise piped in a spiral with parsley leaf at each end of spiral.

Figure 8 (Above)
a) Pimiento center. b) Egg white petals streaked with yellow cream cheese.

LARGE ROUND CUTTER TO OBTAIN 2 CANAPÉS-IN-ONE AND OTHER COOKIE CUTTER SHAPES

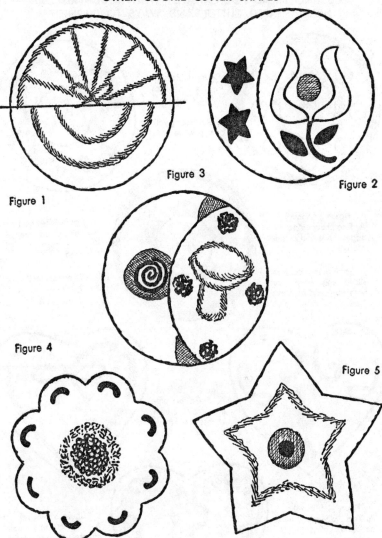

Figure 3

Figure 2

Figure 1

Figure 4

Figure 5

Figure 1. a) Cream cheese piped in thin lines representing spokes in a fan and a ribbon at bottom. b) Half circles of cream cheese. c) Cut on line to make 2 fan-shaped canapes.

Figure 2. a) Cut stars of pimiento freehand or with cutters. b) Circle from thin slice egg yolk. c) Cut-outs from thin slices egg white. d) Green pepper cut-outs. e) Cut apart on line.

Figure 3. a) Anchovy coil. b) Fluff of sieved egg yolk. c) Parsley leaflet. d) Outline of mushroom piped in a mixture of sieved egg yolk and mayonnaise. e) Cut apart on line.

Figure 4. a) Thin strips of pimiento curved to match edge. b) Caviar. c) Chopped onion.

Figure 5. a) Cream cheese or stiff mayonnaise piped. b) Slice of stuffed olive.

CUTTING BREAD FOR CANAPÉS WITH DOUGHNUT OR HEART SHAPED CUTTER, AND WAYS TO GARNISH

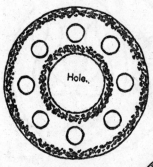

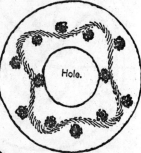

Figure 3 (Below)
A. Thin half-slices stuffed olive.

B. Sieved egg yolk or egg white.

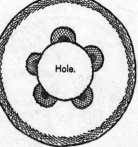

Figure 1 (Above)
A. Fine chopped parsley edges inside and outside of circle.

B. Small rounds cut from sliced egg whites, cut with small end of pastry tube.

Figure 2 (Above)
A. Thin piped line of cream cheese or stiff mayonnaise.

B. Watercress leaflets or parsley.

Figure 6 (Below)
A. Just a thin piping of pink cream cheese or stiff mayonnaise.

Figure 4 (Above)
A. Thin slivers green pepper or pimiento cut in these shapes.

B. Diamonds of pimiento.

Figure 5 (Above)
A. Piping of cream cheese colored green with pimiento strips shaped like a bow.

CANAPÉS CUT FROM LENGTHWISE SLICES OF WHOLE BREAD LOAF
WITHOUT WASTE (Crusts removed first) 4″ x 9½″

A Green pepper triangles

B Radish half-slices

C Cream cheese rose and lines

D Fillets of anchovy

E Wedges from egg slice

F Parsley leaflet

G Tomato slice

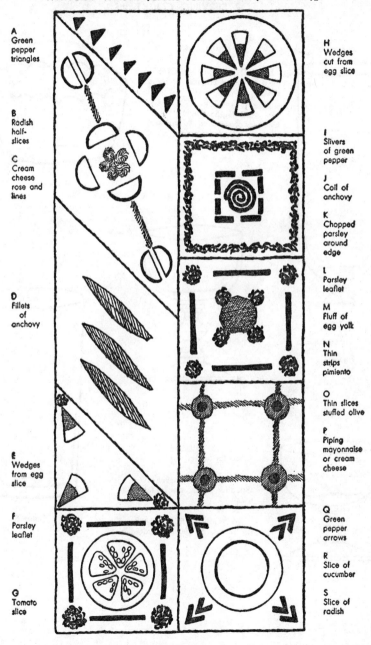

H Wedges cut from egg slice

I Slivers of green pepper

J Coil of anchovy

K Chopped parsley around edge

L Parsley leaflet

M Fluff of egg yolk

N Thin strips pimiento

O Thin slices stuffed olive

P Piping mayonnaise or cream cheese

Q Green pepper arrows

R Slice of cucumber

S Slice of radish

GLASSWARE THAT THE AVERAGE HOUSEWIFE HAS FOR SERVING COCKTAILS

1. TALL TOMATO JUICE GLASS
Ideal for liquid cocktails or for a shrub.

2. GLASS NAPPY
Good for combination like grapefruit sections covered with grape juice or for fruit cups.

Figure 2

Figure 1

Figure 3

3. TALL SHERBET
Good for fruit cups.

4. LOW SHERBET
Good for fruit cups or for fish cocktails.

5. TOMATO JUICE GLASS
For shrubs, or fruit juice cocktails.

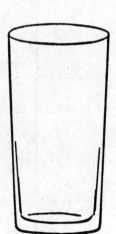

Figure 5

Figure 4

CANAPÉS

Canapés are miniature open-faced sandwiches charmingly decorated. The fillings are nippy-flavored mixtures of cheese, eggs, fish, meat, poultry, etc. These are spread on various bases—tiny cutouts of thinly sliced bread of all varieties toasted on one side, small crisp crackers, potato chips or commercial canapé cases. Canapés are fashioned to be eaten with the fingers, and do not have to be served with alcoholic beverages to be correct and up-to-date as some gourmands would have one believe. Chilled plain tomato and beet juice cocktails, hot plain or tomato bouillon, mulled cider, or plain or blended chilled citrus juices are delightful gastronomic accompaniments. Canapés usually are served on a tray with an assortment of hors d'oeuvres. The recipes which follow are just a few of the many ways to make canapés. Check the recipes for Butters and Fillings, pp 187–191, to see the variety of canapés that are possible. You can then see how to make many new delicious combinations.

AVOCADO CANAPÉS

Scoop flesh from a medium-size, about 8-oz, good quality ripe avocado. Mash with a 3-oz pkg of cream cheese. Season with salt, grated onion and enough mayonnaise to make a medium soft paste. Stir in 3 slices of crisp-cooked crumbled bacon. Serve on toasted cutouts, spread with Lemon Butter, p 188. Suggested garnish: Tiny pimiento triangles and slivers of ripe olive.

BAKED BEAN CANAPÉS

Economical but pretty good!!

½ cup baked beans	Thin slices whole wheat *or*
1 tbsp chili sauce	Boston brown bread
½ tsp prepared mustard	3 tbsp creamed butter
¼ tsp onion juice, p 164	Green onion slices *or*
Dash of salt	chopped cucumber
	Small red radishes

Drain off juice and mash beans fine. Blend in next 4 ingredients. Toast bread on one side, cut 24 strips 1" x 2", or cut circles of brown bread in 4 pie-shaped pieces. Spread with butter, then generously with bean mixture. Suggested garnish: Onion slices or mound of chopped cucumber for pie-shaped pieces, and a row of radish slices stuck into the strips. 20 canapes.

CAVIAR BISCUITS

Many hands will reach for these

Make Baking Powder Biscuit Dough, p 234. Roll ⅓" thick. Cut out with center of doughnut cutter or about size of a quarter. Place an inch apart on baking sheet and bake until brown. Break apart carefully. Heap slightly with thoroughly chilled red caviar, first seasoned with lemon juice, a bit of scraped onion, paprika, and enough thick cream to hold together. Top with a stuffed olive slice.

CAVIAR CANAPÉS

These have authority

Thin slices white bread
2 tbsp soft butter
3 tbsp caviar
½ tbsp lemon juice

1 tbsp very finely chopped onion
1 hard-cooked egg
Parsley

Toast enough bread slices on one side only to make 12 strips 1 x 2 inches. Spread with butter, then with caviar sprinkled with lemon juice. Top each canapé with ¼ tsp onion, then with generous fluff of sieved egg white, a bit of sieved yolk and a parsley leaflet in center. 12 canapés.

CHEESE CONE OR ROLL

A connoisseur's dessert or elegant for snack or stuffing celery

¼ lb American cheese
1¼-oz pkg Roquefort *or* 2-oz
   pkg Blue cheese
3-oz pkg cream cheese

2 tbsp cream
1 tsp sugar
Paprika, parsley
Pilot crackers *or* toast

Grate American cheese into mixing bowl, add crumbled Roquefort and next three ingredients. Blend well with a fork. Cover, chill until stiff enough to handle easily. Shape into a fat cone about 3½" high. Place on pretty glass plate. Smooth cone with knife-blade. Dip tip of a teaspoon into warm water, then press into cone to make rows of scallops around cone. Dash with paprika; stick leaf of parsley into top. Or shape firm cheese into roll about 1" in diameter. Roll gently in finely cut parsley spread on waxed paper to coat roll. Accompany with crackers or toast. Serve with a knife. 10 to 12 servings.

CHICKEN BRAZILIAN PINWHEEL CANAPÉS

1 cup moist cooked chicken
12 Brazil nuts
1 tbsp chopped celery leaves
1 tsp lemon juice

Mayonnaise
1 lb loaf fresh unsliced
   white bread
¼ cup soft butter

Put first 3 ingredients through food chopper using fine blade. Stir in lemon juice and enough mayonnaise to spread. Trim crusts from loaf neatly. Cut a ³⁄₁₆″ thick lengthwise slice from bottom of loaf. Remove slice, cover loaf with damp towel to keep moist. Spread removed slice thinly with butter, then with ⅓ of the filling, spreading uniformly to edge. Begin at narrow end, roll slice up tightly like jelly roll. Wrap roll in waxed paper and chill. Repeat with 2 more bread slices. Just before serving, cut into ¼″ slices and arrange on serving tray. 30 to 36 canapés.

CRABMEAT-ONION CANAPÉS

Remove cartilage from a 6¼-oz can crabmeat. There should be 1⅓ cups. Or use an equal amount of fresh cooked or frozen crabmeat. Flake fine. Stir in ¼ cup mayonnaise and ¼ cup finely chopped pickled onions. Spread on toasted cutouts or crisp crackers. Suggested garnish: Olive slices or flowers made from tiny cutouts of hard-cooked egg white and yolk and green pepper diamond-shaped leaves. See Crabmeat Salad Filling, p 189, for another crabmeat canapé filling.

CREAM CHEESE APPETIZER ROLL

A gourmet's delight

3-oz pkg chilled cream cheese   ⅙ medium clove garlic
3 oz American cheese   Dash of salt
2 tbsp English walnuts   ½ tsp chili powder

Put cheese, nuts, peeled garlic through food chopper using medium blade. Stir in salt and knead smooth. Shape into neat roll 6″ to 8″ long. Sift chili powder on waxed paper, place roll on it, shift back-and-forth to coat roll interestingly. Roll paper around it, tuck in ends; store in refrigerator to ripen. To serve, place on attractive plate; slice thinly. Arrange rows of crackers or toast at the side, or serve cheese slices on round crackers. Keeps 2 or 3 weeks refrigerated. 8 to 10 servings.

DIPLOMAT CANAPÉS

Sardine and egg

Drain oil from a 3¼-oz can small sardines. Mash fish to a paste with 1 tsp lemon juice. Spread on toast rounds or crisp crackers, first spread with Lemon Butter, p 188. Lay a slice of hard-cooked egg on top. Have cream cheese blended with enough beet juice (drained from canned beets) or red food coloring to give an attractive tint, and using tiny star or ribbon decorating tube, pipe around edge of egg slice. Stick tiny crisp parsley leaf in center.

NUTTY CANAPÉS

Delicious and chewy

½ cup ground baked *or* boiled
    lean ham
1 tbsp chili sauce
¼ cup thinly sliced Brazil
    nuts

Mayonnaise
Fresh rye bread slices
Prepared mustard

Blend ham, chili sauce and nuts with enough mayonnaise to spread. Spread bread thinly with mustard, then with ham mixture. Cut twice diagonally to make 4 triangles. Lay canapés on shallow pan and place in a hot oven (475° F) or under broiler to toast until mixture bubbles. Serve hot. 24 canapés.

POPPY SEED CHEESE STRIPS

Delicious, chewy, crunchy canapes

6 slices day-old white bread
6 tbsp snappy cheese spread

2 tbsp poppy seed

Remove crusts from bread. Spread with cheese, then sprinkle with poppy seed. Cut each slice into 3 or 4 strips. Place on greased cookie sheet 1-inch apart. Bake in hot oven (450° F) until cheese bubbles and bread toasts, about 3 min. 18 to 24 strips.

ROQUEFORT CANAPÉS

Cream 2 tbsp butter with ⅓ cup crumbled Roquefort or Blue cheese. Add dash of cayenne, 1 tsp each of lemon juice and Worcestershire or A-1 Sauce. Heap lightly on toast strips or rounds or small crisp crackers. Suggested garnish: Chopped parsley and sprinkling of caviar, or a thin slice of firm red plum tomato centered with parsley leaflet.

SARDINE CANAPÉS

Spread toast strips with Lemon Butter, p 188. On each lay one or more well-drained small sardines. Squeeze lemon juice over fish and garnish with a slice of stuffed olive. For a hot canapé, blend 1 tbsp prepared mustard and ½ cup grated cheese. Dot the sardine with 1 tsp of the mixture. Lay on a shallow pan and toast in a hot oven (450° F) until cheese mixture bubbles and browns. Garnish with stuffed olive slice. Serve hot. 20 canapés.

SHRIMP CANAPÉS

Spread rounds of toast or crisp crackers with mayonnaise, then with Shrimp Butter, p 188. Dip edges of canapé in fine-chopped parsley.

Top each with a small whole curled shrimp first marinated in French dressing and drained. Drop finely chopped stuffed olive or dill pickle in center.

SMOKED TURKEY OR CAPON CANAPÉS

Slice the breast of cooked smoked turkey or capon thin, then cut into circles or strips to fit crackers or toast. Spread toast thinly with mayonnaise, then fit on the turkey or capon slices. Again spread a thin film of mayonnaise over top. Garnish with halves of seeded white grapes or small circles of cranberry jelly. Or spread the commercially canned smoked turkey paste as it comes from can onto toasted cutouts or crackers, or thin it slightly with mayonnaise before spreading. Garnish with thin slivers of ripe olive and pimiento.

TANGY CHIPS

Put ½ cup creamed cottage cheese through sieve. Add 1 tbsp caviar, ¼ tsp onion juice and salt to taste. Cover tightly, chill. Just before serving time, heap on large crisp potato chips or toasted tortillas. (Obtain tortillas from Mexican grocery). Have ready dots or bits of green pepper or pimiento for garnish.

TOASTED CHEESE ROUNDS

¾ cup mayonnaise
½ cup chopped onion
⅓ cup (1½ oz) grated
    Parmesan cheese

Dash Worcestershire sauce
Dash salt and pepper
Toasted bread rounds
Sliced stuffed olives

Combine all ingredients except bread and olives; mix well. Spread mixture on bread; broil until golden brown. Garnish with olives. 30 canapés.

TUNA-OLIVE CANAPÉS

Drain oil from 6½-oz can tuna. Flake fish and mix in ¾ cup finely chopped stuffed olives and 1 tbsp Bahamian or other prepared mustard. Stir in enough mayonnaise for spreading. Spread ¼" thick on rounds or strips of toast or crisp crackers. Suggested Garnish: Sieved hard-cooked egg yolk or white and slivers of green pepper. 30 canapés.

CHEESE TRAYS

A well planned cheese tray is a most attractive appetizer display. For greatest eye and palate appeal, select a variety of cheeses, then prepare and arrange for convenient service. Choose Swiss, aged Cheddar, brick, Liederkranz and a smoked variety which will slice and produce varying shapes, rounds, rectangles, squares and triangles. Overlap slices neatly in straight or curving rows, being guided by the shape of the tray and the design you want to work out on the tray. A small Edam or Gouda with its red paraffin coating makes an attractive center of interest. These little globes of cheese must be readied for easy serving so guests can help themselves just as easily as from the slices. An effective way to prepare these for serving is to use a star or round cookie cutter to cut down about ¼-inch into the center top and remove the paraffin layer neatly. This reveals the cheese in a neat outline. Now take a small French ball cutter and scoop out cheese balls neatly from the interior without disturbing the top star or round design. When a dozen or more balls have been cut out, remove accumulated cheese crumbs, drop balls carefully back into cheese shell. Or from the star-shaped design, use a paring knife to cut out thin wedges of cheese extending to the center. Replace wedges in cheese shell for guests to lift out with a cheese knife. A small wedge or two of Camembert, Roquefort or Blue cheese warmed to room temperature as well as cream cheese can be placed at points on the tray where they fit best between rows of slices. A cheese spread may also be removed from the glass carefully, rolled lightly in chopped parsley and placed on the tray where part of the roll can be sliced and overlapped.

Arrange a variety of crisp crackers attractively around edge of tray in a continuous row or in broken rows. A pretty fruit that goes well with cheese may also serve as a garnish and as a pleasing accompaniment. A red apple sliced thick, the slices overlapped, or left in the shape of the apple is attractive. Brush cut surfaces of apple with lemon juice to prevent discoloration. Bunches of washed, chilled grapes, are also elegant and delicious with cheese.

BASIC CANAPÉ BUTTERS OR SPREADS

Bread cutouts, toasted on one side or not, should first be spread with a seasoned butter to prevent the filling from soaking into the bread. Plain butter is a suitable spread, but seasoned butters give canapés a peppier flavor. Mayonnaise can be used instead of the plain or seasoned butters.

HOW TO PREPARE THE FOLLOWING SEASONED BUTTERS

To make the seasoned butters or spreads, let butter stand at room temperature only long enough to cream easily without becoming oily in appearance. Grind, pound or mash fish, soft cheese, meat or vegetables to a paste. Sieve hard-cooked eggs. Grate firm cheese. Now blend into the creamed butter with the other seasonings.

ANCHOVY BUTTER

For any fish or egg fillings

¼ cup butter
1 tbsp anchovy paste *or*

1 tbsp drained anchovies
pounded to paste

CHEESE BUTTER

For caviar and other fish fillings and stuffing celery

½ cup butter
¼ cup Roquefort, Blue *or*

freshly grated Parmesan
cheese

CHILI BUTTER

For meat and cheese fillings

¼ cup butter
1 tsp chili powder

1 tsp lemon juice

CHIVES, PARSLEY OR MINT BUTTER

Chives and parsley for egg, cheese, meat and liver fillings; mint for fish and lamb fillings

½ cup butter
1 tbsp *or* more finely chopped
chives, parsley *or* mint

1 tsp lemon juice *or* tarragon
vinegar

EGG YOLK BUTTER

For caviar, fish, ham fillings

½ cup butter
4 hard-cooked egg yolks,
sieved

Dash of red pepper
Dash of Worcestershire

GARLIC BUTTER

For fish or meat fillings and making Garlic Bread

½ cup butter
2 peeled medium garlic
cloves

½ tsp salt
Dash of pepper
1 *or* 2 drops tabasco

HORSERADISH BUTTER

For tongue, ham and baked bean fillings

½ cup butter

4 tbsp grated horseradish

LEMON BUTTER

For fish fillings and serving over cooked fish

½ cup butter
1 tbsp *or* more lemon juice

Few gratings lemon rind,
optional

MUSTARD BUTTER

For ham, tuna, sardine and egg fillings

½ cup butter *and*
¼ cup prepared mustard *or*

1 tbsp dry mustard *and*
2 tsp vinegar

OLIVE BUTTER

For fish, meat, egg and chicken fillings

½ cup butter

4 tbsp finely chopped stuffed
olives

PIQUANT BUTTER

For meat or liver fillings

Lemon Butter *plus*
1 tbsp grated horseradish

2 tbsp finely-chopped watercress

SHRIMP, LOBSTER OR CRABMEAT BUTTER

*For hard-cooked egg and avocado fillings and to be topped with whole
shrimp or an anchovy fillet*

½ cup butter
¾ cup cooked shrimp, lobster
or crabmeat mashed with

1 to 2 tbsp fresh lemon juice
Salt to taste
¼ tsp paprika

HOW TO SPREAD FILLINGS ON CANAPÉS

Lightly pile fillings on prepared canapé bases to the thickness of the
bread

CREAM CHEESE-ANCHOVY FILLING

Cream a 3-oz pkg cream cheese with 2 tsp anchovy paste. Stir in 2
tsp finely chopped pickled onions, 1 tbsp each finely chopped parsley,
and lemon juice and salt to suit taste.

CREAM CHEESE-CAVIAR FILLING

Cream a 3-oz pkg cream cheese with 2 tbsp cream, then stir in 1
tbsp caviar or more and a few drops of onion juice.

CREAM CHEESE-TOMATO-NUT FILLING

Cream ¼ cup butter with 3-oz pkg cream cheese. Add salt or seasoning salt to suit taste and enough tomato paste to give desired tint. Then stir in 2 tbsp finely chopped nuts. Good also to stuff celery.

EGG SALAD FILLING

Prepare Egg Salad, p 1218, making sure to chop all ingredients very fine. Good with Chive or Parsley Butter Spreads.

CRABMEAT-CAPER FILLING

Combine flaked crabmeat with enough chopped capers to give peppy flavor and enough mayonnaise to spread easily.

CRABMEAT, LOBSTER, TUNA OR SALMON FILLING

Remove cartilage from a 6½-oz can of crabmeat or lobster, or drain oil from same amount of tuna or salmon. Remove skin from salmon. Flake fish fine. Stir in ½ cup finely chopped celery, 2 tbsp finely chopped green pepper. Season with salt and pepper, add 1½ tsp lemon juice to tuna or salmon (not to crab or lobster mixtures). Then stir in enough mayonnaise for filling to spread easily. Add pepper to suit taste.

SARDINE FILLING

Drain oil from two 3¼-oz cans small sardines. Mash fine and stir in 2 tbsp lemon juice, 1 tbsp each of French Dressing and Mayonnaise, 2 tsp Worcestershire. Season with salt and pepper.

HAM-CHUTNEY-CHEESE FILLING

Combine ground baked or boiled lean ham with equal portions of chutney and grated cheese. Add mayonnaise if needed to make spreadable.

HAM-OLIVE FILLING

Grind ½ lb boiled or baked lean ham with ¼ cup pimiento-stuffed olives and 1 onion size of walnut using fine blade. Stir in 1 to 2 tsp prepared mustard and enough mayonnaise or sour cream to spread easily.

CHICKEN OR CALVES LIVER FILLING

1 lb chicken livers well cleaned and as whole as possible and 3 oz chicken fat. Render fat, p 166. Wash livers, drain. Or remove skin and

veins from calves liver, p 903. Peel and chop fine 2 onions size of eggs. Saute onions and livers in ¼ cup of chicken fat until onion is soft and livers are cooked through. Turn into heavy bowl. Add 2 whole hard-cooked eggs and white of another, 2 tbsp chopped parsley and 1 tsp salt. Chop or mash fine with wooden potato masher or put through food chopper using fine blade. Add pepper and 1 tsp lemon juice and mix. If not soft enough to spread, add enough chicken fat to spread. Just before serving, put into top of double boiler over hot water to heat through. Then shape quickly into a neat mound on warm serving plate. Garnish with leftover hard-cooked egg yolk put through a sieve. Let guests spread on toasted rye bread triangles or crisp crackers. About 2 cups.

PATE DE FOIE GRAS

1 goose *or* 3 chicken livers	Salt to taste
4 tsp mayonnaise	1 hard-cooked egg yolk
1 tsp lemon juice	1 hard-cooked egg white,
½ tsp grated onion	sieved
½ tsp rendered goose *or*	Ripe olives
chicken fat if liver is dry	

Choose well cleaned livers as whole as possible. Wash, drain and *simmer* in enough salted water to completely cover until tender, about 30 minutes for goose and 20 for chicken livers. Drain. Put through food chopper using fine blade. Blend with next 6 ingredients to obtain spreadable paste. Spread on rye crackers or toast. Garnish with sieved egg white and thin slivers of ripe olive. 10 to 12 canapés.

AVOCADO FILLING

Scoop flesh from 1 ripe medium-size avocado. Add 1 tbsp lemon juice or French Dressing, ½ tsp salt, 1 tsp finely chopped onion and mash thoroughly with a silver fork or wooden spoon. Stir in a dash of cayenne and 1 tbsp chili sauce, if desired. This filling is also excellent for stuffing celery.

OLIVE-CELERY FILLING

Cream butter, stir in equal measures of finely chopped stuffed olives and celery to produce a mixture that will just spread. Add enough chopped chives for interesting flavor.

PEANUT BUTTER-BACON FILLING

Combine equal amounts of peanut butter and crumbled crisp bacon. Add just enough chili sauce to make soft enough to heap up slightly on canapés.

PEANUT BUTTER-INDIA RELISH FILLING

Combine equal portions of peanut butter and commercial India relish.

HOW TO GARNISH CANAPÉS

Choose a garnish that harmonizes with the flavor and color of the filling, and with the shape of the canapé. Make garnishes dainty. Tiny leaflets of parsley or cress, or finely chopped fresh parsley are appropriate for many kinds of fillings. Tiny cutouts of pimiento, green pepper, slices of firm red tomato are colorful. Wee wedges from thin slices of lemon, carrot and radishes are easy to cut and are attractive. Slightly thicker slices of stuffed olives and thin strips of ripe olive are also very effective and simple to make. Sieved hard-cooked egg yolks and whites add a lovely fluffy touch. Caviar adds striking contrast and flair. Thin uniform strips of cheese, egg white and ham enable one to make striped and latticed decorations. Pickled pearl onions, small anchovy fillets, lobster coral and shrimp are favorite swank garnishes. Softened cream cheese may be piped from small tubes in many pretty designs. All garnishes should have that "fresh-as-a-daisy" look.

Therefore, it is best to decide what garnishes you want to use, then prepare all of them an hour or so ahead of time. Place between sheets of waxed paper, cover them with an *almost wet* paper towel or cloth, and place in refrigerator all ready to do the decorating job with a speedy "happy-go-lucky" technique.

Tiny cutters for making garnish cutouts from pimiento and green pepper are obtainable in special houseware departments, but these are not essential. With a sharp, thin-bladed knife and sharp-edged small cookie cutters, one can cut out small triangles, diamonds, squares, V-shapes, circles, half-moons, ellipses, etc. The end of a decorating tube can be used to make dots of pimiento and hard-cooked egg whites; and with an olive pitter or top of lip stick container, one can make small circles, half-moons, etc. The canapé illustrations found in this chapter illustrate unlimited possibilities for decorating captivating canapés.

COCKTAILS

Cocktails are of 2 kinds, semi-solid and liquid. The semi-solid include fruit, vegetable and sea food combinations seasoned interestingly. The flavoring for fruit cocktails usually is lemon or lime juice, or ginger-ale. Bland vegetables are marinated in a tart dressing long enough to acquire a stimulating flavor. Fish cocktails are usually served with a lively sauce, lemon wedges and grated horseradish. Cocktails with greatest appeal are colorful, flavorful, cold and have a variation in texture. They are an appropriate first course for luncheons or dinners. A liquid cocktail may be one juice or a blend of juices, either vegetable or fruit. Vegetable cocktails are seasoned with salt, pepper, a dash of tabasco or Worcestershire; and fruit cocktails with lemon juice and sometimes a little sugar.

CANNED JUICES AND NECTARS

Good "hurry-up" cocktails from the pantry shelf

You can buy a great variety of good canned fruit and vegetable juices. Chill them thoroughly in the cans. Some may be served plain as they come from the can while others are improved by adding seasoning or garnish. Float a thin slice of lemon on tomato juice with a sprinkle of chopped parsley or green pepper; a paper-thin slice of orange cut in wedges on cranberry juice, a dash of ginger on carrot juice. Pineapple, apple and grapefruit juices are more attractive when served with a sprig of mint, a red cherry or raspberry. Add lemon or lime juice to pineapple or apple juice as well as to most of the sweet nectars for peppier flavor. Serve them all very cold.

FRESH FRUIT JUICES

Most delectable

Freshly squeezed orange, grapefruit and tangerine juices make delicious cocktails. To enhance them, serve with a sprig of fresh mint or a paper-thin slice of the same fruit. Blends of these juices are also very tasty. For example, a mixture of grapefruit and tangerine juice or grapefruit and orange juice are surprisingly delightful. Most berry and orchard fruit juices extracted for making jelly also make good juice drinks. The darker juices like grape, blackberry and black raspberry may be served with mint sprigs or a twist of lime rind; the brilliant red ones like strawberry, cherry and red raspberry need nothing to enhance them except to be well chilled.

FRESH WINTER FRUIT COCKTAIL

1 lemon *or* lime	1 flavorful apple
Honey	1 Anjou pear
1 medium-size avocado	1 Japanese persimmon

Fruits should be ripe for best flavor and color. Squeeze lemon or lime juice and add an equal amount of honey. Cut avocado in half, strip off peeling, remove seed. Dice small into a bowl. Pare apple and pear, cut in half, remove seeds and dice over the avocado, then cut washed persimmon in half, remove seeds, dice and add. Pour lemon juice mixture over fruit. Toss carefully. Cover and chill. Serve in cocktail or sherbet glasses. 4 servings.

Variety of form and flavor add interest to appetizers. Raw shrimp, hulled and deveined, are simmered in Italian-style dressing to make the delicious hot appetizer in the chafing dish. The Hot Crabmeat Appetizer, p 206, and Toasted Cheese Rounds, p 185, are almost as simple to make. Photo, courtesy Kraft Kitchens.

ABOVE: *On this tray are just a few of the appetizers found in the chapter starting on p 173. In the upper left of the tray are Roly Polys, Tam O'Shanters, and Tuna Fish Canapés. In the lower left are Liver and Bacon Bites, in the center front, Cheese Carrots, and lower right Ham Diamonds. On toothpicks in the grapefruit are Apple Tempters (with a celery cube on the end). Tasty Teasers (with a stuffed olive on end), Glazed Stuffed Shrimp, and Dried Beef Pinwheels. By following the clear instructions in the recipes, you can reproduce this tray exactly, and make an endless combination of other delightful appetizers to highlight every special occasion.*

BELOW: *A blend of chilled Yogurt or sour cream and chilled tomato juice with seasoning, p 198, makes a refreshing cocktail to serve with an assortment of canapés.*

ABOVE: *No beverage can comfort and refresh one more on a hot day than a mint-garnished glass of ice-cold, richly flavored Lemonade, p 217.*

BELOW: *Pineapple Soda in pretty glass mugs, p 222, is almost sure to be welcomed.*

HOW TO MEASURE

Granulated sugar is lightly lifted into a measuring cup with a scoop or spoon, and leveled off with a spatula without tapping or shaking down. Always use the nested set of standard measuring cups that can be filled to the brim and leveled off. (Brown sugar is packed firmly into cups before leveling off.)

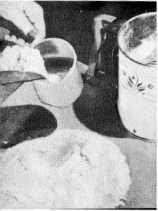

Flour is always sifted once before it is measured. The sifted flour is lifted lightly with a scoop or spoon into a cup until the cup is heaped full. Then without tapping or shaking down, the flour is leveled off with a spatula. Always use the nested set of cups that can be leveled off at the brim. Shaking or tapping undoes the work of sifting.

Oil and syrup are measured like all other liquids. Because of their tendency to cling to the sides of the measuring cup, it is important to use a brush or spoon and scrape every last drop of the oil or syrup out of the measuring cup when adding it to the other ingredients.

Milk and all other liquids are measured in a measuring cup which has the one-cup mark below the rim. The cup must be on a level surface, and then read at eye level to obtain an accurate liquid measure.

HOW TO MEASURE

Cornstarch, baking powder, salt, soda, etc., are measured by first shaking the container to insure a uniform packing of the ingredient. A measuring spoon is then dipped into the container, and filled heaping full. It is leveled off across the top with a straight-edged knife. Always use standard measuring spoons, as the spoons of dinner sets may vary considerably from the standard tsp or tbsp.

Shortening is packed solidly with the back of a spoon into a measuring cup to eliminate all air pockets. It is packed above the rim of the cup, and then leveled off with a spatula or straight-edged knife. The nested set of cups that can be filled to the brim should be used for measuring shortening. It is easier to measure accurately if the shortening is at room temp and not cold and hard.

Photographs Courtesy
Woman's Day Magazine

BELOW: *The paper pattern shown in right-hand corner of picture is used to cut two shell-shapes of pastry for bottom and top of pie. After pie is put together, markings of a fish shell are made with a paring knife handle.*

HOW TO MAKE BAKING POWDER BISCUITS
(See p 234)

2 cups all-purpose flour   ½ tsp salt
3 tsp D.A. baking powder *or*   ⅓ cup shortening
   3¾ tsp tartrate *or* phosphate type   ⅞ cup milk, 1 cup less 2 tbsp

MEMORIZE THE FOLLOWING STEPS TO MAKE DELICATE BISCUITS

Step 1. Measure all ingredients accurately. Never skimp on shortening as it is essential for tenderness. Start oven 10 min before baking; set to hot (450° F).

Step 2. Sift flour, measure, resift 3 times with dry ingredients, the last time into a 3-qt mixing bowl. Three siftings prevent yellow specks on crust caused by incomplete blending of baking powder.

Courtesy of Wheat Flour Institute.

Step 3. Cut shortening into dry ingredients with a pastry blender or 2 knives until particles are size of rice.

Step 4. Make a "well" in the dry ingredients and pour milk in all at once. Stir quickly and vigorously with a dinner fork. (Fork mixes more lightly than a spoon.) When dry ingredients are almost dampened, if dough seems a litle stiff, quickly add another tbsp or so of milk to obtain a soft dough. The dough appears sticky the instant enough liquid is thoroughly stirred into dry ingredients but it soon stiffens up. Unless dough is soft at end of mixing, biscuits will not be delicate.

Step 5. Turn dough out immediately onto a lightly floured pastry cloth, dough board or table. An amateur can knead, roll and cut out the soft dough more easily on a pastry cloth than on a board.

Step 6. Knead quickly 6 to 8 times, then pat out lightly with floured palm of hand or roll out ½- to ¾-inch thick.

Step 7. Cut out biscuits to get as many as possible from the first-rolled dough, then place them on a greased, shallow baking pan. For biscuits crusty-all-around, place them an inch apart on the pan; for biscuits with only tops and bottoms crusty, place them almost together on pan. Lay trimmings on top of each other without kneading, and again pat out with hand or roll to same thickness, then cut out. Lightly press remaining trimmings into biscuit-shape and place on baking pan.

Step 8. For a richer color and more tender crust, brush tops of biscuits (use pastry brush) with cream or melted butter. If biscuits must stand a few min before baking, put in a cool place.

Step 9. Place biscuits in heated oven. Bake 12 to 15 min. Plan your meal so you will be ready to serve biscuits the instant they come from the oven. Only blistering hot biscuits are worth serving.

Step 10. Don't wrap biscuits in a napkin to serve. The napkin holds in the steam which softens the crisp crust you have striven to achieve. Serve on a hot plate, uncovered, or directly from the baking pan. Loosen oven-hot biscuits from pan; you will find most guests delighted to help themselves to the hot biscuits right from the pan. 12 to 15 two-inch biscuits.

(Photo Courtesy of Wheat Flour Institute)

NOTE: To save in cleaning up after biscuits, turn dough onto lightly floured waxed paper. Pat dough out and cut as above. Discard waxed paper. Biscuit dough can be cut in various shapes and used to top meat pies, casserole dishes, etc.

HOW TO REHEAT BISCUITS

To successfully reheat biscuits, place on baking pan close together. Sprinkle lightly with water. Place in a moderately hot oven (425° F) and bake 10 to 12 min, or until crusty and piping hot all the way through.

HOW TO MAKE BASIC WHITE BREAD

This milk bread recipe makes three 1½ lb loaves (See p 269)

9 cups all-purpose flour
2 reg cakes compressed *or*
　2 pkgs dry gran yeast
1 cup lukewarm water
1 tsp sugar

2 cups scalded milk *or* half
　milk, half water
4 tsp salt
¼ cup sugar
¼ cup melted butter *or*
　half shortening

Do not soften yeast in warm milk or bring in contact with shortening before adding some flour to mixture. Fat seems to form a film around yeast cells through which the tiny plants have difficulty in fermenting. Those who melt shortening in the milks as it scalds, and add yeast to this mixture when cooled to lukewarm, are likely to get a slow-rising dough. Best results are obtained by softening yeast in warm water containing a little sugar to start activity of yeast plants. No shortening should be added to batter until about half of flour has been incorporated.

Step 1. Sift flour, measure. Crumble compressed or turn gran yeast into lukewarm water. Stir in 1 tsp sugar and let soften 10 min.

Step 2. Scald milk to destroy enzymes which affect growth of yeast and flavor of dough.

Step 3. Put scalded milk, salt and ¼ cup sugar into 5-qt mixing bowl; cool to lukewarm (about 110° F). If half water is used, add it cold to scalded milk to hasten cooling.

Step 4. Always stir yeast mixture into lukewarm liquid. To overheat yeast at any time injures and destroys it. Yeast that is too cold rises very slowly. The ideal rising temperature for yeast dough is an even, moist warmth from 80 to 85° F., which is a little less than body temp.

Step 5. Add 4 cups of the flour and beat until smooth.

Step 6. Beat in cooled melted shortening.

Step 7. Add enough more flour to make a smooth, soft dough; the softer the dough can be kept without sticking to board or hands, the lighter and more tender bread will be.

Step 8. Sprinkle 1 to 2 tbsp remaining flour evenly over board or pastry cloth. (A linoleum or enamel-topped table, or other modern type table tops are very satisfactory for kneading dough.)

Step 9. Turn dough onto floured board, cover with bowl; let rest 10 min. The dough is very soft as it is turned from bowl; letting it rest causes it to stiffen and makes it easier to handle without adding an excess of flour.

Step 10. Now knead dough until outside is smooth and elastic, from 10 to 15 min. There are 3 basic motions to kneading: (1) Folding dough over on itself toward you. (2) Pushing dough with heels of hands away from you. (3) Then giving dough a quarter turn and repeating. Illustration here shows the first motion of folding dough towards you.

Step 11. Then in easy rhythm of hands, rock back and forth on heels of palms, pressing the dough toward you, then pushing it away from you. This kneading develops the gluten or protein in the dough to give it a strong elastic structure necessary to hold the expanded gas produced by the yeast and keep shape of loaf as it bakes.

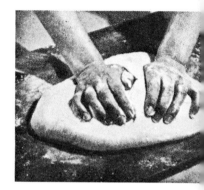

Step 12. Lift up edge of dough and turn it with left hand and at same time fold it over with right. You are now in position to repeat the kneading process started in Step 10. With practice, both hands are used to advantage and an easy rhythmic motion develops. Dough feels satiny and elastic when kneaded sufficiently and does not stick to board or hands.

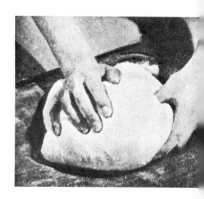

Step 13. Round up dough and return to washed, well-greased mixing bowl; turn once to bring greased-side up. This prevents formation of a thin crust on top which makes streaks in the bread.

Step 14. Cover bowl with a towel, lid, or a 2nd bowl of same size. Place in a warm spot, 80 to 85° F, away from drafts to rise until double. See "Proofing Oven" directions, on following pages.

Step 15. Do not hurry through first rising. It requires from 1½ to 2 hrs. When dough rises sufficiently, the dent made by pressing finger into dough remains.

Step 16. When dough has fully risen, plunge fist into center of dough and fold edges toward center to punch down. Then again turn dough over so smooth side is up. Cover and let rise again until double. The 2nd rising takes less time than the first. One rising produces a satisfactory loaf, but a 2nd rising a superior loaf. After last rising, punch down and turn out on a lightly floured board or pastry cloth.

Step 17. Divide dough into 3 equal portions; round up into balls, cover with bowls and let rest 10 min, then shape into loaves, as on following pages. This "rest period" makes dough easier to handle because the gluten is relaxed.

Step 18. Place loaves in 3 greased 9 x 5 x 3-inch pans. Cover and let rise in a warm place (80 to 85° F) until double, about 1 hr. The process of letting dough rise in a warm place until double is called *"proofing."* For best results there should be an even temp and a certain amount of moisture in the air so loaves will not develop a crust on top. A Homemade Proofing Oven is described in Step 12, *Shaping and Proofing,* on following pages, and can be used with any of the bread recipes in this chapter.

Step 19. Bake in a moderately hot oven (425° F) about 30 min. When done, bread should be well risen with a fully rounded top or "spring." The crust should be golden brown and crisp. Loaves should sound hollow when tapped on the bottom.

Step 20. Turn loaves out of pans immediately onto cake racks to cool for 2 or 3 hrs, uncovered and away from drafts. If cooled too quickly, the crust shrivels, becomes bumpy and soft.

Step 21. When thoroughly cooled, store bread in a metal box with a tight-fitting cover and with small air holes in sides for ventilation. Clean bread box weekly by washing in hot soapy water, rinsing well in hot water, drying well, then airing.

SHAPING AND PROOFING YEAST BREAD LOAVES

Step 1. When dough is ready to shape into loaves, knead down and turn out on board or pastry cloth. Cut with a sharp knife into as many equal portions as there are to be loaves.

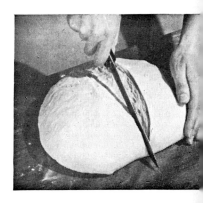

Step 2. Shape portions into smooth balls, cover with bowls or cloth and let rest 10 min; this rest period makes shaping easier.

Step 3. Flatten ball of dough with palms of hands into an oblong shape about 6 x 9 inches. Don't punch or pound the dough.

Step 4. Fold long edge of oblong farthest from you over to the center and press gently to seal.

Step 5. Now fold long edge nearest to you over to center and press gently to seal.

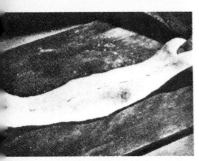

Step 6. Lift folded dough up by both ends and alternately stretch and slap against board until it is twice as long as the baking pan.

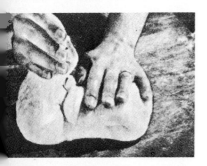

Step 7. Bring ends of folded dough to the center to overlap slightly, then press together to seal.

Step 8. Make an indentation lengthwise through center with edge of hand to mark the next fold.

Step 9. Using the indentation as a marker, fold over the edge of the dough nearest you toward the center.

Step 10. Then fold the other side toward the center, and roll dough gently back and forth with palms of hands to seal the edges and round the loaf into a cylindrical shape.

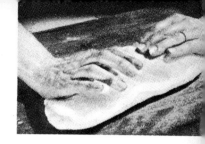

Step 11. Place in greased loaf pan with the seam side of loaf on bottom. Do not press the corners of the loaf into the corners of pan.

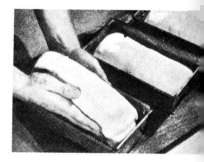

Step 12. Cover loaves with a damp cloth and let rise in a warm place, 80 to 85° F, to double, or improvise a simple Proofing Oven in the following 2 ways:

(1) Use your range baking oven if it is lined with enamel or stainless steel and is one that does not have a pilot light, which would make the oven too warm. Place loaves in cold oven with a large pan of hot water underneath. Close oven door, turn on heat at 400° F. for 1 minute only. Time exactly. Turn off heat and let loaves remain in closed oven 1 hr or until double.

(2) Use a large heavy cardboard box with the folding top attached. Make sure it is clean by wiping out inside thoroughly to be free of dust. Put box on table with open end facing you. Place open jars or pitchers of hot water in the box, close ends securely and cover with a heavy cloth so no cold air gets in and the interior of box warms up before placing bowl of dough or pans of rolls or loaves inside. Check temp of water every 30 min. As air in box cools, replace the hot water. The hot water in the oven or box gives the necessary heat and steam to cause the dough to rise and to keep its surface moist.

Step 13. Perfectly proofed loaves of bread are double the size of the original dough and have a smooth, moist surface.

Step 14. Perfectly baked loaves are symmetrical in shape with an even golden brown crisp crust. The "spring" between the pan line and the top of the bread should be well-rounded with an attractive shred on the side. Remove loaves immediately from pans to cake racks to cool, uncovered and out of drafts for 2 to 3 hrs before cutting. Brush top of hot loaf with melted butter for a soft crust.

HOW TO DO IT DEMONSTRATIONS

Attractive Rolls from Plain and Sweet Roll Dough

See Pages 273–279

Butterfly Rolls   *Butter Horns*

Cloverleaf or Shamrock Rolls   *Crooked Miles*

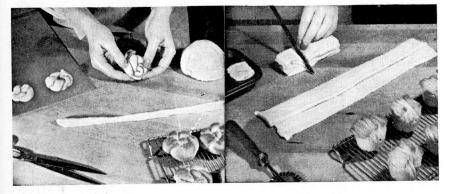

Knots   *Fan Tan Rolls*

Close-ups of interesting Yeast Dough Rolls

Here is the way to get the family to the table quickly when the meal is ready: Tempt them with fragrant, crunchy crusted, tender, sizzling-hot hot bread! Corn sticks, p 241, plain or with cocktail franks buried in the center, and corn meal muffins are tops on the list of favorites. When using self-rising corn meal and flour, omit salt and baking powder. Tamale pie, p 833, is in miniature. Photo, courtesy Self-rising Flour and Corn Meal Program, Inc.

GRAPEFRUIT BRAZILIAN COCKTAIL

Cut 2 medium grapefruit in halves crosswise. Cut out pulpy center with kitchen scissors. Use paring or grapefruit knife to remove seeds and separate sections from dividing membranes. Sprinkle each half with 1 tsp ground Brazil nuts, some finely cut fresh mint and 1 tsp powdered sugar. Chill. Lacking fresh mint, take some juice from hollow of grapefruit, flavor with a drop or two of peppermint extract, then pour over the fruit before adding sugar. 4 servings.

GRAPEFRUIT-GRAPE COCKTAIL

Section 1 medium grapefruit, saving all juice, or use 1 cup canned grapefruit. Wash ½ lb white seedless grapes, and pull from stems. Wash, drain, hull and cut in half ½ pint strawberries. Arrange fruit in layers in bowl. Add enough grapefruit juice to barely cover, a dash of salt and enough sugar and lemon juice to suit taste. Cover, chill. Lift mixture out carefully into sherbet glasses; garnish with fresh sprigs of mint. 4 to 5 servings.

GRAPEFRUIT-GRAPE JUICE COCKTAIL

Serve in shallow glass sauce dishes with spoon

Section 2 medium grapefruit carefully, saving juice. Cover and chill. Chill 1 pt concentrated sweetened grape juice, p 1084, or use frozen grape juice. Just before serving time, arrange sections or diced fruit in serving dishes, add enough grape juice to cover. 4 to 5 servings.

JIFFY FRUIT CUP

Commercial fruit cocktail with fresh fruit added

| No. 2 can fruit cocktail | ½ cup sliced bananas, *or* berries, cherries *or* unpared apple |

Chill fruit in can. Fold in fresh fruit just before serving. 6 servings.

MELON COCKTAIL

| 1 pt cantaloupe balls *or* cubes | 1 pt chilled gingerale |
| 1 pt watermelon balls *or* cubes | Mint |

Choose good flavored melons and chill 2 or 3 hours. Cut into balls or cubes, mix and put into a glass jar. Add chilled gingerale, seal, refrigerate. Serve in cocktail glasses. Garnish with mint. 8 servings.

MELON-PLUM COCKTAIL

Add 1 cup of melon balls or cubes, sprinkled lightly with salt, to 1 cup of sliced peeled sweet red or yellow plums. Cover with slightly sweetened orange juice. Cover, chill. Serve very cold. 4 servings.

PAPAYA COCKTAIL

1 cup diced ripe papaya	Dash of salt
1 cup diced pineapple	1 tsp sugar
3 tbsp lime juice	

Be sure papaya is at right stage of ripeness for finest flavor; skin is green with yellow mottling and flesh is about texture of ripe cantaloupe. Cut in half, remove seeds, pare and dice. Combine all ingredients, cover tightly and chill. Serve in cocktail glasses with a few gratings of fresh lime rind on top, if desired. Do not use papaya seeds as they are harmful. 4 to 5 servings.

PEACH AND ORANGE CUP

4 to 5 fine flavored peaches, chilled	1 cup orange juice squeezed from chilled fruit
	Fresh Mint

Pare and neatly slice peaches; there should be 1 pt. Quickly distribute slices in chilled sherbet glasses, then pour on orange juice. Garnish with mint and serve. 4 servings.

RASPBERRY-CURRANT COCKTAIL

No. 2 can red raspberries	⅔ cup lemon juice, scant
½ cup currant jelly	Dash of cayenne
2 cups cold water	

Drain juice from raspberries, then put berries through fine sieve to remove seeds. Combine purée and juice; there should be about 2 cups. Melt jelly in pan over hot water, slowly add raspberry juice and remaining ingredients. Chill thoroughly. Be careful about cayenne; a little is delightful, too much is too much. Stir thoroughly just before serving. 10 to 12 servings.

FISH COCKTAILS

CLAMS ON THE HALF SHELL

Little Neck or Cherrystone clams are best for eating raw

Rinse and open Cherrystone clams, p 712. Discard flat upper half shells. Loosen meat and remove shell particles. Put 2 tbsp Cocktail

Sauce, p 195, into a small glass or cup. Set in middle of dinner plate and surround with crushed ice, spreading ½" thick to rim of plate. Arrange 6 clams in half shells on the ice. Garnish with lemon wedges and sprigs of parsley. Serve with horseradish, tabasco and crisp crackers. 24 clams serve 4.

CLAM JUICE COCKTAIL

12-oz can clam juice *or* broth   1 tbsp fine-cut celery leaves
1 tbsp tomato catchup   Salt and pepper to taste
⅛ tsp Worcestershire

Mix all ingredients, then chill about 2 hrs. Strain and serve very cold. 4 servings.

CLAM AND TOMATO JUICE COCKTAIL

Combine 1½ cups clam juice or broth (12-oz can) with ¾ cup tomato juice, ⅛ tsp celery salt, and white pepper and salt to taste. Chill. Serve very cold. 5 to 6 servings.

COCKTAIL SAUCE

For clams, oysters, crabmeat, lobster, shrimp

½ cup nippy chili sauce   Dash of pepper
⅓ cup catchup   Few drops of tabasco
1 tsp Worcestershire   2 tsp grated horseradish,
3 tbsp lemon juice   optional
¼ tsp salt

Measure ingredients into a clean glass jar. Stir well, cover and chill thoroughly. 1 generous cup.

CRABMEAT COCKTAIL

Prepare exactly like Shrimp Cocktail except substitute for the shrimp, 1 cup fresh cooked flaked crabmeat or use one 6½-oz can.

CRABMEAT-AVOCADO COCKTAIL OR SALAD

Follow recipe for Crabmeat-Grapefruit Cocktail No. 2 except substitute 2 medium-size ripe avocados for grapefruit, and use 2 to 3 tbsp lemon juice for grapefruit juice. Cut avocados in halves, discard seeds, strip off peeling and cut into neat ½" dice. Add lemon juice, then combine and serve. 8 servings or 4 salads.

CRABMEAT-GRAPEFRUIT COCKTAIL NO. 1

2 medium grapefruit *or*
No. 2 can grapefruit
sections
6½-oz can crabmeat, chilled
Heart leaves lettuce
½ cup mayonnaise *or* salad
dressing, chilled

1 tbsp cider vinegar
1½ tbsp lemon juice
2 tbsp catchup
1 or 2 drops tabasco
Slivered green pepper

Have grapefruit chilled. Pare, section and dice; or drain juice from canned and save. Remove cartilage, and flake crabmeat coarsely. Line cocktail glasses with frill of lettuce. Add fish and fruit in 3 or 4 alternate layers. Blend next 5 ingredients for sauce. Just before serving, pour sauce over cocktails to just moisten. Garnish with green pepper. 6 servings.

CRABMEAT-GRAPEFRUIT COCKTAIL OR SALAD NO. 2

2 small grapefruit
½ cup grapefruit juice
½ cup catchup
¼ tsp tabasco
¼ tsp salt *or* to taste
6½-oz can crabmeat, 1 cup

½ cup fine-diced celery
1 tbsp fine-sheared green
celery leaves *or* green
pepper
Lettuce

Pare grapefruit cutting off all white fiber. Section, then cut sections into 4ths. Squeeze out juice remaining in dividing membranes; there should be ½ cup. Mix juice with next 3 ingredients. Combine grapefruit, flaked crabmeat, celery and leaves or green pepper. Add dressing and toss. Lift lightly into cocktail glasses lined with heart leaves of lettuce, or heap on crisp lettuce arranged on salad plates. 8 servings or 4 salads.

LOBSTER COCKTAIL

Prepare like Shrimp Cocktail except substitute for the shrimp, 1 cup fresh cooked flaked or 6½-oz can lobster meat.

OYSTERS ON THE HALF SHELL

Blue Points are best for eating raw

Rinse and open oysters, p 722. Discard upper half shells. Loosen meat and remove shell particles. Put 2 tbsp Cocktail Sauce, p 195, into a small glass or cup. Set in middle of dinner plate and surround with crushed ice, spreading ½" to rim of plate. Arrange 6 oysters in half shells on the ice. Garnish with lemon wedges and sprigs of parsley. Serve with grated horseradish, tabasco and crisp crackers. 24 oysters serve 4.

SHRIMP COCKTAIL

1 lb large shrimp, cleaned, cooked, p 726	½ cup Cocktail Sauce, p 195
⅓ cup fine-diced celery	Heart lettuce leaves
	Lemon wedges

Chill all ingredients. Just before serving, line small sherbet glasses with lettuce leaves. Now arrange 6 shrimp in each glass with celery in center. Spoon sauce over shrimp. Serve immediately well chilled with wedge of lemon and crisp crackers. 4 to 5 servings.

VEGETABLE COCKTAILS

BEET COCKTAIL

4 cooked beets size large eggs	2 drops tabasco
1 tbsp lemon juice	3 drops Worcestershire
1 tbsp cider vinegar	1 tsp sugar
½ tsp salt	1 tbsp fine-cut parsley
½ tsp grated horseradish	¼ cup fine-diced celery
½ tsp grated onion	Lettuce

Slip skins from beets. Shred beets on coarse grater into mixing bowl. Combine next 8 ingredients and pour over beets. Toss well without breaking up beets. Cover and chill. Just before serving, add parsley and celery, toss lightly. Serve in cocktail glasses lined with a lettuce frill. 5 servings.

BEET JUICE COCKTAILS

1 cup juice from canned beets	½ tsp salt
⅓ cup lemon juice	⅔ cup water
1½ tbsp sugar	1 tbsp cider or tarragon
Dash of cayenne or red pepper	vinegar
	Parsley or cress

Combine first 7 ingredients, cover and chill. Serve very cold in juice glasses. Sprinkle with chopped parsley or cress. 6 servings.

CUCUMBER COCKTAIL

1 cup diced cucumber	1½ tsp lemon juice
1 tsp sugar	⅓ cup fresh sour cream
½ tsp salt	Lettuce
Dash of pepper	Radishes and parsley
Few drops onion juice	

Pare and dice cucumber fine. Combine with next 5 ingredients and fold into sour cream. Cover, chill thoroughly. Serve in sherbet glasses lined with heart leaves of lettuce. Garnish with thin radish slices and a sprig of parsley. 4 servings.

POT LIQUOR COCKTAILS

Do not throw away the flavorful liquid or pot liquor left from cooking vegetables. It contains valuable vitamins and minerals dissolved out of the vegetables. The liquid left from cooking asparagus, peas, green beans, cauliflower and cabbage or greens, alone or in combination, make delectable hot or cold cocktails. Tomato or sauerkraut juice may be added to them for a variation in flavor. Drain off liquid from vegetables as soon as they are tender and before adding butter or other seasonings. Serve immediately while hot, or pour into a jar, cool, cover and chill. Serve within a few hours as these juices deteriorate on standing.

SAUERKRAUT JUICE COCKTAIL

No. 2½ can sauerkraut juice, 3½ cups
3 pimiento stuffed olives
¾ tsp whole caraway seed
1 tsp sugar

Pour juice into a glass jar. Add finely chopped olives, caraway, and sugar, pounded to a powder. Screw on lid and chill until ready to serve, but do not let stand more than a few hours. Strain and serve cold. If desired, tie seed in cheesecloth bag and remove just before serving. 8 to 10 servings.

TOMATO JUICE COCKTAIL

No. 2 can tomato juice, 2½ cups
1½ tsp fine-chopped onion
1 to 2 tsp sugar
2 to 3 tsp lemon juice
½ tsp salt
¼ tsp Worcestershire, optional

Mix, chill, strain and serve very cold. 5 servings.

YOGURT TOMATO JUICE COCKTAIL

1 qt plain tomato juice
½ pt Yogurt
1 tsp lemon juice
1 tsp sugar
1 tsp salt
Dash celery salt *and* pepper

Combine ingredients and beat until blended. Chill and serve cold in juice glasses. 10 servings.

SHRUBS

A shrub is a sprightly flavored cold fruit juice, served in small slender glasses similar to tomato juice glasses. A small scoop of fruit ice or sherbet harmonizing in flavor is floated on top. Serve with a spoon. They are especially pleasant for starting hot weather meals. There are many possibilities for making delicious shrubs.

CRANBERRY SHRUB

Float a scoop of orange ice or sherbet or ginger ice cream on sweetened, chilled cranberry juice.

GRAPE SHRUB

Float a small scoop of grape, lemon or lime ice or sherbet on chilled sweetened grape juice.

ORANGE SHRUB

Float a scoop of lemon or orange ice or sherbet on freshly squeezed chilled orange juice.

RASPBERRY SHRUB

12-oz pkg frozen red raspberries	½ cup lemon juice
1 cup water	1 pt ice water
1 cup sugar	½ pt raspberry ice

Put first 3 ingredients into saucepan, stir and simmer 8 to 10 min. Put through fine sieve rubbing through all pulp. Cover and chill. Just before serving, add lemon juice and ice water. Pour into slender glasses. Float raspberry ice on top. 6 to 8 servings.

Note: Fresh red or black raspberries may also be used to make a shrub. Use 1 qt for the 12-oz pkg frozen.

DIPS OR DUNKS

Dips are highly seasoned mixtures similar to Canapé Fillings except softer in consistency. They should be thick enough *not to drip* when potato or corn chips, pretzels, sticks or crackers are dipped into them. To serve, turn the chilled Dip Mixture into an attractive bowl, place on a serving tray. Arrange rows of chips, sticks, etc. around the bowl.

ALMOND-BACON CHEESE DIP

⅓ cup unblanched almonds, toasted	4 tsp fine-cut green onion
3 strips lean bacon	½ cup mayonnaise
¼ lb aged American cheese, grated	¼ tsp salt

Toast almonds, chop fine. Broil bacon until delicately browned and crisp. Drain and crumble. Combine all ingredients; mix lightly. About 1⅓ cups.

CLAM-CHEESE DIP

1 medium clove garlic	1 tsp Worcestershire
8½-oz can minced clams	1 tsp lemon juice
6 oz cream cheese	½ tsp salt

Rub mixing bowl well with the cut clove of garlic. Discard garlic. Drain juice from clams and save. There should be ½ cup clams. Chop fine or put through food chopper using fine blade or put into electric food blender. Add 1 tbsp of clam juice, then blend thoroughly with remaining ingredients. Cover and chill. Turn into bowl just before serving. About 1⅓ cups.

CREAM CHEESE DIP

Luscious mix for dunking potato chips or pretzels

3-oz pkg cream cheese	Dash of salt
1 tsp grated onion	Dash of pepper
1 tsp chopped capers *or*	1 to 2 tbsp cream
stuffed olives	½ tsp caraway seed, optional

Blend first 5 ingredients, then stir in cream to give a consistency to scoop up with chips. Cover and chill. Just before serving, stir in caraway seed to add crispness and bite. ½ cup.

DEVILED HAM DIP

2½-oz can deviled ham	½ cup mayonnaise *or* salad
5-oz jar pimiento cheese	dressing
	1 tsp grated onion

Have all ingredients at room temperature. Combine and beat with a fork until smooth and well blended. About 1⅓ cups.

GREEN CREAM DIP

1 medium clove garlic	1 tbsp lemon juice
½ tsp salt	1 tbsp tarragon vinegar
2 tbsp fine-chopped anchovies	1 cup mayonnaise *or* salad
or 1½ tbsp anchovy paste	dressing
3 tbsp fine-chopped chives	Coarsely ground black
¼ cup fine-chopped parsley	pepper
½ cup fresh sour cream	

Crush peeled clove of garlic with salt to a fine paste. Blend with next 7 ingredients, then stir in enough pepper to taste. Cover tightly and chill. Turn into bowl just before serving. About 1¾ cups.

HORS D'OEUVRES

Hors d'oeuvres like canapés are high-flavored morsels. Most of them require briskly seasoned mixtures of meat, poultry, fish, cheese, eggs, etc. Hors d'oeuvres differ from canapés in that the mixture is *not* spread on toast or crackers. Some mixtures are rolled in marble-size balls, then fried or broiled, or just tossed in finely chopped parsley or nuts. Other mixtures are stuffed into fruit such as prunes, or into vegetables such as hollowed out beets, plum tomatoes, radishes, mushrooms and grooves of celery. Still other mixtures are spread on thin slices of dried beef or boiled ham, rolled up jelly-roll fashion, cut into ½" lengths, then the resulting pinwheels impaled on picks. Flavorful foods like olives are wrapped in strips of bacon, and broiled and served hot. Most hors d'oeuvres are eaten from a pick, and for this reason special hors d'oeuvres holders with holes to stick picks in are obtainable in china or glassware sections of department stores. These are decorative but not essential. A large grapefruit or apple will serve the same "pin-cushion" purpose.

BACON HORS D'OEUVRES

HOW TO BROIL AND SERVE HOT BACON HORS D'OEUVRES

Wrap medium lean bacon around the chosen food. Usually a strip cut in half crosswise will wrap around food and overlap enough to fasten securely with a pick. It is a good plan to lay these bacon-wrapped foods on a sheet of aluminum foil fitted into a shallow pan that will slip under broiler. These foods may be stored in refrigerator and broiled just before serving. Place 3½" below heat with broiler set at 500° F, which means heat at surface of bacon will be about 325° F. Broil about 5 min, then turn and broil until bacon is crisp, 3 to 5 min longer. Or bake in a mod oven (375° F). Drain quickly on paper toweling or napkin. Replace picks with new ones. Serve piping hot.

Note: Bacon-wrapped hors d'oeuvres may be pan-broiled in a heavy skillet, turning frequently until bacon is crisp all around.

CHICKEN LIVERS BROILED IN BACON

Buy well cleaned chicken livers as whole as possible. Wash, drain. Pat dry with paper toweling or napkin. Cut livers in half. Sprinkle with salt and pepper. Wrap in bacon. Broil.

OLIVES BROILED IN BACON

Wrap half strips of medium lean bacon around medium-size stuffed olives. Broil.

OYSTERS BROILED IN BACON

Pat medium-size oysters gently with absorbent paper toweling or a cloth to remove moisture. Place on waxed paper, sprinkle with salt and pepper. Wrap in bacon. Broil.

PRUNES BROILED IN BACON

Stuff medium-size cooked pitted prunes with a small stuffed olive. Wrap in bacon. Broil.

SHRIMPS BROILED IN BACON

Marinate cooked whole shrimp, sand vein removed, in chili sauce for 2 or 3 hours. Wrap in bacon, leaving a coating of the sauce on the shrimp for best flavor. Broil.

CHEESE HORS D'OEUVRES

DRIED BEEF WHORLS OR PINWHEELS

Take a whirl at these

¼ cup Roquefort *or* Blue cheese	¼ tsp grated onion
2 drops Worcestershire	5 slices drief beef 4″ x 5″
	2 slender carrots, scraped

Mash cheese and blend with next 2 ingredients. Fit dried beef slices together, overlapping some to obtain pieces 4″ x 5″. Spread carefully with cheese mixture, allowing about 2½ level tsp to each piece dried beef. Roll up like jelly roll starting at wide end, and ending with roll 4″ long and about ¾″ thick. Wrap rolls in waxed paper and chill. Cut into ½″ lengths for pinwheels. Stick a thin slice of carrot and a pinwheel on each pick. Stick in special holder or into a grapefruit or apple and serve with other hors d'oeuvres. Another good spread for the dried beef is cream cheese blended with enough grated horseradish to season highly. 40 pinwheels.

FRIED CHEESE BALLS

Excellent with tomato juice cocktail, green or fruit salads

2 cups grated American cheese, ½ lb	2 tbsp dry fine white bread crumbs
2 egg whites	Shortening for frying

Grate cheese on medium grater. Beat egg whites until stiff; fold cheese in thoroughly. Measure mixture by level tsp onto waxed paper.

Roll into balls; then toss in crumbs to cover. Place in frying basket; fry in deep fat heated to 375° F until golden brown, about 1 min. Drain on paper toweling. Serve hot or cold. 24 balls.

CHEESE STUFFED PECANS OR WALNUTS

Make marble-sized balls of plain cream cheese, Roquefort Canapé Cheese Filling, p 184, or use Pate de foie gras, p 190. Press 2 large perfect pecan halves into each ball to hold together sandwich fashion. Chill before serving. ⅓ cup cheese makes about 15.

TANGY CHEESE NUTS

Blend a 3-oz pkg cream cheese with 2 tsp chopped capers and enough grated horseradish to make a paste stiff enough to shape. Make into small balls and roll in coarsely ground or chopped Brazil nuts. Chill. Stick on picks.

COTTAGE CHEESE BLENDS FOR TEMPTING APPETIZERS

To be served with crunchy bread sticks or crisp crackers

1. *Blushing Lady*—Combine lightly but thoroughly 1 cup cold fresh creamed cottage cheese, ¼ cup shredded cooked beets, 4 tsp finely sliced green onion, ½ tsp lemon juice or vinegar, ¼ tsp salt. Turn out loosely into a glass bowl. A dash of cloves is an interesting addition.

2. *Green Cheese*—Delightful and different

2 cups fresh creamed cottage cheese	¼ tsp grated onion
	¼ cup sour cream
¾ tsp salt	8-oz ripe avocado
¹⁄₁₆ tsp white pepper	½ to 1 tsp caraway seed

Put first 5 ingredients into mixing bowl. Cut avocado in half, strip off peel and remove seed. Cut into ¼" lengthwise strips, one at a time, and dice small into mixing bowl. Toss very lightly so as not to break avocado. Turn into serving dish. Cover and chill until serving time. Sprinkle with caraway just before serving to keep seeds crisp. 8 to 10 servings.

3. *Intrigue*—Combine lightly but thoroughly 1 cup cold fresh creamed cottage cheese with 2 tbsp fine-chopped pickled onion, 2 sprigs crisp fresh mint or parsley sheared fine with scissors and a sprinkling of oregano. Turn out loosely into chilled glass bowl. Serve immediately. 4 to 5 servings.

4. *Spring Song*—Combine lightly but thoroughly 1 cup cold fresh creamed cottage cheese with 2 coarsely shredded red radishes, 8 sprigs crisp watercress finely sheared with scissors, ⅛ tsp salt and a dash of

tabasco. Turn loosely into glass bowl and serve immediately. 4 to 5 servings.

Note: Double this quantity for a delicious salad to serve 4.

5. *Waldorf*—Combine lightly but thoroughly—1 cup cold fresh creamed cottage cheese with ⅓ cup diced pared tart crisp apple, ¼ cup finely diced crisp Pascal celery, ½ tsp lemon juice, ½ tsp sugar and ⅟₁₆ tsp salt. Turn out loosely into serving dish. Sprinkle with 2 tbsp chopped pecans just before serving. Serve cold.

EGG HORS D'OEUVRES

DEVILED EGGS

6 hard-cooked eggs, p 663	1½ tsp cider *or* tarragon
½ tsp salt	vinegar
⅛ tsp pepper	2 tbsp sour *or* sweet cream
¼ tsp dry mustard	Parsley *or* paprika
Drop or 2 of onion juice	

Cut cooled peeled eggs in half. Remove yolks carefully, mash; add next 6 ingredients and blend until smooth. Pile lightly into egg whites. Stick parsley leaflet in top or add dash paprika.

For variation, add fine-chopped baked or boiled ham, crisp crumbled bacon, pickles or celery to egg yolk mixture. *Or* blend a little anchovy paste, mashed anchovies or sardines into yolk mixture. But add salt last with anchovy paste or sardines, and taste to see if salt is needed.

EGG SALAD IN CHIPS

2 hard-cooked eggs, p 663	Mayonnaise
1 tbsp chopped ripe olives	Large crisp potato chips
¼ tsp salt	Pimiento, tiny strips
1 tbsp pickle relish	

Chop eggs and olives fine, add salt and relish and stir in mayonnaise to just hold mixture together. Drop a heaping tsp into center of each chip. Garnish with pimiento. Serve at once. 18 to 20 chips.

FISH HORS D'OEUVRES

CAVIAR AND HOW TO SERVE IT

Caviar—a gourmet's luxury—is fish eggs prepared by salting lightly and packing in oil. The highest quality is made of sturgeon roe (eggs) medium in size, gray in color, superior in flavor. Red caviar is prepared from the large eggs of salmon roe. The flavor is not valued as highly as gray caviar. Black caviar is prepared from roe of other fish (labels indicate source of roe). This caviar is small-grained, the flavor is considered better than the red but it does not rate as high as the gray with fastidious gourmets. Carbon is added to give the black color.

Since caviar is potent in flavor, it is served in comparatively small quantities in or on other food. It is usually served as it comes from container with the grains filmed with oil. If this oil is objectionable, put caviar into a fine-meshed sieve, pour hot water through it quickly to remove most of oil. Drain black caviar on a paper towel or napkin to remove excess black liquid to prevent it fading into the lighter colored foods with which it is used. Here are some favorite ways to serve caviar:

1. *For buffet service,* turn chilled caviar into a small bowl; surround with crushed ice. Serve with toast rounds spread with unsalted butter, lemon wedges and a small dish of finely chopped onion. Guests spread desired amount of caviar onto rounds, add a squeeze of lemon and a bit of onion, if desired.

2. *Prepare Deviled Eggs,* p 667. Use pastry bag and star tube to pipe yolk mixture into whites. Leave small depression in top of yolks to fill with caviar.

3. *For a delicious Salad Dressing,* fold into ½ cup chilled mayonnaise or salad dressing, a little lemon juice, finely chopped onion to suit taste and 1 tbsp caviar. Excellent on lettuce, thick slices of tomato or hard-cooked eggs.

4. *Into softened cream cheese,* blend enough red caviar and a few drops of onion juice to give a good flavor. Spread on thin slices of ice box rye bread.

5. *Make Blinis* (tiny buckwheat or white flour pancakes); keep hot in top of double boiler. Serve hot with a blob of sour cream in center, sprinkled with caviar.

BLINIS

⅔ cup rye flour	1 tbsp sugar
⅓ cup all-purpose flour	1 egg
½ tsp salt	1¼ cups milk
2 tsp D.A. baking powder *or*	¼ cup melted butter
2½ tsp tartrate *or* phosphate type	Sour cream, chilled
	Imported caviar, chilled

Sift flours, measure, resift 3 times with next 3 ingredients. Beat egg, add milk and butter; turn quickly into dry ingredients. Beat until smooth. Drop by tsp onto medium hot griddle. Bake until brown on both sides. Remove to top of double boiler placed over hot water. Drizzle each layer of pancakes with melted butter. Serve on hot plates with a blob of sour cream in center, topped with caviar. About 45.

COCKTAIL CROQUETTES

Prepare chicken, lobster or crabmeat mixtures for croquettes, pp 504–7. Shape croquette mixture into marble-size balls. Crumb and egg-dip like croquettes, but the last time dip in fine-chopped nuts instead of crumbs. These croquettes may be prepared and stored in refrigerator until ready to fry. Fry like croquettes until a delicate brown and hot through. Serve on picks. May be kept hot a few minutes in warm oven.

DELUXE PICKLED HERRING

A famous old-time favorite

3 salt herring, 1¾ lb Iceland   ¼ cup sugar
  or Norwegian   ¾ cup 5% cider vinegar
1 qt cold water   3 tbsp water
½ lb onions, peeled, cut in   1 tbsp pickling spice
  ¼" slices

Split herring down belly with kitchen scissors. Remove loose membrane; wash in cold water inside and out. Lay in a flat glass or pottery dish. Add the qt of water, cover, put in cool place 12 hrs to soak. Drain and rinse in cold water. Remove skin by barely cutting through it down the back with kitchen scissors. Using a sharp pointed paring knife, catch hold of skin and strip off carefully so as not to tear flesh. To remove bone, loosen backbone with ribs attached by starting at head-end. Gently pull bones out intact but take care not to tear flesh any more than necessary. Cut away the thin flesh along belly with scissors and discard. Cut trimmed fish neatly into 1" wide crosswise pieces. Arrange fish and onion slices alternately with spice in glass jars. Pour on combined sugar, vinegar and water. Press onion and fish down so vinegar covers them. Seal and store in cool place 2 or 3 days. To serve, place 2 or 3 pieces with some onion rings on lettuce or serve on crackers. 12 to 15 servings.

Note: Keeps several days refrigerated.

HOT CRABMEAT APPETIZER

1 8-oz. pkg cream cheese   ½ tsp cream-style horseradish
1 6½-oz can flaked crabmeat   ¼ tsp salt
2 tbsp finely chopped onion   Dash pepper
1 tbsp milk   ⅓ cup sliced almonds, toasted

Combine all ingredients except almonds, mixing until well blended. Spoon mixture into an 8-inch pie plate or shallow baker; sprinkle with almonds. Bake at 375° F for 15 min. Serves 8.

SMOKED OYSTERS

Buy required amount of oysters. Spread out on shallow pan; place in hot oven (450° F) until piping hot. On another pan, toast a layer of crackers at the same time. Serve on a toasted cracker or serve the cold oysters on hot crackers.

SARDINE SPIRALS

Drain oil from two 3¼-oz cans small sardines. Mash fish with 4 tsp lemon juice and ¾ tsp prepared horseradish, or more to suit taste. Spread mixture on ¼" thick slices fresh bread trimmed of crusts. Roll up, cut in half crosswise and fasten with picks. Brush with melted butter or margarine, sprinkle with grated Parmesan cheese. Place on shallow pan; toast quickly in hot oven (475° F). Replace picks if necessary.

Note: Horseradish in combination with lemon juice perks up any spread.

SARDINE SURPRISES

Make pastry for a one-crust 9" pie, p 928, for 15 to 20 sardines. Roll pastry ⅛" thick keeping shape rectangular. Cut into strips the length of sardines but 2¼ times as wide. Lay drained sardine in middle of each strip, sprinkle with lemon juice, fold pastry over and pinch edges together. Bake on shallow pan in hot oven (450° F) until golden brown, 12 to 15 min. Serve hot.

FRUIT HORS D'OEUVRES

APPLE-CELERY KABOBS

2 tbsp lemon juice	½" thick slice sharp cheese
2 tbsp water	3 or 4 branches Pascal celery
2 tsp sugar	Picks
2 flavorful red apples	

Combine first 3 ingredients. Cut washed unpared apples into ½" cubes. Marinate in lemon mixture an hr, then drain. Meanwhile clean and chill celery. Cut cheese into ½" cubes, celery into ½" lengths. Stick a cheese cube, one of apple, then one of celery onto each pick. Cover and chill until ready to serve. May be made a few hrs ahead of time, since marinated apples do not discolor. Stick the kabobs into a special holder or into a large apple or grapefruit. About 30.

STUFFED GRAPES

Select large firm grapes such as Black Hamburg or White Tokays. Wash and pull carefully from stems. Cut almost through lengthwise and flick out seeds. Have 1¼-oz pkg Roquefort cheese at room temp; add a drop or two of tabasco and sufficient cream to make mixture firm enough to mold into balls, about 1 tsp to each ball. Put balls between grape halves and press together just enough for cheese to show. Cover and chill. 10 to 20.

GARLIC OLIVES

Turn an 8½-oz can of large ripe olives into a glass jar. Peel 2 medium cloves of garlic, cut in half and distribute through jar. Seal, chill for 2 days. Drain just before serving. Insert a pick in each olive. *Or* drain liquid from olives, turn into jar and cover with French Dressing after adding garlic. About 20.

VEGETABLE HORS D'OEUVRES

STUFFED BABY BEETS

Buy canned tiny beets. Use beets uniform in size to stuff. Hollow out centers using a grapefruit knife to make little cups. Marinate cups in French Dressing, keeping covered. Just before serving, drain beets and stuff with Egg Salad, p 1218. Top salad with gray or black caviar and a parsley leaflet.

Note: Use scooped out beet for making soup or in chopped vegetable salad.

STUFFED CELERY

Crunchy and excites hunger

Use sweet-flavored tender celery with fairly deep grooves of either the Pascal or white variety. Separate and wash branches carefully, trimming off damaged tough leaves and stem blemishes. Dry and place in hydrator or plastic bag to chill and crisp. Cut into 3″ to 4″ lengths, leaving a few tender leaves attached. Stuff with the following:

1. *Avocado Filling,* p 190.
2. *Stuff celery grooves* level-full with creamed cheese, then sprinkle liberally with caviar drizzled with onion juice.
3. *Blend cream cheese* with ¼ to ½ as much Roquefort or Blue cheese, season with salt, paprika, lemon juice and Worcestershire.
4. *Roquefort Canape Filling,* p 184.
5. *Cream cheese seasoned* with catchup, Worcestershire and onion juice.
6. *Roquefort blended* with enough whipping cream to heap into grooves, then sprinkled with paprika.

Put any of these mixtures that are smooth into a pastry bag, and with a star tube pipe into the grooves for an attractive fluted surface. Or put filling in with a spoon or fork and smooth it even with the cut edge of the celery lengths, or draw the tines of a fork through it. Stick a tender celery leaf into the celery pieces without leaves. Cover the stuffed celery carefully so as not to spoil surface and chill thoroughly.

MARINATED CELERY ROOT OR CELERIAC

Popular appetizer in German homes and restaurants

3 medium size celery roots	1½ tsp grated onion
½ cup cider vinegar	1½ tsp salt
⅓ cup salad oil	Pepper

Clean, prepare and cook celery root as described under Celery Root with Hollandaise, p 1339. Drain off milk; pat slices dry with a cloth and place in a bowl. Combine remaining ingredients; pour over slices, then turn them carefully in the sauce. Cover and chill for several hrs. Serve cold with crackers or with an assortment of appetizers. A sprinkling of chopped parsley adds a pleasing flavorful touch. 4 servings.

STUFFED CUCUMBERS

Pare small crisp cucumbers. Cut in ½" lengths. Scoop out centers to form little cups, using a grapefruit knife or a small French ball cutter. Fill with deviled ham, or finely chopped shrimp mixed with fine-chopped celery and moistened with mayonnaise. Serve cold on appetizer tray.

STUFFED DILLS

A pretty piquant edible garnish

Use 4" to 5" long dill pickles. Make a lengthwise tunnel through each, using an apple corer. Use scooped out portion for making Tartar Sauce, p 1260, or in sandwich filling. Stuff tunnel lightly with pimiento cheese warmed to room temp. Wrap in waxed paper and chill. To serve, cut into ⅛" slices to garnish fish canapés, or into ¼" slices to garnish cold meat platters or salmon or tuna salad. 25 to 30 thin slices.

LEEK-CHEESE APPETIZER PIE

An intriguing taste teaser

9" baked pastry shell, p 924, or	¼ tsp salt
4 five-inch tart shells, p 1017	¼ lb sharp American *or* fresh
1 cup sliced leeks, 3 medium	Parmesan cheese, grated
1½ tbsp butter	6 tbsp milk

Bake pastry shell. Cool. Wash, trim and cut leeks into ¼" cross-wise slices. Sauté leeks in butter 8 to 10 min over medium heat or until just tender, stirring frequently. Sprinkle with salt and spread evenly in pastry shell. Meantime put grated cheese and milk in top of double boiler, cover, cook over simmering water, stirring frequently until cheese melts and sauce is smooth, 10 to 15 min. Pour sauce over leeks. Place in hot oven (450° F) 8 to 10 min until cheese is set. Serve warm cut into narrow pie-shape wedges. 12 to 15 servings.

BROILED STUFFED MUSHROOMS NO. 1

¼ lb sweetbreads	Salt to taste
½ cup grated aged American	½ tsp Worcestershire
or fresh Parmesan cheese	18 medium-size mushrooms
1 tbsp fine bread crumbs	3 tbsp melted butter
Dash of pepper	

Precook sweetbreads, p 890. Chop fine and mix with next 5 ingredients. Wipe mushrooms with damp cloth or paper toweling. Remove stems and save to make Soup or Sauce, pp 1280, 1259, or add to hamburger. Brush caps all over with butter. Place hollow side up on shallow pan, preferably lined with aluminum foil. Put a heaping tsp of sweetbread mixture into mushrooms, pressing down slightly. Pat melted butter over top with pastry brush. Broil about 3½″ below heat adjusted to 450° F until cheese melts and toasts slightly, 8 to 10 min. Spear with picks to serve. 6 to 8 servings.

BROILED STUFFED MUSHROOMS NO. 2

Quickly made and very delicious

18 medium-size mushrooms	⅓ cup grated American *or*
3 tbsp melted butter	freshly grated Parmesan
10 slices medium lean bacon	cheese

Clean mushrooms as described under Broiled Stuffed Mushrooms No. 1. Brush caps all over with butter. Place hollow-side up on a shallow pan. Chop stems. Pan-broil bacon until done, drain on paper toweling and crumble. Combine stems, bacon and cheese; heap into mushroom caps. Broil 3½″ below heat turned to 450° F 7 to 8 min. Serve hot speared with picks. 9 to 18 servings.

CAVIAR STUFFED RADISHES

Use 24 medium-size round red radishes uniform in size. Wash, cut off root and leaf ends square so radishes stand upright. Scoop out centers with grapefruit knife. Cover with wet paper toweling and chill until crisp. Mash 3 hard-cooked egg yolks, add 4 tsp caviar, 1 tsp fine-chopped parsley, 6 fennel seeds pounded to a powder, ¼ tsp onion juice, ¼ tsp dry mustard, 1½ tsp lemon juice, 1 tsp each mayonnaise and vinegar. Blend and stuff into radish cups. Place in flat pan, cover with waxed paper and chill. Serve on appetizer tray.

STUFFED PLUM TOMATOES

Use rich red but firm plum tomatoes. Wash and dip quickly into hot water just long enough for skins to slip off smoothly. Don't overheat. Skin, then hollow out tomatoes about ⅔ of their length using grapefruit knife. (Use scooped out portion for soup or salad.) Cover and chill. Just before serving time, sprinkle inside with salt and pepper and fill hollows with mixture of whipped or soured cream and horseradish, heaping up slightly.

HORS D'OEUVRES FOR THE BEGINNER

BRAUNSCHWEIGER BALLS

An easy way to take liver

Mash high-grade liver sausage smooth. Measure out tsp onto waxed paper. Pat portions flat in palm of hand and lay a small stuffed olive in center. Mold sausage around olive to cover. Roll balls in finely chopped parsley for color and more flavor. Cover tightly and chill, but do not hold long enough for parsley to lose freshness. Serve on picks.

CERVELAT DUMBBELLS

Serve a lot

Spread thin slices of Cervelat with softened cream cheese. Roll up and stick a pick through roll. Push a tiny pickled onion onto each end of pick close up to the roll.

SALAMI TASTY STICKS

A high-hat way to serve garlic salami

Cut salami into sticks 1½" long, ½" wide and ½" thick. Spread half the length with mayonnaise, then roll mayonnaise-end in grated cheddar cheese. Serve on picks.

Beverages

"Let's have another cup of coffee, let's have another piece of pie." So goes the musical invitation in Irving Berlin's musical "Face the Music." And be sure to make the coffee fresh every time as recommended in the directions in this chapter. We recognize the social value of serving many kinds of beverages but don't forget those which are especially good for the small fry.

A HOT drink on a cold day and a cold drink on a hot one can make important contributions to comfort and morale. They are also practically indispensable for all impromptu between-meal refreshments as well as for planned entertainments.

COFFEE

Most adults consider coffee an important starter for the day, as well as at other meals and "in-between." Therefore, one should be able to make uniformly good coffee every day. This demands a *system* in its making.

The general rules in all methods for making coffee are about the same. *Fresh coffee is the first requirement.* Buy coffee of the *proper grind* for the type of coffee maker used. Buy in fairly small quantities, not more than enough for a week. It is poor economy to buy in larger quantities, as coffee goodness is lost every time container is opened. The best way to keep coffee fresh is in its metal or glass container, or turn it from a bag into a dry, odorless glass jar with air-tight lid and store in the refrigerator. When container is opened, coffee should be quickly removed and lid promptly replaced to preserve fragrance in unused coffee.

Fresh water is the second requirement for good coffee. Always start with freshly drawn cold water. Water preheated or drawn from hot water faucet cannot produce the finest flavored brew. Neither can coffee be made with water containing considerable amounts of minerals or with chlorine. Water with any flavor of its own is not desirable for any cooking and often leaves a mark on pots and pans in the form of a lime deposit or iron rust. A porous stone filter for your faucet is an excellent investment.

A clean coffee maker is the third requirement. Be sure the coffee maker of whatever type—drip pot, vacuum, percolator or old-fashioned coffee pot —is kept perfectly odorlessly clean. Wash with hot soapy water and scald thoroughly with clear water after each using. Once a week fill the pot with hot water, add one teaspoon of soda (never put soda in an aluminum pot), and boil for a few minutes; rinse thoroughly. After coffeee is made never let grounds stand in pot.

In addition to *fresh coffee, fresh water* and *clean coffee maker,* it is necessary to scald coffee maker before using. Measure coffee and water accurately. Serve coffee as soon as possible after brewing. Never *boil* coffee, never re-use grounds and never allow cloth filters, when used, to become dry.

Instant coffee tastes more like coffee made from ground coffee when it is made in larger amounts than one cup and is allowed to stand, covered, over low heat for a short time before serving. A glass carafe is excellent for making instant coffee. *For large quantities,* heat water to boiling in coffee maker; mix instant coffee with just enough cold water to moisten and pour into boiling water (this prevents excessive foaming). Reduce heat to minimum to prevent boiling and let stand about ½ hour.

There are also coffees available from which all or most of the caffeine has been removed. Caffeine is the stimulating element in coffee, so those who drink coffee for its stimulating effect are not satisfied with this type. Beverages made from cereal grains are also used as coffee substitutes, but the flavor is quite different from that of coffee. Some of these preparations sold under trade names are made like regular coffee, while others are made like instant coffee. Some prefer coffee with chicory added for a darker color and heavier body.

OLD-FASHIONED "BOILED" EGG COFFEE

Scald pot with hot water to preheat. Measure 1⅓ level tbsp of regular grind coffee into pot for each 8-oz measuring cup of water. To 5 or 6 tbsp of coffee, stir in about ½ tbsp of beaten egg or egg white, or add the inner linings from 2 egg shells with ¼ cup cold water. Stir well. Add measured amount of fresh boiling water. Place over direct heat and stir a minute or two. Cover, turn off heat (if electricity is used, remove from unit) and let stand to steep 5 to 10 min depending on strength desired. Pour coffee through strainer to serve or strain coffee into hot, scalded pot. (If the coffee and egg mixture is tied loosely in a cloth bag, straining will be unnecessary and the coffee grounds may be removed easily after steeping.) Serve promptly in hot cups.

PERCOLATOR COFFEE

Measure fresh cold water into the pot. Place on heat until water boils, then remove from heat. Measure 1 level tbsp of regular grind coffee into basket for each serving as marked on percolator. Insert basket into percolator, cover, return to low heat and percolate *gently* 6 to 7 min. Remove basket and serve coffee in hot cups. Automatic electric percolators will stop "perking" when coffee is brewed sufficiently and hold it at proper serving temp.

DRIP COFFEE

Preheat pot by scalding with hot water. Measure 1 level tbsp of drip grind coffee for each serving cup of water into filter section of drip pot. Pour in ¼ the required amount of boiling water. After 1 min pour the remaining measured amount of fresh boiling water over coffee and let stand over *very* low heat while water drips through. Heat just sufficient to keep coffee hot, not boiling. Pouring a little of the water over coffee wets and swells it. When remaining water is added, it goes through slowly enough to take with it all the fine coffee flavor and fragrance. Dripping takes about 8 min; never drip the coffee through grounds a second time. Stir brew and serve. If cloth filter is used, wash in cold water immediately after using and keep immersed in cold water until next used. Never use soap in washing filters.

VACUUM COFFEE

Measure required amount of fresh cold water into lower bowl of coffee maker and heat to boiling. While water heats, put filter in place in top of coffee maker and add measured quantity of vacuum grind coffee,* 1⅓ level tbsp for each 8-oz measuring cup of water (1 tbsp per serving cup).

When water boils, turn heat low. If there is a rubber ring on outside of glass tube, moisten it and carefully fit top into lower part. When water rises into upper bowl (some water always remains in lower bowl) stir water and coffee well. Allow water to remain in contact with coffee 1 to 3 min, then turn off heat to let coffee return to lower bowl. If electricity is used, remove coffee maker from heat. When coffee filters through, remove upper bowl and serve immediately in hot cups. If coffee is to be kept hot, place on an asbestos mat over *very low* heat.

ICED COFFEE

For iced coffee, make coffee double strength by any method, using *double* the amount of coffee. Pour the freshly made hot coffee into tall glasses *filled* with ice cubes. Fine flavored iced coffee cannot be made with regular strength coffee or with leftover coffee.

COFFEE STRENGTHS

Note: The standard coffee measuring "spoon" holds 2 tbsp.

One level tbsp of coffee per serving cup (1⅓ tbsp per 8-oz measuring cup) makes coffee of regular or medium strength. If a stronger or weaker coffee is desired, then simply increase or decrease the amount

---

* To enhance coffee flavor, add ¼ tsp butter to the coffee measure for each 3 cups placed in the pot, percolator or vacuum coffee maker. The coffee flavor combines with the butter oil after it comes in contact with the hot water and remains in the brew.

of coffee, but always use the same method. The only satisfactory way to make strong coffee is to use *more* coffee; merely brewing longer will not make fine flavored brew.

DEMITASSE

Make coffee by any of the methods described above, using 4 level tbsp of coffee to each cup—½ pt—of water used. Serve in hot demitasse cups.

FRUIT DRINKS

Fruit punches and various cold fruit drinks are especially refreshing on a hot day, and the fruit juice they contain makes a real contribution to nutrition. The combinations possible are nearly unlimited, as most fruit juices combine harmoniously with one another.

COLD CRANBERRY PUNCH

1 qt fresh cranberries	½ tsp grated orange rind, pkd
4 cups water	2 tbsp lemon juice
1 cup sugar	1 qt apple juice, chilled
5 whole cloves	Thin slices of orange
½ tsp grated lemon rind, pkd	

Wash cranberries, add water and boil gently in a covered 3 qt saucepan until skins pop. Put berries through a sieve or food mill. Stir in sugar, cloves, rinds, cover and chill. Add lemon and apple juice and stir to blend. Serve immediately. Garnish with orange slices. About 2½ qts.

FRUIT FIZZ

½ cup lemon juice	1 pt gingerale, chilled
1 cup orange juice	Ice cubes
¾ cup sugar, *or* to suit taste	

Squeeze lemons and oranges, remove seeds but do not strain juices. Add sugar and shake or beat to mix thoroughly. Add gingerale and serve with an ice cube. 5 cups.

FRUIT JUICE MEDLEY

1½ cups orange juice, 3 medium	1 cup pineapple juice, chilled
	2 cups ice water
⅓ cup lemon juice, 2 medium	Sugar to taste

Combine all ingredients and serve well chilled. 5 to 6 servings.

FRUIT JUICE MERGERS

Almost any combination of fruit juices makes a delicious beverage when well chilled or served over ice cubes. If sweet juice from canned fruit is used, add lemon to improve the flavor. A certain amount of sugar is needed to produce the best flavor in any beverage. A sprig of mint, a slit thick half slice of lemon perched on edge of the glass, or a red cherry dropped into each glass makes a pleasing garnish.

GRAPEFRUIT-CIDER PUNCH

2 cups chilled grapefruit juice
1½ cups chilled sweet cider

1½ cups ice water
½ cup sugar
1 red apple

Combine first 4 ingredients and stir thoroughly. Serve with a garnish of thin crosswise slices of cored apple. 8 servings.

GRAPEFRUIT TANGERINE JUICE

Equal parts of grapefruit and tangerine juice make an extra delicious beverage. No sugar is needed.

GRAPE LEMONADE

½ cup lemon juice, 3 medium
¾ cup orange juice, 2 medium
¼ cup sugar, or to taste
1¼ cups chilled grape juice

1¾ cups ice water
Lemon slices
Mint

Remove seeds from lemon and orange juices, but do not strain. Stir in sugar until dissolved. Add next two ingredients. Place 2 tbsp of crushed ice in each 8-oz glass and fill with the lemonade. Garnish with a lemon slice over rim of each glass and add a sprig of mint. 5 servings.

HOT FRUIT PUNCH

1 cup sugar
2 cups water
1½ cups pineapple juice
1 cup crushed pineapple, 9-oz can

1½ cups grapefruit juice
1½ cups orange juice, 4 medium

Combine first 4 ingredients and heat to boiling. Add grapefruit and orange juice, and reheat just enough to make it steaming hot. Serve immediately in mugs or glasses. About 2 qts.

HOT SPICED OR MULLED GRAPE JUICE

3 cups grape juice	1 4" stick cinnamon
2 cups water	Dash of ginger
2 tbsp sugar	2 tbsp lemon juice

Combine all ingredients, except lemon juice. Heat slowly and stir until sugar dissolves. When hot, stir in lemon juice. Remove cinnamon and serve immediately. 5 cups.

LEMONADE

½ cup freshly squeezed lemon juice, 3 medium	16 large ice cubes, crushed Mint, if desired
½ cup sugar, or to taste	

Cut lemons in half and remove 4 thin slices before squeezing. Remove seeds from juice but do not strain. Add sugar and crushed ice and stir until sugar dissolves and ice is almost melted. Flavor deteriorates on standing, so serve at once, garnished with lemon slices and mint and with a sipper. Amount of both ice and sugar may be varied to suit individual taste. 4 servings.

LEMON SYRUP FOR LEMONADE

1½ cups sugar	1½ cups lemon juice, 9 medium
4 cups water	

Combine sugar and water in a saucepan and heat to boiling; boil briskly for 5 min. Cool. Add unstrained lemon juice, seeds removed, stir thoroughly and pour into a clean glass jar. Cover and store in refrigerator. About 5½ cups.

To prepare lemonade with this syrup, use about ½ cup of syrup for each 8-oz glass of lemonade, filling up with crushed ice. About 11 servings.

Note: Do not keep longer than a few hrs, as syrup loses both flavor and vitamin content on standing. Useful when preparing for a party.

LIMEADE—COLD OR HOT

10 Persian green limes	2 cups ice water
¾ cup sugar, or more	½ tsp grated lime rind

Wash limes and squeeze 9, remove seeds but do not strain juice. Slice remaining lime thin. Combine lime juice, sugar, water and rind; stir until sugar dissolves. Put ⅓ cup crushed ice into each tall glass, add lime liquid. Garnish with slices of lime and serve at once. Or serve hot, diluted with more water, if desired. 5 servings.

ORANGE JUICE

When juice oranges are inexpensive, serve plain orange juice for a refreshing, nutritious and welcome beverage. Chill oranges and squeeze just before serving. If refrigerator space is limited, squeeze juice, put into clean, sterile glass or enamelware container with tight fitting lid. Store in refrigerator, but hold no longer than 2 or 3 hrs for finest flavor. A mint sprig is a glamorous garnish.

SPICED OR MULLED APPLE CIDER (HOT)

1 qt sweet apple cider	1 4" stick cinnamon, if
8 whole allspice	desired
8 whole cloves	Dash of salt
	¼ cup brown sugar, pkd

Put cider into saucepan, add spices, salt and sugar; cover and heat very slowly to boiling. Heat should be so low that cider requires about half hr to reach a boil. Remove from heat, strain and serve steaming hot. 5 servings.

ELABORATION OF COMMERCIAL ICE CREAM

No other food is such a boon to the busy, hospitable homemaker as high quality ice cream available at drug or grocery stores. It is a welcome, nourishing food to everyone from baby to grandma, dished up, as is, or with trimmings. It can be quickly converted into a dozen different roles with specially prepared sauces, flavorsome preserves, jams, nuts, fruit juices or carbonated beverages.

Ice cream can be safely stored in the freezing compartment of a mechanical freezer or in a home food freezer, ready to use for quick dessert or an afternoon or evening refreshment. Children will give mother all the help she needs to prepare elaborate sundaes and parfaits, refreshing coolers, sodas and shakes. These concoctions are popular and wholesome. Recipes for a number of favorites follow.

COOLERS*

APRICOT NECTAR

Into mixing bowl measure 1 cup chilled canned apricot nectar, 2 tsp lemon juice, dash of salt, 1 tbsp sugar and a large scoop vanilla or New York ice cream. Beat until ice cream half melts. Serve at once. 1 serving.

* © National Dairy Council.

CIDER COOLER

Into mixing bowl measure 1 cup chilled cider, 1 tsp sugar, dash of salt and 1 large scoop vanilla or New York ice cream. Beat until ice cream is half melted. Serve at once. Makes 1 serving.

COFFEE COOLER

Into mixing bowl measure 1 cup fresh strong coffee, p 214. Add dash of salt, 3 to 4 small scoops vanilla or New York ice cream and 1½ to 2 tbsp sugar. Beat until ice cream is half melted. Serve at once. Makes 1 serving.

CRANBERRY COOLER

Into mixing bowl measure 1 cup ice water, ¼ cup thick sweetened cranberry jelly, p 1087, dash of salt, 1 tsp sugar, 1 tsp lemon juice and 1 large scoop vanilla or New York ice cream. Beat until ice cream is half melted. Serve at once. Makes 1 serving.

GINGER TEA COOLER

Make 1 cup strong tea by adding 1 teabag and 1 bruised dried ginger root about ½-inch long to 1 cup boiling water and let steep 5 min. Lift out the ginger and tea bag. Cool, add 2 tsp sugar, 1 tbsp lemon juice, dash of salt and 1 to 2 large scoops vanilla or New York ice cream. Add a dash of cinnamon, if desired. Stir until well blended. 1 large serving.

GRAPE COOLER

Into mixing bowl measure 1 cup chilled grape juice, 1 tbsp sugar, dash of salt, 1 large scoop vanilla or New York ice cream. Beat until ice cream is half melted. Serve at once. Makes 1 serving.

LEMON COOLER

Into mixing bowl measure 1 cup ice water, ¼ cup lemon juice, ¼ cup sugar, dash of salt, 1 large scoop vanilla or New York ice cream. Beat until ice cream is half melted. Serve at once. 1 to 2 servings.

PINEAPPLE COOLER

Into mixing bowl measure 1 cup chilled pineapple juice, 1 tbsp lemon juice, dash of salt and 2 large scoops vanilla or New York ice cream. Beat until ice cream is half melted. Serve at once. Makes 2 servings.

PUNCH COOLER

Into a mixing bowl measure 1 cup chilled orange juice, ⅝ cup chilled lime juice, 3 med, ¼ cup chilled lemon juice, 1½ med, 1 cup chilled pineapple juice and ⅔ cup sugar. Add 3 large scoops vanilla or New York ice cream. Beat until half melted. Serve at once. Makes 3 to 4 servings.

SHAKES*

BANANA SHAKE

Measure 1 cup chilled milk into shaker or mixing bowl. Add 1 thoroughly ripe banana pressed through a sieve or mashed, ⅓ cup orange juice, 1 tsp sugar, 1 large scoop ice cream and dash of salt. Shake or beat well. Serve at once. Makes 1 to 2 servings.

BLACK RASPBERRY SHAKE

Measure into shaker or mixing bowl 2 cups chilled milk, 2½ tbsp seedless black raspberry jam, 1 tbsp lemon juice, dash of salt and 3 small scoops ice cream. Shake or beat well. Serve at once. 2 servings.

CHOCOLATE MALTED MILK

Measure into shaker or mixing bowl ½ cup cold Chocolate Syrup, p 223, ¼ cup malted milk powder, 2 cups chilled milk, 1 large scoop vanilla or chocolate ice cream and a dash of salt. Shake or beat until well mixed and frothy. Sprinkle with nutmeg, if desired. Serve at once. Makes 2 servings.

EGGNOG SHAKE

Measure into mixing bowl 1 egg yolk, dash of salt and 1 tsp sugar. Beat until blended. Add ⅔ cup chilled milk, 1 tsp rum extract and 2 large scoops vanilla ice cream. Beat well or put into mixer and shake. Serve at once. Makes 1 serving.

LEMON SHAKE

Measure into shaker or mixing bowl 3 cups chilled buttermilk, ½ cup cold lemon juice, dash of salt, ½ cup sugar, ⅛ tsp lemon rind and 2 small scoops ice cream. Shake or beat thoroughly. Serve at once with a dash of ginger. Makes 4 servings.

* Courtesy of National Dairy Council.

MOLASSES SHAKE

Measure into shaker or mixing bowl 2 tbsp light molasses, 2 tbsp lemon juice, 1 tsp sugar, ¼ tsp grated lemon peel and 1 cup milk. Add a large scoop of vanilla ice cream and shake or beat well. Makes 1 to 2 servings.

PEACH SHAKE

Into shaker or mixing bowl measure ½ cup chilled peaches—canned or fresh cooked—put through a sieve or food mill with syrup, and ⅓ cup chilled milk, dash of salt, 2 or 3 drops almond extract and 1 large scoop vanilla ice cream. Shake or beat well. Serve at once. Makes 1 serving.

PRUNE SHAKE

Into shaker or mixing bowl measure ⅓ cup Prune Purée, p 553, ⅓ cup orange juice, 1 cup chilled milk, dash of salt, 1 tsp lemon juice, 1 tbsp sugar, and 1 large scoop vanilla ice cream. Shake or beat well. Serve at once. Makes 2 servings.

SODAS

BLACK COW

Measure ¼ cup root beer and 1 tsp milk into a 10-oz glass. Add a large scoop of vanilla or New York ice cream and stir slightly. Add ¾ cup more of root beer. 1 serving.

BLACK RASPBERRY SODA

Measure into a 10-oz glass, 2 tbsp seedless black raspberry jam, dash of salt, 1 tsp cream, ¼ cup gingerale and stir vigorously. Add a large scoop vanilla or New York ice cream and stir a few times. Add ¼ cup more of gingerale. 1 serving.

CHOCOLATE SODA

Measure 2 tbsp Chocolate Syrup, p 223, into a 10-oz glass, add 1 tsp milk, ¼ cup carbonated water and stir. Add 1 large scoop of either vanilla or chocolate ice cream and then another ¼ cup carbonated water. Sprinkle with nutmeg, if desired. 1 serving.

GRAPE SODA

Measure ½ cup chilled grape juice, 2 tbsp sugar and 1 tsp milk or cream into a 10-oz glass and stir well. Then add ¼ cup chilled gingerale and 1 large scoop vanilla or New York ice cream and stir well. Add ¼ cup more of gingerale. 1 serving.

MARASCHINO CHERRY SODA

Measure into a 10-oz glass 2 tbsp chopped maraschino cherries and 1 tbsp maraschino juice, stir in 1 tsp cream and ¼ cup gingerale. Add 1 large scoop vanilla or New York ice cream, then another ¼ cup gingerale. Stir slightly. 1 serving.

ORANGE SODA

Measure into a 10-oz glass ¼ cup orange juice, a few shreds grated orange rind, 1 tsp lemon juice, 1 tbsp sugar and 1 tsp milk. Add ¼ cup lime-soda water and a large scoop vanilla or New York ice cream and mix slightly. Add ¼ cup more of lime soda. 1 serving.

PINEAPPLE SODA

Measure into a 10-oz glass 2 tbsp crushed pineapple, 1 tbsp sugar, dash of salt, 1 tsp milk and stir well. Add ¼ cup carbonated water, 1 large scoop vanilla or New York ice cream and stir a few times. Add another ¼ cup carbonated water. 1 serving.

MILK DRINKS

Milk drinks are especially valuable because they are a means of getting more milk into diets of both children and adults. A serving of hot or chilled cocoa or chocolate, malted milks, eggnogs and other flavored milk drinks supply about ¼ of a child's and ½ of an adult's daily requirement of milk. Fruit juices and thin fruit purée combine with milk or buttermilk to make flavorful and refreshing cold drinks. This is an excellent way to use juices drained from canned fruits for use in salads, etc.

Chill all ingredients when making cold milk drinks. After combining, keep cold until served. Never add ice to a milk drink as it dilutes the flavor.

When a very acid fruit juice such as orange or lemon is added to milk, the danger of curdling may be lessened and the richness of flavor increased by adding some cream with the milk. Evaporated milk diluted with an equal amount of water may be used in place of fresh milk. To lessen the tendency of curdling, always stir the fruit juice into the milk. The chance for curdling is increased if the fruit-milk drink is allowed to stand.

ANISE MILK

Appeals to children who dislike milk

1 qt milk	1 tbsp sugar
¼ to ½ tsp anise extract	Dash of salt

Scald milk in top of double boiler. Stir in enough extract to give desired flavor then sugar and salt. Serve hot. 4 to 5 servings.

CHOCOLATE BEVERAGE SYRUP OR SAUCE

5 sqs unsweet chocolate, 5 oz	¼ cup white corn syrup
2 cups boiling water	½ tsp salt
1¾ cups sugar	

Put chocolate and water into saucepan and cook over low heat, stirring constantly until smooth and thick, about 2 min. Add rest of ingredients and boil gently 3 or 4 min, stirring occasionally. There should be 2¾ cups; if less, add boiling water to make this amount. Cool. Pour into clean glass jar. Cover, cool, and store in refrigerator.

For hot or cold chocolate, use 1 tbsp of the syrup to a cup of hot or cold milk or enough to suit taste. For ice cream sauce, stir ¼ cup butter into sauce while hot.

BITTER-SWEET CHOCOLATE SYRUP OR SAUCE

For hot or iced chocolate

½ lb unsweet chocolate	1⅓ cups boiling water
1¾ cups sugar	2 egg yolks, beaten
¼ tsp salt	1 tsp vanilla

Melt chocolate in top of double boiler over hot water. Blend in sugar and salt, and gradually add water, stirring constantly and continue cooking 5 min. Then gradually stir hot mixture into beaten egg yolks. Cool, stir in vanilla. For hot or iced chocolate, add 3 to 4 tsp to each glass of hot or chilled milk. Syrup may be used as a sauce for custards, puddings or ice cream. Store in covered jar in refrigerator. About 2 cups.

HOT CHOCOLATE*

2 sqs unsweet chocolate, 2 oz	1 qt scalded milk *or*
1⅓ cups boiling water	2 cups evaporated milk and
⅓ cup sugar	2 cups boiling water
Dash of salt	½ tsp vanilla

Melt chocolate in top of double boiler over hot water; stir in 1⅓ cups boiling water to obtain a smooth paste. Add next 3 ingredients and

* Chocolate beverage of this strength is not suitable for small children.

heat 5 min longer, stirring often. Add vanilla, whip for a min with rotary beater. Serve hot. Add a marshmallow or a puff of whipped cream for a richer drink. 5 to 6 servings.

CHOCOLATE MALTED MILK

⅓ to ½ cup chocolate syrup,   ½ cup thin cream
   p 223   3½ cups cold milk
¼ cup malted milk powder

Mix chocolate syrup and malted milk powder thoroughly. Add cream and ½ the milk, beat with rotary beater or shake until thoroughly mixed, beat in remaining milk. Serve immediately. 4 to 5 servings.

COCOA FOR ADULTS

3 tbsp cocoa   1 qt scalded milk *or*
3 tbsp sugar   2 cups evaporated milk and
¼ tsp salt   2 cups boiling water
¾ cup boiling water   ¼ tsp vanilla
                           1 tsp butter

Mix cocoa, sugar and salt together and blend to a smooth paste with the ¾ cup boiling water. Heat to boiling and cook 1 min, stirring constantly. Stir in rest of liquid, cover and place over boiling water to keep hot. Just before serving, remove from heat, add vanilla and butter. Whip with a beater until frothy and serve steaming hot. The foam prevents the formation of a "skin" on the cocoa. 4 servings.

Note: See pp 1241–42 Cocoa Sauce for Cocoa.

COCOA FOR CHILDREN

For small children add ½ cup hot milk to each cup of finished cocoa. When making cocoa for the entire family, it is convenient to make it full strength, pour the cocoa for the adults first, then add required amount of milk for the children. In this way, it is not necessary to make separate batches of cocoa.

CHILLED COCOA

To make chilled cocoa, set pan of hot cocoa in cold water to cool quickly. Then pour into a sterile jar or bottle, cover tightly, and place in coldest spot in refrigerator for at least 2 hrs before serving.

FRUIT BUTTERMILK

1½ cups chilled canned fruit   3 tbsp sugar *or* to taste
   juice *or* juice from canned   3 cups chilled buttermilk
   fruit

Combine all ingredients and stir until sugar dissolves. Serve well chilled. Will not curdle on standing. 4 to 5 servings.

Red cherry, apricot, pineapple, peach and grape juice all combine well with buttermilk, or mixed juices may be used. The addition of a little lemon juice is often desirable to pep up the flavor of bland fruit juices.

GRAPE BUTTERMILK

A high calcium beverage due to the addition of dried milk solids

1 pt buttermilk, chilled	2 tbsp sugar
1/3 cup dry milk solids, spray	1/16 tsp salt
process	2 tsp lemon juice
1½ cups grape juice, chilled	

Put buttermilk into a mixing bowl, sprinkle dry milk solids over top and beat with rotary beater until smooth. Add remaining ingredients, whip until frothy. Serve immediately or cover and store in refrigerator until ready to serve. Whip again just before pouring. 4 servings.

HOT CARAMEL MILK SHAKE

1 egg yolk	1 cup hot milk
1 tbsp caramel syrup, p 165	¼ tsp vanilla
Dash of salt	

Beat egg yolk until thick. Then beat in syrup, salt and milk. Stir and heat over hot water until scalding hot. Remove from heat, stir in vanilla and beat until frothy. Serve immediately. 1 serving.

HOT MILK

Soothing and easily digested

1 qt milk	1½ tsp vanilla
2 tbsp sugar	Cinnamon *or* nutmeg
¼ tsp salt	

Heat milk with sugar and salt in top of double boiler until just scalding. Remove from heat and stir in vanilla. Serve hot with a dash of cinnamon or nutmeg over each serving. If preferred, omit the sugar and vanilla, increase salt to suit taste, and sprinkle with nutmeg. 4 to 5 servings.

HOT COCONUT HONEY MILK

¼ cup moist shredded coconut	½ tsp cinnamon
1 tbsp butter	½ tsp nutmeg
1 qt milk	2 tbsp honey

Lightly brown coconut in melted butter in a saucepan, stirring to obtain even color. Add milk, spices and honey, and heat to scalding. Strain out coconut and serve immediately. Or leave coconut in if desired, in which case, chop it fine before browning. 4 to 5 servings.

LEMON-HONEY MILK

1 qt chilled milk	½ cup honey
⅛ tsp salt	¼ cup strained lemon juice

Combine milk, salt and honey and beat until thoroughly mixed. Add lemon juice slowly, beating constantly. Serve at once. 4 servings.

MEXICAN CHOCOLATE

Make hot coffee and mix with an equal amount of hot chocolate. Serve hot.

MOLASSES NOG

3½ cups chilled milk	2 or 3 tbsp light molasses
½ cup coffee cream	Dash of nutmeg *or* ginger
Dash of salt	

Combine first 4 ingredients; stir well. Pour into glasses and sprinkle with preferred spice. 4 servings.

PEPPERMINT BUTTERMILK

2 oz peppermint stick candy—4 small sticks	⅓ cup boiling water
	3 cups chilled buttermilk

Crush candy as fine as possible hammering it between the folds of heavy brown paper; then stir in boiling water and let stand until candy dissolves. Add buttermilk and shake or beat until blended. 3 to 4 servings.

PINEAPPLE BUTTERMILK

2 cups chilled buttermilk	2 to 3 tbsp sugar
2 cups chilled pineapple juice	

Combine milk and juice; stir thoroughly, and add sugar to taste. There is no danger of curdling. Use a larger proportion of buttermilk, if preferred. 4 servings.

PRUNE-MILK PUNCH

1½ cups prune purée, p 553   ½ cup thin cream, Half and
⅓ cup lemon juice   Half
¹⁄₁₆ tsp salt   Sugar to taste
1 qt milk

Stir prune purée, lemon juice and salt into the milk and cream, add sugar to taste, amount depends on the sweetness of the prunes. Chill. Beat with rotary beater before serving. 4 to 6 servings.

SAGE MILK

1 qt milk   Dash of salt
2 tsp sage leaves

Pour milk into a saucepan. Add sage leaves tied in a small cheese-cloth bag with the salt. Heat milk to scalding, stir constantly and press sage with a spoon to extract desired flavor. Remove sage, stir milk and serve hot. 4 servings.

TOMATO BUTTERMILK

2½ cups chilled tomato juice   ½ tsp salt
1½ cups chilled buttermilk   3 or 4 drops Worcestershire

Combine ingredients and mix well. Serve immediately. 4 servings.

TOMATO MILK

A refreshing and nourishing hot weather drink

2¼ cups chilled tomato juice   ¾ cup ice water
1½ cups chilled evaporated   ¾ tsp celery salt
   milk

Slowly add tomato juice to evaporated milk and water, stirring con-stantly. Stir in celery salt. Serve immediately. 4 to 6 servings.

MILK EGG DRINKS

CARAMEL EGGNOG

½ cup sugar   3 cups chilled milk
1½ cups boiling water   ¾ cup chilled evaporated milk
3 egg yolks   ¼ tsp salt

Place ⅓ cup of the sugar in heavy skillet and heat, stirring fre-quently, until amber liquid forms. *Slowly* add the boiling water and stir until caramel dissolves. Remove from heat and cool. Just before

serving, beat yolks until thick and lemon colored, then gradually add
syrup, remaining sugar, milk and salt and beat well. Serve at once. 4 to 5
servings.

EGGNOG NO. 1

2 eggs	1 tbsp rum extract
¼ cup sugar	½ cup whipping cream
Dash of salt	Freshly grated nutmeg
2 cups milk	

Beat eggs, sugar and salt in top of a double boiler. Add milk and
mix well. Cook over hot water with frequent stirring until mixture
barely coats a metal spoon. Chill. Stir in extract. Fold in stiffly beaten
whipped cream. Pour immediately into glasses, and add a dash of nutmeg. 5 to 6 servings.

EGGNOG NO. 2

4 egg yolks*	1½ tsp vanilla
¼ cup sugar	¼ tsp salt
3 cups milk, chilled	Freshly grated nutmeg
1 cup thin cream, chilled	

Beat egg yolks until very thick and light in color. Add sugar, beating
in thoroughly. Stir in milk, cream, vanilla and salt. Serve immediately in
glasses with a dash of nutmeg. 4 to 5 servings.

LEMON EGGNOG

4 egg yolks	¼ tsp grated lemon rind, pkd
½ cup sugar	½ cup whipping cream
½ cup lemon juice, 3 medium	3 cups chilled milk
¼ tsp salt	Nutmeg *or* cinnamon

Beat egg yolks until thick, add sugar, lemon juice, salt, rind and
again beat until thick and light in color. Whip cream and fold into
lemon mixture. Pour into tall glasses. Add milk to almost fill glasses.
Stir well. Add a dash of nutmeg or cinnamon. Serve at once. 4 servings.

PINEAPPLE EGG PUNCH

2 eggs	1 cup chilled crushed
½ cup sugar	pineapple
⅛ tsp salt	½ cup whipping cream
1 qt chilled milk	

* Uses for leftover egg whites will be found on p 659. Reasons for not using
raw, pp 658–9.

Beat eggs until thick and light-colored with sugar and salt. In top of double boiler scald 1 cup of the milk and stir well into the egg mixture. Return to double boiler and stir and cook 2 min longer. Chill. Just before serving, stir in rest of milk and pineapple. Beat cream until stiff, then stir in pineapple mixture until foamy. Pour into tall glasses. Serve at once. 4 to 5 servings.

TEA

Like coffee, tea is aromatic and loses flavor and fragrance rapidly when exposed to air. Therefore, store it in tightly covered container. High-grade tea is the small or medium-sized tender leaves free of stems and dust. Inferior tea selling at a lower price is often poor economy, since even the use of a larger amount will not produce a good flavor. Instant tea makes a good hot or iced beverage. If blended with sugar before adding hot or cold water it dissolves readily.

A glass, china or pottery teapot should always be used for brewing tea. A metal pot imparts some of its own flavor. Two pots may be used or the tea may be brewed in a tightly covered enamel saucepan and strained off into a heated pot for serving. Or place tea ball or tea bag into the pot and pour the boiling water over it. When tea steeps the required time, lift out the ball or bag. Tea made in a cup using a tea ball, bag or strainer is not considered by connoisseurs to have as good flavor or aroma as that brewed by the standard method, though the use of a bag is convenient.

HOT TEA

Choose a good grade of tea of the variety your family prefers. Allow ½ tsp tea for each cup to be brewed. Place in a clean, scalded china pottery or glass teapot. Pour over it the required amount of water that has just reached a vigorous boiling point, cover pot, and let stand 2 to 5 min, or until of desired strength. Serve at once by pouring through a strainer into hot cups. If tea must stand after steeping, strain into a clean pot rinsed in hot water. Serve plain, or with lemon and sugar or cream and sugar. When a number of people are to be served, it is a good plan to provide a pot of hot water for guests to dilute tea to suit their taste.

Note: The strength of tea is determined by the amount of tea used and the length of time it steeps. One-half tsp of tea makes a cup of very strong tea.

ICED TEA

Prepare a strong hot tea as directed above, but use 1 tbsp tea to each cup of boiling water. Pour the freshly made tea through a strainer directly over ice cubes or cracked ice in tall glasses or a pitcher. It is best to make hot tea very strong since it may be diluted easily by adding ice water. If it is too weak it can't be made stronger without brewing more hot tea. Use instant tea also for making iced tea. Serve with lemon or lime wedges or half a calamondin, sugar and a sprig of mint if desired.

OTHER TYPES OF TEA

CAMBRIC TEA

Pacifying and harmless

1 tbsp cream	Dash of salt
1 tsp sugar	1 cup boiling water

Measure cream, sugar and salt into hot cup. Add water. Serve hot. This is a soothing beverage when weary, cold or feeling slightly indisposed. 1 cup.

CAMOMILE TEA

Tea for the jitters

1 cup boiling water	Sugar, about 1 tsp
2 tsp camomile flowers	

Pour water over camomile. Cover tightly and steep 3 min. Strain into hot cup and serve with sugar. 1 cup.

GINGER TEA

An old-timer for colds, cramps, etc.

2 ginger roots, ½″ long by ¼″ wide *or* ½ to ¾ tsp ground ginger	1 cup boiling water Dash of salt Sugar, about 1 tsp

Crush the roots, placed between folds of waxed paper, with a mallet or hammer and put into an enamelware saucepan or teapot. Add water, cover tightly and steep 3 min. Strain into hot cup. Serve hot with sugar to taste. 1 cup.

HOT TEA PUNCH

1 cup strong freshly brewed tea	¾ cup orange juice ¼ cup sugar
¾ cup pineapple juice 2 cups water	Slightly crushed mint

Combine first 5 ingredients and heat slowly, stirring until sugar dissolves. When steaming hot, serve with garnish of crushed mint. 4 servings.

MINT TEA

A pungent warming tea

¼ cup crushed mint leaves
4 cups boiling water

Sugar—about 1 tsp per cup

Put mint into an enamelware saucepan or teapot. Add freshly boiling water, cover tightly and steep 3 min. Strain into cups and garnish with a sprig of fresh mint. Serve with sugar to taste. 4 servings.

RUSSIAN TEA

1 4" stick cinnamon
1½ tsp whole cloves
¼ cup honey
1 cup water
⅔ cup orange juice

¼ cup lemon juice
2 tbsp black tea
6 cups boiling water
1 seedless orange

Simmer spices, honey and the 1 cup water 10 min, then let stand 1 hr. Strain. Add grated rind of 1 orange and 1 lemon, if desired. Squeeze fruit juices. Steep tea in boiling water 1 min. Strain. Add fruit juice and spice mixture to strained tea. Reheat and serve hot. Garnish with thin, crosswise orange slices. 10 servings.

SASSAFRAS TEA

An old-time spring tonic—fragrant, colorful, flavorful

4 pieces sassafras bark, each
    4" x 2"
5 cups boiling water

Sugar, about 1 tsp per cup
Cream, if desired

Use the rosy outer bark from the sassafras roots to make the tea. The bark can be purchased in grocery and drug stores in the early spring. Place washed bark in a clean enamelware saucepan or teapot and pour boiling water over it. Cover tightly and let stand in a warm place to steep 4 or 5 min, or to the desired strength and color. Strain tea into hot cups or into a hot china or pottery teapot. Serve with sugar and cream. 5 servings.

Note: Bark reboiled 2 or 3 times makes good tea.

Breads

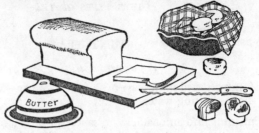

There's nothing like a hot bread to add sparkle to an otherwise ordinary meal. And homemade yeast bread is more popular than ever. Both are easy to make and fun! It's a real thrill to see crusty, golden brown rolls and loaves as good as Grandma's come out of your very own oven. Perhaps that is why more and more women, in cities as well as in rural areas, are serving more homemade breads. Whether made with whole wheat or enriched white flour, breads add much to the family nutrition because they are eaten regularly and in such generous quantities. Read this chapter carefully to get new slants on the "staff of life."

BREADS are of 2 distinct types: (1) *quick breads,* leavened with baking powder or soda. (2) *yeast breads,* leavened with yeast.

Since quick breads are baked immediately after mixing, they can be made on the spur of the moment. Yeast breads require time for rising and shaping, so must be started a few hours before the meal. Yeast breads stay fresh longer than quick breads, so it is practical to bake 2 or 3 days' supply at one time.

QUICK BREADS

Quick breads are popular for breakfast because they can be mixed while the family assembles, and baked while the breakfast fruit is eaten. These breads are also favorites for luncheon and dinner—biscuits, muffins and popovers especially—are right at home in any meal.

The quick bread group also includes griddle cakes, waffles, corn bread, nut and fruit bread, and doughnuts made with baking powder or soda.

The techniques for making quick breads are simple but exacting. Once you learn to make tender, flaky biscuits, light, even-textured muffins and spongy, golden-brown pancakes, it is easier to make them right than wrong.

YEAST BREADS

Homemade bread, the kind Grandmother made to perfume the house once or twice every week in the good old days, is fun to make and so satisfying it is well worth the extra time and attention the dough demands.

Essentials for good bread are fresh dry granular yeast or moist compressed yeast, a good hard wheat or all-purpose flour, salt, liquid, sugar and usually fat. Soft wheat flours also make good breads but a special technique and a different recipe are needed. Butter as the shortening and milk or part milk as the liquid add to flavor and food value. Whole wheat or part whole wheat bread is as easy to make as white bread, and the homemade whole wheat loaf is so good it will help to teach your family to like whole grain breads.

ENRICHED FLOUR, CORN MEAL AND BREAD

Since the average person daily consumes considerable amounts of bread and other bakery products, it is important for breads to carry a good share of the vitamins and minerals necessary for health. In the process of refining flours, meals and cereals, the grains are stripped of the outer coating and the germ which contain almost all the vitamins and minerals.

The enrichment program which was started in 1941 "has played a significant role in the practical elimination of the evidence of vitamin deficiency diseases caused by a lack of the specific nutrients: ariboflavinosis, beriberi and pellagra. Iron was added to help combat the widespread public health problem of simple iron deficiency."* Besides flour, bakery goods, macaroni products, rice and corn meal may be enriched. Today enrichment is required in 30 states and Puerto Rico. But in actual practice, all family flours are enriched as well as about 90 per cent of all commercially baked standard white bread.

TABLE 20   COMPARISON OF NUTRIENTS IN WHEAT FLOUR
AND WHEAT BREAD

Minimum and maximum enrichment levels for the three B vitamins—thiamine, niacin and riboflavin—and iron are given in the table below

One Pound	Protein (grams)	Fat (milligrams)	Calcium (milligrams)	Iron (milligrams)	Thiamine (milligrams)	Riboflavin (milligrams)	Niacin (milligrams)
FLOUR Unenriched (all purpose)	47.6	4.5	73	3.6	.28	.21	4.1
Enriched (all purpose)	47.6	4.5	73	13.-16.5	2.-2.5	1.2-1.5	16.-20.
Whole Wheat	60.3	9.1	186	15.0	2.49	.54	19.7
BREAD Unenriched (white) (3 to 4% nonfat dry milk)	39.5	14.5	381	3.2	.31	.39	5.0
Enriched (white) (3 to 4% nonfat dry milk)	39.5	14.5	381	8.-12.5	1.1-1.8	.7-1.6	10.0-15.0
Whole Wheat (2% nonfat dry milk)	47.6	13.6	449	10.4	1.17	.56	12.9

Sources: Composition of Foods, U. S. Department of Agriculture, Handbook No. 8, Washington, D. C., Revised, December 1963. Definitions and Standards, Part 15, *Cereal Flours and Related Products;* Part 17, *Bakery Products,* Food and Drug Administration, U. S. Department of Health, Education and Welfare.

* From Wheat to Flour. Wheat Flour Institute. 1966.

A food is called *restored* when the same kind and amount of vitamins and minerals taken out of it in the manufacturing process are replaced. A food is called *enriched* when vitamins and minerals not naturally found in the food are added, such as vitamin D, or when natural nutrients are added in larger amounts than the food originally contained, such as vitamin D in milk.

It is the duty of food shoppers to read the labels on flour, meal, bread and breakfast foods and to choose only whole grain, enriched or restored.

QUICK BREADS—BISCUITS

The secret of making good biscuits is a soft but well mixed dough. Such dough is obtained—(1) By accurate measurement of ingredients. (2) By speedy but thorough mixing. A soft dough makes the lightest, tenderest biscuits. Thorough blending contributes to fine, even texture. A few quick kneading motions of a well mixed dough produce flakiness in biscuits.

A baked biscuit should be twice the volume of the raw dough and symmetrical in shape with straight sides and a level top. The crust should be fairly smooth, fragile in appearance, free from specks, tender, crisp and golden brown. The inside should be creamy white, fluffy and flaky, never dry, with a pleasing bland taste, with no trace of baking powder or soda flavor.

BISCUIT MIX

8 cups all-purpose flour	2 tsp salt
3½ tbsp D.A. baking powder	1⅓ cups shortening

Sift flour, measure, resift 3 times with next 2 ingredients, the last time into a 4-qt mixing bowl. Add shortening and with pastry blender, cut it into flour until mixture is a coarse crumbly mass. Put in container with tight fitting cover and store in refrigerator. Keeps a few weeks. *To make biscuits:* Stir ½ cup plus 2 tbsp milk well into 2 cups of mix. Turn out onto floured pastry cloth, knead half a min. Pat or roll out and cut with biscuit cutter dipped in flour. Bake in a 450° F oven about 15 min. Makes 10 to 12 2-inch biscuits.

BAKING POWDER BISCUITS

2 cups all-purpose flour	½ tsp salt
3 tsp D.A. baking powder *or*	⅓ cup shortening
3¾ tsp tartrate *or* phos-	⅞ cup milk (1 cup less 2
phate type	tbsp)

Step 1. Measure all ingredients accurately. Never skimp on shortening as it is essential for tenderness. Start oven 10 min before baking; set to hot (450° F to 500° F).

Step 2. Sift flour, measure, resift 3 times with dry ingredients, the last time into a 3-qt mixing bowl. Three siftings prevent yellow specks on crust caused by incomplete blending of baking powder.

Step 3. Cut shortening into dry ingredients with a pastry blender or 2 knives until particles are size of rice.

Step 4. Make a "well" in the dry ingredients and pour milk in all at once. Stir quickly and vigorously with a dinner fork. (Fork mixes more lightly than a spoon.) When dry ingredients are almost dampened, if dough seems a little stiff, quickly add another tbsp or so of milk to obtain a soft dough. The dough appears sticky the instant enough liquid is thoroughly stirred into dry ingredients but it soon stiffens up. Unless dough is soft at end of mixing, biscuits will not be delicate.

Step 5. Turn dough out immediately onto a lightly floured pastry cloth, dough board or table. An amateur can knead, roll and cut out the soft dough more easily on a pastry cloth than on a board.

Step 6. Knead quickly 6 to 8 times, then pat out lightly with floured palm of hand or roll out ½- to ¾-inch thick.

Step 7. Cut out biscuits to get as many as possible from the first-rolled dough, then place them on a greased, shallow baking pan. For biscuits crusty-all-around, place them an inch apart on the pan; for biscuits with only tops and bottoms crusty, place them almost together on pan. Lay trimmings on top of each other without kneading, and again pat out with hand to same thickness, then cut out. Lightly press remaining trimmings into biscuit-shape and place on baking pan.

Step 8. For a richer color and more tender crust, brush tops of biscuits (use pastry brush) with cream or melted butter. If biscuits must stand a few minutes before baking, put in a cool place.

Step 9. Place biscuits in heated oven. Bake 12 to 15 min. Plan your meal so you will be ready to serve biscuits the instant they come from the oven. Only blistering hot biscuits are worth serving.

Step 10. Don't wrap biscuits in a napkin to serve. The napkin holds in the steam which softens the crisp crust you have striven to achieve. Serve on a hot plate, uncovered, or directly from the baking pan. Loosen oven-hot biscuits from pan; you will find most guests delighted to help themselves to the hot biscuits right from the pan. 12 to 15 two-inch biscuits.

REHEATING BISCUITS

To successfully reheat biscuits, place on baking pan close together. Sprinkle lightly with water. Place in a moderately hot oven (425° F) and bake 10 to 12 min, or until crusty and piping hot all the way through.

Note: To save in cleaning up after biscuits, turn dough onto lightly floured waxed paper. Pat dough out and cut as above. Discard waxed paper. Biscuit dough can be cut in various shapes and used to top meat pies, casserole dishes, etc.

BUTTERMILK BISCUITS

2 cups all-purpose flour
2¼ tsp D.A. baking powder *or*
   2¾ tsp tartrate *or* phosphate type

¼ tsp soda
1 tsp salt
⅓ cup plus 2 tsp shortening
¾ cup thick buttermilk

Sift flour, measure, resift 3 times with next 3 ingredients, the third time into mixing bowl. Cut in shortening with a pastry blender or 2 knives. Add buttermilk all at once, then with a fork stir briskly to thoroughly mix. Turn onto lightly floured board, pastry cloth or wax paper; knead 8 or 10 times. Roll or pat from ½ to ¾-inch thick. Cut with floured cutter, place on greased shallow pan. Brush tops with cream or milk, opt. Bake in hot oven (450° to 500° F) 10 to 15 min. Serve piping hot. About 18 biscuits 2¼-inches in diameter.

CHEESE BISCUITS

Cheesy on top and in the middle

1½ cups all-purpose flour
2¼ tsp D.A. baking powder *or*
   3 tsp tartrate *or* phosphate
   type
½ tsp salt

¼ cup shortening
½ cup milk
¼ cup grated sharp cheese,
   packed and blended with
2 tbsp butter

Sift flour, measure, resift 3 times with baking powder and salt. Cut in shortening with pastry blender or 2 knives until particles are size of rice. Add milk all at once, stir quickly with a fork until dough stiffens. Turn out on lightly floured board or pastry cloth. Quickly knead 8 to 10 times. Roll out ¼-inch thick and cut in 1½-inch rounds. Spread half the biscuits with ⅔ of cheese mixture. Top with rest of biscuits and spread with remainder of cheese. Transfer to greased baking sheet. Bake in a hot oven (450° F) 12 min or until biscuits are golden brown. Serve piping hot. 15 to 18 biscuits.

DROP BISCUITS

2 cups all-purpose flour
3 tsp D.A. baking powder *or*
   3¾ tsp tartrate *or* phosphate type

¾ tsp salt
⅓ cup *plus* 1 tbsp shortening
1 cup *plus* 2 tbsp milk

Sift flour, measure and resift 3 times with baking powder and salt. Cut in shortening with pastry blender until particles are size of rice. Make a "well" and add milk all at once; stir only until just well mixed.

Drop by heaping tbsp 1½ inches apart onto greased baking sheet, shallow pan or into muffin pans. Bake in a hot oven (450° to 500° F) about 15 min or until brown and crusty. Serve hot. 10 to 12 biscuits.

WHOLE WHEAT BISCUITS

Crunchy, chewy with a nut-like flavor

2 cups whole wheat flour	½ tsp salt
2½ tsp D.A. baking powder *or*	⅓ cup shortening
3 tsp tartrate *or* phosphate	1 cup milk
type	

Grease a baking sheet 14 x 10 inches or a shallow pan. Spoon flour into cup to measure, then sift 3 times with baking powder and salt, the last time into a 3-qt mixing bowl; turn bran left in sifter into mixture. Cut in shortening with pastry blender until particles are size of small peas. Make "well" in center, add milk all at once and stir until just mixed. Turn out onto lightly floured board or pastry cloth—do not knead. Roll into a rectangle about ½-inch thick. Cut into 2-inch sqs and place on prepared pan. Bake in hot oven (450° F) 12 to 15 min or until nicely browned. Serve hot. 4 to 5 servings.

BUTTERSCOTCH PINWHEELS

Rich but palate-tickling

Have ready muffin pan with 9 large cups. Measure ¼ cup butter, ½ cup water and ¾ cup brown sugar, packed, into 1-qt saucepan. Heat to boiling and boil 2 min. Then pour syrup into muffin cups and distribute ½ cup walnuts in the syrup. Make 1 recipe Baking Powder Biscuits. Roll dough into a rectangle about 14 x 9 inches. Sprinkle with a mixture of ¼ cup sugar and ½ tsp cinnamon. Roll up like jelly roll starting at narrow end. Cut roll into 1-inch thick slices. Place cut-side down in muffin cups. Bake in hot oven (450° F) 20 to 25 min or until golden brown. Let stand for a min or two, then turn out upside-down onto plate, holding pan inverted a minute for syrup to drain onto biscuits. Serve hot. 9 Pinwheels.

ORANGE PINWHEEL BISCUITS

Real yummy

2 tbsp butter	1 recipe Baking Powder
½ cup orange juice	Biscuits, p 234
½ cup sugar	2 tbsp sugar mixed with ½
1 tsp grated orange rind, pkd	tsp cinnamon

Have ready a baking pan measuring 6 x 10 x 2 inches. Combine first 4 ingredients in saucepan. Heat until butter just melts and mixture is well blended. Pour into baking pan. Mix dough and roll into a 9 x 15 inch rectangle. Sprinkle with sugar-cinnamon mixture. Roll up like jelly roll starting at wide end. Cut into inch-thick slices and lay cut-side down in the syrup. Bake in moderately hot oven (425° F) 20 to 25 min or until golden brown. 15 Pinwheels.

SCONES

A favorite Scotch hot bread

1¾ cups all-purpose flour	½ cup dried currants, washed
3 tsp D.A. baking powder *or*	¼ cup sliced candied cherries
3¾ tsp tartrate *or* phos-	½ cup milk
phate type	1 egg yolk beaten with
1 tsp salt	1 tbsp cream
¼ cup sugar	2 tbsp sugar
¼ cup shortening	½ tsp cinnamon

Sift flour, measure, resift 3 times with baking powder, salt and ¼ cup sugar. Cut shortening into dry ingredients with pastry blender or 2 knives until mixture resembles coarse corn meal. Stir in currants and cherries. Add milk all at once, stir quickly with a fork. Divide dough into 6 equal portions. Knead each portion *very* quickly on a lightly floured board or pastry cloth and pat out into rounds ¼-inch thick and 5 inches in diameter. Place on greased baking sheet. Mark each round with a knife into 4 pie-shaped sections. Brush tops with yolk and cream mixture. Sprinkle with the 2 tbsp sugar mixed with cinnamon. Bake in a hot oven (450° F) 15 min. Serve hot. 6 to 8 servings.

APPLE COFFEE CAKE—STREUSEL TOPPING

Combination coffee cake and pie

1½ cups all-purpose flour	½ cup milk
2¼ tsp D.A. baking powder *or*	¼ cup melted shortening
3 tsp tartrate *or* phosphate	1½ cups chopped tart apples
type	*Streusel Topping:*
½ cup sugar	¼ cup sugar
½ tsp salt	2 tbsp flour
½ tsp cinnamon	½ tsp cinnamon
1 egg	1 tbsp soft butter

Sift flour, measure, resift 3 times with next 4 ingredients. Beat egg, add milk and melted shortening, and pour all at once into dry ingredients; then add apples and mix well. Turn into a well-greased 8-inch sq baking pan. Blend first 3 ingredients for Streusel Topping.

Work in butter to make a crumbly mixture and sprinkle over batter. Bake in a moderately hot oven (400° F) 30 min or until both cake and apples test done. 5 servings.

PLUM KUCHEN

A plumb good coffee cake

1 cup all-purpose flour	⅓ cup milk
2 tsp D.A. baking powder *or*	1 lb Italian blue plums,
2½ tsp tartrate *or* phos-	halved, pitted
phate type	Dash of salt
½ tsp salt	2 tbsp chopped nuts
1 tbsp sugar	¼ cup sugar
3 tbsp shortening	1 tbsp butter

Sift flour, measure, resift 3 times with baking powder, salt and sugar, the last time into a 3-qt mixing bowl. Cut in shortening with a pastry blender or 2 knives until particles are size of rice. Add milk all at once, stir quickly only enough to dampen the dry ingredients. Spread dough in a greased 8-inch layer cake pan. Arrange plums over top, cut-side-up. Blend salt, nuts and sugar and sprinkle over top. Dot with butter. Bake in a moderately hot oven (400° F) 20 to 25 min. Serve warm. 6 servings.

Also good made with sour red plums, but more sugar is needed.

SALLY LUNN

A fluffy cake-like bread

1 cup all-purpose flour	2 tbsp soft butter
2 tbsp D.A. baking powder *or*	3 tbsp sugar
2½ tsp tartrate *or* phos-	1 egg, separated
phate type	½ cup milk
½ tsp salt	½ cup cubed cranberry jelly

Sift flour, measure, resift 3 times with baking powder and salt. Cream butter, add sugar, creaming thoroughly. Add egg yolk and beat until smooth and fluffy. Add flour mixture and milk alternately in 3 portions, beginning and ending with flour and beating well after each. Fold in stiffly beaten egg white. Pour into greased 8-inch sq pan. Bake in a moderately hot oven (400° F) 5 min, then sprinkle cranberry cubes over top of batter and continue baking another 15 or 20 min or until golden brown. Serve warm like coffee cake or muffins with butter. 4 to 5 servings.

CORN BREAD

Corn bread made in different parts of the country has different characteristics because of the variations in ingredients and the methods of baking. People of the South like it made with 100 per cent white corn meal, but as we move farther north, the tendency is to use yellow corn meal and mix it with a good proportion of white flour. Whichever type is made, most people like corn bread with a crisp, crunchy brown crust. This crust is obtained by using a heavy iron or cast aluminum pan (a heavy skillet is perfect). It should be sizzling hot before greasing and pouring in the batter. This starts batter baking immediately and develops the desired crustiness. Or corn bread may be baked in a square, greased aluminum pan if desired. Baking should be done in a hot oven. Corn bread should be served piping hot with plenty of butter.

BUTTERMILK CORN BREAD

1½ cups yellow corn meal	2 eggs, separated
1 tsp salt	1⅓ cups buttermilk
¾ tsp soda	2 tbsp melted shortening

Spoon corn meal lightly into measuring cup and level off. Mix well with salt and soda. Beat egg yolks thoroughly, add buttermilk and beat until well mixed. Add to first mixture and stir until ingredients are blended. Add hot melted shortening, beat again; fold in stiffly beaten egg whites. Turn immediately into a greased piping hot 10-inch heavy skillet, or into a greased 9-inch square pan. Bake in a hot oven, 475° F., 15 to 20 min or until brown and crusty. Serve at once. 5 servings.

Note: For Corn Sticks, bake in greased heated stick pan 12 min. 14 corn sticks.

SWEET MILK CORN BREAD

1 cup yellow corn meal	2 tsp sugar, optional
½ cup all-purpose flour	1 cup milk
1 tsp salt	1 egg
1½ tsp D.A. baking powder *or* 2 tsp tartrate *or* phosphate type	2½ tbsp hot bacon fat *or* shortening

Grease bottom of a 9-inch square pan or heat a 10-inch heavy skillet while mixing batter. Spoon corn meal lightly into measuring cup and level off. Transfer with next four ingredients to mixing bowl and mix well. Combine milk, beaten egg, and melted fat and add all at once to dry ingredients. Mix only enough to moisten. Transfer to greased pan (hot, if skillet is used) and bake in very hot oven, 475° F, for 15 to 20 min or until golden brown. Serve piping hot. 4 to 5 servings.

BACON CORN MEAL MUFFINS

Use muffin pan with 10 to 12 large cups. Criss-cross 2 short strips of half-cooked bacon in each cup. Pour in Sour Cream Corn Bread batter, or Buttermilk Corn Bread batter, to fill muffin cups ⅔ full. Bake in hot oven (450° F) 25 to 30 min or until brown and crusty. Serve hot.

CORN STICKS OR MUFFINS

Any corn bread recipe can be used and baked in corn stick pans or muffin pans to make Corn Sticks or Muffins. Some recipes are better adapted than others, such as the Buttermilk Corn Bread, Sour Cream Corn Bread and Southern Corn Bread, because the egg whites are beaten and added separately, producing a lighter bread. Spoon the batter into greased, hot corn stick pans or muffin pans, filling about ⅔ full. Bake in a hot oven (475° F) 12 to 15 min or until golden brown. Remove from pans immediately and serve at once. 10 to 12 medium muffins.

CRACKLIN' CORN BREAD

1 cup yellow corn meal	1 tsp salt
½ cup all-purpose flour	2 tsp sugar
1½ tsp D.A. baking powder *or*	1 cup buttermilk
2 tsp tartrate *or* phosphate	1 egg
type	½ cup pea-size cracklings
¼ tsp soda	1 tbsp bacon fat

Heat a heavy 10-inch skillet with oven-proof handle in oven 5 to 10 min. While skillet heats, spoon corn meal lightly into measuring cup; level off. Sift flour, measure and resift into mixing bowl with next 4 ingredients. Add corn meal and mix well. Add buttermilk, egg and cracklings and beat hard until well mixed. Remove skillet from oven, add bacon fat and tilt back and forth to coat inside. Pour batter into hot skillet. Bake in hot oven (475° F) 25 to 30 min. Serve very hot. 4 to 5 servings.

SOUR CREAM CORN BREAD

⅔ cup yellow corn meal	1 tsp salt
⅔ cup all-purpose flour	2 tbsp sugar
2 tsp D.A. baking powder *or*	1 egg, separated
2½ tsp tartrate *or* phos-	1 cup soured cream
phate type	3 tbsp shortening
¼ tsp soda	

Heat a 10-inch heavy skillet in the oven 5 to 10 min. Meanwhile, spoon corn meal lightly into cup to measure. Sift flour, measure, and resift with next 4 ingredients into mixing bowl. Add corn meal and mix well. Combine egg yolk and sour cream and beat well. Add to dry ingredients and beat until thoroughly mixed. Now melt shortening in hot skillet, pour into batter and beat well. Beat egg white until stiff but not dry, fold it into batter. Pour batter at once into skillet or a greased 8- or 9-inch square pan. Bake in a hot oven (475° F) 25 to 30 min. Serve very hot. 4 to 5 servings.

SOUTHERN CORN BREAD

1½ cups white corn meal	1⅓ cups buttermilk
¾ tsp soda	2 eggs, separated
1 tsp salt	¼ cup melted shortening

Heat a 10-inch heavy skillet in oven 5 to 10 min. Spoon corn meal lightly into measuring cup, then level off. Add soda and mix well. Add buttermilk to well-beaten egg yolks, add to corn meal mixture and stir just enough to moisten. Add hot melted shortening and beat well. Fold in stiffly beaten egg whites. Turn immediately into the greased hot skillet or a greased 8- or 9-inch square pan. Bake in a hot oven (475° F) 20 to 25 min. Serve very hot with butter. 5 servings.

CRUNCHY FRIED CORN CAKES

Welcome any time, and extra good with a vegetable plate

1½ cups yellow corn meal	1½ cups boiling water
¾ tsp salt	Shortening for frying

Measure meal into mixing bowl, add salt. Pour boiling water in gradually and beat as you add to make a smooth batter stiff enough to shape. Mold neatly into flat oval cakes. Heat ⅓ cup shortening in a 10-inch iron skillet until sizzling but not smoking hot. Lay cakes in and fry moderately fast, until under side is a rich golden brown, 3 to 4 min; don't turn cakes until this rich color develops. Then brown on other side. Serve with butter. 8 cakes.

HUSH PUPPIES

A deep-fat fried Corn Bread that is excellent with fish and a "must" at Southern fish fries

1¾ cups white corn meal	2 tbsp grated onion
⅓ cup all-purpose flour	1 egg
3 tsp D.A. baking powder *or*	½ cup *plus* 1 tbsp buttermilk
3¾ asp tartrate *or* phos-	½ cup tomato juice
phate type	Shortening for frying
1 tsp salt	

Fluff up corn meal by stirring with spoon. To measure, spoon meal into cup, level off. Sift flour, measure, add it with baking powder and salt to meal. Stir thoroughly to mix. Add onion, more or less. Beat egg, stir in buttermilk and tomato juice. Turn liquid into dry ingredients and beat until well blended. Mixture should be a drop batter. Have enough shortening melted in frying kettle or deep skillet to make it 2½ inches deep. Heat to 380° F. To drop batter into hot fat, dip tsp first into hot fat, then into batter. Fry 6 to 8 hush puppies at a time. Fry to rich brown on underside, flip over with fork. When brown and done all way through, lift out with fork onto paper toweling to drain. Cover with sheet of paper toweling until all batter is fried. Serve very hot. 4 to 5 servings.

SPOON BREAD

2¼ cups milk
2 tbsp butter
1 tsp salt

⅔ cup yellow corn meal
3 eggs, separated

Heat milk to scalding; add butter and salt and slowly stir in corn meal. Boil gently for 1 min, stirring constantly. Remove from heat and cool 5 min, then stir into well-beaten egg yolks. Fold in stiffly beaten egg whites and pour into a greased 5-cup casserole. Bake in a moderate oven (375° F) 35 to 40 min. Serve spooned from baking dish with butter. 5 servings.

SPOON BREAD WITH CHEESE

½ cup yellow corn meal
½ tsp salt
¼ tsp dry mustard
Dash of cayenne

1½ cups milk
¾ cup grated American
cheese, pkd
3 eggs, separated

Spoon corn meal lightly into measuring cup, then sift with next 3 ingredients. Add to cold milk measured into a saucepan and stir until smooth, then cook over direct heat until thickened, stirring constantly. Add cheese and remove from heat. Stir until cheese melts. Cool slightly and beat some of the hot mixture into beaten yolks, then return yolk mixture to saucepan and stir well. Remove from heat, cool until luke-warm. Then beat cooled mixture thoroughly and fold in the stiffly beaten egg whites lightly but thoroughly. Pour into well-greased 5-cup glass casserole and bake 35 min in a moderate oven (375° F). Serve hot from baking dish with plenty of butter. 4 servings.

DUMPLINGS—STEAMED OR BOILED

DROP DUMPLINGS

For poultry or meat stews

1½ cups all-purpose flour	½ tsp salt
3½ tsp D.A. baking powder *or*	¾ cup milk
4½ tsp tartrate *or* phosphate type	Chopped parsley

Sift flour, measure, resift 3 times with baking powder and salt, the 3rd time into mixing bowl. Add milk all at once and stir rapidly with a fork until well blended. If desired, stir in about 1 tsp finely chopped parsley. There must be at least 3 cups of boiling liquid to have enough gravy left after cooking dumplings. Drop batter by tsp on top of stewed chicken, beef or lamb stew. Dipping spoon into the hot broth each time before dipping into batter prevents batter from sticking to spoon. As soon as dumplings are all in, cover and boil moderately fast for 12 min without uncovering. Then remove dumplings to a hot platter, arranging them around the outside and the stew in the center. 5 servings.

EGG DROP DUMPLINGS

For chicken or meat stews

1¼ cups all-purpose flour	½ tsp salt
2¾ tsp D.A. baking powder *or*	½ cup milk
3½ tsp tartrate *or* phosphate type	1 egg, slightly beaten

Sift flour, measure, resift 3 times with the baking powder and salt, the last time into a 2-qt mixing bowl. Stir milk into beaten egg and add all at once to flour mixture. Mix lightly with a fork until ingredients are just dampened, but not smooth. Drop by tbsp onto boiling stew. Cover and let boil 12 min without uncovering. Serve immediately. 4 to 6 servings.

MARROW BALL DUMPLINGS

Marrow ball dumplings are best when served in vegetable soup with a beef stock base or in chicken soup

⅓ cup raw marrow, 3 oz	¼ tsp paprika
2 tsp fine-cut parsley	20 soda crackers, rolled fine,
2 eggs, unbeaten	1 cup
½ tsp salt	

Scoop marrow from beef shank bone and press through a coarse sieve. Add remaining ingredients in order given and beat until thoroughly blended. Let stand 2 min to stiffen slightly for easier handling. Shape level tbsp of mixture into balls with hands. Drop into boiling soup, cover and boil gently 5 min. Serve at once in soup. 4 to 5 servings.

POTATO DUMPLINGS

For meat stews, roast pork or Sauerkraut

1 lb potatoes, 3 to 4 medium
1 egg
½ cup all-purpose flour
  Dash of nutmeg
¾ tsp salt

¼ tsp D.A. baking powder *or*
⅓ tsp tartrate *or* phosphate
  type
2 tbsp melted butter

Pare potatoes, add enough water to cover, then cover pan and boil until done. Drain well, rice potatoes into a 2-qt mixing bowl and cool slightly. Drop egg into potatoes, beat well and add next 4 ingredients which have been sifted together. Beat thoroughly. Shape into roll about 1-inch in diameter and cut into 1-inch lengths. Drop pieces into boiling salted water, stirring gently for a min to keep them from sticking to bottom of pan. Dumplings will then rise to top. Cook uncovered 8 to 10 min. Drain dumplings and pour butter over them to keep from sticking together. Serve immediately with meat stew or roast with gravy. Or cook dumplings on top of sauerkraut in a covered pan. Serve with the kraut. 4 servings.

ROLLED BUTTERMILK DUMPLINGS

The kind mamma made for chicken and squirrel stew

1 cup all-purpose flour
1½ tsp D.A. baking powder *or*
  2 tsp tartrate *or* phosphate
  type

¼ tsp baking soda
¼ tsp salt
½ cup buttermilk

Sift flour, measure, resift 3 times with baking powder, soda and salt, the last time into a 2-qt mixing bowl. Add buttermilk and mix lightly with a fork. Turn out on a floured board or pastry cloth. Knead lightly 4 or 5 times and roll or pat out to ¼-inch thickness. Cut into rectangles 1 x 3 inches with a floured knife. Drop onto boiling stew, cover and boil gently 12 min. Do not uncover during cooking. Serve immediately. 12 dumplings or 4 servings.

GRIDDLE CAKES, PANCAKES, FLAPJACKS

GRIDDLE TEMPERATURE

To bake perfect cakes, a griddle must be heated to just the right temp. The skilled cook knows just when the griddle is hot enough; the amateur finds this more difficult. A griddle thermometer is a great help. Contrary to general opinion, the perfect griddle is not smoking hot, but only moderately hot, 300 to 325° F. Lacking a thermometer, the amateur can learn to test the griddle by baking a few small cakes. When the top side is full of bubbles, the bottom side should be baked to a luscious even brown color. If the underside has large white and brown splotches, the griddle is too hot; if the color is an anemic tan, the griddle is not hot enough.

BASIC GRIDDLE CAKES OR PANCAKES

No error in amount of baking powder. These cakes are delicate and delicious

2 cups all-purpose flour	1 tbsp sugar
5 tsp D.A. baking powder *or*	2 eggs
6 tsp tartrate *or* phosphate type	2 cups milk
	⅓ cup melted shortening *or*
1 tsp salt	butter

Sift flour, measure, resift with next 3 ingredients 3 times. Beat eggs in a 3-qt mixing bowl, add milk and mix. Stir in melted shortening; then add flour mixture all at once and beat until perfectly smooth. Have griddle heated only moderately hot, or to a temp of 300 to 325° F on griddle thermometer. Grease griddle *lightly* with unsalted fat. Pour out ¼ cup batter for each cake; bake until top side is full of air bubbles and under side is golden brown, then turn and bake until brown on other side. Turn only once, using a spatula or a pancake turner. Serve at once with butter and hot syrup, honey or sugar, along with sausage or bacon if desired. 25 cakes.

Note: If thinner cakes are desired, add ¼ cup more milk.

BREAD CRUMB GRIDDLE CAKES

1 cup fine dry bread crumbs	2¼ tsp D.A. baking powder *or*
3 tbsp melted butter	3 tsp tartrate *or* phosphate
2 tbsp brown sugar	type
1 tsp cinnamon	½ tsp salt
2 cups milk	3 eggs, separated
1 cup all-purpose flour	

Mix first 4 ingredients in a saucepan and brown slightly stirring frequently. Remove from heat, add half the milk and let stand until milk is absorbed. Sift flour, measure, resift 3 times with baking powder and salt. Beat egg yolks, add remaining cup of milk, then beat in dry ingredients. When smooth, stir in crumb mixture. Then lightly fold in stiffly beaten egg whites. For each cake, pour ¼ cup batter on lightly greased moderately hot griddle (300–325° F). Bake until top side is full of bubbles and under side is golden brown. Then turn and bake until brown on other side. Serve immediately with butter and sugar or hot syrup. 12 to 15 cakes.

BREAKFAST RICE CAKES

3 cups cooked rice, 1 cup raw	1 tsp salt
1 egg	½ tsp nutmeg
¾ cup milk	1 tsp D.A. baking powder *or*
¾ cup all-purpose flour	1¼ tsp tartrate *or* phos-
2 tbsp sugar	phate type

Cook and drain rice, p 433. Beat egg, add milk and cooled rice. Sift flour, measure, resift 3 times with next 4 ingredients. Add to rice mixture and beat well. Pour batter by ¼ cupfuls onto medium hot greased griddle (300–325° F). Bake until golden brown on both sides, turning only once. Serve immediately with butter, syrup or jelly. 16 cakes.

BUTTERMILK GRIDDLE CAKES

1 cup all-purpose flour	¼ tsp soda
½ tsp salt	2 tsp sugar
2 tsp D.A. baking powder *or*	1 egg
2½ tsp tartrate *or* phos-	1 cup thick buttermilk
phate type	¼ cup melted shortening

Sift flour, measure, resift twice with next 4 ingredients, the last time into a 2-qt mixing bowl. Beat egg, stir in milk, add all at once to flour mixture. Beat with egg beater until just smooth, add shortening and beat until well blended. Pour batter by ¼ cupfuls onto ungreased moderately hot griddle (300–325° F). Bake until golden brown on both sides. Serve with butter and syrup. 8 or 9 cakes.

CORN MEAL GRIDDLE CAKES

1½ cups all-purpose flour	1 tsp salt
¾ cup yellow corn meal	2 tbsp sugar
4½ tsp D.A. baking powder *or*	1 egg
5½ tsp tartrate *or* phos-	2 cups milk
phate type	¼ cup melted shortening

Sift flour, measure, resift 3 times with next 4 ingredients, the last time into a 3-qt mixing bowl. Beat egg, add milk and pour all at once into dry ingredients. Beat with rotary beater until smooth. Stir in melted shortening. Bake on a lightly greased, moderately hot griddle (300–325° F) until golden brown on under side and dry-looking on top, then turn and bake until other side browns. Serve immediately with hot syrup. 2 dozen 4-inch cakes.

EVAPORATED MILK GRIDDLE CAKES

1 cup all-purpose flour	2 tsp sugar
1½ tsp D.A. baking powder *or*	¼ cup shortening
2 tsp tartrate *or* phosphate	¼ cup boiling water
type	1 egg, beaten
½ tsp salt	¾ cup evaporated milk

Sift flour, measure, resift 3 times with next 3 ingredients, the last time into a 2-qt mixing bowl. Melt shortening in the boiling water and stir into the beaten egg; add milk, stir, and add all at once to flour mixture. Stir briskly until well mixed. Bake on a moderately hot, slightly greased griddle (300–325° F) until golden brown on both sides. Serve at once with hot syrup. 20—3-inch cakes.

FRENCH PANCAKES

3 eggs, separated	½ cup all-purpose flour
1 tsp sugar	1 tbsp melted butter
½ tsp salt	xxxx sugar
1 cup milk	

Separate eggs and beat yolks until lemon-colored. Add sugar, salt and ½ the milk; beat to mix. Sift flour, measure and stir into yolk mixture. Add remaining milk and beat with rotary beater until smooth. Stir in melted butter. Fold in the stiffly beaten egg whites lightly but thoroughly. Pour ½ cup batter into a heated, lightly greased 8-inch skillet, spread with back of spoon to fill pan. When brown on underside, turn and brown on other side. Spread with jelly and roll. Sprinkle with xxxx sugar, if desired. Serve at once for breakfast, luncheon or as a dessert. Batter is also excellent for regular breakfast-size pancakes. Five 8-inch pancakes.

COMMERCIAL PANCAKE MIXES

In the good commercial pancake mixes the ingredients are so perfectly measured and so scientifically blended it is no trick at all to stir up the batter. It does, however, take careful baking of this batter to produce good cakes. Therefore, the technique of baking must be learned in order to make good cakes. By faithfully following the few simple rules for baking, p 246, one can turn out excellent cakes. After mastering the art of baking cakes from commercial mixes, one should be able to mix and bake homemade pancakes which are even better.

FRUIT AND NUT BREADS

Small wonder fruit and nut breads are so popular; they are flavorful, nutritious, appealing in texture and make most delicious tea and luncheon sandwiches. When a large loaf of any of these breads contains a cup of nuts, little or no shortening is needed, but if nuts are omitted, ¼ to ⅓ cup of shortening should be added, the amount depending on size of loaf.

HOW TO SUCCESSFULLY PREPARE, BAKE AND SLICE FRUIT AND NUT BREADS

1. Assemble all utensils and ingredients and place them at your work space.

2. Prepare fruits and nuts as directed in recipe.

3. Get 2 loaf pans of size stated in recipe. Grease one pan; the other one is used to cover pan containing the batter when it is placed in the oven. Placing a pan over top prevents top of loaf from baking too fast. As long as the top remains soft, the expanding batter pushes up uniformly, making it less likely to crack. *Top pan must be removed after baking 20 min* to give the loaf time to brown attractively on top.

4. Combine ingredients as described in recipe. Turn batter into prepared pan, pushing it well up into corners. Let stand at room temperature 15 to 20 min. Nut and fruit breads are lighter and more uniform in texture if batter stands in pans 15 to 20 min before baking. Batter that stands at room temperature is permeated all thru with gas bubbles released from the leavening agents. When such loaves go into the oven, the difference between the rising on the outside and inside of the loaf is not as great as it is in loaves baked immediately after mixing. Therefore, loaves that stand are less likely to crack on top.

5. Bake at stated temperature. Baking at a higher temperature is liable to scorch fruit and give an "off" flavor. Bake until loaf has developed a rich colored crust and tests done when tried with a cake tester. If not sure of your oven temperature, begin testing for doneness after loaf has baked ¾ of the suggested time.

6. When done, turn loaf out onto cake rack. When cooled thoroughly, wrap in waxed paper and store in bread box.

7. Do not slice until thoroughly cooled. Use a very sharp, straight-edged or scalloped knife (not a saw-tooth) for slicing.

8. Spread with butter or softened cream cheese for sandwiches, and cut in fingers or triangles to make them dainty.

APRICOT NUT BREAD

1 cup dried apricots	1 tsp salt
¾ cup warm water	2 eggs
2½ cups all-purpose flour	¾ cup sugar
4 tsp D.A. baking powder *or*	Milk
5 tsp tartrate *or* phosphate	2 tbsp melted shortening
type	½ cup chopped nuts

Grease a 9 x 5 x 3-inch loaf pan and line neatly with waxed paper. Wash apricots quickly in cold water, then cut in small pieces with scissors, and soak in the warm water 2 hrs. Sift flour, measure, resift 3 times with baking powder and salt. Beat eggs until light, then gradually beat in sugar thoroughly. Drain liquid from apricots, add enough milk to it to make 1 cup and turn into 3-qt mixing bowl. Then stir in egg mixture, the melted shortening and the apricots. Now add the flour and beat well. Stir in nuts. Pour into prepared pan. Let stand 10 min, then cover with another pan of same size and place in moderate oven (350° F). Bake 20 min, then uncover and bake 50 min longer or until loaf tests done with a cake tester. Remove from pan to cake rack to cool before slicing. 1 loaf.

BANANA BREAD

2 cups all-purpose flour	⅓ cup shortening
1½ tsp D.A. baking powder *or*	⅔ cup sugar
2 tsp tartrate *or* phosphate	2 eggs
type	1 cup mashed ripe bananas
½ tsp soda	3 tbsp buttermilk
½ tsp salt	½ cup chopped nuts, opt

Grease a 9 x 5 x 3-inch loaf pan well. Sift flour, measure and resift 3 times with baking powder, soda and salt. Cream shortening and sugar in a 3-qt mixing bowl until smooth and fluffy. Add eggs one at a time and beat well after each addition. Stir in freshly mashed bananas, the buttermilk and nuts. Add flour in 4 portions and beat until smooth after each. Turn into prepared pan and bake like Apricot Nut Bread above. Remove to cake rack to cool before slicing. 1 loaf.

DATE-NUT BREAD

7¼-oz pkg pitted dates	¾ tsp salt
¾ cup boiling water	1 tsp soda
½ cup brown sugar, pkd	1 egg, beaten
¼ cup butter *or* margarine	1 tsp vanilla
1¾ cups all-purpose flour	½ cup walnuts *or* pecans

Grease an 8 x 4 x 2½-inch loaf pan well. Cut dates into 4 pieces using kitchen scissors and drop into a 3-qt mixing bowl. Add boiling water, brown sugar and butter. Stir thoroughly, let cool. Sift flour, measure, resift 3 times with salt and soda. Stir egg into date mixture, then add flour mixture and vanilla and beat well. Stir in chopped nuts. Turn into prepared pan. Bake like Apricot Nut Bread, about 1¼ hrs. 1 loaf.

NUT BREAD

2½ cups cake flour	½ cup sugar
3 tsp D.A. baking powder *or*	1 egg, well beaten
4 tsp tartrate *or* phosphate	1 cup milk
type	1 cup chopped pecans *or*
½ tsp salt	walnuts

Grease an 8 x 4 x 2½-inch loaf pan well. Sift flour, measure, resift 3 times with next 3 ingredients. Combine egg and milk and add all at once to dry ingredients, stirring quickly until flour is dampened but not smooth. Quickly stir in nuts just to distribute. Turn into prepared pan, pushing dough well into corners. Bake in slow oven (300° F) 20 min, then increase heat to moderate (375° F), bake 25 to 30 min longer or until nicely browned. Remove from pan to cake rack to cool before slicing. 1 loaf.

(To prevent a crack from forming on top, see Point No. 3 in directions for fruit and nut breads, p 249.)

OLD-TIME MOLASSES BREAD

Pleasing flavor and aroma—outstanding with butter and cream cheese

2 cups all-purpose flour	½ cup dark molasses
1 tsp salt	⅓ cup sugar
½ tsp soda	3 tbsp melted butter
¾ tsp D.A. baking powder *or*	1½ tsp grated lemon rind, pkd
1 tsp tartrate *or* phosphate	1 tbsp lemon juice
type	½ cup chopped nuts, optional
1 large egg, beaten	⅔ cup buttermilk

Grease a 9 x 5 x 3-inch loaf pan. Start oven 10 min before baking; set to moderate (350° F). Sift flour, measure, resift 3 times with next 3 ingredients. Combine next 6 ingredients in a 3-qt mixing bowl and beat until well blended. Stir in nuts. Add flour mixture alternately with buttermilk to egg mixture in 3 or 4 portions, beginning and ending with flour and mixing well after each portion. Pour batter into prepared pan. Let stand 15 min, then cover with pan of same size and place in heated oven. Bake 20 min, then remove cover and bake 40 min longer or until loaf tests done. Remove from pan to cake rack to cool. 15 to 20 servings.

ORANGE-NUT BREAD

2¼ cups all-purpose flour
2¼ tsp D.A. baking powder *or*
   3 tsp tartrate *or* phosphate
   type
¼ tsp soda
¾ tsp salt

3 tbsp shortening
¾ cup sugar
1 egg, beaten
¾ cup orange juice
½ cup nuts, chopped

Grease a 9 x 5 x 3-inch loaf pan well. Sift flour, measure, resift 3 times with next 3 ingredients. Cream shortening and sugar well, add egg and beat until smooth and fluffy. Add orange juice and sifted dry ingredients alternately in 3 portions, beating until smooth after each. Fold in nuts. Turn into prepared pan, cover with a second pan. Bake in a moderate oven (350° F) 20 min, then uncover and bake 50 min longer. Remove from pan to cake rack to cool. 1 loaf.

PEANUT BUTTER BREAD WITH BUTTERMILK

1¾ cups all-purpose flour
1 tsp soda
½ tsp salt
1 cup brown sugar, pkd

⅓ cup peanut butter
1 egg, well beaten
1 cup thick buttermilk

Grease an 8 x 4 x 2½-inch loaf pan well. Sift flour, measure and resift 3 times with soda and salt. Blend sugar and peanut butter well; add egg and beat until smooth. Add flour mixture and buttermilk alternately in 3 portions beating until smooth after each. Turn into prepared pan. Bake in a moderate oven (350° F) 1 hr or until browned and bread tests done with a cake tester. Remove from pan to cake rack to cool. 1 loaf.

(To prevent the formation of a crack on top of loaf, see Point No. 3 in directions for fruit and nut breads.)

PRUNE-NUT BREAD

1 cup uncooked prunes
½ cup orange juice
   Hot water
½ tsp grated orange rind
2 cups all-purpose flour
3 tsp D.A. baking powder *or*
   3¾ tsp tartrate *or* phosphate type

½ tsp salt
½ tsp cinnamon
¾ cup sugar
1 tbsp melted shortening
2 eggs, beaten
½ cup nuts, chopped

Grease an 8 x 4 x 2½-inch loaf pan well. Cut prune meat from pits with knife or kitchen scissors. Add enough hot water to orange juice to bake 1 cup and pour over prunes and rind. Let stand 10 min. Sift flour, measure, mix well with next 4 ingredients; resift. Add shortening and eggs to softened prunes, then add flour mixture and beat thoroughly. Stir in nuts. Pour into prepared pan. Bake in a moderate oven (350° F) 1 hr or until loaf tests done. Remove from pan to cake rack to cool. 1 loaf.

(To prevent the formation of a crack on top, see Point No. 3 in directions for fruit and nut breads, p 249.)

BOSTON BROWN BREAD

1 cup corn meal	1 tsp salt
1 cup whole rye flour	¾ cup dark molasses
1 cup whole wheat flour	2 cups buttermilk
½ tsp soda	2 tbsp melted shortening
1 tsp D.A. baking powder *or*	1 cup raisins, washed,
1¼ tsp tartrate *or* phos-	drained
phate type	

Stir corn meal, rye and whole wheat flours with a spoon to fluff them up before measuring. Spoon lightly into measuring cup and level off. Mix thoroughly with soda, baking powder and salt. Combine molasses, buttermilk and shortening and stir into dry ingredients until thoroughly mixed. Stir in raisins. Spoon batter into 3 well-greased molds or No. 2 tin cans (2½ cup capacity), filling about ⅔ full. Cover with lids, aluminum foil, or double thickness of waxed paper tied securely in place. Steam 1½ hrs or until springy when pressed and no longer sticky. Cool a few min then remove from molds. Serve warm. To improvise a steamer, place a wire rack on bottom of a deep kettle. Add boiling water to come slightly above the rack, then place molds on rack. Cover tightly. Add more boiling water as water boils away. About 20 servings.

Note: 1-lb metal baking powder cans make excellent molds.

MUFFINS

Muffins require speed in mixing. The principal thing to guard against is *over-mixing*, which causes tunnels, humps, cracks, heaviness and toughness. A perfect muffin has a rounded top—not peaked—with a fragile, tender, pebbly crust. The crumb is even-textured without any tunnels. Add moist raisins, chopped dates or nuts to muffin batter the last few stirs; no extra stirring should be done. Muffin batter may be stored in the refrigerator, covered, for as long as 45 min before baking if placed in the muffin pans before storing.

PLAIN MUFFINS

2 cups all-purpose flour	3 tbsp sugar
3 tsp D.A. baking powder *or*	1 egg
3¾ tsp tartrate *or* phos-	1 cup milk
phate type	3 tbsp melted butter
½ tsp salt	

Grease well muffin pans with 12 medium cups. See sizes of cups in muffin pans below. Sift flour, measure, resift 3 times with next 3 ingredients the last time into a mixing bowl. Beat egg, add milk and melted butter. Make "well" in dry ingredients and add liquid ingredients all at once. Stir quickly until the flour is *just* dampened, then give 4 or 5 more quick stirs. Batter should *not* be smooth, but a little lumpy. Spoon batter quickly into prepared pans, filling cups about ⅔ full. If batter pulls rather than drops cleanly from spoon, it has been overmixed. Bake in a moderately hot oven (425° F) about 20 min until golden brown. Serve immediately uncovered on a hot plate. Loosen surplus muffins, turn on side in muffin pan and return to oven with heat turned off.

Raisin or Date Muffins: Make Plain Muffins, above. With last few stirs fold in ⅔ cup raisins or chopped dates. Bake as directed in recipe.

SIZES OF CUPS IN MUFFIN PANS

LARGE CUPS HOLD ......⅝ cup	SMALL CUPS ....¼ cup
MEDIUM CUPS ....½ cup	TINY CUPS ABOUT ......2 tbsp
MEDIUM SMALL CUPS ...⅓ cup	

BACON MUFFINS

2 slices bacon	½ tsp salt
2 cups all-purpose flour	3 tbsp sugar
3 tsp D.A. baking powder *or*	1 egg
3¾ tsp tartrate *or* phos-	1 cup milk
phate type	2 tbsp bacon fat

Grease muffin pans with 12 medium cups. Pan-broil bacon until done, drain and *crumble*. Sift flour, measure, resift 3 times with next 3 ingredients, the last time into 3-qt mixing bowl; add crisp bacon and stir to distribute. Beat egg, stir in milk and melted fat. Add to dry ingredients all at once, stir quickly until flour is just dampened; then give 4 or 5 more stirs. Batter should not be smooth. Spoon into prepared pans, filling cups ⅔ full. Bake in moderately hot oven (425° F) 20 min or until browned. Serve piping hot.

BLUEBERRY MUFFINS

Make Twin Mountain Muffins, p 258. With last few stirs fold in 1 cup washed, drained blueberries. Bake as directed in recipe.

BANANA MUFFINS
Add distinction to any meal

1½ cups all-purpose flour
1¼ tsp D.A. baking powder *or*
    1½ tsp tartrate *or* phos-
    phate type
½ tsp soda
1 tsp salt
3 tbsp sugar

2 small eggs
2 medium bananas, ½ lb
¼ tsp grated lemon rind, pkd
1 tsp lemon juice
3 tbsp buttermilk
3 tbsp shortening

Grease muffin pans with 8 to 10 medium muffin cups. Start oven 10 min before baking; set to moderately hot (400° F). Sift flour, measure, resift 3 times with next 4 ingredients, the last time into a 3-qt mixing bowl. Beat eggs, add sliced bananas and crush with silver fork to size of small peas. Add lemon rind, juice and buttermilk, then stir in shortening. Add liquid all at once to dry ingredients; stir quickly and vigorously until *flour is just dampened, but no more*. Stirring should take about 20 seconds. Spoon into prepared pans. Place in heated oven and bake about 30 min or until well browned. Serve hot.

BRAN MUFFINS

1 cup buttermilk
2 cups shredded whole bran
1 cup all-purpose flour
1 tsp D.A. baking powder *or*
    1¼ tsp tartrate or phos-
    phate type
½ tsp soda

½ tsp salt
⅓ cup shortening
⅓ cup dark brown sugar, pkd
1 egg
3 tbsp dark molasses
⅓ cup plumped raisins, opt

Grease muffin pans with 12 medium cups. Start oven 10 minutes before baking; set to moderately hot (400° F).

Measure buttermilk into a bowl. Stir in bran and let stand a few minutes. Sift flour, measure, resift 3 times with next 3 ingredients. Beat shortening and sugar until creamy using rotary beater. Add egg, beat until smooth and fluffy. Beat in molasses. Clean off beater, use wooden spoon. Add flour and bran mixture alternately in 3 portions, beating until smooth after each addition. Fold in raisins. Spoon into prepared pans. Bake 20 minutes or until golden brown. Serve hot.

CORN MEAL MUFFINS
(See recipes p 241)

CRANBERRY MUFFINS

1 cup chopped raw
    cranberries
½ cup sugar
2 cups all-purpose flour
3 tsp D.A. baking powder *or*
    3¾ tsp tartrate *or* phos-
    phate type

½ tsp salt
2 tbsp sugar
1 egg
1 cup milk
¼ cup melted shortening

Grease well muffin pans with 12 large or 16 medium cups. Wash cranberries, chop and stir in the ½ cup sugar. Sift flour, measure, resift 3 times with next 3 ingredients. Beat egg, then beat in milk and melted shortening; add all at once to dry ingredients and stir quickly until flour is just dampened; batter is not smooth. Fold in cranberries with the last few stirs. Quickly spoon batter into prepared pans, filling ⅔ full. Bake in a moderately hot oven (400° F) 20 to 25 min. Serve hot.

GRAHAM GEMS

An old-time name for delicious whole wheat muffins

1½ cups whole wheat flour	1 tsp soda
1 cup all-purpose flour	¼ cup shortening
1 tsp D.A. baking powder *or*	½ cup sugar
1¼ tsp tartrate *or* phos-	2 eggs, beaten
phate type	1½ cups buttermilk
1 tsp salt	

Grease muffin pans with 15 to 18 medium cups. Start oven 10 min before baking; set to moderately hot (425° F). Spoon whole wheat flour into cup to measure. Sift all-purpose flour, then measure. Resift flours 3 times with next 3 ingredients, the last time into mixing bowl. Add bran left in sifter to dry ingredients. Cream shortening and sugar, add beaten eggs and beat until fluffy. Add flour mixture and buttermilk alternately in 3 or 4 portions, beginning and ending with flour and mixing until just blended after additions, then beat 5 or 6 times. Spoon batter into prepared pans, filling ⅔ full. Place in heated oven and bake 20 min or until golden brown. ½ cup chopped nuts or raisins may be folded in with last few stirs, if desired.

POTATO FLOUR MUFFINS

A deluxe puffy crusty hot bread

½ cup potato flour	½ tsp salt
1 tsp D.A. baking powder *or*	4 eggs, separated
1¼ tsp tartrate *or* phos-	2 tbsp sugar
phate type	2 tbsp ice water

Grease heavily muffin pans with 10 large cups—these muffins stick easily. Spoon unsifted potato flour lightly into cup to measure. Add baking powder and salt, sift 3 times. Beat egg whites until stiff but not dry, add sugar in 2 portions and beat just to blend after each. Beat yolks thoroughly, then fold into whites. Add flour mixture gradually by sprinkling a tbsp at a time over the top and cut-and-fold in lightly and carefully until flour is incorporated. When all flour is added, sprinkle a few drops of water at a time over the top and continue folding in until all the water is absorbed. Spoon lightly into the prepared pans. Bake in a moderate oven (375° F) 18 to 20 min. Serve hot with butter.

RICE MUFFINS

1 cup all-purpose flour	½ tsp salt
1 tbsp sugar	1 egg
2 tsp D.A. baking powder *or*	⅔ cup milk
2½ tsp tartrate *or* phosphate type	1 cup cold boiled rice, p 433
	3 tbsp melted shortening

Grease well muffin pans with 12 medium cups. Sift flour, measure, resift 3 times with next 3 ingredients. Beat egg thoroughly in a 2-qt mixing bowl, then stir in milk, rice and shortening. Immediately add flour mixture and stir quickly until flour is just dampened; then stir 4 or 5 more times, but not until smooth. Spoon quickly into prepared pans, filling ⅔ full. Bake in a moderately hot oven (425° F) 20 min or until nicely browned. Serve hot.

ROLLED OAT MUFFINS

1 cup milk	½ tsp soda
1 cup quick rolled oats	1 tsp salt
4 tbsp shortening	⅓ cup moist brown sugar, pkd
1 cup all-purpose flour	
1 tsp D.A. baking powder *or*	½ cup moist raisins
1¼ tsp tartrate *or* phosphate type	1 egg, well beaten

Grease muffin pans with 12 medium cups. Heat milk to scalding over hot water; stir in oats and shortening and cool. Meanwhile, sift flour, measure, resift 3 times with baking powder, soda and salt, the last time into mixing bowl. Add brown sugar and raisins and mix well. When oat mixture is lukewarm, add egg and stir quickly into dry ingredients until just mixed but not smooth. Spoon quickly into prepared pans, filling ⅔ full. Bake in a moderately hot oven (425° F) 18 to 20 min. Serve hot.

SOY MUFFINS

1½ cups all-purpose flour	½ tsp salt
½ cup soy flour	¼ cup butter
4 tsp D.A. baking powder *or*	¼ cup sugar
5 tsp tartrate *or* phosphate type	1 egg, beaten
	1 cup milk

Grease muffin pans with 12 medium small cups. Sift flours, measure, resift 3 times with baking powder and salt. Cream butter, add sugar

gradually, creaming well. Beat in egg until fluffy. Stir in milk, then add
flour mixture all at once and stir quickly until dry ingredients are just
dampened, but not smooth. Spoon into prepared pans, filling about ⅔
full. Bake in a moderately hot oven (425° F) 20 min or until nicely
browned. Serve hot.

TWIN MOUNTAIN MUFFINS

2 cups all-purpose flour
3 tsp D.A. baking powder *or*
   3¾ tsp tartrate *or* phosphate type
½ tsp salt

⅓ cup butter or shortening
⅔ cup sugar
1 large or 2 small eggs, beaten
¾ cup milk

Grease muffin pan with 12 medium cups. Start oven 10 min before
baking; set to moderately hot (425° F). Sift flour, measure and resift
3 times with baking powder and salt. Cream soft butter, add sugar
gradually and blend thoroughly. Add egg and beat until fluffy. Add flour
mixture alternately with milk in 3 portions, beginning and ending with
flour and beating well after each addition. Spoon batter into prepared
pans, filling ⅔ full. Place in heated oven and bake 18 to 20 min or until
delicately browned. Serve hot.

WAFFLES

CHARACTERISTICS OF GOOD WAFFLES, AND RULES
FOR BAKING

Good waffles are beautifully browned on both sides, crisp, tender and
delicious in flavor. Good waffle batter resembles griddle cake batter but contains less leaven and more eggs. The egg yolks are combined with the milk
or cream, the egg whites are beaten until just stiff, then folded into the batter
at the last. The batter should be barely thin enough to pour. The less sugar
in the batter, the crisper the waffle.

Most waffle irons have a temperature indicator which tells when the iron
is hot enough to bake. If the iron has no indicator, connect and pour 1 tsp
of water into center of iron, close quickly, and when steam stops coming
from iron, it is hot enough for baking. Most waffle batters contain enough
shortening to make greasing iron unnecessary. Be sure to *learn* the amount
of batter needed to bake a waffle that fills the iron evenly. For a round,
4 compartment 7-inch waffle iron, a scant half cup of batter is sufficient.
Therefore, quickly pour in about 2 tbsp of batter into center of each compartment. Close and bake until waffle puffs and stops steaming. Open
iron and let waffle remain a few seconds to crisp. Remove waffle, pour in

more batter immediately, then serve the baked waffle and continue with this procedure.

Note: Creamed foods are delicious served on hot waffles instead of toast, in which case, increase shortening ¼ to make them more crisp. Chocolate Waffles take the place of cake when served with ice cream.

TREATMENT AND CARE OF ELECTRIC WAFFLE IRONS

A new waffle iron must be greased and heated before waffles are baked, but it will not need greasing thereafter if given proper care. To grease, use a pastry brush to rub a thin coat of salad oil over the entire baking surface of both bottom and top grids. Immediately connect iron with current, close iron and heat exactly 10 min, no longer. Time this heating accurately. If the iron becomes too hot, it may be injured, and if batter is poured into it then, the waffle will scorch in spots; if batter is poured in before iron is hot enough the waffle will stick. Discard the first waffle baked in a new iron.

When the indicator shows the iron to be hot enough, pour in batter and close iron at once. Do not open until waffle stops steaming. If it is opened too soon, the waffle splits crosswise, one half sticking to the top and the other to the bottom grid. After waffle stops steaming, open iron, let waffle remain just a few seconds, then remove to hot plate. But before serving waffle, immediately pour in batter for the next one; close iron and bake, then serve waffle. Repeat this routine of pouring in batter immediately after removing waffle as long as baking.

CLEANING WAFFLE IRON

Should a waffle stick, lift off all loose bits, then use a wire brush to remove bits stuck to the grids. Use a soft brush to remove crumbs from iron left from waffles that bake normally. Use a soft dry cloth to wipe the edges and sides of the grids. Use a damp cloth only to wipe batter from the outside of the iron. Never put an electric waffle iron in water to wash as this would damage the heating element. When you finish baking waffles, leave the iron open until it is cold, then clean, close and store.

BASIC WAFFLES

2 cups all-purpose flour	3 eggs, separated
2 tsp D.A. baking powder *or*	2 tsp sugar
2½ tsp tartrate *or* phosphate type	1¼ cups milk
½ tsp salt	⅓ cup melted shortening

Sift flour, measure and resift 3 times with baking powder and salt, the last time into mixing bowl. Beat egg whites to a stiff froth, not dry; add sugar and beat until mixture stands in soft peaks. Beat egg yolks, add milk and shortening and pour into flour mixture. Beat quickly with a wooden spoon until smooth. Now fold whites into batter lightly but thoroughly. Bake in a hot iron, using ½ cup batter for each waffle. When waffle is done, let remain in iron a few seconds to crisp. Serve immediately with butter and hot syrup. Seven or eight 7-inch waffles.

BANANA WAFFLES

2 cups all-purpose flour	3 eggs
3 tsp D.A. baking powder or	1½ cups milk
3½ tsp tartrate or phos-	⅓ cup melted shortening
phate type	1 cup mashed ripe
1 tbsp sugar	bananas, 2
¾ tsp salt	

Sift flour, measure and resift 3 times with remaining dry ingredients. Beat eggs, add milk and shortening. Pour into dry ingredients, add bananas and beat until smooth. Use ½ cup batter for each waffle. Bake in a hot waffle iron until golden brown. Serve immediately with butter and hot syrup. Six 7-inch waffles.

BUTTERMILK WAFFLES

2¼ cups all-purpose flour	1 tsp salt
2¼ tsp D.A. baking powder or	3 eggs, separated
3 tsp tartrate or phosphate	2 tsp sugar
type	2 cups thick buttermilk
½ tsp soda	⅓ cup melted shortening

Combine ingredients and bake like Basic Waffles, p 259. 8 waffles.

CORN MEAL WAFFLES

1¾ cups all-purpose flour	1 tsp salt
1 cup yellow corn meal	2 tsp sugar
2 tsp D.A. baking powder or	3 eggs, separated
2½ tsp tartrate or phos-	2½ cups thick buttermilk
phate type	⅓ cup melted shortening
½ tsp soda	

Combine ingredients and bake like Basic Waffles. 8 waffles.

FEATHERY WAFFLES FOR DESSERT

2 cups cake flour	4 eggs, separated
3 tsp D.A. baking powder or	¼ cup sugar
3¾ tsp tartrate or phos-	1 cup milk
phate type	¼ cup melted shortening
½ tsp salt	

Sift flour, measure, resift 3 times with baking powder and salt. Beat egg whites to a stiff froth, add sugar gradually and continue beating until mixture stands in soft peaks. Beat yolks, add milk and shortening and add to flour mixture. Beat with wooden spoon until smooth, then fold in whites lightly but thoroughly. Use ½ cup batter for each waffle. Bake in a hot iron until golden brown. Serve immediately with ice cream, cooked fruit or Butterscotch Sauce, p 642. Seven 7-inch waffles.

PECAN WAFFLES

Follow Recipe for Basic Waffles, p 259. Immediately after pouring batter into waffle iron, sprinkle with a few chopped pecans.

APPLE WAFFLES

Follow Recipe for Basic Waffles, p 259, except fold into batter ¾ cup finely chopped apples just before folding in egg whites.

CHOCOLATE WAFFLES

Make Red Devil's Food Cake Batter, p 339. Bake like Basic Waffles, p 259. Seven 7-inch waffles.

POPOVERS

Popovers are a most delicious hot bread and very easy to make. Unlike muffins, there is no danger of overbeating the batter. Batter should be beaten vigorously to develop gluten in the flour. The gluten holds in the steam which expands batter while baking.

Heavy iron or cast aluminum popover pans were originally recommended, but excellent popovers may be baked in ordinary muffin pans or glass custard cups. There does, however, seem to be a definite advantage in heating the pans before batter is poured into them.

Good popovers have the appearance of having tried to "pop over." As they bake, batter expands 4 or 5 times in size and becomes hollow, golden-brown shells. The inside of the shell should have a slightly moist thin layer, which should never be thick, wet or soggy. Puncturing popovers with a skewer before they are removed from the oven helps to reduce this moistness.

BASIC POPOVERS

Pans should be heated 3 or 4 min to get sizzling hot before pouring in batter

1 cup all-purpose flour	1 cup milk
½ tsp salt	2 eggs, beaten
1 tsp sugar, optional	1 tbsp melted butter

Start oven 10 min before baking; set to hot (475° F). Grease well deep muffin pan with cups holding ⅓ cup, *or* popover pan with 9 to 12 medium cups, *or* use custard cups. Sift flour, measure, add salt and sugar and resift into mixing bowl. Now place prepared pans in oven to heat 3 or 4 min. Combine milk, eggs and butter, add to flour mixture, then beat thoroughly with rotary beater a min or two. Quickly pour batter into sizzling hot muffin pan, filling cups half full. Place in hot oven. Bake 12 min, then reduce heat to moderate (350° F) and bake 15 min longer. Two or 3 min before end of baking time, quickly pierce popovers with sharp steel skewer. Serve immediately on a hot plate.

Note: When using custard cups, place on cookie sheet to bake.

CHEESE POPOVERS

Good hot or cold and excellent with fruit salad

½ cup grated aged
American cheese, 2 oz

Make Basic Popovers and grease muffin pans more liberally. Fill hot muffin pan cups ¼ full, sprinkle 1 tsp grated cheese over batter in cups, add remaining batter and top with rest of cheese. Bake like Basic Popovers.

TOAST

There are two types of toast, *dry* and *French*. The dry includes plain toast, Melba toast, toast cups, croutons and croustades or bread cases. Any of these variations may be brushed with melted butter or margarine before toasting to add rich color and flavor. This also makes the toast more tender. The toasting process changes the starch on the surface of the bread into dextrin, which gives it a sweeter flavor than untoasted bread.

French toast is slices of plain bread, preferably stale, dipped into a mixture of milk and beaten eggs, then slowly browned in shallow fat. French toast is moist, has richer flavor and greater food value than the dry varieties.

CINNAMON TOAST

Mix 1 part cinnamon with 3 parts granulated sugar. Sprinkle mixture generously over hot buttered toast and serve hot. *Or* toast bread on one side in the broiler, then butter untoasted side and sprinkle with the cinnamon-sugar mixture. Return to broiler until browned and butter bubbles. Serve hot.

CROUTONS

For a delicious rich tender crouton, spread whole bread slices with butter, then cut slices in ½-inch strips, and cut strips into cubes. Spread in a single layer in a shallow baking pan, then brown in a moderate oven (350° F) shaking pan occasionally.

CROUSTADES OR BREAD CASES

A specialty for party and guest meals, and as elegant as Puff Pastry Patty Shells

Croustades or bread cases are excellent edible containers for creamed foods. They are made from whole or partly sliced loaves of 2- or 3-day-old bread. The most bread-saving shapes for croustades are squares, rectangles and diamonds. To make, trim off all crust. Cut the loaf lengthwise into 2-inch thick slices, then cut slices into 2½-inch sqs, or 2 by 3-inch rectangles, or 3½-inch long diamonds. Cut out round croustades which are more wasteful of bread, with a large, deep round biscuit cutter, cut and remove an inside circle to within ⅓-inch from bottom with a smaller round cutter. When the insides are removed, these bread shapes are "boxes" with bottom and side walls of uniform thickness, about ⅓-inch. To make the "boxes," use a sharp paring knife to cut along a straight line parallel to the outer edge of the bread ⅓-inch from the edge, then cut down to within ⅓-inch from the bottom of the bread. Use a fork to remove bread from center to form the "box." It takes a little practice to shape croustades neatly, but once the trick is learned, the work is easy. (Dry the bread removed from inside the "boxes" to make all white crumbs.)

Cut and scoop out bread shapes a few hrs before mealtime; place on a baking sheet, cover carefully with a slightly dampened towel so as not to distort shapes. Ten to 15 min before serving, brush inside and outside of these "bread boxes" with melted butter. Toast in a moderate oven (375° F) to an even brown on all sides, turning 2 or 3 times. When these crisp, hot, tender croustades are filled with tasty chicken, fish or mushroom concoctions, they are most attractive and delicious.

Note: Croustades may be fried in deep fat (375° F) to a golden brown, then drained on absorbent paper before filling with creamed mixtures.

FRENCH TOAST

3 eggs	7 slices 2 to 3 day old bread
1 cup milk	½ cup butter *or* margarine
1 tbsp sugar	xxxx sugar
½ tsp salt	

Beat eggs, then stir in next 3 ingredients. Cut bread slices in half. Heat half the butter in a heavy skillet. Dip bread in egg mixture a few seconds to coat both sides, then lift into skillet and fry until golden brown on both sides. Add more butter as required. Sprinkle with sugar and serve at once with syrup. 4 to 5 servings.

MELBA TOAST

For true Melba toast, slice white or ice box rye bread from ⅛- to ¼-inch thick. Remove crusts if desired. Lay on a shallow baking pan and place in a very slow oven (250–300° F) until perfectly dry and crisp. Toast should be very light brown and not curled. Serve with butter.

Ordinary sliced bread may be toasted in the same way to produce a kind of zwieback. This keeps hard and crisp for several days in a tightly covered tin container.

MELBA BOWKNOTS

Tie inch-wide, 6-inch long thin strips of very fresh bread into a loose knot before toasting.

MELBA CHEESE TOAST

Spread the thinly sliced bread with soft butter, then sprinkle with grated Parmesan cheese before toasting.

MILK TOAST

Heat to scalding, 1 cup milk for each 2 slices of toast. Toast, then butter white, whole wheat or rye bread. Place in warm soup plates. Pour scalding milk over toast, add a dash of salt and pepper, if desired. Serve immediately.

A slice of crisp bacon and a poached egg served on top of the toast make a heartier dish. Some like milk toast with a sprinkling of sugar over it.

PUFFY FRENCH TOAST

12 slices 2-day old bread	2 eggs, separated
Soft butter	1 cup milk
¾ cup brown sugar, pkd	3 tbsp melted butter
1¾ cups all-purpose flour	Shortening for frying
½ tsp salt	xxxx sugar
1¼ tsp D.A. baking powder *or*	
1½ tsp tartrate *or* phosphate type	

Spread bread slices with butter then sprinkle half the slices with brown sugar, 2 tbsp to a slice. Cover with remaining slices, butter-side down, then cut into quarters. Sift flour, measure and resift with rest of dry ingredients into mixing bowl. Drop egg yolks onto flour, then add milk and melted butter. Beat with a rotary beater until smooth. Fold in stiffly beaten egg whites. Dip bread squares into batter until covered well. Have fat heated in skillet to a depth of 1-inch. Fry squares over medium heat in hot fat until browned on both sides. Turn once during cooking. Serve sprinkled with xxxx sugar, if desired. 4 servings.

SKILLET TOAST JOHN BIXBY

| 4 slices bread | 3 tbsp soft butter *or* margarine |

Spread both sides of bread with the butter. Heat 9-inch heavy iron skillet over moderate heat. Lay in buttered bread and brown to a toast color, about 2 min on each side. Serve with jelly or jam. 2 servings.

TOAST CUPS—INEXPENSIVE PATTY SHELLS

| Slices fresh bread, trimmed | Melted butter |

Fresh pliant bread slices of regular thickness are needed to make "cups" of attractive shape. Trim crust thinly from slices. Brush both sides with butter, then press slices carefully into muffin cups to form "cups" with 4 uniform points. Place in a slow oven (300° F) and toast until crisp and golden brown. Fill immediately with hot creamed fish, poultry, meat, vegetable or cheese mixtures.

Note: Bread slices may be prepared and fitted into muffin pans 2 or 3 hrs before needed. Cover with a damp towel. Ten to 15 min before serving, place in heated oven and brown.

YEAST BREAD

Good homemade bread has such tantalizing aroma, tempting flavor and is so satisfying to eat that everyone should be able to enjoy it now and then. Homemade bread is well worth the effort which yeast dough requires, and it's a pleasure to delight the family with such a treat. Bread making is a gratifying job, and once the fundamentals are learned, it is doubly so.

YEAST DOUGHS

There are 3 basic types of yeast dough for making bread and rolls: (1) A water dough for crusty French Bread and Crusty Water Rolls. (2) A milk dough for richer bread and rolls. (3) A sweet dough for fancy breads, rolls, coffee cakes, doughnuts, etc. These types differ not only in liquid, but in the amount of shortening, sugar and eggs used. There are many ways to elaborate each of these doughs. See Table No. 21 on how to use them interchangeably.

The experienced cook knows how to elaborate the 3 basic doughs into the numerous variations illustrated in chart on following page. Study this chart for better understanding of the Yeast Bread Family. The heavy arrows indicate Basic Dough Recipes used to make the authentic variations of rolls, coffee cakes, etc. The broken arrows indicate recipes that are good substitutions for making excellent variations.

TABLE 21

YEAST BREAD DOUGHS AND POSSIBLE VARIATIONS

Bread Sticks

Vienna Rolls

Cloverleaf Rolls
Crooked Miles
Fan Tans
Knots
Parkerhouse Rolls
Puff Balls
Herb Bread

Orange Pinwheels
Plum or Apple Kuchen
Raised Doughnuts
Schnecken
Swedish Tea Ring

Hasty Apple Coffee Cake

FRENCH BREAD
(Water Bread)

WHITE BREAD
(Milk Bread)

PLAIN ROLL DOUGH
(Egg Bread)
(Egg added, less flour)

RICH ROLL DOUGH
(Sweet Roll Dough)

KNEADLESS DROP DOUGH

Drop Rolls

SPECIAL RECIPES
(Other Ingredients Added or Special Manipulation Required)

Quick Streusel Coffee Cake

Braided Rolls
Butterfly Rolls
Butterhorn Rolls
Cinnamon Coffee Cake
Cinnamon Whirl
Cinnamon Rolls
Clothespin Rolls

Bismarks
Cottage Cheese Kuchen
Jule Kake
Kolachy
Old Fashioned Streusel
Coffee Cake
Orange Butterfly Rolls

		Part (50%) Whole Wheat Bread	Whole Wheat Bread	Refrigerator Rolls
		Rye Bread		Quick Bread
		Prune Bread		Swedish Limpa
		Pumpkin Bread		Whole Wheat Bread
Buckwheat Pancakes	Kolachy			
Buttermilk Rolls	Stollen			
Danish Pastry	Nut Bread			
English Muffins	Oatmeal Bread			

YEAST PACKAGE SIZES

There are 2 types of yeast available—*Compressed and Dry Granular. Compressed* comes in 2 sizes, Regular and Household. Regular cakes are smaller and weigh from ½ oz to a trifle more, depending on brand; the Household cake weighs about 1 oz and is equal to 2 cakes of the Regular *Compressed* or 2 packages of *Dry Granular. Dry Granular* yeast comes in packages of varying sizes and weights ranging from 7 to 7½ grams, which is about ¼ oz.

A cake of *Compressed* yeast weighs more than a package of *Dry Granular* because it contains moisture, but both have the same leavening power and may be used interchangeably. *Compressed* yeast is very perishable and requires refrigeration; *Dry Granular* has a much longer life, and while it is usually stored at room temperature, it remains "lively" much longer if stored in refrigerator. In recipes in this book, *Compressed* yeast is designated by reg cakes and *Dry Granular* by packages (pkg).

WATER YEAST DOUGH

In olden times water was the only liquid used to make bread and rolls in rural communities of America and Europe, and little or no shortening or sugar was added. This type of dough is used in French and Vienna Bread as well as in the popular hard, crusty water rolls and crunchy bread sticks. Bread made from this dough does not have the nutritional value of that made with milk, eggs, shortening and sugar, but it does have a wonderful flavor and is particularly appreciated for its crustiness.

CRUSTY FRENCH BREAD

4 cups all-purpose flour in summer, 3¾ in winter	2 tsp sugar
	1½ tsp salt
1 reg cake compressed *or*	1 tbsp shortening
1 pkg dry gran yeast	2 egg whites, unbeaten
1 cup lukewarm water	1 tbsp water
(110° F)	Corn meal

Sift flour and measure. Crumble compressed or turn dry granular yeast into ¼ cup of the water and let soften 10 min. Put remaining water into 4-qt bowl, add sugar, salt, shortening and 1 cup of the flour and beat until smooth. Then beat in yeast mixture, then 1 egg white. Now *beat* and *stir* in remaining flour to make a stiff dough. Turn out on lightly floured board or pastry cloth and knead until smooth and satiny, about 10 min. Return to washed, well greased bowl, turn once to bring greased side up. Cover and let rise in warm place until double, about 1 hr, then knead down. Turn out on board or pastry cloth, cover with bowl and let rest 10 min. To make Vienna or French Bread, form dough into a narrow, rounded loaf about 14 inches long tapered at both ends. Place on greased baking sheet sprinkled with corn meal. With a very sharp knife, make 5 or 6 diagonal cuts about ⅛-inch deep across top. Slightly beat remaining egg white with water and brush loaf well. Cover with damp cloth and let rise in warm place until double. Start oven 10 min before baking; set to moderately hot (425° F). Place shallow pan of boiling water on floor of oven to produce crustiness. Now place loaf in oven and bake 10 min, then reduce heat to moderate (350° F). Remove loaf from oven and again brush lightly with egg white mixture. Bake another 10 min and repeat brushing with egg white. Continue baking 20 to 25 min until golden brown and crusty—entire baking time 40 to 45 min. Remove immediately to cake rack to cool. 1 large loaf.

Note: A Vienna Bread loaf is wider and shorter than a French.

BREAD STICKS

Salt and seed sticks

Use Crusty French Bread dough, p 267, or White Bread dough, p 269. After 2nd rising cut off pieces of dough and shape into uniform size balls about 1½ inches in diameter. Lay on lightly floured board or pastry cloth, cover, let rest 10 min. Grease fingers lightly, then roll each ball lightly back-and-forth until it is a roll uniform in thickness 10 to 12 inches long and ⅜-inch thick. Lay on greased backing sheet. Cover, let rise in warm place until double, about 45 min. Using light pressure, brush with 1 slightly beaten egg white blended with 1 tbsp water. Leave plain or make very shallow diagonal cuts across top with razor blade or sharp knife. Sprinkle with poppy or sesame seed, or large flat salt crystals, if desired. Bake in moderate oven (375° F) until golden brown—8 to 10 min. Place a shallow pan of hot water on bottom of oven to produce a crisp crust and attractive color. For fancy bread sticks, make dough strips ¼-inch thick and 10 inches long and braid 3 together. Cut off ends neatly. Let rise until double and bake in same way.

CRUSTY WATER ROLLS

Dumbbells, Twin Rolls, Vienna Rolls

Make Crusty French Bread dough, p 267, and after 2nd rising, punch down and turn out on lightly floured board or pastry cloth. Cover with bowl and let rest 10 min. Then cut dough into 16 to 20 equal pieces, then roll quickly into balls.

Dumbbells. To shape Dumbbells, cut the balls of dough in half and roll each portion into a ball. Place 2 balls *close together* on greased baking sheet sprinkled with corn meal, then brush with cold water. Let rise in warm place until double, about 1 hr. Bake in a moderately hot oven (425° F) 10 min, then brush with cold water or Egg White Mixture and sprinkle with sesame, caraway or poppy seed, if desired, then bake 10 min longer or until golden brown. A shallow pan of water on floor of oven during baking helps produce a thick, crisp crust and golden brown color.

Twin Rolls. To shape Twin Rolls, pat balls of dough out into round, flat "cakes." Place on greased baking sheet sprinkled with corn meal, then with greased scissors, cut all the way across roll through top and almost to the bottom. Let rise in warm place until double. Bake like Dumbbells.

Vienna Rolls. To shape balls into Vienna Rolls, use outstretched fingers of both hands and roll back-and-forth lightly until ball becomes a 4-inch oval tapered at both ends. Place on greased baking sheet sprinkled with corn meal. Let rise and bake like Dumbbells.

BASIC WHITE BREAD

Because bread is eaten so regularly it should be made as nutritious as possible for good health. Adding milk and using enriched flour has greatly improved the nutritional value of white bread. True white bread does not contain egg, but excellent bread can be made from the Plain Roll Dough, p 273. Bread which contains milk browns more quickly and keeps moist longer than bread made with water. As a rule, Basic White Bread dough is used to make loaves, but it may also be used to make all the varied rolls in this chapter.

The following Basic White Bread recipe, if accurately followed, will produce the kind of homemade bread that can win prizes at county fairs and praises from the family.

BASIC WHITE BREAD

This milk bread recipe makes three 1½ lb loaves

9 cups all-purpose flour	2 cups scalded milk *or* half
*2 reg cakes compressed *or*	milk, half water
2 pkgs dry gran yeast	4 tsp salt
1 cup lukewarm water	¼ cup sugar
1 tsp sugar	¼ cup melted butter *or*
	half shortening

Do not soften yeast in warm milk or bring in contact with shortening before adding some flour to mixture. Fat seems to form a film around yeast cells through

*See p 267 for yeast package sizes.

which the tiny plants have difficulty in fermenting. Those who melt shortening in the milk as it scalds, and add yeast to this mixture when cooled to lukewarm, are likely to get a slow-rising dough. Best results are obtained by softening yeast in warm water containing a little sugar to start activity of yeast plants. No shortening should be added to batter until about half of flour has been incorporated.

Note: Best rising conditions for yeast dough are moist air and a temperature of 80 to 85° F and out of a draft, see Step 12, p 272.

Step 1. Sift flour, measure. Crumble compressed or turn granular yeast into lukewarm water. Stir in 1 tsp sugar and let soften 10 min.

Step 2. Scald milk to destroy enzymes which affect growth of yeast and flavor of dough.

Step 3. Put scalded milk, salt and ¼ cup sugar into 5-qt mixing bowl; cool to lukewarm (about 110° F). If half water is used, add it cold to scalded milk to hasten cooling.

Step 4. Always stir yeast mixture into lukewarm liquid. To over-heat yeast at any time injures and destroys it. Yeast that is too cold rises very slowly. The ideal rising temperature for yeast dough is an even, moist warmth from 80 to 85° F, which is a little less than body temperature.

Step 5. Add 4 cups of the flour and beat until smooth.

Step 6. Beat in cooled melted shortening.

Step 7. Add enough more flour to make a smooth, soft dough; the softer the dough can be kept without sticking to board or hands, the lighter and more tender bread will be.

Step 8. Sprinkle 1 to 2 tbsp remaining flour evenly over board or pastry cloth. (A linoleum or enamel-topped table, or other modern type table tops are very satisfactory for kneading dough.)

Step 9. Turn dough onto floured board, cover with bowl; let rest 10 min. The dough is very soft as it is turned from bowl; letting it rest causes it to stiffen and makes it easier to handle without adding an excess of flour.

Step 10. Now knead dough until outside is smooth and elastic, from 10 to 15 min. There are 3 basic motions to kneading: (1) Folding dough over on itself toward you. (2) Pushing dough with heels of hands away from you. (3) Then giving dough a quarter turn and repeating.

Step 11. Then in easy rhythm of hands, rock back and forth on heels of palms, pressing the dough toward you, then pushing it away from you. This kneading develops the gluten or protein in the dough to give it a strong elastic structure necessary to hold the expanded gas produced by the yeast and keep shape of loaf as it bakes.

Step 12. Lift up edge of dough and turn it with left hand and at same time fold it over with right. You are now in position to repeat the kneading process started in Step 10. With practice, both hands are used to advantage and an easy rhythmic motion develops. Dough feels satiny and elastic and when kneaded enough does not stick to board or hands.

Step 13. Round up dough and return to washed, well-greased mixing bowl; turn once to bring greased-side up. This prevents formation of a thin crust on top which makes streaks in the bread.

Step 14. Cover bowl with a towel, lid, or a 2nd bowl of same size. Place in a warm spot, 80 to 85° F, away from drafts to rise until double. See "Proofing Oven" directions, Step 12, p 272.

Step 15. Do not hurry through first rising. It requires from 1½ to 2 hrs. When dough rises sufficiently, the dent made by pressing finger into dough remains.

Step 16. When dough has fully risen, plunge fist into center of dough and fold edges toward center to punch down. Then again turn dough over so smooth side is up. Cover and let rise again until double. The 2nd rising takes less time than the first. One rising produces a satisfactory loaf, but a 2nd rising a superior loaf. After last rising, punch down and turn out on a lightly floured board or pastry cloth.

Step 17. Divide dough into 3 equal portions; round up into balls, cover with bowls and let rest 10 min, then shape into loaves. This "rest period" makes dough easier to handle because the gluten is relaxed.

Step 18. *Place loaves in 3 greased 9 x 5 x 3-inch pans. Cover and let rise in a warm place (80 to 85° F) until double, about 1 hr.

Step 19. Bake in a moderately hot oven (425° F) about 30 min. When done, bread should be well risen with a fully rounded top or "spring." The crust should be golden brown and crisp. Loaves should sound hollow when tapped on the bottom.

Step 20. Turn loaves out of pans immediately onto cake racks to cool for 2 or 3 hrs, uncovered and away from drafts. If cooled too quickly, the crust shrivels, becomes bumpy and soft.

Step 21. When thoroughly cooled, store bread in a metal box with a tight-fitting cover and with small air holes in sides for ventilation. Clean bread box weekly by washing in hot soapy water, rinsing well in hot water, drying well, then airing.

SHAPING AND PROOFING YEAST BREAD LOAVES

Step 1. When dough is ready to shape into loaves, knead down and turn out on board or pastry cloth. Cut with a sharp knife into as many equal portions as there are to be loaves.

Step 2. Shape portions into smooth balls, cover with bowls or cloth and let rest 10 min; this rest period makes shaping easier.

*The process of letting dough rise in a warm place until double is called "proofing." For best results there should be an even temperature and a certain amount of moisture in the air so loaves will not develop a crust on top. See Step 12 Shaping and Proofing.

Step 3. Flatten ball of dough with palms of hands into an oblong shape about 6 x 9 inches. Don't punch or pound the dough.

Step 4. Fold long edge of oblong farthest from you over to the center and press gently to seal.

Step 5. Now fold long edge nearest to you over to center and press gently to seal.

Step 6. Lift folded dough up by both ends and alternately stretch and slap against board until it is twice as long as the baking pan.

Step 7. Bring ends of folded dough to the center to overlap slightly, then press together to seal.

Step 8. Make an indentation lengthwise through center with edge of hand to mark the next fold.

Step 9. Using the indentation as a marker, fold over the edge of the dough nearest you toward the center.

Step 10. Then fold the other side toward the center, and roll dough gently back and forth with palms of hands to seal the edges and round the loaf into a cylindrical shape.

Step 11. Place in greased loaf pan with the seam side of loaf on bottom. Do not press the corners of the loaf into the corners of pan.

Step 12. Cover loaves with a damp cloth and let rise in a warm place, 80 to 85° F, to double, or improvise a simple Proofing Oven in the following 2 ways:

(1) Use your range baking oven if it is lined with enamel or stainless steel and is one that does not have a pilot light, which would make the oven too warm. Place loaves in cold oven with a large pan of hot water underneath. Close oven door, turn on heat at 400° F. for 1 min only. Time exactly. Turn off heat and let loaves remain in closed oven 1 hr or until double.

(2) Use a large heavy cardboard box with the folding top attached. Make sure it is clean by wiping out inside thoroughly to be free of dust. Put box on table with open-end facing you. Place open jars or pitchers of hot water in the box, close ends securely and cover with a heavy cloth so no cold air gets in and the interior of box warms up before placing bowl of dough or pans of rolls or loaves inside. Check temperature of water every 30 min. As air in box cools, replace the hot water. The hot water in the oven or box gives the necessary heat and steam to cause the dough to rise and to keep its surface moist.

Step 13. Perfectly proofed loaves of bread are double size of original dough and have a smooth, moist surface. Bake. Step 19, p 271.

Step 14. Perfectly baked loaves are symmetrical in shape with an even golden brown crisp crust. The "spring" between the pan line and the top of the bread should be well-rounded with an attractive shred on the side. Remove loaves immediately from pans to cake racks to cool, uncovered and out of drafts for 2 to 3 hrs before cutting. Brush top of hot loaf with melted butter for a soft crust.

YEAST ROLL DOUGHS

Plain Rolls, Sweet Rolls, Refrigerator Rolls, Etc.

As a rule Roll Doughs are usually a little softer than dough for bread, and may be made of different liquids and varying amounts of egg, sugar and shortening. Water Rolls made from Crusty French Bread dough, p 267, contains very little shortening and sugar, and a little egg white. Plain Roll Dough, below, includes a moderate amount of egg, sugar and shortening. Sweet Roll Dough, p 279, requires a larger amount of egg, sugar and shortening. Even White Bread dough, p 269, makes delicious Pan Rolls. All these doughs may be used to make the various shaped rolls described in this chapter. Kneadless (no-knead) Rolls are an innovation to keep step with the speed of modern living. They require a maximum amount of yeast, a minimum amount of flour, and vigorous beating.

HOW TO MAKE ROLLS OF UNIFORM SIZE

Punch dough down after 2nd rising. Turn out onto lightly floured board or pastry cloth and shape into a long "rope" 1-inch in thickness. To do this, use about a lb of dough and roll it back-and-forth with palms of hands. With a sharp knife, cut off an inch of dough and shape into a ball to see if the inch-length gives the right size ball. When right length is determined, cut the "rope" quickly into the length determined. Shape immediately into rolls.

BROWN-AND-SERVE ROLLS

Use plain dough recipe (below), shaping as desired. When risen about half as much as usual, bake at a lower temp, 275° F, about 25 min or until they are rigid but not browned. (Rolls will rise more in oven because the lower temp does not kill the yeast as soon.) After cooling, rolls may be placed in plastic bag and frozen. To use, bake 5 to 7 min at 450° F.

WHY BRUSH ROLLS WITH MELTED FAT?

Coating the rolls with a thin film of fat helps to retain the shape as well as the lines of separation throughout rising and baking.

PLAIN ROLL DOUGH AND VARIATIONS
About 4½ lbs dough

8 to 8¾ cups all-purpose
  flour
2 reg cakes compressed *or* 2
  pkgs dry gran yeast
¼ cup lukewarm water
1 tsp sugar

2 cups milk, scalded
2 tsp salt
½ cup sugar
2 eggs, beaten
⅓ cup melted shortening

Sift flour and measure. Crumble compressed or turn gran yeast into lukewarm water, stir in the 1 tsp sugar; let soften 10 min. In a 4-qt bowl combine hot milk with salt and sugar and cool to lukewarm. Then add yeast mixture and eggs and stir thoroughly. Beat in half the flour until smooth, then the cooled shortening. Stir in all but 2 tbsp of remaining flour and mix in thoroughly with hand. Turn out on board or pastry cloth sprinkled with rest of flour; cover dough with bowl, let rest 10 min. Then knead until dough is smooth and elastic, about 10 min, adding no more flour for kneading. Shape into ball, place in the washed, greased bowl, turn once to bring greased side up. Cover with a damp cloth, let rise in warm place until double, about 1½ hrs. Punch down, turn dough over, cover and again let rise until double. Then shape into rolls as desired. This amount of dough makes 1 Cinnamon Coffee Cake, p 290, 1 loaf Cinnamon Whirl Bread, p 295, and 1½ dozen rolls, or all the dough makes 4 to 5 dozen rolls.

Note: Shape this dough into loaves, p 272, for nutritious egg bread. 3 loaves.

BRAIDS

After 2nd rising of Plain Roll Dough, turn out onto lightly floured board or pastry cloth. Cut off pieces of dough about "golf ball" size for each strip used in the braid. With outstretched fingers of both hands, roll into 10-inch lengths of pencil-size thickness. Place 3 strips side by side on the board, press far ends firmly together. Now braid in usual way. Cut crosswise in half, press ends firmly together. Place braids on greased baking sheet, brush with melted butter, cover and let rise in warm place until double. See *Step 12*, p 272. Bake in moderately hot oven (400° F) 12 to 15 min. Serve hot.

BUTTERFLY ROLLS

Make ¼ recipe of Plain Roll Dough, p 273, or ½ Sweet Roll Dough, p 279. After 2nd rising, turn out on lightly floured board or pastry cloth and roll into two 7-inch wide rectangles a little less than ¼-inch thick. Spread thinly with soft butter. Begin at wide end, roll up tightly like jelly roll. Cut into slices 1¼-inch wide. Firmly press handle of wooden spoon or knife down center of each slice parallel to cut edges. When handle is lifted, roll takes butterfly shape. Place on greased baking sheet; brush with melted butter, cover, let rise in warm place until double. Bake in moderately hot oven (400° F) 15 to 20 min or to a golden brown. Serve warm.

BUTTERHORNS

After 2nd rising of ¼ recipe Plain Roll dough, p 273, or ½ recipe Sweet Roll Dough, p 279, turn out on lightly floured board or pastry cloth, cover, let rest 10 min. Then roll out enough dough to make a 12-inch circle about ¼-inch thick. Brush with soft butter. Cut into 12 pie-shape pieces. Begining at wide end, roll up, stretching dough slightly as you roll. Lay straight or in crescent-shape on greased baking sheet with tip of dough underneath. Brush with melted butter, cover, let rise in warm place until double. Bake in moderately hot oven (400° F) 12 to 15 min.

CINNAMON ROLLS

After 2nd rising of ¼ recipe of Plain Roll Dough, p 273, or ½ of Sweet Roll Dough, p 279, turn out on lightly floured board or pastry cloth, shape into a ball, cover, let rest 10 min. Roll into an 8 x 14-inch rectangle. Brush with 2 tbsp melted butter, sprinkle with ¼ cup sugar mixed with 2 tsp cinnamon and ½ cup moist raisins. Roll up like jelly roll starting at wide end, pinching edge to roll to seal. Cut into 1-inch lengths. Place close together in a greased pan, cut-side down. Brush with melted butter, cover, let rise in a warm place until double, about 45 min. Bake in a moderate oven (375° F) 25 to 30 min. 14 rolls.

CLOTHESPIN ROLLS

After 2nd rising of ¼ recipe of Plain Roll Dough, p 273, turn out on lightly floured board or pastry cloth, cover with bowl, let rest 10 min. Roll into a long rectangle about ¼-inch thick and about 8 inches wide. Spread thinly with soft butter. Fold ½ of dough crosswise over other half; trim edges of dough to square corners. Cut into strips 8 inches long and ¼-inch wide. Wind strips around greased wood clothespins starting just below knob; tuck both ends in to prevent unwinding. Place on greased baking sheet; brush with melted shortening. Cover, let rise in warm place until double. Bake in moderately hot oven (400° F) 12 to 15 min. While warm, carefully slip clothespins out of rolls. 18 rolls.

CLOVERLEAF OR SHAMROCK ROLLS

After 2nd rising of Plain Roll Dough, or Sweet Roll Dough, cut off small pieces of dough and roll into smooth balls varying in size from small walnuts to large marbles, depending on size of muffin cups. Place 3 in each greased muffin cup. Brush lightly with melted shortening, cover, let rise in warm place until double. Bake in a moderately hot oven (400° F) 12 to 15 min. Two larger or 4 small balls may be used for each roll, if preferred. Mixing balls of white and whole wheat dough in the same muffin cup makes an attractive variation.

CROOKED MILES

After 2nd rising of Plain Roll Dough, cut off pieces of dough large enough to make "ropes" 7 inches long and ⅜-inch thick. Make Rolls by tying a loose knot at one end of the "rope," then pull rest of "rope" *loosely* through center and wind through center until it is all used up. Place on greased baking sheet; brush with melted butter. Cover, let rise in warm place until double. Bake in moderately hot oven (400° F) 15 to 20 min.

FAN TAN ROLLS

After 2nd rising of ¼ recipe of Plain Roll Dough or ½ of Sweet Roll Dough, turn out onto lightly floured board or pastry cloth, round up into ball, cover with bowl, let rest 10 min. Roll into rectangle 22 x 9 inches. Brush with melted butter. Cut into strips 1½-inches wide, making 6 strips 22-inches long. Pile strips on top of each other, turning top strip butter-side down. Press lightly into even width and height. Let stand a min, then cut into 1¼-inch wide pieces. Lay cut-side down into greased muffin cups 2¾-inches across. Cover, let rise in warm place until double, about 45 min. Bake in moderately hot oven (400° F) 12 to 15 min.

KNOTS

After 2nd rising, remove ¼ of Plain Roll Dough, p 273, or ½ of Sweet Roll Dough, p 279, to lightly floured board or pastry cloth. Divide into 12 equal pieces. Roll pieces on board back-and-forth with the palms to form ropes about ½-inch thick and 10 inches long. Cut ropes crosswise in half. Hold rope by both ends, stretch lightly and tie into a loose knot. Place on greased baking sheet, brush with melted butter, cover and let rise in warm place until double. Bake in a moderately hot oven (400° F) 12 to 15 min.

PAN ROLLS

Pan Rolls are easy to shape and bake. Use ⅓ of the Plain Roll Dough, p 273, to make 18 rolls. Shape dough into a long rope. Cut into 18 even-size pieces. Shape into balls. Place balls to just touch in a greased 10-inch skillet or pan—metal or glass, sq or round. Brush with melted butter, cover with "supported damp cloth" (cloth should not rest on rolls) and let rise in warm place until double, about 1 hr. Bake in a moderately hot oven (400° F) 20 to 25 min or until nicely browned.

PARKER HOUSE ROLLS

A famous dinner roll credited to the old Parker House in Boston

After 2nd rising of Plain Roll Dough, p 273, turn dough out on lightly floured board or pastry cloth. Roll out to about ⅓-inch thickness. Cut out with floured biscuit cutter. Lift out trimmings and place them on top of each other, cover, let rest 10 min before re-rolling and cutting. Cover cut-out rolls with towel; let rest 10 min. With a thin knife handle, make a deep crease across each roll a little above center. Brush surface with melted butter. Using both hands, pick up rounds and stretch them a little to make ovals, then fold at crease, pressing longer side over shorter one. Place 1-inch apart, long-side up on a lightly greased baking pan. Brush tops with melted butter. Cover, let rise in warm place until double. Bake in a moderately hot oven (400° F) 12 to 15 min. Serve hot.

PUFF BALLS

Interesting little hat-shaped rolls

After 2nd rising of Plain Roll Dough, p 273, turn out on lightly floured board or pastry cloth. Roll out about ¼-inch thick. Cut out with doughnut cutter dipped in flour, putting the cut-out "holes" to one side. Now lift out trimmings, place them on top of each other, cover and let rest 10 min, then re-roll and cut. Lift doughnut-shapes to a greased baking sheet; brush with melted butter. Now roll 2 of the cut-out "holes" or an equal amount of trimmings into a ball and drop into centers of doughnut cut-outs. Brush with melted butter, cover and let rise until double. Bake in a moderately hot oven (400° F) 12 to 20 min. Serve hot.

BUTTERMILK YEAST ROLLS

Buttermilk does something for these topnotch rolls

2¾ cups all-purpose flour
1 tsp D.A. baking powder
1 tsp salt
¼ tsp soda
1 reg cake compressed *or* 1 pkg dry gran yeast

¼ cup lukewarm water
1 tbsp sugar
1 cup lukewarm buttermilk
3 tbsp melted shortening

Sift flour, measure and resift 3 times with next 3 ingredients. Crumble compressed or turn granular yeast into lukewarm water and let stand 10 min. Then stir in the sugar and buttermilk. Beat in half the flour mixture, then shortening. Now stir in all but 2 tbsp of remaining flour. Turn out on lightly floured board or pastry cloth sprinkled with the 2 tbsp flour, cover dough with bowl and let rest 10 min. Knead thoroughly for 10 min. Again cover with bowl and let rest 20 min. Shape into rolls, p 273, and place in greased pans. Cover, let rise in a warm place until double, about 1¼ hrs. Bake in a moderately hot oven (400° F) 15 to 20 min, depending on size of rolls. 24 medium size rolls.

CORN MEAL ROLLS

4½ to 5 cups all-purpose flour
2 cups milk
½ cup sugar
1 tsp salt
1 cup corn meal white *or* yellow

1 reg cake compressed *or* 1 pkg dry gran yeast
½ cup lukewarm water
2 eggs, beaten
½ cup melted shortening
2 tbsp melted shortening, cooled

Sift flour and measure. Measure milk, sugar and salt into top of double boiler. Place over direct heat, then sift in corn meal gradually, stirring to keep smooth. Heat to boiling, then place over boiling water and cook 10 min, stirring frequently. Now turn into 4-qt mixing bowl and cool to *lukewarm* with occasional stirring. Crumble compressed or turn dry gran yeast into *lukewarm water* and let soften. Stir eggs and yeast into corn meal mixture, then half the flour, beating thoroughly. Now beat in cooled shortening and enough of remaining flour to make a soft dough. Turn out on lightly floured board or pastry cloth, cover with bowl and let rest 10 min. Then knead until smooth and elastic, about 10 min. Round up dough, place in washed, greased bowl, turning once to bring greased side up. Cover and let rise in warm place until double. Punch down, turn out on board or pastry cloth, cover and let rest 10 min. Cut dough into 3 equal pieces. Shape each piece into a rope 27 inches long. Cut ropes into ¾-inch long pieces, then shape quickly into balls. Dip balls lightly in the 2 tbsp shortening and place 3 balls into each greased cup of muffin pans. Cover, let rise in warm place until double. Bake in moderately hot oven (400° F) 20 to 25 min or until golden brown. Remove to cake racks. Serve warm. 3 dozen.

Do not soften yeast in warm milk or bring in contact with shortening before adding some flour to mixture. Fat seems to form a film around yeast cells through which the tiny plants have difficulty in fermenting. Those who melt shortening in the milk as it scalds, and add yeast to this mixture when cooled to lukewarm, are likely to get a slow-rising dough. Best results are obtained by softening yeast in warm water containing a little sugar to start activity of yeast plants. No shortening should be added to batter until about half of flour has been incorporated.

Note: Best rising conditions for yeast dough are moist air and a temp of 80 to 85° F and out of a draft.

KNEADLESS DROP ROLLS

Quick easy way to make delicious hot rolls and coffee cake

3½ cups all-purpose flour
1 cup milk
1 reg cake compressed *or* 1
  pkg dry gran yeast
¼ cup lukewarm water
⅔ cup sugar
⅓ cup shortening

1 tsp salt
3 eggs, beaten
1 tsp vanilla
Melted butter
3 tbsp sugar and
1 tsp cinnamon, mixed

Sift flour and measure. Scald milk in top of double boiler and pour into 3-qt mixing bowl to cool to lukewarm. Crumble compressed or turn gran yeast into lukewarm water, stir in 1 tsp of the sugar and let soften 10 min. Then stir yeast mixture into milk and beat in 1½ cups of the flour until smooth. Cover and let rise in warm place until light, about 45 min. Cream shortening, salt and remaining sugar in another 3-qt bowl until smooth, add yeast batter gradually, stirring to mix well. Beat in eggs and vanilla thoroughly. Add remaining flour and beat until thoroughly mixed. Spoon batter into well greased muffin pans with large size cups, filling about ⅓ full. Cover and let rise in warm place until double, about 1 hr. Brush gently with melted butter and sprinkle with sugar-cinnamon mixture. Bake in moderately hot oven (400° F) about 18 min. 24 rolls.

Note: Also use this batter to make Quick Old-Time Streusel Coffee Cake and Hasty Apple Coffee Cake.

SWEET ROLL DOUGH AND VARIATIONS

Rich Dough:

(For rolls, Jule Kake, Cinnamon Loaf, Raised Doughnuts, Raisin Bread, Swedish Tea Ring, etc.)
4¼ to 5 cups all-purpose flour
2 reg cakes compressed *or* 2
  pkgs dry gran yeast
¼ cup lukewarm water
½ cup sugar
¾ cup milk, scalded
1 tsp salt
2 eggs *or* 4 yolks
1 tsp grated lemon rind, pkd
⅓ cup butter *or* margarine
½ tsp mace *or* ground cardamon, optional

Richer Dough:

(For Rich Rolls, Pecan Rolls, Coffee Cakes, etc.)
4¼ to 4¾ cups all-purpose flour
2 reg cakes compressed *or* 2
  pkgs dry gran yeast
¼ cup lukewarm water
½ cup sugar
⅔ cup milk, scalded
1 tsp salt
2 eggs *or* 4 yolks
1 tsp grated lemon rind, pkd
½ cup butter *or* margarine
½ tsp mace *or* ground cardamon, optional

Sift flour once, then measure, and use the 1st amount for coffee cakes, rolls, etc., the 2nd amount for bread. Crumble compressed or turn gran yeast into lukewarm water, stir in 1 tsp of the sugar and let soften 10 min. Put milk with rest of sugar and salt in top of double boiler and place over hot water to scald. Cool to lukewarm in a 4-qt mixing bowl, then stir in yeast mixture and beaten eggs. Add half the flour and beat hard with rotary beater or electric mixer, then beat in cooled shortening, rind, and spice if used. (Cardamon is especially nice in coffee cake.) Gradually stir in all but ¼ cup of remaining flour until well mixed in. Cover, let stand 10 min to stiffen, then turn out onto board or pastry cloth sprinkled with remaining ¼ cup flour. Knead thoroughly, at least 5 min. The dough is soft but its richness prevents its adhering to board if kneading is done fast. The dough must be soft to make delicate, light flaky rolls and coffee cakes; adding more flour makes a bready product. Place dough in a lightly greased bowl, turn once to bring greased side up. Cover with a damp cloth and let rise in a warm place or Proofing Oven, until double, 1½ to 2 hrs. Punch down, turn over, cover and again let rise until double, about 30 min. (One rising produces very satisfactory products but a 2nd rising superior ones.) Now punch down and turn onto a lightly floured board or pastry cloth; cover with bowl, let rest 10 min. Shape into rolls and place in greased pans or spread dough in greased layer cake pans for coffee cake, and finish as desired. Makes about 2⅛ lbs dough—enough for one 9" coffee cake and 9 or 10 rolls.

REFRIGERATOR ROLLS

Ingredients for refrigerator rolls differ slightly from those in regular rolls. Any dough, however, that contains a little extra yeast may be successfully held overnight or 24 hrs before baking. If the dough is to be kept longer than 2 days, it is best to use water instead of milk as the liquid. The dough should be made from cold ingredients and not allowed to rise.

Here is how to keep dough from rising: (1) Start with cold ingredients. (2) Roll kneaded dough out thin, place on waxed paper, cover with a towel and lay directly on metal refrigerator shelf to chill through fast. (3) When chilled, remove paper and place dough in chilled bowl, cover tightly and return to refrigerator. Some rising takes place even in chilled dough but at a greatly retarded rate. About 3 hrs before rolls are required, remove dough from refrigerator. Shape immediately, place in pans, grease tops and let rise in warm place until double, then bake. The dough keeps well for 5 or 6 days. Fresh hot rolls may be served each day from this dough.

Note: Best rising conditions for yeast dough are moist air and a temp of 80 to 85° F and out of a draft.

PLAIN REFRIGERATOR ROLLS

6 to 6¼ cups all-purpose flour	¼ cup lukewarm water
1¼ cups water	½ cup sugar
2 reg cakes compressed *or* 2 pkgs dry gran yeast	2 tsp salt
	2 eggs, well beaten
	⅓ cup melted shortening

Sift flour and measure. Heat water to boiling, set in pan of ice water and stir occasionally until very cold. Crumble compressed or turn gran yeast into lukewarm water measured into a 4-qt bowl and let stand 10 min. Now add cold water, sugar, salt, eggs and 3 cups of the flour; beat vigorously until well blended. Add cooled shortening and beat well. Stir in all but ¼ cup of remaining flour. Turn dough out on board or pastry cloth sprinkled with remaining flour, cover with bowl; let rest 10 min. Now knead until smooth and elastic, about 10 min. Flatten dough out into a thin sheet; place between 2 towels and lay directly on metal shelf in refrigerator to chill thoroughly. Then quickly shape into a ball and place in a clean, greased, chilled bowl, turning once to bring greased-side up. Cover tightly with a lid greased on inside to fit bowl. Store in refrigerator until ready to use. Remove required amount from refrigerator as needed. Let stand until dough warms to room temp, then form into desired shapes, pp 273–77. Place in greased pans, cover and let rise in warm place until double, about 1¼ hrs. Bake in a moderately hot oven (400° F) 10 to 12 min. 36 medium Cloverleaf rolls.

POTATO REFRIGERATOR ROLLS

For best flavor, do not hold this yeast dough containing milk longer than 36 to 48 hrs. If a longer hold-over time is desired, make Plain Refrigerator Rolls, above.

6¼ cups all-purpose flour	1 cup milk, scalded
1 reg cake compressed *or* 1 pkg dry gran yeast	1 cup hot riced cooked potatoes, pkd
¼ cup lukewarm water	2 eggs, beaten
⅓ cup sugar	⅔ cup melted butter *or* shortening
2 tsp salt	

Sift flour and measure. Crumble compressed or turn gran yeast into lukewarm water in a 4-qt bowl, stir in 1 tsp of the sugar and let soften 10 min. Stir remaining sugar, and salt into the hot milk, then add ¼ cup of it to the hot potatoes and beat until smooth. Cool to lukewarm. Blend remaining cooled milk with yeast thoroughly. Stir in potatoes and eggs. Beat in half the flour thoroughly, then cooled shortening and remaining flour. Turn out onto lightly floured board or pastry cloth, cover with bowl and let rest 10 min. Then knead until smooth and elastic, about 10 min, using no more than 2 tbsp flour for kneading. Place in greased bowl, turn dough once to bring greased side up. Grease inside of a lid which fits bowl and cover bowl, then wrap in a damp cloth and place in refrigerator overnight or for several hrs. When ready to make rolls, take all or part of dough from refrigerator and shape immediately into rolls, pp 274–77. Cover, let rise in a warm place until double, 1½ to 2 hrs, touching tops lightly with warm water if crust forms. Bake in a moderately hot oven (400° F) 10 to 12 min. 54 Parker House or Cloverleaf rolls.

Note: Half of this dough may be used one day and the other half kept chilled another 24 hrs and then baked.

FANCY ROLLS, BUNS, BISMARCKS AND DOUGHNUTS

BUTTERSCOTCH ROLLS

Follow recipe for making and baking Pecan Rolls or Schnecken, p 287, except reduce brown sugar to ½ cup. Spread sugar-butter mixture in a 9-inch sq baking pan then sprinkle with ⅓ cup chopped nuts, if desired. Arrange rolls cut-side down almost together over the sugar mixture.

CINNAMON CROWN ROLLS

½ recipe Sweet Roll Dough,
    p 279
3 tbsp melted butter

⅓ cup fine-cut pecans
⅓ cup sugar mixed with
1 tsp cinnamon

After second rising of dough, punch down and turn out on lightly floured board or pastry cloth. Cover with bowl and let rest 10 min. Cut dough into 4 equal pieces; shape each piece into an 8-inch long "rope." Now cut each "rope" into 8 pieces, making 32 pieces. Roll into balls size of walnuts. Put melted butter in one small bowl, the nuts in a 2nd bowl and the sugar-cinnamon mix in a 3rd. Toss each ball in melted butter until well covered, then in nuts and last in sugar-cinnamon mixture. Place in well-greased 9-inch ring mold (7-cup capacity) about 1-inch apart, slightly toward inside of mold; place 2nd row of coated balls over the first, but toward outside of pan and in the inch space left between. Sprinkle any leftover coating mixture over rolls. Let rise in warm place until double, about 1 hr. Bake in moderate oven (350° F) 25 to 30 min. Turn out on plate and serve hot, pulling apart with fork. 5 to 6 servings.

Note: Bake rolls from a full recipe of Sweet Roll Dough in a well-greased 10-in tube cake pan.

HOT CROSS BUNS

New method, easy handling, moist and delicious

3¾ cups all-purpose flour	½ cup melted butter, cooled
¾ cup milk	½ cup currants, washed,
½ cup sugar	plumped, p 165
1 tsp salt	¼ cup moist citron, cut fine
2 reg cakes compressed *or* 2	1 tsp cinnamon
pkgs dry gran yeast	1 egg white mixed with 1
¼ cup lukewarm water	tbsp water
2 eggs, beaten	

Sift flour and measure. Scald milk in top of double boiler, add sugar and salt, stir thoroughly and pour into a 4-qt mixing bowl to cool to lukewarm. Soften yeast in lukewarm water for 5 min. Now add to cooled milk and beat in 1¼ cups of flour with rotary beater until smooth, then the eggs, then shortening. Stir in remaining flour with wooden spoon and beat 5 min. Cover and let rise in warm place until double, about 1½ hrs. Add currants, citron and cinnamon and knead until fruit is distributed and cinnamon streaked through dough. Cover and place in refrigerator 2½ hrs to rise slowly and to chill for easier handling. Turn out onto lightly floured board or pastry cloth and knead a min. Cut dough into 4 equal portions; shape portions into uniform rolls, then cut each roll into 4ths. Shape into 16 buns. Place on greased 15½ x 10½-inch cookie sheet. Brush with egg white mixture. Cover with damp cheesecloth and let rise in warm place until double, about 1¾ hrs. Bake in moderate oven (350° F) 18 to 20 min. Make crosses of Confectioners' Icing on buns. Serve warm or cold. 2½ lbs dough or 16 large buns.

Note: If desired, use a sharp knife to cut a shallow cross into top of each bun just before baking.

CONFECTIONERS' ICING

½ cup confectioners' sugar,	1 tsp white corn syrup
pkd	¼ tsp vanilla
1 tbsp milk	Few grains salt

Combine ingredients and mix until smooth. Using star tube, pipe icing onto warm buns to make crosses, or pour from tip of teaspoon. Sufficient icing for 16 buns.

KOLACHY

Kolachi or Kolache

Real Bohemian Kolachy are made according to following recipe, but excellent Kolachy can be made with Sweet Roll Dough, p 279.

After 2nd rising, turn dough out on a lightly floured board or pastry cloth, cut in half and round up portions; cover with bowls, let rest 10 min. Roll out ¼-inch thick and cut into 2¼-inch rounds with a biscuit cutter lightly dipped in flour. Place on a greased baking sheet. With thumb, make wide, deep indentation in center of each round and fill with any of the Kolachy Fillings. Cover, let rise until double in a warm place, about 15 min. Bake in a moderately hot oven (400° F) 15 to 20 min. Remove to cake rack to cool. Sprinkle with xxxx sugar. About 3 dozen.

Note: Another way to shape Kolachy is to roll dough ⅜-in thick; cut into 3-in sq. Put a tbsp of filling in center, bring corners to center over filling and pinch together.

BOHEMIAN KOLACHY DOUGH

3 cups all-purpose flour	¼ cup soft butter
¾ cup milk, scalded	¼ cup sugar
1 reg cake compressed *or* 1	½ tsp salt
pkg dry gran yeast	1 egg yolk
¼ cup lukewarm water	½ tsp grated lemon rind, pkd
1 tsp sugar	xxxx sugar

Sift flour and measure. Scald milk and cool to lukewarm. Crumble compressed or turn dry gran yeast into lukewarm water, stir in 1 tsp sugar and let soften 10 min. In a 3-qt mixing bowl, cream butter, add next 4 ingredients and beat until smooth. Stir in yeast mixture, then add the flour and milk alternately in 3 portions, stirring and beating after each to form a smooth, soft dough. Round up dough and return to washed, greased bowl, turning once to bring greased side up. Cover and let rise in warm place until double, about 2 hrs. Turn out on lightly floured board or pastry cloth and roll out ¼-inch thick. Cut out with a 2½-inch biscuit cutter and place on a greased cookie sheet. Let rest 10 min, then make wide, deep indentation in center of each round with greased thumb. Fill with 1 tbsp desired Kolachy Filling. Let rise in warm place until a little more than double, about 15 min. Bake in a moderately hot oven (400° F) 15 to 20 min. Remove to cake rack, and while warm, sprinkle with xxxx sugar. About 2 dozen.

APRICOT FILLING FOR KOLACHY

½ lb dried apricots	1½ cups water
⅓ cup sugar	1 tbsp butter

Wash apricots quickly in cold water. Place in saucepan with sugar and water, heat to boiling, reduce heat, cover and simmer 45 min. When cool, press fruit and juice through a food mill or coarse sieve. Stir in butter. 1½ cups purée.

COTTAGE CHEESE FILLING FOR KOLACHY

½ lb creamed cottage cheese   ⅛ tsp mace
2 egg yolks, beaten   Dash of salt
2 tbsp sugar   ¼ cup golden raisins,
1 tbsp melted butter   plumped, p 165

Combine all ingredients and mix just enough to blend well.

PRUNE FILLING FOR KOLACHY

½ lb prunes $\frac{1}{16}$ tsp cloves
¼ cup sugar   ⅛ tsp allspice
1½ cups water   1 tbsp butter
½ tsp grated lemon rind

Wash prunes, place in saucepan with sugar and water. Heat to
boiling, reduce heat, cover and simmer 45 min. Cool, drain off juice
and save. Pit prunes and put fruit through food mill or press through
coarse sieve. Stir remaining ingredients into purée. If filling is too thick,
thin with some prune juice.

GLAZED ORANGE BUTTERFLY ROLLS

Rolls: *Glaze:*
Sweet Roll Dough, p 279   ½ cup xxxx sugar, pkd
⅓ cup soft butter   1 tbsp orange juice
½ cup sugar mixed with   2 tsp white corn syrup
2 tsp grated orange rind   Dash of salt
            1 tsp grated orange rind

Make the dough, but omit the mace or cardamon. After 2nd rising,
punch down and turn out on lightly floured board or pastry cloth. Cut
in half, round up portions and cover with bowls; let rest 10 min. Roll
out each portion into a rectangle 9 x 15 inches. Spread each with half
the butter, sprinkle with half the sugar-rind mixture. Roll up snugly
like jelly roll stretching slightly while rolling. Moisten edge and pinch
it to roll to seal. Cut into 1¼-inch wide slices, or 12 slices to each roll.
Hold handle of wooden spoon or knife parallel with cut edge of roll;
press down hard across center of rolls to produce butterfly shape. Place
on greased baking sheet; cover, let rise in a warm place until double,
about 45 min. Bake in a moderate oven (375° F) 18 to 20 min or until
golden brown. Remove to cake racks to cool slightly. To make glaze,
combine and heat last 5 ingredients just to boiling. Then brush over
rolls about 5 min after removing from oven to obtain a clear, shiny
glaze. Delicious warm; good cold. 24 rolls.

ORANGE MARMALADE PINWHEELS

An easy economical roll with a dressed up look and flavor

Sweet Roll Dough, p 279   ¾ cup orange marmalade
3 tbsp soft butter

Grease generously muffin pans with 24 medium cups measuring
2¾ inches across. After 2nd rising of dough, punch down, turn out on
lightly floured board or pastry cloth, round up, cover with bowl, let
rest 10 min. Roll out into a 12 x 18 rectangle. Spread with soft
butter, then with marmalade. Roll up snugly like jelly roll starting at
wide end. Cut into ¾-inch slices. Place cut-side down in prepared
muffin pans. Cover and let rise in warm place until double, about 1 hr.
Bake in a moderate oven (375° F) about 20 min or until golden brown.
Remove from pans at once. Serve warm. 24 Pinwheels.

ORANGE POCKETBOOK ROLLS

Spring a surprise with these different delightful rolls

Sweet Roll Dough, p 279   ¼ cup sugar mixed with
3 seedless medium oranges   1 tsp cinnamon

After 2nd rising of dough, punch down and turn out on lightly
floured board or pastry cloth; cover with bowl, let rest 10 min. Meanwhile section the oranges. Roll dough out ¼-inch thick; cut into
circles with a 3½-inch cookie cutter. Place an orange section on one
side of each circle, sprinkle with 1 tsp cinnamon mixture; fold over,
press edges together and lay on a greased baking sheet 2 inches apart.
Cover, let rise in warm place until double. Bake in a moderately hot
oven (400° F) 20 min or until nicely browned. Serve warm. 15 rolls.

PINEAPPLE BUTTER BUNS

Dough: ½ cup well-drained crushed
  ½ Recipe Sweet Roll Dough,   pineapple
    p 279   *Filling:*
Pan Dressing: 2 tbsp soft butter
  ½ cup soft butter   ½ cup drained crushed pine-
  ½ cup sugar   apple
  1 tsp lemon juice

After 2nd rising of dough, punch down, turn out on lightly floured
board or pastry cloth, cover with bowl and let rest 10 min. Meanwhile
prepare Pan Dressing: Combine butter and sugar in a 9-inch sq pan
and place over low heat just long enough to blend well. Remove from
heat and stir in lemon juice and pineapple. Now roll dough into a 16 x

9-inch rectangle. Spread evenly with the 2 tbsp butter, then the pineapple for filling. Start at wide end and roll up snugly like jelly roll. Cut into 1-inch slices. Lay rolls over Dressing in pan. Cover, let rise in warm place until double, about 1 hr. Bake in a moderate oven (375° F) 20 to 25 min or until golden brown. Cool in pan on cake rack 2 min, then invert on plate. Serve warm. 16 rolls.

ROYAL RUSKS

Royal Rusks—sweet dough made in Parker House Roll shapes

1 Recipe Sweet Roll Dough,   Melted butter
  p 279

After 2nd rising, punch dough down and turn out on lightly floured board or pastry cloth. Cover with bowl, let rest 10 min, then roll out ⅓-inch thick. Cut and shape like Parker House Rolls, p 277, brushing with melted butter between fold and on top. Cover and let rise in a warm place until double. Bake in moderately hot oven (425° F) 12 to 15 min or until golden brown. 3 to 4 dozen.

SCHNECKEN OR PECAN ROLLS

Use ½ Sweet Roll Dough,   6 tsp white corn syrup
  or ¼ Plain Roll Dough,   Pecan halves
  p 273 or 279   *Dough Spread:*
Pan Spread: ¼ cup soft butter
  ⅔ cup moist brown sugar, pkd   ¼ cup granulated sugar
  ¼ cup soft butter   ½ tsp cinnamon
     Melted butter

Grease muffin pans with 12 deep cups 2¾ inches across. Cream brown sugar and butter until smooth and place 1 tbsp of the mixture in bottom of each muffin cup, then add ½ tsp of the syrup and 6 to 8 pecan halves to each cup.

After 2nd rising of dough, turn out on lightly floured board or pastry cloth, round up, cover with bowl and let rest 10 min. Then roll dough into a 15 x 8-inch rectangle, about ⅓-inch thick. Spread with butter and sprinkle with sugar mixed with cinnamon. Now start at wide side, roll up snugly like jelly roll, stretching dough slightly while rolling. Moisten edge and pinch to roll to seal. Cut into 1¼-inch slices. Place cut-side-down into prepared muffin pan. Brush with melted butter. Cover lightly and let rise in warm place until double, about 1 hr. Bake in a moderate oven (375° F) 25 min. Remove from oven; let stand a half min, then loosen edges with a knife and turn upside down onto serving plate. Hold pan over rolls a min for syrup to drain out on rolls. Serve warm nut-side-up.

BANANA DOUGHNUTS

5 cups all-purpose flour
3 tsp D.A. baking powder *or*
   4 tsp tartrate *or* phosphate
   type
1 tsp soda
2 tsp salt
1 tsp nutmeg
¼ cup shortening
1 cup sugar

1½ tsp vanilla
3 eggs, well beaten
¾ cup mashed bananas,
   2 good-sized bananas
   combined with
½ cup buttermilk
½ cup flour for rolling
Shortening for frying*

Sift flour, measure, and resift 3 times with baking powder, soda, salt and nutmeg. Cream shortening, blend in sugar, add vanilla and eggs, and beat until light and fluffy. Add combined bananas and buttermilk and stir until well mixed. Add flour mixture in 3 or 4 portions, stirring just enough to mix after each addition. Chill before rolling. Remove one-fourth of dough from refrigerator at a time, knead it lightly 4 or 5 times, roll out on floured pastry cloth to ⅜-inch thickness, and cut with floured 2½-inch doughnut cutter. Fry in deep fat heated to 360° F, p 738, until golden brown, then lift out and drain on absorbent paper. If desired, the dough may be covered tightly and kept in the refrigerator for 1 or 2 days, to be fried as needed. About 42.

BUTTERMILK DOUGHNUTS

3½ cups all-purpose flour
   4 tsp baking powder *or*
     5¼ tsp tartrate *or* phos-
     phate type
½ tsp salt
¼ tsp nutmeg
1 tsp soda

2 eggs
1 cup sugar
½ tsp vanilla
1 cup buttermilk
2 tbsp melted butter
Shortening for frying*

Sift flour, measure and resift 3 times with baking powder, salt, nutmeg and soda. Beat eggs, add sugar and vanilla and beat well for about 2 min. Stir in buttermilk and butter, then the flour mixture until dough is smooth. This dough is too soft to handle immediately, but first must be chilled in refrigerator for two or three hrs. Rub flour into pastry cloth for rolling. Remove one-fourth of the chilled dough from refrigerator. Roll out quickly to a little more than ¼-inch in thickness. Cut with doughnut cutter. Remove trimmings carefully and pile on top of each other. Re-roll these, using as little flour as possible. Lift doughnuts carefully into frying basket. Lower into hot fat (360° F). Turn as soon as browned on lower side and fry until brown on other side. Remove doughnuts with a fork or skewer and drain on absorbent paper.

*See Frying with Deep Fat, p 738.

If sugar-coated doughnuts are desired, they may be dropped into a paper sack containing several spoonfuls of powdered or granulated sugar and shaken to coat. Repeat rolling and frying until dough is used up—3 dozen.

DROP DOUGHNUTS

Shortening for frying*	½ tsp nutmeg
3 cups all-purpose flour	2 tbsp soft butter
3 tsp baking powder,	1 cup sugar
see p 112	2 eggs or 4 yolks, beaten
½ tsp salt	1 cup buttermilk
½ tsp cinnamon	

Put shortening into 3-qt frying kettle and hook thermometer onto the inside of kettle. Sift flour, measure and resift 3 times with next 4 ingredients. Cream butter, blend in sugar, then add eggs or yolks and beat thoroughly. Add flour mixture and milk alternately in 3 or 4 portions, stirring until just blended after additions. Heat shortening to 370° F. Quickly drop by teaspoonfuls (no more) into hot fat until 7 or 8 are in kettle; fry until golden brown and cooked through, about 3 minutes. Lift out with slotted spoon or fork onto paper toweling to drain. Tumble in sugar while warm, if desired. About 40.

HASTY CHERRY, PLUM OR PEACH COFFEE CAKE

Prepare Kneadless Drop Batter, p 279 as for Hasty Apple Cake, p 290. Use 3 to 4 cups fresh pitted cherries, halved pitted fresh plums or pared sliced fresh peaches. Sprinkle ¾ to 1 cup sugar evenly over the fruit. These same fruit toppings may also be used on Coffee Cake made from Sweet Roll Dough. 2 coffee cakes.

BISMARCKS OR JELLY DOUGHNUTS

1 Recipe Sweet Roll Dough	2 lbs fat for frying
Scant ½ cup tart stiff jam	½ cup granulated sugar

Make Sweet Roll Dough according to directions. After first rising, turn dough out on lightly floured board or pastry cloth and cut in half. Quickly round up portions and cover with bowls; let rest 10 min, then roll out to ¼-inch thickness. Let rest 5 min. Cut out rounds with 2½-inch cutter lightly dipped in flour and again let stand 5 min. Place about 1 tsp jam in center of half the rounds, top with remaining rounds, sandwich fashion. Seal edges firmly by pressing together with a fork or fingers. Again, let rise in a warm place uncovered until double, from

* See Frying with Deep Fat, p 738.

25 to 30 min. Use pancake turner to lift bismarcks and slide into deep fat heated to 370° F. Fry until brown and crisp on both sides, about 3 min, turning once. Drain on absorbent paper, then shake while warm in paper bag containing sugar. 20 Bismarcks.

RAISED DOUGHNUTS

Make Sweet Roll Dough according to directions. After first rising, turn out on lightly floured board or pastry cloth and cut in half. Quickly round up portions and cover with bowls; let rest 10 min. Then roll out ½-inch thick. Dip a 3-inch doughnut cutter in flour and cut out doughnuts. Let rise on lightly floured board in warm place until very light, about 45 min. Do not cover as the light crust that forms makes it easier to lift and slide doughnuts from pancake turner into hot fat. Fry in deep fat heated to 370° F until golden brown on both sides, about 3 min, turning once during frying. Drain on absorbent paper. Shake while warm in a paper bag containing granulated sugar. These are elegant warm but also good cold. About 24.

Note: To reheat doughnuts, place in a paper bag and put into hot oven for a few minutes.

CINNAMON TWIST COFFEE CAKE

Use ⅓ of Sweet Roll Dough, or ⅙ of Plain Roll Dough, for each coffee cake. After 2nd rising, shape into a ball, cover with bowl and let rest 10 min. Roll out to an 8 x 14 inch rectangle. Spread with 2 tbsp soft butter and sprinkle with a mixture of 1 tsp cinnamon and ⅓ cup sugar. Roll up snugly like a jelly roll starting at wide end; moisten edge and pinch neatly to roll. Lay straight, sealed edge underneath, on a greased baking sheet 10½ x 15½ inches. With scissors, cut about ¾ths way through roll at 1-inch intervals. Twist cut sections so they lie flat, then turn one section to the right, the next to the left, then to right, etc. There will be 2 rows of overlapping sections of rolls, each attached in the center. Brush with melted butter, cover and let rise in warm place until double, about 1 hr. Bake in moderately hot oven (400° F) about 30 min. Cool on sheet on cake rack 10 min, then drizzle with Confectioners' Icing, p 283. Serve warm. 6 to 7 servings.

HASTY APPLE COFFEE CAKE

Kneadless Drop Roll   1 tbsp melted butter
Batter, p 279   ¾ cup sugar mixed with
8 medium-size tart apples   2 tsp cinnamon

Make Kneadless Drop Roll Batter as directed. Spread into 2 well-greased pans 11 x 7 x 1½ inches, or two 10-inch round layer cake pans.

Pare apples, cut in quarters, core, cut quarters into 4 wedges. Pat dough with melted butter; lay apples close together, pressing core-side slightly into batter. Sprinkle sugar-cinnamon mixture evenly over apples. Cover, let rise in a warm place until double, about 1 hr. Cover pan with an inverted 2nd pan of same size to thoroughly cook apples. Bake 10 min in moderately hot oven (400° F), then remove covers and bake about 20 min longer or until apples are tender and cakes are done. Serve warm. 10 to 15 servings.

DANISH KRINGLER

¾ cup (1½ sticks) butter, softened
1 package active dry yeast
¼ cup warm water
⅓ cup milk, scalded
¼ cup sugar
¼ tsp salt

½ tsp lemon extract
1 egg
2¼ cups regular all-purpose flour
⅔ cup apricot filling
Egg white, slightly beaten
Granulated sugar

Divide butter in half; on waxed paper spread each half to measure 7 x 7 in. Chill. In large mixing bowl combine yeast and water; cool milk to lukewarm and add to yeast mixture. Add salt, sugar, lemon extract and egg; beat until sugar is dissolved. Gradually add flour; mix until smooth. On well floured board, roll dough to an 8 x 12-in rectangle. Place one of the butter squares, butter side down, to cover ⅔ of dough; peel off waxed paper. Fold unbuttered third of dough over center third; then fold remaining third over top. (3 layer rectangle measures 8 x 4 in.) Fold one end over middle third and fold other end over doubled layer. (9 layer rectangle measures 4 x 2⅔ inches.) Wrap in waxed paper and chill 30 min. Roll dough again to an 8 x 12-inch rectangle; add remaining butter square and fold as before. Chill several hours or overnight. Cut dough into two equal pieces. Roll each, one at a time, to measure 20 x 6 in. Spread center with ⅓ cup apricot filling. Fold one lengthwise edge over middle; moisten with water and fold other edge over top to make dough 20 inches long and 2 inches wide. Place on buttered baking sheet, sealed edge down, to form circle. Seal joining ends, brush top with egg white and sprinkle with granulated sugar. Bake at once in a preheated 350° F oven, 25 to 30 minutes or until golden brown. 2 kringlers.

COTTAGE CHEESE KUCHEN

½ recipe Sweet Roll Dough, p 279
Filling:
12 oz creamed cottage cheese
3 eggs, separated
½ cup mace
⅛ tsp mace

⅛ tsp salt
1 tsp grated lemon rind, pkd
1 tbsp lemon juice
2 tbsp flour
¼ cup cream
½ cup golden raisins, plumped

Make Sweet Roll Dough, and after 2nd rising turn out onto lightly floured board or pastry cloth; cut in half, round up each half, cover with bowls and let rest 10 min. Roll out into rectangles large enough to fit snugly over bottom and up sides of two 11 x 7 x 1½-inch pans. Prick well with fork, cover, let rise in a warm place 15 to 20 min. Meanwhile prepare Filling by pressing cheese through a fine strainer into a 3-qt mixing bowl. Add beaten egg yolks with next 8 ingredients and stir thoroughly. Fold in stiffly beaten egg whites. Pour into the dough-lined pans. Bake in a moderate oven (350° F) 45 min. Serve while slightly warm. 8 to 12 servings.

PLUM KUCHEN No. 1

Canned Plums

¼ recipe Sweet Roll Dough	⅛ tsp grated lemon rind, pkd
No. 2 can blue plums	⅛ tsp cinnamon
1 tbsp corn starch	⅛ tsp salt
1 tsp lemon juice	

Make dough and after 2nd rising, punch down and turn out on a lightly floured board or pastry cloth. Round up, cover with bowl and let rest 10 min. Roll into a circle to fit into bottom and up sides of a 9-inch layer cake pan. Dough is about ¼-inch thick. Prick dough in bottom with a fork. Lay drained plums, pitted and halved, cut-side up over dough. Combine corn starch with a little of the plum juice to make smooth paste, stir in remaining juice and cook with constant stirring until mixture thickens and is clear. Stir in remaining ingredients and *cool,* then pour over plums. Let rise until double, about 1 hr. Bake in a moderate oven (375° F) 25 min or until rim is golden brown. Cool 5 min then serve warm from pan. 4 servings.

PLUM KUCHEN No. 2

Fresh blue plums

Follow recipe for Plum Kuchen No. 1, except use 12 fresh plums. Wash, halve and pit plums and lay cut-side up over dough. Then strew Confectioners' Sugar Streusel, p 294, over top. Let rise and bake like Plum Kuchen No. 1.

LACED-UP APPLE-RAISIN COFFEE CAKE

Follow recipe for making Laced-Up Apricot Coffee Cake. Instead of Apricot Purée, use sweetened stiff tart apple sauce combined with a few raisins and flavored with cinnamon or allspice.

LACED-UP APRICOT COFFEE CAKE

A distinctive, refreshing, gold-striped beauty

½ recipe Sweet Roll Dough,
  p 279
2 tbsp soft butter
⅔ cup stiff Apricot Purée,
  p 551

⅔ cup sugar
¼ tsp salt
Melted butter
Confectioners' Icing, p 283

After 2nd rising of dough, punch down, turn out onto floured board or pastry cloth, cover with bowl, let rest 10 min. Roll out into 10 x 14-inch rectangle. Spread with butter. Combine purée, sugar and salt and spread a 3-inch wide strip lengthwise down center to within 1½ inches of each end. Fold dough up at both ends 1½ inches over apricot mixture; this prevents filling from running out while baking. Now with sharp paring knife make cuts through the dough on each side of the filling 1½ inches apart and 2 inches long. To lace, start at one end and lift strips alternately up over the filling, crossing them at the center; the end of each strip should be covered neatly with the succeeding pair of strips. Stretch the last 2 strips enough to tuck neatly underneath end fold. Use 2 pancake turners to lift the coffee cake carefully onto a greased 10½ x 15½-inch cookie sheet with a rim all around. Gently press top and sides to level and evenly shape the cake. Brush with melted butter or milk. Cover with damp cloth that is supported so as not to touch cake. Let rise in warm place until double, about 1 hr. Bake in a moderate oven (375° F) 25 to 28 min or until done. Cool in pan on cake rack. Drizzle with Confectioners' Icing while warm. The icing may be made with juice drained from cooked apricots instead of water. Serve warm or cold. 8 to 10 servings.

LACED-UP PRUNE COFFEE CAKE

Follow recipe for Laced-Up Apricot Coffee Cake, except use Sweetened Prune Purée, p 553, and ¼ cup chopped nuts.

QUICK OLD-TIME STREUSEL COFFEE CAKE

Easy to make, lacy-textured snack special

Batter:
  Kneadless Drop Roll
  Batter, p 279
½ tsp ground cardamon *or*
1 tsp grated orange rind, pkd

Streusel:
¼ cup flour
¼ cup sugar
2 tbsp soft butter

Make dough using the cardamon or orange rind instead of vanilla. Spread batter into 2 well-greased 11 x 7 x 1½-inch pans or two 10-inch round layer cake pans. Mix flour and sugar, blend in butter with pastry blender until crumbly particles are size of peas, then sprinkle over top of batter. Let rise in warm place until double. Bake in a moderately hot oven (400° F) 18 to 20 min or until golden brown. Serve warm. 10 to 15 servings.

SWEDISH TEA RING

½ recipe Sweet Roll Dough,
  p 279
2 tbsp soft butter
1 tsp cinnamon mixed
  with ¼ cup sugar
¼ cup raisins, plumped,
  p 165

Melted butter
Confectioners' Icing,
  p 283
½ cup blanched slivered
  toasted almonds, optional

Make dough and after 2nd rising, punch down and turn out on lightly floured board or pastry cloth; round up, cover with bowl, let rest 10 min. Roll into a 15 x 8-inch rectangle. Spread with the butter, sprinkle with cinnamon-sugar mixture and raisins to within ½-inch of edge. Roll up snugly like jelly roll, starting at wide-side. Moisten edge, then pinch it firmly against roll. Place roll on greased baking sheet with sealed edge on bottom. Stretch slightly, curve into a ring and join the ends of roll by slipping them inside each other, pinching together to seal. Now press ring from both inside and out to shape into a perfect circle. Start at *outside* of ring, and with scissors make cuts toward center about ¾th the way through ring and 1-inch apart for each section. Now turn sections on their sides all in same direction, overlapping slightly. Brush with melted butter. Cover lightly; let rise in warm place until double. Bake in a moderate oven (375° F) 30 to 35 min. Cool on sheet on cake rack 5 min, then slide onto cake rack with spatula. Cool 5 min longer, then spread with Icing and sprinkle with almonds. Serves 10 to 12.

CONFECTIONERS' SUGAR STREUSEL

A topping for rich sweet rolls and coffee cake

¾ cup xxxx sugar, pkd
½ cup flour
  Dash of salt
¼ cup soft butter

1 egg yolk
¼ cup ground almonds,
  optional

Measure sugar, flour and salt into mixing bowl and stir to blend. Add butter well blended with egg yolk, then with pastry blender cut into sugar mixture until particles are size of peas. Or rub the butter-yolk mixture in with tips of fingers. Stir in almonds. Sprinkle over coffee cakes or sweet rolls after shaping, or just before placing in oven. Enough for two 9-inch coffee cakes or 24 rolls.

OLD-FASHIONED STREUSEL NUT COFFEE CAKE

Sweet Roll Dough	2 tsp cinnamon
Streusel Topping:	Dash of salt
⅔ cup brown sugar, pkd	¼ cup soft butter
½ cup flour	⅔ cup chopped nuts

After 1st or 2nd rising of dough, punch down and turn out on lightly floured board or pastry cloth; cut in half, round up, cover with bowls and let rest 10 min. Roll each portion out to fit a 7 x 11 x 1½-inch pan or a 10-inch round cake pan. Cover with a damp cloth and let rise in warm place until double. Meanwhile mix sugar, flour, cinnamon and salt thoroughly; work in soft butter with pastry blender or with finger tips to obtain a coarse crumbly mixture, then stir in nuts. Sprinkle over coffee cake before rising or just before placing in oven. Bake in a moderately hot oven (400° F) 25 to 30 min. Serve warm. 10 to 12 servings.

SPECIAL BREADS

CINNAMON WHIRL BREAD

Use ⅔ Sweet Roll Dough, p 279, or ⅓ Plain Roll Dough, p 273, for each loaf. After 2nd rising, turn out onto lightly floured board or pastry cloth, round up, cover with bowl, let rest 10 min. Roll out into an 8 x 15-inch rectangle. Brush with 2 tbsp of cream or soft butter and sprinkle with 1 tsp cinnamon mixed with ⅓ cup sugar to within ¼-inch of edge. Start at narrow end, roll up snugly like jelly roll, stretching dough slightly while rolling; seal edge by moistening and pinching to the roll. Place in a greased loaf pan 9 x 5 x 3 inches with sealed edge on bottom. Brush top with melted shortening. Cover, let rise in a warm place until double, about 1 hr. Bake in a moderate oven (375° F) 35 to 40 min. (If glass baking pan is used, bake at 350° F.) Remove from pan to cake rack to cool. Frost with Confectioners' Icing, p 283, while still warm, if desired.

Note: Spreading dough with butter makes a richer loaf but the whirls may tend to separate in places.

GARLIC BREAD

Perfect with Tossed Salad

1 medium clove garlic, peeled	1 loaf long French *or* Vienna bread
⅓ cup butter, room temp	

Pound garlic to paste. Stir in butter thoroughly. Slash bread diagonally into inch-thick slices, being careful *not to cut through bottom crust.*

Separate slices slightly and spread both sides *thinly* with the butter. Place on a baking sheet in a moderately hot oven (425° F) 10 to 12 min or until blistering hot and edges are toasted. Serve in a long basket lined with napkin for guests to break off pieces as desired. 5 to 6 servings.

HERB BREAD

Use Recipe for Plain Roll Dough, p 273, or White Bread, p 269. Make according to directions but add the following spices to scalded milk: 1 tbsp caraway seed, 1 tsp nutmeg and 1 tsp crumbled sieved sage. This bread is wonderful for meat or chicken sandwiches, either plain or toasted.

POPPY SEED OR NUT ROLLS

Hungarian

Dough:
1 cup milk
1 tbsp sugar
1 reg cake compressed *or* 1 pkg gran yeast
3 cups all-purpose flour
¼ tsp salt

½ cup cold butter
3 egg yolks
Filling:
2 cups poppy seed *or* finely ground nuts mixed with
1 cup sugar
1 egg, beaten slightly

Start oven 10 min before baking; set to moderate (350° F). Grease baking sheet lightly. Scald milk, add sugar and *cool to lukewarm,* then crumble in yeast to soften 10 min. Sift flour, measure into a 3-qt mixing bowl. Add salt and butter, then cut into flour with pastry blender as for pastry. Beat egg yolks; stir into milk-yeast mixture, then add gradually to flour, mixing well to a stiff dough. Divide dough into 3 equal portions and let rest 10 min. Roll out each portion to a 10-inch square on a lightly floured pastry cloth. Sprinkle each with ⅓ of poppy seed mixture. Roll up like jelly roll, pinch edges together to seal. Place on prepared sheet seam-side down. Cover and let rise 1 hr in a warm place (85° F). Beat egg and brush over rolls. Bake 20 min. Remove from oven to cake rack to cool.

NUT BREAD

This bread is delicious toasted or wonderful for party sandwiches

3½ cups all-purpose flour
1 reg cake compressed *or*
1 pkg dry gran yeast
¼ cup lukewarm water
⅓ cup sugar
1 cup milk, scalded

¾ tsp salt
2 tbsp melted shortening
1 egg white, stiffly beaten
1¼ cups coarsely chopped walnuts *or* pecans

Sift flour and measure. Crumble compressed or turn granular yeast into the lukewarm water with 1 tsp of the sugar and let soften 10 min. Combine hot milk with rest of sugar and the salt in a 4-qt mixing bowl, stir and cool to lukewarm, then stir yeast into milk mixture. Beat in 1½ cups of the flour to a smooth batter, then the cooled shortening. Stir in egg white and nuts. Add all but ¼ cup of remaining flour and mix until smooth. Turn dough out onto lightly floured board or pastry cloth, cover with bowl and let rest 10 min. Then knead for 5 min, using only enough of remaining flour to prevent sticking to board or hands. Round up and return to washed, greased bowl, turning once to bring greased side up. Cover, let rise in warm place until double, about 1½ hrs. Punch down, turn out on lightly floured board or pastry cloth. Cut in half, round up portions, cover with bowls, let rest 10 min. Shape into loaves, p 271. Place in 9 x 5 x 3-inch greased pans. Cover and let rise in warm place until double, about 1 hr. Bake in moderately hot oven (400° F) 30 to 35 min. Remove from pans to cake racks to cool uncovered and out of a draft. 2 loaves.

OATMEAL BREAD

An appetite-satisfying bread and makes excellent toast

5 cups all-purpose flour	1 reg cake compressed *or*
2½ cups rolled oats	1 pkg dry gran yeast
⅓ cup molasses	¼ cup lukewarm water
2 tsp salt	1 tsp sugar
2 tbsp shortening	1 cup milk, scalded
1¼ cups boiling water	

Sift flour and measure. Measure next 4 ingredients into 4-qt mixing bowl. Pour boiling water over mixture, stir well; let stand 1 hr. Soften yeast in lukewarm water with sugar, let stand 10 min. Combine yeast and lukewarm milk and stir into oatmeal mixture. Beat in about ½ the flour, then add all but ¼ cup of remaining flour and mix to a stiff dough. Turn out on board or pastry cloth sprinkled with remaining flour. Cover dough with bowl; let rest 10 min, then knead until smooth and elastic, about 10 min. Place in the washed, greased bowl, turn once to bring greased-side up. Cover, let rise in a warm place until double, about 2 hrs. Turn out on lightly floured board, cut in half, quickly round up and cover with bowls; let rest 10 min. Shape into loaves, p 271. Place in 9 x 5 x 3-inch greased loaf pans. Cover and let rise in warm place until double, about 1 hr. Bake in a moderate oven (375° F) 40 to 45 min. Remove from pans to cake rack to cool. Two 2-lb loaves.

Note: Best rising conditions for yeast dough are moist air and a temp of 80 to 85° F and out of a draft.

CURRANT OATMEAL BREAD

Follow directions for making Oatmeal Bread, except stir in ¾ cup washed, drained dried currants after the first half of flour is beaten in. The bread may have Confectioners' Icing, p 283, brushed over the top while still slightly warm.

PRUNE OR RAISIN BREAD

A favorite fruit bread—plain, toasted or for sandwiches

6½ cups all-purpose flour
1 reg cake compressed *or*
1 pkg dry gran yeast
¼ cup lukewarm water
⅓ cup sugar
2 tsp salt

1¾ cups milk, scalded
¼ cup melted shortening
1 egg, beaten
1 cup chopped cooked
prunes *or* raisins

Sift flour and measure. Crumble compressed or granular yeast into the lukewarm water with 1 tsp of the sugar and let soften 10 min. Stir remaining sugar and salt into hot milk in a 4-qt mixing bowl, and cool to lukewarm. Now stir yeast into milk, then beat in 2½ cups of the flour. Stir in cooled shortening, then egg and beat vigorously. Stir in prunes and all but ¼ cup of remaining flour and mix thoroughly. Turn dough onto board or pastry cloth sprinkled with remaining flour; cover with bowl, let rest 10 min, then knead 10 min. Return to washed, greased bowl, turn once to bring greased side up. Cover and let rise in warm place until double. Punch down, turn out on board, cut dough in half, round up halves, cover with bowls and let rest 10 min. Shape into loaves, p 271. Place in two 9 x 5 x 3-inch greased pans. Cover, let rise in warm place until double, about 1¼ hrs. Bake in moderate oven (375° F) 50 min. Remove from pans to cake racks to cool uncovered and out of draft. 2 loaves.

PUMPKIN OR SQUASH BREAD

Pumpkin adds to bread a rich golden color, surprisingly good flavor and extra food value

8 to 8½ cups all-purpose
flour
2 reg cakes compressed *or*
2 pkgs dry gran yeast
¼ cup lukewarm water
¼ cup sugar

1¾ cups milk, scalded
1 tbsp salt
2 cups pumpkin *or* squash
purée, p 1390, *or* canned
¼ cup melted shortening

Note: Best rising conditions for yeast dough are moist air and a temperature of 80 to 85° F and out of a draft.

Sift flour and measure. Crumble compressed or granular yeast into lukewarm water, stir in 1 tsp of the sugar and let soften 10 min. Pour hot milk into 4-qt mixing bowl, stir in salt and remaining sugar and cool to lukewarm. Beat in 2½ cups of the flour until batter is smooth, then pumpkin and cooled shortening. Add about 6 cups more flour to make a stiff dough, then turn out onto board or pastry cloth sprinkled with flour, cover with bowl and let rest 10 min. Then knead until smooth and elastic, about 10 min. Return to washed, greased bowl, turn once to bring greased side up. Cover and let rise in warm place until double, about 1 hr. Punch down, turn over in bowl and let rise again until double, about 45 min. Turn out onto board and cut into 3 equal portions. Round up portions, cover with bowls and let rest 10 min. Shape into loaves, p 271. Place in 9 x 5 x 3-inch greased pans. Cover and let rise in warm place until double and tops are well-rounded, about 1 hr. Bake in a moderately hot oven (400° F) 35 to 40 min or until well browned. Turn out on cake racks to cool uncovered and out of a draft. 3 loaves.

Note: Make a variation of this bread to please pumpkin pie enthusiasts as follows: Use 1¼ cups milk and ½ cup orange juice for the liquid. Mix into the flour 1 tsp ginger, 2 tsp cinnamon, 1 tsp nutmeg and 1 tsp grated orange rind.

PUMPERNICKEL BREAD

1½ cups all-purpose flour
5½ cups rye flour
  1 reg cake compressed *or*
    1 pkg dry gran yeast
  1 cup lukewarm water

1 cup milk, scalded
1 tbsp salt
3 tbsp molasses
2 tbsp melted shortening
1 to 2 tbsp corn meal

Sift flours and measure separately. Crumble the compressed or granular yeast into the lukewarm water and let soften 10 min. Combine next 3 ingredients in 4-qt mixing bowl and cool to lukewarm. Stir in the yeast mixture, then beat in the all-purpose flour with a rotary beater, then the shortening. Now gradually add the rye flour beating and stirring in with wooden spoon. Turn dough out onto lightly floured board or pastry cloth, cover with bowl and let rest 10 min. Then knead until smooth and elastic, about 10 min. Return to washed, greased bowl, turning once to bring greased side up. Cover and let rise in a warm place until double, about 2 hrs. Punch down, cover and again let rise until light, about 30 min. Now turn out on floured board, cut in half, cover, let rest 10 min, then shape into round, flat loaves. Place in well-greased 8-inch layer cake pans with corn meal sprinkled on bottom. Cover and let rise in a warm place until double, about 1 hr. Bake in a moderate oven (375° F) about 1 hr. Remove from pans to cake racks to cool. Two 1-lb loaves.

QUICK YEAST BREAD

6¼ cups all-purpose flour
2 reg cakes compressed *or*
2 pkgs dry gran yeast
¼ cup lukewarm water
2 tbsp sugar

1 cup milk, scalded
2 tsp salt
1 cup water
1 tbsp melted shortening

Sift flour and measure. Crumble compressed or dry granular yeast into the lukewarm water, stir in 1 tsp of the sugar; let soften 10 min. Put hot milk into 4-qt mixing bowl, stir in remaining sugar and salt and the 1 cup water. Cool to lukewarm. Now stir in yeast, then beat in 3 cups of the flour until smooth, then the shortening. Add all but 2 tbsp of remaining flour, mixing thoroughly. Turn dough onto board or pastry cloth sprinkled with remaining flour, cover with bowl and let rest 10 min. Knead until smooth and elastic, about 10 min. Cut dough in half, round up portions, cover with bowl, let rest 10 min. Shape into loaves, p 271. Place in 9 x 5 x 3-inch greased pans. Grease top lightly, cover and let rise in warm place until double, about 1 hr. Bake in a moderately hot oven (400° F) 30 to 35 min. Remove from pans to cake racks to cool uncovered and out of draft. 2 loaves.

SWEDISH LIMPA BREAD

A pleasing, high-flavored Swedish Rye

3¼ cups all-purpose flour
3 cups rye flour
1 reg cake compressed *or*
1 pkg dry gran yeast
¼ cup lukewarm water
1 tsp granulated sugar
2 tsp caraway seed

1 tbsp salt
⅓ cup brown sugar, pkd,
  or dark molasses
1½ tsp grated orange rind, pkd
1¼ cups milk, scalded
½ cup water
3 tbsp melted shortening

Sift flours, then measure separately. Crumble compressed or turn dry granular yeast into the lukewarm water, stir in the 1 tsp sugar and let soften 10 min. Add next 4 ingredients to hot milk in a 4-qt mixing bowl and cool to lukewarm. Stir yeast and the ½ cup water into milk mixture. Beat in all but ¼ cup of all-purpose flour, then the cooled shortening. Stir in rye flour gradually to make a stiff dough. Turn dough onto board or pastry cloth sprinkled with rest of all-purpose flour. Cover with bowl and let rest 10 min. Knead lightly for 10 min, then round into ball and return to washed, greased bowl, turning once to bring greased side up. Cover and let rise in warm place until double, about 1½ hrs. Now turn dough out on lightly floured board, cut in half, round up

Note: Best rising conditions for yeast dough are moist air and a temp of 80 to 85° F and out of a draft.

portions, cover with bowls, let rest 10 min. Shape into loaves, p 271. Place in 9 x 5 x 3-inch greased pans. Cover and let rise in warm place until double, about 1½ hrs. Bake in a moderately hot oven (400° F) 40 to 45 min or until done. Remove at once to cake rack to cool uncovered and out of draft. 2 loaves.

BOHEMIAN RYE BREAD

6 cups Bohemian Style rye and wheat flour	2 tbsp shortening
1 reg cake compressed *or*	3 tbsp dark molasses
1 pkg dry gran yeast	1 tsp caraway seed, optional
1 cup lukewarm water	Egg white diluted with
1 cup milk, scalded	1 tbsp water
1 tbsp salt	1 tbsp corn meal

Sift flour and measure. Soften yeast in the lukewarm water; let stand 10 min. Combine next 4 ingredients, cool to lukewarm, then stir in yeast mixture thoroughly. Add flour and caraway seed and mix well. Turn onto a floured board or pastry cloth, cover with bowl, let rest 10 min. Knead until smooth and elastic, 7 to 10 min. Place dough in a 4-qt greased bowl, turn once to bring greased side up. Let rise in a warm place until doubled, about 1½ hrs. When sufficiently risen, dough retains impression of fingers. Punch down, let rise again until light, about 30 min. Turn onto floured board, cut in half, cover, let rest 10 min. Shape into loaves about 14 inches long. Place on well-greased baking sheet with corn meal sprinkled over area occupied by loaves. Cover, let rise in a warm place about 1 hr. Beat egg white and water slightly and brush over top to glaze. With a very sharp knife, cut 3 shallow gashes into each loaf. Bake in moderate oven (375° F) 50 to 60 min. Remove from pan to cake rack to cool. Two 1¼ lb loaves.

MILWAUKEE RYE BREAD

6 cups rye flour	2 tbsp shortening
2 cups all-purpose flour	2 tsp caraway seed, opt
¾ cup white or yellow corn meal	1 reg pkg compressed or dry granular yeast
1½ cups cold water	¼ cup lukewarm water
1½ cups boiling water	2 cups smooth mashed potatoes
4 tsp salt	1 tbsp corn meal
1 tbsp sugar	

Sift flours, then measure separately. Measure the ¾ cup corn meal into saucepan. Stir in cold water slowly to keep smooth then add boiling water. Heat to boiling and simmer 2 min stirring constantly. Add next 4 ingredients and let stand until lukewarm. Soften yeast in lukewarm water for 10 min then add to lukewarm corn meal mixture.

Stir in potatoes and both flours to make a smooth dough. Turn out onto
a lightly floured board or pastry cloth, cover with bowl, let rest 10 min.
Knead until smooth and elastic, about 10 min. Place in lightly greased
bowl, turn over to bring greased side up. Cover and let rise until double,
about 1½ hrs. Now punch dough down; turn out on lightly floured
board, cut in half, round up, cover with bowls and let rest 10 min.
Shape in oval loaves 14" long and place on greased baking sheet
sprinkled with the 1 tbsp corn meal. Cover and let rise in a warm place
until double. Bake in moderate oven (375° F) from 50 to 60 min.
Remove to cake racks to cool. 2 loaves.

WHOLE WHEAT BREAD—50%

5 to 6 cups all-purpose flour
5 to 6 cups whole wheat flour
2 reg cakes compressed *or*
  2 pkgs dry gran yeast
¼ cup lukewarm water
1 tsp sugar

3 cups milk, scalded, *or* half
  water
4 tsp salt
½ cup brown sugar, pkd,
  or molasses
¼ cup melted shortening,
  cooled

Sift all-purpose flour and measure. Measure smaller amount for
strong gluten flour, larger amount for flour with less gluten. Spoon
whole wheat flour lightly into cup to measure. Crumble compressed
or granular yeast into lukewarm water, stir in 1 tsp sugar and let
soften 10 min. In a 5-qt mixing bowl, combine hot milk, salt and brown
sugar; cool to lukewarm, then stir in yeast. Beat in 2 cups of each flour
thoroughly, then the shortening, then remaining all-purpose flour; then
add whole wheat flour last and mix well. Turn out on lightly floured
board or pastry cloth, cover with bowl and let rest 10 min. Knead until
smooth and elastic, about 10 min, using no more flour for kneading
than necessary. Return to washed, greased bowl; turn once to bring
greased side up. Cover and let rise in warm place until double, about
1 hr. Then turn out on board or pastry cloth, cut in quarters, round up,
cover with bowls, let rest 10 min. Shape into loaves, p 271. Place in well
greased 9 x 5 x 3-inch pans. Grease tops, cover and let rise until double,
about 1½ hrs. Bake in moderately hot oven (400° F) 40 min or until
done. Remove from pans to cake racks to cool uncovered out of a draft.
4 loaves.

WHOLE WHEAT BREAD—100%

6½ to 7½ cups whole wheat
  flour
2 reg cakes compressed *or*
  2 pkgs dry gran yeast
⅔ cup lukewarm water

½ cup brown sugar, pkd
1 tbsp salt
2 cups milk, scalded
2 tbsp melted shortening
2 tbsp all-purpose flour

Spoon flour lightly into cup to measure. Crumble compressed or granular yeast into lukewarm water, stir in 1 tsp of the sugar and let soften 10 min. Add remaining sugar and salt to hot milk and cool to lukewarm in a 4-qt mixing bowl. Then stir yeast well into milk mixture. Beat in 3 cups of the flour, then the shortening. Add remaining flour gradually, mixing thoroughly. Turn out on board or pastry cloth sprinkled with the all-purpose flour and knead 10 min. Return to washed, greased bowl, turn once to bring greased side up. Cover and let rise in warm place until double, about 1 hr. Turn out on board again, cut in half, round up portions, cover with bowls, let rest 10 min. Then shape into loaves, p 271. Place in 9 x 5 x 3-inch well greased pans. Cover, let rise in warm place until double and rounded tops come above sides of pans, about 1 hr. Bake in a moderately hot oven (400° F) 40 min or until done. Remove from pans to cake racks to cool uncovered out of a draft. 2 loaves.

SPECIAL RECIPES

Brioche, Buckwheat Pancakes, Danish Pastry and English Muffins differ from the usual yeast breads in that they require special manipulation to obtain their typical texture or crust.

BRIOCHE

It's rewarding every now and then to make some fancy bread or coffee cake for your family. The following recipe tells how to bake the famous old-time rich bread called Brioche. The traditional brioche baking pan was a round, bowl-shaped mold, usually fluted. Today few women have or can buy such molds. Muffin pans, however, are excellent substitutes. Brioche dough is rich and quite soft—qualities needed for delicate, tender bread. Such dough is most easily handled when chilled, and it must be handled quickly as it gets sticky when manipulated too long. Brioche is baked at a high temperature as the small amount of dough in the muffin pans would dry out if baked slowly. Brioche is buttery on the outside, tender, soft and fine-textured on the inside. Any leftovers reheated are equally good the next day. The flavor is not sweet but slightly salty which comes from the butter or margarine. If eaten with butter, unsalted or sweet butter is delightful on them. Tiny brioche baked in the tiniest muffin pans make unusual hors d'oeuvres by removing the crown and scooping out a little of the crumb from the lower portion, then filling with a nippy cheese, fish, or ham mixture. Then replace crown by securing with a little butter. Muffin-size brioche is excellent split in half crosswise and filled with creamed chicken or turkey.

BRIOCHE

*Shiny and crisp on outside, tender, soft and fine-textured on inside.
Especially delicious with unsalted butter*

3 cups all-purpose flour	1 tbsp sugar
1 reg cake compressed *or*	¼ tsp salt
1 pkg dry gran yeast	3 eggs, unbeaten
¼ cup lukewarm water	⅓ cup milk
1 tsp sugar	1 egg yolk mixed with
¾ cup soft butter *or*	1 tbsp milk
margarine	

Sift flour and measure. Crumble compressed or turn dry granular
yeast into lukewarm water measured into 1-qt bowl. Stir in 1 tsp sugar
and ½ cup of the flour, then beat thoroughly until smooth. Shape into
a ball; cut a cross into the top with scissors. This cut exposes more
surface to warm air which encourages rising. Cover and set in a warm
place 15 to 20 min to become a sponge. Meanwhile put 1½ cups of the
flour in a 4-qt mixing bowl. Add ½ of the butter, the tbsp of sugar, salt
and 1 egg; mix and beat with wooden spoon, adding milk gradually to
make a smooth paste. Add remaining butter, another egg, the remaining
1 cup flour and beat again until paste is smooth and no longer sticky.
Now form a hollow in center, add the sponge and the last egg, then
knead well in bowl until smooth, about 5 min. Place in a clean, greased
bowl, cover with a pan or supported cloth so it won't stick to dough
and let rise in warm place about 1½ hrs. Turn out on lightly floured
board and beat down with palm of hand. Return to bowl, cover, set in
refrigerator overnight to ripen. Chilling changes dough to right consistency for shaping. Before shaping, turn out on very lightly floured
board and again beat down with palm of hand. Cut off ¼ of the dough
and return it to refrigerator. Mold remaining dough into 16 balls about
egg-size. Place in well-greased muffin pans with cups measuring 3-inches
across. Now remove dough from refrigerator and shape into same
number of balls about marble-size. Then cut a crisscross with scissors
in top of each ball in pan. Now push dough from center out to make
a hollow large enough to insert a small ball to make the crown of each
brioche. Again cover with pan or supported cloth and let rise in warm
place until double, about 1¼ hrs. Then brush gently with yolk mixture.
Bake in hot oven (425° F) until brioche is shiny and brown, from
20 to 25 min. Remove from pans to cake racks immediately. 16 Brioche.

GRANDMA'S BUCKWHEAT CAKES

4 cups buckwheat flour	1 tsp D.A. baking powder *or*
1 cup all-purpose flour	1¼ tsp tartrate *or* phos-
¼ cup corn meal	phate type
1 reg cake compressed *or*	1 tsp soda
1 pkg dry gran yeast	1½ tsp salt
4 cups lukewarm water	2 tbsp molasses
2 tbsp sugar	⅓ cup milk
1 egg, beaten	

Sift flours, then measure. Spoon corn meal into cup to measure and stir into the flours. Crumble compressed or granular yeast into the lukewarm water in a 4-qt heavy mixing bowl or stone jar. Stir in sugar, then flours and corn meal and beat well. Cover and set in a warm place overnight. Next morning, stir in last 6 ingredients. (Add a little more soda if batter is too sour and more milk if batter needs thinning.) Bake on a moderately hot greased griddle (300–325° F). Serve hot with warm syrup and butter. 36 five-inch cakes.

Variations: Make BLINIS, a popular appetizer from this batter, from prepared pancake mixes or any griddle cake batter made by recipes in this book. Fry 2- to 3-inch pancakes. Serve hot with blob of sour cream in center sprinkled with caviar.

Note: To serve Buckwheat Cakes every morning for several days, use 1 cup of the batter as a *starter* for the next morning's batch of cakes. Use this batter in place of yeast and add the same amount of water, corn meal and flour as specified above. Beat well and let stand overnight. Next morning add remaining 6 ingredients, mix and bake as before. A cup of batter on the second morning may be used as a *starter* for the next morning's batch of cakes, and on and on as long as Buckwheat Cakes are desired.

DANISH PASTRY

5¼ cups all-purpose flour	2 eggs, beaten
⅓ cup sugar	1 tsp vanilla
3 reg cakes compressed *or*	1¼ cups or 2½ sticks unsalted
3 pkgs dry gran yeast	butter, well chilled
¾ cup lukewarm water	1 egg white beaten with
1 tsp salt	1 tbsp cold water
¾ cup milk, scalded	Sugar
¼ cup melted shortening	

Sift flour and measure. Stir 1 tbsp of the sugar and the yeast thoroughly into the lukewarm water; let soften 10 min. Stir salt and remaining sugar into hot milk in a 4-qt bowl and cool to lukewarm. Then stir in yeast mixture. Beat in 2 cups of flour until smooth, then cooled shortening, then eggs and vanilla. Gradually add all but ¼ cup of remaining flour, mixing thoroughly. Turn out on lightly floured board or pastry cloth, cover with bowl; let rest 10 min. Knead thoroughly for

5 min, using remaining flour. Return to washed, greased bowl, turning once to bring greased side up. Cover, let rise in warm place until increased ¼ in bulk, from 20 to 30 min. Now turn out on lightly floured board or pastry cloth and roll into a rectangle about 14 x 18 inches. Cut ½ the butter into small bits over *center third* of dough. Fold over one side of dough to cover butter; press edge against dough to seal in butter, then cut remaining butter in bits over top. Fold remaining *third of dough* over the butter, and again press edge against dough to seal firmly. Now turn dough so wide-side is toward you, and again roll into a 14 x 18-inch rectangle. Fold each end of dough to center, then fold in half to bring open-ends together. Place folded dough between 2 lightly floured sheets of waxed paper and chill in refrigerator 45 min. Roll out once more into a 14 x 18-inch rectangle, and again fold as before. Wrap in waxed paper, then in a damp cloth and chill in refrigerator 4 to 5 hrs or overnight. Rolling and folding spreads the chilled butter between thin sheets of dough to produce the puffy layers characteristic of Danish Pastry. Dough must be thoroughly chilled and handled quickly to keep butter in dough very firm. Remove only ¼ of dough at a time, returning balance to refrigerator. Work quickly so layers of butter do not soften. Roll out again to about ½-inch thickness and cut out desired shapes. Star or round cut-outs, snails, Braids, p 274, or Butterhorns, p 274, are suitable shapes for this pastry. Place on greased baking sheet, cover, let rise in warm place until double, about 1 hr. Brush lightly with egg white mixture and sprinkle with sugar. Bake in a moderate oven (375° F) 15 to 18 min, depending on size of rolls. Remove immediately from pan to cake rack. Brush at once with Confectioners' Icing, p 283, and sprinkle with chopped nuts, if desired. 2 to 4 dozen.

HINT: Chilling dough board before rolling dough is a big help to amateurs.

ENGLISH MUFFINS

4 cups all-purpose flour
1¼ cups milk
¾ tsp salt
1 reg cake compressed *or*
1 pkg dry gran yeast

¼ cup lukewarm water
1 tsp sugar
3 tbsp melted shortening
Corn meal

Sift flour and measure. Scald milk with salt and cool to lukewarm in 4-qt mixing bowl. Crumble compressed or granular yeast into the lukewarm water, stir in sugar and let soften 10 min. Then stir yeast into milk, then add half the flour gradually, beating in with wooden spoon until batter is well mixed. Beat in cooled shortening until smooth, then rest of flour to make a smooth, soft dough. Now turn dough into clean, greased bowl of same size; pat top with a little water. Cover and let rise in warm place until double, about 2 hrs. Then turn out on lightly floured board or pastry cloth and knead. Again cover with bowl and let rest 10 min. Now roll out ½-inch thick. Cut in 3- or 4-inch rounds and place on board sprinkled with corn meal. Cover, let rise in warm place until muffins start getting light, about 45 min. To bake, heat griddle moderately hot (300° F) then grease lightly. Use pancake turner to transfer muffins to griddle. Bake about 20 min, turning 2 or 3 times. Place unbaked muffins in refrigerator while first batch bakes. When ready to serve, split cold muffins and toast each half on both sides. Spread with butter, serve piping hot. 18 4-inch muffins.

CHRISTMAS STOLLEN

½ cup milk
½ cup sugar
1 tsp salt
2 pkgs active dry yeast
½ cup warm water
2 eggs, slightly beaten
½ cup (1 stick) butter, softened
4½ cups regular all-purpose flour
1 cup seedless raisins
½ cup candied citron

½ cup red glacé cherries
1½ tsp grated lemon rind
¼ tsp nutmeg
Butter, melted
2 tbsp butter, melted
¼ cup sugar
½ tsp cinnamon
Confectioners frosting
Chopped walnuts
Chopped red and green glacé cherries

Scald milk; in mixing bowl with ½ cup sugar and salt; cool to lukewarm. Soften yeast in water; add to milk mixture along with eggs and butter; stir until smooth. Gradually add flour and mix thoroughly. Add raisins, citron, cherries, lemon rind and nutmeg. On lightly floured board, knead until smooth and elastic. Place in buttered bowl; brush top with melted butter and allow to rise until double in bulk. Knead down and divide dough in half. On lightly floured board roll each half into an 8-inch circle; make crease down center and fold over. Moisten edges to seal. Place on large buttered baking sheet; brush with 2 tablespoons melted butter. Combine ¼ cup sugar and cinnamon; sprinkle over tops. Allow to rise until double in bulk. Bake in preheated 350° F oven 30 to 40 min. Cool; frost tops with confectioners frosting and sprinkle with walnuts and cherries.

Cake

The popular song "If I'd known you were coming I'd have baked a cake," sums up the idea that CAKE is the most complimentary of desserts to prepare for guests. Evidently it is this idea that fortifies a hostess to spend hours baking, frosting and decorating a cake. However, cake baking is not always a happy experience as many failures arise in this glamorous cooking venture. Therefore, women are constantly searching for answers to questions such as these: Why is angel food cake almost always baked with a hole in the middle? What is the best way to prepare a cake pan so the cake won't stick to the bottom? Why do cake recipes always advise beginning and ending with flour when adding the dry and liquid ingredients alternately? If you are the kind of person who likes to know WHY before adopting a new technique, this chapter will have a special appeal to you.

CAKE TYPES

THERE are 2 general types of cake: Butter Cakes, containing shortening, and Sponge or Angel Food Cake which does not contain shortening. A slight overlapping occurs in Butter Sponge and Chiffon Cakes.

Butter cakes include most layer cakes and all Pound Cakes and Fruit Cakes. Butter Cakes are baked in many forms: Layers, loaves, sheets and cupcakes. Custom often determines the form as in Pound Cake, which is usually baked in a loaf. As a rule, the recipe specifies the type of pan in which the cake is baked. Sponge and Angel Food Cakes are usually baked in tube pans. The tube provides for heat penetration in the center equal to that on the outside of the pan. This equal heat penetration insures uniformly baked, tender, moist cake. Sponge Cakes are also baked in layers, as for Boston Cream Pie, and in thin sheets for Jelly and Cream Rolls.

FACTORS CONTRIBUTING TO SUCCESSFUL CAKE MAKING

1. *High quality ingredients.* Use a proven brand of flour, fine-grain sugar or moist brown sugar free of lumps, fresh butter or shortening, fresh

eggs, good live baking powder, fresh milk and a dependable brand of flavorings or spices.

2. *A tested proven recipe.* Have recipe before you and be so familiar with its directions you can follow each step in mixing without interruption.

3. *Have all ingredients assembled and at room temp,* and all equipment at hand. This prevents delays in mixing which might cause a cake failure.

4. *Accurate measurement* of all ingredients. Use standard measuring cups and spoons and make all measurements level.

5. *Good mixing technique.* Follow to the letter the directions given in your tested recipe.

6. *Adjusting oven racks and starting oven.* Adjust oven racks for uniform baking. Bake layers, sheets and cupcakes on oven rack placed in middle of oven. Bake Angel Food and Sponge Cakes in tube pans on lower rack. Use stated baking temp. Make sure oven is regulated for accurate heat control; if oven has no heat control, use an accurate oven thermometer to check the heat.

7. *Proper baking technique.* (a) Use correct size pans—the size specified in recipe. The material of which the pan is made influences the baking temp. Bake batter in *glass pans* 25 degrees lower than in *aluminum pans.* (b) Place pans on oven rack so there is space between pans as well as space between pans and oven walls. (c) Bake cake the stated length of time—until just done—no longer. Start testing for doneness 2 or 3 min before end of stated baking time. Over-baking ruins cakes just as much as under-baking.

BAKING IN THE SOUTH or AT HIGH ALTITUDES

COOKIES, PASTRY, QUICK BREADS, YEAST BREADS, DESSERTS

In the South—Increase the flour a little or decrease the liquid a little.

In High Altitudes—Follow recipes in this book if altitude is 3000 feet or less. In higher altitudes see page 1440 for necessary changes.

MEASURING UTENSILS FOR INGREDIENTS

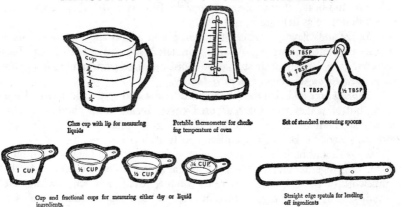

Glass cup with lip for measuring liquids

Portable thermometer for checking temperature of oven

Set of standard measuring spoons

Cup and fractional cups for measuring either dry or liquid ingredients.

Straight edge spatula for leveling off ingredients

HELPFUL HINTS FOR MEASURING

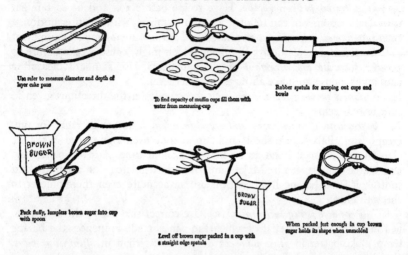

Use ruler to measure diameter and depth of layer cake pans

To find capacity of muffin cups fill them with water from measuring-cup

Rubber spatula for scraping out cups and bowls

Pack fluffy, lumpless brown sugar into cup with spoon

Level off brown sugar packed in a cup with a straight edge spatula

When packed just enough in cup brown sugar holds its shape when unmolded

WHY ARE FUNCTION AND QUALITY OF INGREDIENTS IMPORTANT?

Both sponge and butter cakes require high quality ingredients to produce quality cakes.

Flour contributes greatly to the framework of cake, and while many good cakes are made with all-purpose or bread flour, cake flour is better for delicate cake baking. Cake flour is a soft wheat flour put through a special milling process. It contains more starch and less gluten than all-purpose or bread flour, and produces a more delicate texture. When it is necessary to substitute all-purpose for cake flour, *use 2 tbsp less flour per cup than recipe calls for,* and beat batter as little as possible. But even with these 2 changes, cake will not be as delicate in texture.

Sugar adds flavor, increases tenderness and affects the texture of cake; it also promotes browning. A fine granulated sugar is essential for fine-textured cake. Brown sugar should be moist and free from lumps; *it should be pressed through a coarse sieve if lumpy.*

Shortenings add richness, make cake tender and some add flavor. High grade butter makes the finest flavored cakes; bland, fresh shortening also makes excellent cakes, but salt should be slightly increased. Vegetable oil, too, makes good cakes such as chiffon and fruit.

Eggs should be fresh for good flavor and savory odor. They help to bind ingredients together and add flavor as well as protein. This contributes to the framework of the cake. Eggs increase volume, particularly when whites are beaten separately. Use eggs of medium size unless recipe specifies otherwise.

One medium egg white measures about 2 tbsp; 1 medium yolk about 1½ tbsp. *Eggs separate easiest when cold; therefore, separate whites from yolks on removing from refrigerator, but use neither whites nor yolks until they warm to room temp.* Egg whites at room temp beat up to greater volume than when just removed from refrigerator.

Leavening increases volume and produces light, tender cake. Baking powder, soda and beaten egg whites supply the leavening in cake. In sponge and angel food cakes, air beaten into eggs or egg whites is usually the only leavening. In butter cakes, baking powder or soda is the chief leavening. Be sure baking powder is "alive" to have full leavening power. The air beaten into batter also acts as leavening—see p 112. Soda is generally used in sour cream, buttermilk or molasses cakes.

Liquid dissolves the sugar and salt. It also is needed to swell the gluten and starch in the flour. Sweet milk and buttermilk are the liquids most used in cakes; like eggs they also contribute protein and fat which influences the texture. Water and fruit juices are sometimes used for the liquid. "Soured" pasteurized milk should not be substituted for buttermilk. In pasteurization, the number and kinds of organisms which cause natural souring of milk are so altered along with the destruction of harmful bacteria, that this milk sometimes develops an objectionable flavor on "souring." It sours more slowly than raw milk and sometimes tastes "spoiled" rather than "sour." Commercial buttermilk is made by adding natural souring organisms to pasteurized milk, and the result is buttermilk of fairly uniform flavor and thickness. *Raw unpasteurized milk,* either sweet or sour, is dangerous and should not be used.

Flavoring. Always use *fresh,* high quality flavoring extracts and spices. An inferior extract or an old spice can produce only poor flavor in the finished product. The amount of flavoring should be slighty more when bland shortening is used than when butter is used. Combinations of extracts and spices are interesting and add variety when used discreetly.

WHY MEASURE INGREDIENTS ACCURATELY?

Exact measurement of all ingredients is necessary for success in all carefully tested recipes. Greater-than-usual care in measuring needs to be taken in cake making as cake success depends to a large extent on an accurate balance between the various ingredients.

Proper measuring techniques and equipment are so important that we have written a separate Chapter on them. In the Chapter on *"Measurements and Equivalents,"* p 154, are found directions and tables of equivalents that help everyone—from the inexperienced to the skilled cook. The inexperienced cook can make sure good habits of measuring are developed from the very beginning; the skilled cook can check her habits with the latest accepted techniques.

Measurement of dry and solid ingredients is best done by using nested sets of *standard measuring spoons and cups*. The cups come in heavy tin, aluminum and plastic ware. The metal utensils are usually more accurate; they cost a little more but last longer. The sets of cups contain 1 cup, ½ cup, ⅓ cup and ¼ cup measures; each holds an accurate measurement when filled to the brim and leveled off. For liquid measure, a glass measuring cup is convenient, as the top *measuring mark* is below the rim of the cup—this avoids overflowing.

Measuring Spoon Sets contain 1 tablespoon, 1 teaspoon, ½ teaspoon and ¼ teaspoon measures. These are essential to accurately measure small quantities.

WHY HAVE INGREDIENTS AND EQUIPMENT AT HAND?

Assemble ingredients and equipment. The first step in making a cake is to collect all ingredients, baking pans, mixing and measuring equipment. *Ingredients should be at room temp. The term "soft butter" used in recipes in this book, means butter at room temp,* about 70° F.

Preparing cake pans. Use pans spotlessly clean of proper size.

Angel Food and Sponge Cake pans must be free from grease. Just a trace of grease is sufficient to prevent the cake from rising fully. These batters need to cling to a clean non-skid metallic surface to rise to greatest height. After *"Butter Cakes"* are baked in such pans, they should be scrubbed thoroughly in hot soapy water, then rinsed in boiling water.

Butter Cake pans that are free from scratches, need only a thoroughly uniform greasing. Line bottoms of layer cake pans, and especially scratched ones, neatly with *heavy waxed paper*. To line pans neatly, place pan to be used onto as many sheets of waxed paper as number of liners needed. Then with pencil, mark tightly against pan. Now pin layers of paper together to keep from slipping, then with scissors, cut carefully *just inside the marked circle*. Lay paper circle into lightly greased pan, press out smoothly, then grease paper *or use 2 layers of thin waxed paper*. Sides of layer cake pans may or may not be greased. Some experienced bakers believe greater cake volume results when sides of pans *are not greased*. However, when sides are greased, cakes have smoother sides for icing. Cakes baked in pans greased with unsalted shortening come out of pans easier than from pans greased with butter. Many homemakers however, use butter because they want a butter-flavored cake crust. Use a pastry brush or crumpled waxed paper to spread grease over pans.

Sheet or loaf cake pans. Line bottoms of oblong or square pans with heavy waxed, typewriter or smooth brown wrapping paper, then grease paper and sides of pans. Line bottoms and sides of loaf pans neatly with heavy waxed, smooth brown wrapping or parchment paper, then grease paper. See method to cut linings for loaf pans neatly, p 366.

Cupcake or muffin pans. Grease cups liberally or line bottoms of *cups in muffin pans* with circles of heavy waxed paper, then grease paper and sides of muffin cups thoroughly. Or for cupcakes for lunch packing, place paper baking cups of proper size in the muffin cups. In this case, grease neither the muffin pans nor the paper cups.

Heating oven. Well-insulated ovens take from 4 to 10 min to heat to required temp; a poorly insulated oven may take 20 min or longer. Therefore, start oven and set temp control 10 min before cake is ready to go into oven, so temp will be correct by the time batter is mixed.

Preparing ingredients. Cut fruit, chop nuts or melt chocolate first. Then sift flour once, measure and resift 3 times with salt, leavening and any spices; when soda is used, sift mixture from 4 to 6 times. Sifting may be done conveniently on 2 sheets of waxed paper as follows:

SIFTING FLOUR

1. Have 2 pieces of waxed paper ready. Sift unmeasured flour once into bowl or onto 1 piece of paper.

2. *To measure,* set sifter on 2nd piece of paper. Now spoon sifted flour lightly into correct measuring cup or cups, level off with knife or spatula, then turn measured flour into sifter. Now measure and add to the sifter any additional ingredients to be sifted with the flour.

3. Return any unused sifted flour on first piece of paper to flour container, so paper can be used in the sifting process.

4. Now sift ingredients in sifter onto paper, then place empty sifter on first piece of paper. Pick up paper containing flour and turn flour into sifter; then sift through onto paper. Repeat sifting desired number of times from one paper to other, leaving flour in sifter on paper after last sifting. Now sift flour into cake mixture, adding in 3 or 4 portions—be sure to use all the flour in sifter and on paper under it. Waxed paper may be folded and stored in sifter for next baking.

STANDARD METHOD OF MIXING SPONGE-TYPE CAKES

Have all ingredients at room temperature

In Angel Food and true Sponge, the 2 main types of sponge cakes, the only leavening is *air* beaten into the egg yolks or whites or air incorporated into the flour in sifting. In these cakes the aim is to beat the maximum amount of air into the yolks or whites, then handle them so lightly that most of this air is retained while adding remaining ingredients. The expansion of this air during baking is what makes the cake light; if air is lost while combining ingredients, the cake will be compact in texture and small in volume. The mixing methods for the 2 types are as follows:

TRUE SPONGE CAKE

Sift flour, measure, resift 3 times. With a rotary beater, beat egg yolks until very thick and lemon-yellow, then gradually beat in half the sugar, then flavoring. Clean off and wash beater. Sift in flour in 3 or 4 portions, and with wooden spoon cut-and-fold in until smooth—*do not beat.* Now quickly beat egg whites with clean beater until foamy, sift in salt and cream of tartar and beat until soft rounded peaks form, add remaining sugar gradually and continue beating until pointed peaks curving at tips form. Then cut-and-fold yolk mixture into whites until well blended, about 40 fold-over strokes. Flow batter immediately into ungreased tube pan. Bake according to recipe.

TRUE ANGEL FOOD

Sift flour, measure, add half the fine granulated sugar, then resift 6 times. For a 10-inch cake, use a 4-qt bowl for beating whites. Sift salt and cream of tartar over whites and beat with a wire whip until stiff enough to form pointed glossy peaks, then gradually beat in remaining sugar then the flavoring. Now fold in flour-sugar mixture in 4 or 5 portions carefully but thoroughly. Flow batter into ungreased tube pan and bake according to recipe.

COOLING THE CAKES

Cool *Sponge* and *Angel Food Cakes* completely in the pan inverted. A well-designed tube pan stands on the tube which is higher than sides of pan, or has side supports to hold it up from the table in an inverted position. If cake is cooled upright or is removed from pan while warm, the delicate cells which do not have time to become firm collapse under their own weight.

HOW TO USE ELECTRIC MIXER TO MIX SPONGE-TYPE CAKES

This is not the Quick-Mix Method. See p 348

For Sponge Cake. Sift flour, measure, resift 3 times. Put yolks and any liquid into large mixer bowl and beat on *Medium Speed* until thick and spongy, 4 to 5 min. Gradually add half the sugar and beat again until thick and spongy. Add flavoring. Turn mixer to *Lowest Speed,* add flour mixture in 4 or 5 portions, beating until batter is just smooth, scraping bowl with rubber scraper while beating. Clean off beaters and remove bowl from platform. With a rotary beater, beat whites in a 3- to 4-qt mixing bowl to a stiff foam, add rest of sugar gradually, beating until glossy pointed peaks curve at tips. Cut-and-fold yolk mixture into whites by hand with wooden spoon until well blended, about 40 fold-over strokes. Now quickly flow batter into pan. Bake according to recipe.

For Angel Food Cake. Sift flour, measure, add half the sugar, resift 6 times. Put whites in large mixer bowl, add salt and cream of tartar and make sure to beat all of the whites on *Medium Speed* until they stand in stiff, glossy peaks, 2 to 3 minutes. Add remaining sugar in 4 or 5 portions and continue beating until glossy pointed peaks curve at tips. Add flavoring at end of beating. Clean off beaters and remove bowl from platform. With wire whip cut-and-fold in flour-sugar mixture in 5 portions, the first 4 portions using 20 fold-over strokes after each portion, and the last one 40 strokes. Flow batter into ungreased tube pan and bake according to directions.

CAUSES OF SPONGE-TYPE CAKE FAILURES

Why Is Cake Undersized and Compact?
1. Egg whites too cold
2. Overbeaten—air beaten out
3. Oven too hot
4. Too large a pan
5. Cake removed from pan too soon

Why Is It Rubbery and Tough?
1. Overbeaten
2. Too hot or too cold an oven

Why Is It Coarse Grained?
1. Eggs underbeaten
2. Ingredients not thoroughly blended

Why Does It Have a Hard or Sticky Crust?
1. Too much sugar
2. Oven too hot
3. Overbaked or underbaked

SPONGE TYPE CAKES

ANGEL FOOD CAKE

Angel Food Cake has greater volume and more tender texture when egg whites are beaten with a wire whip than when beaten with a rotary or electric beater. Follow this recipe exactly, and the result will be a handsome, high, moist, tender, delicious cake.

For a 10-inch Flat-top Cake:
    1 cup cake flour
    1½ cups fine granulated sugar
    1⅓ cups egg whites, 10 to 11
    1¼ tsp cream of tartar
    ¼ tsp salt
    1 tsp vanilla
    ¼ tsp almond extract

For a 10-inch High Rounded-top Cake:
    1 cup *plus* 1 tbsp cake flour
    1½ cups fine granulated sugar
    1½ cups egg whites (12 to 13)
    ⅜ tsp salt
    1½ tsp cream of tartar
    1½ tsp vanilla
    ¼ tsp almond extract

Have all ingredients at room temp. Have ready 10-inch tube pan, preferably with removable bottom—do not grease. Bake on bottom rack of oven. Start oven 10 min before baking; set to slow (300° F).

Sift flour, measure, resift 6 times with half the sugar. Turn whites into 4-qt mixing bowl; sprinkle salt and cream of tartar over whites. Now hold bowl slightly tipped, turn it slowly and beat with a *flat wire whip* until whites are stiff enough to hold *pointed, glossy peaks.* Now set bowl flat on table, and add remaining sugar in 6 portions, sifting it over whites, beating about 20 strokes after each portion. Then beat in flavorings with 10 more strokes. Add flour-sugar mixture in 5 portions, sifting each portion over whites, and turning bowl slowly, fold in gently but thoroughly with *wire whip* using 20 complete fold-over strokes after first 4 portions, then use 40 strokes to blend in last portion. Now flow batter quickly but gently into pan, turning pan slowly to even up batter. With a knife, cut gently around through batter with a wave-like motion to break air bubbles, to level top and to push batter a little higher around tube. Place in center of oven rack. Bake 65 to 70 min or until cake is delicately browned and springs back when lightly touched with finger. Remove from oven; invert at once over large funnel or large bottle if pan does not stand on tube or side supports. Leave upside down until just cooled. To remove cake, use spatula or thin-bladed knife to loosen carefully around sides and tube, using *straight down-and-up* strokes—not sliding spatula around the cake. Then lift out by tube and run spatula carefully under bottom of cake. If bottom of pan is not removable, rap edge of pan sharply against edge of table to loosen. To serve cake unfrosted, place *top-side-up* on plate; if frosted, place *bottom-side-up* on plate. Frost with Thin Butter Icing, p 395, or Confectioners' Icing, p 392, substituting orange juice for the liquid. 12 to 15 servings.

Note: This cake bakes satisfactorily in a moderately slow oven (325° F) in 50 to 60 min, but deeper cracks develop on top. If richer brown crust around tube is desired, heat pan in oven 3 or 4 min before pouring in batter.

BUTTER SPONGE LAYER CAKE

Looks like pie, tastes like cake

1¾ cups cake flour	3 eggs, room temp
1¼ tsp D.A. baking powder *or*	½ tsp salt
1½ tsp tartrate *or* phos-	1½ tsp vanilla
phate type	1½ cups sugar
¾ cup lukewarm milk	Cocoa Filling, p 397
1½ tbsp butter	½ pt whipping cream

Line bottoms of two 8-inch layer cake pans with waxed paper—grease paper lightly. Start oven 10 min before baking; set to moderate (350° F).

Sift flour, measure, resift 3 times with baking powder. Scald milk in top of double boiler, remove from heat, add butter and cool to lukewarm.

In a 3-qt mixing bowl, beat eggs with salt and vanilla until thick and lemon-colored, gradually add sugar and beat until thick and spongy. Then quickly stir in lukewarm milk. Add flour all at once, then beat until batter is smooth. Turn into prepared pans. Bake 30 min or until cake tests done. Cool in pans on cake racks 5 min, then turn out on racks, loosen paper and turn right-side up to cool. Spread Cocoa Filling between layers and over top of cake. Spread sides with ⅔ of the stiffly whipped cream, then pipe rest of cream lattice-fashion over top of Cocoa Filling. 10 servings.

CHOCOLATE CREAM SPONGE ROLL

Sponge Cake:
- ¼ cup xxxx sugar, pkd
- 1 cup cake flour
- 1 tsp D.A. baking powder *or*
- 1¼ tsp tartrate *or* phosphate type
- ¼ tsp salt
- 4 eggs, separated
- 1 cup sugar
- 1 tsp vanilla

Cream Filling:
- 1 tbsp gelatin
- ¼ cup cold water
- 1 sq unsweet chocolate
- 1 tbsp water
- ⅓ cup sugar
- Dash of salt
- ½ cup milk
- ½ tsp vanilla
- ½ cup whipping cream

Line a 12 x 18-inch jelly roll pan with waxed paper—grease paper. Prepare a towel by sprinkling evenly with xxxx sugar. Start oven 10 min before baking; set to moderate (375° F).

Sponge Cake. Sift flour, measure, resift 3 times with next 2 ingredients. Beat egg yolks with rotary beater until thick; gradually add ½ of the sugar and vanilla, beating until thick and light-colored. Remove and wash beater to beat whites until they form soft shiny peaks, then gradually beat in remaining sugar until shiny peaks curve at tips. Remove beater. With a wire whip, fold yolk mixture gradually into whites, then gradually fold in dry ingredients lightly but thoroughly. Flow batter gently down center of pan from one end to other, then spread ever so lightly to edges. Bake 12 to 15 min or until cake springs back when lightly touched. Remove to cake rack and quickly loosen edges with thin-bladed knife. Turn out on prepared towel and quickly strip off paper. Start at *wide side,* roll up gently, then roll up in towel. Cool on cake rack.

Cream Filling. Soften gelatin in cold water. Melt chocolate in top of double boiler over hot water; stir in the 1 tbsp water, sugar and salt. Add milk gradually and cook until smooth and thick, stirring constantly. Remove from heat. Stir in gelatin until dissolved, then vanilla. Chill until consistency of thin custard. Whip cream until stiff, then *fold* it gently into cold chocolate mixture.

Unroll cooled cake. Spread carefully with Chocolate Cream Filling and re-roll gently. Wrap in waxed paper and chill in refrigerator at least an hr. 8 to 10 servings.

GOLD SPOT ANGEL FOOD OR DAFFODIL CAKE

Beautiful as a daffodil. High, tender and moist like Angel Food

White Part:	Yellow Part:
½ cup cake flour	¾ cup cake flour
2⅔ tbsp fine gran sugar	⅓ cup fine gran sugar
¾ cup egg whites	6 egg yolks
⅛ tsp salt	1 tsp lemon extract
½ tsp cream of tartar	¾ cup egg whites
½ cup fine gran sugar	⅛ tsp salt
1 tsp vanilla	½ tsp cream of tartar
	½ cup fine gran sugar

Have ready a 10-inch tube pan—do not grease.

Sift flour for *both* parts. Measure ½ cup flour, add 2⅔ tbsp sugar, resift 5 times, last time onto waxed paper, placing it near bowl for mixing White Part. Measure the ¾ cup flour, add ⅓ cup sugar and resift 5 times, last time onto waxed paper, placing it near bowl for mixing Yellow Part. Have 3 bowls ready. Measure the 2 portions of egg whites into two 3-qt mixing bowls, and yolks into a 1-qt bowl.

White Part. With wire whip, beat whites until foamy, sprinkle salt and cream of tartar over them, and beat until soft rounded peaks form, then beat in the ½ cup sugar, 2 tbsp at a time, using about 15 strokes after each, or until whites form shiny peaks that curve at tips. Beat in vanilla with 5 strokes. Sift sugar-flour mixture over whites in 4 portions, cutting-and-folding in first 3 portions with 20 complete fold-over strokes after each, then use 40 strokes to fold in last portion.

Yellow Part. With a rotary beater, immediately beat yolks until thick and lemon-colored, beating in lemon extract with last few turns. Now beat whites with wire whip until foamy; sift salt and cream of tartar over them, then beat until whites form soft rounded peaks. Now beat in sugar, 2 tbsp at a time, using about 15 strokes after each portion or until they form shiny peaks that curve at tips. Now gently pour yolks over whites, scraping bowl with rubber scraper, then with wire whip, cut-and-fold in until blended, using about 20 strokes. Now sift sugar-flour mixture over in 4 portions, cutting-and-folding in with 15 to 20 strokes after first 3 portions, then use 35 to 40 strokes after last. Quickly but gently dip alternate large spoonfuls of yellow and white batter into pan. *Place pan on lowest rack in cold oven.* Start oven immediately; set to moderately slow (325° F). Bake 1 hr or until cake tests done. Remove from oven; invert at once over bottle or large funnel and let hang until cool. Remove from pan and serve plain or spread with Confectioners' Icing, p 392, using orange juice instead of the boiling water. 12 servings.

JELLY ROLL

xxxx sugar	2 tbsp water
¾ cup cake flour	4 eggs, separated
¾ tsp D.A. baking powder *or*	¾ cup sugar
1 tsp tartrate *or* phosphate	½ tsp vanilla
type	1 cup tart red jelly
¼ tsp salt	

Line bottom of 15½ x 10½ x ⅝-inch jelly roll pan with waxed paper—grease paper and sides of pan lightly. Prepare a towel by sprinkling evenly but lightly with xxxx sugar. Start oven 10 min before baking; set to moderately hot (400° F).

Sift flour, measure, resift 3 times with next 2 ingredients. Put water and egg yolks into a 3-qt mixing bowl and place *over hot water,* then beat with a rotary beater until very thick and light-colored. Add ½ of the sugar gradually and continue to beat until thick. Remove bowl from hot water. Beat in vanilla. Remove beater. Now sift flour in 4 or 5 portions over yolk mixture, folding in with wire whip until smooth after each. Beat egg whites with clean rotary beater until soft shiny peaks form, then gradually beat in remaining sugar until shiny pointed peaks curve at tips. Fold yolk batter into whites lightly but thoroughly with wire whip. Quickly flow batter gently down center of pan from one end to the other, then spread lightly to edges. Bake on center rack of oven 8 to 9 min or until cake springs back when lightly touched. Remove to cake rack and quickly loosen edges with thin-bladed knife. Turn out on prepared towel and immediately strip off paper carefully. Then roll up from *narrow side* into an even roll; then roll up in towel. Cool on cake rack. Unroll gently and spread evenly with jelly, slightly broken up with a fork. Reroll and wrap in waxed paper. Serve the day baked. 8 servings.

LEMON JELLY ROLL

Follow recipe for *Jelly Roll* above, except spread with Lemon Filling, p 398.

MOSS ROSE CAKE

A beautiful and delicious Milk Sponge Cake

2 cups cake flour	2 cups sugar
2 tsp D.A. baking powder *or*	4 eggs
2½ tsp tartrate *or* phos-	½ tsp almond extract
phate type	1 cup milk, scalded
½ tsp salt	

Line bottoms of two 8 x 8 x 2-inch pans with waxed paper—grease paper. Start oven 10 min before baking; set to moderate (350° F).

Sift flour, measure, resift 3 times with baking powder and salt. Use deep bowl for thorough mixing. Put sugar in 1-qt deep bowl, or small mixer bowl if electric mixer is used, turn unbeaten eggs over sugar. Beat with rotary beater or electric mixer on *Medium Speed* 10 min, or until mixture is thick, smooth and fluffy. Use a rubber scraper to transfer mixture gently to a 3- or 4-qt bowl. Fold in flour in 3 portions thoroughly with wire whip or rubber scraper. Now add extract and the barely hot milk all at once; beat vigorously with a wooden spoon about ½ min until thoroughly blended. Pour this thin batter immediately into prepared pans. Bake 30 min or until cake springs back when lightly touched. Cool in pans on cake racks 10 min, then loosen sides and turn out on racks; loosen paper and turn right-side up on racks, to finish cooling. Frost with Moss Rose Icing, p 393. 12 to 14 servings.

Note: May also be baked in three 8-inch or two 9-inch round layers.

QUICK-MIX SPONGE CAKE

Easy to make and excellent. For different occasions bake it in various forms such as Boston Cream Pie, Whipped Cream Sponge Loaf and Strawberry Shortcake

1½ cups cake flour	6 medium eggs, separated
1½ tsp D.A. baking powder *or*	¼ cup cold water
2 tsp tartrate *or* phosphate type	2 tsp lemon juice
	1 tsp vanilla
½ tsp salt	½ tsp grated lemon rind, pkd
1½ cups sugar	

Use a 10-inch tube pan—*do not grease.* Start oven 10 min before baking; set to moderately slow (325° F).

Sift flour, measure, resift 3 times with baking powder, salt and ½ the sugar. Put egg whites into a 4-qt mixing bowl. Put yolks into large mixer bowl, add water and lemon juice, then beat on *Medium Speed* until thick and spongy, 4 or 5 min. Without stopping beaters, add ½ cup of remaining sugar gradually and vanilla and beat until mixture is again thick and spongy. Now turn mixer to *Lowest Speed* and add flour in 4 portions, scraping sides and bottom of bowl constantly with rubber scraper. Beat until batter is just smooth. Now stop beating; remove and clean off beaters. Add lemon rind to yolk mixture. Now with rotary beater, quickly beat egg whites until stiff enough to form shiny peaks, then beat in remaining ¼ cup sugar gradually until whites form shiny pointed peaks that curve at tips. With a rubber scraper, cut and fold yolk mixture into whites, lightly but thoroughly. Flow batter into pan. Bake 1 hr or until cake springs back when lightly touched. Remove from oven and invert over large funnel or bottle. When just cooled, remove from pan like Angel Food, p 315. Spread thinly with Orange or Lemon Butter Frosting, p 387, or thickly with Sweetened Whipped Cream. 10 to 12 servings.

STANDARD SPONGE CAKE

The delicate texture of this cake makes it a winner

1 cup cake flour	¼ cup cold water
6 medium eggs, separated	1 tsp cream of tartar
1 cup sugar	½ tsp salt
1 tsp vanilla	Orange Butter Frosting,
½ tsp lemon extract	p 387 *or* whipping cream

Use a 10-inch tube pan—*do not grease.* Start oven 10 min before baking; set to moderately slow (325° F).

Sift flour, measure, resift 3 times. Put egg whites into a 4-qt bowl. Put yolks into a 3-qt bowl; gradually beat in ½ the sugar with a rotary beater until so thick beater is difficult to turn, at least 5 min. With a wooden spoon, beat in flavorings. Now add flour and water alternately in 3 or 4 portions, beating vigorously after each. Now sift cream of tartar and salt over whites, and beat with clean rotary beater until stiff enough to form soft shiny peaks, then add rest of sugar gradually and beat until the shiny meringue forms pointed peaks that curve at tips. Use a rubber scraper to quickly fold yolk mixture into the whites lightly but thoroughly. Now flow batter into pan. Bake cake on bottom rack 1 hr or until it springs back when lightly touched with finger. Remove from oven; invert at once over large funnel or bottle if pan does not stand on tube or side-supports. When just cool, remove from pan like Angel Food. Spread thinly with Orange Butter Frosting or generously with Sweetened Whipped Cream. Serves 10 to 12.

SUNSHINE CAKE

The most delicate and luscious of all sponge cakes

1 cup *plus* 2 tbsp cake flour	1 tsp cream of tartar
¼ tsp salt	½ tsp lemon extract
1½ cups fine granulated sugar	½ tsp orange extract
6 egg yolks	Orange Butter Frosting,
1 cup egg whites, 8 or 9	p 387

Use a 10-inch tube pan—*do not grease.* Bake cake on bottom oven rack. Start oven 10 min before baking; set to moderately slow (325° F).

Sift flour, measure, resift 5 times with salt and ½ cup of the sugar. Beat yolks with rotary beater or on electric mixer until thick and lemon-colored, adding flavorings at last. Remove beater. Beat whites with wire whip in a 4-qt mixing bowl until foamy, then sift cream of tartar over top and beat until stiff enough to stand in soft peaks. Now add remaining sugar in 6 to 8 portions, using 10 cutting-and-folding-over strokes after each. Turn yolks over whites, then cut-and-fold in with wire whip until well blended, using about 25 cutting-and-folding-over strokes. Now add flour mixture in 5 or 6 portions with 10 cutting-and-folding-over strokes after each. Flow batter gently into pan. Bake about 1 hr or until cake tests done. Hang cake inverted over large funnel or bottle only until cooled. Loosen sides of cake with thin-bladed knife or spatula just like Angel Food Cake. Lift out of pan, then loosen around tube and bottom, keeping as much of the brown crust on cake as possible. Turn cake carefully bottom-side up on cake plate. Spread top, sides and inside hole thinly with Orange Butter Frosting. If cake is served unfrosted, place on plate top-side up and sprinkle with xxxx sugar. 12 to 15 servings.

MODERN BOSTON CREAM OR WASHINGTON PIE

This is a delicious Sponge Cake dessert. For Authentic Boston Cream or Washington Pie see p 332.

Line bottom of 1½-inch deep 9-inch layer cake pan with heavy waxed paper—grease paper and sides of pan. Make ½ recipe of either the *Standard or Quick-Mix Sponge Cake,* pp 320, 321, and flow batter into prepared pan. Bake in moderately hot oven (425° F) about 12 min or until cake springs back when lightly touched. Cool in pan on cake rack 5 min, then turn out on rack, strip off paper and invert to finish cooling. Split cake to make 2 uniform layers. Spread Cream Filling, p 397, or Lemon Filling, p 398, between layers. Sprinkle xxxx sugar over top, or spread with Thin Butter Icing, p 395. Serve the day cake is baked. 5 to 6 servings.

WHIPPED CREAM SPONGE LOAF CAKES

Flow the *Quick-Mix Sponge Cake* batter, p 320, into 2 ungreased 9½ x 5¼ x 2½-inch loaf pans. Bake at 325° F for 40 min. Invert pans to hang on edges of 2 other pans or bowls to cool. Then remove from pans carefully. Split loaves lengthwise into 3 layers of equal thickness. Spread sweetened Gelatin Whipped Cream, p 396, thickly between layers and over top and sides. Store in refrigerator until serving time. If desired, shave some sweet or semi-sweet chocolate lightly over top. 16 to 20 servings.

BUTTER CAKES

The OLD-TIME CREAMING METHOD OF MAKING "BUTTER" CAKE often called the STANDARD or CONVENTIONAL METHOD

This good old way of cake-making has been developing through the years and has been used to make *Plain Yellow, White, Chocolate and Spice cakes.* Each generation has made improvement in the quality of these cakes. There are several reasons for this improvement.

1. *Refinement of ingredients* such as flour, sugar, molasses, shortening, baking powder and flavorings.

2. *Mixing equipment,* baking pans and heat-controlled ovens which have been standardized for efficiency.

3. *The accumulated experience* of home and trained laboratory bakers has developed the present high standards for cake.

Unless cake has good volume, uniform shape, attractive color, pleasing aroma, delicate light texture, satisfying moistness and excellent flavor, it does not rate high with the millions of discriminating cake eaters.

The findings of research as well as home bakers is now organized, and with this information any home cook can make cake of high quality. The *steps* outlined under *Basic 2-Egg Cake,* p 326, are based on these findings.

All so called *"Butter"* Cakes, however, are not made according to the technique described under these *steps.* For example, the *Quick-Mix cakes* described on p 348, and which belong to the *"Butter"* type cakes use a very different method from the old-time creaming method.

To use the old-time creaming method successfully, have all ingredients at room temp. *(The term "Soft Butter" used in recipes in this book means butter at room temp—about 70° F).* At this temp butter or shortening creams readily, eggs beat up to greater volume and all ingredients blend easily into a batter of uniform consistency. Sift all dry ingredients, except sugar, together at least 3 times to completely distribute leavening and all other ingredients, and to give even color and flavor to cocoa and spice cakes.

The *creaming method* begins with creaming the butter, then follows by adding part or all of the sugar with continued creaming until well blended, adding flavoring, beating in eggs until smooth and fluffy, *alternately* adding the flour mixture and milk and mixing after each portion until batter is smooth. Then turn batter quickly into prepared pans. Bake according to recipe used. See steps in detail, p 326.

HOW TO USE ELECTRIC MIXER TO MIX BUTTER CAKES USING OLD-TIME RECIPES

This is not the Quick-Mix Method, see p 348

Mixing cakes on an electric mixer saves time and a lot of energy, and it is possible to make as good cakes as the best old-time hand-mixed ones. The technique of mixing is simple, and closely follows that used in hand-mixing. *Here is how to proceed:*

Have all ingredients at room temp. Sift the flour once, measure, resift 3 times with leavening, salt and any spices. If cocoa is used, sift it with the dry ingredients. Measure the milk or other liquid. Measure the sugar. When beaten egg whites are folded into batter at last, save out ¼ of the sugar specified in the recipe to beat into whites to make a shiny meringue. Now put soft butter or shortening into mixer bowl and cream on *Medium Speed* until shiny, then without stopping beaters, add sugar gradually and cream thoroughly, scraping bottom and sides of bowl with rubber scraper. Now stop beating, add whole eggs, yolks or unbeaten whites and flavoring and continue to beat on *Medium Speed* 5 min or until very smooth and fluffy, scraping down sides of bowl while beating. If chocolate is added, have it melted and cooled, and beat in at this point until just blended. From this point on, the mixing may be done in one of two ways:

1. Turn mixer to *Lowest Speed,* then add dry ingredients and liquid alternately in 3 or 4 portions, beginning and ending with flour and beating until just smooth after each portion, scraping sides and bottom of bowl while mixing.

2. *Here change to hand stirring.* Stop beating, remove beaters and clean off. Now remove bowl from platform to table. *With a wooden spoon,* stir in flour and milk alternately in 3 or 4 portions, beginning and ending with flour and mixing until barely smooth after each portion. When adding the flour and liquid, there is less danger of over-mixing by hand than with the mixer. Over-mixing produces a less delicate cake.

If stiffly beaten egg whites are added at the last, cut-and-fold the meringue in lightly but thoroughly into the batter whether finished by mixer or mixed by hand.

CAUSES OF BUTTER CAKE FAILURE

Any one or a combination of the following factors may cause a cake failure.

Why Does Cake Fall?
1. Too much shortening, sugar or leavening
2. Too many egg whites
3. Too slow an oven
4. Underbaked

Why Is Cake Dry?
1. Too much flour or leavening
2. Not enough shortening
3. Baked too long
4. Temp too low

Why Is Cake Coarse-Grained?
(*Large holes or tunnels*)
1. Not creamed enough
2. Too little sugar
3. Too much leavening
4. Egg whites not combined thoroughly

5. Soda produces in a few cakes some holes, but this is OK
6. Not scraping spoon and sides of bowl during the mixing
7. Putting cake in oven before it is heated to right temp
8. Baking at too low a temp

Why Is Top Not Level?
1. Too much flour
2. Oven rack not level
3. Oven heat uneven
4. Pans too close to oven sides

Why Is Crust Moist and Sticky?
1. Too much sugar
2. Too much liquid

Why Does Cake Shrink?
1. Too much shortening
2. Ingredients too warm; in hot

weather use milk and eggs just from refrigerator

3. Too hot oven
4. Overbaking

Why Does Cake Crumble?

1. Too much shortening or leavening
2. Too little egg
3. Too much air beaten in
4. Undermixing
5. Putting in oven before it is heated to right temp

Why Is Cake Heavy and Compact?

1. Mixed too slowly after adding milk
2. Too much shortening
3. Too little baking powder
4. Baked too slow or too fast

Why Is Cake Undersized?

1. Ingredients too cold
2. Too small a recipe
3. Batter not thoroughly combined
4. Wrong leavening—not using D.A. baking powder, or not adding single-action baking powder the last minute of mixing
5. Too large a pan or too hot an oven

Why Top Cracks?

1. Too much flour, or overmixing if all-purpose flour used
2. Too hot an oven

Why Does Cake Have Heavy Layer on Bottom?

1. Inferior shortening
2. Too much liquid
3. Ingredients too warm; in hot weather use milk and eggs right from refrigerator
4. Wrong leavening—not using D.A. baking powder or not adding single-action powder the last minute of mixing
5. Undermixing
6. Too low a temp

What Causes Toughness?

1. Too little shortening
2. Too little sugar
3. Too much flour
4. Putting cake in oven before it is heated to right temp

Why Does Cake Stick to Pans?

1. Pan insufficiently greased, or pan not lined with waxed paper
2. Too low oven temp
3. Cake stands in pan too long before removing to cake rack
4. Too much liquid
5. Underbeating

Why Raisins, Nuts, Etc. Sink to Bottom?

1. Using recipe where they don't belong
2. Pieces are too large
3. Using wrong type of flour
4. Putting cake in oven before it reaches the proper temp

Note: To prevent cake failure, use a proven recipe, quality ingredients, accurate measurements, proper mixing technique and a well-regulated oven.

Good Idea: When cakes are baking take time to study Glossary of Terms at end of Volume II, or Diet Pattern in front of Volume I. You'll find lots of useful information.

YELLOW OR WHOLE EGG CAKES
USING BAKING POWDER

In mixing any type of *Butter Cake* batter, it is important to know how to correctly use both types of baking powder.

WORDS OF CAUTION: Read the Label! Know the 2 types of baking powder! Here is How to Use Them:

1. Double Action (D.A.) or Sulphate-phosphate type. Since so many homemakers use a D.A. type of baking powder the amount indicated in all cake recipes in this chapter is for the D.A. type such as *Calumet, Clabber Girl, KC, Crescent, Davis OK* and *Hearth Club.* This powder is always sifted 3 or more times with the flour.

2. Tartrate and Phosphate type. To use a *tartrate powder* such as *Royal,* or a *phosphate* powder such as *Rumford, Dr. Price,* or *Jewel Tea* use ¼ more than D.A. powder. For example, if 2 tsp of D.A. baking powder are called for in the recipe use 2½ tsp of either a Tartrate or Phosphate powder *but do not sift it in with the flour* as is advised when using D.A. powder. Instead sprinkle the powder *over the batter* the last min of beating, then beat for ½ to 1 min, or until the powder is well blended through the batter. See p 113.

BASIC 2-EGG CAKE WITH SWEET MILK

A moist yellow cake of fine texture and very palatable

1¾ cups *plus* 2 tbsp cake flour	¼ cup soft butter
2 tsp D.A. baking powder *or*	¼ cup shortening
2½ tsp tartrate *or* phos-	1 cup *plus* 2 tbsp sugar
phate type	1 tsp vanilla
½ tsp salt	¾ cup sweet milk
2 eggs	

Grease two 8-inch layer cake pans; line bottoms with heavy waxed paper—grease paper. Start oven 10 min before baking; set to moderate (350° F). Bake 25 to 30 min.

STEPS IN MAKING BY THE OLD-TIME CREAMING METHOD

Step 1. Sift flour once before measuring to assure accurate measurement, then resift 3 times with leavening, salt and spices. See *Sifting,* p 313. The 3 siftings insure even distribution of leavening, salt and spices through flour as well as through batter. Sifting also incorporates some air into the flour which adds to lightness of finished cake. *The following 2, 3 and 4 steps are the creaming technique:*

Step 2. Cream shortening until smooth and shiny. Thorough creaming is important for smooth, uniform blending with other ingredients. This produces smooth uniform batter and fine-textured cake.

Step 3. Add the sugar gradually, creaming well. When recipes direct adding beaten egg whites last, *set aside ¼ of the sugar* called for in the recipe to beat into the egg whites later. Creaming shortening and sugar thoroughly incorporates air, giving cake volume, fine texture and velvetiness. Research shows it makes no difference whether mixture is creamed thoroughly before or after eggs are added, but it is important that thorough creaming be done.

Step 4. Add whole eggs one at a time and beat vigorously until thick, fluffy and light color, or separate eggs adding egg yolks only one at a time and beat until thick, fluffy and light color. See Step 7 for adding egg whites. When beating is done thoroughly, most of the sugar dissolves, at least very little graininess remains apparent. Thorough beating at this point also makes batter thick and fluffy and cake light and large in volume. Up to this point, it is almost impossible to *overbeat*—slighting this beating has an unfavorable effect on texture and volume of the finished cake.

Step 5. Now add extracts to creamed mixture. Here the *mixing technique starts.* Extracts should always be added to the creamed mixture rather than to the finished batter, *because fat and egg absorb and hold the flavor better than sugar, milk or flour.* Cake retains more flavor when flavoring is added at this point.

Step 6. Add sifted dry ingredients and liquids alternately. Add dry ingredients in 3 or 4 portions, and the liquid in 2 or 3—*always begin and end with flour,* and beat until *smooth after* each addition. When liquid is added first, the fat in the creamed mixture tends to separate out, producing a curdled appearance. After flour is added, it still does not produce a smooth batter. Adding flour first and last, prevents batter from becoming excessively thin at any point during mixing. This binds the ingredients together and produces a smooth batter and a fine-texture cake. On contact with liquid, leavening loses some gas, so after starting to add the liquid, *mixing should proceed as rapidly as possible.*

Step 7. When adding egg whites last, beat them with ¼ the sugar called for in recipe. Egg whites properly beaten and folded into batter incorporate considerable air, adding to volume and lightness of cake. Whites must be at room temp and in a bowl, *ready for beating before cake mixing starts.* Have ready ¼ of the sugar specified in recipe to beat into whites. Adding sugar to whites helps retain air beaten into them, and the smooth meringue is easier to fold into batter than plain, stiffly beaten whites. *Beat whites and add to batter this way:* Beat whites until just stiff enough to form soft, shiny peaks, then gradually beat in sugar to a stiff shiny meringue. Now quickly slide meringue onto the batter, and with a *wire whip,* cut-and-fold it in lightly. It is important that this cutting-and-folding be done quickly and thoroughly. If flecks of white show in batter, cake will have coarse texture; if cutting-and-folding is *overdone,* cake will have less volume.

Step 8. Pour batter immediately into prepared pans. (Weigh batter into pans if you have a scale.) Use rubber scraper to scrape all batter quickly from bowl into pans. When batter is thick, use rubber scraper to gently swirl it out from center so it is slightly higher around edge of pan than in center—in rising, the layer levels-out instead of rounding-up in center. If batter is thin, it will level itself. After batter is in pans, it is not affected by standing a few min, but if it stands in mixing bowl a few minutes before it is poured into pans, handling at this point tends to work out gas and reduces the volume of cake.

Step 9. Place pans in oven correctly for number of pans used. Adjust oven rack as near center of oven as possible. Place pans on rack so cakes are not close to door, top of oven or floor of oven. Pans should not touch each other or be too near oven walls—and one pan should *never be directly above another.* Heat must circulate freely around pans for even baking. When one pan is used, place it so center of cake is in center of oven. Set 2 pans on rack placed in middle of oven, neither touching each other nor oven walls. For 3 pans, adjust 2 racks as near to middle of oven as possible so lower cakes won't rise and touch rack above; place 2 pans on lower rack and 1 pan on upper rack, but not above either of the 2 lower pans. For 4 pans, place 2 pans on each rack, staggering so no 2 pans are directly above one another.

Step 10. Start testing for doneness 3 or 4 min before end of specified baking time. Ovens differ and may vary slightly in temp. Using a different size pan than is called for in recipe, or a different make of pan, influences baking time. Baking is faster in glass than in metal pans; *use a temp 25 degrees lower when baking in glass.* Cake dries out if overbaked, or falls if underbaked. Always test cake for doneness, and learn how to recognize when it is done. Do not remove cake from oven to test. Common tests are:

(a) Remove cake from oven at once when it just begins to pull away from sides of pan; it is overbaked when it has *pulled away from sides of pan in oven.* Most cakes pull away from sides of pan noticeably when out of oven a few minutes.

(b) Quickly stick a clean tooth pick or cake tester into center; if any uncooked batter adheres, cake is not done. Continue baking a few minutes, then repeat test, and bake *only* until tester comes out clean.

(c) Press cake very lightly with finger tip; if imprint does not remain, cake is done.

Step 11. Cool cakes in pans on cake racks 5 min before removing from pans. Warm cake is delicate, and if removed immediately from pans, it will break or crumble. Cakes that cool completely in pans become soggy. The average 5-min cooling period firms cake enough to be handled and allows enough cooling time out of the pan to prevent sogginess.

Step 12. Frost or ice cake as soon as oven heat is gone. This seals in moistness that is a *"must" quality* of any good cake. Have frosting or icing made before mixing the cake, or mix while baking cake, or start mixing it immediately after cake is removed from oven. See *directions for frosting or icing cake,* p 382.

Step 13. Store cake to keep it fresh. The kind of Frosting, Icing and Filling used determines the place of storing the cake. Cake with whipped cream or French Butter Icing should be stored in the refrigerator, and covered if possible. Other cakes keep well under cake covers. Or set cake on flat surface such as a table, cover with large, deep bowl. Wring a clean towel out of water, fold several times, then wrap around bottom of bowl to keep out air. Re-wet towel when it dries. When slices are removed from cake, retain moisture in remaining cake by placing a wad of wet paper toweling on plate in the open wedge.

HOW TO FREEZE CAKES

Either *Butter* or *Sponge-Type cakes* may be frozen very successfully. This is a sweet boon for the busy homemaker. She can make and decorate cakes for a party, a birthday or guest meals a week or so ahead at her convenience.

As soon as the cake cools, frost or ice it, then place in the freezer long enough to become firm enough to wrap securely without marring the icing. Then remove and wrap in moisture-proof cellophane as nearly airtight as possible, sealing edges with locker tape. Return to freezer as is or in a box. Remove cake from freezer ½-hr or so before serving time to warm up. Cake looks and tastes as though freshly baked.

BASIC 3-EGG CAKE WITH SWEET MILK

2½ cups cake flour	⅓ cup soft butter *and*
2½ tsp D.A. baking powder *or*	⅓ cup shortening
3 tsp tartrate *or* phosphate	1½ cups sugar
type	1½ tsp vanilla
¾ tsp salt	1 cup milk
3 eggs, medium	

Grease two 9-inch layer cake pans; line bottoms with heavy waxed paper—grease paper. Start oven 10 min before baking; set to moderate (350° F).

Follow directions exactly for mixing and baking *Basic 2-Egg Cake with Sweet Milk.* Bake 22 to 23 min.

Note: This makes 30 medium cupcakes. Bake in greased muffin pans at 375° F about 16 min.

BASIC 2-EGG CAKE WITH BUTTERMILK

Follow direction for making and baking *Basic 2-Egg Cake with Sweet Milk,* p 326, except *reduce* the baking powder to 1 tsp, and add ⅜ tsp soda, which is ¼ tsp and ½ of ¼ tsp, then sift with flour, baking powder and salt 6 times instead of 3 times. Use ¾ cup plus 1 tbsp thick buttermilk instead of the ¾ cup sweet milk. Note: This makes 30 to 32 medium cupcakes. Bake in moderate oven (375° F) 12 to 15 min.

BASIC 3-EGG CAKE WITH BUTTERMILK

Follow directions for making *Basic 3-Egg Cake with Sweet Milk,* p 329, except reduce baking powder to 1¼ tsp and add ½ tsp soda. Then sift with flour, baking powder and salt 6 times instead of 3 times. Use 1 cup plus 1 tbsp thick buttermilk in place of the 1 cup sweet milk.

*HONEY IN CAKES

In cakes and cookies honey can be substituted for the sugar. However, the liquid called for in the recipe must be reduced *¼ cup for each cup of honey used,* or in the same proportion for fractions of a cup. For example—*If ½ cup of honey is used, reduce the liquid by 2 tbsp; for ¼ cup honey, reduce the liquid by 1 tbsp.*

Better textured cake is usually obtained if only half the sugar in the recipe is replaced with honey, but the liquid in the recipe *still must be reduced* ¼ cup for each cup of honey used. Omit vanilla in honey cakes; the flavor is better without it. Cardamon blends well with honey flavor—this combination dates back hundreds of years.

The adjustments made in the liquid portion of a cake when honey is substituted for half, or all of the sugar, are illustrated in the following *Plain Butter Cake Recipe.* (1 cup equals 16 tbsp.)

PLAIN BUTTER CAKE WITH HONEY VARIATIONS

Ingredients	All-Sugar Cake	½ Sugar ½ Honey Cake	All-Honey Cake
Cake flour	3 cups	3 cups	3 cups
Milk	1 cup	13 tbsp (¾ cup plus 1 tbsp)	⅝ cup or 10 tbsp
Shortening	½ cup	½ cup	½ cup
Sugar	1½ cups	¾ cup	None
Honey	None	¾ cup	1½ cups
Eggs	3	3	3
Baking powder	3 tsp	3 tsp	3 tsp
Vanilla	1 tsp	None	None
Salt	¾ tsp	¾ tsp	¾ tsp

*Circular 528 Univ. of Illinois Extension Service in Agriculture and Home Economics.

Cakes baked by the 2 honey recipes above were entirely satisfactory. A medium-thick delicately flavored clover honey was used in both these recipes. There is no reason to suppose that other honeys of similar thickness and pleasing flavor would not give equally good results.

The All-Honey cakes were slightly closer in texture than cakes made with half honey, and they had a more pronounced honey flavor, a darker interior color and were less velvety. The old-time creaming method of mixing the batter, p 322, was found satisfactory. In this method, the shortening and honey are creamed together until smooth and fluffy. Then the eggs, one at a time, are beaten into the mixture, then the sifted dry ingredients and the milk are added alternately, the flour in thirds and the milk in halves.

APPLE SAUCE CAKE

A delicious moist cake—retains good flavor after standing a day or two

2¼ cups all-purpose flour	½ cup *plus* 1 tbsp shortening
1 tsp salt	2 tbsp white sugar
1½ tsp soda	3 tbsp molasses
¾ tsp cinnamon	1 tsp lemon extract *or*
½ tsp nutmeg	½ tsp grated lemon rind,
¼ tsp cloves	pkd
¾ cup plumped raisins, cut	1 egg, beaten
⅓ cup walnuts, cut	1½ cups stiff unsweetened
1 cup brown sugar, pkd	apple sauce

Grease a 12 x 7½ x 2-inch glass baking pan. Line bottom with heavy waxed paper—grease paper. Start oven 10 min before baking; set to moderately slow (325° F). Or bake half the recipe in a 7 x 7 x 1¼-inch tin pan at moderate (350° F).

Sift flour, measure, resift 5 times with next 5 ingredients. Mix ¼ cup of this flour mixture with raisins and nuts. Put brown sugar through coarse sieve to remove lumps. Cream shortening with wooden spoon, add brown sugar gradually creaming well. Stir in white sugar, molasses and extract. Beat in egg until mixture is fluffy. Now add flour alternately with unsweetened apple sauce in 3 or 4 portions, beginning and ending with flour and beating until smooth after each. Stir in raisins and nuts. Turn batter into prepared pan, pushing it up a little higher around edge than in center. Bake large cake 47 to 50 min and the small cake 25 min, or until cake tests done. Cool in pan on cake rack 10 min, then turn out onto rack, quickly loosen paper and remove for steam to escape. Wash and dry pan; place over cake and invert, then finish cooling in pan. When cool, spread thinly with Lemon Confectioners' Icing, p 394, or Quick Caramel Frosting, p 390. Best when just cooled. Wrap pan with leftover cake in several layers of waxed paper and store in bread box. Large cake serves 12 to 15; small one 6 to 7.

AUTHENTIC BOSTON CREAM PIE (2 Pies)

Follow directions for baking *Basic 2-Egg Cake,* p 326. When cool, use a long, sharp thin-bladed knife to split each cake into 2 uniform layers. Remove top layer. Spread a ¼-inch thick layer of Cream Filling, p 397, over bottom layers. Replace top layers, matching them. Spread thin Chocolate Butter Frosting, p 384, over tops, or sprinkle with xxxx sugar. Serve fresh. 12 servings.

AUTHENTIC WASHINGTON CREAM PIE (2 Pies)

An aristocratic delicious rich dessert

Follow directions for baking *Basic 2-Egg Cake,* p 326. When cool, use a long, sharp thin-bladed knife to split each cake into 2 uniform layers. Lift off top layers carefully and place cut-side up onto waxed paper. Spread the 4 layers with *Gelatin Whipped Cream,* p 396. Let set 10 to 15 min, then spoon a thin layer of raspberry jam over cream on bottom layers. Now replace top layers, cream-side down, matching layers. Sift xxxx sugar evenly over top. Store in refrigerator until serving time. Serve same day. 12 servings.

BANANA-NUT LAYER CAKE

An outstanding cake with exceptionally good flavor

1¾ cups cake flour	½ cup buttermilk
1 tsp soda	½ cup shortening
½ tsp salt	1½ cups sugar
⅔ cup mashed well-ripened bananas, 2 medium	2 eggs
	1 tsp vanilla
1 tsp lemon juice	⅓ cup fine-chopped pecans

Grease two 8-inch layer pans; line bottoms with waxed paper—grease paper. Start oven 10 min before baking; set to moderate (350° F).

Sift flour, measure, resift 4 times with soda and salt. With silver fork, quickly crush bananas to fine paste, add lemon juice and stir in buttermilk. Cream shortening with wooden spoon, add sugar gradually and cream thoroughly. Add eggs, one at a time, beating well after each addition. Stir in vanilla. Add dry ingredients alternately with banana mixture in 3 or 4 portions, beginning and ending with flour and beating well after each. Fold in nuts. Turn into prepared pans. Bake 28 to 30 min. Remove to cake racks and cool in pans 8 to 10 min, then turn out on racks, loosen paper but leave on cake, then invert cake to finish cooling. Put layers together with Whipped Cream-Banana Topping.

Topping:

½ pt whipping cream	½ tsp vanilla
2 tbsp xxxx sugar	2 large ripe bananas

Chill bowl and rotary beater in refrigerator. Whip cream until stiff; add sugar and vanilla and beat to blend. Place 1 layer of cake on serving plate bottom-side up. Spread with whipped cream, then add a layer of sliced bananas, then another layer of whipped cream. Now carefully place 2nd layer top-side up on cream filling, and repeat with cream, bananas, then cream. Banana slices between layers of whipped cream do not discolor. Serve promptly, store leftover cake in refrigerator. 10 to 12 servings.

BURNT SUGAR CAKE

A great favorite—made too infrequently

½ cup sugar	1 tsp salt
½ cup water	1 cup shortening, half
1 cup milk, about	soft butter
3½ cups *plus* 1 tbsp cake flour	2 cups sugar
3 tsp D.A. baking powder *or*	1 tsp vanilla
3¾ tsp tartrate *or* phos-	3 eggs *or* 5 egg whites
phate type	

Grease three 9-inch layer cake pans; line bottoms with waxed paper —grease paper. Start oven 10 min before baking; set to moderate (350° F).

Put the ½ cup sugar into hot skillet, and with constant stirring, heat until sugar turns to a light brown syrup (caramel). Do not cook too brown—this causes a bitter flavor. Remove from heat. Add water cautiously, replace over heat and simmer until caramel just dissolves. Remove from heat and pour into measuring cup—there should be ½ cup syrup. Cool to room temp, then add milk to make 1½ cups.

Sift flour, measure, resift 4 times with baking powder and salt. With wooden spoon, cream shortening and butter until shiny, add sugar gradually and cream thoroughly. Stir in vanilla. Clean off spoon and remove. Now with rotary beater, beat in eggs one at a time (or whites in 3 portions) until satiny and fluffy. Clean off beater; remove. Add flour and milk alternately in 4 or 5 portions, beginning and ending with flour and beating with wooden spoon until smooth after each. Turn batter into prepared pans. Bake 24 to 26 min, or until cake tests done. Cool in pans on cake racks 5 min, then turn out on racks, loosen paper and quickly invert. When just cool, spread Penuche Frosting, p 389, between layers and over top and sides. 12 to 15 servings.

Note: Cake made with whole eggs is richer, but cake made with whites has a more delicate flavor and quality crust.

Note: The term "Soft Butter" used in recipes in this book means butter at room temp—about 70° F.

CRUMB CAKE

A quick busy-day cake with delightful flavor and fragrance. Especially good warm

1 cup seedless raisins	1 cup granulated sugar
2 cups all-purpose flour	¾ cup margarine *or*
1 tsp cinnamon	shortening
½ tsp nutmeg	2 eggs, beaten
½ tsp salt	1 cup buttermilk
½ cup all-purpose flour	1 tsp vanilla
1 cup brown sugar, pkd	1 tsp soda

Grease a 9 x 9 x 2-inch pan, line bottom with heavy waxed paper —grease paper, or bake half the recipe in a 7 x 7 x 1¼-inch pan. Start oven 10 min before baking; set to moderate (350° F).

Wash raisins, plump, p 165. Cool. Sift flour, measure 2 cups and resift with next 3 ingredients, the last time into a 3-qt mixing bowl. Now measure and set aside the ½ cup flour. Put lumpy moist brown sugar through coarse sieve into mixing bowl. Add granulated sugar and shortening and blend with pastry blender or rub together with fingers until mixture is size of small peas. Now take out 1 cup of this crumb-like mixture for topping. Add the ½ cup flour to ingredients in mixing bowl and blend until mixture is like coarse corn meal. Combine eggs, buttermilk and vanilla, then stir in soda, and quickly add to dry ingredients. Beat with rotary beater until smooth. Turn half the batter into prepared pan, quickly sprinkle half the raisins over top, add remaining batter, then rest of raisins. Sprinkle top with reserved crumbly mixture. Bake about 35 min or until cake tests done. Cool in pan on cake rack 10 min, then turn out onto rack, remove paper. Wash and dry pan, then turn it over cake and invert. Serve warm or cold. Serves 10 to 12.

DOLLY VARDEN CAKE

An heirloom recipe that is still prized

3 cups cake flour	1 cup milk
1½ tsp D.A. baking powder *or*	½ tsp vanilla
2 tsp tartrate *or* phosphate	½ cup currants, plumped,
type	p 165
½ tsp salt	½ cup fine-cut moist citron
¾ cup soft butter	2 tsp cinnamon
2 cups sugar	½ tsp cloves
4 eggs	½ tsp nutmeg

Line bottoms of two 8 x 8 x 2-inch pans with waxed paper—grease paper. Start oven 10 min before baking; set to moderate (350° F).

Sift flour, measure, resift 3 times with baking powder and salt. Use wooden spoon to cream butter until shiny, add sugar gradually and cream well. Clean off spoon, remove. Beat in eggs, one at a time with rotary beater until smooth and fluffy. Remove beater, use wooden spoon. Add flour and milk alternately in 4 or 5 portions, beginning and ending with flour and beating until smooth after each. Now carefully divide batter into 2 equal portions. Add vanilla to 1 portion, stirring just enough to mix, then turn batter into 1 of the prepared pans. To the other portion, add the fruit and spices, stirring to distribute thoroughly. Turn into the 2nd pan. Bake the yellow layer about 30 min; bake the dark layer 35 min or until both cakes test done. Cool in pans on cake racks 5 min, then turn out on racks, remove paper and invert to finish cooling. Use Spice Layer for bottom layer. Spread 7-Minute Icing, p 392, or Basic Butter Frosting, p 383, between layers and over top and sides. Cut with a very sharp knife. 10 servings.

DOUBLE ORANGE CAKE

This unusual cake has delicious flavor and attractive color

1 medium navel orange	1 tsp salt
½ cup raisins, plumped,	¾ tsp soda
p 165	½ cup shortening
½ cup pitted dates	1¼ cups sugar
½ cup pecans	2 eggs
2 cups cake flour	½ cup buttermilk

Grease two 8-inch layer pans, line bottoms with waxed paper—grease paper. Start oven 10 min before baking; set to moderate (350° F).

Wash orange and squeeze out juice—there should be ⅓ cup. Put rind through finest blade of food chopper once, then measure ¼ cup pkd. Now re-grind the ¼ cup rind with raisins, dates and nuts 2 more times. Stir the ⅓ cup orange juice into the ground mixture until well blended and smooth. Sift flour, measure, resift 4 times with salt and soda. Cream shortening, add sugar gradually and cream well. Add eggs, one at a time, beating thoroughly after each. Add flour mixture alternately with buttermilk in 4 or 5 portions, beginning and ending with flour and beating until smooth after each. Beat in fruit mixture thoroughly. Turn into prepared pans. Bake 30 min or until cake tests done. Cool in pans on cake racks 10 min, then turn out on racks, loosen paper and quickly invert. When just cool, spread cake with Orange Butter Frosting, p 387. 12 servings.

Note: The term "Soft Butter" used in recipes in this book means butter at room temp—about 70° F.

GRAHAM CRACKER CAKE

A different and delightful cake

15 Graham crackers	½ cup butter *or* shortening
1 cup cake flour	¾ cup sugar
2 tsp D.A. baking powder *or*	1 tsp vanilla
2½ tsp tartrate *or* phos-	2 eggs, separated
phate type	1 cup milk
½ tsp salt	

Line two 8-inch layer cake pans with waxed paper—grease paper. Start oven 10 min before baking; set to moderate (350° F).

Roll crackers into fine crumbs or put through food mill; there should be 1 cup and 2 tbsp. Sift flour, measure, resift 3 times with baking powder and salt. Cream soft butter with wooden spoon until shiny, add sugar gradually and cream thoroughly. Add vanilla, then egg yolks one at a time and beat until smooth and fluffy. Add milk and flour alternately in 2 or 3 portions, beginning and ending with flour and beating well after each. With rotary beater beat egg whites until they *form* shiny pointed peaks. Now fold cracker crumbs and whites alternately in 2 or 3 portions into the batter until just well blended. Turn batter into prepared pans. Bake about 25 min or until cake tests done. Cool in pans on cake racks 5 min, then turn out on racks, loosen papers and turn cakes right-side up. This delicate cake should be handled carefully. When cool, spread with Lady Baltimore Icing, p 394. 10 servings.

MARASCHINO CHERRY CAKE

2½ cups cake flour	1 cup sugar
3 tsp D.A. baking powder *or*	2 eggs
3¾ tsp tartrate *or* phos-	⅔ cup milk *and*
phate type	⅓ cup cherry juice
¾ tsp salt	½ cup sliced cherries
½ cup butter *or* shortening	7-Minute Icing, p 392

Grease two 8-inch layer cake pans; line bottoms with waxed paper —grease paper. Start oven 10 min before baking; set to moderate (350° F).

Sift flour, measure, resift 3 times with baking powder and salt. With wooden spoon, cream soft butter until smooth and shiny, add sugar gradually and cream thoroughly. Remove and clean off spoon. Add eggs, one at a time, and beat with rotary beater until light-colored and fluffy. Remove beater. Add flour and liquid alternately in 3 or 4 portions, beginning and ending with flour and beating with wooden spoon until smooth after each. Fold in cherries. Turn into prepared pans. Bake 25 to 30 min or until cake tests done. Cool in pans on cake racks 5 min, then turn out on racks, loosen paper and invert cake to finish cooling. Spread 7-Minute Icing between layers and over top and sides of cake. Decorate with maraschino cherry halves, if desired. 10 to 12 servings.

PEANUT BUTTER CAKE

Surprisingly good! Fluffy, flavorful and nutritious

2 cups *plus* 2 tbsp cake flour
¾ tsp soda
¾ tsp salt
1 tsp D.A. baking powder *or*
    1¼ tsp tartrate *or* phos-
    phate type
⅓ cup butter *or* margarine

⅓ cup homogenized
    peanut butter
1⅓ cups sugar
2 medium eggs
⅔ cup buttermilk
⅓ cup orange juice

Grease two 9-inch layer pans, line bottoms with waxed paper—grease paper. Start oven 10 min before baking; set to moderate (350° F).

Sift flour, measure, resift 5 times with soda, salt and baking powder. With wooden spoon cream soft butter and peanut butter until smooth, add sugar gradually and cream well. Scrape off spoon, remove. Beat in eggs one at a time with rotary beater until satiny and fluffy. Remove beater, use wooden spoon. Add flour and buttermilk mixed with the orange juice in 3 or 4 portions, beginning and ending with flour and beating until smooth after each. Turn batter into prepared pans. Bake 25 to 27 min or until cake barely tests done. Cool in pans on cake racks 5 to 10 min, then turn out on racks, loosen paper and invert to finish cooling. When cool, spread Creamy Chocolate Frosting, p 385, between layers and over top and sides. 12 servings.

SOUR CREAM CAKE

1½ cups cake flour
¾ tsp soda
¼ tsp cream of tartar
½ tsp salt
¼ cup butter *or* shortening

¾ cup sugar
1 egg
1 tsp vanilla
¾ cup sour cream

Grease two 8-inch layer cake pans; line bottoms with waxed paper —grease paper. Start oven 10 min before baking; set to moderate (350° F).

Sift flour, measure, resift 4 times with next 3 ingredients. Use wooden spoon to cream soft butter and sugar until smooth and shiny, add egg and vanilla and beat until light-colored and fluffy. Add flour mixture and sour cream alternately in 2 or 3 portions, beginning and ending with flour and beating thoroughly after each. Turn into prepared pans. Bake about 20 min or until cake tests done. Cool in pans on cake racks 5 min, then turn out on racks, loosen paper and invert to finish cooling. When barely cool, spread with Strawberry 7-Minute Icing, p 394, or any desired icing. 10 servings.

SPICY SPLENDOR CAKE

Well behaving, good eating, fine textured, moist and tender

3 cups cake flour
1½ tsp soda
½ tsp salt
1½ tsp cinnamon
½ tsp each, nutmeg, cloves, allspice

2¼ cups moist light brown sugar, pkd
½ cup soft butter *and*
¼ cup shortening
3 eggs, beaten
1½ cups buttermilk

Grease two 9-inch layer cake pans; line bottoms with waxed paper —grease paper. Then also grease muffin pan with 6 medium cups. Start oven 10 min before baking; set to moderate (350° F),

Sift flour, measure, resift 6 times with next 6 ingredients. Put sugar through coarse sieve to remove lumps. Cream butter and shortening with wooden spoon until smooth and shiny, add sugar gradually and cream thoroughly. Scrape off spoon, remove. Add eggs, one at a time and beat with rotary beater until satiny and fluffy. Remove beater. Now add flour alternately with buttermilk in 4 or 5 portions, beginning and ending with flour and beating with spoon until smooth after each. Spoon batter into muffin pan to half fill cups, then turn remaining batter into prepared pans. Set muffin pan in cool place. First bake layers 25 min or until cakes test done. Cool in pans on cake racks 10 min, then turn out on racks, loosen papers and invert to finish cooling. Meanwhile, increase oven temp to moderately hot (400° F) and bake cupcakes 10 min. Cool in pan 5 min, then remove. Spread Rum Butter Frosting, p 388, between layers and over top of cake. 12 to 14 servings.

Note: There is a little more batter than needed for two 9-in layers. Batter in muffin pan can stand while layers bake. Serve warm cupcakes for first meal.

CHOCOLATE CAKES

COCOA CAKE

This is a very good cake!

2 cups cake flour
¼ tsp soda
1½ tsp D.A. baking powder *or*
    2 tsp tartrate *or* phosphate type
½ tsp salt
⅓ cup cocoa

⅔ cup butter *or* shortening
1½ cups sugar
2 eggs, beaten
1 tsp vanilla
½ cup buttermilk
½ cup boiling water

Line bottoms of two 8-inch layer pans with waxed paper—grease paper. Start oven 10 min before baking; set to moderate (350° F). Sift flour, measure, resift 3 times with next 4 ingredients. Use wooden spoon to cream soft butter and sugar thoroughly, add eggs, one at a time, beating vigorously until smooth and fluffy after each. Stir in vanilla. Add flour mixture alternately with buttermilk in 3 or 4 portions, beginning and ending with flour and beating well after each. Now add boiling water all at once and quickly stir until smooth. Turn into prepared pans. Bake 25 to 30 min. Cool in pans on cake racks 5 min, then turn out on racks, strip off paper, invert to finish cooling. Spread with Coconut Icing, p 392. 10 servings.

GERMAN SWEET CHOCOLATE CAKE

1 pkg German sweet chocolate	1 tsp vanilla
	½ tsp salt
½ cup boiling water	1 tsp soda
1 cup (2 sticks) butter	2½ cups sifted cake flour
2 cups sugar	1 cup buttermilk
4 egg yolks, unbeaten	4 egg whites

Melt chocolate in boiling water. Cool. Cream butter and sugar until light and fluffy. Add egg yolks, one at a time, beating after each addition. Add chocolate and vanilla. Sift together salt, soda and flour. Add alternately with buttermilk to chocolate mixture, beating well after each addition. Beat until batter is smooth. Beat egg whites until stiff peaks form. Fold into batter. Then pour into three 8- or 9-inch layer pans, lined on bottoms with wax paper. Bake in moderate oven, 350 F, 30 to 40 min. Cool. Frost tops only.

Coconut-Pecan Frosting: Combine 1 cup evaporated milk, 1 cup sugar, 3 egg yolks, ¼ lb butter and 1 tsp vanilla in a saucepan. Cook and stir over medium heat until mixture thickens, about 12 min. Add about 1⅓ cups grated coconut and 1 cup chopped pecans. Beat until cool and thick enough to spread. Makes 2⅔ cups, enough to cover tops of three 9-inch layers.

RED DEVIL'S FOOD CAKE

Good color, texture and flavor

2 cups cake flour	1½ cups sugar
1 tsp soda	2 eggs, beaten
¼ tsp salt	1 tsp vanilla
1½ to 2 sqs unsweet chocolate	½ cup buttermilk
½ cups butter *or* shortening	½ cup boiling water

Line bottoms of two 8-inch layer pans with waxed paper—grease paper. Start oven 10 min before baking; set to moderate (350° F). Sift flour, measure, resift 3 times with soda and salt. Melt chocolate over hot water; cool. Use wooden spoon to cream soft butter until smooth and shiny, gradually add sugar and cream thoroughly. Add eggs, one at a time, and beat until smooth and fluffy; stir in vanilla and cooled chocolate. Add flour and buttermilk alternately in 4 or 5 portions, beginning and ending with flour and beating until smooth after each. Add boiling water all at once and beat until just smooth. The batter is thin. Turn into prepared pans. Bake 25 to 30 min or until cake springs back when lightly touched. Cool in pans on cake racks 5 min, then turn out on racks, strip off paper and invert to finish cooling. When cool, spread with desired frosting. 10 servings.

WHITE CAKES

BASIC 3-EGG WHITE CAKE WITH SWEET MILK

Moist, delicate texture, good volume

2¼ cups cake flour
2½ tsp D.A. baking powder *or*
   3 tsp tartrate *or* phosphate
   type
¾ tsp salt
¼ cup soft butter *and*
¼ cup shortening

1⅓ cups sugar
½ tsp each almond and lemon
   extract *or*
2 tsp vanilla
3 egg whites, unbeaten
1 cup milk

Grease two 8-inch layer pans, line bottoms with waxed paper—grease paper. Start oven 10 min before baking; set to moderate (375° F). Sift flour, measure, resift 3 times with baking powder and salt. Cream butter and shortening with wooden spoon until smooth and shiny, add sugar gradually, creaming thoroughly. Stir in flavoring. Scrape off spoon and remove. Add egg whites in 2 portions and beat vigorously with rotary beater after each until fluffy. Remove beater. Now add flour and milk alternately in 3 or 4 portions, beginning and ending with flour and beating with wooden spoon until smooth after each. Turn into prepared pans. Bake 20 to 22 min or until cake tests done. Cool in pans on cake racks 5 min, then turn out on racks, quickly loosen paper and invert. When barely cool, spread with chocolate or desired frosting. 12 to 15 servings.

BASIC 4-EGG WHITE CAKE WITH SWEET MILK

3 cups cake flour
3 tsp D.A. baking powder *or*
   3¾ tsp tartrate *or* phosphate type
1 tsp salt
⅓ cup soft butter *and*
⅓ cup shortening

1¾ cups sugar
½ tsp almond and 1¼ tsp
   lemon extract *or*
2 tsp vanilla
4 egg whites, unbeaten
1⅓ cups milk

Grease two 9-inch layer pans for thick layers or three 9-inch pans for medium layers; line bottoms with waxed paper—grease paper. Start oven 10 min before baking; set to moderate (375° F).

Follow directions exactly for mixing and baking *Basic 3-Egg White Cake with Sweet Milk*. Bake the 2 layers 23 min and the 3 layers about 20 min or until cake tests done.

BASIC 3-EGG WHITE CAKE WITH BUTTERMILK

Excellent flavor and volume—stays moist

Follow directions exactly for making *Basic 3-Egg White Cake with Sweet Milk*, substituting buttermilk for sweet milk. Reduce baking powder to 1 tsp and add ½ tsp soda. Now sift 6 times with flour and salt, instead of 3 times. Bake in two 8-inch layers in moderate oven (375° F) 20 to 22 min.

BASIC 4-EGG WHITE CAKE WITH BUTTERMILK

Follow directions exactly for making *Basic 4-Egg White Cake with Sweet Milk*, substituting buttermilk for sweet milk. Reduce baking powder to 1½ tsp and add ½ tsp soda. Now sift 6 times with flour and salt instead of 3 times. Bake in two 9-inch layers in moderate oven (375° F) 23 to 25 min.

BRIDE'S CAKE—4 TIER

Moist white cake of fine texture and good flavor. A strong arm or electric mixer is needed to mix it, and 2 workers to assemble it

Decorative Frosting, p 386
4 cups cake flour
2 tsp D.A. baking powder *or*
   2½ tsp tartrate *or* phosphate type
1 tsp cream of tartar
½ tsp salt
2 cups soft butter *or*
   half shortening, 1 lb
2⅓ cups xxxx sugar, sifted
   and pkd
2 tsp vanilla

(No liquid used)
2 cups egg whites, 18
Apricot Filling, p 344
or
Orange Filling, p 399
Glossy White Icing, p 393
White heavy cardboards
cut to fit under each cake
4 sizes Cellophane Lace
Doilies
Pleated ribbon, optional

To make this 4-tier Bride's Cake, double recipes for cake, filling and frosting, but *make only one recipe of cake at a time.* However, mix and bake the 2nd batch of cakes immediately after the first so all will be of equal freshness. The *top tier* may be a small *Groom's Cake*, p 370, or Fruit Cake made by any recipe in this chapter. When cake is cut, the top tier of Fruit Cake is usually lifted off intact, tightly wrapped, boxed and kept for the First Wedding Anniversary.

Make a plan for decorating the cake. Estimate how many roses, orange blossoms, leaves, etc. you will need. Be sure to have decorating tubes, nails and bags required for this work, as well as information and skill for doing it. A few days before baking cake, make Decorative Icing, then make flowers and leaves. Store these in one layer in a shallow box —a suit box lined with a soft cloth is ideal. Cover to keep clean and dry. Also make *Filling* and store in refrigerator in covered container.

Have ready 4 pans 2 inches deep: a 12-, a 9-, a 6- and a 4-inch or a 1 lb (5-inch) coffee can. Prepare pans by lining with parchment or smooth brown wrapping paper cut to fit bottom, p 312. Grease bottoms of pans lightly, fit in linings, then grease linings.

MIXING THE CAKE

Sift flour, measure, resift 6 times with next 3 ingredients. Cream butter until smooth and shiny, add sugar gradually, creaming thoroughly. Stir in vanilla. Add ¾ cup of the unbeaten egg whites in 3 portions, beating well after each portion. Now add flour and remaining whites alternately in 4 or 5 portions, beating until batter is smooth after each.

Weighing the batter—One recipe of this batter weighs 4 lbs.

1st batch—Weigh 3½ lbs batter into the 12-inch pan, and the remaining ½ lb batter into the 4-inch pan, or into the 1 lb coffee can.

2nd batch—Weigh 2½ lbs batter into the 9-inch pan, and the remaining 1½ lbs into the 6-inch pan.

Quickly swirl batter so it is a little higher at edge of pans than in center—this prevents humping in center. Bake all cakes in a moderately slow oven (325° F). Put the 12-inch and the 4-inch layers into oven. Bake the 4-inch layer about 20 min and the 12-inch layer 40 to 45 min. Put the 9-inch and 6-inch layers into oven. Bake the 6-inch layer about 25 min and the 9-inch layer 30 min or until cakes test done. Cool cakes in pans on cake racks 10 min, then remove all cakes except the 12-inch layer to racks and strip off paper lining carefully, turn right-side up to finish cooling. Turn the 12-inch layer out on a towel spread over a thick fold of newspapers, as this cake is too wide for a cake rack and its weight makes it more difficult to handle. Strip off paper. Slip hand underneath newspaper and turn cake carefully right-side up onto the bottom of the 12-inch layer pan. Let cakes stand until cool, but no longer, then *ice promptly.*

FINISHING THE CAKE

Make Glossy Icing. If there are slight humps in center of cakes, slice them off to level layers to prevent finished cake from leaning. Split the cakes, one at a time, into 2 uniform layers, using a sharp thin-bladed long knife. Lift off top-half carefully and turn upside-down on waxed paper beside the bottom half. Spread filling, Apricot or Orange, over cut surfaces of both halves evenly, then let stand about 10 min. Now put the halves together as they originally were, being sure to match sides. Press together gently. Spread top of layer with the same filling—do not spread on sides of layers as this might cause Glossy Icing to slide. Let stand 30 min for filling to set. Place on the 12-inch heavy cardboard a slightly larger paper lace or cellophane lace doily. Over doily, lay four 4-inch strips of waxed paper in a hollow-square form to keep doily from being smeared with icing. On this, place the filled 12-inch layer. Spread sides and top of this cake smoothly with Glossy Icing. Now split the 9-inch layer, separate the 2 halves and spread with Filling, handling same as previous layer. Place on a doily-covered cardboard of same diameter. Spread Glossy Icing on sides and top as for first layer, then use spatulas or pancake turners to place this layer with cardboard onto exact center of lower layer. Pull spatulas out carefully so as not to mar icing on lower layer. Repeat the cake-splitting, spreading with filling then icing and laying together like the first 2 layers until cake is finished. Now put some Glossy Icing in pastry bag fitted with desired tube (with which we hope you have practiced) and pipe a border around the bottom and top edges of each layer. Always work from top layer down when piping. Straight line or festoon borders may be used. Now press the roses, orange blossoms or lilies of the valley and leaves previously made from Decorative Icing, or bought, into the Glossy Icing where they add the most glamorous touch. Now pleat enough white ribbon to fit around bottom of cake and slip it under edge of doily, but first carefully pull out the 4 protective strips of waxed paper. Now set the Bride-and-Groom figurine in center of top tier. Obtain figurine from bakery or novelty stores.

CUTTING THE CAKE

The bride cuts the first piece of cake from the bottom layer or layer above it. Then the caterer or a member of the family cuts the cake for serving. The 4- or 5-inch top tier is removed and served, or saved, depending on whether it is a Bride's or a Groom's Cake. The 6-inch layer is lifted off to the side with the cardboard under it and cut into wedges 3 inches long. The 9-inch layer is next removed with cardboard under it. Then a circular up-and-down cut is made all the way through the cake following the imprint of the outer rim of the removed 6-inch layer. Cut this outer 1½-inch wide circle of cake into 2-inch-wide pieces. Cut remaining inner 6-inch circle of cake into inch-wide wedges. The 12-inch or bottom layer is cut up-and-down around the imprint left by the 9-inch layer. Cut the outer 1½-inch circle into 2-inch-wide pieces. Cut the remaining inner 9-inch circle into wedges 2 inches wide.

APRICOT FILLING FOR BRIDE'S CAKE AND PETITS FOURS

Prepare ahead of time and store in covered container. Double this recipe for a 4-tier Bride's Cake

2 cups dried apricots, ½ lb
2½ cups water
1½ cups sugar

1 cup water
¼ tsp salt
½ tsp almond extract

Wash apricots, put into saucepan, add the 2½ cups water, cover and soak 45 min. Heat to boiling, cover, reduce heat, simmer 15 to 20 min or until fruit is soft. Put through food mill or sieve. There should be 2¼ cups purée. Cook sugar and the 1 cup of water to a thin syrup— 5 to 6 min; add purée and beat with rotary beater until smooth. Remove beater. Heat to boiling; boil 2 to 3 min or until slightly thick, stirring constantly with a wooden spoon. There should be 2¾ cups filling. Remove from heat, stir in salt and extract. Cool. The consistency should be like stiff jam. If too stiff to spread, warm up over hot water. Spread between layers and over tops of cakes. This prevents crumbing, insures moistness and makes cutting easy. After spreading, let set 20 to 30 min before covering with Glossy Icing. Enough for 2-tier Bride's Cake.

HICKORY NUT CAKE

Follow recipe for mixing and baking *Basic White Cake,* p 340, but reserve 2 tbsp of flour mixture to toss with ½ cup broken hickory nut-meats. Add nuts with the last few stirs. Spread with Browned Butter Frosting, p 384, adding ½ cup broken hickory nutmeats, if desired. 8 to 10 servings.

Note: Butternuts or pecans may be used instead of hickory nuts.

LADY BALTIMORE CAKE

Follow recipe for *Basic 3-Egg White Cake* with either sweet milk or buttermilk, pp 340, 341. Spread with Lady Baltimore Icing, p 394. 10 to 12 servings.

PETITS FOURS No. 1

This is a neat new method of dipping Petits Fours, and is especially adapted to refrigerators with freezing compartments

Make batter for two 9-inch layers of White Cake with either sweet milk or buttermilk. Pour batter into two 13 x 9-inch pans lined with waxed paper—grease paper. Bake in moderate oven (375° F) about 20 min or until cake tests done. Cool in pans on cake racks 5 min, then turn out on racks, loosen paper and turn right-side up. When cool, cut cake crosswise into 3 equal pieces. Place each piece on a waxed-paper-covered cardboard, cut to fit the piece. Now split each piece to make 2 layers. Remove top layer. Spread bottom layer with French Butter Cream Frosting, or Apricot Filling, p 391 or p 344. Replace top layer exactly. Store the cake slices singly in freezing unit. Freeze firm. When ready to dip, remove one piece at a time. With a sharp knife, trim off ends of crusts so corners are square, then cut pieces into 8 crosswise strips; now cut these strips in half crosswise, making Petits Fours 2 x 1-inch, or cut into 2-inch squares. The frozen Petits Fours do not crumble when dipped in frosting. Have Petits Fours Frosting made. Place frosting in double boiler over warm water to soften to a pouring consistency. Place a frozen Petit Four on tines of fork top-side-down and lower into frosting just enough to come barely to top. Lift up, drain a few seconds, then turn right-side up on cake rack for frosting to set. When set, pipe desired designs, such as initials, etc. on top.

PETITS FOURS No. 2

Bake White, Plain Yellow or Golden Gate Cake in sheets, or bake tiny cream puffs or éclairs, pp 936, 937. Plan shape and size of Petits Fours desired—small squares, diamonds or oblongs. A good plan is to make a paper pattern the same size as cake pan, then with a ruler mark off the size of Petits Fours desired. Now stick tooth picks into the 4 edges of sheet cake to measure off size and as a guide to cut cake. Use a long, sharp, thin-bladed knife to cut shapes neatly with clean-cut edges, then spread top and sides thinly with Apricot Glaze, p 368, and let set. Or fill Cream Puffs or Éclairs with Cream Filling, p 397.

Arrange Petits Fours on cake rack in neat rows 1-inch apart. Set rack in jelly roll or a shallow pan—see that no crumbs are in pan. Place a 2nd similar pan along side. Have Fondant or Petits Fours Frosting, p 389, softened to pouring consistency (and tinted if desired) over hot water in double boiler. Pour Frosting *quickly* down the rows, then *quickly* turn pan around and pour Frosting down the rows again so all 4 sides are covered. Now quickly lift rack into 2nd pan, and with rubber scraper, quickly return frosting in first pan to double boiler to again soften to pouring consistency.

Note: If 2 or 3 tints of frosting are desired, start with white first, and heat only a third of the frosting at a time so the amount leftover from each batch will be small. When barely firm, remove Petits Fours carefully from rack with a spatula and place on waxed paper, and with a sharp knife, trim off any rough edges on bottom. Serve as soon as possible for best appearance and delicate eating.

WHIPPED CREAM CAKE

A luxurious cake, expensive, but worth the price. If you are looking for a "conversation piece," here it is

2 cups cake flour
3 tsp D.A. baking powder *or*
    3¾ tsp tartrate *or* phos-
    phate type
1½ cups fine grain sugar
3 egg whites
½ tsp salt

1 pt whipping cream
1 tsp vanilla
½ cup cold water
2 tbsp xxxx sugar
¾ tsp vanilla
Chocolate decorettes *or*
shaved sweet chocolate

Line bottoms of two 9-inch layer pans with waxed paper—grease paper lightly. Start oven 10 min before baking; set to moderate (350° F).

Sift flour, measure, resift 5 times with baking powder and 1 cup of the sugar. Put egg whites into bowl, add salt and beat until they form soft peaks, add remaining ½ cup sugar gradually and beat to a stiff glossy meringue. Pour half the whipping cream (1 cup) into cold bowl, beat with rotary beater until stiff, adding vanilla the last few turns. Carefully fold whipped cream into meringue with wire whip, then add flour mixture and water alternately in 6 portions, beginning and ending with flour, and cutting-and-folding in 10 times after first 5 portions, then use 30 fold-over strokes after the last. Turn into prepared pans. Bake 15 min, then reduce heat to 325° F and bake 12 to 15 min longer. Cool in pans on cake racks 5 min, loosen sides and invert on racks, loosen paper and turn cakes right-side up on racks to finish cooling. Whip remaining cream until stiff, fold in sugar and vanilla. Spread thinly between layers, over top and sides of cake. Sprinkle with Chocolate decorettes or shaved chocolate. Store in refrigerator until serving time. 15 servings.

Note: A soft 7-Minute Icing or thin Butter Frosting is also appropriate for this cake.

EGG YOLK CAKES

GOLD LOAF CAKE

This Quick-Mix cake has fine texture, good flavor, is moist and easy to slice

2¼ cups cake flour
2½ tsp D.A. baking powder *or*
    3 tsp tartrate *or* phosphate
    type
1 tsp salt
1⅓ cups sugar

½ cup shortening
1 tsp grated lemon rind, pkd
1 cup milk
1 tsp vanilla
5 eggs yolks, ⅓ cup

Line a 9 x 5 x 3-inch loaf pan neatly with waxed paper—grease paper. Start oven 10 min before baking; set to moderately slow (325° F).

Sift flour, measure, resift 3 times with next 3 ingredients, the last time into large mixer bowl. Add shortening, lemon rind and ¾ cup of the milk. Beat 2 min on *Medium Speed* on electric mixer, scraping bowl constantly with a rubber scraper while beating, or beat 200 strokes by hand with a wooden spoon. Stop beating and clean off beaters or spoon. Add remaining ¼ cup milk, vanilla and egg yolks. Again beat 2 min, scraping bowl constantly while beating, or beat 200 strokes by hand. Turn batter into prepared pan. Bake 20 min, then increase heat to moderate (350° F) and bake 30 min longer. This cake has typical Pound Cake crack down center. Cool in pan on cake rack 15 min, then turn out on rack, leaving paper lining attached. May be iced, if desired, but it is not necessary. 15 to 20 servings.

GOLDEN GATE CAKE

A delicious cake and a good way to use leftover yolks from Angel Food

1½ cups cake flour	1 cup sugar
2 tsp D.A. baking powder *or*	8 egg yolks, scant ⅔ cup
2½ tsp tartrate *or* phosphate type	½ tsp lemon extract
½ tsp salt	½ tsp orange extract
½ cup soft butter	½ cup milk

Grease a 12¼ x 9 x 2-inch baking pan; line bottom with waxed paper—grease paper. Start oven 10 min before baking; set to moderate (350° F). Sift flour, measure, resift 3 times with baking powder and salt. Cream butter until smooth and shiny with wooden spoon, add sugar gradually and cream thoroughly. Scrape off spoon, remove. Add well-beaten yolks and beat with rotary beater until light-colored and fluffy, then beat in extracts. Clean off beater, remove, use wooden spoon. Add flour and milk alternately in 3 or 4 portions, beginning and ending with flour and beating well after each. Turn into prepared pan. Bake 22 to 25 min or until cake tests done. Cool in pan on cake rack 5 min, then turn out on rack to evaporate steam and remove paper. Wash and dry pan, replace over cake and invert. Finish cooling on rack. Spread top with Fool-Proof Chocolate or Rum-Nut Frosting, pp 387, 388. 15 servings.

REMEMBER: Increase flour a little or decrease liquid a little when baking in the South.

GOLDEN GATE CAKE, ENLARGED

2 cups cake flour
2½ tsp D.A. baking powder *or*
   3 tsp tartrate *or* phosphate
   type
¾ tsp salt
¾ cup soft butter *or* part
   shortening

1½ cups sugar
12 egg yolks, 1 cup
¾ tsp lemon extract
¾ tsp orange extract
¾ cup milk

Bake in a 12¼ x 9 x 2-inch greased baking pan at 350° F 35 min or until cake tests done.

LORD BALTIMORE CAKE

Follow recipe for Golden Gate Cake, p 347. Turn batter into two 8-inch layer pans. Bake in moderate oven (350° F) 23 min or until cake tests done. Spread Lord Baltimore Icing, p 394, between layers and over top and sides. 15 servings.

QUICK-MIX CAKES—ONE-BOWL METHOD

All ingredients must be at room temperature

This *Modern or 1-bowl Method* usually means all dry ingredients are sifted into large mixer bowl. Shortening and more than half the liquid are then added, then mixed at *Medium Speed* for 2 min, scraping bowl constantly with rubber scraper, or beating 200 strokes by hand. Then beating is stopped. Rest of liquid, eggs and flavorings are added, then mixing is continued on *Medium Speed* another 2 min, scraping bowl while mixing, or beating 200 strokes by hand. When beating by hand, rest a few seconds 2 or 3 times, counting strokes only while beating.

Step 1. Sift flour, measure, resift 3 times with baking powder, salt and sugar, the last time into large mixer bowl.

Step 2. Add shortening and about ¾ of the liquid. Stir with a spoon to blend.

Step 3. Beat at medium speed for 2 min, scraping bowl constantly. Time exactly.

Step 4. Stop beating and scrape beaters to clean them.

Step 5. Now add remaining liquid, eggs and flavoring and again beat on medium speed for 2 min, scraping bowl while beating.

Step 6. Use rubber scraper to flow batter into prepared pans. Bake, cool and frost as directed in the recipe.

CHERRY CHOCOLATE CAKE

Quick-Mix—A surprisingly good cake dotted with cherries

1 sq unsweet chocolate	½ tsp salt
2 tbsp water	⅔ cup buttermilk mixed with
½ cup shortening	2 tbsp cherry juice
1½ cups cake flour	1 egg
1 cup sugar	¼ cup well-drained mara-
1 tsp soda	schino cherries cut in 8ths

Grease an 8 x 8 x 2-inch pan, line bottom with waxed paper—grease paper. Start oven 10 min before baking; set to moderate (350° F). Put chocolate and water into a custard cup and set in hot water to melt. When melted, stir until smooth, then cool. Measure shortening into mixer bowl. Sift flour, measure, resift 3 times with sugar, soda and salt, the last time into bowl. Add buttermilk and cherry juice. Beat on *Medium Speed* of electric mixer 2 min, scraping sides and bottom of bowl constantly with rubber scraper while beating, or beat 200 strokes by hand. Stop beating. Quickly scrape beaters or spoon with scraper. Add egg and cooled chocolate. Beat 2 min more on mixer, constantly scraping bowl while mixing, or 200 strokes by hand with wooden spoon. Quickly turn batter into prepared pan. Sprinkle cherries evenly over top of batter. Bake about 35 min. Cool in pan on cake rack 5 min, then turn out on rack and strip off paper. Quickly wash and dry pan, then replace cake in it. When cool, spread top with ½ recipe Coffee Butter Frosting, p 385.

CHOCOLATE MARBLE CAKE

Quick Mix

2 cups all-purpose flour	1 cup milk
3½ tsp D.A. baking powder *or*	1 tsp vanilla
4½ tsp tartrate *or* phos-	2 eggs
phate type	1 sq unsweet chocolate,
1 tsp salt	melted
1¼ cups sugar	½ tsp soda
½ cup soft butter	2 tbsp hot water

Have all ingredients at room temp. Line bottom of 9 x 9 x 2-inch pan with plain or waxed paper—grease paper lightly. Start oven 10 min before baking; set to moderate (350° F).

Sift flour, measure, resift 3 times with next 3 ingredients, the last time into large mixer bowl. Add butter, milk and vanilla and stir with wooden spoon to blend. Scraping bowl constantly with rubber scraper, beat at *Medium Speed* on electric mixer 2 min, or 200 strokes by hand with wooden spoon. Stop beating and scrape off beaters or spoon. Add eggs and beat 2 more min, scraping bowl constantly, or 200 strokes by hand. Pour ⅔ of this batter into prepared pan, then quickly add cooled chocolate and soda dissolved in the water to remaining batter and beat ½ min. Run chocolate batter over the light batter, then quickly *cut through with knife 2 or 3 times* for marble effect. Bake 35 to 40 min or until cake tests done. Cool on cake rack 10 min, then turn out on rack and remove paper. Quickly wash and dry pan and replace cake in it. When cool, spread with Creamy Chocolate Frosting, p 385. 10 to 12 servings.

DEVIL'S FOOD CAKE

Quick Mix

3 sqs unsweet chocolate	½ cup shortening
2 cups cake flour	1 cup milk
1 tsp soda	1 tsp vanilla
1 tsp salt	2 eggs
1⅓ cups sugar	

Line bottoms of two 9-inch layer pans with waxed paper—grease paper but *not* sides of pans. Start oven 10 min before baking; set to moderate (350° F).

Melt chocolate over hot water, then stir and cool. Sift flour, measure, resift 3 times with next 3 ingredients, the last time into large mixer bowl. Add shortening, ¾ cup of the milk and vanilla. Beat on *Medium Speed* 2 min, constantly scraping bowl with rubber scraper while beating, or beat 200 strokes by hand with wooden spoon. Stop beating and scrape off beaters or spoon. Quickly add rest of milk, eggs and cooled chocolate, and again beat 2 min on mixer, scraping bowl constantly, or 200 strokes by hand. Pour batter into prepared pans, pushing it up around edge of pans. Bake 20 min or just until cake tests done. Cool in pans on cake racks 5 min, then turn out on racks, strip off paper and invert to finish cooling. Spread White Mountain Icing, p 395, between layers, over top and sides. 12 to 15 servings.

FRESH COCONUT CAKE

A superb Quick Mix white cake for the most festive occasions

1⅔ cups cake flour	½ cup coconut milk, p 122
1 cup sugar	¼ cup sweet milk
¾ tsp salt	3 egg whites, unbeaten
3 tsp D.A. baking powder *or*	1 tsp vanilla
3¾ tsp tartrate *or* phosphate type	7-Minute Icing, p 392
⅓ cup *plus* 1 tbsp shortening	3 cups fine-grated coconut

Line bottoms of two 8-inch layer pans with waxed paper—grease paper and sides of pans lightly. Start oven 10 min before baking; set to moderate (350° F). Have all ingredients at room temp. Sift flour, measure, resift 3 times with next 3 ingredients, the last time into large mixer bowl. Add shortening and coconut milk; beat on *Medium Speed* 2 min or 200 strokes by hand, scraping sides of bowl with rubber scraper while beating. Stop beating and scrape off beaters or spoon. Add the ¼ cup milk, egg whites and vanilla. Beat 2 min on mixer or 200 strokes by hand, constantly scraping down sides of bowl to keep batter smooth. Turn into prepared pans. Bake 25 min or until cake tests done. Cool in pans on cake racks 5 min, then turn out on racks to finish cooling. Spread Lemon Filling, p 398, or 7-Minute Icing, p 392, between layers, then spread top and sides with 7-Minute Icing. Sprinkle generously with coconut. 8 to 10 servings.

Note: This cake may also be made very satisfactorily by hand using old-time creaming method, p 322.

SILVER WHITE CAKE

Quick Mix

2 cups cake flour	1¼ cups sugar
2½ tsp D.A. baking powder *or*	½ cup shortening
3¼ tsp tartrate *or* phosphate type	¾ cup milk
	1 tsp vanilla
¼ tsp salt	3 egg whites, unbeaten

Line bottoms of two 8-inch layer pans with waxed paper—grease paper. Start oven 10 min before baking; set to moderate (375° F).

Have all ingredients at room temp. Sift flour, measure, resift 3 times with next 3 ingredients, the last time into the large mixer bowl. Add shortening and ½ cup of the milk. Stir with wooden spoon to blend, then clean off and remove spoon. Now beat 2 min with electric beater on *Medium Speed,* or 200 strokes by hand with a wooden spoon, scraping sides and bottom of bowl while beating. Stop beating; add remaining ¼ cup milk, vanilla and egg whites. Again beat 2 more min on mixer or 200 strokes by hand, scraping while beating. Turn batter into prepared pans. Bake 25 to 30 min or until cake tests done. Cool in pans on cake racks 5 min, then turn out onto racks, strip off paper and invert to finish cooling. Spread Lemon Filling, p 398, between layers and over top. When firm, spread top and sides with 7-Minute Icing, p 392. 10 servings.

Note: Review Quick Mix Method, p 348

LOAF CAKES

CHOCOLATE LOAF CAKE

This chocolate loaf is unusual. A thick slice is delicious as is, but capped with ice cream, it's TOPS!

1 cup brown sugar, pkd	⅔ cup butter *or* margarine
½ cup sweet milk	1 cup brown sugar, pkd, put
2 egg yolks	through coarse sieve
3 sqs unsweet chocolate	2 whole eggs
2 cups cake flour	2 tsp vanilla
½ tsp salt	½ cup buttermilk
1 tsp soda	

Line a greased 10 x 5 x 2¾-inch or 9 x 5 x 3-inch pan with heavy waxed paper—grease paper lightly. Start oven 10 min before baking; set to moderately slow (325° F). Put first 3 ingredients into top of double boiler, beat well, then place over simmering water, add chocolate and cook and stir until chocolate melts. Remove from heat; cool to room temp. Sift flour, measure, resift 5 times with salt and soda. Cream soft butter with wooden spoon, add next cup of sugar and cream thoroughly. Scrape off spoon; remove. Add eggs and flavoring and beat with rotary beater until smooth and fluffy, then add chocolate mixture and again beat until smooth. Clean off, remove beater. Now add flour mixture and buttermilk alternately in 3 or 4 portions, beginning and ending with flour and beating hard with wooden spoon until well blended after each. Turn batter into prepared pan, pushing it higher around edge of pan than in center. Bake 20 min, then increase heat to moderate (350° F) and bake 40 to 45 min longer. Cool in pan on cake rack 10 min, then remove with paper attached to rack to finish cooling. Wash and dry pan; return cooled cake to it. Spread top with Basic Butter Frosting, p 383, if desired.

CURRANT LOAF CAKE

A first-class Pound Cake of yesteryear. This cake requires long, hard beating, so a strong arm or an electric mixer is needed

2 cups cake flour	1¼ cups sugar
¾ tsp salt	½ tsp orange extract
¾ cup currants, plumped	½ tsp lemon extract
¾ cup butter *or* margarine	4 eggs, unbeaten

Have all ingredients at room temp. Grease lightly a 9 x 5 x 3-inch loaf pan, and line with waxed paper cut to fit neatly on inside. Do not grease inside of paper. Start oven 10 min before baking; set to moderately slow (325° F). Sift flour, measure, resift with salt. Reserve 1 tbsp of the flour. Wash currants quickly and carefully, put in colander or sieve and place over hot water, cover and steam about 5 min to plump up. Cream soft butter in mixer bowl at *Medium Speed* until smooth and shiny; gradually add sugar, scraping bowl constantly with rubber scraper; beat 2 min or 200 strokes by hand. Add extracts, then eggs, one at a time, beating 1 min after each egg on mixer or 100 strokes by hand. Add flour in 4 or 5 portions, mixing on *Low Speed* by mixer or by hand just enough to blend in well. Toss currants in reserved flour and *fold while hot* into batter until well distributed. Turn batter into prepared pan, pushing it up an inch higher around edge than in center. Bake 15 min, then increase heat to moderate (350° F) and bake 45 min longer or until cake tests done, p 328. Cool in pan on cake rack 5 min, then lift cake with paper attached from pan to rack to finish cooling. Store like Pound Cake, p 355, 15 to 20 servings.

MRS. EDGAR'S BUTTERMILK CAKE

You'll want to bake this cake again and again because you can't forget its fine flavor, texture and color

4⅓ cups all-purpose flour
1¾ cups butter—3¼ sticks
3⅓ cups fine granulated sugar
8 eggs

¼ tsp baking soda
1 tbsp vanilla
½ cup buttermilk

Have all ingredients at room temp. One needs a strong arm or an electric beater when making this cake.

Adjust rack 6 to 7 inches above bottom of oven. Start oven 10 min before baking; set to moderately slow (325° F). Butter well a loaf pan 10 x 5 x 3-inches, then dust with flour, gently tapping against tabletop to remove excess. Sift flour then measure. Measure butter and soda into a 4-qt mixing bowl and cream until smooth and soft. Add vanilla, then sugar gradually, creaming thoroughly. Cream with rotary beater if you do not use an electric beater. Add eggs one at a time, beating well after each. Now clean off beater, remove and use wooden spoon. Then add flour and milk alternately in 2 or 3 portions beginning and ending with flour and beating until thoroughly blended after each portion. Turn batter into prepared pan, pushing well up into corners and around sides so it is almost an inch higher around edge than down the center. This helps cake to bake level. Bake an hr and 15 to 20 min or until cake tests done when a toothpick or cake tester is stuck into center. Start testing 5 min before time is up. Remove to cake rack and immediately turn out onto cake rack carefully to cool right-side up. May be sliced as soon as cold or may be stored wrapped in waxed paper like pound cake. 24 to 30 servings.

Note: This cake may be baked in small loaf pans 6 x 3½ x 2¼-inches, holding 12 oz batter each. These loaves require from 50 to 55 min to bake.

OLD-FASHIONED MARBLE SPICE CAKE

This original marble cake can't be beat for flavor

Dark Part:
- 2¼ cups cake flour
- 1 tsp soda
- ⅜ tsp salt
- 1½ tsp cinnamon
- 1 tsp cloves
- ¾ cup butter *or* shortening
- ¾ cup brown sugar, pkd
- 3 egg yolks, beaten
- 3 tbsp molasses
- ¾ cup buttermilk

Light Part:
- 2 cups cake flour
- 1 tsp D.A. baking powder *or*
- 1¼ tsp tartrate *or* phosphate type
- ¼ tsp soda
- ⅜ tsp salt
- ⅓ cup soft butter
- 1 tsp vanilla
- ¾ cup granulated sugar
- ¾ cup buttermilk
- 3 egg whites

Grease a 3½-inch high 9-inch tube pan; line bottom with heavy waxed paper. Start oven 10 min before baking; set to moderately slow (325° F). Mix cake as follows:

For dark part: Sift flour, measure, resift 3 times with soda, salt and spices.

For light part: Sift flour, measure, resift 3 times with baking powder, soda and salt.

Next: Measure other ingredients for both parts, keeping them separate. Mix dark part first, then quickly mix light part so dark will not stand long.

Dark part: Cream soft butter until smooth and shiny with a wooden spoon, add sieved brown sugar gradually, creaming thoroughly. Clean off and remove spoon. Beat in egg yolks with rotary beater, then molasses until fluffy. Remove beater. Add flour and buttermilk alternately in 4 or 5 portions, beginning and ending with flour and beating well with wooden spoon after each addition.

Light part: Cream butter, add vanilla and sugar and cream thoroughly with wooden spoon. Scrape off spoon, remove. With rotary beater, beat in egg whites until smooth and fluffy. Remove beater and use spoon. Add flour mixture and buttermilk alternately in 4 or 5 portions, beginning and ending with flour and beating well after each portion. For marbled effect, dip alternate spoonfuls of light and dark batter into prepared pan. Bake 1 hr or until cake tests done. Cool in pan on cake rack 10 min, then loosen sides and around tube with thin-bladed knife. Turn out on rack and quickly turn top-side up and cool before cutting. Spread with frosting, if desired, but none is necessary on this delicious cake. 10 servings.

Try pound cake à la mode with chocolate sauce.

POUND CAKE

The authentic old-time kind. You need a strong arm or an electric mixer for making perfect pound cake

1 lb cake flour, *or* 4½ cups
  sifted once
1½ tsp salt
½ tsp mace
1 lb soft butter *or* margarine,
  2 cups

1 lb sugar *or* 2¼ cups
1½ tsp vanilla *or* brandy
  extract
1 lb eggs—9 or 10, *or* 2 cups,
  slightly beaten

Line bottoms and sides of three 8¾ x 4¾ x 2½-inch loaf pans with smooth brown or parchment paper—do not grease. Have all ingredients at room temp—about 75° F. Weigh or measure ingredients, but best to weigh. Start oven 10 min before baking; set to moderately slow (325° F).

Sift flour with salt and mace 2 times. Beat butter or margarine until smooth and shiny (on *Speed 3* if mixer is used). Add sugar gradually and continue to beat until very smooth and fluffy, scraping bowl constantly throughout beating with rubber scraper. Add flavoring, then eggs in 4 or 5 portions, beating thoroughly after each. A curdled appearance may result with addition of eggs, but this can be overcome by thorough mixing. Add about ½ cup flour at a time, using *Speed 1,* and mix well after each addition. Turn batter into prepared pans, quickly pushing it higher around edge of pan than in center. Place in oven on lower rack. Bake 20 min, then increase heat to moderate (350° F) and bake about 40 min longer, or until "crack" on top is slightly browned and shows no moistness. Cool in pans on cake racks 5 min, then remove cakes from pans to racks to finishing cooling. Do not remove paper. When cool, wrap cakes with paper attached snugly in waxed paper. Store in bread box. The cake may be eaten immediately, but flavor improves after 24 hrs. Do not remove attached paper from cake as it is sliced. Re-wrap any unused cake and store in bread box. 35 to 40 servings.

Note: It takes 10 to 12 min to mix this cake on an electric mixer, or 15 to 20 min by hand.

SILVER WHITE LOAF CAKE

2⅔ cups cake flour
2½ tsp D.A. baking powder *or*
  3 tsp tartrate *or* phosphate
  type
½ tsp salt
2⅔ cup soft butter *or* half
  shortening

2 cups sugar
2 tsp brandy extract *or*
  vanilla
⅔ cup egg whites, unbeaten
1 cup milk

Line a greased 10 x 5 x 2¾-inch or a 9 x 5 x 3-inch pan with heavy waxed paper—grease paper lightly. Start oven 10 min before baking; set to moderately slow (325° F).

Sift flour, measure, resift 3 times with baking powder and salt. Cream soft butter with wooden spoon until smooth and shiny, add sugar gradually and cream thoroughly. Stir in flavoring, then with rotary beater, beat in egg whites in 2 portions until satiny and fluffy. Remove beater, use spoon. Add flour mixture alternately with milk in 4 or 5 portions, beginning and ending with flour and beating well after each. Turn into prepared pan. Bake 20 min, then increase heat to moderate (350° F) and bake about 40 min longer, or until cake tests done. Cool in pan on cake rack 10 min, then remove with paper attached to rack to finish cooling. Wash and dry pan; return cooled cake to it. Spread top with Chocolate Butter Frosting, p 384, if desired.

Note: For half this recipe, use an 8¼ x 4½ x 2¾-inch pan. Bake at 325° F 15 min, then at 350° F 25 min longer or until cake tests done.

CUPCAKES

Unadorned warm cupcakes are delicious, but with a thick swirl of Vanilla or Chocolate Butter Frosting, they are topnotch

BANANA-NUT CUPCAKES

Follow recipe for *Banana-Nut Cake*, p 332. Spoon batter into greased muffin pans with 15 or 16 medium cups, filling cups a little more than half full. Bake in moderate oven (375° F) 15 to 18 min, or until cakes test done. Cool in pans on cake racks 5 min, then remove to racks to finish cooling.

CHOCOLATE CUPCAKES

1 cup cake flour	½ cup margarine *or* butter
½ tsp salt	1 tsp vanilla
2 tsp D.A. baking powder *or*	1 cup sugar
2½ tsp tartrate *or* phos-	2 eggs
phate type	½ cup milk
2 sqs unsweet chocolate	

Grease muffin pans with 16 medium cups. Start oven 10 min before baking; set to moderate (375° F). Sift flour, measure, resift 3 times with salt and baking powder. Melt chocolate over hot water, then cool. With wooden spoon, cream soft margarine until smooth and shiny, add vanilla, then sugar gradually, creaming thoroughly. Clean spoon, remove. With rotary beater, beat in eggs, one at a time, until fluffy, then add chocolate and beat thoroughly. *Remove beater, use spoon.* Add flour mixture and milk alternately in 3 or 4 portions, beginning and ending with flour and beating well after each. Spoon batter into prepared pans, filling ½ full. Bake 15 min. Cool in pans on cake rack 5 min, then remove to racks. Spread with Basic Butter Frosting, p 383, flavored with vanilla or a drop of peppermint extract.

CHOCOLATE CHIP CUPCAKES

2½ cups cake flour
2¼ tsp D.A. baking powder *or*
  3 tsp tartrate *or* phosphate
  type
½ tsp salt
½ cup soft butter
 1 cup strained honey

½ cup sugar
 3 eggs, separated
1 tsp vanilla
½ cup milk
1 cup semi-sweet chocolate
  chips

Have ingredients at room temp and manipulate batter as little as possible to prevent chips from sinking to bottom.

Line muffin pans with paper baking cups, or grease the muffin cups well. Start oven 10 min before baking; set to moderate (375° F).

Sift flour, measure, resift 3 times with baking powder and salt. With wooden spoon, cream butter and honey until well blended, then add ¼ cup of the sugar and egg yolks and beat until smooth and fluffy. Stir in vanilla. Add flour and milk alternately in 4 or 5 portions, beginning and ending with flour and beating until smooth after each. Beat egg whites until stiff enough to form soft shiny peaks, then gradually beat in remaining sugar. *Fold* whites lightly but thoroughly into batter. Now *fold* in chocolate chips until *just distributed* to prevent chips from sinking to bottom. Spoon batter into prepared pans, filling cups about ⅔ full. Bake about 20 min or until cakes just spring back when lightly touched. Cool in pans on cake racks 5 min, then remove to racks. Best while a little warm. 24 cupcakes.

GINGERBREAD CUPCAKES

Follow recipe for *Buttermilk Gingerbread,* p 360. Spoon batter into greased muffin pans with medium cups, filling cups about ½ full. Bake in a moderate oven (375° F) 20 to 25 min. Cool in pans on cake racks 5 min, then remove to racks. Best eaten while a little warm.

GOLDEN CUPCAKES

Another good way to use egg yolks

1½ cups cake flour
½ tsp salt
 2 tsp D.A. baking powder *or*
  2½ tsp tartrate *or* phosphate type
⅓ cup shortening

¾ cup sugar
½ tsp vanilla
½ tsp orange extract
 4 egg yolks, well beaten
½ cup milk *or* milk and water
  mixed

Grease muffin pans with 12 medium cups. Start oven 10 min before baking; set to moderate (350° F). Sift flour, measure, resift 3 times with salt and baking powder. Cream shortening, gradually add sugar, then extracts and cream well. Beat egg yolks with rotary beater, add to creamed mixture, beat well. With wooden spoon, stir in dry ingredients in 4 or 5 portions, beating well after additions. Scrape spoon off, then gradually stir in the milk. When all milk is added, beat 1 min with rotary beater or vigorously with spoon. Spoon batter into prepared pan. Bake 15 to 18 min or until done. Cool in pan on cake rack 5 min, then remove to rack. Spread with Basic Butter Icing, p 383, if desired.

Note: Double ingredients for two 9" layers of cake. Bake at same temp.

HONEY SPICE SOUR CREAM CUPCAKES

Rich color, pleasing flavor and fluffy texture

2 cups cake flour	1 cup moist brown sugar, pkd
½ tsp salt	½ cup shortening
1 tsp soda	1 cup honey
¾ tsp cloves, scant	3 eggs
¾ tsp allspice, scant	1 cup thick sour cream
¾ tsp cinnamon	

Grease muffin pans with 28 medium cups, then line bottoms of cups with small circles of waxed paper. Start oven 10 min before baking; set to moderate (350° F).

Sift flour, measure, resift 4 times with salt, soda and spices. Press sugar through coarse sieve to remove lumps. Cream shortening and sugar thoroughly with a wooden spoon, then beat in honey. Clean off spoon, remove. Add eggs, one at a time and beat with rotary beater until smooth and fluffy. Clean off beater, use wooden spoon. Add flour mixture alternately with sour cream in 3 or 4 portions, beginning and ending with flour and beating until smooth after each. Spoon batter into prepared pans, filling cups ½ full. Bake 15 min or until cakes test done. Cool in pans on cake racks 5 min, then remove to racks. Wash and dry pans quickly, then return cakes to pans. Serve warm plain, or spread when barely cool with Basic Butter Frosting, p 383.

ORANGE CUPCAKES

1½ cups cake flour	¾ cup sugar
2 tsp D.A. baking powder *or*	1 egg
2½ tsp tartrate *or* phos-phate type	¼ cup melted butter, cooled
¼ tsp salt	¼ cup coffee cream
	¼ cup fresh orange juice

Grease muffin pans with 16 medium cups. Start oven 10 min before baking; set to moderate (375° F). Sift flour, measure, resift 3 times with next 3 ingredients, the last time into mixing bowl. Beat egg, add butter, cream and orange juice; add to dry ingredients and stir with wooden spoon until just wet, *then beat hard 1 min only.* Spoon batter into prepared pans, filling but ½ full. Bake 15 to 20 min. Cool in pans on cake rack 5 min, then remove. Serve warm or frost with Orange Butter Frosting, p 387.

ORANGE-RAISIN CUPCAKES

A wooden spoon and rotary beater mix these tasty unusual cupcakes

2 cups cake flour	1 cup sugar
½ tsp D.A. baking powder *or*	2 eggs, beaten
¾ tsp tartrate *or* phosphate	1 tsp vanilla
type	½ cup fine-cut plumped
½ tsp salt	raisins, p 165
½ tsp soda	2 tbsp grated orange rind
½ cup shortening	⅔ cup buttermilk

Grease muffin pans with 18 medium cups, p 254. Start oven 10 min before baking; set to moderate (375° F). Sift flour, measure, resift 5 times with next 3 ingredients. With wooden spoon, cream shortening, add sugar gradually and cream thoroughly. Clean off spoon; remove. Add eggs and vanilla and beat with rotary beater until satiny and fluffy. Remove beater. Again use spoon to stir in raisins and rind. Add flour mixture and milk alternately in 3 or 4 portions, beginning and ending with flour and beating until smooth after each portion. Spoon batter into prepared pans, filling cups half full only. Bake 15 min or until done. Cool in pans on cake rack 5 min, then remove to rack to finish cooling. Spread with Basic or Chocolate Butter Frosting, pp 383, 384.

WHITE CUPCAKES

Follow recipe for either *Basic 3- or 4-Egg White Cake,* p 340. Grease muffin pans with medium cups, p 254. Fill cups only half full of batter—no more. Bake in moderate oven (375° F) 15 to 16 min. The *3-Egg Cake* batter makes 20 to 22 cupcakes; the *4-Egg White Cake* batter makes 30 cupcakes.

BUTTERMILK WHITE CUPCAKES

Follow recipe for either *Basic 3- or 4-Egg White Cake with Buttermilk.* Grease medium muffin cups. Fill muffin cups only half full—no more. Bake in moderate oven (375° F) 15 to 16 min. The *3-Egg White*

Cake batter makes 20 to 22 cupcakes; the *4-Egg White Cake* batter makes 30 cupcakes.

YELLOW CUPCAKES

Follow recipe for *Basic 2-Egg Cake,* p 326. Spoon batter into greased muffin pans with 24 medium cups, filling cups only half full. Bake in moderate oven (375° F) 16 min or until cakes test done.

GINGERBREAD

BUTTERMILK GINGERBREAD

1½ cups all-purpose flour *or*	½ tsp allspice
1⅔ cups cake flour	½ cup soft butter
¼ tsp salt	½ cup sugar
½ tsp soda	1 egg
½ tsp cinnamon	½ cup molasses
¾ tsp ginger	½ cup *plus* 2 tbsp buttermilk

Line bottom of an 8 x 8 x 2-inch baking pan with waxed paper—grease paper and sides of pan lightly. Start oven 10 min before baking; set to moderate (350° F).

Sift flour, measure, resift 3 times with salt, soda and spices. With rotary beater, cream butter until smooth, add sugar and egg and beat until smooth and fluffy; add molasses and beat vigorously 2 min longer. Clean off beater and remove. Add flour mixture and buttermilk alternately in 3 or 4 portions, beginning and ending with flour and beating with wooden spoon until smooth after each. Turn batter into prepared pan. Bake 25 to 30 min. Cool in pan on cake rack 5 min, then turn out on rack, strip off paper quickly and invert. Serve warm with whipped cream, apple sauce or melted marshmallows. If glass baking pan is used, bake at 325° F. 6 to 8 servings.

GEORGE WASHINGTON GINGERBREAD

Has genuine old-time flavor that will never go out of date

2¼ cups all-purpose flour	2 eggs
1¼ tsp ginger	¾ cup brown sugar, pkd
1¼ tsp cinnamon	¾ cup molasses
½ tsp each, cloves, nutmeg *and* salt	¾ cup melted shortening
	½ tsp soda
2 tsp D.A. baking powder *or* 2½ tsp tartrate *or* phosphate type	1 cup boiling water

Line bottom of 9 x 9 x 2-inch pan with waxed paper—grease paper and sides of pan. Start oven 10 min before baking; set to moderate (350° F).

Sift flour, measure, resift 3 times with next 6 ingredients. Beat eggs in 3-qt mixing bowl with rotary beater, then beat in sieved sugar, molasses and shortening until mixture is very creamy. Clean off beater, remove and use wooden spoon. Stir in flour mixture in 2 portions until well mixed. Add soda dissolved in boiling water, then beat with rotary beater until smooth. Pour into prepared pan. Bake 35 min or until cake tests done. Cool in pan on cake rack 5 min, then turn out on rack, strip off paper carefully and quickly invert. Serve warm plain, or with whipped cream into which is folded half as much sweetened stiff tart apple sauce. 9 servings.

HONEY GINGER CAKE

Two tone in color, delicate in texture with rich appealing honey flavor

2¼ cups cake flour	½ cup brown sugar, pkd
2 tsp soda—yes, 2	1 egg
1 tsp salt	1 cup honey
1 tsp ginger	1 cup buttermilk
1 tsp cinnamon	½ pt whipping cream
½ cup shortening	Walnuts, broken

Line bottoms of two 9-inch layer pans with waxed paper; grease paper and sides of pans. Start oven 10 min before baking; set to moderate (350° F).

Sift flour, measure, resift 3 times with next 4 ingredients. Cream shortening, add sieved sugar gradually and cream thoroughly. With rotary beater, beat in egg until smooth and fluffy, then honey until blended. Clean off and remove beater. Add flour mixture and milk alternately in 3 or 4 portions, beginning and ending with flour and beating with wooden spoon until blended after each. Turn into prepared pans. Bake about 30 min or until cake tests done. Remove to cake racks to cool in pans 5 min, then carefully turn out on racks, remove paper and quickly turn right side up to finish cooling. Whip cream stiff, sweeten with 1 tsp honey and spread between layers and over top. Sprinkle with walnuts. Store in refrigerator an hour or two before serving. 10 servings.

Remember: This encyclopedia of cooking is more than a book. See the information on Diets, Menus, Buying Hints, can sizes, etc., in the front of this volume. Read the social use of food, table setting and service, picnics and special meals, buffet service at the end of Volume II.

UPSIDE-DOWN CAKES

APRICOT UPSIDE-DOWN CAKE

Turns out beautifully. Distinctive in appearance, and rates "tops" in Upside-Downs

1 cup moist dried apricots, 28 to 30 large halves
½ cup boiling water
⅓ cup butter
½ cup brown sugar, pkd
3 tbsp white corn syrup
1 cup all-purpose flour

1¼ tsp D.A. baking powder *or* 1½ tsp tartrate *or* phosphate type
¼ tsp salt
¼ cup shortening
½ cup sugar
2 eggs
¼ tsp almond extract
Apricot juice and milk

Wash apricots quickly in cold water; put into bowl, add boiling water, cover and let stand 2 or 3 hrs. Drain off juice—there should be ¼ cup, if not, add milk to make ¼ cup.

Have ready an 8 x 8 x 2-inch pan. Start oven 10 min before baking; set to moderate (350° F). Put butter and moist brown sugar in pan over very low heat to blend and cook until mixture just bubbles. Add corn syrup, then remove from heat. Arrange apricot halves cut-side up in sugar-butter mixture. Sift flour, measure, resift 3 times with baking powder and salt. Cream shortening and sugar in a 2- or 3-qt bowl with a rotary beater, beat in eggs one at a time until smooth and fluffy, then the almond extract. Clean off beater, remove and use a wooden spoon. Stir in flour and liquid alternately in 2 or 3 portions, beating until smooth after each. Spoon batter carefully over apricots, then spread out gently. Bake 35 min or until cake tests done. Cool on cake rack 10 min, then invert onto serving plate, letting all juice drip over cake. Serve warm, plain or with whipped cream. 4 to 6 servings.

Note: Halved fresh or drained canned apricots may be used in place of the dried.

GINGERBREAD-PEAR UPSIDE-DOWN CAKE

Blend 2 tbsp melted butter, ¼ cup sugar and 2 tbsp white corn syrup. Spread over bottom of a 9-inch skillet. Arrange 6 small pear halves on mixture. Pour Buttermilk Gingerbread Batter, p 360, over pears. Bake in moderately slow oven (325° F) about 1 hr.

It will pay you to review the Homemaker's Handbook, p 69, occasionally.

PINEAPPLE CRUSH UPSIDE-DOWN CAKE

More economical than the Pineapple Wheel Cake, but it's a glazed beauty and delicious

1½ cups crushed pineapple
1 cup sugar
2½ tbsp cornstarch
3 tbsp butter
2 tbsp white corn syrup
8 drained maraschino cherries, cut in half
1½ cups all-purpose flour

2 tsp D.A. baking powder *or* 2½ tsp tartrate *or* phosphate type
½ tsp salt
⅓ cup shortening
½ tsp vanilla
2 eggs
½ cup milk
Whipping cream, optional

Use a 10-inch heavy skillet with oven-proof handle. Start oven 10 min before baking; set to moderate (350° F).

Turn pineapple into a sieve placed over bowl to drain—save juice. Blend ⅓ cup of the sugar and cornstarch in skillet, stir in pineapple juice, place over heat and stir constantly until sauce boils and is clear. Remove from heat, stir in butter, syrup and drained pineapple, then spread evenly over bottom of skillet; arrange cherry halves, round-side down, in a pattern over pineapple.

Sift flour, measure, resift 3 times with baking powder and salt. Use rotary beater to cream shortening and remaining ⅔ cup sugar, add vanilla, then eggs one at a time, beating vigorously until smooth and fluffy. Clean off and remove beater; use wooden spoon. Stir in flour alternately with milk in 3 or 4 portions, beginning and ending with flour and beating well after each. Spoon batter lightly over pineapple, then spread out gently. Bake 40 to 45 min or until cake tests done, p 328. Cool in pan on cake rack 10 min, then turn out on a serving plate. Serve warm with whipped cream, if desired. 6 to 8 servings.

PINEAPPLE WHEEL UPSIDE-DOWN CAKE

This sponge-type cake turns out perfectly—has glamour, but surely will increase the girth

⅓ cup butter *or* margarine
½ cup brown sugar, pkd
8 slices pineapple, No. 2 can
4 maraschino cherries *or* 8 pecan halves
1 cup all-purpose flour

1 tsp D.A. baking powder *or* 1¼ tsp tartrate *or* phosphate type
¼ tsp salt
2 eggs
⅔ cup sugar
¼ cup pineapple juice *or* milk

Use a 9- or 10-inch heavy skillet with oven-proof handle. Start oven 10 min before baking; set to moderate (350° F).

Put butter and moist brown sugar into skillet and place over low heat to blend and cook until mixture bubbles, then remove from heat and arrange pineapple slices neatly over sugar mixture. Drop half a cherry or nut in center of each pineapple slice. Sift flour, measure, resift 3 times with baking powder and salt. Break eggs into a 3-qt mixing bowl, beat with rotary beater until thick and fluffy, then add sugar in 2 or 3 portions and beat until thick and spongy. Clean off beater, remove. With wooden spoon, fold in flour mixture and liquid alternately in 3 or 4 portions, beginning and ending with flour and *cutting-and-folding-in* until smooth after each. Spoon batter lightly over pineapple, then spread out gently. Bake cake in 9-inch skillet about 25 min and in 10-inch about 22 min or until cake tests done, p 328. Cool in skillet on cake rack 10 min then invert onto serving plate. Best served warm, plain, or with whipped cream. 6 servings.

FRUIT CAKES

FACTS YOU SHOULD KNOW TO MAKE AND SERVE PERFECT FRUIT CAKE

Fine fruit cake is really expensive but is so delicious and has such wide appeal that most homemakers want to know how to make it. Several factors contribute to success. Most important is a recipe calling for well-proportioned ingredients and clear-cut directions. This chapter offers several excellent fruit cake recipes with but one set of complete directions which apply to all. By reading these recipes and the set of directions which follows, one can ascertain the cost of ingredients, equipment needed and time and work required.

This information helps one to plan the number of fruit cakes to make and to decide on their weight and shape. They may be baked in various containers, but it is practical to use pans of the same size and shape for cakes to bake perfectly in the same time. Small cakes that weigh about a lb are appropriate for the average-size family, or for nice little gifts. This small cake serves 8 to 10 without leftovers. Other containers such as loaf pans of different sizes, coffee cans, tube cake pans, ring molds, casseroles, etc. may be used, but the most practical are loaf pans and coffee cans.

The average kitchen usually has necessary mixing equipment and parchment or smooth unglazed brown wrapping paper for lining the pans, however, one needs to take an inventory of these essentials. If some item is lacking, buy it when you shop for ingredients.

THE TIME TO MAKE FRUIT CAKE

Fruit cake for the holidays or special occasions should be baked at least 3 or 4 weeks beforehand. This enables the homemaker to work leisurely and carefully and allows time for cakes to ripen and mellow to their best flavor and texture.

SELECTION OF INGREDIENTS

Choose fresh ingredients—nuts, moist candied fruits, eggs, shortening, etc. Dried-out, hard or rancid nuts produce cake inferior in aroma and flavor. Shelled nuts are usually a better buy than those in the shell, and are less trouble to prepare.

High quality candied fruits are expensive, but they give fruit cake its most luscious flavor. To cut the cost of fruit cakes, some cooks substitute inexpensive raisins and currants for part of the candied fruit. Too many raisins and currants give the cake a bitter or scorched flavor. Assorted ready-cut candied fruits are usually available and cost little more than fruit not cut. But small cans of such fruit are very expensive. The ready-cut fruit saves considerable time in the cake making, but one objection to it is, it is cut into small cubes. When a high proportion of fruit is used, these small cubes do not give the cake a texture easy to cut into thin slices. Fruit cut into narrow, match-like strips weaves through the cake and holds it together so that it cuts into thin slices which hold together.

SELECTION OF EQUIPMENT

The best kind of pans to buy are loaf pans in various sizes which are usually obtainable in department or hardware stores. Three ideal sizes are: The 5¾ x 3⅛ x 2¼-inch, tiny loaf pans hold 1 pt and take from 1 to 1¼ lb batter. The No. 6 pan, 8 x 4 x 2⅜-inch holds 2 pts and takes about 2¼ lb batter. The No. 11 pan, 8½ x 4½ x 2¾-inch holds 3 pts and takes 3 to 3¼ lb batter. A large jelly roll pan, preferably tin, and with a rim all around is also essential.

Parchment or smooth brown unglazed wrapping paper is best for lining pans. Paper insulates the pans and protects the cake batter from scorching. Fruit cake contains a high percentage of sugar and scorches easily. Line pans with one layer of heavy parchment or smooth brown paper or 2 layers of white typewriter paper. Fit paper closely into inside of greased pans to preserve pan-shape of cake. Grease paper lightly.

GETTING READY TO MAKE CAKE—PREPARING FRUIT AND NUTS

Weigh or measure fruits and nuts specified in recipe. Prepare fruits first. A thin-bladed sharp knife and a cutting board are needed to cut fruit into thin, match-like strips. Cut citron hollow-side down into thin slices about 1/16-inch thick. Pile 8 to 10 slices on top of each other and cut into thin, narrow strips, a trick that speeds up the work. Put one lemon or orange peel inside another, hollow-side down, and cut into thin crosswise slices;

then cut slices into short lengths. Cut candied pineapple slices crosswise into 3 slices, then pile slices on top of each other and cut down into thin strips. Cut candied cherries in halves or quarters. Break walnuts or pecans into 4 or 5 pieces. Blanch almonds, p 121, and while soft, cut into thin broadside slices. Combine fruits, nuts, syrup, brandy, juice from pickled peaches, lemon or orange juice specified in recipe. Mix thoroughly with hands or wooden spoon until fruit and nuts are well-coated with liquids. Cover tightly and let stand overnight, but mix 2 or 3 times while standing as liquid settles in bottom and lower layer of ingredients becomes more saturated. A 2½ to 3-gallon enamelware or stainless steel dishpan or bowl of similar size is ideal to mix a big batch of fruit cake.

CUTTING PAPERS AND LINING PANS

Make pattern for inside liners of pans as follows: Measure a sheet of paper as long as bottom and ends of pan, plus one inch, and as wide as the bottom and the two sides, plus one inch. Now hold pan upside down, lay paper over bottom and down over sides, then press paper down over ends, and with scissors cut closely against corners of pan. This pattern fits neatly inside the pan and extends ½-inch above edge. Trace this pattern on a sheet of thin cardboard, and cut out a cardboard pattern. Lay cardboard pattern over 5 or 6 sheets of paper and trace around it. Pin sheets together, cut around tracing. Repeat, using paper economically to obtain liners required. Next, grease pans lightly but evenly and fit liners into pans. If paper is thin, grease inside liner and fit a second liner into pan. The half-inch of paper extending above edge of pans all around protects cakes from browning too fast on top and aids in removing cakes from pans.

MIXING CAKE

Have ingredients at room temp. Measure dry ingredients. Combine flour and spices with any leavening and sift 3 times to mix thoroughly. Measure butter or shortening into a large bowl or large electric mixer bowl; cream until smooth and shiny. Add sugar and cream thoroughly. (To be sure lumps are out of moist brown sugar, put through a coarse sieve.) Then add whole eggs and beat until smooth and fluffy. If molasses or jelly is used, stir in after the sugar. Add flour in 4 or 5 portions (alternately with milk if used) and mix well between additions. Turn this batter over fruit mixture, scraping out with rubber scraper. Mix with hands by lifting fruit mixture up into batter until fruit is well coated. Weigh batter at once into pans; push up well into corners for good shape, then smooth and level tops with spatula or knife. Rap pan on table top 2 or 3 times to pack batter down evenly. Fill pans with batter to within ⅛ to ¼-inch of top. Pat a thin film of milk over tops. This produces an attractive shine to top crust and reduces browning to a minimum.

BAKING CAKES

Place cakes of same size and shape on large tin jelly roll pan. Keep cakes at least ½-inch apart for heat circulation. Pour hot water into pan to a depth of ¼-inch. As water evaporates, replace with boiling water. Place cookie sheet with cakes on lower rack of slow oven (250° F) and bake until done, p 328. Small pans holding 1¼ lb batter require about 2½ hrs. Coffee cans holding 1⅔ to 1¾ lb batter bake in about 3 hrs. The No. 6 pans require about 3 hrs, the No. 11 pans about 3½ hrs. Only enough cakes to fill 1 rack should be baked at one time. Only 8 pans holding 1¼ lb batter will go on a 17¼ x 11½ x ½-inch jelly roll pan ½-inch apart. This pan fits into a 16 x 18-inch oven. Therefore, make up at one time *no more* than 12 to 14 lbs of batter. Six coffee cans stand on this pan and take about 12 lbs of batter. No. 6 and No. 11 pans should *stand directly on oven rack*. Rack takes 6 No. 6 pans, holding about 12½ lbs batter or 6 No. 11 pans, holding about 14 lbs batter. When pans are placed directly on oven rack, put jelly roll pan on floor of oven and fill with water for steam to keep cakes moist.

When cakes are done, remove to racks to cool thoroughly in pans, then lift cakes out with paper attached onto racks. At this point, glaze and decorate.

HOW TO GLAZE FRUIT CAKES

Use Apricot Glaze or Corn Syrup Glaze, p 368. Brush cooled cakes with hot glaze. Decorate, then brush again with hot glaze. Dry before wrapping or storing. Apricot Glaze adds pleasing flavor.

HOW TO DECORATE FRUIT CAKES

Perfect whole blanched almonds or pistachios, pecan halves, candied fruits and moist candied citron are the most commonly used decorative materials. Candied cherries may be left whole, cut in halves or in petal-shaped pieces to make designs that resemble poinsettias, daisies or other flowers. The cherries may be coarsely chopped then groups of these pieces used for "holly berries." Candied pineapple is also used to make flower petals or leaves. Moist candied citron may be sliced thin, then cut into shapes of berries and leaves to form wreaths of holly and mistletoe. Tiny metal cutters obtainable in the better department stores are ideal for doing this work. Use these cut-outs in their natural color or tint by letting them stand in the following syrup: Boil 1 cup sugar, ½ cup water and 1 tbsp white corn syrup 3 min, add food coloring to produce the required tint. Remove from heat and add cut-outs. Let stand until of desired shade, then lift out with fork onto waxed paper to drain. Move 2 or 3 times to clean paper. Plan a design for decorating the cake, then draw it on paper. The most attractive motifs usually have the largest design in the center. For example, use whole almonds to make petals of a flower, then heap chopped citron in the center to simulate pollen. From this central flower may radiate a festoon or wreath of leaves. When design is decided upon, brush a thin film of hot glaze over cake, let dry slightly, then place fruits and nuts on cake according to design. Now pat more hot glaze lightly over nuts and fruits with a brush, being careful not to disturb design. Let stand uncovered until glaze is thoroughly dry. Wrap and store until needed for gifts or serving.

WRAPPING AND STORING FRUIT CAKE

Trim off edges of lining paper and wrap cakes in moisture-proof cellophane, sealing airtight with Scotch tape. Or wrap snugly in aluminum foil. Store in a box with a cover—a cardboard suit box is ideal because cakes should not be stacked on top of each other. Ripen in a cool place, but not cold enough to freeze.

SERVING FRUIT CAKE

Two or 3 days before serving, refrigerate cakes or store them in a place about 40° F. When chilled, cakes made by our recipes do not crumble but cut into thin *whole* slices. Most people enjoy eating fruit cake plain, sliced thin, others like it with a puff of whipped cream or Custard Sauce. Wrap leftover cake snugly in waxed paper, then in aluminum foil and store in refrigerator. When fruit cake dries out, steam it until moist, but not wet. Such cake, however, is never as good as cake which retains original moisture.

APRICOT GLAZE FOR FRUIT CAKE

¼ lb dried apricots   1 cup white corn syrup
1½ cups cold water

Wash apricots, add water and soak several hrs or overnight. Cook in the same water until tender, about 15 min. Drain off juice through a sieve or food mill, and rub only half the apricots through the sieve. Use unsieved fruit as sauce. Measure juice and puréed fruit—there should be ½ cup. Add corn syrup, boil rapidly 2 or 3 min or until mixture is clear. Remove from heat. Apply immediately to fruit cake with a pastry brush. If desired, apply decorations after first coat of glaze, then add a second coat over decorations after first coat is set. Reheat glaze to boiling each time it is used. Allow glaze to dry thoroughly before wrapping or storing cakes. Enough to double-coat 12 to 15 lb fruit cake.

CORN SYRUP GLAZE FOR FRUIT CAKE

Boil equal amounts of water and white corn syrup vigorously 1 min, starting to count time when boiling actually begins. Flavor with lemon extract or brandy. Use like Apricot Glaze.

BANANA FRUIT CAKE

½ lb pitted dates, cut in 4ths
2 cups candied cherries, 1 lb
2 cups broken pecans, 1 lb
1 lb candied pineapple, diced
1 cup golden raisins
1 lb chopped mixed fruit,
  citron, figs, etc.
3 cups cake flour
¾ tsp soda

½ tsp salt
1 tsp nutmeg
¾ cup soft butter, 1½ sticks
2 cups sugar
1 tsp vanilla
4 eggs
4 large full-ripe bananas
½ cup buttermilk

Prepare cake pans, p 366. Prepare fruit and nuts, leaving cherries and raisins whole. Put into a 5- to 6-qt mixing bowl or dish pan. Sift flour, measure, add soda, salt and nutmeg and resift 3 or 4 times. Cream butter, add sugar and vanilla gradually creaming well. Then add eggs one at a time and cream until smooth and fluffy. Now add flour mixture in 3 or 4 portions, beat until smooth after each. Peel bananas, crush fine and beat into batter. Now turn batter over fruit and with wooden spoon lift fruit up through batter until well blended. Now add buttermilk and continue mixing in by lifting cake mixture up through milk until well blended. Put batter neatly into pans. Smooth top. Place pans on shallow jelly roll pan. Pour water around pans, see p 367. Bake in a 300° F oven for 2 hrs. About 7½ lbs cake.

BLUE RIBBON FRUIT CAKE

Cake slices perfectly and tastes perfectly wonderful

*1 cup medium syrup
½ lb candied citron
½ lb candied pineapple
½ lb candied cherries
2 15-oz pkg golden raisins
2 lbs whole dates, pitted
1 medium orange, juice and
  grated rind
1 medium lemon, juice and
  grated rind

1 pt syrup or juice from
  pickled peaches or watermelon or from canned
  peaches
2 lbs pecan meats
4 cups sifted all-purpose flour
1 tsp soda
1½ tsp salt
¾ lb butter or margarine
2¼ cups granulated sugar
6 eggs, beaten
1 cup buttermilk

* To make syrup, heat ½ cup sugar and 1 cup water to boiling, then simmer 5 min. Add 1 tbsp white corn syrup and cool. Follow directions found in *Facts You Should Know to Make and Serve Perfect Fruit Cake,* p 364. 12 lb.

GROOM'S CAKE

Often used as top tier on Bride's Cake—also good fruit cake for any occasion

1½ lbs currants, 4½ cups	½ tsp nutmeg
*½ cup Medium Syrup	1¼ tsp salt
4 cups all-purpose flour	¾ cup shortening
2½ tsp D.A. baking powder *or*	1½ cups sugar
3 tsp tartrate *or* phosphate	5 eggs
type	½ cup apricot *or* peach
½ tsp soda	juice
½ tsp cinnamon	1 cup coffee cream

Line two 9½ x 5½ x 2¾-inch loaf pans with smooth brown paper; grease paper well. Start oven 10 min before baking; set to moderately slow (325° F).

Wash and drain currants, then stir in syrup and let stand 1 day to plump, stirring occasionally. Sift flour, measure, resift 3 times with next 5 ingredients. Toss currants in 1 cup of the flour mixture. Use rotary beater to cream shortening, add sugar gradually, creaming thoroughly. Beat in eggs one at a time until light-colored and fluffy. Clean off beater, remove; use wooden spoon. Add flour mixture alternately with combined juice and cream in 3 or 4 portions, beginning and ending with flour and beating well after each addition. Stir in currants until evenly distributed. Turn into prepared pans. If cake is to be eaten immediately, place a jelly roll pan of hot water in bottom of oven; if it is to be stored, bake without water. Bake 80 to 90 min. Cool in pans on cake racks 15 min, then remove from pans with paper snugly attached and cool thoroughly. Let cake stand 24 hrs before decorating. Glaze and decorate like Fruit Cake, p 367. 40 to 50 servings.

HOLIDAY LIGHT FRUIT CAKE

A 23 lb reception cake for your most discriminating guests

*1 cup medium syrup	1 pt peach pickle juice
2 lb golden raisins	2 lb pecan meats, broken
2 lb candied cherries, red	1 lb almonds, blanched,
1 lb candied cherries, green	sliced
½ lb candied orange peel	2 lb soft butter
½ lb candied lemon peel	8 cups sifted all-purpose flour
2 lb candied citron	1 tbsp salt
1 lb candied pineapple	2 lb eggs, 16
1 lb moist white figs	4½ cups sugar
2 oz moist candied ginger	4 tbsp vanilla

*To make syrup, heat ½ cup sugar and 1 cup water to boiling, then simmer 5 min. Add 1 tbsp while corn syrup and cool. Follow directions found p 364.

NO-BAKE FRUIT CAKE

Excellent to make when you forget to bake fruit cake in time

½ cup seedless raisins   ½ cup blanched almonds
½ cup golden raisins   ½ cup soft butter
½ cup candied cherries   ½ cup honey
½ cup pitted dates   ½ tsp cinnamon
½ cup moist light figs   ¼ tsp mace
½ cup candied pineapple   1 tsp salt
½ cup candied orange peel 1 tsp vanilla
½ cup candied lemon peel 2 tsp lemon juice
½ cup candied citron   ½ lb Graham crackers, 20

Wash raisins, drain well. Cut raisins and cherries in half, the dates in quarters and rest of fruit into thin match-like strips, p 365. Slice almonds thinly. Cream butter, stir in honey, spices, salt and flavorings. Pour over the cut fruit and nuts, mix and let stand two hrs. Work in the rolled cracker crumbs thoroughly with a wooden spoon. Pack firmly into a 7½ x 3½ x 2¼-inch loaf pan, neatly lined with waxed paper, as described in directions *Facts You Should Know to Make and Serve Perfect Fruit Cake.* Cover with waxed paper and store in a cool place. If possible, store in refrigerator, but a very cool cellar that keeps butter fresh is also suitable. May be served within a few days or will keep several months if properly stored. Slice and serve cake while it is cold. 3 lb.

OLD-FASHIONED DARK FRUIT CAKE

Fine flavored, rich dark cake

*2 cups medium syrup   1½ tsp salt
15-oz pkg seedless raisins   2 tsp cinnamon
2 15-oz pkgs golden raisins ½ tsp cloves
2½ lb whole dates, pitted   ½ to 1 tsp allspice
2 lb candied citron   ½ tsp nutmeg
1 lb candied pineapple   ½ tsp mace
¼ lb candied orange peel ½ lb butter *or* margarine
¼ lb candied lemon peel   ½ lb brown sugar, 1 cup *plus*
½ lb candied red cherries   2 tbsp, pkd
½ lb almonds, blanched   4 eggs
1½ lb all-purpose flour,   1 cup currant jelly
    6 cups sifted   1 cup light molasses
2 tsp soda   1½ cups buttermilk

*To make syrup, heat 1 cup sugar and 2 cups water to boiling, then simmer 5 min. Add 2 tbsp white corn syrup and cool. Follow directions found in *Facts You Should Know to Make and Serve Perfect Fruit Cake,* p 364. 14 lb.

Note: These are big cake recipes. Make ½ or ¼ to suit your needs.

REFRIGERATOR OR ICE BOX CAKE

Refrigerator Cakes are ideal party desserts because they are usually made the day before they are served. A time-saver on party day is an energy saver. These desserts are easily made glamorous with plain whipped cream or cream tinted with a drop of food color, and by adding fruit or nuts. A spring form pan is generally recommended, but a glass loaf pan, casserole or tube cake pan serves equally well, and when cakes are molded in these shapes and the party touch is added, they are just as elaborate.

STUFFED ANGEL FOOD—CHOCOLATE

Expensive but worth the compliments

Angel Food Cake—10 inches   1 cup milk
   in diam and 4 inches high   2 tbsp plain gelatin
4 sqs unsweet chocolate   ½ cup cold water
1 cup xxxx sugar, pkd   2½ cups whipping cream
¼ tsp salt

Use Angel Food Cake at least 1 day old. Cut into 3 equal crosswise slices. Put chocolate into top of double boiler and place over boiling water to melt. When melted, stir in sugar and salt until blended. Then stir in milk slowly and continue to cook and stir until mixture is perfectly smooth. Meanwhile soften gelatin in cold water for 5 min. Remove mixture from heat and stir in gelatin thoroughly. Stand in pan of cold water until the consistency of unbeaten egg whites. Beat the cream until stiff but still smooth. Fold cream lightly but thoroughly into the chocolate mixture. As soon as mixture shows sign of beginning to stiffen, spread thickly about ¾-inch thick between layers of cake and over top and sides, watching to keep the slices standing up straight in their original way. Refrigerate until serving time. 12 servings.

BANANA-VANILLA WAFER PUDDING

An attractive, satisfying old-timer

1 cup sugar   4 tbsp butter
6 tbsp all-purpose flour   1 tsp vanilla
¾ tsp salt   5 oz pkg vanilla wafers
4 cups milk   4 large ripe bananas
4 eggs   Whipping cream, opt

Blend sugar, flour and salt in top of double boiler, stir in milk and cook over hot water until thick, about 10 min, stirring frequently. Beat eggs, then stir in about ½ cup of the hot mixture and return to double boiler, stir and cook 4 to 5 min. Remove from heat. Add butter and vanilla and beat smooth with rotary beater. Lightly butter an 8-cup round glass casserole. Arrange wafers in bottom, then spoon ½-inch thick layer of custard over wafers. Slice 2 bananas over custard and spoon a thin layer of custard over bananas. Lay on wafers, then slice the 2 remaining bananas over them. Spread remaining custard over top, completely covering bananas. Crush remaining wafers fine and sprinkle over custard. Cover and chill 6 to 8 hrs. Serve with whipped cream, if desired. 8 servings.

CHEESE REFRIGERATOR CAKE No. 1

Crust:
- 5-oz pkg zwieback
- ¼ cup sugar
- 1 tsp cinnamon
- ¼ cup melted butter

Filling:
- 1 tsp lemon rind, pkd
- 3 tbsp lemon juice
- 12 oz creamed cottage cheese
- 3 eggs, separated
- ¾ cup sugar blended with
- 1 tbsp corn starch

Crust: Butter an 8-inch spring form pan. Start oven 10 min before baking; set to moderately hot (400° F). Roll zwieback into fine crumbs, then measure into mixing bowl with sugar and cinnamon and stir well. Add butter and mix *well* with fingers, then pat firmly in a thin layer over bottom and up sides of prepared pan. Bake 10 min. Remove to cake rack to cool while mixing filling.

Filling: Grate lemon rind and squeeze juice. Press cheese through a medium sieve into top of double boiler. Stir in well-beaten egg yolks and sugar-corn starch mixture. Cook over boiling water with frequent stirring until thickened, about 15 min. Remove from heat and cool slightly, then stir in lemon rind and juice. With rotary beater, beat egg whites until stiff, then fold them gently but thoroughly into cheese mixture. Turn into prepared crust. Cover loosely with waxed paper, chill at least 2 hrs before serving. 6 to 8 servings.

CHEESE REFRIGERATOR CAKE No. 2

- Bread Crumb Pastry Shell, p 930
- 4 tsp plain gelatin
- ¼ cup cold water
- 2 eggs, separated
- ¼ tsp salt
- ½ cup milk

- ½ cup sugar
- 12 oz creamed cottage cheese
- 1 tsp grated lemon rind, pkd
- 3 tbsp lemon juice
- ½ teaspoon vanilla
- 1 cup coffee cream
- Strawberries, optional

Line an 8-inch spring form pan with the bread crumb pastry. Set in refrigerator. Sprinkle gelatin over cold water to soften 5 min. Beat egg yolks in top of double boiler; stir in salt, milk and sugar and cook and stir over hot water until mixture is slightly thickened. Remove from heat, add gelatin and stir until dissolved; cool. Rub cottage cheese through a sieve; add egg mixture, lemon rind, juice, vanilla, and cream and mix well. Fold in stiffly beaten egg whites. Turn into pan. Chill until firm. Remove sides of pan and serve with fresh strawberries for garnish, if desired. 8 to 12 servings.

CHOCOLATE REFRIGERATOR CAKE

4 to 6 oz sponge cake
2 tsp plain gelatin
¼ cup cold water
6½ oz pkg semi-sweet chocolate bits

½ cup milk
1 tsp vanilla
3 eggs, separated
½ pt whipping cream

Cut sponge cake into ¼-inch slices, then cut into lengths the height of loaf pan. Reserve a few even slices for top. Have ready a 5 x 9 x 3-inch loaf pan and arrange "cake lengths" closely together around sides and bottom. Soften gelatin in cold water. Heat chocolate and milk in top of double boiler over boiling water; stir to a smooth paste. Stir in gelatin until dissolved. Remove from heat. Beat egg yolks well; stir into chocolate, add vanilla and beat until smooth. Beat egg whites until just stiff, then fold into chocolate mixture. Cool. Beat half the cream until stiff and fold into chocolate mixture. Now pour half the mixture into prepared pan. Add a layer of the left-over uneven cake slices, then pour in rest of chocolate. Top with reserved slices. Chill in refrigerator a few hrs or overnight. To serve, unmold and garnish with remaining cream whipped stiff. 6 to 8 servings.

FRUIT REFRIGERATOR CAKE

1 cup walnuts
1 cup candied cherries
⅓ cup candied orange peel
⅓ cup candied lemon peel
¾ cup candied citron
1½ cups seedless raisins,
washed and cut in half
1½ cups unsweetened Prune
Purée, p 553

1 cup unsweetened Apricot
Purée, p 551
1 cup sugar
1 cup orange juice
1 tsp each, cinnamon,
allspice, nutmeg
1 tsp brandy flavoring
4 tbsp plain gelatin
½ cup cold water
1½ pts whipping cream

Chop nuts and candied fruit fine. Cut cherries in 4ths. Use a 10-inch tube pan and sprinkle half the nuts over bottom. Combine fine-cut fruits and purées with next 6 ingredients, cover and let stand 1½ hrs. Soften gelatin in cold water 5 min. Then heat fruit mixture to boiling, stirring constantly. Remove from heat and stir in gelatin until dissolved, then cool thoroughly. Whip cream until thick but not stiff, then gently *fold cold fruit mixture into it.* Pour into prepared pan over the nuts, then sprinkle remaining nuts over top. Cover and store in refrigerator overnight. Remove from pan as described on p 1155. Slice and serve. 20 servings.

LEMON ICE BOX CAKE

A year-round glamour dessert—rich and refreshing

12 oz loaf sponge cake, bought *or* homemade	2 cups xxxx sugar, sifted and pkd
½ cup butter *or* margarine	¼ cup milk, scalded
1 tsp grated lemon rind, pkd	½ pt whipping cream
¼ cup lemon juice	1 tbsp pistachio nuts, sliced

Line bottom and sides of an 8¾ x 4½ x 2½-inch glass loaf pan with waxed paper, extending paper ½-inch over sides by which to lift cake out easily. Cut cake into 12 uniform ⅓-inch thick slices. Cream soft butter with lemon rind until smooth, then stir in lemon juice and sugar alternately. Add hot milk gradually, beating until fluffy. Arrange 3 cake slices flat on bottom of pan in an even layer. Spread ⅓ of filling evenly over cake. Repeat with cake and filling until all are used, finishing with cake. Cover snugly with waxed paper, and fasten with rubber band to hold in place. Chill 5 or 6 hrs. To serve, lift cake to serving plate. Pull paper from sides and cut it off. Leave plain, or spread top and side with stiffly whipped cream, swirling it; or spread cream smoothly and crisscross it with tines of fork. Sprinkle with pistachio nuts. 8 servings.

TORTES

BLITZ TORTE

An attractive German-type cake with a crunchy meringue top. Easier to make . . . and to eat . . . than you think

½ cup almonds, blanched	⅓ cup soft butter
1 cup cake flour	1¼ cups sugar
2 tsp D.A. baking powder *or* 2½ tsp tartrate *or* phosphate type	1 tsp vanilla
	4 egg yolks
	5 egg whites
¼ tsp salt	¼ cup milk

Grease two 9-inch layer cake pans, line bottoms with waxed paper —grease paper. Start oven 10 min before baking; set to moderate (350° F).

Blanch almonds, p 121. While moist and soft, slice thinly lengthwise; cover with damp paper until ready to use. Sift flour, measure, resift 3 times with baking powder and salt. Cream butter until shiny, gradually add ½ cup of the sugar, creaming well with wooden spoon. Stir in vanilla. Scrape off spoon; remove. Beat in egg yolks one at a time with a rotary beater until fluffy. Clean off and remove beater. Add flour mixture and milk alternately in 3 or 4 portions, beginning and ending with flour and beating with wooden spoon until smooth after each. Spread batter in prepared pans. Bake 10 min. Meanwhile, beat egg whites to a stiff foam, add remaining ¾ cup sugar gradually and continue to beat until stiff. Remove the partially baked cake to top of stove. (Keep oven door closed.) Quickly swirl meringue over cakes to within ¼-inch of edge; sprinkle with almonds and return immediately to oven to bake 15 min longer, or until cake tests done. Cool in pans on cake racks 10 min. Very carefully loosen cakes around edge with a thin-blade knife, then lift out gently with a wide spatula to racks to finish cooling right side up. When cool, remove paper from bottom. Place one layer, meringue-side down on cake plate. Spread with Lemon or Sour Cream Filling, p 398, or below. Top with remaining layer, meringue-side up. Cut with a very sharp knife, wiping and dipping it quickly in water before cutting each slice. 10 servings.

SOUR CREAM FILLING FOR BLITZ TORTE

2 tbsp sugar	1 cup thick sour cream
1 tbsp corn starch	1 egg yolk
Dash of salt	½ tsp grated lemon rind, pkd

Blend sugar, corn starch and salt in top of double boiler; add cream and egg yolk and beat with rotary beater until smooth. Remove beater. Place over boiling water, cook and stir until mixture is smooth and thickened. Remove from heat and stir in rind. Cool over cold water, stirring frequently. Spread between layers of torte. Enough for two layers.

DOBOS TORTE

The "queen" of all tortes—7 thin layers of Special Sponge Cake with smooth-as-satin Filling between layers, over top and sides. Ritzy, high-powered and delicious

½ cup *plus* 2 tbsp cake flour	¾ lb xxxx sugar, 1⅝ cups,
⅛ tsp salt	sifted and pkd
7 egg yolks	1½ tsp lemon juice
	5 large egg whites, ⅔ cup

Grease well three 8-inch layer cake pans, or as many as will fit easily on 1 rack of your oven, then sprinkle pans with flour and shake out excess to obtain a thin coat over greased surface. Start oven 10 min before baking; set to hot (450° F).

Sift flour, measure, resift with salt. Sift the xxxx sugar to remove lumps. Beat yolks until lemon-colored, then add sugar and beat 5 min at *Medium Speed* on electric mixer or 10 min by hand with rotary beater. Add flour gradually and continue to beat on mixer 4 min or 8 min by hand. Fold in the lemon juice. With clean rotary beater, beat egg whites until they form soft pointed shiny peaks, then cut-and-fold yolks into the whites until well blended, from 25 to 30 cutting-and-folding-over strokes. Gently spread enough batter over bottom of pans to barely cover. Bake 4 to 5 min only, or until delicately browned. Cool in pans on cake racks 5 min, then loosen carefully around edges. Now hold pan up on edge, start loosening cake carefully from one side and gradually ease it away from pan, placing right-side up on rack. Repeat process until all cake batter is baked. When cakes are cool, spread Chocolate Torte Filling between layers and over top and sides. Place in refrigerator until firm, then cover with a hood made of waxed paper, by placing a band of folded waxed paper around the cake and pinning, then laying a piece across the top. Store in refrigerator until serving time. This cake is best after standing at least 24 hrs. 12 to 15 servings.

CHOCOLATE TORTE FILLING

When made right, this Filling is as smooth as whipped butter. It is as elegant on other cakes as on Dobos Torte

½ lb sweet or semi-sweet chocolate
¼ cup whipping cream
3 eggs, well beaten

1½ cups xxxx sugar, pkd
½ lb sweet butter (unsalted)
½ tsp vanilla

Put chocolate and cream into top of double boiler; place over gently boiling water and stir until chocolate melts and blends with cream. Then remove from heat and stir in eggs, then the sugar. Return to heat and cook with constant stirring until mixture is thick and smooth. Remove from heat and cool in a pan of cold water, stirring frequently. When cool, add butter bit by bit in pieces size of regular pats, beating hard with rotary beater or electric mixer until smooth and fluffy, then beat in vanilla. Spread immediately. Store in refrigerator. Enough for 7 torte layers.

GRAHAM CRACKER TORTE

Looks and tastes like rich pie—but it's Torte!

¾ cup fine-cut dates
¼ cup broken nuts
12 graham crackers
¼ cup melted butter
3 egg yolks
⅓ cup sugar

2½ tbsp all-purpose flour
¼ tsp salt
2 cups milk
½ tsp lemon extract
3 egg whites
6 tbsp sugar

Cut dates with scissors and break nuts medium fine. Roll crackers to fine crumbs—there should be 1 cup. Blend crumbs with butter thoroughly and turn into 9-inch glass pie plate; press firmly over bottom and sides to uniform thickness. Start oven 10 min before baking; set to slow (300° F). Beat egg yolks, then beat in sugar, which has been blended with the flour and salt, add milk and mix thoroughly. Turn into top of double boiler and place over boiling water. Cook and stir until smooth and thickened. Stir in extract. Pour hot custard into crumb-lined pan, then sprinkle with dates and nuts. Beat egg whites with rotary beater to a stiff foam, then add 6 tbsp sugar in 3 portions, beating until shiny and stiff after each. Spread meringue over torte, swirling top. Bake 20 to 25 min or until beautifully browned. Cool on cake rack to lukewarm before serving. Serves 6 to 8.

SCHAUM TORTE

1 cup sugar	1 tsp vanilla
4 egg whites, room temp	1 cup whipping cream
1 tsp vinegar	1 qt strawberries

Draw 2 circles size of 8-inch layer pan on white or smooth brown wrapping paper and place on baking sheet. Start oven 10 min before baking; set to slow (275° F). Sift sugar and measure. With rotary beater, beat whites slowly at first, then increase speed and beat until stiff. Add sugar in 5 portions, beating well after each. Then beat in vinegar and vanilla. Spoon meringue onto paper circles, keeping it ¼-inch inside of edge. Spread to uniform thickness, making swirls over top. Bake 60 min. Remove from oven. Carefully slide a thin-bladed sharp knife under meringue to separate from paper. When cool, place 1 layer on serving plate, spread with whipped cream, then with sweetened sliced berries. Top with 2nd torte layer and swirl remaining cream over top. Garnish with remaining berries. Serve at once. 8 servings.

Note: For individual tortes, bake in greased muffin pans with 6 cups (3¼″ diam) at same temp and time.

CHEESE CAKES

COTTAGE CHEESE CAKE

Crust:

5 to 6-oz pkg zwieback	½ tsp cinnamon
¼ cup sugar	½ cup melted butter

Grease an 8-inch spring form pan with soft butter. Start oven 10 min before baking; set to slow (300° F). Roll zwieback into fine crumbs

—there should be 2 cups. Mix crumbs with remaining ingredients thoroughly, and with fingers pat uniformly thick over bottom and up sides of prepared pan to form a thin crust. Chill while mixing filling.

Filling:
3 eggs, separated
1 cup sugar
¼ cup all-purpose flour

1½ lb dry cottage cheese
1 tsp vanilla
1½ tsp grated lemon rind, pkd
½ pt whipping cream

Beat egg yolks until thick and lemon-colored. Blend sugar and flour together, add to beaten yolks and mix well. Rub cheese through a sieve into yolk mixture, then beat well. Stir in vanilla and lemon rind. Whip cream until stiff and lightly fold into cheese mixture, then fold in stiffly beaten egg whites. Turn mixture into crumb-lined pan. Bake 1¼ hrs. Remove to cake rack to cool. Remove sides of pan just before serving. 8 servings.

CREAM CHEESE CAKE

Smooth-as-Satin

Crust:
5 to 6-oz pkg zwieback
2 tbsp sugar
⅓ cup melted butter
Filling:
15 oz cream cheese, room temp

½ pt cream, 1 cup
½ tsp salt
1 tsp vanilla
1 cup sugar
4 eggs, separated

Grease a 9-inch spring form pan with soft butter. Start oven 10 min before baking; set to slow (300° F). Roll zwieback into fine crumbs, then mix well with the 2 tbsp sugar and melted butter. Pat all but ½ cup of this mixture uniformly over bottom and up sides of prepared pan for a thin crust. Cream the cheese until smooth, then add cream gradually, beating with rotary beater until smooth and fluffy. Add salt, vanilla and 1 cup sugar and continue beating until thoroughly mixed. Now wash beater and beat whites until stiff enough to form shiny pointed peaks that curve at tips. Then beat yolks until thick and light in color, then beat them into cheese mixture well. *Fold in beaten whites lightly* but thoroughly. Flow mixture into crumb-lined pan, then sprinkle lightly with the ½ cup crumbs. Bake 1 hr. Turn off heat and leave in oven 1 hr longer. Remove from oven to cake rack to cool. To loosen sides, use spatula to make straight down-and-up strokes against side of pan, then release sides of spring form. Now slide cake on bottom of spring form onto serving plate. 10 to 12 servings.

SOUR CREAM CHEESE CAKE

Quick-baked, two-tone, high-toned cheese cake

12 Graham crackers	⅛ tsp cinnamon
¼ cup melted butter	12 oz creamed cottage cheese
3 eggs	1 pt sour cream
⅓ cup sugar	6 drops almond extract
⅛ tsp maple extract	3 tbsp sugar
⅛ tsp vanilla	Jelly
Dash of salt	

Grease well with soft butter a 9-inch spring form pan. Start oven 10 min before baking; set to moderate (350° F).

Roll Graham crackers into fine crumbs—there should be 1 cup. Add butter, mix thoroughly with fingers and pat uniformly thick over bottom and up sides of prepared pan. Beat eggs with rotary beater, add next 6 ingredients and beat until well blended. Pour into crumb-lined pan. Bake 30 min, then remove from oven. Now increase oven heat to hot (475° F). Immediately beat sour cream with flavoring and sugar and pour over cheese cake; return to hot oven for only 5 min. Cool in pan on cake rack, then place in refrigerator to chill. When chilled, run a knife around edge of cake to loosen, then release sides of spring form. Garnish each serving with a tsp of tart jelly. 6 to 8 servings.

FROSTINGS, ICINGS, TOPPINGS AND FILLINGS FOR CAKES

The names, *Frostings* and *Icings* are usually considered synonymous, however, in a strict sense, they are different:

A *Frosting* is a thicker mixture, cooked or uncooked, and is used on cakes only.

An *Icing* may be *fluffy* or *thin*. *Fluffy Icing* is a cooked sugar mixture containing egg whites or yolks, and is stiff enough to spread in swirls over cake.

A *Thin Icing* contains only sugar and liquid; it may be cooked or uncooked, and is thin enough to spread with a pastry brush or to drizzle. It is used on fancy breads, coffee cakes, Danish pastry, etc.

Since the mixtures are different and have different uses, we have divided our recipes into the following groups:

BUTTER FROSTING: Uncooked mixtures made by creaming butter, xxxx sugar, a small amount of liquid and flavorings.

COOKED FROSTINGS: Sugar and liquid are combined, then cooked like candy, and require the same temp attention. Fudge Frosting is in this group.

FLUFFY ICINGS: Sugar, corn syrup, or other syrup, water and unbeaten raw egg whites are combined and beaten over boiling water until mixture stands in glossy pointed peaks. Seven-Minute Icing is the best-known in this group. Or sugar and water are boiled to a "thread" stage, and then gradually beaten into stiffly beaten egg whites. White Mountain Icing is also in this group.

THIN ICINGS: Confectioners' (xxxx) sugar is blended with just enough liquid, such as water, milk, cream or fruit juices, to spread thinly. A little melted butter or corn syrup is often added to make icing shiny. Confectioners' Icing is in this group.

TOPPINGS: Various ingredients such as nuts, coconut, streusel, semi-sweet chocolate, etc., are combined and sprinkled on a cake before or after baking. Whipped cream spread on a cooled cake is also included in this group.

FILLINGS: Cooked, thickened mixtures spread between layers of cake or in Cream Rolls such as custards, fruit fillings, poppy seed and nut fillings. They may also be spread on top of cakes just before adding frosting.

BUTTER FROSTINGS AND HOW TO MAKE THEM SHINY

These amounts of glycerin, fondant and corn syrup apply to recipes in this book.

1. Stir in ¼ tsp or a little more glycerin into 1 recipe of frosting. Buy glycerin from druggist.

2. Stir in a tbsp or more of soft fondant, either homemade or buy fondant from bakery, confectionery or grocery.

3. Stir in a tbsp or two of white corn syrup, then beat hard.

FROST OR ICE THE CAKE PROMPTLY

Frosting or icing should be spread on cake as soon as it is barely cool. At this stage cake has its maximum moistness. Covering it with frosting or icing at this point helps to retain moisture.

GETTING CAKE READY FOR FILLING AND FROSTING

Layers of cake should be uniform in thickness and level. Should there be a hump on top of layer, carefully slice it off to make level. Brush loose crumbs from sides of layers to keep spatula clean when spreading frosting.

PREPARING PLATE AND PLACING CAKE ON IT

Prepare plate by laying four 3-inch wide strips of waxed paper on it to form a "hollow square." This protects plate from smears and is easily slipped out after cake is frosted. Lay first cake layer on plate *bottom-side-up* . . . bottom is always level and this insures a straight-standing cake. You are now ready to spread the filling.

SPREADING THE FILLING

Spoon about 1 cup of filling onto center of a 9-inch layer, then with a 6- or 7-inch blade spatula, quickly spread filling in uniform thickness to edge of cake. Filling should be about 3/16-inch thick for best eating. Let filling set for a few minutes. Now lay on 2nd layer *top-side-up* if cake is a 2 layer; if it is a 3-layer, lay 2nd layer on *bottom-side-up,* and again spread with filling and let set a few minutes to firm. Then add 3rd layer *top-side-up.* Top of cake may also be spread thinly with filling for a richer, moister cake. If filling is spread on top of cake, let it set well before spreading with frosting or icing.

SPREADING THE FROSTING OR ICING

Spread Frosting or Icing between layers of cake when Filling is not used, but a thin layer of Fluffy Icing spread over Filling makes an extra-delicious cake.

Be sure frosting or icing is of good spreading consistency. It should not flow or move when spread. First, spread sides of cake. With a 6- or 7-inch blade spatula, dip up about a heaping tbsp of frosting at a time. Starting at the bottom of the cake, spread with an upward stroke and *bring some of the frosting up over edge of top layer,* making a narrow rim all around top edge of cake. Turn cake while spreading sides with a uniform thick layer of frosting. For up-and-down swirls, make *up strokes* with the frosting overlapping slightly where each spatulaful of frosting is added. *Always* move spatula in the same direction, and with same pressure, to keep sides of cake perpendicular. To finish cake base, hold spatula at an angle, and run tip of blade around bottom of cake to cover unfrosted spots. Now pile remaining frosting on top-center of cake, then quickly swirl out in a uniform layer to slightly *overlap the rim of frosting* made when spreading the sides. The fewer strokes used to spread frosting, the more attractive the cake will be; going over it with dabbing strokes gives an overhandled appearance—this is especially true of *butter and cooked frostings.* Before starting to spread frosting, decide on shape and depth of swirls you want, then once you quickly make the strokes you had in mind, *stop stroking.* The swirls of frosting may not be exactly as planned, but they will look better than if you do them over and over. Frosting technique improves with practice and observation.

STORE CAKE TO KEEP IT AS FRESH AS POSSIBLE

Store uncut cake spread with frosting or icing in a cool place under a cake cover, which is almost, but not quite airtight. After cutting such cakes, lay a wad of dampened, not wet, paper toweling or paper napkin in space on plate where cake was removed. Be sure paper does not touch cake. *Always store in refrigerator* cakes covered with French Cream Frosting, whipped cream and cakes put together with cream fillings. Store large sheet cakes

(cakes baked in large pans from 2 to 2½ inches deep) in the pans in which they baked. Cool such cake in the pan on cake rack 5 min, then turn onto rack for steam to escape. Leave the cake bottom-side-up. Quickly wash and dry pan, then replace it over cake. Now grasp pan with rack and turn it right-side-up in the pan. Frost or ice promptly, and when set, wrap waxed paper around pan snugly, then wrap in several folds of dry towel. Store in cool place. If cake is unfrosted, wrap waxed paper around pan, then wrap in a dampened towel instead of a dry one.

CAKE FROSTINGS—UNCOOKED

CAUTION: The term "soft butter" means butter at room temp—about 70° F

ALLEGRETTI FROSTING

Use Basic Butter Frosting, below, or 7-Minute Icing, p 392, and spread on cake as directed. Melt 2 sqs unsweet chocolate over warm water, beat in ¼ tsp butter. When cooled, pour chocolate neatly from a spoon around top-edge of cake, dripping it down sides in a natural way. Leave center-top of cake white, and the sides just partially covered with chocolate—this gives a strikingly beautiful brown-and-white effect. Let chocolate become firm before cutting cake.

BASIC BUTTER FROSTING (VANILLA)

Put xxxx sugar through sieve or flour sifter before measuring, then pack firmly into cup.

¼ cup soft butter
2 cups xxxx sugar, sifted and
   firmly pkd
¼ tsp salt

1 tsp vanilla
2 to 3 tbsp cream
1½ tbsp corn syrup

Cream butter until shiny, add sugar gradually, creaming thoroughly. Stir in salt and vanilla. Gradually beat in cream and white syrup, using just enough to produce a smooth spreading consistency. Spread on cake. Covers two 8-inch layers or 20 cupcakes.

ANISE BUTTER FROSTING

Follow directions for making above Basic Butter Frosting, except substitute a few drops of anise extract for the vanilla. Frosting with this flavor is harmonious on chocolate cake.

BUTTER-NUT FROSTING

Follow directions for making Basic Butter Frosting. Stir in ½ cup chopped pecans, butternuts, walnuts, etc. Good on Banana, Chocolate or White Cake.

BROWNED BUTTER FROSTING

¼ cup butter
2 cups xxxx sugar, sifted and
  pkd
2 tbsp cream

1½ tsp vanilla
2 tsp white corn syrup
1½ tbsp hot water

Melt butter, then keep over low heat until golden brown—do not scorch. Remove from heat and beat sugar and cream alternately into butter in the hot saucepan. Stir in vanilla and white syrup, then add hot water, and beat until cool and of good spreading consistency. Add ½ cup chopped hickory nuts, if desired. Enough for between and over top and sides of two 8-inch layers.

CHOCOLATE BUTTER FROSTING

Follow directions for making Basic Butter Frosting, p 383. Stir in ½ to 1 sq of unsweet chocolate, first melted over hot water and cooled. Good on Chocolate, Peanut Butter, Yellow or White Cakes.

CHOCOLATE CREAM CHEESE FROSTING

3 oz pkg cream cheese
1 sq unsweet chocolate,
  melted
2 cups xxxx sugar, sifted and
  pkd

Dash of salt
½ tsp vanilla
2 to 4 tbsp cream

Have cheese at room temp and stir until smooth and soft. Blend in cooled chocolate, then gradually add sugar, beating until smooth after each addition. Stir in salt, vanilla and enough cream or milk to give a smooth spreading consistency. Spread on barely cooled cake. Good on Yellow or Orange Cake. Enough for two 8-inch layers.

CHOCOLATE HOBNAIL FROSTING

¼ cup milk
1 cup xxxx sugar, sifted and
  pkd
2 egg yolks
3 tbsp shortening

1 tsp vanilla
1½ to 2 sqs unsweet chocolate,
  melted, cooled slightly
¼ tsp salt

Set a 1½- to 2-qt mixing bowl in ice water, then add milk, sugar and yolks. Beat vigorously with rotary beater to blend, then add remaining ingredients and beat until creamy, thick and of good spreading consistency. To obtain hobnail effect, press tip of tsp into frosting, then draw out quickly. Enough for one 10-inch Sponge Cake or two 8-inch layers.

ABOVE: *For a truly delicious, tender and moist cake you can't do better than this mildly flavored German Sweet Chocolate Cake,* **p** *339. The go-with frosting adds to its glory. Photo, courtesy American Dairy Association.*

BELOW: *Traditionally served for Christmas breakfast in Germany, Stollen,* **p** *307, is equally at home as an afternoon or evening treat with coffee. Chopped parsley forms the star that decorates the butter, shaped for buffet service. Photo, courtesy American Dairy Association.*

ABOVE: *Popcorn balls, candied orange peel and fresh pears provide refreshments for all sizes and strengths of appetites. A snowman candle and a colorful parsley and real cranberry garnish at the stem-end of the pears add an appealing seasonal touch.*

BELOW: *This interesting Confection Tray has a row of Creamy Chocolate Fudge Squares around the outside. In the center are dates stuffed with softened lemon-flavored fondant mixed with shredded coconut. The toasted pecans provide a treat for the candy abstainer. In the upper left corner are tenderized prunes stuffed with tenderized dried apricots, then rolled in the Fruit Cake Glaze, p 368.*

QUICK-MIX CAKES—ONE-BOWL METHOD

All ingredients must be at room temperature

This *MODERN OR 1-BOWL METHOD, p 348,* usually means all dry ingredients are sifted into large mixer bowl. Shortening and more than half the liquid are then added, then mixed at *MEDIUM SPEED* for 2 min, scraping bowl constantly with rubber scraper, or beating 200 strokes by hand. Then beating is stopped. Rest of liquid, eggs and flavorings are added, then mixing is continued on *MEDIUM SPEED* another 2 min, scraping bowl while mixing, or beating 200 strokes by hand. When beating by hand, rest a few seconds 2 or 3 times, counting strokes only while beating. The Mixer Method is demonstrated in the following 6 illustrations:

1. Sift flour, measure, resift 3 times with baking powder, salt and sugar, the last time into larger mixer bowl.

2. Add shortening and about ¾ths of the liquid. Stir with a spoon to blend.

3. Beat at medium speed for 2 min, scraping bowl constantly. Time exactly.

4. Stop beating and scrape beaters to clean them.

5. Now add remaining liquid, eggs and flavoring and again beat on medium speed for 2 min, scraping bowl while beating.

6. Use rubber scraper to flow batter into prepared pans. Bake, cool and frost as directed in the recipe.

HOW TO MAKE A CAKE

Old Time Creaming Method

Step 1. Sift flour once before measuring to assure accurate measurement, then resift 3 times with leavening, salt and spices. See *Sifting, p 313.* The 3 siftings insure even distribution of leavening, salt and spices through flour as well as through batter. Sifting also incorporates some air into the flour which adds to lightness of finished cake. *The following 2, 3 and 4 steps are the creaming technique:*

Step 2. Cream the shortening until smooth and shiny. Creaming shortening is important for smooth and uniform blending with the other ingredients. This produces a smooth uniform batter and a fine-textured cake.

Step 3. Add the sugar gradually, creaming well. When recipes direct adding beaten egg whites last, *set aside ¼ of the sugar* called for in the recipe to beat into the egg whites later. Creaming shortening and sugar thoroughly incorporates air, giving cake volume, fine texture and velvetiness. Research shows it makes no difference whether mixture is creamed thoroughly before or after eggs are added, but it is important that thorough creaming be done.

Step 4. Add whole eggs or egg yolks (beaten or unbeaten as recipe directs) *and beat vigorously until thick, fluffy and light color.* When beating at this stage is done thoroughly, most of the sugar dissolves, at least very little graininess remains apparent. Thorough beating at this point also makes batter thick and fluffy and cake light and large in volume. Up to this point, it is almost impossible to *overbeat*—slighting this beating has an unfavorable effect on texture and volume of the finished cake.

Step 5. Now add extracts to creamed mixture. Here the *mixing technique starts.* Extracts should always be added to the creamed mixture rather than to the finished batter, *because fat and egg absorb and hold the flavor better than sugar, milk or flour.* Cake retains more flavor when flavoring is added at this point.

Step 6. Add sifted dry ingredients and liquids alternately. Add dry ingredients in 3 or 4 portions, and the liquid in 2 or 3—*always begin and end with flour,* and beat until *smooth* after each addition. When liquid is added first, the fat in the creamed mixture tends to separate out, producing a curdled appearance. After flour is added, it still does not produce a smooth batter. Adding flour first and last, prevents batter from becoming excessively thin at any point during mixing. This binds the ingredients together and produces a smooth batter and a fine-texture cake. On contact with liquid, leavening loses some gas, so after starting to add the liquid, *mixing should proceed as rapidly as possible.*

Step 7. When adding egg whites last, beat them with ¼ the sugar called for in recipe. Egg whites properly beaten and folded into batter incorporate considerable air, adding to volume and lightness of cake. Whites must be at room temp and in a bowl, *ready for beating before cake mixing starts.* Have ready ¼ of the sugar specified in recipe to beat into whites. Adding sugar to whites helps retain air beaten into them, and the smooth meringue is easier to fold into batter than plain, stiffly beaten whites. **Beat whites and add to batter this way:** Beat whites until just stiff enough to form soft, shiny peaks, then gradually beat in sugar to a stiff shiny meringue. Now quickly slide meringue onto the batter, and with a *wire whip,* cut-and-fold it in lightly. It is important that this cutting-and-folding be done quickly and thoroughly. If flecks of white show in batter, cake will have coarse texture; if cutting-and-folding is *overdone,* cake will have less volume.

Step 8. Pour batter immediately into prepared pans. (Weigh batter into pans if you have a scale.) Use rubber scraper to scrape all batter quickly from bowl into pans. When batter is thick, use rubber scraper to gently swirl it out from center so it is slightly higher around edge of pan than in center—in rising, the layer levels-out instead of rounding-up in center. If batter is thin, it will level itself. After batter is in pans, it is not affected by standing a few min, but if it stands in mixing bowl a few min before it is poured into pans, handling at this point tends to work out gas and reduces the volume of cake.

Step 9. Place pans in oven correctly for number of pans used. Adjust oven rack as near center of oven as possible. Place pans on rack so cakes are not close to door, top of oven or floor of oven. Pans should not touch each other or be too near oven walls—and one pan should *never be directly above another.* Heat must circulate freely around pans for even baking. When one pan is used, place it so center of cake is in center of oven. Set 2 pans on rack placed in middle of oven, neither touching each other nor oven walls. For 3 pans, adjust 2 racks as near to middle of oven as possible so lower cakes won't rise and touch rack above; place 2 pans on lower rack and 1 pan on upper rack, but not above either of the 2 lower pans. For 4 pans, place 2 pans on each rack, staggering so no 2 pans are directly above one another.

Step 10. Start testing for doneness 3 or 4 minutes before end of specified baking time. Ovens differ and may vary slightly in temp. Using a different size pan than is called for in recipe, or a different make of pan, influences baking time. Baking is faster in glass than in metal pans; *use a temperature 25 degrees lower when baking in glass.* Cake dries out if overbaked, or falls if underbaked. Always test cake for doneness, and learn how to recognize when it is done. Do not remove cake from oven to test. Common tests are:

(a) Remove cake from oven at once when it just begins to pull away from sides of pan; it is overbaked when it has *pulled away from sides of pan in oven.* Most cakes pull away from sides of pan noticeably when out of oven a few min.

(b) Quickly stick a clean toothpick or cake tester into center, if any uncooked batter adheres, cake is not done. Continue baking a few min, then repeat test, and bake *only* until tester comes out clean.

(c) Press cake very lightly with finger tip; if imprint does not remain, cake is done.

Step 11. Cool cakes in pans on cake racks 5 minutes before removing from pans. Warm cake is delicate, and if removed immediately from pans, it will break or crumble. Cakes that cool completely in pans become soggy. The average 5-minute cooling period firms cake enough to be handled and allows enough cooling time out of the pan to prevent sogginess.

Step 12. Frost or ice cake as soon as oven heat is gone. This seals in moistness that is a *"must" quality* of any good cake. Have frosting or icing made before mixing the cake, or start mixing it immediately after cake is removed from oven. See *Directions for Frosting or Icing Cake, p 382.*

Step 13. Store cake to keep it fresh. The kind of frosting, icing and filling used determines the place of storing the cake. Cake with whipped cream or French Butter Icing should be stored in the refrigerator, and covered if possible. Other cakes keep well under cake covers. Or set cake on flat surface such as a table, cover with large, deep bowl. Wring a clean towel out of water, fold several times, then wrap around bottom of bowl to keep out air. Re-wet towel when it dries. When slices are removed from cake, retain moisture in remaining cake by placing a wad of wet paper toweling on plate in the open wedge.

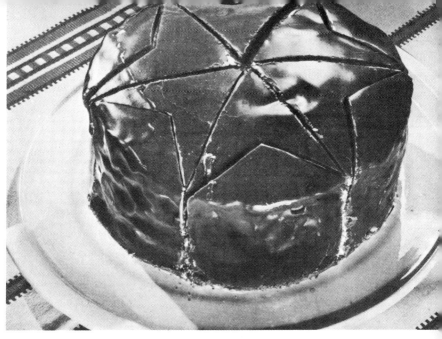

Almost any kind of cake would taste better dressed up in this glossy Dark Chocolate Frosting, p 385. The cake is the Basic 2-Egg described on p 326.

The finest Bride's cake is one made at home by a home cook who follows a dependable recipe, p 341. Use a pastry bag and the simple tubes that come with it to make the cake shown here. Decorative frosting, p 386, is used.

ABOVE: *These beautiful cookies, the leaf-shaped tray on which they are arranged, the steaming cups of coffee, all put one in a fine autumnal mood.*

BELOW: *These luscious Cocoa Indians, p 458, are tempting to the eyes and almost too tempting to the palate. With a glass of milk, they make a most satisfying between-meal snack for the worker as well as for energetic, fast-growing children.*

Griddle Cakes, stacked three high and topped with whipped butter and maple syrup, make a Sunday breakfast worth getting up for. Sour cream with brown sugar is another delectable, smile-winning topping.

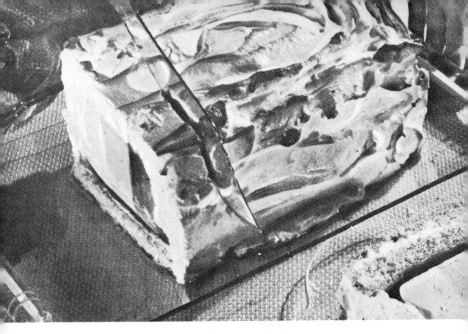

ABOVE: *You'll never fail to stimulate the interest of the most passive person at your table when you bring on a Baked Alaska, p 610. There is no secret about the preparation—it's just using care to employ insulating principles intelligently.*

BELOW: *Scoops of vanilla ice cream dropped into Chocolate Blanc Mange, p 626, that is still warm enough to start the ice cream melting.*

HOW TO BAKE CUSTARD

1. Heat milk with sugar and salt to scalding point, that is when little beads begin to form at edge. Pour slowly over slightly beaten eggs, stirring thoroughly. Add flavoring. Strain into baking dish, dot with butter and sprinkle with nutmeg.

2. Place baking dish in pan of hot water. Add water until it reaches the same height as custard. Bake in moderately slow oven, 325° F, for about 30 to 35 minutes or until done.

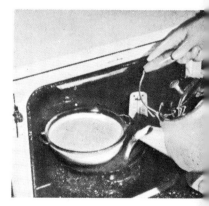

3. A perfect baked custard has a smooth, jelly-like consistency and does not whey or curdle. If you use a glass baking dish, you can easily see that there are no beads of water bubbling out on the sides of the dish.

Photographs Courtesy
Woman's Day Magazine.

HOW TO MAKE SOFT CUSTARD

1. Heat milk, sugar and salt to scalding point. Add milk slowly to slightly beaten eggs, stirring constantly. Return mixture to top part of double boiler to cook over simmering water.

2. Do not have more than one inch of water under the custard. Stir often and cook until custard coats a metal spoon, being very careful not to overcook the custard. Stop the cooking at once and remove from water.

3. Chill custard before serving. Good soft custard is thick enough to be eaten plain, yet thin enough to be used as a sauce for other desserts. When soft custard is topped with uncooked meringue, it is called Floating Island.

Photographs Courtesy
Woman's Day Magazine.

HOW TO MAKE STEAMED CUSTARD

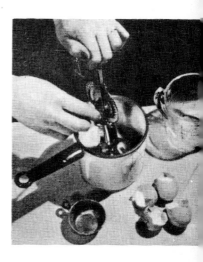

1. Butter inside of top part of double boiler. Add milk then remaining ingredients. Beat with rotary beater. Cover and cook over 1 inch of simmering water.

2. Cook covered without stirring for 15 minutes. Uncover and continue cooking until custard is set and leaves the sides of pan when it is tilted.

3. Remove top part of the double boiler from hot water and carefully set aside to cool undisturbed. Spoon out lightly and serve plain or with crushed fruit sauce or whipped cream.

Photographs Courtesy
Woman's Day Magazine.

ABOVE: *Steamed Fruit Pudding, p 633, which is festive and delicious enough all by itself, takes on new lusciousness and charm when served with a rich, golden Foamy Sauce, p 1243, or a Brandy Sauce, p 1238.*

BELOW: *More ways to shape and decorate Basic Sugar Cookies, p 486, a supplement to any light dessert. Here the garnishes are blanched almonds and colored sugars, added after cookies are brushed with slightly beaten diluted egg white, which holds the nuts and sugar fast.*

ABOVE: *On Valentine's day, this Snow Pudding,* p 587, *made into heart-shaped molds, and decorated with bits of ribbon and lace, will delight the youngsters. It's airy-light, pretty and delicious—good eating for the whole family.*

BELOW: *Snow Pudding,* p 587, *unmolded in a shallow glass bowl already containing the accompanying Custard Sauce is a delicately light, floating dessert that is especially good for hot days when the appetite is so easily discouraged.*

This Cheese Soufflé, p 439, light as a feather, is surprisingly easy to make. Perfect for a guest luncheon, it finishes baking unattended while you leisurely greet your guests. Equally delicious for family meals. Photo, courtesy Kraft Kitchens.

COFFEE OR MOCHA BUTTER FROSTING

A fresh strong infusion is needed for true coffee flavor—never use leftover coffee

⅓ cup medium grind coffee
1 cup cold water
¼ cup soft butter

2 cups xxxx sugar, sifted and pkd
¼ tsp salt
1 tbsp white corn syrup

Add coffee to water and heat just to boiling; remove from heat, cover and let stand 2 min, then strain through fine sieve or cheesecloth to remove all grounds. Cool before adding to frosting. Cream butter until smooth and shiny, gradually blend in sugar alternately with about 3 tbsp of the coffee. Then beat in salt and the white corn syrup until mixture has good spreading consistency. Appropriate for Chocolate, White and Yellow Cakes. Covers tops and sides of two 8-inch layers.

COFFEE-CHERRY-NUT FROSTING

To Coffee Butter Frosting above, add 2 tbsp each, chopped candied cherries and sliced blanched pistachios. Good on White Cake.

CREAMY CHOCOLATE FROSTING

¼ cup butter
3 sqs unsweet chocolate
2¼ cups xxxx sugar, sifted and pkd

¼ tsp salt
⅓ cup milk, scalded
1 tsp vanilla

Melt butter and chocolate over hot water and stir to blend. Measure sugar and salt into 2-qt mixing bowl, add hot milk and stir until completely dissolved. Stir in chocolate. Beat while hot and thin with a wooden spoon until of proper spreading consistency, then beat in vanilla when mixture begins to thicken. Spread on cake when thick and creamy. Good on Golden Gate Cake. Enough for 8¼ x 12-inch sheet cake.

DARK CHOCOLATE FROSTING

Heating after mixing makes this frosting dark, glossy and smooth—just like the beautiful frostings in fancy bakeries

1½ cups xxxx sugar, sifted and pkd
¼ cup cocoa

¼ cup soft butter
3 tbsp cream *or* milk, about
½ tsp vanilla

Sift sugar, measure, then resift twice with cocoa. Cream butter until shiny, then add sugar-cocoa mixture alternately with cream, beating thoroughly. Stir in vanilla. *To darken color,* turn frosting into saucepan and place over very *low heat,* stirring constantly until frosting is dark and glossy—about 5 min. Spread on cake immediately or cool a min or two to proper spreading consistency. Good on Yellow Cake or Eclairs. Enough for two 8-inch layers.

DECORATING BRIDE'S AND PARTY CAKES

Use Decorative Frosting only for decorating Wedding or Bride's Cakes. Use Basic Butter Frosting, Glossy Icing or Basic 7-Minute Icing for borders on Brides' Cakes, and to do impromptu decorations on Birthday and Party Cakes

First, study directions that come with the pastry bag and decorating tubes, and if possible watch a skilled worker. Start by making simple flowers and borders. A good way to practice is to put some shortening in a pastry bag fitted with tube, then press decorations out on back of layer cake pan. Use spatula to return shortening to bag for further trials. With observation and practice, it is easy to make simple decorated Birthday, Party or Holiday Cakes. An elaborate cake such as wedding cakes require more skill and planning.

The ornamental motifs on wedding cakes are usually made a few days ahead of time. Decorative Frosting is piped from a pastry bag fitted with ornamenting tubes onto waxed paper or flower nails into stars, roses, forget-me-nots, etc. and allowed to dry before storing in a covered box until needed. To do impromptu decorations, press out flowers, leaves, stars, borders, or write Birthday Greetings directly from the tube onto cake after frosting has set.

DECORATIVE FROSTING

This frosting is used only to make flowers, leaves and other ornaments for decorating Wedding Cakes. It becomes very white and shell-like and too hard to eat

2½ to 3 cups xxxx sugar, sifted and pkd	2 tsp melted Cocoa Butter (buy from druggist)
1 egg white, slightly beaten	2 tsp cream *or* milk
⅓ cup soft butter	Food color, if desired
1 tsp vanilla	Pastry bag and tubes
⅛ tsp salt	

In a 2-qt mixing bowl, blend 1 cup of the sugar with egg white, then thoroughly beat in butter, flavoring, salt and cocoa butter. Now beat in remaining sugar and the cream alternately. Stir in a few drops of food color, if desired. To test, put a little frosting into a spare decorating tube, then press out with finger onto waxed paper to see if it holds shape, and presses out smoothly. Add a few drops of cream or more sugar, if necessary for right consistency. Then put frosting into pastry bags fitted with proper tubes.

FOOL-PROOF CHOCOLATE FROSTING

Easy to make, easy to spread—has a wonderful flavor and beautiful sheen that never dulls

2 sqs unsweet chocolate	$\frac{1}{16}$ tsp salt
14 or 15-oz can sweetened	1 tsp vanilla
condensed milk	1 tbsp butter

Put first 3 ingredients in top of double boiler. Stir frequently and cook over (not in) boiling water 8 to 10 min or until chocolate melts and mixture is smooth and thick. Remove from heat. Stir in vanilla and butter. Replace hot water in bottom of double boiler with cold to cool frosting, stirring frequently, or beat with rotary beater. Thin with a little cream, if necessary. Covers tops and sides of two 9-inch layers.

GLOSSY CREAM CHEESE FROSTING

2 3-oz pkgs cream cheese at room temp	½ tsp grated orange rind, pkd
⅛ tsp salt	1¾ cups xxxx sugar, sifted and pkd
1 tbsp orange juice	1 tsp cocoa butter

Stir cheese until smooth, then blend in salt, orange juice and rind. Now beat in the sugar. Melt cocoa butter (from druggist) over hot water, add a little of the icing to it in the hot pan, then scrape out quickly. Beat thoroughly. Good on Double Orange, p 335, or White Cake, p 340. Covers tops and sides of two 8-inch layers.

LEMON BUTTER FROSTING

Follow directions for making Basic Butter Frosting, p 383, except substitute lemon juice for half the cream and ½ tsp grated lemon rind, pkd for the vanilla. Good on yellow cake and gingerbread. A thinner frosting made by adding more liquid is delicious on Angel Food or Chiffon Cake.

ORANGE BUTTER FROSTING

Follow directions for making Basic Butter Frosting, except substitute 2 tbsp orange juice for the cream and 1 tsp grated orange rind for the vanilla. Suitable for Yellow or White Cake, and when made thinner, for Angel Food or Sponge Cakes.

RUM-NUT BUTTER FROSTING

2 tbsp soft butter
2 tbsp cream
1 egg yolk
Dash of salt

2 cups xxxx sugar, sifted and pkd
2 tbsp white corn syrup
1 tsp rum extract
¼ cup chopped nuts

Cream butter until shiny; blend in cream and egg yolk well. Stir in salt and about ½ cup of the sugar and beat until very smooth. Then add rest of sugar and white corn syrup alternately in 3 or 4 portions and stir until smooth and of right spreading consistency. Stir in extract and nuts; spread on cake. (Omit nuts if desired.) Good on Yellow or White Cake. Enough for two 8-inch layers.

STRAWBERRY BUTTER FROSTING

¼ cup soft butter
Dash of salt
3½ cups xxxx sugar, sifted and pkd

¼ cup strawberry juice
2 tbsp cream
Sliced berries

Cream butter until shiny, add salt. Blend in 3 cups of the sugar alternately with strained strawberry juice and cream to produce a smooth spreading consistency. Remove ½ cup of the frosting, and spread remainder on cake. Add rest of sugar to reserved frosting to make stiff enough to hold shape. Turn into pastry bag with star tube and make rosettes in center or around edge of cake. Garnish with slices of strawberry. Pleasing on White or Angel Food Cakes. Enough for two 8-inch layers or 16 decorated frosted cupcakes.

CAKE FROSTINGS—COOKED

3-MINUTE COCOA FROSTING

Smooth and easy to cut

2 egg yolks, beaten
1 cup sugar
¼ cup cocoa
¼ tsp salt

¼ cup cream
1 tsp butter
1 tsp white corn syrup
1 tsp vanilla

Combine first 5 ingredients in a saucepan. Place over low heat, stir constantly and heat to bubbling, then cook 3 min. Remove from heat, add butter, white syrup and vanilla. Cool by placing saucepan in cold water, if desired, then beat until thick and smooth. If too thick to spread easily, thin with a little cream. Double recipe for two 9-inch layers.

CHOCOLATE FUDGE FROSTING

Make *Chocolate Fudge*, p 403. When fudge is beaten until it stiffens, add cream a little at a time and beat until it will spread easily and smoothly. Spread between layers and swirl over top and sides of cake. Let stand until set before cutting. Covers two 8-inch layers, tops and sides.

Note: Prepared Fudge Mixes make satisfactory Fudge Frostings when directions on packages are followed.

FONDANT OR PETITS FOURS FROSTING

A thin shimmering finish for rich delicate sheet cake or Petits Fours. This frosting is poured, never spread

1 cup bought *or* homemade
    Fondant, p 404
2 to 3 tsp hot cream *or* water
½ tsp butter

⅛ tsp almond extract *or* ½ tsp vanilla
Food color, optional

Measure first 4 ingredients into top of double boiler, then place over (not in) barely simmering water. *Do not beat or stir—beating and stirring prevents frosting from being creamy.* With a small wooden spoon or tongue depressor, blend ingredients gently together. Add just enough color to give a delicate tint. When consistency is like thin corn syrup, pour over cake for a thin coating. If used on a sheet cake that is in pan, pour Fondant Frosting over top, then shift back-and-forth to obtain a uniform thin layer. Now put some fondant of contrasting color into a pastry bag fitted with *small-hole decorating tube* for drawing fine lines, then pipe double lines over the frosting to make small squares or oblongs. When cake is cut between these double lines, every piece is edged with a delicate line. Put a little frosting in another bag fitted with a star or leaf tube and make little decorations in center of each piece of cake.

PENUCHE FROSTING

This frosting is expensive, but it's good enough to be! Neither flavoring nor salt is needed, but nuts may be added for extra goodness

2 cups brown sugar, pkd
2 cups granulated sugar
2 cups cream or half milk

2 tbsp corn syrup
½ cup butter, room temp
Cream for thinning

Measure first 4 ingredients into 3-qt saucepan; place over medium heat and heat to boiling, stirring frequently with wooden spoon until sugar dissolves. When syrup reaches a steady brisk boil, add butter in 4 or 5 portions so not to stop the even boiling. Continue the brisk even boiling (syrup stays about 1½-inch from top of pan) 20 to 22 min, or until thermometer registers 234° F. Or test by dripping a little syrup into cup of cold water; when drops fall to bottom and can be formed into a soft, not sticky ball; remove from heat at once. Quickly turn into another saucepan of same size to eliminate grainy accumulation. (Saucepan is best, in case frosting needs to be reheated.) Cool without stirring to about room temp. If frosting must be hurried, set pan into cold water, changing water 3 or 4 times, but do not stir. When thick and cool, set saucepan on wet cloth, and beat with electric mixer at high speed or with rotary beater 3 or 4 min until light-colored. Remove beater. Now with wooden spoon, beat slowly until thick and cool, beating in a tsp or 2 of cream for good spreading consistency. *Do not spread frosting, if it thickens while still warm;* but *continue to beat, adding a little cream until it cools, spreads easily and holds shape.* Should frosting thicken too fast, add cream a little at a time and keep beating—a very creamy frosting results, so don't get panicky and spread it too quickly. Covers tops and sides of two 9-inch layers. *Note:* If frosting is undercooked and not spreadable after 7 or 8 min of beating, *place over high direct heat,* heat a min or two stirring until mass follows spoon. Again set in cold water and beat until cold. This procedure may be repeated 2 or 3 times, and it works! This is an easy frosting to make if you use an electric mixer or rotary beater the first 3 or 4 min of beating, then a wooden spoon. Final beating need not be hard, but it should be fairly constant.

QUICK CARAMEL FROSTING FOR APPLE SAUCE CAKE

½ cup brown sugar, pkd	2 tbsp shortening
½ cup granulated sugar	⅛ tsp salt
⅓ cup milk	1 tsp butter
1 tsp white corn syrup	¼ tsp vanilla

Measure first 6 ingredients into a 1-qt saucepan, stir and place over medium heat. Stir constantly and heat to boiling, then cook at rolling boil 3 to 4 min, or until soft ball forms when a little syrup is dripped into a cup of cold water. Remove from heat. Add butter and vanilla, do not stir. Place saucepan in bowl of cold water for 3 or 4 min to cool, then beat until creamy and of spreading consistency. If too thick, add a few drops of cream or more butter. Spread over Apple Sauce or other sheet cakes.

Don't Forget: To big and little children the frosting is as important as the cake.

FRENCH BUTTER CREAM FROSTING

A luscious, easy-to-spread topping for Chocolate Cake and worth the price if you want something really luxurious!

⅔ cup sugar	¾ cup milk
¼ cup all-purpose flour	½ lb cold unsalted butter
¼ tsp salt	1 tsp vanilla *or* rum extract

Measure first 3 ingredients into saucepan and mix thoroughly, then stir in milk until smooth. Place over medium heat and cook with constant stirring until *very thick.* If not smooth when partially cooked, beat with rotary beater, then continue cooking and stirring. Remove from heat and turn into a 2- or 3-qt mixing bowl. Cool to room temp by placing bowl in cold water, if desired. Mixture should not be warm enough to melt butter. Remove a stick of the butter at a time from refrigerator—cut in half lengthwise, then crosswise into ½-inch pieces. With electric mixer or rotary beater, beat in the firm butter, about 2 tbsp at a time, beating until smooth after each addition. When all butter is in, beat in flavoring. Entire beating takes 8 to 10 min. Frosting will spread more evenly if chilled 5 or 10 min after mixing. Spread this fluffy stiff Frosting on cooled cake. Thickly covers three 9-inch layers. Store cake in refrigerator until serving time.

FRENCH BUTTER CREAM BURNT SUGAR OR CARAMEL FROSTING

Good on any cake but excellent on Burnt Sugar or White Cake

½ cup Caramel syrup, p 165	½ tsp salt, scant
¼ cup flour	¼ cup cream
½ cup sugar	½ lb cold unsalted butter
	1 tsp vanilla

Caramelize sugar and make syrup. In a 1-qt saucepan, blend flour, sugar and salt, then stir in caramel syrup and the cream until smooth. Place over medium heat, and with constant stirring, cook until very thick and smooth, about 5 min. Remove from heat and turn into 3-qt mixing bowl and set in cold water to cool to room temp. With rotary beater or electric mixer, beat in butter 1 tbsp at a time, beating until smooth after each. When all butter is in, beat in flavoring, then spread on cake. Covers two 9-inch layers, tops and sides. Store cake in refrigerator.

This book will show you thousands of ways to a man's heart.

CAKE ICINGS

FLUFFY AND CONFECTIONERS' BASIC 7-MINUTE ICING

Corn syrup in this icing retards crust formation

1 egg white	¾ cup sugar
⅛ tsp cream of tartar	½ tsp vanilla
Dash of salt	1 to 2 tsp white corn syrup
3 tbsp cold water	

Put first 5 ingredients in top of double boiler, then place over boiling water—upper pan should not touch surface of water. Beat with rotary beater 7 *minutes,* or with electric beater 4 min, or until icing stands in pointed stiff peaks. Remove from heat. Change hot water for cold and replace top of double boiler. Add vanilla and syrup, then continue beating until icing stands in shiny peaks stiff enough to hold shape. Spread on cake immediately. Enough for top and sides of two 8-inch layers. Double recipe for three 8-inch or two 9-inch layers.

BROWN MOUNTAIN ICING

Good on Chocolate or Spice Cake—stays shiny

1 cup brown sugar, pkd	¼ tsp salt
½ cup granulated sugar	2 egg whites
¼ cup white corn syrup	1 tsp vanilla
½ cup water	

Put first 5 ingredients into a 2-qt saucepan. Proceed as for White Mountain Icing, p 395. Covers tops and sides of two 9-inch layers.

COCONUT ICING

Frost cake with *Basic 7-Minute,* or *White Mountain Icing,* p 395, and immediately sprinkle with freshly grated, p 122, or canned, moist-pack coconut, being sure to sprinkle sides as well as top of cake.

CONFECTIONERS' ICING

To enhance Coffee Cakes, Buns, Doughnuts and simple layer cake. Orange juice instead of water makes tangy icing

1½ cups xxxx sugar, sifted and pkd	Dash of salt
2½ tbsp boiling water	1 tsp vanilla
1 tsp butter	1 tbsp white corn syrup

Measure sugar into 2-qt mixing bowl. Combine water and butter; when melted, add salt and vanilla and stir into the sugar, then beat in syrup until smooth. Add more boiling water drop by drop if necessary to produce a smooth spreading consistency. Beat 2 or 3 min until very creamy, keeping sides of bowl scraped down. Drizzle immediately on slightly warm baked goods. Strained lemon or any other fresh fruit juice may be substituted for the water and vanilla, if desired. Enough for two 8-inch coffee cakes.

EGG YOLK ICING

2 egg yolks
⅛ tsp cream of tartar
Dash of salt
2 tbsp cold water

1 tbsp lemon juice
¾ cup sugar
¼ tsp grated lemon rind, pkd

Place egg yolks, cream of tartar, salt, water, lemon juice and sugar in the top of a double boiler. Place *over* boiling water (upper pan should not touch surface of water) and beat with a rotary beater or electric mixer for 7 min or until mixture is thick and fluffy and holds its shape. Remove from heat. Stir in lemon rind. Spread on cake. This icing is especially suitable for a white cake. Enough for one 8-inch layer.

MOSS ROSE ICING

Follow directions for making *Coconut Icing,* except soak the coconut in 2 or 3 tbsp of orange juice to which ¼ tsp of grated orange rind and 1 tsp of sugar have been added. Squeeze moisture out of coconut, fluff it up and sprinkle over icing. Use on Moss Rose Cake, p 319.

GLOSSY WHITE ICING

Here's an icing that stays shiny

1 cup *plus*
2 tbsp sugar
⅓ cup water
2 egg whites, ¼ cup
Dash of salt

¼ tsp cream of tartar
3 tbsp xxxx sugar, sifted and
    firmly pkd
1 tsp vanilla

Blend sugar and water in saucepan, place over low heat. Brush down sides of saucepan frequently with a wet pastry brush. Turn egg whites into 3-qt mixing bowl and set bowl on wet cloth to keep from sliding. Add salt and beat with a wire whip to a foam, then add cream of tartar and beat until stiff, gradually adding the xxxx sugar as you beat. Mixture should beat into moist, shiny peaks when all sugar is added. When sugar and water syrup cook to 236° F, p 402, then pour slowly but continuously over whites while beating. Continue beating until cold. Beat in vanilla. Covers tops and sides of two 9-inch layers.

LADY BALTIMORE ICING

Follow directions for Glossy White, or White Mountain Icing, pp 393, 395, except substitute 1 tsp rum flavoring for the vanilla. Then fold in ½ cup chopped moist raisins, 3 thinly sliced light moist dried figs and ¼ cup chopped pecans.

LEMON CONFECTIONERS' ICING

For apple sauce cake, sweet rolls, etc.

¼ cup xxxx sugar, sifted and firmly pkd	½ tsp white corn syrup
1½ tsp lemon juice	Dash of salt
½ tsp soft butter	1 tsp cream

Combine all ingredients and beat hard to blend. Drizzle over top of cake or rolls. This icing adds flavor and helps to retain moisture in the product. Enough for 1 small Apple Sauce Cake. Double recipe for full size cake.

LORD BALTIMORE ICING

White Mountain Icing, p 395	¼ cup pecans broken small
2 grated crisp almond macaroons	2 tbsp blanched almonds slivered and toasted, pp 121, 415
6 well-drained maraschino cherries, sliced	½ tsp orange extract *or* ¼ tsp grated orange rind, pkd

Make White Mountain or 7-Minute Icing substituting ½ tsp orange extract for the vanilla. When almost cool and very thick, remove ⅓ of icing to a small bowl. Fold remaining ingredients into this and spread between layers of Golden Gate Cake, p 347. Spread remaining icing over top and sides.

STRAWBERRY 7-MINUTE ICING

Good on white or plain yellow cake

3½ tbsp strawberry purée	Dash of salt
1 egg white	¾ cup sugar
⅛ tsp cream of tartar	1 tsp white corn syrup

Crush about ½ cup washed, hulled ripe berries, then press through fine sieve to remove seeds from purée. Combine first 5 ingredients in top of double boiler. Stir to mix and beat with rotary beater or electric mixer over, not in, boiling water until mixture stands in firm peaks, about

7 min. Remove from heat. Replace hot water with cold, add syrup and beat until mixture is cool and very stiff. Enough for two 8-inch layers.

THIN BUTTER ICING

For coffee cakes, tea rings, Jule Kake and plain layer or cupcakes

2 tbsp butter
1 cup xxxx sugar, sifted and firmly pkd

1½ tbsp milk
½ tsp vanilla

Melt butter in bowl over hot water; then add sugar and milk alternately, a little at a time, stirring until smooth after each addition. Stir in vanilla. When smooth, pour over cake and let stand until set before cutting. Enough for one 8-inch layer.

Note: Fruit juice may be used in place of milk and vanilla and a tsp of white corn syrup adds shine.

WHITE MOUNTAIN ICING

An "old-timer" and hard to beat for flavor and shine

½ cup sugar
¼ cup white corn syrup
⅛ tsp salt

2 tbsp water
2 egg whites
½ tsp vanilla

Measure first 4 ingredients into a 1-qt saucepan. Put egg whites into a 2-qt mixing bowl and set bowl on wet cloth to keep from sliding. Place sugar mixture over heat, and when syrup starts to boil, brush down sides of saucepan with a wet pastry brush. Boil moderately fast until syrup spins a thread 5 to 6 inches long, or 242° F. Three to 4 min after sugar starts boiling, beat egg whites with rotary beater until they form soft peaks. Leave beater in bowl. When syrup cooks to right stage, pour about half of it in a thin stream around over the whites, using rotary beater like a spoon to beat as you pour in syrup. Quickly set remaining syrup back on stove to keep hot and pourable. Then beat icing hard with beater until thick and fluffy, then add rest of syrup and continue beating until stiff, shiny peaks form. Add vanilla and beat icing until it is shiny and stiff enough to hold deep swirls when spread. Enough for top, sides and between two 8-inch layers.

CAKE TOPPINGS

BAKED CAKE TOPPING

2 egg whites, room temp
¼ tsp salt

2 cups brown sugar, pkd
¼ cup chopped nuts

Beat egg whites and salt to stiff foam, gradually add half moist brown sugar and continue beating until blended. If turning rotary beater becomes too difficult, stir in rest of sugar with a spoon, then fold in nuts. Strew over cake batter in pan before placing in oven. If preferred, sprinkle nuts over topping after it is spread on cake. Bake at the temp specified and until cake tests done. Enough for two 9-inch round layers or one 8 x 12-inch sheet.

BROILED CAKE TOPPING

⅓ cup butter, melted   ¼ cup cream *or* milk
⅔ cup moist brown sugar, pkd   ½ cup moist coconut

Mix ingredients together thoroughly. Spread on cake just removed from oven. Set Broiler Control at 300° F and have broiler rack as far as possible from source of heat. Place cake on rack and cook until topping bubbles all over and becomes nicely toasted, but watch carefully to prevent scorching. Enough for an 8- or 9-inch sq cake or 7 x 11-inch sheet.

COCOA WHIPPED CREAM

Adding gelatin to whipped cream firms it so it will hold up 2 or 3 hrs after spreading on cake. Cake topped with whipped cream and served immediately needs no gelatin

1 tsp plain gelatin   ⅓ cup cocoa
4 tsp cold water   Dash of salt
⅓ cup xxxx sugar, sifted and   ½ pt whipping cream
     firmly pkd   ¼ tsp vanilla

Have cream, mixing bowl and beater cold. Soften gelatin in cold water 5 min, then place over hot water to melt. Cool. Sift sugar, cocoa and salt together 3 times. Whip cream to a thick foam, add vanilla then pour gelatin quickly in a thin stream over cream while stirring in. Now sift in cocoa mixture gradually and beat until stiff enough to spread —*do not overbeat*. Spoon cream immediately over cake and spread quickly. Enough for an 8 x 12-inch cake or two 8-inch layers.

GELATIN WHIPPED CREAM

For cakes that must be stored 3 or 4 hrs before serving or for making borders with decorating tubes

Follow directions for Plain Whipped Cream, but add 1 tsp plain gelatin softened in 4 tsp cold water 5 min, then melt over hot water and cool. Beat cream until slightly thickened, then pour gelatin quickly in a thin stream over cream while stirring in with beater. Now beat until well distributed. Add sugar and flavoring and beat until smooth and thick enough to mound up or to retain swirls. *Do not overbeat.*

PLAIN WHIPPED CREAM

½ pt whipping cream　　　　½ tsp vanilla *or* desired
2 tbsp xxxx sugar　　　　　　flavoring

Chill 2-qt mixing bowl and rotary beater a few minutes in refrigerator, if possible. Turn chilled cream into bowl and beat until
slightly thickened. Add sugar and flavoring and beat until smooth, shiny
and thick enough to mound. *Do not overbeat* as this gives a buttery
flavor and coarse texture. Granulated sugar may be used, but the xxxx
sugar gives a little smoother texture. Cake spread with Plain Whipped
Cream should be stored in refrigerator and served within an hour or two.

CAKE FILLINGS

Apricot filling for bride's cake and petits fours, see p 344

CHOCOLATE CREAM FILLING

Use Filling for Chocolate Cream Sponge Roll, p 317. Spread between two 8- or 9-inch layers of Chocolate or Yellow Cake.

COCOA FILLING

Good on chocolate or white cake

¼ cup cocoa　　　　　　　1½ cups milk, scalded
⅔ cup sugar　　　　　　　1 egg, beaten
½ tsp salt　　　　　　　　2 tbsp butter
3 tbsp flour　　　　　　　½ tsp vanilla

Blend first 4 ingredients in top of double boiler, stir in milk and
place over boiling water. Cook and stir until mixture thickens, then
cook 10 min with frequent stirring. Stir a little of the hot mixture into
beaten egg, then return to pan and cook 2 min longer, stirring constantly. Remove from heat. Stir in butter and vanilla. Cool, stirring
occasionally to prevent "skin" forming on surface. Spread between two
8- or 9-inch layers.

CREAM FILLING

For layer cake, Blitz Torte or Boston Cream Pie

1 tbsp flour　　　　　　　1¾ cups milk
1½ tbsp corn starch　　　　1 egg, slightly beaten
½ tsp salt　　　　　　　　2 tbsp butter
½ cup sugar　　　　　　　1 tsp vanilla

Mix dry ingredients in top of double boiler. Add milk gradually
and stir to blend, then heat to boiling over direct medium heat, stirring
constantly. Now stir some of the hot mixture into egg and return to

double boiler, beating thoroughly. Cover, place over hot water and cook 15 min, stirring frequently. Remove from heat and stir in butter and vanilla. Cool before spreading. Enough to spread between and over top of two 8-inch layers.

DATE FILLING

Good on white or yellow cake

1 cup pitted dates, cut in 4ths	⅓ cup sugar
¾ cup water	2 tbsp lemon juice
⅛ tsp salt	1 tbsp butter

Put first 4 ingredients into saucepan, heat to boiling and cook gently with constant stirring until thick and smooth, about 5 min. Remove from heat. Stir in lemon juice and butter, then cool. Enough for two 8- or 9-inch layers.

LEMON BUTTER JELLY

This rich, lemony filling made with whole eggs or yolks keeps well. It may be made 3 to 4 days before using. Delicious for layer cakes, filled cookies and tarts

½ cup butter	2 tbsp flour
3 eggs *or* ⅔ cup yolks, beaten	½ cup *plus* 1 tbsp strained lemon juice, 3 lemons
2 cups sugar	½ tsp grated lemon rind, pkd

Melt butter in top of double boiler. Blend sugar and flour, add eggs and beat well, then stir into the melted butter. Now stir in lemon juice. Cook *over gently boiling water,* stirring constantly until mixture is thick and clear, from 10 to 12 min. Remove from heat; stir in rind. Cool, then pour into a clean jar. Cover and store in refrigerator. 2½ cups filling. Enough to spread between and over tops of three 9-inch layers of cake, or fills fourteen 3½-inch tarts. After spreading cake with filling, cover filling with 7-Minute Icing, p 392. Spread the tarts with whipped cream, or fold some whipped cream into filling before spooning into tart shells for extra-special filling.

LEMON FILLING

¼ cup corn starch	Dash of salt
1 cup sugar	¼ cup lemon juice
1¼ cups cold water	1 tsp grated lemon rind, pkd
2 egg yolks, slightly beaten	1 tbsp butter

Blend corn starch and sugar in a 1-qt saucepan—stir in cold water gradually, and cook over medium heat until mixture boils and thickens, stirring constantly to keep from sticking. Add some of the hot mixture to yolks, stir well and return to pan and cook and stir 2 more min.

Remove from heat, add remaining ingredients and stir until well blended. Cool thoroughly before spreading on cooled cake. Enough to spread between two 8-inch layers and on top.

MARSHMALLOW FILLING

For white cake or putting between cookies

10 marshmallows	2 tbsp chopped nuts
¼ cup moist raisins	½ tsp grated orange rind, pkd
1 tbsp cream	

Put marshmallows in top of double boiler with raisins, place over hot water and stir with wooden spoon until marshmallows melt. Remove from heat and blend in cream thoroughly. Stir in nuts and rind to distribute evenly. Spread between two 8- or 9-inch layers.

ORANGE FILLING No. 1

A high-flavored filling for white or yellow cake

1½ cups sugar	⅔ cup strained orange juice
⅓ cup flour	4 tsp lemon juice
Dash of salt	1½ tsp grated orange rind, pkd
2 tbsp soft butter	¼ tsp grated lemon rind, pkd
2 eggs, beaten	

In a 1-qt saucepan blend sugar, flour, salt and butter thoroughly. Add eggs and orange juice and beat until well-blended. Cook over medium heat until thick and smooth, stirring constantly. Remove from heat, add lemon juice and rinds. Cool slightly before spreading on cake. Enough for two 8- or 9-inch layers.

ORANGE FILLING No. 2

4 tbsp corn starch	1 tbsp grated orange rind
1 cup sugar	⅓ cup orange juice
½ cup water	¼ tsp lemon juice
¼ cup orange juice	2 tbsp butter
¼ tsp salt	

Blend corn starch and sugar in a 1-qt saucepan; stir in water, ¼ cup orange juice and salt. Place over low heat and stir until mixture is smooth and thick—about 5 min. Remove from heat, add rest of ingredients and stir until well blended. Cool without stirring until stiff and jelly-like. Enough to spread between two 9-inch layers and over top. When set, spread with 7-Minute Icing, p 392; then sprinkle with coconut, if desired.

SOUR CREAM FILLING FOR BLITZ TORTE

See p 376.

Candy

This chapter is good news for the younger generation, for it not only contains recipes for many delicious candies but also the information that under the PROPER CIRCUMSTANCES, candy is good for children! As for yourself, Mother—just take a good look in the mirror and make your own decision!

ALMOST everyone likes candy. It is a source of the quick energy that is needed during times of strenuous activity, and since children are almost always playing and using up calories at a rapid rate, wholesome candy may *at times* satisfy a definite need in their diets.

Candy that is made with pure ingredients, and eaten in moderation at a time that will not interfere with regular meals, has a place in the diet. The ingredients of even the least expensive commercial candies must be pure, to conform to the pure food and drug laws, but it must be remembered that the habitual eating of even the purest candy is sure to put pounds of weight on adults, and is equally sure to dull the appetite of both children and adults for the other foods which they need for buoyant health. The largest percentage of the nutritional value of candy is in its energy or caloric content. Other nutrients are present, of course, but in relatively small amounts when compared to some other foods of equal caloric content. In addition, all sweet foods tend to dull the appetite. The practice of eating sweet foods for dessert has become established because they give the feeling of satisfaction and completeness to the meal. Candy is an excellent dessert and can be served frequently at the end of a meal in place of other desserts. When sweet foods are eaten before meals, however, they can destroy the desire for other foods to such an extent that the diet may suffer.

It is particularly desirable that the candy eaten generally by both adults and children have some nutritive value in addition to calories. Candies which consist of pure sugar with a little flavoring, such as plain fondant, have little additional nutritive value. On the other hand, candies with a good proportion of dried or glacéd fruit contain substantial amounts of both minerals and vitamins. Between these extremes are candies containing milk, dried cereals, nuts or fruits, and those made with brown sugar or molasses. These ingredients contain varying amounts of valuable nutrients as well as calories.

In normal health, sugar is one of the most easily and quickly digested and assimilated of all foods. But it should be remembered that white sugar is a pure carbohydrate and contains no protein, minerals or vitamins—only calories. Two scant tbsp of sugar yield 100 calories. So candy should never be allowed to take the place of any of the foods listed in the diet pattern, but should be used only for extra fuel or energy value.

HINTS ON MAKING CANDY AT HOME

The two types of candy—crystalline and non-crystalline or amorphous—require different handling. To obtain the tiny crystals necessary for creaminess in crystalline candy such as fudge and fondant, sugar grains must not be permitted to collect on the sides of the pan during cooking, but must be wiped down with a damp cloth wrapped around the tines of a fork. Such crystals grow slowly into large ones, thus making the candy "grainy."

If you have been having trouble with graininess in candy, and if there is any sign of graininess on the sides of the pan at end of cooking, pour it into a clean pan or bowl immediately on removal from the heat, with no scraping whatever. Then cool the syrup enough so that the pan can be held on the palm of the hand without discomfort, before beating. Cooling may be hastened by setting the pan in a bowl of cool water, but no stirring should be done until it is cooled. This cooled candy requires a long beating to start the sugar crystals to form, but once they start, they form all at once and are all very tiny. And when all the crystals are tiny, the candy has the creamy quality which is so desirable. Non-crystalline candies, such as caramels and butterscotch, should not be beaten, except for stirring in the flavoring, after removal from the heat. They should be poured directly into a buttered pan and allowed to cool and become firm undisturbed.

Flavoring should be added to the candy after cooking since all flavorings are volatile and are dissipated rapidly in hot liquids. When candy is to be beaten, the flavoring may be added after the candy is cooled. Because the flavoring must be added to non-crystalline candy that is not beaten just as soon as it is taken from the heat, a slightly larger amount of flavoring is usually needed to compensate for the loss in the hot syrup.

Nuts or other ingredients that are added to candy must be fresh and of good quality. Stale or withered nuts will spoil the flavor and defeat all the care given to make the candy good.

Candy that is to be kept for any length of time or that is intended for a gift should be wrapped in individual pieces. This prevents pieces from sticking together, and it helps keep the candy fresh and moist. Use a good heavy-waxed paper, or moisture-proof cellophane. Ordinary cellophane, the kind used for wrapping gift packages is not moisture-proof and will stick.

When making candy at home, you will be more successful if you choose a clear, dry day. A humid atmosphere or excessively hot weather adds to the difficulties of making almost any kind of candy. This is especially true when making caramels and toffee, and dipping chocolates.

ADVANTAGES OF A CANDY THERMOMETER

In making any candy, a candy thermometer is a valuable piece of equipment, particularly for a beginner. It takes experience to recognize the traditional home tests for "doneness," such as dropping small amounts of the hot syrup into cold water and "spinning a thread" from the syrup. The only way to be sure of getting identical results every time is to use a candy thermometer in addition to the other tests. A reliable candy thermometer should be used with the bulb placed well below the surface of the boiling syrup, but not touching the bottom, and the reading taken at eye level. Learning to judge the various stages as described below will help to overcome many difficulties caused by variations in humidity and altitude.

TABLE 22.   COOKING TEMPERATURES FOR CANDY*

Thread stage ....230–234° F	Hard ball stage ......250–265° F
Soft ball stage ....234–238° F	Soft crack stage ....265–272° F
Medium ball stage ....238–245° F	Medium crack stage ....272–290° F
Firm ball stage ....245–250° F	Hard crack stage ......290–310° F
Caramel stage ....320–345° F	

* For making candy at high altitudes, see between pages 1442–1443.

THE COLD WATER TEST

Whether you use a candy thermometer or not, the cold water test is an invaluable aid in determining when the candy is done, since it reflects atmospheric conditions and temperature does not. Make the test as follows:

Into a cupful of cold but not ice water, let fall several drops of the boiling hot candy. Test immediately by forming the drops into a ball with the fingers. At the *soft ball stage,* the drops form a ball that just can be picked up but will collapse when removed from the water. At the *medium ball stage,* the ball in water is fairly firm but loses its shape when lifted out; at the *firm ball stage* the ball in water has a putty-like feel and holds its shape out of water. At the *hard ball stage,* the ball when removed from water is so hard it makes a sound when tapped against a plate.

At the *soft crack stage* the candy is too hard to shape into a ball in water, but the firm ribbon it forms will bend when lifted out. At the *medium crack stage* it holds its shape out of water without being brittle. At the *hard crack stage* it remains brittle when removed from the water. The *caramel stage* begins at the point where the color becomes a light amber, and continues through a dark amber color; if allowed to progress too far, the caramel develops a disagreeably burned flavor.

Caution: Remove pan of candy from heat while the *cold water test* is being made; otherwise there is danger of overcooking while testing is done.

BEATEN CANDIES

CHOCOLATE FUDGE

2 sqs unsweet chocolate	¼ tsp salt
2 cups sugar	2 tbsp butter
1 cup milk	1 tsp vanilla
1 tsp white corn syrup	½ to 1 cup chopped nuts

Cut or break chocolate into small pieces, put into a heavy 3-qt saucepan with sugar, milk, corn syrup, salt and butter; stir until well mixed and place over direct heat. Brush sides of pan down frequently with a pastry brush dipped in water to prevent crystals from forming and stir occasionally. Cook to soft ball stage (234° F), being sure to remove the pan from the heat while making cold water test. When done, remove from heat and place pan on a cake rack to cool without further stirring or shaking of pan. When cool enough to hold hand on bottom of pan comfortably, add vanilla and beat fudge vigorously until it begins to stiffen and loses its shine. Stir in nuts. Turn out into a buttered 8-inch sq pan, pressing into a uniform layer. Mark in squares and cool thoroughly. 1¼ lbs.

To Make Marshmallow Fudge:

Increase chocolate in Chocolate Fudge to 3 sqs. Cook, cool and beat as in Chocolate Fudge. When thoroughly beaten, quickly pour over 1 cup marshmallows cut into quarters that are spread out in the buttered 8-inch sq pan. Finish as above.

To Make Fudge Balls:

Add chopped nuts and chopped dates, figs or cherries to beaten fudge and work together until just blended. Using about a tbsp of fudge, mold with the hands into even sized balls. Roll in finely ground nuts, or dip in chocolate, p 408.

DIVINITY

First Part:	Second Part:
1 cup chopped nuts	2 cups sugar
1 cup sugar	⅔ cup white corn syrup
½ cup water	¼ tsp salt
⅛ tsp cream of tartar	¼ cup water
3 egg whites, room temp	1 tsp vanilla

First Part: Chop nuts. Measure sugar, water and cream of tartar into a 1-qt saucepan and put the egg whites into a 3-qt mixing bowl. Have a wet pastry brush ready. Butter an 8 x 8 x 2-inch pan.

Second Part: Put the first 4 ingredients into a 3-qt saucepan.

First Part: Stir ingredients in the saucepan well then place over brisk heat and boil rapidly without stirring to a medium ball (240° F) or until syrup spins a 6-inch long thread from a fork. Brush sides of pan down frequently with the wet brush to prevent crystals from forming on sides of pan. Meanwhile beat egg whites until stiff. When syrup cooks to 240° F, remove from heat and put the second saucepan over medium heat, stirring occasionally. Now pour the hot syrup slowly over egg whites, beating continuously until very stiff and shiny. Now remove beater and clean off.

Second Part: Boil the syrup to the medium crack stage (280° F), remove from heat and pour slowly over mixture in bowl, beating constantly until very stiff, using a food fork. Now stir in flavoring and nuts. Turn into prepared pan and spread to uniform thickness. When set, mark into squares. Candied fruits such as cherries and pineapples may also be folded in with the nuts. About 2 lbs.

FONDANT

3 cups sugar   1½ cups boiling water
⅓ tsp cream of tartar

Put all ingredients into a 3-qt saucepan and stir until sugar dissolves. Now place over heat and boil briskly without stirring. Wrap a wet cloth around tines of a fork and wipe down crystals that form around sides of pan while cooking. Cook to soft ball stage (238° F), about 20 min. Remove from heat and cool just until bubbles disappear, then pour into a large shallow platter. *Do not scrape the pan.* Place platter on cake rack for syrup to cool from bottom as well as surface. Cool until platter can be held on palm of hand comfortably. Then beat with a wooden spoon until mass loses stickiness and becomes lumpy and crumbly in appearance. Now scrape the mass together, then gather up in hands and knead until smooth, creamy and plastic. Place in a clean container. Cover first with a damp cloth, then with a tight fitting lid. Let stand at least 24 hrs to ripen before using. Fondant will keep for weeks on the pantry shelf if tightly covered. A corn syrup or shortening can makes a good container. 1¼ lbs.

HOW TO USE FONDANT FOR BON BON CENTERS

Remove as much of the cold fondant from the jar as needed. Add the desired coloring and flavoring and knead well into the cold fondant to obtain uniform color and flavor throughout the mass. Keep both color and flavoring delicate. Many combinations of extracts and essences may be added to obtain delightful flavors for bon bon centers: vanilla, almond, rose or lemon may be used. A combination of wine and rose, or one of vanilla and almond are elegant variations. Fresh lime extract is delicious in fondant. To make, add a little lemon juice to fresh grated lime rind; let stand 2 min, then squeeze out and use juice. Lemon and orange rind similarly treated with lemon juice and squeezed out give equally gratifying flavors. A concentrated coffee or tea brew also make tempting flavors.

After fondant is colored and flavored, roll it out into a long rope on waxed paper, not more than a half inch in diameter, keeping thickness uniform. Now cut the rope into ¼-inch lengths for uniform size bon bon centers. If *solid centers* are required, quickly form them into small balls which will be a trifle soft. Place on another sheet of waxed paper and dry slightly to form a thin shell on the outside to make them easier to dip.

If *liquid centers* are desired, use the quarter-inch lengths cut from the rope of fondant, flatten out slightly and place pieces of fruit in the center such as a half or quarter of a maraschino cherry, a small seedless white grape, or a quarter of a fresh strawberry, then quickly wrap the fondant around the fruit. Make sure the fruit is covered or the juice in the fruit will leak out and the bon bon will be difficult to dip. Let dry for a few min, then dip.

HOW TO USE FONDANT TO DIP BON BONS AND POUR ON PETITS FOURS

If coloring is used, be careful to keep it very delicate. Both color and flavor may be kneaded into the cold fondant as for bon bon centers. Place 1 cup of the colored, flavored fondant in top of a 2-cup double boiler and set over hot, not boiling water. Turn the mass over occasionally with a wooden paddle, but do not stir as this may start crystallization. When lumps of solid fondant have disappeared, it should have consistency of corn syrup. If not, paddle in hot water drop by drop to give this consistency. It is now ready to dip bon bon centers or pour over petits fours, p 344.

MEXICAN ORANGE CANDY

1 cup sugar	1 cup evaporated milk
¼ cup boiling water	1 tsp grated orange rind,
2 cups sugar	pkd
Dash of salt	1 cup chopped nuts

Caramelize 1 cup sugar to a rich amber color, p 165; add boiling water and boil, stirring occasionally until caramel is entirely dissolved. Add the 2 cups sugar, salt and milk, stir well and cook to soft ball stage (236° F). Just before candy is done, add orange rind. Remove from heat and cool as for Chocolate Fudge, p 403. Beat until candy begins to stiffen, then stir in nuts. Drop by teaspoonfuls onto buttered waxed paper. 1¾ lbs.

NOUGAT

Part I   Mazette Stock
1½ cups sugar
1¼ cups white corn syrup

¼ cup water
3 small egg whites

Put the sugar, corn syrup and water into a 3-qt saucepan. Stir until thoroughly blended and wipe down any sugar crystals on sides of the pan. Adjust the candy thermometer onto the side of the pan and place over heat. Cook without stirring to 238° F (medium ball stage). When the syrup reaches the 230° F mark (thread stage), beat the egg whites until they stand in peaks. When syrup reaches 238° F, add slowly to the beaten whites and continue beating until the mixture is lukewarm and thick. This Mazette stock will keep several days if it is well covered with waxed paper. When making a variety of candies that are to be dipped in chocolate, it is an advantage to make this first part a few days ahead. Makes from 5½ to 5¾ cups.

Part II
3 cups sugar
3 cups corn syrup
4 tsp vanilla

½ cup melted butter
1 tsp salt
3 cups blanched, delicately
    toasted almonds

Put the sugar and corn syrup into a 4-qt saucepan. Stir to blend, then wipe down any sugar crystals. Adjust thermometer on sides of the pan and place over the heat. Cook to 275° F (medium crack stage). Have the Mazette stock in a large mixing bowl and pour this hot syrup over it all at once, and mix well with a heavy wooden spoon. Next add the vanilla and butter slowly, continuing to mix with the spoon. Then add the salt and the nuts and again mix. Turn out into two 9-inch sq pans and flatten the top with buttered hands. Let stand several hrs, then turn out onto a board and cut. If plain nougat is desired, wrap in heavy waxed paper to retain the shape. Or dip the slender rectangular pieces immediately into chocolate. (See p 408.) Makes about 5 lbs.

Note: If Part II is too large an amount to handle, make only half the quantity and use just half of the Mazette stock.

ORANGE-COCONUT CREAMS

1 tbsp butter
2 cups granulated sugar
¼ cup water
½ cup evaporated milk
2 tsp orange flower water

2 tsp orange juice
¼ tsp grated orange
    rind, pkd
2 cups moist shredded
    coconut

Melt butter in a 3-qt heavy saucepan. Add sugar, water and milk and boil to soft ball stage—236° F, stirring constantly. Cool and beat like Chocolate Fudge, p 403. Add flavoring, orange juice, rind and coconut and knead into candy until creamy. Using about a tbsp of candy, mold with hands into even size balls. Roll in additional coconut. 1½ lbs.

Note: Obtain orange flower water from druggist.

PANOCHA

Also spelled penuche and penuchi

1¾ cups light brown sugar, pkd	¾ cup evaporated milk
Dash of salt	¼ cup water
1 tbsp corn syrup	1 tsp vanilla
1 tbsp butter	⅔ cup chopped nuts

Combine first 6 ingredients in a heavy 3-qt saucepan and cook to the soft ball stage—234° F, stirring constantly. Cool and beat like Chocolate Fudge, p 403, adding vanilla and nuts just before turning into buttered pan. 1⅛ lbs.

PRALINES

1 cup brown sugar, pkd	½ cup water
2 cups gran sugar	2 tsp mapleine
3 tbsp corn syrup	1 cup pecans, chopped
¾ cup evaporated milk	½ cup pecan halves

Measure all ingredients, except nuts, into a 3-qt heavy saucepan. Cook to soft ball stage—236° F, stirring frequently with a wooden spoon. Remove from heat and cool to lukewarm. Then add nuts and beat until stiff and creamy. When mixture is stiff, drop rapidly from spoon onto buttered waxed paper in patties about 4 inches in diameter. Press pecan halves into top of each praline. Candy should stiffen immediately. Wrap in waxed paper. 1¾ lbs, 12 pralines.

SEA FOAM

2 egg whites, room temp	½ cup water
2 cups brown sugar, pkd	½ tsp salt
½ cup gran sugar	1 tsp vanilla
⅓ cup white corn syrup	½ cup broken walnuts

Put egg whites into a 3-qt mixing bowl, then set bowl on wet cloth to keep it from slipping when beating. Put the next 5 ingredients into a 3-qt saucepan, stir thoroughly and place over medium heat. Boil to hard ball stage—256° F, frequently wiping sugar crystals down sides of pan with a wet pastry brush. Do not stir. Remove from heat to cool while beating egg whites until stiff, then slowly add syrup, beating in thoroughly. Now remove beater and use egg whip or a food fork and continue to beat with slower rhythm, stopping a minute or two now and then. It usually takes 8 to 10 min of beating. The beating must continue until candy is past the "pully" stage and starts to get creamy and holds shape. Then add vanilla and nuts and beat until candy holds swirls. Quickly drop candy from tsp in mounds on waxed paper or turn into a buttered 8 x 8-inch pan. Candy that is beaten sufficiently will not spread when dropped into mounds. 1¼ lbs.

CHOCOLATE DIPPING

Buy a good quality of *dipping chocolate*. Ordinary chocolate used in cooking will not do. Milk, Vanilla and Bitter Chocolate, obtainable from special confectioners or grocers, is prepared especially for dipping. A blend of Bitter and Milk Chocolate makes a fine coating for caramels, while Milk and Vanilla is excellent for fruit centers and puddings.

Put enough lukewarm water (110°–115° F) into the lower part of a double boiler to come just below the upper part when it is set in place. Set in the upper part containing the chocolate cut into fine pieces. Place double boiler over very low heat. When chocolate is over-heated, the fat rises and separates out causing light streaks which spoil the appearance of the chocolate. Chocolate should be melted slowly, stirring often. Keep the temp of the water constant at the simmering point, 185° F, using a thermometer to check the temp frequently. Melt at least a pound of chocolate at a time, and more if possible. The larger the quantity used, the longer the temp will remain just right for dipping. Allow plenty of time; it requires an hr or two to melt a lb or two of chocolate.

Chocolate must not come in contact with steam or water because even a trace of moisture spoils it.

As chocolate melts, stir vigorously to distribute the fat thoroughly and to make it perfectly smooth.

Shape bon bon centers and let stand on waxed paper while chocolate melts. The thin crust formed on the surface facilitates dipping.

Dipping may be done from the upper part of the double boiler, but such an arrangement makes it difficult to remove bon bons. A more convenient way is to pour a cupful into a small bowl or onto a marble slab. Work back and forth with the fingers until chocolate feels cool (85°–90° F). To test for proper temperature, allow chocolate to string from the hand into the chocolate melted for dipping. It it holds a ruffly appearance on the surface for a few seconds as if so much narrow string had fallen from the hand, it is ready for dipping.

Dipping may be done with the fingers, a fork, or a regular candy dipper. (The amateur usually prefers the dipper.) Place centers in the chocolate one at a time. Roll around gently but quickly with the dipper until well covered. Slip the dipper under the center. Scrape off any excess chocolate against the edge of the bowl, the edge of double boiler, or the crusty rim of the pool of chocolate on the marble slab. Drop right side up on waxed paper. As the candy drops from the dipper, twist the thread of chocolate clinging to dipper to make a swirl across the top. With a little practice this swirl becomes professional looking.

The coating should harden immediately after the swirl is formed. If the design does not remain intact, the coating is too warm. If it breaks or the piece coats rough, the chocolate is too cold.

Chocolate that becomes too cold may be re-melted in the double boiler. This should be done as slowly and as carefully as at first.

The room in which the dipping is done should not be below 58° F and not higher than 68° F. In summer, dipped candy may be placed in a dry refrigerator for a few min to harden, but never next to the ice or in a damp place, because sweating spoils chocolate.

FRUIT CANDIES

CANDIED APPLES

Candying Fruit:	*Glazing Fruit:*
2½ lbs, Jonathan *or* Northern Spy apples	2½ cups sugar
7 cups sugar	¾ cup water
½ cup white corn syrup	

Candying Fruit: Use very firm apples. Pare thinly, remove cores and cut quarters into ½-inch slices. Put fruit into 3-qt saucepan and barely cover with boiling water. Place over heat and as soon as water starts to boil, note time and boil *exactly 3 min.* Drain, saving water. Now make a syrup using 2 cups of the drained off water and 2½ cups sugar. Heat syrup and as soon as sugar dissolves, add drained apples and again bring just to a boil, because longer boiling will soften fruit too much. Now turn fruit and syrup into a clean glass or enamelware bowl and let stand uncovered 24 hrs. Again drain syrup from fruit, and add ½ cup sugar and the ½ cup corn syrup to it and place over heat just long enough to dissolve sugar, then return fruit to syrup and again heat just to boiling. Now return syrup and fruit back to bowl and let stand uncovered another 24 hrs. Again drain off syrup, add 1 cup sugar and heat until sugar dissolves, then return fruit to syrup and heat just to boiling, then return fruit and syrup back to bowl to stand 24 hrs. Repeat draining and adding 1 cup sugar, heating just to boiling and letting stand 24 hrs 3 more times. The fruit should stand in the syrup the last time about a week and at this time the syrup should be as thick as honey. Now drain fruit in a wire basket or colander, and after it drains well, dip basket or colander with fruit in it for a few seconds in gently boiling water to remove excess syrup. Now lay pieces of fruit on waxed paper to drain and dry. After draining and drying 3 or 4 days, glaze fruit.

Glazing Fruit: Put sugar and water into a 3-qt saucepan and boil 3 or 4 min. While boiling, dip the fruit into the hot syrup, then remove, drain and spread out on waxed paper to dry and become glazed. This glazing produces a non-sticky candy. The leftover syrup may be used on pancakes or waffles.

This method of candying fruit was developed by the New York State College of Agriculture at Cornell University and the N. Y. Experiment Station at Geneva.

CANDIED ORANGE OR GRAPEFRUIT PEEL

Tender, translucent, moist, sugar crusted peel is attractive, delicious candy

6 *or* 7 medium-size grape-fruit	6 cups sugar
	½ cup water

Use thick-peel, clear yellow fruit as free from blemishes as possible. Wash in cold water using a scouring pad and a paring knife to scrub and scrape off dirt and discolorations. Rinse thoroughly. Cut in half lengthwise for best shaped strips for candying. Squeeze out juice for punch, or remove sections for breakfast fruit, salad, etc. Cover, place in refrigerator and use within a few hrs. Now hold fruit shells under cold running water and with tsp, scrape out all loose fiber to obtain clean shells of even thickness. Then use kitchen scissors to cut into lengthwise, canoe-shaped strips about ½-inch wide at middle, dropping into a 4-qt heavy aluminum or enamelware pan. Cover with cold water, place over heat, cover pan and heat to boiling. Then drain off all water. Repeat with the adding of cold water, heating to boiling and draining 6 or 7 times or until the peel has just a slight, pleasant bitterness left. Let the last cooking continue 10 to 15 min until peel is just tender. Drain quickly and measure. There should be 1½ qts of peel pkd only medium firm. Now return peel to same heavy pan in which it was cooked and while hot, add the sugar and water. Toss around gently to distribute sugar. Cover, place over very, very low heat. Continue shaking pan and tossing peel until sugar dissolves. Now uncover and *simmer* shaking pan occasionally to prevent sticking until syrup reaches temp of 238° F. Remove immediately from heat. At this time, peel should be perfectly translucent. This slow cooking requires from 2 to 2½ hrs. Now turn peel into colander placed over bowl to drain. When lukewarm, remove a few strips of peel at a time and toss in granulated sugar spread out on a plate. Lay coated strips on a tray and cool until surface is crusty. When cold, pack in box with air-tight cover with waxed paper between layers. When dry, strips may be dipped in chocolate, p 408.

CHOCOLATE CARAMEL APPLES

1 cup brown sugar, pkd	2 tbsp butter
¼ cup white corn syrup	4 Jonathan apples, washed
¼ cup milk	4 wooden skewers
1 sq unsweet chocolate	

Measure sugar, syrup, milk and chocolate into top of double boiler. Place over direct heat and cook until a drop in cold water forms a hard ball—250° F. Stir occasionally to prevent sticking. Add butter and cool 2 to 3 min. Place over boiling water to keep warm while dipping apples. Push a skewer through core of apple at stem-end, then holding by skewer, dip caramel syrup over top of apple to coat. Twirl apple in syrup to coat bottom half evenly and twirl a few times out of syrup to remove excess. Stand upright on greased sheet of waxed paper to cool.

OLD-FASHIONED CANDIED FRUIT ROLL

½ lb seedless raisins	½ lb pecans *or* walnuts
¼ lb dried figs	3 tbsp butter, melted
¼ lb dried apricots	2 cups sugar
½ lb dates	¾ cup water
¼ lb candied pineapple	3 tbsp vinegar
½ lb moist coconut, 2 cans	

Choose fresh dried fruits when making this confection. Wash raisins, figs, and apricots and shake in a cloth to remove excess moisture. Remove seeds from dates and combine with washed fruits, pineapple and coconut. Put fruit-coconut mixture through a food grinder, using the coarse blade. Combine ground mixture with coarsely chopped nuts and spread out on a flat pan which has been spread with the melted butter. Put sugar, water, and vinegar into a saucepan, mix well, and wipe down sugar from sides of pan before heating. Cook without stirring to the soft ball stage (234° F). Remove from heat and pour over the fruit. (Do not scrape any syrup out of the pan.) Let cool; then knead the mixture until well mixed. Form into two rolls about 2 inches in diameter. Wrap in waxed paper or a dampened, clean cloth and place in a refrigerator for about 3 hrs or until it slices well. If it is to be served later on or packed for gifts, wrap in several layers of heavy waxed paper or moisture-proof cellophane, store in a tightly covered box and keep in a cool place. Cut in ¼-inch slices to serve. 3½ lbs.

HARD CANDIES AND BRITTLES

BUTTERSCOTCH PATTIES

1 cup gran sugar	1 tsp vinegar
1 cup white corn syrup	½ cup butter

Put syrup and sugar into saucepan and heat until sugar dissolves. Then add vinegar. Continue boiling without stirring until it reaches 260° F (hard ball stage). Add butter and continue cooking to 270° F (soft crack stage). Remove from heat. Drop ½-tsp of the candy onto well buttered pans to form patties. Let cool before removing from pans. Makes about 40 patties.

CANDIED PUFF BALLS

1 cup sugar	1 tsp butter
¾ cup water	¼ tsp vanilla
¼ cup light molasses	1 lg pkg puffed cereal,
Dash of salt	4½ oz
1 tsp vinegar	⅓ cup salted peanuts

Cook sugar, water, molasses and salt to 256° F (hard ball stage). Add vinegar and continue to cook rapidly for ½ min. Remove from heat, add butter and vanilla and quickly pour over the cereal and peanuts, measured into a greased bowl, mixing well. Form into balls when partially cooled. When thoroughly cool, wrap in waxed paper. Makes 1 dozen 2-inch balls.

OATMEAL TOFFEE

2 cups rolled oats	½ tsp salt
⅓ cup melted butter *or*	1½ tsp vanilla
margarine	1 cup semi-sweet chocolate
½ cup brown sugar,	chips
pkd firmly	¼ cup finely chopped nuts
¼ cup dark corn syrup	

Stir oats into the butter. Add sugar, syrup, salt, and vanilla and pour into a greased 8-inch square pan and bake in a hot oven (450° F) for about 12 min until golden brown. Turn off heat, remove from oven, sprinkle on the chocolate chips, return to hot oven for about 2 min until chocolate is melted. Remove from oven and spread the melted chocolate evenly over candy and sprinkle with nuts. Allow to cool, then cut into squares. About 16 sqs.

OLD ENGLISH NUT TOFFEE

1 lb butter	½ cup coarsely chopped
1 lb gran sugar (2 cups)	almonds (leave skins on)

Combine all ingredients in a 3-qt heavy saucepan. Heat slowly to boiling point and boil gently until mixture reaches 305° F (hard crack stage) or until it is a golden brown color. Stir constantly while candy is cooking. When required temp is reached, pour out on a well oiled marble slab or large baking sheet. Spread flat with an oiled knife. Let stand several min, loosen bottom and mark into squares. Then, if desired, candy may be covered with a thin layer of melted dipping chocolate, p 408, and sprinkled with additional nuts. When cool, carefully break into pieces. Keep in tightly covered container. The flavor improves if candy is allowed to mellow for several days. 80 pieces or 1⅝ lbs.

PEANUT BRITTLE

2 cups sugar	$\frac{1}{16}$ tsp salt
1 cup water	½ lb shelled peanuts

Combine sugar, water and salt in a 3-qt saucepan, stirring until sugar dissolves. Bring to a boil, cover tightly and boil 3 min; remove cover and continue cooking until syrup takes on a rich caramel color— 320° F. Have peanuts spread out on a 12½ x 19-inch buttered shallow enamelware pan, a marble slab or an enamel kitchen table top. Pour caramel syrup over peanuts and let cool thoroughly before breaking in pieces. About 1½ lbs.

CARAMEL POPCORN

As delicious as you can buy ANYWHERE

6 qts popped corn	½ cup boiling water
¾ cup salted skinned peanuts	1 tbsp butter
2 cups sugar	½ tsp soda
¼ tsp cream of tartar	

Have corn fresh and crisp. Turn into a large dishpan or a 6-qt bowl. Stir in peanuts. Measure sugar and cream of tartar into a 3-qt saucepan. Stir in boiling water thoroughly. Place over moderate heat, cover pan and boil gently for 5 min, stirring occasionally. Then uncover pan and continue cooking without stirring but watch closely until syrup takes on a bright caramel color. Do not cook to a dark caramel or there will be a bitter flavor. Remove from heat at once, stir in butter and soda until thoroughly mixed and pour immediately in a thin stream quickly all over top of corn. Then quickly use two forks to stir and lift thoroughly until all corn and nuts are coated with the candy. As soon as corn can be handled, lift out portions loosely as large as a fist onto sheets of waxed paper. Do not press together. When corn is cold, break apart into small nuggets and store in a closely covered container or cellophane bags. Serves 10 to 12.

POPCORN BALLS

10 qts freshly popped corn	1 cup sugar
1 cup molasses	2 tbsp butter *or* margarine

Put the popped corn into a large kettle holding at least 6 qts. Measure molasses, sugar and butter into a 3-qt saucepan and cook with occasional stirring to crack stage, 273° to 274° F. Drizzle the mixture over the popcorn while another person tosses and mixes the corn with 2 long handled forks. Be careful not to drip any of the hot molasses on hands because at this high heat it would make a bad burn. Rub additional butter or margarine on the hands and quickly shape into balls, using only light pressure. After all the popcorn balls are made, cover balls loosely with waxed paper. The secret of keeping the balls crisp is to store them at room temp, never in the refrigerator whether they are wrapped or not. 36 medium balls.

NUT CONFECTIONS

CHOCOLATE CLUSTERS

½ lb dipping chocolate *or* Plain chocolate bars	½ lb Spanish peanuts, *or* raisins

Break the chocolate in several pieces. Melt in top of double boiler over warm water stirring occasionally until just melted. Do not overheat (see p 408). Keep water at 185° F; check with a thermometer. Remove from heat but let remain over warm water. Add nuts. Cool slightly and drop from tsp onto sheet of waxed paper and let remain until firm. Store in cool place. Makes 3 dozen.

Note: Other nuts or combinations of nuts and raisins may be used in the same way.

GLAZED ALMONDS

½ cup sugar	1 cup blanched almonds
⅓ cup water	(¼ lb) *or* walnuts may be
1 tbsp butter	substituted

Place sugar and water in small heavy skillet and heat slowly to form a light brown caramel syrup. Add butter and almonds and stir constantly until almonds are nicely toasted and coated with syrup. Be very careful not to burn either almonds or sugar-syrup. Pour out on greased enamel or aluminum surface (enamel top table or large baking sheet). Spread almonds apart quickly with two forks. Cool. Makes ½ lb.

TOASTED ALMONDS NO. 1

1 cup almonds, blanched   ½ cup vegetable oil

To blanch almonds, pour boiling water over them to cover. Let stand 3 to 5 min or until the brown skin can be easily slipped off between the fingers. Drain and remove the skins. Dry well. Place oil in a small pan and heat until hot, between 325° F and 350° F. Drop in almonds. Stir continually until they turn a light toasted color. Remove from oil with a fork. Drop on paper towel to drain. Sprinkle with salt, if salted almonds are desired. ¼ lb.

TOASTED ALMONDS NO. 2

Blanched, dried almonds may also be drizzled with enough melted butter to thinly coat them, then spread on a shallow pan and toasted in a moderate oven (350° F) until they are a golden color. Sprinkle with salt while hot.

TOASTING COCONUT

Spread shredded coconut loosely in a thin uniform layer in a shallow pan. Place in a moderately slow oven (325° F), stirring and lifting frequently with a fork until a pale golden color.

POURED CANDY

CREAMY CARAMELS

2 cups granulated sugar   2 cups evaporated milk *or*
  Dash of salt   cream
2 cups white corn syrup   1 tsp vanilla *or* 2 tbsp rum
½ cup butter   flavoring

Put sugar, salt and corn syrup into a 3 to 4 qt heavy saucepan, heat to boiling, and boil to firm ball stage—245° F stirring occasionally. Gradually add the butter and milk so slowly that mixture does not stop boiling at any time; continue to cook rapidly, with constant stirring to medium ball stage—242° F. The candy will stick and scorch easily toward the last, so be careful to stir constantly. Remove from heat and stir in flavoring. Pour into a buttered 9″ square baking pan. Cool thoroughly before cutting. When cold, turn out onto a molding board covered with waxed paper. Cut with a sharp, heavy knife, using a sawing motion. Wrap in waxed paper or in moisture-proof cellophane (ordinary cellophane will stick). Makes 2 lbs.

CHOCOLATE CARAMELS

Melt 3 sqs (3 oz) unsweetened chocolate over hot water in the pan in which the candy is to be cooked; to this add the sugar, salt and corn syrup, and proceed as for Creamy Caramels, above.

NUT CARAMELS

Just before pouring Creamy Caramels (above) into pan, add ½ cup coarsely chopped pecans or walnuts.

FRUIT NUT CARAMELS

1 cup brown sugar, firmly pkd	3 cups seedless raisins (15 oz pkg)
1 cup white corn syrup	1 tsp salt
1⅓ cups evaporated milk	1 cup chopped nuts
2 tbsp butter	1½ tsp vanilla

Combine sugar and corn syrup and boil 5 min without stirring. Add milk gradually so as not to stop boiling at any time. Then add butter. Boil to a medium ball stage (240° F) stirring constantly. Remove from fire. Add washed, drained raisins, salt, nuts, and vanilla. Stir just enough to blend and turn into buttered pan. Cool. Makes 2½ lbs.

PULLED CANDY

HONEY TAFFY

2⅓ cups sugar	¼ tsp salt
2⅓ cups honey	2 tsp vanilla
1⅔ cups water	

Combine sugar, honey, water and salt and cook rapidly to 280° F (medium crack). Stir in vanilla and pour into a buttered pan to cool enough to be handled. Then pull until light. With the last few pulls, draw out into a rope about ½ inch in diameter. While still pliable quickly cut into ½-inch lengths using kitchen scissors with blades rubbed with softened butter. Wrap each piece in heavy waxed paper. 2 to 2½ lbs.

Note: Do not stir candy while cooking.

SALT WATER TAFFY

1 lb confectioners' sugar	1½ cups corn syrup
¼ cup water	1 tbsp glycerine, opt
¼ lb butter	1 tsp vanilla
1 tsp salt	

Put sugar and water in saucepan, stir to moisten sugar. Then add next 4 ingredients, cook from 265° to 270° F (soft crack stage). Add vanilla, pour into shallow buttered pan. As soon as candy is cool enough to handle, pull until white and porous. Then quickly draw out into a rope about half an inch in diameter. Quickly cut into half-inch lengths using kitchen scissors with blades rubbed with oil or softened butter. Lay each piece on small squares of heavy waxed paper. Roll up paper and twist ends lightly. Makes 1 to 1½ lbs.

Note: Do not stir taffy while cooking.

TAFFY SWEDISH STYLE

3⅓ cups sugar	1 tsp peppermint extract
1⅓ cups cold water	Few drops red vegetable
1 tbsp vinegar	coloring

Put sugar, water and vinegar into a 2-qt saucepan. Stir until sugar is partly dissolved; then wipe sides down with a damp cloth to remove any crystals. Heat rapidly to boiling and cook briskly without any stirring to 270° F (soft crack stage). Immediately pour onto a lightly buttered marble slab or shallow platter or shallow enamel pan, reserving ½ cup. To the ½ cup add enough red coloring to give a red raspberry color; allow only one or two drops for coloring it. Pour this into a lightly buttered saucer and place over a pan of warm water to keep slightly soft. Just as soon as the edges of the uncolored syrup begin to stiffen, draw the edges toward the center, using the buttered tines of a fork. As soon as candy is cool enough to be handled, add the peppermint extract, and begin pulling in hands. While the candy is still hot, put it down frequently and butter the hands. Continue pulling the candy until it is snowy white and porous in appearance. Lay candy down on slab and pull out into a rope of even thickness, about 18 inches long. Transfer the colored candy to a buttered platter or to the slab; divide into 4 equal portions, and draw each one out into a strip as long as the uncolored piece. Quickly press 2 of the strips into the surface of the uncolored candy; turn over and press the other 2 into the other side. Now draw out the whole piece about 6 feet long, so it is of uniform thickness. With a pair of buttered kitchen scissors, cut quickly into 1-inch pieces resembling puffy striped pillows. Let stand on buttered slab until hardened, then wrap in waxed paper or moisture-proof cellophane squares, twisting ends together. Makes 1½ lbs.

QUICK AND UNCOOKED CANDIES

BAKED COCONUT KISSES

½ cup evaporated milk	¼ tsp almond extract
½ cup gran sugar	2 cups shredded coconut

Combine first three ingredients, blending thoroughly. Fold in the coconut. Drop from a tsp onto a well oiled (not buttered) baking sheet. Bake in a slow oven (300° F) 15 min. Remove from pan while hot to avoid crushing. Makes 18 kisses.

PEANUT BUTTER PINWHEELS

1 egg white	2 cups sifted xxxx sugar, firmly pkd
½ tsp grated orange rind	
2 tsp lemon juice	2 tbsp xxxx sugar
Dash of salt	¼ cup soft peanut butter

Beat egg white until stiff, and stir in the orange rind, lemon juice, salt and 2 cups sugar until well blended. Sprinkle the 2 tbsp sugar over a piece of waxed paper, and turn the mixture out onto this. Using a rolling pin rubbed with more sugar, roll out about ⅛ inch thick. Carefully spread the peanut butter over this sheet like jelly on a jelly roll. Roll the sheet up carefully like a jelly roll, and wrap it in the waxed paper. Lay the wrapped roll on a piece of cardboard to keep it straight, and chill in the refrigerator. After 1 hour, transfer to a covered candy box. When ready to serve, cut in slices about ¼ inch thick. Makes about ¾ lb.

POTATO KISSES

⅔ cup hot cooked potato	1 tsp vanilla
2 tsp butter, melted	Dash of salt
1 lb xxxx sugar, sifted	½ lb moist coconut, 2 cans
2½ tbsp cocoa *or* 1½ sqs unsweet chocolate	

Put hot potatoes through a ricer to remove all lumps, and beat in melted butter. Put potato in a mixing bowl, add sugar and beat until thoroughly blended. Add cocoa, or melted chocolate which has been cooled, and beat thoroughly. Mix in vanilla, salt and coconut, and drop by teaspoonfuls onto waxed paper. Keep the mounds of candy rather regular in shape and size. Place in a refrigerator or other cool place for a short time to harden. Hardened candy should be kept in a tightly covered container. About 1½ lbs.

QUICK CHOCOLATE CREAMS

2 sqs unsweet chocolate, 2 oz	1⅓ cups sweetened condensed milk, 1 can
	1 cup chopped nuts

Heat chocolate and sweetened condensed milk in top of double boiler until chocolate melts. Stir until well blended and continue beating until very thick. Allow to cool enough to be able to handle. Drop from teaspoon into bowl of chopped nuts. Form into balls and place on waxed paper. Chill in refrigerator before serving. Makes about 3 dozen.

UNCOOKED CREAM MINTS

2 tbsp butter	2 cups sifted xxxx sugar, firmly pkd
2 tbsp vegetable fat	
2 tbsp warm water	

Butter and vegetable fat are both needed for proper flavor and consistency of these mints. Do not use a substitute for either. Cream butter and vegetable fat and add warm water. Beat until creamy. Flavor and color to suit taste (few drops of mint, peppermint, etc., and pink, yellow or green pure food coloring). Add sifted xxxx sugar gradually and blend well into creamed mixture until a roll may be shaped. Wrap roll in waxed paper. Chill. Slice for serving. About 2 dozen.

A SPECIAL CANDY

ALMOND PASTE

1 lb almonds, blanched, p 121	2 egg whites
2 cups sugar	xxxx sugar
1 cup water	¼ tsp rosewater, opt

Blanch almonds and while moist put through a fine shredder or a regular nut grinder to obtain a fine meal. (Putting through a food chopper gives a waxy product very difficult to blend smoothly with the sugar mixture.) Boil sugar and water without stirring to 240° F. Pour while hot slowly over the stiffly beaten egg whites, beating continuously until mixture is smooth and stiff. Quickly stir in the almond meal, then turn out onto a board over which is generously sprinkled xxxx sugar and knead until smooth, adding the rosewater the last few motions. Press into a pie pan making an even layered cake. Wrap snugly with waxed paper. To serve, cut in small pie shaped pieces.

Cereals

When the word "cereal" is used, most Americans promptly think of breakfast foods; but properly speaking, any food made principally from cereal grains or flour is a cereal food. Thus spaghetti, rice, and popcorn are really cereals, just like your favorite packaged breakfast food. For the purpose of simplification, flours and meals are discussed in the "Homemakers Handbook" section, page 109.

ALL cereals have one characteristic in common—they are an inexpensive source of energy since all contain a large proportion of the carbohydrate—starch. They also contain protein in different amounts, some more than others, and varying amounts of minerals and vitamins. The whole grain cereals are also valuable for the type of cellulose or roughage they contribute to the diet, as well as minerals and vitamins.

A wide variety of cereal products helps the menu planner to add interest to every day meals at breakfast, luncheon or dinner, and enables her to extend the flavor and energy value of more expensive foods and thereby stretch her food dollars.

BREAKFAST CEREALS

Many forms of breakfast cereals using copyrighted trade names are on the market. They are made of corn, wheat, oats, rice and barley or combinations of these grains; they are uncooked or ready-to-eat; whole grain, enriched or restored; puffed, toasted, "exploded," shredded or in other ways altered to make them appealing in appearance, flavor and texture, or to increase their nutritive value. The whole grain cereals retain the nutrients of the whole unprocessed grains and have the natural proportions of bran, germ and endosperm. Refining takes away nearly all of the roughage, minerals and vitamins through the removal of the outer coatings and germ proteins. Now, however, under the leadership of nutritional groups and manufacturers, many brands of refined cereals have been "restored or enriched."

A *"restored cereal"* is refined from whole grain or portions of one or more grains with sufficient thiamine, niacin and iron added to "restore" the accepted whole-grain level of these nutrients as found in the original grain or grains. An *"enriched cereal"* is one to which other vitamins or minerals not noticeably present in the original grain (such as vitamin D) have been added, or to which the minerals and vitamins have been added in greater amounts than would be found in the original whole grain. *The original whole grains and whole grain cereals in general are still superior in protein content and supply roughage that is not found in the refined cereals even though enriched or restored.*

The legislative bodies of many states are recognizing the nutritional advantages of supplying minerals and vitamins in cereals at a level approximating that of the natural grains, and are *requiring* the enrichment or restoration of some cereal products. And many manufacturers are improving the nutritional value of their products even in the states where it is not required. It is definitely important to your family's health to read the labels and choose the cereal products that provide the highest nutritional values.

TYPES OF BREAKFAST CEREALS

The manufacturing processes of the various types of breakfast cereals are varied and extremely complex, and their description is not suitable for a book of this type. However, some general information will prove helpful in providing day-to-day variety.

BREAKFAST CEREALS TO BE COOKED—

Oats: Rolled oats are made by softening the oat grains with steam, flattening them between steel rollers and drying. Quick-cooking rolled oats are made by cooking the grains partially with steam, rolling and drying.

Farina: There is a dark and light farina. The dark is the particles of ground hard wheat which are left when the flour is sifted out. Dark farina has a high percentage of the protein of the wheat germ and is also known as "midlings." Light farina is refined dark farina.

Wheat cereals: Wheat cereals are usually designated as rolled wheat, cracked wheat, or wheat meal. They usually consist of the entire wheat grain that has been treated in various ways to make it cook more quickly and give it richer flavor.

Corn: Corn meal is made by grinding either white or yellow corn. Ordinarily the germ is first removed, which improves the keeping quality of the meal. Stoneground meal, which is also available, retains the germ and is superior in flavor and nutritional value, although it does not keep as well as regular meal.

Hominy: Hominy is made by loosening and removing the husk and the germ of white flint corn either with lye or soda. It may be whole or cracked. Hominy grits are produced by grinding the whole grains of hominy.

READY-TO-EAT CEREAL—

Ready-to-eat cereals include those made from corn, oats, rice, wheat, barley and combinations of these grains. They are treated in a variety of ways, cleaned, flavored with various syrups, cooked or steamed under pressure, dried, then toasted, rolled, puffed, flaked or treated in whatever way necessary to produce the desired forms. The one thing they all have in common is that they may be served directly from the box without further preparation. The whole grain or enriched type should always be chosen.

MACARONI AND RELATED PRODUCTS

There are more than a hundred forms of macaroni, spaghetti, noodles and similar products. Artificial coloring is prohibited by law, the color being contributed by the ingredients only, gluten or egg as the case may be. Macaroni, spaghetti, and vermicelli are made from semolina flour (Durum wheat), farina flour (hard wheat other than Durum) or from other wheat flours. Mixtures of two or all three types of flours are also used. Water, sometimes egg, and a small amount of salt are the only additions. Semolina or farina flours contain chiefly the gluten part of the hard wheat kernel and little starch, and the products made from them are deep cream in color and hold their shape and texture well after cooking. Soft wheat products contain less gluten, are softer when cooked, and are dull white or gray in color. The products made from Semolina or farina flour are usually considered higher quality, but some prefer the softer texture of the other type. Learn to read the labels to select the kind you prefer.

TYPES OF MACARONI AND RELATED PRODUCTS

The most common types of macaroni products are listed and described as follows:

Macaroni—Straight long hollow tubes.

Spaghetti—Straight long solid strands, smaller in diameter than macaroni.

Vermicelli—Straight long solid strands thinner in diameter than spaghetti.

Elbow Macaroni—Short lengths of macaroni bent in an arc.

Curly Spaghetti—Spaghetti strands that have been twisted.

Coiled Vermicelli—Vermicelli strands bent in a three-quarter circle.

Sea Shells—Shell-shapes made from macaroni paste.

Butterflies—Rectangular pieces of macaroni that have been pinched in the middle to form a butterfly shape.

NOODLES—

Egg noodles—Made from wheat flour and at least 5 per cent egg solids, either whole eggs or just the yolks. The latter gives the deeper yellow color. This percentage of egg solids is equivalent to about 2 eggs per pound of noodles.

Plain noodles—Made of flour and water anly.
Soup rings—Tiny doughnut-shaped noodle rings.
Alphabets—Letters of the alphabet made from noodle dough.

OTHER CEREAL PRODUCTS

COOKIES—

National manufacturers provide a wide choice in the selection of cookies. These "bought" cookies are desirable for many uses in the modern busy home. Branded types are of uniform quality and a variety that fits your particular requirement is not difficult to find.

CRACKERS—

Crackers for every course in the meal and for every possible occasion are available. Many, such as butter wafers, may be used not only as an accompaniment for soup or salad, but also as the basis for canapes and sweet tidbits. Selected types may be rolled for crumbs and used in many ways. Whole grain crackers such as rye crisps, shredded wheat wafers, and graham crackers contribute more nutritive value than the highly refined types.

RICE—

Cultivated rice is available in this country in two main varieties: *head rice* with long slender grains and *blue rose* rice with shorter plump grains. Broken rice of both types is made up of grains which were cracked in factory processes. Several grades of each are on the market. There are many other varieties of rice, in fact, there are more than a thousand over the entire world.

Brown rice has the hulls removed but it is unpolished, and a light bran coating and the germ are retained. It contains a higher proportion of vitamins and minerals than white rice and has a nut-like flavor and a slightly chewy texture. It requires a little more liquid and cooking time than regular milled rice. One cup uncooked rice yields 4 cups cooked rice.

Regular milled white rice may be either short, medium or long grain. The brown coat and germ are removed and the kernels polished with soft brushes. It is cleaned during the milling process and is ready-to-cook without washing. One cup uncooked rice yields 3 cups cooked rice.

Parboiled rice. By a special steam-pressure process, the grains of rice are parboiled before milling. This treatment aids in the retention of much of the natural vitamin and mineral content. However, parboiled rice takes longer to cook than regular rice and requires 2½ cups water to 1 cup rice in cooking. After cooking, the grains will be fluffy, separate and plump. One cup parboiled rice yields 4 cups cooked rice.

Pre-cooked rice is regular milled rice which has been cooked after milling and has then been dehydrated. It requires a minimum of preparation time.

There is also a *Quick Brown Rice* on the market now which cooks in 15 min.

USES OF VARIOUS TYPES OF RICES

The short and medium grain rice have a greater tendency for the grains to cling together and hence are best used in croquettes, puddings, rice rings, etc. Long grain rice which is 4 to 5 times as long as the grain is wide, tends to be more light and fluffy with each grain distinct and so is preferred for curries, chicken, fish and meat dishes.

Wild rice is the seed of a tall grass grown in shallow water. It is also known as water rice or Indian rice. It has no treatment after being harvested. The grains are long and slender with a greenish cast and the rice has an unusual flavor. It is considered a delicacy and is more expensive than either brown or white rice. Wild rice is particularly relished when served with wild game or poultry.

SAGO—

Sago is made from the starchy pith in the stems of the sago and other tropical palms. It is sold in pearl form. The grains are fairly small and it is used like tapioca.

TAPIOCA—

Tapioca is made from the starch of the roots of the cassava plant (also known as manioc), a large tropical shrub. The roots resemble sweet potatoes and are from one to four feet long. Tapioca starch is formed into granules or the larger pearls. It is used for thickening gravies and soups and in making desserts.

STARCHES—

Edible starch may be made from corn, wheat, rice and other grains, also from potatoes. Laundry starch is similar to edible cornstarch but is not purified or pulverized. *Arrowroot* is a very finely powdered starch made from the roots of the small tropical arrowroot plant. It is used for making delicate custards, blanc manges and other puddings.

COOKING AND SERVING CEREALS

BREAKFAST CEREALS

There are 2 kinds of breakfast cereals—those that must be cooked and the ready-to-eat. The 5 types that must be cooked are *Farina, Brown Granular Wheat Cereal, Rolled Oats, Rolled Wheat* and *Wheat-Oat Cereal.* They may be either type, quick-cooking or regular cooking.

There are 3 reasons for cooking cereal: (1) To improve flavor. (2) To improve digestibility. (3) To soften the cellulose which improves the texture. In cooking, the starch granules, which are of different sizes and shapes in different cereal plants, absorb water and become greatly enlarged. That is why cereal increases so much in bulk during cooking, and unless the cereal is cooked in sufficient water, the starch granules will not swell completely, and the cereal will not thicken like it should as it cooks.

The flavor of cereal is developed to the highest point when the starch grains swell to maximum size and the cellulose is softened just enough to make the texture pleasing. Longer cooking does not make the cereal more digestible, nor does it improve the flavor. Research also indicates that cereals cooked until the starch swells to its fullest and the cellulose is just softened, retain more thiamine than cereals that are cooked longer.

Cooking directions on modern cereal packages specify the cooking time which makes the product most enjoyable for eating and conserving thiamine. The cooking time for cooking the regular or old-fashioned type and the quick-cooking type cereals, of course, differs. The quick-cooking cereals have been processed by various methods so a few minutes of cooking is all that is needed. Some of these processes which make a cereal quick-cooking include further grinding or cutting, a special steam cooking, and in some instances, the addition of disodium phosphate. This disodium phosphate converts the cooking water to the alkaline side, which causes the starch granules to gelatinize more quickly.

Ready-to-Eat Cereals: The prepared cereals which are nutritionally most desirable are those made from whole grains, but the others—the many delicious enriched and restored flakes and puffed grains and shreds—are also valuable and bring variety into the diet.

Crispness is the most important characteristic of these cereals, and they retain their crispness well until their air-tight seal is broken. After they are once opened, however, the best precautions cannot prevent them from absorbing moisture and becoming tough. Ready-to-eat cereal can be easily freshened by spreading it on a baking sheet and placing in a slow oven for a few minutes. On cooling it will become as fresh and crisp as ever.

Fresh fruit is often used with prepared cereals. Sliced bananas, various kinds of berries, and sliced peaches are favored varieties. This fruit needs to be prepared just before serving to have its fullest fresh color and flavor.

RICE, SPAGHETTI, MACARONI AND OTHER PASTA

Rice, spaghetti, macaroni and other pasta have been used for generations in the American diet chiefly as an alternate for potatoes. Formerly, their contribution to the diet was chiefly calories. Now that rice is processed to retain more minerals and vitamins and many of the pastas are enriched, they can contribute valuable nutrients to the diet. Rice no longer needs to be washed before and after cooking which wasted soluble starch, minerals and vitamins. And it is much better to toss a little melted butter with macaroni and spaghetti to keep the strands from sticking together than to rinse them with hot water.

It would be very difficult to find on the market any of the old-process rice which requires washing to remove the loose starch with which it is coated. The rule was to wash the rice in enough changes of cold water until the last rinse water was clear. This treatment is now known to be wasteful of both minerals and vitamins. In recent years, nutritionists and food chemists who have had an appreciation of the value of rice, spaghetti, and macaroni to great numbers of people all over the world have been making studies of the production of rice in different parts of the world and have been comparing the food values of the rice. The result has been the development of this new converted rice.

Laboratory tests show that the modern milled rice which requires no rinsing and is cooked in a minimum of water has a much richer vitamin content than rice which is rinsed and cooked in a large amount of water. In the old method of washing rice three times in water, it lost a considerable amount of its vitamins. The method of cooking is also important. For example, when 1 cup of rice is cooked in a double boiler with 2½ cups of water and all the water is absorbed and the rice is not rinsed, only a trifle more than 3% of the thiamine, about 2% of the niacin and 2¾% of the riboflavin is lost. When 1 cup is cooked in the old way by adding 10 cups of water and the excess is drained off after cooking, 14⅓% of the thiamine, about 18% of the niacin and a little more than 11% of the riboflavin is lost. Therefore, there is as great a need for improvement in the method of cooking as there has been in processing. These food losses in the old method of cooking explain why undernourishment exists among so many of the people of nations that consume enormous quantities of rice. All of us should cook rice in a way that insures the fewest possible nutrient losses.

GENERAL METHODS FOR COOKING CEREALS

Each family has its own standards for breakfast cereal. In general, when preparing a new kind of cereal, it is well to have it fairly thick, since it can then be thinned to the desired consistency by adding boiling water, whereas it can be thickened only by prolonged cooking. After a few trials the exact amount of water can be determined.

GENERAL DIRECTIONS FOR COOKING CEREALS

It is well to become familiar with directions on cereal packages. They have been tested to produce the best possible product. The points to be remembered for the general cooking of all cereals are as follows:

(1) *Measure* the water and salt accurately.

(2) *Heat the water* to boiling point before adding cereal and salt.

(3) *Measure cereal* accurately by letting the cereal flow from package into cup, then level off with a knife or spatula.

(4) *Sprinkle the cereal* from the cup slowly but steadily into the boiling water so boiling does not stop, and stir constantly while adding the cereal.

(5) *Continue to stir* cereal while it thickens to keep it from sticking to the pan.

(6) *Heat should be reduced* while cooking continues for the required time, according to directions on package; or cook the cereal from this point in a double boiler. Many cereals cook in a surprisingly short time.

HOW TO COOK BREAKFAST CEREAL

Rolled Oats or Rolled Wheat

3 cups boiling water   1¼ cups rolled cereal
¾ tsp salt

GRANULAR CEREALS

Corn Meal, Grits and Farina

5 cups boiling water   1 cup cereal
1½ tsp salt

Direct Heat Method: To the measured amount of rapidly boiling salted water, slowly but steadily sprinkle in the measured cereal, stirring constantly. Now reduce heat and cook over direct heat, with frequent stirring, from 15 to 20 min. This method requires more attention than the Double Boiler Method. Serves 4.

Double Boiler Method: (Direct heat with completion in double boiler.) Fill lower part of double boiler ⅓ full of water and heat to boiling. Place upper part of double boiler with the measured amount of boiling water and salt over direct heat, then heat to boiling point. Now slowly but steadily sprinkle the cereal into the water, stirring constantly. Cook over direct heat with constant stirring until cereal begins to thicken, then place over lower part of double boiler and cook for the time specified on the package, which ranges from 15 to 30 minutes, depending on the particular cereal.

There is no point in cooking cereals in a *Pressure Saucepan.* The reason is that most cereals bought now belong to the quick-cooking variety, and pressure cooking has no advantage. And modern methods of cooking cereals have been so simplified that cooking the cereals by the *Direct Heat* or *Double Boiler* methods takes less time than putting the cereal into the pressure saucepan and obtaining the required pressure.

SERVING SUGGESTIONS

Both hot and ready-to-eat cereals respond to a bit of edible garnish.

For Hot Cereal:

(1) *Add thinly* sliced or chopped moist dried apricots, moist dates, moist dried figs, prunes or raisins to the hot cereal the last few min of cooking.

(2) *Drop a tsp* or so of bright red jelly or strawberry preserves into the center of light farina to replace the sugar.

(3) *Add a few tbsp* of honey or molasses to cereal the last few min of cooking for appealing new flavor.

(4) *Serve cereal* with Vanilla Eggnog.

For Ready-to-Eat Cereal:

(1) *Serve enough fresh fruits* such as sliced peaches, raspberries and strawberries over cereal, thus combining breakfast fruit and cereal.

(2) *Serve the cereal around* a handsome baked apple.

(3) *Heat bite-size shredded wheat* in a shallow pan with melted butter drizzled over it, then sprinkled with moist brown sugar. Heat in a moderate oven (375° F) a few minutes.

(4) *Dip shredded wheat* quickly in boiling salted water, remove from water and drain, then serve at once with hot or cold milk.

CORN*

FRIED CORN MEAL MUSH

Cook corn meal by either Direct Heat or Double Boiler Method, see p 427. Pour the mush into a greased loaf pan or baking powder can and cool thoroughly; it may be covered and kept in the refrigerator for a day or two, if desired. When ready to cook, remove mush from the mold, slice ¼ to ½ inch thick. The thinner the slice, the crisper the finished product. Dip slices of mush in corn meal. Fry in heavy skillet. If slices are fried in 10-inch skillet, use 3 tbsp fat, less in a smaller

*Recipes using corn and corn meal, such as corn bread, etc., will be found in the related chapters. See Index for exact pages.

skillet. Heat fat until moderately hot, add slices and fry until brown and crisp on both sides. Serve hot with butter.

POPPED CORN

1 cup shelled popcorn	⅓ to ½ cup butter
¼ cup lard *or* vegetable shortening	Salt to suit taste

One cup of the best of popcorn will yield 28 cups of popped corn.

Pop ⅙ to ¼ cup of the corn at a time, the amount depending on the size of the container used for popping. If an old-fashioned wire popper is used, put in enough corn barely to cover the bottom. Shake slowly over moderate heat until the corn starts popping; then shake faster until all the corn is popped. If a heavy kettle, skillet or metal popper (electric or not) is used, melt in the pan or popper 1 tbsp of the lard for each ¼ cup corn. When hot, add corn, cover, and place over moderate heat. Shake the pan, or turn the crank of the popper until corn stops popping. Pour popped corn into a large bowl and pour melted butter over it, allowing about 2 tbsp butter for each ¼ cup of corn used. Mix thoroughly and sprinkle with salt, tossing to distribute it. 5 to 6 servings.

Note: If dried out popcorn pops to only one third the normal yield for the variety, add 2½ tbsp water to 1 lb shelled corn in a qt jar, then seal. If yield is only two thirds normal, add 1 tbsp water to 1 lb corn.

LYE HOMINY

Olden Time Farm Style

Put a scant tbsp of lye (caustic potash) into an iron kettle, never aluminum. Cautiously add one gallon of water. When lye comes into contact with water, it boils up, and produces a solution caustic enough to cause dangerous burns to skin and flesh. Add 2 qts dry shelled large kernel corn (preferably white). Stir, let stand overnight. Use only an enamelware or stainless steel spoon. Next morning, place over fire and heat to boiling; stir thoroughly; then simmer about 20 minutes, or until husks on corn are loosened. To test, lift out a spoonful of corn; let cold water run over it until it is well rinsed; then rub a few kernels with fingers to see if outside husks are loosened. When loose, drain off lye water, fill kettle with cold water, drain again, and repeat this process 2 or 3 times. Turn hominy into an enamelware colander or on a wire screen, and place under running water to rinse 15 or 20 min. Lift up from time to time with the spoon to expose the hominy uniformly to the water. This washing process should remove most of the lye and husks. Turn hominy into dishpan, and fill up with water to loosen the husks; then drain again to remove more of the husks. Repeat until the corn is free from husks. Now turn back into the same kettle in which corn was originally cooked, and which has been scrubbed clean. Cover well with water, heat to boiling, reduce heat to simmering, cover, and cook until corn is tender all the way through, about 3 hrs for kernels of average size. Add more boiling water from time to time if needed. When tender, turn hominy with liquid into containers, and cover. Mason jars with their lids screwed on loose are ideal. Put into a cold place until ready to use.

Note: Just a tiny trace of lye flavor should remain in the hominy for the good old-time quality.

MACARONI, NOODLES, ETC.

Recipes for various noodle, macaroni and spaghetti dishes will be found in the related chapters, such as meat, cheese, vegetables, etc. See Index for exact pages.

TO COOK MACARONI, SPAGHETTI AND NOODLES

Gradually add the macaroni, spaghetti, or noodles, left whole or broken in short lengths, to a large amount of rapidly boiling salted water. For a 7- or 8-oz package, at least 3 qts water and 3 tsp salt should be used in a 4 or 5 qt saucepan. Cook rapidly until tender. Time ranges from 8 to 10 min for noodles, 15 to 20 min for spaghetti, and 20 to 25 min for macaroni. Different brands of all three products require different cooking times. Follow directions on package, if any are given, or test frequently for tenderness. When done, drain in a colander. Rinse if desired by letting hot water run through it for a min, then drain thoroughly.

To serve buttered, as an alternate for potatoes, add melted butter and toss about until each piece is coated, allowing about ¼ cup butter to a 7-oz package.

To keep spaghetti whole, put ends into boiling water first; as they soften, press rest of strands down into water.

½ lb of macaroni, spaghetti or noodles serves 4 to 5.

CRISP FRIED NOODLES

2 cups fine noodles,   2 tsp salt
    about 4 oz   Shortening for frying
2 qts boiling water

Drop noodles into rapidly boiling water to which the salt has been added. Boil briskly for 5 min; then drain noodles in colander and rinse by running hot water through them. Spread noodles out loosely on waxed paper or paper toweling, and cover lightly with cheesecloth; let stand for several hrs until dried off but not hard. Or spread the noodles on a baking sheet and dry off for about 30 min in a slow oven (300° to

325° F). Fry noodles a few at a time in a fine meshed frying basket, in deep fat heated to 360° F, until they are crisp and a delicate golden brown. Lift out and drain thoroughly on paper toweling. Sprinkle with salt. Serve with Chop Suey, Veal à la King, creamed fish, etc. 3 to 5 servings.

GOLDEN NOODLES

⅞ cup all-purpose flour
½ tsp salt
½ tsp baking powder

3 egg yolks
4 tsp water

Sift flour, measure, and resift with salt and baking powder. Beat egg yolks and water, and add flour gradually to yolk mixture by using a fork for mixing. Knead this stiff dough well until smooth, 3 or 4 min. Cover, let stand 10 min to relax. Roll out almost to paper-thin thickness or to a 17 to 18-inch sq or circle. Cut into 3 to 3¼-inch sqs. Or, this dough may be rolled up tight and cut in wide or narrow noodles. Open cut rings to prevent sticking and to dry before storing. After drying for 6 to 8 hrs, store in covered jar with punctured top. These can be used in any dish calling for noodles. ½ lb noodles.

HOME-MADE NOODLES

¾ cup *plus* 2 tbsp sifted
    all-purpose flour
½ tsp salt
½ tsp baking powder

⅛ tsp poultry seasoning, if
    desired
1 large egg, beaten

Sift flour, measure and resift with remaining dry ingredients. Add gradually to beaten egg, mixing until thoroughly blended. Roll paper-thin on a floured board keeping the shape rectangular as much as possible. Allow to stand 20 min. Roll up and slice ⅛-inch wide for fine noodles or ½-inch for broad ones. Toss *lightly* to separate strands and spread out to dry for several hrs. Makes ½ lb of dried noodles. When ready to use, cook as directed, p 430.

POPPY SEED NOODLES

Drain fresh-cooked noodles quickly. Then turn into a heated bowl and drizzle with enough melted butter, or warmed sour cream, that when tossed gently, noodles will be thinly coated. Now sprinkle with poppy seed to add an interesting crunchiness and pleasing flavor. Serve at once.

SAUTÉED NOODLES

8-oz. pkg noodles

2 to 3 tbsp bacon drippings
or other fat

Cook noodles as directed, p 430, until tender, from 8 to 10 min. Drain well. Heat fat in a skillet, add noodles, and sauté, turning frequently until delicately browned. 5 to 7 servings.

STUFFED NOODLES

Something very different, but very good

1 recipe Golden Noodle
dough, p 431
2 qts good strength chicken
broth diluted with 1 pt
water
½ cup cottage cheese
3 tbsp grated American
cheese

6 tbsp fine dry bread crumbs
Red pepper
Few dashes ground
marjoram
¼ tsp grated lemon rind, if
desired
Chopped parsley

Make up noodles and roll out to a 17 to 18-inch square. Let rest and cut into 3 to 3¼-inch sqs. Have chicken broth in a 4-qt kettle on stove ready to heat. Combine cottage cheese and next 5 ingredients, and mix thoroughly. Arrange 2 tsp of mixture on one corner of noodle squares, but keep it back about ½-inch from edge. Brush edge of dough with a pastry brush dampened in cold water. Fold dough over to form triangle, and press edges together with fork tines. Heat broth to boiling, add noodles, and boil gently until dough is done—10 to 12 min. Serve immediately in soup bowls; divide broth and noodles evenly. Sprinkle chopped parsley over each bowl. Makes 20 to 24 noodles or 4 servings.

RAVIOLI WITH TOMATO SAUCE

A well-known Italian dish made easy for American cooks

Tomato Sauce, p 1261
Dough:
1½ cups all-purpose flour
¼ tsp salt
1 egg
1 tbsp soft butter
¼ cup lukewarm water
Filling:
½ cup finely chopped cooked
chicken *or* veal
½ cup finely chopped raw
spinach, pkd

¼ cup fine dry bread crumbs
3 tbsp grated fresh Parmesan
cheese, not dry pkg type
1 egg, unbeaten
¼ medium clove garlic
chopped very fine
¼ tsp salt
Dash of black pepper
Fresh grated Parmesan
cheese
½ cup fine-cut cooked chicken
or veal

Make tomato sauce.

Dough: Sift flour, measure, resift with salt into mixing bowl. Make a well in center, add egg and butter, then *gradually* add water and mix with a fork to a smooth stiff dough. Now knead dough 2 or 3 min until very smooth, then divide in half, cover and let rest 10 min.

Filling: Combine first 8 ingredients for filling and stir until thoroughly mixed. Now roll 1 portion of the dough very thin on a lightly floured pastry cloth, making it as nearly a 16-inch sq as possible. Slip it onto a large cookie sheet without disturbing the shape. Roll 2nd portion of dough out to same size and shape. With knife, lightly mark dough on pastry cloth into 2-inch sqs. Put ½ tsp of filling neatly onto center of each sq. Use narrow-edge of pastry brush wet in cold water, to brush down between filling each way. Now carefully lay dough on cookie sheet exactly over the filled dough. Then press down firmly between rows of filling each way to seal in and make square pockets. Cut apart with a knife or pastry wheel. If no pastry wheel is available, press edges of sqs together with tines of a fork. Drop half the ravioli into 2 qts rapidly boiling water, to which 2 tsp salt have been added. Boil 10 to 12 min. Lift out with slotted spoon or wide-tined food fork into colander to drain 2 or 3 min. Cook rest of ravioli and drain in same way. Serve on heated plates. Add chicken to Tomato Sauce, reheat thoroughly, spoon over ravioli and sprinkle generously with Parmesan cheese. 4 servings.

RICE

Recipes using rice and various rice dishes will be found in the related chapters. See Index for exact pages.

METHODS OF COOKING REGULAR MILLED RICE

(*Rice on market today does not need to be washed*)

CHINESE METHOD (so-called)

Measure 2⅓ cups water, 1 tsp salt and 1 cup regular milled rice into a 3-quart saucepan that has a tight-fitting cover. Bring to a boil and stir once or twice. Lower heat to simmer, cover tightly and cook without lifting cover for 20 min, being sure heat is low enough to let liquid barely simmer. Turn heat off and let stand in warm place 10 min before serving. All water will be absorbed and rice will be dry and fluffy.

OVEN METHOD

Measure 1 cup rice into a baking pan or dish which has a cover. Heat 2 cups water* and 1 tsp salt to boiling, pour over rice and stir. Cover tightly and bake at 350° F about 25 min or until rice is tender and liquid is absorbed.

* Chicken or beef broth or consommé may be used, in which case, omit salt. If parboiled or brown rice is used, increase liquid to 2½ cups and time to 45 to 50 min.

DOUBLE BOILER METHOD

Place 1 cup rice in top of double boiler with 2½ cups milk and 1 tsp salt. Heat to boiling over direct heat; then place over boiling water, cover tightly and cook 40 min or until milk is absorbed.

OLD-FASHIONED BOILED METHOD

(*not recommended as too much food value is lost*)

Measure 2 or 3 qts of boiling water into a 4-qt saucepan. Place over heat, add 2 tsp salt to each qt of water used, then drop in 1 cup rice slowly so boiling does not stop. Stir rice frequently but lightly with a fork to prevent sticking. Boil until grains of rice are soft when pressed between thumb and finger—from 15 to 20 min, the time depending on variety of rice. When done, pour rice into a colander to drain, then rinse with hot water. Now cover colander with a cloth and set the colander over a pan of hot water placed over low heat. This swells and drys the grains to make them fluffy.

To Make Rice Snowy White, add 1 tsp lemon juice, a tbsp of vinegar or ¼ teaspoon cream of tartar to the cooking water for 1 cup rice. One cup raw rice makes 3 to 4 cups cooked.

RICE COOKED IN MILK

1 cup rice   **3½ cups scalded milk**

Follow package directions for washing. Place rice, milk and 1 tsp salt in top of double boiler, cook over boiling water about 40 min, or until rice is soft and milk absorbed. This method of cooking is especially desirable for cereal for small children. 5 servings.

WILD RICE

Wash 1 cup wild rice through several cold waters until rinse water is clear. Drain and place in a large sauce pan. Add 2 qts boiling water and 1 tsp salt; boil at a moderate rate for 1 hr, or until rice is thoroughly tender, adding more boiling water as it is needed. Drain; do not rinse. This is a delicious stuffing for roast duck; or it may be buttered and served with the duck or with creamed poultry or meat.

Cheese

A taste for mild cheese is usually acquired at an early age, but a liking for the nippier cheeses often develops more gradually as one's tastes become more sophisticated. Cheese is such a valuable food, both nutritionally and socially, that an appreciation for it should be encouraged by every homemaker. The recipes in this chapter provide practical help.

CHEESE is an appealing food either eaten as is, or when it is added to a variety of other foods to contribute delicious rich flavor and pleasing texture. Since it is made principally from milk, it is one of the most valuable of foods. It contains the high-quality protein and calcium of milk in concentrated form. For example, 4 to 5 ozs of American cheese provides almost the same amount of protein and calcium as a full qt of whole milk. Other cheeses provide varying amounts depending on the fraction of milk they contain and the treatment they receive. In converting milk into cheese, there are some losses in all of the vitamins except in vitamin A. In fact, ordinary American cheese contains more vitamin A than an equivalent amount of whole milk.

The characteristic textures and flavors of the various cheeses depend on the agent used to form the curd (either rennet or lactic acid), the kind of milk (cow, goat or sheep), the amount of moisture and salt, and the kind of spices added, the size of the cheese, temp and conditions of ripening and the particular molds or bacteria which are present. Young, "unripened" cheeses, such as cottage and cream cheese, are bland in flavor and very soft. Cured cheeses are aged from a few weeks to several years before they reach their full flavor. In general, the longer they are aged, the sharper the flavor and the more characteristic the texture—dry and crumbly or almost liquid depending on the kind of cheese.

Cheese making has a history that dates back farther than any other prepared food now in use, and at one time the ingredients and methods were guarded secretly by certain localities and even by families for generations. In many cases, the exact ingredient that accounted for a typical flavor or texture was neither known nor understood . . . for example, a certain cave might have been used for ripening, and in this cave would be found all factors responsible for the cheese's individuality . . . a constant temp and humidity, and the colonies of bacteria or mold required.

Dairy scientists who have specialized in cheese making have discovered to a great extent conditions necessary for manufacture of most kinds of cheeses. At present many cheeses originally made elsewhere in the world are successfully produced in this country. In addition, America has produced several distinctive varieties not found elsewhere. The original name of the European cheese may have been altered or changed, or sizes have been reduced, but for the most part, quality has been retained in domestic reproductions. Most domestic cheeses are made from pasteurized milk, and are produced under very sanitary conditions, which is not true of all European varieties. *Table 23, page 448, answers your questions about cheese,* lists the most common domestic and European cheeses, *and* gives a hint of how they are made and suggests uses.

COOKING CHEESE

There is one rule to remember when cooking cheese—do not overcook! Cook at a low temp or for a very short time at a higher temp. Cheese cooked at too high a temp or too long becomes rubbery, stringy and flavor and texture are greatly impaired. Grated dry, aged cheese used to top "au gratin" dishes may be browned quickly at quite a high temp with no ill effects. Therefore, a double boiler, a low temp oven or a watchful eye on the broiler or hot oven are in order when cooking cheese.

The various kinds of cheddar or American cheese are the most commonly used for cooking. Almost any degree of sharpness and gradation of flavor can be found in cheeses of this type, from the mild Longhorn to the sharper Herkimer County cheese. Families vary in their preferences, but in general, a sharper, longer aged cheese contributes more flavor and a better texture to cooked dishes than a young, mild one.

CHEESE PUMPKINS FOR PIE GARNISH

Use processed yellow cheddar cheese, mild or sharp or cheese spreads that come in glasses. If cheese is firm, grate, then work with spoon or knead until plastic. Measure cheese out by level tablespoonfuls. Roll into balls, flatten them a little at both ends. Make a depression in top and bottom. Hold flattened ball in hollow of left hand, gently press edge of a flat-handled silver knife up and down into ball to simulate ridges on a pumpkin. Make sure creases meet in center of top and bottom depressions. With practice these pumpkins become quite realistic. Press a clove into center of top depression for stem. Clever edible garnishes for apple, cherry or pumpkin pie.

BAKED CHEESE DISHES

CHEESE AND SHRIMP CUSTARD

2 tbsp fine-cut onion	1⅓ cups grated American
½ cup fine-diced celery	cheese, ⅓ lb
¼ cup butter	2 eggs, beaten
4 slices bread, cubed ½-inch	1½ cups milk
½ lb cooked shrimp, p 726	½ tsp salt

Sauté onion and celery lightly in hot butter for 5 min or until soft. Add bread cubes and toss to coat lightly with butter. Turn ⅓ of bread mixture into a 6-cup greased casserole. Add ½ the shrimp, then ⅓ of the cheese; then repeat with bread, shrimp and cheese, and top with remaining bread mixture. Combine eggs, milk and salt and pour over layers, then sprinkle with rest of cheese. Bake in a moderately slow oven (325° F) 45 min. 4 servings.

CHEESE-EGG FLOAT

3 tbsp butter	½ tsp celery salt
3 tbsp flour	5 eggs
1½ cups milk	1 cup grated cheese, ¼ lb
½ tsp salt	5 slices hot toast
1 tsp grated onion	

Melt butter in saucepan, blend in flour, then add milk and seasonings, stirring constantly over low heat until sauce boils and thickens. Pour into a 10¼ x 6 x 2-inch buttered baking dish. Break eggs and slide onto hot sauce, then sprinkle with cheese. Bake in a moderately slow oven (325° F) 12 to 15 min or until eggs are of desired doneness and cheese nicely browned. Spoon carefully onto hot buttered toast. 5 servings.

CHEESE FONDUE

2 cups milk	1 tsp salt
½ lb sharp American cheese,	Dash of pepper
grated *or* cubed	3 eggs, separated
1 tbsp butter	4 slices toasted bread, cubed

Scald milk and remove from heat. Stir in cheese, butter and seasonings until cheese melts. Beat egg yolks thoroughly and slowly stir into milk mixture. Beat egg whites until just stiff, then fold cheese mixture lightly but thoroughly into them. Place toast cubes in an 8″ square or a 6 x 10 x 2-inch buttered baking dish. Pour cheese mixture over toast. Bake in a moderate oven (350° F) 25 to 30 min or until a thin, pointed knife inserted in center comes out clean. 5 servings.

CHEESE PUDDING WITH SPANISH SAUCE
Cheese Pudding

8 slices toast	3 eggs
¼ cup butter	2¼ cups milk
1 tsp chopped chives	1 tsp salt
½ lb sharp American cheese, 2 cups grated	Dash of pepper

Spread toast with butter, then cube and toss with the chives. In a buttered 6-cup casserole, make alternate layers of toast and grated cheese, topping with toast cubes. Beat eggs, stir in milk and seasonings and pour over the layers. Bake in a moderately slow oven (325° F) 1 hr.

Spanish Sauce

3 tbsp shortening	2 cups canned *or* fresh tomatoes, puréed
2 tbsp fine-cut onion	¼ tsp dry mustard
1 tbsp flour	1 tsp salt
¼ cup fine-cut green pepper	Dash of pepper
½ cup fine-cut celery	

Melt shortening, add onion and sauté until soft, then blend in flour until smooth. Add remaining ingredients and cook with constant stirring until mixture boils and thickens. Serve hot over Cheese Pudding. 4 servings.

CHEESE-RICE LOAF WITH MUSHROOM SAUCE

¼ cup butter	½ cup fine dry bread crumbs
1 cup milk	¼ cup fine-cut celery
3 eggs	2 tsp fine-cut onion
1½ cups cooked rice, ½ cup uncooked	1 tbsp each chopped parsley and green pepper
1½ cups grated sharp cheese, 6 oz	¾ tsp salt
	½ tsp prepared mustard

Melt butter in 1-qt saucepan, add milk and heat to scalding, stirring frequently. Beat eggs, add rice, cheese and crumbs, then the hot milk. Add remaining ingredients and mix well. Turn into a buttered 8¼ x 4½ x 2¾-inch loaf pan bottom lined with waxed paper to aid in removal of loaf. Bake in a moderately slow oven (325° F) 1 hr. Turn out and serve hot with piping hot Mushroom Sauce. 6 servings.

Mushroom Sauce:

¼ cup butter	1½ cups milk
½ lb mushrooms, sliced	½ cup cream
¼ cup flour	1 tsp salt

Melt butter in top of double boiler, add mushrooms, cover and sauté 5 min over direct low heat. Now sprinkle flour over mushrooms and blend until smooth. Stir in remaining ingredients. Place over boiling water and cook until mixture thickens, stirring to keep smooth. Canned mushrooms may also be used. 3 cups sauce.

CHEESE SOUFFLÉ

¼ cup butter	1½ cups milk
¼ cup flour	½ lb sharp American cheese,
1 tsp salt	grated
Dash of cayenne	6 eggs, separated
Dash of dry mustard	

Have ready 2-qt casserole—do not grease. Start oven 10 min before baking; set to slow (300° F).

Melt butter in top of double boiler over boiling water, blend in flour and seasonings until smooth. Add milk gradually and cook and stir until mixture thickens. Add cheese, cover and cook, stirring frequently until cheese is melted and well blended. Beat egg yolks thoroughly, then gradually stir hot cheese sauce into them. Now cool slightly, then lightly but thoroughly fold into egg whites, which have been beaten until stiff enough to form shiny peaks that curve at the tips. Turn carefully into casserole. Now use a teaspoon to make a track all around in the soufflé about 1-inch inside the casserole. This helps the crack to break in a more even line during baking. Place in oven with rack adjusted as near center as possible. Bake 1 hr or until puffed high and a rich golden brown. Serve at once. Tomato Sauce or broiled tomatoes go well with this soufflé. 5 to 6 servings.

CHEESE RING

2 tbsp butter	¾ tsp salt
3 tbsp flour	Dash of cayenne
1 cup milk	4 eggs, slightly beaten
¼ lb American cheese, grated	1 cup soft bread crumbs,
¼ lb Swiss cheese, grated	2 to 3 slices

Melt butter in top of a double boiler and blend in flour. Add milk gradually and cook over hot water until mixture is smooth and thick, stirring constantly. Add both kinds of cheese and seasonings and continue to cook until cheese is melted; stir occasionally. Pour gradually over eggs, and mix well. Fold in crumbs lightly but thoroughly and pour into a well-greased 4 to 5-cup ring mold that has a waxed paper lining. (See Note.) Set in a second pan of hot water, bake in moderate oven (350° F) 30 min. Turn out, fill center with creamed vegetables or fish, or buttered vegetables. 5 servings.

Note: To line a ring mold, place the bottom of the mold on a piece of plain white paper, outline the outer edge and inner hole. Cut out and snip around both edges of the paper ring so that the snipped paper will slightly overlap to fit snugly against rounded bottom side. Grease mold first, fit in paper and grease paper.

PIZZA

Crusty French Bread
Dough, p 267
Salad oil
2 six oz cans tomato paste,
basil flavored
or No. 2 can tomatoes
or 6 medium fresh
tomatoes
Sweet basil

½ lb cheese—Mozzarella,
cheddar or Swiss
¼ lb cooked lean ham
or ½ lb Italian garlic
sausage
or ¾ lb pork link sausage
½ cup chopped onion
2 oz grated Romano cheese
Salt, pepper, orégano

Prepare dough for Crusty French Bread. Let rise until it doubles in bulk and has a slightly sour, yeasty odor. Cut into 4 portions, cover, let rest 10 min. Roll out into 8-inch circles. Lift into pie pans. Press out gently until it is uniformly ¼ inch thick in bottom and slightly thicker on sides. Brush dough with salad oil. Quickly spread tomato paste or tomatoes over bottom. Sprinkle ⅛ tsp sweet basil over canned or fresh tomatoes. Sprinkle in grated cheese, then the slivers of ham or half-cooked sausage, the onion and last the grated Romano cheese. Use pastry brush to pat thin film of salad oil over top. Sprinkle with salt, pepper, and about ¾ tsp of crumbled oregano. Bake immediately in a hot oven (450° F) until thoroughly done, about 20 min. Serve blistering hot, cut in wedges. 4 to 6 servings.

POLENTA

An inexpensive, hearty Mexican 1-dish meal

1 qt boiling water
1 tsp salt
1 cup yellow corn meal
1 cup fresh-grated Parmesan
cheese

2 tbsp milk
½ cup corn meal
½ cup shortening

Measure water into top of double boiler, add salt and slowly sift in the 1 cup of meal, stirring constantly to keep smooth. Cover, place over gently boiling water and cook 1 hr, stirring often. Remove from heat and stir in cheese until melted. Pour immediately into 2 greased 9-inch cake or pie pans. Cool until firm enough to cut. Just before serving, cut into pie-shaped pieces; dip pieces in milk, then in corn meal to coat. Heat shortening in heavy skillet until hot but not smoking, lay in Polenta and fry until golden and crisp—about 10 min to each side. Serve plain with crisp bacon or Tomato Sauce, p 1261. 4 servings.

TOMATO CHEESE FONDUE

1 cup tomato juice
1 cup coarse soft bread
   crumbs
1 cup sharp American cheese,
   grated, ¼ lb

1 tbsp butter, melted
½ tsp salt
4 eggs, separated

Pour tomato juice over bread crumbs and let stand until well soaked. Stir in cheese, melted butter and salt. Beat egg yolks thoroughly and stir into bread crumb mixture. Beat egg whites until stiff and fold in lightly but thoroughly. Turn into buttered 6-cup casserole, and bake in a moderate oven (325° F) 45 min to 1 hr, or until a sharp knife inserted in the center comes out clean. 5 servings.

See Recipes for CROQUETTES—RICE AND CHEESE and
HOMINY AND CHEESE, p 502 and 503

MACARONI AND NOODLE DISHES

BAKED MACARONI AND CHEESE NO. 1

Has what it takes to make it a satisfying meat alternate

8-oz pkg macaroni
3 tbsp butter *or* margarine
2 tbsp flour
3 cups milk
2 egg yolks
2 cups grated cheddar cheese,
   ½ lb

½ tsp salt
   Few dashes pepper
2 tsp chopped parsley *or*
   chives
2 tsp chopped pimiento, opt
¼ cup fine dry bread crumbs

Drop short length macaroni into 2 qts boiling water to which 2 tsp salt are added. Boil about 15 min or until tender, p 430. Drain and rinse in cold water. Let macaroni cool. Meanwhile melt butter in saucepan, blend in flour. Then add milk gradually, stirring constantly and boiling gently to a smooth thickened sauce. Remove from heat. Beat egg yolks, add a little of the hot sauce, stir well, then return to saucepan with 1½ cups of the cheese. Stir until cheese just melts. Then stir in salt, pepper, parsley and pimiento. Fold in macaroni. Turn into buttered glass baking dish 8″ x 8″ x 2″. Toss remaining cheese with crumbs and sprinkle over top. Place in hot oven (450° F) and bake 10 to 12 min or until mixture bubbles and top is browned appetizingly. Serves 4 to 5.

A wonderful place to use leftover chicken and roasts, cut fine.

BAKED MACARONI AND CHEESE NO. 2

A 1-dish meal welcomed by most everyone when well-made—and don't skimp on the cheese

3 qts boiling water	½ lb sharp American cheese
1 tbsp salt	*or* ½ lb tangy Cheese Food,
7 or 8-oz pkg macaroni	crumbled
Salt	1 large *or* 2 small eggs
3 tbsp butter	1¾ cups milk

Heat water to boiling in a 4-qt saucepan, add salt, then macaroni and boil uncovered from 8 to 20 min or until tender, the time depending on brand of macaroni. Stir and lift up macaroni with fork occasionally to prevent sticking. Turn into a colander to drain, then run hot water through macaroni to rinse well. Arrange ⅓ of macaroni in a buttered 8-cup casserole, sprinkle lightly with salt, then dot with ⅓ of the butter, then sprinkle with ⅓ the grated cheese. Repeat with macaroni, butter and cheese until all are used. Beat egg, stir in milk and pour over the macaroni. Press macaroni gently down with fork until liquid comes up over top layer. Add a little more milk, if necessary. Bake in a moderately slow oven (325° F) 30 to 40 min or until bubbly and top is a tempting golden brown. Serve hot. 5 servings.

QUICK BAKED MACARONI AND CHEESE

3 qts boiling water	2 tbsp flour
1 tbsp salt	2 cups milk
7 or 8-oz pkg macaroni	1 tsp salt
2 tbsp butter	½ lb sharp American cheese

Heat water to boiling in a 4-qt saucepan, add salt and macaroni and boil 8 to 20 min, the time depending on the macaroni. Stir frequently with a fork to prevent sticking. Drain in a colander, then run hot water through to rinse well. Melt butter in top of double boiler over boiling water, blend in flour and add milk gradually, stirring until sauce is smooth and thick. Add salt and grated cheese, and stir until cheese melts. Arrange hot macaroni and cheese sauce in layers in a 6-cup buttered casserole. Bake in a moderately hot oven (400° F) until toasted on top, 10 to 15 min. 5 servings.

BAKED MACARONI LOAF

8-oz pkg long macaroni	1 tbsp chopped pimiento
1 tbsp salt	3 eggs, beaten
2 qts boiling water	1½ cups milk
1 tbsp chopped green pepper	1½ cups dry bread crumbs
2 tbsp chopped onion	½ tsp salt
½ cup finely chopped celery	½ lb American cheese, grated
¼ cup butter	

Dip ends of macaroni into boiling salted water, pushing rest in as ends soften. Cook uncovered until tender, about 20 min, occasionally lifting macaroni gently with a fork to prevent sticking. Drain, rinse with hot water. Sauté pepper, onion and celery in butter in a saucepan 1 min. Stir in next 6 ingredients. Lay ¼ of macaroni in lengthwise layers in greased loaf pan 8¼ x 4½ x 2¾ inches. Pour in ¼ of cheese mixture. Repeat until all ingredients are used. Bake in moderate oven (325° F) 1 hr. Turn out on a platter, serve with piping hot Tomato Sauce (p 1261). 6 servings.

Variation: Bake in buttered ring mold, turn out and serve with creamed vegetables, chicken or tuna.

JIFFY NOODLES

8 oz pkg broad noodles	⅓ cup chili sauce
2 tsp salt	¼ cup melted butter
1½ cups grated sharp Ameri-	Salt to taste
can cheese, ⅜ lb	Parsley

Drop noodles into 2 qts rapidly boiling water, add salt and boil rapidly until tender, about 10 min. Drain thoroughly and turn hot noodles into a hot serving dish. Add next 4 ingredients and toss gently like a salad until cheese melts. Garnish with parsley. Serve immediately. Spaghetti or macaroni may be used in place of noodles. 5 servings.

LASAGNE

A popular Italian hub-of-the-meal dish with exciting flavor and rich nutrients

Tomato-Meat Sauce:	¼ tsp oregano, pkd
2 tbsp olive oil	Filling:
1 medium clove garlic	2 qts boiling water
⅓ cup chopped celery	2 tsp salt
½ lb ground beef chuck	7 oz pkg broad noodles
2 cups canned tomatoes	¼ lb Mozzarella or Scamorze
3 tbsp tomato paste	cheese
1½ tsp salt	6 oz Ricotta cheese, ¾ cup
¹⁄₁₆ tsp black pepper	⅓ cup freshly grated
	Parmesan cheese, 1 oz

Put olive oil in a 3-qt saucepan. Add peeled, finely chopped garlic and celery and sauté until soft and yellow. Add meat, stir with fork to separate; cook until meat is a gray color. Add next 5 ingredients. Stir, cover and *simmer* 1 hr, stirring occasionally. About 20 min before sauce is done, start to cook filling. Heat water to boiling, add salt and noodles; boil briskly 7 to 8 min or until noodles are tender. Drain noodles in colander. Meanwhile finely dice Mozzarella cheese; press Ricotta through a coarse sieve and coarsely grate Parmesan. Turn ¼ of the Tomato-Meat Sauce into a buttered 10 x 6 x 2-inch glass baking dish; add a layer of

⅓ of the noodles, sprinkle diced Mozzarella over noodles; add another layer of noodles and the Ricotta; now add ¼ more of the sauce. Add rest of noodles and sprinkle Parmesan over top. Bake in a moderate oven (375° F) 15 to 20 min, or until cheese browns and exposed noodles are slightly crisp. Serve at once, cut into squares with rest of reheated Tomato-Meat Sauce over top. 4 servings.

QUICK MACARONI MEAL

¼ cup fine-cut celery
2 tsp fine-cut green pepper
2 tsp fine-cut onion
¼ cup butter *or* margarine
¼ cup flour
2 cups milk

6 oz sharp American cheese, 1½ cups, grated
¾ tsp salt
¾ tsp Worcestershire
¼ tsp dry mustard
8 oz pkg macaroni, cooked
½ lb thin-sliced cooked ham

Sauté vegetables lightly in butter in top of double boiler 5 min over direct heat. Remove vegetables and blend flour into butter remaining in pan. Add milk gradually and cook and stir until mixture thickens and is smooth. Now stir in cheese, salt, Worcestershire and mustard. Then place over boiling water and cook slowly until cheese melts, stirring often. Drain freshly cooked macaroni; rinse with boiling water. Drain well, then turn onto hot platter. Top with sautéed vegetables; pour hot cheese sauce over all. Garnish with hot frizzled ham and serve at once. 4 servings.

SAUCES, RABBITS,* AND SPREADS

BASIC CHEESE SAUCE

3 tbsp butter, melted
¼ cup flour
2 cups milk
⅜ tsp salt

½ lb sharp American cheese cut in ½-inch cubes
1 tsp lemon juice, if desired

Melt butter in top of double boiler over direct heat. Blend in flour, add milk gradually and cook over boiling water until thick. Stir constantly to keep smooth. Add salt and cheese and cover and continue to cook over hot water until cheese is melted. Stir occasionally. Stir in lemon juice. Serve hot over toast with bacon or ham, or use as a cheese sauce for cooked vegetables.

Variations: 1. Add ½ cup sliced ripe or stuffed olives and heat thoroughly. Pour hot sauce over slices of either tomato, hard-cooked egg, turkey, or chicken arranged on hot buttered toast.

2. Add ½ cup raisins, heat thoroughly and pour over hot, freshly cooked vegetables such as broccoli or cauliflower.

*Also erroneously spelled and pronounced "Rarebit."

3. Pour hot sauce over hot Rice Croquettes, p 503, top with jelly.

4. When cheese is melted, pour a small amount of hot mixture over 1 beaten egg. Mix thoroughly and return to hot mixture. Continue to cook for 2 min, stirring constantly. Serve hot over toast.

CHEESE CHICKEN DELUXE

1 tbsp butter	1 cup grated sharp American
1 tbsp flour	cheese, ¼ lb
1 tsp dry mustard	1 egg, beaten
½ tsp salt	½ lb thinly sliced, cold,
⅛ tsp paprika	cooked chicken
1¼ cups milk	Parsley

Melt butter in top of double boiler over boiling water. Blend in flour and seasonings and gradually add milk, stirring constantly. Continue to cook over boiling water until mixture is smooth and thickened. Stir to keep smooth. Add cheese, cover and let stand over hot (not boiling) water until cheese is melted and well blended. Stir occasionally. Slowly add part of the hot mixture to egg, stir to mix well and return to double boiler. Cook for 2 min longer, stirring. Remove from heat but keep over hot water. Split and toast buns; arrange chicken slices on top, pour cheese sauce over all. Garnish with dash of paprika, a sprig of parsley, serve immediately. 4 servings.

CHEESE HAM BAKE

Handsome, palatable, fine for using leftover ham

2 tsp butter	1 tsp finely chopped parsley
8 slices enriched bread	1½ cups aged, grated American
1⅓ cups ground cooked ham,	cheese, 6 oz
boiled *or* baked—½ lb	1½ cups milk
1½ tsp prepared mustard *or*	3 eggs, slightly beaten
½ tsp dry mustard mixed	¼ tsp salt
with 1 tbsp milk	1/16 tsp pepper

Butter an eight-inch glass baking dish. Trim crusts from bread and fit 4 slices into dish. Combine ham with either kind of mustard and parsley, and mix thoroughly. Spread ham evenly on half the bread; then sprinkle cheese evenly over ham. Top with remaining four slices of bread which have been cut in half diagonally. Use a sharp knife to cut through ham-cheese mixture and the lower slice of bread. Combine milk with eggs, add seasonings, stir thoroughly, and pour mixture slowly over bread so that entire surface of bread is wet with mixture. Let stand one-half hr for bread to absorb all liquid. Bake in a moderately slow oven (325° F) 50 to 60 min. Remove dish to chop plate. Garnish center with sprig of crisp parsley and serve immediately. 4 generous servings.

CHEESE TOASTIES

½ lb sharp American cheese, grated	6 hamburger buns
1 tsp prepared mustard	Soft butter
2 to 4 tbsp milk	Pan-broiled bacon, p 855
Dash of salt	Tomato slices
	Water cress

Measure first 4 ingredients into a mixing bowl, then mix well. Split buns in half, toast or not, as desired, then spread cut surfaces with butter, then with cheese mixture. Place under broiler and toast until cheese is puffy and golden brown. Garnish with hot bacon, a tomato slice and a sprig of cress. Serve hot. 6 servings.

Note: Cheese toasties made with thick slices of French or Vienna bread, or split Vienna rolls are a delicious accompaniment for salad luncheons. The use of Parmesan cheese is another excellent variation.

CHEESE-TOMATO SANDWICH SPREAD

A versatile spread for many types of sandwiches, appetizers or snacks

2 tbsp each of fine-cut green pepper and onion	1 lb sharp American cheese cut into small cubes
10½ oz can condensed tomato soup	1½ tsp Worcestershire
½ tsp salt	Pepper
	2 eggs, well beaten

Combine first 5 ingredients in top of double boiler and cook over hot water until cheese melts, stirring frequently. Combine next 3 ingredients, and stir in some of the hot cheese mixture, then return to double boiler and cook 2 min longer, stirring constantly. Remove from heat and cool. This mixture stored in a clean, tightly covered container in the refrigerator keeps several days. About 3½ cups.

When ready to make sandwiches, place 1 slice of boiled or baked ham and a generous portion of cold slaw, mixed with mayonnaise, between each 2 slices of toast. Spread tops of sandwiches generously with Cheese Spread. Toast under broiler until lightly browned. Serve immediately. This Spread may be used on single slices of bread for toasted open-face sandwiches.

CORN AND CHEESE RABBIT

2 tbsp chopped green pepper	11-oz can (1 cup) cream style corn
2 tbsp chopped onion	
1 tbsp butter	½ lb cheese, diced
½ tsp salt	½ tsp Worcestershire
Dash of pepper	2 eggs, beaten
⅛ tsp paprika	Toast
⅔ cup milk	10 slices frizzled dried beef, p 835

Sauté green pepper and onion in butter until soft over direct heat in top of double boiler. Add seasonings, milk and corn, and simmer 10 min. Place over boiling water and stir in cheese and Worcestershire sauce. When cheese is melted and well blended, gradually stir a small amount of the hot mixture into beaten eggs. Mix well and return to cheese mixture in double boiler, and cook 2 min longer, stirring constantly. Serve on toast, garnish with parsley and slices of hot frizzled beef. 5 servings.

PIMIENTO CHEESE

1 lb longhorn cheese
4-oz can pimientoes

½ cup Special Salad Dressing, p 1206

Grate the cheese. Drain pimientos, chop, and add to cheese. Add dressing and blend together thoroughly. Chill before using. Serve on lettuce or cabbage as salad, as a sandwich spread, or as stuffing for celery. About 1 qt.

TOMATO RABBIT

2 tbsp butter
3 tbsp flour
¾ cup milk
1 cup grated sharp cheese,
  ¼ lb
1 tsp sugar

1 tsp salt
½ cup canned *or* fresh
  tomatoes, puréed
5 slices buttered toast
5 slices pan-broiled bacon

Melt butter in top of double boiler over boiling water. Blend in flour and stir constantly while adding milk, then continue to stir until sauce thickens. Stir in grated cheese, sugar, salt, cover and allow cheese to melt, stirring occasionally. Add puréed tomatoes gradually, stirring to mix well. Serve immediately on hot buttered toast. Garnish with crisp bacon. 5 servings.

WELSH RABBIT

¾ cup thin cream
½ lb American cheese, cut
  into small cubes
½ tsp salt
Dash of cayenne

¼ tsp prepared mustard
1 egg, slightly beaten
Toast
Paprika

Combine cream and cheese in top of double boiler. Add salt, cayenne and mustard. Cook over hot water (not boiling) until cheese is melted, stirring occasionally. Gradually add some of the hot sauce to egg, stir well and return to double boiler. Cook for 1 or 2 min until sauce thickens, stirring constantly. Pour over hot toast, dash with paprika and serve immediately. Makes about 1 cup. A thick slice of tomato, crisp bacon, or slices of frizzled ham make appropriate edible garnishes. 4 or 5 servings.

TABLE 23   THE ANSWERS TO YOUR QUESTIONS ABOUT CHEESE

Name of Cheese	Where Manufactured	Kind of Milk and Special Agents or Ingredients Added	Conditioning and Flavor	Color and Other Characteristics	Uses
American Cheddar Longhorn Prints Daisies Flats Twins "Coon Cured" Herkimer County	Originated in America if sold under these names. Principally in United States and Canada. Wisconsin and New York produce most (90%) of this nation's supply.	Whole Milk Rennet	Aged for more pronounced flavor from 2 or 3 months to 2 years. Young cheeses are mild; aged cheese sharp.	Pale yellow to deep orange. Firm, even texture when young. Aged cheese has more tendency to crumble. Various forms, depending on type, but all are either round flat cakes or cylinders of different size.	Versatile. Can be used plain, toasted or in cooked foods in a great variety of ways. Aged cheeses best for cooking.
Bleu or Blue Vein	Domestic version of Roquefort except that it is made from cow's milk. See Roquefort.				
Brick	Originated in America and mostly made here.	Whole Milk Rennet	Ripened for a mild sweet flavor for at least 8 weeks. If cured longer, has a more pronounced flavor.	Light straw color. Moist, soft, slightly elastic.	Excellent for sandwiches and appetizers. If aged, also served with crackers for dessert.
Brie	Originated in France, now also made in America.	Whole milk or partly skimmed. Rennet. Mold-ripened.	Stored until surface is covered with mold (8 days), then ripened from 2 to 4 weeks until pronounced odor and sharp characteristic flavor developed.	Red color on surface. Interior varies from waxy to semi-liquid. (Similar to Camembert.)	Served mainly with crackers as appetizer or dessert, or with salads.
Camembert	France originally, now also made in America.	Whole Milk. Rennet. Mold-ripened.	Ripened for 4 to 6 weeks to develop the characteristic odor and flavor.	Greyish outside rind, light yellow, color inside. Waxy to semi-liquid when fully cured.	With crackers as appetizer or dessert, or with salads.

	Origin	Ripening	Milk	Characteristics	Uses
Cheddar	Orginal process started in Cheddar, England. A modification of this process is used to make American cheese.				
Cheshire	Cheddar-type cheese originally made in Chester, England. Colored deep yellow with annatto and usually ripened for an extended period to develop a sharp flavor.				
Cottage Cheese often called Dutch Cheese Schmeerkäse	Made extensively in America. Made on farms all over the world for immediate use. Also made commercially here.	Not ripened. Very perishable, needs same care as fresh milk. (If cream is added, it is called "creamed cottage cheese.")	Skimmed Milk. Lactic acid cultures.	Soft white fluffy curds. Very mild.	Eaten as is, or in salads or used in cooking to make cheese cake, custards, etc.
Cream Cheese	America	Not ripened. Very perishable. Needs same care as fresh milk. Most sanitary if bought factory-wrapped or in jars.	Thick sour cream or Milk with cream added. Lactic acid cultures.	Soft, white, creamy. Mild and rich.	Versatile. Can be served plain with crackers or used in salads, sandwiches, cheese cake, pies, and as topping for fruit and other desserts.
Edam Also called Block Edam	Originated in Netherlands. Now also made in America.	Ripened for 3 weeks to 3 months. Flavor is similar to Cheddar and becomes sharper and more pronounced with longer aging.	Skimmed milk. Rennet.	Round ball with red outer coating. Firm, slightly crumbly, semi-hard. Softer types are similar to brick cheese.	Appetizers, desserts, salads, or grated for flavoring.
Emmenthaler	The original Swiss type cheese made in Emmental, Switzerland. See Swiss.				
English Dairy	Cheddar type, harder than American with a sharper flavor. Grates well and particularly desirable for au gratin dishes.				
Gorganzola	Italian version of Roquefort type except that it is made from cow's milk. In this country made the same as Blue Cheese.				
Gouda	Netherlands originally, now also made in America.	Ripened 6 to 8 weeks to develop a slightly sweet nut-like flavor.	Whole milk or partly skimmed. Rennet.	Red coated, round ball. Golden color inside. (Baby Gouda is bun-shaped.)	Sandwiches, appetizers, desserts, salads, grated for flavoring.

Name of Cheese	Where Manufactured	Kind of Milk and Special Agents or Ingredients Added	Conditioning and Flavor	Color and Other Characteristics	Uses
Gruyère	Emmenthaler type of cheese made in France. Name originated from Gruyère, Switzerland. Now also made in America.	Usually partly skimmed milk. Skimmed and whole milk also used.	Similar to Swiss. Mildly salty, nut-like flavor.	Circular cake or individual wedge portions wrapped in foil. Firm texture.	Appetizers, desserts, salads, on crackers.
Hand	Originated in Germany, now made in America and all other countries where Germanic races are.	Skim milk plus buttermilk. Natural souring. Caraway sometimes added.	Originally shaped by hand which accounts for the name. Ripened until very sharp and pungent odor and taste develop.	All variety of shapes and sizes. Fairly firm texture.	This cheese is enjoyed principally only by those accustomed to eating it.
Hvid Gjedeost	Orginated in Norway.	Goat's milk.	European cheese made primarily for local consumption. Rather uncommon in America.	Chocolate brown, too hard to be sliced.	Shaved thin and served with very hard crackers.
Italian Cheese Salame Provoloni Provoloncinni Provolette Cacio Cavallo and others	There are more than 20 types of Italian cheese made in Wisconsin alone. Many are cured or smoked to give a salty, tangy flavor. They are all made by practically the same method, the difference being in shape and age. Used for table use when fresh, but more commonly used for flavoring soups, salads, macaroni, etc., after considerable aging. Made from cow's milk and in some localities buffalo milk. They are molded into a variety of shapes by hand.				
Jack	Originated in Monterey, California.	Similar in manufacture and use to American cheese. It is not colored. Made and sold only in California under this name. Ripened for 3 weeks.			
Liederkranz	Manufactured in Ohio under a copyright.	Ripened by red-mold growth on surface. Somewhat resembles Limburg.			

Limburg	Originated in Belgium, then made in Germany, Austria and now in America.	Whole sweet milk. Rennet. Bacteria ripened.	Ripened for 2 or 3 months during which a reddish brown rind forms on brick and pungent flavor develops.	Soft textured. If rind is removed, much of the odor is lost.	Sandwich spread, on crackers, appetizer, dessert. (Recommend it with potatoes boiled in jackets.)
Loaf Cheese	See footnote (1). Same as process cheese.				
Muenster	Originated in Germany, a limited quantity is made in America.	Whole milk. Rennet. Caraway or anise usually added.	Ripened 2 or 3 months to develop pronounced flavor. Mild when fresh.	Soft, light tan color. Outside brown or red.	Sandwich spread, appetizers, desserts.
Mysost also called Primost	Originated in Norway, Sweden and Denmark. Now made to a limited extent in America.	Whey.	Not ripened. Molded into desired forms. Unique sweetish taste, very mild.	Light brown color, buttery consistency.	Spread for crackers, appetizer, dessert.
Neufchatel	Originated in France, now also made in America.	Made like cream cheese except that it is made from whole or skim milk. Used as base for some cheese spreads such as pimiento.			
Nokkelost also called Spiced Leyden	Originated in Norway.	Similar to Edam with caraway seed added.			
Parmesan	Originated in Lombardy, Italy. (A similar cheese but of better quality is made in Emilia, Italy, called Regianno.)	Skimmed milk.	Ripened for 1 to 4 years until hard and dry.	Exterior is dark green or black. Very hard, excellent for grating.	Used in soups, salads, macaroni, etc.

(1) Processed cheeses are the heated (pasteurized) and blended products made from one or more lots of cheese. The ripened cheeses are ground together, or are cut into cubes and a small quantity of emulsifier added. Then the mixture is heated with constant stirring to the desired consistency. It is then poured into suitable molds, cubes, boxes, etc., and generally wrapped in foil or some other protective paper. In this way a more plastic cheese is obtained that has resistance to mold development as long as it is not unwrapped. All processed cheeses are somewhat similar in texture and plasticity and usually are milder in odor and flavor than the original cheeses from which they are made.

Name of Cheese	Where Manufactured	Kind of Milk and Special Agents or Ingredients Added	Conditioning and Flavor	Color and Other Characteristics	Uses
Pear also called Scarmorze	Originated in Italy, now also made in America.	Buffalo milk. Rennet.	Hand shaped, comes in pairs.	Light tan in color	Sliced ¼ inch thick crossways and fried in olive oil.
Primost	See Mysost.				
Pineapple	Originated in Connecticut.	Whole milk. Rennet.	Ripened for several months, surface rubbed with oil to make it smooth and hard. Made like American only heated longer.	Shaped like a pineapple with diamond-shaped corrugations on surface. Hard cheese, bright yellow color.	Sandwiches, appetizers, dessert, on crackers.
Ricotta	Originated in central Europe, now made in America.	Whey may have skimmed milk added.	Salty taste.	Pure white, small rounds with flat top.	Used in soups, salads, macaroni, etc.
Romano	Originated in Italy, now also made in America.	Similar to Parmesan and used for same purpose. Made from sheep's milk or cow's milk depending on where made.			
Roquefort	Originated in France, now also made here from cow's milk as Bleu cheese.	Sheep's milk. Rennet. Mold-ripened.	Layers of cheese and dry, ground bread crumbs (specially baked and allowed to mold for 4 to 6 weeks) are salted and ripened for 1 to 5 months to develop salty flavor. Holes are punched through cake to promote interior mold growth.	Soft uncolored, open textured with streaks of blue-green mold mottled throughout interior. Crumbly when fully aged. Large cakes or individual wedges.	Salads, desserts, appetizers, on crackers.

Sage	Originated in America in the New England states.	Cheddar or American cheese is made according to the regular process except that green sage leaves are mixed with the curd to give a mottled green appearance and a characteristic sage flavor. At present, sage extract is used for flavor, and green corn ground and used for the mottled appearance.	
Sap Sago	Originated in Switzerland.	Sour skim milk with buttermilk and whey added. Natural souring.	Ripened 3 to 6 weeks, then ground and mixed with an aromatic species of clover, which gives it its characteristic flavor.	Hard green cheese, usually grated.	Sprinkled on bread or crackers, Appetizers, Salads, Desserts.
Stilton	Originated in England.	Whole milk with cream added. Rennet.	Similar to Roquefort and Gorgonzola. Ripened about 2 years to have the best piquant flavor.	Often ground and put into glass jars. Characteristic blue-green mold throughout interior.	Same as Roquefort.
Swiss	Originated in Switzerland, now made in every civilized country.	Whole milk. Lactic acid bacteria of bulgaricus group added. Rennet.	Cheese cake is soaked in brine solution about 3 days, then ripened for 3 to 6 months to develop characteristic sweet or salty flavor, (ripened 6 to 10 months or longer in Switzerland). During ripening, gas bubbles developed which form holes or "eyes" in the cheese.	Firm bodied cheese with well developed "eyes." Domestic products compare very favorably to imported in spite of general prejudice to the contrary. Usually in large round cakes.	Sandwiches, appetizers, dessert. In cooking. When dry can be grated over soups, salads, and other main dishes.

Cookies

Just the mention of cookies brings back happy childhood memories to most folks, for cookies seem to have been invented especially for children. Most likely, Grandma made her reputation for cookies with a single recipe. But today, even a bride can make a dozen different kinds of cookies that would make Grandpa gasp, if she studies this chapter carefully. These recipes will help your favorite small boys and girls build up a marvelous store of cookie memories.

COOKIE VARIETIES

BY definition, *Cookies are Small, Flat, Sweet Cakes.* They may be crisp, soft, thick, thin, dark, light, plain, full of fruit and nuts, frosted, filled or decorated. Whichever way cookies are made, and whatever the kind or cost, people of all ages enjoy them—especially when they are homemade. The cookies in this Chapter belong to 8 types, which are as follows:

1. *Bar Cookies.* Made from soft dough, spread or pressed out in a baking pan, then baked and cut into bars.

2. *Drop Cookies.* Made from soft dough, then dropped in desired size from a spoon onto a baking sheet, then baked.

3. *Meringue Cookies.* Made from a mixture requiring no flour. Egg whites are beaten stiff with sugar, then nuts, fruit or cereal flakes are folded in, then dropped from a spoon onto baking sheet and baked.

4. *Molded or Stamped Cookies.* Made from moderately soft dough that can be molded into balls, then stamped out with the bottom of a wet, cloth-covered glass, or with tines of a fork, or shaped into crescents with the hands, then baked.

5. *Pressed Cookies.* Made from rich dough that is put into a Cookie Gun, then pressed out to form definite shapes which remain after baking.

6. *Refrigerator (Ice Box) Cookies.* Made from moderately stiff dough and shaped into rolls or bars, thoroughly chilled, then sliced with a sharp knife and baked.

7. *Rolled Cookies.* Made from moderately stiff dough—sometimes chilled; then rolled and cut out into desired shapes before baking.

8. *Holiday Cookies.* Made from any of the above types of dough, then shaped or cut into some traditional form, then decorated and baked, or

baked then decorated. Many of these cookies originated in foreign lands and are made during the Holiday Season only.

CAUTIONS

1. The term "soft butter" means butter at room temperature—about 70° F.
2. Increase flour or decrease liquid a little when making cookies in the South.

QUALITY OF COOKIES DEPENDS ON INGREDIENTS

Cookies require good fresh ingredients. Butter makes the most delicious cookies because of its flavor; margarine also makes very good cookies, and by slightly increasing the salt and other flavoring, excellent results can be obtained with vegetable shortening or bland lard. All-purpose rather than cake flour is generally used. Use fresh eggs and milk, and nuts sweet and free from rancidity. Use moist raisins or other dried or candied fruits, or steam them if dry to regain their normal moistness. Use fresh extracts and spices. It is unfortunate that some cooks think baking is a grand way to utilize bits of fruit, nuts, milk, eggs or shortening no longer suitable for table use. No cookie is better than the quality of any ingredient that goes into it.

MIXING COOKIES

Mixing of cookies will move quickly and easily if you follow the system outlined in the Recipes in this Chapter. This system is as follows:

1. *Collect all ingredients* and utensils. Have shortening, eggs and milk at room temperature. However, *in very warm weather,* use these ingredients directly from the refrigerator.

2. *Prepare baking pans*—grease, flour, or line with waxed paper as recipe directs.

3. *Chop nuts,* cut fruit, melt chocolate, etc.

4. *Measure all ingredients.* And sift dry ingredients together from 1 to 4 times for good distribution of leavening and spices.

5. *Combine ingredients* to make the dough as outlined in recipe. All cookie doughs are relatively soft—a soft dough produces the tenderest cookies. Use as little flour on pastry cloth or dough board for rolling and cutting as possible. In very warm weather, chill dough before rolling, dropping or molding to make it firmer, less sticky and easy to handle without adding more flour.

PLACING COOKIES ON BAKING SHEET

(Place cookies at least 1 inch from edge of baking sheet to prevent scorching.)

1. *Drop Cookies.* Measure the dough uniformly and drop from spoon

into neat mounds of same height so all bake done in same length of time. Drop the distance apart suggested in recipe so they will not run together.

2. Molded or Stamped Cookies. Measure dough and mold or stamp uniformly thick on cookie sheet for all cookies to bake done in same length of time.

3. Refrigerator Cookies. Slice cookies uniformly thick so all bake done in same length of time.

4. Rolled Cookies. A *Pastry Cloth and Stockinet-covered Rolling Pin* are a great help in rolling cookie dough, and the cookies are more easily removed than from a dough board. Roll dough uniformly thick so all cookies bake done in the same length of time. Use a wide-bladed spatula to lift cookies from *Pastry Cloth* to baking sheet immediately after cutting.

BAKE COOKIES ON A SHEET RIGHT SIZE FOR OVEN

Caution: Do not use a baking sheet too large for your oven for best heat circulation. A 15½- by 11-inch baking sheet is the best size for a 16- by 18-inch oven, and a 16½- by 14-inch sheet is better for a larger oven. Cookies bake best on a rimless pan.

1. Bake only 1 sheet of cookies at a time in an average-size oven, and at the temperature specified in the recipe. Start checking for doneness a minute or two before stated baking time expires.

2. Remove baking sheet from oven to a cake rack the *instant the desired color* is obtained. For easy removal of cookies from baking sheet, note in recipe the time indicated they should remain on sheet before removing. Use a wide-bladed spatula to loosen cookies, then slide them onto cake rack.

STORING AND "RESTORING" COOKIES

Store cookies in a suitable container—a tightly-covered cookie jar of pottery, glass or china, or a tin box with a tight-fitting lid. Store only one kind of cookie in the jar at a time, and wash jar thoroughly between bakings so there will be no interchange of flavors. Should cookies become soft after storing, restore crispness by placing on an ungreased baking sheet in a slow oven (300° F.) for 3 to 5 minutes. Cool thoroughly before storing.

BAR COOKIES

Bar Cookies are baked in a layer, then cut into squares or oblongs, such as Brownies. They are easy to make as dough is spread or pressed into a greased pan, then baked. After baking, cookies may be frosted, sprinkled with xxxx sugar or left plain, then cut. This type of cookie is best eaten fresh. For best keeping, do not cut until ready to serve, but leave in baking pan and wrap well.

BROWNIES

A quickly made de luxe cookie

½ cup butter *or* margarine	2 eggs
2 sq unsweet chocolate	1 cup sugar
¾ cup all-purpose flour	1 tsp vanilla
¼ tsp D.A. baking powder *or*	¾ cup chopped nuts
⅓ tsp tartrate *or* phosphate type, optional	

Lightly grease an 11 x 7 x 1½-inch or 9-inch square pan. Start oven 10 min before baking; set to moderate (350° F). Put butter and chocolate in top of double boiler, place over hot—not boiling—water to melt. When melted, stir thoroughly, then cool. Sift flour, measure, resift 3 times with baking powder. With rotary beater, beat eggs until thick and fluffy, add sugar in 3 portions, beating well after each, then beat in chocolate and vanilla. Remove beater; use wooden spoon. Stir in flour mixture, then nuts. Turn into prepared pan and spread evenly. Bake 20 min—*do not overbake.* Remove from oven to cake rack, and while hot, mark into squares with tip of sharp pointed knife to obtain clean-cut edges. Cool in pan on rack, then finish cutting squares just before serving. To store, leave brownies in pan and wrap in waxed paper to keep moist. 16 squares.

BLOND OR BUTTERSCOTCH BROWNIES

A moist, chewy nut-filled cookie with rich butterscotch flavor

¾ cup all-purpose flour	1 cup brown sugar, packed
¼ tsp D.A. baking powder	2 eggs, beaten
½ tsp salt	½ tsp vanilla
½ cup butter *or* margarine	¾ cup walnuts *or* pecans

Grease an 8 x 8 x 2-inch pan. Start oven 10 min before baking; set to moderate (350° F). Sift flour, measure, resift with baking powder and salt. Melt butter in a 1-qt saucepan over low heat, add sugar and stir with wooden spoon until smooth, then remove from heat. Cool slightly, then beat in eggs until well blended. Beat in vanilla, then flour mixture until smooth. Stir in broken nuts. Spread batter in prepared pan to even thickness. Bake 20 to 22 min or until barely done. Mark, cool in pan on cake rack, then cut and store like Brownies, above. 16 Brownies.

COCOA BROWNIES

Quick Mix and very good Brownies

¾ cup all-purpose flour	½ cup soft butter
1 cup sugar	2 eggs
¼ tsp salt	1 tsp vanilla
¼ cup cocoa	½ cup chopped nuts

Grease an 8 x 8 x 2-inch pan. Start oven 10 min before baking; set to moderate (350° F). Sift flour, measure, resift 3 times with next 3 ingredients, the last time into a 3-qt mixing bowl, or the large mixer bowl. Add butter, eggs and vanilla. Use wooden spoon and beat 100 strokes per min for 3 min by hand, or 2 min on *Medium Speed* on mixer. Clean off beater and remove. Stir in nuts with a wooden spoon until just distributed. Turn into prepared pan and spread out to even thickness. Bake 20 to 22 min or until barely done. Mark, cool in pan on cake rack, then cut and store like Brownies, p 457. Sixteen 2-inch Brownies.

COCOA INDIANS

A luscious type of Brownie with raisins instead of nuts

⅔ cup golden raisins
1 cup all-purpose flour
¼ tsp D.A. baking powder *or*
  ⅓ tsp tartrate *or* phosphate
  type
⅜ tsp salt
¼ cup cocoa

½ cup *plus* 2 tbsp soft butter
  or margarine
1 cup sugar
2 eggs
½ tsp vanilla
¼ cup milk

Grease a 7 x 11 x 1½-inch pan. Start oven 10 min before baking; set to moderate (350° F). Plump raisins, p 165. Sift flour, measure, resift 3 times with next 3 ingredients. Cream butter in a 3-qt mixing bowl until soft and shiny, add sugar in 2 portions, creaming well. Beat in eggs, one at a time until fluffy, then stir in vanilla. Now add flour mixture and milk alternately in 2 or 3 portions, beating until smooth after each. Stir in raisins. Spread batter in pan to uniform thickness. Bake 23 to 25 min or until just done. Remove from oven and mark into 4 strips each way with pointed knife. Cool on cake rack, then finish cutting. Store like Brownies, p 457. 16 Indians.

COCONUT FINGERS

A quick sweet for children's snacks

8 slices day-old white bread
1 cup sweetened condensed
  milk

1½ cups moist shredded
  coconut

Remove crusts from bread, then cut each slice into 4 strips. Dip strips into milk, then into coconut, covering all sides. Place on a greased baking sheet. Bake in a moderately slow oven (325° F) 10 to 15 min or until delicately browned. Remove from pan at once to cake rack to cool and crisp. Ground nuts may be used with, or in place of the coconut. 32 fingers.

DATE OATMEAL SQUARES

Rich and good!

Filling:
- 7¼-oz pkg pitted dates *or*
- ½ lb moist whole dates
- ⅔ cup boiling water
- 1 tsp lemon extract
- ½ cup *or* more chopped nuts

Cookie Dough:
- ⅔ cup all-purpose flour
- ½ tsp soda
- ½ tsp cinnamon
- ¼ tsp salt
- ⅔ cup brown sugar, packed
- 1½ cups quick oats
- ⅓ cup melted butter

Grease an 8 x 8 x 2-inch pan. Start oven 10 min before baking; set to moderate (375° F). Cut dates small, dropping into 1-qt saucepan, add water and cook and stir over medium heat to a medium-thick paste. Remove from heat; stir in extract and nuts. Cool. Sift flour, measure, resift 4 times with soda, cinnamon and salt; with a fork, stir in sugar and oats until blended. Now drizzle butter over mixture and toss until well mixed. Spread half the mixture in pan evenly, then pat with hand to make smooth. Now spread date mixture evenly over top. Crumble remaining oat mixture over dates and pat down gently. Bake 20 to 22 min. Remove to cake rack to cool in pan, then cut into 6 strips each way. To store, leave in pan and wrap in waxed paper. 36 squares.

FORK-PRINT COOKIES

An old-world type of cookie. Interesting, very good, chewy, yet tender. The dough retains imprint of marking throughout baking.

- 1¼ cups all-purpose flour
- ¼ tsp D.A. baking powder *or*
  - ⅓ tsp tartrate *or* phosphate type
- ⅛ tsp salt

- ½ cup *plus* 2 tbsp soft butter
- ½ cup *plus* 2 tbsp sugar
- ½ an egg
- 1 tsp vanilla

Grease a 9½ x 13½ x ¾-inch jelly roll pan; sprinkle lightly with flour, then overturn and tap to remove excess flour. Start oven 10 min before baking; set to slow (300° F). Sift flour, measure, resift 3 times with baking powder and salt. Cream butter until smooth and shiny, add sugar and cream well. Add the half egg, beat until fluffy. Stir in vanilla, then flour and beat until well blended. Turn batter into pan and spread out with spatula to even thickness and until top is smooth. Now draw a 4-tine fork over dough to make straight, shallow lines 1½ inches apart both ways for a crisscross pattern. Bake 30 min or to a pale golden color. Remove to cake rack and immediately cut into 5 strips each way to obtain bars. Let cool in pan on cake rack, then remove carefully. Store in container with tight-fitting cover. 25 bars.

FRUIT BARS

Cookies with Fruit Cake flavor and texture—expensive but delightful. Use moist fruit

¼ lb moist candied citron
¾ cup pitted dates, packed
½ cup golden raisins, packed
½ cup moist figs, packed
1 cup pecans *or* walnuts
½ cup light molasses *or* honey
1 tsp brandy extract
1½ cups all-purpose flour

½ tsp D.A. baking powder *or*
⅔ tsp tartrate *or* phosphate type
¼ tsp salt
½ tsp cinnamon
¼ tsp nutmeg
⅓ cup soft butter
½ cup sugar
2 eggs
2 tbsp buttermilk

Grease a 9½ x 13½ x ¾-inch jelly roll pan, then sprinkle with flour and shake out excess. Start oven 10 min before baking; set to moderate (350° F). Slice citron thin, then cut fine. Cut rest of fruit medium-fine with scissors. Break nuts medium-fine. Combine fruit and nuts in bowl, add molasses and flavoring and stir enough to blend. Sift flour, measure, resift 3 times with next 4 ingredients. Cream butter with wooden spoon in a 3-qt mixing bowl until smooth, add sugar and cream well. Beat in eggs one at a time until fluffy. Add flour and buttermilk alternately in 2 portions, stirring until just smooth after each. Stir in fruit-nut mixture until well distributed. Spread batter in pan to even thickness. Bake 20 min. Remove to cake rack and mark immediately into 6 strips one way and 5 the other, then cut into bars. Finish cooling in pan on rack. When cool, wrap pan snugly in waxed paper, or remove bars to a box with tight-fitting cover, placing waxed paper between layers. 30 bars.

PEPPERMINT CREAM BROWNIES

Two layers of fudgy cake with zesty pink frosting between make top-notch cookies

2 sq unsweet chocolate
⅔ cup all-purpose flour
¼ tsp D.A. baking powder *or*
⅓ tsp tartrate *or* phosphate type
⅛ tsp salt

⅓ cup butter *or* margarine
½ tsp vanilla
¾ cup sugar
2 eggs
1 tbsp milk
½ cup chopped walnuts

Grease two 8 x 8 x 2-inch pans; line bottoms with waxed paper—grease paper. Start oven 10 min before baking; set to moderate (350° F). Melt chocolate over hot water, then cool. Sift flour, measure, resift 3 times with baking powder and salt. Cream soft butter and vanilla until smooth, add sugar gradually, creaming well. Beat in eggs, one at a time until fluffy. Stir in chocolate, then milk and flour until well blended, then nuts until just distributed. Divide dough in half and spread to an even thickness in prepared pans. Bake 20 min or until barely done. Remove to cake rack to cool 3 min, then turn out on rack, loosen paper and invert, leaving paper underneath. When barely cool, turn over, remove paper and spread bottom of *1 layer* evenly and clear to the edge with Peppermint Butter Cream. Top with other layer right-side up, and press gently together. Cut the filled Brownies into 6 strips 1 way and 3 the other way, using sharp thin-bladed knife. 18 bars.

PEPPERMINT BUTTER CREAM

2 tbsp soft butter
1 cup sifted xxxx sugar,
firmly packed
1 tbsp hot milk
Dash red food color

⅛ tsp peppermint extract *or*
2 drops oil of peppermint
2 tsp white corn syrup
Dash of salt

Cream butter, add sugar gradually with the hot milk, then add enough color to give a delicate pink. Stir in syrup, salt and enough flavoring to suit taste. Beat to a smooth, spreading consistency. Enough for 2—8-inch squares.

WALNUT STICKS

Interesting in shape, texture and color—chewy and good-flavored

Part 1:

1¼ cups all-purpose flour
½ cup butter *or* margarine

½ cup moist brown sugar,
packed

Grease a 13½ x 9½ x ¾-inch jelly roll pan. Start oven 10 min before baking; set to moderate (350° F). Sift flour and measure. Cream soft butter until shiny, add sugar, creaming well. Add flour in 3 or 4 portions, working it in with a wooden spoon to form a smooth, stiff dough. Turn dough into prepared pan; pat out and press into a thin even layer; smooth edges and top well with spatula. Bake 15 min, then remove to cake rack to cool, then add

Part 2:

¼ cup shredded coconut,
packed
½ cup chopped walnuts
¾ cup brown sugar, packed
2 tbsp flour

½ tsp D. A. baking powder *or*
⅔ tsp tartrate *or* phosphate
type
1 egg
½ tsp vanilla
¼ tsp almond extract
xxxx sugar

Shear moist coconut into short shreds. Chop walnuts. Press sugar through coarse sieve to remove lumps, then stir with flour and baking powder to blend. Beat in next 3 ingredients with rotary beater. Remove beater. Use wooden spoon to stir in coconut and nuts. Spread mixture evenly over *Part 1*—the cooled baked layer. Return to oven and bake 15 to 18 min. Top appears slightly underbaked. Cool slightly in pan on cake rack, then sift xxxx sugar lightly over top. Cut into 6 strips lengthwise, then 4 crosswise for 3¼ x 1½-inch bars. When cool, remove strips of bars to container with tight-fitting cover with waxed paper between layers. 24 sticks.

DROP COOKIES

These are the cookies to send to your Soldier Boy

Drop cookies are quick and easy to make. Their spicy fragrance, rich moist nutty-fruity interiors and informal shapes make them most popular. They keep and pack well—so are excellent to mail as gifts. They may be made any size, *small* for Teas, *medium* for family meals and *big* for children's snacks. A good feature of Drop Cookies is that dough can be mixed in the evening, left in the bowl, covered, and stored in refrigerator, then baked next morning, or as needed.

APPLE SAUCE COOKIES

Delectable—and especially so when they have just lost oven heat. Tender and rich

1 cup very thick sweetened apple sauce	½ tsp each—cinnamon, nutmeg and cloves
1 cup moist seedless raisins	¾ cup soft margarine *or* butter
¾ cup chopped walnuts	
2¼ cups all-purpose flour	⅓ cup moist brown sugar, pkd
1 tsp soda	½ cup granulated sugar
½ tsp salt	2 eggs

Make sweetened apple sauce thick enough when cold to remain in shape when heaped up. Or cook a No. 2 can of commercial sauce in a 3-qt saucepan with constant stirring over brisk heat about 15 min or until there is just 1 cup of sauce when cooled. Start oven 10 min before baking; set to moderately hot (400° F). Plump raisins, p 165. Chop nuts. Grease baking sheet lightly.

Sift flour, measure, resift 4 times with next 5 ingredients. Cream margarine until shiny, add sugars and cream well. Beat in eggs one at a time until fluffy after each. Stir in cooled apple sauce, then flour in 2 or 3 portions, mixing until smooth after each portion. Stir in raisins and nuts until distributed. Drop heaping teaspoonfuls 2 inches apart in neat mounds on baking sheets. Bake 10 to 12 min or until nicely browned. Remove from pan to cake racks immediately. When cool, store in container with tight-fitting cover and with sheets of waxed paper between layers. 3½ dozen.

CHOCOLATE CHIP COOKIES

1½ cups all-purpose flour
½ tsp soda
⅓ tsp salt
⅔ cup soft butter *or* half shortening
½ cup granulated sugar
½ cup brown sugar, packed
1 tsp vanilla
1 large egg *or* 2 small
1 tbsp cream
½ cup chopped nuts
6 or 7-oz pkg chocolate chips, bits or morsels

Grease baking sheets lightly. Start oven 10 min before baking; set to moderate (375° F). Sift flour, measure, resift 4 times with soda and salt. Cream butter until smooth and shiny, add sugars and cream well. Stir in vanilla, then beat in egg until fluffy. Add flour in 2 portions, mixing until smooth after each. Stir in cream, then nuts and chocolate chips. Drop level dessert spoonfuls onto prepared sheets 2½ inches apart, using rubber scraper to push dough from spoon. Shape quickly into round mounds with tsp. Or chill dough, then spoon out onto waxed paper and roll into balls. Bake about 10 min or until delicately browned. Remove from oven; let stand a min, then remove cookies to cake racks. 4 dozen.

DOUBLE CHOCOLATE DROP COOKIES

Attractive deliciously rich cookies

2 cups all-purpose flour
½ tsp salt
½ tsp soda
1 cup moist brown sugar, pkd
½ cup chopped nuts
2 sq unsweet chocolate
½ cup shortening—half soft butter
1 tsp vanilla
1 egg
¾ cup milk

Grease baking sheets lightly. Start oven 10 min before baking; set to moderately hot (400° F). Sift flour, measure, resift 4 times with salt and soda. Put brown sugar through coarse sieve to remove lumps. Chop nuts. Put chocolate in large custard cup and stand in hot water to melt, then cool. Cream shortening until smooth and shiny, add sugar gradually and cream well. Stir in vanilla. Beat in egg until fluffy, then beat in cooled chocolate. Add flour mixture and milk alternately in 3 or 4 portions, beating smooth after each portion. Stir in nuts. Drop from dessert spoon into neat mounds on baking sheet. Bake about 10 min or until cookies are just done—*don't overbake*. Let stand on baking sheet a min before removing to cake racks to cool. When barely cool, swirl Chocolate Icing over tops. Let stand on cookie sheet until icing is firm. Store 1-layer deep in covered box. 36 cookies.

CHOCOLATE ICING

¼ cup butter, melted	¼ cup thin cream
2 sqs unsweet chocolate	½ tsp vanilla
2 cups xxxx sugar, sifted	1 egg yolk
and pkd	2 tbsp white corn syrup

Measure butter into 2-qt mixing bowl and stand it over hot water to melt. Put chocolate in large custard cup and set in hot water to melt, then cool. Add xxxx sugar alternately with cream to melted butter, beating until smooth after each portion. Beat in vanilla, then chocolate, egg yolk and syrup until smooth and shiny. Enough to spread 36 cookies.

CHOCOLATE SOUR CREAM DROP COOKIES

2 sq unsweet chocolate	⅔ cup soft butter *or*
1¾ cups all-purpose flour	margarine
1 tsp D.A. baking powder *or*	1⅓ cups sugar
1¼ tsp tartrate *or* phos-	1 tsp vanilla
phate type	1 egg
½ tsp soda	½ cup sour cream
½ tsp salt	½ cup broken nutmeats

Grease baking sheets lightly. Start oven 10 min before baking; set to moderately hot (425° F). Put chocolate in a large custard cup and set in a pan of hot water to melt; when melted, remove to cool. Sift flour, measure, resift 4 times with baking powder, soda and salt. In a 2-qt mixing bowl, cream butter until smooth, add sugar in 2 portions, creaming well. Stir in vanilla, then beat in egg until fluffy. Stir in cooled chocolate until blended, then sour cream. Add flour mixture and mix well. Stir in nuts. Drop by heaping teaspoonfuls 2 inches apart onto prepared sheets. Bake 9 to 10 min or until barely done. Let stand on sheet on cake rack a min or two, then remove to rack to cool. Store in box with tight-fitting cover with waxed paper between layers. 4 dozen.

SOFT CHOCOLATE DROP COOKIES

Make exactly like Chocolate Sour Cream Drop Cookies, above, except substitute 1⅓ cups moist brown sugar, packed, for the 1⅓ cups sugar and reduce chocolate to 1½ squares.

GUMDROP COOKIES

¾ cup gumdrops	⅜ tsp salt
½ cup blanched almonds	⅓ cup soft butter
1 cup all-purpose flour	⅔ cup sugar
½ tsp D.A. baking powder *or*	½ tsp vanilla
⅔ tsp tartrate *or* phosphate	1 egg
type	2 tbsp milk

Grease baking sheets lightly. Start oven 10 min before baking; set to moderately hot (400° F). Cut gumdrops small with scissors dipped in hot water, dropping on waxed paper to keep pieces separate. Blanch almonds; split in half lengthwise, p 121. Sift flour, measure, resift 3 times with baking powder and salt. Cream butter until smooth with wooden spoon, add sugar in 2 portions, creaming well. Stir in vanilla and beat in egg until fluffy. Add flour mixture alternately with milk in 2 portions, mixing until smooth after each, then stir in gumdrops. Drop by rounded teaspoonfuls onto prepared sheets 2 inches apart. Stick 4 almond halves into each. Bake 10 min or until lightly browned. Remove to cake racks immediately to crisp. 2 dozen.

HERMITS

A little different flavor but very well liked

⅔ cup raisins, plumped,
   p 165
½ cup chopped nuts
1 cup brown sugar, packed
1¾ cups all-purpose flour
½ tsp salt
½ tsp soda

½ tsp cinnamon
½ tsp nutmeg
½ cup butter *or* shortening
1 egg
¼ cup fresh cold coffee

Grease baking sheets lightly. Start oven 10 min before baking; set to moderately hot (400° F). Plump raisins and cool. Chop nuts. Put sugar through coarse sieve. Sift flour, measure, resift 4 times with next 4 ingredients. Cream margarine, add sugar and cream well. Beat in egg until fluffy. Add flour mixture and coffee alternately in 2 or 3 portions, mixing until smooth after each. Stir in raisins and nuts. Drop heaping teaspoonfuls on prepared sheets. Bake 10 to 12 min. Cool on sheet on cake rack a min, then remove to rack to cool. Store in container with tight-fitting cover with waxed paper between layers. 4 dozen.

MINCEMEAT COOKIES

Beautiful color, tantalizing aroma and fine flavor

1 cup chopped walnuts
3 cups all-purpose flour
1 tsp salt
2 tsp soda
¾ cup soft margarine

1½ cups sugar
3 eggs
1 cup moist mincemeat
3 tbsp brandy, peach pickle
   juice or buttermilk

Grease baking sheets lightly. Start oven 10 min before baking; set to moderately hot (400° F). Chop nuts. Sift flour, measure, resift 4 times with salt and soda. Cream margarine until shiny, add sugar, creaming well. Then beat in eggs one at a time until fluffy after each.

Stir in mincemeat and brandy, then flour in 3 or 4 portions, mixing until smooth after each. Stir in nuts. Drop 2 inches apart by heaping teaspoonfuls onto baking sheet in neat mounds. Bake 9 to 10 min or to a luscious brown. Remove at once from pan to cake racks. Store in container with tight-fitting cover. 4 dozen.

MOLASSES DROP COOKIES No. 1

Excellent! A moist fruit-nut filled cookie you will be proud to serve on any occasion, but serve them fresh

1 cup raisins, plumped, p 165	¼ cup brown sugar, pkd
½ cup chopped nuts	½ cup soft butter *or*
2 cups all-purpose flour	margarine *plus*
1 tsp soda	2 tbsp shortening
¼ tsp salt	1 egg
⅛ tsp ginger	½ cup dark molasses
½ tsp cloves	½ cup thick buttermilk
½ tsp cinnamon	

Grease baking sheets. Start oven 10 min before baking; set to moderately hot (400° F). Wash raisins and plump, then cool. Chop nuts. Sift flour, measure, resift 4 times with next 5 ingredients. Press brown sugar through a coarse sieve to remove lumps. In a 3-qt mixing bowl, cream butter and shortening with a wooden spoon until smooth, add sugar and cream well. Scrape off spoon, remove. Beat in egg with rotary beater until fluffy, then beat in molasses until satiny. Remove beater and use spoon. Stir in flour mixture and milk alternately in 2 or 3 portions, beginning and ending with flour and mixing until smooth after each portion. Stir in raisins and nuts until well distributed. Drop by heaping teaspoonfuls onto prepared sheet. Bake about 10 min or until delicately browned. Remove at once from sheet to cake rack. When cool, store in jar or box with tight-fitting cover with sheet of waxed paper between layers. 3 dozen.

MOLASSES DROP COOKIES No. 2

Soft, simple to make—quick to disappear

4 cups all-purpose flour	¾ cup sugar
3 tsp soda—yes 3	2 eggs
1½ tsp salt	¾ cup thick sour cream
¾ tsp each, cinnamon, ginger,	¾ cup dark molasses
cloves, nutmeg	2 cups seedless raisins,
¾ cup shortening, *or* cold	plumped, p 165
poultry fat, p 166	1 cup broken nutmeats

Grease baking sheets lightly. Arrange rack in middle of oven, then start oven 10 min before baking; set to moderate (375° F). Sift flour, measure, resift 3 times with soda, salt and spices. Measure shortening and sugar into a 4-qt mixing bowl. Beat with rotary beater until creamy, then beat in eggs, then cream and molasses. Remove beater, use wooden spoon. Add flour mixture in 3 or 4 portions, beating until smooth after each. Stir in raisins and nuts. Drop by heaping teaspoonfuls onto prepared sheets. Bake about 12 min. Remove from oven and let stand on baking sheet a min, then remove to racks to cool. Store in tightly covered container with waxed paper between layers. 6½ dozen.

OATMEAL DROP COOKIES No. 1

Tiptop cookies—crisp, crunchy and flavorful

½ cup seedless raisins	½ tsp nutmeg
⅓ cup water	⅔ cup butter *or* half lard
½ cup chopped walnuts	1 cup sugar
2 cups all-purpose flour	1 egg
¼ tsp salt	2 tbsp molasses
1 tsp soda	2 tbsp raisin water
1 tsp cinnamon	2 cups regular oats

Grease baking sheets lightly. Start oven 10 min before baking; set to moderately hot (400° F). Wash raisins, add water and simmer 3 minutes; drain, saving water. Chop nuts. Sift flour, measure, resift 4 times with next 4 ingredients. With wooden spoon, beat melted butter and sugar thoroughly, then beat in eggs, then molasses. Add flour mixture and raisin water alternately in 2 or 3 portions, mixing until smooth after each. Stir in large flake oats, raisins, and nuts. Measure heaping teaspoonfuls of dough onto waxed paper; roll quickly and lightly into balls. Place 2 inches apart on prepared sheet. Flatten with tines of fork, keeping shape as round as possible. Bake 10 to 11 min or to a light brown. Let stand on sheet a min, then remove to cake rack to cool. Store in container with tight-fitting cover with waxed paper between layers. 3½ dozen.

OATMEAL DROP COOKIES No. 2

These cookies will win compliments—they are moist with good old-time flavor

1 cup seedless raisins	½ tsp nutmeg
½ cup chopped nuts	½ cup butter *or* margarine
1½ cups all-purpose flour	1 cup sugar
1 tsp soda	1 egg
¼ tsp salt	⅔ cup buttermilk
1 tsp cinnamon	1½ cups quick oats

Grease baking sheets. Start oven 10 min before baking; set to moderately hot (400° F). Plump raisins, p 165. Chop nuts. Sift flour, measure, resift 4 times with next 4 ingredients. Cream soft butter until shiny, add sugar in 2 portions and cream well. Beat in egg until fluffy. Add flour and buttermilk alternately in 2 or 3 portions, mixing until smooth after each. Stir in oats, raisins and nuts. Drop by heaping teaspoonfuls onto prepared sheets 2 inches apart. Bake 10 to 12 min or to a light brown. Cool on sheet a min, then remove to cake racks to cool. Store in container with tight-fitting cover with waxed paper between layers. 3 dozen.

OLD-FASHIONED LACE COOKIES

As much like candy as cookies—delicious, lacy and crisp—can be shaped interestingly. They are mixed in a saucepan

1 cup all-purpose flour	¾ tsp D.A. baking powder *or*
1 tsp cinnamon	1 tsp tartrate *or* phosphate
¹⁄₁₆ tsp nutmeg	type
¼ tsp salt	½ cup butter *or* margarine
½ tsp soda	½ cup sugar
	½ cup light molasses
	1 tsp lemon extract

Grease baking sheets, then dust with flour to coat with a thin film for easy removal of cookies. Start oven 10 min before baking; set to moderately slow (325° F). Sift flour, measure, resift 3 times with next 5 ingredients. Heat butter, sugar and molasses in a 1-qt saucepan over low heat, stirring until mixture bubbles. Remove from heat, cool a min, then beat in extract and flour until smooth. Now place saucepan over hot water for 5 min, then remove. Drop by level teaspoonfuls 3 inches apart onto prepared sheet. Bake 10 min or to a reddish brown. Cool 1 or 2 min, then remove quickly from sheet to rack by sliding spatula under cookies. While warm and pliable, curve cookies gently into scoop-shapes, scrolls or little ruffled baskets. Store when cool and crisp in tightly covered box with waxed paper between layers. About 5 dozen.

Note: If cookies become too brittle before shaping, return to oven on baking sheet a few seconds to soften, then shape quickly.

ROCKS No. 1

Excellent when fresh—they become firm on standing but retain fine flavor

1 cup moist currants	¼ tsp salt
⅔ cup chopped nuts	½ tsp soda
1½ cups all-purpose flour	½ cup butter *or* margarine
¼ tsp allspice	¾ cup sugar
½ tsp cinnamon	2 eggs
½ tsp nutmeg	

Grease baking sheets lightly. Start oven 10 min before baking; set to moderately hot (400° F). Wash currants, then plump, p 165, and cool. Chop nuts. Sift flour, measure, resift 4 times with next 5 ingredients. Cream soft butter until shiny, add sugar and cream well. Beat in eggs one at a time until fluffy. Add flour in 2 portions, mixing until smooth after each. Stir in currants and nuts. Drop by heaping teaspoonfuls onto sheets in neat mounds 2 inches apart. Bake about 10 min or until nicely browned. Remove from pan immediately to cake racks to cool. Store with waxed paper between layers. 2 dozen.

ROCKS No. 2

Poultry fat

2⅓ cups all-purpose flour	⅛ tsp ginger
½ tsp soda	⅔ cup rendered poultry fat,
1 tsp D.A. baking powder *or*	p 166
1¼ tsp tartrate *or* phos-	1 cup brown sugar,
phate type	firmly pkd
1½ tsp cinnamon	2 eggs, beaten
¾ tsp salt	⅔ cup chopped walnut meats
¼ tsp allspice	⅔ cup seeded raisins

Start oven 10 min before baking; set to moderate (350° F). Sift flour, measure and resift 3 times with remaining dry ingredients. Cream fat, add sugar gradually and continue beating thoroughly. Add eggs and beat well. Add flour and stir until thoroughly blended. Stir in nut meats and raisins. Drop by teaspoonfuls onto an ungreased baking sheet. Bake 12 to 15 min. Cool on cake racks. 4 dozen.

SOUR CREAM COOKIES

Appreciated more today than when developed years and years ago

2 cups all-purpose flour	¼ tsp nutmeg
½ tsp D.A. baking powder	1 cup brown sugar, packed
or ¾ tsp tartrate *or*	½ cup margarine *or* butter
phosphate type	1 egg
¼ tsp soda	½ cup thick sour cream
¼ tsp salt	½ cup chopped nuts *or* raisins

Grease baking sheets lightly. Start oven 10 min before baking; set to moderately hot (400° F). Sift flour, measure, resift 3 times with next 4 ingredients. Put brown sugar through coarse sieve. Cream margarine, add sugar gradually, creaming well. Beat in egg until fluffy. Add dry ingredients and the cream alternately in 2 or 3 portions, beating until smooth after each. Stir in nuts. Drop heaping teaspoonfuls 2 inches apart onto greased sheets. Bake 8 to 10 min or until no imprint is left when pressed lightly. Remove at once to cake rack to cool. 3 dozen.

VANILLA CRISPS

The secret of obtaining good shape is to drop dough onto a flour-dusted baking sheet

1⅓ cups all-purpose flour	½ cup shortening
1 tsp D.A. baking powder	*or* half butter
or 1¼ tsp tartrate *or*	1 cup sugar
phosphate type	2 tsp vanilla
½ tsp salt	2 eggs

Sprinkle ungreased baking sheet with flour, then tilt sheet and tap lightly to leave a thin film of flour. Start oven 10 min before baking; set to moderately hot (400° F). Sift flour, measure, resift 3 times with baking powder and salt. Cream shortening, add sugar in 2 or 3 portions, creaming well. Stir in vanilla, then beat in eggs one at a time until fluffy. Stir in flour in 2 portions, mixing until smooth after each. Drop by teaspoonfuls 1½ inches apart onto prepared sheet. Bake about 8 min or until delicately browned. Remove from baking sheet immediately to cake rack to cool. About 5 dozen.

MERINGUE COOKIES

These are the bouffant glamour members of the Cookie Family. They are delicate and fragile and add beauty and variety to the Cookie Tray. They are best eaten the day baked.

COCOA MACAROONS

3 tbsp cocoa	1½ cups corn flakes tossed with
¼ tsp salt	½ cup moist shredded
¾ cup sugar	coconut, packed, 1½ oz
⅓ cup egg whites, room temp	

Have baking sheet lined with smooth brown wrapping or typewriter paper—do not grease. Start oven 10 min before baking; set to moderately slow (325° F). Sift cocoa, salt and sugar together 3 times. Beat whites with wire whip until just stiff enough to hold moist rounded peaks. Add cocoa mixture gradually, *folding* in gently. Drizzle over corn flake-coconut mixture in another bowl, then toss with 2 forks until well mixed. Drop heaping tablespoonfuls of mixture from fork onto prepared sheet about 2 inches apart. Bake 20 min or until dry enough to hold shape. Slide paper with macaroons onto a wet towel; let stand 5 min or until macaroons lift off paper, then place on cake rack to crisp. 1½ dozen.

COCONUT MACAROONS WITH CONDENSED MILK

Delicate, rich, sweet, chewy and moist—eat while young, they harden with age

2 cups moist shredded coconut, 5½ to 6 oz	1 tsp lemon juice
½ tsp grated lemon rind, packed	¼ tsp salt
	½ cup sweetened condensed milk

Grease baking sheet. Start oven 10 min before baking; set to moderately slow (325° F). Fluff up coconut and turn into a 3-qt mixing bowl. Stir grated rind, lemon juice and salt into condensed milk, then drizzle over coconut. Now toss gently but thoroughly with 2 forks until coconut is evenly coated. Drop heaping tablespoonfuls from fork 1 inch apart onto prepared sheet. Push coconut into the mounds around base. Bake 12 to 15 min or to a delicate brown. Remove from sheet at once to cake rack to cool. 1½ dozen.

CORN FLAKE KISSES

Best eaten fresh

½ cup chopped pecans	⅔ cup sugar
2 egg whites, room temp	1½ cups crisp corn flakes
¼ tsp salt	

Lay typewriter or smooth brown wrapping paper on baking sheet —do not grease. Start oven 10 min before baking; set to slow (300° F).

Chop nuts. Turn whites into 2-qt mixing bowl, add salt and beat with rotary beater until stiff enough to hold soft rounded peaks. Add sugar in 4 portions, beating until shiny peaks that curve at tips form. Remove beater; use fork. Fold nuts in gently, then corn flakes until just distributed. Drop heaping teaspoonfuls from fork 2 in. apart onto prepared sheet. Bake 25 to 30 min or until just golden brown and dry enough to hold shape. Remove at once from paper to cake rack to cool. Store no longer than a day. 2½ dozen.

CREOLE MAPLE KISSES

Serve the day baked

½ cup chopped nuts	⅛ tsp salt
¾ cup brown sugar, packed	1 tsp vinegar
½ cup granulated sugar	1 tsp vanilla
3 egg whites, room temp	

Lay white typewriter or smooth brown wrapping paper on baking sheet—do not grease. Start oven 10 min before baking; set to very slow (250° F).

Chop nuts. Put moist brown sugar through coarse sieve to remove lumps, then blend thoroughly with granulated sugar. Beat whites and salt in a 2-qt mixing bowl with rotary beater until stiff enough to form pointed peaks that curve at tips. Sprinkle sugar over whites in 6 portions, beating well after each. Now beat in vinegar and vanilla until pointed peaks curve at tips. Remove beater and use fork to *gently* fold in nuts. Drop rounded teaspoonfuls about 1 inch apart onto prepared sheet and spread to silver dollar-size. Bake 18 to 20 min or until outside is crisp. Remove immediately from paper to cake rack to cool. Put flat-bottoms of 2 Kisses together with *Maple Butter Cream*. 24 filled Kisses.

MAPLE BUTTER CREAM

Spread between Creole Kisses or plain cookies to make them extra-special!

⅓ cup sifted xxxx sugar,
   firmly packed

2 tbsp soft butter
¼ tsp maple extract

Cream butter until smooth and shiny. Blend in sugar thoroughly, then the extract. Spread bottom of 1 cookie then press bottom of another cookie into icing.

MACAROONS, ALMOND

A luxury cookie for special parties—even the crumbs are decorative, crunchy and flavorful "MUSTS" in some desserts, such as Biscuit Tortoni, etc.

½ cup almond paste, ¼ lb
   (Buy at bakery *or* fancy
   grocery)
⅔ cup granulated sugar
3 tbsp sifted xxxx sugar, pkd

1 tbsp all-purpose flour
Dash of salt
¼ tsp vanilla
2 unbeaten egg whites

Line baking sheet with smooth brown wrapping paper—do not grease. Start oven 10 min before baking; set to slow (300° F). Blend almond paste and granulated sugar in a 1-qt mixing bowl with fingers thoroughly, then work in sugar, flour, salt and vanilla. Now stir in egg whites thoroughly with wooden spoon. Drop from teaspoon onto prepared baking sheet or from pastry bag fitted with plain, round-hole tube. Cover with greased waxed paper and let stand 3 hr at room temp. Then dip fingers in cold water and lightly pat tops of cookies. Bake 20 min or until delicately browned; watch closely the last 5 min as they scorch easily. Have cake rack spread with cloth wrung from cold water; slide paper onto wet cloth and let stand until macaroons can be removed easily, about 5 min. 24—1½-inch macaroons.

MERINGUE KISSES AND VARIATIONS

3 egg whites, room temp	1 tsp vinegar
1 cup sugar, sifted	1 tsp vanilla

Lay smooth brown wrapping paper on baking sheet—do not grease. Start oven 10 min before baking; set to very slow (250° F). Turn whites into 2-qt mixing bowl. Beat with rotary beater until stiff enough to form pointed peaks curved at tips. Now add sugar in 6 portions and beat until blended in after each, then beat in vinegar and vanilla until meringue forms pointed peaks that stand straight. Put mixture into pastry bag fitted with plain round-hole tube. Press out onto prepared sheet 1 inch apart into silver dollar-size rounds, about ¾-inch high, or drop mixture by heaping teaspoonfuls. Bake 25 to 30 min or until a pale cream color. Outside should be crisp and fragile and centers slightly soft. Remove from paper at once to cake rack to cool. 3 to 4 dozen.

ORANGE CREAM KISSES

Follow directions exactly for mixing and baking *Meringue Kisses,* above. When cold, put 2 Kisses together with *Orange Cream Filling,* bottoms facing.

ORANGE CREAM FILLING

2 tbsp soft butter	½ tsp orange rind, packed
⅓ cup sifted xxxx sugar, firmly packed	1 tsp orange juice

Cream butter, blend in sugar thoroughly. Stir in grated rind and orange juice. Spread bottom of 1 cookie, then place another one over it and press together.

MOLDED AND STAMPED COOKIES

These cookie doughs are firm enough to hold shape well after molding with the hands into cylinders, crescent or balls. Then these shapes may be baked as is, or stamped with a glass, thumb or tines of a fork, and such impressions are retained in detail throughout baking because little or no leavening is used.

ALMOND CRESCENTS

½ cup almonds, blanched	⅓ cup sifted xxxx sugar, pkd
¾ cup plus 2 tbsp all-purpose flour	½ tsp vanilla
⅛ tsp salt	¼ tsp almond extract
½ cup butter *or* margarine	xxxx sugar

Have baking sheet ready—do not grease. Start oven 10 min before baking; set to moderately slow (325° F). Put almonds through nut or food chopper using coarse blade. Sift flour, measure, resift with salt. Cream soft butter until shiny, add sugar, put through sieve; cream well. Stir in flavorings, then almonds and flour. Knead dough to blend smoothly. Divide dough in half, then lay on board and with palms of hands roll each into a rope 15 inches long. Cut ropes into 1-inch lengths, then roll each piece between palms until 2 inches long. Place on baking sheet, curving into crescent-shape. Bake 15 to 17 min or until a pale golden color. Remove at once to cake rack, then sift xxxx sugar over tops. Attractive, crunchy, good keepers if you can keep them. 30.

BUTTER NUTTIES

Attractive, good butter flavor and worth all they cost—a lovely party cookie

2½ cups all-purpose flour (No salt)	1 tsp grated lemon rind, packed
1 cup chopped walnuts	1 cup soft butter
12 to 15 candied cherries	¾ cup sugar
	2 eggs, separated

Grease baking sheets lightly. Start oven 10 min before baking; set to moderate (350° F). Sift flour, measure. Chop nuts to size of split peas. Cut cherries in half. Grate lemon rind. Cream butter until shiny, add rind, then sugar gradually, creaming well. Beat in egg yolks until fluffy, then stir in flour in 3 or 4 portions, mixing until just smooth after each. Cover and chill dough an hr or so. Beat egg whites *very slightly* and pour into a shallow pan. Put part of the nuts into a shallow pan, adding rest as needed. Measure dough by level tablespoonfuls onto waxed paper, then quickly shape into balls. Put 5 or 6 balls into egg whites, shift pan around to coat balls, then roll in the nuts. Place 1½ inches apart on prepared sheet, then press a half cherry into center of each. Bake 20 to 23 min or until golden brown. Remove to cake rack to cool on pan a min, then carefully slide onto rack to cool. About 30.

EASY SUGAR COOKIES

The name means what it indicates—the attractive finish makes them look difficult

2 cups all-purpose flour	1 tsp vanilla
¾ tsp D.A. baking powder *or* 1 tsp tartrate *or* phosphate type	½ tsp almond extract
	1 egg
½ tsp salt	1 egg white slightly beaten with
½ cup soft butter	1 tsp cold water
½ cup sugar	Sugar crystals *or* nuts

Grease baking sheets. Start oven 10 min before baking; set to moderately hot (400° F). Sift flour, measure, resift 3 times with baking powder and salt. Cream butter until shiny, add sugar in 2 portions, creaming well. Stir in flavorings, then beat in egg until fluffy. Add flour in 3 or 4 portions, mixing until smooth after each. Cover dough and chill at least an hr. Measure dough by level tbsp onto waxed paper. Quickly shape into balls and place on prepared sheet. Press twice with tines of fork to about ⅛-inch thick, or with a flat-bottom glass covered with a piece of cloth wrung out of cold water. Brush cookies lightly with egg mixture, then sprinkle with sugar or chopped nuts. Bake 10 min or until delicately browned. Remove from sheet immediately to cake rack to cool. 2 to 3 dozen.

LEMON SUGAR COOKIES

Crisp and sweet with a definite lemon twang. Nice with dessert of contrasting flavor

2⅛ cups all-purpose flour	½ cup shortening
¾ tsp D.A. baking powder *or* 1 tsp tartrate *or* phosphate type	1 cup sugar
	1 egg *or* 2 yolks
	2 tsp lemon juice
¼ tsp salt	1 tsp grated lemon rind, packed
½ cup soft butter and	

Grease baking sheets lightly. Start oven 10 min before baking; set to moderately hot (400° F). Sift flour, measure, resift 3 times with baking powder and salt. Cream butter and shortening until shiny and smooth, add sugar in 2 portions, creaming well. Beat in egg until fluffy, then stir in lemon juice and rind. Stir in flour in 2 or 3 portions, mixing until smooth after each. Measure level tablespoonfuls of dough onto waxed paper, quickly shape into balls. Place 3 inches apart on prepared sheet. Cover flat-bottomed glass with a piece of clean cheesecloth wrung out of cold water, and stamp cookies out to even thickness, about ⅛-inch. Bake 6 to 8 min or until delicately browned around edges. Remove immediately to cake racks to cool. 4 dozen.

PEANUT BUTTER COOKIES

Children's favorite. Tender, crisp and flavorful

1¼ cups all-purpose flour	½ cup peanut butter, room temp
¼ tsp soda	
½ tsp D.A. baking powder *or* ⅔ tsp tartrate *or* phosphate type	½ cup granulated sugar
	½ cup moist brown sugar, packed
¼ tsp salt	1 egg
½ cup soft butter *or* margarine	1 tsp vanilla

Have baking sheets ready—do not grease. Start oven 10 min before baking; set to moderate (375° F).

Sift flour, measure, resift 3 times with soda, baking powder and salt. With wooden spoon, cream both butters until light, add both sugars and cream very thoroughly. Beat in egg, then stir in vanilla. Add flour in 2 or 3 portions, mixing until smooth after each. Chill dough for an hr or so. Measure level tablespoonfuls of dough onto waxed paper; shape quickly into balls. Place 2 inches apart on baking sheet. Press twice with tines of fork, first dipped in cold water, to make crisscross pattern on top. Bake 10 to 12 min or until delicately browned. Remove immediately from baking sheet to cake racks to cool. 2¾ dozen.

PRALINE COOKIES

Crunchy, rich-flavored and good keepers

1⅓ cups *plus* 1 tbsp all-purpose flour	1 cup coarsely chopped pecans
¼ tsp D.A. baking powder *or* ⅓ tsp tartrate *or* phosphate type	1½ cups brown sugar, packed
	¾ cup butter *or* margarine
	1 egg
	1 tsp vanilla

Grease baking sheets lightly. Start oven 10 min before baking; set to moderate (375° F). Sift flour, measure and resift with baking powder. Chop nuts. Put brown sugar through a coarse sieve to remove lumps. Cream soft butter in a 3-qt mixing bowl until shiny, add sugar in 2 portions, creaming well. Beat in egg until fluffy, then stir in vanilla. Add flour in 2 or 3 portions, mixing until smooth after each. Stir in nuts. Measure dough by level tablespoonfuls onto waxed paper, then quickly roll into balls. Place 2 inches apart on baking sheet. Flatten to about ⅛-inch thickness with a flat-bottomed glass, bottom covered with dampened cheesecloth. Bake about 12 min or until nicely browned. Cool on pan a min, then remove to cake rack. 3 dozen.

3-WAY GINGER COOKIES

Puff up in baking, then settle down. Beautiful brown, chewy, good flavor

2 cups all-purpose flour	*or* half shortening
¼ tsp salt	1 cup sugar
1 tsp soda	1 egg
1 tsp ginger	¼ cup dark molasses
½ cup soft butter	1 tbsp vinegar

Grease baking sheets lightly. Start oven 10 min before baking; set to moderate (375° F). Sift flour, measure, resift 4 times with next 3 ingredients. Cream butter until shiny, add sugar gradually and cream well. Beat in egg until fluffy. Stir in molasses, then vinegar. Add flour in 2 portions, mixing until smooth after each portion.

1-Way—Drop by level dessertspoonfuls onto waxed paper; shape into balls, rolling lightly between buttered palms of hands. Arrange on prepared sheets. Bake 12 to 13 min or until delicately browned. Let stand on sheet a min, then remove to cake racks to cool. 4 dozen 2½-inch cookies.

2-Way—After shaping dough into balls, dip into ½ cup chopped nuts spread on waxed paper. Place on baking sheet, nut-side up and bake as above.

3-Way—Shape balls as above. Dip into a mixture of 3 tbsp granulated sugar and 1 tbsp grated orange rind. Place on baking sheet, sugar-side up. Bake as above.

COOKIE PRESS DOUGH

This is a special rich-type dough. No leavening is used. Spritz has made this type of cookies famous. The dough must be soft enough to press compactly into a cookie press. When correctly made, this dough comes out of cookie press smoothly and retains fine lines of design perfectly throughout baking. There are 3 tricks that help in pressing dough shapes out perfectly:

1. Press out dough for 1 or 2 cookies on pan to eliminate air in tube, then return this when next refilling press.

2. Have cookie sheet cold and ungreased to prevent cookies from lifting up from sheet when Cookie *Press* or *Gun* is lifted.

3. Cookie Press should be lifted as soon as emerging dough is visible, then moved quickly from cookie to cookie in fast rhythm.

Chilled Spritz Dough may be rolled out, cut into fancy shapes and baked for Holiday Cookies.

ALMOND SPRITZ COOKIES

¾ cup grated almonds, packed	¾ cup sugar
2¼ cups all-purpose flour	1 small egg plus 1 yolk
1 cup soft butter, ½ lb	¼ tsp almond extract

Have all ingredients at room temp. Have baking sheets ready—do not grease. Start oven 10 min before baking; set to moderate (375° F). Use unblanched or blanched almonds, as desired. Put almonds through nut grater, or food mill a few at a time to obtain fine gratings; if screw is left loose, almonds grate easily. Sift flour and measure. Cream butter until shiny, add sugar and cream well. Beat in egg and yolk until fluffy, then stir in extract, then flour in 3 or 4 portions, mixing until smooth after each. Stir in grated nuts. Cover dough and chill an hr, then knead slightly to make smooth. Fill cookie press fitted with star tube, packing into press firmly. Press out small wreaths onto baking sheet. Bake 8 to

10 min or until delicately browned. Slip spatula under cookies and slide onto cake rack at once to cool. 5 dozen.

BASIC SPRITZ COOKIES

2½ cups all-purpose flour	3 egg yolks
1 cup soft butter, ½ lb	½ tsp almond extract
¾ cup sifted sugar	*or* 1 tsp vanilla

Have baking sheets ready—do not grease. Start oven 10 min before baking; set to moderately hot (400° F). Sift flour and measure. Cream butter until shiny, add sugar gradually, creaming well. Beat in yolks until fluffy, then flavoring. Stir in flour in 3 or 4 portions until smooth. If dough is soft, chill an hr. Now shape dough into a cylinder and drop into cookie press, fitted with desired design plate. Press dough out onto cold baking sheet about 1-inch apart. Bake about 8 min or until a delicate brown. Remove from pans immediately to cake racks to cool. If difficult to remove from pans, return to oven a minute. Cool thoroughly. 4½ dozen medium cookies.

CHOCOLATE SPRITZ COOKIES

Follow directions exactly for mixing and baking Basic Spritz Cookies, except add immediately after creaming butter and sugar, 1½ sqs unsweet chocolate, melted and cooled, and use 1 tsp vanilla for the flavoring.

REFRIGERATOR (Ice Box) COOKIES

Refrigerator cookie dough is only a trifle softer than rolled cookie dough. As soon as dough is mixed, pack it into cookie molds or shape into a roll. Wrap in waxed paper and chill until firm enough to slice. Reshaping once may be necessary. *Or* place waxed-paper-wrapped roll on a piece of thin cardboard similar to shirt cardboard, roll up into a cylinder, then fasten with 2 or 3 rubber bands. This roll will not have to be reshaped. Chill several hrs. When ready to bake, remove cookie roll, slice and bake as many cookies as desired. If roll is well wrapped and kept thoroughly chilled, dough should keep in good condition 5 or 6 days.

BASIC NUT REFRIGERATOR COOKIES

Rich, appealing flavor, fine color—stay crisp if you can keep them

2¾ cups all-purpose flour	½ cup brown sugar, packed
¾ tsp salt	⅔ cup granulated sugar
½ tsp soda	1 tsp vanilla
1 cup soft butter *or*	2 eggs, beaten
half shortening	½ cup chopped nuts

Have ingredients at room temp. Have baking sheets ready—do not grease. Start oven 10 min before baking; set to moderately hot (400° F).

Sift flour, measure, resift 3 times with salt and soda. Cream butter until smooth, add sugars gradually, creaming thoroughly. Put lumpy brown sugar through coarse sieve. Stir in vanilla, then eggs one at a time, and beat until well blended. Add flour in 3 portions, mixing well after each. Stir in nuts. Chill dough until stiff, then divide in half and place on 2 sheets of waxed paper. Quickly shape into 2 uniform rolls about 2 inches in diameter, then roll up in the paper. Lay on piece of cardboard to keep level and store in refrigerator until very firm—from 4 to 6 hrs. If rolls flatten out the first hr, quickly remold into round rolls. When firm, slice with a sharp knife into ¼-inch thick cookies. Keep thickness uniform for perfect baking. Place an inch apart on baking sheet. Bake 8 to 10 min to a pale golden color. Remove from pan to cake rack to cool thoroughly before storing in an airtight container with waxed paper between layers. 40 cookies.

CHOCOLATE NUT REFRIGERATOR COOKIES

Follow directions for making *Basic Nut Refrigerator Cookies*, except add 2 sqs melted and cooled unsweet chocolate to dough just after adding eggs, and beat thoroughly. Slivered almonds may be substituted for pecans. 40 cookies.

DATE-NUT REFRIGERATOR COOKIES

Follow directions for making *Basic Nut Refrigerator Cookies*, except substitute 1 tsp freshly grated orange rind, packed, for the vanilla, and add ¾ cup finely cut moist dates to dough when nuts are added. 45 cookies.

CHERRY-CITRON NUT REFRIGERATOR COOKIES

Follow directions for making *Basic Nut Refrigerator Cookies*, except substitute ⅛ tsp anise extract for the vanilla, and add ¼ cup *each* of thin-sliced moist candied cherries (not maraschino) and citron when nuts are added. 45 cookies.

LEMON-COCONUT REFRIGERATOR COOKIES

Follow directions for making *Basic Nut Refrigerator Cookies*, except substitute 1 tsp freshly grated lemon rind, packed, and ½ tsp lemon extract for the vanilla, and substitute 1 cup moist shredded coconut, packed, for the nuts. 45 cookies.

CHECKERBOARD OR RIBBON COOKIES

These cookies require *2 colors* of dough. Divide each dough equally into 2 or 3 portions for uniform, thick layers. The most attractive layers are between ¼- and ⅓-inch thick. Have molds ready—the cardboard boxes which waxed paper rolls come in or square-cornered freezing trays make excellent molds. Line molds neatly with heavy waxed paper. Measure a portion of the freshly mixed dough into the lined mold, then *press down* compactly into an even layer with a spatula or pancake turner, smoothing the top. Place mold in freezing unit until very firm, then add next layer of soft dough of contrasting color, *pressing down and smoothing top.* It is important that layers be level and of same thickness for perfect stripes and checks. Return mold to freezing unit for soft layer to become firm, repeating until desired number of layers have been added. For Checkerboard Cookies there must *always* be an *even number of* layers, such as 4 or 6. When the last layer is added, cover mold with waxed paper and place in coldest spot in refrigerator (not freezing unit) to become very firm. Slice and bake like *Basic Nut Refrigerator Cookies,* p 478.

CHECKERBOARD AND RIBBON COOKIES

It takes a little time to mold these mystery cookies, but it is easy once the trick is understood

1 sq unsweet chocolate	¼ tsp salt
2½ cups all-purpose flour	¾ cup shortening, half butter
¾ tsp D.A. baking powder *or*	1 cup sugar
1 tsp tartrate *or* phosphate	1 tsp vanilla
type	2 eggs

Grease baking sheets lightly. Start oven 10 min before baking; set to moderate (375° F). Line mold neatly with waxed paper—square-cornered 9 x 5 x 3-inch loaf pans or 10 x 5 x 2-inch freezing trays are suitable.

Melt chocolate over hot water, then cool to lukewarm. Sift flour, measure, resift 3 times with baking powder and salt. Cream shortening until smooth and shiny, add sugar in 2 or 3 portions, creaming well. Stir in vanilla, then beat in eggs, one at a time until fluffy. Add flour in 3 portions, mixing until smooth after each. Divide dough exactly in half. Add chocolate to 1 portion, kneading it in with back of spoon until well blended. Pack exactly half the chocolate dough into mold compactly with pancake turner or spatula to make a uniformly thick layer, smoothing the top. Place in freezing unit until layer is firm. Now add exactly half the soft plain dough; spread out and pack in an even layer, then return to freezing unit until firm. Repeat until the 4 layers are added. Then cover with waxed paper and store in refrigerator (not freezing unit) overnight. See below how to use this Molded Dough for Ribbon or Checkerboard Cookies.

For Ribbon Cookies—Unmold cookie dough; remove waxed paper and cut with sharp knife into ⅛-inch slices. Bake 8 to 10 min.

For Checkerboard Cookies—Unmold cookie dough, remove waxed paper and slice the layered dough *exactly as thick as the individual layers*. Now lay 4 slices carefully on top of each other, reversing slices so when viewed from the end, each chocolate stripe lies exactly above a white stripe. Quickly wrap this bar of dough in waxed paper so as not to spoil shape and return to refrigerator to become firm. Repeat laying 4 slices together until desired number of cookie dough bars have been put together, wrapped and chilled. To slice, remove waxed paper, hold bar with the paper and cut from checked-end into ⅛-inch slices. Carefully lift with spatula to baking sheet to preserve shape. Bake 8 to 10 min. Remove from pan to cake rack immediately to cool. 4 to 5 dozen.

CHERRY CHEWS

A colorful crisp party cookie of good flavor

1¼ cups cake flour	*¾ cup xxxx sugar, pkd
⅛ tsp salt	¼ tsp almond extract
¼ cup candied cherries	¼ tsp vanilla
½ cup soft butter	1 tsp cream *or* milk

Grease baking sheets. Start oven 10 min before baking; set to moderately hot (400° F). Sift flour, measure, resift with salt. Cut cherries lengthwise into 4ths, then cut 4ths into halves. Cream butter until shiny, add sugar and cream well. Stir in flavorings and cream. Add flour in 2 or 3 portions, mixing until smooth after each. Pat dough out on heavy waxed paper to ½-inch thickness, then sprinkle with cherries; roll up like jelly roll to distribute cherries. Shape into a uniform roll about 8-inches long and 1½-inches in diameter. Wrap in waxed paper and chill in coldest spot in refrigerator until firm enough to slice easily. Remove roll to cutting board, and with sharp, thin-bladed knife, cut with saw-like motion into slices about ⅛-inch thick. Place on prepared baking sheet. Bake 7 to 8 min or to a pale golden color. Cool on pan on cake rack a min, then slip spatula gently under cookies to loosen, then slide onto rack to cool. Store in container with tight-fitting cover with waxed paper between layers. About 3 dozen.

* Put xxxx sugar through sieve or flour sifter, then pack firmly into cup.

CHOCOLATE PINWHEELS

*If you will closely observe the colored picture, see opposite page 385,
you can see exactly how to achieve these beautiful cookies*

1 sq unsweet chocolate	½ tsp salt, scant
2 cups *plus* 1 tbsp all-purpose flour	¾ cup soft butter
½ tsp D.A. baking powder *or*	1 cup *plus* 2 tbsp sugar
⅔ tsp tartrate *or* phosphate type	1½ tsp vanilla
	1 large egg
	1½ tbsp milk

Grease baking sheets lightly. Start oven 10 min before baking; set to moderately hot (400° F).

Melt chocolate over hot water, then cool to lukewarm. Sift flour, measure, resift with baking powder and salt. Cream butter until smooth and shiny, add sugar in 2 or 3 portions, creaming well. Stir in vanilla, then beat in egg until fluffy. Add flour and milk alternately in 2 or 3 portions, mixing until smooth after each. Now divide dough into 2 parts, with a little more in one than the other. Blend chocolate into the smaller portion with a wooden spoon. Chill both portions of dough about an hr. Now shape each portion into a rectangular bar about 5 by 6 inches. Return light dough to refrigerator. Place chocolate dough on lightly floured pastry cloth and roll out with floured, stockinet-covered rolling pin into a rectangle about 12 x 15 inches. Use a 12 x 15 inch sheet of waxed paper as a guide to roll out this rectangle. Now lay another 12 x 15 sheet of waxed paper on *bottom of a baking sheet,* then set baking sheet on dough. Now quickly invert pastry cloth with its dough onto *back of baking sheet.* Lift off pastry cloth and place baking sheet of dough in refrigerator.

Next, roll out light dough on pastry cloth to same size—12 x 15 inches. Now remove rolled-out chocolate dough from refrigerator; place another baking sheet carefully over top of this dough. Bring the 2 baking sheets to edge of light dough, then *gradually* lower over light dough, pulling out the *inside baking sheet* as the chocolate dough falls exactly into place on top of light dough. Remove waxed paper from top. Now carefully roll up double layer of dough snugly, starting at the narrow-end. Wrap roll in waxed paper, twisting ends together tightly. Now roll up in thin cardboard and fasten with 2 or 3 rubber bands. (Shirt cardboard is ideal.) Place in refrigerator to chill until very firm. To bake, cut into slices ⅛-inch thick. Place on prepared sheets. Bake 8 to 9 min or until delicately browned. Remove immediately from baking sheet to cake racks to cool. 4 to 4½ dozen.

REMEMBER: Increase flour a little or decrease liquid a little when baking in the South.

DATE PINWHEELS

Chewy, rich in flavor and attractive

Cookie Dough:
- 1¼ cups all-purpose flour
- ¼ tsp soda
- ½ tsp salt, scant
- ¼ cup brown sugar, packed
- ½ cup butter *or* margarine
- ¼ cup granulated sugar
- 1 egg
- ½ tsp vanilla

Date Filling:
- ½ lb whole fresh dates *or*
- 7¼-oz pkg pitted dates
- ⅓ cup water
- ¼ cup sugar
- ½ cup fine-cut nuts
- 2 tsp lemon juice
- ½ tsp grated lemon rind

Grease baking sheets. Start oven 10 min before baking; set to moderately hot (400° F).

Dough: Sift flour, measure, resift 3 times with soda and salt. Put moist brown sugar through coarse sieve. Cream soft butter until shiny, add sugars and cream well. Beat in egg until fluffy, stir in vanilla, then flour and mix until smooth. Cover and place dough in refrigerator while preparing Filling.

Filling: Pit whole dates, and cut either kind small, dropping into a 1-qt saucepan. Add water and sugar, place over moderate heat and cook and stir to a medium-thick paste, from 3 to 4 min. Remove from heat; cool to lukewarm, then stir in nuts, lemon juice and rind. Lightly flour a pastry cloth and roll cookie dough into a 10 x 14-inch rectangle. Now spread *Date Filling* carefully over dough in a uniformly thick layer. Begin at narrow end, roll up like jelly roll, using cloth to facilitate rolling. Now wrap roll in waxed paper, then in thin cardboard and fasten with rubber bands and chill in refrigerator until very firm. Remove to cutting board, remove paper, and with a sharp knife, cut into slices about ³⁄₁₆-inch thick. Place about 1-inch apart on prepared sheets. Bake about 7 min or until a golden brown—*do not overbake*. Remove to cake rack to cool on baking sheets about a min, then remove to rack. 3 dozen.

ORANGE-PECAN REFRIGERATOR COOKIES

Delicate orange flavor and color—very crisp and tender

- 1½ cups all-purpose flour
- ¼ tsp salt
- ¼ tsp soda
- ½ tsp D.A. baking powder *or*
  - ⅔ tsp tartrate *or* phosphate type
- ⅔ cup butter *or* margarine
- ¾ cup *plus* 1 tbsp sugar
- 1 tbsp orange juice
- 1 tsp lemon juice
- ½ tsp grated orange rind, packed
- 1 egg
- ½ cup fine-cut pecans

Grease baking sheets lightly. Start oven 10 min before baking; set to moderately hot (400° F).

Sift flour, measure, resift 4 times with next 3 ingredients. In a 3-qt mixing bowl, cream soft butter until smooth, add sugar in 2 portions, creaming well. Add orange and lemon juice and rind and beat well, then beat in egg until fluffy. Stir in flour in 2 portions until well mixed after each, then stir in nuts. Cover bowl, place in refrigerator until dough is firm. Now shape quickly into a roll about 10 inches long. Wrap in waxed paper, then in a piece of thin cardboard and hold in shape with rubber bands. Store in refrigerator overnight or until very firm. Slice with a sharp knife into cookies about $\frac{3}{16}$-inch thick. Place on prepared sheet. Bake about 8 min or to a delicate golden color. Remove from pan to cake rack immediately to cool. 3¾ dozen.

ROLLED COOKIES

Rolled Cookies are what got cookies rolling! They are the Originals! They require more time, more equipment and more work than other cookies but provide greater opportunity for making original and attractive shapes. The Cookie Cutter plays an important role here. See Directions for Cutting Cookies, next page.

Now that Pastry Cloths and Refrigerators are available to most home-makers, the problem Grandma had of rolling and cutting soft dough is practically eliminated. Now, with a refrigerator, the dough can be mixed, then chilled until very firm, then only enough removed at a time for a pan of cookies. Chilled dough rolls out easily with a stockinet-covered rolling pin on a pastry cloth with very little additional flour, thus retaining the softness required for delicate cookies. Most rolled cookie doughs can be covered and stored in the refrigerator, then baked as needed. Roll dough uniformly thick for even baking and cut as many cookies as possible from the dough, using same size cutter for each panful for uniform baking. Different shapes on a baking sheet do not bake done in the same time.

RE-ROLLING COOKIE DOUGH

Lay leftover dough scraps together on pastry cloth, overlapping edges well. Then press with rolling pin to stick pieces together. Now roll very lightly and cut as before. Cookies re-rolled this way are as tender as those baked from first-rolled dough. Wadding and kneading dough scraps together toughens the cookies.

DIRECTIONS FOR CUTTING OUT ROLLED COOKIES

Always dip cutters in flour before cutting dough

It takes more imagination than anything else to do a masterful job of cutting cookies. With a long straight knife one can cut squares, oblongs and diamonds of various sizes; with a pastry jagger one can cut these same shapes with scalloped edges. Large circles can be cut out with the *removable rim* from a coffee can, or with a No. 2½ tin can cut open smoothly. With a knife these circles may then be cut in halves, or quarters for fan-shapes. These same cutters can be used to nick out an oval or a half-moon from each large round cut-out. With a 2- or 3-inch plain round cutter, cut a circle out of the coffee rim circle, making a ring or wreath. Biscuit and doughnut cutters make good cookie cutters. With a little ingenuity, it is unnecessary to buy a lot of cutters to make attractive cookies. Here are some cutters, however, that every homemaker should have:

1. Bold scalloped round cutters in 2 or 3 sizes. Bold designs are retained throughout the baking, while shallow designs are lost in the baking.

2. Heart, diamond and star-shape cutters in 2 or 3 sizes.

3. Gingerbread men, Santa Claus, Christmas tree and animal cutters, such as duck, chicken and rabbit, if there are children in the home.

Shapes like hatchets, bells and stockings may be cut from thin white cardboard, then lay these shapes on the dough and trace around with the tip of a knife. Use a spatula or small pancake turner to lift the cookies to the baking sheet as soon as they are cut. When one has 2 or 3 sizes of cutters in one shape, it is easy to produce some unusual effects. For example, small heart-shapes cut from thin-rolled dough laid on a larger heart-cut-out bake very satisfactorily. This baked cookie may then have only the small heart spread with frosting, or sprinkle it with colored sugar before baking. Or a small heart may be cut from a larger heart, and heart-shaped-rim laid on a heart cut-out of the same size to give a picture-frame effect. The 2 sizes of star and scalloped cutters can be used in the same way. After cutting cookies with a doughnut cutter, overlap the small left-over rounds in a circle for wreaths, or overlap the edges of 5 of these cut-outs to look like petals of a flower, pressing together in the center. A little tuft of coconut dropped in the center will simulate stamens.

BASIC SUGAR COOKIES

A great favorite—delicate sweet crunchy cookies

2½ cups all-purpose flour	1⅓ cups sugar
½ tsp soda	½ tsp vanilla
1 tsp cream of tartar	½ tsp lemon extract
¼ tsp salt	2 eggs
½ cup soft butter	1 to 2 tbsp milk
⅓ cup shortening	Raisins, nuts, if desired

Grease baking sheets lightly. Start oven 10 min before baking; set to moderately hot (425° F).

Sift flour, measure, resift 5 times with next 3 ingredients. Cream butter and shortening until shiny, then add sugar gradually and cream well. Stir in flavorings, then beat in eggs until fluffy. Add flour in 2 or 3 portions, mixing until smooth after each portion. Stir in milk. Cover bowl and place in refrigerator to chill an hr. Remove ⅓ of the dough at a time (keep rest chilled). Roll out on a lightly floured pastry cloth with floured stockinet-covered rolling pin to a thickness between ⅛- and ¼-inch. Cut out as close together as possible. Place on prepared baking sheet. Leave plain, or sprinkle with sugar, or press a raisin, or nut lightly into center of cookies. Brush with egg white beaten slightly with 1 tbsp of water, if desired. Re-roll leftover dough, p 484. Bake 8 to 10 min to a light golden brown. Let stand on baking sheet a half min, then remove to cake racks to cool. 5 dozen 2¼-inch cookies.

BUTTERSCOTCH COOKIES

Substitute 1⅓ cups moist brown sugar packed for the granulated in Basic Sugar Cookie Recipe, and stir in ½ cup chopped pecans after the flour is added. Otherwise make and bake as directed.

LEMON-COCONUT COOKIES

Omit vanilla from Basic Sugar Cookie Recipe. Add 1 tsp grated lemon rind, packed and ½ cup moist, fine-cut shredded coconut, firmly packed. Otherwise make and bake as directed.

MAPLE-PECAN COOKIES

Omit extracts from Basic Sugar Cookie Recipe. Add ½ tsp maple extract. Stir in ½ cup chopped pecans after adding flour. Otherwise make and bake as directed.

ORANGE COOKIES

Omit milk and vanilla from Basic Sugar Cookie Recipe, and for it substitute 1 to 2 tbsp orange juice and ½ tsp grated orange rind. Otherwise make and bake as directed.

SAND TARTS

Make Basic Sugar Cookie dough as directed. Roll out and cut with 2-inch cookie cutter. Brush with slightly beaten egg white, then sprinkle with a mixture of 2 tbsp sugar and ¼ tsp cinnamon. Otherwise make and bake as directed.

SPICE COOKIES

Omit vanilla. Substitute moist brown sugar packed for granulated in Basic Sugar Cookie Recipe. Sift flour, measure, resift 3 times with baking powder, salt, ½ tsp cinnamon, ¼ tsp cloves, and ¼ tsp nutmeg. Otherwise make and bake as directed.

BEST ORANGE COOKIES MADE WITH POULTRY FAT

1 tsp grated orange rind, pkd	¾ tsp salt
2 tbsp orange juice	⅓ cup cold poultry fat, p 166
2 cups all-purpose flour	1 cup sugar
2 tsp D.A. baking powder *or*	4 egg yolks, beaten
2½ tsp tartrate *or* phos-	
phate type	

Grease baking sheets lightly. Start oven 10 min before baking; set to moderately hot (400° F).

Wash orange, grate rind and squeeze juice. Sift flour, measure, resift 3 times with baking powder and salt. Cream fat, sugar and orange rind well. Beat in yolks and orange juice vigorously until well blended. Add sifted dry ingredients and stir until well mixed. Divide dough into 3 portions; wrap in waxed paper and chill. Remove 1 portion at a time and roll out with floured stockinet-covered rolling pin on lightly floured pastry cloth, about ⅛-inch thick. Cut with 2-inch cutter. Sprinkle with sugar, if desired. Lift with broad-blade spatula to prepared sheet. Bake 8 to 10 min or until delicately browned. Cool on pan on cake rack a min or two, then remove to rack to cool. Store in container with tight-fitting cover with waxed paper between layers. 5 dozen.

BRANDY SNAPS

These wafer-like cookies are delicious with ice cream or beverages

2¾ cups all-purpose flour	¾ cup white corn syrup
½ cup butter	⅛ tsp salt
1⅓ cups brown sugar, packed	1½ tsp ginger

Grease baking sheets. Start oven 10 min before baking; set to moderately hot (400° F). Sift flour and measure. Measure next 5 ingredients into top of double boiler; place over boiling water and stir until butter melts and ingredients are well blended. Remove from heat and cool slightly. Stir in flour in 2 or 3 portions, mixing well. Remove dough to waxed paper and chill thoroughly, then divide dough into 4 portions. Remove one portion at a time and roll out with a floured stockinet-covered rolling pin on a lightly floured pastry cloth to a very thin sheet, about $\frac{1}{16}$-inch thick. Cut into 2-inch rounds. Lift carefully with spatula and place about ½-inch apart on prepared baking sheet. Bake 5 min. Let cool on pan on cake rack a min or two, then remove to rack. Stored in a tightly covered container, these cookies keep several months. About 11 dozen.

COTTAGE CHEESE COOKIES

These intriguing cookies look like little square pillows. They are
luscious and nutritious. Storing is no problem

2 cups all-purpose flour	1 cup creamed cottage cheese
¼ tsp D.A. baking powder *or*	Stiff red jelly *or* well-
⅓ tsp tartrate *or* phosphate	drained strawberry *or*
type	cherry preserves
1 cup soft butter, ½ lb	

Have baking sheets ready—do not grease. Start oven 10 min before
baking; set to moderately hot (425° F). Sift flour, measure, resift with
baking powder. Cream butter until shiny, add cheese and cream until
well blended. (Press cheese with large curds through coarse sieve.) Add
flour in 3 or 4 portions, mixing until smooth after each. Shape into a
ball; wrap in waxed paper and chill about an hr. Remove half the dough
at a time. Shape into a rectangle; pat and roll out carefully on a lightly
floured pastry cloth into a 10 x 15-inch rectangle about ⅛-inch thick.
Cut into 6 strips one way and 4 the other to obtain 24—2½-inch
squares. Place a scant tsp of jelly or preserves in center of each square
(do only a few sqs at a time), then fold corners of dough up to center,
pressing all meeting edges together *firmly*. It is important edges be sealed
together well so jelly won't run out onto sheet. Place filled squares
onto baking sheet. Bake about 12 min or until delicately browned. Remove immediately from pan to cake racks to cool. 4 dozen.

DELICATE BUTTER COOKIES

Fragile, golden, delicious butter-flavored cookies

2½ cups *plus* 1 tbsp all-purpose	⅔ cup sugar
flour	1 tsp vanilla
¾ tsp D.A. baking powder *or*	1 tsp lemon extract
1 tsp tartrate *or* phosphate	1 egg
type	(No salt)
1 cup butter, room temp	

Have baking sheets ready—do not grease. Start oven 10 min before
baking, set to moderately hot (425° F).
Sift flour, measure, resift 3 times with baking powder. Cream butter
until smooth and shiny, add sugar gradually, creaming thoroughly. Stir
in flavorings, then beat in egg until fluffy. Add flour in 2 or 3 portions,
mixing only until smooth after each portion. Cover and place in refrigerator 1 hr to chill. Remove ⅓ of dough at a time (keep rest chilled).
Roll out on a lightly floured pastry cloth with floured stockinet-covered
rolling pin to a thickness of about 1⁄16-inch. Cut as close together as
possible and place 1-inch apart on baking sheet. Bake from 4 to 5 min
to a delicate golden color. Remove to cake racks to cool. To store, lay

one-layer deep between sheets of waxed paper in covered box to prevent tender cookies from breaking. 7 dozen 2¼-inch cookies.

FRUIT FILLED COOKIES

Not a rich but a delicious hearty cookie—enjoyed by children as well as adults

Fruit Filling:
 1 cup pitted moist dates
 ½ tsp lemon rind, packed
 2 tbsp lemon juice
 1 cup sugar
 1 tbsp flour
 1 cup seedless raisins
  Dash of salt
 ¾ cup water

Cookie Dough:
 4½ cups all-purpose flour
 2 tsp D.A. baking powder
  or 1½ tsp tartrate *or*
  phosphate type
 ½ tsp salt
 1 cup shortening *or* half
  butter, half lard
 2 cups sugar
 2 eggs
 2 tsp vanilla
 ⅓ tbsp thick cream

Filling: Use kitchen scissors to cut dates small. Grate lemon rind and squeeze juice. Blend sugar and flour in a 1-qt saucepan, add remaining ingredients and mix well. Place over low heat, stir constantly and cook until well-blended and thick, boiling about 3 min. Cool.

Cookie Dough: Grease baking sheets lightly. Start oven 10 min before baking; set to moderately hot (400° F).

Sift flour, measure, resift 3 times with baking powder and salt. Cream shortening until shiny, add sugar gradually and beat well. Beat in egg until smooth and fluffy, then vanilla. Stir in flour and cream alternately in 2 or 3 portions, beginning and ending with flour and beating well after each. Cover and chill dough at least an hr. Roll out about ⅛-inch thick on a lightly floured pastry cloth. Cut out with 2-inch heart-shape cutter, or any desired shape. Place half of the cut-outs on prepared baking sheet. Now place a tsp of *Fruit Filling* in center of each cut-out, then cover with another cut-out, sandwich fashion. Press edges together firmly with tip-end of knife handle. Bake 10 to 12 min or until delicately browned. Remove immediately from pan to cake rack to cool. 4 to 5 dozen.

Note: Any tart firm jelly, preserves or mincemeat are suitable for filling. Other delicious fillings are those for kolachy, p 285.

GINGER CRISPS

These cookies keep crisp as long as they last

½ cup butter *or* margarine   2 cups all-purpose flour
½ cup light molasses   1 tsp cinnamon
½ cup sugar   ½ tsp ginger
 1 tbsp vinegar   1½ tsp soda

Grease baking sheets. Start oven 10 min before baking; set to moderate (375° F). Measure first 4 ingredients into 1-qt saucepan. Stir well and place over moderate heat and boil gently exactly 3 min, stirring constantly. Remove from heat and cool. Meanwhile sift flour, measure, resift 3 times with rest of ingredients. Add dry ingredients to cooled molasses mixture in 2 or 3 portions, mixing until smooth after each. Shape dough into a ball; wrap in waxed paper and chill overnight or for several hrs. Roll out thin—about 1/16-inch on lightly floured pastry cloth with stockinet-covered rolling pin. Cut with a 2-inch round cutter. Place 1½ inches apart on prepared baking sheet. Bake about 7 min or until a rich brown. Immediately remove from pan to cake rack to cool. 8 to 9 dozen.

GROUND OATMEAL COOKIES

Interesting, delicious, crisp and nutritious

1 cup quick rolled oats	½ cup granulated sugar
½ cup moist pitted dates	½ cup butter *or* margarine
1 cup all-purpose flour	1 egg
½ tsp soda	½ tsp vanilla
¼ tsp salt	¼ cup chopped nuts
½ cup brown sugar, packed	

Grease baking sheets. Start oven 10 min before baking; set to moderately hot (400° F). Put oats through food chopper using coarse blade, putting through a little at a time. Then put dates through chopper. Sift flour, measure, resift 4 times with soda and salt. Put moist brown sugar through coarse sieve, then stir into granulated sugar. Cream soft butter until shiny, then add sugars in 2 portions and cream well. Beat in egg until fluffy, then stir in vanilla and dates. Add flour mixed with oatmeal in 2 portions, mixing until smooth after each. Now stir in nuts, mixing well. Roll out on a lightly floured pastry cloth about ¼-inch thick. Cut with a 2¼-inch round cutter. Place on prepared sheet. Bake 9 to 10 min. Remove immediately to cake rack to cool. 2½ dozen.

HUNGARIAN JELLY-FILLED CRESCENTS

2 cups all-purpose flour	½ cup sour cream
¼ tsp salt	½ cup stiff tart jelly
½ cup firm butter	1 egg yolk beaten with
1 tbsp lard	3 tbsp milk
2 small egg yolks	xxxx sugar

Grease baking sheets lightly. Start oven 10 min before baking; set to moderately hot (400° F).

Sift flour, measure, resift with salt into 3-qt mixing bowl. Add firm butter sliced into pats and the lard, then with a pastry blender or 2 knives cut ingredients together until consistency of coarse corn meal. Now mix in the 2 yolks and sour cream until just smooth. Shape dough into a ball, wrap in waxed paper and chill overnight. Roll out on lightly floured pastry cloth to ⅛-inch thickness. Cut into 3-inch rounds. Place ½ tsp jelly ½-inch from edge on each round; then fold the ½-inch edge over jelly to completely cover it, then press edges down to seal in jelly. Now roll up like jelly roll. Place on waxed paper with open edge on bottom; shape into crescents. Brush with yolk-milk mixture and place on prepared sheet. Bake 10 to 12 min or to a light golden color. Remove from baking sheet at once to cake rack to cool. Sprinkle with xxxx sugar. 2 dozen.

LEMON CREAM CHEESE COOKIES

2¼ cups all-purpose flour	1 cup sugar
1 cup soft butter or half	2 egg yolks
shortening	1 tsp vanilla
¼ tsp salt	1 tsp grated lemon rind,
3-oz pkg cream cheese	packed

Grease baking sheets lightly. Start oven 10 min before baking; set to moderately hot (400° F). Sift flour and measure. Put butter, salt and cream cheese into mixing bowl; cream until very smooth. Add sugar in 2 or 3 portions, creaming well. Beat in yolks until fluffy, then stir in vanilla and lemon rind. Stir in flour in 2 or 3 portions, mixing well. Chill dough about 1 hr, then roll out ⅓ of dough at a time on a lightly floured pastry cloth about ³⁄₁₆-inch thick. Cut out with 2½-inch cutter as close together as possible. Place 1 inch apart on prepared baking sheet. Bake 10 to 12 min, or to a pale golden color. Remove immediately to cake rack to cool. 3½ dozen.

ROLLED SOFT GINGER COOKIES

2¼ cups all-purpose flour	½ cup sugar
½ tsp soda	1 egg, beaten
1½ tsp ginger	¼ cup dark molasses
¼ tsp salt	¼ cup buttermilk
½ cup soft butter	

Grease baking sheets lightly. Start oven 10 min before baking; set to moderate (375° F). Sift flour, measure, resift 4 times with next 3 ingredients. Cream butter until shiny, add sugar gradually, creaming well. Beat in egg until fluffy, then molasses. Add flour and buttermilk alternately in 2 or 3 portions, beginning and ending with flour and beating until smooth after each portion. Turn dough out onto waxed paper, *press* together and chill several hrs. To bake, divide into 3 portions, removing 1 portion at a time. Roll out on lightly floured pastry cloth about ¼-inch thick. Cut with 2-inch cutter. Place on baking sheet. Bake 10 to 12 min or until lightly browned. Remove to cake racks to cool. 4 dozen cookies.

ROLLED SOUR CREAM COOKIES

Good cookies with delicate butter-cream flavor, crisp and tender. Retain shape of deep scalloped cutters perfectly

2⅓ cups all-purpose flour	1 tbsp shortening
¼ tsp soda	½ tsp orange extract
¾ tsp D.A. baking powder *or*	¼ tsp lemon extract
1 tsp tartrate *or* phosphate	1 cup sugar
type	1 egg
½ tsp salt, scant	⅓ cup sour cream
½ cup butter *plus*	

Grease baking sheets lightly. Start oven 10 min before baking; set to moderate (375° F).

Sift flour, measure, resift 4 times with next 3 ingredients. Cream butter and shortening until smooth; stir in flavorings. Then add sugar in 2 or 3 portions, creaming well. Beat in egg until fluffy, then stir in flour mixture and the cream alternately in 2 or 3 portions, mixing until just smooth after each. Roll out on a lightly floured pastry cloth or board about ³⁄₁₆-inch thick. Cut out with a 2½-inch cutter. Place on prepared sheet and bake 13 to 15 min. Remove from pan to cake rack immediately. About 4 dozen.

Variation: Brush cookies with egg white blended with 1 tbsp water, then sprinkle with sugar. Place a blanched almond in center of each before baking for an attractive finish.

SCOTCH SHORTBREAD

Made famous in Scotland. Mildly sweet with delicate butter flavor—a crunchy thick cookie

2¼ cups all-purpose flour	1 cup soft butter
¼ tsp D.A. baking powder *or*	½ cup *plus* 1 tbsp sugar
⅓ tsp tartrate *or* phosphate	
type	

Have baking sheets ready—do not grease. Start oven 10 min before baking; set to moderately slow (325° F). Sift flour, measure, resift 2 times with baking powder. Cream butter until shiny, add sugar gradually, creaming well. Stir in flour in 2 or 3 portions, mixing until smooth after each portion, then knead a few times to blend well. Roll out on a

Remember: All baking powder designated in recipes in this book is the Double Action, the Sulphate-Phosphate Type. See p 113 for using other types in these recipes.

lightly floured pastry cloth ¼-inch thick, keeping shape as nearly rectangular as possible. Prick dough all over with a large tined fork, or mark shallow crisscross lines over top with tines of fork; or press any other desired design over top. Cut into 2-inch sqs. Place on baking sheet ½-inch apart. Bake 18 to 20 min or to a very delicate golden color. Remove from pans immediately to cake racks to cool. 3 dozen.

Note: Rolled out shortbread dough may be cut to fit an 8 or 9-inch cake pan. Use knife handle or knitting needle to mark these circles deeply into pie-shaped wedges. Or the small plain squares may be marked with thumb-print all around edge.

SHORTBREAD FANS

2⅛ cups all-purpose flour	⅔ cup brown sugar, packed
¼ tsp D.A. baking powder *or*	1 cup soft butter
⅓ tsp tartrate *or* phosphate type	1 egg yolk mixed with
	2 tbsp milk

Have baking sheets ready—do not grease. Start oven 10 min before baking; set to moderately slow (325° F).

Sift flour, measure, resift twice with baking powder. Put moist sugar through coarse sieve to remove lumps. Cream butter until shiny, add sugar gradually, creaming well. Add flour in 2 or 3 portions, mixing until smooth after each. Knead dough until smooth. Roll out ¼-inch thick on lightly floured pastry cloth with floured stockinet-covered rolling pin. Cut with a round, plain or scalloped cutter 4 to 5 inches in diameter. Then cut each round into quarters. With handle of a knife, mark each quarter with lines to represent splints in a fan. Brush with egg yolk mixture. Place on baking sheet ½-inch apart. Bake 20 to 25 min or until delicately browned. Remove from pans immediately to cake racks to cool. 2½ dozen.

SOFT MOLASSES ROLLED COOKIES

A Yankee favorite

5¼ to 5½ cups all-purpose flour	1 cup lard, melted
	1 cup sugar
1½ tsp cream of tartar	1 cup molasses
1½ tsp ginger	2 tsp vanilla
1½ tsp cinnamon	1 egg, beaten
½ tsp cloves	4 tsp soda
¾ tsp salt	¾ cup hot water

Grease aluminum baking sheets lightly, then dust with flour to prevent cookies from spreading. Start oven 10 min before baking; set to moderately hot (400° F).

Sift flour, measure, resift 3 times with next 5 ingredients. Heat lard until barely melted, cool slightly, then pour over sugar in a 4-qt mixing bowl. With rotary beater, beat until blended, then beat in molasses, then vanilla and egg, beating very hard. Dissolve soda in the hot water and stir into molasses mixture. Now stir dry ingredients into molasses mixture in 3 or 4 portions, stirring after each until thoroughly blended. Cover dough with waxed paper and chill in refrigerator 20 min or more for easier handling. Remove ¼ of dough at a time. Roll out on lightly floured pastry cloth about ¼-inch thick and cut with a 3½-inch cutter. Place on prepared sheets. Bake about 10 min. Remove from oven to cake rack, let cool on pan a min or two, then remove to racks to cool. 36 to 40—3½-inch cookies.

SOFT SUGAR COOKIES

A memorable pioneer day cookie. The secret of softness is cutting thick and baking at high temp

4 cups all-purpose flour	1 cup soft butter *or use*
1 tsp D.A. baking powder	⅓ cup each, margarine, lard
or 1¼ tsp tartrate *or*	and shortening
phosphate type	1½ cups sugar
1 tsp soda	2 tsp vanilla
¾ tsp salt	2 eggs
¾ tsp freshly grated nutmeg	¾ cup sour cream

Grease baking sheet lightly. Start oven 10 min before baking; set to hot (450° F) . . . *Yes,* 450° F. Use a 3-qt mixing bowl and mix with a wooden spoon.

Sift flour, measure, resift 4 times with next 4 ingredients. Cream butter or combination of shortenings until smooth, add sugar gradually, creaming well. Stir in vanilla, then beat in eggs until fluffy. Add flour mixture alternately with cream in 2 or 3 portions, mixing until smooth after each. Scrape off spoon, remove. Cover bowl and chill in refrigerator an hr or so to firm dough for easier rolling. Remove ⅓ of dough at a time. Roll out on a lightly floured pastry cloth with stockinet-covered rolling pin ¼-inch thick. Cut out with a 3½-inch cutter. Place on prepared baking sheet. Sprinkle with sugar, if desired. Bake 9 to 10 min. Remove at once to cake rack to cool. Store in tight-covered cookie jar or box with waxed paper between layers. 40 cookies.

VIENNA CREAM CHEESE TARTS

1 cup all-purpose flour	1 egg yolk mixed with
½ cup soft butter	2 tbsp milk
3-oz pkg cream cheese	¼ cup chopped walnuts
¼ cup stiff tart jelly	xxxx sugar

Have all ingredients at room temp. Grease baking sheets lightly. Start oven 10 min before baking; set to moderately hot (400° F).

Sift flour and measure. Cream butter and cheese until smooth and fluffy. Stir in flour, then knead into a smooth dough. Wrap in waxed paper and chill several hrs. Roll dough out on a lightly floured pastry cloth into a rectangle ⅛-inch thick. Cut into 2-inch squares. Place ¼ tsp jelly in one corner of each square. Now begin at this corner, and *fold over the corner* to just completely cover the jelly; press down to seal in jelly, then from this point roll the square diagonally, pinching together slightly. Place on waxed paper with seam-side down. Brush with yolk mixture, then sprinkle with nuts, or dip brushed surface in nuts. Place on prepared baking sheet, curving into crescent shape. Bake 12 to 15 min. Remove immediately from pan to cake racks to cool. Sprinkle with xxxx sugar. 2½ dozen.

HOLIDAY COOKIES

These cookies originated in many lands and are made from *all types* of cookie dough. From European countries come the Lebkuchen, Cinnamon Stars, Pfefferneusse, Spritz and Springerlie, but America claims the Gingerbread Man! Spritz Dough and our Sugar Cookie Dough are generally used to make traditional Christmas and New Year emblem cookies, such as trees, stockings, bells and stars. The same doughs are used to make Children's Party Cookies such as boy-and-girl cut-outs, or oblongs with children's names written on them for Party Favors; and Easter Cookies cut in shapes such as ducks, chickens and rabbits. These cookies must be *rolled thicker* to be less fragile.

CINNAMON STARS

Famous Christmas Cookie—expensive and elegant, but worth the cost once a year

1 lb unblanched almonds	6 egg whites, room temp
Grated rind of 1 lemon	1 tsp cinnamon
1 lb sifted xxxx firmly packed sugar	xxxx sugar

Rub baking sheet very lightly with melted paraffin. Start oven 10 min before baking; set to slow (300° F).

Shake almonds in a clean dry cloth to rub off any loose material, but do not blanch. Grate almonds fine in a nut grater or put a few at a time through a food mill, leaving bottom screw loose. This grating requires time and patience, but the characteristic quality can be obtained only from *grated almonds*. Grate off only the yellow portion of

Remember: All baking powder designated in recipes in this book is the Double Action, the Sulphate-Phosphate Type. See p 113 for using other types in these recipes.

lemon rind, then fold it in waxed paper to keep fragrant and moist. Beat egg whites until stiff but not dry, then gradually beat in sugar until shiny pointed peaks that curve at the tips form. Now fold in lemon rind until distributed. Remove ¼ of the mixture and reserve. To remainder, add almonds and cinnamon, folding in until just blended. Now turn out mixture onto pastry cloth or board sprinkled generously with sugar. Roll out ¼-inch thick. Cut out with a star cutter. Now on each cut-out, drop a teaspoonful of *reserved meringue,* and with handle of spoon, draw it out into each point of the star. Transfer carefully to prepared baking sheet. Bake 40 to 50 min or until lightly browned and crusty. Remove immediately from pan to cake racks to cool. 2 to 4 dozen stars, depending on size.

GINGERBREAD MEN

Fun Cookies—Fun to make, to give and to get!

2¾ cups all-purpose flour	¾ cup light molasses
½ tsp soda	1 egg, beaten
1 tsp ginger	½ tsp grated lemon rind,
½ tsp cinnamon	packed
½ tsp salt	1 tsp hot water
½ cup shortening	1 tsp vinegar
¼ cup moist brown sugar, pkd	

Grease baking sheets lightly, then sprinkle with flour, then tilt and tap lightly to coat with thin film. Start oven 10 min before baking; set to moderate (350° F). Sift flour, measure, resift 4 times with next 4 ingredients. With rotary beater, cream shortening until shiny, add moist sugar in 2 or 3 portions and cream well. Now beat in molasses and egg until fluffy. Clean off beater, remove; use wooden spoon. Add flour in 2 or 3 portions, mixing until smooth after each, then stir in lemon rind, water and vinegar until well blended. Cover dough and chill until firm. Divide into 4 portions. Remove 1 portion at a time from refrigerator and roll out ¼-inch thick on a lightly floured pastry cloth. Use Snowman or Santa Claus cutter, or make a cardboard pattern to lay on dough and trace around with knife to cut out cookies. Use pancake turner to lift cut-outs from pastry cloth and a spatula to carefully slide onto prepared baking sheet. Bend arms and legs to give action poses such as running, fighting, etc. Bake about 20 min or until nicely browned. Remove from pan immediately to cake racks to cool. Decorate cookies with *Confectioners' Icing* or *Butter Frosting,* pp 392, 383, making hair, beard, fur on coat and stockings. Use currants, candies and pieces of candied cherries to make eyes, nose, mouth, buttons, etc. Store in metal box with tight-fitting cover 1-layer deep. About 12 six-inch gingerbread men.

DARK LEBKUCHEN

½ lb almonds, blanched,
  p 121
⅓ cup candied orange peel
¾ cup moist candied citron
½ cup candied cherries
1¼ cups honey
2 cups moist brown sugar,
  pkd
¼ cup water

7 cups all-purpose flour
½ tsp soda
¼ tsp each, cloves and nutmeg
1 tsp cinnamon
2 eggs
1 cup sifted xxxx sugar,
  firmly packed
1 tsp white corn syrup
Hot water

Grease baking sheets. Start oven 10 min before baking; set to moderate (350° F). Blanch almonds and cut in slivers while moist. Cut moist orange peel, citron and cherries fine, then measure. Measure honey, sugar and water into a 3-qt saucepan, stir to mix; place over medium heat and boil gently 5 min, then cool. Sift flour, measure, resift 4 times with soda and spices. Remove about 1 cup of flour mixture and sprinkle over nuts and fruit, tossing well to dredge. Use a wooden spoon to beat in eggs, one at a time, into cooled honey mixture, then stir in flour in 4 portions, mixing until smooth after each. Now add fruit mixture and knead thoroughly. Wrap dough in several layers of heavy waxed paper and store 3 or 4 days in a cool place—not refrigerator. When ready to bake, divide dough in 4 parts. Roll out 1 part at a time on a lightly floured pastry cloth or board about ¼-inch thick, keeping shape rectangular. Cut into oblongs 2 x 3 inches. Place on prepared sheets. Bake 12 to 15 min or until nicely browned. Remove from pan to cake rack immediately to cool. Now combine xxxx sugar and corn syrup, and add water by teaspoonfuls, mixing well to obtain an icing that spreads easily but does not run. Spread thinly on cookies and let stand until icing is firm. Store in an airtight container with waxed paper between layers to "ripen" for at least a month. About 10 dozen.

LIGHT LEBKUCHEN

¼ lb almonds, blanched,
  p 121
¼ lb candied citron
1 tsp grated lemon rind, pkd
4 cups all-purpose flour
½ tsp salt

2 tsp cinnamon
4 eggs, room temp
2 cups sugar
1 small cube ammonium
  carbonate, crushed—1 scant
  tsp

Grease baking sheets. Start oven 10 min before baking; set to moderately slow (325° F). Blanch almonds and cut fine while moist. Slice citron thin crosswise, then cut fine. Grate lemon rind. Sift flour, measure, resift 3 times with salt and cinnamon. Separate eggs. Beat whites with rotary beater until just stiff, then add yolks and sugar and beat with rotary beater or on *Low Speed* on electric mixer 10 min. Now remove beater, clean off and use wooden spoon. Stir in ammonium carbonate and rind, then stir in flour mixture in 4 portions, mixing well after each. Stir in almonds and citron last. Divide dough into 2 portions. Roll each out on a lightly floured pastry cloth or board to a little less than ¼-inch thick, keeping shape of dough as rectangular as possible. Cut into 3 x 2-inch oblongs, or other desired shapes. Lift cookies onto a lightly floured board, cover with cloth and let stand overnight. Next morning lift cookies from board, brush *bottom* first with a dry pastry brush, then with a brush dipped in cold water. Place wet-side up on prepared baking sheet. Bake 15 to 18 min or to a delicate golden brown. Remove from pan to cake rack immediately to cool. Store in an airtight container with waxed paper between layers. Let "ripen" at least a month before serving. Lebkuchen improve with age. About 8 dozen.

DARK PFEFFERNEUSSE

1st Part:

1¼ cups strained honey
¾ cup light molasses
2 tbsp butter *and*
½ cup lard *or* other
 shortening
1½ tsp cinnamon

¾ tsp cloves
½ tsp grated lemon rind,
 packed
6¼ cups all-purpose flour
1½ tsp soda
2 tbsp boiling water

Grease baking sheets lightly. Start oven 10 min before baking; set to moderate (350° F). Measure first 6 ingredients into a 3-qt saucepan, stir thoroughly. Place over medium heat and heat just to boiling. Remove from heat and cool slightly, then stir in lemon rind and 3 cups of the flour until well-mixed. Now dissolve soda in the hot water and stir in until well-mixed; then mix in well 3 more cups of the flour. Turn dough out on a pastry cloth or board sprinkled with part of the remaining ¼ cup flour. Knead until smooth, sprinkling more flour on cloth or board as needed. Wrap dough in several layers of heavy waxed paper, then wrap in a towel and put in a warm place (like back of stove) for 4 or 5 days.

2nd Part:

2 cups sugar
½ cup milk
1 egg, beaten
2½ cups all-purpose flour

Almonds or candied
cherries
xxxx sugar

Measure sugar and milk into a 1-qt saucepan; stir well and place over medium heat and heat just to boiling, then cool. Again heat to boiling, cool slightly and pour into a 4-qt mixing bowl. Beat in egg thoroughly and stir in flour in 2 or 3 portions, mixing well. Now remove towel and paper from first dough and add it to this freshly mixed dough.

Knead thoroughly until well mixed. Then turn out onto lightly floured pastry cloth or board and again knead, using as little flour as possible. To roll, divide dough into 3 portions. Roll each portion out ¼-inch thick. Cut out in diamond or other desired shapes. Place on prepared baking sheets. Decorate with whole blanched almonds or a piece of cherry. Bake 15 to 20 min or until nicely browned. Remove from pans to cake racks immediately to cool. Sprinkle with xxxx sugar, if desired. Store in an airtight container with waxed paper between layers. About 5 dozen 2 x 3¾-inch diamond-shaped cookies.

Note: Or roll dough into a long rope about 1 inch in diameter, then cut into ¼- to ⅓-inch lengths; roll pieces lightly between fingers to make balls. Place on prepared baking sheets. Bake 20 min. 20 dozen balls.

LIGHT PFEFFERNEUSSE

½ cup candied citron
½ tsp grated lemon rind, pkd
⅓ cup orange juice
2 cups all-purpose flour
½ tsp salt

½ tsp D.A. baking powder *or*
  ⅔ tsp tartrate *or* phosphate
  type
⅛ tsp white pepper
2 eggs, separated
1 cup sugar
Sugar

Grease baking sheets. Start oven 10 min before baking; set to moderately slow (325° F). Cut citron in thin slices, then cut fine. Grate lemon rind. Squeeze orange juice, cover and store in refrigerator. Sift flour, measure, resift 3 times with next 3 ingredients. Beat egg whites until stiff, add yolks and sugar and beat with rotary beater or at *Low Speed* on electric mixer for 10 min. Remove beater, use wooden spoon. Stir in lemon rind, then flour in 3 portions, mixing until smooth after each. Stir in citron. Wrap dough in waxed paper and chill. When ready to bake, pinch off pieces of dough about half the size of walnuts and roll into balls. Dip tops in the orange juice, then in sugar, either granulated or xxxx. Place sugar-side up about 2 inches apart on prepared sheets. Bake about 20 min or until a delicate brown. Remove immediately from pans to cake racks to cool. Store in airtight container with waxed paper between layers. 5 dozen.

MANDEL KAKAS

Elegant fragile Scandinavian pressed cookies for special occasions

½ cup fine-cut almonds
2 cups all-purpose flour
1 cup soft butter, unsalted

⅔ cup sugar
1 small egg white or yolk
¼ tsp almond extract

Have tiny 3¼-inch tart pans or 2½-inch bold scalloped gelatin molds ready—do not grease. Start oven 10 min before baking; set to moderate (375° F). Blanch almonds; chop fine while moist. Sift flour and measure. Cream butter until smooth and shiny, add sugar, creaming well. Beat in egg white until fluffy. Stir in extract, then flour to form a smooth, stiff dough. Measure by level tablespoonfuls onto waxed paper, quickly roll into balls. Now put balls inside of tart pans or molds, and with fingers, carefully press dough over bottom and *only half way up sides* of pan to uniform thickness. Molding dough into balls helps to obtain more uniform scallops around edge. Sprinkle ½ tsp almonds over dough, then press in gently. Set pans or molds on baking sheets. Bake 9 to 10 min to a pale gold color. Cool in pans on cake racks 2 or 3 min, then very *gently* shake from pans into hand and place on racks to cool. Store in waxed paper lined box with tight-fitting cover in one layer. 4 dozen.

SPRINGERLIE

German cookies made at Christmas—brittle and hard, yet when correctly made, are light, fragile and shell-like

Anise seed	1 cube ammonium carbonate
1 tsp grated lemon rind, pkd	(from druggist)
4 cups all-purpose flour	20 drops oil of anise
4 eggs	Corn starch
2 cups sugar, sifted	

Grease baking sheets and sprinkle lightly with anise seed. Start oven 10 min before baking; set to very slow (275° F).

Grate lemon rind. Sift flour and measure. Separate eggs; put yolks into 3-qt mixing bowl and whites into a 2-qt mixing bowl. Beat yolks until foamy with a rotary beater, then beat in the sugar thoroughly. Clean off and wash beater. Beat whites until stiff. Now turn whites onto yolk mixture and beat slowly with rotary beater or at *Low Speed* on electric mixer for 10 min. Remove beater and use wooden spoon. Crush ammonium carbonate and fold at once with anise oil and lemon rind into egg-sugar mixture. Now fold in flour in 4 portions until just smooth after each. Cover dough and chill 2 or 3 hrs. Meanwhile, tie a tbsp of corn starch loosely in a piece of cheesecloth and dust the Springerlie Board well. Now divide dough into 4 portions. Remove 1 portion at a time from refrigerator and roll out ¼-inch thick on a lightly floured pastry cloth or board. With Springerlie Board, stamp the rolled-out dough firmly so as to leave deep, clear impressions of the designs. Repeat dusting board each time cookies are stamped. Cut cookies apart between picture designs. Lift cookies carefully to a lightly floured board or baking sheet; cover with towel and let stand overnight. Before baking, brush flour from underside of Springerlie, and with finger, rub underside carefully with cold water. Place on prepared sheet. Bake 40 min or to a delicate straw-color. Cool on pans on cake racks 10 min, then remove to racks. Store in box with tight-fitting cover. May be eaten immediately, but improve with age. 6 to 8 dozen.

Croquettes

DON'T underestimate Croquettes! They are not a "refrigerator clean-up food." When carefully prepared by the tested recipes in this book, they are a dramatic entree. And when attractively garnished and served with an appropriate sauce or accompaniment, they become a gastronomic delight. Plan to have them for guest meals, too!

If deep fat frying is too expensive or impractical in your kitchen, you can bake many kinds beautifully. Prepare in usual way, except substitute Buttered Crumbs, p 162 for the dry ones. Place "dried off" croquettes on a cookie sheet and bake in a moderately hot oven (400° F) to a rich brown, from 15 to 20 min. Cylindrical croquettes bake to a more even color than the cones.

Hint: For dainty luncheons, measure croquette mixture in ¼ cup portions. This makes more croquettes and therefore requires more crumbs for coating.

GENERAL DIRECTIONS FOR MAKING CROQUETTES

Ingredients: To make delicious croquettes chop food so it is identifiable, never grind it. Adding a little finely chopped celery or green pepper to some mixtures gives croquettes a pleasant crunchy "bite."

To make croquettes, you will need Croquette White Sauce, appropriate seasonings (see individual recipes), chopped cooked meat, poultry, fish, eggs, etc., fine dry bread or cracker crumbs, egg beaten with water to coat croquettes and shortening for frying.

Measuring, shaping, coating, drying-off: Measure out mixture by ¼ or ⅓ cupfuls onto waxed paper spread with crumbs, and placed on cookie sheet. Spreading crumbs on waxed paper saves dishes and time. Place in refrigerator to chill. When cold and firm, shape measured portions neatly into cone or cylinder shapes. Roll in the crumbs, then in egg mixture and again in crumbs. To produce a crisper crust on croquettes, stand ½ hr in a cool place or refrigerator for coating to dry off.

Frying: Just before serving time, heat shortening from 360° to 365° F. Place croquettes, cones upright, cylinders on side, in frying basket and lower into hot fat, adjusting heat to keep at a constant temp around 350° F. Fry to a rich brown, from 3 to 4 min, time depending on size. Lift basket up and gently turn croquettes out onto absorbent paper placed in a shallow pan to drain, then place in slow oven (250° F) to keep hot until serving time, not more than 10 to 15 min for best eating quality. Serve with appropriate sauce, if desired.

Hint: Cover leftover croquettes and store in refrigerator. Reheat next day on an open shallow pan in a moderately hot oven (400° F) for 12 to 15 min. As good as freshly fried ones.

CROQUETTE WHITE SAUCE

Did you know a few twirls of a rotary beater give a smooth finishing touch to White Sauce?

½ cup butter, margarine *or* chicken fat
½ cup flour
2 cups milk

1 tsp salt
¼ tsp pepper
1 egg, beaten

Melt butter in saucepan over low heat, add flour in 2 portions, blending until smooth. Add milk gradually stirring constantly to keep smooth. Continue stirring until sauce boils, then simmer 5 min. Stir in seasonings. Remove from heat and beat in the egg, then cook and stir another 2 min. About 2 cups.

Hint: Cool White Sauce by covering and setting saucepan in cold water. Change water occasionally and stir sauce frequently to prevent "skin" or film from forming.

CHEESE CROQUETTES

HOMINY CHEESE CROQUETTES

¾ cup hominy grits
3 cups water
¾ tsp salt
1½ cups grated sharp American Cheese, 6 oz
1½ tbsp butter, melted

2 egg yolks, beaten
⅔ cup fine dry bread crumbs
1 egg beaten with
1 tbsp water
Shortening for frying

Put hominy in top of double boiler, add water and salt and soak for 3 or 4 hrs. Then place over boiling water, cover and cook until hominy is tender, from 30 to 45 min stirring occasionally. Cool slightly and combine lightly but thoroughly with cheese, butter and egg yolks. Measure ⅓ cup portions onto the crumbs spread on waxed paper. Chill. When firm, shape portions neatly into cones or balls. Coat cones, dry off and fry at 365° F as described under *General Directions,* p 501. Serve hot with Tomato Sauce, p 1261. 5 servings.

Note: An equal quantity of crushed cooked whole hominy may be used in place of the grits.

RICE-CHEESE CROQUETTES

1 cup raw rice
1½ cups grated sharp American cheese, 6 oz
2 egg yolks, beaten
1½ tsp salt

Pepper
⅔ cup fine dry bread crumbs
2 eggs beaten with
2 tbsp water
Shortening for frying

Cook rice according to directions on pkg. Do not rinse. Cool to lukewarm. Mix lightly but thoroughly with cheese, egg yolks, salt and pepper. Measure ⅓ cup portions onto crumbs spread on waxed paper. Chill. When firm, shape portions neatly into cones or balls. Coat cones, dry off and fry at 365° F as described under *General Directions,* p 501. Serve hot with any tart jelly or Tomato Sauce, p 1261. 4 to 5 servings.

SWISS CHEESE CROQUETTES

½ recipe Croquette White Sauce, p 502
½ tsp hot English type mustard
1 tbsp fine-cut green pepper *or* stuffed green olives

1 cup fine-diced Swiss cheese, 6 oz
1 egg beaten with
1 tbsp water
½ cup fine dry bread crumbs
Shortening for frying

Make White Sauce. Stir in mustard and green pepper, then cool to room temp. Now fold in cheese and measure ⅓ cup portions onto the crumbs spread on waxed paper. Chill thoroughly until firm, then form into cone-shapes. Roll in crumbs, then in egg-water mixture to coat well, then again in crumbs. Place in refrigerator until frying time. Fry in shortening heated to 365° F until golden brown. Lift out, drain and serve very hot with slices of broiled tomatoes. 6 croquettes.

EGG CROQUETTES

EGG CROQUETTES

Crispy outside, creamy inside, pleasant flavor

6 hard-cooked eggs, p 663
¼ cup butter *or* margarine
⅓ cup flour
1½ cups milk
1 tsp salt
⅟₁₆ tsp pepper
⅓ tsp grated onion

¾ tsp monosodium glutamate, optional, p 131
1 cup fine dry bread crumbs
1 egg beaten with
2 tbsp milk
Shortening for frying
Parsley

Hard cook eggs correctly. Make a cream sauce of next 5 ingredients. Cool. Fold diced eggs, onion and M S G into cream sauce. Measure out mixture by ⅓ cupfuls onto waxed paper spread with the crumbs. Place in refrigerator to chill. When cold and firm, shape measured portions neatly into cone-shapes. Roll in the crumbs, then in egg mixture and again in crumbs. Allow croquettes to stand for ½ hr in a cool place or in refrigerator to dry off. Fry in shortening heated to 365° F about 3 min or until golden brown. Drain on absorbent paper. Serve immediately with parsley garnish. 8 croquettes.

Note: Crumbled crisp bacon added to egg mixture makes a delicious variation.

FISH CROQUETTES

CRABMEAT CROQUETTES

½ recipe Croquette White Sauce, p 502
1 tbsp lemon juice
Few dashes of cayenne
⅓ cup finely chopped celery
½ tsp sherry extract, optional

6 oz can crabmeat *or* 1 cup fresh cooked
½ cup fine dry bread crumbs
1 egg beaten with
1 tbsp water
Shortening for frying

Make Croquette White Sauce. Stir in next 4 ingredients. Drain and discard liquid from crab; flake fish coarsely, removing cartilage. Fold into sauce mixture. Measure ¼ cup portions onto the crumbs spread on waxed paper. Chill. When firm, shape portions neatly into cones. Coat cones, dry off and fry at 365° F as described under *General Directions,* p 501. Serve hot with Egg Sauce, p 1255, if desired. 6 croquettes.

LOBSTER CROQUETTES

Follow directions for making Crabmeat Croquettes above by substituting lobster for the crabmeat.

SALMON CROQUETTES

½ recipe Croquette White Sauce, p 502
1 tbsp lemon juice
1 tsp onion juice, optional
1 lb can pink *or* red salmon

⅔ cup fine dry bread crumbs
1 egg beaten with
1 tbsp water
Shortening for frying

Make Croquette White Sauce using the juice from salmon as part of liquid. Stir in next 2 ingredients. Discard skin from salmon. Fold the flaked fish and crushed bones into white sauce. Cool mixture. Measure ⅓ cup portions onto the crumbs spread on waxed paper. Chill. When firm, shape portions neatly into cones, balls or cylinders. Coat cones, dry off and fry at 365° F as described under *General Directions.* Serve with Egg, Tartar or Tomato Sauce, pp 1255, 1260-61. 4 to 5 servings.

MEAT CROQUETTES
HAM CROQUETTES NO. 1

½ recipe warm Croquette
White Sauce, p 502
½ tsp prepared brown mus-
tard
1 tsp finely chopped parsley

2 cups finely diced baked *or*
boiled ham
½ cup fine dry bread crumbs
1 egg beaten with
1 tbsp water
Shortening for frying

Make Croquette Sauce. Put first 4 ingredients into mixing bowl and fold together until well blended. Cool mixture. Measure ⅓ cup portions onto the crumbs spread on waxed paper. Place in refrigerator to chill for an hr or so. Remove and shape portions neatly into cone shapes. Roll in crumbs, then in egg mixture and again in crumbs. Let croquettes stand ½ hr in refrigerator or cool place for coating to dry off. Fry at 365° F according to *General Directions,* p 501. Serve with Sauté Banana, p 561, or Egg Sauce, p 1255. 4 servings.

HAM CROQUETTES NO. 2

1 cup ground lean cooked
ham
2 cups cold stiff mashed
potatoes
1 egg, beaten

½ cup dry bread crumbs
1 egg beaten with
1 tbsp water
Shortening for frying

Combine ham, potatoes and egg until well blended. Divide into ⅓ cup portions, shape, coat and fry just like *Ham Croquettes* No. 1.

LAMB CROQUETTES

Follow directions for making *Chickeny Chicken Croquettes,* p 507, by substituting 2½ cups chopped braised or roast lamb for the chicken. Use lamb gravy or broth for making the sauce. Add 1 tbsp finely chopped mint to croquette mixture. Cool. Measure ⅓ cup portions onto the crumbs spread on waxed paper. Chill. When firm, shape portions neatly into cones. Coat cones, dry off and fry at 365° F as described under *General Directions.* Serve very hot with mint jelly. 5 or 6 servings.

LIVER AND BACON CROQUETTES
A pleasant way to sneak liver into the diet

½ recipe Croquette White
Sauce, p 502
9 slices bacon
2 tbsp bacon fat
¾ lb sliced beef *or* pork liver
¾ tsp salt

Pepper
⅓ cup fine dry bread crumbs
⅔ cup fine dry bread crumbs
1 egg beaten with
1 tbsp water
Shortening for frying

Make Croquette White Sauce. Pan-fry bacon until done. Remove to absorbent paper to drain and crisp. Remove skin and veins from liver. Sauté in the bacon fat until barely cooked through. Sprinkle with salt and pepper. Cool. Chop fine on a board. There should be 1½ cups. Fold the ⅓ cup of crumbs into the sauce then the crumbled bacon and liver. Cool. Measure scant ¼ cupfuls of mixture onto waxed paper spread with the ⅔ cup of crumbs. Shape into cones, then roll gently in crumbs, then in egg mixture and again in crumbs. Repeat rolling in egg and crumbs if a thick crusty shell is desired. Let stand ½ hr in refrigerator or in a cool place for coating to dry off. Fry at 365° F according to *General Directions*, p. 501. Serve hot. 8 croquettes.

Note: Leftover cooked bacon and liver may be used.

SWEETBREAD CROQUETTES

2 cups chopped pre-cooked
  sweetbreads, 1 lb raw
1½ cups Croquette White
  Sauce, p 502
½ to 1 tsp scraped onion and
  juice, p 164
6 drops tabasco sauce

¼ cup finely diced celery *or*
1 tbsp finely chopped parsley
1 egg beaten with
1 tbsp water
⅔ cup fine dry bread crumbs
Shortening for frying

Pre-cook sweetbreads as described on p 890. When cool, cut into ⅓-inch dice. Make ¾ recipe Croquette White Sauce. Stir in next 3 ingredients, then fold in sweetbreads. Cool mixture. Measure ⅓ cup portions onto the crumbs spread on waxed paper. Chill. When firm, shape portions neatly into cones. Coat cones with next 3 ingredients, dry off and fry at 365° F as described under *General Directions*. 8 croquettes.

VEAL CROQUETTES

½ recipe Croquette White
  Sauce, p 502
1 tsp scraped onion and
  juice, p 164
6 dashes cayenne
1½ cups chopped cooked veal
⅓ cup chopped pecans *or*
  walnuts

½ cup thin sliced green
  celery, sautéed in
1 tsp butter
⅔ cup fine dry bread crumbs
1 egg beaten with
1 tbsp water
Shortening for frying

Make Croquette White Sauce. Stir in onion, juice and cayenne; then fold in veal, nuts and celery. Cool mixture. Measure ⅓ cup portions onto the crumbs spread on waxed paper. Chill. When firm, shape portions neatly into cones. Coat cones with crumbs and egg mixture, dry off and fry at 365° F as described under *General Directions*. 6 to 8 croquettes.

POULTRY CROQUETTES

CHICKEN CROQUETTES

There need be no last minute rush when you serve croquettes. The mixture can be prepared a few hrs in advance

½ recipe warm Croquette
  White Sauce, p 502
2 cups finely diced moist
  cooked chicken, pkd, no
  skin
½ cup blanched slivered almonds *or*

½ cup mushrooms, sautéed,
  p 1356
Salt and pepper
½ cup fine dry bread crumbs,
  p 151
1 large egg beaten with
1 tbsp water
  Shortening for frying

Make White Sauce. Turn sauce and next 3 ingredients into mixing bowl and fold together until well blended. Season to taste, then cool. Measure ⅓ cup portions onto crumbs spread on waxed paper. There should be 6 or 7 portions. Slip a cookie sheet or a piece of clean cardboard under waxed paper and place in refrigerator to chill for an hr. Remove and shape portions neatly into cones. Roll carefully in crumbs, then in egg mixture and again in crumbs. Let croquettes stand ½ hr in refrigerator or cool place for coating to dry off. Fry in shortening heated to 365° F according to *General Directions,* p 501. 4 servings.

CHICKENY CHICKEN CROQUETTES

Delicious!

⅓ cup chicken fat *or* butter
½ cup flour
1¼ cups rich chicken broth,
  p 1289
2 egg yolks
¾ cup coffee cream
2½ cups finely diced moist
  cooked chicken, p 1041-2,
  no skin

Salt and pepper to taste
⅔ cup fine dry bread crumbs
1 egg beaten with
1 tbsp water
  Shortening for frying
  Parsley

Heat fat in top of double boiler over direct heat. Blend in flour, add broth slowly stirring to keep smooth. Cook and stir until sauce boils and thickens. Beat egg yolks, add cream, stir until smooth, then add to sauce. Stir in chicken and seasonings; cook gently over boiling water 10 min, stirring occasionally. Remove from heat; set pan in cold water to cool. Measure cooled mixture by ¼ cupfuls onto waxed paper spread with the crumbs. Chill thoroughly in refrigerator. One hr before serving time, quickly shape into cones or cylinders. Roll in the crumbs, then in egg mixture and again in crumbs. Let stand about ½ hr in refrigerator to dry coating. Just before serving time, heat shortening to 365° F. Fry until golden brown and piping hot all the way through, from 3 to 4 min. Lift basket out, remove croquettes gently to shallow pan lined with absorbent paper and place in slow oven (250° F) to keep hot until all croquettes are fried. Arrange on hot platter and garnish with parsley. A thickened gravy made with extra chicken fat or a creamed vegetable such as peas are delicious with these croquettes. 5 to 6 servings.

TURKEY CROQUETTES

Substitute diced cooked turkey for chicken in *Chickeny Chicken Croquettes,* and proceed in same way.

Note—General Directions for Croquettes, p 501 also see Deep-Fat Frying, p 739.

Desserts

One function of desserts is to produce a sense of complete satisfaction at the end of the meal. The delicious flavor and beauty of a special dessert also add glamour to an otherwise ordinary meal. All of which is good enough reason for trying every one of the recipes in this chapter. But you'll probably need no coaxing to do this, for where is the hostess who doesn't love to hear the oh's and ah's that are sure to greet a particularly delectable dessert?

WHETHER we are born with certain basic likes and dislikes or not, one of our natural and universal food preferences is certainly dessert. The youngest members of the family light up with pleasant anticipation at the sight of their rennet custard dessert or a bowl of sparkling, quivery gelatin. Junior will eat his spinach without any grumbling when he knows it will hasten the moment that the chocolate pudding is set before him. And all the grown-ups from Aunt Mary to Grandpa Jones retain much of this youthful anticipation of the treat in store that surely follows the "spinach."

Under the general heading of *dessert,* there are all degrees of richness, lightness, sweetness, and simplicity. Although technically a dessert is the food that is served at the end of a meal and would therefore include pies, pastries, and cakes as well as custards, puddings, ice creams, etc., most generally the first three desserts are called by their own names and the word *Dessert* applies to fruits, either raw or cooked, whips and meringues, custards, puddings, frozen desserts, baked fruit desserts, gelatin desserts, and miscellaneous desserts such as cheese, omelettes, fritters and deep fat fried rosettes.

For a dessert to serve its purpose best, it must be chosen to suit the meal it follows. After a hearty meal, a steamed pudding or some other very rich and heavy dessert would make the eater feel stuffed and uncomfortable and might even give him the impression that the particular dessert was "indigestible." When actually the same dessert served after a lighter meal would be just the necessary addition for that feeling of satisfaction after eating. The dessert should not be more of the same kind of food in a different form that was served previously in the meal; for example, a custard should not follow a creamed soup or chicken a la king, an apple betty should not follow a Waldorf salad, and meringue shells should not follow an omelet or souffle.

In planning menus, choose a light dessert to follow a heavy meal, and a richer dessert to follow a light meal and choose foods that go into that dessert that are different from the foods served in the meal. Then even the richest desserts can be used when they are suitable and the meal will not only be more enjoyed and more easily digested, but will be better nutritionally. Most desserts provide a generous serving of fruit, milk or eggs, and when chosen wisely make a substantial contribution to the diet pattern, p 3.

HOW TO USE THE VARIOUS TYPES OF BAKING POWDER IN DESSERT RECIPES

In all dessert recipes calling for baking powder, the amount designated is for double action, the sulphate-phosphate type. When using a tartrate or phosphate type, increase the amount one-fourth teaspoon for each teaspoonful used. Please read p 113.

BAKED FRUIT DESSERTS

Brown Bettys or Scalloped Fruit—are made by alternating layers of *sweetened whole fruit* such as berries or sliced or chopped *sweetened fruit* such as apples or peaches with buttered bite-size bread crumbs. A small amount of fruit juice or water is poured over the mixture. Baking dish is covered until the fruit is cooked about tender, then it is uncovered and cooking continued for 15 min to brown and crisp top.

Crumbles, Crunches, Crisps, etc.—are casseroles of sweetened sliced fruit topped with a streusel-like mixture, then baked until fruit is soft and top is crunchy.

APPLE BROWN BETTY

When well made, this dessert is a great favorite. Using cider instead of water for the liquid accentuates the apple flavor

6 slices 4- to 5-day-old bread from 1 lb loaf, *or* equal quantity of sweet rolls	¾ cup light brown sugar, pkd
	½ tsp cinnamon
	¼ tsp salt
¼ cup melted butter	½ cup water *or* apple cider
6 cups sliced pared tart apples, 2 lbs	Whipping cream, optional

Butter a 9 x 9 x 2-inch baking dish. Start oven 10 min before baking; set to moderately hot (400° F).

Pull bread into bite-size crumbs; toast lightly in shallow pan, then turn into 2-qt bowl. Drizzle butter over crumbs and toss with fork to coat well; turn ⅓ of them into prepared pan. Cover with half the apples. Blend sugar, cinnamon and salt. Sprinkle half the mixture over apples. Add another layer of crumbs, remaining apples and rest of sugar mixture. Top with remaining crumbs. Drizzle water or cider over all. Cover with lid or aluminum foil. Bake 30 min, then uncover and bake 10 min longer, or until top is richly browned and crusty. Serve warm or cold with plain or whipped cream. 5 servings.

Note: For a change in flavor, substitute white for brown sugar, and add 1 to 2 tbsp lemon juice to the water or cider.

PLUM BROWN BETTY

Piquant, pleasing summertime dessert. Serve lukewarm for best eating

6 slices 4- or 5-day-old bread
   from 1 lb loaf
1 lb *red* plums, 8 to 10,
   washed

⅞ to 1 cup sugar
¼ cup melted butter *or*
   margarine
Cream, optional

Butter a 10¼ x 6¼ x 2-inch glass baking dish, or a 6-cup casserole with cover. Start oven 10 min before baking; set to hot (450° F).

Trim brown crusts from bread thinly, using scissors or sharp knife. Stack slices together on board and with sharp knife, cut through both ways to make ¼-inch cubes. There should be 4 cups slightly pressed down. Spread cubes on cookie sheet and toast *lightly* under broiler or in the hot oven, turning cubes with fork 2 or 3 times. Cool, then turn into 3-qt bowl. Drizzle with butter, tossing to coat well; sprinkle ¼ of them into prepared pan. Stir sugar into rest of crumbs. With sharp paring knife, cut plum flesh cleanly from pits in 5 or 6 pieces, dropping into bowl. Spread half the plums evenly over crumbs in pan, then sprinkle with half the sugar mixture. Repeat with rest of plums and sugar mixture. Cover with aluminum foil, pressing it snugly against outside of pan; or cover casserole. Bake 20 min or until fruit is cooked and starts bubbling up; uncover and bake until crumbs are richly browned, about 10 min longer. Remove to cake rack to cool. Serve lukewarm, with or without slightly sweetened cream sprinkled with cinnamon. 4 servings.

RHUBARB FIG BAR BETTY

Rhubarb blends surprisingly well with fig bars

1 lb tender juicy rhubarb
¼ cup sugar
½ tsp grated lemon rind, pkd
7¾-oz pkg fig bars, *or* ½ lb
   bulk

2 tbsp butter
1 to 3 tbsp water, depending
   on juiciness of rhubarb

Butter a 5- to 6-cup casserole with cover. Start oven 10 min before baking; set to moderate (375° F).

Wash rhubarb, trim off and discard leaf and root ends; cut into ½-inch lengths, dropping into bowl. Add sugar and lemon rind and stir to distribute. Cut fig bars into ½-inch cubes, 3 strips each way. Put ⅓ of cubes in casserole, spreading evenly. Add half the rhubarb, then another ⅓ of cubes and rest of rhubarb; top with cubes. Dot with butter. Add water at side of casserole. Cover and bake 20 min, then remove cover and bake 5 to 10 min longer until rhubarb is boiling and tender, and top is crusty. Remove to cake rack to cool; serve lukewarm. 5 to 6 servings.

APPLE CRUNCH

⅔ cup all-purpose flour
¾ cup granulated or light brown sugar, pkd
⅓ cup butter or margarine

5 or 6 medium size, tart apples about 1¾ lbs, 4 cups pared, sliced
1 tsp cinnamon, opt

Butter a baking dish 10 x 6½ x 2-inches. Start oven 10 min before baking; set to moderate (375° F). Measure flour, sugar and cinnamon into a 2-qt mixing bowl. Add butter and with pastry blender or 2 knives cut together to make a crumbly mixture. Pare apples thinly, quarter, core, slice thinly, measure into prepared pan, spreading level. Sprinkle sugar mixture over top. Bake about 20 to 30 min or until top is golden brown and crunchy and apples are tender. 5 servings.

Note: ½ light brown and ½ granulated sugar may be used. A teaspoon of lemon juice drizzled over apples adds good flavor.

Pandowdies—Dutch Apple Cakes, Sally Lunn and Grunts are closely related to a Pandowdy—Made from batter ranging in sweetness and richness from a Plain Muffin to a Cottage Pudding batter. There are 3 ways of combining batter and fruit: (1) Whole fruit such as berries or chopped or sliced fruit like apples or peaches are folded into the batter. (2) Batter is poured into baking pan, then fruit is arranged over top, then sprinkled with sugar and sometimes spice. (3) Fruit is arranged over bottom of buttered baking pan, sprinkled with sugar and spice if desired, then batter is poured over fruit. No matter how these desserts are put together, they are baked in a moderate oven like cake until batter is baked done and fruit is tender.

An apple dessert is no better than the apples used. A tart apple is the one that adds tang. See p 97 for best varieties.

APPLE GRUNT

*A delightful fruity cake—quickly mixed, quickly baked. Eat warm.
Serve as a hearty dessert or coffee cake*

Topping:
    ⅓ cup moist brown sugar,
      pkd
    1 tbsp flour
    ½ tsp cinnamon
    2 tbsp firm butter *or*
      margarine

Cake Part:
    2¼ cups sliced juicy tart
      apples, 3 large—¾ lb

1¼ cups all-purpose flour
1 tsp D.A. baking powder
  or 1¼ tsp tartrate *or*
  phosphate type
½ tsp soda
½ tsp salt
3 tbsp soft butter
½ cup sugar
1 egg
½ cup buttermilk

Butter well a 10¼ x 6¼ x 2-inch baking pan. Adjust rack about 5 inches from bottom of oven. Start oven 10 min before baking; set to moderately hot (400° F).

Topping: Measure ingredients for topping into 1-qt bowl. Cut in butter with pastry blender until mixture is crumbly, the size of peas.

Cake Part: Wash apples, pare thinly, cut in quarters, core, then slice quarters thinly. Cover with wet paper toweling to prevent discoloring. Sift flour, measure and resift 3 times with baking powder, soda and salt. Cream butter in a 2-qt mixing bowl, add sugar gradually and cream well. Beat in egg thoroughly. Add flour mixture and buttermilk in 2 or 3 portions, beginning and ending with flour and beating well after each. Now fold in apples. Turn into prepared pan. Sprinkle with topping. Bake 30 min or until cake tests done and top is bubbly and brown. Remove to cake rack. Serve warm, plain, or with cream or Vanilla Sauce, p 1249. 5 to 6 servings.

APPLE PANDOWDY

A thrifty good old-time dessert

1 tbsp soft butter
1¼ lbs tart cooking apples
¼ tsp salt
½ cup sugar

¼ tsp nutmeg
Cottage Pudding batter,
  p 618 using
¼ tsp each of lemon and
  vanilla extracts

Butter bottom and sides of an 8 x 8 x 2-inch baking pan. Start oven 10 min before baking; set to moderate (350° F).

Wash apples. If skins are tough, pare, otherwise do not. Quickly shred apples directly into baking pan using coarse shredder to obtain match-like julienne strips. Or slice thin and cut into thin strips. Spread apples in a uniform layer over bottom of pan. Quickly sift salt over them to prevent discoloration, then sprinkle on the sugar mixed with nutmeg. Cover and place in oven for 10 min while preparing Cottage Pudding batter. Remove pan from oven and quickly spread batter evenly over hot apples. Bake 30 to 35 min or until pudding tests done. Remove to cake rack to cool 5 min, then loosen sides and invert onto serving plate. Serve warm with "Soft Hard Sauce," p 1245, or Cinnamon or Nutmeg Dip, pp 1240-41. 5 to 6 servings.

Pandowdy is done when a toothpick or cake tester stuck in center comes out clean.

DUTCH APPLE CAKE—SUMMER APPLES

It beats the Dutch how much of this you can eat!

Topping:
    1 lb tart cooking apples,
      5 medium
    1 tbsp melted butter
    ¼ cup sugar
    1 tsp cinnamon
Batter:
    2 cups all-purpose flour

3 tsp D.A. baking powder
  or 3¾ tsp tartrate *or*
  phosphate type
½ tsp salt
¼ cup margarine *or*
  shortening
½ cup sugar
1 egg
1 cup milk

Butter well a 7 x 11 x 1½-inch or a 9-inch square baking pan. Start oven 10 min before baking; set to moderately hot (400° F), or 25 degrees lower if baked in glass.

Topping: Pare, quarter and core apples, then cover with damp cloth or paper toweling until ready to slice. Blend sugar and cinnamon together thoroughly.

Batter: Sift flour, measure, resift 3 times with baking powder and salt. Cream margarine until soft in a 3-qt mixing bowl, add sugar and egg, then beat with rotary beater until smooth and creamy. Clean off beater, remove and use wooden spoon. Add flour and milk in 3 or 4 portions, beginning and ending with flour and beating until smooth after each. Turn into prepared pan, spreading level. Quickly cut quartered apples into 3 lengthwise slices. As you cut apples, press slices core-side down close together slightly into dough in 3 or 4 lengthwise parallel rows. Brush apples gently with butter and sprinkle with sugar-cinnamon mixture. Bake 30 min or until apples are tender and cake tests done. Cool slightly on cake rack but serve warm, as coffee cake or with Hard or Lemon Sauce, p 1245 as dessert. 6 servings.

For a change use Cottage Pudding Batter p 618 instead of one given above.

DUTCH APPLE CAKE—FALL APPLES

A family type good old-time dessert

Topping:
5 medium size tart cooking apples, Jonathan, Northern Spy, etc.
1 tbsp melted butter
2 tbsp water
¼ cup sugar
1 tsp cinnamon

Batter:
2 cups all-purpose flour
½ tsp soda
½ tsp salt
¼ cup soft margarine *or* butter
½ cup sugar
1 egg
1 cup buttermilk

Butter a 7 x 11 x 1½-inch baking pan. Start oven 10 min before baking; set to moderately hot (400° F).

Topping: Pare, quarter and core apples, then cut quarters into half lengthwise. Heat butter in 9-inch skillet, add apples and water, cover and "steam" over medium heat, shaking skillet occasionally to heat evenly until water just evaporates and apples are hot through. Remove from heat; turn out on plate to cool. Blend sugar and cinnamon.

Batter: Sift flour, measure and resift 3 times with soda and salt. Cream margarine with rotary beater, add sugar and egg and beat until smooth and fluffy. Clean off beater; use wooden spoon. Add flour and buttermilk alternately in 3 or 4 portions, beginning and ending with flour and beating until smooth after each. Turn into prepared pan; spread level. Quickly press apple slices close together, core-side down, slightly into dough in 3 or 4 lengthwise parallel rows. Sprinkle with cinnamon-sugar mixture. Bake 35 to 40 min or until apples are tender and cake tests done. Cool a few min on cake rack. Serve warm or with Nutmeg or Vanilla Sauce, pp 1247 or 1249. 6 servings.

BLACKBERRY SALLY LUNN

No. 303 can wild blackberries
Buttermilk
1¾ cups all-purpose flour
2 tsp D.A. baking powder *or*
2½ tsp tartrate or phosphate type
¼ tsp soda
½ tsp salt
⅓ cup butter or margarine
⅔ cup sugar
1 large egg
1 tbsp lemon juice

Grease a 10 x 6 x 1¾-inch glass baking dish. Start oven 10 min before baking; set to moderately hot (400° F). Drain juice from berries —about ⅔ cup and add enough buttermilk to make 1 cup. Sift flour, measure, resift 3 times with baking powder, soda and salt. Cream margarine with rotary beater; add sugar and egg and beat until smooth and creamy. Clean off beater and remove. Stir in lemon juice with wooden spoon, then stir in flour mixture and berry liquid alternately in 2 or 3 portions, beginning and ending with flour and beating until smooth after each. Now fold in drained berries until distributed. Turn into prepared pan, gently spreading level. Bake 30 to 40 min, or until cake tester comes out clean. Remove to cake rack to cool slightly. Serve lukewarm with Lemon Hard Sauce, p 1245.

For Fresh Blackberry Sally Lunn, use 1 cup buttermilk for liquid and fold into batter 1 pint washed, drained berries. 6 servings.

CANNED BOYSENBERRY PANDOWDY

Delicious served as coffee cake, or as a cake for dessert. This Pandowdy is the "berries"!

2 cups canned boysenberries in heavy syrup, No. 303 can *or* jar	¼ tsp soda
	½ tsp salt
	⅓ cup butter *or* margarine
1 tbsp lemon juice	
2 cups all-purpose flour	⅔ cup sugar
2 tsp D. A. baking powder *or* 2½ tsp tartrate *or* phosphate type, p 326	2 eggs
	2 tbsp milk
	2 tbsp sugar for top

Butter well a 7 x 11 x 1½-inch baking pan. Adjust rack 5 to 6 inches above bottom of oven. Start oven 10 min before baking; set to moderate (375° F).

Drain berries in sieve set over a pint-size glass measuring cup—there should be 1 cup berries and 1¼ cups berry syrup. Squeeze lemon juice and add to berry syrup. Sift flour, measure, resift 3 times with baking powder, soda and salt. Cream shortening, add sugar and cream well. Beat eggs in one at a time with rotary beater; clean off and remove beater. Use wooden spoon to stir in flour mixture alternately with syrup in 3 or 4 portions, beginning and ending with flour and beating until smooth after each. Beat in milk to blend well. Turn into prepared pan. Scatter drained berries gently over top. Sprinkle with the 2 tbsp sugar. Bake 40 min or until cake tests done when pricked with a toothpick or top springs back when lightly touched. Cool slightly on cake rack but serve warm cut in squares. 8 servings.

REMEMBER: Increase flour a little or decrease liquid a little when baking in the South.

FRESH BLUEBERRY BUCKLE

Old-time Blueberry Buckle is a streusel-topped blueberry cake. It is delicious as coffee cake for breakfast or cake for dessert

Topping:
1 pt fresh blueberries
2 tsp lemon juice
⅓ cup sugar
⅓ cup all-purpose flour
½ tsp cinnamon
¼ cup firm butter

Cake:
2 cups all-purpose flour

½ tsp salt
2½ tsp D.A. baking powder
    or 3¼ tsp tartrate *or*
    phosphate type
½ cup shortening
½ cup sugar
1 egg
½ cup *plus* 2 tbsp milk

Line a 9 x 9 x 2-inch baking pan with waxed paper; butter paper and sides of pan. Start oven 10 min before baking; set to moderate (350° F).

Topping: Look over berries, discarding stems and imperfect ones. Wash through 2 cold waters, lifting last time into colander to drain. Then turn into a bowl, add lemon juice and toss. Measure next 4 ingredients into a 2-qt bowl. Cut mixture together with a pastry blender until consistency of small peas.

Cake: Sift flour, measure, resift 3 times with salt and baking powder. Cream shortening in a 3-qt bowl, add sugar gradually, creaming well. Add egg and beat until smooth and fluffy. Add flour and milk alternately in 3 or 4 portions, beginning and ending with flour and mixing well after each. Turn into prepared pan, spreading a little higher around edge of pan than in center. Now sprinkle berries evenly over top, then the sugar-cinnamon mixture over berries. Bake about 1 hr or until cake tests done. Remove to cake rack to cool slightly in pan before inverting to turn out on another cake rack. Quickly remove waxed paper. Then quickly place cake pan in which buckle was baked over buckle and invert so it will be right side up. Serve warm. 6 to 8 servings.

COBBLERS

Plain pastry, rich biscuit dough or a muffin-like batter is used. The pastry or dough is rolled out from ⅛ to ¼-inch thick and is used in 2 ways: (a) It may be rolled large enough to cover bottom and sides and extend an inch or more beyond rim of baking dish. The sweetened fruit is arranged in the lined pan, and extending dough is folded up over the top of the fruit to almost meet in center. (b) The sweetened fruit is arranged in a buttered baking dish, and the rolled-out pastry or dough with gashes for steam vents is laid over the top.

When batter is used, it is poured over the fruit arranged in a buttered baking dish. In either way, the cobbler is baked in a moderately hot oven until crust is brown and crisp and fruit is tender.

APPLE COBBLER

A notable dessert with forthright, unaffected goodness

Pastry for 9-inch double crust, p 924	½ cup water
	1 tbsp butter
5 cups thin-sliced juicy tart apples	½ tsp cinnamon *or* nutmeg, optional
1 cup sugar	Sugar for sprinkling
1 tbsp flour	

Adjust rack to be in center of oven. Start oven 10 min before baking; set to hot (425° F). Make pastry; roll ⅔ of it and line a 3-in. deep 10-inch casserole. Pastry should hang over edge about 1-inch. Wash apples, pare thinly, quarter, core and slice lengthwise. Blend sugar and flour. Sprinkle 2 tbsp of it over bottom of casserole. Stir rest into the apples. Turn apples into casserole. Pour water all over fruit, dot with butter, sprinkle with the spice. Roll out rest of pastry into a 7 or 8-inch circle. Cut design in center for wide-open steam vents and lay over top to cover exposed apples. Sprinkle with sugar. Bake about 20 min or until pastry begins to brown, then reduce heat to moderate (350° F) and continue baking until fruit is tender, pastry is brown and juice oozes up through vents. At this point remove cobbler to cake rack to cool, or take a spoon and chop up and down through cobbler thoroughly to mix the fruit and crust. Sprinkle top with a little more sugar and return to oven to cook another 10 or 15 min, or until top begins to get crusty. Cool to lukewarm. Serve plain or with cream. 5 to 6 servings.

FRESH APRICOT COBBLER

Don't let anyone tell you fresh apricots won't make delicious cobbler

Pastry for 8-inch double crust, p 924	2 or 3 drops almond extract
	1 tbsp firm butter
1 cup sugar	¼ cup white corn syrup
1½ lb fresh meaty apricots, 3½ cups sliced	2 tsp cream
	1 tbsp sugar

Have ready a 10¼ x 6¼ x 2-inch glass or aluminum baking pan. Adjust rack about 5 inches above bottom of oven. Start oven 10 min before baking; set to hot (450° F). Make pastry. Roll ¾ of it out into a 10 x 14-inch rectangle. Fold in half, then gently lift into pan; unfold carefully so as not to tear, then fit into angles. Dough will extend about 1½-inches over sides of pan. Sprinkle bottom with ¼ cup of the sugar.

Wash apricots, cut in half, remove pits, then cut in quarters. Leave 2 or 3 pits in for flavor. Turn into pan over the sugar, spreading level. Sprinkle with remaining sugar, add extract and dot with butter, then drizzle with syrup. Bring extending dough up over apricots. Cut small squares of dough out of corners so it will fold neatly. There should be about a 7 x 4-inch rectangle of fruit uncovered. Roll out remaining pastry into a rectangle. Cut into ½-inch wide strips. Place strips of right length crisscross over apricots. Cover strip ends with 4 strips, making a "framed window." Brush top with cream, then sprinkle with 1 tbsp sugar. Bake 17 to 20 min then reduce heat to moderate (375° F) and bake 25 to 30 min longer or until well browned and juice bubbles up between strips. Remove to cake rack to cool. Serve lukewarm. 6 servings.

BLACKBERRY COBBLER

Although this is a simple family dessert, the most discriminating company will enjoy it.

1 qt blackberries	⅔ cup sugar blended with
Pastry for 8-inch double	1 tbsp cornstarch *and*
crust, p 924	⅛ tsp salt
2 tbsp fine dry white bread	1 tbsp lemon juice
crumbs, p 168	1 tbsp butter
	1 tbsp thin cream *or* milk
	2 to 3 tsp sugar

Adjust rack to be in middle of oven. Start oven 10 min before baking; set to hot (450° F). Have ready a 10¼ x 6¼ x 2-inch baking pan.

Pick over berries, then wash by swishing gently through 2 cold waters, the last time lifting into colander to drain.

Make pastry. Roll out ¾ of it into a rectangle about 14½ x 10½ inches. Fold in half and lift carefully into pan, then gently unfold so as not to tear pastry and fit well into angles. Dough will extend about 1½ inches over rim of pan. Sprinkle bottom with crumbs, then with ¼ cup of the sugar mixture. Turn berries into pan, leveling top. Drizzle on lemon juice, then sprinkle with rest of sugar mixture. Dot with butter. Now fold extending dough *up over berries*—this leaves an area of berries about 3 x 7 inches uncovered. Now roll out rest of dough to about 5 x 8 inches; trim off edges neatly. Cut a long design down middle of this pastry for steam vents, then lay over top of cobbler to cover exposed berries. Brush top of cobbler with cream and sprinkle with sugar. Bake 15 min, then reduce heat to moderately slow (325° F) and bake 15 to 18 min longer, or until pastry is well browned and juice oozes up through vents. Remove to cake rack to cool an hour or more. Serve warm, 4 to 6 servings.

FRESH RED CHERRY COBBLER

May I have another helping, please?

Filling:
- 1 qt sour red cherries
- 1 cup sugar
- ⅛ tsp salt
- 2 tsp cornstarch

Dough:
- 1½ cups all-purpose flour
- 1 tsp sugar
- ¼ tsp salt
- 1 tsp D.A. baking powder *or* 1¼ tsp tartrate *or* phosphate type
- ⅓ cup shortening
- ½ cup *plus* 1½ tbsp milk
- 1 tsp melted butter

Have ready a glass or aluminum pan about 10¼ x 6¼ x 2 inches. Adjust rack about 5 inches above bottom of oven. Start oven 10 min before baking; set to hot (450° F).

Filling: Wash cherries *with stems on* (important to remove spray chemicals) through 3 or 4 cold waters, lifting last time into colander to drain. As you pull out stems, use loop-end of a sturdy wire hairpin, or a No. 1 paper clip opened to an S-shape to pry out pits. This method of pitting keeps cherries plump and retains all the juice. One quart of sound, well developed cherries makes 3½ to 4 cups pitted fruit. Blend sugar, salt and cornstarch in a bowl.

Dough: Sift flour, measure, resift 3 times with salt, sugar and baking powder, the last time into a 2-qt mixing bowl. Cut in shortening with pastry blender until particles are size of rice. Now add milk all at once and stir vigorously with a fork to mix. Turn out ¾ of the dough onto a floured pastry cloth. Shape into a rectangle, then roll out to about 13½ x 12 inches. Fold dough through center and lift into baking dish, then carefully unfold and fit into angles of pan. There should be about an inch of dough extending over rim of dish. Now sprinkle ⅓ of sugar mixture over bottom of dough, then add cherries, spreading level. Sprinkle on rest of sugar, then dot with butter. Fold extending dough up over fruit. This leaves a strip of cherries uncovered in center. Roll out rest of dough slightly larger than exposed cherries, and cut design in center for steam vents. Lay over cherries, overlapping other dough a little. Bake 15 min, then reduce heat to slow (325° F) and bake 10 to 15 min longer or until richly browned and cherries are tender. Cool on cake rack to lukewarm. 4 to 5 servings.

Note: Sprinkle top of cobbler with sugar before baking for interesting crusty change.

Pans in which cobblers are baked should be no deeper than finished cobbler in order to brown beautifully.

GOOSEBERRY COBBLER

Crisp, tender crusted, juicy and delicious

Biscuit Dough, p 234
4½ cups stemmed, washed
  gooseberries *or* equal
  amount barely thawed
  frozen

2 cups sugar for fresh berries
  or 1 cup for frozen
1 to 2 tsp cream, and sugar

Butter lightly a 10¼ x 6¼ x 2-inch glass or aluminum pan. Adjust rack to be in middle of oven. Start oven 10 min before baking; set to moderately hot (400° F).

Make Biscuit Dough. Roll out ¾ of it into a 14½ x 10½-inch rectangle. Fold dough crosswise through center, lift into pan and unfold carefully so as not to tear dough; fit well into angles. Dough will extend over pan. Turn berries into pan, spreading level. Sprinkle sugar over berries. Fold extending dough neatly up over berries. Cut out a little square of the dough at each corner to prevent crust from being too thick. Tuck in ends at 4 corners neatly. There will be an area of about 6 x 2 inches of berries in center exposed. Roll out rest of dough into a 3 x 7-inch rectangle. Trim off edges neatly and cut a long design in center for generous steam vents. Lay this dough over center to cover berries. Brush entire top lightly but completely with cream, then sprinkle evenly with sugar. Bake 35 to 40 min or until crust is a luscious brown and berries are tender. Serve lukewarm for greatest appetite appeal. 5 to 6 servings.

GUAVA COBBLER

One must taste this dessert to believe how good it really is

Pastry for 9-inch double
  crust, p 924
1 qt prepared guavas
1¼ cups sugar *or* more

1 cup water
2 tbsp butter
Few dashes nutmeg
Thin cream and sugar

Adjust rack to be in center of oven. Start oven 10 min before baking; set to moderately hot (425° F).

Prepare pastry. Roll out ⅔ of it to line a 3-inch deep 10-inch diam. casserole and hang over edge 1 inch. Wash guavas, pare thinly. Cut in halves crosswise, scrape out seedy portion into a food mill and rub through to obtain all purée possible. Slice the fleshy guava shells into the puree to measure. Stir sugar and water into guavas, then turn into pastry-lined casserole and spread out evenly. Dot with butter, then sprinkle with nutmeg. Now turn overhanging pastry forward over fruit. Roll out rest of pastry into a circle, cut design in center for wide-open steam vents, then lay over top to cover exposed fruit. Brush top with cream, then sprinkle with sugar. Bake about 20 min or until pastry begins to brown, then reduce heat to moderate (350° F) and bake 25 to 30 min longer or until crust is nicely browned and juice starts bubbling up through vents. 6 to 8 servings.

Note: 1 qt of canned guavas may be used in place of the fresh to prepare equally good cobbler.

FRESH PEACH COBBLER

Make this simple but luscious dessert several times during peach season —the family will lick it up!

1 cup *plus* 2 tbsp sugar	2½ lb ripe juicy freestone
⅛ tsp salt	peaches, 12 to 14 egg-size
1 tbsp flour, optional	1 tbsp butter
Pastry for 8-inch double	1 to 2 drops almond extract
crust, p 924	Thin cream and sugar
2 tbsp fine dry white bread	
crumbs, p 168	

Have ready a 10¼ x 6¼ x 2-inch glass or aluminum baking pan. Adjust rack to be in middle of oven. Start oven 10 min before baking; set to hot (450° F).

Blend sugar, salt and flour—use flour only if peaches are very juicy. Make pastry. Roll out ¾ of it into a rectangle about 14½ x 10½ inches. Fold in half to lift easily into pan. Unfold carefully so as not to tear pastry, fitting well into angles of pan. Pastry will extend about 1½ inches over pan edge. Sprinkle bread crumbs over bottom of pastry-lined pan, then ¼ cup of the sugar mixture. Pare peaches, then cut from pits in 6 to 8 lengthwise slices, discarding pits. There should be about 5 cups sliced fruit. Turn peaches into pan, spreading level. Dot with butter and add almond extract. Sprinkle with rest of sugar. Fold extending dough neatly up over peaches; cut out a little square of dough at each corner to prevent the pastry from being too thick. Tuck in ends at the 4 corners neatly. There will be an area of about 2 x 6 inches of peaches in center that will not be covered with pastry. Roll out rest of pastry into a rectangle about 3 x 7 inches. Trim off edges neatly and cut a long design down center for generous steam vents. Lay this pastry over center to cover peaches. Brush entire top lightly but completely with cream, then sprinkle evenly with sugar, a tsp or so, for an interesting surface. Bake 15 to 17 min or until crust starts browning. Now reduce heat to moderately slow (325° F) and bake 25 min longer, or until bottom and top crusts are a rich brown and juice starts bubbling up through vents. Remove to cake rack to cool. Serve lukewarm, plain or with cream. 6 servings.

FRESH RED PLUM COBBLER
Another sure-to-get-eaten dessert

1 lb red plums, 8 to 10	1¼ tsp D.A. baking powder
¾ to ⅞ cup sugar	*or* 1½ tsp tartrate *or*
1 tbsp cornstarch	phosphate type
Dash of salt	2 tsp sugar
1 cup all-purpose flour	¼ tsp salt
	¼ cup shortening
	⅓ cup milk

Adjust rack 4 to 5 inches above bottom of oven. Start oven 10 min before baking; set to hot (450° F). Have ready an 8-inch pie pan.

Wash plums. With a sharp paring knife, cut fruit cleanly from pits in 5 or 6 pieces, dropping into bowl. Blend sugar, cornstarch and salt. Sift flour, measure, resift 3 times with baking powder, 2 tsp sugar and salt, the last time into a 2 or 3-qt mixing bowl. Cut shortening into flour with pastry blender until particles are size of rice. Add milk all at once and stir with fork until well mixed. Turn out on floured pastry cloth; knead 3 or 4 times, then roll into a circle about 12 inches in diameter. Fold over and lay exactly in center of pie pan, then unfold and fit snugly into angles of pan. About a 2-inch rim of dough will hang over edge. Sprinkle ⅓ of sugar mixture over bottom, then stir rest into the fruit. Turn fruit into lined pan, spreading level. Bring extending dough carefully up over fruit toward center, forming a slightly ruffled edge, leaving a 3 or 4-inch center circle of plums uncovered. Bake 10 min, then reduce heat to moderate (350° F) and bake 10 to 12 min longer or until attractively browned. Remove to cake rack to cool to lukewarm. Serve as is or with cream. 4 servings.

RAISIN COBBLER
Don't pass this up

Filling:
- ⅔ cup sugar
- 2 tbsp cornstarch
- ⅔ cup orange juice
- ⅔ cup water
- 2 cups seedless raisins
- 1 tbsp butter
- 1 tsp lemon juice
- ¼ tsp salt
- 1 small seedless orange, quartered and thinly sliced
- Whipped cream

Pastry:
- 1 cup all-purpose flour
- ½ tsp salt
- ⅓ cup shortening
- 3 tbsp ice water

Blend sugar and cornstarch in a saucepan. Stir in orange juice, water and raisins and cook with constant stirring until liquid is just clear and thickened. Remove from heat. Stir in butter, lemon juice and salt, then fold in orange slices. Turn into a pie pan 7 inches in diameter and 1½-

inches deep. Prepare pastry according to directions, p 924. Roll out as for pie in a round shape to fit the pan. Cut a design in top for steam vents. Lay carefully over top of raisin mixture. Trim pastry. Flute edge. Bake in a hot oven (450° F) 15 min, then reduce heat to moderate (350° F) and bake 15 to 20 min longer. Cool cobbler on cake rack to lukewarm. Cut in wedges, top with whipped cream. 6 servings.

BLACK RASPBERRY COBBLER

Belongs in the top bracket of delicious simple desserts

Pastry for 9-inch single crust *or*	1 qt black raspberries
	2 tbsp flour
½ Biscuit dough recipe, p 928 or 234	1 tbsp lemon juice
	½ to ⅔ cup sugar

Adjust rack to center of oven. Start oven 10 min before baking; set to hot (450° F).

Make pastry and roll out into a 9-inch circle. Cut design in center, making wide-open steam vents. Look over berries, discarding hulls. Wash carefully in cold water, then lift out into colander to drain a few minutes. Butter a deep round 9-inch pie pan 1¼ inches deep. Combine sugar and flour. Turn berries into pie pan, sprinkle with sugar mixture, then drizzle with lemon juice. Place pastry over top of fruit and press edges neatly against edge of pan. Bake 15 min, then reduce heat to moderately slow (325° F) and bake about 20 min longer or until pastry is nicely browned and juice bubbles merrily up through vents. Remove to cake rack to cool to lukewarm. 4 to 5 servings.

TEXAS YAM COBBLER

This hearty dessert is highly prized in the southern yam growing country

Pastry for 9-inch double crust, p 924	3 tbsp flour blended with ¼ cup sugar
1½ lbs yams	1 cup water from cooked yams
1½ cups boiling water	
½ tsp salt	2 tbsp butter
1 cup crushed pineapple, 9-oz can	

Have ready an 8 x 8 x 2-inch glass baking pan. Start oven 10 min before baking; set to moderately hot (425° F).

Make pastry. Wash yams then cover with boiling water. Now take hot yams one by one from water and quickly pare. Cut into ⅓-inch thick slices and drop immediately into boiling salted water to prevent discoloring. Cover and boil gently 10 min or until barely tender. Drain; save water.

Roll out about ⅔ of the pastry into a 12-inch sq on a floured pastry cloth. Fit it snugly into baking pan. About ¾-inch of pastry *will hang over pan rim.* Arrange yam slices in pan, then spread pineapple over top. Sprinkle with flour-sugar mixture. Pour yam water over top and dot with butter. Now carefully fold *extending pastry* neatly up over yam filling. Roll out remaining pastry into about a 7-inch sq. Cut design for steam vents and lay over uncovered filling in center. Bake 35 to 40 min or until nicely browned. Serve warm. 6 to 8 servings.

CUSTARDS

Baked, Stirred, and Steamed

True custards consist only of milk, eggs, and a small amount of sugar for sweetening and flavoring. One egg or 2 egg yolks will thicken 1 cup of milk, but more eggs may be used if the custards are to be unmolded. They may be baked, stirred or steamed, but the basic ingredients and the principles of cooking are the same. Cooking at too high a temperature or for too long a time causes eggs to toughen and milk to curdle, and an overcooked baked or steamed custard will have a porous texture and will tend to weep or whey on standing; the solid portions will be tough and rubbery instead of smooth, quivery and jelly-like. An overcooked stirred custard will be lumpy instead of smooth.

Baked Custards. The eggs are beaten slightly just enough to mix the yolk and the white but never enough to make the eggs frothy, and the milk is stirred in. If the milk is scalded before adding to the eggs, the baking time is reduced considerably. This mixture is usually poured through a strainer into the baking dishes to remove any stringy bits of egg white, but unless the thick "strings" of white (chalaza) are very apparent, it is not necessary. The baking dishes are placed in a slow oven in a pan of hot water. The water must come almost up to the top of the containers for the custard to bake evenly throughout and not become too hot on the surface. The length of baking time will depend on the proportion of eggs used, the temperature of the milk and the size of the container. Baked custard should be removed from the oven when a small portion in the very center is still liquid; there will be enough heat retained in the custard to continue cooking the center after it is removed from the oven. A dot of butter or dash of nutmeg or cinnamon is often added for flavor and an attractive surface.

Stirred Custards. Stirred custards are also called soft or "boiled" custards and are always cooked on top of the stove over simmering water, stirring constantly until the desired consistency is obtained. They are often made with egg yolks only, using 2 or 3 yolks to 1 cup of milk. The water in the lower part of the double boiler should be only about 1 inch deep so that the upper part of the double boiler is not sitting in the hot water. The cooking is continued over simmering water until the custard just coats a metal spoon (see p 534). As soon as this point is reached, it should be taken from over the hot water at once and set in a pan of cold water to prevent further cooking or curdling, or poured into a clean chilled bowl for cooling. If a custard shows signs of curdling, it should be removed immediately from the heat—placed over cold water, and beaten vigorously with a rotary beater to restore the smoothness. The stirred custard will thicken somewhat as it cools and may be served plain or with fruit, cake, ice cream or with meringue for "floating island."

Steamed Custards. Steamed custards are similar to both baked and stirred custards; they are cooked on top of the stove but they are cooked without stirring. When the custard is done, it is set and leaves the sides of the pan in a solid mass when the pan is tilted. The custard is still quivery in the center but will become firm as it is allowed to cool undisturbed. Steamed custards may be served plain, with cream, or with crushed fruit sauce. (See p 535.)

HOW TO BAKE CUSTARD

Step 1. Put milk, sugar and salt into top of double boiler; place over boiling water, cover and heat to scalding or until bubbles begin to form at edge. Pour slowly over slightly beaten eggs, stirring thoroughly. Add flavoring. Strain into baking dish, dot with butter and sprinkle with nutmeg.

Step 2. Place baking dish in pan of hot water. Add water until it reaches the same height as custard. Bake in moderately slow oven, (325° F), for about 30 to 35 min or until done.

Step 3. A perfect baked custard has a smooth, jelly-like consistency and does not whey or curdle. If you use a glass baking dish, you can easily see that there are no beads of water bubbling out on the inside of the dish.

Testing baked custard for doneness: Insert a sharp-pointed knife into one of the custards in two places—at center and half way between center and side of cup. First point may be slightly underdone, indicated by semi-liquid custard adhering to knife; second point should be done, indicated by knife coming out clean. Or shake the custard gently to note the area of the quivery liquid in the center. If there is only about an inch circle of semi-liquid in the center, the custard is done. Custard cup holds sufficient heat to complete cooking of custard after removal from oven.

BAKED CUSTARD

*1 qt milk	4 eggs, beaten slightly
½ cup sugar	1 tsp vanilla
¼ tsp salt	Nutmeg *or* cinnamon

*Substitute 1 cup cream for 1 cup of the milk for a richer custard.

Start oven 10 min before baking; set to moderately slow (325° F). Butter 6 custard cups. Put milk, sugar and salt into top of double boiler; place over boiling water, cover and heat to scalding. Stir milk slowly into beaten eggs; add vanilla. Strain and pour all but ½ cup into cups. Beat this ½ cupful until very foamy then pour it carefully over cups. Add a dash or two of nutmeg. Set cups in a shallow pan. Pour in enough hot water to come up almost to top of cups. Set on center rack in oven. Bake until done, 25 or 30 min. This short baking time is possible only if custard mixture is actually hot when poured into cups and placed in oven immediately. Just before baking time is up, begin test for doneness, and continue baking only until custard tests done. Do not overbake, as baking too long or at too high a temp results in wheying or "weeping." Use tongs to lift custard cups from hot water to cake rack. Serve directly from individual cups, or unmold into individual serving dishes. Serve with any desired dessert sauce on top. 6 servings.

BAKED CUSTARD VARIATIONS

LEMON CUSTARD

Make and bake exactly like Baked Custard except add 1 tsp grated lemon rind, and use mace for nutmeg, to custard mixture after the ½ cup has been removed for beating until foamy. Pour into buttered cups without straining and bake as directed.

MINCEMEAT CUSTARD

Make and bake exactly like Baked Custard except reduce sugar to ⅓ cup and add ½ cup prepared mincemeat. Pour into cups without straining and bake as directed.

BROWN SUGAR BAKED CUSTARD

Make exactly like Basic Baked Custard, except substitute ⅔ cup dark brown sugar, packed, for the ½ cup granulated sugar. A few chopped nuts may be dropped into cups before adding custard.

BUTTERSCOTCH BAKED CUSTARD

10 Butterscotch patties	¼ tsp salt
3 cups milk	3 eggs
⅓ cup sugar	1 tsp vanilla

Start oven 10 min before baking; set to moderately slow (325° F). Butter well 5 custard cups each ¾-cup capacity. Drop 2 crushed butterscotch patties—1 heaping tsp into each cup. Set cups in a 1½-inch deep baking pan or skillet.

Scald milk in top of double boiler over hot water, then stir in sugar and salt. Beat eggs *slightly* in a 2-qt bowl, then stir in hot milk and vanilla. Strain into cups. Pour hot water into pan to come up ½ inch from top of cups. Bake 30 min, or until custard tests done, p 526. Remove from oven, then from hot water to cake rack to cool. Serve warm or chilled, in cups or unmolded, as desired. 5 servings.

CASSEROLE CARAMEL CUSTARD

A practical way to cook this dessert. Excellent as is and exquisite topped with Whipped cream

⅞ cup sugar—¾ cup *plus* 2 tbsp	¼ tsp salt
½ cup water	3 cups milk
4 eggs, slightly beaten	1 tsp vanilla
	Whipping cream, optional

Start oven 10 min before baking; set to moderately slow (325° F).
Butter a 6-cup casserole and have ready a 12 x 7½ x 2-inch glass baking pan or a similar sized enamel pan in which to set casserole.

Heat a 9-inch skillet, preferably aluminum, hot. Sift ½ cup of the sugar gradually into hot skillet, shaking skillet over heat vigorously. Continue to heat, and stir with a wooden spoon until sugar melts and takes on a *pale golden amber color*. Remove at once from heat and cautiously add water, then 2 tbsp of remaining sugar. Boil down gently to exactly ½ cup syrup. This amount is important for caramel sauce to be of right consistency. If caramel boils down more than this, add hot water to make ½ cup. Pour caramel into casserole. Beat eggs slightly, stir in the remaining ¼ cup sugar, the salt, milk and vanilla. Strain carefully over caramel in casserole. Set casserole in baking pan, pour 3 cups hot water around casserole. Bake 35 to 40 min, or until custard just tests done. Remove immediately to cake rack to cool to lukewarm or until cold. To serve, spoon custard into serving dishes with some of caramel sauce in bottom over each serving. Add a plop of whipped cream, if desired. 6 to 7 servings.

CHOCOLATE POTS DE CRÈME

The name isn't appealing, but the creamy dessert is unusual and distinctive

1½ cups 12% cream— Half and Half	1 tsp vanilla
1½ sqs unsweet chocolate	3 egg yolks
⅛ tsp salt	6 tbsp sugar

Have ready 4 buttered custard cups holding about ¾ cup each. Start oven 10 min before baking; set to moderately slow (325° F).

Put cream into top of double boiler and add the chocolate cut in 8 to 10 pieces. Cover and place over simmering water. Stir occasionally until chocolate melts and blends smoothly with cream. Then stir in salt and vanilla. Beat egg yolks well with rotary beater, then add sugar and hot cream mixture slowly, beating to blend well. Now pour into custard cups. Set in a tin or glass pan 7 x 7 x 2-inches and add hot water to come up almost to top of cups. Bake about 30 min, or until *just set*. When cups are shaken, Crème waves like soft jelly. The interior should be consistency of thick sour cream when cold. Remove to cake rack to cool. Serve in cups, plain or with a few chopped pistachios or a tsp of whipped cream. 4 servings.

COFFEE POTS DE CRÈME

A rich sophisticated dessert. A good way to use up egg yolks

1½ cups 12% cream—	⅟₁₆ tsp salt
Half and Half	⅓ cup fresh boiling water
4 egg yolks	2 tsp instant coffee
¼ cup sugar	

Have ready 4 buttered custard cups holding about ¾ cup each. Start oven 10 min before baking; set to moderately slow (325° F).

Scald cream in top of double boiler. Meanwhile beat yolks with rotary beater, then beat in sugar and salt, then slowly add the hot cream. Stir coffee into boiling water, then stir into cream mixture. Pour into custard cups. Set in a tin or glass pan about 7 x 7 x 2-inches; add hot water to come up almost to top of cups. Bake about 30 min, or until *just barely set.* Test by gently shaking pans—if Crème waves like soft jelly, it's done. Remove to cake rack to cool, then chill before serving. Serve plain right from the cups, or with a tsp of whipped cream, however, no garnish is needed for this delicate dessert. 4 servings.

Note: ⅓ cup freshly made double strength coffee may be used in place of the water and instant coffee.

CRUNCHY CARAMEL PEACH CRÈME

Try this, it's deliciously different! Most of the preparation can be done the day before

Crème:	Caramel:
¼ cup all-purpose flour	½ cup sugar
2 tbsp sugar	½ cup boiling water
1½ cups milk	*Topping:*
1½ cups 12% cream—	1 lb well ripened peaches,
Half and Half	or 2 cups neatly sliced
6 egg yolks, beaten	2 tbsp xxxx sugar
	1 cup whipping cream

Have ready 8 low sherbets or an 8 x 8 x 2-inch glass baking pan. Also butter well a 9-inch square aluminum or tin pan.

Crème: Blend flour and sugar in top of double boiler, then slowly stir in about ½ cup of the milk until smooth, then add remaining milk and cream. Place over boiling water and cook and stir constantly with wooden spoon until thickened, about 10 min. Beat yolks, stir in a little of the hot mixture, then add to double boiler and cook and stir 2 min longer until just thickened. Remove from heat and beat 1 min with rotary beater until very smooth and creamy. Pour into sherbets or 8-inch pan. Cool thoroughly on cake rack, then chill at least an hr or so.

Caramel: Put the ½ cup sugar and boiling water into a 1-qt saucepan, stir and heat to boiling, then cover and cook 10 to 15 min until syrup is *just a delicate amber* color. Remove cover last 2 or 3 min of cooking to watch, and stir gently. Pour into buttered 9-inch pan, scraping out saucepan with rubber scraper, then shift pan back and forth to flow syrup out in a very thin sheet over bottom of pan. Let harden until brittle, then tap caramel with metal knife handle to break into pieces. Then put between 2 sheets of waxed paper and crush by tapping with wooden spoon or any hard object. No piece should be larger than a dime. Caramel can be made a day or two in advance and stored in a tightly covered jar.

Topping: To assemble, pare and slice peaches thinly. Sprinkle with xxxx sugar; let stand 2 or 3 min to drain, then arrange slices closely together over custard. Return to refrigerator while whipping cream. Whip cream until stiff, then spread over peaches. Sprinkle with crushed caramel. Serve immediately or cover and chill 2 or 3 hrs before serving. 8 servings.

CRÈME BRULÉE No. 1

French Custard, p 532
½ cup granulated sugar

½ cup boiling water
Whipping cream

Make Custard and turn into a shallow bowl 8 or 9 inches in diameter. Chill without moving until a "skin" forms over top. Butter a 9 or 10-inch layer cake pan. Meanwhile, put sugar and water into a 1-qt saucepan. Stir well and place over moderate heat. Cover and boil until syrup starts to thicken, then uncover. Now *watch closely* and boil syrup to a *delicate amber,* moving pan back and forth to keep color even. *Do not scorch.* When a light tan, pour into buttered pan. Immediately shift pan back and forth to spread caramel into a thin even layer over bottom of pan. If it starts to harden, pull edges out with a spatula or fork. Pull it as thin as possible. It hardens quickly.

Just before serving Brulée, tap caramel sharply with knife handle to shatter into dime-size pieces. Caramel keeps for days in an airtight container. Sprinkle generously over Custard. Quickly drop mounds of whipped cream over caramel, dish up and serve immediately. 5 to 6 servings.

CRÈME BRULÉE No. 2

Make French Custard, p 532, and pour into an 8-inch metal cake pan. Chill until "skin" forms on top—do not break this.

Preheat oven to broiling temp (550° F). Place chilled custard on sheet of aluminum foil, pressing it around sides of pan. Now press ⅓ cup light brown sugar, packed, through a coarse sieve evenly over top. Place custard under broiler so top surface is 3-inches below heat. Watch and remove the instant sugar melts or is caramelized. *Do not scorch.* Remove to cake rack and remove foil, then place in refrigerator to chill. To serve, tap caramel with spoon to break into small pieces. Garnish with whipped cream and serve at once.

FLOATING ISLAND

The aristocrat of old-time desserts—you will have a hard time finding a better one. Make it for plain or most elaborate meals

Custard:
2 cups milk
¼ cup sugar
¼ tsp salt
4 egg yolks
1 tsp vanilla

Islands:
2 egg whites
Dash of salt
1 tbsp *plus* 1 tsp sugar
Guava Jelly, shaved chocolate *or* decorettes, caramel syrup

Custard: Scald milk with sugar and salt in top of double boiler over *simmering* water. Beat yolks in a 2-qt bowl, then slowly stir in hot milk. *Strain* back into double boiler. Cook and stir *over,* not in, *simmering* water until custard just coats a metal spoon, not more than 2 or 3 min. Remove from heat at once. Stir in vanilla. Turn into a large shallow glass bowl or individual serving dishes. Cool, then chill.

Islands: Heat 1½ qts water in a 10-inch iron skillet barely to simmering. Meanwhile, add salt to egg whites and beat until fluffy, then beat in sugar in 2 portions and beat until shiny and stiff. Drop heaping tablespoonfuls of meringue carefully on top of water an inch apart. Cover and poach 1½ to 2 min. Do not let water boil. Lift out and drain on slotted spoon or food fork and slide onto custard. A rim of custard should show all around the "island." Leave plain, or garnish "islands" with bits of bright jelly, shaved sweet chocolate or decorettes or drizzle with caramel syrup. Chill until ready to serve. 5 servings.

FRENCH CUSTARD

A versatile satin-smooth custard. Delicious as is, or as a basis for elegant desserts. Keeps a day or two when well chilled

1 tbsp butter	⅓ cup sugar
1 tbsp flour	⅛ tsp salt
2 cups milk	6 egg yolks, beaten
1 cup 12% cream—	1 tsp vanilla
Half and Half	

Melt butter in top of double boiler *over boiling water*. Blend in flour with a wooden spoon, then the milk and cream slowly to keep very smooth. Cook and stir until slightly thickened, about 10 min. Now stir in sugar and salt. Remove from heat and slowly stir hot mixture into beaten yolks. Now *strain* mixture back into double boiler. Again place over *gently boiling* water and cook and stir, watching until custard *just coats* a metal spoon, not more than 2 or 3 min. *Do not overcook*. Remove from heat at once and stir in vanilla. If desired, set top of double boiler into cold water for 2 or 3 min to quickly stop cooking custard. Beat well with rotary beater. Turn into bowl, glass jar or serving dishes. Cool to room temp, then cover and chill before serving. 5 servings.

WAYS TO SERVE: 1. Serve over Baked Apples, Prune Whip or other Fruit Puddings.

                   2. Pour over a slice of flavorful firm jelly such as guava, currant, etc.

                   3. Top with a blob of sweetened whipped cream; sprinkle with chocolate decorettes or chopped nuts, or drizzle with caramel syrup.

Note: If a slightly thinner custard is preferred, use 5 egg yolks.

LEMON CAKE CUSTARD

A refreshing delicate dessert—cake on top, custard on bottom

1½ tsp butter	1 cup sugar
½ tsp grated lemon rind	¼ tsp salt
¼ cup lemon juice, 1 large	2 eggs, separated
lemon	1 cup milk
4 tbsp all-purpose flour	Whipped cream, optional

Divide butter equally among 5 custard cups, each holding ¾-cup. Start oven 10 min before baking; set to slow (325° F). Have ready a glass or enamel baking pan 12 x 7½ x 2-inches. Wash lemon, grate rind, squeeze juice and measure. Sift flour, measure and turn into a mixing bowl. Stir in sugar, salt, then lemon juice. Add egg yolks and beat well with rotary beater. Remove and wash beater. Stir in rind and milk into lemon mixture with rubber scraper. Then beat egg whites until stiff and immediately turn them into lemon mixture and cut and fold them thoroughly into mixture with scraper until they form a soft spongy mass throughout. Spoon the mixture quickly into prepared cups. Set cups in the shallow glass baking pan. Pour hot water around cups to a depth of 1 inch. Bake 45 to 50 min or until custard tests done, p 526. Remove cups from pan to cake rack to cool. Serve lukewarm or cold, plain or with puff of whipped cream.

LIME CAKE CUSTARD

If you enjoy lime, you'll like this

1½ tsp butter	1 cup sugar
1 tsp grated lime rind	¼ tsp salt
¼ cup lime juice	2 eggs, separated
¼ cup all-purpose flour	1 cup milk

Prepare exactly like Lemon Cake Custard. 5 servings.

ORANGE CAKE CUSTARD

1½ tsp butter	¼ cup all-purpose flour
1 tsp grated orange rind, pkd	1 cup sugar
	¼ tsp salt
¼ cup orange juice, strained	2 eggs, separated
1 tbsp lemon juice	1 cup milk

Prepare exactly like Lemon Cake Custard. 5 servings.

PINEAPPLE CAKE CUSTARD

1½ tsp butter	¾ cup sugar
1 tsp grated lemon rind	¼ tsp salt
1 tbsp lemon juice	2 eggs, separated
¼ cup drained crushed pineapple	½ cup milk blended with
¼ cup all-purpose flour	¼ cup pineapple juice drained from crushed pineapple

Prepare like Lemon Cake Custard. 5 servings.

PEANUT BUTTER CUSTARD

A child's favorite because it contains flavorful peanut butter

2 cups milk	3 eggs
¼ cup peanut butter	⅓ cup sugar
½ tsp vanilla	¼ tsp salt

Butter 4 or 5 custard cups, then arrange in a 9-inch iron skillet or a glass or enamelware baking pan. Bake on top oven rack for delicate browning. Start oven 10 min before baking; set to moderately slow (325° F).

Scald milk in top of double boiler over simmering water, p 526. Remove from heat. Stir in peanut butter until well blended, then vanilla. Beat eggs *slightly* in a 2-qt bowl. Stir in sugar and salt, then the milk mixture. Strain through medium coarse strainer into cups. Pour hot water around cups to within ½-inch from top. Bake 28 to 30 min, or until custard tests done, p 526. Remove from oven, then with tongs remove from skillet to cake rack to cool. Serve lukewarm or cold, plain or with Chocolate Sauce. 5 servings.

PUMPKIN CUSTARD

For those who like pumpkin pie filling but not the crust

2 eggs	Dash of ginger *and*
½ cup moist brown sugar, pkd	½ tsp cinnamon blended with
½ tsp salt	1 tbsp boiling water
1 cup canned *or* home-cooked	1 cup thin cream *or* rich milk
pumpkin puree, p 1390	⅛ tsp grated orange rind, pkd

Start oven 10 min before baking; set to moderately slow (325° F). Butter 4 or 5 custard cups, then arrange in a 9-inch iron skillet or a glass or enamelware baking pan. Bake on top oven rack for delicate browning.

Beat eggs slightly with rotary beater, then beat in sugar, salt and pumpkin. Add spices mixed to a paste in the boiling water. Remove beater. Use wooden spoon to stir in cream and rind. Pour into cups. Bake about 40 min, or until custard tests done, p 526. Serve as is or with plain whipped cream. 4 to 5 servings.

HOW TO MAKE STIRRED OR SOFT CUSTARD

Step 1. Put milk, sugar and salt into top of double boiler. Place over boiling water and heat to scalding point. Meanwhile beat eggs slightly, add hot milk slowly, stirring constantly. Return mixture to top part of double boiler to cook over simmering water.

Step 2. Water in lower part of double boiler should not be more than 1-inch deep. The water should never touch the bottom of the upper part of double boiler. Stir often and cook until custard just coats a metal spoon. Stop the cooking at once and remove from water.

Step 3. Chill custard before serving. Good soft custard is thick enough to be eaten plain, yet thin enough to be used as a sauce for other desserts. When soft custard is topped with cooked or uncooked meringue, it is called Floating Island.

SOFT OR STIRRED CUSTARD

3 cups milk	3 eggs, beaten slightly
⅓ cup sugar	1 tsp vanilla
¼ tsp salt	

Put milk, sugar and salt in top of double boiler. Cover, place over hot water and heat to scalding. Beat eggs slightly and slowly stir in the hot milk. Strain if desired and return to double boiler. Place over lower part of double boiler, containing simmering water 1-inch deep, stirring constantly until mixture just coats a metal spoon. Custard will thicken somewhat on cooling, so do not cook it until thick; to do so will cause it to curdle. Remove immediately from heat and set pan of custard in cold water; add vanilla, and chill before serving. Serve in sherbet glasses or sauce dishes, or as a sauce for cake or pudding. 5 servings.

Note: Custard which has begun to curdle can often be restored by placing it quickly over cold water to stop cooking immediately, then beating vigorously with a rotary beater until smooth. Do not reheat.

JAM MERINGUE PUFF

Delicate, glamorous, good

Custard:	Puff:
1 cup milk	3 egg whites
3 tbsp sugar	⅓ cup tart jelly *or* jam
⅛ tsp salt	Dash of salt
3 egg yolks	
¼ tsp vanilla	

Custard: Scald milk in top of double boiler with sugar and salt. Beat egg yolks until well mixed, then stir in the scalded milk thoroughly. Turn back into top of double boiler, stirring constantly until custard coats a metal spoon. Remove immediately from heat and stir in vanilla. Pour into bowl and cool, then chill.

Puff: Wash double boiler. Now beat egg whites until stiff. Then beat in the jam or jelly and salt (Kumquat marmalade is excellent) until well blended. Turn carefully into double boiler, and put on lid with its inside rubbed with butter. Place over gently boiling water for 25 to 30 min. Now turn into a serving dish and cool slightly out of a draft. Serve with custard sauce poured over top. 5 servings.

HOW TO MAKE STEAMED CUSTARD

Step 1. Butter inside of top of double boiler. Add milk, then remaining ingredients. Beat with rotary beater. Cover and place over lower part of double boiler containing simmering water 1-inch deep.

Step 2. Cook covered without stirring for 15 min. Uncover and continue cooking until custard sets and when tilted leaves the sides of pan.

Step 3. Remove top part of the double boiler from hot water and carefully remove to cake rack to cool undisturbed. Spoon out lightly and serve plain or with crushed fruit sauce or whipped cream.

STEAMED CUSTARD

½ tsp butter	⅛ tsp salt
1½ cups milk	1 tsp vanilla *or*
3 eggs	¼ tsp grated orange rind, pkd
¼ cup sugar	lightly

Rub inside of top part of double boiler with the butter. Add milk then remaining ingredients. Beat with rotary beater for 1 min. Cover and place over lower part of double boiler containing boiling water no more than 1-inch deep. Water should not touch bottom of top part. Quickly reduce heat so that water barely simmers. Cook without removing cover for 15 min. Then remove cover and continue cooking 5 to 10 min longer or until custard is set and leaves the side of pan when tilted. Center of custard should still be quivery when cooking is stopped. Remove top of boiler to a cake rack to cool undisturbed. Dip out into individual serving dishes and serve with cream if desired. 4 servings.

BREAD PUDDING

Bread Pudding. Bread pudding is a custard base with enough bread, whole wheat or white, added to give it body. The bread should soak up practically all the custard. Toasting and buttering the bread and then arranging it in slices or neat strips produces a more attractive appearance than if the bread is torn into uneven crumbs and arranged in a hodge-podge manner. Unlike custards however, bread pudding is baked directly on a rack rather than in a pan of hot water. This produces a slightly browned surface all around and adds to the appetite appeal. Bread pudding is done when a knife inserted in the center comes out clean, and should be served when it has just lost its oven heat.

BREAD PUDDING

We believe bread pudding baked the old fashioned way directly on oven rack (not in water bath) is the most attractive and tastiest kind

5 ⅝-inch thick slices 2- *or* 3-day-old bread from 1-lb loaf	3 cups milk, scalded 3 eggs ¼ tsp salt
2 tbsp soft butter *or* margarine	½ cup sugar ½ tsp vanilla
½ cup moist raisins	¼ tsp cinnamon

Butter a 10 x 6½ x 1¾-inch glass baking dish. Adjust rack 6 to 7 inches above bottom of oven. Start oven 10 min before baking; set to moderate (350° F). Toast bread lightly, then spread with butter while hot. Cut slices in half or quarters. Fit neatly in prepared dish, over-lapping slightly. Sprinkle raisins between slices, not over top. Scald milk. Beat eggs slightly in a 2-qt bowl. Stir in salt and all but 2 tbsp of the sugar, then hot milk and vanilla. Pour over toast and let stand 10 min, pressing toast down lightly once or twice to soak up milk mixture. Blend cinnamon with remaining sugar and sprinkle over top. Bake directly on oven rack 25 to 30 min, or until pointed knife inserted in center comes out clean and top is an appetizing brown. Serve warm or cold, plain or with cream. 4 to 5 servings.

CAKE-CRUMB CUSTARD WITH LEMON GINGER SAUCE

An easy good dessert from leftover cake crumbs

Custard:
2 cups leftover crumbs from pound, yellow, *or* white butter *or* sponge cake, lightly pkd
1 cup scalded milk
¾ cup moist shredded coco-nut, lightly pkd
½ tsp salt
2 eggs, separated

Sauce:
1 cup white corn syrup
⅓ cup sugar
½ tsp ground ginger
2 tbsp firm butter
½ tsp grated lemon rind, pkd
¼ cup lemon juice

Custard: Butter well the inside of top part of double boiler with a rounded bottom. Break cake into crumbs and put into a 2 or 3 qt mixing bowl. Scald milk and pour over crumbs. Let stand 10 min, or a little longer for stale crumbs. Cut coconut in short lengths with scissors and add to crumbs, then beat yolks well and scrape them into crumb mixture. Add salt and mix well using a rubber scraper. Beat whites until stiff enough to hold shiny pointed peaks and turn im-mediately into the crumb mixture. Use scraper to cut and fold whites thoroughly into crumb mixture. Turn mixture very gently into the prepared top of double boiler. Place over very gently boiling water, cover and cook from 40 to 45 min, or until custard will leave side of pan when tilted, and a pointed paring knife inserted into center comes out clean. Turn out carefully onto serving plate. Serve hot with sauce.

Sauce: Put corn syrup, sugar blended with ginger into saucepan and heat to boiling. Remove from heat, beat in butter, then stir in lemon rind and juice. Serve warm over cake crumb custard. 5 or 6 servings.

COCOA BREAD PUDDING

1½ cups evaporated milk
2½ cups milk
2 tbsp butter
2 cups sifted dry bread
  crumbs
½ cup sugar

¼ cup cocoa
2 eggs, slightly beaten
½ tsp salt
1 tsp vanilla
Cream

Start oven 10 min before baking; set to moderate (350° F).

Butter a 6-cup shallow baking dish. Combine milks in top of double boiler, add butter, place over boiling water and heat to scalding. Pour over bread crumbs, stir well. Mix sugar and cocoa thoroughly and add to beaten eggs, add the next 2 ingredients, continuing to beat until well mixed. Combine thoroughly with milk and crumb mixture, and pour into baking dish. Bake 45 min, or until custard tests done, p 526. Serve warm or cold with cream. 6 to 8 servings.

LEMON CRACKER MERINGUE PUDDING

A "pinch hitter" for lemon pie using leftover crackers

Pudding:
  ½ tsp grated lemon rind, pkd
  2 tsp lemon juice
  ⅔ cup crushed crisp crackers
    —13 thin 2-inch square
    crackers
  ⅔ cup sugar
  ¼ tsp salt
  2 cups milk, scalded

2 egg yolks
2 tbsp melted butter

Meringue:
  2 egg whites
  Dash of salt
  ¼ cup sugar
  ½ tsp vanilla

Butter a 4-cup glass baking dish and set in a 1½-inch deep larger glass or tin pan. Start oven 10 min before baking; set to moderate (350° F).

Pudding: Grate lemon rind and squeeze juice. Combine crackers, sugar, salt, lemon rind and juice in a 2-qt bowl. Slowly stir in hot milk and let stand 10 min. Then stir in beaten yolks and butter. Turn into prepared dish and set in oven. Pour hot water around dish to almost fill pan. Bake 35 min. Make meringue last 5 min of baking.

Meringue: Beat egg whites and salt until stiff, add sugar in 2 or 3 portions and vanilla and beat until stiff and shiny. Remove pudding from oven; pile meringue over top, then swirl, touching sides of dish all around. Return to oven and bake 12 to 15 min, or until delicately browned. Remove to cake rack. Serve warm or cold. 5 servings.

LEMON GRAPE-NUT PUDDING
Good pudding

¼ cup soft butter *or* margarine	⅓ cup grape-nuts
¾ cup sugar	¼ tsp grated lemon rind, pkd
2 egg yolks	1½ tbsp lemon juice
2 tbsp flour	Dash of salt
¾ cup milk	2 egg whites
	Cream

Butter a 4-qt casserole. Start oven 10 min before baking; set to moderately slow (325° F).

Beat butter with rotary beater until creamy, then add ½ cup of the sugar gradually, beating thoroughly. Beat in yolks until fluffy. Clean off, wash and dry beater. Use wooden spoon to stir in flour, milk and grape-nuts, then lemon rind and juice. Add salt to egg whites and beat until stiff, then gradually beat in remaining ¼ cup sugar to a stiff shiny meringue. Fold meringue lightly but thoroughly into grape-nut mixture. Turn into prepared pan. Bake 40 min or until pudding is a rich golden brown. Remove to cake rack to cool. Serve warm with cream. 5 servings.

ORANGE MARMALADE BREAD PUDDING

5 slices 3-day-old bread, toasted	1¾ cups milk
3 tbsp soft butter	1 tbsp lemon juice
¾ cup orange marmalade	⅛ tsp nutmeg
3 eggs, slightly beaten	Cream, or Lemon Sauce, p 1243 or 1246

Start oven 10 min before baking; set to slow (300° F). Butter a shallow 6-cup baking dish. Spread toast (do not remove crusts) with the butter and marmalade. Cut bread in cubes and turn into baking dish. Mix eggs with milk, lemon juice and nutmeg, and pour over toast cubes. Bake 45 min, or until custard tests done, p 526. Serve warm or cold, plain or with cream, or lemon sauce. 5 servings.

DUMPLINGS

Dumplings, Baked—Plain pastry or rich biscuit dough is used. It is rolled from ⅛ to ¼-inch thick, then cut into 5 to 7-inch squares, or rounds or rectangles of similar size. Fruit is heaped in center of the individual cut-outs, then sprinkled with sugar and sometimes spice. Pastry or dough is brought up over fruit and pinched together to seal fruit in. Dumplings are placed on a flat baking sheet to bake until brown and fruit is tender; or they may be placed in an inch-high rim pan containing syrup; this low rim permits tops to brown well. The lower part of dumplings poach in the syrup and form a thickened sauce to serve over them.

Dumplings, Steamed—Biscuit dough is used. It is rolled out about ¼-inch thick and used to enclose the fruit the same as for Baked Dumplings. They may be put in custard cups or laid directly on a perforated pan which fits into a kettle containing boiling water. The steam circulating around them cooks dough until puffy and done and fruit is tender. They are drained and served at once with cream or a harmonizing sauce.

Dumplings, Boiled—These are 2 types: *drop and molded.* (1) Drop, made from a slightly sweet drop dumpling batter. They are poached in a tightly covered pan in a simmering Thin Sugar Syrup, Sweetened Fruit Sauce or Fruit Juice. The cooking liquid is served as a sauce over the dumplings. (2) Made from Potato Dumpling Dough. Shaped into a long roll, then cut into even lengths. These lengths are patted out and molded around sweetened fruit to seal it in well and cover it about ⅛-inch thick. Dumplings are dropped carefully into boiling water to cook until dough is done and fruit is tender.

Fruit Rolls, Roly Polys, etc.—Biscuit or pastry dough rolled into a rectangle, then spread thickly with fruit, sprinkled with sugar and melted butter, then rolled up and baked whole, or sliced like cinnamon rolls, then baked or baked in syrup.

APPLE DUMPLINGS No. 1

These Apple Dumplings are a treat

Pastry for Dessert
Dumplings, p 933
8 to 9 medium size tart
apples, 2 lbs
9 tbsp sugar, ½ cup *plus*
1 tbsp

Dash of cinnamon *or*
nutmeg, *or* both
2 tbsp firm butter
Caramel *or* Orange Sauce,
pp 1239 or 1247

Have ready a 10½ x 15½ x ½-inch jelly roll pan. Adjust rack 5 to 6 inches above bottom of oven. Start oven 10 min before baking; set to hot (450° F).

Make pastry. Wash apples, pare thinly, cut in quarters, remove cores, then cut into 2 lengthwise slices. Cover with wet paper toweling to prevent discoloring. Roll pastry into a 14 x 21-inch rectangle on a *well-floured* pastry cloth. Cut in *half lengthwise* and in *thirds crosswise* to make six 7-inch squares. Arrange 3 apple slices flat in center of pastry square to make an *open triangle,* then add 7 or 8 more slices compactly to stand upright inside of triangle. Sprinkle each dumpling with 1½ tbsp sugar, dash of cinnamon and dot with butter. Moisten edges of pastry with brush or fingers. Now bring *2 opposite corners* of pastry up over fruit to just overlap on top and press together, then bring up remaining 2 corners in same way and *pinch or press all 4 corners* together firmly. Now pinch open edges firmly together to seal, making 4 seams. (Dumplings are square.) Transfer dumplings with pancake turner to jelly roll pan, placing an inch apart. Bake 20 min, then reduce heat to moderate (350° F) and bake 25 to 30 min longer. Watch, and if any juice runs out of dumplings, reduce heat to keep it from scorching. Remove to cake rack to cool slightly, but serve warm, plain with cream or Caramel or Orange Sauce. 6 servings.

APPLE DUMPLINGS BAKED IN SAUCE No. 2

7 or 8 medium-size tart
    apples
    Pastry for 9-inch Double
    Crust, p 924
1¼ cups granulated sugar

2 tbsp firm butter
1¼ cups hot water, apple juice
    or cider
⅛ tsp salt
½ tsp lemon juice

Butter a 7 x 11 x 1½-inch baking pan. Adjust oven rack to 5 to 6 inches above bottom of oven. Start oven 10 min before baking; set to hot (450° F).

Wash apples, pare thinly, quarter, core and cut quarters into 2 or 3 lengthwise slices; cover with wet paper toweling or cloth to prevent discoloring.

Make pastry; roll out on floured pastry cloth into a 12 x 18-inch rectangle. Cut into six 6-inch squares. Heap ⅙ of the apple slices in center of each square; sprinkle each heap with 1 tbsp sugar and dot with butter. Moisten edges of squares. Now bring *2 opposite corners* of pastry up over apples to slightly overlap and pinch together gently, then bring up the 2 remaining corners and pinch or press all 4 corners together on top-center of dumpling. Now pinch open sides together to seal in fruit, making 4 fluted seams. Place dumplings in prepared pan. Prick tops 2 or 3 times with fork. Combine remaining sugar with next 3 ingredients and pour around dumplings. Bake 12 min or until lightly browned, then reduce heat to moderately slow (325° F) and bake 25 min longer or until apples are tender when pierced with a cake tester or toothpick, and pastry is richly browned. Remove to cake rack to cool to lukewarm. Serve with sauce in pan spooned over dumplings. 6 servings.

Note: Biscuit Dough, p 234, may be used in place of pie pastry.

GRANDMA'S BOILED APPLE DUMPLINGS

Syrup:
    ½ cup light brown sugar, pkd
    1½ cups water
    ¼ cup butter
    ¼ tsp salt
    2½ cups finely diced tart apples
Dumplings:
    1 tbsp lemon juice

1 cup all-purpose flour
2 tsp D.A. baking powder
    or 2½ tsp tartrate *or* phos-
    phate type
2 tbsp sugar
¼ tsp salt
⅓ cup *plus* 1 tbsp milk

Syrup: Measure first 4 ingredients into a 3-qt saucepan. Pare apples thinly, quarter and core, then cut quarters into 3 lengthwise slices; hold the 3 slices together and slice thinly into a quart bowl or cup. Now cut through apples with a sharp knife in the bowl until pieces are about size of peas. Remove and add 1 cup of the chopped apples to ingredients in saucepan, then heat to boiling and *simmer* 5 min.

Dumplings: Meanwhile, quickly stir lemon juice into remaining 1½ cups apples. Sift flour, measure and resift 3 times with baking powder, sugar and salt, the last time into a 2-qt mixing bowl. Add lemon-apple mixture then milk, and quickly stir to just blend well. Drop dumplings into syrup this way: First dip dessert spoon into the boiling syrup, then into the dough to fill spoon heaping and drop into syrup. Repeat dipping into syrup then into batter until all dumplings are added. Boil gently uncovered for 5 min, then cover tightly and boil 15 min longer. Remove from heat; lift off cover and let cool a few min before serving. Spoon dumplings into dishes with some of the sauce over them. Serve warm plain or with thin cream. 6 servings.

BANANA CRESCENTS

A good and different dessert

Pastry for 8-inch double crust, p 924	$\frac{1}{16}$ tsp mace
	¼ tsp grated lemon rind
3 large, 10 to 11″ *or* 6 small, 4 to 5″ long bananas	1 tbsp sugar
	1 egg white beaten with
1½ tbsp lemon juice	2 tbsp water

Start oven 10 min before baking; set to hot (425° F).

Make pastry. Roll into a 10 x 15-inch rectangle. Cut into six 5-inch squares. Peel and dip bananas in lemon juice and place diagonally on squares (cut large bananas in half). Sprinkle each banana with ½ tsp of mixture of next four ingredients. Roll up like jelly roll by starting at one corner. Shape into crescents and pinch open ends together. Place on ungreased cookie sheet. Brush with egg white. Bake 15 to 20 min, or to a golden brown. Serve warm with Lemon Sauce.

LEMON SAUCE

¼ cup sugar	Dash of salt
2 tbsp cornstarch	⅓ cup lemon juice
1¼ cups boiling water	1 tsp grated lemon rind
½ cup white corn syrup	1 tbsp butter

Blend sugar and cornstarch. Stir in boiling water thoroughly. Add syrup and salt, and cook and stir until mixture is thick and clear. Add remaining ingredients, and cook over low heat until well blended. 2 cups sauce.

BLACKBERRY DUMPLINGS MOHAWK

This good recipe comes from an American Indian woman. It dates before ovens

Berry Sauce:
- 1 qt blackberries
- ½ cup sugar
- ¼ cup water
- Dash of salt
- 1 tbsp lemon juice

Dumplings:
- 1 cup all-purpose flour
- 1 tbsp sugar
- ¼ tsp salt
- 1½ tsp D.A. baking powder *or* 2 tsp tartrate *or* phosphate type
- 1½ tbsp firm butter
- ½ cup *plus* 1 tbsp milk

Berry Sauce: Pick over berries discarding imperfect ones. Wash, then put undrained berries into a 3-qt saucepan with a tight-fitting cover. Add next 4 ingredients and stir into berries gently. Cover and simmer 3 min.

Dumplings: Sift flour, measure and resift 3 times with next 3 ingredients. Cut in butter with pastry blender until size of rice. Add milk all at once and stir vigorously for half a minute with a fork. Drop from tsp onto simmering berries, dipping spoon each time into hot sauce before dipping into batter. Cover tightly. Simmer over very low heat 20 min. Do not uncover during this cooking period. Spoon dumplings into individual dishes and pour sauce and berries over top. Serve warm. 8 dumplings or 4 servings.

Note: If barely ripe wild blackberries are used, omit lemon juice.

CHERRY DUMPLINGS MOHAWK

Follow recipe for Blackberry Dumplings, substituting 1½ qts sour red cherries that have been pitted, add ¾ cup sugar and omit lemon juice.

BLUEBERRY ROLY POLY

A delicious curlicue dessert—don't skimp on the fruit

1 pt box blueberries, 2½ cups

Dough:
- 2 cups all-purpose flour
- 3 tsp D.A. baking powder *or* 3¾ tsp tartrate *or* phosphate type
- ½ tsp salt
- 1 tbsp sugar
- ⅓ cup shortening
- ⅔ cup *plus* 1 tbsp milk

Filling:
- 2 tbsp soft butter
- ½ cup sugar
- 1 tbsp lemon juice
- 1 tbsp cream
- 1 tbsp sugar

Butter lightly an 11 x 7¼ x 1½-inch baking pan. Start oven 10 min before baking; set to moderately hot (400° F). Pick over, wash and drain berries.

Dough: Sift flour, measure, resift 3 times with next 3 ingredients, the last time into a 2-qt mixing bowl. Add shortening and cut in with pastry blender until particles are size of rice. Add milk all at once and stir quickly with a fork until well blended. Turn dough out onto floured pastry cloth; shape into a square, then roll out to a 15 x 10-inch rectangle, keeping edges as straight as possible.

Filling: Spread dough with softened butter, then sprinkle with sugar. Now strew 2 cups of the berries evenly over sugar to within ¾-inch of the edge. Drizzle with lemon juice. Now start at wide side, roll up carefully like jelly-roll, pinching edge of roll to seal, then pinch ends together. Roll should be 15 inches long. Cut into inch-wide crosswise slices. With pancake turner or spatula transfer carefully to prepared pan. Press remaining berries into slices where berries are skimpy. Use pastry brush to pat top with cream, then sprinkle with sugar. Bake 30 to 35 min. Remove to cake rack to cool slightly, but serve warm. Serve plain or with cream. 5 to 6 servings.

BLUEBERRY ROLY POLY—VARIATIONS ETC.

Variation No. 1: Transfer the whole berry filled roly poly with 2 pancake turners to a 13½ x 9¾ x ¾-inch jelly roll pan and bake as above, about 35 to 40 min.

Variation No. 2: Roly Poly may be laid on buttered pan or platter, then placed in a roasting pan containing a trivet. Add enough hot water to come up to trivet. Cover and steam over top stove heat 50 to 60 min. Serve warm within a few minutes after removing from steamer. Serve with cream or stewed blueberries.

GOOSEBERRY DUMPLINGS

Hold on to your gooseberries with a custard cup. As easy to eat as pie, but easier to make

1 recipe Baking Powder Biscuits, p 234	5 cups stemmed, freshly washed goosberries
2 cups sugar mixed with	

Have ready a shallow glass custard cup holding ¾ cup. Butter a 6¼ x 10¼ x 2-inch glass or aluminum baking pan. Start oven 10 min before baking; set to hot (425° F).

Make biscuit dough. Roll out on a floured pastry cloth into a 12 x 18-inch rectangle. Cut into 3 strips one way and 2 the other to make 6 sqs. Now lightly fit a square into the custard cup; dough will extend over cup. Heap ⅙ of the sugared berries into each. Moisten edges of square, then bring opposite corners of dough over top of fruit, lapping slightly and pressing together, then bring up the other 2 corners likewise. Now pinch open edges together firmly to seal to make 4 fluted seams. Now turn dumpling carefully from cup into hand, *place right-*

side up in prepared pan. Proceed in same manner with rest of dumplings. Prick tops with fork. Bake 30 to 35 min. Remove to cake rack to cool in pan. Serve warm. 6 servings.

Note: Use this good custard cup trick when making dumplings with any rolling small fruit.

PEACH DUMPLINGS

A nice little dessert and a pleasant change from pie

Pastry for 9-inch double
 crust, p 924
2½ lbs juicy ripe freestone
 peaches, 13 large egg-size

1 cup sugar
Few dashes of salt
3 tsp firm butter
¼ cup water

Have ready an 11 x 7 x 1½-inch baking pan. Start oven 10 min before baking; set to hot (450° F).

Make pastry. Shape into a small rectangle on floured pastry cloth or board, then roll out to a 12 x 18-inch rectangle. Cut pastry lengthwise into 2 even strips, then crosswise into 3 even strips to make six 6-inch squares. Pare peaches thinly, cut in half. Slice 3 peach halves onto center of each square; keep slices *heaped high.* Add 2 tbsp sugar, dash of salt and ½ tsp butter to each heap. Moisten edges of sqs all around with pastry brush. Now bring *2 opposite corners* of pastry *up over peaches* to slightly overlap and pinch corners together gently; now *bring up remaining 2 corners* and pinch or press all 4 corners together firmly on top-center of dumpling. Now pinch open side edges together firmly to seal. (Dumplings are sq.) Transfer dumplings to pan carefully, keeping them separated. Dice rest of peaches; add remaining ¼ cup sugar and the water, stir and pour around dumplings. Bake 20 min, then reduce heat to moderate (350° F) and bake 15 to 20 min longer. Remove to cake rack. Serve lukewarm with cream or Custard Sauce, p 1243, flavored with almond. 6 servings.

SKILLET PEACH DUMPLINGS

Any bride can make this dessert and the groom will think it is just like mother made

Sauce:
 ⅓ cup butter *or*
  margarine
 ¾ cup sugar
 1 tbsp water, opt
Biscuit Dough:
 1¼ cups all-purpose flour
 2 tsp D.A. baking powder
  or 2½ tsp tartrate *or* phosphate type

2 tsp sugar
¼ tsp salt
¼ cup shortening
¾ cup milk
Filling:
 2¼ lb ripe, juicy
  freestone peaches—12 egg-size
 ¼ cup sugar

Have ready a heavy 10-inch (⚹8) iron or aluminum skillet with a heat-proof handle. Adjust rack to be 5 to 6 inches above bottom of oven. Start oven 10 min before baking; set to hot (450° F).

Measure first 3 ingredients into skillet; place over low heat and cook and stir until mixture bubbles. Remove from heat. (Omit water if peaches are very juicy.)

Sift flour, measure, resift 3 times with next 3 ingredients, the last time into 2-qt mixing bowl. Cut in shortening with pastry blender until particles are size of rice. Pare peaches, cutting flesh away from pits in 6 to 8 lengthwise slices, dropping into a quart measure. There should be a generous quart of sliced fruit. Turn fruit into skillet, spreading level. Sprinkle with remaining ¼ cup sugar. Now stir milk quickly into flour mixture with fork until just well blended. Spoon blobs of dough all over peaches, then with rubber scraper gently spread out dough to almost cover peaches. Bake 15 min, then reduce heat to moderate (325° F) and bake 5 to 8 min longer, or until biscuit topping is browned and peaches are tender. Remove to cake rack to cool until warm. Spoon carefully into serving dishes, keeping biscuit part on top. Serve plain, with cream or a small scoop of ice cream. 5 to 6 servings.

BOILED BLUE PLUM DUMPLINGS

A favorite Bohemian dessert. Different, delicious and sure to give a lot of eating pleasure

Dough:
½ cup all-purpose flour
    Dash of nutmeg
½ tsp salt
¼ tsp D.A. baking powder *or*
    ⅓ tsp tartrate *or* phosphate
    type
1 lb potatoes, 3 medium—
    accurate amount is impor-
    tant
1 tsp salt
1 egg, beaten

Filling:
½ tsp grated lemon rind, pkd
¼ cup sugar
¼ tsp cinnamon
10 medium-size blue plums,
    10 oz, washed
Topping:
2 tbsp butter *or* margarine
½ cup dry white bread
    crumbs, p 168
    Cream and sugar

Dough: Sift flour, measure, add next 3 ingredients and resift.

Pare potatoes. Put into a 1½-qt saucepan, add 1 tsp salt, barely cover with water, cover and boil gently until tender, about 20 min. (Prepare Filling while potatoes cook.) Drain potatoes, and rice or put through food mill, into a 2-qt mixing bowl. Cool 5 min, then add egg and beat well, then beat in flour mixture. Now shape dough on a lightly floured sheet of waxed paper into a 10-inch roll.

Filling: Grate lemon rind, then blend with sugar and cinnamon.

Slit plums on one side; remove pits carefully. Fill each cavity neatly with 1 tsp of sugar mixture, then close plum and lay on plate.

Assembling and cooking: Have ready a 4-qt saucepan; add 2 qts water and ¾ tsp salt. Heat to boiling over moderate heat. Cut dough roll into 10 equal pieces. With floured hands, flatten pieces between palms into about 3½-inch patties. Holding patty in one hand, put a plum in center; press edges of dough up around it, pinch together and mold into a *smooth ball.* When all dumplings are made, slide easily into the boiling water; and as each is added, move it gently with spoon to keep from sticking to bottom. Dumplings remain on bottom at first, then rise to top. Boil, uncovered, moderately fast for 10 min. Lift out with slotted spoon to serving dishes.

Topping: While dumplings cook, melt butter, add crumbs and stir until browned lightly. Remove from heat. Stir in any sugar mixture left over from filling. Sprinkle over hot dumplings. Serve warm with cream and more sugar, if desired. 4 to 5 servings.

BAKED RED PLUM DUMPLINGS

A delightful quick dessert

Pastry for 9-inch double crust, p 924	Cream
	Cinnamon
1 to 1¼ lb red plums, 10 large	Water or eggwhite
1¼ cups sugar	

Grease lightly a 13½ x 9½ x ½-inch jelly roll pan, or a pan of almost similar size with not too high a rim as this retards browning. Start oven 10 min before baking; set to hot (450° F).

Make pastry and divide in half. Roll first half into a 10 x 15-inch rectangle. Now cut it into 3 strips one way and 2 the other, making six 5-inch sqs. Roll 2nd half into same size rectangle and cut in same way.

Wash plums. Cut into plums and twist paring knife slightly as you cut to remove flesh cleanly from pits in 2 pieces. Put ½ of plum, cut side up, in center of pastry square. Heap a level tbsp of sugar in the hollow, then top with other plum half, hollow-side up, and add another tbsp sugar. Moisten edges of pastry with water or egg white. Now bring 2 opposite corners of pastry up over top of fruit, lapping slightly and pressing together, then bring up the other 2 corners likewise. Pinch the open edges together firmly to seal. Place on prepared pan so dumplings do not touch. Prick top once or twice with fork. Bake 15 min, then reduce heat to moderate (350° F) and bake 15 min longer or until nicely browned. Remove to cake rack to cool to lukewarm. Serve plain or with sweetened cream with a dash of cinnamon, if desired. 5 to 6 servings.

DELICIOUS BAKED RAISIN DUMPLINGS

Syrup in which dumplings bake develops into a rich sauce

Raisin Sauce:
½ cup brown sugar, pkd
½ cup granulated sugar
¼ tsp salt
¼ tsp cinnamon
¾ cup seedless raisins, washed
1 tbsp butter
1½ cups water
1 tsp vanilla

Drop Batter:
¾ cup all-purpose flour

1 tsp D.A. baking powder
or 1¼ tsp tartrate *or* phosphate type
¼ tsp salt
⅓ cup coarsely broken nuts
2 tbsp soft butter *or* margarine
⅓ cup granulated sugar
⅓ cup milk
Cream, plain or whipped, optional

Butter well a 7 x 11 x 1½-inch baking pan. Start oven 10 min before baking; set to moderate (350° F).

Raisin Sauce: Blend sugars, salt and cinnamon in 1-qt saucepan, add raisins (remove any stems), butter and water. Heat to boiling, then boil gently about 10 min. Remove from heat and stir in vanilla.

Drop Batter: Meanwhile, sift flour, measure and resift 3 times with baking powder and salt. Break nuts. Cream butter in a 2-qt mixing bowl, add sugar gradually and cream thoroughly. Now combine flour and sugar mixtures and with a pastry blender or food fork, work together until well blended. Add milk all at once and beat hard to a smooth batter. Drop from tbsp *into prepared pan* into 6 mounds an inch apart. Pour the hot sauce *around* mounds. Sprinkle with nuts. Bake 25 to 30 min to a golden brown. Remove to cake rack. Serve warm or cold with cream. 6 servings.

FRITTERS

BATTER FOR FRUIT FRITTERS AND GENERAL DIRECTIONS FOR FRYING. Batter for Meat, Fish and Vegetable Fritters, see p 1349

1 cup all-purpose flour
1 tsp D.A. baking powder *or*
1¼ tsp tart. or phos. type
½ tsp salt
3 tbsp sugar
1 egg

⅓ cup milk
1 tsp melted butter
½ to 1 cup of drained sweetened fruit
Shortening for frying

Sift flour, measure and resift 3 times with next 3 ingredients. Beat egg, add milk, stir in butter quickly, then add flour and beat to a smooth batter. Fold in fruit until just distributed. It doesn't hurt batter to stand a few min.

General Directions for Frying: In a 3-qt frying kettle, heat shortening to 360° F. No frying basket is needed for fritters. Dip spoon into hot fat and quickly dip up a heaping tsp of batter, and with a second spoon quickly push it into the fat. Work fast so 6 or 7 fritters can fry at the same time. Temp drops quite fast but try to maintain it around 350° F throughout frying. Turn fritters when brown on underside. It requires from 4 to 5 min to fry fritters of this size to a golden brown and to cook all the way through. Lift out quickly with food fork or slotted spoon onto absorbent paper to drain. Sprinkle with xxxx sugar if desired. Serve hot like pancakes with sugar or syrup, or serve sprinkled with xxxx sugar for afternoon tea or coffee. 24 fritters.

Hint: To save fat, strain while hot through one layer of cleansing tissue or cheesecloth placed in a coarse sieve over a shortening or coffee can. Cool. Store in refrigerator for next frying.

Hint: Fritters—fat or flat, depend on the way you fry them; in deep fat, they come out globular, in shallow fat, they come out flat. Good either way. See also Frying with Deep Fat, p 738.

APPLE FRITTERS

1 recipe Batter for Fruit Fritters, p 548	1 cup grated pared tart apples, 2 *or* 3 medium

Make batter. Grate apples and fold immediately into batter before apples discolor. Fry at 360° F according to *General Directions for Frying,* p 548. Sprinkle with xxxx sugar. Serve like doughnuts with tea or coffee, or with syrup for dessert. 4 to 5 servings.

APRICOT FRITTERS

1 recipe Batter for Fruit Fritters, p 548	1 cup drained sweetened dried apricots

Make batter. Cut apricot halves into quarters with kitchen scissors and fold into batter. Fry at 360° F according to *General Directions for Frying,* p 548. Serve same as Apple Fritters. 4 to 5 servings.

BANANA FRITTERS

1 recipe Batter for Fruit Fritters, p 548 2 good sized ripe bananas	2 tsp lemon juice 2 tbsp xxxx sugar

Make batter. Cut peeled bananas into ¼-inch dice. Sprinkle with lemon juice and sugar. Fold into batter. Fry at 360° F according to *General Directions for Frying,* p 548. Serve same as Apple Fritters. 4 to 5 servings.

BLUEBERRY FRITTERS, Shallow Fat Fried

Shallow fat frying is necessary to hold onto the berries. Good hot or cold, plain or dusted with sugar. Delicious with beautifully clouded interiors.

1 recipe Batter for Fruit Fritters, p 548	½ cup blueberries, fresh *or* thawed frozen
2 tsp lemon juice, optional	½ cup shortening
¼ tsp cinnamon, optional	

Make batter. Stir in lemon juice and cinnamon. Fold in blueberries. In a heavy 10-inch skillet heat shortening to about 350° F. Drop batter by tablespoonfuls into fat. Fry until golden brown on underside, then turn with pancake turner or spatula and fry until brown on other side. Frying requires 4 to 5 min. Serve warm for breakfast instead of pancakes, or with Orange Sauce, p 1247, for luncheon dessert. 12—3-inch fritters.

CRANBERRY FRITTERS, Shallow Fat Fried

1 recipe Batter for Fruit Fritters, p 548	½ cup sweetened cranberry sauce
	½ cup shortening

Make batter. Fold in cranberry sauce. Heat shortening to about 350° F in a heavy 10-inch skillet. Drop batter by tablespoonfuls into the fat. Fry until golden brown on underside, then turn with pancake turner or spatula and fry until brown on other side. Frying requires 4 to 5 min. Serve warm for breakfast instead of pancakes, or with Orange Sauce, p 1247, for luncheon dessert. 12 fritters.

JACK HORNER'S PLUM FRITTERS

1 recipe Batter for Fruit Fritters, p 548	⅓ cup diced sweetened cooked prunes
	⅓ cup diced peeled orange

Make batter. Fold in the fruits. Fry at 360° F according to *General Directions for Frying,* p 548. 20 fritters.

Hint: Whole pitted prunes may be stuffed with sections of a small orange, chunks of pineapple or moist candied cherries, then dipped into the batter and fried.

ORANGE BIT-OF-GOLD FRITTERS

1 recipe Batter for Fruit Fritters, p 548	1 tsp grated orange rind, pkd
	1 cup diced peeled oranges

Make batter, stir in orange rind, then fold in fruit. Fry at 360° F according to *General Directions for Frying,* p 548. 16 fritters.

PEACH FRITTERS

1 recipe Batter for Fruit Fritters, p 548	1 cup sliced fresh fine flavored peaches

Make batter. Fold in peaches. Fry at 360° F according to *General Directions for Frying*, p 548. Serve warm with Sugar-Syrup, p 169, flavored with almond. 16 to 18 fritters.

DRIED FRUIT

STEWED DRIED APPLES

A simple good dessert, or a tasty filling for baked or fried pies

1 lb dried apples 5 cups cold water	½ cup sugar

Look over apples; cut away with scissors any dark spots and remaining cores. Quickly wash in cold water. Place in a 4-qt saucepan, add cold water, cover and soak 3 or 4 hrs. Then heat to boiling over moderate heat, then reduce heat, cover and simmer 15 to 20 min or until soft, but not mushy. Now stir in sugar and simmer 5 min longer. Remove from heat. Cool to lukewarm or chill. 6 cups thick sauce.

STEWED DRIED APRICOTS

1 lb dried apricots 6 cups cold water	1 cup sugar Dash of salt, optional

For attractive appetizing results, use bright true-colored, clean fruit. Pick over fruit, snipping out any dark spots with scissors. Wash quickly but thoroughly in cold water. When apricots stand several min in water because of slow washing, they lose considerable fine flavor. Put fruit in a 3-qt saucepan, add water, cover and let stand 1 to 2 hrs. Then place over moderate heat and when fruit begins to boil vigorously, reduce heat immediately to a simmer and cook 12 to 15 min longer or until just soft. Now add sugar and salt and let simmer another 5 min. Remove from heat to cool to lukewarm, or chill to serve plain or with cream.

DRIED APRICOT PURÉE

Excellent for making ice cream, fruit whip or to serve to babies or oldsters

Stew apricots as described above. Add sugar or leave unsweetened, depending on how purée is to be used. Turn apricots into a sieve or food mill placed over a bowl. Let stand until syrup drains off. Pour syrup into a container and save for making fruit cocktail or for a beverage. Now rub fruit through sieve or food mill to obtain all the purée. There should be 2 cups stiff purée. If a thinner purée is desired, thin it with some of the juice drained off.

STEWED DRIED FRUIT—ANY KIND

Peaches, pears and figs may be cooked in the following way to make a simple good dessert.

Prepare exactly like Stewed Dried Apricots, except add sugar to suit taste, allowing from ⅓ to ⅔ cup sugar to each pound of fruit. Amount depends on tartness of fruit and personal taste. Some prefer to add no sugar at all.

STEWED DRIED PRUNES

Correctly cooked, prunes are handsome, delicious and nourishing

1 lb moist prunes	Sugar, optional
Lukewarm water	

Wash prunes quickly but thoroughly in cold water, lifting them out into a 3-qt saucepan. Barely cover with lukewarm water, about 2½ cups. Then cover and cook over low heat, never above simmering point, until fruit is tender. The slower the cooking the better the product. It takes from 30 to 40 min. Add sugar, if desired. The addition of sugar gives a thicker, more attractive syrup. Serve lukewarm or chilled, plain or with cream. 5 to 6 servings.

PRUNES WITH LEMON SLICES

Prepare exactly like Stewed Dried Prunes, except add ½ lemon sliced very thin when they start to cook with ¼ to ⅓ cup sugar. Serve lemon slices with the prunes.

PRUNES WITH ORANGE

Prepare exactly like Stewed Dried Prunes, except add sliced or diced pared oranges to prunes when they are served.

SOAKED PRUNES

Attractive and very good

Wash prunes and drop into a clean glass jar. Cover with lukewarm water, cover jar and place in refrigerator several days to soak and plump up fruit until it is tender. A day or so before they are to be served, ⅓ cup sugar and ¼ cup white corn syrup may be added.

PURÉE OF ANY DRIED FRUIT

Excellent for baby food or for oldsters and for making fruit whips

1 lb moist dried fruit	⅔ to 1⅓ cups sugar, depend-
1½ cups water	ing on tartness of fruit

Wash fruit quickly but thoroughly in cold water, lifting out into a 3-qt saucepan. Add water which should come 1-inch above top of fruit. Cover and let soak 1 to 3 hrs. Cook in same water in which fruit soaked. Now heat to boiling over moderate heat, then reduce heat and simmer until tender, 15 to 20 min. Stir in sugar last 5 min of cooking, and cook until sugar dissolves. Remove from heat and cool to room temperature then drain, saving juice. Pit prunes then turn fruit into a sieve or food mill and rub through thoroughly to obtain all purée. Or, put fruit into a bowl and use kitchen scissors or biscuit cutter to chop the fruit fine. If purée is thicker than desired, add enough of the drained-off juice to give desired consistency. A stiff purée is preferred for cake fillings and a medium one for fruit whips. Store in a sterilized jar with tight fitting cover in refrigerator. About 2½ cups. Use leftover juice over fruit cups or for beverage.

STEWED RAISINS

Better than you think

½ lb seedless raisins	Sugar, optional
Lukewarm water	

Wash raisins quickly in cold water, lifting out into a 1-qt saucepan. Add enough lukewarm water to cover. Cover pan and let stand 1 hr, then place over low heat and *simmer* 5 to 10 min or until plump and tender. Add 1 to 2 tbsp sugar and simmer another 2 min. Remove from heat and serve lukewarm or chilled with plain cookies or buttered toast. 4 servings.

DRIED FRUIT COMPOTE

An unusually good uncooked dessert

½ cup moist dried apricots	½ cup pitted dates
½ cup moist seedless raisins	⅓ cup lemon juice
½ cup moist dried figs	¼ cup honey
½ cup moist dried prunes	Cream, coffee or whipping

Use bright colored apricots. Wash apricots, raisins, figs, and prunes quickly but thoroughly in cold water. Drain, then pat dry on absorbent paper. Remove pits from prunes and put through food chopper alternating the fruit as you chop them so they will be somewhat mixed, dropping them into a mixing bowl. Drizzle lemon juice and honey over fruit and mix well. Cover tightly and place in refrigerator for a day or so for fruits to soften and for flavors to blend. To serve, heap cold mixture lightly in sherbet glasses and pour plain cream around fruit heap or top with a puff of whipped cream. 5 to 6 servings.

LIME HONEY FRUIT COMPOTE

Intriguing flavor and high in nutritive value

½ tsp grated green lime rind, pkd
¼ cup lime juice, 2 green limes
4 medium size apples
¼ cup honey

¼ cup seedless raisins
1 doz moist medium size prunes
1 doz pitted dates
¼ cup pecans *or* walnuts
Thin cream

Grate lime rind just before needed. Squeeze and measure lime juice. Wash apples, remove blossom and stem ends, then grate on a coarse grater, skin and all. Drop grated apple immediately into lime juice. Add honey, raisins, then prunes and dates cut small. Mix well, cover and chill 12 to 24 hrs for flavors to blend. Just before serving stir in nuts. Heap lightly into serving dishes and serve with cream. 4 servings.

Note: The mixed dried fruit may be used to make this dessert.

BLACKSTONE WINTER FRUIT COMPOTE

A simple but attractive and refreshing fruit dessert or cocktail

1 lb mixed dried fruit, pears, peaches, apricots, prunes
3 cups water

¾ cup sugar
Dash of salt
¼ cup white corn syrup

Wash fruit quickly but well in cold water; put into a 3-qt saucepan. Add water, cover and heat to boiling, then reduce and *simmer* 20 min. Add sugar and salt the last 5 min of cooking. Remove from heat and add syrup. Keep covered while cooling, then chill. The fruit should be whole but tender and the syrup clear and thick. 7 to 8 servings.

COOKED FRUIT

Cooked fruit. A few fruits are even more delicious when they are cooked by stewing, poaching, baking, broiling or frying and some may be cooked just for an enjoyable variation from the fresh. Stewed fruit is usually cut into slices and either cooked to obtain a mushy sauce or to retain the shape of the slices. Poached fruit is the whole fruit either pared or unpared that is simmered slowly in a syrup. Baked fruits may be pared if desired and then baked until tender, but with their original form intact. Broiling is often used for grapefruit or oranges with a dot of butter added to give a bubbly, golden-brown surface.

Certain varieties of some fruits are more suitable for cooking than others, and the degree of ripeness, conditions of the growing season, as well as the kind of finished product preferred will all influence the selection of fruit for cooking. Certain varieties of apples, for example, will cook to a mush readily and are therefore best for sauce, while others hold their shape well and are best for beautiful stewed apple slices or baked apples.* In general, the same varieties that are best for canning are best for cooking. In order for fruit to have the best flavor after it is cooked, it must be fully ripened before cooking. Pears, peaches and plums should begin to feel just a trifle soft and should be dripping with juice; berries, cherries, and apples should be fully ripe and bright in color. Fruit that matures in a dry season will require more water for cooking than fruits that grow in a rainy one, and your own experience will be the best guide for the proper amount of water to use.

Certain cooking procedures will also influence the appearance and flavor of the finished fruit. Fruits may be left unpeeled if the skins will cook tender, but most often it provides more pleasant eating to have the skins removed. The peel should be removed however in the thinnest possible layer, to preserve as much of the flavor, form and food value as possible. If fruit is cooked whole, the core is sometimes removed and seeds or pits are often discarded. Fruit for sauce can be cut into irregularly shaped slices, but they should all be approximately the same thickness so the sauce will cook readily. But if the fruit is to be served in pieces, the slices should be neatly and evenly cut for the best appearance and most uniform cooking. A saucepan that is stained or darkened or chipped and pitted should never be used to cook fruit. Most fruits contain a fairly high percentage of acid, and most of the darkening on pans or the exposed surfaces in chipped or pitted pans react with this acid. This reaction dissolves some of the darkened portions of the pan giving a gray color and off flavor to the finished product.

When fruit is cooked in plain water, the water tends to soak into the fruit and cause it to puff up or cook to a mush. However, when fruit is cooked in a syrup the fruit tends to hold its shape and remain slightly firm. Therefore, if a sauce is desired, the fruit should be cooked first in water and then a minimum of sugar added so as not to mask the true fruit flavor, and if solid pieces with clean cut edges are desired, the fruit should be dropped into a thin to medium sugar syrup. (Quince, which is a very hard fruit, is the only exception.) When cooking sauce, only enough water should be added to prevent the fruit from scorching and to mush up the fruit, but not so much that the fruit will be watery. If fruit is to retain its shape in cooking, then more water is needed, but still just enough to produce luscious juice that will just barely cover the fruit. The fruit should always be cooked in a covered pan over moderate heat to prevent excess evaporation of liquid and fragrance.

Overcooking will darken the color and dissipate the flavor of cooked fruits. At the instant enough juice is coaxed out of berries, peaches and pears to almost cover the fruit, it is usually cooked soft enough to please most

*See pp 77–78.

palates. As soon as fruit is soft enough to be pierced easily with a toothpick, it is usually cooked done enough to be enjoyed by most everyone.

In addition to sugar, lemon is sometimes added to cooked fruits to make the colors, particularly the reds, more brilliant and to give a piquant flavor. Sometimes fruits are combined to obtain a red color. A little food coloring, cinnamon candies or mint are sometimes added for both flavor and color. Most cooked fruits can be enjoyed when served either warm or chilled, and topped with cream, whipped cream, ice cream, sauces or served plain.

"DRESSING UP" CANNED APPLE SAUCE

The quality of canned apple sauce has improved much in the last few years. It is however, usually made from bland flavored apples. Therefore the flavor may be made peppier and more interesting in appearance in a number of ways. To make it more tart add a little lemon juice and more sugar. Or combine a little lemon juice with some grated lemon rind and sugar and sprinkle it over the servings. A mixture of sugar and cinnamon sprinkled over the sauce adds color and pleasing spicy flavor. Half a cup of plumped raisins folded into a No. 2 can of sauce just before serving is good. Serve the sauce chilled or reheat and serve warm.

APPLES FOR APPLE SAUCE

Early summer apples make the most delicious apple sauce. Red Junes, Early Transparent, Duchess and Greenings are the choice varieties for sauce. Apples should be cooked in a minimum of water without sugar until mushy, then sugar should be stirred in and cooking continued only long enough for sugar to dissolve and blend with the apples. No spice is needed when apples have a natural fine flavor of their own.

STANDARD APPLE SAUCE

Apple sauce is so good. Many enjoy eating it as a vegetable with meat. It is generally served, however, as a delicious refreshing dessert.

2 lbs tart juicy apples, 8 to 9 medium	apples—1 cup needed for most
½ to 1 cup water, amount depending on juiciness of	Dash of salt ½ cup sugar *or* to taste

Wash apples, pare thinly, quarter, core and cut quarters into 3 or 4 slices, dropping into a 3-qt saucepan. There should be 6 cups. Add water and salt, cover closely and place over moderate heat. Cook *without stirring*, but shake pan across heat unit often to prevent sticking. When apples are mushy, beat vigorously with rotary beater to break up any lumps, then stir in sugar. Cover and simmer a min or two longer. Remove from heat. Again whip with beater to a smooth sauce, then turn into serving dish. Serve lukewarm or chilled. 3 cups or 4 to 6 servings.

FOOD MILL APPLE SAUCE

Wash apples well. If dirty, scrub in lukewarm soapy water, then rinse thoroughly in cold water. Use paring knife to trim out stem and blossom ends and any blemishes. Cut in quarters, dropping into saucepan. Cook as above, but instead of beating with rotary beater, put through food mill.

APPLE AND CRANBERRY SAUCE

A stimulating change and delightful blend of fruit flavors

1½ lbs tart cooking apples,   ¾ cup water
  p 97   1¼ cups sugar
½ lb cranberries

Wash, pare, quarter, core and slice apples, dropping them into a 3-qt saucepan. Pick over cranberries, discarding soft ones. Wash and add to apples, then add water. Cover pan, place over heat and after boiling starts, cook at moderate speed, from 15 to 20 min, shaking pan frequently to prevent sticking. As soon as fruits are tender, add sugar, stir in very gently and cook 2 or 3 min longer, or until juice is syrupy. Remove from heat and chill before serving. 5 to 6 servings.

APPLECOT SAUCE

Different and appetizing

¼ lb dried apricots   ½ cup sugar
1½ lbs tart cooking apples

Use bright colored apricots. Wash quickly in cold water. Put into a 3-qt saucepan, add enough water to cover, about 1½ cups. Cover and let soak 1 to 2 hrs. Then place over moderate heat and simmer 5 min. Meanwhile wash, pare, quarter, core and slice apples and turn them over the apricots. Again cover pan and boil gently until apples are tender, from 10 to 15 min. Now stir in sugar and simmer for 2 or 3 min. Put through food mill or leave as is. Serve hot or cold. 5 to 6 servings.

BAKED APPLES NO. 1

Nicely baked apples are a perfect dessert for a heavy meal. Use Rome Beauty, Jonathan, Northern Spy, McIntosh

6 large perfect apples—   ⅓ cup seedless raisins *or* nuts,
  3-inches in diameter   optional
½ to ⅔ cup sugar, depending   2 tbsp butter, optional
  on tartness

Use baking dish 6½ x 10¼ x 1¾ inches. Start oven 10 min before baking; set to mod (350° F).

Wash, then core carefully using apple corer. Fit apples stem side up in baking dish. It is important that apples fit snugly in baking pan for perfect baking. Fill holes with sugar, and raisins or nuts. Dot with butter. Pour enough water *around* apples to barely cover bottom of pan. Bake 45 min to 1 hr or until apples test tender when pierced with toothpick or fork. Remove to cake rack to cool. Serve lukewarm or cold. 6 servings.

BAKED APPLES NO. 2

The quickest way to bake apples. They are glazed, juicy and plumper than regular baked apples

6 large apples—3-in in diameter	½ cup water
1 cup sugar	½ lemon cut in thin slices, optional

Use baking dish 6½ x 10¼ x 1¾ inches. Start oven 10 min before baking; set to mod (350° F).

Wash and core apples. Heat sugar and water to boiling in a deep aluminum skillet or a 2 or 3-qt shallow saucepan. Add lemon slices and then apples. Cook apples gently about 5 min, turning the apples over and over to heat them through. Lift apples out into baking dish, then pour syrup and lemon slices over apples. Bake 15 to 20 min or until apples are tender, basting them twice with the syrup in pan during baking. Remove to cake rack to cool. Serve with syrup and lemon slices lukewarm or cold, plain or with cream. 6 servings.

BAKED APPLES NO. 3—OLDEN DAY METHOD

Delicious served as a vegetable for a meat accompaniment or as dessert

10 medium-size tart baking apples	½ cup sugar

Use a shallow baking pan about 11 x 7 x 2 inches. Start oven 10 min before baking; set to moderate (350° F).

Wash apples, cut in half lengthwise, then with paring knife cut out a shallow wedge to remove core. Dip cut surface of apples quickly in water or cider, then in sugar placed in a saucer so that a thick sugar coat adheres to the apple. Place halves, sugar-side up, snugly together in a baking pan. Sift rest of sugar over top of apples. Bake until tender, from 40 to 50 min. These apples are soft in the center but the cut surface has a tough leathery skin which is appreciated by many people. Remove to cake rack. Serve lukewarm. 5 to 6 servings.

Note: When these apples have cut side turned down in baking pan and ¼ cup water is poured over apples, they will bake more quickly—in from 20 to 30 min.

MINCEMEAT STUFFED APPLES

Prepare exactly like Baked Apples No. 1, except use ½ cup mincemeat to fill the holes in the apples instead of the sugar and the raisins.

PINEAPPLE STUFFED BAKED APPLES

Prepare exactly like Baked Apples No. 1, except use ½ cup drained crushed pineapple and ¼ cup light brown sugar to fill holes in apples instead of the sugar and raisins.

CINNAMON APPLES

A beautiful edible garnish for meat or poultry, or on a lettuce leaf topped with mayonnaise they make a delicious salad, and with cream a fine dessert

6 Rome Beauty apples *or*	1½ cups water
8 large Jonathans	⅓ cup cinnamon drops
¾ cup sugar	

Wash apples, pare thinly, then use apple corer to remove core neatly. Put sugar, water and cinnamon drops into a 3-qt saucepan. Place over heat and cook until sugar and candy dissolve. Add apples one at a time. Boil gently uncovered, turning apples over carefully from time to time until they are tender when tested with a toothpick. Now lift apples out into a shallow dish. Continue boiling the syrup until it is thick like honey when dropped from spoon. Now spoon syrup over apples a little at a time to glaze them. When all syrup has been spooned on, place in refrigerator to chill. These apples may be stuffed with chopped nuts before glazing with the syrup. 6 to 8 servings.

FRIED APPLES

For the most delicious fried apples use barely ripe ones. *Such apples come out of the skillet with a thin jelly-like coating*

2 lbs apples, Jonathan *or*	3 tbsp butter *or* bacon fat
Northern Spy	½ cup sugar, *or* more

Use tart flavorful apples. Wash but do not pare. Cut into quarters, remove cores, stem and blossom-ends, then cut into 2 or 3 lengthwise slices, number depending on size of apples. Have butter melted in a 10-inch heavy skillet over low heat. Add apples before they discolor. Cover skillet tightly and cook gently 4 to 5 min, or until apples are puffed, slightly cracked and very wet with juice. Now turn fruit over with a pancake turner. Sprinkle with ⅓ cup of the sugar. Cover, reduce heat and cook another min or two until sugar is absorbed and slices are translucent and under-side is a delicate brown. Now sprinkle with rest of sugar, and lift out carefully onto plate. Serve hot with bacon or sausage or for dessert. 4 to 5 servings.

POACHED APPLE RINGS

A beautiful edible garnish for ham, sausage or bacon

1 cup water
1½ cups sugar
½ cup white corn syrup

3 tbsp lemon juice, 1 lemon
2 lbs tart, just ripe red apples

Put first 4 ingredients into a 10-inch aluminum skillet or a shallow saucepan, stir thoroughly, place over heat and simmer 5 min. Meanwhile, wash apples, remove stem and blossom ends, core then cut apples crosswise into ⅜-inch thick slices. Immediately slide slices into boiling syrup and continue simmering until apples are tender and translucent. Lift out with spatula or pancake turner. Use leftover syrup again by adding a little more water, sugar and corn syrup. 5 servings.

POACHED ORANGE SLICES

Prepare exactly like Poached Apple Rings except substitute clear-yellow, medium size seedless oranges for the apples. A most attractive garnish for baked ham or to eat as dessert.

SCALLOPED APPLES

Good dessert with an oven-meal

2 lbs tart apples—
    Greenings, Jonathans *or*
    Duchess
½ cup sugar

3 tbsp butter
Grated sharp cheese, optional

Bake in a moderate oven (350° F). Butter an 8-cup casserole with a cover.

Wash apples, pare thinly, or leave unpared, quarter, core and cut quarters into 2 or 3 lengthwise slices. Arrange apples in layers in casserole, sprinkling each with sugar and dotting with butter. Cover and bake 30 to 40 min or until just tender. Serve with sprinkling of cheese, hot, or chill before serving. 4 to 5 servings.

STEWED APPLES

Apples in one of their most beautiful and tempting forms. Serve as vegetable or dessert

3 lbs lively flavored apples,
    12 medium
1⅓ cups sugar
1⅓ cups water
⅓ cup white corn syrup

Dash of salt
⅛ tsp nutmeg *or* 4-inch stick cinnamon *or* ½ lemon sliced paper-thin, optional

Use Jonathan, Northern Spy or Baldwin apples. Put next 5 ingredients into a 4-qt saucepan, stir well, then place over very low heat.

Wash apples, pare thinly, quarter, core and add to hot syrup. Cover loosely, heat to boiling, then reduce heat and *simmer* 15 to 20 min, or until tender and translucent in appearance. Turn gently into a bowl. Serve lukewarm or cool, or cover and chill. 6 to 7 servings.

BAKED BANANAS

An attractive way to obtain a delicious but different banana flavor and texture

5 medium size bananas, green-tipped	1½ cups crushed cornflakes, about
3 tbsp lemon juice	Lemon Sundae Sauce, p 645

Butter a 6½ x 10¼ x 1¾-inch baking dish. Start oven 10 min before baking; set to moderate (350° F).

Squeeze lemon juice and measure into a pie plate. Peel bananas carefully. Do not scrape. Roll in lemon juice then in cornflakes spread on piece of waxed paper. Lay in baking dish. Bake 20 to 25 min or until top is brown and crisp and bananas are soft. Remove to cake rack. Use pancake turner to lift bananas onto platter carefully. Serve lukewarm with the Lemon Sundae Sauce for dessert or serve plain for a vegetable.

BAKED BANANAS IN CRANBERRY SAUCE

A good meat accompaniment or a good dessert

1 cup sugar	1 pt cranberries, ½ lb
Dash of salt	2 large well-ripened bananas
1 cup water	Whipped cream, optional

Have ready a 9-inch glass pie pan. Start oven 10 min before baking; set to moderately hot (350° F).

Measure sugar, salt and water into a 3-qt saucepan. Place over heat and stir until sugar dissolves. Add picked-over, washed cranberries. Heat to boiling, then reduce heat, cover and *simmer* 3 to 4 min. Peel bananas; slice lengthwise in half and place in pie pan. Pour hot cranberries over them. Bake 15 min. Remove to cake rack to cool. Serve plain or with whipped cream. 4 to 5 generous servings.

BANANA SAUTÉ

Worth trying for the different delicate flavor and texture

5 medium-size bananas	½ lemon
⅓ cup butter	¼ cup tart red jelly

Use all-yellow or green tipped bananas. Heat butter in a heavy 9-inch skillet until just bubbling. Meanwhile peel bananas and cut in half lengthwise. Lay cut-side down close together in the hot butter. Quickly squeeze lemon juice over bananas. Cook only moderately fast until fruit is delicately browned on under side. Then reduce heat and carefully turn bananas over using a pancake turner or large spatula so as not to break them. Continue cooking until other side is browned, then use pancake turner to lift out carefully onto a hot platter. Pour leftover butter in skillet over top, then decorate by dropping a teaspoon of jelly in center of each half. Cooking may continue until bananas are very soft and well browned. A sweeter more delicate but less attractive product results.

STEWED BLACKBERRIES

This is a quick and pleasant dessert to serve lukewarm in berry season

1 qt blackberries	Dash of salt
½ cup sugar	1 tbsp lemon juice, opt
¼ cup water	

Pick over berries, removing any hulls or stems. Wash berries carefully, swishing them through cold water, then lift out of water on outstretched fingers into a 3-qt saucepan. Add remaining ingredients. Cover and heat slowly to boiling, then simmer only 3 or 4 min, shaking pan occasionally to prevent sticking. In dry weather, ½ cup water will be needed. Remove from heat and turn gently into bowl. Serve warm or chilled, plain or with cream. If barely ripe wild blackberries are cooked, no lemon juice is required. A plain sugar cookie or a warm buttered roll makes a delightful accompaniment. 4 to 5 servings.

STEWED SOUR RED CHERRIES

A colorful, lively flavored quick dessert

1 qt sour red cherries	½ cup water
1 cup sugar	Dash of salt

Wash and pit cherries as described under Sugared Cherries, p 573. Put sugar, water and salt into 3-qt saucepan. Heat to boiling, then simmer 2 or 3 min. Add cherries and *simmer* 5 min or until fruit is barely tender. Remove from heat; turn into a bowl, cool, then cover and place in refrigerator for 2 or 3 hrs for the sugar syrup to permeate and sweeten cherries all the way through. Serve plain or with cream. A sugar cookie is a pleasing accompaniment. 4 to 5 servings.

STEWED SOUR RED CHERRY PANCAKE OR PUDDING SAUCE

Good on waffles or Cottage Pudding. Pancakes filled with creamed cottage cheese, then rolled and served with this sauce are attractive and delicious

1 recipe Stewed Red Cherries, above	2 tbsp butter
1½ tsp cornstarch	Drop *or* 2 almond extract

Blend 2 tbsp juice from stewed cherries smoothly with the cornstarch, then stir into cherries. Cook with constant stirring until sauce is thickened and clear. Remove from heat. Stir in butter and extract. Serve warm for sauce or as simple dessert. 5 to 6 servings.

CRANBERRY SAUCE

1 lb cranberries, about 1 qt	2 cups sugar
1 cup boiling water	Dash of salt

Look over berries, discard soft ones and remove stems. Wash in cold water, lift berries into a 3-qt saucepan. Add water, cover and place over vigorous heat. When berries begin to boil, reduce heat enough to boil gently for 10 min. Now add sugar and salt and continue cooking until sugar is dissolved, 4 or 5 min. Remove from heat and cool. Serve lukewarm or cold. 3¼ cups sauce.

CRANBERRY JELLY

Cranberries have to be pureed before they will jell

Follow the Cranberry Sauce recipe above, cooking berries first until soft, 10 to 12 min, then put berries and juice through a food mill or a sieve to obtain all puree. Return puree to saucepan, add sugar and salt and cook and stir about 4 min. Now pour puree into a 3-cup mold or into small molds for individual servings. Makes 3 cups jelly.

HONEYED APPLES AND CRANBERRIES

Excellent with fowl or pork

4 medium-size firm cooking apples	1 cup sugar
2 cups cranberries	¼ tsp salt
1½ cups water	2 four-inch long sticks cinnamon, optional
½ cup honey	

Wash, pare and core apples. Leave whole, place in 3-qt saucepan. Pick over cranberries, discarding damaged ones. Wash and add to apples. Then add water, cover, heat to boiling then reduce heat and cook gently

5 min. Then gently turn apples over to obtain even red color. Add remaining ingredients and cook gently until apples are tender, 15 to 20 min. Then lift apples carefully out into serving dish and pour cranberries over apples and let cool. Chill before serving. 4 servings.

OLD-TIME CRANBERRIES

This method keeps berries whole

2 cups sugar	1 qt cranberries, 1 lb
2 cups water	Dash of salt

Pick over cranberries, discarding damaged ones. Then wash in cold water and drain. Measure sugar and water into a 3-qt saucepan. Heat to boiling then reduce heat and boil gently for 5 min. Now add berries and salt, cover and *simmer* for 5 min without stirring. Remove from heat to cool in pan, keeping covered. 1 qt.

BROILED GRAPEFRUIT

2 medium-size heavy grape-	2 tbsp butter
fruit	Few dashes nutmeg, op-
⅓ cup light brown sugar	tional

Wash grapefruit, cut crosswise in halves. Clip around core with kitchen scissors and lift out. Flick out any seed. Use grapefruit knife or paring knife to cut sections loose around sides and away from dividing membranes. Sprinkle with the sugar, dot with butter and sprinkle with nutmeg. Arrange grapefruit on a rack or baking sheet and slide under the broiler about 6-inches below heating unit to glaze the top and barely heat the grapefruit through. Remove to serving plate to serve as breakfast fruit or for light dessert. 4 servings.

Note: To avoid heating the broiler, try top-stove pan broiling. For 2 grapefruit heat 4 tbsp butter in skillet, sprinkle in ¼ cup brown sugar. Place over moderate heat, lay in the 4 grapefruit halves, cut-side down, and heat *gently* to melt sugar and warm fruit. To serve lift out onto plates and pour syrup from pan over fruit. To vary the flavor, use maple syrup or honey with butter; or heat the grapefruit in butter, then place on serving plates while very hot, add a spoonful of currant or mint jelly or creme de menthe. 4 servings.

BAKED GUAVAS

Elegant in appearance, tantalizing in flavor and texture

5 large pink-fleshed guavas	2 tbsp lemon juice
½ to ⅔ cup sugar	1 tbsp butter
Dash of salt	2 tbsp water

Use a 6½ x 10¼ x 1¾-inch baking dish. Start oven 10 min before baking; set to moderate (350° F).

Wash guavas, pare thinly and cut crosswise into halves. Use spoon to carefully scoop out seedy pulp. Put this portion through food mill or sieve to remove seed and obtain puree. Stir sugar, salt and lemon juice into puree. Put the guava half shells, hollow side up, in the baking dish. Fill shells with puree. Dot each half with butter. Pour water around fruit, cover with a piece of aluminum foil and bake 20 to 25 min, or until tender. Remove to cake rack to cool to lukewarm. Serve plain or with cream. 5 servings.

NECTARINE-RASPBERRY COMPOTE

This high-class simple dessert is impressive

⅔ cup sugar
Dash of salt
⅔ cup water

1¼ lbs ripe nectarines, 8 medium
1 pt red raspberries, washed, drained

Put sugar, salt and water into a 1½-qt saucepan. Heat to boiling, then simmer 3 or 4 min. Wash nectarines; pierce 2 or 3 times with a skewer or fork and drop into syrup. Cover and simmer until just tender, 10 to 12 min. Lift fruit out with slotted spoon into bowl. Add raspberries and simmer only 2 or 3 min. Turn into a fine-meshed sieve held over nectarines. Rub all pulp through with back of spoon, leaving only seeds in sieve. Stir fruit and puree gently. Cool, then cover and chill. 4 servings.

FRESH BAKED PEACHES

A peachy way to prepare peaches for a simple but distinctive dessert

2 to 2¼ lbs just ripe good flavored peaches, 9 to 10 good size
½ cup sugar

¼ tsp cornstarch *or* ½ tsp flour, optional
¼ cup water

Butter well a flat-bottomed 8-cup casserole with cover. Adjust rack about 5 inches from bottom of oven. Start oven 10 min before baking; set to moderate (375° F).

Pare peaches thinly and leave whole. Place in casserole stem-end up. Blend sugar and flour; sprinkle over peaches, leaving as much of mixture on fruit as possible. Pour water in at side. Cover and bake about 40 min. Carefully turn fruit once during baking. Remove to cake rack and again gently flip fruit over. Cool uncovered about 15 min then cover. Serve lukewarm or chilled, plain or with cream. 4 to 5 servings.

STEWED FRESH PEACHES

Very simple but incredibly good

½ to ⅔ cup sugar
⅔ cup water

1½ lbs ripe, juicy cling *or* freestone peaches

Put sugar and water into a 3-qt saucepan. Heat slowly to boiling, then simmer 2 or 3 min. Meanwhile, wash peaches, pare thinly, and cut fruit away from seeds in halves. Drop into the hot syrup, cover, reheat to boiling, then simmer 10 min or until just tender. Time depends on size of peaches. Remove from heat and when lukewarm or chilled, serve plain or with cream. 4 to 5 servings.

STEWED PEACHES IN RED PLUM PURÉE

An invigorating summertime dessert. Ideal for either sick or well stomachs

¾ cup sugar	1¼ lbs freestone peaches, 5 medium
1 cup water	½ lb red plums, 5 medium

Heat sugar and water in a 2-qt saucepan to boiling, then simmer 5 min. Meanwhile, pare peaches thinly, cut in half and discard pits. Drop fruit into the syrup and boil gently 5 to 6 min or until barely tender. Lift out into bowl with slotted spoon. To syrup in pan, add plums which have been washed and cut in half, pits left in. Cover and boil gently 6 to 7 min or until tender. Pour plums into a coarse strainer held over peaches and rub fruit through strainer with back of spoon. Stir fruit gently. Serve lukewarm or chilled. 1 pt or 4 servings.

BAKED PEARS

A simple satisfying dessert. Serve with sugar cookies or hot buttered toast

2 lbs Bartlett *or* Bosc pears, appx 5	2 tbsp lemon juice
	¼ cup water
2 tbsp sugar	2 tsp butter

Use a 6½ x 10¼ x 1¾-inch baking dish. Start oven 10 min before baking; set to moderately slow (325° F).

Wash, pare and halve pears. Remove cores neatly with a teaspoon or a melon-ball cutter. Arrange cut-side down in baking dish and sprinkle with sugar and lemon juice. Pour water around pears and dot them with butter. Cover dish with a piece of aluminum foil and bake from 45 to 60 min, time depending on type of pear. 5 servings.

BAKED GINGERED PEARS

Old-time favorite dessert. When baked, pears are slightly more flavorful than when poached

¼ cup brown sugar, pkd	½ tsp grated lemon rind, pkd
½ cup white corn syrup	1 tbsp lemon juice
⅜ tsp ginger—¼ plus ⅛ tsp	3 to 4 firm ripe pears, 1 lb
½ cup water	1 tbsp butter

Butter well a 10 x 6 x 1½-inch glass baking dish. Start oven 10 min before baking; set to moderate (350° F).

Combine first 6 ingredients in a 1-qt saucepan. Pare pears thinly, cut in half, remove cores with French ball cutter or tip of spoon. Add pears and butter to saucepan. Heat to boiling, then *simmer* uncovered 5 min. Arrange pears in one layer, cut-side up in prepared pan. Pour syrup over pears. Bake 25 to 30 min, or until tender, basting 3 or 4 times with the syrup. Remove to top of stove to keep warm, basting occasionally until serving time. Serve warm. 3 to 4 servings.

CRANBERRY GLAZED PEARS

A colorful scrumptious satisfying dessert

¾ lb cranberries, 2½ cups	1½ cups hot water
2 lbs winter pears, 4 *or* 5 medium	1½ cups sugar
	Dash of salt

Have 8-cup casserole with cover ready. Start oven 10 min before baking; set to moderately hot (400° F).

Pick over, wash and drain cranberries; turn half of them into casserole. Pare pears thinly, cut in half and remove core with tip of tsp. Arrange hollow-side up in casserole. Sprinkle rest of cranberries over pears. Combine water, sugar and salt and stir. Pour over fruit. Cover and bake 10 min or until juice starts to bubble up, then uncover and bake 20 min longer or until pears are just tender. Baste 2 or 3 times during baking to glaze pears with cranberry juice. Cool before serving. 8 servings.

POACHED PEARS

Versatile elegant way to serve pears

½ cup water	½ cup sugar
½ lemon, sliced thinly	1 tsp vinegar
4 large Bartlett *or* Bosc pears	8 whole cloves

Measure water into a 3-qt saucepan, add sliced lemon and simmer gently for 5 min. Meanwhile wash pears, leave unpared, or pare off thin strip of peeling about 1-inch wide all around stem end for interesting appearance, but remove and replace blossom ends with 4 of the cloves. Now add remaining ingredients to water and lemon slices, add pears laying them on their sides. Cover kettle and gently simmer them for about 45 min or until tender enough to be easily pierced with toothpick. Turn over 2 or 3 times during the cooking. When done, lift out onto a plate to cool. Let the liquid left in pan cook another 5 min or until quite a thick syrup. Pour over pears and cool. While cooling, occasionally spoon syrup over pears to give them a glazed coating. Serve as salad, a garnish for meat or with cream for dessert. 4 servings.

POACHED GINGERED PEARS

Follow directions for Baked Gingered Pears, except cook pears in covered saucepan until fork tender, from 15 to 20 min. Remove from heat but keep warm until serving time. Pears may be prepared ahead of time and stored in refrigerator, then reheated before serving.

POACHED PEARS SABAYONE

This dessert qualifies for your "show off" meals

1 cup sugar	½ cup apricot purée, p 551
1 cup water	blended with 3 tbsp syrup
Dash of salt	from Poached Pears
3 ripe Anjou pears	Sabayone Sauce, p 1249

Measure sugar, water and salt into a 3-qt saucepan. Stir and heat to boiling, then simmer 3 or 4 min. Pare pears carefully, cut in half, scoop out cores neatly with tip of teaspoon, then cut out stem fiber with knife. Slide pears gently into the syrup and simmer until just tender when pricked with a toothpick. Lift pears carefully from syrup onto dessert plates. Heap apricot purée mixture into pear hollows. Now flow Sabayone Sauce generously over top. A tbsp or more syrup may be poured around the fruit. Serve warm or cold. 6 servings.

STEWED PEARS

These end a hearty meal pleasantly

1 cup sugar	4 large *or* 5 medium Bartlett
1½ cups water	*or* Bosc pears
1 lemon sliced thin, optional	

Put sugar and water into a 3-qt saucepan. Add lemon slices and heat slowly to boiling. Wash pears, pare thinly, cut in half and remove cores neatly with tip of teaspoon or a melon ball cutter. Cut each pear half lengthwise into 4 slices. Drop immediately into hot syrup, cover and simmer until tender, from 8 to 15 min, depending on size of pears. Serve pears with the lemon, lukewarm or chilled in the syrup. 4 to 5 servings.

Note: Slightly underripe pears never make as luscious a dessert as well-ripened fruit.

STEWED RED PLUMS

Attractive and luscious

¾ to ⅞ cup sugar	1 lb red plums, 8 *or* 9
⅔ cup water	

Heat sugar and water to boiling in a 1½-qt saucepan. Wash plums, prick each several times with a skewer, cake tester or fork and drop into syrup to preserve shape. Cover and boil gently 15 to 18 min or until plums are tender. Turn into bowl. Serve lukewarm or chilled with sugar cookies. 1 pt or 4 servings.

BAKED QUINCES

Has extraordinary flavor—goes in oven pale yellow, comes out red

6 medium-size sound quinces,   ⅓ cup water
   1½ lbs   Cream, optional
⅔ cup granulated sugar

Have ready a 6-cup casserole with its cover. Start oven 10 min before baking; set to moderately slow (325° F).

Wash quinces. Pare thinly, cut in quarters and pull out the cores (seed sacs) with tip of paring knife, dropping quarters into casserole. Sprinkle on sugar as pieces are added. Add water, cover and bake about 1½ hrs, or until tender and a rich red color. Serve lukewarm or cold, plain or with cream. 4 to 5 servings.

STEWED QUINCES

Treat yourself to this rare ultra delicious dessert once or twice during the short quince season

6 medium-size sound quinces,   Dash of salt
   1½ lbs   ⅔ cup sugar
2¾ cups hot water

Wash quinces. Pare thinly, cut in quarters and pull out the cores (seed sacs) with tip of paring knife and discard. Cut quarters into 5 or 6 lengthwise slices, dropping into a 3-qt saucepan containing the water to prevent discoloration. Heat to boiling, cover, reduce heat and *simmer* until almost tender, about 20 min. Add salt and sugar, cover and continue simmering 15 or 20 min longer, or until juice is richly flavored. Remove from heat; cool slightly and turn into bowl. Serve lukewarm or cold. 5 to 6 servings.

RHUBARB

Zesty, tangy stewed rhubarb *sweetened just right* is a delicious spring-time dessert. But don't expect as delicious a sauce from rhubarb which stands a day or so in a store and becomes limp, or which is out of season. Only fleshy tender stalks, freshly pulled in the spring and cooked within a few hrs makes sauce that is rare in color, consistency and flavor. Hothouse rhubarb that comes to the market late in winter is expensive but delicious. A good variety of home-grown rhubarb such as McDonald, which is fertilized to grow rapidly is the best.

STEWED FRESH RHUBARB

2 lbs fresh tender rhubarb	2 to 3 tbsp water
1 to 1¼ cups sugar	Cream, if desired

Wash rhubarb stalks thoroughly. Trim off and discard leaf and root ends. Do not peel off skin unless tough as skin gives attractive color. Cut stalks into inch lengths, dropping into a 3-qt saucepan. Add sugar and water, then toss to distribute. Cover saucepan and cook slowly, shaking pan occasionally to prevent sticking. Cook until tender, from 5 to 7 min. Turn into bowl. Serve lukewarm or cold, plain or with cream. 5 to 6 servings.

Note: It will require more water to cook rhubarb in summer or in dry weather— at least a half cup for 2 lbs. This product has much more fiber than when made from tender juicy rhubarb.

FRUIT FOR DESSERT

RAW

One of the simplest of all desserts is fresh fruits of all kinds, either raw or cooked. These same fruits may also be used in many baked desserts and puddings, custards, or gelatin mixtures, but they make superior desserts for an otherwise hearty meal when they are served alone.

Raw fruit. Any fruit that is eaten raw can be served that way for dessert. All should be ripe and at the peak of their flavor and beauty. They should all be washed carefully and then served at the temperature at which they are most enjoyed. Most berries have their finest flavor when they are taken from the refrigerator just long enough to be cool but not cold, and a slight sprinkling of sugar added a few minutes before serving draws out enough juice to make the fruit most palatable. Cantaloupes and muskmelons have their most potent flavor and aroma when they are taken from the refrigerator long enough ahead of serving time to be almost at room temperature, but most other melons, particularly watermelon, are generally preferred chilled. Usually a dash of salt or a wedge of lemon or lime to squeeze over the melon is the only addition necessary for the utmost eating enjoyment.

Peaches, bananas, pears and mangoes are usually peeled and sliced directly into the serving dish and then served at once with either a light sprinkling of sugar, some cream, or a fruit juice such as orange or pineapple poured over them. Peaches may be cooled or chilled. Bananas are always best at room temperature and they should never be stored in the refrigerator. Pears and mangoes have excellent flavor at either room or refrigerator temperature.

Fresh pineapple probably requires more advance preparation than any other fresh fruit. There are several methods of preparation so that either cones of it may be eaten from the fingers or wedges or cubes eaten with a spoon. Generally the addition of a small amount of sugar makes the fruit juicier and more enjoyable to most people. Also the flavor is most characteristic if the fruit is removed from the refrigerator long enough ahead of serving time to be cool but not ice-cold.

Other fruits that are often eaten from the hand, such as apples, pears, and grapes may be arranged attractively and served from a fruit bowl. Then the diners can select their preferred fruit and eat it from the hand or pare and cut it with a knife. Very often a bowl of fruit of this type is served with an assortment of cheese and crackers, and although it is one of the most simple desserts to serve, it can very correctly follow a very formal meal.

Citrus fruits, such as grapefruit and oranges, can be served for dessert either cut in half to be eaten with a spoon or pared and cut into sections. Tangerines are usually peeled and the easily divided sections eaten with the fingers. Sugar is commonly used on grapefruit and some oranges, but if you've never tried a sprinkling of salt instead, you have a treat in store.

AMBROSIA

A great favorite, especially in the South. Wonderful finish for heavy meal

6 large oranges	½ cup grated fresh *or* moist
1 large well ripened banana	canned coconut, cut fine
2 tbsp sugar *or* to taste	3 or 4 strawberries *or*
	maraschino cherries, opt

Pare oranges in a continuous strip around and around so as to remove all white fiber. Section oranges, removing any seeds, then cut crosswise into ¼-inch pieces. Cover and chill. Just before serving, peel banana, then cut crosswise into ¼-inch slices, dropping into large serving dish. Turn oranges over banana, sprinkle with sugar and coconut. Toss lightly so as not to break banana slices. Garnish with few slices of berries or cherries. Bring to table to serve in small glass serving dishes. 4 servings.

Note: A sectioned grapefruit and ⅓ cup broken pecans may be added to Ambrosia just before tossing to perk up flavor and add interest. Tangerines may be used with oranges or in place of oranges. If Ambrosia is not juicy enough add extra orange or tangerine juice.

SUGARED FRESH APRICOTS AND RED PLUMS

Really luscious. They combine well and are appropriate for breakfast fruit or dinner dessert

6 ripe meaty apricots	1½ to 2 tbsp sugar,
3 large ripe red plums	*or* to taste

Wash fruit carefully but well. Cut apricots in half; flick out pit, then cut halves in quarters or smaller, dropping into serving dishes or bowl. Sprinkle with half the sugar. Cut the juicy plums away from pits in 5 or 6 pieces, dropping onto apricots so juice will coat apricots. Sprinkle with remaining sugar. Toss gently. Serve at once or set in refrigerator to chill an hr or so before serving. 2 servings.

BANANAS AND CREAM

The quickest, freshest looking dessert ever served. And it's tops in flavor and food value

Use full-ripe bananas—those that are rich yellow flecked with brown spots. Do not chill the fruit, but you can chill serving dishes and cream. Do not prepare until dessert is ready to be served. Strip peeling from bananas carefully and do not scrape the bananas after peeling if they are perfect, for to do so takes away from their delightfully fresh appearance. Cut crosswise in slices at least ³⁄₁₆-inch thick, letting slices fall directly into serving dishes. Do not touch after slicing. Serve immediately, letting each person add sugar and cream to suit his own whim.

COCONUT CREAM FOR BANANAS

This doesn't sound pretentious, but it isn't ordinary

½ cup finely grated fresh coconut, pkd
½ cup coconut milk
½ cup thin cream, 12%

Dash of salt
1 tbsp sugar
Bananas

Combine all ingredients except bananas and turn into a clean glass jar. Close tight and let stand in refrigerator a few hrs. Strain out coconut by pressing out all the liquid, or turn mixture into a food mill with bottom screw loosened. Press practically all the coconut through to obtain a fine-grated creamy liquid. Serve over sliced, thoroughly ripe bananas, chocolate pudding or any dessert harmonious with coconut. 4 to 5 servings.

SUGARED BERRIES

The most gorgeous and colorful of desserts. So simple yet never served often enough

The berries most elegant for sugaring are strawberries, raspberries, loganberries, boysenberries, blackberries and blueberries.

Choose berries full-ripe but not over-ripe. Look over, remove hulls or caps. Wash quickly in cold water, handling carefully so as not to break. Lift out into colander to drain. Cut strawberries in half, but leave all others whole. Then turn into bowl to chill an hr before serving. Shake berries from bowl into serving dishes so as not to break them. Sift granulated sugar over top and serve immediately, either plain or with cream. 3 servings for 1-pt berries.

CANTALOUPE FOR DESSERT

Wonderful for Calorie Counters. It's filling and full of Vitamin A and C

Place washed cantaloupe in refrigerator only long enough to cool but not until it becomes icy cold. Cut in half, scoop out seeds. Serve immediately plain or with a few red raspberries or strawberries dropped into hollow, or for a more substantial dessert with a scoop of ice cream.

HOW TO BUY CANTALOUPE

Choose a "full-slip" cantaloupe. When cantaloupe is ready for good eating, it separates from the vine of its own accord, leaving a slightly sunken, smooth, well-callused scar. This is the "finger-print" of well ripened melons. These full-ripe melons can be delivered in perfect condition anywhere in the U.S. under modern methods of refrigerated shipping.

Consider the netting. The netting of properly matured cantaloupe is coarse, corky, and grayish in color. This netting is well developed and stands out in bold relief all over surface of melon.

Beware of the "pincher." Slight softening at the blossom end *may* indicate ripe, mature melons, but it is not an infallible test. In self-serve stores where everyone is permitted to select his own melon, pressing it at the blossom end may soften even unripe melons and you are misled. Don't be a "pincher." Depend upon the "full-slip" and quality of netting to guide you in choosing cantaloupe.

SUGARED SOUR RED CHERRIES

A delightfully high-flavored, sparkling dessert as well as a wonderful breakfast fruit

1 qt sour red cherries	1 cup sugar

Wash cherries with stems on through 3 or 4 cold waters, lifting the last time into a colander to drain well. Then as you pull out stems, use loop-end of sturdy wire hairpin or loop-end of an open paper clip to pry out seeds. Drop cherries into bowl. There should be 3 cups pitted fruit. Sprinkle on sugar. Cover and let stand a few min at room temp or place in refrigerator a few hrs. Then stir gently and serve while the brilliant red color lingers, preferably in glass dishes. 4 to 5 servings.

SUGARED CURRANTS

As beautiful as rubies with a wonderful perky flavor. A perfect breakfast starter or meal ender

1 qt ripe red currants	¾ to 1 cup sugar

Choose freshly picked, well-ripened currants. Wash carefully through 2 or 3 cold waters, then lift into colander to drain well. Now strip currants gently from stems, dropping into bowl. Sift sugar over fruit, then toss with a fork to distribute, purposely crushing a few of the currants. Serve immediately or cover and store in refrigerator to chill an hr or so for some of the sugar to dissolve. Serve preferably in glass dishes. 5 to 6 servings.

FRUIT COMBINATION DESSERTS

A dessert that is hard to beat where there are children is a single fruit or a combination of fruits with cookies such as:

1. Crushed or diced pineapple with stewed dried apricots or canned apricots
2. Sliced bananas and sweetened strawberries
3. Strawberries and pears
4. Red raspberries and fresh sliced peaches
5. Sliced or diced oranges and canned peaches
6. Frozen or bottled grape juice over sectioned grapefruit

These are all twangy combinations which give a change from the ordinary fruit sauce. When cookies are lacking, try fresh sugared berries —over strips of hot buttered toast. Fresh warm apple sauce is also delicious over the toast, too.

FRUIT CUPS

Fruit cups are not only good meal starters but good meal finishers

Almost any combination of chilled fruits, fresh or canned, is delicious. Here are some ideas to put your creative talent to work.

1. Sliced bananas, seedless white grapes, diced pared oranges, pomegranate seeds.
2. Sliced bananas, sectioned grapefruit, sliced strawberries, canned sliced peaches.
3. Sliced strawberries, diced fresh or canned pineapple, honeydew melon diced or in balls.
4. Sliced fresh peaches, raspberries, diced cantaloupe.
5. Sectioned oranges, diced avocado, sliced red or blue plums, diced raw pears.
6. Diced apples, halves of seeded Tokay grapes, diced oranges, diced canned peaches.

When canned fruit is used, add a little lemon juice to give pleasing tartness. Maraschino cherries are an attractive addition, one to a serving being sufficient. A small amount of juice from the Maraschino cherries or some grenadine contributes attractive color and flavor. When fruits are not sufficiently juicy, add orange juice, left over canned juice or cider. Moist packed grated coconut, broken unsalted nuts such as pecans and walnuts or a puff of whipped cream make interesting toppings for garnish.

SUGARED GUAVAS

Delicious as strawberries but a better eye-opener

Use full-ripe pink fleshed guavas. Chill. Just before serving wash carefully and snip off a thin slice from both blossom and stem ends. Arrange 2 or 3, depending on size on serving plate and add a little mound of granulated sugar. Dip an end of guava in the sugar to coat surface of exposed flesh, then E-A-T!

MANGOES

This fruit appears in large city markets about last of June

Mangoes are another superb semi-tropical fruit. When well developed and full-ripe they have a most tempting and naturally sweet satisfying flavor. The texture of the flesh is smooth and reminds one of the most luscious of juicy peaches, but the flesh clings to the large flat seed much more tenaciously than the flesh of a cling peach. When ripe, the flesh yields a little to pressure and the pale green skin is splotched with rose and yellow. To serve, wash fruit, and chill in order to pare very thinly and smoothly. Slice flesh away from seed in 2 large lobes as from a cling peach. Serve 1 or more halves to a person, depending on size of fruit which varies from ½ to 1½ lbs. Serve plain for a high calorie dessert, with cream and sugar.

SUGARED FRESH PEACHES

The simplest and most delicious summertime dessert or breakfast fruit. Elbertas, Hale-Havens, South Havens and fine textured J. H. Hales are excellent for sugaring

2 to 2½ lbs freestone peaches,	Sugar
8 to 10 medium	

Choose well-ripened juicy fruit free of bruises. Fruit with a carmine color around seed cavity makes the most attractive dessert. Have peaches chilled or at room temp. Flavor is less intense in chilled fruit, but many prefer chilling even if flavor is sacrificed. Just before serving, pare fruit thinly and slice neatly from pits, dropping into bowl or serving dishes. Sprinkle sugar over peaches *immediately* after slicing. Do not stir. Serve at once for the most attractive color. Some like to let the sliced sugared fruit stand in a bowl until some of the sugar dissolves—10 to 15 min, but longer standing darkens the fruit and slices become limp. 4 to 5 servings.

HOW TO SELECT AND PREPARE FRESH PINEAPPLE

To determine whether fresh pineapple is ripe, pull out 2 or 3 leaves. If they come out easily and have a distinctive pineapple aroma, the fruit is ripe. If pineapple is not ripe, to hasten ripening, wrap it in heavy paper and hold at 65° F temp. An easy way to prepare pineapple is to cut it in ½-inch crosswise slices with a heavy sharp knife. Pare slices thinly with a paring knife, and use the point to cut out "eyes" remaining in rims of slices. Now cut slices in half and cut out center tough core and discard, then cut into wedges or dice.

SUGARED FRESH PINEAPPLE

Delectable and refreshing

2 lb pineapple yields 2½ to 3 cups diced fruit	Use 2 or 3 tbsp sugar to each cup fruit, depending on sweetness

Prepare fruit, measure and turn into bowl. Sprinkle with sugar to taste. Stir gently to mix. Cover and let stand an hr or so before serving for juice to flow and sugar to dissolve. Fruit may be placed in refrigerator, but flavor is more pronounced if served not too cold.

PINEAPPLE CONES TO EAT FROM FINGERS

No paring the pineapple here!

An easy way to cut cones from unpared fresh pineapple is to use an apple corer or sharp paring knife. Stick the corer or knife into the fruit crosswise, making a shallow cut around each "eye." Now push the corer or knife through to the tough center core, turning as you push. Then pull out the cone. After a few cones are pulled out, the rest are easy to pry loose. Arrange cones around a mound of sugar on glass plates. Dip cones in sugar and eat from fingers.

FRESH PINEAPPLE IN THE SHELL

Served this way, pineapple provided its own artistic garnish

This method of preparation appeals, because it eliminates the pesky paring. Chill pineapple and just before serving time, cut carefully in half lengthwise through the fruit as well as through leafy top, then cut each piece in half through lengthwise to obtain 4 quarters. Leave leaves attached. With the skin side down, use a sharp paring knife to slice the hard core neatly away from each section. Now use a grapefruit knife to cut the flesh loose from the peeling, close to the eyes. Again use paring knife to cut loosened fruit into 3 or 4 lengthwise strips, then cut the strips crosswise into bite-size pieces. Leave pineapple sections intact in their skins. Lift onto plates and at the table serve with sugar.

GOLDEN SAPOTE

One of the most delicious of semi-tropical fruits

Golden sapote resembles giant green gage plums and their smooth, pale yellow flesh has a slight resemblance to that of avocado. They have a most appealing flavor and they are very palatable without adding either salt or sugar. To serve, wash fruit, cut in half, lift out seed. To eat, scoop the flesh from the skin with a spoon, or cut halves in 3 or 4 lengthwise sections and eat from hand.

GELATIN DESSERTS

Gelatin desserts are made and unmolded the same as gelatin salads, except that they are almost always made with fruit and very frequently have whipped or plain cream folded into them or it is served over them. Rich cream mixtures that are thickened with just enough gelatin to permit them to be molded are known as Bavarian Cream, Charlotte Russe, etc. These desserts are particularly well adapted to summertime meals; they can be rich without being stodgy and are cool and refreshing to eat as well as to make. Attractively shaped metal, glass or pottery molds are interesting to have for making molded desserts, but with a little imagination these desserts can be molded beautifully in shallow pans, small mixing bowls, custard cups, etc. Once the gelatin has set, the molds should always be covered tightly to prevent the food from getting dry on the surface or pulling away from the sides of the mold.

DRIED APRICOT BAVARIAN

Attractive in color, rich, delicious

2 tbsp plain gelatin
⅓ cup cold water *or* apricot
   juice left from cooking
   apricots
¾ cup dried Apricot Purée
   sweetened, p 551

¼ cup sugar
¾ cup whipping cream,
   chilled
2 tsp lemon juice

Sprinkle gelatin over cold water measured into a custard cup. Let soften 5 min, then melt to a clear liquid by standing cup in hot water. Turn purée into a mixing bowl, stir in sugar thoroughly, then stir in melted gelatin and lemon juice. Set aside to cool until it is consistency of unbeaten egg white. Now beat cream until just stiff but not until lumpy. Quickly scrape cream lightly onto top of apricot mixture and with rubber scraper cut and fold cream lightly into apricot mixture. It may be folded in thoroughly or only long enough to leave interestingly streaked. Cover and chill. To serve, heap lightly into sherbet glasses. Garnish with whipped cream or with slivered toasted almonds or both. 5 servings.

CHARLOTTE RUSSE

A delicate appealing dessert when made with 1½ tsp gelatin

Cup Liners:
3 commercial sponge shortcake cups, *or*
12 lady fingers, split
⅛ tsp grated lemon rind,
optional

Cream Filling:
½ cup milk, scalded

1½ tsp gelatin *in*
1 tbsp cold water
⅛ tsp salt
3 tbsp xxxx sugar
1 tsp vanilla
½ pt whipping cream
Sweet chocolate, chopped
nuts *or* toasted cake crumbs

Cut cakes into ¼-inch strips. Line 4 tall custard cups, ¾-cup capacity, evenly with 8 strips of cake so strips do not overlap. Cut 2 of the strips short enough to fit snugly into bottom of cup. Sprinkle cake with a few gratings of lemon rind. Scald milk. Soak gelatin in cold water, then dissolve in hot milk. Stir in salt, sugar and vanilla. Set in cold water to thoroughly cool, stirring occasionally. Whip cream until stiff, and gradually fold in gelatin mixture cooled to a soft jelly consistency, using a rubber scraper or wooden spoon to fold. Spoon into cake lined molds, tapping molds to fill completely. Chill at least 2 hrs before serving. To unmold, run a thin bladed knife between cup and dessert and turn out into serving plate or compote. Sprinkle with finely chopped nuts, shaved sweet chocolate or toasted fine cake crumbs. 4 servings.

CHOCOLATE BAVARIAN

Delicious but less rich with evaporated milk

1 tbsp plain gelatin
¼ cup cold water
1 sq unsweet chocolate, 1 oz
½ cup boiling water
⅛ tsp salt

1½ cups whipping cream *or*
evaporated milk
½ cup sugar
1 tsp vanilla

Sprinkle gelatin over ¼ cup of the cold water measured into a custard cup. Let soften 5 min. Put chocolate into a saucepan and set over hot water to melt. Now stir in boiling water and salt and ½ cup of the cream, then the sugar. Place directly over moderate heat and cook and stir about 5 min or until smooth and thickened. Remove from heat and stir in softened gelatin until dissolved. Add vanilla and cool to consistency of unbeaten egg white. Now beat remaining cream or milk until stiff. Quickly scrape cream onto top of chocolate mixture and cut and fold it in lightly but thoroughly. Turn into mold or individual serving dishes and chill until set. 6 servings.

CHOCOLATE COOKIE CRUST BAVARIAN
Attractive, delicate, rich refrigerator dessert

Crust:
    1½ cups crisp chocolate cookie
        crumbs
    ⅓ cup melted butter
Filling:
    1 tbsp plain gelatin
    ¼ cup water
    1 cup milk, scalded

3 eggs, separated
½ cup sugar
¼ tsp salt
1 tsp vanilla
¾ cup whipping cream
    Small bar sweet chocolate,
        chilled

Butter an 8 x 8 x 2-inch baking pan, or a 9-inch glass pie pan.

Crust: Use 18 to 20 thin crisp commercial cookies about 3-inches in diameter, or the 2-inch double cookies stuck together with thin icing. Roll cookies fine or break up and put through food mill. Turn crumbs into bowl, add butter and work with hands until crumbs pack when squeezed together. Turn into prepared pan. Press an even layer of crumbs on sides of pan with spatula or rubber scraper and on bottom of pan with bottom of a glass. Chill at least 30 min.

Filling: Soften gelatin in cold water. Scald milk in top of double boiler. Beat egg yolks slightly in a 1-qt bowl, add sugar and salt, then while stirring, slowly pour hot milk into yolks. *Strain* back into double boiler and cook and stir over gently boiling water until mixture coats a metal spoon, from 2 to 3 min. Remove from heat and stir in gelatin until dissolved, then vanilla. Beat egg whites until stiff with rotary beater, then fold them into warm gelatin mixture, and again beat *until just* smooth. Chill until *slightly thickened.* Whip cream until barely stiff, then fold lightly into gelatin mixture until just blended. Turn into crumb-lined pan. Grate chilled chocolate evenly and generously over top. Chill several hrs or overnight. Cut into rectangles or wedges. 8 servings.

Note: To lift servings from pan easily, dip pan into warm water for a second.

COCONUT CHARLOTTE
Dainty and delicious

1½ tsp soft butter
¾ cup grated fresh coconut
4 tsp plain gelatin
¼ cup cold water
½ cup coconut milk
½ cup milk

¾ cup sugar
¼ tsp salt
1 cup whipping cream
Lemon Sauce, p 1246
10 to 12 handsome strawberries

Rub inside of 6-cup mold with butter to coat evenly. Pat ½ of he coconut uniformly over bottom and sides of mold. Sift gelatin over old water, and let soak 5 min. Combine next 4 ingredients in saucepan and heat to simmering. Remove from heat. Stir in gelatin until dissolved. Cool until thick and syrupy. Whip cream until just stiff, not stiff enough for granular appearance. Use beater to whip gelatin to a soft foam, then quickly *cut-and-fold* gelatin into cream, lightly but thoroughly. Turn immediately into prepared mold. Sprinkle rest of coconut over top. Cover, place in refrigerator to stiffen. Unmold and serve same day with Lemon Sauce. Garnish with fresh strawberries. Serves 5 to 6.

GRAPE BAVARIAN

6-oz can frozen concentrated grape juice	4 tsp lemon juice
1 tbsp plain gelatin	3 tbsp sugar
$\frac{1}{16}$ tsp salt	$\frac{2}{3}$ cup whipping cream

Pour grape juice into a measuring cup and add enough water to make 1 pint. Turn into a 3-qt mixing bowl. Remove $\frac{1}{4}$ cup of grape juice to a custard cup, sift gelatin over juice and let stand 5 min to soften. Then place cup over hot water or set cup in hot water until gelatin melts. Now stir gelatin well into grape juice, then next 3 ingredients. Set in refrigerator or bowl of ice water until consistency is like unbeaten egg white. Now use rotary beater and beat until light and foamy. Quickly wash beater and beat cream until just stiff. With rubber scraper, remove all cream to grape-juice mixture and cut and fold together until completely blended or leave mixture nicely streaked purple and white. Turn carefully into 2-qt mold rinsed in cold water. Chill until firm. Unmold and serve on cold plates. 5 to 6 servings.

NESSELRODE PUDDING

A distinguished delicious dessert for holiday or party meals

1 tbsp plain gelatin	$\frac{1}{4}$ tsp salt
$\frac{1}{4}$ cup cold water	$\frac{1}{2}$ cup commercial Nesselrode
$1\frac{1}{3}$ cups milk	Fruit Mix, $\frac{1}{2}$ of 10-oz
$\frac{1}{4}$ cup sugar	bottle
$\frac{1}{4}$ cup washed seedless raisins	$\frac{1}{2}$ tsp vanilla
2 egg yolks	1 cup whipping cream

Sift gelatin into cold water to soften for 5 min. Put milk, sugar and raisins in top of double boiler, place over boiling water and heat to scalding. Beat egg yolks, add some of hot milk, stir well then return to double boiler and continue cooking and stirring until mixture coats a metal spoon. Remove from heat and add salt and gelatin, stirring until gelatin dissolves. Meanwhile measure Nesselrode Fruit Mix, and with scissors snip the larger pieces to size of raisins; add to gelatin mixture with vanilla. Set in a pan of cold water to cool to consistency of soft jelly with occasional gentle stirring. Beat cream until stiff, then cut and fold gelatin mixture lightly but thoroughly into it. Turn at once into pudding mold, melon or other shape holding 6 cups, rinsed in cold water, or ripple mixture into sherbet glasses. Cover, place mold or sherbets in refrigerator to congeal which will require at least 2 hrs. When ready to serve, unmold the mold on a handsome plate. Garnish with macaroons or other delicious cookies or slices of cake to serve with pudding. 6 to 8 servings.

Note: If Nesselrode Mix is not available, use the following instead: Combine 3 tbsp chopped maraschino cherries, 2 tbsp crushed pineapple, 2 tbsp chopped cooked chestnuts or almonds, ¼ cup sugar, ⅓ cup water, simmer 5 min. Remove from heat and add 2 tsp rum extract.

FRESH ORANGE BAVARIAN
Tangy and refreshing

¼ tsp grated orange rind, pkd	Dash of salt
1 cup orange juice	½ cup sugar, or more
1 tbsp lemon juice	1 cup whipping cream,
1 tbsp plain gelatin	chilled
¼ cup cold water	1 seedless orange, diced

Have ready a 4 to 5-cup mold, or a glass loaf pan.

Wash orange, grate rind then squeeze orange and lemon juice. Combine rind with juices, let stand 2 min, then strain, discarding rind. Soften gelatin in cold water then set container in hot water until gelatin melts. Stir salt and sugar into fruit juice, then gelatin mixture. Taste for sweetness. Chill until thick and syrupy. Whip ¾ of the cream until just stiff. Whip syrupy gelatin mixture with same beater until fluffy. Remove beater. Use rubber scraper to quickly fold in whipped cream lightly but thoroughly. Turn into mold first rinsed with cold water. Chill until firm. To serve, unmold, p 1155, onto a chilled serving plate. Garnish with remaining ¼ cup cream whipped, and diced orange. 5 servings.

PERSIMMON BAVARIAN

3 medium sized Japanese persimmons, 1¼ lbs	1⅓ tbsp plain gelatin
¼ cup sugar	3 tbsp cold water
⅛ tsp salt	½ tsp grated lemon rind
1½ cups milk	5 tsp lemon juice
4 egg yolks	1 cup whipping cream, ½ pt

Persimmons should be thoroughly ripe and soft with wrinkled skins. Wash, remove calyx, cut in quarters, and snare out the seeds. Put fruit through a food mill or sieve to obtain purée. There should be 2 cups. Put sugar, salt and milk into top of double boiler, heat to scalding and stir occasionally. Beat egg yolks, slowly pour in hot milk and stir as you pour. Return mixture to top of double boiler and cook with almost constant stirring until custard coats a metal spoon. Soften gelatin in cold water 3 or 4 min and stir into hot custard until dissolved. Fold in persimmon purée, grated lemon rind and juice. Cool, chill until mixture starts congealing. Fold in stiffly whipped cream lightly but thoroughly. Cover and again return to refrigerator to chill. Serve in chilled sherbets. A garnish of toasted coconut may be added. 7 to 8 servings.

PINEAPPLE BAVARIAN

1 tbsp plain gelatin
¼ cup cold water
9-oz can crushed pineapple,
 1 cup
1 cup whipping cream,
 chilled

Dash of salt
¼ to ⅓ cup sugar
3 tbsp lemon juice, 1 lemon
Strawberries or maraschino
cherries, optional

Sift the gelatin over the water measured into a custard cup. Let stand 5 min to soften. Meanwhile turn pineapple into a 2-qt mixing bowl. Stir in lemon juice, salt, and sugar, the amount depending on sweetness of pineapple. Set custard cup of gelatin in a pan containing hot water and let stand until it melts to a clear liquid, then stir gelatin into pineapple mixture. Set aside or in refrigerator until mixture becomes consistency of thick unbeaten egg white. Have cream whipped until just stiff, but not lumpy. Quickly scrape cream onto top of pineapple mixture, then using the scraper, quickly cut and fold in the cream lightly but thoroughly. Cover and place in refrigerator to chill. Serve heaped lightly in sherbets. Garnish with a red-ripe strawberry with sugar sifted over it or a maraschino cherry. 5 to 6 servings.

FRESH RED RASPBERRY BAVARIAN

1 pt red raspberries
⅔ cup sugar
 Dash of salt
1 tbsp lemon juice

¼ cup cold water
1 tbsp plain gelatin
1 cup whipping cream

Pick over berries, wash gently in cold water, then drain. Stir in sugar and salt. Cover and let stand in refrigerator a few hrs or until sugar dissolves. Turn berries into a fine-meshed sieve, placed over a bowl. Rub juice and pulp through thoroughly with back of a spoon. There should be 1½ cups puree. Stir in lemon juice. Measure water into custard cup; sift gelatin into it and let soften 3 or 4 min. Now set cup in hot water until gelatin melts, then stir it into berry mixture. Set in cool place until syrupy. Whip cream until stiff but not until buttery, then fold berry mixture into cream lightly. Turn into a mold. Cover and chill in refrigerator until firm. Unmold to serve. May be garnished with a puff of whipped cream and a few choice whole berries, or serve plain. 6 servings.

Note: Frozen raspberries may be used. Thaw and press through sieve. Decrease sugar.

RUSSIAN CREAM

1 tbsp gelatin	1 cup fresh sour cream
½ cup cold water	¼ tsp salt
1 cup coffee cream	½ tsp vanilla
¾ cup sugar	Red raspberries

Sprinkle gelatin over cold water to soften 5 min. Turn coffee cream and sugar into top of double boiler and place over hot water until warm, stirring to dissolve sugar, then remove from heat. Now stir in gelatin until dissolved. Chill. When mixture cools to a consistency of unbeaten egg whites, whip until stiff, then fold in sour cream, slightly beaten, salt and vanilla. Pour into molds and place in refrigerator until firm. Unmold and serve cold with red raspberries, fresh or frozen. 6 servings.

STRAWBERRY BAVARIAN

A blushing beauty and delicious

1 qt strawberries	¼ tsp salt
1 tbsp plain gelatin	1 tbsp lemon juice
2 tbsp water	1 cup whipping cream
⅔ cup sugar *or* more	

Wash strawberries carefully, swishing them gently in cold water. Lift out into colander to drain. Hull, save 7 or 8 small berries for garnish; then crush the rest and add sugar to suit taste. Rub berries through a sieve or food mill to obtain purée. There should be 1⅔ cups. Now sprinkle gelatin into cold water measured into a custard cup and let soften 5 min. Then melt to a clear liquid by standing cup in hot water. Stir gelatin into strawberry purée thoroughly, stir in salt and lemon juice; let cool until the consistency of unbeaten egg whites. Now beat cream until stiff, but not lumpy. Quickly scrape cream into strawberry mixture and with rubber scraper cut and fold in lightly but thoroughly. Turn into a mold or let congeal in bowl. Garnish with sweetened whole berries. 7 to 8 servings.

VANILLA BAVARIAN OR CRÈME VANILLE

A delightful dessert

1 tbsp plain gelatin	¼ tsp salt
¼ cup water	2 cups milk
3 egg yolks	1 cup whipping cream,
1 whole egg	chilled
½ cup sugar	1½ tsp vanilla

To soften gelatin sprinkle over cold water measured into a custard up. Now heat milk to scalding in top of double boiler. Beat egg yolks and egg thoroughly, then beat in sugar and salt until well blended. Add scalded milk gradually, stirring constantly. Return to double boiler, and cook and stir over gently boiling water until mixture coats a metal spoon. Remove from heat and stir in gelatin until it melts. Let cool to consistency of thick unbeaten egg whites. At this point have the cream beaten until just stiff but smooth. Turn cream and vanilla into custard mixture and with rubber scraper cut and fold in lightly but thoroughly. Turn immediately into a mold. Chill until firm. Unmold and serve at table plain or with crushed sweetened berries or with Caramel syrup, p 643. 8 to 10 servings.

LEMON FLUFF

A delightful lemon colored dessert with a chiffon texture. Wonderful to finish a heavy meal

1½ tsp grated lemon rind, pkd	4 eggs, separated
⅓ cup lemon juice, 2 medium lemons	1 cup sugar
4 tsp plain gelatin	¼ tsp salt
⅔ cup cold water	Whipping cream
	Pistachios *or* almonds

Wash lemons, grate rind and fold it up in waxed paper. Squeeze lemon juice. Soften gelatin in half the water. Place over hot water until melted. Put remaining water and ⅔ cup of the sugar into a saucepan and boil gently for 5 min. Meanwhile beat egg yolks, add remaining sugar and salt and beat until thick; then stir in the lemon rind and juice. Wash egg beater and beat whites to a stiff foam. Then set whites in a bowl of hot water, add the boiling syrup slowly and continue beating until mixture is stiff, shiny, smooth and warm. Remove from heat, add the gelatin slowly, beating constantly until well blended and very smooth. Then cut and fold the yolk-lemon mixture in thoroughly. Turn immediately into a 6-cup mold or glass loaf pan rinsed with cold water. Cover and chill until firm. Unmold, see p 1155. Pile sweetened whipped cream lightly over top and sprinkle with sliced pistachios or almonds. 6 servings.

MARSHMALLOW PUDDING

With Lemon Sauce this pudding looks like clean, drifted snow drenched with sunshine

1 tbsp plain gelatin	2 egg whites
¼ cup cold water	Dash of salt
½ cup boiling water	½ tsp vanilla
¾ cup sugar	Lemon Sauce, p 1246

Soften gelatin in the cold water for 5 min; then set over hot water to melt. Put boiling water and sugar in the top of a double boiler, stir thoroughly, and add egg whites. Place over gently boiling water, and start beating immediately; continue beating with a rotary beater until mixture is stiff, smooth, shiny and warm. Remove from heat, and slowly add melted gelatin with constant beating until mixture is well blended. Add salt and vanilla, and again beat until blended. Turn immediately into an 8-inch sq cake pan rinsed with cold water. Place in refrigerator until firm. Cut out in squares, and serve with sauce. 4 to 5 servings.

MOCHA WHIP

1 tbsp plain gelatin	½ cup sugar
2 tbsp cold water	Dash of salt
½ cup very strong coffee	2 tsp vanilla
3 eggs, separated	Cream

Soften gelatin in the cold water for 5 min, then set in hot water to melt. Make the strong coffee by adding 6 tbsp medium grind coffee to 1 cup boiling water and heat just to boiling. Then turn off heat, cover and let stand 3 min; strain through several thicknesses of cheesecloth and cool slightly. Beat the egg yolks in the top of a double boiler, then beat in the sugar and salt. Add the ½ cup coffee and cook and stir over hot water until the mixture coats a spoon. Stir in the vanilla, then gelatin. Fold in stiffly beaten egg whites lightly but thoroughly. Pour into 4-cup glass mold or into smaller individual glass ones. Chill until firm. When ready to serve, unmold and serve with cream. 4 cups.

Note: Instant coffee may be used.

ORANGE SPANISH CREAM

4½ tsp plain gelatin	¼ tsp lemon rind, pkd
1¼ cups milk	1 cup orange juice
½ cup sugar	2 tbsp lemon juice
¼ tsp salt	1 seedless orange, sliced for
2 eggs, separated	garnish
¼ tsp grated orange rind, pkd	

Soften gelatin in ½ cup of the cold milk for 5 min. Put remaining milk in the top of double boiler and place over boiling water to scald. Add gelatin and stir until it dissolves. Add the sugar and salt. Pour part of hot mixture over slightly beaten egg yolks, stirring vigorously. Return to double boiler and cook and stir for 3 min. Remove from heat. Add grated rinds and juices. Cool slightly and fold in the stiffly beaten egg whites. Pour into 4 individual molds. Chill until firm. The pudding separates with a clear jelly layer on the bottom. Garnish with a border of pared orange cut in crosswise slices, then in half. 4 servings.

PINEAPPLE SNOW

Prepare night before for a ready delicious dessert next day

1 tbsp plain gelatin   Dash of salt
¼ cup cold water   ¼ cup sugar
1 cup crushed pineapple,   ¼ cup water
   9-oz can   2 egg whites
3 tbsp lemon juice, 1 lemon

Soften gelatin in the cold water for 5 min. Place over hot water to melt. Turn pineapple into mixing bowl. Add lemon juice and salt, then add the melted gelatin slowly and stir thoroughly to blend well. Place in refrigerator until mixture is a thick syrup. Meanwhile combine sugar and water in top of double boiler. Add egg whites, place over gently boiling water, start beating immediately with a rotary beater and continue beating until mixture is stiff, shiny, smooth and warm. Remove from heat and immediately begin adding the syrupy pineapple mixture gradually, and cut and fold in until thoroughly blended. Pour immediately into a 4-cup mold rinsed with cold water. Chill until firm. Unmold, p 1155. Serve with Custard Sauce, p 1243, if desired. 5 servings.

FRESH RED RASPBERRY FLUFF

A dainty light dessert for hot weather. Ideal for the employed home-maker

½ pt fresh red raspberries   2 tsp plain gelatin
½ cup sugar   2 egg whites, beaten
2 tbsp lemon juice   Dash of salt
2 tbsp cold water   1 tbsp sugar

Pick over, wash and drain berries. Sprinkle sugar over berries, cover and let stand in refrigerator a few hrs. To assemble, stir berries carefully to crush as few as possible. Then with a rubber scraper fold in lemon juice. Measure cold water into custard cup, then sprinkle in gelatin and let stand 3 or 4 min to soften. Now set cup in hot water until gelatin melts, then stir it gently into berry mixture. Now beat egg whites until stiff, then beat in salt and 1 tbsp sugar until very smooth. Now cut-and-fold berry mixture lightly but thoroughly into beaten whites. Heap mixture into sherbets, glass cups or leave in bowl. Cover and place in refrigerator until firm, at least 3 hrs. When served in sherbets, add a blob of whipped cream and a few choice whole berries, or a spoonful of crushed sweetened raspberries. 4 servings.

RASPBERRY MALLOW CREAM

A snap to make, easy to eat and rich

1 pt fresh red raspberries,	12 marshmallows
2 cups	2 tbsp sugar
½ pt whipping cream	3 tbsp sugar
2 tsp lemon juice	

Pick over, wash, *drain and chill* berries. Have cream, bowl and beater chilled. Squeeze lemon juice. Cut marshmallows in 6 to 8 pieces with scissors. Beat cream until it begins to thicken, then add lemon juice and 2 tbsp sugar; continue beating until stiff, but still smooth. Now gently fold in marshmallows and 1½ cups of the berries. Cover bowl and chill until very stiff, at least 2 hrs. Crush remaining berries lightly; stir in rest of sugar and chill. To serve, spoon cream mixture into sherbets, then spoon sweetened berries over top. 5 to 6 servings.

Note: A nice variation is to fold in ½ cup moist cold cooked rice into the cream just before adding raspberries.

SNOW PUDDING

Wonderful hot weather meal finish

2 tsp plain gelatin	Dash of salt
¼ cup cold water	⅓ cup lemon juice, 2 lemons
1 cup boiling water	2 egg whites, room temp
¾ cup sugar	Custard Sauce, p 1243

Have ready a 4 to 5-cup mold, loaf pan or individual molds. Sprinkle gelatin on the cold water and let soften 5 min. Then add ½ the boiling water, ½ of sugar, the salt and lemon juice and stir until sugar and gelatin dissolve. Chill until mixture is consistency of unbeaten egg whites. Put rest of boiling water and sugar into saucepan and boil gently 3 min. Beat egg whites until stiff, add hot syrup slowly, stirring in vigorously with egg beater, then beat until stiff and shiny. Now slowly add gelatin syrup and beat until well-blended. Turn into mold rinsed in cold water. Chill until set. Serve with Custard Sauce. 5 servings.

SPANISII CREAM

A delicate, two-layer dessert

1 tbsp plain gelatin	3 eggs, separated
¼ cup cold water	¼ to ½ tsp salt
3 cups milk	1 tsp vanilla
⅓ to ½ cup sugar	

Soften gelatin in cold water for 5 min. Scald milk in top of double boiler. Add sugar and gelatin and stir until dissolved. Stir a small amount of mixture into the slightly beaten yolks, return to double boiler and cook and stir over hot water until mixture coats a spoon. Remove from heat, add salt and vanilla and fold in the stiffly beaten egg whites lightly but thoroughly. Pour into cups that have been rinsed in cold water. Chill until firm. 4 to 8 servings.

BANANA GRAPE MOLD

Different and very palatable

1 tbsp plain gelatin	¾ cup cold water
¼ cup cold water	1 tsp lemon juice
½ cup boiling water	¼ cup sugar
6-oz can frozen concentrated	3 full-ripe bananas
grape juice, ¾ cup	Whipping cream

Sprinkle gelatin over cold water measured into a custard cup. Let soften 5 min. Then dissolve in the boiling water. Now add next 4 ingredients and stir until sugar dissolves. Pour a little of the mixture into the bottom of a mold and place in refrigerator to congeal. When congealed, peel a banana, cut into ¼-inch slices and arrange over congealed gelatin in a pattern. Drop a spoonful of gelatin over banana slices so as not to disturb and return to refrigerator. When rest of grape mixture is thick and syrupy, fold in rest of freshly sliced bananas, pour into mold and chill until firm. Unmold onto chilled serving plate. Serve with whipped cream. 5 servings.

FRUIT-NUT JELLY

Delicious as a salad or as rich dessert that seems light

1 pkg fruit-flavored gelatin, cherry *or* raspberry preferred, *or* a mixture of each	½ cup whipping cream
	1 large, well-ripened banana
	⅓ cup pecans
1 cup boiling water	1 tbsp sugar
1 cup cold water	

Have ready a glass or aluminum loaf pan 9¼ x 5¼ x 2¾-inches. Brush lightly with salad oil. Turn gelatin into a 2-qt mixing bowl. Add boiling water, stir until gelatin dissolves, then stir in cold water. Let mixture stand until it thickens to consistency of unbeaten egg whites. Meantime whip cream until it will just stand in ripples, not until stiff. Beat in sugar. Then cut the peeled, scraped banana into crosswise slices, dropping them into cream, and *folding* them carefully in to prevent discoloration. Turn nuts over cream. When gelatin reaches the raw egg-white consistency, fold in banana nut mixture just enough to streak it through gelatin. Turn into prepared pan. Some of the whipped cream should be streaked interestingly over top. Chill until firm. Invert onto serving plate. Cut into slices. Serve plain for dessert or with mayonnaise for salad.

JELLIED FRUIT DELIGHT

1 tbsp gelatin	½ tsp orange rind, pkd
¼ cup cold water	⅛ tsp salt
1½ cups unsweetened apple sauce, p 556	2 seedless oranges, peeled, diced
⅓ cup sugar	Sauce
1 tbsp lemon juice	

Soften gelatin in cold water for 5 min. Heat apple sauce, remove from heat and stir in gelatin until completely dissolved. Stir in sugar, lemon juice, orange rind and salt. Chill slightly before folding in orange sections. Pour into individual molds and chill until firm. Serve cold with following sauce: ½ cup milk, ½ cup coffee cream, ⅛ tsp nutmeg, ⅛ tsp cinnamon and 1 tbsp sugar. Mix well and pour some over each serving. 4 to 5 servings.

MELON MOLD

1 medium-sized cantaloupe	1 tsp sugar
½ pkg lemon-flavored gelatin	Dash of salt
½ cup boiling water	½ cup Bing cherries, ¼ lb
1 tbsp lemon juice	

Cut cantaloupe in half, scoop out seeds and fiber from center. Put the gelatin into a bowl, add the boiling water and stir until dissolved. Add lemon juice, sugar and salt and stir until dissolved. Chill until consistency of unbeaten egg white. Enlarge the cavity of the cantaloupe by scooping out about ½-inch of the flesh. Cube the scooped-out portion, about 1 cup, and add this and the pitted, halved cherries to the thickened gelatin mixture. Fill the two cantaloupe halves with the mixture. Put the cantaloupe in a deep pan, a bread loaf pan will do. Wrap all in waxed paper and place in the refrigerator to congeal. Cut cantaloupe must be well wrapped to keep aroma from penetrating other foods in refrigerator. To serve, cut each half in two. Serve well chilled. 4 servings.

MOLDED PLUM PUDDING

¼ cup moist shredded candied citron, pkd	1 tbsp plain gelatin
¾ cup seedless raisins, plumped, chopped, p 165	¼ cup cold water
½ cup chopped pecans or walnuts	1¾ cup boiling cider, apple juice or peach juice from canned peaches
½ cup chopped moist dates	⅛ tsp salt
3 tbsp lemon juice	Hard Sauce, p 1245 or Whipping cream

Have ready 8 or 9 (⅓ cup capacity) gelatin molds. Combine citron, raisins, nuts and dates in a 2-qt mixing bowl. Stir in lemon juice.

Soften gelatin in the cold water for 5 min. Then stir this into the hot fruit juice. Then stir in salt and fruit mixture. Let cool until the consistency of unbeaten egg white. Spoon mixture into molds. Set molds in a flat shallow pan and place in refrigerator to congeal. When ready to serve, unmold, p 1155, on small serving plates. Top with Hard Sauce or sweetened whipped cream flavored as desired. 8 to 9 servings.

ORANGE JELLY

4½ tsp plain gelatin
¼ cup cold water
1 cup boiling water
1 tsp grated orange rind, pkd
½ tsp grated lemon rind, pkd

1¾ cups orange juice
¾ cup sugar
½ cup lemon juice
Dash of salt
Cream

Soften gelatin in the cold water for 5 min; then add boiling water, stirring until gelatin dissolves. Add grated rinds to 3 tbsp of the orange juice and let stand 5 min. Strain off liquid into rest of orange juice, pressing thoroughly. Discard rind. Add next 3 ingredients and stir until well blended. Cool, turn into a 4-cup mold which has been rinsed in cold water, cover and place in refrigerator to congeal. Serve plain, or with plain or whipped cream. 5 to 6 servings.

ORANGE BUTTERMILK JELLY

½ cup strained orange juice
1 tbsp lemon juice
1½ cups fresh buttermilk
Dash of salt
About ⅓ cup sugar, or to suit taste

1 tbsp plain gelatin
3 tbsp cold water
2 seedless oranges, pared, sectioned
Whipping cream

Stir orange and lemon juice into buttermilk, then salt. Add sugar to suit taste, depending on sweetness of orange juice. Soften gelatin in cold water; then heat over hot water until melted. Stir into buttermilk mixture. Pour into a mold or bowl and chill until firm. Unmold and garnish with orange sections, and serve with whipped cream if desired. 5 servings.

FROZEN DESSERTS

Ice cream and its frozen relatives are among the most popular desserts which grace the American table, and are probably the most typically American of all foods with the possible exception of pie.

It is difficult to classify frozen desserts because there is very little uniformity in the ingredients used in products called by the various names, however, a general classification that will help to differentiate between the various desserts is as follows:

Ice Cream: Plain or Philadelphia ice cream is a mixture of thin cream, a sweetener and flavoring that is stirred while frozen and may or may not have some type of binder added, such as gelatin, eggs, etc.

New York or French ice cream has enough egg yolks added to give the ice cream a definite yellow color.

Custard ice cream has a base of whole egg and milk that may be cooked or uncooked.

Regular ice cream contains either flour, cornstarch or gelatin as the thickening and may contain egg in a smaller proportion than the New York type.

Unstirred ice cream (made in the mechanical refrigerator) usually contains richer cream and a relatively large amount of some binder or stabilizer.

Ices: An ice consists of sweetened fruit juice or purée that is usually diluted with water and may contain beaten egg white.

Sherbets: A sherbet is sweetened fruit juice or purée that is usually diluted with milk instead of water and may contain beaten egg white.

Mousse: A mousse contains sweetened, flavored whipped cream that is molded and frozen without stirring.

Frappé: A frappé is the same as an ice except that it is frozen only to a mush.

Frozen desserts are simply frozen liquids with various substances added for flavor, texture, and color. As water freezes, it becomes a solid hard block of ice that is too hard to spoon into. If the water is stirred as it is frozen, it will have a milky appearance due to tiny air bubbles that are frozen into its interior and a slightly less solid consistency, although it will still be too hard to be spooned out. The addition of sugar lowers the freezing point of the water sufficiently that the frozen mass will not be solid and will be the consistency of the frozen dessert known as an *Ice*. In fact, a true ice is simply a sweetened fruit juice that is diluted with water and frozen with continual stirring.

The ice crystals in an *Ice* are still fairly large, and on standing these crystals grow to form still larger ones. If particles of fat (as in milk and cream), or egg (either white or yolk or both), gelatin or starch (flour or cornstarch) is added to the mixture, these particles keep the ice crystals from coming together to form large crystals and therefore keep the frozen dessert creamy and smooth-textured and give it enough body so that it does not thaw immediately when taken from the freezer. All of these added ingredients are known as binders, stabilizers or interfering substances. They also add viscosity to the original liquid and make it possible to beat more air into the mixture, which gives a lighter, fluffier dessert, a creamier texture and a greater volume. This increase in volume is known as overrun.

Very satisfactory desserts can be made without stirring, but the proportion of interfering substances must necessarily be high. This usually makes a very rich dessert. If too rich a cream is added, the consistency has an unpleasant cloying tendency that is not enjoyable, so it is better to use a cream of medium fat content and to add other substances such as eggs or gelatin.

The ingredients added to frozen desserts must always be of the highest quality. Freezing will never improve the flavor of a rancid nut, an overripe piece of fruit, or old milk and cream. It is poor economy to spoil the flavor of a whole freezer of ice cream by trying to salvage a cup of overripe berries.

ICE CREAMS

Directions for Freezing Ice Cream

About 5 lbs (4 qts) of chipped ice and 2 cups coarse salt will be needed for freezing ice cream in a 2-qt freezer. That much more additional salt and ice will be needed if the ice cream is to be packed in the freezer to ripen. This proportion is about 8 cups finely chopped ice to each cup of coarse salt.

Pour boiling water over the washed cream can and the beater of the freezer; drain and set aside to cool.

Any mixture should be thoroughly chilled before it is poured into cream can for freezing. Fit the dasher and can into place before pouring in the chilled ice cream mixture. Pour in ice cream mixture, then fit lid and crank into place. If the parts are fitted together correctly, the crank will turn freely and the dasher as well as the can will revolve when the crank is turned clockwise. Pack layers of ice then layers of salt around can with a wooden spoon. Turn crank several times while packing so ice doesn't pack enough to keep freezer can from turning easily. Continue adding ice and salt until ice chamber over top of cream can is filled. Turn the crank slowly (about 40 revolutions per min) for the first three min, then turn rapidly until it is very difficult to turn. For best results the turning must be continuous.

When cream is frozen, clear away the salt and ice to about 1 inch below the lid of the cream can. Wipe the lid carefully to remove all ice and salt; take lid off. Take out the beater and scrape clean. The cream may be transferred to freezing pans of mechanical refrigerator or left in the cream can to "ripen" for a few hrs before serving. If left in the can, push ice cream gently down into can, replace the lid and fit it with a cork or pack cover to keep any brine from seeping in. Drain the water from the ice chamber. Repack with ice and salt to come up over top of can. Cover with several thicknesses of newspaper and damp cloth and put in a cool place to ripen, not longer than 2 or 3 hrs. If packed in cold refrigerator trays, pack down gently and cover with a sheet or two of heavy waxed paper. Return quickly to freezing compartment to ripen.

APRICOT ICE CREAM—REFRIGERATOR

1 cup dried apricots, about 6 oz	2 egg whites
1 cup hot water	⅔ cup whipping cream *or* evaporated milk, chilled
½ cup sugar	⅛ tsp almond flavoring
¼ cup water	

Wash apricots thoroughly but quickly in cold water. Lift out into a 3-qt saucepan. Add the hot water, cover and let soak 2 or 3 hrs; then cook in same water for 5 to 10 min, or until soft. Put through food mill or purée sieve; there should be 1 cup of pulp and liquid. If not, add water to make 1 cup. Cool; then chill about 15 min. Boil sugar and ¼ cup water together until syrup threads; pour hot syrup over stiffly beaten egg whites, and beat until smooth and thick with rotary beater. Chill 15 min. Meanwhile, put chilled cream or milk in bowl surrounded by chipped ice and whip until very thick; then add almond flavoring and continue whipping until stiff. Fold in chilled apricot purée; then fold in the egg white mixture lightly but thoroughly. Turn into freezing tray of mechanical refrigerator and freeze until firm. If frozen in hand-turned ice cream freezer, the cream or evaporated milk need not be whipped. 5 generous servings.

AVOCADO ICE CREAM

2 medium size, well-ripened, but not over-ripe avocados	1 cup cream
¼ cup lemon juice	1 cup milk
¾ cup sugar	1 tsp plain gelatin
¼ tsp salt	1 tbsp cold water

Cut avocados in half. Strip off peel and remove pit. Purée through a fine meshed sieve or food mill, or mash fine with a silver fork. Immediately add the lemon juice, sugar and salt and stir until sugar is dissolved. Add the cream and milk. Soften gelatin in water for 5 min. Stand over boiling water to melt, then stir very thoroughly into avocado mixture. Turn into the freezer can. Pack in ice and salt and freeze according to directions. 1 qt.

BANANA ICE CREAM

If you like bananas, you'll love this

½ cup sugar	½ cup whipping cream
1 tbsp flour	4 good sized well ripened
⅛ tsp salt	bananas
1 cup milk	1 tbsp lemon juice
1 cup 12% cream—Half and Half	2 tbsp sugar

Blend the sugar, flour and salt in top part of double boiler, then stir in milk until smooth. Place over boiling water and cook and stir until milk is steaming hot and the flour is cooked, about 10 min. Remove from heat and set in ice water, stirring occasionally until custard is cold. Meanwhile peel bananas and put through food mill or sieve quickly to obtain purée. There should be 1½ cups purée. Stir purée, and

Note: Ice cream freezing directions, p 592.

rest of ingredients immediately into the cold custard thoroughly until well blended. Turn at once into freezer can and freeze according to directions. 1¼ qts.

BUTTERSCOTCH ICE CREAM

1¼ cups light brown sugar, pkd
¼ cup butter
1 cup water
4 egg yolks

1 cup coffee cream
14½-oz can evaporated milk
¼ tsp salt
1½ tsp vanilla

Put sugar and butter into a skillet. Heat slowly, stirring occasionally until sugar melts. Add water slowly, stir and simmer about 5 min. Beat yolks and pour hot syrup over them, beating vigorously. Return to very low heat and stir continuously until mixture thickens slightly, 2 or 3 min. Remove from heat and cool. Add cream, evaporated milk, salt and vanilla. Mix well and chill. Turn into freezer can and freeze according to directions. 2 qts.

CHOCOLATE ICE CREAM

2 cups milk
2 sqs unsweet chocolate, 2-oz
1 cup sugar
2 tbsp flour

¼ tsp salt
2 eggs
2 tsp vanilla
2 cups coffee cream

Heat milk and broken chocolate in top of double boiler until chocolate melts. Combine sugar, flour and salt. Add eggs, beat thoroughly. combine with chocolate mixture and cook over direct heat until mixture thickens, stirring constantly—about 2 min. Strain and cool. Add vanilla and cream. Turn into freezer can and freeze according to directions. About 1½ qts.

COFFEE ICE CREAM—REFRIGERATOR

2 cups milk
5 tbsp medium grind coffee
1½ tsp plain gelatin
¼ cup cold water

$\frac{1}{16}$ tsp salt
¾ cup sugar
2 tsp vanilla
2 cups whipping cream, 1 pt

Put milk and coffee into top of double boiler, place over boiling water and heat for 15 min, stirring occasionally. Soften gelatin in cold water for 5 min. Strain coffee through several folds of cheese-cloth. Add softened gelatin, salt and sugar to the hot strained coffee mixture and stir thoroughly. Chill in refrigerator tray until the mixture is consistency of unbeaten egg white. At this point, fold coffee mixture and the vanilla extract into the stiffly whipped cream. Return immediately to the re-

Note: Ice cream freezing directions, p 592.

frigerator tray to freeze. If a hand-turned freezer is used, substitute coffee cream for the whipping cream and freeze according to directions. 1½ qts.

Note: High quality instant coffee may be used in place of the coffee that has been brewed.

GUAVA ICE CREAM

Folks who enjoy guavas believe there is no better ice cream than this

1 cup milk	2 tsp lemon juice
⅔ cup sugar	1 cup 12% cream, Half and
⅛ tsp salt	Half
3 egg yolks, beaten	1 cup whipping cream
Ripe, pink-flesh guavas for	
1½ cups purée	

Put milk, sugar and salt into top part of double boiler; stir well and place over boiling water long enough for milk to scald. Pour hot milk over beaten egg yolks, stirring to keep smooth, then return to double boiler and cook and stir until custard just coats a spoon. Remove from heat and set in ice water, stirring often until custard is cold. Meanwhile wash guavas, pare, slice and rub through a food mill enough to make 1½ cups purée. Stir purée with rest of ingredients into the cold custard. Now turn into freezer can and freeze according to directions. 1½ qts.

LEMON ICE CREAM

Every bite a delight—smooth as velvet

1 cup sugar	1 cup whipping cream
1 tbsp flour	2 tsp grated lemon rind, pkd
⅛ tsp salt	4 tbsp lemon juice
1 cup milk	Few drops yellow coloring
1 cup 12% cream—Half and	
Half	

Blend sugar well with flour and salt in top of double boiler, then stir in milk slowly. Place over boiling water. Cook and stir until milk is steaming hot and flour is cooked, about 10 min. Remove from heat and set in a pan of ice water, stirring frequently until custard is cold. Then stir in rest of ingredients. Now turn into freezer can and freeze according to directions. 1 qt.

MINCEMEAT ICE CREAM—REFRIGERATOR

¼ cup milk	2 tsp lemon juice
¼ cup water	½ tsp vanilla
⅓ cup sugar	1 cup prepared mincemeat
2 egg yolks, well beaten	1 cup whipping cream
Dash of salt	

Put the first 3 ingredients into top of double boiler and heat over boiling water to scalding. Pour slowly over egg yolks, stirring constantly. Return to double boiler and continue to stir over boiling water 5 min longer. Remove from heat, stir in salt, lemon juice and vanilla, and add mincemeat prepared according to directions on the package. Chill. Whip the thoroughly chilled cream until stiff. Fold mincemeat mixture into the whipped cream and turn into freezing tray of a refrigerator to freeze for 6 to 8 hrs. 6 servings.

NESSELRODE ICE CREAM

Prepare exactly like Nesselrode Pudding, p 580, except reduce gelatin to 1½ tsp. Freeze in usual way.

ORANGE ICE CREAM

Possesses a subtle bouquet

1 cup milk	1 cup whipping cream
½ cup sugar	1 cup fresh orange juice
⅛ tsp salt	1½ tsp grated orange rind, pkd
3 egg yolks	4 tsp lemon juice
½ cup 12% cream, Half and	3 tbsp sugar
Half	¼ tsp orange extract

Put first 3 ingredients into top part of double boiler. Stir thoroughly and place over boiling water. Cover and heat long enough for milk to scald. Meanwhile, beat yolks, stir in the hot milk mixture slowly to keep smooth. Then return to double boiler and cook and stir with metal spoon until mixture just coats the spoon. Remove from heat at once and set in a pan of ice water and stir often until custard is cold. Now stir in remaining ingredients thoroughly, then turn into freezer can and freeze immediately according to directions.* 1¼ qts.

PEACH ICE CREAM—REFRIGERATOR

1½ cups purée from juicy-ripe peaches	Dash of salt
1¼ cups whipping cream	1 cup xxxx sugar
2 tsp lemon juice	⅛ tsp almond extract

Pare, slice and put enough peaches through sieve or food mill to make 1½ cups purée. Thoroughly chill cream and whip with rotary beater in a chilled bowl until thick, add salt and lemon juice and continue beating until very stiff. Beat in the sugar and fold in the peach purée blended with extract. Turn into refrigerator tray immediately and freeze for about 2 hrs. 6 servings.

* Ice cream freezing directions, p 592.

PEANUT BRITTLE ICE CREAM

1½ tsp plain gelatin	½ cup sugar
2 tbsp milk	¼ tsp salt
1 qt coffee cream	½ lb peanut brittle, crushed

Soften gelatin in the milk for 5 min. Scald ½ cup of the cream, add sugar, and softened gelatin and salt. Stir until sugar and gelatin dissolve. Cool and combine with remaining cream. Pour into freezer can and freeze according to directions. When partially frozen, remove cover, then add peanut brittle. Replace cover; continue freezing until firm. 1½ qts.

BUTTER PECAN ICE CREAM

Excellent!

½ cup sugar	1 cup whipping cream
1 tbsp flour	1 tbsp vanilla
⅛ tsp salt	½ to ¾ cup pecans
1 cup milk	2 tbsp butter
1 cup 12% cream—Half and Half	

Blend the first 3 ingredients in top of double boiler, then stir in milk until smooth. Place over boiling water and cook and stir until milk is steaming hot and flour is cooked, about 10 min. Remove from heat and set pan in ice water, stirring until custard is cold. Meanwhile melt butter in skillet until it foams, then add nuts and stir constantly about 3 min, until butter and nuts become slightly browned, but not scorched. Remove from heat and turn out on paper toweling for paper to absorb excess fat for 2 or 3 min. Now add nuts with rest of ingredients to custard, stir well and turn into a freezer can and freeze according to directions. 1 qt.

PEPPERMINT STICK ICE CREAM NO. 1

2 cups milk	¼ lb peppermint stick candy
¾ cup sugar	1 cup whipping cream,
¼ tsp salt	chilled
2 eggs, beaten	

Put milk, sugar and salt into top of double boiler. Cover; place over boiling water and heat milk to scalding. Now stir hot mixture gradually into eggs; then return to pan and cook over hot water, stirring constantly until mixture just coats a metal spoon. Cool thoroughly. Stir in finely crushed candy. Beat chilled cream until stiff and fold in the peppermint custard. Turn into either freezing tray or into a hand-turned freezer, and freeze according to directions. 5 servings.

Note: Ice cream freezing directions, p 592.

PEPPERMINT STICK ICE CREAM NO. 2

1 qt coffee cream	1 tsp plain gelatin
½ lb peppermint stick candy	2 tbsp cold water
¼ tsp salt	

Put cream into a 2 qt mixing bowl, add crushed candy, cover and place in the refrigerator several hrs or until candy dissolves. When ready to freeze, add salt. Soften gelatin in cold water for 5 min then place over hot water to melt, then stir into cream mixture until thoroughly blended. Strain into freezer can and freeze according to directions. About 2 qts.

PEPPERMINT CANDY ICE CREAM—REFRIGERATOR

½ lb peppermint stick candy	2 cups whipping cream,
1 cup milk	chilled
⅟₁₆ tsp salt	

Crush the peppermint stick candy finely using a rolling-pin or potato masher. Turn into a 2-qt mixing bowl. Add milk and salt and pour into a refrigerator tray to freeze to a mushy consistency. Remove the partially frozen mixture to a chilled bowl and beat well with a rotary beater, and quickly fold in cream whipped until stiff. Return mixture immediately to chilled refrigerator tray, and finish freezing. 8 servings.

PRUNE ICE CREAM

1 cup whipping cream,	¾ tsp grated lemon rind
chilled	¾ lb prunes, cooked, pitted,
3 tbsp lemon juice	chopped, 1½ cups
¼ cup sugar	¼ cup chopped nuts, opt.
⅛ tsp salt	

Turn cream into a chilled bowl. Add lemon juice and beat with a rotary beater until fluffy and stiff. Beat in the sugar, salt and lemon rind. Now fold in prunes and nuts. Immediately turn into cold refrigerator tray and place in freezing compartment for 6 to 8 hrs. 6 to 8 servings.

RASPBERRY ICE CREAM

¼ lb marshmallows, 16	¼ tsp salt
1 pt red raspberries	1 cup whipping cream,
¼ cup water	chilled
⅓ cup sugar	3 tbsp lemon juice

Put marshmallows in top of double boiler with washed, well-drained raspberries and water; place over boiling water and heat until marshmallows are melted but are still fluffy, stirring frequently. Stir in sugar and salt and chill until syrupy. Whip cream until very thick; then add lemon juice and continue whipping until stiff. Now fold raspberry mixture into cream lightly but thoroughly. Turn immediately into cold refrigerator tray and freeze at the lowest temp until firm, then return to normal temp and allow cream to ripen until ready to serve. Stirring is not necessary. 4 servings.

STRAWBERRY ICE CREAM

1 qt well-ripened strawber-ries, washed, hulled	1 tsp plain gelatin
1 cup sugar	1 tbsp cold water
1 tbsp lemon juice	1 cup whole milk
¼ tsp salt	3 cups coffee cream

Crush berries and rub through a fine sieve or a food mill to obtain fine purée; there should be 1¾ cups purée if berries are of good quality. Add sugar, lemon juice and salt, stirring well; cover and place in refrigerator. Soften gelatin in the cold water and dissolve in milk heated to scalding. Cool. Combine with strawberry purée. Add cream. Turn into freezer can and freeze according to directions. Serve plain or with a puff of whipped cream. 10 servings.

VANILLA ICE CREAM NO. 1

1 cup milk	2 eggs
1 tbsp cornstarch	2 cups coffee cream
½ cup sugar	2 tsp vanilla
¼ tsp salt	

Scald milk in top of double boiler. Blend cornstarch, sugar and salt and stir in hot milk slowly to keep smooth. Return to double boiler and cook and stir until thick and smooth. Beat eggs slightly; add small amount of hot mixture, beat slightly, then combine with remaining hot mixture, and cook and stir 1 min longer—now strain and cool. Stir in cream and vanilla. Turn into freezer can and freeze according to directions. 1 qt.

VANILLA ICE CREAM NO. 2

1½ qts milk	4 cups cream, 1 qt
4 eggs	1½ tbsp vanilla
2½ cups sugar	½ tsp salt

Scald milk in top of double boiler. Beat eggs until light and fluffy and add sugar gradually, beating well after each ¼ cup addition. When the mixture becomes stiff and difficult to beat, stir in milk. Return to double boiler and cook and stir 2 min longer. Remove from heat and cool. Then stir in cream, vanilla, and salt thoroughly. Then pour into a gallon freezer. Freeze according to directions. 1 gallon.

VANILLA ICE CREAM—AMERICAN TYPE

½ cup sugar
1 tbsp flour
⅛ tsp salt
1 cup milk

1 cup 12% cream,
Half and Half
1 cup whipping cream
1 tbsp vanilla *or*
1 tsp vanilla bean powder

Blend the first 3 ingredients in the top of a double boiler, then stir in milk slowly. Place over boiling water and cook and stir until milk is steaming hot and flour is cooked, about 10 min. Remove from heat and set in a pan of ice water and stir often until custard is cold. Then stir in rest of ingredients, turn into freezer can and freeze according to directions. 1 qt.

VANILLA ICE CREAM—FRENCH TYPE

The universal favorite

1 cup milk
½ cup sugar
⅛ tsp salt
3 egg yolks

1 cup 12% cream,
Half and Half
1 cup whipping cream
1 tbsp vanilla, *or*
¾ tsp vanilla bean powder

Put milk, sugar and salt into top of double boiler; stir well and place over boiling water, cover and heat long enough to scald milk. Beat yolks well, stir in scalded milk mixture, then return to top of double boiler and cook and stir with metal spoon until custard just coats the spoon. Remove at once from heat and stand in ice water, stir often until custard is cold. Now add rest of ingredients, stir well and turn into freezer can. Freeze according to directions. 1 qt.

OLD-FASHIONED VANILLA ICE CREAM

1½ tsp cornstarch
¼ tsp salt
¾ cup sugar
3 cups whole milk

2 eggs, beaten
2 cups whipping cream
1½ tsp vanilla

Blend cornstarch, salt and sugar well in top of double boiler. Stir in 2 cups of the milk slowly to keep smooth. Cook over boiling water for 20 min, stirring occasionally. Beat eggs until light, gradually stir in a small amount of the hot mixture, then return to the double boiler and cook and stir 2 min longer. Remove from heat and cool. Then strain and stir in rest of milk, cream and vanilla. Pour into freezer can and freeze according to directions. 8 to 10 servings.

Note: Ice cream freezing directions, p 592.

BISCUIT TORTONI
A classy French old-time ice cream dessert

¾ cup fine-chopped blanched
    toasted almonds
⅔ cup dry almond macaroons
¾ cup sugar
⅓ cup hot water
5 egg yolks, ⅜ cup

2 tbsp warm water
Dash of salt
1 tbsp vanilla *or* Sherry
    flavoring
1 pt whipping cream
5 candied cherries

Have ready ten 3½ x 2-inch frilly paper boxes or souffle cups 2¾ inches in diameter and 1-inch deep. Blanch, toast and chop almonds. Grate macaroons. Put sugar and hot water into a 1-qt saucepan. Boil to 238° F, or until syrup spins a thread 3 to 4 inches long. Remove from heat. With rotary beater, beat egg yolks, warm water and salt thoroughly, then turn into top of double boiler using rubber scraper to scrape bowl clean. Now continue to beat yolk mixture rapidly while slowly adding the hot syrup. Then place over gently boiling water and cook and stir with a wooden spoon until just thickened, 6 to 8 min. Remove from heat and cool thoroughly, stirring frequently. Stir in flavoring and nuts, then *fold in* stiffly whipped cream. Pour into boxes or cups, filling to top. Sprinkle tops with macaroon crumbs. Place in freezing compartment of refrigerator 3 or 4 hrs until firm. Garnish with half cherry. 10 servings.

FREEZES

LEMON CREAM FREEZE
Easy and Excellent!

14½-oz can evaporated milk
½ cup lemon juice
¾ cup sugar

1/16 tsp salt
1¼ tsp lemon rind, pkd

Pour milk into a refrigerator tray and freeze to an icy mush; remove to a cold bowl, add juice and beat with rotary beater until stiff. Beat in sugar and salt gradually. Remove beater, then fold in rind. Turn immediately into chilled tray and freeze. 6 servings.

RASPBERRY FREEZE

1 cup evaporated milk
1 tbsp lemon juice
¼ tsp lemon rind
Dash of salt

¾ cup seedless black rasp-
    berry jam, homemade *or*
    commercial

Pour evaporated milk into refrigerator tray and freeze to an icy mush. Now turn milk into a cold bowl, add lemon juice and beat with a rotary beater until stiff and fluffy. Add remaining ingredients and continue beating until thoroughly blended. Turn mixture back into chilled freezing tray and freeze 6 to 8 hrs. Very good. 4 to 6 servings.

VELVA FRUIT*

Quick, easy, delicious

6 cups fresh fruit purée	¼ tsp salt
1½ to 2 cups sugar	2 tbsp plain gelatin
2 tbsp lemon juice, omit for acid fruits	½ cup cold water

Prepare purée according to directions. Add sugar, lemon juice if used, and the salt to purée and stir thoroughly. Soften gelatin in water 5 min, then melt by placing over hot water. Have the fruit purée around 70° F room temp, when the gelatin is added. If the purée is too cool, the gelatin will congeal before it can be thoroughly blended into the purée. If it is too warm, it will expand too much when whipped in the freezer. Add purée mixture slowly to the dissolved gelatin, stirring continuously. Pour into ice cream freezer and freeze with 8 parts of chipped ice to 1 part of coarse salt for 20 min, or until the crank turns hard and the frozen velva clings to the dasher. Remove dasher, and serve either soft-frozen, or place in the refrigerator tray and harden for several hrs. Or pack at once into moisture-vapor-resistant cartons, seal and place in the freezer locker or cabinet immediately. 1 gallon.

TO MAKE FRUIT PURÉE

Berries, except strawberries: Pick over berries, wash and drain. Press berries through sieve, fine colander, or food mill. Four qts whole fresh fruit make about 6 cups purée.

Cantaloupe: Select fully ripe cantaloupe. Pare and slice. Press through sieve or fine colander. Six lbs whole melon make about 6 cups purée.

Cranberries: Pick over berries, wash and drain. Cook in a little water until skins break. Press through sieve, fine colander, or food mill. Three qts whole fresh berries make about 6 cups purée.

Grapes, Concord type: Wash and stem grapes. Place in pan and crush; cover and heat to simmering until juice begins to flow and seeds are loosened from pulp. Press through sieve, fine colander, or food mill. Six lbs whole fresh fruit make about 6 cups purée.

Peaches, also apricots, nectarines: Select fully ripe, rich-flavored fruit. Pare; remove any bruised portions. Cut into quarters and place in a boiling syrup (1 cup sugar to 8 cups water) for 3 min to keep fruit from darkening. Remove, drain and press through sieve or fine colander. Cool. Six lbs whole fresh fruit make about 6 cups purée.

Rhubarb: Wash and cut rhubarb into pieces as for sauce. Do not remove the skin which gives the product its pretty pink color. Heat in a double

*Adapted from U. S. Department of Agriculture Bulletin.

boiler or in a pan over boiling water until rhubarb is soft. Press through sieve, fine colander, or food mill. Cool. Four lbs cut rhubarb make about 6 cups purée.

Strawberries: Select fully ripe strawberries, avoiding overripe berries that give an off-flavor. Wash strawberries, drain and hull. Press through a sieve, fine colander, or food mill, but don't force through the last pulp which contains most of the seeds, which are bluish in color. They also give a woody texture to purée or Velva Fruit when stored. Five qts whole fresh fruit make about 6 cups purée.

TO STORE FROZEN PURÉE

Instead of making fruit purée immediately into Velva Fruit, you can preserve it by freezing and make it up a few months later, as follows:

Mix 6 cups fruit purée with 1½ to 2 cups sugar depending on sweetness of fruit. Stir until sugar is completely dissolved. Seal in glass jars or tin cans to preserve fresh fruit flavor (R-enamel cans for red or dark purées). Leave 1-inch head space for swelling. Freeze and store at 0° F or lower.

TO USE FROZEN PURÉE

When using frozen sweetened purée to make Velva Fruit, remove purée from freezer. Put sealed container in cold or lukewarm, not hot, water; shake occasionally to speed thawing. A quart of purée will thaw in about 2 hrs. When purée reaches room temp, about 70° F, add salt, and lemon juice if desired. Then add purée to the melted gelatin and continue as directed in the Velva Fruit recipe, p 602.

ICES AND SHERBETS

GRAPE ICE No. 1

2 tsp plain gelatin	4 tbsp lemon juice
¼ cup cold water	¾ cup sugar
1½ pt bottle grape juice	⅛ tsp salt

Sift gelatin onto the cold water and let soften 5 min; then place over hot water to melt. Combine grape and lemon juice, stir in sugar, salt and the gelatin thoroughly. Freeze according to directions*. About 1½ qts.

GRAPE ICE No. 2

⅓ cup white corn syrup	6-oz can frozen concentrated
½ cup sugar	grape juice diluted with
¾ cup cold water	¾ cup cold water
2 tsp plain gelatin	⅓ cup orange juice
¼ cup cold water	⅛ tsp salt
	2 egg whites

* Ice cream freezing directions, p 592.

Put syrup, sugar and the ¾ cup of water into a 1 qt saucepan and boil gently 10 min. Sprinkle gelatin over remaining cold water and let soften 5 min. Now add gelatin to hot syrup and stir until dissolved. Cool and add the juices and salt. Pour into freezing tray of refrigerator, set at coldest temp and freeze. When mixture becomes mushy, loosen from sides of tray, remove to a chilled bowl and beat hard with a rotary beater for a few seconds, then add stiffly beaten egg whites and again beat hard until well blended. Return immediately to freezer tray and finish freezing. 5 to 6 generous servings.

Note: This mixture may be frozen in hand freezer. See directions, p 592.

LIME ICE
Elegant dessert for a heavy meal

1½ tsp plain gelatin	¾ cup strained lime juice,
1 tbsp cold water	6 to 8 limes
3 cups water	½ tsp grated lime rind, pkd
1½ cups sugar	7 or 8 drops of green food
⅛ tsp salt	coloring
	2 egg whites, stiffly beaten

Soften gelatin in the 1 tbsp of water for 5 min. Combine the 3 cups of water, sugar and salt in a saucepan and boil gently for 5 min. Remove from heat, add softened gelatin and stir until dissolved. Cool. Add lime juice, rind and coloring and pour into freezer can. Freeze to a soft mush according to directions. Then open freezer can and add the egg whites and continue to freeze until firm. About 2 qts.

ORANGE ICE

1½ tsp grated orange rind, pkd	¼ cup cold water
2 cups orange juice	1½ cups sugar
½ cup lemon juice	1 cup water
2 tsp plain gelatin	2 egg whites, stiffly beaten

Combine rind and juices and let stand 5 min. Then strain off juice and discard rind and pulp. Sprinkle gelatin into cold water and let soften 5 min. Add sugar to water, heat to boiling and boil syrup gently for 2 min. Remove from heat, add gelatin and stir to dissolve. Add fruit juices, cool mixture and freeze according to directions. Mixture may be turned into tray of refrigerator, in which case the beaten egg whites should be folded in when the ice freezes to a mushy consistency. 3 pts.

PINEAPPLE ICE

1 cup sugar	¼ cup lemon juice, 1 large
3 cups water	lemon
9-oz can crushed pineapple,	⅛ tsp salt
1 cup	2 egg whites

Combine sugar and water in a 2-qt saucepan and boil 5 min. Cool thoroughly. Add next 3 ingredients and mix well. Pour into refrigerator trays, and freeze at coldest temp to a mush. Beat egg whites until stiff. Turn ice from freezing tray quickly into a chilled bowl, add egg whites and beat hard and fast, then return to tray and freeze until firm. Or turn into freezer can and freeze according to directions. 5 servings.

BLACK RASPBERRY ICE
Another exquisite dessert

2 tsp plain gelatin
¾ cup cold water
¾ cup sugar
1⅔ cups concentrated black
raspberry juice, p 1080

¼ cup lemon juice
½ tsp grated lemon rind
Dash of Salt
2 egg whites

Sprinkle the gelatin over ¼ cup of the water and let soften 5 min. Combine remaining water with ½ cup of the sugar and heat to boiling. Remove from heat, add gelatin and stir until dissolved. Cool. Add fruit juices and lemon rind. Pour quickly into clean can of ice cream freezer and freeze according to directions to a stiff mush. Add salt to egg whites and beat until stiff. Add remaining ¼ cup sugar gradually and beat until thick and smooth. Add to mixture in freezer and continue according to directions. About 1½ qts.

THREE-FRUIT ICE

1¼ cups water
1 cup sugar
⅛ tsp salt
½ cup orange juice,
1 large orange

3 tbsp lemon juice, 1 lemon
2 well-ripened bananas,
mashed, about ¾ cup

Put half the water and the sugar and salt into a 1-qt saucepan and heat to boiling; remove from heat and add rest of water, fruit juices, and mashed bananas. Pour into freezing tray of refrigerator and freeze until thick and mushy. Then turn into a chilled bowl and beat quickly and thoroughly. Return immediately to chilled freezing tray and place in the refrigerator to finish freezing until firm. Or if desired, turn into freezer can and freeze according to directions. 5 servings.

CRANBERRY APPLE MILK SHERBET

½ lb cranberries, about 2 cups
1 cup water
1 cup thick, tart applesauce

1 cup sugar
¼ cup orange juice
⅔ cup whipping cream

Note: Ice cream freezing directions, p 592.

Wash and pick over cranberries, add water and cook in covered pan until soft; put through food mill or sieve, cooking water and all, discarding skins. Combine cranberry purée with applesauce, sugar and orange juice. Beat chilled cream until very stiff. Fold into cold fruit mixture thoroughly but lightly and turn into refrigerator tray or into hand-turned freezer and freeze according to directions. When freezing in hand freezer do not whip cream. 5 servings.

CREAMY LEMON SHERBET

2 tsp plain gelatin	⅔ cup strained lemon juice
2 tbsp cold water	¼ tsp grated lemon rind, pkd
1½ cups sugar	firmly
¼ tsp salt	1 cup whipping cream
2½ cups milk, scalded	

Soften gelatin in cold water for 5 min. Add sugar, salt and softened gelatin to hot milk and stir until dissolved; cool. Add lemon juice and rind and pour into a freezing tray of the refrigerator, and freeze to an icy mush. Stir and fold in stiffly beaten cream. Return to refrigerator and freeze until firm. 8 servings.

Note: If hand freezer is used, omit gelatin and cold water. Combine all ingredients but the lemon juice and freeze to a mush. Then add lemon juice and freeze until firm according to directions.

PINEAPPLE BUTTERMILK SHERBET

1 qt fresh buttermilk	1/16 tsp salt
9-oz can crushed pineapple,	1 cup sugar
1 cup	2 egg whites, stiffly beaten
1 tsp lemon juice	

Mix together thoroughly all ingredients except egg whites and pour into freezing tray of refrigerator. Set refrigerator at coldest temp and freeze mixture until mushy. Pour into chilled bowl and beat until smooth with rotary beater. Fold in stiffly beaten egg whites thoroughly and immediately return to chilled trays and continue freezing until firm. Return controls to normal freezing temp and allow to ripen until ready to serve. 8 to 10 servings.

MARLOWS

CHERRY MARLOW

½ lb marshmallows, about 32	⅛ tsp salt
No. 2 can sour red cherries	¼ tsp almond extract
or 2½ cups fresh pitted	1 cup whipping cream
cherries, sweetened	1 tbsp lemon juice

Put marshmallows and juice drained from cherries into top of double boiler and place over boiling water until marshmallows melt but are still fluffy. Remove from heat and stir in the finely chopped cherries. Add salt and almond extract; mix well, chill thoroughly. Then whip cream until thick; add lemon juice and continue whipping until stiff. Fold cherry mixture into whipped cream, pour into freezing tray of refrigerator and freeze at lowest temp until firm, stirring once or twice if cherries tend to sink to the bottom. 5 to 6 servings.

Note: If fresh cherries are used, add ¼ cup water to them and simmer in a covered pan until tender. Cool and drain before chopping.

PRUNE MARLOW

1 cup richly flavored prune juice, sweetened	¼ cup prune purée, p 553
16 marshmallows, ¼ lb	2 tbsp lemon juice
	1 cup whipping cream

Heat prune juice (use liquid in which dried prunes were cooked) to boiling. Remove from heat, add marshmallows and beat with rotary beater until they are melted and mixture is smooth. Beat in prune purée and lemon juice and turn into freezing tray of refrigerator; freeze about 1 hr, then remove to a chilled bowl and beat well. Fold in whipped cream. Return immediately to chilled tray and continue freezing until firm. Or turn into the can of a hand freezer and freeze until firm according to directions. 5 servings.

RHUBARB MARLOW

1 cup whipping cream*	¼ tsp salt
3 cups diced rhubarb	¼ lb marshmallows, 16
1 tbsp water	2 tbsp lemon juice
¾ cup sugar	Few drops red coloring

Chill cream thoroughly. Place rhubarb and water in saucepan, cover and cook over moderate heat. As soon as juice flows, add sugar and cook until rhubarb is tender but not mushy. Remove from heat. Add salt and marshmallows which have been cut into quarters with scissors dipped in hot water. Stir to distribute and let chill. Remove cream to a chilled bowl, add lemon juice and whip with rotary beater until very stiff. Fold coloring into the rhubarb mixture, then fold gently but thoroughly into the whipped cream. Turn immediately into chilled freezing tray. Freeze at coldest temp until firm—about 3 hrs. Then return temp to normal refrigerator temp and keep in freezing unit until ready to serve. 4 to 6 servings.

*Evaporated milk may be used in place of the cream.

MOUSSES

CARAMEL MOUSSE

½ cup sugar, caramelized	1 tbsp butter
½ cup boiling water	⅟₁₆ tsp salt
3 egg yolks	¾ cup whipping cream
¼ cup milk	½ tsp vanilla

Caramelize the sugar to a rich amber color, and carefully stir in the boiling water gradually. Increase the heat and continue stirring until caramel dissolves and syrup is slightly thickened. Beat yolks until thick and lemon-colored; stir in milk. Pour the slightly cooled syrup over yolk mixture, stirring constantly. Then return to the skillet and cook and stir 2 or 3 min over low direct heat until smooth and slightly thickened. Remove from heat, stir in butter and salt and cool. Now whip chilled cream until stiff. Fold the cooled custard mixture and vanilla gently but thoroughly into the cream. Turn into chilled freezing trays and place in refrigerator, turning control to coldest point. Freeze until firm; then return controls to normal freezing temp and let ripen until ready to serve. Or place mixture in freezer can, close tightly and surround with a mixture of 1 part salt to 4 parts cracked ice; let stand without turning until frozen hard, 2 or 3 hrs. Do not remove from freezer until ready to serve. 5 servings.

CHOCOLATE MOUSSE

1½ tsp gelatin	¾ cup sugar
2 tbsp cold water	¼ tsp salt
1 cup milk	1 tsp vanilla
1 to 1½ sqs unsweet chocolate	2 cups whipping cream

Sprinkle gelatin over cold water and let soften. Heat milk to scalding, add broken chocolate, cook and stir until chocolate melts. Remove from heat, stir in sugar, salt, vanilla and gelatin until gelatin and sugar dissolve. Strain and cool. Whip cream until stiff and fold it in lightly but thoroughly into chocolate mixture. Turn into freezing tray, place in freezing compartment and freeze at the lowest temp until firm. Then return to normal refrigerator temp and let ripen until ready to serve. 5 servings.

GOLDEN MOUSSE

1 cup whipping cream	¼ tsp grated lemon rind, pkd
¼ lb marshmallows	½ cup peach jam, commercial
¼ cup milk	¼ cup orange marmalade
2 tsp lemon juice	Dash of salt

Chill cream thoroughly. Put marshmallows and milk into top of double boiler; cover and place over hot water until marshmallows melt; remove from heat and cool. Beat cream in a cold bowl, add lemon juice and beat with a rotary beater until fluffy and stiff. Fold in the cooled marshmallow mixture and remaining ingredients lightly but thoroughly. Freeze in refrigerator tray until firm, 8 to 10 hrs, or overnight. 4 to 6 servings.

PINEAPPLE MOUSSE

1 cup whipping cream
2 tsp plain gelatin
3 tbsp cold water
1 cup pineapple juice

⅛ tsp salt
3 tbsp lemon juice
1¼ cups crushed pineapple

Chill cream thoroughly. Meanwhile soften gelatin in cold water for 5 min. Heat pineapple juice to simmering. Remove from heat, add gelatin and stir until gelatin dissolves. Add salt and cool. Then add lemon juice and pineapple. Chill until thick. Remove cream to a cold bowl and beat until stiff. Fold lightly but thoroughly into pineapple mixture. Turn into chilled refrigerator tray, set refrigerator at coldest temp and freeze for several hrs, or until firm. Return controls to normal refrigerator temp to ripen until ready to serve. Serve in chilled dishes. 8 to 12 servings.

STRAWBERRY MOUSSE

1⅔ cups whipping cream
2 tsp plain gelatin
2 tbsp cold water

1 qt well-ripened sound strawberries
¾ cup sugar
3 tbsp lemon juice

Chill cream thoroughly. Soften gelatin in cold water 5 min. Wash, hull, drain and crush or press strawberries through a coarse sieve or a food mill. There will be from 1½ to 2 cups purée. If berries are sour, ¼ cup more sugar will be required. Add sugar to purée and stir occasionally until it dissolves. Stand softened gelatin over hot water until it melts, add ½ cup strawberry mixture and stir thoroughly until blended, then return this to strawberry mixture and again stir very thoroughly. Whip cream until very stiff. Fold in lemon juice and strawberry mixture lightly but thoroughly. Turn at once into cold freezing trays and freeze at lowest temp until firm. Then return controls to normal refrigerator temp to ripen until ready to serve. 3 pints.

A good idea: Mousse mixtures poured into paper souffle cups save on freezing time and serving dishes.

MISCELLANEOUS DESSERTS

Certain foods that are served occasionally for dessert do not fit into the usual classification of desserts. Such desserts are Crêpes Suzette, Swedish Rosettes, Baked Alaska and Meringue Glacé. Many famous chefs have made their reputations on an unusual dessert specialty, and many homemakers can win the same praise by becoming proficient at one of the unusual recipes in this section.

BAKED ALASKA

A culinary marvel

Fresh sponge cake baked in
a sheet, p 320
1 qt brick of ice cream
firmly frozen

5 egg whites
Dash of salt
⅔ cup sugar

Start oven 10 min before baking; set to very hot (500° F). This dessert must be served the instant it comes out of the oven. Cut sponge cake 1 to 1½ inches thick in a rectangle that is 1 inch wider and 1 inch longer than the brick of ice cream. Place cake on a piece of aluminum foil wrapped around a small, thick wooden board. Beat egg whites and salt until stiff. Add sugar gradually and beat until mixture is thick, smooth, glossy and stands in firm peaks. Place very hard brick of ice cream on cake and quickly spread meringue to completely and thickly cover top and sides of ice cream and cake. Place in the hot oven and bake 3 to 4 min or until meringue is golden brown. Remove from oven, immediately loosen from board and slide onto serving dish. Slice and serve immediately while meringue is warm. 6 to 8 servings.

COTTAGE CHEESE AND HONEY

A delicious dessert consists of creamed cottage cheese served with cream and honey. Pour on the thin cream or top milk and drizzle honey over the top. Fresh strawberries or raspberries are a pleasing addition, and so is fresh pineapple. When fruit is added, combine honey with the cream, 1¼ cup honey to 1 cup cream.

CRÊPES SUZETTE

½ cup all-purpose flour
1 tsp sugar
¼ tsp salt
2 eggs, separated

⅞ cup milk
½ tbsp melted butter
xxxx sugar

Sift flour, measure and add sugar and salt and sift again into a 2-qt mixing bowl. Beat egg yolks, add milk and melted butter and beat well.

Add the flour and beat until very smooth. Fold in stiffly beaten egg whites. For each pancake, pour about ¼ cup of batter onto a moderately heated griddle (325° F) and bake until under side is lightly browned. Turn and bake until brown on other side. (See information on griddle temp, p 246.) Remove from pan, spread with 2 tbsp of the hot Orange Butter Sauce; roll, sprinkle with confectioners' sugar.

Orange Butter Sauce:

¾ cup butter	3 tbsp lemon juice
1½ cups xxxx sugar, pkd	⅓ cup orange marmalade
½ tsp grated orange rind, pkd	¾ cup orange sections, free
¼ tsp grated lemon rind, pkd	of membrane
⅓ cup orange juice	Brandy

Cream butter and confectioners' sugar. Add grated orange and lemon rind and juices and the marmalade. Mix well. Heat to boiling. Spread 2 tbsp of this mixture on each pancake. Roll, sprinkle with confectioners' sugar. If necessary to reheat, place in pan and set in hot oven (400° F) a few min to heat through. To serve, place on a heat resistant dish. Pour 2 tbsp brandy over each pancake, turn pancakes over so they are covered with brandy. Light brandy and spoon over pancakes as it burns. To the remaining orange butter sauce, add the ¾ cup orange sections cut into small pieces. Heat to boiling. When flame from brandy has burned out, pour orange sauce over pancakes. Serve with a tbsp of combined sauces. 8 to 9 crêpes.

MERINGUE GLACÉ

A dramatic classic dessert

Have meringue shells baked in small egg-shape, egg-size mounds. Put a large scoop of vanilla ice cream into a cold glass nappy, compote or dessert plate, then press 2 meringue shells firmly into ice cream on opposite sides. Spoon sweetened sliced strawberries or crushed red raspberries generously over ice cream. Top with whipped cream.

MERINGUE SHELLS

Soft or crisp

3 egg whites	¾ tsp cream of tartar
⅜ tsp salt	¾ cup sugar

Have egg whites warmed to room temp. Add salt and cream of tartar and beat until mixture forms rounding peaks. Beat in sugar in portions of 1 tbsp at a time and continue beating until sugar is dissolved and glossy pointed peaks form. Shape into mounds, cups or any desired form on ungreased heavy wrapping paper or other unglazed paper on a baking sheet. A pastry bag is useful in shaping meringues. Bake in a very slow oven (250° F) 30 min for soft shells; bake 1 hr for dry, faintly browned shells. At the end of baking period, turn off heat and allow meringues to remain in oven until they cool. Serve with ice cream, whipped cream, berries or other fruit. 5 servings.

SWEDISH ROSETTES OR PATTY SHELL CASES

Shortening, about 2 lbs
¾ cup of all-purpose flour
¾ tsp salt
2 tsp sugar

2 egg yolks
⅔ cup milk
1 tbsp salad oil
xxxx sugar

Put shortening into a deep-fat frying kettle and place over low heat. Sift flour, measure and resift 3 times with salt and sugar, the last time into a 2 qt mixing bowl. Add egg yolks to the milk and beat with a rotary egg beater. Stir in the salad oil. Combine dry ingredients with the liquid and beat to a smooth batter. Now heat shortening to 370° F. To fry rosettes: Heat the rosette iron first by immersing it in the hot fat. Then dip the hot iron to one-half its height in the batter, then dip it again in the hot fat. Cook for about 40 seconds or until rosette is a delicate brown. Lift out at once and remove rosette carefully from the iron with a fork. Reheat iron in the fat and repeat the process. Drain rosettes on absorbent paper and serve them sprinkled with xxxx sugar. If patty shells are to be made, omit the xxxx sugar.

COTTAGE CHEESE RENNET-CUSTARD

12-oz pkg creamed cottage
  cheese
2 cups milk*

1 pkg vanilla rennet powder
Strained honey

Divide cottage cheese among 5 sherbet glasses or custard cups. Heat milk until just lukewarm (110° F) in top of a double boiler. Immediately remove from heat and quickly stir in the rennet powder until entirely dissolved. Quickly pour over the cottage cheese in the sherbet glasses and let stand without moving at room temp for 10 min, or until firm. Chill in refrigerator. Before serving, add a spoonful of honey to each custard. 5 servings.

PEPPERMINT RENNET-CUSTARD

⅛ lb peppermint stick candy
2 cups milk*
1 rennet tablet

1 tbsp cold water
Chocolate Syrup, p 223

Crush candy into fine crumbs and add to milk; stir and let stand in refrigerator for 1 hr. Dissolve rennet tablet in cold water. Turn milk and candy mixture into top of double boiler, stir until candy is all dis-

*Do not use evaporated or soft curd milk in rennet-custard, as it will not thicken.

solved, then heat until lukewarm (110° F). Remove from heat and stir in dissolved rennet tablet. Pour immediately into sherbet glasses or custard cups. Let stand undisturbed for 10 min at room temp; then chill in refrigerator. Just before serving, garnish with a spoonful of thick Chocolate Syrup. 5 servings.

STRUDEL

A famous dessert that has memorable goodness

2¼ cups all-purpose flour	1½ cups sugar
½ tsp salt	2 tsp cinnamon
3 tbsp lard	½ tsp grated lemon rind, pkd
1 egg, unbeaten	2½ to 3 lb tart, juicy apples
⅔ cup warm water	¼ cup melted butter for
¾ to 1 cup raisins	brushing
2 cups fine, dry bread crumbs	1 cup finely chopped walnuts,
(no crusts)	if desired
½ cup butter	

This is an authentic old-time strudel recipe, and requires a technique for *stretching* the dough to obtain the thin tissue-like sheets. Many modern recipes indicate to *roll* the dough thin but this method does not produce the *very* thin almost transparent sheets that are necessary for the best strudel. Learning the proper manipulation will require a little practice if it has never been tried before, but the effort will be well rewarded by the enthusiastic reception this pastry will receive from those who remember it and those who have never tasted it before.

Sift the flour, measure and add salt. Add lard and cut in with a pastry blender or two knives until consistency of corn meal. Make a well in the center of the mixture and drop in the egg. Slowly add water, working mixture with the fingertips until all the water has been added. Continue to knead in the bowl about 5 min. Dough will be quite sticky. Turn out on a lightly floured board and continue to knead until a satin-smooth ball of dough is obtained. Place on a well floured spot on board, roll lightly to flatten top and form a flat disc. Brush with melted butter and let stand uncovered for 30 min.

Meanwhile prepare remaining ingredients by plumping raisins (p 165), preparing bread crumbs, and mixing with the ½ cup butter. Mix sugar, cinnamon and lemon rind thoroughly. Pare and grate apples into a bowl and cover. Melt butter for brushing. Prepare a table for stretching dough by placing a piece of clean sheeting over it, having at least 2 feet of cloth hanging over edge. A breakfast table is about the right size, and a round table is ideal.

Begin stretching dough by picking it up with finger tips, then laying it over the back of the two fists. Then by raising and lowering the fists alternately just enough to stretch the dough slightly in the center, and turning the dough at the same time to stretch it evenly, the patty of dough will be enlarged until it can no longer be held on the back of the fists. It is then placed in the middle of the cloth. Take hold of the edge of the dough and stretch gently walking around the table to stretch the dough evenly in all directions. Stretch until sheet of dough is paper-thin and about 56 inches in diameter. There will still be a heavy edge of dough all around the outside of the circle; this can be removed by pulling it off in the palm of the hand and rolling the strip of dough around the hand in one continuous length as it is pulled off. Let this ball of dough rest 30 min, first greasing top, and then it can be stretched like the first ball to make a smaller strudel. Let the thin stretched dough dry a few min, fanning to hasten drying, until it has texture of damp tissue paper. With a pastry brush sprinkle melted butter (3 tbsp) over entire surface, pick up 4 sides overhanging the table with the aid of the cloth, fold over one at a time onto top of table, making a 30 x 36 inch rectangle.

This rectangle of dough is ready to be spread with filling. Spread filling ingredients in following order in continuous strip 4 inches wide down entire length of dough about 2 inches from one edge. This leaves a large area of dough that can be wrapped around the filling several times to form the delicate layers characteristic of strudel. First, sprinkle ¾ cup bread crumbs, then add three-fourths of grated apples on top of crumbs. (Heap to about 1-inch thickness.) Sprinkle apples with heavy layer of sugar-cinnamon mixture, saving out about ¼ for second smaller strudel. Top with three-fourths of raisins and nuts, sprinkle again with ¾ cup bread crumbs. Using the cloth to help lift thin sheet of dough, fold the 2-inch strip of dough over filling to seal outer edge. Fold over two short ends to seal ends of roll. By pulling the cloth and roll of dough toward you, and lifting so the strudel will roll over, the sheet of dough can be rolled up completely, jellyroll fashion (except that all filling is in center). Cut in lengths to fit shallow, well-greased baking pans. Brush tops with melted butter, bake in hot oven (400° F) 20 to 25 min. Loosen from pans while still hot. Cool on cake rack. Sprinkle with powdered sugar, cut into serving portions. Treat small ball of dough in same way. Makes 5 rolls, 12 to 15" long and about 3" wide.

BAKED PUDDING

Baked puddings, delicious at any time, are particularly practical as desserts with oven meals, because most of them are baked in a moderate oven (350 or 375° F). It's easy to get them to turn out "just right" every time. Here are some very simple hints for success:

Baking dishes of glass bake the pudding faster than does either aluminum or tin. So if glass dishes are used when not specified in the recipe, the baking temp should be reduced 25 degrees.

Sauces always enhance a baked pudding, no matter how delicious it may be in itself. Plan to make the sauce ahead of time, or during the baking.

Serving temperatures are really important. Most puddings are at their most appealing stage when still warm—not chilled. Leftover pudding can usually be reheated without loss of quality if a sheet of aluminum foil is folded around it before placing in a moderate oven for about 10 min.

APPLE CHARLOTTE

A fancy, delicious dessert made from the simplest ingredients

1¼ lbs tart cooking apples,
    preferably Jonathans
1 tbsp water
⅓ cup sugar
¼ tsp cinnamon
¼ cup moist seedless raisins

6 to 8 slices day-old bread
⅔ cup melted butter *or*
    margarine
Apricot Glaze for Fruit
Cake, p 368

Use a plain round pudding mold about 6 inches high and 4 inches in diameter; a No. 3 tin can with its lid will serve for a mold. Start oven 10 min before baking; set to moderate (375° F).

Wash apples, pare thinly, quarter, core and cut quarters lengthwise into 3 slices if apples are medium size, 4 or 5 slices if large; drop into 3-qt saucepan. Add water and sugar and stir very gently. Cover pan, place over moderate heat, heat to boiling. Reduce heat and cook *very slowly* until slices are transparent at edges—4 to 6 min; shake pan occasionally to prevent sticking. Remove from heat and drain off 1 tbsp apple juice; add cinnamon to make paste. Add raisins and cinnamon to apples; stir gently to avoid breaking apples. Cool uncovered. Meanwhile trim crusts from bread and cut out 2 circles to fit bottom and top of mold snugly. Cut rest of bread into inch-wide strips lengthwise, fitting them vertically around sides of mold. Remove strips and dip both strips and rounds into melted butter, coating both sides but not permitting them to soak up butter. Fit coated circle into bottom and strips up sides of mold. Turn in apple mixture and pack rather firmly to the top. Top with remaining bread circle, pressing down firmly. Put on lid of mold, set mold in shallow pan and place on center rack of oven. Bake about 40 min. Remove from oven, take off lid, and immediately invert onto serving plate. Carefully lift off mold. Brush pudding carefully, while hot, with the fruit glaze. Cool to lukewarm and serve with whipped cream. 4 servings.

Note: The two circular pieces of bread may be cut into quarters before putting into mold, to make serving easier.

CARROT PUDDING

A real surprise in cottage puddings! Light, tender, delicate

½ cup finely shredded carrots,
  pkd
1¾ cups all-purpose flour
1½ tsp D.A. baking powder *or*
  2 tsp tartrate *or* phosphate
  type
½ tsp salt

¼ tsp baking soda
⅓ cup shortening
1 cup sugar
1 tsp lemon extract
1 egg
1 cup buttermilk

Have all ingredients at room temp. Grease a 9 x 9 x 2-inch pan with butter. Start oven 10 min before baking, setting to moderate (375° F).

Scrape, clean, wash carrots and grate on medium fine grater. Measure packed tightly in cup. Sift flour, measure and resift 3 times with next 3 ingredients. Cream shortening in a 3-qt mixing bowl, add sugar gradually, creaming well. Stir in lemon extract, add egg, and beat until smooth and fluffy. Add flour and buttermilk alternately in 3 or 4 portions, beginning and ending with flour and beating until smooth after each addition. Sprinkle in carrots and fold in just enough to distribute evenly. Turn into prepared pan, spreading a little higher at edge of pan than in center. Bake 30 to 35 min or until pudding tests done. Remove to cake rack, cool to lukewarm. Cut in serving portions, lift onto dessert plates and serve with Citrus or Nutmeg Pudding Sauce, pp 1241, 1247. 6 to 8 servings.

UPSIDE-DOWN FRESH CHERRY PUDDING

This dessert is a pleasing adventure in cherry goodness. It makes its own delicious sauce as it bakes

Sauce:
  1 qt sour red cherries *or*
    No. 2 can sour red pitted
  ¾ cup sugar
  ½ cup boiling water, omit if
    canned cherries are used
Batter:
  1½ cups all-purpose flour
  1½ tsp D.A. baking powder *or*

2 tsp tartrate *or* phosphate
  type
¼ tsp salt
½ cup soft butter *or*
  shortening
1 cup sugar
⅛ tsp almond extract
1 egg, beaten
1 cup milk

Have ingredients at room temp. Grease an 8 x 8 x 2-inch glass baking dish with soft butter. Adjust rack 5 to 6 inches above bottom of oven. Start oven 10 min before baking; set to moderate (350° F).

Sauce: Wash, drain, stem and pit cherries, p 573. There should be 3½ cups. Turn into a 1½-qt saucepan with the sugar and water. Heat to boiling, then reduce heat and *simmer* 3 to 4 min, stirring occasionally. Remove from heat, but keep hot.

Batter: Sift flour, measure, resift 3 times with baking powder and salt. Cream butter until smooth, add sugar gradually, creaming well. Stir in almond extract; beat in egg until smooth and fluffy. Add flour and milk in 3 or 4 portions, beginning and ending with flour and beating well after each addition. Turn into prepared pan, spreading level. Gently pour hot cherries and juice over batter. Bake 35 to 40 min, or until top springs back when lightly pressed with fingertips. Remove to cake rack; cool to lukewarm. Spoon warm pudding into dishes, and sauce over it. 7 to 8 servings.

UPSIDE-DOWN CHOCOLATE PUDDING

This luscious dessert separates into a rich chocolate cake topping with a creamy chocolate sauce underneath

Pudding:
½ to ⅔ cup broken nutmeats
1 sq unsweet chocolate
2 tbsp butter
1¼ cups cake *or* 1 cup all-purpose flour
2 tsp D.A. baking powder *or* 2½ tsp tartrate *or* phosphate type
¾ cup sugar
¼ tsp salt

½ cup milk
1 tsp vanilla

Topping:
¾ cup granulated sugar
¼ cup moist brown sugar, pkd
2 tbsp cocoa
1 cup cold water
Whipping cream *or* Half-and-Half

Have pudding ingredients at room temp. Grease an 8 x 8 x 2-inch baking dish or pan with butter or margarine. Start oven 10 min before baking, setting to moderate (350° F).

Pudding: Break pecans or English walnuts coarsely. Put chocolate and butter into shallow glass custard cup; set in pan of hot water. When melted, blend until smooth and remove cup from water to cool. Sift flour, measure and resift 3 times with next 3 ingredients, last time into a 2-qt mixing bowl. Stir in milk thoroughly; add vanilla, then chocolate mixture, beating until smooth. Stir in nuts until just distributed. Turn into prepared pan, spread smooth.

Topping: Quickly blend granulated and brown sugar with cocoa and sift evenly over batter; pour cold water gently all over the top. Bake 40 to 50 min. Remove to cake rack to cool to lukewarm. Spoon warm pudding into serving dishes, then sauce around pudding. Serve with whipped or plain cream. 6 to 8 servings.

Puddings are as delicious as pie or cake, but are easier to make.

COTTAGE PUDDING

Although an old-timer, this is always a most delicious dessert. It's ten times better warm than cold! Re-warm the cake by heating it for a few minutes in a hot oven in a paper sack

1¾ cups all-purpose flour
  2 tsp D.A. baking powder *or*
    2½ tsp tartrate *or* phos-
     phate type
¼ tsp salt
¼ tsp baking soda

⅓ cup soft butter *or*
  shortening
⅔ cup sugar
1 egg
1 tsp vanilla
1 cup buttermilk

Have all ingredients at room temp. Grease a 9 x 9 x 2-inch baking pan, or dish. Start oven 10 min before baking, setting to moderate (375° F), if using an aluminum pan; if a glass dish, set to 350° F.

Sift flour, measure and resift 3 times with next 3 ingredients. Cream butter in 2- or 3-qt mixing bowl until smooth; add sugar gradually, creaming well. Add egg and beat until smooth and fluffy. Stir in vanilla. Add flour and buttermilk alternately, in 3 or 4 portions, beginning and ending with flour and beating till smooth after each addition. Turn batter into prepared pan and spread level. Bake 25 to 30 min or until golden brown, not longer. Remove to cake rack to cool to lukewarm. Cut into serving portions and serve warm with lukewarm Citrus or Nutmeg Pudding Sauce, pp 1241, 1247. 6 to 8 servings.

DATE CAKE PUDDING

Easy to make and has wonderful flavor

1 cup dates, 6-oz pkg, pitted
3 tbsp shortening *or*
  butter
1 tsp soda
½ tsp salt
1¼ cups boiling water
¾ cup nuts, cut

1½ cups cake flour
1 cup brown sugar, pkd
1 egg
1 tsp vanilla
Whipping cream or Lemon
Whipped Cream Sauce,
p 1246

Butter a 9 x 9 x 2-inch baking pan. Start oven 10 min before baking; set to moderate (350° F).

Snip dates into 3 or 4 pieces with scissors. Put in a 1-qt bowl and add shortening, soda and salt, then the boiling water. Stir well; let cool 10 min, then add nuts. Meanwhile sift flour and measure. Measure sugar into a 2-qt mixing bowl, add egg and beat until light with rotary beater; clean off beater and remove. Stir in vanilla with a wooden spoon. Now add flour and date mixture alternately in 2 or 3 portions, beginning and ending with flour and beating until just smooth after each portion. Batter is thin. Turn into prepared pan. Bake 25 to 30 min, or until cake tests done when pricked with a toothpick. Serve warm plain, or cold with whipped cream. 8 servings.

DATE GRAHAM CRACKER TORTE

Simple—and simply luscious

1 cup graham cracker crumbs	4 egg whites, ½ cup
(10 to 11 crackers)	¼ tsp salt
½ cup dates cut small, pkd,	1 tsp vinegar
about 10 pitted	¾ cup sugar
¼ cup moist grated coconut	1 tsp butter
1 tsp D.A. baking powder	¾ cup whipping cream

Have all ingredients at room temp. Grease 9-inch glass pie plate with soft butter. Start oven 10 min before baking; set to moderate (350° F).

Lay crackers on sheet of waxed paper, fold paper over crackers and crush fine with rolling pin. Measure. Cut dates with kitchen scissors onto same sheet of waxed paper. Sprinkle about ⅓ of cracker crumbs over dates and toss until date pieces are separated. Add coconut; again toss to mix. Blend baking powder with rest of crumbs. Turn egg whites into 3-qt mixing bowl; sift salt over them and beat until foamy. Add vinegar and continue beating until stiff enough to stand in soft peaks. Add sugar in 3 or 4 portions, beating well after each addition. Clean off and remove beater. Add crumb mixture in 3 or 4 portions, cutting and folding in lightly with rubber scraper. Fold in date mixture. Turn into prepared pie plate; spread level. Bake 15 min; then reduce heat to moderately slow (325° F), and bake 15 min longer. Remove to cake rack to cool. Meanwhile whip cream. Cut in wedges and serve lukewarm with a puff of whipped cream. 5 to 6 servings.

DATE PUDDING WITH BRANDY CRÈME SAUCE

Rich and very palatable

½ lb pitted dates	½ tsp baking soda
½ cup boiling water	½ cup sugar
1 tbsp butter	1 egg, well beaten
¾ cup all-purpose flour	½ tsp vanilla
¼ tsp salt	⅓ cup pecans, chopped

Have all ingredients at room temp. Grease a 10 x 6½ x 2-inch glass baking dish with soft butter; set it in jelly roll pan. Start oven 10 min before baking; set to moderately slow (325° F).

Cut dates into 3 pieces each, dropping into 2-qt bowl. Add boiling water and butter, stir and let stand 10 min. Sift flour, measure and resift 3 times with salt and soda. Stir sugar into date mixture; then add egg, beating until fluffy. Add vanilla, then flour, mixing well. Stir in nuts until well distributed. Pour into prepared baking dish. Place in oven and pour

¼ inch of hot water into the jelly roll pan; this prevents pudding from becoming crusty on bottom. Bake 35 min. Remove to cake rack; cool a few min, then cut in squares. Serve lukewarm or cold with Brandy Crème Sauce, p 1238. 8 servings.

SAUCY DATE PUDDING

Pudding that makes its own good sauce as it bakes

1 tsp soft butter
¾ cup dates, cut small, 15 to
   16 pitted
¼ tsp grated lemon rind, pkd
¾ cup all-purpose flour
⅓ cup sugar
½ tsp salt
  2 tsp D.A. baking powder *or*
  2½ tsp tartrate *or* phosphate type

⅓ cup *plus* 1 tbsp milk
1½ cups boiling water
  1 tbsp butter
⅔ cup brown sugar, pkd
½ tsp vanilla
⅛ tsp salt

Have all ingredients at room temp. Grease a 6-cup casserole well with soft butter. Start oven 10 min before baking; set to moderate (350° F).

Cut dates and measure. Grate lemon rind. Sift flour, measure and resift 3 times with next 3 ingredients. Add dates and lemon rind; toss enough to distribute evenly. Add milk all at once and stir until well blended. Turn batter into prepared casserole. Combine boiling water with remaining ingredients and stir until sugar dissolves. Pour over batter in casserole. Bake 25 to 30 min. Remove to cake rack to cool slightly. Serve pudding lukewarm, spooning it into serving dishes and sauce over it. 5 to 6 servings.

INDIAN PUDDING

A famous New England dessert

4 cups milk
¾ tsp salt
¼ cup yellow cornmeal
  2 tbsp quick-cooking tapioca
⅔ cup brown sugar, pkd

½ tsp ginger
½ tsp cinnamon
2 tbsp butter
Ice Cream, Hard Sauce,
p 1245, *or* Thin Cream

Start oven 10 min before baking; set to slow (300° F).

Butter a 6-cup casserole. Measure 3 cups of the milk into top of double boiler; cover, place over boiling water and heat to scalding point. Now add salt, then cornmeal and tapioca gradually, stirring with wooden spoon and cooking until smooth and thickened. Add sugar blended with spices and the butter and beat to mix thoroughly. Turn into prepared casserole, pour remaining cup of cold milk over top and bake for 3 hrs, stirring occasionally. Remove to cake rack and serve lukewarm with a scoop of ice cream in center of each serving or with hard sauce or plain cream. 5 to 6 servings.

Note: One-half cup of light molasses may be used in place of the brown sugar.

ORANGE MERINGUE PUDDING

A very unusual dessert—delicate and flavorful

Pudding:
6 to 7 oz Angel Food Cake*
½ tsp grated lemon rind, pkd
1 tsp lemon juice
1 cup orange juice
¾ cup sugar
2 tbsp cornstarch
¼ tsp salt
½ cup water
2 egg yolks
Meringue:
2 egg whites
Dash of salt
¼ cup sugar

Note: If desired, fit half the cake slices into dish, then pour on half the sauce; top with remaining cake slices and rest of sauce.

Have ready a 4-cup casserole or small glass loaf pan. Start oven 10 min before baking; set to moderate (350° F).

Pudding: Cut the 6 to 7 ounces of cake into 12 slices 2¼-inch sq and ½-inch thick. Fit slices in casserole, overlapping neatly. Grate lemon rind, then squeeze lemon and orange juice and combine with rind. Blend sugar, cornstarch and salt in a 3-qt saucepan. Stir in juice mixture and water until smooth. Place over direct moderate heat and cook and stir until thick and clear. Remove from heat. Beat egg yolks, then stir cooked mixture into them thoroughly. Pour while warm over cake slices.

Meringue: Add salt to egg whites and beat until almost stiff, then add the ¼ cup sugar in 2 or 3 portions and beat to a stiff meringue. Pile lightly over cake mixture, swirling over top and touching edge of dish all around. Bake 12 to 15 min, or until nicely browned. Remove to cake rack to cool. Serve warm or cold. 5 to 6 servings.

FRESH PEACH PUDDING

A different, good dessert. Doubles for coffee cake and between-meal snack

1¼ lbs ripe freestone peaches,
6 egg-size, *or* 2 cups diced,
pkd
1 cup all-purpose flour
1 tsp D.A. baking powder *or*
1¼ tsp tartrate *or* phosphate type
½ tsp salt
½ cup soft butter *or*
margarine, 1 stick
½ cup sugar
⅛ tsp almond extract *or* ½
tsp vanilla
2 eggs
⅔ cup sugar
½ tsp cinnamon

*Half of a 10-oz commercial Angel Food Cake 7-inches in diameter and 2¼-inches high is the amount needed for this dessert.

Have ingredients at room temp. Grease an 8 x 8 x 2-inch baking pan
with soft butter. Start oven 10 min before baking; set to moderate
(350° F).

Pare peaches; cut into ¼-inch lengthwise slices, then *across* slices
to make ¼-inch dice; drop into 2-cup measure. Cover with wet paper
toweling to prevent discoloring. Sift flour, measure, and resift 3 times
with baking powder and salt. Cream butter or margarine, add sugar
gradually and cream until fluffy. Blend in flavoring. Beat in eggs one
at a time until fluffy, using rotary beater. Clean off and remove beater;
with wooden spoon, stir in flour in 2 or 3 portions, beating until smooth
after each. Spread half the batter in prepared pan; sprinkle with ⅓ cup
of the sugar and spread diced peaches evenly over batter; spoon on and
spread out remaining batter. Combine rest of sugar with cinnamon
and sprinkle over top. Bake 30 to 35 min or until pudding tests done.
Remove to cake rack to cool; serve warm with cream or Custard Sauce,
p 1243. 6 to 8 servings.

WILD PERSIMMON PUDDING

Surprisingly tasty, with a custardy consistency

2 qts wild persimmons	1 egg
2 cups milk	1 cup sugar
3 cups all-purpose flour	1 tsp vanilla
1 tsp salt	½ tsp lemon extract
½ tsp cloves, scant	¼ cup butter, melted
½ tsp nutmeg	1 tsp baking soda in
1 tsp cinnamon	1 tbsp hot water
1½ tsp D.A. baking powder *or*	
2 tsp tartrate *or* phosphate	
type	

Have ingredients at room temp. Grease 12 x 7½ x 2-inch baking
dish or pan. Start oven 10 min before baking, set to moderate (350° F)
for aluminum pan or to slow (325° F) if glass dish is used.

Use thoroughly ripe fruit, preferably picked after frost. Wash carefully and drain. Remove calyx or cap. Rub fruit through colander or
food mill to obtain all purée possible. There should be at least 3 cups
thick purée. Stir milk into purée. Sift flour, measure and resift 3 times
with next 5 ingredients. Beat egg, gradually add sugar and continue
beating with rotary beater until creamy. Stir in flavorings and beat in
butter thoroughly. Add persimmon mixture alternately with flour in
3 or 4 portions, beginning and ending with flour and beating well after
each. Add soda to hot water; stir quickly into pudding mixture and beat
until well blended. Turn at once into prepared pan. Bake 45 to 50
min, or until cake tester tests done. Serve warm or cold with whipped
cream or softened Hard Sauce, p 1245. 12 servings.

PINEAPPLE COTTAGE PUDDING

But be generous with the sauce—Yummy!

½ cup crushed pineapple,
  with its juice
1¾ cups all-purpose flour
2 tsp D.A. baking powder *or*
2½ tsp tartrate *or* phosphate type
¼ tsp baking soda
¼ tsp salt

⅓ cup soft butter *or*
  margarine
2 tsp lemon juice
¼ tsp grated lemon rind, pkd
⅔ cup sugar
1 egg
¾ cup buttermilk

Have ingredients at room temp. Grease a 9 x 9 x 2-inch baking pan. Start oven 10 min before baking, set to moderate (375° F).

Measure out pineapple. Sift flour, measure, resift 3 times with next 3 ingredients. Cream butter in 2- or 3-qt mixing bowl; stir in lemon juice and rind, then add sugar gradually, and cream well. Add egg and beat until smooth and fluffy. Add flour and buttermilk alternately in 2 or 3 portions, beginning and ending with flour and beating until smooth after each portion. Fold in pineapple and immediately turn into prepared pan, spreading out so batter is slightly higher around edges than in center. Bake 30 min. Remove to cake rack and serve lukewarm with Citrus Sauce, p 1241. 6 to 8 servings.

BAKED PRUNE PUDDING

This fine rich pudding is a delightful climax to any light meal

1 cup pitted cooked prunes
  cut in 3 or 4 pieces, pkd
¼ tsp grated lemon rind, pkd
¼ cup coarsely broken
  walnuts
½ cup cracker crumbs, 8
  2-inch sq
⅓ cup sugar

¾ tsp D.A. baking powder *or*
1 tsp tartrate *or* phosphate
  type
¼ tsp salt
½ cup milk, room temp
1 tsp vanilla
1 tbsp melted butter
Cream

Butter an 8½ x 4½ x 1¾-inch glass loaf pan or a 4-cup casserole. Start oven 10 min before baking; set to moderate (375° F).

Pit and cut prunes with a paring knife. Prepare lemon rind and nuts and add to prunes. Put crackers through food mill or roll fine; turn into a 2-qt mixing bowl. Stir in sugar, baking powder and salt, then stir in milk, vanilla and butter. Now fold in prune mixture thoroughly. Turn into prepared pan. Bake uncovered 35 min or until pudding has a thin brown crust over top and around sides. Serve warm with cream. 4 servings.

EVERYDAY RAISIN PUDDING

1 cup seedless raisins	2¼ cups all-purpose flour
½ tsp cloves	¼ tsp salt
1 tsp cinnamon	1 tsp D.A. baking powder or
½ cup butter or margarine	1¼ tsp tartrate or phos-
1 cup sugar	phate type
1 cup boiling water	1 tsp baking soda

Have all ingredients at room temp. Grease a 9 x 9 x 2-inch pan. Start oven 10 min before baking, set to moderate (350° F).

Wash raisins quickly in cold water, lifting with outstretched fingers into 3-qt saucepan. Add next 5 ingredients, place over moderate heat, stir thoroughly and heat to boiling. Reduce heat, cover pan and simmer 5 min or until raisins are just tender. Remove from heat; set pan in cold water to cool raisins to room temp. Meanwhile sift flour, measure and resift 3 times with remaining ingredients. Add to raisin mixture and beat until smooth. Turn into prepared pan and bake 35 to 40 min. Remove to cake rack to cool. Serve lukewarm with 1890 Pudding Sauce, p 1249. 6 to 8 servings.

RHUBARB STRAWBERRY MERINGUE

1½ lbs rhubarb	1 pt strawberries, washed
2 tbsp flour	and hulled
1¼ cups sugar	2 eggs, separated
2 tbsp water	

Trim off and discard leaves and root end of rhubarb; wash, drain and cut stems into ½-inch lengths. There should be about 3 cups cut. Turn into a saucepan with the flour and 1 cup of the sugar blended together, add water and simmer for 10 min, stirring frequently. Add strawberries. Remove from heat and *slowly* stir in the well-beaten egg yolks. Turn into an 8-inch sq casserole and bake in a moderate oven (350° F) for 10 min. Beat egg whites until stiff, gradually add remaining sugar and continue to beat until smooth and thick. Pile lightly over pudding; return to oven reduced to 300° F (slow) and bake 15 min longer or until meringue is delicately browned. If preferred, meringue may be applied to the cooled pudding with a pastry tube or in puffs dropped from a spoon, and baked. 6 to 8 servings.

MRS LAURA WALLING'S SWEET POTATO PUDDING

2½ lbs sweet potatoes or yams	2 eggs, unbeaten
⅔ cup sugar	¼ cup evaporated milk or
¾ tsp salt	cream
¼ cup *plus* 1 tbsp soft butter	½ tsp nutmeg

Butter a 9-inch heavy skillet. Start oven 10 min before baking; set to moderately hot (400° F). Use sound sweet potatoes free from blemishes. Pare thinly and dip into hot water to prevent discoloration. When potatoes are pared, lift out of hot water and quickly grate on a medium fine shredder into a 3-qt mixing bowl. Stir in sugar and salt immediately, then the butter and rest of ingredients. Beat thoroughly with a wooden spoon, then turn into prepared skillet. Bake 10 min, then reduce heat to moderate (350° F) and bake from 2 to 2½ hrs longer. Remove to cake rack to cool. Serve lukewarm plain or with cream. 7 to 8 servings.

BLANC-MANGE OR OLD-FASHIONED CORNSTARCH PUDDING

It is unfortunate that so many homemakers of today are too "busy" to make simple Blanc-Mange Puddings. These old-time cornstarch-milk combinations are superior in flavor and nutrition, and less expensive too, than the packaged commercial pudding mixes. A good Blanc-Mange is a fitting climax to the finest of meals. Follow any of the Blanc-Mange recipes in this book and treat your family to some of the old-time goodness. We warn you, though —they will never go back to the store variety.

CARAMEL BLANC-MANGE

The goodness of this dessert is unforgettable. Even when made the day before, it retains its soft, velvety texture

⅓ cup sugar	¼ tsp salt
½ cup hot water	½ cup cold milk
2 cups milk, scalded	½ tsp vanilla
¼ cup cornstarch	Cream
½ cup sugar	

Make caramel syrup by sifting ⅓ cup sugar into a 9-inch skillet, then heat with constant stirring until sugar melts to a rich amber liquid. Do not scorch. Cautiously add the hot water, then cook and stir over *low heat* until caramel dissolves. Remove from heat. Scald milk in top of double boiler over boiling water. Blend cornstarch with sugar and salt, then blend in cold milk until smooth. Stir cornstarch mixture into scalded milk, then stir in the caramel syrup. Now cook and stir until smooth and thickened, then cover and cook about 15 min with occasional stirring. Remove from heat. Stir in vanilla. Turn into individual dishes or serving bowl. Cool, then cover and chill. Serve plain or with cream. 5 servings.

CHOCOLATE BLANC-MANGE

Serve this economical delicate pudding without apologies. It is just stiff enough to barely hold shape when turned from individual molds, but creamy when spooned into

3 cups milk, scalded	¼ tsp salt
2 sqs unsweet chocolate	1 tsp vanilla
2 tbsp butter	1 tbsp firm butter
⅓ cup cornstarch	Cream
¾ cup sugar	

Scald milk. Put chocolate and butter into top of 2-qt double boiler and place over *simmering* water to melt. Blend next 3 ingredients and stir into chocolate with a wooden spoon. Then stir in hot milk gradually to keep smooth. Beat with rotary beater, if necessary. Cook and stir over gently boiling water until smooth and thickened, then cover and cook about 15 min, stirring occasionally. Remove from heat. Stir in vanilla, then the tbsp of butter. Turn into family-size dish or individual ones. Good lukewarm or cold. Cover with aluminum foil or waxed paper before chilling. Serve with plain or whipped cream, or flow a thin layer of cream over tops of individual servings. 5 to 6 servings.

Ways To Serve: For an especially delicious treat, pour while still warm into individual serving dishes. Place a generous scoop of vanilla ice cream in each serving, and serve at once. 6 to 8 servings.

SWEET CHOCOLATE BLANC-MANGE

Follow directions for Chocolate Blanc-Mange, but substitute ½ cup (3 oz) semi-sweet chocolate chips for the unsweetened chocolate, and reduce sugar to ⅓ cup plus 1 tbsp.

CINNAMON BLANC-MANGE

2½ cups milk	⅜ tsp salt
¼ cup cornstarch	1 tsp cinnamon
⅓ cup brown sugar, firmly pkd	1⁄16 tsp almond extract
	1 tbsp butter

Scald 2 cups of the milk in top of double boiler. Combine cornstarch, sugar, salt and cinnamon and mix until smooth with remaining cold milk. Stir carefully into the scalded milk and cook over boiling water, stirring occasionally, about 15 min or until thick and smooth. Add flavoring and butter, mixing well. Serve warm or cold with cream if desired. A spoonful of tart red jelly makes a colorful, tasty garnish. 5 servings.

ELEGANT CHOCOLATE CUSTARD PUDDING

Egg yolks make this pudding delicate, rich and smooth

3 sqs unsweet chocolate	5 egg yolks, beaten
1 cup sugar	1 tbsp firm butter
1 tbsp flour	½ tsp vanilla
¼ tsp salt	Cream, plain or whipped
2 cups milk, scalded	

Melt chocolate in top of double boiler over hot water. Blend sugar, flour and salt and stir into chocolate with wooden spoon. Gradually stir in hot milk, then *cook and stir* until mixture thickens. Beat yolks with rotary beater in a 2-qt bowl, then add chocolate mixture gradually, beating well. Quickly *strain* mixture back into double boiler. Place over boiling water and cook and stir 3 or 4 min, until just thickened. Remove from heat. Stir in butter until melted, then vanilla. Turn into serving dish or sherbets. Cool, then cover and chill. 5 servings.

Ways To Serve: 1. Serve plain, or flow a little cream over top of custard in sherbets for appealing contrast.

        2. Spoon a blob of whipped cream over pudding.

        3. Sprinkle with a few nuts. Pistachios are especially elegant.

        4. Drop a canned pear half cut-side down on top of custard in sherbet glass, or spoon over sliced bananas.

CHOCOLATE MARSHMALLOW PUDDING

This brown and white marbled dessert is rich and full of flavor

12 marshmallows, quartered	2½ cups milk, scalded
2½ sqs unsweet chocolate	1 egg, well beaten
½ cup sugar	½ tsp vanilla
¼ cup all-purpose flour	Cream—Nuts
¼ tsp salt	

Use scissors dipped in hot water to cut marshmallows, dropping them onto waxed paper. Melt chocolate in top of double boiler *over* boiling water. Blend sugar, flour and salt and stir into chocolate, then gradually stir in milk until smooth. Cook and stir until thickened, about 10 min. Stir a little of the chocolate mixture into egg, then return to double boiler. Beat with rotary beater; remove beater. Cook and stir with wooden spoon about 2 min. Remove from heat and stir in vanilla. Fold marshmallows lightly into hot mixture. Cover and let stand 5 min. Now gently fold mixture over 2 or 3 times, then turn into serving dish or sherbets. Serve warm or cold with cream and a few chopped nuts, if desired. 5 to 6 servings.

CORNSTARCH PUDDING

Blanc Mange

⅓ cup cornstarch	3½ cups milk
½ tsp salt	2 tbsp firm butter
¾ cup sugar	1 tsp vanilla

Blend cornstarch, salt and sugar in a bowl. Stir in 1 cup of the cold milk until smooth. Scald rest of milk, add the cornstarch mixture, and stir constantly over direct heat until it boils and thickens. Place over boiling water, cover and cook 10 min longer, stirring occasionally. Remove from heat, stir in butter and vanilla, and pour into large bowl or individual molds, such as custard cups to cool. Unmold if desired and serve plain or with any preferred sauce or with preserves or fresh fruit, such as crushed sugared strawberries or sliced bananas. 5 servings.

FRESH FRUIT CREAM PUDDING

Rhubarb or Cherry

Cream Pudding:

2 tbsp cornstarch	2 cups milk
½ cup sugar	3 eggs, beaten
⅛ tsp salt	

Blend cornstarch, sugar and salt in top of a double boiler. Add cold milk and stir until smooth. Cook over direct heat, stirring constantly until mixture boils and thickens. Slowly stir part of the hot mixture into the beaten eggs. Return to hot mixture in top of double boiler, then cook over boiling water for 2 min, stirring constantly to keep smooth. Remove from heat and cool. Prepare Rhubarb or Cherry Cream Pudding as described below to serve with this cooled cream pudding.

Rhubarb Cream Pudding:

1 lb rhubarb	½ cup sugar
1 tbsp water	1 tbsp cornstarch

Wash rhubarb, discard stem ends and leaves. Slice stalks in 1-inch lengths. Add water, cover and cook slowly until rhubarb is soft. Mix sugar and cornstarch thoroughly, and stir into the rhubarb; stir constantly over low heat until mixture boils and thickens. Chill. When ready to serve, stir rhubarb sauce into chilled cream pudding. 5 servings.

Cherry Cream Pudding:

Thaw 1 pt slightly sweetened frozen cherries in refrigerator. One pt of canned cherries may be substituted. Keep covered during thawing to prevent fruit from darkening. Drain off juice and stir 1 tsp of cornstarch into each ⅓ cup of juice. Cook over medium heat until thick and clear, stirring constantly. Add cherries and chill. When ready to serve, spoon cherry mixture into bottom of 5 individual serving dishes, then add the above cream pudding chilled to cover. Top with whipped cream if desired. 5 servings.

LEMON CREAM PUDDING

1 cup sugar	3 eggs, separated
⅛ tsp salt	½ cup lemon juice
¼ cup cornstarch	½ tsp grated lemon rind, pkd
1 cup cold water	Currant jelly
¾ cup milk	

Thoroughly blend sugar, salt and cornstarch in top of double boiler. Add cold water and milk and blend until smooth. Stir constantly over direct heat until mixture boils and becomes transparent-looking. Place over boiling water, cover, and cook 15 min. Separate eggs and beat the yolks; stir in lemon juice and rind. Stir a little of the hot mixture into the egg yolks, then return to the double boiler and cook 2 min longer, stirring constantly. Remove from heat. While still warm, fold in the egg whites which have been beaten until just stiff. Chill and serve in sherbet glasses with a currant jelly garnish. 5 to 6 servings.

Note: If jelly garnish is omitted, an additional 2 tbsp of sugar may be desirable.

MINCEMEAT PUDDING

⅛ tsp salt	2 eggs, separated
1 tbsp flour	¼ cup orange juice
2 tbsp cornstarch	1 tbsp butter
⅓ cup sugar	4 to 5 oz (½ pkg) mince-
1½ cups milk	meat made by directions

Blend salt, flour, cornstarch and half the sugar in top of double boiler. Add about ½ cup of the cold milk and stir until smooth. Add remaining milk and cook and stir over hot water until mixture is smooth and thickened. Beat egg whites until stiff, add dash of salt and remaining sugar. Continue to beat until very stiff. Pour a small amount of hot custard over beaten egg yolks and return to double boiler. Add orange juice, butter and prepared mincemeat. Then fold in half the beaten egg whites and spread the remainder over the top. Cover and cook over hot water for 3 min. Cool. This pudding is soft and should be spooned into sherbets to serve. 4 large servings.

ORANGE FLOAT

½ cup sugar	½ cup orange juice
¼ tsp salt	½ tsp grated orange rind, pkd
2 tbsp cornstarch	1 tbsp lemon juice
1 cup cold water	Orange sections
1 egg, separated	

Blend sugar, salt, and cornstarch thoroughly in saucepan; add water and stir until smooth. Cook over direct heat until mixture boils and thickens, stirring constantly. Stir part of hot mixture into beaten egg yolk; return to double boiler and cook over hot water for 3 min longer. Combine orange juice and rind with lemon juice and stir in gradually. Remove from heat. Beat egg white until stiff, then fold it into the hot mixture lightly and quickly until well mixed. Pour into serving dishes and garnish each with 3 or 4 orange sections. 5 servings.

FRESH BLUEBERRY REFRIGERATOR PUDDING

This dessert sounds commonplace, but it's intriguing and surprisingly good

1 pt fresh blueberries	1½ tbsp cold water
⅓ cup sugar	4 slices from 1-lb loaf fresh
¼ cup water	home-style firm white bread
2 tbsp lemon juice	2 tbsp soft butter
1½ tsp cornstarch	½ cup whipping cream

Cut a 9 x 9-inch sq of parchment paper and line the long sides and bottom of a 9 x 5 x 2½-inch glass loaf pan. Pick over berries, wash and drain. Put sugar and the ¼ cup water in a 1½-qt saucepan, stir and heat to boiling. Add berries, again heat to boiling, then *simmer* 3 or 4 min. Stir in lemon juice and the cornstarch blended with cold water. Cook and stir until smooth, clear and thickened. Remove from heat; cool to lukewarm.

Trim crusts from bread, then spread with butter. Cut each slice in quarters. Fit 2 slices bread snugly over bottom of prepared pan, butter-side up. Now spread with half the berries. Top with remaining bread and spread with remaining berries. Cover with waxed paper and store in refrigerator at least 2 or 3 hrs, or overnight. When ready to serve, lift from pan by paper to serving plate. Spread top and sides with whipped cream. Slice and serve on dessert plates. 4 to 5 servings.

Note: Buttered slices may be cut into 16 sqs each, then the bread and berries arranged in 4 large custard cups. Serve pudding in the cups with whipped cream on top.

RÖD GRÖD OR DANISH RED PUDDING

A colorful delicious dainty dessert—a little on the expensive side but if you grow your own berries, don't skip this!

1¼ cups stemmed washed red currants, p 573	¾ cup sugar
	⅛ tsp salt
1 cup washed red raspberries	2 or 3 tbsp cornstarch
⅔ cup and ¼ cup water	Whipping cream

Put currants, raspberries and ⅔-cup water into 3-qt saucepan. Cover, heat to boiling, reduce heat and simmer 8 to 10 min. Now turn into a fine-mesh sieve placed over a bowl; press juice and pulp through with back of a spoon, adding the ¼ cup water as pulp is pressed through. There should be 3 cups juice. Now blend sugar, salt and cornstarch in 3-qt saucepan. Stir in fruit juice until smooth, then cook and stir until thick and clear, 3 or 4 min. Remove from heat and cool slightly. Pour into molds or sherbet glasses, then chill. To serve, flow a thin layer of unwhipped or half-whipped cream over dessert. 4 servings.

Note: Double recipe for party or guest meals. When covered, it keeps several days in refrigerator. Dessert is not stiff enough to mold when smallest amount of cornstarch is used. Pour into sherbets and chill.

VANILLA PUDDING WITH CRISPY TOPPING

⅓ cup sugar
¼ tsp salt
3 tbsp cornstarch

2 cups milk
1 egg, separated
½ tsp vanilla

Blend sugar, salt and cornstarch thoroughly in the top of a double boiler. Add the milk gradually and blend well. Place over hot water and cook and stir until mixture is smooth and thick. Cover and cook for 15 min. Remove from heat and pour hot mixture over slightly beaten egg yolk; fold in vanilla and stiffly beaten egg white lightly but well. Pour into individual serving dishes or large bowl. This pudding may be eaten warm or cold. Just before serving, sprinkle with Crispy Topping.

Crispy Topping:
1 tbsp butter
1½ tbsp brown sugar
½ cup cornflakes

2 tbsp chopped nuts
Dash of salt

Melt butter and blend in brown sugar. Cook until thick and smooth, stirring constantly. Stir in cornflakes, nuts and salt. Cool. 5 servings.

STEAMED PUDDINGS

Steamed puddings may be quite solid and firm, like plum pudding; or they may be fluffy and cake-like in texture. To be sure that their texture is just right, and lacks sogginess, here are simple precautions:

Cover molds tightly. Molds with their own tight-fitting lids are ideal; but any type of tin can may be used if it is covered with parchment paper held firmly in place with a stout rubber band, and if the parchment is also covered with a square of aluminum foil snugly pressed down around the sides. The object of course is to exclude condensing steam. The inside of the lid or parchment cover should be greased to prevent sticking.

Allow room to rise. Never fill molds more than from ⅔ to ¾ full. Otherwise the rising batter might push the cover off.

Never cover mold with water. The molds should stand on a rack in the steamer, and only enough water should be used to cover about the bottom third of the molds. This amount of water—1 or 2 qts—produces plenty of steam, yet there is no danger of its bubbling up and getting inside the molds.

Keep it steaming. The water in the steamer should never stop boiling. If it gets too low, add more. As a rule it is permitted to boil vigorously for the first hr or so, then turned down and boiled gently the rest of the time. Don't try to keep the pudding warm by letting it stand in the hot water after boiling stops.

Serve puddings hot or re-heat before serving. Steamed puddings keep well if wrapped in waxed paper and stored in the refrigerator, so it's practical to make more than one at a time. They should always, however, be served hot for greatest appeal. Fortunately they re-heat very well if the wrapping is removed and the pudding placed in the steamer again for ½ to 1 hr, depending on size.

★   ★   ★   ★

CHOCOLATE PUDDING

Fluffy in texture, excellent in flavor

1½ sqs unsweet chocolate	3 eggs, separated
1 tbsp butter	¾ cup sugar
1¼ cups all-purpose flour	½ cup buttermilk
1 tsp D.A. baking powder *or*	1 tsp vanilla
1¼ tsp tartrate *or* phos-	¼ cup chopped pecans
phate type	Sterling *or* Hard Sauce,
½ tsp soda	pp 1249 *or* 1245
½ tsp salt	

Grease three 1-pt pudding molds with soft butter and dust with flour; tap against table to shake out excess. Have steamer ready. About 10 min before needed, add 1 to 2 qts water; place over low heat.

Put chocolate and butter into glass custard cup and set in simmering water to melt; remove from heat, stir well and cool. Sift flour, measure and re-sift 3 times with next 3 ingredients. Beat egg yolks with rotary beater until light and foamy; add sugar gradually and continue to beat until light colored and fluffy. Clean off and wash beater. Using wooden spoon, beat in the vanilla, then chocolate until well blended, then the flour and milk alternately in 2 or 3 portions, beating until well blended after each addition. Stir in nuts. Beat egg whites until stiff enough to hold pointed peaks, but still shiny. Fold into chocolate mixture lightly but thoroughly. Turn at once into prepared molds. Cover molds and steam 1½ hrs. Lift out and remove covers or lids; immediately turn upside down on parchment or waxed paper laid over cake racks. (Parchment covers may be re-used in this way.) Carefully lift off molds. Serve immediately with any desired sauce. 10 to 12 servings.

DATE-FIG PUDDING

Very good!

1 tbsp flour	1 tsp salt
1½ cups ground chilled suet, pkd lightly	1 tsp cinnamon
	¼ tsp ginger
1 lb moist light-colored dried Smyrna figs	¼ tsp allspice
	¼ tsp nutmeg
6-oz pkg moist pitted dates, chopped	½ cup sugar
	2 eggs
2½ cups all-purpose flour	½ cup honey
1 tsp soda	1 cup buttermilk
1 tsp D.A. baking powder *or* 1¼ tsp tartrate *or* phosphate type	1 tsp vanilla

Grease two 1-qt molds with soft butter and dust with flour; invert and tap against table to shake out excess. Have steamer ready. About 10 min before needed, add 1 to 2 qts water and place over low heat.

Remove all tough stringy membrane from suet and while *cold,* put through food chopper using fine blade. Prepare figs and dates. Sift flour, measure, and resift 4 times with next 8 ingredients, last time into 4-qt mixing bowl. Add fruit and use hands to toss and mix until pieces of fruit are coated and separate. Add suet and again mix with hands. Beat eggs until foamy; stir in honey, buttermilk and vanilla thoroughly, and gradually add to fruit mixture, stirring only until well blended. Turn batter into prepared molds; it should fill molds a trifle more than ⅔ full. Cover molds with lids or parchment paper tied down, and steam 3 hrs. Then lift puddings out, remove lids or covers, and immediately invert on parchment paper placed on cake racks. (Parchment covers may be re-used in this way.) Carefully lift off molds. Serve warm with Brandy or Hard Sauce (pp 1238 or 1245) which has stood at room temp until soft enough to spread over warm pudding. 3½ lbs or 15 to 20 servings.

FRUIT-NUT PUDDING

Purty good pudding!

2 tbsp fine dry breadcrumbs	1 cup golden raisins, plumped, p 165
1 cup ground chilled suet, lightly pkd	½ cup finely cut moist citron
2 cups all-purpose flour	½ cup slivered blanched almonds
1½ tsp soda	
¼ tsp allspice	½ cup fine dry breadcrumbs
½ tsp cinnamon	1¼ cups buttermilk
⅛ tsp cloves	2 eggs
1 tsp salt	¾ cup light brown sugar, pkd
	1 tbsp brandy extract

Grease two 1-qt pudding molds with soft butter; then dust with the 2 tbsp crumbs. Have steamer ready. About 10 min before needed, add 1 to 2 qts hot water and place over low heat.

Clean suet by peeling out all tough stringy membrane, and while *cold,* put through food chopper, using fine blade. Prepare raisins, citron and almonds. Put the ½ cup crumbs into mixing bowl, stir in buttermilk, and let stand 10 min to soften. Sift flour, measure and resift 3 times with next 5 ingredients. Add fruit and nuts to flour mixture and toss lightly to coat and separate pieces. Add suet and again toss lightly until well mixed. Beat eggs, stir in crumb and buttermilk mixture, sugar and extract, and gradually add to flour mixture, stirring just enough to blend. Pour into prepared molds. Cover molds with own lids or with sqs of greased, floured parchment paper fastened down with rubber bands. Steam 4 hrs. Remove to cake rack, remove covers or lids, and immediately invert onto racks which have been covered with parchment paper. (Parchment covers may be re-used in this way.) Serve immediately or let stand until thoroughly cooled, then wrap snugly in waxed paper and place in refrigerator. Before serving, steam at least 1 hr, unwrapped, until hot through. Serve warm with Hard, Foamy or any desired sauce, pp 1243 or 1245. 15 to 20 servings.

ELEANOR COSTELLO'S PLUM PUDDING

Excellent in flavor; tastes almost like mild-flavored, fruity fruit cake

1 cup ground chilled suet, lightly pkd	1 cup seedless raisins, washed and plumped, p 165
½ cup fine dry breadcrumbs	½ cup candied cherries, cut in 4ths
2½ cups all-purpose flour	
1 cup sugar	½ cup candied pineapple, cut same size as cherries
½ tsp salt	
2 tsp cinnamon	½ cup pitted dates, cut same size
¼ tsp cloves	
1 small tart apple, pared and diced fine	1 tsp baking soda
	1 cup buttermilk

Grease two 1-qt pudding molds with soft butter; sprinkle buttered surface with flour, shaking to distribute evenly; then invert and tap gently against table top to remove excess flour. Have steamer ready. About 10 min before needed, add 1 to 2 qts water; place over low heat.

Clean suet by peeling out all stringy, tough membrane; while still cold, put through food chopper, using fine blade; add some of breadcrumbs now and then to clean suet from chopper. Or put suet through Mouli shredder. Prepare all the fruit. Sift flour, measure and resift 3 or 4 times with next 4 ingredients, the last time into a 4-qt mixing bowl. Add fruit to flour mixture; use hands to lift through flour until every piece is coated and separated. Add crumbs, cold suet, and again mix lightly and well. Stir soda quickly into buttermilk and add gradually to mixture, stirring only until well blended. Dip batter lightly into prepared molds, filling about ⅔ full. Cover molds with own lids, or with buttered parchment paper fastened down with strong rubber bands and covered with aluminum foil fitted snugly around edges to keep any water out of pudding. Place molds in steamer and steam 4 hrs. Be sure water in steamer boils vigorously for first 2 hrs, or until puddings have risen fully; then reduce heat to steam at moderate rate for remaining time. Add boiling water to steamer as needed. When done, take puddings from steamer, remove covers or lids, and immediately turn upside down on parchment or waxed paper laid on cake racks. (Parchment covers may be re-used in this way.) Carefully lift off molds and serve immediately or let puddings stand until thoroughly cooled. Wrap snugly in waxed paper and store in refrigerator. To serve, reheat pudding by placing unwrapped on plate in steamer for 1 hr. Serve warm with desired sauce.

Note: Stiff, tart applesauce may be used in place of diced apple. Puddings will keep for months in refrigerator. They may be served like fruit cake if preferred.

RAISIN CRUMB PUDDING

An old-time moist, tasty, inexpensive pudding

1 tbsp fine dry breadcrumbs	1 tsp soda
1 cup seedless raisins, washed, plumped, p 165	⅛ tsp cloves
¾ cup fine dry breadcrumbs	¼ cup soft butter
1 cup buttermilk	½ cup moist brown sugar, pkd
⅓ cup all-purpose flour	2 tbsp light molasses
½ tsp cinnamon	1 egg, beaten

Grease a 4 to 5 cup mold well with soft butter, then dust with the 1 tbsp crumbs, shaking to distribute evenly. Have steamer ready. About 10 min before needed, add 1 to 2 qts water; place over low heat.

Prepare raisins, cool and dry off. Put the ¾ cup crumbs in mixing bowl, stir in buttermilk, and let stand 10 min to soften. Sift flour, measure and resift 3 times with next 3 ingredients. Stir in raisins. Cream butter and sugar thoroughly; beat in molasses until smooth and fluffy. Beat in egg well; stir in crumb mixture and flour-raisin mixture just until well blended. Pour batter into prepared mold; it should be about ¾ full. Cover mold with lids or sqs of greased, floured parchment paper, fastened securely with rubber band. Steam vigorously for 1 hr; reduce heat and steam at moderate rate for 2 hrs longer. Lift out onto cake rack; remove lid or cover, and immediately invert puddings on cake rack covered with parchment paper. (Parchment covers may be re-used in this way.) Carefully lift off molds. Serve warm; or cool thoroughly, wrap in waxed paper, and store in refrigerator until ready to serve. Then reheat by steaming. Serve with Brandy or Hard Sauce, pp 1238 or 1245. 6 to 8 servings.

RICE PUDDINGS

RICE PUDDING

¼ cup raw rice	¼ tsp salt
2 cups milk, scalded	1 tsp vanilla
2 eggs, separated	Cream
½ cup sugar	

Follow directions on box for preparing rice, p 433. Add to milk in top of double boiler, and cook covered over boiling water until rice is tender, about 50 min. Stir occasionally with a fork during first part of cooking to keep rice from sticking. Beat egg yolks thoroughly, add 3 tbsp of the sugar and the salt, and stir in some of the hot rice mixture; return to rest of hot rice and cook 2 min longer; stirring constantly. Remove from heat and cool slightly. Then stir in vanilla. Beat egg whites until stiff, and gradually beat in the remaining sugar until smooth. Fold into rice custard. Chill and serve with cream or top milk with a garnish of jam or jelly on each serving, if desired. 5 servings.

RICE PUDDING MERINGUE

3 cups milk, scalded	3 tbsp lemon juice
½ cup raw rice	2 eggs, separated
¾ tsp salt	Dash of salt for meringue
¾ cup sugar	Cinnamon
1 tsp grated lemon rind	

Combine milk, rice, salt, and ½ cup of the sugar in the top of a double boiler, cover and cook over boiling water for 50 min, or until rice is tender. Stir occasionally during the first part of the cooking. When rice is tender, add lemon rind and juice. Beat the egg whites until stiff, add salt and gradually add the ¼ cup of sugar and continue to beat until the mixture is very stiff. Beat the yolks slightly and pour a small amount of the hot rice over them. Mix and stir into rice in double boiler. Fold in ¼ of the beaten whites and spread the remainder over the custard. Sprinkle with cinnamon. Cover and cook over boiling water for 5 min, or until meringue is set. Serve warm or cooled. 4 large servings.

CHOCOLATE RICE PUDDING

2 cups milk	½ cup Chocolate Syrup, p 223
½ cup raw rice	2 eggs, separated
¾ tsp salt	1 tsp butter

Scald milk in top of double boiler, add rice and salt; cover and cook over hot water until rice is tender and all water is absorbed, about 50 min. Stir with a fork occasionally to separate rice kernels. When rice is tender, blend in the chocolate syrup; then pour part of hot mixture over slightly beaten egg yolks. Return to double boiler and cook for 3 min, stirring constantly. Remove from heat, add butter and fold in the stiffly beaten egg whites immediately. Serve warm or cold. 4 to 6 servings.

ELEANOR'S FLUFFY CREAMED RICE

This good pudding will be popular with family and guests

1 cup rice	3 egg yolks
4 cups cold water	½ cup sugar
1 tsp salt	1 tsp vanilla
2 cups milk	3 egg whites

Put rice into a sieve and run enough cold water through to rinse it. Turn rice into a 3-qt saucepan and add the cold water and salt. Place over high heat and heat to boiling, stirring frequently. Now reduce heat to boil *very gently. Cover* and cook 30 min, lifting up grains and stirring frequently with fork to prevent sticking. At this point the rice should have absorbed most of the water. Now add milk, stir carefully and continue cooking over medium heat about 10 min, stirring frequently. Then beat yolks, stir in sugar, then stir this slowly but gently into rice. Continue cooking for about 3 min, stirring constantly. Stir in vanilla and remove from heat. Stir so as not to break up rice grains. Now beat egg whites until just stiff and shiny. Quickly but gently fold rice mixture into whites, keeping mixture fluffy. (There is enough heat in rice to cook whites.) Serve warm or cold. 8 to 10 servings.

Note: If only half of dessert is desired, use half the recipe and only 2 small eggs.

GLORIFIED RICE

A substantial, tasty, fluffy textured dessert and attractive

2 cups cooked rice, p 433	½ cup whipping cream
16 marshmallows, ¼ lb	¼ cup sugar
9-oz can crushed pineapple, 1 cup	6 strawberries *or* maraschino cherries

Turn the warm drained rice into a 3-qt mixing bowl, spreading out to make as much surface as possible. Use kitchen scissors to cut the marshmallows into eighths, dropping them all over the rice. Use a fork to toss rice to keep marshmallows separated. Now whip cream until almost stiff, then add sugar in 2 or 3 portions and continue whipping until just stiff. Clean off beater and use rubber scraper to turn cream over rice mixture. Cut and fold cream into rice, then add the drained pineapple and fold in just enough to distribute. Cover bowl and place in refrigerator to chill. To serve, spoon into sherbets or nappies. Top with crushed sweetened berries or a maraschino cherry. 5 to 6 servings.

OLD-FASHIONED RICE PUDDING

This soft, creamy pudding never goes out of style

1 qt milk	¼ tsp grated lemon rind, pkd,
¼ cup raw rice	optional
⅛ tsp salt	1 tsp vanilla
¼ cup sugar	⅛ tsp grated nutmeg
	½ cup thin cream

Have ready a 6-cup casserole. Start oven 10 min before baking; set to 275° F (slow).

Put first 4 ingredients in top of double boiler, place over boiling water, cover and heat until milk scalds. Remove from heat, stir in lemon rind, vanilla and nutmeg. Turn into casserole; do not cover. Place on middle oven rack and bake 2½ to 3 hrs. Stir with fork 3 times during first hr, to keep rice from settling. After 1½ hrs, stir in half the cream; remainder at end of 2 hrs. Bake until rice is perfectly tender. Remove to cake rack, cool. Serve warm or cold. 4 servings.

For *Raisin Rice Pudding,* stir in ⅓ cup seedless raisins after the first hr of cooking.

TAPIOCA PUDDINGS

BAKED APPLE TAPIOCA PUDDING

Economical but popular, and good for everybody

¼ cup quick cooking tapioca	1¼ lbs tart juicy quick cooking
½ cup granulated sugar	apples, 3½ cups sliced
⅛ tsp salt	¼ cup light brown sugar, pkd
2 cups boiling water	1 tbsp butter

Butter well a 10¼ x 6¼ x 2-inch glass baking dish. Start oven 10 min before baking; set to hot (450° F).

Blend tapioca, sugar and salt in a 1½-qt saucepan. Stir in boiling water and place over moderate heat. Cook and stir with wooden spoon 5 to 6 min, or until clear and thick. Pare apples thinly, quarter, core and cut quarters into thin slices. Turn into buttered pan, spreading level. Sprinkle with brown sugar and dot with butter. Pour tapioca over apples, pressing apples down with spoon. Bake 25 min, pressing apples down 2 or 3 times during cooking. Remove to cake rack to cool. Serve warm with cream. 4 to 5 servings.

BUTTERSCOTCH TAPIOCA PUDDING

Prepare exactly like *Tapioca Pudding,* except substitute dark brown sugar, pkd, for the granulated.

TAPIOCA PUDDING

1 egg, separated	¼ tsp salt
3 cups milk	1 tsp vanilla
¼ cup quick-cooking tapioca	Cream
⅓ cup sugar	

Beat egg yolk in top of a double boiler. Stir in the next 4 ingredients thoroughly, place over boiling water and cook and stir for 10 min. Now remove from heat and stir in vanilla. Beat egg white until stiff but still shiny and turn it onto pudding and cut and fold it in lightly but thoroughly. Chill or serve lukewarm, plain or with cream. Strawberry or raspberry jam or preserves makes a pleasing edible garnish. 5 servings.

FRESH FRUIT TAPIOCA

1½ cups sliced *or* crushed fresh fruit	¼ cup quick-cooking tapioca
½ cup sugar *or* to suit taste	¼ tsp salt
Water	2 tbsp lemon juice, *or* to suit taste

Strawberries, sour red cherries, raspberries, or any fresh fruit may be used in this recipe. When fruit has been sliced or crushed, add desired amount of sugar and let stand ½ hr. Turn into a colander and drain off juice for 3 min, then measure, and add enough water to make 2 cups of liquid. Add the tapioca and salt to this liquid and heat to boiling over direct heat. Immediately remove from heat, add drained fruit and lemon juice. Chill, stirring occasionally as it cools. Serve plain or with cream. 5 servings.

TAPIOCA LIME FLUFF

¼ cup plus 1 tbsp quick-cooking tapioca	½ tsp salt
2½ cups water	2 egg yolks
¾ cup plus 2 tbsp sugar	¼ cup lime juice
2 tbsp butter	½ tsp grated lime rind, pkd
	2 egg whites

Measure first 5 ingredients into a 3-qt saucepan. Stir thoroughly, place over moderate direct heat. Cook and stir until mixture boils. Remove from heat, slowly stir in beaten yolks. Return to heat, cook and stir 2 min longer. Remove from heat, stir in lime juice and rind. Beat egg whites until stiff. Pour hot tapioca mixture slowly over them, beating well while pouring. Cool; then chill thoroughly before serving. 5 servings.

LOGANBERRY TAPIOCA

⅓ cup quick-cooking tapioca
½ cup sugar
¼ tsp salt
12-oz bottle loganberry juice

¾ cup water
4½ tsp lemon juice
Coffee cream

Mix tapioca, sugar, salt, loganberry juice and water; stir well and cook over direct heat, stirring constantly until it reaches a full rolling boil. Remove from heat and stir in lemon juice. Chill, stirring occasionally as it cools. It becomes much thicker when cold. Serve with cream. 5 servings.

Note: Any berry, cherry, currant or grape juice may be used in place of the loganberry juice.

ORANGE TAPIOCA

A true orange flavored dessert. Keeps perfectly in refrigerator for next day's meal

1½ cups boiling water
⅓ cup quick cooking tapioca
½ cup sugar
¼ tsp salt

1 tsp grated orange rind, pkd
1 cup freshly squeezed orange juice, about 3 medium
½ cup whipping cream

Measure water into top of double boiler. Blend tapioca, sugar and salt and gradually stir into water. Place over direct heat and cook and stir to a brisk boil. Now place *over briskly boiling water* and cook 6 to 7 min, stirring often. Remove from heat and cool about 5 min. Mixture will become clear and thicken as it cools. Meanwhile, wash and grate rind from 1 orange, then squeeze oranges; remove seeds with fork and measure juice. Stir rind into juice, then gradually stir mixture into tapioca. Chill thoroughly. Whip cream until stiff, then fold it gently into tapioca mixture. Turn into serving dish or pile lightly into sherbet glasses. Cover and store in refrigerator. Serve plain, or garnish with 2 or 3 wedges cut from round slices of orange dipped in xxxx sugar. 5 to 6 servings.

BAKED PEACH TAPIOCA PUDDING

A different and welcome dessert in peach season

¼ cup quick cooking tapioca
¾ cup sugar
¼ tsp salt
1½ cups boiling water

1¼ lb ripe juicy freestone peaches, 3 cups sliced
1 tbsp butter
⅛ tsp almond extract
Nutmeg, optional

Butter well a 10¼ x 6¼ x 2-inch glass baking pan. Start oven 10 min before baking; set to hot (450° F).

Blend tapioca, ½ cup of the sugar and salt in a 1½-qt saucepan, then stir in boiling water. Place over moderate heat and cook and stir until clear and thickened, about 8 min. Pare peaches thinly; cut from pits in 8 to 10 lengthwise thin slices. Turn into buttered pan, spreading level. Sprinkle with rest of sugar and dot with butter. Drip extract over peaches. (Sprinkle nutmeg over peaches if used.) Pour on tapioca, and with wooden spoon press peaches down. Bake 30 to 35 min, pressing peaches down 2 or 3 times during cooking. Top should be delicately mottled with brown. Remove to cake rack to cool slightly, but serve warm. Serve with cream. 4 to 5 servings.

Note: May be cooked in double boiler. Add peaches and remaining ingredients to tapioca after it cooks 8 min, then cover and cook over hot water until thickened and fruit is tender.

PINEAPPLE OR FRUITED TAPIOCA

A wholesome old-fashioned delicate dessert. Pineapple chunks add texture

2¼ cups scalded milk
¼ cup quick-cooking tapioca
2 medium-size eggs, separated
¼ tsp salt, scant

⅓ cup sugar
1 tsp vanilla
½ cup well drained pineapple in chunks *or* crushed

Scald milk in top of double boiler over hot water. Stir in tapioca and cook, stirring frequently until tapioca is transparent, 4 to 5 min. Beat egg yolks, then beat in salt and half the sugar; add a little hot tapioca to yolks, then quickly combine with hot mixture. Cook and stir a min or two until custard coats a spoon. Remove from heat. Stir in vanilla. Beat whites until stiff, then beat in remaining sugar until stiff but still shiny. Fold into tapioca lightly but thoroughly, cool 2 or 3 min, then fold in pineapple. Turn into bowl. Serve lukewarm or cold. Do not cover until cool, then cover and refrigerate 2 or 3 hrs, if desired. 5 to 6 servings.

ELABORATION OF COMMERCIAL ICE CREAM

No other food is such a boon to the busy, hospitable homemaker as high quality ice cream that is available at almost any corner drug store. It is a delicious nourishing food to serve anyone from baby to grandma. And it can be quickly converted into a dozen different roles with the help of some specially prepared sauces, flavorsome preserves or jam, nuts, fruit juices or carbonated beverages.

Ice cream can be safely stored in the freezing compartment of a mechanical refrigerator or in a home food freezer ready to use for a quick dessert or an afternoon or evening snack. And the children will soon give mother all the help she needs to prepare elaborate sundaes and parfaits, or refreshing coolers, sodas and shakes. Because these concoctions are so popular and so wholesome, recommendations for elaboration are included in this as well as in the Beverage Chapter.

BUTTERSCOTCH SAUCE

Vanilla ice cream or freshly made plain cake, topped with this sauce is really elegant

1½ cups light brown sugar, pkd	⅔ cup thin cream *or* evaporated milk
⅔ cup white corn syrup	rated milk
⅓ cup water	Dash of salt
¼ cup butter *or* margarine	½ tsp vanilla

Measure first 4 ingredients into a 1½-qt saucepan; stir well to blend. Place over moderate heat and with frequent stirring, cook to soft ball stage (236° F). Remove from heat and cool 10 to 15 min. Now stir in the cream gradually, then the salt and vanilla. Pour into a clean jar with tight fitting cover. Store in refrigerator. Serve warm or cold over ice cream or any appropriate pudding. To heat, stand jar in hot water long enough to become warm. 2 cups.

CARAMEL SAUCE FOR ICE CREAM OR DESSERTS

This sauce lifts many desserts into top rating—ice cream, canned pears, apple dumplings, etc.

1 cup sugar	Dash of salt
1½ cups 12% cream *or* coffee cream	½ tsp vanilla

Heat a heavy skillet just enough that when a little sugar is sifted in, it will melt in a few seconds to an almost clear syrup. If it melts into an amber color immediately, the skillet is too hot. When skillet is right temp, continue to sprinkle sugar in slowly and shake skillet vigorously, but leave it on burner to heat sugar uniformly. When a little more than half the sugar is in, begin to stir the caramel with a wooden spoon to caramelize it evenly. When all the sugar is melted and is *a very pale amber* color, draw the skillet from the heat and slowly add the cream. (If amber color becomes too pronounced, the sauce will taste scorched.) The caramel quickly hardens as cream is added, so return skillet to very low heat and stir caramel as it dissolves and the sauce thickens to a thin gravy consistency—from 8 to 10 min. Remove from heat. Stir in salt and flavoring. Cool a few min, then pour into a clean jar with tight fitting cover. Cover and cool, then store in refrigerator. Serve cold over ice cream. If too thick, thin with cream to desired consistency. 1½ cups.

CARAMEL SYRUP

Easy to make and it's grand to have on hand to add glamour and extra goodness to Baked or Boiled Custard or ice cream

⅔ cup sugar	⅓ cup sugar
1 cup water	

Place a heavy skillet, preferably a bright shiny one to readily see when caramel is right color, over moderate heat. When hot, sift in the ⅔ cup sugar slowly, stirring slowly but continuously with a wooden spoon until sugar liquefies and the syrup is a rich amber color. Do not heat to a dark amber or syrup will have a scorched flavor. Remove from heat immediately, lift up spoon and add water cautiously. Now return skillet to heat and cook with occasional stirring until all the hard caramel dissolves. Then add remaining sugar, stir to mix, and remove spoon. Now simmer slowly until syrup boils down to one cup. Pour into measuring cup. If there is more than one cup, boil down more, if there is less than 1 cup stir in boiling water to make just 1 cup. Pour into jar with tight fitting cover and keep in refrigerator. 1 cup.

CHOCOLATE SAUCE

One that plays any chocolate role well

1 tbsp butter	1 cup sugar
1 tbsp shortening	1 tbsp cornstarch
2 sqs unsweet chocolate	¼ tsp salt
¾ cup boiling water	1 tsp vanilla
2 tbsp white corn syrup	

Measure first 3 ingredients into top of double boiler. Place over hot water until chocolate melts. Slowly blend in boiling water and corn syrup. Place over direct heat, add next 3 ingredients blended well. Heat to boiling, reduce heat and boil gently 10 min, stirring occasionally. Remove from heat, stir in vanilla. Serve over cake, ice cream or in chocolate milk. May be kept several weeks if placed in tightly covered jar in refrigerator. 1½ cups sauce.

Note: If a thicker sauce is wanted, cook a min or two longer.

CHOCOLATE MARSHMALLOW SUNDAE*

Pour over each large serving of vanilla or New York ice cream 2 tsp marshmallow crème, then add 2 tsp chocolate syrup.

*Courtesy of National Dairy Council.

CHOCOLATE PEANUT BUTTER SAUCE

For ice cream sundaes

½ cup water
⅓ cup sugar
1 tbsp white corn syrup
⅛ tsp salt

1 sq unsweet chocolate
⅛ tsp vanilla
2 tbsp peanut butter

Put the first 4 ingredients into a 1 qt saucepan. Add chocolate cut into bits and place over moderate direct heat and boil slowly for 3 min, stirring to blend the chocolate evenly and thoroughly. Remove from heat, stir in vanilla and peanut butter to blend. Serve hot or cold over New York or vanilla ice cream. 1 cup.

CHOCOLATE PEPPERMINT SAUCE

For ice cream sundaes or puddings

⅓ cup milk
⅓ cup coffee cream
2 egg yolks
⅓ cup sugar

⅛ tsp salt
1 sq unsweet chocolate
⅓ cup crushed peppermint
  stick candy

Put milk, cream and yolks in top of double boiler. Beat with rotary beater until well blended. Add sugar, salt, and chocolate that has been grated or cut in pieces. Place over boiling water and cook and stir until chocolate is melted and mixture is thick, about 7 min. Add candy and stir well. Let cool. If the crunchy consistency of candy is desired, add candy to cold sauce just before serving. Serve over New York or vanilla ice cream. ¾ cup.

COFFEE SAUCE

For ice cream sundaes or puddings

¼ cup sugar
2 tsp cornstarch
¼ cup very strong, freshly
  brewed coffee

¼ cup milk
¼ cup coffee cream
Dash of salt
⅛ tsp vanilla

Blend sugar and cornstarch. Make the strong coffee by pouring ¾ cup of boiling water over ½ cup medium grind coffee. Heat just to boiling and let stand 1 min, then strain through several thicknesses of cheesecloth. Stir ¼ cup of the coffee, the milk and cream into the sugar mixture until smooth. Place over moderate heat and cook and stir about 3 min or until thick and smooth. Remove from heat, stir in salt and vanilla, and cool. Use while fresh over vanilla ice cream. ¾ cup.

Note: The strong coffee may be made from instant coffee.

FRESH FRUIT SUNDAE*

Raspberries, strawberries and fresh peaches make exceptionally good sundaes. Wash berries, drain and hull. Crush only slightly. For each cup add from ¼ to ⅓ cup sugar and stir to distribute. Pare peaches, slice away from pits, then chop medium fine and add to each cupful of fruit ⅓ cup sugar and stir. Add 2 or 3 tbsp of sweetened fruit over each large serving of vanilla or New York ice cream.

GUAVA SYRUP

For ice cream sundaes, waffles

2¾ lbs guavas, soft but not discolored
1½ cups boiling water

2½ cups sugar
1 tsp lime or lemon juice
⅛ tsp salt

Wash guavas thoroughly in cold water. Remove thin slice from stem and blossom ends; then slice thin into a bowl or saucepan. Use a heavy biscuit cutter to chop fruit very fine. Add boiling water, and use a wooden potato masher or wooden spoon to crush fruit well. Turn into jelly bag, and squeeze out all juice. (Use a massaging motion.) There should be 1 qt very thick juice. Turn into saucepan (5 to 6 qt). Stir in sugar, lime or lemon juice, and salt. Boil moderately fast or until thick and syrupy. Pour into hot sterile jars. Cover with hot paraffin. Seal. 4 half pints.

HONEY CHOCOLATE DOT SUNDAE*

Pour over each large serving of vanilla or New York ice cream 1 tbsp of chocolate dot sauce, made as follows: Heat honey by standing container in hot water until a little more than lukewarm. For each tbsp honey, add 2 tsp semi-sweet chocolate bits. Serve at once.

HONEY NUT SUNDAE*

Over each large serving of vanilla or New York ice cream, drizzle ½ tbsp honey, then sprinkle ½ tbsp chopped pecans or walnuts over the top.

LEMON SUNDAE*

For each large serving of vanilla or New York ice cream, blend 1 tbsp white corn syrup, $\frac{1}{16}$ tsp grated lemon rind, pkd, and ¼ tsp lemon juice and turn over ice cream. Sprinkle ½ tsp toasted coconut over the top.

*Courtesy of National Dairy Council.

LEMON-ORANGE SAUCE

½ cup sugar
1 tbsp cornstarch
¾ cup cold water
2 tbsp butter
3 tbsp lemon juice

½ tsp grated lemon rind
½ tsp grated orange rind, pkd
1 seedless orange, pared, diced
Dash of salt

Blend sugar and cornstarch in a 1 qt saucepan. Add water and stir to form a smooth paste. Place over moderate direct heat and cook and stir until mixture is clear, about 3 min. Remove from heat and stir in remaining ingredients. Cool. 1½ cups.

FRESH LIME SAUCE

For ice cream sundaes

¼ cup sugar
2 tsp cornstarch
¼ cup water
¼ cup fresh lime juice

⅛ tsp grated lime rind, pkd
2 drops green coloring
2 tbsp honey

Combine sugar and cornstarch. Then add water and lime juice and stir until smooth. Place over direct heat and heat until boiling, stirring constantly. Boil slowly for 1 min or until thick and transparent. Remove from heat, add rind, coloring and honey. Stir well and cool. Serve over New York or vanilla ice cream. About ⅔ cup.

CRISPY NUT TOPPING

For ice cream sundaes

2 tsp butter
½ cup chopped pecans
½ cup crushed crisp cereal

¼ cup brown sugar, firmly pkd
Maple syrup

Heat butter in skillet slowly until melted, then add nuts and brown lightly, tossing with a fork to prevent scorching. Remove from heat, add cereal and sugar and mix. Serve as topping for ice cream over which a serving of maple syrup, or any desired sauce has first been poured. Serve over vanilla or New York ice cream. 1 cup.

MARSHMALLOW NUT SUNDAE*

Cut ¼ cup pecans or almonds into slivers. Turn into a shallow 1 qt pan containing 1 tbsp butter. Heat slowly until nuts take on a toasted color. Remove from heat and add 2 tbsp brown sugar and a dash of salt.

*Courtesy of National Dairy Council.

Stir to blend. Pour over each large serving of vanilla or New York ice cream, 2 tsp marshmallow crème and over this sprinkle 1 tbsp of the toasted nuts.

SHORTCAKES

GRAPEFRUIT SHORTCAKE

Surprisingly attractive and delicious

Fruit:
- 2 medium size grapefruit
- 2 tbsp chopped maraschino cherries

- ¼ cup shortening
- ⅓ cup *plus* 1 tbsp milk
- 2 tbsp melted butter

Shortcake:
- 1¼ cups all-purpose flour
- 1½ tsp D.A. baking powder *or* 2 tsp tartrate *or* phosphate type
- ½ tsp salt

Sauce:
- ¼ cup butter
- 1½ tsp flour
- 1/16 tsp salt
- ¼ cup sugar
- ¾ cup grapefruit juice

Grease lightly a jelly roll pan 13½ x 9½-inches. Start oven 10 min before baking; set to hot (450° F).

Fruit: Pare and section grapefruit. Cut sections neatly into 4 pieces. There should be about 2¼ cups. Drain off juice. There should be ¾ cup; if not, add water to make ¾ cup. Cut cherries into 4ths.

Shortcake: Sift flour, measure, resift 4 times with baking powder and salt, the last time into a 2-qt mixing bowl. Cut shortening into flour with pastry blender until particles are pea size. Now add milk all at once and stir with a fork until well blended. Turn dough out on floured pastry cloth, knead a few times. Divide in half. Shape each quickly into flat rounds and roll out to about 7 inches in diameter. Lay one round onto prepared pan. Brush with melted butter, then lay other round of dough on top and brush with butter. Bake 15 to 17 min, or to a rich brown. Remove to cake rack. While shortcake bakes make sauce.

Sauce: Melt butter carefully in saucepan. Stir in flour until smooth, then stir in salt, sugar and grapefruit juice slowly. Cook and stir until thickened, from 3 to 4 min; remove from heat. Now break hot shortcake open, lay bottom part onto serving plate. Cover with half the grapefruit and half the hot sauce. Now replace top shortcake and add remaining fruit, sprinkle with the cherries, then drizzle rest of hot sauce over top. Serve warm. 5 servings.

Remember: Shape shortcake dough in as many interesting and practical ways as you can before baking for family style; shape in 2 rounds for twin shortcakes for impressive guest meals; in large biscuits for individual servings for party meals.

ORANGE SHORTCAKE
A year-round strong competitor of strawberry shortcake

Sauce:
6 seedless oranges, medium size
¾ cup sugar
2 tbsp cornstarch
¼ tsp salt
¾ cup water
⅓ cup butter
¾ cup orange juice and
½ tsp grated rind, pkd
1½ tbsp lemon juice

Shortcake:
2 cups all-purpose flour
3 tsp D.A. baking powder *or*
   3¾ tsp phosphate *or* tartrate type
½ tsp salt
1 tbsp sugar
½ cup shortening
⅞ cup milk—1 cup *less* 2 tbsp

Butter a 9-inch layer cake pan. Start oven 10 min before baking; set to moderately hot (425° F).

Sauce: Grate orange rind, wrap in waxed paper. Pare oranges, cutting off all white fiber. Section oranges, then squeeze out juice left in dividing membranes, there should be ¾ cup. Cut orange sections into thirds—there should be 1 qt. Blend sugar, cornstarch and salt in a 1 qt saucepan, stir in water, place over direct moderate heat and cook and stir until mixture is smooth, clear and thickened. Remove from heat and stir in butter, then orange juice. Add orange rind to lemon juice; let stand 2 min, then strain off juice into sauce. Stir well; fold in diced oranges. Cover, set on stove to keep warm.

Shortcake: Sift flour, measure, resift 3 times with next 3 ingredients, the last time into a 3-qt mixing bowl. Cut shortening in with pastry blender until particles are size of peas. Add milk all at once and stir well. Turn into prepared pan. Push dough higher around edge of pan than in center. Bake 25 min, or to a rich brown. Remove to cake rack to cool 2 or 3 min, then lift onto plate. Split into 2 even layers using a sawtooth knife. Lift off top layer and spoon warm orange sauce generously over lower layer, then add top layer, crust side down and spoon rest of sauce over top. Serve warm for the best eating. 7 servings.

RHUBARB SHORTCAKE

Make exactly like Orange Shortcake, except substitute for the Orange Sauce 3 cups of freshly cooked, sweetened pink rhubarb.

STRAWBERRY OR PEACH SHORTCAKE

2 cups all-purpose flour
3 tsp D.A. baking powder *or*
   3¾ tsp tartrate *or*
   phosphate type
½ tsp salt
½ cup shortening
1 cup milk *less* 2 tbsp
2 or 3 tbsp melted butter
1 tbsp sugar

Grease a 9-inch layer cake pan. Start oven 10 min before baking; set to hot (450° F).

Sift flour, measure, resift 3 times with baking powder and salt, the last time into a 3-qt mixing bowl. Cut in shortening with pastry blender or 2 knives until particles are size of rice. Add milk all at once and mix lightly and quickly with a fork. Turn into prepared pan, and with lightly floured hand, pat out to uniform thickness. Brush with butter and sprinkle with sugar. Bake 15 to 18 min, or until a rich crusty brown. Split while warm and drizzle melted butter over cut surfaces. Spoon sweetened berries or peaches generously over lower layer, then top with remaining layer, cut-side-up and spoon on more berries and juice. Serve immediately plain or with cream. 4 to 6 servings.

Variation: Or turn this dough out on a lightly floured board, knead quickly and lightly 8 to 10 times, pat or roll out to ½-inch thickness. Then cut with a 2½-inch cutter. Transfer half the rounds to a greased baking sheet, brush with melted butter, top with remaining rounds. Brush tops with melted butter and sprinkle with sugar. Bake as directed for shortcake. 6 individual shortcakes.

Note: A good way to split a warm big shortcake is to cut it apart with a white sewing thread, using a sawing motion. Shortcake may also be cut into individual serving portions before laying together with fruit. Leftover shortcake may be reheated successfully like biscuits, p 235.

SNOWS, SOUFFLÉS, WHIPS AND FOOL

APPLE SNOW

A delicate dessert, nice for small children or oldsters or anybody

4 medium-size tart apples	3 egg whites
¼ to ⅓ cup water *or* an	1 tbsp lemon juice
8½-oz can apple sauce	Custard Sauce, p 1243
¾ cup sugar	Red jelly, optional
¾ cup hot water	

Wash, pare, core and slice apples into a 2-qt saucepan; add water, cover and cook slowly until mushy, shaking pan frequently to prevent sticking. When done, remove from heat, beat until smooth. There should be 1 cup stiff sauce. Cover to keep hot. Measure sugar into sauce pan, add hot water, cover and place over high heat. After boiling 1 min, uncover and cook until syrup spins a thread from 6 to 8 inches long. Remove from heat, but keep hot. Quickly beat whites until they form shiny peaks, then immediately pour hot syrup in a thin stream over whites, beating constantly with rotary beater, but using it to beat as with a spoon until all syrup has dripped in. Now use both hands to beat whites until very stiff. Add apple sauce and lemon juice to syrup pan, return to heat to mix clinging syrup into sauce. Now add sauce gradually to the whites, and beat until very stiff. Cover lightly and place in refrigerator to chill. Serve spooned lightly into sherbets or nappies. Flow stream of sauce over snow, then top with a fleck of red jelly. 5 servings.

CHOCOLATE SOUFFLÉ

A delicate, rich, spongy textured dessert. Also nutritious and simple to make

¼ cup butter or margarine	¾ cup sugar
⅓ cup sifted all-purpose flour	4 eggs, separated
1½ cups milk	1 tsp vanilla
¼ tsp salt	Custard Sauce, p 1243 *or*
2 sq unsweet chocolate, 2 oz	Whipped cream

Have ready a 6 or 7-cup casserole, also a glass pan 12 x 7¼ x 2-inches in which to set casserole. Start oven 10 min before baking; set to moderately slow (325° F). Heat butter over direct medium heat in top of a 2-qt double boiler until just melted. Remove from heat, stir in flour until smooth, then add milk gradually stirring to keep smooth. Now place over boiling water, add the salt and chocolate cut in 6 to 8 pieces; then cook and stir until mixture is smooth and thick and chocolate is melted. Stir in half the sugar. Beat egg yolks well, then stir in a little of hot mixture; then add to double boiler and cook and stir 2 min longer. Remove from heat, add vanilla, then beat mixture thoroughly with rotary beater. Now wash beater and beat whites until barely stiff; then add the rest of sugar gradually and beat until whites form shiny pointed peaks. Now cut and fold the whites gently but thoroughly into the chocolate mixture. Turn mixture ever so gently into the ungreased casserole. Set casserole in glass baking dish, pour 3 or 4 cups of hot water around casserole and bake 65 to 70 min. Remove from oven, lift casserole from water onto cake rack to cool a little out of a draft. Have custard sauce made or cream whipped. Spoon the warm soufflé gently into serving dishes and flow stream of sauce over top or add a puff of whipped cream. Serve at once. 6 to 8 servings.

ORANGE MARMALADE SOUFFLÉ

An imposing dessert

Souffle:	Custard:
4 eggs, separated	1½ cups milk
½ cup stiff orange marmalade	⅛ tsp salt
	2 tbsp sugar
¼ tsp salt	1 tbsp flour
3 tbsp sugar	½ tsp vanilla
	½ cup blanched toasted almonds

Soufflé: Butter inside of top and lid of a double boiler. One with rounded bottom is preferable. Beat egg whites very stiff with wire whip. Fold in marmalade, salt and sugar very lightly but thoroughly. Turn into prepared double boiler. Cover and cook over *simmering* water about 80 min or until done. When a cake tester inserted in center comes out clean, the soufflé is done.

Custard: While Soufflé cooks, put milk, salt and sugar into a second double boiler and place over hot water to scald, stirring frequently. (If a second double boiler is not available, scald milk in a heavy saucepan directly over low heat, watching closely not to overheat.) Beat yolks well, add flour and beat until smooth. Now pour a little of the hot milk into yolks, stir well and return to double boiler, stirring vigorously. Cook over *simmering* water with constant stirring until custard just coats a spoon, see p 534. Remove from heat, cool slightly, then stir in vanilla. When Soufflé is done, turn it out onto a serving plate and pour Custard Sauce over it. Garnish with slivered salted almonds, if desired. Serve at once. 5 to 6 servings.

MERINGUE WITH COCOA CUSTARD

Arouses culinary interest and pleases palates

Cocoa Custard:
    ¼ cup cocoa
    ½ cup sugar
    ⅛ tsp salt
  1¾ cup milk
    3 egg yolks
    2 tbsp firm butter

1 tsp vanilla
Meringue:
    ⅓ cup sugar
    ⅓ cup boiling water
    3 egg whites
    ⅛ tsp salt

Custard: Blend first 3 ingredients in top of double boiler then gradually stir in milk to keep smooth. Place over boiling water and cook and stir until mixture thickens, about 10 min. Beat egg yolks well, slowly stir in some of the hot mixture, then stir back into mixture in double boiler and continue cooking and stirring 2 min longer. Then remove from heat, beat in butter until it melts, then stir in vanilla. Cover and cool to room temp, then chill.

Meringue: Put sugar and water into a 1-qt saucepan, stir well and place over medium heat. Cover and heat to boiling and boil 2 or 3 min, then uncover and cook without stirring until syrup spins a thread 6 to 8 inches long. Withdraw from heat, quickly beat egg whites with salt until just stiff, then pour hot syrup in a thin stream over whites, using the rotary beater first like a spoon to beat, then use both hands to beat the meringue hard until it is stiff, shiny and will hold sharp pointed peaks. Clean off beater, remove. Serve immediately by heaping meringue lightly into serving dishes. Flow a stream of the cocoa custard over meringue to partly cover and run down sides and around meringue.

Or easier still, the raw egg whites, sugar and water may be put into top of double boiler, then placed over gently boiling water and beaten with either a rotary or electric beater until meringue is stiff enough to hold sharp pointed peaks. This is just like making Seven-Minute Icing. Then remove and serve. 5 servings.

PEACH MERINGUES WITH ORANGE SAUCE

Furnishes ocular as well as palate satisfaction. A pleasing way with canned peaches

No. 2½ can cling peach
halves in heavy syrup

Sauce:
2½ tbsp cornstarch
¼ to ⅓ cup sugar
⅛ tsp salt
Juice drained from peach
halves
½ cup orange juice

2 egg yolks
3 tbsp lemon juice, 1 lemon
2 tbsp butter

Meringues:
Drained peach halves
1 egg white
¼ cup sugar
½ tsp vinegar

Sauce: Blend cornstarch, sugar and salt in a 2 to 3-qt saucepan. Stir in the juice drained from the peaches. There should be 1¼ cups juice—use no more. Then stir in orange juice. Place over medium heat and cook and stir until thickened and smooth, then simmer 2 or 3 min to thoroughly cook starch. Now remove from heat. Beat egg yolks well, stir in lemon juice, then some of the hot mixture. Now stir yolk mixture into mixture in saucepan and return to heat and cook and stir 2 or 3 min. Remove from heat, beat in butter. Cover and keep warm.

Meringues: Place peach halves in buttered shallow glass pan 10 x 6½ x 2 inches hollow side up. Beat egg white until stiff, then add sugar gradually beating until meringue forms shiny pointed peaks, now beat in vinegar. Spoon meringue neatly into hollows of peaches. Bake 12 to 15 min (350° F) or until peaches are hot through and meringue is brown. With spoon lift hot peach halves carefully into serving dishes and stream some of the sauce carefully over meringue. 7 to 8 servings.

BAKED APRICOT WHIP

Really is good

1 cup sweetened dried
apricot purée, p 551
⅛ tsp salt
1½ tsp lemon juice

¾ cup whipping cream,
chilled
2 egg whites, room temp
¼ cup sugar

Butter a six-cup glass casserole and have ready a 9″ glass pie pan. Start oven 10 min before baking; set to moderate (350° F).

Turn purée into a 2-qt mixing bowl. Stir in salt and lemon juice. Use rotary beater to whip cream until just stiff. Fold it lightly but thoroughly into apricots, using rubber scraper. Wash beater and beat egg whites until they just form peaks, then sift in sugar in 2 or 3 portions, beating until meringue is stiff and shiny. Scrape whites onto apricot mixture and cut and fold in lightly but until just well blended. Now turn lightly into prepared casserole. Set casserole in the glass pie pan, pour in 1 cup hot water around casserole or enough to come to within ¼ inch of top of pie pan and bake for 20 min, then reduce heat to slow (300° F) and bake 20 min longer. Remove from oven and serve immediately. This dessert may be chilled and served uncooked. 5 servings.

GOOSEBERRY FOOL

A favorite pioneer dessert with fluff and lively flavor

1 pt stemmed green *or* ripe gooseberries	1 tbsp butter
	⅛ tsp salt
¾ cup water	2 eggs, separated
½ cup sugar	¼ cup sugar

Stem berries, wash in cold water and drain. Put into enamelware or aluminum saucepan with water, cover pan, heat to boiling and boil gently until berries are soft—8 to 10 min. Put through colander or food mill making sure to push through all pulp. Return purée to saucepan, add sugar, butter and salt and stir to mix. Beat egg yolks well and stir into the purée. Beat egg whites to stiff foam, gradually add sugar and beat until stiff and shiny. Place purée over heat; stir constantly until mixture bubbles and thickens. Quickly pour hot berry mixture over whites; cut and fold in until thoroughly blended. Cover; chill in refrigerator. Serve in chilled sherbet glasses with a topping of whipped cream, a sliced strawberry or finely chopped nuts. 4 servings.

PEANUT BRITTLE WHIP

Crunchy, rich and tasty

1 cup whipping cream	16 lady fingers *or* crisp
½ tsp vanilla	sweet wafers
Dash of salt	Maraschino cherries
¼ cup crushed peanut brittle	

Whip chilled cream until barely stiff, then fold in flavoring, salt, and brittle. Stand lady fingers or wafers up around sides of sherbet glasses. Heap whipped mixture lightly into sherbets. Top with maraschino cherry, if desired. 4 servings.

BAKED PRUNE WHIP

Simple, but incredibly good

Whip:
1 cup prune purée, p 553
½ tsp grated lemon rind, pkd
½ cup chopped pecans *or*
    walnuts
⅛ tsp salt
  4 egg whites—½ cup, room
    temp

⅓ cup sugar
Sauce:
2 eggs yolks
3 tbsp sugar
Dash of salt
1 cup milk
1 tsp vanilla

Start oven 10 min before baking; set to moderate (350° F). Have a six-cup glass casserole ready.

Whip: Cook prunes, pit, put through food mill or rub through coarse sieve, or chop very fine. Grate lemon rind, chop nuts. Add salt to egg whites, beat just until stiff enough to hold peaks, then gradually add sugar and beat until shiny and meringue holds sharp pointed peaks. Clean off beater and use rubber scraper. Add prune purée mixed with lemon rind gradually and cut and fold in gently until just well distributed. Add nuts the last few cutting and folding motions. Turn very gently into casserole. Set casserole into a glass baking dish 12 x 7½ x 2-inches. Pour enough hot water around casserole to come up 1 inch deep. Place in oven on lower rack and bake 30 to 35 min. Remove to cake rack to cool slightly out of a draft.

Sauce: While Whip bakes make sauce. Scald milk in double boiler. Beat egg yolks with sugar and salt, stir in the milk thoroughly, then pour back into double boiler and cook and stir gently over boiling water until sauce just coats a metal spoon. Remove from heat immediately. Stir in vanilla. Cool. Sauce may be made before prune whip, if it is desired cool. 5 to 6 servings.

PINEAPPLE DATE WHIP

Rich, easy to make, and very good

½ cup moist pitted dates,
  chopped
1 tbsp lemon juice
9-oz can crushed pineapple,
  1 cup

⅔ cup whipping cream
1 tbsp sugar *or* to suit taste
$\frac{1}{16}$ tsp salt
4 marshmallows, optional

Cut dates into pieces size of peas. Pour lemon juice over them. Turn pineapple into a sieve to drain, saving juice to use in beverages or gelatin desserts. Pour cream into a 2-qt mixing bowl, whip until about stiff then add sugar and salt and whip until stiff. Now fold in the pineapple and dates until just well distributed, using a rubber scraper. Cut marshmallows into 8ths using scissors, dropping into a mixing bowl. Turn the pineapple date whip carefully over the marshmallows. Use marshmallows only if date whip is to stand in refrigerator to absorb any liquid which forms. If dessert is served immediately no marshmallows are needed. 5 servings.

PRUNE WHIP No. 1

Easy to make. Rich but delicate

¾ cup cut cooked prunes, pkd	1 cup whipping cream
¼ cup sugar	½ tsp vanilla
⅛ tsp salt	¼ cup broken pecans

Pit prunes and cut with small paring knife or scissors. Turn into mixing bowl. Stir in sugar and salt to blend well. Whip cream until just stiff, then gently fold prune mixture into it; then vanilla and nuts until barely distributed. Keep mixture fluffy. Pile lightly into sherbets or cover and chill until serving time. Serve within an hr or two after combining. 5 servings.

Note: 1 cup evaporated milk may be substituted for cream in Prune Whip, but add 2 to 3 tsp lemon juice to milk while whipping.

PRUNE OR APRICOT WHIP

Light, delicious dessert easy to make

1 cup pitted, stewed prunes, p 552, *or*	2 tbsp prune *or* apricot juice
	2 tsp lemon juice *and*
¾ cup stewed, dried apricots, p 551, chopped fine	⅛ tsp grated lemon rind, pkd
	¼ cup sugar
2 egg whites	¹⁄₁₆ tsp salt

Prepare fruit. Put egg whites, juices, sugar and salt into top of double boiler. Stir well. Place over gently boiling water and immediately start beating with a rotary or electric beater as in making Seven-Minute Icing and continue beating about 7 min with rotary beater or 4 min with electric, or until meringue holds stiff pointed peaks. Remove pan from boiling water. Lift out beater and clean off. Now use rubber scraper to fold in fruit as it is gradually added until just distributed. If apricots are used, omit lemon juice and use a few drops almond extract instead. Turn whip gently into a serving dish or heap lightly into sherbets and serve immediately or place in refrigerator to chill. 4 to 5 servings.

Note: For an uncooked Prune or Apricot Whip, the egg whites may be whipped until almost stiff and the sugar added gradually and beating continued until very shiny and stiff. Then the prunes and juices may be folded in carefully.

Eggs

Have you ever wondered why slices of hard-cooked egg in food photographs have their yolks in the exact center, and why the pictured yolks are radiantly yellow from rim to rim? And does this make you wonder why yolks in your hard-cooked eggs list heavily to one side, and why they have dark circles around them? You will find the answers to these and other questions in this chapter, as well as complete directions on how specialists in egg cookery cook eggs and egg dishes to make them attractive and delectable.

EGGS are one of the most important foods in cookery. No housewife could very well get along without using eggs as eggs, eggs in custards, omelets, soufflés, sauces, cakes, etc. They are very valuable nutritionally, because they make substantial contributions of good quality protein, iron, phosphorus, vitamins A and D and the B-Complex vitamins. It is no wonder that a good dietary plan recommends at least 3 or 4 eggs a week, and one a day if possible, whether one is reducing, gaining or just maintaining good health. Eggs also have flavor, color, leavening power and a dozen other characteristics which make them valuable to the cook as well as to the "eater."

EGGS—AVAILABLE IN SEVERAL GRADES

Eggs are graded on the basis of outside appearance, weight and interior quality. Interior quality is judged by candling. Candling consists of holding and turning the egg before a beam of light strong enough to observe the interior. Eggs may be graded according to federal, state or private standards. The federal standards use the letters AA, A, B for designation. Many fine graded eggs are sold under a brand or trademark name without a "letter" grade.

Graded eggs carry the grade, the size and in some cases the date of candling on the carton. Graded eggs are not always available in all markets.

The choice of quality should be determined by the use and the price. High quality eggs are ideal for cooking in the shell, poaching and frying. Grade B eggs may be economically used for other cooking.

EGG QUALITY IS EASILY DETERMINED

The position of the yolk, the condition of the thick and thin white and the size of the air cell determine interior quality. A high quality egg when broken out on a plate has a high curved yolk, well centered and banked in a thick white. There is a very little thin white. These are the characteristics of a fresh egg. As the egg loses quality, the air cell becomes larger due to moisture loss. There is less thick white. The yolk floats to the side or top of the egg. The lower quality egg when broken out on a plate has a flattened yolk and the white is watery and thin.

Biological abnormalities sometimes appear in eggs as blood spots—bright fatty or dark specks. They occur very infrequently. They may be lifted out of the egg before cooking. They do not alter the nutritive value or the cooking performance.

EGG CARE

Eggs should spend their entire lives under refrigeration—both in the store and in the home. This not only keeps them fresh for a longer time, but aids in keeping the yolks in the center, which is so important for hard-cooked eggs to be deviled or sliced for use as a garnish. In summertime especially, the dealer should be as careful of his eggs as he has to be of his butter, and the consumer has a right to demand that they be kept in his refrigerator, at 40 to 45° F, until purchased.

For many cooking purposes, however, it is a good plan to remove from the refrigerator the eggs that are to be used and let them warm up for half an hour. This helps prevent the shell from cracking when the eggs are put into hot water to cook. Egg whites at room temp produce more volume when beaten, than do chilled whites. But since eggs separate more easily when chilled, try separating them immediately on removal from the refrigerator; then allow the whites to warm up for 15 to 20 min before beating. Yolks may be used cold.

CARE OF LEFTOVER EGG YOLKS

Care, of course, should be used to obtain unbroken yolks when they are separated from the whites. To do the best job of separation, be sure eggs are fresh and cold. Slide yolks gently from the shell into a clean, sterile jar of the right size. Cover jar tightly and place in refrigerator. Yolks should never stand around at room temp, as they develop a "skin" on the top and this dried-out area cannot be beaten up smoothly with the remainder of the yolks. If you have no lid that fits the jar, lay a sq of dampened paper toweling over top of jar; then place another sq of waxed paper or aluminum foil over the top, and fasten it down tightly with a rubber band. Use yolks within 2 or 3 days for the best flavor.

USES FOR LEFTOVER EGG YOLKS

1. Make *French Custard,* p 532.
2. Add 1 or 2 yolks to *Parsley Sauce,* p 1234.
3. Make *Mousseline Sauce,* p 1258.
4. Make *Egg Wash* for brushing over rolls and Puff Pastry, p 935.
5. Add a few drops of yolk to *French Dressing* and shake to keep stable emulsion, p 661.
6. Make *Boiled Salad Dressing* No. 2, p 1198.
7. Make *Pie Filling* like Chocolate, p 960 and Lemon Meringue, p 952, and instead of meringue, spread with whipped cream, p 397.
8. Make *Egg Yolk Icing,* p 393.
9. Make *Eggnog No. 2* with only yolks, p 228.
10. Make *Gold Loaf Cake,* p 346.
11. Add an extra yolk or two to *Baked Custard Recipe,* p 526.
12. Put yolks into a small greased bowl, place over simmering water, cover and cook until yolks are firm. Cool. Mash yolks and season like yolks for *Deviled Eggs,* p 667, and use for sandwich spread. Or press yolks through a sieve and use as a *garnish* for green vegetables or fish dishes.
13. Add 1 or 2 yolks to a Six-egg *Scrambled Egg* Recipe, p 675.
14. Stir 1 or 2 well beaten yolks into *chicken* or *fish soup* to add fine color and more nutrients. Do not boil after adding.
15. *Blanquette* of *Veal,* p 876.
16. *Spritz Cookies,* p 478.
17. *Golden Cup Cakes,* p 357.
18. *Hollandaise Sauce,* p 1256.
19. *Custard Sauce,* p 1243.
20. *Allemande Sauce,* p 1250.
21. *Lobster Newburg,* p 721.
22. *Bitter-Sweet Chocolate Syrup,* p 223.

CARE OF LEFTOVER EGG WHITES

Where egg yolks are consumed regularly, the accumulation of egg whites becomes a problem. Eggs should be separated when very cold so the danger of getting a bit of yolk in the whites is prevented. Whites containing the least amount of yolk will never beat up to a full-volume stiff white meringue. Turn the cold whites into a clean, dry jar with a tight fitting lid and store in refrigerator. But do not hold more than a few days at most.

USES OF LEFTOVER EGG WHITES

1. Slip 1 or 2 whites into a 5- or 6-egg *omelet* or scrambled eggs.
2. Add an extra white to make handsomer *pie or pudding meringue.* Increase sugar.

3. An extra white in *baked custard* makes it firmer, more nutritious.

4. Steam or bake whites slowly until barely firm. Chop or rice. Add to *soup* mixtures, *white* or *cheese sauce* for fish, vegetables or chipped beef.

5. Meringue *Cookies*, p 470, and *Meringues*, p 1027.

6. *Angel Food* Cake, p 315.

7. One-half tsp added to each cup of *French Dressing* and shaken thoroughly helps much to hold dressing in an emulsion.

SHOULD EGG WHITES BE EATEN RAW?

For many years several physiological chemists have objected to *raw egg white in the diet* because their observations indicated that it was indigestible. And nutritionists also have observed a characteristic dermatitis in animals and humans when fed experimental diets containing *large* amounts of raw white. The dermatitis is due to a factor in egg white called avidin, which inactivates the vitamin biotin. But since the average diet contains adequate amounts of biotin, and since raw white appears in the average diet so irregularly and in such *small* amounts, no biotin deficiency should result.

In recent studies, nutritionists found the co-efficient of digestibility of raw white to be 80%, cooked white 86%, and a rate between these two for the *beaten* white. In view of these findings, our best known nutritionists now raise no objection to occasional foods containing average amounts of beaten raw egg white.

DRIED EGGS

Relatively few eggs were dried in this country until World War II presented its gigantic feeding problem. This concentrated form of egg helped supply the military forces as well as the peoples of the allied nations with the dietary benefits of eggs, and using a minimum of shipping and storage space. Dried eggs, however, have long been used commercially in candy, ice cream, bakery products and other foods. Now they are used extensively in all the Quick Mixes, such as Cake, Muffins, etc. They are especially important in all types of emergency feeding programs.

Dried whole eggs contain most of the nutritive value of the whole eggs, but 96 to 98 per cent of the water is removed, leaving a dry powder. This powder keeps fairly well in a cool, dry place in a covered container, but it should be refrigerated if possible.

Dried eggs must be reconstituted—mixed with water—before they are used. They are usually reconstituted before mixing with other ingredients in which case the reconstituted egg can be used just like the fresh. However, if a recipe calls for sifting dry ingredients together, the powdered eggs may be added to the dry ingredients, and the water for reconstitution purposes added to the other liquid. The powder will be reconstituted when the ingredients are mixed. To measure, sift the dried egg powder once, then pack firmly into measuring spoon or cup, and level off. For practical purposes, ¼ cup of powdered egg (1 oz) and ¼ cup of water equals 2 whole eggs. Add the powder to the water, cold or barely lukewarm, placed in a deep bowl, then blend to a smooth thick paste free from lumps with a rotary beater, wire whisk or spoon. Add remaining water and stir and blend slowly to avoid splashing.

Reconstitute dried yolks or dried whites in a similar way. One tbsp of dried white and two tbsp of water is equivalent to one fresh egg white. Reconstituted whites can be used for angel food cakes, meringues, candy and in other similar dishes. One and one-half tbsp of dried yolk and one tbsp of water is equivalent to one fresh yolk. Used in custards and general cooking. Because of the possible danger of salmonella poisoning, buy only the highest quality of dried egg yolk; cook thoroughly, preferably by baking.

HOW TO FREEZE EGGS

Eggs may be frozen whole or separated before freezing but should never be frozen in the shell. For greatest convenience in using, pack them in quantities to be used at one time.

Use only perfect, uncracked eggs for freezing (use cracked eggs immediately). Wash and dry eggs before breaking. Break each one separately.

Whole Eggs. After correct number have been broken (10 whole large eggs make 1 pint), beat with rotary beater just enough to mix thoroughly but not enough to whip in air. Add salt (1 tsp per 1 pint eggs) for eggs to use for scrambling or salad dressing or sugar (1 tbsp per pint eggs) for desserts or baking to prevent gumminess. Strain through sieve, pack in cartons.

Egg yolks. Measure yolks, add 1 tbsp sugar or ½ tsp salt for each cup of yolks, and mix with rotary beater as above.

Egg Whites. Fill carton with unbeaten egg whites. Add nothing.

Packaging. Use tight, moisture-vapor-proof package or container. For small amounts plastic cups may be used; when frozen, remove from cups, label, and store several in one large package. Freeze as rapidly as possible.

To use frozen eggs. Thaw amount to be used at one time. Do not refreeze after thawing. Thaw in refrigerator or under cold running water. Use as fresh eggs. Frozen eggs may be stored 6 months.

Equivalents: 2 tbsp thawed white = 1 egg white
1⅓ tbsp thawed yolks = 1 egg yolk
3 tbsp thawed whole egg = 1 whole egg

THE USES OF EGGS IN COOKERY

Eggs for Leavening. The ability of eggs to leaven or lighten batters, doughs and other mixtures is familiar to everyone and yet not entirely understood by anyone. When the egg is beaten, it forms a foam of tiny bubbles that have the ability to hold up under considerable handling. When these bubbles are incorporated into a mixture, and heat is applied, they expand and raise or lighten the product. When heat is applied gradually, the tiny walls of each bubble coagulate thus preventing the finished product from collapsing as it cools. Whole eggs can be whipped to increase their volume about 6 times, egg whites will increase in volume 7 to 8 times, and egg yolks about twice. Once eggs are whipped to their maximum volume, their power to expand is spent. Further whipping only reduces the volume.

Eggs as Interfering Substances. When a substance freezes, ice crystals form, and if a clear liquid is frozen without stirring, it forms a solid block. If the mixture is stirred as it is frozen (as in an ice cream freezer), the crystals are smaller and do not form a solid block, especially if there is some interfering substance to prevent small crystals from coming together. Beaten egg, especially the white, acts as such an interfering substance, and is used in frozen dishes to create a pleasing texture especially in those that are not stirred continually to incorporate air. Egg white and sometimes yolk have a similar effect in candy and in some kinds of frosting by interfering with the formation of large sugar crystals and helping to keep the candy creamy.

Eggs as Emulsifiers. Certain substances such as oil and water (or vinegar) will not mix together, and yet in the presence of other substances called emulsifiers, the tiny globules of fat will remain suspended in the water and will not easily separate out. The emulsifier seems to coat the fat globules and keeps them from combining with each other and separating from the mixture. Mayonnaise is an emulsion of oil and vinegar that is held together by egg yolk or whole egg as the emulsifying agent. Egg yolk is the most efficient emulsifying agent known, and one egg yolk can emulsify from 1 to 1½ cupfuls of oil or from 19 to 27 times its own weight. Eggs act in the same way in many other foods such as cakes which contain fats. Egg whites also have the ability to emulsify, but not to as great an extent as the yolk.

Eggs as Thickening Agents. Egg can be used to thicken gravies, soups, sauces, fillings, and custards. One egg when mixed and heated properly with 1 cup of milk forms a jelly-like baked custard, or a smooth thickened stirred custard. One whole egg, or two yolks have about equal ability to thicken 1 cup of milk and lightly beaten ones thicken better than those well beaten.

Eggs as a Binding Agent. In meat loaves and vegetable molds, as well as in cakes, etc., eggs are well mixed with the other ingredients. During cooking the eggs become firm and help bind mixtures together and hold their shape.

Eggs as Adhesive Agents. Beaten egg is slightly sticky so when croquettes, chops, chicken pieces are first dipped in egg, then in crumbs, the egg holds crumbs tightly and keeps them in place during cooking and serving.

Eggs as Decoration. Eggs, hard-cooked and sliced, quartered, halved, chopped or sieved, poached, whipped, or baked are used by clever cooks to not only beautify but to add to the nutritive value and texture of a numberless variety of salads, casseroles, appetizers, desserts, etc.

Eggs as Clarifying Agents. A slightly beaten egg can be added to soup or coffee to make it very clear. As the egg cooks and coagulates, it entangles the solid particles that make liquid cloudy, then they can be strained out.

Eggs as Eggs. A plain egg, cooked in the shell, poached, fried, scrambled or baked is still a favorite of everyone. Eggs are one of those staple foods that can be served in such endless variety that they never become monotonous even though they are served daily.

EGG COOKERY

There is one rule that should be followed in every type of egg cookery, and that is, eggs should be cooked at a *low to moderate temp* to assure appealing and uniformly tender eggs and egg dishes. *High temp and long cooking* make the egg white tough, less digestible and darkens the surface of the yolk. Whole eggs coagulate or cook to firmness when they reach 149° to 158° F, egg whites at 140° to 149° F and egg yolks at 149° to 158° F. All these temps are considerably below the boiling temp of water 212° F. A properly cooked egg is delicate and tender and one of the most easily digested of all foods. A *hard-cooked egg,* if cooked at a low temp for the right length of time is *no less digestible* than a soft-cooked egg.

Foods made with eggs as the principal ingredient as in custards and soufflés, when cooked at a high temp soon lose their eye and palate appeal because they soon droop and "weep," indicating that the protein coagulated too rapidly and too completely.

EGGS COOKED IN THE SHELL

Boiling: A "boiled" egg should not be boiled at all, but *simmered.* Simmering means cooking just below the boiling point. There are 2 types of "boiled" eggs correctly called (1) Soft-cooked and (2) Hard-cooked.

SOFT-COOKED EGGS

Cold Water Method: Always cook eggs in a glass or enamel pan; cooking eggs in an aluminum pan always turns it black. Place eggs (4 or less) in pan and cover them with cold or lukewarm water to come ½-inch above eggs. Bring rapidly just to boiling, then turn off heat, and if necessary set pan off burner to prevent further boiling. Cover and let stand 2 or 4 min, depending on individual preference. *Cool eggs promptly* in running cold water to prevent further cooking, and to make them easy to handle.

Boiling Water Method: Heat water in pan just to a rapid boil, using enough water to come ½-inch above eggs. Meanwhile warm very cold eggs (4 or less) slightly in warm water to avoid cracked shells. Transfer eggs to boiling water with a spoon, turn off heat, and if necessary set pan off burner to prevent further boiling. Cover and let stand 6 to 8 min. Cool as above.

Cooking More than 4 Eggs: Use either the Cold or Boiling Water method. Do not turn off but reduce heat to keep water below *simmering.* Hold 4 to 6 min. Cool as above.

HARD-COOKED EGGS

Cold Water Method: Always place eggs in a glass or enamelware pan, then add enough cold or lukewarm water to come ½-inch above eggs. Heat rapidly just to boiling. Then turn off heat, and if necessary set pan off burner to prevent further boiling. Cover and let stand 15 min. Cool promptly and thoroughly in cold water—this makes shells easier to remove and helps prevent dark surface on yolks.

Boiling Water Method: Heat water in pan just to a rapid boil, using enough water to come ½-inch above eggs. Meanwhile warm very cold eggs slightly in warm water to avoid cracked shells. Transfer eggs to boiling water with a spoon. Now reduce heat to keep water *below simmering.* Cover and hold at *simmering* 20 min. *Cool promptly* and thoroughly in cold water as above.

To Remove the Shell: It is very difficult to smoothly peel hard-cooked new laid eggs—those a few days old peel smoothly. To remove shells smoothly, put the cooked eggs immediately under cold water to chill. As eggs cool, tap egg gently against a hard surface, turning over and over from end to end to crack shell in numerous small pieces, then roll lightly between hands. Now hold under running water and start peeling at large-end of egg. The water helps ease off the shell.

Causes for Dark Surfaced Egg Yolks: There are 4 ways to prevent formation of dark surface on hard-cooked egg yolks: (1) Use only fresh eggs. (2) Cook at a low temp. (3) Do not overcook. (4) Be sure to chill the cooked eggs promptly and thoroughly, then crack shells immediately.

HARD-COOKED EGGS FOR GARNISHING OR STUFFING

How to cook eggs with yolks in the center

Very fresh eggs of the best quality will have the yolks in the center, and they will usually stay there during cooking. Eggs that are not entirely fresh and have a less firm white will need to be turned over and over during the first few min of cooking to keep yolks in center. Even with care, a very poor egg may not cook with the yolk in the exact center. Place eggs in cold water to cover well, and keep stirring gently so as to turn the eggs over and over until the water reaches the *simmering point.* Now reduce heat and continue to stir another min or two, then let cook at this *below simmering temp* for 15 to 20 min. As the eggs are turned *over and over* the first few min of cooking, the yolks shift back and forth and at the same time the whites coagulate from the outside toward the center, and the result is that yolks are held in the center of the eggs.

BAKED EGG DISHES

BAKED OR SHIRRED EGGS

Break the desired number of eggs into a shallow greased baking dish or pan, or into individual greased custard cups or casseroles. Dot with butter and sprinkle with salt and pepper. A tbsp of cream or milk may be poured over each yolk to prevent the yolk from shriveling during the baking and to cause the white to bake with a delicate custard-like texture. Bake in a moderate oven (325° F) uncovered from 12 to 20 min, or covered for 10 to 15 min, or until of the desired firmness. Serve at once, directly from the baking dish. Baked eggs will continue to cook in the hot dish after they are removed from the oven, so they should be served at once, or removed from oven when they are just slightly softer than desired.

BAKED EGGS IN TOMATO CUPS

5 medium-size tomatoes	5 eggs
½ tsp salt	5 slices bacon
2 tbsp butter	Parsley

Wash tomatoes, remove core at stem end, and scoop out enough of the pulp to provide space for the egg. Save pulp. Sprinkle salt inside of tomatoes. Divide butter and put a portion into each tomato. Place in shallow greased baking pan and bake in a moderately hot oven (400° F) for 7 to 8 min. Remove from oven and quickly break an egg into each tomato cup. Pour removed tomato pulp around tomatoes. Return to oven and cook eggs to desired consistency (5 to 10 min). Meanwhile pan-broil bacon until crisp. Arrange tomatoes on hot platter, garnish with bacon and parsley. 5 servings.

EGGS BAKED IN BACON RINGS

8 slices bacon	Salt and pepper to taste
2½ slices bread	Parsley
5 eggs	

Pan-broil bacon in a heavy skillet until half done, remove to a plate. Pour off all drippings except 1 teaspoonful. Cut bread in rounds with a biscuit cutter to fit into bottom of rings in a muffin pan and brown on both sides in drippings. Place in bottom of muffin rings. Line side of each ring with 1½ strips of bacon. Break an egg into each ring and season with salt and pepper. Pour ¼ tsp bacon drippings over the top of each egg. Bake in a moderately slow oven (325° F) for 20 min, covered or uncovered to the desired stage of doneness. Remove carefully with spatula to serve. Garnish with parsley. 5 servings.

EGGS IN POTATO NESTS

¼ cup scalded milk
2 tbsp butter
4 medium potatoes, cooked
  and mashed
Salt and pepper to taste

1 egg, beaten
4 tsp catchup
4 eggs
4 slices bacon

Add hot milk and butter to hot potatoes. Beat until light and fluffy. Add seasonings, the beaten egg and again beat hard. Spread lightly in a greased glass pie plate, about 8½ inches in diameter. Make 4 depressions in surface and put 1 tsp catchup in each. Break an egg into each depression. Lay strips of bacon over top, so each egg is covered and bake in moderately slow oven (325° F) until bacon is browned and eggs are cooked to preferred stage of doneness, about 20 to 25 min. 4 servings.

HARD-COOKED EGG DISHES

See Hard-Cooked Eggs, p 663

CREAMED EGGS

6 Hard-Cooked Eggs, p 663
2 cups medium White Sauce,
  p 1262

5 slices hot buttered toast
Paprika
Parsley *or* cress

Shell eggs and slice or cut lengthwise into halves, quarters or eighths. Quickly but carefully arrange eggs on hot buttered toast or toasted muffins. Pour a generous amount of piping hot white sauce over eggs. Add a dash of paprika and a garnish of crisp parsley or cress. Serve at once. 4 to 5 servings.

Variation: Eggs in Cheese Sauce. Arrange hard-cooked eggs on toast as described above. Pour Basic Cheese Sauce, p 444 or Welsh Rabbit, p 447 over eggs. Garnish with a slice of Pan-Broiled Tomato, p 1406. Serve immediately.

CREAMED EGGS AND ASPARAGUS ON TOAST

3 tbsp butter *or* bacon
  drippings
3 tbsp flour
1½ cups milk
1 tsp salt

5 hard-cooked eggs
1 lb cooked, fresh *or* frozen
  asparagus
5 slices buttered toast
Pimiento

Melt butter in top of double boiler over direct heat. Blend in flour and gradually add milk (liquid drained from asparagus may be substituted for part of the milk), stirring constantly until sauce boils and thickens. Add salt, eggs which have been shelled and cut into sixths or sliced, and the drained asparagus. Heat over boiling water before serving on buttered toast. Garnish with strips of pimiento. 5 servings.

CREAMED MUSHROOMS AND EGGS ON TOAST

¼ cup finely diced celery
2 tbsp butter
1 tbsp flour
1½ cups milk
10½ oz can mushroom soup

6 hard-cooked eggs, diced
½ tsp salt
Dash of pepper
1 tsp chopped parsley
4 slices buttered toast

Sauté celery in butter in a skillet until soft, about 5 min. Blend in flour. Add milk gradually and cook over low heat, stirring constantly until mixture boils and thickens and becomes smooth. Now add the mushroom soup and blend until smooth. Add to the celery mixture and heat to boiling, stirring constantly. Gently fold in the eggs and seasonings. Serve piping hot over hot crisp toast with a sprinkling of parsley. 4 servings.

CREAMED EGGS AND DEVILED HAM

3 tbsp butter
3 tbsp flour
½ tsp salt
1½ cups milk
4 Hard-cooked Eggs, p 663

¾ cup thin-sliced celery
4 slices toast
3 oz can deviled ham
1 tbsp chopped parsley

Make a cream sauce of the first 4 ingredients. Fold in 3 of the eggs which have been diced and the celery and let stand over low heat while spreading toast with deviled ham. Pour hot egg sauce over toast, then top with slices of remaining egg and the parsley. Serve immediately. 4 servings.

CURRIED EGGS

6 Hard-cooked Eggs, p 663
¼ tsp prepared mustard
⅛ tsp salt
½ tsp vinegar
2 tbsp mayonnaise
1 tsp chopped onion
2½ tbsp flour

¼ cup butter
1¼ cups milk
1 chicken flavored bouillon cube
¼ tsp curry powder
2 slices bread, cut in cubes
1 tbsp finely chopped onion

Start oven 10 min before baking; set to moderate (350° F).

Remove shells from eggs and cut in half lengthwise. Carefully remove yolks and mash with a fork or force through a sieve. Add mustard, salt, vinegar, mayonnaise and the 1 tsp of onion to the egg yolks. Mix well and heap lightly back into the egg white halves. Arrange the halves in the bottom of greased shallow baking dish. Make white sauce from flour, 2½ tbsp of the butter, and the milk. To the hot white sauce add the bouillon and curry. Pour over the egg halves and top with bread cubes that have been tossed with the remaining 1½ tbsp melted butter and the 1 tbsp onion. Bake 15 min, or until crumbs are toasty. Serve at once directly from casserole. 4 servings.

DEVILED EGGS NO. 1

6 hard-cooked eggs	¼ tsp sugar
¼ tsp salt	Dash of pepper
¾ tsp prepared mustard	2 to 3 drops of Worcester-
½ tsp vinegar	shire sauce, if desired
¼ tsp fresh onion juice	Paprika, parsley, chives *or*
1 tbsp mayonnaise	pimiento

Cut hard-cooked eggs in half lengthwise. Remove yolks carefully and force through coarse sieve. Add next eight ingredients and whip until smooth and fluffy. Heap spontaneously into egg whites. Do not pack or pat surface smooth. Sprinkle with paprika, chopped parsley, finely chopped chives, or a strip of pimiento. Serve immediately. Makes 12 halves.

DEVILED EGGS NO. 2

6 hard-cooked eggs	¼ cup cream
¼ tsp salt	1 tsp finely chopped chives
½ tsp dry mustard	¼ tsp sugar
2 tsp lemon juice	Dash of red pepper

Prepare as directed in Deviled Eggs No. 1, above. Makes 12 halves.

Note: For other deviled egg recipe, see p 204.

EGGS À LA GOLDENROD

6 hard-cooked eggs, p 663	5 slices toast, buttered if
2 cups medium white sauce	desired
	Parsley *or* cress

Have eggs cooked just in time to be ready for use. Then shell eggs and separate whites from yolks; chop the whites coarsely and add to the hot white sauce. Reheat until whites are hot, and pour over hot toast. Rub the egg yolks through a sieve onto the creamed whites. Garnish with parsley or cress, and serve immediately. 4 to 5 servings.

Variation. Put the hard-cooked egg whites through a ricer, combine with white sauce, and pour over toast arranged on a platter. Place a whole egg yolk in the center of each slice of toast and add a dash of paprika for color. Garnish platter with a sprig of parsley at each end.

EGGS À LA KING

1 cup sliced mushrooms	2 tsp chopped pimiento
3 tbsp butter	6 hard-cooked eggs cut in
¼ cup flour	wedges
2 cups milk	Bite size shredded wheat
2 tsp chopped green pepper	biscuits
1 tsp salt	Parsley

Sauté mushrooms in heated butter for 5 min. Push mushrooms aside and blend flour into butter until smooth. Add milk gradually, stirring constantly and continue to cook and stir until mixture is smooth and thickened. Add green pepper, salt, pimiento, and eggs, and heat thoroughly stirring very gently to prevent sticking. Stir carefully to avoid breaking egg wedges. Serve hot over hot crisped shredded wheat biscuits, which have been salted if desired. Garnish with freshly chopped parsley. 4 servings.

EGGS AND ASPARAGUS AU GRATIN

¼ cup butter
4 slices toasted white bread, cut in small cubes
2 tbsp flour
1½ cups milk
1 tbsp chopped parsley
¼ tsp celery salt

¾ tsp salt
½ cup grated American cheese, 2 oz
12-oz pkg frozen asparagus tips cooked or cooked, fresh asparagus
4 hard-cooked eggs

Melt butter in saucepan over low heat, remove 1 tbsp and toss with ½ the bread cubes. Add flour to remaining butter in saucepan and blend well. Add milk slowly, stirring constantly to make a smooth sauce. Cook until mixture boils and thickens. Add parsley, salts and cheese, stir to blend. Sprinkle the remaining half of toast cubes in greased oblong casserole (6-cup). Arrange alternate layers of asparagus and sliced eggs. Pour hot cheese sauce over layers, top with bread cubes which have been tossed in melted butter. Bake 15 min in moderate oven (375° F) until toasted on top. Serve at once. 4 servings.

EGG CUTLETS

¼ cup butter
½ cup flour
1 cup milk
1 egg, beaten
½ tsp salt
Dash of pepper

$\frac{1}{16}$ tsp curry powder
1½ tsp lemon juice
6 hard-cooked eggs, chopped
½ cup bread crumbs
3 tbsp shortening for frying

Melt butter in top of double boiler and blend in flour. Add milk gradually, stirring constantly until mixture thickens. Pour part of hot mixture onto beaten egg, stirring constantly. Pour back into double boiler, mix well and cook 2 min longer. Add rest of ingredients except bread crumbs and shortening. Blend well and chill thoroughly in refrigerator. Shape into cutlets and roll in bread crumbs. Chill again. Panfry in shortening until a golden brown on both sides. Serve with Tomato Sauce, p 1261, if desired. 8 small cutlets, or *this same mixture can be shaped into croquettes and fried in deep fat.*

Note: Directions for Hard-cooked Eggs on p 663.

EGGS IN MUSTARD SAUCE

3 tbsp butter
¼ cup flour
2 cups milk
1½ tsp sugar
1 tsp salt
1½ tsp dry mustard

¼ cup vinegar
6 hard-cooked eggs, peeled
  and sliced
Chinese noodles
Parsley

Make a white sauce of the butter, flour and milk, p 1262. Mix together sugar, salt, mustard and vinegar and add to the white sauce. Then fold in the eggs carefully. Heat thoroughly and serve over Chinese Noodles. Garnish with parsley. 4 servings.

EGGS TETRAZZINI

¼ cup finely chopped onion
¼ cup finely chopped celery
2 tbsp almonds, blanched
  and slivered
2 tbsp chopped green
  pepper
2 tbsp butter
1 cup cold water

2½ oz pkg dry mushroom
  soup mix
1 cup milk
4 hard-cooked eggs, diced
2 cups hot cooked Spaghetti,
  p 430
Chopped parsley

Sauté onion, celery, almonds and green pepper in the butter for 5 min. Meanwhile, gradually add the water to the soup mix in a saucepan. Stir until well blended and smooth; add milk and heat to boiling over medium heat, stirring constantly. Simmer for 5 min; stir occasionally. Add sautéed ingredients and the eggs. Heat thoroughly and pour over hot drained spaghetti. Garnish with parsley and serve immediately. 4 servings.

HARD-COOKED EGGS WITH WATERCRESS SAUCE

3 tbsp butter
3 tbsp flour
1 cup milk
½ tsp salt
1¼ tsp vinegar

$\frac{1}{16}$ to ⅛ tsp prepared mustard
½ cup finely shredded
  watercress
6 hard-cooked eggs
Toast points

Make a white sauce of the first 4 ingredients. Add vinegar, mustard, and watercress. Heat thoroughly, but do not boil. Shell and cut eggs in half as soon as cooked (do not cool). Arrange on toast and pour watercress sauce over them immediately. Serve at once. 4 servings.

Note: Directions for Hard-cooked Eggs on p 663.

HOT DEVILED EGGS

2 tbsp butter
2 tbsp flour
1 cup milk
½ tsp salt
2 tsp prepared mustard
Dash of red pepper

1 tsp grated onion
1 tbsp catchup
6 hard-cooked eggs
4 slices hot toast
1 tsp finely cut chives

Melt butter and blend in flour until smooth. Gradually add milk, stirring constantly and continue to cook until sauce boils and thickens. Add the seasonings, onion, and catchup. Slice the eggs and place on the slices of toast. Pour the hot sauce over eggs. Sprinkle with chives and serve hot. 4 servings.

HOT STUFFED EGGS SUPREME

2 tsp finely chopped onion
1½ cups chopped fresh mushrooms
3 tbsp butter
8 hard-cooked eggs
2 tbsp mayonnaise
Dash of salt

1½ tsp prepared mustard
⅟₁₆ tsp salt
Generous dash of pepper
1½ cups sour cream
Paprika
Chopped parsley

Sauté onion and mushrooms in butter for 10 min. Remove from heat, cool. Peel eggs, cut in half lengthwise. Carefully remove yolks and add them with the mayonnaise and salt to the mushroom mixture. Mix thoroughly and refill into hollows of egg whites. Press halves together and carefully place in a small baking dish (3-cups). Blend mustard, salt and pepper with sour cream and pour over eggs. Set dish in a pan of hot water and bake in a moderate oven (350° F) for 15 to 20 min until eggs are heated thoroughly and tops are temptingly browned. Add paprika and parsley and serve immediately. 4 servings.

LOBSTER STUFFED EGGS IN TOMATO SAUCE

4 hard-cooked eggs
2 tbsp mayonnaise
1 tbsp milk
½ tsp salt
1 tsp lemon juice

1 cup Fresh Cooked *or*
canned lobster meat
chopped, see p 720
2 slices bread, quartered and
toasted
¼ cup sharp grated cheese

Remove shells from eggs and cut in half lengthwise. Carefully remove yolks and press through a sieve. Add mayonnaise, milk, salt and lemon juice to sieved yolks and blend thoroughly. Add lobster meat. Lightly heap lobster mixture back into egg whites and place on slices of toast arranged in a single layer in a glass baking dish. Pour Tomato

Sauce (below) over all. Sprinkle with cheese and bake in a moderate oven (375° F) for 15 to 20 min. Serve immediately. 4 servings.

Tomato Sauce:

½ tsp green pepper	⅛ tsp onion juice
1 tbsp finely chopped celery	10½ oz can tomato soup
2 tbsp butter	½ tsp salt
	½ tsp sugar

Sauté green pepper and celery in butter until soft, about 5 min. Add remaining ingredients and stir to blend well. Heat to boiling.

SPANISH EGGS ON TOAST

4 Deviled Eggs, p 667	2 tbsp sharp grated
4 slices of hot toast	cheese
Tomato Sauce (above)	Parsley

Prepare deviled eggs as directed in recipes No. 1 or No. 2, p 667 and p 204. Lay slices of toast on bottom of 4-cup greased casserole, or cut slices to fit bottom of 4 individual baking casseroles. Arrange eggs on top of toast. Pour hot Tomato Sauce as prepared in Lobster Stuffed Eggs, p 670 around eggs. Sprinkle with grated cheese. Bake in moderate oven (375° F) 15 min, or until cheese melts and is slightly toasted. Garnish with extra toast triangles and parsley and serve at once. 4 servings.

FRIED EGG DISHES

Method 1: Frying eggs means cooking them in very shallow fat. The fat should not be very hot for a tender, delicate fried egg. However, some like the crisp, lacy edge produced by fat that is quite hot. Eggs may be fried "Over or Up." "Over" means the egg is turned and cooked on both sides. "Up" or "sunny-side-up" means that it is fried on one side only. The egg white film that remains over the yolk of an egg cooked "sunny-side-up" should be cooked by spooning hot fat over it. Butter, bacon or ham drippings, lard and vegetable shortening are all used for frying eggs.

Method 2: Another pleasing method of frying eggs is to use just enough fat to grease the bottom of the skillet. Cook the egg in this to set the bottom surface, then add ½ tsp water for 1 egg, and a little less for each additional egg in the skillet. Cover tightly and cook over low heat until eggs are cooked to desired doneness. Eggs cooked in this manner are somewhat like poached eggs.

Method 3: Eggs occasionally are fried in deep fat heated to a moderate temp, about 360° F. The egg should be broken into a saucer and slipped carefully into the hot fat. The *French-fried* egg should be cooked only until just brown, then removed immediately with a slotted spoon.

Frying is one of the least desirable ways of cooking eggs from a dietetic standpoint. Not only does the high temp necessary for good frying toughen the white, but the coating of fat slows down the digestion rate. For this reason fried eggs are not recommended for children. However, so many adults like their eggs fried better than any other way, so on the principle that it is much better to eat fried eggs than not eat eggs at all, frying should not be ruled out.

DRESSED-UP HAM AND EGGS

4 half-inch slices bread
4 ⅛-inch thick slices
  boiled ham
4 eggs

Salt and pepper
4 tbsp butter *or* margarine
Parsley

Cut centers out of bread slices using a biscuit cutter. Place ham slices on lightly greased shallow pan. Lay bread on top. Break egg into hole in bread. Sprinkle with salt and pepper. Lay cut-out rounds of bread on pan. Drizzle melted butter or margarine over all. Bake in moderate oven (350° F) until eggs are cooked to desired stage, and bread is toasted. Serve with toast rounds and parsley garnish. 4 servings.

EGGS LYONNAISE

2 tbsp butter
4 medium onions
¾ tsp salt
4 eggs

¼ cup top milk *or* cream
Pepper
Chopped parsley

Heat butter in a skillet. Add peeled onions that are cut into ¼-inch thick slices and ½ tsp of the salt. Cover and cook over low heat until onion slices are transparent, about 15 min. Turn over carefully with a pancake turner so as not to spoil the shape of the onion slices. Carefully slide eggs onto onion slices from a saucer. Add top milk, sprinkle with remaining salt, and pepper, cover and continue to cook over medium heat until eggs are cooked to the desired firmness. Sprinkle with parsley and serve immediately. 4 servings.

POACHED EGG DISHES

POACHED EGGS

Method 1: Poaching means cooking eggs removed from shell in *simmering* water. To preserve the shape, the egg is sometimes broken into a metal poacher placed over, or in hot water. If poacher is not used, the egg should be broken into a saucer and carefully slipped into the hot water. When done to the desired firmness, usually when the white has just coagulated, the egg should be carefully lifted from water with a slotted spoon or pancake turner, letting it drain a moment. Poached eggs may be served on hot toast, buttered rice or noodles,

ABOVE: *Crisp, thin, almost candy-like Brandy Snaps, p 487, are perfect with ice cream. They have unusual texture and flavor which are retained for months if stored in a tightly covered metal container.*

BELOW: *Date Pinwheel Cookies, p 483, Ribbon Bars, p 480, and Lemon-Coconut Refrigerator Cookies, p 479, make a perfect accompaniment for Hot Mulled Cider, p 218, on a cold winter evening.*

ABOVE: *When jelly runs out and scorches the edge of your cookies, try the trick pictured here. The jelly is sealed into the corner of the Vienna Tart, p 494, before it is rolled and shaped into a crescent, then it stays "put" during baking.*

BELOW: *Fruit Filled cookies, p 489, are something that children and adults loudly cheer. You put the filling on half of the cut-out cookies, lay the others over them, and seal the edges together with a knife handle.*

ABOVE: *Crisp, fragile crusted shortcake, p 648, with a white, fluffy, tender crumb on the biscuit laid together generously with crushed and whole sugared strawberries and then rimmed heavily with whipped sweetened cream is a dessert that will be rated as one of the most delicious as long as the world stands.*

BELOW: *A beautiful bowl of sugared fruit—fresh strawberries combined with frozen peaches only partially thawed. The tiny bunches of crystals that still cling to the peach wedges is part of the unthawed syrup that adds glitter and refreshing chilliness as well as delightful eating quality.*

ABOVE: *A perfectly baked golden cheese soufflé, p 439, can be brought to the table with justifiable pride. The trick of running a spoon around the edge develops the even break around the top and adds considerably to its attractive appearance. The beauty is fleeting however, so take it from the oven directly to the table, and have the family ready to eat it without a moment's delay.*

BELOW: *Jelly in the top of these rice croquettes, p 503, stays "put" because small depressions were made in the croquettes when they were shaped.*

ABOVE: *A wonderful Cheese Pudding, p 438. This is a hearty luncheon casserole for hungry people.*

BELOW: *The three steps in making Quick Baked Macaroni and Cheese, p 442. An easy meal, and most satisfying.*

A satisfying luncheon or Sunday night supper may be arranged conveniently on a single big platter for buffet service. Whole tomato roses with whole hard-cooked egg centers, leaf lettuce and sliced cucumbers may be combined into a salad by each guest; there's the dressing in the center bowl. Everybody may carve his own portion of cream cheese from the big loaf which is helpfully scored into eighths and decorated with sliced ripe olives. Two-tone bread and butter sandwiches are provided, and so is a pitcher of iced tea.

ABOVE: *If the idea of serving chilled slices of red ripe tomatoes for breakfast is new to you, there is a treat in store. Served on the same platter with the breakfast eggs and bacon, they provide the morning fruit to the main dish.*

BELOW: *Scrambled eggs, p 675. A fluffy mound of scrambled eggs, cooked to perfection—neither too moist nor too dry—surrounded with golden crisp slices of bacon and thick slices of garden-ripe chilled tomatoes presents the breakfast fruit, eggs and bacon in a new and highly acceptable form.*

Barbecued Ribs, p 860, whet the appetite, outdoors or in. Add beautiful tossed salad and corn on the cob and you can't miss. Photo, courtesy American Dairy Associaiton.

Courtesy Poultry and Egg National Board, Chicago, Ill.

ABOVE: *Eggs Benedict,* **p** *673. Serve Hollandaise sauce,* **p** *1256, separately, and ladle it over the poached eggs, pan-fried ham, and hot toast while the family is gathered around the table. Eat it at once to capture the peak of its goodness.*

BELOW: *This is a modern twist to serving "poached eggs on toast." It appears like something perfectly new with a real old-timey flavor. All that it is, is steaming hot, soft poached eggs atop hot crispy cereal flakes.* *Courtesy Cereal Institute, Chicago*

ABOVE: *One way to begin making beautifully puffy, tender omelets, p 676, is to start off with the Sta-puff variety, p 678. Following our recipe to the letter will quickly build up confidence in your ability to achieve.*

BELOW: *One of the simplest and most effective ways to use eggs for a garnish is to hard cook them so the yolks will be in the center, p 663, then slice them crosswise. An arrangement of overlapping slices around the top of a baked casserole and an accent of crisp parsley completes the picture.*

EGGS

RETAIL GRADES and USES

GRADES	AA	A	B	C
USES	Excellent Table Eggs	Fine Table Eggs	Table, Cooking and Baking Eggs	Cooking and Baking Eggs
CANDLING APPEARANCE				
SHELL	Clean and sound	Clean and sound	Clean, sound, may be abnormal	Clean, sound, may be abnormal
YOLK	Outline slightly defined	Outline fairly well defined	Outline well defined, slight defects permitted	Plainly visible (appears dark) some defects permitted
WHITE	Clear and firm	Clear and reasonably firm	Clear but slightly weak	Weak and watery, small meat spots permitted
AIR CELL	1/8 inch deep, regular or slightly wavy	1/4 inch deep, regular or slightly wavy	3/8 inch deep, movement up to 3/8 inch	3/8 inch deep, may be bubbly or free

SIZE

Weight Requirements per Dozen for Above Grades are as Follows:
JUMBO (28 oz.), EXTRA LARGE (26 oz.), LARGE (24 oz.), MEDIUM (21 oz.), and SMALL (18 oz.)

BROKEN OUT

SIDE VIEW				
AREA COVERED	Small	Moderate	Wide	Very wide
YOLK	Round and upstanding	Round and upstanding	Somewhat flattened	Very flattened, breaks easily
THICK WHITE	Large amount, standing very well around yolk	Large amount, standing up well around yolk	Medium amount, flattened	Small amount
THIN WHITE	Small amount	Small amount	Medium amount	Large amount

HARD COOKED

YOLK	Well Centered	Just Off Center	Off Center	Not Centered; Outline Irregular

FRIED

WHITE	Upstanding	Somewhat spread out	Spread widely; mostly thin	Spread out over large area
YOLK	Round, upstanding	Round, upstanding	Somewhat flattened	Very flat

ABOVE: *There are so many kinds of good cold cuts that are available these days and the size, shape, color, and flavor vary so that a great many combinations and arrangements are possible. Deviled Eggs, p 667, go well with any of them, and so does Potato Salad, p 1188.*

BELOW: *Eggs in Casserole, p 683. "Float" savory deviled eggs in a "sea" of tomato sauce and you have the making of a satisfying and nutritious luncheon or supper dish.*

ABOVE: *Why not serve food in the same lovely skillet in which it cooked? Fish fillets,* **p** *698, poached in a pottery skillet can come to the table in unbroken pieces, with the savory Spanish sauce,* **p** *1260, bubbling hot.*

BELOW: *Have your favorite fish made into fillets to make these interesting fish "roll-ups." Prepare them according to the directions for French-Fried Fish,* **p** *736, but after they are covered with cornmeal, simply roll them up and tie with a piece of string. Then fry as usual. Serve with green beans and Dill Sauce.*

ABOVE: *Baked fish with the crisp golden crust of "fried fish" and a moist, tender, juicy inside can be made in the oven by the "Quick Spencer Method,"* **p** 701. *The oil is drizzled over each piece before baking—and it won't burn.*

BELOW: *Small, whole fish like brook trout are ideal for pan frying,* **p** 707. *But they must be promptly cleaned, sprinkled generously with salt, then rolled in cornmeal and promptly fried until the outside is crisp and brown, the inside is cooked all the way through. For greatest palate appeal, fish must be served sizzling hot.*

mashed potatoes, buttered vegetables like spinach and asparagus and corned beef hash.

Method 2: Lightly grease the bottom of a glass or iron skillet. Add water to give a depth of at least 1 inch over the eggs and heat to simmering. Break very fresh eggs one at a time into a saucer and slip into the hot water, reducing heat as low as possible, so water does not even simmer. Do not crowd the eggs. Cook very slowly until the white is firm and the yolk filmed over, occasionally spooning the hot water over the yolk if necessary. Lift eggs out carefully, one at a time, with a slotted pancake turner, permitting them to drain thoroughly. Slide carefully onto a slice of hot buttered toast to serve.

Note: English muffin rings, or large cookie cutters that are open on the top, may be placed in the skillet, and an egg slid into each ring. When the white begins to coagulate, the ring may be lifted out and the cooking continued to the desired doneness. This gives the cooked eggs a perfectly round even rim. (An ingenious person could cut muffin rings from clean, used No. 1 or 2 tin cans with a metal shears.)

EGGS À LA ROCKEFELLER

1 tbsp butter	Salt to taste
1 tbsp flour	2 tsp butter
½ cup milk	4 poached eggs, see above
¼ cup grated sharp American cheese, 1 oz	4 slices whole wheat bread, toasted and buttered
¼ tsp salt	1 tbsp chopped parsley
1 large tomato, cut into 4 crosswise slices	

Melt butter, blend in flour, add milk gradually stirring constantly. Cook and stir until smooth and thickened. Remove from heat. Add cheese and ¼ tsp salt and stir until cheese is melted and well blended. Sprinkle tomato slices with salt, dot with ½ tsp butter on each slice. Broil until tops are slightly browned. Meanwhile poach eggs. Assemble by placing a slice of tomato on a slice of hot toast; top each with a hot poached egg. Pour cheese sauce over at once, sprinkle with parsley and serve immediately. 4 servings.

EGGS BENEDICT

6 ham slices, cut thin *or* canned pork loaf	6 poached eggs
Pork *or* bacon drippings	⅔ cup Hollandaise Sauce, p 1256
3 large English muffins, *or* 6 slices hot toast	Parsley

Pan-broil ham in drippings until edges are curly and ham is delicately browned. Have muffins split in halves and toasted. Place hot ham slices on hot toasted muffins, top with hot poached eggs and pour Hollandaise Sauce over all. Garnish with sprigs of parsley. Serve hot. Makes 4 to 6 servings.

EGGS POACHED IN MILK

1 cup milk	5 eggs
1 tbsp butter	Buttered toast
Salt to suit taste	Bacon
	Parsley

Heat milk slowly in a shallow glass or iron skillet. Melt butter in the milk, and stir in a little salt. Break eggs in a saucer and slide one at a time into hot milk and let stand over low heat until desired firmness. Lift eggs out onto buttered toast and pour remaining milk over them. If a small pan is used, do not try to cook all 5 eggs at the same time. This is a hearty and satisfying breakfast dish. Serve with hot crisp bacon. Garnish with parsley. 5 servings.

POACHED EGGS IN POTATO NESTS

Drop poached eggs into nests made of hot Mashed Potatoes, p 1378, for a supper dish. Garnish with strips of crisp hot bacon, or browned slices of canned pork loaf, and parsley or cress.

EGGS POACHED IN TOMATOES

No. 2½ can of tomatoes,	5 eggs
3½ cups	Salt and pepper
1 tbsp chopped onion	1½ cups toasted coarse
1 tsp sugar	bread crumbs
3 tbsp butter	

Heat first 4 ingredients to boiling. Turn into 10½ x 6½ x 2-inch glass baking dish. Break 5 eggs and slide into tomatoes so as not to break the yolks. Season with salt and pepper. Sprinkle top with bread crumbs. Bake in moderate oven (375° F) until eggs are desired doneness, from 10 to 15 min. Serve with additional toast. 5 servings.

TASTY SAUCED EGGS

An appealing German dish called "Sour Eggs" or "Lost Eggs"

1 tbsp butter	1 egg yolk
1 tbsp flour	4 eggs
1 cup water	Hot toast
1 tsp vinegar	Chopped parsley
½ tsp salt	

Melt butter in a 9-inch skillet. Blend in flour, and add water slowly with constant stirring to keep mixture smooth. Heat to boiling, and stir in vinegar and salt. Beat egg yolk, add some hot sauce, beat well; then return this to hot mixture and stir thoroughly. Have sauce barely simmering, and slip eggs one at a time into sauce. Cover tightly and poach 2 or 3 min. Remove lid and baste eggs with sauce until they cook to desired consistency. Serve eggs on toast with sauce over top. Shower with parsley. 3 to 4 servings.

SCRAMBLED EGG DISHES

The most usual way of preparing scrambled eggs is to break them into a bowl, add seasonings and 1 tbsp of milk or cream per egg, then beat them slightly. Then they are poured into a heated skillet containing a small amount of fat and gently folded over from bottom and sides as they coagulate. Or they may be cooked without fat, or with very little, over hot water in the top of a double boiler. Constant stirring should be avoided. Scrambled eggs may be either soft or firm. Another method of scrambling is to break the whole eggs into hot fat in a skillet, then stir lightly with a fork; this results in streaking the yellow part of the eggs interestingly with the white. Various chopped foods such as crisp bacon, ham, dried beef, grated Cheddar cheese, chopped cooked vegetables or flaky cottage cheese folded into scrambled eggs when nearly done are delightful.

EGG SPINACH SCRAMBLE

½ lb raw spinach, washed, drained, shredded, 2½ cups, lightly pkd	½ tsp salt
	¼ tsp prepared horseradish
	Dash of pepper
2 tsp chopped onion	2 medium-size tomatoes,
2 tbsp butter *or* margarine	sliced, broiled
6 eggs, slightly beaten	5 thin slices boiled ham

Sauté spinach and onion in the butter for 5 min. Combine eggs with seasonings and add to the spinach. Cook over low heat, stirring occasionally but very gently with a spatula or fork as egg cooks at the bottom of pan. As soon as egg is of the desired firmness, remove from heat at once. Slide out carefully into the center of a hot platter and surround with hot broiled tomato slices and sprinkle top with ham slices cut in strips and pan fried until fat edges are browned. 4 servings.

HEARTY SCRAMBLED EGGS

To make a heartier dish of Scrambled Eggs, stir ½ cup cottage cheese, chopped cooked ham, liver, or shredded dried beef into the egg mixture just as it is beginning to coagulate. If a sufficient quantity is added, this makes a fine main dish for a simple family dinner.

PARSLEY EGG SCRAMBLE

Add 1 tbsp coarsely chopped parsley to the beaten eggs and proceed as for Scrambled Eggs. 5 servings.

TOMATO SCRAMBLE

1 tbsp butter	½ tsp sugar
2 tbsp fine chopped onion	½ tsp salt
1 tbsp all-purpose flour	Dash of pepper
2 or 3 tomatoes, ¾ lb	4 eggs

Melt butter in a saucepan, add onion and sauté until soft, about 5 min. Blend in the flour thoroughly, then add the skinned, quartered tomatoes. Add seasonings and carefully stir the tomatoes into the flour mixture. Cover and continue to cook over low heat for 5 to 10 min until tomatoes are cooked but not mushy. Keep mixture over low heat and add the whole eggs, stir gently with a fork as they cook. Serve at once on slices of toast if desired. 4 servings.

OMELETS

There are 2 types of omelets: (1) The French type similar to scrambled eggs. (2) The puffy or American type resembles a soufflé. In the French omelet, the yolks and whites are beaten together, poured into a hot skillet with fat, after cooking a few minutes, a spatula is used to gently lift (never stir) cooked portions to permit the uncooked mixture to flow underneath. In the puffy omelet, the whites are beaten separately until stiff, then the beaten seasoned yolks are folded into them. The mixture is cooked in a greased skillet without stirring or other manipulation, first on top of the stove until bottom is cooked to a delicate brown and then in the oven until completely set.

BACON OMELET

Make a Puffy Omelet as directed. Have ⅓ lb bacon broiled until crisp and a delicate brown; drain thoroughly. Chop or crumble coarsely and keep hot. When omelet is done, sprinkle bacon over half the surface, cut omelet quickly in half, fold over and carefully slide onto hot platter. Garnish with parsley or pan-broiled tomatoes. Serve immediately. 5 servings.

CHEESE OMELET

Make French Omelet or Puffy Omelet and just before folding, sprinkle surface with from ½ to 1 cup coarsely grated sharp American cheese. Serve at once.

FRENCH OMELET

6 eggs	⅓ cup water *or* milk
¾ tsp salt	3 tbsp butter
Few grains pepper	Parsley *or* cress

Beat eggs until mixed but not foamy; stir in seasonings and water. Melt butter in a heavy skillet and turn mixture into the moderately hot skillet. Cook omelet slowly, pricking and lifting with a fork during cooking period. Cook until firm to the touch of finger (8 to 10 min). The omelet may be cooked entirely on top of the range or put in the oven part of the time to dry the top. Fold or roll omelet, turn onto a hot platter, and serve immediately. Garnish with parsley or cress. 4 servings.

Variations. Spread omelet with jelly or preserves before rolling or folding, or serve with hot broiled fruit such as tomato slices, halves of peaches or apricots. Omelets may also be served with any one of a number of suitable sauces: Cheese Sauce, p 1253, Tomato Sauce, p 1261, Spanish Sauce, p 1260, and a Medium White Sauce, p 1262 with a vegetable, cooked chicken or fish added.

MUSHROOM OMELET

Sauté 1 cup sliced fresh mushrooms in butter until heated through. Fold into French or Puffy Omelet mixture just before turning into skillet, or make either omelet as directed and just before folding, sprinkle surface with the sautéed mushrooms.

PARSLEY OMELET

Add 1 tbsp finely chopped parsley to the beaten eggs and proceed as for French Omelet (above).

PUFFY OMELET

6 eggs, separated	2 to 4 tbsp butter
3 tbsp cold water	Parsley *or* cress
1 tsp salt	

Beat egg whites until frothy, add water and continue beating until stiff. Beat egg yolks with salt until very thick and light in color, and fold into the whites lightly but thoroughly. Have a large skillet moderately hot, melt the butter, and pour in the egg mixture. Cook very slowly over low heat for about 20 min, or until bottom of omelet appears nicely browned and crisp when gently lifted from side with a knife. Do not stir at any time. Then slip skillet containing omelet into a moderate oven (325° F) for 2 to 5 min, or until top is dry but not browned. Loosen quickly around edges, make a quick cut through the center, fold over and slide omelet onto a hot serving plate. Garnish with parsley or cress. Serve immediately. 5 servings.

Variations. All of the variations of French Omelet are also suitable for Puffy Omelet and Sta-Puff Omelet (following page).

STA-PUFF OMELET

⅓ cup butter *or* margarine	2 tbsp shortening for
⅓ cup flour	skillet
1½ cups milk	1 lb fresh-cooked *or* canned
1 tsp salt	shrimp
4 eggs, separated	Chopped parsley
¾ tsp salt	

Prepare a thick white sauce from the first four ingredients. Cool. Beat the egg yolks slightly, add ⅔ cup of the thick white sauce and reserve remaining sauce for shrimp. Add the ¾ tsp salt and beat thoroughly to blend. Then fold in the stiffly beaten egg whites. Heat shortening over low heat in an 8-inch skillet. Pour in the omelet mixture. Level surface gently, and cover with a domed-shaped lid, greased on the inside. This will allow the omelet to rise without sticking to the top. (An inverted pie pan will also serve as a cover.) Cook over very low heat for 15 to 20 min or until a light brown crust is formed on the bottom. Lift slightly at the side with a spatula to make sure omelet is cooked through. Loosen the omelet from sides of skillet, cut through center to crust but not through it, slide onto a hot platter. Pour creamed shrimp on one half of omelet, carefully fold other half over. Sprinkle with parsley. Serve immediately. 4 servings.

Note: To prepare creamed shrimp, add ½ cup cooked milk to remaining white sauce. Add cleaned shrimp and season with 1 tsp grated onion and a dash of pepper. Reheat over hot water while omelet is cooking.

GREEN OMELETS—CAUSE AND PREVENTION

Green color on the bottom of an omelet is due to hydrogen sulfide of egg whites combining with iron in yolks to form iron sulfide which has green color. It is harmless but unattractive. This happens because the egg separates out either after beaten whites and yolks are combined and stand awhile before cooking, or whites are insufficiently beaten, or whites and yolks are not well blended. To prevent it, beat whites *thoroughly* but not until dry appearing, blend them immediately and thoroughly with beaten yolks. Start cooking promptly. There is less chance of obtaining green color if omelet is cooked on top of stove. Omelets require longer cooking in oven and give eggs more chance to separate out, developing green color.

SOUFFLÉS

Soufflé is the French word for "puffed up," and this is an exact description of what happens to this dish in cooking. Basically, a soufflé consists of a white sauce with egg yolks added and with stiffly beaten egg whites folded in. During baking the beaten egg expands and sets.

Various ingredients such as cheese,* chopped meat, fish or vegetables may be added to the basic mixture. There are also sweet dessert soufflés such as lemon, orange, chocolate and rum.

The secret of making good soufflés is to organize the procedure, combine ingredients correctly, bake correctly, serve promptly. The white sauce should be smooth, and while hot the beaten egg yolks should be stirred thoroughly into it. Egg whites should be whipped until stiff enough for the peaks to hold their shape, but remain shiny and soft enough to bend over. Whites so beaten fold in easily. If beaten stiff and dry, they are difficult to fold in and they can't hold air and expand. Fold them in gently but thoroughly, then turn mixture gently into an *ungreased* casserole. Set casserole on 2 shallow jelly roll pans (½" deep), one nested within the other. Air space between pans control heat for perfect browning. Place immediately in a moderately slow oven (325° F), bake at least an hr. Once done, serve promptly, because they start falling as soon as they start cooling.

CELERY SOUFFLÉ

3 tbsp butter	¾ tsp salt
1 cup fine-diced celery	Dash of pepper
4 tbsp flour	4 eggs, separated
1 cup milk	

Start oven 10 min before baking; set to moderately slow (325° F). Melt butter in saucepan, add celery, cook and stir 2 or 3 min. Blend in flour, add milk gradually stirring to keep smooth. Cook over direct heat, stir constantly until sauce boils and thickens. Add seasonings. Remove from heat. Beat egg yolks thoroughly and slowly stir them into hot sauce. Cook and stir 2 min longer. Cool slightly. Beat egg whites until stiff and slide onto sauce and fold in lightly but thoroughly. Turn into a 6-cup ungreased casserole and bake 50 to 55 min. Serve immediately. 4 servings.

CHICKEN OR MEAT SOUFFLÉ

3 tbsp butter	3 eggs, separated
3 tbsp flour	1 cup fine-chopped cooked
½ tsp salt	chicken *or* meat
1 cup milk	

Melt butter, blend in flour and salt. Add milk gradually and stir constantly over direct heat until mixture boils and thickens. Stir hot sauce slowly into the well-beaten egg yolks, then fold in chicken and cool a few min. Beat egg whites until stiff and fold lightly but thoroughly into chicken mixture. Turn into an ungreased 6-cup casserole. Bake in a moderately slow oven (325° F) about 1 hr, or until a rich brown. Serve immediately. 5 servings.

* Cheese Soufflé may be found on p 439.

DRIED BEEF SOUFFLÉ

3 tbsp butter	4 eggs, separated
¼ cup flour	4 oz dried beef
1¼ cups milk	Pepper, opt

Preheat oven to moderately slow (325° F). Have ready a 6-cup casserole. Do not grease. Melt butter in a saucepan, blend in flour. Add milk gradually, stirring to keep smooth. Cook over moderate heat, stirring constantly until smooth and thick. Stir slowly into well beaten yolks. Cool slightly. Separate beef slices and pour hot water over them. Let stand a min, no more. Drain and with scissors cut fine, dropping into egg yolk mixture. Fold beef in. Beat egg whites until stiff, then pour yolk mixture over them and cut and fold together carefully. Flow mixture gently into casserole. Bake about 1 hr. Serve immediately. 5 servings.

MUSHROOM SOUFFLÉ

¼ cup butter	¼ cup flour
1½ cups sliced fresh mush-rooms, ½ to ¾ lb	1 cup milk
	2 chicken bouillon cubes
¼ cup finely diced celery	4 eggs, separated

Melt butter in a skillet. Add mushrooms and celery and sauté for 5 min. Push vegetables to one side and blend flour into butter. Add the milk gradually and then the bouillon cubes. Heat to boiling over low heat, stirring constantly until smooth and thickened. Beat egg yolks thoroughly. Gradually beat in cream sauce mixture. Cool slightly and fold in the stiffly beaten egg whites. Turn into ungreased 6-cup casserole. Bake in a moderately slow oven (325° F) about 1 hr. Serve immediately plain or with creamed chicken or sweetbreads. 5 generous servings.

OATMEAL SOUFFLÉ

2 tbsp butter	2 tbsp chopped pimiento
1 cup milk	½ tsp salt
½ cup quick-cooking rolled oats	2 slices bacon, cooked and chopped
½ cup grated sharp cheese	3 eggs, separated
Dash of dry mustard	

Add butter to milk and scald. Stir in oats gradually and cook 5 min, stirring constantly. Remove from heat and stir in cheese. When cheese is melted, add mustard, pimiento, salt, bacon, and then stir into beaten egg yolks. Cool slightly. Beat whites until stiff and fold into oat mixture. Turn into an ungreased 6-cup casserole, bake in a moderately slow oven (325° F) about 1 hr, or until a rich brown. Serve immediately. 5 servings.

Note: Read method for Soufflés, p 678.

SPAGHETTI RING SOUFFLÉ WITH CREAMED HAM

¾ pkg spaghetti (5 to 6 oz)	3 eggs, separated
2 tbsp butter	3 cups medium White Sauce,
3 tbsp flour	p 1262
1 tsp salt	2½ cups diced cooked ham
Dash of pepper	Salt and pepper
1½ cups milk	

Drop broken spaghetti into 1½ qts boiling salted water and boil uncovered until just tender, about 20 min. Drain, rinse well with hot water and again drain. Melt butter, blend in flour, salt and pepper. Add milk gradually and stir over direct heat until sauce boils and thickens. Cool and stir into beaten egg yolks; fold in spaghetti. Beat egg whites until stiff and fold in lightly but thoroughly. Turn into well-greased 6-cup paper-lined ring mold, see note p 439; bake directly on rack in a moderately slow oven (325° F) for 45 to 50 min, or until a sharp knife inserted in the center comes out clean. Combine unseasoned white sauce with the ham, heat and season to taste. Unmold spaghetti soufflé onto hot platter and serve with creamed ham. Macaroni may be used in place of spaghetti, and ring may be served with creamed chicken or tuna instead of the ham. 5 servings.

TUNA SOUFFLÉ

¼ cup butter	¼ tsp salt
⅓ cup flour	Dash of pepper
1¼ cups milk	2 tbsp chopped parsley
4 eggs, separated	7 oz can tuna
1 tsp chopped onion	

Melt butter and blend in flour until smooth. Gradually add the milk and cook over low heat until sauce boils and thickens, stirring constantly to keep smooth. Thoroughly beat egg yolks. Add white sauce gradually, stirring to keep smooth. Add the onion, salt, pepper, parsley and flaked tuna. Cool slightly. Carefully fold in the stiffly beaten egg whites. Turn into ungreased 6-cup casserole. Bake in a moderately slow oven (325° F) about 1 hr, or until puffy and high and delicately browned on top. Serve immediately. 5 generous servings.

Don't forget: (1) Soufflés go into ungreased casseroles—they want a rough not a sleek surface to hang onto as they puff up and rise high. (2) If you have an extra egg white or two stored in the refrigerator, add them to the whites of eggs the recipe calls for and fold into mixture. The extra whites add volume and nutritive value to the soufflé.

Note: Read method for Soufflés, p 678.

MISCELLANEOUS EGG DISHES

CREOLE EGGS

2 tbsp butter
2 tbsp flour
1 cup tomato juice
¼ cup finely chopped celery
2 tbsp finely chopped green
  pepper

1 tsp finely chopped onion
¼ tsp salt
Dash pepper
⅛ tsp allspice
6 hard-cooked eggs
2 tbsp chopped parsley

Melt butter in a saucepan, blend in flour until smooth. Add tomato juice gradually, stirring constantly, then add remaining ingredients in the order listed, except eggs and parsley. Cook, stirring constantly until mixture boils and is thickened. Chop or rice the hard-cooked egg whites and add to the tomato mixture. Serve hot on toast or hot biscuits. Garnish with sieved egg yolks and parsley. 4 servings.

EGG AND FISH LOAF

3 slices bacon, cut into
  small pieces
1 tsp chopped onion
1 cup cooked fish, flaked,
  leftover
1 cup cold boiled rice

½ cup milk
1 egg, slightly beaten
Salt to taste
½ tsp paprika
4 hard-cooked eggs

Pan fry bacon and onion until bacon is lightly browned and onion is slightly transparent about 5 min. Stir in fish and rice. Combine milk, beaten egg, and seasonings and add to first mixture. Dice the hard-cooked eggs and add to fish mixture. Stir to blend. Turn mixture into a 4-cup greased loaf pan and bake 30 min in a moderate oven (350° F). Turn out on a hot platter and serve with Tomato Sauce, p 1261. 4 servings.

EGG AND RICE SURPRISE

3 slices bacon
2 tbsp onion
1 beef bouillon cube
1 tbsp water
3 cups Cooked Rice,
  p 433 1 cup raw

2 tbsp chopped parsley
½ tsp salt
⅛ tsp pepper
1 tbsp butter
2 tomatoes
4 eggs

Cut bacon with kitchen scissors directly into a skillet. Add onion and sauté until bacon is lightly browned. Soften the bouillon cube in the water; add to the bacon along with the rice, parsley, salt and

Note: Directions for Hard-cooked Eggs on p 663.

pepper. Heat thoroughly. Butter the sides and bottoms of 4 individual covered casseroles or ramekins. Cut tomatoes into thin slices. Place 2 slices in the bottom of each casserole—fill each one with the hot rice mixture, make a slight depression in the rice and break an egg into each. Top with 2 slices of tomato, sprinkle lightly with more salt. Cover and bake in a moderate oven (350° F) for 10 to 15 min or until whites of eggs are just set. 4 servings.

EGG CASSEROLE

¼ cup butter	1½ cups milk
1 cup finely diced celery	2 tbsp finely chopped parsley
2 tbsp chopped onion	6 hard-cooked eggs
1 tbsp chopped green pepper	1 slice bread, cut in cubes
3 tbsp flour	2 tbsp melted butter
1 tsp salt	

Melt butter in saucepan; add celery, onion and green pepper and sauté for 5 min. Blend in the flour and salt. Gradually add the milk, stirring constantly and heat until mixture just boils and thickens. Add the parsley and pour sauce over the eggs which have been cut in half crosswise and placed in the bottom of a greased 5-cup casserole. Toss the bread cubes in the 2 tbsp melted butter and sprinkle on top of casserole. Bake at 400° F (moderately hot oven) for 15 min. Serve immediately. 4 servings.

CHINESE EGG ROLLS

Popular appetizer or main dish

Roll Filling:

⅓ cup water	2½ cups bean sprouts washed and drained, ½ lb
2 cups green cabbage chopped medium fine	*1 lb commercial Egg Roll Skins, 7-inch sq
⅔ cup celery chopped medium fine	*Batter for Dipping Rolls:*
½ lb ground lean pork	½ cup all-purpose flour
½ cup fine-cut green onions and tops	1 tsp D.A. baking powder *or* 1¼ tsp tartrate *or* phosphate type
1 tsp salt	¼ tsp salt
2⅔ tbsp soy sauce	1 small egg, slightly beaten
1 tbsp sugar	½ cup cold water
2 tsp peanut butter	3 cups shortening *or* oil
1½ tsp monosodium glutamate	

Filling: Heat water in saucepan to boiling, add cabbage and celery and cook 4 to 5 min, stirring lightly to prevent sticking. Vegetables should still be crisp. Remove from heat and drain. Heat heavy skillet

*Note: Buy Egg Roll Skins from Chinese grocery.

over low heat without fat, add pork and cook until gray in color, tossing with fork to keep meat separated, then add cabbage-celery mixture and the next 6 ingredients. Heat 2 or 3 min, stirring with fork to blend seasonings. Remove from heat and stir in bean sprouts. Vegetables should still be crisp. Pile 1 to 2 tbsp pork mixture diagonally across each egg roll skin 2 inches from corner nearest you and to within 1 inch from sides. Start with corner nearest you, and roll skin tightly around filling once; fold in the ends and finish rolling. Place a drop of batter on corner to seal the roll. Egg rolls may be made 2 or 3 hrs ahead of time and kept in refrigerator until ready to fry.

Batter: Sift flour, measure, resift with baking powder and salt. Beat egg slightly, add water, then stir in dry ingredients and beat until smooth. Heat fat in 10-inch skillet to 375° F. Dip egg rolls in batter with wide-tined fork and fry until golden brown, 2 to 3 min on each side. Drain on paper toweling. Serve piping hot. 10 rolls 4 to 5 inches long.

CHINESE EGG FOO YEUNG

A very popular Chinese dish

3 water chestnuts	¾ tsp monosodium glutamate
¼ cup green onions	¾ tsp salt
1 dry onion size egg	1 tsp sugar
1 medium size tomato	2-oz can sliced mushrooms,
2 cups fresh *or* canned bean	drained
sprouts	5 eggs
*¼ lb lean ground beef	2 tbsp shortening *or* oil
1 tbsp soy sauce	1 tsp sugar

Peel chestnuts and slice thin crosswise. Clean green onions, then cut with scissors into ¼-inch lengths with some of the green tops. Peel onion; cut in half lengthwise, then cut halves into ⅛-inch wide lengthwise strips. Wash tomato and cut into thin lengthwise wedges; remove and discard seeds. Rinse bean sprouts in cold water and drain. Put meat into 2-qt bowl and break apart with a fork; then add next 4 ingredients and all vegetables, except tomatoes and bean sprouts. Mix lightly with silver fork or chop sticks. Break eggs over meat mixture, then beat lightly until meat particles are separated. Heat shortening in heavy skillet hot enough for cakes not to spread much. For a 4-inch Egg Foo Yeung, pour ⅓ cup of egg mixture into hot skillet. After mixture cooks about a min, spread over top of each cake ½ cup bean sprouts, ¼ of the tomato slices and sprinkle with ¼ tsp of the sugar. Cook until cakes are nicely browned on under side—about 3 min. Then carefully turn with pancake turner, holding bean sprouts in place with spatula, and

*Finely diced cooked chicken, pork or shrimp may be substituted for the beef.

Note: Buy water chestnuts and bean sprouts canned, or fresh from Chinese grocery or restaurant.

brown other side. Cook cakes until edges are a little crisp and brown. Serve with Thickened Soy Sauce, below. 4 servings.

EGG FOO YEUNG

3 tbsp flour	½ cup Chinese mixed
1¼ tsp salt	vegetables
4 eggs, well beaten	1 cup diced cooked chicken
2 tsp chopped onion	*or* veal
½ cup bean sprouts	Fat for frying

Blend flour and salt thoroughly with the eggs. Add remaining ingredients, except fat. The melted fat in skillet should be at least ¼-inch deep. Using a ¼-cup to measure, carefully pour one portion of the mixture at a time into the hot fat. It will run slightly at first, but as it cooks, carefully fold edges back toward center of each patty with a spoon. Brown over medium heat until underside is firm, turn and brown slightly on second side. Remove from skillet and keep hot while cooking remainder of patties. Serve hot with soy sauce (below). Makes about 12 patties.

Note: Egg Foo Yeung may also be cooked in this way: dip a ladle into heated deep fat, then into egg mixture. Hold ladle full of egg mixture into hot fat until firm and crisp at edges. Loosen mixture from ladle and drop carefully into fat to finish cooking.

Leftover bean sprouts and Chinese mixed vegetables may be used to prepare Chop Suey, p 870, Sub Gum, p 881, or Swiss Steak, p 815.

Soy Sauce:
1½ tsp cornstarch	¾ cup water
1½ tsp sugar	1 tbsp soy sauce

Mix cornstarch and sugar in a small saucepan. Add water gradually and blend until smooth. Heat to boiling, add soy sauce and simmer 1 min. Serve hot.

EGG PANCAKES WITH CHERRY SAUCE

Cottage Cheese Filling:
- 1 lb creamed cottage cheese
- ¾ tsp grated lemon rind
- 2 tbsp sugar
- Dash of salt

Thin Egg Pancakes:
- 1 cup milk
- 3 eggs, beaten
- 1 cup sifted all-purpose flour
- ¾ tsp salt
- 1 tbsp sugar
- 3 tbsp shortening

Filling: Combine all ingredients above to make filling.
Pancakes: Stir ½ cup of the milk into the eggs. Add the flour, salt

and sugar all at once and beat with a rotary beater until smooth; add remaining milk and mix thoroughly. Heat 1 tsp shortening in a 9-inch skillet and add ¼ cup of the batter. Rotate skillet slightly so that the batter runs to edges all around. Bake until delicately brown on each side, turning once. Remove to a large plate, quickly spread with 3 tbsp of cottage cheese filling and roll. Cover finished pancakes to keep hot. Repeat baking, filling, and rolling until batter is used up. Arrange rolls on hot platter. Serve promptly with cherry sauce made as follows:

Simmer ½ lb pitted sour red cherries with 1 cup water, ⅓ cup sugar and 2 to 4 tbsp lemon juice, depending on sweetness of cherries, for 5 min. Stir in 2 tbsp cornstarch blended to a thin paste with a tbsp of cold water. Cook until slightly thickened and clear. 10 pancakes.

OLD TIME EGG PANCAKES

High Puffed Rims

3 eggs	¼ tsp salt
⅓ cup milk	2 tbsp shortening
⅓ cup flour	¼ cup thinly sliced apples

Start oven 10 min before baking, set to moderately hot (400° F). Beat eggs slightly. Add milk, then combined flour and salt, beating with a rotary beater until smooth. Have shortening heated in a heavy 10-inch skillet, tilt skillet from side to side so all surfaces will be coated with the fat. Quickly turn egg mixture into hot skillet and sprinkle apple slices over top. Bake uncovered, 20 min. Remove from oven and turn out onto a hot dinner plate and serve immediately with a sprinkling of sugar or sugar combined with cinnamon. 2 servings.

Fish

Of course, the ideal way to cook fish is to build a fire alongside a trout stream and have the frying pan sizzling hot for the big ones that did not get away. But don't despair if you can't achieve this goal for today you can go to market and "catch" your favorite fish that has been kept fresh by adequate refrigeration during transportation (often by air) or with its fresh goodness frozen in. In this chapter you'll learn to cook each fish in the way that suits it best, which is not always in a frying pan.

AT ONE time fish could be enjoyed regularly only by those people who lived close to the source of supply: salt water fish near the coast or fresh water fish brought in by the amateur fisherman of the family. And even then there was no year-round supply, for fresh varieties of fish are produced in abundance and in good quality only at certain seasons in any one locality.

Now, however, the vastly improved methods of refrigeration and air transportation have made fresh fish in their season available to all parts of the country. In addition, freezing processes have made it possible to obtain most of the popular varieties during most of the year even out of season. Quick (sharp) freezing makes no appreciable change in the appearance, quality or food value of freshly caught fish. And frozen fish, after it is thawed, can be cooked by the same methods just as successfully as fresh.

The United States ranks very low with other countries in the consumption of fish. This is unfortunate because fish not only makes greater variety in our meals possible (there are over 140 available varieties of edible fish on the market), but they are very important from a nutritional standpoint. *Fish* is not a substitute for meat, it *is meat*. It is a complete protein food, and contains the B-vitamins—thiamine, riboflavin, and niacin, and the fatter fish also contain vitamins A and D. Fish also supply certain minerals—phosphorus, iron, copper, and magnesium (and calcium if the bones are eaten as in canned salmon). The food value of fish varies depending upon the kind of fish, the amount of fat present, and the producing area. (See p 691.)

Salt-water fish have special nutritional value because of their iodine content. This mineral is also present in the soil in sea coast areas, and is therefore found in the vegetables, etc., but in the middle states, the area west of the Alleghenies and east of the Rockies, and especially around the Great Lakes (the goiter belt*) there is very little if any iodine in the soil or in the locally grown products. The regular use of salt water fish** supplies the diet with iodine which is hard to find naturally in other foods.

Information in this chapter adapted from publications of U. S. Department of Interior Fish and Wild Life Service, Washington, D. C.

FORMS OF MARKET FISH

Study the following sketches to learn the various ways the dealer prepares fish for the market. Purchasing various forms of even the same kind of fish from time to time and adapting the form to the method of cooking is one of the surest ways of keeping the family as interested in fish as in meat. Here are the most important forms of fresh and frozen fish and what they mean:

1. Whole (or round) fish are fish as they come from the water. Fish sold whole are usually varieties that keep best without being dressed, but such fish should have gills removed when caught, *as this is where spoilage*

begins. These fish must be scaled, drawn, then thoroughly washed inside and out in *cold water.* Drain quickly, then pat dry inside and out with paper toweling or cloth. Rub inside of fish with lemon juice, using 1 tbsp per lb, if desired to add pleasing flavor and decrease "fishy odor." Wrap fish in waxed or parchment paper, lay on tray and store in refrigerator.

2. Drawn fish are fish which have been eviscerated (entrails removed). These include small fish such as butterfish, dabs and croakers, and larger fish such as bluefish or Spanish mackerel. They must be scaled and washed thoroughly. Heads may be removed and the fins cut out with scissors. Fish cooked with heads on and fins in are juicier and more flavorful than when heads and fins are removed. They may be split or cut in serving pieces for quick cooking. Rub with a little lemon juice before cooking, if desired.

*There is more than one type of goiter, and the need for iodine is to be considered a *prevention* not a cure. When a goiter has developed, it should be treated only under the advice of a physician.
**Iodized salt is the only other practical source of iodine in this area.

2

3. *Dressed fish* are scaled, drawn and usually have heads, tails and fins

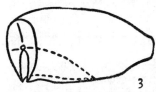

removed. When washed, small dressed fish are ready for cooking, or they may be split open. Large dressed fish, after washing, may be baked whole, but frequently are split or cut into steaks or fillets.

3

4. *Pan-dressed fish* have scales, entrails, head, tail, and sometimes the backbone removed. This includes fish such as yellow perch, scup, whiting,

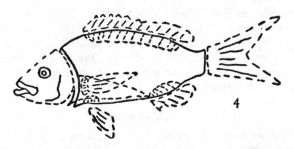

4

flounder and sole. After washing, they may be split open along either the belly or back. They are then ready for cooking.

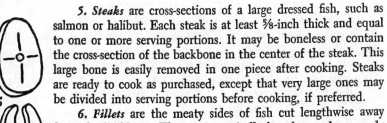

5. *Steaks* are cross-sections of a large dressed fish, such as salmon or halibut. Each steak is at least ⅝-inch thick and equal to one or more serving portions. It may be boneless or contain the cross-section of the backbone in the center of the steak. This large bone is easily removed in one piece after cooking. Steaks are ready to cook as purchased, except that very large ones may be divided into serving portions before cooking, if preferred.

5

6. *Fillets* are the meaty sides of fish cut lengthwise away from the backbone. They are practically boneless and are ready for cooking with no further preparation. If the skin (with scales removed) is left on, the fish will be juicier and have more flavor. Fillets are usually cut from fish weighing 1½ to 4 lb. They are sold in three different forms—

a. A single fillet is one side of a fish, and may weigh from several oz to a lb or more, depending on the size and thickness of the fish. This is the type usually marketed.

b. A butterfly fillet is the two sides of the fish, held together by the uncut belly of the fish.

6 a

c. Sticks are at least inch-thick pieces cut either crosswise or lengthwise from fillets of larger fish. (Indicated on Sketch 6b as B).

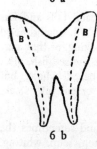

WEIGHT OF FISH TO ALLOW PER SERVING

(1) Whole—not dressed—1 lb per serving, about.
(2) Dressed Fish—1 lb for 2 generous servings.
(3) Steak or Fillets—1 lb for 3 average servings.

6 b

HOW TO SALT FISH BEFORE COOKING

If practical, an hour before cooking, rub salt inside and outside of fish, using 1 tsp to each lb. If fish is cut into steaks, fillets or sticks, sprinkle salt over fish, using 1 tsp salt to each lb. Place salted fish on plate or enamel tray, then wrap in waxed or parchment paper and store in refrigerator until cooking time. To conserve flavor and juices, never salt fish before freezing or before thawing frozen fish.

SHELLFISH

Shellfish are bought in 4 general ways: 1. Alive in shell. 2. The cooked meat without shell. 3. Shucked. 4. Frozen cooked meat or frozen uncooked in shell.

Alive in shell. Crabs, lobsters, clams and oysters purchased in the shell should be very much alive, see pp 711, 715, 719, 722.

Cooked meat. The edible portions of cooked shellfish, picked from the shells and ready to eat. Crabs, shrimp and lobsters are the shellfish that are marketed in this way.

Shucked. The raw fish are removed from the shells and kept on ice until sold. Oysters, clams, shrimps and scallops are often sold this way.

Buy following amounts of shellfish for average servings:

One lb of shelled clams serves 6.

A 2-lb lobster in the shell yields 2 average servings. One chicken lobster (about ¾ lb) serves 1.

One lb cooked lobster meat removed from shell serves 6.

One lb of fresh unshucked shrimp serves 3.

One qt of shucked oysters or 4 dozen in the shell serves 6.

KNOW YOUR FISH

TABLE 24

Kind	Producing Area	Season	Description	Cooking Methods	Fuel Value (Calories) Per Pound	Approximate Size (Lb.)
Salt Water						
Alewife	N. Atl., S. Atl.	All year	Fairly lean	Broil*, boil, steam, deep fat or pan-fry	550	5-60
Barracuda	Atl., Pac. (smaller)	Feb.-June	Fat (variable)	Broil, bake*, boil or steam	510	1-7
Bluefish	Atlantic, Gulf	All year	Fat	Broil, bake*, deep fat or pan-fry	535	½-¾
Blue Runner	Gulf	All year	Fat	Broil*, bake, deep fat or pan-fry	445	¼-1¼
Butterfish	N. Atl., Mid. Atl., Chesapeake	Apr.-Dec.	Fat	Broil, deep fat or pan-fry*, bake	745	
Cod	N. Atl., N. Pac.	All year	Lean	Broil*, bake, boil or steam, chowder	315	2½-10
Croaker	Atlantic, Gulf	Feb.-Nov.	Lean	Broil, bake, boil or steam, deep fat or pan-fry*, chowder	415	1-11½
Cusk	Atlantic	All year	Very lean	All methods, bake best	315	5
Drumfish	Ches., S. Atl., Gulf	Dec.-Oct.	Lean	Bake*, boil or steam, chowder	345	2-25
Eel, common	North Atlantic	All year	Fat (variable)	Broil, deep fat or pan-fry*	710	¼-10
Flounders						
a. Blackback	N. Atl., Mid. Atl., Chesapeake	All year	Lean	Broil, bake, boil or steam, deep fat or pan-fry*, chowder	290	¾-2
b. Dab	N. Atl., Mid. Atl.	All year	Lean	Bake, broil, pan-fry*	395	¾-2½
c. Fluke	Atlantic	All year	Lean	Broil, bake, boil or steam, deep fat or pan-fry*, chowder	290	2-12
d. Sole	N. Atl., Mid. Atl.	All year	Lean	Broil, bake, boil or steam, deep fat or pan-fry*, chowder	345	1-10
Groupers	South Atl., Gulf	Nov.-Apr.	Lean	Broil, bake*, boil or steam, chowder	380	5-15
Haddock	N. Atl., Mid. Atl.	All year	Lean	Broil*, bake, boil or steam, chowder	325	2½-6
(Finnan Haddie)	(Made from Haddock)	Fall, Winter, Spring				
Hake	N. Atl., Mid. Atl.	All year	Lean	Bake*, boil or steam, chowder	340	3-10
Halibut	N. Atl., N. Pac.	All year	Fat †	Broil*, bake, boil or steam, chowder	550	10-300
Herring, sea	Atlantic, Pacific	All year	Fat (variable)	Broil*, bake	620-825	1

* Best Cooking Method
† Often sold with fat trimmed out.

Kind	Producing Area	Season	Description	Cooking Methods	Fuel Value (Calories) Per Pound	Approximate Size (Lbs.)
Horse Mackerel	Pacific	March-Oct.	Fat	Broil*, boil or steam	620	3/4-3
King Fish	Atlantic	Jan.-June	Fairly lean	Broil*, bake, deep fat or pan-fry	360	2-20
King Mackerel	S. Atl., Gulf	Oct.-May	Fat	Broil*, bake	900	5-20
Lincod	N. Pac., S. Pac.	All year	Fairly lean	Broil, bake*, boil or steam	355	1/2-21/2
Mackerel	N. Atl., Mid. Atl.	Apr.-Nov.	Fat	Broil*, bake, boiled or steamed	715-900	1/2-21/2
Mullet	S. Atl., Gulf of Cal.	All year	Fat	Broil*, bake, boil or steam, chowder	530	1/2-5
Ocean Perch (See Rosefish)						
Pollock	N. Atl., Mid. Atl.	All year	Lean	Broil, bake, boil or steam*, chowder	425	21/2-12
Pompano	S. Atl., Gulf	All year	Fat	Broil*, bake, boil or steam	730	11/2-3
Porgy (Scup)	Atlantic	All year	Fat	Broil*, bake, deep fat or pan-fry	520	1/2-11/2
Red Snapper	S. Atl., Gulf	All year	Lean	Broil*, bake*, boil or steam	395	2-15
Rockfish	Pacific	All year	Fairly lean	Broil, bake, deep fat or pan-fry*	375	2-5
Rosefish (Ocean Perch)	North Atlantic	All year	Fat	Broil*, deep fat, or pan-fry	455	11/2-2
Sablefish	North Pacific	All year	Fat (variable)	Broil, bake*, boil or steam	900	5-15
Salmon	N. Atl., N. Pac., Pacific	All year	Fat	Broil*, deep fat, pan-fry, bake or boil	600-990	5-30
Sea Bass						
Black	Atlantic	All year	Fairly fat	All methods, broil best	395	11/2-4
White	Pacific	All year	Fat (variable)	Broil*, bake, deep fat or pan-fry	410	11/2-4
Sea Trout						
Grey	Atlantic	Nov.-May	Fairly fat	Broil*, bake, deep fat or pan-fry	390	1-6
Spotted	S. Atl. and Gulf	Dec.-July	Fairly fat	All methods	455	1-10
Shad	Atlantic, Pacific		Fat	Broil, bake*	740	11/4-5
Sheepshead	Atlantic	All year	Fairly lean	Broil, bake, deep fat or pan-fry*	490	1-15
Smelt	Atlantic	Sept.-May	Fairly lean	Broil, deep fat or pan-fry*	395	1/8-1
	Pacific	Sept.-May	Fat (variable)	Broil, deep fat or pan-fry*	900	1/8-1
Spanish Mackerel	Ches., S. Atl., Gulf	Nov.-Apr.	Fat	Broil*, bake, deep fat or pan-fry	900	1-4
Spot	Mid. Atl., Ches., South Atlantic	June-Nov.	Lean	Broil*, deep fat or pan-fry	455	1/4-11/4

Striped Bass	Atl. (Now also N. Atlantic)	All year	Fat	Broil, bake, deep fat or pan-fry*	455	2-15
Sturgeon	North Atlantic	July-Sept.	Fairly lean	Broil or bake*	405	60-700
Swordfish	N. Atl., Mid. Atl., South Pacific		Lean	Broil*, bake	520	
Tautog	N. Atl., Mid. Atl.	All year	Fairly lean	Broil*, bake, deep fat or pan-fry	380	
Tilefish		Oct.-May	Fat	Broil, bake*, boil or steam	340	4-18
Tomcod	Atlantic	All year	Fairly lean	Broil, bake, deep fat or pan-fry	330	
Tuna	N. Atl., S. Pac.	All year	Fat	Broil, bake*, boil or steam	570-770	10-700
Weakfish	N. Atl., Mid. Atl.	All year	Lean	Broil, bake, pan-fry*	515	4-14
White Perch	Atlantic	May-Dec.	Fairly lean	Broil, bake, deep fat or pan-fry*	340	½-1½
Whiting	N. Atl., Mid. Atl.		Lean	Broil, bake, deep fat or pan-fry*		
Wolfish	Atlantic	Aug.-Dec.	Fairly lean	All methods	455	8
Yellowtail	Pacific	All year	Fat (variable)	Broil*, bake, deep fat or pan-fry	600	8-50
Fresh Water						
Blue Pike	Gt. Lakes and rivers	All year	Lean	Broil, bake, deep fat or pan-fry*	360	¾-1
Buffalofish	Rivers and Lakes, Mississippi	Sept.-May	Fat	Broil, bake, deep fat or pan-fry*	430	3-25
Carp	Gt. Lakes, all coasts, Mississippi river	All year	Lean	Broil, bake*, deep fat or pan-fry	420	2-8
Catfish (Bullhead)	Gt. Lakes, all coasts, Mississippi river	All year	Lean	Broil, deep fat or pan-fry*, chowder	445	1-40
¹ Eel	Mississippi river					
Lake Herring	Gt. Lakes and rivers	All year	Fat	Broil, deep fat or pan-fry*	615	⅓-1
Lake Trout	Gt. Lakes and rivers	Apr.-Nov.	Fat	Broil, bake*, deep fat or pan-fry	745	1½-10
Pickerel	Gt. Lakes and rivers	All year	Lean	Broil, bake, deep fat or pan-fry*, chowder	360	1½
Sauger Pike	Great Lakes	Nov.-May	Lean	Broil, bake, deep fat or pan-fry*	355	1 to 1½
Sheepshead	Great Lakes, Mississippi river	All year	Fairly lean	Broil, bake, boil or steam	445	1½-8

¹ Eel is common in the Mississippi and all its tributaries. See salt water chart.

Kind	Producing Area	Season	Description	Cooking Methods	Fuel Value (Calories) Per Pound	Approximate Size (Lb.)
Smelt	Gt. Lakes and rivers	Sept.-May	Fairly fat	Broil, bake, deep fat or pan-fry*	395	8 to 20 per lb.
Suckers	Gt. Lakes, Miss. riv.	Apr.-Dec.	Fairly fat	Broil, bake, deep fat or pan-fry*	420	1½
Whitefish	Gt. Lakes and rivers	All year	Fat	Broil, bake*, deep fat or pan-fry	680	1½-6
Yellow Perch	Gt. Lakes and rivers	All year	Lean	Broil, bake, deep fat or pan-fry*	370	½-1
Yellow Pike	Gt. Lakes & its riv.	All year	Fairly Lean	Broil, bake, deep fat or pan-fry*	360	1½ to 10
Shellfish						
Clams (Hard and Soft)	Atl., Pacific coasts	All year	Lean	All methods, small sizes eaten raw	344-355	
Crabs (Hard and Soft)	Atl. and Gulf, Pac.	All year	Lean	All methods except chowder	370	(av. 5-inch spread)
Lobster, Common	North Atlantic Mid. Atl., Pacific	All year	Lean	All methods except frying or deep fat fry	380	1-20
Oysters	Atl., Gulf, Pacific	Sept.-Apr.	Lean	All methods, small sizes eaten raw	365	
Scallops	Atlantic	All year	Lean	All methods	335	Cape (marble size)
Shrimp	S. Atl., Gulf Pacific	All year	Lean	All methods except broil	370	Sea (walnuts)

* Best Cooking Method.

BUYING FISH

Never compromise on the quality of fish . . . when you buy it, buy the best! Not necessarily the most expensive, but most emphatically buy top quality, whether fresh or frozen. And cook it the same day, if possible.

Frozen fish that is prepared by a reliable concern, and transported and stored by a reliable dealer so that it is at zero temp at all times, will be as fresh as the day it was frozen.

Fresh fish of top quality has a *fresh* appearance and no objectionable odor. The flesh of the fish should be firm, moist and elastic, and the eyes bright and full and never sunken. If the gills have not been removed (a practice that is very highly recommended for good keeping), they should be reddish pink. Form the habit of always making these observations when purchasing, and perhaps even more important, choose a reliable dealer on whom you can depend for top quality and honest judgment. Beware of fish "bargains."

Fish is one of the most perishable of foods. Enzyme action within the fish and air borne bacteria cause it to spoil quickly unless it is handled with the greatest of care and is adequately refrigerated.

Buy fresh fish of various varieties when they are in season in your locality; that is when they are least expensive, best. Frozen fish is available most of the year. (See chart No. 24, previous pages.)

Try less familiar varieties when they are abundant and inexpensive. The demand for favorite varieties may increase their price to a point where less well-known varieties are much better values, and will be equally enjoyed by your family.

Purchase the size of fish which is the best buy. Large fish of a given variety may be available in abundance only at certain seasons. Smaller sizes may be less expensive, just as easy to prepare, and more tasty in many cases.

Take advantage of the ready-to-cook cuts (steaks, fillets and sticks) if you need to save time and labor in preparing fish.

Buy the kind of fish that suits your needs. Lean fish are best for steaming, boiling, frying, or for soups. Baking or broiling requires a fish with more fat or the addition of oil or butter (see chart No. 24, previous pages). Dealers are glad to recommend varieties and to suggest the most practical form for you.

Buy the right amount to serve your family adequately.

Oysters and Clams. When buying oysters and clams, make sure the shells are tightly clamped together. Do not buy them if the shells are gaping. This means the shellfish are dead and no longer good. If you are buying shucked clams, oysters or scallops, purchase only from a dealer you know is dependable; these fish keep well only if they are adequately iced and properly handled. Frozen shucked shellfish is also available, and the same rules of storage apply to it as to frozen fin fish (above).

Crabs and Lobsters. Crabs and lobsters must be alive when purchased in the shell. If they are already cooked, make sure the retailer has kept them on ice and that they were cooked alive. Test by straightening out their tails; if the tails spring back into a curled position and are not limp, you can be sure they were cooked alive.

HOW TO CLEAN, PREPARE AND STORE FISH*

1. Remove gills from freshly caught fish at once and from bought fish as soon as possible to preserve freshness. Spoilage starts at the gills. The sooner they are removed, the longer fish remains fresh smelling.

2. When *cleaning fish,* wear plastic coated gloves or dip hands in salt to prevent fish from slipping from your grasp.

3. Hold fish firmly near tail and scrape off scales with a saw-tooth knife, working from tail toward head. Soak whole fish in water a few seconds before beginning and scales will come off easier.

4. Do not trim the fins off, but cut into flesh on each side of the base of the fin. This permits easy removal of the fin and fin bone either before or after cooking.

5. Cut a slit in the fish's belly from head to tail, then lift out entrails intact. Be sure to remove the heavy vein (blood line) that runs down the back bone.

6. Wash quickly in cold water. Drain thoroughly.

7. Cut off head and tail if desired.

8. To bone fish or make fillets, start at the tail and run a sharp knife close to the backbone the entire length of the fish. Then by working the knife carefully down towards the abdominal side, hugging it against the bone, the entire side may be stripped away. Repeat on other side.

9. Wrap fish tightly in waxed paper and store in the meat compartment, or directly below the ice compartment. Plan to use fish the same day whenever possible.

10. Frozen fish may be held in the freezing compartment for a day or so and then allowed to thaw in the refrigerator just before ready to use. Do not refreeze when once thawed.

11. Chill hands in cold water before handling fish. To remove fish odors from hands and utensils, rub with moistened salt *before* using any soap. Rub hands with lemon rind for the final touch.

12. Leftover fish, raw or cooked, should be stored tightly covered in the refrigerator. Form the habit of using cold leftover fish flaked in salad rather than reheating.

CLEANING CATFISH AND EEL

Catfish, eel and other tough-skinned fish must have skin removed to obtain attractive, fine flavored fish. Catfish are so sleek they cannot be held

*For further information on care of fish in the home, see p 147.

firmly in the hands. To skin them, drive a sturdy nail in the body of a tree or into a heavy board, or a 2 x 4 in an outside building. With a sharp knife, barely cut through skin all around base of head. Hang fish by its tough throat over the nail. With pliers, grip skin that runs up to a point at back of head. Pull down strongly, stripping off skin and leaving smooth, clean, white flesh. Eviscerate fish. To sever head easily which is attached with strong hard bone, hold back of fish with the point where you want to separate head from body squarely over edge of a tub or a similar narrow, firm edged object. Very sharply hit the fish against this edge. This breaks the bone quickly and it is easy to finish removing head with knife. Clean eel in same way.

SKINNING CARP—TO IMPROVE FLAVOR

Carp is often sold alive, though it may also be purchased dressed and ready for cooking. A very sharp, thin, pointed knife is needed if the fish is to be dressed in the home. First, kill fish by sticking knife halfway through the body back of the head, just behind the gills. This will permit free and thorough bleeding. Then cut out the back fin. Remove scales and outer skin by grasping fish by the tail and shaving off the scales and outer skin in thin strips; work the knife toward the head without cutting into the flesh. Then split the belly from back to front, being careful not to cut into the entrails, which may then be removed as a whole. Cut off the head back of the front fins. Cut away the tail and other fins and wash the fish thoroughly in plenty of cold water. Drain thoroughly.

A simpler method of removing the entire skin is to plunge the fish into boiling water, allowing it to remain about half a min after boiling starts again. The skin may then be easily rubbed off while the fish is hot, and the flesh rinsed in cold salt solution. Boiling, however, must not be prolonged beyond the point where the skin slips off easily, or the flesh will break apart.

To improve the flavor of carp, prepare the following dressing: Mix ½ cup salt, ½ cup grated or ground onion (with its juice), 1 tbsp vinegar, ½ tsp black pepper, and a pinch of mace. Place the dressed carp in a deep dish and cover with the dressing. Let it stand for 1 hr and then rinse thoroughly, discarding the dressing. Wash the fish in a pan of cold water for about 1 min to remove all salt from the surface. It may then be fried, broiled, baked or boiled like any other fish.

HOW TO COOK AND HANDLE FISH

1. Keep fish fresh by storing in refrigerator until last possible moment before cooking.

2. Allow frozen fish to thaw in refrigerator before cooking.

3. If you buy packaged or wrapped fillets or steaks, note on the wrapper whether they have been salted. If salt has been used, not so much additional salt is required in cooking.

4. Fish cooks quickly but it should be cooked thoroughly and still not be overcooked. Use short cooking periods at high temp or longer periods at low temp. Properly cooked fish is always flaky and slightly moist, overcooking makes fish dry and hard.

5. If you use fat or oil in cooking fish, don't let the fat smoke. It not only means that the heat is too high, but it carries the fish odor to other parts of the house.

6. Prepare fish stock from heads and bones left from filleting fish. Use it as soon as possible for making chowders, sauces and molded sea food salads.

7. Refer to chart No. 24 to learn the best method for cooking fish you have bought. A lean fish may often be successfully broiled or baked by adding cooking oil or some other fat, and fat fish may be boiled or used in chowder by first removing all visible fat.

8. Refer to next ten pages for the recommended methods for baking, boiling, broiling, and frying fish.

9. "Fishy" dishes should be washed in a strong solution of salt and water to remove the odor before using soap. Scald thoroughly.

BAKED FISH

BAKED WHOLE FISH WITH STUFFING

Weight from 3 to 5 lbs

Kinds to Bake: Barracuda (small), Bass, Bluefish, Carp, Cod, Drumfish, Grouper, Lake Trout, Ling Cod, Pompano, Red Snapper, Sablefish, Salmon, Shad, Spotted Sea Trout, Tilefish, White Fish.

Amount to Serve: Buy 7 to 8 oz for each person.

Temp to Bake: 400° F.

Time to Bake: 45 to 60 min time depending on weight and thickness of fish.

Tests for Doneness: Fish breaks apart into flakes when a fork is stuck into it and slightly twisted.

When to Serve: Immediately, while sizzling hot.

Make sure you know weight of your fish, so you will know how much salt to use and how to plan cooking time to fit serving time.

Clean the fish. Wash thoroughly in cold water and drain well; then pat dry inside and out with a clean cloth or paper toweling. Rub inside of fish with lemon juice; use ½ tsp juice to each lb of fish. Lemon juice brings out the best in fish flavor. Now sprinkle ¾ tsp salt to each lb of fish on the inside. Wrap fish in parchment or waxed paper and place in refrigerator 30 min or more to allow salt to penetrate into flesh. Meanwhile, make the desired stuffing. See recommendations below. Prepare only enough stuffing to fill cavity loosely. So take time to carefully estimate amount of stuffing you will need. Stuff fish, then close cavity with small skewers or strong tooth picks and lace together with twine. Lay a sheet of aluminum foil, or cheesecloth folded several times so as to be as wide and long as the fish, or lettuce leaves on a shallow baking pan; a jelly roll pan with a rim all around is ideal. Place fish on foil, cloth or lettuce, and brush both sides with melted butter, then sprinkle with salt, using ¼ tsp to each lb. Bake until fish tests done. It will be tastier and brown more attractively if it is basted 2 or 3 times during baking with a mixture of ½ cup hot water and 2 tbsp butter. When done, lift fish out onto a hot platter, using 2 pancake turners or wide spatulas. Quickly remove skewers and twine and if head was left on, cut it off neatly with poultry or kitchen scissors. Garnish head end with a bouquet of crisp parsley, watercress, celery leaves or fresh dill. Serve immediately. Slices of lemon or lime dashed with chopped parsley or paprika are also attractive garnishes.

BAKED FISH BIRDS

Kinds of Fish to Use: Cod, Croaker, Flounder, Grouper, Haddock, Mackerel, Pollock, Red Snapper, Rockfish, Salmon, Sea Bass, Sheepshead, Whiting, Yellow Pike.

½ recipe Bread Stuffing, p 700	Pepper
or Oyster Stuffing, p 1074	5 strips lean bacon
1½ lb fish fillets	Chopped parsley
1 tsp salt	

Start oven 10 min before baking; set to moderate (350° F).

Prepare the stuffing. Remove skin from fillets and cut into serving-size portions. Sprinkle fillets with salt and pepper. Place a small ball of stuffing on the end of each fillet, roll up neatly around the stuffing and fasten with toothpicks or small skewers, or wrap twine around and tie. Arrange the birds in a well-greased, shallow baking pan. Lay a half slice of bacon over top of each bird, or brush with butter. Bake in moderate oven (350° F) for 30 min, or until fish tests done. Remove toothpicks, skewers or twine; place carefully on a hot platter. Garnish with parsley and serve plain or with any desired fish sauce. Serves 5.

BAKED WHOLE FISH WITHOUT STUFFING

Many prefer fish without stuffing. Prepare fish, season, brush with butter, bake and baste in same way as described above. Use same test for doneness. Fish without stuffing takes a little less time for baking.

Recommended Fish Stuffings: Bread (next page), Celery, p 1072, Oyster, p 1074.

Recommended Fish Sauces: Almond-Butter, p 1257, Drawn Butter, p 1255, Dill, p 1254, Egg, p 1255, Lemon Butter, p 1257, Spanish, p 1260, Tartar, p 1260, Tomato, p 1261.

BREAD STUFFING FOR BAKED FISH

Sufficient for a 2½ to 3 lb white fish

⅔ cup chopped celery
2 tbsp chopped onion
1½ tsp butter
3½ cups coarse fresh bread
    crumbs, 4½ slices from
    1 lb loaf

½ tsp seasoning salt, p 132
¼ tsp salt
⅛ tsp pepper
3 tbsp water *or* milk

Sauté celery and onion in butter until soft and yellow. Prepare crumbs, add seasonings, toss until blended, then add sautéed vegetables, combined with liquid and toss again to blend.

EGG SAUCE FOR BAKED FISH

2 tbsp sweet pickle relish
½ to ¾ tsp salt

1½ cups medium white sauce,
    p 1262
2 hard cooked eggs, diced

Stir relish and salt into hot white sauce. Then fold in eggs. 4 servings.

SAVORY BAKED HALIBUT STEAKS

Other Kinds of Steaks to Bake: See Guide to Baking Fish, p 698

2½ lb halibut steaks, 1-inch
    thick
1½ lb ripe tomatoes
1½ tbsp finely chopped onion
1 tbsp finely chopped green
    pepper

Pepper
2½ tsp salt
2 tbsp flour
⅓ cup melted butter
Chopped parsley

Start oven 10 min before baking; set to moderate hot (400° F).

Wipe fish steaks off with a damp cheesecloth; lay half on well greased sheet of aluminum foil placed in shallow baking pan. Then lay ¼-inch thick peeled tomato slices over fish; spread onion and green pepper over tomatoes, sprinkle with pepper and 1 tsp of salt. Lay remaining steaks over top. Use small skewers or strong toothpicks to hold upper and lower steaks together. Combine rest of salt with pepper and flour. Brush sides and top of fish with butter, then sprinkle with seasoned flour. Bake 40 min, or until fish tests done and is attractively browned. Baste fish twice during baking with remaining melted butter. Lift onto hot platter; remove skewers. Pour pan gravy around fish. Garnish with parsley, serve sizzling hot. 4 to 5 servings.

FISH BAKED IN PARCHMENT

This special method of baking fish conserves a maximum of fish juices to serve with the fish.

Start oven 10 min before baking; set to moderate (350° F).

Use small, cleaned whole fish or fillets of large fish. Wash whole fish thoroughly in cold water, then drain; or wipe fillets with a damp cloth. Cut parchment paper 3 times as wide as the fish, and 1½ to 2 inches longer. Rub paper well on inside with soft butter and sprinkle fish with salt, 1 to 1¼ tsp per lb. Place fish on paper, sprinkle generously with lemon juice and paprika. Fold paper neatly over fish, finishing with a "hem" around 3 edges. Fasten with wire paper clips or pins. Bake 20 min. When done, slide packets onto hot platter. With scissors, cut and remove parchment, letting juices flow over fish. Serve immediately, with garnish of lemon and cucumber slices and crisp watercress. 2 lbs serves 4.

QUICK-BAKED FISH SPENCER METHOD

This second special method for baking fish must be done exactly according to directions for perfectly baked fish. Don't substitute flour, cornmeal, or cracker crumbs for breadcrumbs as they do not brown evenly. Be sure fish is well coated with crumbs. One-half cup of whole milk may be used in place of evaporated milk and water. The fish won't burn—don't add water or additional oil!

2 lb fish	2 tsp salt
¼ cup evaporated milk	2 cups fine dry bread crumbs
¼ cup water	Salad oil

Start oven 10 min before baking; set to very hot (500°–600° F).

Use cleaned small whole fish fillets or thick steaks. Bake small steaks and small fillets whole. Have steaks cut ¾-inch thick. Cut large fillets into serving portions. Dip fish in mixture of evaporated milk, water and salt, then into bread crumbs until thickly coated. Place on oiled, shallow baking pan; drizzle each piece lightly with oil. Allow 2 tbsp oil for all the fish. Put fish into oven, uncovered, bake 10 min. Do not add water or turn fish while baking. When done, fish will be brown and dry on outside, tender and juicy on inside. Remove to hot platter, using pancake turner. Garnish with parsley and overlapping slices of cucumber or lemon. Serve at once. 5 servings.

BOILING FISH

"Boiled" fish like "boiled" eggs is a misnomer since the water must *never boil. Simmering* fish produces the best flavor, texture, and appearance. Simmering should continue only long enough for fish to be cooked through and still hold its shape.

Kinds of Fish to Boil: Cod, Hake, Pike, Pollock, Red Snapper, Salmon, Trout, White Fish.

PLAIN BOILED FISH

Use whole fish, thick slices of large fish, fillets or steaks. Wipe with dampened cloth, then wrap in cheesecloth, cooking parchment paper, or lay in an oiled wire basket. Pour water into kettle estimating amount to barely cover fish. Add 1 tbsp of salt and 1 tbsp lemon juice to each qt of water. A slice of onion, a little celery, carrots, and a sprig of parsley or a bit of bay leaf or other seasoning may be added to water for extra flavor. Heat water to boiling and boil 5 to 10 min to improve flavor. Then reduce heat and place fish in liquid. Cover and simmer very slowly until fish is tender. Never let water boil! Simmer 10 min per lb for thin fish, 10 to 20 min per lb for thick fish. Lift fish from broth, handling gently. Unwind cheesecloth carefully, and place fish intact on a hot platter. Garnish with cress or parsley and serve hot, or let chill in broth and serve cold with Tartar, p 1260 or Egg, p 1255 sauce.

BOILED FISH DINNER

1 lb green cabbage, shredded	Few dashes of red pepper
4 small potatoes	1½ lb Northern pike, *or* 1 lb
4 small carrots	shucked cleaned green
1 medium onion	shrimp
3 tbsp butter	1 cup fresh, frozen *or*
2 tsp salt	canned peas
1 cup boiling water	

Trim off soiled leaves of cabbage and discard. Shred cabbage finely. Peel potatoes, cut in fourths; scrape carrots, wash, slice thin; peel onion and chop. Melt butter in a large saucepan, add onion, and simmer until soft. Add rest of vegetables, arranging cabbage and peas on top, add salt, water and pepper; cover and simmer 10 min. Now remove about half the cabbage and peas. Have the fish cut neatly into serving-size portions and lay skin side down over vegetables; or add shucked, cleaned but uncooked shrimp. Cover with cabbage and peas that were removed; then cover the pan tightly, and simmer 5 to 10 min, or until fish is done. Drain off all liquid and add enough boiling water to make 1 cup. Blend 1½ tbsp flour with 3 tbsp cold water to make a smooth paste; add to hot broth and cook over direct heat, stirring constantly until sauce boils and thickens. Stir in 2 tsp lemon juice. Place fish and vegetables carefully on a hot platter, pour sauce over all, and sprinkle with 1 tbsp finely chopped parsley, if desired. 4 servings.

BOILED SALMON WITH EGG CAPER SAUCE

Easy to do, attractive and very good

1½ lb salmon, cod *or* hake

Egg Caper Sauce:
2 tbsp butter
2 tbsp flour
½ tsp salt
Few dashes of red pepper
2 cups milk
¾ tsp dry mustard
3 hard-cooked eggs, p 663
1 to 2 tsp chopped capers

Court Bouillon:
½ cup each of sliced carrots, celery and onion
1 tbsp salt
Pinch of thyme, not too much
½ tsp whole peppers
2 whole cloves
1½ qts water *or* fish stock
¼-inch thick slice lemon

Fish to be boiled should always be in one piece.

Sauce: Melt butter, blend in flour, salt and pepper in top of double boiler over direct heat; then stir in the milk slowly, and cook with continued stirring until the sauce boils and thickens. Stir in mustard; then fold in the coarsely chopped eggs and the capers. Place over hot water and cover to keep hot.

Court Bouillon: Heat ingredients for court bouillon in a 4-qt saucepan to boiling; reduce heat, cover and boil gently 15 min. Wipe fish with damp cloth, tie in a double thickness of cheesecloth, lower it into the court bouillon and press down evenly beneath surface of liquid. Cover and simmer 18 to 20 min or until the fish flakes when a fork is stuck into it and twisted slightly. Lift fish out onto a plate, remove cloth; then to make fish attractive, peel off the skin carefully to preserve the shape. Use a spatula or pancake turner to transfer fish to hot platter. Pour the hot sauce over the fish and serve at once. 4 or 5 servings.

COLD BOILED FISH

Whole trout *or* salmon
2½ to 3 lbs
1 qt water
1 medium onion

1 large carrot
2 tbsp chopped parsley
1 tbsp vinegar *or* lemon juice
2½ tsp salt

Clean fish, bone if desired, then wrap in cheesecloth. Put water in a pan large enough to lay the whole fish in straight; add remaining ingredients. Heat to boiling and boil gently 10 min. Reduce heat, place fish in liquid and simmer gently about ½ hr until fish is tender but firm and whole. Cool thoroughly in liquid, place in refrigerator as soon as practical after removing from heat. Before serving, remove from liquid to a platter, carefully remove cheesecloth and all skin. Pour Relish Dressing or Sour Cream Sauce over fish. 4 servings.

See next page for recipes for Relish Dressing and Sour Cream Sauce

Relish Dressing:
 1 hard-cooked egg, chopped
 ¾ cup chopped celery
 ¼ cup chopped green onion
 ¼ cup chopped green pepper
 ¼ cup chopped sweet pickle

or 3 tbsp chopped parsley
 2 tbsp lemon juice
 ¾ cup Boiled Salad Dressing,
  p 1198
 ¼ cup chili sauce
 3 tomatoes

Combine all ingredients except tomatoes and chill thoroughly. Cover entire fish with cold dressing. Garnish with thick slices of tomato.

Sour Cream Sauce:
 1 cup sour cream
 2 tbsp horseradish
 3 tbsp chopped stuffed olives

½ tsp salt
 2 tomatoes, sliced
 1 cucumber, sliced

Combine first 4 ingredients and chill thoroughly. Serve sauce over cold fish. Garnish with tomatoes and cucumbers.

DELICIOUS BOILED FISH

2½ lb fish, pike, salmon, cod,
  perch, haddock, etc.
2½ cups boiling water
 24 whole black peppers
 2 sprigs parsley
 1 small bay leaf

2¼ tsp salt
 1 tbsp lemon juice
 2 tsp sugar
 2 tbsp flour
 2 tbsp cold water
 1 egg yolk

Remove scales from fish, wash, pat dry with cloth. Leave small fish whole; cut large ones into serving portions. Lay fish in a heavy 3-qt saucepan. Add next 5 ingredients, cover, place over low heat and simmer 30 min. Drain off liquid and strain. There should be 1½ cups. Put this into another saucepan, add lemon juice, sugar, and flour mixed to a smooth paste with cold water. Cook slowly, stir constantly to keep smooth until mixture boils. Beat egg yolk, stir in a little of the hot sauce, return to mixture in saucepan; continue cooking and stirring another min. Serve fish in a hot dish with sauce poured over it. Garnish with parsley. 5 servings.

BROILED FISH

Kinds to Broil: Alewife, Blue Runner, Cod, Haddock, Halibut, Sea Herring, Horse Mackerel, Kingfish, King Mackerel, Mullet, Pompano, Porgy or Scup, Rosefish, Salmon, Sea Bass, Sea Trout, Spanish Mackerel, Spot, Swordfish, Sheepshead, Tautog.

Amount to Serve: Buy 8 oz of dressed fish or 6 oz of steaks or fillets for each person.

Temp to Broil: 550° F.

Time to Broil: 8 to 15 min per lb, time depends on thickness.

Test for Doneness: It flakes when fork stuck into it is twisted.

When to Serve: Immediately while fish is blistering hot.

Broiling is a quick way to cook fish deliciously. It takes no more than 15 min for fish to move from the refrigerator to the table by the "broiler route." Any lean or fat fish can be broiled, but those listed above broil best. Lean fish, see Table 24, p 691, must be brushed with oil, melted butter or French dressing to prevent drying out on surface during broiling. Broil fresh fish as promptly after securing as convenient for finest flavor and juiciest texture. But thaw frozen fish completely, and thaw in the refrigerator. Thawing at room temp results in loss of considerable juice, which causes cooked fish to be dry. Broil promptly after thawing for best results. Cuts most frequently broiled are fillets, steaks, small whole, pan-dressed, drawn or dressed fish, split or cut portions of larger fish.

If necessary, wash fish quickly in cold water. Drain well, then pat dry with a clean cloth or paper toweling. Lay fish on parchment or waxed paper and sprinkle both sides with salt, using ¾ tsp of salt for each lb of fish. Sprinkle with pepper and flour also, if desired. Wrap paper around fish and place in refrigerator 15 to 20 min for it to absorb salt. Preheat broiler at 550° F for 10 min, or follow broiler directions of your stove manufacturer.

When broiler is hot, oil broiler rack and place fish on it, skin-side down if split fish is used. Quickly brush top-side with oil or fat, as desired. Slide broiler rack under heat so surface of fish is about 3 inches from source of heat. Broil until fish tests done with a fork. Do not turn fish. The preheated broiler rack browns under side sufficiently. Brush fish with oil or fat every 3 min. Test thin fillets for doneness after 6 or 7 min, and 2-inch thick whole fish, fillets or steaks after 8 to 10 min. When done, use pancake turner to lift fish to a hot platter. Garnish with lemon slices and parsley.

BROILED SALT MACKEREL

2 lb salt mackerel fillets	2 tsp cut parsley
¼ cup melted butter	1 lemon, cut in wedges

Lay fish in a flat pan, flesh-side up, cover with cold water; cover tightly and soak in refrigerator 12 hr. Drain, pat dry with clean cloth or paper toweling. Brush with melted butter and place on an oiled hot broiler rack, skin-side down. Broil as directed above. Slide carefully onto hot platter, sprinkle with parsley, drizzle with more butter. Serve piping hot with lemon for garnish. 5 servings.

FILLET OF SOLE AND OYSTERS PARMESAN

½ pt oysters, 16 medium	Pepper
4½ tbsp butter	2 tsp fine-cut parlsey
1 lb fillet of sole	1¼ cups bread crumbs, pea size
3 tbsp flour	1 cup fresh grated
1½ tsp salt	Parmesan cheese
1½ cups milk	

In 1-qt saucepan, heat oysters in their liquid over low heat only until plump and edges curl. Remove from heat and strain off all the liquid into another saucepan. Add 1½ tbsp of the butter to drained oysters and 1½ tbsp to the liquid. Lay fish, cut into serving pieces, into liquid. Place over low heat 3 or 4 min until fish cooks just enough to flake when pierced with fork and slightly twisted. Lift fish out carefully into an 8 x 8-inch glass baking dish. Make a white sauce of remaining butter, flour, salt and milk, p 1262. Stir in pepper and parsley. Pour sauce over fish. Add crumbs to oysters and toss, then arrange over top of fish. Sprinkle with cheese. Broil 3½ inches below heat (450° F) 10 min or until cheese melts and crumbs are crunchy. Serve at once from baking dish. 4 servings.

BROILED SHAD ROE

2 pair shad roe, medium size,	1 tsp salt
1¼ lb	Pepper
2 tsp lemon juice	8 thin strips lean bacon
2 tbsp butter, melted	

If roe is frozen, thaw out in refrigerator, but cook promptly.

Wipe roe and cut tissue connecting pair with kitchen scissors. Sprinkle both sides of roe with lemon juice, brush well with butter and lay in a shallow pan lined with aluminum foil. Broil under high heat (550° F) about 3 inches from source of heat 5 min, sprinkle with salt and pepper, turn and season other side. Add bacon at this point and broil 5 min; then turn bacon and remove any pieces that are crisp to hot serving plate. Turn roe and broil 3 or 4 min longer on each side until done and slightly golden. Roe requires about 15 min to cook if it is removed from refrigerator when completely thawed. Brush with butter and serve with 2 pieces of crisp bacon and a wedge of lemon. 4 servings.

BROILED SWORDFISH

1 lb frozen swordfish, 1½	¾ tsp salt
to 2-inches thick	Dash of pepper
2 tsp lemon juice	2 tbsp butter

Thaw fish thoroughly in refrigerator just in time to be broiled. Wipe fish with damp cloth, sprinkle both sides with lemon juice, salt and pepper; then dot with half the butter. Place on aluminum foil in shallow pan or on broiler rack about 3 inches from source of heat. Set broiler at 550° F, broil 12 min, then turn, dot with remaining butter, and continue cooking 10 to 12 min longer or until fish is lightly browned. Baste 2 or 3 times with the juice which accumulates. Serve with Egg Caper Sauce, p 703. 4 servings.

Note: It is important that frozen fish be completely thawed before cooking, and that it be cooked immediately after thawing.

BROWN BUTTER SAUCE FOR BROILED FISH

3 to 4 tbsp butter   2 tbsp lemon juice

Carefully heat butter in small pan so it browns well but does not burn. Remove from heat. Stir in lemon juice, and immediately pour over any preferred hot broiled fish cooked according to preceding directions. Garnish with parsley. Serve at once. 4 servings.

PAN AND DEEP-FAT FRIED FISH

See directions for Frying with Deep Fat, p 738

PAN-FRIED FISH

Choose fillets or steaks, pan-dressed fish or drawn or dressed fish, split or cut into serving portions. Blend ½ cup cornmeal and 2 tsp salt. Beat 1 egg and stir in 2 tbsp milk or water. Dip fish, first in egg mixture, then in meal. Melt enough shortening, lard or bacon drippings in a heavy skillet to be ¼-inch deep, then heat until hot but not smoking. Place coated fish in hot fat and cook 3 to 5 min, or until nicely browned on under side. Cover skillet and remove from heat about 2 min to permit fish to cook in its own steam. Then remove cover, turn fish and return skillet to heat. Cook until under side is browned to desired color. Fish less than ⅝-inch thick require less cooking time; thicker fish require longer. 5 servings.

FRENCH-FRIED FISH (See p 736)

FRIED FILLETS OF LAKE PERCH OR PIKE

It's hard for one to find fault with this fish

1½ lb perch *or* pike fillets	⅓ cup flour
1 tsp salt	1 egg
⅛ tsp pepper	2 tbsp lemon juice
¾ cup fine cracker crumbs	½ cup shortening or bacon fat

Cut fish in single fillets, scrape off any scales, cut off fins, etc. and wipe clean with a damp cloth; sprinkle with salt and pepper. Crush saltine crackers with rolling pin or put through food mill. Put crumbs in 1 pie pan, flour in another. Break egg into shallow pan, add lemon juice and beat slightly with fork. Coat fish in flour well, then with egg mixture, then in cracker crumbs, patting crumbs on firmly. Lay on a platter, cover with waxed paper and store in refrigerator until ready to fry—2 or 3 hrs, or fry immediately. Heat shortening in heavy skillet until sizzling but not smoking hot; put fish in and fry 4 or 5 min or until brown and crisp, then turn carefully with broad-blade spatula and brown other side. Cooking takes 8 to 10 min. Drain on paper toweling and serve on hot platter. 4 to 5 servings.

Note: A little additional lemon juice may be sprinkled on fish with the seasonings.

FRIED SHAD ROE

2 pair shad roe, medium size, 1¼ lb	2 tsp lemon juice
	1 tsp salt
8 strips lean bacon	Pepper

If shad roe is frozen, thaw out completely in refrigerator.

Wipe roe with damp cloth and cut tissue connecting pairs with kitchen scissors. Brush with lemon juice. Pan-fry the bacon until crisp and remove to serving platter. Add roe to skillet, cover and cook over medium heat, about 5 min, or until nicely browned on under side. Season with salt and pepper, turn, season other side, cover and cook another 5 min, or until under side is nicely browned. Roe removed from refrigerator will require additional time to cook thoroughly; so turn and cook an additional 2 min on each side, but leave cover off the last 4 min of cooking to crisp. Serve with 2 slices of bacon and lemon wedges, or melt 2 tbsp butter and add 2 tsp lemon juice and serve over the roe. 4 servings.

FRIED SMELTS

Don't let the tiny size of smelts cause you to pass them up for bigger fish which are available all the year round. Smelts are a cinch to clean. They have few scales which are loose and easy to remove. They are no trouble to cook, they are easy to eat and no fish has a more delicious flavor. While the backbone is tiny and delicate, it lifts out all in one piece with just a flick of the fork. The rest of the fish is boneless and the crisp tail is as edible and good flavored as the flesh. When you buy smelts, get enough of them. Allow at least 6 to 8 smelts which weigh about half a lb for each person. *To clean smelts:* fold newspapers so they will be thick enough to prevent the fish odor from getting through to the table or board on which cleaning is done. Over newspaper lay waxed paper or the white parchment paper in which fish was wrapped. Lay fish on paper, hold by tail and scrape toward head. Next cut off the head, then split belly carefully from one end to the other and lift out entrails. A small wad of dampened paper toweling makes an ideal mop for wiping out any loose colored or silvery membrane. Rinse fish quickly, one at a time in cold water. Never let them stand in water to soak out the fine flavor. Drain and if there is not time to drain well, lay on paper toweling and pat gently to dry. *Frying:* either shallow or deep is the best method of cooking, but the former method is more economical unless the deep fat can be used repeatedly for the cooking of fish. The fat should be clarified after cooking each mess of fish. See directions for pan-frying, p 707, or deep-fat frying, p 738.

SPECIAL RECIPES

FISH WITH DILL AND TOMATOES

This tasty fish can be prepared any day in the year

1 lb fillets *or* steaks, pike, whiting, haddock, halibut
1 tbsp flour
1 tbsp corn meal
1 tsp salt
Few dashes of pepper
2 tbsp bacon fat *or* shortening

1 small onion, walnut-size, sliced
6 heads fresh dill, *or* ½ to 1 tsp dill seed
2 cups canned, *or* 4 medium size fresh tomatoes, peeled, sliced
Dill heads *or* parsley

Use clean fresh or just thawed frozen fish. Pat dry with paper toweling. Blend flour, meal, salt and pepper in pie pan or on waxed paper. Dip fish in flour mixture until well coated. Heat fat in 9-inch skillet until just sizzling. Add fish and brown well on both sides. Sprinkle remaining flour mixture over fish; add onion, tomatoes and dill heads or seeds. Cover and cook over medium heat 25 to 30 min. Taste and season with additional salt and pepper, if needed. Serve immediately. Lift fish onto plate with pancake turner; pour sauce over it. Garnish with fresh dill heads or parsley. Serve with boiled or mashed potatoes. 4 servings.

FISH CAKES

3 medium potatoes
2 cups fish flakes, 11½ oz can
½ cup top milk *or* thin cream

¾ tsp salt
Dash of pepper
Shallow fat for frying

Boil potatoes in jackets until tender. Remove skins and mash (cold mashed potatoes also may be used). Add fish, milk, and seasonings and mix thoroughly. Cool mixture. Shape into small flat cakes and pan-fry in moderately hot fat until brown and crusty on both sides. May be served with Dill Sauce, p 1254 or Tartar Sauce, p 1260. 5 to 6 servings.

FISH CHOWDERS
See recipes in chapter on "Soups," p 1264.

FISH CREOLE

¼ cup butter	⅓ cup water
2 tbsp chopped onion	1 bay leaf
⅔ cup chopped celery	¾ lb cooked fish, flaked, *or*
2 tbsp chopped green pepper	2 cups boiled shrimp
¼ cup flour	½ tsp salt *or* to taste
2½ cups canned tomatoes, No. 2 can	

Melt butter in skillet, add onion, celery and green pepper, and simmer about 5 min, stirring frequently. Blend in flour, add tomatoes and water, and stir until sauce boils and thickens. Add bay leaf, fish and salt, cover and simmer about 15 min. Remove bay leaf. Serve hot over Mashed or Baked Potatoes, p 1378 or pp 1372–73, or Boiled Rice, p 433. 4 servings.

SMOKED FISH

1 lb smoked fish, 4 medium	Dash of pepper
½ cup water	1 tbsp butter *or* margarine,
2 tbsp lemon juice	melted
⅛ tsp sugar	2 tbsp chopped parsley
⅛ tsp salt	

Carefully remove head, tail and back bone from fish. Discard. Place in a skillet, add next 5 ingredients. Cover and cook over medium heat for 10 min or until fish are heated through and the liquid has evaporated. Place hot fillets on a platter, drizzle with melted butter and sprinkle with parsley. 4 servings.

THREE WAY HERRING

2 lb cleaned, boned herring, 3 cups ground	1 tbsp grated onion
3 eggs, well beaten	1 tbsp salt
	1½ cups milk

Choose freshly caught, firm-fleshed herring; clean and wash thoroughly inside and out. Remove bones (see directions for preparing fish fillets, p 696) and then remove meat from the skin in one whole piece, using an ordinary paring knife for scraping. Put boned, skinned fish through food chopper twice, or pound to a fine paste with a wooden potato masher. Add well-beaten eggs, stir in onion, salt, then add milk slowly, beating hard with a wooden spoon until a stiff dough-like consistency is produced. Cook as follows:

1. *Fish Cakes.* Drop by spoonfuls into shallow hot fat. Shape into

cakes with a spoon. Sauté 6 or 7 min or until brown on under side. Turn and brown on other side. Serve immediately.

2. Fish Balls. Make a seasoned fish stock by simmering fish bones and skin, one slice each of onion and lemon and a small carrot in enough water to cover for 1½ hrs. Strain off stock into another pan, reheat. Dip spoon first into hot stock, then quickly into the fish mixture, shaping the spoonfuls into an oval. Drop into stock, cover, simmer 15 min or until cooked through. Lift out with slotted spoon. Cooked balls resemble peeled hard-cooked eggs. Serve with Tomato Sauce, p 1261.

3. Fish Pudding. Turn mixture into a buttered 5-cup casserole or loaf pan and bake in a moderate oven (350° F) 1¼ to 1½ hrs. Unmold onto hot platter, serve hot with Tartar Sauce, p 1260.

The entire mixture makes 12 to 15 servings.

KIPPERED HERRING WITH SCRAMBLED EGGS NO. 1

Remove paper from herring can, lay can in saucepan. Cover with cold water, heat to boiling, boil 5 min to be sure to heat herring thoroughly. Meanwhile scramble eggs, p 675. When ready to serve, place key from can over tongue on can, turn upside down holding cloth over can while opening to prevent spurting out of juice. Remove cloth, open in usual way and serve with eggs. A 3½-oz can serves 2.

Variation: Serve heated herring with potatoes boiled in jackets.

KIPPERED HERRING WITH SCRAMBLED EGGS NO. 2

A favorite English breakfast dish—made with either canned or cellophane-wrapped kippers

9-oz pkg kippered herring fillets, 2 fish	2 tsp lemon juice
	1 tbsp melted butter
1½ cups cold water	Scrambled Eggs, p 675

Wipe fish with damp cloth, then separate fillets by cutting apart with scissors. Place in skillet skin-side down, add water, heat to boiling, reduce heat, cover and simmer 10 min. Lift fish from liquid with pancake turner to hot platter. Brush with lemon juice and butter. Serve with Scrambled Eggs. 4 servings.

CLAMS

SPECIES OF CLAMS

1. Hard-shell or quahaug clams from the Atlantic coast have the most general distribution. The large ones of this variety are used in making broths and chowders. The small ones, such as Little Necks and Cherry Stones, are good served raw on the half shell, in cocktails, and also steamed or broiled.

2. *Soft-shell clams* come from both Atlantic and Pacific coasts. They are good for clam bakes, frying, steaming, roasting and broth.

3. *Razor clams* from the Pacific coast make good chowders.

Clams bought alive in the shell are sold by the dozen. To determine whether they are alive, try to open the shell with the fingers. A live clam holds its shell tightly closed.

CLEANING CLAMS

Scrub clams with a stiff brush, wash thoroughly in cold water. Change water as often as it becomes dirty. To remove all sand from clams, hold them a few min under cold running water.

To open clams for serving on half-shell, insert a strong, sharp slender knife between shells and cut around clam through the muscle. Twist knife slightly to pry shell open. There is a special knife for this purpose. Loosen meat in shell. To use in Chowder, turn juice and meat into a bowl. If sand adheres to meat, rinse off quickly in cold water. If sand is in juice, let stand for sand to settle, then drain off juice and use with clam meat.

CLAM CHOWDER

See recipes in chapter on "Soup," p 1265, 1270.

CLAM FRITTERS

Wash and open 12 clams; drain off liquor, save. Split clams, discard dark stomach contents. Put clams through food chopper. Sift all-purpose flour, measure 1 cup, resift with 1 tsp baking powder, ½ tsp salt, ⅛ tsp pepper and dash of nutmeg. Add ⅓ cup clam liquor, 2 beaten eggs, ⅓ cup milk, beat until smooth. Fold in 2 tsp melted butter and chopped clams. Drop by tablespoonsfuls into deep fat, heated to 375° F. Fry until brown. Drain. Serve hot with lemon wedges. 4 servings.

CLAMS ON THE HALF SHELL

See recipe in chapter on "Appetizers," p 194.

STEAMING CLAMS

Choose Little Neck hard-shell clams and clean as described above, but do not open. Place the unopened clams hinge-side down in a shallow pan in a steamer and steam until shells open, then remove immediately. Remove one shell of each clam and discard. Serve the clams on the remaining shells on a hot plate. Provide melted butter for dipping the clams, also salt and pepper. The broth in the pan may be served along with the clams in cups. Allow 2½ to 3 dozen for 5 servings.

ROASTING CLAMS

Clean the clams thoroughly and place in a baking pan. Roast in a moderately hot oven (425° F) until the shells open. Remove immediately and serve like steamed clams. Allow 2½ to 3 dozen for 5 servings.

WASH BOILER "CLAM BAKE"

A clean, old-time sturdy washboiler with a tight fitting lid is ideal for this cooking job. Have three hard wood racks made to fit into it one above the other about 8 inches apart. Make a sturdy stone support around a deep bed of coals over which to place the boiler, or put it on a kitchen stove. Lay fresh lobster and clams on lower rack, put washed sweet or white potatoes and washed eggs in their shells on the second rack. Place husked ears of corn and chicken that has been half broiled on top rack. Add not more than 2 cups water to the boiler for an amount of food to serve 6 to 8 people. Cover tightly and place over heat which is just sufficient to keep food steaming thoroughly all the time. Cook at this rate 45 min to 1 hr. Keep cover tightly fitted during entire cooking. Serve foods very hot with butter, salt and pepper; pour the savory juice collected in bottom of kettle into cups to serve each person to drink as a hot appetizer or to drink with the meal.

CODFISH

TO FRESHEN CODFISH

Method 1. Leave codfish in large pieces. Let cold water run over codfish for 15 min, then place in saucepan, cover with cold water and heat slowly just to boiling—*Do Not Boil.* Pour off water and repeat this process until fish tastes fresh.

Method 2. Leave codfish in large pieces. Let cold water run over it for 15 min, then warm water for 5 min. Drain, cover with cold water and soak overnight.

Method 3. Leave codfish in large pieces. Soak codfish in cold water 3 or 4 hrs, changing water every hr.

CREAMED CODFISH

½ lb salt codfish	3 cups milk
¼ cup butter	Dash of pepper
¼ cup flour	

Freshen codfish as described above. Drain, break apart in bite-size pieces. Melt butter in top of double boiler; blend in flour, add milk gradually and cook over direct heat, stirring constantly until sauce boils and thickens. Add fish, and pepper to suit taste. Place over boiling water, cover, cook 20 to 30 min. Serve on toast or over boiled potatoes. 5 servings.

CODFISH AU GRATIN

Prepare Creamed Codfish, p 713. Add 1 cup grated cheese to the white sauce just before adding codfish, stirring until blended. Instead of continued cooking in double boiler, pour creamed fish into shallow baking dish, sprinkle with buttered bread crumbs. Bake in moderate oven (350° F) until nicely toasted, 20 to 30 min. 5 servings.

CODFISH BALLS

A perennial favorite. Work for the golden fringed effect

½ lb frozen *or* dried salt
  codfish
4 medium boiling potatoes
3 tbsp milk

1 tbsp butter
2 eggs, well beaten
Salt and pepper to taste
3 or 4 drops tabasco

Freshen cod, see p 713. Cut codfish into several pieces and place in saucepan over pared, quartered potatoes. Barely cover with boiling water, heat to boiling. Reduce heat, cover and simmer until potatoes are tender, about 20 min. Drain off any liquid that remains. Mash potatoes and codfish together, add milk and butter and whip until smooth and fluffy. Add the eggs and beat well. Season to taste with salt, pepper and tabasco. If desired, ¼ tsp of fennel or other herb seasoning may be added. With a fork, form mixture into rough irregular balls, letting the shreds of codfish fringe out from the "ball." Fry until golden brown in deep fat heated to 375° F. Drain on absorbent paper and serve on hot platter with parsley sauce made by adding ⅓ cup finely cut parsley to 1½ cups seasoned medium White Sauce, p 1262. 4 servings.

CODFISH CASSEROLE

½ lb salt codfish
3 tbsp butter
3 tbsp flour
1 cup canned *or* cooked
  fresh *or* frozen peas
Milk

1 tbsp chopped pimiento
  (optional)
1 cup grated cheese, ¼ lb
Salt and pepper to taste
⅓ cup fine dry bread crumbs
2 tbsp melted butter

Freshen codfish, p 713. Drain and flake the fish. Melt butter, blend in flour, and add liquid drained from peas to which enough milk has been added to make 2 cups. Stir constantly over direct heat until thickened; then add grated cheese. Add seasonings. (Salt may not be needed if fish retains enough salt.) Fold in drained peas, pimiento, and flaked codfish and turn into a 4-cup buttered casserole. Stir crumbs into melted butter and sprinkle over top. Bake in a moderately slow oven (325° F) for 45 to 50 min. 5 servings.

FRIED CODFISH WITH MAYONNAISE SAUCE

2 tbsp butter *or* margarine	Dash of salt
3 tbsp flour	1½ lbs frozen codfish fillets,
1 cup milk	thawed in refrigerator
½ cup Mayonnaise, p 1202	⅓ cup corn meal
2 tbsp lemon juice	⅓ cup shortening
¼ tsp sugar	

Blend melted butter and flour in the top of double boiler. Add milk gradually, cook over direct heat, stirring constantly until mixture boils and thickens. Add mayonnaise, lemon juice, sugar and salt and mix. Keep hot over hot water. Divide codfish into serving pieces, dip into cornmeal and fry on both sides in the hot shortening until brown and crisp and done through. Serve immediately with the hot sauce. 4 servings.

CRABS

HOW TO BUY CRABS

The most common varieties are blue crabs from the Atlantic and Gulf coasts, and the larger Dungeness crabs from the Pacific coast. All varieties have both hard and soft-shelled stages. Normally, crabs are hard-shelled, but as they grow the shells must be enlarged, so the old shell is discarded from time to time and a new one forms. If the crab is caught just before the new shell hardens, it is called a soft-shelled crab. Hard-shelled crabs are available all year, but are most plentiful in the summer. Soft-shelled crabs are in season from May to October. Crabs are purchased alive by the dozen and should be kept alive in moist seaweed until they are cooked. Some markets sell fresh crabmeat (cooked) by the lb.

COOKING HARD-SHELLED CRABS

Only live crabs should be cooked. Boil them in sea water if it is available because it contains the amount of salt that gives the best flavor. Or boil them in enough plain salted water to cover (add 1 tbsp salt to each qt of water used). Actually boil the crabs for 20 min, or steam them for 25 min. Crabs turn red during cooking. Drain and plunge into cold water just long enough to cool slightly. Again drain, then remove the meat.

The sweet, edible meat is found in the claws, legs and body of the crab. After cooking, pull off the claws and legs, and crack the shells. Break off the segment that folds under the body at the rear. Holding the crab in the left hand with the back toward you, slip fingers of the right hand under the top shell and pull the body downward so as not to break it. (The top shell is sometimes used for baking deviled crabmeat.) Holding the crab under cold running water, remove the digestive tract. Then split the crab along the central crease. Hold half the body in the left hand, and with a sharp knife cut the hard membranous covering along the outside edge. With a nutpick, remove the tender sweet meat in each cavity, being careful not to break off pieces of shell into the meat. Pick the meat out carefully so it will not be necessary to wash it off, for washing results in a loss of both flavor and food value.

CLEANING AND COOKING SOFT-SHELLED CRABS

Use only live crabs. Soft-shelled crabs should be dressed before cooking. Place the live crab with its back up on a board, and kill by cutting off the head ½ to ¾-inch back of the eyes. Turn back the tapered pointed ends of its back about half way, and scrape out the spongy material that is exposed. Then peel off the tail or "apron" which laps under the crab, together with the spongy mass under it and discard. Wash the crab in cold water.

Soft-shelled crabs are cooked by frying. Have deep fat heated to 360° F. While it heats, let the crabs stand in a salt solution of 2 tbsp salt to 1 cup water for about 2 min; then drain, dip into beaten egg, and roll in fine bread crumbs. Arrange crabs 1 layer deep in a wire frying basket and lower into the hot fat. Fry until golden brown, turning over once. Lift out onto absorbent paper or paper toweling to drain, and serve with Tartar Sauce, p 1260. The entire soft-shelled crab is edible. Allow 5 large, 10 medium or 15 small crabs for five servings.

FRENCH-FRIED SOFT SHELL CRABS

Easier than you think; better than you think. Extra special luncheon, dinner or late supper delight

1 dozen soft shell crabs, 1½ to 2 lb	½ to ⅔ cup fine cracker crumbs, p 151
1 tsp salt	1½ to 2 lb shortening
Pepper	Tartar Sauce, p 1260
Flour to coat	Parsley *or* cress
1 large *or* 2 small eggs	

Clean crabs as directed above. Wash quickly in cold water. Drain. Sprinkle with salt and pepper. Dip in flour to coat, then in slightly beaten egg and finally in crumbs to cover well. Lay on cake rack or plate and place in refrigerator to dry off for a few minutes. Just before serving time, place one-layer deep in frying basket, lower into fat heated to 360° F. Keep heat constant and when crabs become rich brown on underside, turn to brown other side. Frying requires about 3 min. Lift basket out, turn crabs onto paper toweling or brown paper to drain. Serve at once on hot plates with Tartar Sauce. Garnish with parsley or cress. 4 servings.

CRABMEAT CAKES

⅓ cup butter
1 clove garlic
¼ cup flour
1 cup milk
¾ tsp salt
   Few grains of pepper
½ tsp Worcestershire sauce

¾ cup dry fine bread crumbs
6½-oz can crabmeat, 1⅔ cups
   flaked
1 egg, beaten, diluted with
1 tbsp water
¼ cup milk
1 hard-cooked egg, p 663

Melt half the butter in a saucepan with clove of garlic which has been sliced into several pieces. Remove pieces of garlic when butter is melted. Blend in flour and add the milk, stirring constantly until the sauce boils and thickens. Add salt, pepper, and Worcestershire sauce to the white sauce. (There should be 1¼ cups sauce.) To ½ of the sauce, add ¼ cup of the bread crumbs, and crabmeat from which cartilage has been removed. Mix well, cover tightly, and chill in refrigerator. Shape mixture into 10 small patties, dip patties into remaining bread crumbs, beaten egg, and again in crumbs. Pan-fry in remaining butter in a moderately hot skillet for about 5 min. Serve hot with remaining white sauce thinned with the ¼ cup of milk and reheated with the chopped hard-cooked egg. 5 servings.

DEVILED CRABS

¼ cup butter
2 tbsp flour
½ cup milk
2 cups cooked crabmeat,
   flaked *or* canned
½ tsp salt
½ tsp paprika

¼ tsp pepper
½ tsp prepared mustard
1 tbsp chopped parsley
1 tbsp lemon juice
   Yolks of 3 hard-cooked
   eggs, mashed
⅔ cup buttered crumbs

Melt butter in a saucepan, blend in flour. Add milk gradually, and cook over low heat stirring constantly until sauce boils and thickens. Fold in remaining ingredients except buttered crumbs, and mix until well blended but do not mash. Turn mixture into a greased 6-cup casserole, or into individual casseroles or cleaned crab shells. Sprinkle with buttered crumbs (2 tbsp of butter) and bake in a moderately hot oven (400° F) for 5 to 10 min or until crumbs are temptingly brown and mixture is heated through. Serve at once directly from casserole. 4 servings.

CRABMEAT MORNAY

A delightful French method to stretch crabmeat for a luncheon favorite

1 cup crabmeat, 7½-oz can
1 tbsp butter

1 tbsp lemon juice
1 cup Mornay Sauce, p 1258

Drain liquid from crab, look over fish and discard any cartilage. Divide into 4 well-buttered fish shells or shallow individual ramekins. Sprinkle with the lemon juice and spoon ¼ cup Mornay Sauce over each. Bake in moderately hot oven (400° F) 10 to 12 min until light brown and bubbly. Or place under 350° F broiler 3 inches from source of heat; broil until browned and bubbly, 8 to 10 min. 4 servings.

FINNAN HADDIE

CREAMED FINNAN HADDIE

2 cups medium-thin White Sauce, p 1262	¾ lb finnan haddie Parsley or cress

In making white sauce, use 1½ tbsp flour per cup of milk, and omit salt. Place over boiling water. Cut finnan haddie into inch cubes, using kitchen scissors for convenience. Fold into the hot White Sauce, cover, and heat over boiling water for 20 to 30 min. Serve on toast or boiled or baked potatoes. Garnish with parsley. 5 servings.

FINNAN HADDIE AND POTATO CASSEROLE

¾ lb finnan haddie 4 medium potatoes, pared and diced	2½ cups milk 2 tbsp butter Chopped parsley

Cut finnan haddie into serving-size pieces, and put into saucepan with potatoes and milk. Heat slowly until milk begins to simmer. Turn into a shallow baking dish and dot with butter. Bake in a moderate oven (350° F) until potatoes are tender, about 30 to 35 min. Sprinkle with parsley and serve at once. 5 servings.

FINNAN HADDIE SUPREME

This satisfying fish dish comes from Scotland

13-oz can finnan haddie, about 2½ cups	¹⁄₁₆ tsp white pepper
¼ cup butter *or* margarine	1½ cups milk
¼ cup flour	2 hard-cooked eggs, sliced
⅜ tsp salt	1 tbsp capers
	2 tbsp chopped sweet pickle

Drain liquid from fish and discard. Rinse fish, then flake into large pieces, removing any bone and skin. Melt butter in top of double boiler over direct heat, blend in flour, salt and pepper, then add milk gradually, stirring constantly. Cook until thick and smooth—about 5 min. Carefully fold in fish. Place over boiling water, cover and reheat 5 min. Turn into hot serving dish. Arrange overlapping egg slices down center, then sprinkle capers and pickles along side of eggs. Serve with potatoes boiled in jackets or toast. 4 servings.

FROG LEGS

FRENCH-FRIED FROG LEGS

2 lb frog legs	2 tbsp water
2 tsp salt	1 cup fine bread crumbs *or*
¼ tsp pepper	corn meal
2 eggs, beaten	Fat for frying
4 tsp lemon juice	

If frog legs are large, cut apart through backbone. Never wash as the delicate flavor is easily lost. If necessary, cut off feet and wipe with a damp cloth. Dry on paper towel. Season with salt and pepper. Combine egg, lemon juice and water. Dip frog legs into egg mixture and then roll in crumbs. Fry in deep fat at 350° F for 6 to 10 min or golden brown and until tender. Serve immediately. 4 to 5 servings.

PAN-FRIED FROG LEGS

2 lb frog legs	¼ cup flour *or* corn meal
1 tsp salt	¼ cup butter *or* margarine
⅛ tsp pepper	1 tsp freshly grated onion

If frog legs are large, cut apart through backbone. Wipe with a damp cloth but do not dip in water as delicate flavor is easily soaked out. Cut off feet. Dry on paper towels. Combine salt, pepper, and flour, dip frog legs into flour mixture to coat well. Fry in the hot butter and onion until delicately browned. Cover and cook over low heat until tender—about 15 to 18 min. Serve piping hot. 4 servings.

LOBSTERS

HOW TO BUY LOBSTERS

Lobsters are in season all year, but are most plentiful in summer. Only live lobsters, or fresh-cooked lobster meat should ever be bought. Live lobsters have dark green shells with red specks; when cooked, the shells become bright red. Two types are found on the market: the North Atlantic variety which have large claws, and the Florida or California variety which have no claws but have large antennae protruding from the head.

A lobster weighing 1 lb is called a "chicken lobster." One and one-fourth lb lobsters are called "mediums," and those weighing more are called "selects." Any lobster that is heavy for its size will be full of tender sweet meat. The white flesh of the claws, body and tail, and the roe and liver are the edible parts of a lobster. The lungs, stomach and intestinal vein are not edible, and should be removed before or after cooking. The female lobster's roe is called coral, and is considered a great delicacy by some people who therefore prefer the female; but the male has firmer flesh and a more brilliant red shell when cooked. The male lobster has a narrower tail than the female, and the two uppermost fins within his tail are stiff and hard. Female lobsters with the eggs attached are said to be "berried," and their sale is prohibited in most states because of conservation laws. Frozen lobster tails can also be bought. These come from Florida, the Bahamas and Africa. One lobster serves 1 to 2 persons. See p 690 for other information on buying.

BOILING LOBSTERS

Only live lobsters should be used, and they should be boiled as soon as they are delivered. Half-fill a large kettle (2½ gallon capacity) with boiling water. Cover, and bring to a full rolling boil. Add 1 cup salt, then put in the live lobster, grasping it by the middle of the back. (The lobster should have its claws pegged by the dealer for the protection of those who are less skilled in handling lobster and might otherwise get pinched.) Put it in head first; it will be instantly killed. Cover pot and boil rapidly 4 to 5 min, then simmer 20 to 30 min, the time depending on size. Then lift the lobster out and lay on its claws to drain.

To open boiled lobster: Twist off the 2 large claws first, then the 4 pairs of small claws. With a hammer or a nutcracker, break each of the large claws and remove the meat from each in 1 piece. Separate tail from body at the joint by holding 1 part in each hand and pulling until they come apart. Hold the tail in the palm of the left hand, hard shell side down, and with kitchen scissors, make a slit the full length of the tail. Pull apart and break the white meat loose in 1 large piece. Run a small sharp knife down the length of this piece of meat to the center *where a dark line* will be found. This is the *intestine* and should be removed carefully. Then take the body shell in the left hand and draw out the body meat carefully with the right hand, so as not to remove *the stomach or "lady"* which should be discarded along with the spongy lungs at the sides of the body. The green liver has excellent flavor and is very nutritious. It is used in preparation of sauce or to garnish the lobster platter. Break the body meat into several pieces and pick out the flesh around the bones. The eggs or roe (coral) should be used for garnishing. Be careful not to let any of the tough feathery gill-like particles under the shell become mixed with the meat.

BROILED LOBSTER

Adjust broiler rack so top of lobster will be about 3 inches from source of heat. Start broiler 10 min before broiling; set to very hot (550° F). Prepare live lobster with pegged claws on its back on a cutting board. Now kill by inserting a sharp knife between the body and tail segments, thus cutting the spinal cord. Cross the large claws. Starting at the head, make a deep cut lengthwise through the body and tail, being careful not to cut the stomach or "lady," which is a sack lying just back of the head. Pull the 2 halves apart without breaking. *Remove the "lady,"* and also the intestines which run the length of the body and tail. Crack the large claws. Brush the meat with melted butter, and sprinkle with salt and pepper. Spread lobster, shell-side down on the thoroughly heated broiler rack. Broil slowly for 20 min. When done, meat is shrunken slightly from shell. Remove to serving platter and drizzle melted butter, made tart with lemon juice, over lobster. Garnish with lemon slices and parsley. Serve immediately. Serves 1 to 2.

BROILED LOBSTER TAILS

4 frozen lobster tails, 1½ lb   ¼ cup salt
2 qts boiling water   ¼ cup melted butter

Drop lobster tails into boiling water, add salt and heat to boiling again. Reduce heat, cover and simmer 20 min. Drain. With sharp knife or kitchen scissors, remove soft shell-like covering on underside of tail. Make a deep cut through center of flesh and remove dark vein. Drizzle part of butter over lobster meat, place on rack 4 to 6 inches from broiler heat and broil 6 min. Serve in the shell with remaining butter. 4 servings.

LOBSTER NEWBURG

2 cups diced boiled lobster   1 cup thin cream
    meat, fresh cooked *or*   2 egg yolks, beaten
    canned   ¼ tsp salt
1 tbsp sherry extract   1 tsp lemon juice
¼ cup melted butter   Paprika
1 tbsp flour   Water cress

Heat the lobster thoroughly with the extract and 3 tbsp of the butter, being careful not to brown the butter. In another saucepan, blend the remaining butter with the flour, then add the cream and stir constantly until the sauce boils over direct heat. Remove from heat. Stir into the beaten egg yolks and return to the saucepan, cooking over low heat with constant stirring for about 2 min or until thickened. Add the heated lobster and seasonings and mix well, but do not heat again or the sauce may curdle. Serve immediately on hot toasted crackers or crisp toast. Garnish with cress or parsley. 5 servings.

LOBSTER THERMIDOR

4 frozen lobster tails, 1½ to   ¼ tsp black pepper
    2 lb *or* 2 medium-sized live   ¼ cup Madeira *or* other
    lobsters   white wine
¼ cup butter   1 cup cream
½ cup sliced mushrooms   3 egg yolks
½ tsp salt   1 tbsp Parmesan cheese

Cook lobster tails in 2 qts water with ¼ cup salt added for 20 min at simmering temp. Then remove meat as from boiled lobster according to directions, p 720. Remove soft shell-like covering on underside of lobster tail and scoop out meat from shell. Remove dark vein, and cut meat into inch pieces. Melt butter in top of double boiler over direct heat. Add mushrooms and sauté for 2 or 3 min. Add lobster meat, salt, pepper and wine. Cook for 2 min over direct heat or until wine is absorbed, then place over boiling water and add the cream and yolks which have been beaten together. Cook with constant stirring until slightly thickened. Pile lobster mixture into shells, sprinkle with cheese and broil for about 5 min or until meat is well heated through and cheese is slightly browned. Serve piping hot. 4 servings.

OYSTERS

HOW TO BUY OYSTERS

No food is of more consistently high quality than oysters, because their cultivation, production, handling, transportation and marketing are subject to rigid government supervision. The oyster industry is carried on by every coastal state in the country. The best-known varieties are "Blue Points" and "Rockaways" from Long Island, "Cotuits" from Massachusetts and "Lynnhavens" from Virginia. Pacific coast oysters, grown mostly in Puget Sound, are world-famous for their fine flavor.

The old idea that oysters can be eaten only in months with an "R"— that is, from September through April—is largely superstition. The belief arose from the fact that oysters are not desirable for food during the spawning season, which was supposed to be from May 1st to September 1st. However, the spawning season differs in different localities and with different varieties, and oysters of prime quality are available from some source all year. The price is higher during the summer due to their perishability. Some cities and localities prohibit their shipping and sale during the hot months.

Oysters may be purchased shucked by the pt, qt or gallon or in the shell by the dozen. Oysters purchased in the shell are usually the small "Blue Point" oysters which are desirable for eating raw on the half shell, p 196.

HOW TO OPEN OYSTERS

Insert the point of a thin-bladed sharp knife between the shells just back of the hinge which is at the pointed side of the oyster. Cut through the large muscle that holds the shells tightly together. Separate the shells and loosen the oyster meat. Be sure to save the liquor from the oysters to use in cooking.

HOW TO CLEAN SHUCKED OYSTERS

Turn oysters into a sieve or colander placed over a saucepan to catch liquor. Set oysters over a second pan and pour cold water over them, allowing *not more* than ½ cup cold water to each qt of oysters. Then pick up each oyster separately and examine it to remove any bits of broken shell. Never let oysters stand in water. The water and liquor in the saucepans may be strained and used with the oysters if they are to be stewed or escalloped.

OYSTERS AU GRATIN

1 pt oysters	Dash of pepper
⅓ cup butter *or* poultry fat	Dash of poultry seasoning
4 tbsp flour	Few drops onion juice, p
Milk	164
1¼ tsp salt	⅔ cup fine dry bread crumbs

Start oven 10 min before baking; set to moderate (350° F). Heat oysters in their liquor until they curl, then strain off liquid; measure, add milk to make 2⅔ cups. Heat 3 tbsp of the butter in a saucepan, blend in flour, add milk mixture gradually and cook and stir until smooth and thickened. Add seasonings and oysters. Turn into buttered individual baking dishes, shells or an 8-inch pie plate. Heat remaining butter in skillet, add crumbs and toss to mix well. Spread evenly over oysters. Bake 18 to 20 min, or until bubbly and crumbs are a rich brown. Serve at once. 4 to 5 servings.

ESCALLOPED OYSTERS

1 pt oysters	½ tsp salt
2 cups coarse cracker crumbs	Pepper
¼ cup melted butter	½ cup milk *or* chicken broth

Pick over oysters to remove any bits of shell. Chop the oysters coarsely (cutting in 3 or 4 pieces with kitchen scissors is a convenient method) and combine with their liquor. Mix cracker crumbs and melted butter, and arrange a layer of half the buttered crumbs in bottom of a 9-inch round shallow baking dish. Pour oysters over them in a uniform layer and sprinkle with the salt and pepper. Cover with remaining crumbs and pour milk over all. Bake in a moderately hot oven (400° F) for 20 min. 5 servings.

Variation: If a larger proportion of crumbs is desired, substitute 4 cups toasted coarse bread crumbs and increase the milk to 1 cup.

OYSTER FRITTERS

1 recipe Batter for Shellfish	⅛ tsp pepper
Fritters, p 1349	1 cup oysters

Make batter. Stir in pepper. Look over oysters, drain off liquid and discard. Cut oysters into 4 or 5 even pieces with kitchen scissors. Fold into batter. Fry at 360° F according to *General Directions for Frying,* p 1349. Serve hot for luncheon or supper. Serve with creamed celery, peas or chicken. 3 to 4 servings.

FRENCH-FRIED OYSTERS

The easy, quick way to prepare crusty oysters

24 large oysters	Cracker crumbs *or*
2 tbsp lemon juice	corn meal
¾ tsp salt	1 to 1½ lb shortening
Pepper	Lemon wedges
Flour to coat	Parsley
1 egg, beaten	Tartar Sauce, p 1260

Look over oysters for pieces of shell. Drain thoroughly. Pat dry between folds of cloth or paper toweling. Sprinkle with lemon juice, then with salt and pepper. Coat with flour, then dip in slightly beaten egg, then in crumbs or meal. Lay on cake rack or plate and place in refrigerator for an hr to dry off. Just before serving time, place 1 layer deep in frying basket and lower into shortening heated to 365° F. Adjust heat to keep temp constant and fry until golden brown, from 1½ to 2 min. Lift out basket, turn oysters onto absorbent paper. Serve at once on hot plates. Garnish with lemon wedges and parsley. Serve with Tartar Sauce. 4 servings.

OYSTER SANDWICHES

Toast white bread, spread with Tartar Sauce. Lay 4 sizzling hot French-Fried Oysters between 2 slices of toast. Serve with a thick slice of tomato.

PAN-FRIED OYSTERS

Prepare oysters as for French-fried Oysters (above), but fry in a skillet in shallow hot fat about ¼ inch deep until delicately browned on both sides. Serve on hot platter with lemon slices and garnish of cress.

RAW OYSTERS ON HALF SHELL

See recipe in chapter on "Appetizers," p 196.

OYSTER STEW AND OYSTER BISQUE

See recipes, chapter on "Soups," p 1272.

OYSTERS ROCKEFELLER MODERNE

½ lb fresh spinach
¼ cup parsley leaves, pressed down
½ cup celery leaves, pressed down
¼ cup tender green onion tops *or* chives

1 small bay leaf
1 tsp Worcestershire sauce
¼ tsp salt
¼ cup shortening
½ cup grated dry bread crumbs
½ pt fresh oysters

Start oven 10 min before baking; set to hot (400° F). Put spinach, parsley, celery, onion and bay leaf through food chopper using medium fine knife. Mix any juice that is expressed back into the spinach mixture. Add Worcestershire sauce and salt; mix well. Heat 3 tbsp of the shortening in skillet, add spinach mixture and simmer for 5 min. Mix together crumbs and remaining shortening. Line bottom of greased 9-inch casserole with crumbs. Lay oysters in layer over this. Spread spinach mixture over all and sprinkle top with crumbs. Bake 20 min. Serve at once. 4 servings.

SCALLOPS

HOW TO BUY SCALLOPS

Scallops are mollusks like clams and oysters, but they are seldom seen in their shells. The part which is marketed is the single large muscle that opens and closes the shell; clams and oysters both have similar muscles, but much smaller. Small "Long Island" scallops from the coastal bays are about ¾-inch thick and pinkish white; they are in season from September through April. The larger white deep sea scallop is in season all year; it may be as large as 2 inches in diameter. The small scallops are considered to have the sweetest flavor. Deep sea scallops are available frozen as well as fresh.

FRENCH-FRIED SCALLOPS

1 qt scallops
Fine dry bread crumbs
2 eggs, beaten

Pepper, if desired
Shortening for frying

If scallops are large, split across the grain and cut into ¾-inch cubes. Immerse scallops for 3 min in cold salted water, 1 tbsp salt to each cup of water. Drain thoroughly. Roll in bread crumbs, then dip into beaten egg seasoned with pepper, and again roll in crumbs. Place one layer deep in a wire frying basket, and lower into deep fat heated to 375° F. Fry about 4 min or until richly browned and tender. Drain and serve piping hot with Tartar Sauce, p 1260, if desired. 5 servings.

PAN-FRIED SCALLOPS

For pan-frying, scallops may be dipped in egg and crumbs as for French-fried Scallops, p 725, or pan-fry without any coating. Have about ⅛-inch layer of butter or other fat melted in a hot skillet. Cook the scallops for 4 min over low heat, turning when about half done. Serve piping hot. A sauce may be made for the uncrumbed scallops, if desired, by adding a couple of tbsp of water to the residue in the skillet and stirring over low heat until it is dissolved.

SHRIMP

HOW TO BUY SHRIMP

Shrimp are crustaceans like lobster and crab. They come to the market with heads removed, packed in ice. They may be sold either in this green form or boiled, with or without the shells. Shrimp are graded according to the number per lb as follows: *jumbo,* under 25 per lb, *large* 25 to 30, *medium* 30 to 42, *small* 42 and over per lb. One lb makes 3 or 4 servings in most cooked dishes. Shrimp are found in all coastal waters, but the most abundant shrimp fisheries are located in Puget Sound. Prawns are similar to shrimp but much larger, often attaining a length of 7 inches, and they are much less common.

Shrimp may be bought "green"—uncooked and shucked or unshucked and frozen. They have little color before cooking, but become pink to bright red when boiled. Canned shrimp are available packed in either tin cans or glass jars. They are ready for use except that in most brands the dark sand vein down the back needs to be removed.

PREPARING FRESH SHRIMP

2 cups water	¼ medium onion, sliced
1 cup sliced celery	2½ lb green shrimp
1½ tsp whole black peppers	2 slices lemon
2 tsp salt	

Heat water to boiling, add next 4 ingredients; simmer 30 min. Meanwhile, shuck shrimp by breaking under shell and opening from front to back and peeling off shell. Remove dark sand vein from center-back of shrimp by making a shallow cut from end to end along back just deep enough to reveal vein, then gently pull it out in one piece. Rinse quickly in cold water. Add lemon slices to simmering liquid; boil 5 min, then strain. Discard seasonings and vegetables. Measure liquid, add water to make 1½ qts, and return to kettle. Heat to boiling, add shrimp, reheat to boiling, reduce heat, cover and simmer 5 to 10 min until tender, time depending on size. Cool shrimp quickly in the liquid by standing pan in cold water, then drain and quickly rinse in cold water. Two and one-half lb green shrimp make 2½ cups after shucking and cooking. If shrimp are stored an hr or so before using, cover and chill to keep juicy and plump.

Variation 1: Shuck and clean shrimp as described above. Drop into enough boiling salted water to cover—1 tsp salt to 1 qt water—reheat to boiling, reduce heat, cover and simmer 5 to 10 min. Drain and use in desired way.

Variation 2: Wash unshucked shrimp in cold water, then drop into boiling salted water—1 tsp salt to 1 qt water. When water boils again, lower heat and simmer 5 min. Remove from heat, drain and place under cold running water. When cool, remove shucks and veins as described above. This method produces attractive shrimp, but sand veins are more difficult to remove.

CREAMED SHRIMP

2 lb green shrimp *or* 2	2 tbsp finely chopped
5-oz cans shrimp	sweet pickle
2 cups medium White Sauce,	Buttered hot toast
p 1262	Watercress

Clean and cook shrimp as described above. Or remove sand veins from canned shrimp and rinse in cold water. Fold cooked or canned shrimp into hot white sauce in top of double boiler and continue heating over boiling water until they are hot through, about 15 min. Serve shrimp over hot toast. Sprinkle pickle or capers over top. Garnish with cress and serve immediately. 5 servings.

CURRIED SHRIMP

Follow recipe for Chicken Curry, p 1047 substituting 2 cups cleaned, cooked shrimp for the chicken. More lemon juice may be desired in the shrimp curry.

FRENCH-FRIED SHRIMP

2 lb green shrimp *or* 3	1 tsp sugar
5-oz cans wet-pack shrimp,	½ tsp salt
drained and cleaned	1 egg
½ cup flour	¼ cup water
¼ tsp D.A. baking powder	

Clean but do not cook fresh shrimp. Sift flour, measure and resift with baking powder, sugar and salt into mixing bowl. Beat egg, add water and add to flour mixture, stir just enough to blend. Drop 3 or 4 raw, cleaned shrimp into batter at a time. Lift out into frying basket, then lower into deep fat heated to 360° F; fry to a delicate golden brown. Lift out onto absorbent paper to drain a few min. Serve while piping hot with Tartar, p 1260, Soy, p 685, or Barbecue Sauce, p 1250. 6 servings. If cooked shrimp are used for dipping in batter, fry at 375° F.

SHRIMP À LA KING

1 lb green shrimp	⅓ cup flour
1¾ tsp salt	2¼ cups milk
1 cup boiling water	2 tsp chopped pimiento
3 tbsp butter	2 hard-cooked eggs, diced
1 cup chopped celery	Crisp waffles *or* toast
1 tbsp chopped green pepper	

Shuck shrimp and remove dark sand vein from backs; rinse in cold water. Add 1 tsp of salt to the water, heat to boiling, add shrimp and simmer 5 to 10 min in a covered saucepan. Remove from heat, drain, rinse quickly in cold water. Melt butter in top of double boiler, add celery and green pepper and sauté 5 min, then blend in flour. Add milk gradually and cook over direct heat, stirring constantly until sauce boils and thickens. Add pimiento, diced eggs, shrimp and rest of salt and reheat over boiling water. Serve over crisp hot waffles or toast. 4 to 5 servings.

SHRIMP COCKTAIL (See "Appetizers," p 197)

SHRIMP JAMBALAYA

This enjoyable dish originated in New Orleans, where fine Creole cooks combined the best in French and Spanish cooking. Use fresh, fresh-frozen or canned shrimp

3 slices bacon	1 tbsp tomato catchup
⅔ cup diced celery	1 tbsp Worcestershire sauce
½ cup chopped onion	½ cup water
½ cup chopped green pepper	2 cups fresh *or* canned shrimp
11-oz can cream of tomato soup, undiluted	Salt to taste
	4 cups hot cooked rice

Cut bacon into short lengths with scissors, then sauté until done. Add celery, onion and pepper, and cook until vegetables are soft. Now add soup, catchup, Worcestershire sauce and water. Simmer 10 min, then add shrimp and continue simmering 20 min. Season with salt. Serve with steamed rice. 4 servings.

SHRIMP PASTE

1 lb green shrimp	1⅔ tbsp vinegar
½ cup salad dressing	¼ tsp salt
1 tsp seasoning salt	¼ cup soft butter

Clean and cook shrimp according to directions, p 726. When shrimp cools, drain off liquid and discard. Put shrimp through a food chopper; add remaining ingredients and mix thoroughly. Use paste for sandwich filling or spread for canapés. About 1½ cups.

SHRIMP CREOLE

2 med onions, sliced
4 stalks celery, chopped
2 tbsp bacon drippings
1 tbsp flour
1 tsp salt
2 tbsp chili powder
1 cup water

2 cups tomatoes
2 cups peas
1 tbsp vinegar
1 tsp sugar
1½ cups cooked shrimp,
  p 726

Sauté onions and celery in bacon drippings until crisply tender but not browned. Add flour, salt and chili powder and blend. Slowly add water, stirring to make smooth sauce. Cook slowly, covered, 15 min. Add remaining ingredients and cook until shrimp are heated through. Serves 6.

SHRIMP DE JONGHE

2 lbs shrimp
½ lb (2 sticks) butter
1 clove garlic, minced
1 tsp salt

⅓ cup parsley, chopped fine
1½ cups bread crumbs, toasted
¼ cup grated Parmesan cheese

Wash shrimp, remove shells and devein. Drain well and dry. Melt 1 stick butter in skillet and reserve ¼ cup. Split shrimp lengthwise and sauté in butter left in skillet, about 5 min. Cream remaining stick of butter until fluffy in electric mixer. Add garlic, salt, parsley and bread crumbs; mix well. Arrange shrimp evenly over bottom of shallow baking dish, about 9 x 12 inches. Sprinkle crumbs over shrimp, sprinkle on cheese, then drizzle reserved melted butter over all. Bake 30 min at 325°F. If crumbs are not crisp, brown under broiler. Serves 6 to 8.

QUICK SHRIMP NEWBURG

1 (7-oz) pkg frozen, shelled,
  deveined shrimp
½ tsp salt
¼ cup water

1½ tbsp butter
1 tbsp flour
1 cup half-and-half cream
2 eggs

Place frozen shrimp, salt and boiling water in saucepan, cover and simmer 2 min. Drain, saving liquid if desired. Make white sauce of butter, flour and cream, substituting cooking liquid for equal amount of cream if desired. Beat eggs slightly, stir in about half of hot mixture, a little at a time; then return to remaining sauce and cook over low heat a couple of min. Add shrimp and cook only until heated through. Serves 2 or 3.

CANNED SALMON AND TUNA

CREAMED SALMON

15½-oz can red *or* pink salmon
2 cups medium White Sauce,
  p 1262
1 tbsp chopped parsley

½ tsp fine-grated onion
Toast slices
Cress *or* parsley

Drain salmon but save liquid to add to white sauce. Remove skin and discard. Flake fish coarsely with a fork and crush the bones. Have White Sauce in top of double boiler over hot water. Add onion and fish with its juice and heat thoroughly, about 10 min. Add parsley just before serving. Serve on toast triangles. Garnish with cress. 5 servings.

SALMON AND MACARONI CASSEROLE

7 oz macaroni, broken
3 tbsp butter
3 tbsp flour
1-lb can red *or* pink salmon
  Milk
¾ tsp salt

Dash of pepper
½ cup sliced pared
  cucumber
¼ cup bread crumbs, blended
  with 2 tbsp melted butter
¼ cup grated cheese, 1 oz

Cook macaroni until barely tender. Drain, rinse with hot water. Melt butter, blend in flour, add juice drained from salmon plus enough milk to make 1½ cups. Stir over direct heat until sauce boils and thickens. Add seasonings and macaroni. Discard salmon skin; crush bones, combine with fish and flake. Arrange in alternate layers with macaroni mixture in 6-cup greased casserole, beginning and ending with macaroni. Top with layer of cucumbers. Mix buttered bread crumbs with cheese, sprinkle over top. Bake in moderate oven (375° F) for 20 to 25 min. Serves 5.

SALMON AU GRATIN

1-lb can red *or* pink salmon
1 tbsp lemon juice
1 tbsp butter
1 tbsp flour
1 cup milk

½ tsp celery salt *or* ½ cup
  drained, cooked celery
Salt and pepper to taste
¼ cup fine dry bread crumbs
¼ cup grated American cheese

Drain salmon, remove bones and skin, discard skin. Flake fish. Crush bones and add to salmon. Add lemon juice. Melt butter, blend in flour, and fish juice and milk, stir over direct heat until sauce boils and thickens. Add salmon, celery salt or cooked celery, salt and pepper as desired. Turn into a 6-cup buttered casserole and sprinkle bread crumbs and cheese mixed together over the top. Bake in a moderately hot oven (400° F) for about 20 min. 5 servings.

SALMON LOAF

1-lb can red *or* pink salmon	1½ cups coarse dry bread
1 tbsp lemon juice	crumbs
Dash of cayenne	½ tsp baking powder
1 tsp salt	½ cup evaporated milk
2 eggs, beaten	½ cup fish liquid and
⅔ cup chopped celery	water

Drain salmon and save liquid; discard skin and crush bones when flaking fish. Add remaining ingredients, then mix well. Pack firmly into a 9 x 4½ x 2½-inch buttered glass loaf pan. Bake in a moderate oven (350° F) until brown and firm, from 30 to 40 min. Unmold onto hot serving platter. Serve with Tomato, p 1261 or Cheese Sauce, p 444. Salmon Loaf mixture may be made into patties and pan-fried. 5 servings.

SALMON CAKES

1-lb can red *or* pink salmon	Salt and pepper to taste
2 eggs, slightly beaten	1 tbsp lemon juice
1 cup cold mashed potatoes	¼ cup shortening

Drain salmon, save juice. Remove skin and bones, discard skin. Mash salmon. Crush bones; add to fish. Stir in eggs, fish juice and potato; blend well. Add seasonings and lemon juice, mixing thoroughly. Divide in ¼-cup portions and shape in flat patties about ½-inch thick. Heat shortening in heavy skillet, lay in patties and brown slowly on both sides to a rich golden color. Remove to a hot platter and garnish with parsley and lemon wedges if desired. May be served with Tartar, p 1260 or Celery Sauce, p 1252. 5 servings.

Note: ¼ tsp scraped onion may be added to cakes.

SALMON AND RICE CASSEROLE

½ cup raw rice	1 tsp salt
2 eggs	2 tbsp lemon juice
1 cup milk	¼ cup butter, melted
1-lb can red *or* pink salmon	½ cup fine dry bread crumbs
2 tbsp chopped parsley	

Cook old or new process rice as in directions, p 433. Beat eggs thoroughly and combine with milk and the hot rice. Remove skin and bones from salmon. Discard skin, flake salmon, crush bones and add. Stir flaked salmon into the rice mixture and add parsley, salt and lemon juice. Turn into a 6-cup greased baking dish or into individual custard cups. Toss butter and crumbs together and sprinkle over the top. Bake in a moderately slow oven (325° F) for 30 to 40 min. Serve hot. 5 servings.

SALMON SOUFFLÉ

¼ cup butter
⅓ cup flour
1½ tsp salt

2 cups milk
4 eggs, separated
1-lb can red *or* pink salmon

Melt butter in top of double boiler; blend in flour, add salt and milk gradually, and cook over direct heat, stirring constantly until sauce boils and thickens. Beat egg yolks until light, stir in a little of the hot sauce, and pour back into rest of sauce; cook over boiling water, stirring constantly for 2 min. Remove from heat. Drain salmon, remove skins and bones, discard skin, and flake salmon. Crush bones and add to fish. Mix fish and juice with sauce. Beat egg whites until stiff and fold lightly but thoroughly into the mixture. Pour into an ungreased 8-cup casserole and bake in a moderately slow oven (325° F) for 1 hr. See method for baking, p 678. Serve immediately. 5 servings.

Note: Any leftover cooked fresh fish may be used in place of the salmon.

CREAMED TUNA FISH

Two 7-oz cans tuna fish

2 cups medium White Sauce, p 1262

Drain off oil and flake fish coarsely. Combine flaked fish with the hot white sauce and reheat over boiling water for 10 min. Serve on mashed potatoes, hot boiled rice, noodles, or toast. One tbsp chopped pimiento and ½ cup sautéed mushrooms may be added for richer color and flavor. 5 servings.

FISH COBBLER

¼ cup chopped celery
½ tbsp chopped green pepper
½ tbsp finely chopped onion
3 tbsp butter
3 tbsp flour
1½ cups milk

7-oz can tuna, flaked
5¾-oz can shrimp, cleaned
½ tsp salt
Dash of pepper
½ tsp finely cut pimiento

Sauté celery, green pepper and onion in the butter for 5 min. Blend in the flour; then add milk gradually and stir constantly over direct heat until the mixture boils and thickens. Add tuna, shrimp, seasonings and pimiento, and pour into a well-greased 4-cup casserole. Prepare baking powder biscuit dough as follows:

1 cup sifted all-purpose flour
1 tsp D.A. baking powder *or*
   1¼ tsp tartrate *or* phosphate type

½ tsp salt
¼ cup shortening
⅜ cup, 6 tbsp, milk

Sift flour, baking powder and salt together 3 times. Cut in shortening with pastry blender or 2 knives and add milk all at once, stirring with a fork just until the dough stiffens. Turn out onto a lightly floured board and knead lightly about 8 times; then roll about ⅜-inch thick, and cut to fit top of casserole. Cut a few gashes in it and place over hot fish mixture. Bake in a hot oven (450° F) for 20 to 30 min, or until crust is well browned and cooked through. 4 to 5 servings.

TUNA AND CELERY FONDUE

1¼ cups milk	1 cup finely diced celery
1 tbsp butter	7-oz can tuna
1 cup soft bread crumbs	3 eggs, separated
½ tsp salt	1 tbsp lemon juice

Scald milk, add butter, crumbs, salt, celery and tuna, which has been drained and flaked. Beat egg yolks well, and stir in a little of the hot mixture, then return to saucepan and heat for about 3 min or until thickened, stirring constantly. Remove from heat and fold in lemon juice and stiffly beaten egg whites. Turn into 6-cup buttered casserole, bake in a moderately slow oven (325° F) for 1 hr, or until a knife inserted in the center comes out clean. (If desired, the celery may be sautéed in a small amount of butter for 5 min before combining with other ingredients; otherwise it will remain slightly crisp even after baking.) 5 servings.

TUNA FISH AND EGGS À LA KING

3½-oz can tuna	2 tsp chopped green pepper
Butter *or* margarine	2 tsp chopped pimiento
3 tbsp flour	2 hard-cooked eggs, p 663
½ tsp salt	quartered
1½ cups milk	

Drain oil from the canned tuna, add enough butter or margarine to make 3 tbsp. Place in top of double boiler over direct heat, add flour and salt and blend. Add the milk gradually, stirring constantly until the mixture boils and thickens. Add the flaked fish, green pepper, pimiento and eggs, and reheat over boiling water. Serve piping hot on toast with a garnish of parsley. 4 servings.

TUNA AND NOODLE CASSEROLE

7-oz can tuna	8 oz noodles
3 cups medium White Sauce, p 1262	½ cup buttered bread crumbs

Drain oil from tuna, flake fish, and add to white sauce; heat over boiling water. Meanwhile cook noodles in 2 qts boiling salted water, boiling vigorously until tender, p 430. Drain well. Arrange in alternate layers with the creamed tuna in a buttered casserole. Sprinkle buttered bread crumbs on top and bake in a moderate oven (350° F) about 20 min, or until golden brown. 5 servings.

Variation: Add 1 cup grated cheese, or 1 chicken bouillon cube to white sauce (with salt omitted) and proceed as above. Cooked sliced potatoes may be used in place of the noodles.

TUNA AND NOODLE CASSEROLE SUPREME

A Meal in a Jiffy

8 oz noodles
2 hard-cooked eggs
7-oz can tuna
1 cup drained, canned, *or*
  leftover cooked peas

10½-oz can cream of mushroom
  soup
¼ cup grated cheese

Cook noodles in 2 qts boiling salted water, boiling vigorously until soft. Drain well in a colander and rinse with hot water. Peel and slice eggs. Meanwhile drain oil from tuna and discard. Arrange layers of noodles, sliced egg, flaked tuna and peas in a greased 6-cup casserole, beginning and ending with noodles. Heat mushroom soup (in same pan used to cook the noodles) and add enough liquid drained from peas (or milk) to fill mushroom soup can. Stir to keep smooth and heat to boiling. Pour over the tuna and noodle mixture in the casserole, pushing mixture very gently aside with a fork to allow liquid to run down to bottom. Top with grated cheese and bake in a moderately hot oven (375° F) for 15 to 20 min, or until mixture is hot through and cheese is a temptingly brown color. Serve at once directly from casserole. 5 servings.

Note: One cup crumbled potato chips may be substituted for the grated cheese for an unusually flavorsome topping.

TUNA TURNOVERS

¼ cup butter *or* margarine
⅓ cup flour
½ tsp salt
1½ cups milk
7-oz can tuna, drained
2 hard-cooked eggs, chopped

1 tsp finely chopped onion
¼ cup finely chopped celery
1 cup coarsely grated carrot
Pastry for double crust
pie, p 924

Melt butter in saucepan and blend in flour until smooth. Add salt, then milk gradually stirring to keep smooth. Cook over direct heat, stirring constantly until mixture boils and thickens. To ½ cup of this white sauce (reserve remainder for relish sauce, below), add the drained, flaked tuna, hard-cooked eggs, onion, celery and carrot. Mix lightly until thoroughly blended. Roll out pastry to ⅛-inch thickness into a rectangle

20 x 10 inches. Cut into eight 5-inch rounds and place a large spoonful of the tuna mixture on each round. Moisten edges of pastry with water, fold over to form a semi-circle. With tines of a fork, press edges firmly together. Prick top of turnover in several places, or cut a design to allow for escape of steam. Place on ungreased baking sheet, bake 20 min in a hot oven (425° F). Serve hot with Relish Sauce. 4 servings.

Relish Sauce:

1 cup thick white sauce, reserved from turnovers,
above
¼ cup milk

2 tbsp India relish
½ tsp prepared mustard
Dash of salt

Combine all ingredients. Heat thoroughly in the top of double boiler and serve over the hot tuna turnovers.

WAYS TO SERVE COLD CANNED RED SALMON

A main dish requiring minimum time for serving

If possible, chill salmon in the can several hrs before serving. Open can, drain. Unmold carefully on serving dish. Remove skin and discard.

1. Serve with lemon wedges.
2. Serve with a sprinkling of finely chopped onion.
3. Unmolded salmon may be garnished with piquant salad dressing, and sprinkled with chopped parsley or paprika.
4. Heat ripe olives in their own juice, drain, and allow 3 or 4 olives to a serving. Place attractively around the salmon.
5. Serve with sliced tomatoes or tomato wedges.

PLANKED FISH

3 lb shad, whitefish *or*
haddock*
Melted butter
Salt and pepper
1 qt hot fluffy mashed
potatoes

1 egg
1 pt freshly cooked peas
1 pt cooked julienned carrots
2 to 3 ripe tomatoes, medium
Parsley *or* cress
Lemon wedges

Method 1: Clean and split fish. Lay skin side down on buttered, heated, prepared plank, see p 1437. Brush well with melted butter, sprinkle with salt and pepper. Place on broiler 2 inches below flame, cook until fish is nicely browned and done. It is done when it breaks apart into moist flakes. Garnish with parsley, lemon wedges; serve vegetables separately.

Method 2: Leave fish whole, lay on a narrow buttered strip of aluminum foil or parchment paper placed on shallow pan. Brush with

* These are the fish commonly planked.

melted butter, sprinkle inside and out with salt and pepper. Place under broiler or in moderately hot oven (400° F), cook until fish is browned nicely on top. Slide broad spatula or pancake turner under foil or paper, lift fish, carefully inverting it onto heated, buttered, prepared plank. Lift off paper carefully. Have egg beaten well into mashed potatoes and put into a pastry bag with a rose tube. Quickly pipe potatoes around fish, leaving spaces for other vegetables. Cut tomatoes in half crosswise, slip into spaces allowed. Brush fish and tomatoes with butter, sprinkle with salt and pepper. Return to broiler or oven, cook until fish is browned and well done and potatoes are beautifully edged with golden brown. Speedily slip rest of vegetables into their spaces, garnish with greens, serve at once. 5 servings.

FRENCH-FRIED FISH

1½ lbs small fish fillets	1 egg, beaten
½ cup corn meal	2 tbsp milk or water
2 tsp salt	2½ lbs shortening for frying

The best fish for French frying are small Pike, Whitefish, Perch, Rock Bass, Croppy. These directions are for fresh or frozen fillets weighing 3 or 4 oz and not thicker than ½ inch or thinner than 3/16 inch.* Frozen fillets should stand until they are just thoroughly thawed through. Make sure all scales are removed. Do not wash fillets; wipe clean with a damp cloth. Blend corn meal and salt. Combine egg and milk. Dip fish first in egg mixture, then toss in meal mixture. Have enough fat when melted to fill kettle a little more than ⅓ full heated to 375° F (no hotter) in a frying kettle holding at least 3 qts. Place not more than 9 or 10 oz of fillets in the frying basket at one time. Lower into fat. If the dipped fish has warmed up to almost room temp, there will be little drop in temp of the fat. In fact, the temp may rise and in this case, turn heat lower so temp does not rise above 375° F. Fry for 3 min or until fish is golden brown and surface crisp and crunchy. At this stage, fish of this size should be thoroughly cooked, but the flesh should be moist and juicy. Serve immediately sizzling hot. 4 to 5 servings.

*For larger fillets that are as thick as 1 inch, cut into pieces that weigh no more than 4 or 5 oz each, treat in the same way as described above, but fry it at 350° F instead of 375° F for 4 to 5 min.

REMEMBER: This book is arranged ALPHABETICALLY by chapter; ALPHABETICALLY by subject within chapters; ALPHABETICALLY by recipe within subjects. Also CROSS-REFERENCED by page number in recipes. Completely indexed at page 1475

Was I embarrassed!!
Glossary!! Page 1423
What is:
Forcemeat
Boullibaisse
Bechamel
Andalouse
Bearnais
Papillot
Cocotte

Picnic
Sunday—
Buffet if it
Rains
See Pages
1439-1442

CLEAN STAINS
from Saucepans
2 Qt Alumir
small white
Enamel
Stainless
Steel
Cooker

Beauty Note—
Better check
Calorie Chart pg.16-17
and
Nutrition Charts
pg. 16-40 before
Shopping!